Players Plans & Pawns

The Campaign and Battle of Gettysburg, Volume I

Players Plans & Pawns

A Comprehensive Narrative of Military Operations, Planning and Dramatis Persona in the Eastern Armies January to June – 1863

Kevin A. Campbell

Copyright © 2014 by Kevin A. Campbell.

Library of Congress Control Number:		2014915314
ISBN:	Hardcover	978-1-4990-6229-8
	Softcover	978-1-4990-6230-4
	eBook	978-1-4990-6231-1

All rights reserved. No part of this book may be reproduced or transmitted in any form or by any means, electronic or mechanical, including photocopying, recording, or by any information storage and retrieval system, without permission in writing from the copyright owner.

Any people depicted in stock imagery provided by Thinkstock are models, and such images are being used for illustrative purposes only.
Certain stock imagery © Thinkstock.

This book was printed in the United States of America.

Rev. date: 09/08/2014

To order additional copies of this book, contact:
Xlibris LLC
1-888-795-4274
www.Xlibris.com
Orders@Xlibris.com
650901

Contents

Preface xi
Acknowledgements xxiii
Introduction xxv
Prologue   To Save the Nation 3

Book I: Players and Plans

1   Death of an Icon 11
2   Joe Hooker Gets an Army 67
3   An Unremarkable Pennsylvanian 111
4   "The Best Soldier I Ever Saw" 133
5   Confederate Players 159
6   The Federals Come Full Circle 207
7   North to Victory 249

Book II: Pawns

8   The Game Begins 285
9   Hooker Hunts for Lee 385
10   Hooker's Command 429
11   Lee's Long Arm and Hooker's Superiority 537
12   The Gunners 565
13   The Boys of '63 625
14   The Federal Horsemen 679
15   Stuart Concentrates 717

Epilogue   Intentions 761
Appendix A   Organization of the Army of
                  The Potomac – 3 June 1863 767
Appendix B   Organization of the Army of
                  Northern Virginia – 3 June 1863 805
Abbreviations 835
Bibliography 837

Images, Maps and Charts

Theater of operations	10
Stonwall Jackson	19
Jackson Deploys	27
The Wonding of Jackson	45
Guiney's Station	63
Joseph Hooker	75
John F. Reynolds	90
Dan Sickles	96
John Sedgwick	99
Oliver O. Howard	102
Henry W. Slocum	107
Henry W. Slocum	109
George G. Meade	127
John B. Floyd	153
Robert E. Lee	157
James Longstreet	178
Richard S. Ewell	187
Ambrose Powell Hill	197
James Ewell Brown Stuart	204
George Stoneman	220
George Henry Sharpe	225
Winfield Scott Hancock	241
Zebulon Vance	268
Lee Shifts to Culpeper	284
George Pickett	295
John Bell Hood	317
Robert E Rodes	330
Jubal Anderson Early	340
William Dorsey Pender	362
Richard H. Anderson	367
Harry Heth	377
Group of Army of the Potomac Scouts	394
Albion Parris Howe	403
Vermont Brigade Crosses the Rappahannock	406
Lewis Grant	407
Pontoon bridge at deep run	410
George Sykes	420

John Newton	435
James Samuel Wadsworth	445
Abner Doubleday	454
William Henry French	472
David Bell Birney	480
Francis Channing Barlow	505
Alpheus Starkey Williams	522
George Sears Green	533
William Farquhar Berry	542
Artillery Battery	545
Robert Ogden Tyler	566
John Caldwell Tidball	569
Edward Porter Alexander	596
Regiment in line of battle	667
Alfred Pleasonton	688
John Buford	694
David McMurtrie Gregg	709
Hugh Judson Kilpatrick	712
Wade Hampton	733
William H. F. Lee	743
John D. Imboden	758

This work is dedicated to

Susan:

Who taught a broken man to live laugh and love again

Preface

I have noticed over the years that it is customary for any author/historian who presents another publication regarding some aspect of the Gettysburg Campaign to apologize and make an effort to justify his/her reason for contributing an additional work to the already massive amount of preexisting literature on the campaign and battle. I have only one thing to say to this phenomenon. I have no intention of apologizing for doing something I love.

A Man's Journey
My first visit to the Gettysburg battlefield took place when I was a young man on my first pilgrimage away from the security of my boyhood home. I, along with a group of other young men, was traveling to the National Boy Scout Jamboree in western Pennsylvania. Arrangements had been made for our troop to spend a few days prior to the jamboree touring some of the historical locations in the Philadelphia and Washington DC area. One of these locations was the battlefield of Gettysburg and our tour bus arrived on the famous site late one morning.

Now you can imagine a large group of youngsters between the ages of twelve and seventeen had other things to do that summer day. Tramping the same ground that some old guys in blue and gray did one hundred and fourteen years earlier was not on the list. Still, we managed to see a few of those hallowed sights. The position of the Twentieth Maine was pointed out to us. The Trostle Farm was next, and then some place called the Wheatfield and a place where there were a large number of big boulders that were built for climbing. Finally we made our way to a place called The Angle. Our tour guide informed us the location was called The Angle due to the ninety-degree jog in the stonewall the Union troops were positioned behind. Our day ended there for we had to drive to Baltimore that night to our low-cost hotel.

Needless to say I paid scant attention to the tour guide and more attention to horsing around. I gathered up a few souvenirs at the local gift shop and went on my merry way. Owing to my limited years, I was not capable of understanding or comprehending what had taken place on the ground around me. I did not take the time to ponder the events of those three days in July or what they should have meant to me. Then again it is difficult for a teenager to comprehend mortality or what may be present in a man's beliefs that drive him forward in the face of a hailstorm of lead. To believe in a cause so strongly as to sacrifice one's life was something that at the time my fellow Boy Scouts and I could not grasp. As our trip progressed, and finally came to an end with our return home, the afternoon we spent at Gettysburg drifted into the recesses of my mind. Every so often it would be extracted during a retelling of the adventure but, when the tale was complete it would be tucked back to the niche from which it came.

I returned to my life, the memory of my trip a wonderful one. I enjoyed the experience greatly and as time passed and I began to reflect on the trip. I began to think more about the events which had taken place on that southern Pennsylvania battlefield. Then one day a flyer arrived in the mail. It touted a new series of books from *Time-Life*. The subject was the Civil War. Reading through the contents heightened my interested. At the time I wasn't in a good position monetarily and did not have money to throw around. After some contemplation and thoughts of my trip to Gettysburg, I filled out the form and sent it in.

Waiting for the first issues was more agonizing than I had expected. I was not sure why. I didn't know it at the time but I was traveling the road that other Civil War buffs had traveled when they had realized their passion. I began to research some events. My curiosity for not only Gettysburg but the entire Civil War grew. I began reading and visiting the library on a regular basis. Unfortunately, there are not many outlets available for a young man living on the west coast, thousands of miles for the seat of rebellion. Finally, after five agonizing weeks my first book arrived in the mail. To my surprise and great pleasure it was the Gettysburg volume. I read it that night and was hooked. I couldn't wait for the next volume.

My first major read on Gettysburg, like most budding Gettysburg buffs I guess, was Edwin Coddington's *The Gettysburg Campaign.* My brother, who managed to figure out I was transforming, purchased a copy for me as a Christmas present. After rapidly opening the rest of my gifts I began to read the work immediately. In fact I read the preface while still sitting among the family opening their gifts. As I proceeded through the work I was fascinated by the detail presented. As I read on I began to think of Coddington as a deity. Was this kind of detail available? I certainly look forward to finding out. While Coddington's work was groundbreaking, as I discovered additional details of the battle I have since placed some of the elements under more serious scrutiny.

I could not get enough, spending time scouring every possible location I could think of where Civil War literature may be available. I subscribed to *Civil War Times Illustrated* and began a collection, which is still growing today. I joined a history book club selecting Shelby Foot's three volume work as my introductory set. The construction of my library had begun. While perusing a copy of *CWTI*, I discovered an advertisement for the Whole Grail of Civil War sets, the Official Records. The offer consisted of an introductory volume and then five volumes per month for $83.00 a month. Even though I could not afford it, I filled out the form and sent it. I was living in an apartment at the time paying less than $100 a month for rent. You can imagine the status of the place. When the first volume arrived I was in heaven again. It contained over one thousand pages covering the first battle along Bull Run and other events in Virginia. As additional volumes arrived I began to read in earnest. I specifically remember reading about the battle of Balls Bluff and the demise of Colonel Edward Baker, Lincoln's friend and a senator from my home state.

As time passed I progressed in my real career. In the early 1990's I had an opportunity to travel in relation to my job. One such trip sent me to the Baltimore area. Seeking to take advantage of the opportunity, I scheduled the journey for late in the week so as to spend the weekend visiting the battlefields in the area. Early on a Friday morning I headed out of Baltimore to the northwest toward the place I had visited thirteen years earlier. As I rolled into the southern Pennsylvania town I began to plan my adventure. It was going to be a beautiful late spring day. No clouds were in the sky and not a single branch on any tree was moving under the breath of the wind.

First, I would venture to the fields west of town to see the famous railroad cut and the places where the Iron Brigade lived up to their moniker. Then I traveled north to Oak Hill and across the battlefield north of town, where the men of Howard's Eleventh Corps wrote another chapter in their heroic but maligned performance record. I worked my way over to Culp's Hill to see the wooded slopes where the Confederates may have squandered their greatest opportunity to drive the Federals from their evening position on July 1. Back through town I went. Finding Steinwehr Avenue I headed south out of town. Glancing to the left I could see the famous Angle and the Copse of Trees marking Lee's target on the fateful final day. Ahead was the Codori farm, with its red structures shining in the sun's warmth.

Passing the structures I went down the now paved Emmitsburg Road past the legendary Peach Orchard. Turning left I worked my way to the rock covered ground of Devils Den. Standing between the boulders it was easy to see how the area received its name. Cracks and gaps were everywhere. I could just imagine Union troops hiding among the rocks taking aim at the oncoming Rebels. Then being utterly surprised as other Rebels sprung upon them from the tops of the boulders. To the east rose Big and Little Round Top, the latter being one of the major goals of my quest.

After driving to the top of the hill, I parked my small rental car, noted the time at near 3 p.m., jumped out of the car and head in the direction of the trail to the extreme left of the Union line. Finding the path, I started down it hoping to find that famous patch of ground on the hillside. I had not traveled far before I noticed a small white cube on the ground just off the trail. On closer inspection I discovered that it was a marker denoting the position of the left end of the 83rd Pennsylvania. I was getting closer to the object of my quest. Returning to the trail I moved on to the east keeping a sharp eye out for the marker, which would tell me the location of the 20th Maine's position on July 2. I was looking for the place where Chamberlain's boys made their heroic stand against Colonel Oates' hard charging 15th Alabama.

After what seemed a long time I found what I was looking for. There I was standing on the same slope that was held so stubbornly by those soldiers of Maine. At the time of my visit to the site I was not aware of particulars. All I knew was what I had read in Coddington's work and other minor recollections I had managed to lay my hands on. But that did not matter. There I was standing in the spot, positioned on the same tree cover, rocky hillside.

I don't know how long I stood there. The wind was still. There was no sound other than the sweet chirping of birds in the branches above. Finding a good sized rock I sat down and my mind began to wander. Closing my eyes I could almost see the long blue line formed between the trees. The sound of discharging weapons, the smell of gunpowder heavy in the air. Minié balls whizzing past like angry bumblebees and the horrific thud of one, which finds its target. Then that terrifying screeching known as the Rebel yell fills the air, and a line of gray moves quickly up the hill toward the withering boys in blue.

I could even hear the voices from long ago. Most were screams in agony. Others were calm and orderly, shouting commands and direction through the maelstrom of battle. And other voices too. They seemed quiet and happy. Finally, drifting back to the present, I realized there were other people walking toward me down the path. It was time to go. I did not know how long I had set there but I could tell by the position of the sun that it was getting late and I still had one more stop to make. My previous journey up the trail seemed longer than the trip back to the car. When I reached my vehicle I noticed that it was half past four. It had not seamed that long since I parked the car.

Pointing the car north I headed back toward town, passing the numerous monuments positioned along the side of the road. Down Sedgwick and Hancock Avenues I went, past the Pennsylvania Memorial and finally to the turn out at the Copes of Trees. After leaving the car once again, I walked to the large concrete platform in the center of which was positioned the large bronze monument to Pickett's Charge. The first time I heard it referred to as Longstreet's Assault was when I read the memorial plaque near the trees. I was also shocked at how small and insignificant the group of trees really was. How could such an insignificant little patch of woods become so famous? It was no different than any other patch of woods. It's branches had no discernible quality. The trunks were those of common trees. Not bent in any way to draw distinction to them. Even the crowns of the trees seemed to be common. I would suppose the trees had been well cared for since their rendezvous with immortality. They looked much the same as they did in the numerous period photographs I had seen, seeming to change little over the previous century.

Walking out from behind the trees I looked across the open space between the trees and Seminary Ridge. It was shocking to see how far it was across the fields to the Virginia Memorial, which was difficult to see as the sun was making its way toward the horizon in the west. I tried to imagine the gray clad troops jumping off from the far tree line, making their way across the expanse all the way up to the short rock wall in front of me. What would make men cross that opening into the teeth of death? At the time I did not have the answer and to this day I am still not sure. To believe in a cause so strongly that one would march to his demise to see it done is something that our modern society has lost the ability to understand.

Walking onward toward the wall I passed the monument to Cushing's Battery. I could almost see Armistead standing with one hand on the rim of the cannon wheel while the other held his sword aloft, his hat now impaled on the blade, halfway to its base. I reached up and put one hand on the cannon wheel. I could almost feel the vibration as if the sound of battle was still resonating in the ornamental weapon. Walking on I passed the shining white monument to the 71st Pennsylvania and up to the stone wall.

The first thing one notices about the wall is that it is not tall. It is about mid thigh in height or less. It had looked taller in a number of the photographs I had seen, obviously succumbing to time and weather. The stones used to construct it are not unique. They resemble the material used to construct thousands of rock walls. Some of the stones however, may not have been part of the original wall, having possibly been replaced over the years. The wooden fence, which complimented the wall in many period photographs, was gone. It is not the material however, that makes the wall particular. There seems to be an aura, which floats in the air near the short little inconspicuous barrier.

Looking out across the open expanse beyond I could visualize the mass of men clad in gray trudging onward through the hail of steel and lead toward their objective. The tree line across the valley could be seen clearly but the details were difficult to discern due to the sun slowly lowering itself toward the horizon. The automobiles traveling down the Emmitsburg Road seemed out of place. Glancing to the left they could be followed until they passed behind the Codori farm buildings only to emerge a short time later.

To the right was the corner of the Angle. Walking over to the corner I stood in the shadow of the tree that had sprouted there. It seemed like a good place to take a breather. After a moment I stepped over the pile of stones and sat down under the tree. I had been walking all day and my legs and feet were reminding me of the distance they had traveled. I remember wondering how the soldiers of Gettysburg managed to tramp all those miles. They surely must have had sore feet and legs. It felt good to sit and relax; my long day of reliving history was near an end.

As with my visit to the position of the 20th Maine, I'm not sure how long I sat under the tree. The sun was now hitting my legs as it had dipped far enough to slip its beams under the rim of the tree. Not even a wisp of wind had been present all day to dry a little of the perspiration from a person's skin. Now as I sat in that place I had wanted to visit for the past few years it seemed as if someone knew I was there. Slowly a rustling could be heard. In low tones first it grew and became more audible. Glancing up I noticed the leaves were moving slightly in the shallow breath of wind which had come up. For a moment I thought "where were you when I needed you." Then suddenly a thought came to me, "maybe it wasn't the wind at all." Turning, I looked over my left shoulder at the Copes of Trees. I could not tell if the breath of wind was having the same effect on them. I sure didn't look as if it was.

Suddenly I felt different. I seemed to have gotten choked up. This wasn't something that happened to me a lot. It was not something that a guy liked to discuss. It was the same feeling that one gets when the great events of their life are unfolding. Such as the birth of a child, or the remembrance of a recently departed loved one. It was both joy and sadness rolled into one emotion. No other person other than my dearly departed first wife was ever made aware of how I was feeling at that moment. Before I knew what was happening something cool ran down my cheek. I quickly wiped it away not wanting anyone to see the tear. Then another showed up. I brushed it aside quickly. Composing myself, I sat for a few additional minutes in the vanishing shade of that special tree. Then, gathering my thoughts, I got up and made my way back to the car. My day was done.

At the time I was not sure what drove my emotions to the brink of a tear. Later after formulating a few thoughts I think I have managed to come to a conclusion. Our society these days is one of immediate gratification. We never stop to think about things just expect things to be the way we wish them to be. We don't dwell in the past we live for the moment. And, in reality what hardships do we have? Yes, there are certain segments of our society which may not have all the "comforts" of others but those luxuries are there for those who overcome their obstacles. We live in a world where our cell phone is as important to us as eating dinner, and we expect to get both whether we earn the privilege or not. Our society's biggest concern on any particular day may be getting to the DVD vending machine before the newest releases are gobbled up by those who preceded us.

We have lost the ability to understand what the participants in the great conflict of our nation's history went through to do what they thought was "right." And, in a larger sense, both sides believed they were right. Both Northern and Southern soldiers believed in their hearts they were correct. Both sides believed so strongly in their cause that they were willing to risk death for that belief. I suppose it was my understanding of this concept that brought the tear to my eye. Generally, we cannot comprehend the hardships of those times or what families went through. The willingness of the common man to endure hardships unto his death to establish what is right in his mind is powerful. This concept is something which our on demand society seems to have misplaced.

The events of history shape us as a civilization. They define the conciseness and sole of us as a people. They may divide us in the moment but in the long term bring us together to form a stronger, more cohesive Union. Our history is littered with these events. One of the two seminal moments was the founding of our nation. The founders risked their lives to bring us together and the citizens risk theirs by fighting to establish our nation. The Civil War, our second major event, nearly destroyed all that had been achieved. Once again the citizens risk their lives and endured unthinkable hardships to save our great experiment in a representative republic.

I believe that the understanding of these events and the adversity the common man endured to keep the Union whole is the reason sitting at the Angle had such an effect on me. Men fighting and dying because it was the right thing to do has always defined us as a society. While the understanding of this may not be as strong today as it has been in the past, at our core, we still comprehend it. The older one gets the more a person begins to appreciate the rights and freedoms they have been granted by those who have sacrificed so much. I guess you may call this appreciation wisdom. Unfortunately in today's society too many of us simply sit back and become spectators as the freedoms these men sacrificed everything for are withered away by power hungry entities and an overbearing government which under the auspice of protecting us from such atrocities does the same.

As I drove back to the local hotel, I wondered if I would ever return to Gettysburg. Since my visit which prompted the paragraphs above, many defining events in my life have occurred, the major one being the passing of my first wife. She taught me two things before we where parted. The first was that we can never know what God has in store for us. The second is that the key to happiness centers on following your passions. To that end I began the task of writing a history of the campaign and great battle of which this work is the first installment. My library of Civil War books and periodicals has grown to include around 4,500 entries and while it has not grown as fast over the last few months it still is expanding at a hasty rate.

Before she left me my late wife provided the greatest joy of my life, our daughter. Although she is of special needs I hope to someday instill in her an understanding of the sacrifice made but those heroic soldiers of the nineteenth century. I have returned to Gettysburg many times since my first wife's passing and make annual trips to that hollowed place to do research. I look forward to the day when I can walk to the same spots I visit each year with my daughter. Showing her the places where brave men died so that the nation she was born into could grow into the greatest, most caring and free country she will grow to love. Walk with her across McPherson's Ridge where Buford's boys covered themselves with glory. Show her the Virginia Monument with Robert Lee sitting on his trusted horse Traveller. Then to Devils Den to see the great boulders, which I'm sure she will want to climb on. Up Little Round Top to look out over the battlefield. Then, to where Pickett's boy and the North Carolinians were defeated at the Angle. I hope to walk with her out to the stone wall and sit on the wall under the tree just as I had done years earlier. Yes, I want to share all these things with her. Maybe we will even share a tear together.

Purpose of this Work

It is the purpose of this work to act as a preamble to the campaign and battle of Gettysburg. This overture is intended to set the stage for additional volumes of what is perceived to be a multi-volume work covering the planning, execution, combat, retreat and fallout of the campaign. The author anticipates nine volumes with general topics to include:

Volume 1 (this volume) – Preparation, planning and biographical data
Volume 2 – The opening battles of the campaign including:
        Brandy Station
        Second Winchester
Volume 3 – The movements and engagements to midnight 30 June
Volume 4 – 1 July.
Volume 5 – 2 July: Longstreet's assault on the Federal left
Volume 6 – 2 July: The fighting on the Federal right
Volume 7 – 3 July: Longstreet's Assault and cavalry actions
Volume 8 – The retreat of Lee's army and Meade's pursuit
Volume 9 – The results of the campaign including:

Controversies
Lives of the participants through the remainder of the war
Post war period

This work is intended to tell the story of the Gettysburg Campaign from the viewpoint of the participants, from the highest levels of each army's command structure to the private fighting on the battle line. Historically there have been two schools of thought in telling the story of the Civil War. The first, and the method which is the oldest, is to characterize the events by dealing generally with leaders and scrutinizing strategy and tactics. The modern focus to battle history is to address the soldier's existence and his relation to his environment and social matters. Combining these two philosophies obviously present a massive undertaking and clearly not every shred of every participant's tale can be included. To think one could accomplish such a feat would not only be ludicrous but would take multiple lifetimes. O. B. Curtis, historian of the 24th Michigan once noted that "[e]ach soldier's experience is a volume in itself." This, as I have discovered, is an absolute truth. As such, I have attempted to include elements which I believe will have the greatest impact on the reader. Whether success has been achieved will be up to the individuals who chose to outlay their hard earned capital.

British writer and critic Lytton Strachey once observed, "[t]he historian is like a person adrift in a small boat: he will row out over that great ocean of material, and lower down into it, here and there, a little bucket, which will bring up to the light of day some characteristic specimen, from those far depths, to be examined with a careful curiosity." He also noted that "[i]gnorance is the first requisite of the historian - ignorance, which simplifies and clarifies, which selects and omits, with a placid perfection unattainable by the highest art." In simpler terms, historians are sometimes wrong. Or stated differently, they document the facts, evaluate them and form opinions to fill in the holes in the story. The opinions formulated are based on their knowledge of additional facts and their understanding of the personal characteristics of the participants. This method of analysis injects an air of uncertainty in the evaluation and, therefore provides the opportunity for error. Hence, historians can never be correct one hundred percent of the time. In fact the only individuals who have the ability to be correct about historic events are those who were there, and even those who participated can be suspect. Time and the decay of memories affect those who partook causing the injection of errors or untruths from those who are revered as expert. This is simply the job of the historian. Their evaluations and thoughts are not intended to be erroneous. They are required by their trade to interpret the facts, and then fill in the fissures to provide a clearer picture whenever possible.

This is not a bad thing. The opinions formed spur conversation, discussion and, hopefully, cordial disagreement, which help drive everyone toward the one truth of the event. This is the fascination of history. While there is only one true history, the pursuit of it is what holds the interest of not only the professional historian but the amateur as well. The thrill of the hunt is what drives the investigator. Finding that small tidbit of information, which answers a long pondered question, is an adventure in its own right. It provides a euphoric conclusion to the quest and brings the hunt to an end. This is what interests me regarding the Civil War. I imagine the insatiable quest for knowledge possessed by mankind has manifested itself in me in the form of a desire to know more about the Gettysburg Campaign and the great conflict in general.

Before the reader arrives at the body of this work, I would like to clear up a couple of matters. I am not a historian and I do not claim to be one. I have no education within the topics that interest me, other than the schooling I have provided myself. That makes me more of what many would consider a buff, or to be more formal, an independent researcher. I also do not consider myself a writer. In fact my most challenging subject as a youngster was learning to write the English language properly, something to which many friends and family members will attest. Thank God for editors and the advent of computer software with a spelling checker. Knowing this the reader may be prompted to ask, "then why write a book." My only answer to such a question would be "because I wish too."

The other obvious question is why write about the most documented battle of the great conflict? Over the decades since the war the amount of printed material on Gettysburg and the campaign leading to the clash, has grown to massive proportions. In fact there have been publications devoted to documenting all the published material on the battle. The majority of new material is in the form of micro studies regarding segments of the campaign or the republishing of previously existing, out of print writings. In fact the only complete and fresh looks at the overall campaign and battle published in recent years are Stephen Sears' fine study, Noah Andre Trudeau's *Gettysburg: A Testing of Courage* and Allen C. Guelzo's *Gettysburg The Last Invasion*. Armed with the bevy of new information, I felt it was time for a new look at the campaign from the point of view of the participant, whom I have discovered usually possess thoughts and positions outside the mainstream of modern consideration.

I have tried, unsuccessfully at times, to remove my own opinions regarding specific events or decisions in order to tell their story. As usual, good intentions are more often than not just that, intentions. There are some topics which require some form of opinion. However, I have tried to keep these to a minimum.

The opinions expressed in this work, when they do appear, while they may agree or disagree with others, are my own. I am a firm believer in doing all possible to determine facts, evaluating them and coming to a conclusion. While it is the historian's job to fill in the holes of any event, it is not his/her job to skew history with preconceived or personal opinions. Within this work I have tried to evaluate the facts and come to logical conclusions devoid of as much speculation as possible. We live in a society today where it has become increasingly difficult to determine fact from fiction. It is common knowledge that political correctness and revisionist thinking runs amuck in our daily lives. In addition, pundits, who profess to be knowledgeable on specific subjects, provide poor if not atrocious submissions to the lexicon of history for their own self-promotion thus precipitating falsehood and myth as fact. These contributions to the historical narrative breed a misinformed society and are the basis by which we as a society loose our history and as such it is rewritten by those who have a financial or political agenda. In addition, it is human nature to disregard or rewrite unflattering elements of our past. Although we as a society may secretly wish that such events were not part of our history, many of those unbecoming episodes define who we are as a nation and as such must be taken in their historical context not within the context of a pundits' opinion or a special interest group who wishes to advance their own agenda. It is refreshing to realize the facts of history, while they can be assaulted by such elements, cannot be altered by the attack. There is only one true history no matter how hard news organizations, educational institution, political figures or special interest groups attempt to re-write events to their advantage. The job of the historian is to find the facts, investigate them and determine, as accurately as possible, the true history and not bow to the altar of political correctness or worry about who will be offended by his/her findings.

The pivotal campaign of the war has fascinated me for years. Investigating the topics and documenting the findings is my chosen method of educating myself on the subject. I have also discovered that no matter how much one may know regarding a specific situation, there is always more to be learned and others who have opinions. Unfortunately my location (west coast, southern Oregon to be exact) does not lend itself to providing access to original documents and firsthand accounts. While every effort has been made, short of regular flights or relocation to the east coast, to acquire information from primary sources, I reserved myself to the fact that secondary sources sighting primary sources would need to be relied on to make this work a reality. When including information from secondary sources I have made every effort to utilize only information, which can be attributed to a primary source.

I have tried to approach this work from a centrist point of view. After the conclusion of the war thousands of accounts where written documenting all aspects of the fight. Most general accounts where written from the top down. These accounts where developed from the highest points of the political establishment and military command structure with minimal coverage of the events and activities at the lower levels of the armies. Other accounts where written from the bottom up, providing detailed remembrances, of the trials and tribulations of the common soldier. Many of these "bottom up" accounts, while poorly written by sometimes uneducated men, provide significant detail as to what the foot soldier was required to endure. During the development of this work I have tried to drive the account from both directions to create a narrative which allows the reader to identify and understand the upper echelon while still being able to relate to the common soldier. Whether I have been successful will be left to the reader.

This work is also about men at war and the tempest of battle. The purpose of this manuscript is to include depictions, which relay the chaos and appalling elements of war from the highest echelons to the lowest private. The Civil War contains thousands of instances of heroic men and the units they belonged to or commanded. However, it also contains a much greater number of sad and brutal realities of combat. It is hoped that the reader will discover what it was like to be involved in those great battles, standing shoulder to shoulder with a friend on the battle line one minute and the next instant watching them die, while hoping you where not the next one to suffer the same fate.

It is also about the men who sacrificed everything, including their livelihood, land, families and lives to a cause, right or wrong, which they believed strongly enough in to endure the hardships of armed conflict. How it would have been to be present in the room or around the campfire when the high level decisions were made, while knowing that many of those decisions may determine the fate of thousands.

As I have previously mentioned, I am not a professional writer and never planned to be one. My only desire is to relate to the reader what it was like to be a participant, to instill an understanding of the men, the time, and the personalities that shaped events. I have made an effort to present these events based on the facts and determine responsibility for failure or compensation for success. I encourage the reader to evaluate the events or facts and come to their own conclusions which I am sure in many instances will be different than mine. I hope you find this work as interesting and entertaining to read as I did in creating it.

Kevin A Campbell
2014

Acknowledgements

I have always read and been told that no one writes a book alone. And, while I whole heartily agree with this, one cannot avoid feeling isolated when attempting to write a history about events which occurred 2,700 miles from his home.

Over the previous twenty or so years, an immense number of individuals whom I have never met, have spent a great deal of time money and energy making out of copyright material such as original regimental histories and government publications available in electronic form via the Internet. These publications have been a great help in the creation of this work and your efforts are greatly appreciated.

I would like to thank the kind folks at Kaaterskill Books in East Jewett New York for allowing me to purchase their broken set of the New York rosters two volumes at a time in order that I may afford them.

There are many places in and around the Gettysburg Battlefield I enjoy visiting. Without a doubt my favorite is the Doubleday Inn Bed and Breakfast. I would be remiss if I failed to thank Todd and Christine Thomas, the innkeepers at the Doubleday. Their kind hospitality over the previous five years during my annual visits to the area has been nothing but pleasurable. My time there has always been relaxing and provided me a much appreciated respite from the grind of daily life. If you are ever in the Gettysburg area and need a quiet place to unwind, I would strongly recommend you visit the Doubleday and partake in its warmth. And who knows, you may even get to play with Molly, the innkeepers lovable Golden Retriever.

I would also like to express a great deal of thanks to Stuart Dempsey. Stuart, a resident of the Gettysburg area, is a licensed battlefield guide and operates Battleground Tours which specializes in not only Civil War excursions but Revolutionary War and World War II as well. Stuart has guided me around various portions of the Gettysburg field for a few years now and I am always amazed at his insight and knowledge on not only Gettysburg but Civil War history in general. Many thanks.

I would like to express my gratitude to the wonderful staff at the United States Army Heritage and Education Center in Carlisle Pennsylvania. They were always cordial and helpful while I was plowing through their archival material.

Thanks are also extended to John Heiser at the Gettysburg National Military Park. His patience in putting up with my long list of archival materials I would hand to him each time I visited the library was much appreciated.

I would be remiss if I did not include the late Bob Younger. Bob would probably not have remembered me if he had bumped into me on the street, but I would have remembered him. I had the opportunity to speak with him on two occasions when I was passing through Dayton, Ohio. I was on my way from Columbus to Champaign, Illinois and stopped to spend time at my second favorite place (the first being Gettysburg), Morningside. His sharp wit and no holds barred commentary on any topic, including the books he had for sale in his shop, always kept me interested and entertained. I credit him with fueling my passion for Gettysburg. Without him this project would probably not have been undertaken. I wish I had lived closer so that I could have visited his shop more often and enjoyed his company and commentary more frequently.

I would also like to personally thank Patty Stringfellow, director of the Jasper County Public Library for providing permission to utilize one of the letters contained within the libraries extensive collection of papers in the Robert H. Milroy Collection.

I am also thankful for the editorial work of Katrina Myers. Katrina put up with my poor grammar, syntax and butchering of the English language for nearly two years as I fed her segments of the manuscript. She was always cordial and interested in my work and I appreciated her honesty and editorial assistance.

When word got out at my real place of employment that I had undertaken such a task in addition to those of my occupation, I received nothing but support from those whom I spend nearly thirty percent of my life with. Thanks for all your support. You know who you are.

Being a full time husband and father of a special needs child is a heavy task in itself. I would like to express loving gratitude to my wife Susan who over the last two and a half years has kept me grounded and provided me greater clarity regarding my life and responsibilities to not only my daughter but to myself as well.

Thanks to my late parents Richard and Vickie who, although I rebelled on many occasions, managed to raise me right. I will see you again someday.

Finally, I would like to thank all the gallant veterans who endured the hardships, the resolute historians who documented their experiences, the editors who skillfully polished their work and the dogged documenters who gathered and organized the records. I wish to thank them for the plethora of data and mountains of primary and secondary, published and unpublished sources from which this manuscript was created. The time spent on this project and the experiences it has provided me have been some of the richest events of my life.

Thanks to all.

Introduction

By the spring of 1863 the American Civil War was two years old. The Southern Confederacy had seen a string of successes in the east while their efforts in the western regions had seen a number of setbacks. The North had seen nothing but defeat and disappointment in the east. It had started at Bull Run and had come to a head at Fredericksburg in December 1862.

Although the Confederacy had achieved a number of victories, they had been at great cost to its resources, in particular the reduction in the manpower needed to fight the war. With a total population of slightly more than nine million it would be impossible to replace the losses. If the south was going to achieve success it would have to come soon. Attempting to attain its independence through force of arms was the cause of the decline in manpower. Victory could not come through armed conflict with an administration in Washington which had determined to preserve the Union at all cost. Only by convincing the Lincoln administration that it was in the best interests of the Washington political machine, and the North in general, to let the Southerners go in peace would the South achieve its freedom. The only way to create such a situation would be to make the Northern population suffer the same ravages of war which the South had been enduring since the beginning of the conflict. This could only be accomplished by taking the war into the untouched regions of the Northern Union, bringing it to the doorstep of the citizenry. During the spring of 1863 that's exactly what the commander of the Confederacy's finest army, the Army of Northern Virginia, prepared to do.

Players Plans & Pawns

For heroes have the whole earth for their tomb; and in lands
far from their own, where the column with its epitaph declares
it, there is enshrined in every breast a record unwritten
with no tablet to preserve it, except that of the heart.

Pericles 430 BC

Prologue

To Save the Nation

> "As to the policy I 'seem to be pursuing'"[1]
> *Lincoln to Horace Greeley*
> *22 August 1862*

During the first summer of the American Civil War, President Abraham Lincoln called a special session of the thirty-seventh Congress. One result of the gathering was the passing and signing of the First Confiscation Act. The act provided to the Federal Government the authority to confiscate all property held by those who were actively participating in the rebellion against the United States. The law itself was not groundbreaking. It was a restating of current recognized laws of warfare. It sanctioned the government to seize any property which was used to wage war, including slaves, which were still considered within the language in the bill, a possession. Shortly after the first battle at Bull Run, when many in the North first began to understand the war would be more than a simple affair, Lincoln signed the bill into law.

When Congress reconvened in December 1861, the confiscation issue once again became the object of heated debate. The first act, in the minds of many hard line radicals, had no teeth and was not having the desired effect regarding the granting of freedom to liberated slaves. The act gave no instructions to Federal army officers on how to treat any slave who may wander into the army's camps, or who had been liberated by force of arms. Some commanders freed slaves and send them northward, while others simply sent them back from whence they came.

As the returning legislators began to debate additional regulations to better define the authority granted to army officers, arguments over the extent of their power erupted. The debate was indeed frustrating as it pitted Senators and Congressmen against one another. The ultimate question was one of Constitutional authority. Did the Constitution of the United States allow for the seizure of property if the parties in question disagreed with the course chosen for the nation as a whole? Could the government, under the Constitution, confiscate the property of a Southerner, who had not taken up arms against the United States, but simply expressed his disagreement with Washington and supported the Confederacy's right to exist? The discussions were anything but peaceful. Illinois radical Republican Senator

---

[1] Nicolay, John G. & Hay, John, ***Complete Works of Abraham Lincoln***, vol.8, p.15.

Lyman Trumbull introduced the first version of a second bill which contained language that provided for the seizure of all property from anyone identified as being in rebellion against the country. Taking the lead, and joined by other radicals, including Massachusetts Senator Charles Sumner, Trumbull pushed his bill but received severe opposition, some of it coming from within his own party. Illinois' other Republican Senator, Orville Browning, a good friend to the president, led a more conservative group. With both sides firmly entrenched, the arguments within the two legislative bodies began in earnest. Deciding the endless debate would accomplish nothing, a group of moderates, led by John Sherman of Ohio began work on a compromise bill. Senator Sherman's group rewrote Trumbull's bill, and after nearly eight months of debate, a compromise was approved. On 17 July 1862, President Lincoln signed the bill into law.[2]

The first paragraph of the legislation defined the crime required to elicit confiscation of one's property and the punishments to be handed down.

> *Be it enacted by the Senate and House of Representatives of the United States of America in Congress assembled,* That every person who shall hereafter commit the crime of treason against the United States, and shall be adjudged guilty thereof, shall suffer death, and all his slaves, if any, shall be declared and made free; or, at the discretion of the court, he shall be imprisoned for not less than five years and fined not less than ten thousand dollars, and all his slaves, if any, shall be declared and made free; said fine shall be levied and collected on any or all of the property, real and personal, excluding slaves, of which the said person so convicted was the owner at the time of committing the said crime, any sale or conveyance to the contrary notwithstanding.

Also included were fourteen sections defining issues such as the inability of a person convicted of any crimes under the new law to hold public office. Other sections discussed what was to be done with confiscated property, what conditions had to be met before someone could receive amnesty from the president, and a number of other details. Two of the most prominent sections were those dealing with the issue of slavery.

> SEC. 9. *And be it further enacted,* That all slaves of persons who shall hereafter be engaged in rebellion against the government of the United States, or who shall in any way give aid or comfort thereto, escaping from such persons and taking refuge within the lines of the army; and all slaves captured from such persons or deserted by them and coming under the control of the government of the United States; and all slaves of such person

---

[2] Faust, Patricia L., ***Historical Times Illustrated Encyclopedia of the Civil War***, p.157.

found on [*or*] being within any place occupied by rebel forces and afterwards occupied by the forces of the United States, shall be deemed captives of war, and shall be forever free of their servitude, and not again held as slaves.

SEC. 10. *And be it further enacted*, That no slave escaping into any State, Territory, or the District of Columbia, from any other State, shall be delivered up, or in any way impeded or hindered of his liberty, except for crime, or some offence against the laws, unless the person claiming said fugitive shall first make oath that the person to whom the labor or service of such fugitive is alleged to be due is his lawful owner, and has not borne arms against the United States in the present rebellion, nor in any way given aid and comfort thereto; and no person engaged in the military or naval service of the United States shall, under any pretence whatever, assume to decide on the validity of the claim of any person to the service or labor of any other person, or surrender up any such person to the claimant, on pain of being dismissed from the service.[3]

It was now clear to all involved what the disposition of escaped and liberated slaves would be. However, the Lincoln administration did little to ensure the act was enforced. The president's uninspiring support quickly drew fire from hot headed radicals pressing for the emancipations of all slaves. Within a month, Lincoln began receiving demands from radicals in his own party to follow through on the legislation and enforce the new law. Foremost in the onslaught was Horace Greeley, editor of the *New York Tribune*, whose paper was standard reading for the Republican Party.

Greeley was born into a poverty stricken family in New Hampshire. He learned the printer's trade early in his life and at the age of twenty traveled to New York City to seek his fortune. Ten years later he founded the *Tribune* and through hard work built it into one of the most powerful papers of its day. When the war broke out, Greeley's publication was daily reading for nearly 300,000 subscribers. His disdain for the institution of slavery, which he considered an immoral practice and economically regressive, was shown to the public when he opposed the Compromise of 1851 and the Kansas Nebraska Act. Greeley was slow to support Lincoln, but once elected, he backed the new president. However, he expressed great disappointment with Lincoln's failure to immediately emancipate the slaves.[4]

In an open letter to the president entitled "The Prayer of the Twenty Millions," published in the 19 August 1862 edition of the *Tribune*, Greeley took Lincoln to task. He implying that the president was bowing to, among other things, political

---

[3] ***Electronic Source:*** http://www.history.umd.edu/Freedmen/conact2.htm. Last Accessed: 6/9/08.

[4] Faust, ***Encyclopedia***, p.322.

pressure and the policies he "seem[ed] to be pursuing" were contradicting those which helped him achieve election. Greeley's nine point document was a long worded reminder to Lincoln that, in Greeley's opinion, the abolitionists who got him elected were not pleased with his delays in abolishing the immoral practice.

Lincoln responded to Greeley three days later. In typical Lincoln manner, the president used few words to define his stance on the situation and what ultimate goal he intended for his administration.

>Executive Mansion,
>Washington, August 22, 1862.
>
>Hon. Horace Greeley:
>Dear Sir.
>
>   I have just read yours of the 19th. addressed to myself through the New-York Tribune. If there be in it any statements, or assumptions of fact, which I may know to be erroneous, I do not, now and here, controvert them. If there be in it any inferences which I may believe to be falsely drawn, I do not now and here, argue against them. If there be perceptable [sic] in it an impatient and dictatorial tone, I waive it in deference to an old friend, whose heart I have always supposed to be right.
>   As to the policy I "seem to be pursuing" as you say, I have not meant to leave any one in doubt.
>   I would save the Union. I would save it the shortest way under the Constitution. The sooner the national authority can be restored; the nearer the Union will be "the Union as it was." If there be those who would not save the Union, unless they could at the same time *save* slavery, I do not agree with them. If there be those who would not save the Union unless they could at the same time *destroy* slavery, I do not agree with them. My paramount object in this struggle *is* to save the Union, and is *not* either to save or to destroy slavery. If I could save the Union without freeing *any* slave I would do it, and if I could save it by freeing *all* the slaves I would do it; and if I could save it by freeing some and leaving others alone I would also do that. What I do about slavery, and the colored race, I do because I believe it helps to save the Union; and what I forbear, I forbear because I do *not* believe it would help to save the Union. I shall do *less* whenever I shall believe what I am doing hurts the cause, and I shall do *more* whenever I shall believe doing more will help the cause. I shall try to correct errors when shown to be errors; and I shall adopt new views so fast as they shall appear to be true views.

> I have here stated my purpose according to my view of *official* duty; and I intend no modification of my oft-expressed *personal* wish that all men everywhere could be free.
> Yours,
> A. Lincoln.[5]

Lincoln left no doubt as to his goals and responsibility. In his mind, he was tasked with saving the Union by restoring the authority of the Federal Government. If the slavery issue could be used as a tool to do so, he would utilize it but only at the proper time. If slavery could not be used as an effective tool, he would not use it. If he could free all the slaves and save the Union, Lincoln noted to Greeley, he would do so. Greeley must have been pleased when a month later; Lincoln issued the Emancipation Proclamation, a first draft of which had probably already been written when Lincoln penned his letter to Greeley.

Like Greeley, Robert E. Lee, the epitome of Southern Aristocracy, also opposed slavery on moral grounds. But, unlike Greeley, Lee was not willing to do anything to force its end or lobby for its extinction. Instead, Lee held to his five basic beliefs about the institution which were not far from the core beliefs of most Americans in the mid-nineteenth century. First, Lee believed that slavery was a political and moral malevolence which hung around the neck of America like a great albatross. In a letter to his wife Mary, which he wrote in late 1856, Lee articulated his opinion.

> "In this enlightened age, there are few I believe, but what will acknowledge, that slavery as an institution, is a moral & political evil in our Country."[6]

Secondly, Lee felt that blacks in America were better off than if they were in their native Africa. He believed that their situation, difficult as it was, provided them a better moral and social environment and allowed them to grow and evolve in those areas.

Third, Lee believed in a racial hierarchy which by today's standards would be extremely controversial but during Lee's time was an accepted concept. He considered the white man to be at the top of this evolutionary ladder. Just below the white man were the Mexicans. Next were the Blacks, followed only by the American Indian. This hierarchy was critical to Lee's ideas on how society functioned. It allowed him to justify his somewhat abstract loathing of the institution of slavery.

Next, and probably most controversial, was Lee's belief that the Blackman's servitude was necessary for his advancement as a race and that Lee hoped it would lead them to better things. "The painful discipline they are undergoing," he wrote

---

[5] Nicolay & Hay, ***Complete Works of Abraham Lincoln***, vol.8, pp.15-16.

[6] Thomas, Emory M., ***Robert E. Lee***, p.173. This passage is often cited by historians in an effort to establish Lee's disapproval with slavery.

Mary, "is necessary for their instruction as a race, & I hope will prepare & lead them to better things."

Finally, Lee felt it was not his responsibility to make any effort to bring the practice to an end. He believed the decision to place Blacks in bondage and the length of time they would be held so, was a verdict rendered by God. "How long their subjugation may be necessary is known & ordered by a wise Merciful Providence." Lee believed that slavery would eventually be stricken from the earth but it was not up to him to decide when and where.

> "While we see the [c]ourse of the final abolition of human [s]lavery is onward, & we give it all the aid of our prayers & all justifiable means in our power, we must leave the progress as well as the result in his hands who sees the end; who [c]hooses to work by slow influences; & with whom two thousand years are but as a single day." [7]

Whether Lee ever considered the possibility that his Deity was working his purpose by inaugurating war in the spring of 1861 is not known. The final outcome was still very much in doubt. While Lee's Confederacy had achieved most of the success in the east, Lincoln fought on, determined to preserve the Union. It remained to be seen if the Union would be restored, and if it was, would Horace Greeley's vision of it being free of the scourge of slavery come to pass? Or, would the Confederacy be successful and the young country split in two, allowing Lee's God to determine the hour of the Blackman's liberation? Unknown to all three was the fact that the summer of 1863 would bring the titanic campaign and battle of the American Civil War. Also unknown to them was that God had already begun to wave his mighty hand.

---

[7] *Ibid.*

Book I
Players and Plans

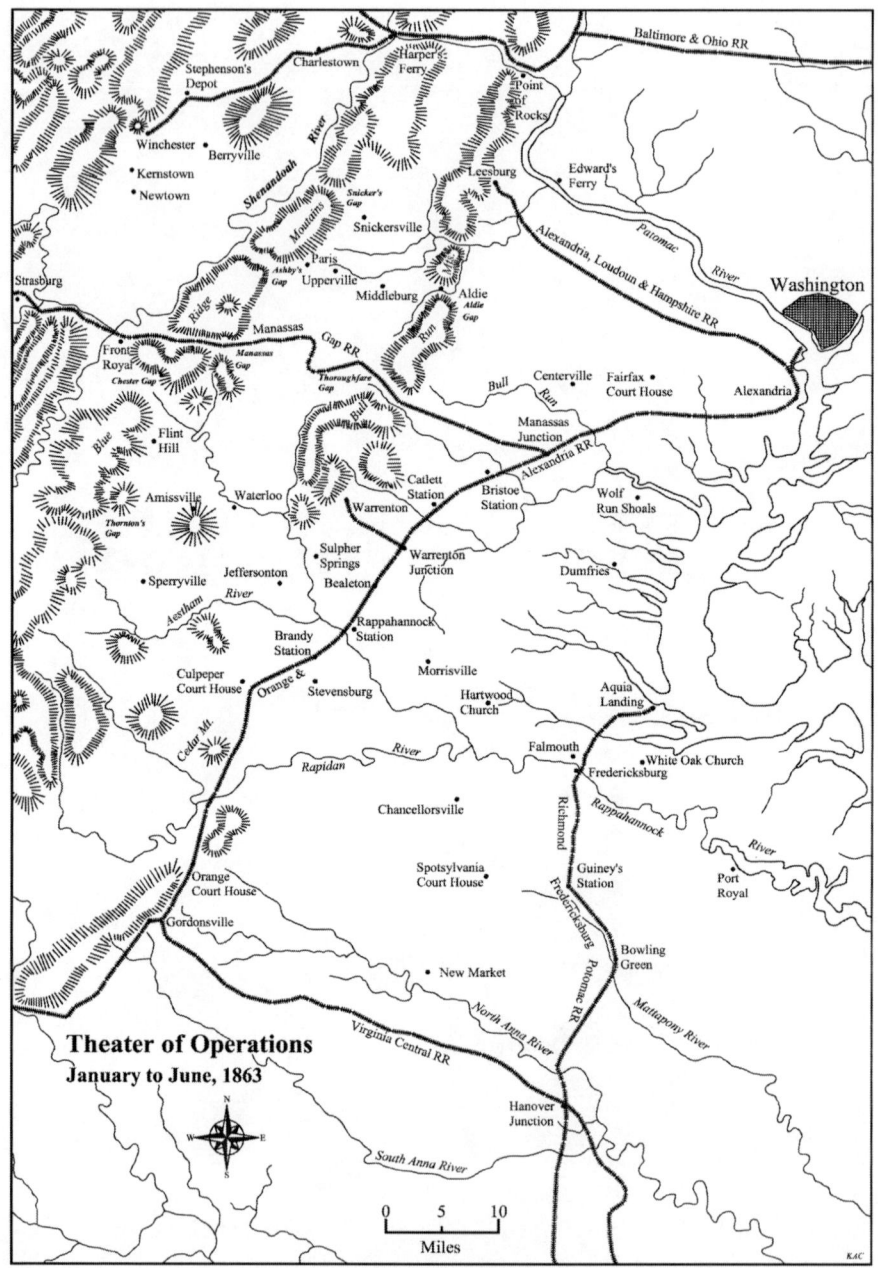

Theater of operations

Chapter I

Death of an Icon

> "I do not know how to replace him."[1]
> *Lee to his son Custis*
> *regarding the loss of*
> *Thomas (Stonewall) Jackson.*

By late April 1863, Robert E. Lee was feeling confident but reserved. During the first two years of the war, Lee developed a keen sense of reading and understanding Union generals. Three had been placed at the head of the Union's grand Army of the Potomac. All had been summarily dismissed after tangling with Lee and his mighty Army of Northern Virginia. First there had been George McClellan. Little Mac, as his troops called him due to his short stature, had been an excellent organizer. His propensity for having everything in its place before taking action allowed Lee to push him away from the gates of Richmond and off the Virginia peninsula. Then there was John Pope. Lee had little if any respect for Pope, and showed it by dividing his army and ending Pope's career in the east with a sound thrashing at Second Manassas. To rejuvenate the battered Federal army, Lincoln placed McClellan in command again. Knowing Little Mac suffered from what his president called the "slows", Lee divided his army once more and marched across Maryland. If not for a misplaced order, he would have no doubt defeated McClellan again. As it was, the outnumbered Confederates fought the Federals to a bloody standstill along Antietam Creek. Finally, there was Ambrose Burnside and the slaughter of Fredericksburg. Yes, Lee had been very successful in judging the capabilities and tendencies of his opponents.[2]

Joe Hooker, who had replaced Burnside, was now on the move and reports were beginning to filter in. The previous day a message arrived from Jeb Stuart, Lee's cavalry corps commander, which reported Federal soldiers moving up the Rappahannock to the west. As morning broke along Stonewall Jackson's front

---

[1] Dowdey, Clifford & Manarin, Louis H., *The Wartime Papers of Robert E. Lee*, p.484.

[2] Sears, Steven W., *Chancellorsville*, pp.27-28; Jones, Wilber D., Stonewall Jackson, his Courier, and Special Order No. 191, *Civil War Regiments* (hereafter *CWR*), vol.5 no.3, pp.1-26; Sears, Steven W., *Landscape Turned Red – The Battle of Antietam*, p.16. The loss of Special Order 191 is one of the enduring mysteries of the Civil War. It is quite likely, baring the discovery of a document confessing the loss by one of the participants, it will never be solved.

south of Fredericksburg, more troops were seen negotiating the river under a heavy fog to reach the south bank. After personally venturing to the front, Lee sent a telegraph to Confederate President Jefferson Davis. "Taken with the reports received from our left," he wrote, "it looks like a general advance; but where his main effort will be made, can not say." By 10 a.m., a second dispatch from Stuart provided more specific information. General Oliver O. Howard's Eleventh Corps was crossing upriver at Kelly's Ford. As the morning progressed, with the fog lifting, Lee began to see the events south of town more clearly. The force on the river was large, prompting Lee to send an additional telegram to Richmond. "He is certainly crossing in large force here, and it looks as if he were in earnest. I here of no other point at which he is crossing, except below Kelly's Ford, where General Howard has crossed with his division [corps], said to be 14,000, six pieces of artillery, and some cavalry." While Stuart had managed to identify elements of what he believed to be three Federal corps up river, Lee was still not convinced the main effort against him would be on his left. Where was the force upriver going? Were they headed for Gordonsville, or worse yet, Richmond? Was their objective Lee's communication and supply line, or was it the rear of his army? There were still a number of questions to answer before Lee would feel comfortable enough to make a countermove.[3]

As the day wore on, Lee began to realize the force on the river was not the main effort. "No demonstration was made opposite any other part of our lines at Fredericksburg," he wrote in his report, "and the strength of the force that had crossed and its apparent indisposition to attack indicated that the principal effort of the enemy would be made in some other quarter." At 6:30 p.m., reports began to filter in from rogue cavalry scouts that Federal infantry and cavalry were crossing the Rapidan River at Germanna and Ely's Fords. This left no doubt in Lee's mind that the target of the upriver force was his army's rear. Fifteen minutes later, Lee sat down to dictate his first orders of the Chancellorsville Campaign.

Hooker's movements on 28 and 29 April surprised Lee. It was the first time since his elevation to command of the Army of Northern Virginia he had been truly outfoxed by the Federals. Even though he was still somewhat in the dark, there were a few things he could do. He quickly began recalling his dispersed army, which had been scattered to cover numerous points from which Hooker could threaten his position. Lee had direct control over General Richard A. Anderson's Division since Anderson's immediate superior, First Corps commander General James Longstreet, was on a foraging expedition in southeastern Virginia with a portion of his corps. "Draw in your brigade from United States Ford," Lee wrote to Anderson, "and throw your left back so as to cover the road leading from Chancellorsville down to the river, taking the strongest line you can, and holding it to the best advantage." Lee instructed Anderson to go forward personally and oversee the gathering and deployment of his five brigades. Although heavily outnumbered, Anderson could at least deny Hooker an unobstructed march to Lee's

---

[3] Stackpole, Edward J., ***Chancellorsville***, pp.128-129; Bigelow, John, Jr., ***Chancellorsville***, pp.206-207.

rear. The order however was slow in reaching Anderson. When it finally arrived, around 9 p.m., the division commander proceeded to carry them out promptly.[4]

Richard "Dick" Anderson quickly sent for his brigades, which were scattered about the vicinity of Fredericksburg and the Rappahannock River. One brigade, Brigadier General A. R. "Rans" Wright's outfit, had started the day the furthest away from the intended rendezvous. Previous orders had already put Wright on the march, and he had closed much of the gap by midday. Now at midnight he received additional orders from Andersen to march to Chancellorsville and report to his division commander. Two more of Anderson's brigades were on their way as well. Brigadier General's Carnot Posey and William Mahone had been posted up the Rappahannock near United States Ford. When reports began coming in from their pickets posted at the upriver fords that Federals were crossing in strength, the two generals had a decision to make. After a short discussion, it was decided to leave a small covering force near the fords and fall back to Chancellorsville. After posting five companies of the 19th Mississippi and another regiment from General Mahone's brigade, the two generals pulled back to a point one half mile from Chancellorsville along the Ely Ford road. It was in this position that Anderson found them around midnight. After a short consultation, it was decided their current position was not strong enough and the brigades should be pulled back even further. By the morning of the 30th, Wright's brigade found them and together Anderson ordered them to fall back to the intersection of the Mine Road and the Old Orange Turnpike near Zoan Church. From his new position Anderson, minus his remaining two brigades, would form the initial defensive position west of Fredericksburg. His force, once his two tardy brigades arrived, would consist of just over 8,000 battle-hardened Confederates. They would initially face 60,000 Federal soldiers. After having William P. Smith, General Lee's acting chief engineer evaluate the position, Anderson deployed his brigades and began to dig in.[5]

While Anderson repositioned his force near the crossroads, five miles to the east, Stonewall Jackson rose early. Once again, the morning began cold and foggy along the river. Soon Jackson met Lee and the two commanders ventured forth to observe developments along the water's edge. As the fog began to clear, the inactive Federals became visible. The situation was now much the same as Jackson had faced last December during the Fredericksburg fight. It would be difficult for the Confederates to get at the enemy, just as it had been a few months ago. Lee, realizing this, thought it best to let the Union army come to him, if that was indeed their intention. Jackson however, was not interested in waiting. With the enemy poised on the riverbank he saw opportunity. "If you think it can be done, I will give orders for it," Lee responded to Jackson's request to attack. To formulate his plan, Jackson needed time to reconnoiter the terrain. Lee at once granted his

---

[4] Bigelow, *Chancellorsville*, pp.207-209; *The War of the Rebellion: A Compilation of the Official Records of the Union and Confederate Armies* (hereafter *OR*) vol.25, pt.1, pp.796. All citations refer to Series I unless noted; *OR* vol.25, pt.2, pp.759; Freeman, Douglas S., *Lee's Lieutenants, A Study in Command*, vol.2, p.526.

[5] *OR* vol.25, pt.1, pp.849, 862, 865, 871; Freeman, *Lee's Lieutenants*, vol.2, pp.529-530.

request, and Jackson spent the better part of a dreary, rainy Virginia day studying the ground and the Federal position. As the day wore on, it became increasingly evident to Jackson that any attack toward the river would be a costly one. Finally, he admitted to himself that Lee was correct. Seeking out Lee, Jackson informed him "It would be inexpedient to attack here." By this time, Lee had become firmly convinced that the Federal units along the river were simply a holding force. When Jackson inquired as to what to do, Lee was prepared with a response. "Move then, at dawn tomorrow up to Anderson," Lee ordered, "make arrangements to repulse the enemy."[6]

Jackson Moves Up

Now, with the rainy day close to an end, Jackson went to work. Earlier in the day, he had requested Jedediah Hotchkiss, his topographical and mapmaking expert, to supply for him eight maps of the area. The map intended for his use, was to be larger, encompassing the terrain as far as Stevensburg to the northwest. With the topography element taken care of, Jackson chose Major General Jubal Early's division to remain behind and hold the Federal force on the river. The fiery Early would be required to defend a five mile long front with 10,000 men against a force four to five times his own. The force designated to move on Chancellorsville would include the remainder of Jackson's corps plus Isaac Trimble's division. With Trimble off convalescing from a previous wound, command of his division fell to Brigadier General Raleigh Colston. Three of Lafayette McLaws' four First Corps brigades would press forward just past midnight. Jackson's force would follow. Lee and Jackson were gambling on the main Federal strike taking place near the crossroads. The risk was great, but if the battle went well and Hooker did what Lee expected him to, a grand victory could be won.[7]

The final piece of Jackson's preparation was more difficult to put in place. He needed to know the area. Hotchkiss' maps could only provide minimal information about major roads and landmarks. The General needed to understand in detail the surrounding area and required guides to navigate through the mass of forest, which was the Wilderness. Seeking out corps chaplain, Reverend Beverly Tucker Lacy, Jackson inquired about the roads in the area. Lacy, who had lived in the area for a couple of years, responded stating there were three main roads. Jackson inquired whether Lacy was confident enough to lead the troops in the dark to Chancellorsville, and if he was not, did he know of anyone who may possess the knowledge to do so. Thinking for a moment, Lacy recalled that one of William Yerby's boys knew the country west of Fredericksburg quite well. Jackson had not visited the Yerby home since the morning he was roused by news of the Federals crossing the river. Lacy had been to visit the family more recently, having been sent by the general to see off his wife and infant child, who had recently spent

---

[6] Freeman, *Lee's Lieutenants*, vol.2, pp.526-527; Robertson, James I., *Stonewall Jackson: The Man, The Soldier, The Legend*, p.703.

[7] Freeman, *Lee's Lieutenants*, vol.2, p.527; Robertson, *Stonewall Jackson*, p.703.

time there. The visit had been the first time the general had seen his new daughter. "Let us go to Mr. Yerby's, I have not called on them for some days," Jackson said.[8]

By the time the two horsemen reached William Yerby's home, it was late and the family had turned in for the night. Choosing not to wake them, Jackson and Lacy turned around and rode back toward the front. The return trip was filled with conversation of the upcoming movement and the situation near the crossroads. The general was now certain that Anderson's Division would be attacked. If the situation was so direr, Lacy wondered why Jackson could not move his troops at night. With the moon being near full and the distance short, would it not be possible to do so, Lacy asked? Pondering the thought for a moment, Jackson responded stating he would rather not march the troops at night but "the reason you suggest is weighty." With that, the general sent Lacy off in search of a suitable guide for the task at hand. Contemplating Lacy's comment, Jackson decided to split the difference. Leaving at dawn, as Lee had ordered may make him too late to help Anderson. Even though McLaws would be on his way shortly, their combined commands would not be sufficient to hold off three Federal Corps if Hooker decided to get aggressive. Jackson would step his corps off at 3 a.m. with Rodes' men off first, Hill's next and Colston bringing up the rear. Shortly after midnight, the general crossed the threshold of his tent and dressed in his full uniform. After his attire was acceptable, he ordered the troops awakened.[9]

After the general had his corps on the road, he rode ahead toward Anderson's position, arriving around 8 a.m. Anderson, who had been supported earlier in the morning by the arrival of McLaws' Division, was arrayed facing west on a front nearly a mile long. After surveying the ground, and armed with the knowledge that his corps was on its way, Jackson made a fateful decision. There would be no more digging in. Working quickly, preparations were made to begin advancing toward the enemy. First, Anderson still had two brigades on the river upstream from Fredericksburg. Jackson gave orders to recall them, and the brigades of Perry and Wilcox began marching to join their division. By 11 o'clock Mahone's brigade was on its way up the Old Orange Turnpike. Jackson rode at the front of the advance. It wasn't long before the marching Rebels ran into the vanguard of Major General George Sykes' Second Division of the Fifth Corps. To the south, Posey and Wright's brigades advanced down the Orange Plank Road. Two miles down the road the Confederates encountered a large enemy force. The fight was on.[10]

---

[8] Robertson, ***Stonewall Jackson***, p.703, Robertson cites Lacy's narrative as the source for the late evening trip to Yerby's.

[9] *Ibid*, pp.703-704. The moon was full at 2:53 p.m. on 3 May.

[10] Freeman, ***Lee's Lieutenants***, vol.2, pp.531-532; ***OR*** vol.25, pt.1, p.850. The Old Orange Turnpike and the Orange Plank Road were two distinct routes but for a distance of about two miles between Chancellorsville and the Wilderness Church, they followed the same path. For the purpose of this narrative the term Plank Road will be used to designate the Orange Plank Road and the Old Orange Turnpike when they are the same thoroughfare. When the two roads do not follow the same roadbed, they will be designated Orange Plank Road and the Old Orange Turnpike, whichever name is pertinent to the narrative.

As the day wore on, both armies battered each other to a standstill with no significant progress by either side. While the Confederates managed to push the Union men back toward the crossroads, the Northerners still held a strong position. Humphreys' Third Division of the Fifth Corps held the Union left, anchored on the Rappahannock. Griffin's First Division filled the gap between there and the crossroads. Sickles' Third Corps and Slocum's Twelfth Corps held the crossroads behind a well-established position. Jackson had seen it from the top of a hill looking westward earlier that day. From the hill, in the open ground around the area, Jackson observed three lines of battle drawn up and ready to fight. The line was supported by some hastily erected but stout earthworks. Further to the west, out of sight, were Howard's Eleventh Corps troops positioned parallel to the Old Orange Turnpike.[11]

Darkness Falls, Plans Form

As darkness began to settle over the field, Jackson sent Major T.M.R. Talcott, Lee's aide-decamp, in search of the commanding general to report news from the front. The advance of the Federals had been blocked, and they were now in force at Chancellorsville. He then rode to the area where the Plank Road crossed the road leading to Catharine Furnace to the southwest. It was there that General Lee found him. Jackson saluted his commander and both men retired to a sheltered area among the trees to escape a Federal sharpshooter who, as of yet, had not been dispatched from his perch in a pine tree. Once in the deepening shadows of the woods, Lee sat on a fallen tree trunk and invited Jackson to sit with him. The commanding general was interested in what Jackson knew about the left flank. Jackson outlined what he knew for Lee but expressed that it was of passing importance. Jackson went on to relay his thought that Hooker would pull back during the night and would cross back over the river. "By tomorrow morning," he said, "there will not be any of them this side of the river." Lee shook his head. While Lee hoped that his subordinate was correct, he did not agree. Hooker's main effort would be here. The Federals had established a strong position and they would not abandon it freely. Fighting Joe, as the papers called him, would have to be driven from it.[12]

Lee had already conducted a reconnaissance to the right and found the woods of the Wilderness too thick and overgrown for an attack to have positive results if made from that quarter. A push there, between the river and the Old Turnpike, was out of the question. With one option eliminated, the discussion turned to what possibilities there may be in the center. It was believed the center was strongly held. Jackson had seen it earlier in the afternoon from his elevated position. An effort there however would not be completely discarded until a proper reconnaissance could be conducted. Major Talcott, who had returned to the crossroads, was tapped out by Lee. Jackson would provide the young James Keith Boswell, his Captain of Engineers. The two reconnaissance officers collected themselves, departed the shelter of the trees, and entered the gathering darkness.

---

[11] Freeman, ***Lee's Lieutenants***, vol.2, p.537.

[12] *Ibid*, p.538; Talcott, Thomas M. R., General Lee's Strategy at the Battle of Chancellorsville, **Southern Historical Society Papers** (hereafter **SHSP**), vol.34, pp.16-17.

After the two men departed, Lee and Jackson renewed their discussion about possibilities on the left. One thing was certain; if they were to turn Hooker's right they needed to know where it was. In short order General Stuart rode up, dismounted and joined the conversation. Grinning from ear to ear, Stuart relayed a remarkable development. General Lee's nephew, General Fitzhugh Lee, one of Stuart's brigade commanders, had reported that while reconnoitering to the west, the troopers had found the right end of Hooker's line. Amazingly, it was hanging in the air just to the west of the Wilderness Church along the Old Turnpike, positioned on no discernible geographical feature. It seemed to be as long as there were soldiers to man it, and then abruptly ended. Stuart also reported the presence of any menacing Federal cavalry covering the exposed position seemed to be nonexistent. Conversations about a move to the left now began in earnest. Were there adequate roads in the area? If so, were they concealed from the enemy's view? These things had to be discovered before the movement of a large force to strike Hooker's exposed right flank could even be attempted. Stuart did not know the answers, but he would make the effort to find out. The cavalryman jumped up into his saddle once more and pounded off down the road toward the Catherine Furnace.[13]

The moon was bright as Boswell and Talcott made their way toward the Federal line. Talcott was not sure of the hour which their reconnaissance expedition began, but it was surely sometime between eight and nine o'clock. As the two made their way through the undergrowth, they came upon a sight which Talcott would remember for the remainder of his days. There, on the ground lay a dead Confederate soldier. The dead man was not a man at all but looked to be a young boy. The corpse appeared to be shorter in years than Boswell's age of twenty-four. A sliver of moonlight cast an eerie glow upon the dead boy's face, which was turned upright facing the heavens. Until the day he died, Talcott would vividly remember the young boy lying motionless in the moonlight and think of his companion that night. The scouting mission to the Federal center was the only instance Boswell and Talcott would be in close association with each other. The dead boy's upturned face and the events of the following evening would be engrained in Talcott's mind forever.[14]

The two men returned from their reconnaissance work around 10 p.m. and reported the center of the Federal line well defended. They observed heavy entrenchments and thick woods bristling with guns and additional fortifications under construction. The report decided the course of action. A process of elimination had determined their course. The Confederates would make an effort to hit the Federal right.[15]

"How can we get at those people?" Lee said leaning over a map of the area. The question was asked of himself in addition to the individuals present. "You know best," responded Jackson. "Show me what to do, and I will try to do it." Lee began to trace

---

[13]   Talcott, General Lee's Strategy, **SHSP**, vol.34, p.16; Freeman, *Lee's Lieutenants*, vol.2, p.538; Robertson, *Stonewall Jackson*, p.710.

[14]   Talcott, General Lee's Strategy, **SHSP**, vol.34, p.17.

[15]   Freeman, *Lee's Lieutenants*, vol. 2, p.540; Robertson, *Stonewall Jackson*, p.711.

a line of march along the roads around the Federal right. If Jackson could manage to position his assaulting force in secret, Lee could pinch Hooker between that force and the remaining troops, much in the fashion first envisioned by the Union commander in his original battle plan. Lee turned to Jackson and told his Second Corps commander the responsibility for turning the Federal right would be his. This was just what Jackson wanted to hear, and a grin spread across his face. The responsibility for getting the job done was now in his hands. "General Stuart will cover your movement with his cavalry," Lee added. Jackson stood and snapped a salute to Lee, "My troops will move at four o'clock," he said. Lee responded with a nod of his head and informed Jackson that if he had any misgivings about the Federals still being in position, he could fire a salvo with one of Stuart's guns to check.[16]

No orders were issued that night. With the plan in place, the group broke up and each man departed for the locations selected for that night's minimal amount of shuteye. Lee, placing a saddle blanket on the ground near the foot of a tree, was soon asleep with his overcoat pulled up around him for warmth. Jackson walked back into the trees and did the same, placing his saddle blanket on the ground as well. He then removed his sword and stood it against a tree. As he prepared to get some sleep, "Sandie" Pendleton, a member of Jackson's staff and son of Lee's artillery chief General William Nelson Pendleton, noticed Jackson possessed minimal clothing to protect him from the night chill. He offered Jackson his overcoat for warmth. The general declined. Then Sandie offered his cloak. Jackson finally accepted the garment and both men sank to the ground for some much needed sleep.

Less the two hours later, Jackson rose with a twinge of a bad cold in his head and chest. Perhaps waiting in the rain on the platform at Guiney's Station to meet his wife Anna and their new baby a few days earlier had exposed him sufficiently to allow the cold to take hold. The morning, like the wait on the platform, was cold and wet. Thinking he should not keep Sandie's cloak any longer, he walked over to where the youth was sleeping and carefully placed the garment over him, being mindful not to wake the young man. A small fire was still burning a short distance away. Wrapping his rubber overcoat around him for warmth, he went to the fire and sat on an old Federal hardtack box, left by the enemy. Stretching his hands out to the flames, he gathered as much heat as the small blaze would give.[17]

---

[16] Talcott, General Lee's Strategy, *SHSP*, vol.34, p.16. Talcott admits he may be in error as to when the "How can we get at those people?" conversation took place. He notes that he and Boswell had returned from their recon mission prior to the discussion. However, the exchange he was privy to may have been a restating of a previous conversation witnessed by Major Charles Marshall of Lee's staff.

After the war, a silly controversy arose regarding who formulated the plan for turning the Federal right. Supporters of Jackson argued that the idea originated with Jackson. Others insisted that Lee was the originator. It is obvious that the plan was a combination of ideas and circumstances, which indicated the Federal position was vulnerable on its right. Various individuals provided intelligence to Lee who was responsible for the decision to make the movement. Lee, exercising his typical command strategy, left the details to Jackson.

[17] Freeman, *Lee's Lieutenants*, vol.2, pp.542-543.

Thomas Jonathan "Stonewall" Jackson, *LOC*

Shortly after Jackson sat, Reverend Lacy walk to the meager flames. He was just who Jackson needed to see. "Come, sit down," he said. "I wish to talk with you." After Lacy had taken a seat, Jackson inquired as to the availability of any roads which would provide a path to Hooker's flank or rear. To the right there were none, Lacy said, but to the left there were a number of good and bad roads, which could provide the required path. Jackson pulled Hotchkiss' map from his pocket. Handing Lacy a pencil, he asked the reverend to draw the route around the left. Lacy sketched the course on the map, but it was too near the enemy's position for Jackson. "It goes within the line of the enemy's pickets," he said. Did Lacy know of any other roads that lead further south, well beyond the Federal lines? No, the preacher responded but surely there must be another road leading south from the vicinity of Catharine Furnace around to the Plank Road. "…[W]here can you find this out certainly?" Jackson inquired. Lacy thought for a moment. The proprietor of the furnace, Colonel Wellford would certainly know. In fact, Lacy continued, the colonel's son would make a good guide. Jackson's eyes twinkled. Leaving the fire, he walked over and rousted Jed Hotchkiss. Once Hotchkiss was awake Jackson instructed him as to his wishes. Jed would ride with Reverend Lacy around to the left and find Mr. Wellford. Once in contact, Hotchkiss, with Wellford's help, would determine if there was a path available leading around the right end of the Federal army. If it did exist, its length and whether it was suitable for artillery needed to be determined. With that, Lacy and Hotchkiss mounted their horses and rode off into the darkness toward the furnace.[18]

After the riders left, Jackson returned to the fire, sitting down once again on the old cracker box. After a short time, Colonel Armistead L. Long, a member of

---

[18] *Ibid*, p.543-544.

Lee's staff, came to the fire. Standing next to the fire, Long noticed that Jackson was shivering from the cold. A short distance away, camp cooks were up and about. Acquiring a hot cup of coffee, he returned to the fire and offered it to Jackson. The general took the steaming tin cup in his hands, thanked Long, and took a sip of the hot liquid. Suddenly, a clanking sound broke the stillness of the morning. Looking toward the area where Jackson had slept, Long discovered the general's sword had fallen from its position against the tree. The colonel picked up the sword and handed it to Jackson who buckled it on. Later Long would note, "[I]t strongly impressed me at the time as an omen of evil. This feeling haunted me the whole day." The events of the next twenty-four hours would provide strong support for the old medieval superstition of a falling sword portending bad luck.[19]

It was nearly 3 a.m. when Lacy and Hotchkiss arrived at the Wellford residence south of Catharine Furnace. Dismounting, they went to the door and woke the sleeping occupants. As Lacy spoke to the family, Hotchkiss pulled the colonel aside and began quizzing him about a possible route to the Federal right. Was there a way, he inquired, to pass around Chancellorsville and connect with the Old Turnpike near the Wilderness Tavern? "Yes," Wellford replied. In fact, he himself had just constructed a road in that direction to transport wood and iron ore to the furnace. Anxiously Hotchkiss pulled out his map and ignoring the darkness, Wellford traced the route on it. Once the line was on the map Wellford offered to act as a guide if one was needed. After a few apologies for the early morning interruption, Lacy and Hotchkiss jumped on their mounts and rode into the darkness again in the direction they had come.[20]

By the time the reverend and Hotchkiss returned from their reconnaissance, the first hints of dawn were beginning to show themselves. Both Lee and Jackson crouched at the dwindling fire as Hotchkiss made his report. There was a way around to the Federal right. Taking another cracker box, he pulled the map from his pocket and spread it out for the two commanders as he traced the route. Jackson's eyes never left the map as the path was explained.[21]

There were two critical spots in the route. The first would be encountered just before the column reached the furnace. There, on the east side of Lewis Creek, the road crested a rise before descending to the stream. The hill was devoid of foliage and could be seen clearly from the north and south. If the Federals were paying attention, as they no doubt would be, the column would be seen as it crossed the edge of the hill and moved down to the creek. At Catharine Furnace, the westerly path turned southwest for nearly two miles before it struck the Brock Road. Here, the second and most critical point in the route would be encountered. The logical direction to turn would be back toward the north. Doing so would put the marching troops within clear view of the Union lines on a course toward the Federal position,

---

[19]   Long, Armistead L., *Memoirs of Robert E. Lee*, p.558.

[20]   Henderson, G.F.R., *Stonewall Jackson and the American Civil War*, vol.2, pp.431-432; Robertson, *Stonewall Jackson*, p.713. Henderson cites a personal letter from Hotchkiss as his source.

[21]   *Ibid*, p.432.

tipping the hand of the Southerners. Instead, the column had to turn to the south, traveling another 600 yards away from the enemy before making a sharp right turn back to the north. The marching men would then be on a parallel road, shielding them from the prying eyes of the opponent. Two miles further, the line of march found the Brock Road once again. An additional three miles would put the column along the Old Turnpike about two miles west of Howard's camping Eleventh Corps. The total distance was nearly twelve miles.[22]

Lee stood by quietly as Hotchkiss explained the route to Jackson. When the particulars had been outlined, and as Jackson pondered the map, Lee quietly inquired, "General Jackson, what do you propose to do?" Lee knew the answer before he asked the question. Jackson placed his finger on the map and traced Hotchkiss' path around to the Federal right. "Go around here," he said.

Then came the question for which Lee did not know the answer. "What do you propose to make this movement with?" he inquired.

"With my whole corps," Jackson responded.

"What will you leave me?"

"The divisions of Anderson and McLaws."

Jackson's force would contain fifteen brigades of infantry and supporting artillery. Close to 30,000 men would make the march. This left Lee with about 17,000 men to face the bulk of Hooker's army on his front. It was indeed a bold move, but Jackson had been bold in the past. Lee had grown accustomed to the aggressive actions of his Second Corps commander whose daring movements, on most occasions, had produced results. There was no reason to doubt this proposal would not provide an opportunity for great success as well. Lee made his decision. In a tranquil voice Lee uttered the words that sealed the fate of Hooker's army at Chancellorsville. "Well, go on," he said.[23]

The Confederates Step Off

The morning was in full bloom when the first brigade of Jackson's flanking force put their feet to the road. The lead division would be Daniel Harvey Hill's old command under Brigadier General Robert E. Rodes. Close to 8 a.m., Brigadier General Alfred H. Colquitt led his men down the Plank Road. The marching men were intermixed with wagons, artillery and ambulances. Reaching the road to the furnace, the column was ordered to turn left. It was obvious to Colquitt his destination was the flank of Hooker's army. About an hour later, the head of the column neared the first trouble spot in the march. The road opened out onto the knoll overlooking Lewis Creek and Catharine Furnace. Breaking from the cover of the trees, the column descended toward the brook. It wasn't long before Federals spied the marching Southerners.

---

[22] Robertson, ***Stonewall Jackson***, pp.713-714; Freeman, ***Lee's Lieutenants***, vol.2, pp.544-545; Stackpole, ***Chancellorsville***, pp.214-215. Robertson places the distance at twelve miles. Freeman puts it at "a fraction more than 9 miles," to the intersection of the Brock and Plank Roads. A review of period maps confirms the distance to the Plank Road as stated by Freeman and the distance to the Federal right very close to Robertson's twelve miles.

[23] Freeman, ***Lee's Lieutenants***, vol.2, pp.546-547; Bigelow, ***Chancellorsville***, p.475.

To the north, Brigadier General David Birney noticed the column and reported it to his corps commander General Daniel E. Sickles. Sickles suggested that Birney fire a few artillery rounds in the direction of the procession. Quickly ordering Captain A. Judson Clark's Battery B, 1st New Jersey Artillery forward, Birney commanded the guns to fire from the crown of an open hill near a dilapidated house. Clark opened up at a range of sixteen hundred yards. As the shells began bursting, a number of Confederates took cover in the trees to avoid being hit. Soon the order came for the Rebels to double quick across the open hillside, giving the impression to the Federals that all was in confusion in the column. Clark was so pleased with the results that he ran two additional guns up and added them to the barrage.[24]

The column continued to double quick down the road and across Lewis Creek. With the Federals now aware of the Confederate column, it was necessary to take the proper steps to protect it from assault by ambitious Yankees. Just before the furnace, a side road departed the main thoroughfare. The road provided the Federal troops a path directly to the flank of the column. Jackson, recognizing the threat from the north, ordered General Rodes to detach some men from the column. Rodes selected the 23rd Georgia from General Colquitt's lead brigade to deploy and protect the column's flank.[25]

Colonel Emory F. Best commanded the Georgia boys. According to Best, he was given authority by General Jackson to order additional troops to his support if attacked by a force large enough to justify assistance. Pushing forward, Best established his position some 200 yards from Clark's Battery. To cover his exposed flanks, the colonel thought it prudent to deploy three companies as skirmishers in addition to the one deployed to his front, leaving only five companies in his main force. Best was in the same position when, around 1 p.m. he was assaulted by an enemy force which drove in his pickets. Unable to maintain his position, Best ordered his men to retire, and the regiment fell back toward the rear of Jackson's column, taking position in a railroad cut on the left of the road south of Catharine Furnace. As the men fought from the cut, General James J. Archer arrived and took command, ordering Best and his men to hold the line until ordered to leave. Archer then went about providing additional troops to support the Georgians. Best and his support held off the Yankees long enough for the Rebel column to move out of reach. Soon afterward, Archer sent orders for the 23rd to retire, but Best did not receive the command until the left end of the railroad cut had been wrestled from his grasp. Finally, the Colonel gave the order to fall back, but it was too late. The regimental colors were saved, but the regiment was not. Only a handful of men managed to escape. Three were wounded and 296 where captured. For his work that day, Best would be court-martialed and drummed out of the army, an unjust fate for a man who did all he could to maintained the covertness of Jackson's column.[26]

---

[24] *OR* vol.25, pt.1, pp.386, 408, 443; Freeman, ***Lee's Lieutenants***, vol.2, p.549.

[25] Freeman, ***Lee's Lieutenants***, vol.2, p.549-550.

[26] *OR* vol.25, pt.1, pp.940,979-980; Sears, ***Chancellorsville***, pp.255-256.

Jackson Finds the Federal Right

After Jackson's column passed the furnace, the Yankees caused no additional irritation. With Wellford showing the way, the column turned south on the Brock Road instead of north to remain hidden. A short distance down the side road and then the sharp right, just as Wellford had traced on Hotchkiss' map, sent the column north toward the enemy. With Jeb Stuart's cavalry patrolling all the roads, which entered from the east, Jackson's men pressed on. An additional two miles brought the column to the Brock Road once again. With the 5th Alabama leading the way, the hidden flanking column pushed onward toward the Plank Road. It was nearly 2 p.m. before the column came within sight of the intersection.[27]

Helping to screen General Rodes' advance was Colonel Thomas Munford's 2nd Virginia Cavalry. To protect the column's flank, Munford had turned his men east onto the Plank Road to reconnoiter the thoroughfare. As they moved down the road, the troopers bumped into a Yankee cavalry picket. The Northerners turned and fled with the Rebels hot on their heels. A mile and a half later, Munford's boy halted their chase. Remembering their orders to observe only, the horsemen threw out their own picket line and waited. With the pickets, in position the men began to mill about. To the left of the road was a knoll barren of foliage at its summit. A captain ventured up the hill to take a look at the surrounding countryside. The view was amazing. So wonderful in fact that the captain wasted no time in descending the hill and riding back down the road at a full gallop to find his brigade commander, Fitzhugh Lee. After hearing the trooper's news, Lee quickly rode forward and ascended the hill himself. As he broke from the cover of the trees, he saw the same sight the captain had seen. "What a sight presented itself before me." He would later write. His first thought was of finding General Jackson.[28]

Jackson was at the head of Rodes' infantry column when Fitzhugh Lee found him. "General," Lee said, "if you will ride with me, halting your column here, out of sight, I will show you the enemy's right." Jackson, bringing along only a courier, followed Lee to the knoll. After climbing the path to the summit and entering the clearing, Jackson saw what had impressed Munford's trooper and Fitz Lee. There spread out before the general no more than 700 yards in the distance was the right flank of Hooker's army, and it was indeed in the air. Jackson couldn't actually see the end of the line, for dense woods closed in, hiding it from view. He could however, see about a mile of the line as it ran along the Old Turnpike, past its intersection with the Plank Road, facing to the south. "There were the lines of defense, abates in front, and long lines of stacked arms in rear," Lee recalled.

---

[27] Bigelow, ***Chancellorsville***, p.289; Bigelow says the head of the column reached the Old Turnpike at 2:30. This would place the column near the intersection with the Plank Road shortly before 2 pm. The Plank Road obtained its name for the plank construction used for the roadbed.

Many post war accounts utilize the term plank road as a description of the road and not a proper name while others utilize the term Plank Road as a proper name. For the purpose of this narrative the terms are presented as they appear in the writings of the participants.

[28] Sears, ***Chancellorsville***, p.257; Lee, Fitzhugh, Chancellorsville-Address of General Fitzhugh Lee before the Virginia Division, A.N.V. Association, October 29th, 1879, ***SHSP***, vol.7, p.572.

The Union soldiers were gathered in groups behind their position. From the looks of it, the Yankees were content with participating in the typical events of camp life, smoking, playing cards and engaging in general conversation. The sight was amazing to Lee. Toward the rear, some soldiers were even butchering cattle, no doubt for the evening's meal. Lee expected to be praised for his discovery, but Jackson uttered no words. After spending five minutes examining the Union position and silently moving his lips as if in pray, Jackson realized that moving on the Yankees down the Plank Road would result in a frontal attack on their position. Without saying a word, Jackson sought his lone courier. "Tell General Rodes to move across the Old plank-road, halt when he gets to the Old [Orange] turnpike, and I will join him there," Jackson instructed the courier. Jackson knew attacking down the Orange Turnpike would place the assault squarely on the flank of the Union position. Whirling his horse around, the courier was off quickly with his message, Jackson hot on his heels, the general's elbows bouncing with the motion of Little Sorrel. Lee later expressed his disappointed with Jackson not congratulating him on his discovery. He may not have felt so dissatisfied watching Jackson bound down the hill if he had realized it was the last time he would ever see him. "Alas! I had looked upon him for the last time," he would say later.[29]

By the time Jackson arrived back at the column, General Rodes had already pushed the head of the long winding snake beyond the Plank Road. Jackson's tenor was different after he returned from the reconnaissance, recalled Edward P. Alexander. "When he came back from the view, there was a perceptible increase in eagerness in his air, and he hurried the head of the column," Alexander wrote. Sitting down on a stump along the Brock Road, Jackson took a pencil in hand and, either checking the time or making a guess, he wrote a hurried note to General Lee.

Near 3 PM
May 2, 1863

General,
    The enemy has made a stand at Chancellor's which is about two miles from Chancellorsville. I hope as soon as practicable to attack. I trust that an everkind Providence will bless us with great success.

                  Respectfully,
                  T. J. Jackson, Lieutenant General

Then, as an afterthought Jackson added, "The leading division is up, and the next two appear to be well closed." It would be his last contact with General Lee on a battlefield.[30]

---

[29] Lee, Chancellorsville-Address, **SHSP**, vol.7, pp.572-573.

[30] Alexander, Edward Porter, *Fighting for the Confederacy – The Personal Recollections of General Edward Porter Alexander*, p.202; Smith, James Power, Stonewall Jackson's Last Battle, **Battles and Leaders of the Civil War** (hereafter **B&L**), vol.3, p.206.

While Jackson was writing his note to General Lee, the commanding general's son, cavalryman William H. F. "Rooney" Lee was writing one of his own to his commander, General Stuart. When the message was complete, he handed it to a courier for delivery. The note was entrusted to a young man who would have a great deal to do with how the events of the next few hours unfolded. Private David Kyle of the 9th Virginia Cavalry was to deliver the note and after being warned to be leery of the roads due to Yankee patrols, the nineteen-year-old headed off in the direction of General Stuart's last known whereabouts. Kyle was the perfect man for the job. If avoiding Federal troops infesting the roads was a requirement, he was well-equipped as his home was the nearby Bullock farm. His front door was no more the three or four miles from where Rooney Lee handed him the dispatch. In 1857, after spending two years at the Dowdall residence, young David moved just down the road to live with his sister Catharine, her husband Oscar Bullock, and their two children. As the events of the evening began to unfold, Private Kyle was better equipped and probably the only person close to the Confederate high command who knew exactly where he was at all times.[31]

To avoid the Yankee patrols, Kyle decided to head cross-country toward Parker's Store. After passing the marching Confederate column, which was still on the Brock Road, he turned north and headed toward the Rapidan River. The young private made his way past Lacy's Mill to Ely's Ford along the banks of the river. He found Stuart near the Ely home and handed him the dispatch. Evidently it had taken Kyle longer than Stuart thought it should have because the General inquired as to his unhurried navigation of the distance. After Kyle explained the need to take the roundabout path, Stuart questioned the youngster as to his knowledge of the local countryside. Kyle attempted to answer but before he could another local youth, Tom Chancellor, who happened to be nearby, chimed in. "He knows every hog-path," the boy stated in a reassuring tone. Stuart understood the value Kyle would be to Jackson and inquired if the youth thought his horse was up for another journey. After Kyle responded affirmatively, Stuart quickly wrote a note and sealed it in a large envelope. He handed the envelope to Kyle with instructions to deliver it to General Jackson. "You will find General Jackson on the plank road somewhere between the Brock [R]oad and the line of battle," Stuart said. "Keep behind the firing and don't let them capture you. If General Jackson wants you for a guide, stay with him." With another document now in his charge, Private Kyle headed off to the southwest. It was 6:30 p.m.[32]

---

[31] Krick, Robert K., *The Smoothbore Volley That Doomed the Confederacy*, p.10; Kyle, David J., Jackson's Guide when Shot, *CV*, vol.4, p.308. Robert Krick's work in tracking down family information for David Kyle should be commended. His research into the young man that guided Stonewall Jackson that night has shed new light on his knowledge of the area and fixed Kyle's narrative of the evening's events as being the most authoritative. Kyle's handwritten narrative is ten pages long. A typed version of it is housed at the FSNMP in Fredericksburg, Virginia. The account was first published in *Confederate Veteran* in 1896. Others who had recounted the events of 2 May discounted it. Douglas Southall Freeman was the first to utilize Kyle's narrative.

[32] Kyle, Jackson's Guide, *CV*, vol.4, p.308.

The Battle Line Forms

General Rodes turned his men to the right after striking the Old Orange Turnpike and marched the column about a mile before it was halted one-half mile from the right flank of Howard's Eleventh Corps. The afternoon was fading into early evening as Rodes began to file his division off the road, sending brigades to both the left and right of the thoroughfare. Colquitt took his brigade to the right while Brigadier General Alfred Iverson, who was missing a number of men, filed his troops off to the left. The absent men had been deployed as skirmishers earlier that morning before the march began and were not recalled in time to join the movement. Colonel Edward A. O'Neal, in command of Rodes' old brigade, followed Iverson while Brigadier General George Doles' men moved to the right behind Colquitt, forming the left and right center of the line respectively. The last brigade in Rodes' Division, commanded by Brigadier General Stephen D. Ramseur, was held back and would form up with the units in the second line. Once Rodes' Division was in place, the battlefront stretched for nearly two miles with the Old Orange Turnpike bisecting the line. Sharpshooters were arrayed in front of the line about 400 yards in advance. The distance placed them about half way between the forming lines and the Federal flank. The sharpshooters were charged with preventing any communication with the enemy. They had to be vigilant for a failure of any kind could mean discovery.

The second battle line formed behind the first at a distance of about 150 yards. Ramseur's men filed off to the right and took position behind Colquitt. Brigadier General Colston's fourth division, under General Trimble, minus Elisha F. Paxton's Brigade, filled in the reminder of the second wave. As the second line filed into position, Iverson deployed the 23rd North Carolina as flankers to protect the left of the battle line. Brigadier General Francis R. T. Nicholls' brigade from Colston's command accidentally slipped into the third line, failing to align with its companion Fourth Division members. Nicholls' boys moved to the left, pushing the end of the third battle line north of the turnpike beyond the end of the first and second lines. Joining Nicholls in the third line was Brigadier General William D. Pender's Brigade from A. P. Hill's Division. Pender arrayed his brigade with his right resting on the turnpike. Brigadier General Henry Heth's command from Hill's Division was ordered to form on the left end of the second line but before "Harry" could get his men into place, the line stepped off. Heth ended up in the third line between Pender and Nicholls. Artillery would be used to support the advance. Two guns from the Stuart Horse Artillery were placed in the road to advance with the foot soldiers. Captain James Breathed, who commanded the guns, was ordered to keep his two remaining pieces back as a reserve. Two additional guns under Captain Marcellus N. Moorman were also held in reserve. The reserve section would be brought forward to relieve the two forward guns as the advance progressed, allowing the sections to "leap frog" each other as the advanced moved forward.[33]

---

[33] Bigelow, *Chancellorsville*, pp.291-292; *OR* vol.25, pt. 1, pp.1049; Krick, *Smoothbore*, p.4.

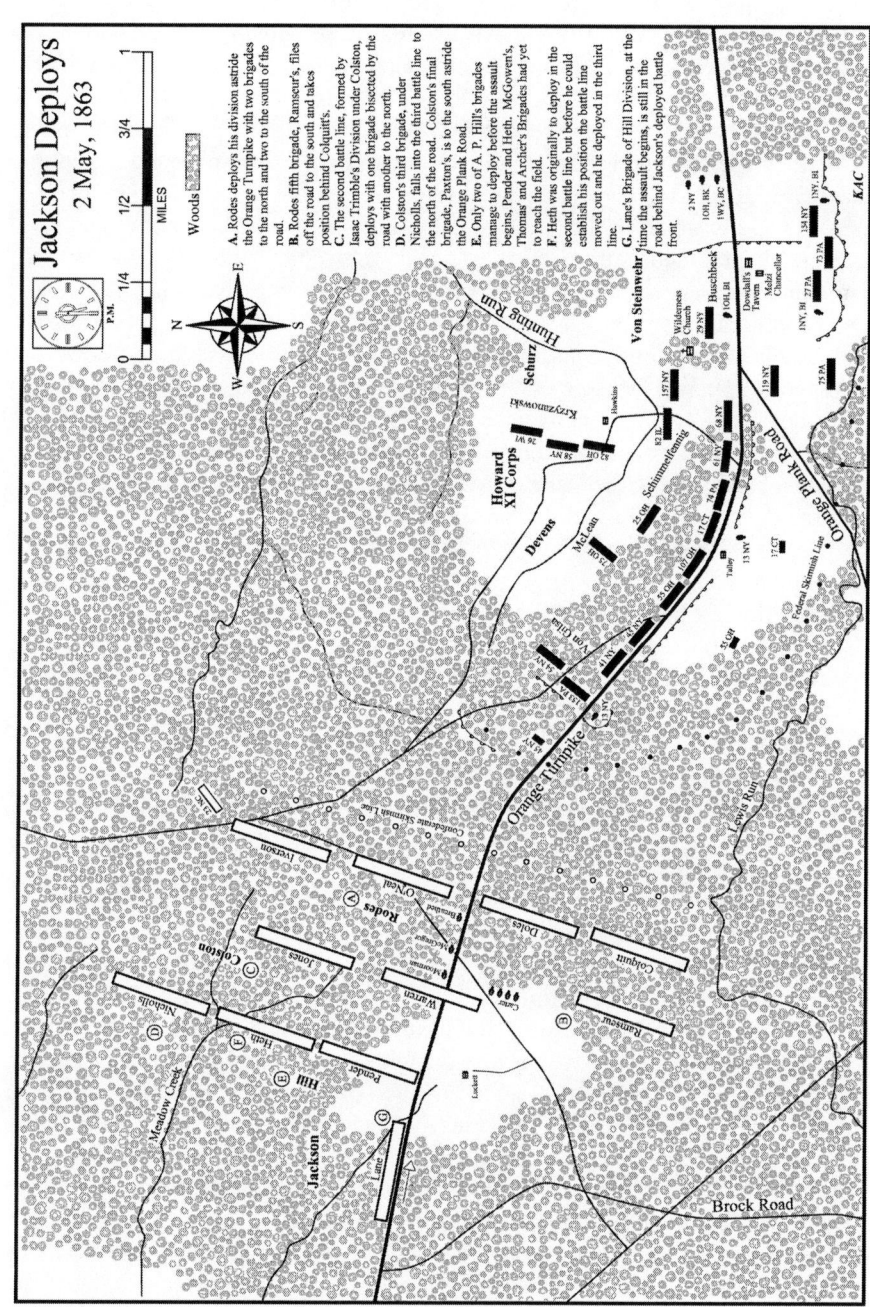

Jackson Deploys

Bringing up the rear were Lane and McGowan's Brigades of Hill's Division. Hill's last two units would not arrive in time to be deployed in support of the main attack. The North and South Carolinians would continue their tramping for another two miles before being placed in line of battle as darkness settled over the woods. Near Lane's marching men were positioned a number of reserve cannon, including those of Captain Moorman. Moorman, who commanded the Lynchburg Beauregard Rifles, felt it was odd that his guns had not been ordered to retire since his command was part of the horse artillery. Looking around, he noticed General Jackson, dismounted, sitting by the side of the road. Riding over, Moorman dismounted and approached the general. Jackson knew the captain well. He had been Moorman's instructor at the Virginia Military Institute. The captain walked up, saluted, and inquired regarding his disposition with the assaulting troops.

"Yes, Captain," Jackson said, "I will give you the honor of going in with my troops." The two men conversed for a few minutes as Rodes and Colston's lines formed. As they talked, fire was heard off to the east. Moorman wondered aloud who it was doing the firing. "How far do you suppose it is?" Jackson asked. Moorman guessed that it was five or six miles.

"I suppose it is General Lee," Jackson responded. He then asked Moorman what time it was.

"Five forty," Moorman replied.

The General thanked Moorman and said, "Time we were moving." He mounted Little Sorrel and trotted off to find General Rodes. The captain of artillery mounted his horse as well and returned to his guns.[34]

Jackson found General Rodes astride his horse near the front. Riding to a stop, he reached under his raincoat, which he still wore although the weather had warmed, and checked his watch. Eying Rodes, Jackson asked, "Are you ready, General Rodes?"

"Yes sir," responded Rodes.

"You can go forward then," Jackson calmly replied.

It was sometime between 5:15 and Caption Moorman's 5:40 when General Rodes turned to Major Eugene Blackford of the 5th Alabama, who was in command of the sharpshooters on the skirmish line. All that was needed was a nod. The order was given and a bugle was blown. The line of battle stepped off. There were close to twenty thousand men arrayed across the Old Orange Turnpike as the battle line surged forward. The skirmish line, in advance of the main battle line, for some reason did not get the order to advance. As the main line approached, there was confusion. A general halt was called and the line paused. After a few moments, the men on picket got into line and the whole front began to move together. The Confederate line holding its ranks, moved toward the exposed right of Howard's Eleventh Corps. Howard had assumed the underbrush and growth in the woods to the west was so thick it could not be navigated. While the going was difficult, the

---

[34] Moorman, Marcellus N., Narrative of Events and Observations Connected with the Wounding of General T. J. (Stonewall) Jackson, **SHSP**, vol.30, p.111.

Confederates remained in line and continued to push slowly forward. Howard's assumption was a miscalculation that would cost the Federals dearly.[35]

Whether or not Jackson spent any time developing a strategy for the initial attack must be left to conjecture. If the strategy was not by design, its execution was simple and automatic. With the flanks of the line extending far beyond the road, and the end of the Federal line anchored on it, the center of Jackson's assault would strike the Federals perpendicular to their position on the Old Turnpike. The center of the Confederate line advancing down the road would make contact first. Slowed by encountering the Yankees, the center of the line would form a vertex, allowing the wings to naturally swing inward and close around the encamped Federals. If Howard's men stood their ground and made a stand, the wings would encase them. Once the attack had crushed Hooker's right wing, Jackson planned to push on and interpose his force between the Federals and the river, establishing a position which would deny Hooker access to the Rapidan River. A movement of this nature would cut the Federals off from the river, and trap them on the south side of the waterway. With the Union army isolated, Jackson could reinforce his position and dig in. Working together with Lee, he would be able to encircle and destroy Hooker's force. The elimination of the Army of the Potomac would, at a minimum, create panic in Washington and could possible bring about the end of the war. It would also allow Lee to gather his forces and contemplate marching on the Northern capital unchallenged by an army in the field and unhindered by politics in Richmond. The thought of marching north unopposed would have brought a smile to Jackson's normally stern face.[36]

A Great Stampede

Positioned on the extreme right of the Eleventh Corps were the regiments of Colonel Leopold von Gilsa's First Brigade of the corps' First Division. Two regiments plus two companies of another were refused to the right at a ninety-degree angle to the road with their front facing the setting sun. From the right of the line, it was three miles to the Rapidan and no Federal troops were covering the gap. The open space could have easily been closed by Federal cavalry had most of Hooker's horse soldiers not been out on a raid to disrupt Lee supply line and escape route. The 153rd Pennsylvania under Colonel Charles Glanz, a nine-month regiment that had never been in battle before, was positioned with its left resting on the Old Orange Turnpike. To their right was Lieutenant Colonel Charles Ashby's 54th New York. Von Gilsa aligned his 41st and 45th New York along the road with their rear toward the area behind the two regiments angled away from the road. The right of the 45th was in a position to be enfiladed by any fire parallel to the road. The entire brigade, numbering around fourteen hundred men, had been charged with covering the Army of the Potomac's flank. The position concerned von Gilsa.

---

[35]   *OR* vol.25, pt. 1, p.941; Sears, ***Chancellorsville***, p.272. It is highly unlikely a bugle was used to signal the start of the advance.

[36]   McGuire, Dr. Hunter, General T.J. ("Stonewall") Jackson, His Career and Character, ***SHSP***, vol.25, p.110.

He realized if attacked by a superior force he would not be capable of holding it. His requests for a reserve force to be sent were not acted on, and he remained unsupported throughout the afternoon. Late in the day, shots were heard from the Federal skirmish line shortly after a patrol from the 45th New York reported a buildup of enemy troops to their front. It was just prior to 6:00 p.m.[37]

The storm broke upon the Federal right as Rebels burst from the trees screaming and yelling. Moving forward quickly, they fired heavy volleys into the unsuspecting Yankees whose arms were stacked while they busied themselves preparing their evening meal. Von Gilsa wrote in his after action report that his men "stood coolly and bravely, fired three times, and stood still after they [Confederates] had outflanked me...." The Colonel must have been referring to the Pennsylvania boys or the 54th New York because his two regiments along the road seemed to break and run without firing a shot. The Confederates advanced parallel to the road, allowed the Rebels to slam into the Federal units facing the thoroughfare from the flank. A few of these men formed up behind the regiments facing the attack and tried to lend a hand. Francis Stofflet of the 153rd Pennsylvania recorded the experience in his diary. "I fired into the thicket, others did likewise, reloaded and fired again," he noted. Stofflet however, did not stay in position long. General Doles ordered the 21st Georgia to advance toward the Union left and turn the Federal flank. This the Georgians did in splendid fashion driving the New Yorkers from their position, sending them scurrying to the rear. The rout was on.[38]

Colonel von Gilsa had deployed his two pieces of artillery in the road. As the enemy advanced, the guns were brought into action, firing on the mass of advancing men. The gunners managed to get off a number of shots, but the tide could not be checked. Further resistance would only result in capture or death. Working feverously, the crews desperately tried to limber up their weapons and depart. Realizing the guns were preparing to leave, the Confederates took aim at the horses. All the animals were shot down, and the Southerners claimed their prize. A testament to how quickly von Gilsa's brigade departed its position was its relatively light casualties. Only one hundred and thirty three of its fourteen hundred men were killed or wounded, a relatively low number for such an engagement.[39]

Colonel Robert Reily of the 75th Ohio heard the firing to his right. Reily's Buckeyes were positioned further to the east and in the rear of the regiments on the road. Quickly he barked orders instructing the men to wheel right and face the sound of the firing, but Reily had little time. Before the regiment could get into line, fleeing troops from von Gilsa brigade began running through his forming ranks. Confusion ensued and the formation of the battle line was delayed. Some of the retreating men, after running some four hundred yards, stop to join ranks with the Ohio men, but the majority of the departing men passed through the relocating regiment. Just as the Ohio soldiers got into position, the Confederates fell upon

---

[37] *OR* vol.25, pt.1, pp.941, 636; Sears, ***Chancellorsville***, p.272; Stackpole, ***Chancellorsville***, p.220.

[38] Sears, ***Chancellorsville***, p.272; *OR* vol.25, pt.1, pp.636, 966; Bigelow, ***Chancellorsville***, p.296.

[39] Bigelow, ***Chancellorsville***, p.296; *OR* vol.25, pt.1, p.182.

them. The brave Ohioans engaged two brigades of Confederates and two pieces of artillery, belching canister, for ten minutes. Captain Benjamin Morgan noted that, "after firing three rounds, men falling fast, and heavily pressed by overwhelming numbers, the order was given by Colonel Reily to about-face…" As the regiment worked hard to hold its positions and perform a fighting retreat, Colonel Reily was hit and killed.[40]

Further to the east, the Second Brigade was deployed fronting the road. Colonel John C. Lee, commander of the 55th Ohio, hearing the fire, leapt aboard his horse and rode to find his division commander, Brigadier General Charles Devens. Lee found Devens sitting on his horse near the Talley House. The general seemed unsure as to what should be done. With his corps commander two miles away, there was no one to help him. Lee requested permission to change his units facing to the right. "Not yet," replied Devens. Lee did not plead his case. He turned and immediately rode back to his regiment. When he arrived, he discovered the unit being devastated by fire. The incoming rounds were parallel to the road, slamming the right end of his line. From their current position, the Ohio boys could not return it. Again, Lee rode to Devens requesting a change of position. Once again, with the tempest developing around him, Devens dismissed Lee with a wave of his hand. Lee would not return to his command after his second dismissal, as his horse received a wound. The frightened animal bolted and nearly carried the colonel into the onrushing Confederates. After regaining control Lee managed to get the animal headed toward the rear.[41]

The 55th, along with the 25th and 107th Ohio and the 17th Connecticut formed a line and tried to stem the tide. The 75th Ohio, as it worked its way to the rear, took position with its fellow second brigade regiments. Once formed up, the brigade did an admirable job. Standing in the face of overwhelming odds, they engaged a Confederate force three times their size. Men began to melt away. Colonel Seraphim Meyer of the 107th was shot down. Both Colonel William Nobel and Lieutenant-Colonel Charles Walter of the 17th were wounded. No one saw what happened to Major James Stevens of the 55th. Somehow he was lost in the maelstrom and presumed missing. Finally, after taking heavy losses, the brigade was forced to fall back from its position near the Talley House. As the brigade began its withdrawal, it became apparent that it would be impossible to halt and reform the battle line owing to the huge number of fleeing soldiers from other commands. No one knew how or if the Confederates could be stopped. It seemed as if they were on their way to Washington.[42]

"…we had ridden right into the enemy…"

Shortly before Jackson turned loose his hard driving Confederates, Major Pennock Huey rode at the head of his 8th Pennsylvania Cavalry. Huey's riders,

---

[40] *OR* vol.25, pt.1, pp.637, 643; Bigelow, ***Chancellorsville***, p.296.

[41] *OR* vol.25, pt. 1, p.642; Bigelow, ***Chancellorsville***, p.296.

[42] *OR* vol.25, pt. 1, p.638; Bigelow, ***Chancellorsville***, p.297.

as part of Colonel Thomas C. Devin's Federal cavalry brigade, had been ordered forward to support General Sickles as the general's Third Corps probed what was perceived to be a Confederate retreat near Catharine Furnace. Accompanied by General Alfred Pleasonton, Huey's command and the remainder of the brigade, found Sickles right where they expected. The brigade remained for only a short time before it was sent back to Hazel Grove with instructions to "stand to horse" in order to respond rapidly if needed. Huey, however, was ordered to remain with Pleasonton and await orders for an expected assault upon the retreating Confederates. While riding to find Sickles, Pleasonton informed Huey of their mission. "The impression was," Pleasonton told Huey, "that the enemy were [sic] retreating, and that we were going to charge through their lines, open communications with General Sedgwick, and harass the rear of the enemy's column."[43]

As prisoners from the 23rd Georgia were lead to the rear, they encountered members of Huey's regiment. The horsemen had been informed of the retreating Rebel column to the south and were sympathetic to the prisoners' sacrifice which had allowed Lee's army to escape. This was more than one Rebel could stand. "You may think you have done a big thing just now, but wait until Jackson gets round on your right," the irritated soldier commented. This brought outbursts of laughter from the cavalry. According to Major Huey, no one in the regiment was aware that there was trouble on the right of the Federal Line. By the end of the day, the horsemen would discover the man's comment was no laughing matter.[44]

Huey remained with Sickles and Pleasonton for what the major noted as "a long time after the cavalry had been sent back" awaiting instructions. What took so long, Huey did not record. Suddenly, a courier arrived and made a quick report to Sickles. Huey, Pleasonton and the Third Corps commander turned their horses and started for Hazel Grove. Upon reaching their destination, a second messenger arrived. The new man, more animated than his predecessor, quickly informed General Sickles that the Eleventh Corps had been flanked and General Howard required the services of a cavalry regiment. Turning to Huey, Pleasonton ordered him to take his regiment and report to General Howard as quickly as possible. When Huey inquired as to where he might find Howard, Pleasonton, no doubt making an educated guess, responded "near the Old Wilderness Church." Huey quickly turned his horse and rode off to find his boys. It was 6:30.[45]

When Huey's regiment arrived back at Hazel Grove, boredom quickly set in. Lieutenant Andrew B. Wells, in order to conquer the monotony, suggested a rousing game of cards. After rounding up Major Peter Keenan, Lieutenant J. Haseltine Haddock and Captain William A. Daily, Wells flipped over a hardtack box, covered it with a blanket, and under the shade of a nearby tree, started

---

[43] Huey, Pennock, *A True History of The Charge of the 8th Pennsylvania Cavalry at Chancellorsville*, p.13.

[44] Collins, John L., When Stonewall Jackson Turned our Right, *Battles & Leaders of the Civil War* (hereafter *B&L*), vol.3, p.183; Huey, *8th Pennsylvania Cavalry*, p.16.

[45] Huey, *8th Pennsylvania Cavalry*, p.14.

dealing. The four men had been at it for a little over two hours when an excited officer rode up and inquired as to who was in command. With Major Huey absent, Major Keenan, from his seated position next to Wells spoke up. "I am, what's the trouble?" he asked. "General Howard wants a cavalry regiment," the man replied. Then, as quickly as he arrived, the courier spurred his horse around and departed. If Keenan was perplexed regarding what to do, his concern evaporated when Major Huey arrived and ordered the men to mount up. "Major," Keenan sarcastically remarked, "you have spoiled a damned good game."[46]

Quickly the regiment mounted and with Major Huey at its head rode north along a side road from Hazel Grove toward the Plank Road. With Huey rode Keenan, Captain Charles Arrowsmith, who commanded the first squadron and Lieutenant J. Edward Carpenter, in charge of the second company. Lieutenant Haddock, Huey's adjutant, also rode next to the Major. The road taken was so narrow and encroached upon by undergrowth that Huey's regiment was forced into columns of two, a formation that would be required until the wider and more open Plank Road was reached. In addition, the woods to both the left and right were so thick that any group of horsemen would be forced to break formation if driven from the road. Although the firing of muskets could be heard in the distance, no one within the regiment, except for possibly Major Huey, was anticipating any danger.

As the Pennsylvanians approached the Plank Road, their side road veered slightly to the west, arching in a direction which would take the horsemen onto the Plank Road at an acute angle. It was not long before the members of the 8th Pennsylvania began to wonder if the captive from the 23rd Georgia had not been lying to them. Within a short distance of the Plank Road, the head of the column met a rather large mass of men from the Eleventh Corps. Passing through Howard's retreating ranks, Huey kept his course. With the undergrowth and trees so heavy it would be difficult to identify or see any threat that might be to his front. Suddenly, rounding a turn in the road, the Pennsylvanians came face to face with a heavy Confederate battle line. "When we arrived almost at the plank road," Major Huey recorded later, "we discovered that we had ridden right into the enemy, the plank road in our front being occupied by them in great force, and that we were completely surrounded, the woods at that point being filled with the flankers of Jackson's column, who were thoroughly hidden from our view by the thick undergrowth." A retreat was not possible, the road being so narrow that such an order would throw the regiment back upon itself, instigating confusion and panic. Quickly Huey did the only thing he could do. "It was here that I gave the command to 'draw sabre and charge…'"[47]

Sabers were extracted and raised aloft as spurs were put to horses. The Pennsylvanians bolted forward toward the advancing Confederates. The Rebels, shocked to see horsemen at their front, wavered slightly and paused. Huey led his galloping horses into the mass of Southerners showing no mercy to their cries as his men slashed left and right with their sabers and trampled Rebel soldiers under

---

[46] Wittenburg, Eric J., *The Union Cavalry Comes of Age*, p.163.

[47] Collins, Turned our Right, *B&L*, vol.3, p.183; Huey, *8th Pennsylvania Cavalry*, p.17.

their horses' hooves. Huey recorded the melee years later as if it had occurred only minutes before.

> "The scene at this point was one which can never be effaced from the memory of those present. The order to charge, followed by its instant execution, had such an overwhelming and paralyzing effect upon the enemy that for the space of a few seconds those nearest to us seemed utterly to lose the power of motion. Many throwing down their arms, raising their hands, and pleading for mercy and surrender, they doubtless thinking they had unawares [sic] run into the main part of the Union army. But in such a moment mercy shuns the path of war. We, deaf to their cries, dashed madly through and over them, trampling them under our horses' feet, and using our sabres right and left on all within our reach. Surrounded and cut off, every man of us, thinking it was his last minute on earth, resolved to sell his life as dearly as possible. Arriving at the plank road, we found it filled with men unable to retreat or escape, the road behind being so clearly packed with their comrades. Scores were trampled to death beneath our horses' feet as we went plunging and dashing over them. It was not until we had faced to the left on the plank road that the head of our column received any check. Although the flank of the regiment was suffering severely from the enemy, who were so close as to be able to use their bayonets with terrible effect on our men and horses as they came dashing past them, the charge on the plank road had the fortunate effect of opening a possible means of retreat for our men."[48]

The charge was directed at an angle that took the Confederate line in a somewhat perpendicular direction to its advance. The riders dispersed, with the bulk of the unit looping around to hit the front of the enemy's line while two groups assaulted its rear. According to Huey, the charge of the 8th Cavalry "completely" checked the Rebel advance. While the force of the impact may have halted Jackson's line, his opinion would be shown to be pure fantasy. The shock of mounted troops slowed the Confederates but it did not stop them in their tracks. For about 100 yards Huey's riders cut their way through Jackson's front, before they broke out the rear of the first battle line. When they exited the rear of the line, a rude surprise awaited them. Jackson's second battle line, with time to prepare, had leveled their weapons. Hundreds of muskets exploded in the faces of the charging Keystone States. The volley decimated what remained of any organization Huey's column had managed to maintain. Chaos ensued as the Confederate line erupted, firing into the mounted men at close range. As Confederate bullets began to fly, Peter Keenan realized the Rebel battle line was too deep to penetrate. Keenan was a large stout man, and,

---

[48] Huey, *8th Pennsylvania Cavalry*, p.18-19.

flashing his saber, he cut left and right, wildly defending himself in hand to hand combat with any of the hated Rebels he could reach. A quick scan of the front showed the line to be thinner to the right, so Keenan quickly ordered his battalion in that direction. As the words "to the right" left his mouth the initial volley exploded striking him down with multiple hits. Keenan, riding next to Huey, fell "against me [Huey]… lighting on the ground under my horse." Huey, miraculously managed to avoid being struck by rounds from the initial volley. Lieutenant Carpenter saw Keenan go down. "He was actually among the bayonets of the enemy, in their line of battle, which was badly thrown out of order by our charge," Carpenter recorded. "He fell forward, pitching headlong in the direction of the enemy, and in the direction in which his horse was moving." Keenan's body would be found a few days later were he had fallen, pierced by thirteen bullets. The same volley which struck down Keenan also killed Adjutant Haddock and Captain Arrowsmith. "Captain Arrowsmith," Carpenter noted, "rode a bay horse, and fell with his horse, both horse and rider striking down together." At the instant Carpenter saw Arrowsmith fall, his horse was hit in the chest cutting the breast strap and causing the steed to rear. Men and horses went down in bunches. Major Huey struggled mightily to extricate his command from the deadly situation. By the time he was able to pull what was left of his command back toward Chancellorsville, he had taken thirty men as casualties and lost eighty horses.[49]

Captain William A. Corrie rode toward the rear of the column with Huey's second squadron. As they approached the Plank Road, Corrie observed the first squad break into a trot and a gap of about twenty-five yards developed between the two detachments. He soon heard the command "draw sabers" and observed the men ahead of him draw their blades. Soon the second squadron was following the example and Corrie watch as his group drew their weapons and received orders to move forward at the trot. Rounding a bend in the road, he came upon a sight which he would never forget. Before his squadron was the remnants of the beleaguered first, cutting and slashing their way through what seemed to be the entire Rebel army. Quickly Corrie charged forward with his command. "After charging over the dead men and horses of the first squadron we charged into Jackson's column, and, as luck would have it, found them with empty guns – thanks to our poor comrades ahead. The enemy was as thick as bees, and we appeared to be among thousands of them in an instant." Lieutenant Wells, who had previously spent time at the infamous Libby Prison, had no intention of going back. Slashing left and right at anyone wearing an enemy uniform, he heard some Rebels yell "I surrender," but the lieutenant took no time to take any prisoners for fear of being made one himself. As Jackson's masses surged forward, Corrie and the reminder of the second squadron became cut off from the Plank Road, making an obvious route of retreat unavailable to them. Circumstances forced the group to turn northeast and cut their way through the heavy trees and undergrowth toward the crossroads at Chancellorsville.[50]

[49] *Ibid*, pp.19-20; **OR** vol.25, pt.1, pp.784-785; Wittenburg, **The Union Cavalry**, p.164; Bigelow, **Chancellorsville**, p.297.

[50] Wittenburg, **The Union Cavalry**, p.165; Huey, **8th Pennsylvania Cavalry**, pp.19-20.

Trooper John L. Collins had a much different opinion than Huey regarding the initial contact with the Confederates. "We struck it as a wave strikes a stately ship," he wrote of hitting Jackson's line, "the ship is staggered, maybe thrown on her beam ends, but the wave is dashed into spray, and the ship sails on as before." Centered in the pandemonium, Collins reined his horse into a full gallop turn. As the steed began to bank, it was hit and dropped. Collins pitched over the falling horse's neck and landed in a dusty heap alongside the road. Struggling to his feet he quickly determined he was unhurt. All around were Confederates, working hard to get back into line after the impact. In the other direction were the departing horses of his regiment. Gathering his wits and realizing where he was, survival instincts took over as his concern now became escaping with his life. Running toward the woods on the right of the Plank Road, Collins passed the Rebel line just as it fired a volley at the backs of the retreating cavalry. While the Rebels were reloading, he ran past them at top speed, trying to put some distance between his enemy and his back. As another volley exploded along the line, he dropped down behind some fallen trees escaping the hail of bullets. Once again, as the fire died, Collins jumped up and ran at fast as he could through the woods. Repeating the process, he made good his escape.[51]

In the midst of his retreating Eleventh Corps rode General Howard. Collins, now retreating with the mass, reported seeing him astride his horse attempting to rally the members of his shattered command. The general had been severely wounded at the battle of Seven Pines. The result was the amputation of his right arm. Under the stump of his arm was a stand of colors which had been abandoned by its unit. Very few of the fleeing soldiers paid any attention to him. With a tear in his eye, Howard tried desperately to slow the men. The scene moved Collins. "I could not go past the general," he wrote, "he seemed worthy to stand by. I hooked up my saber and fell into the little line that had gathered about him." Howard's little band fired off a few rounds after waiting for the approaching Rebels to come into range. Soon, retreating soldiers filled the space between the advancing battle line and the rallied men. Seeing the troops moving toward him, Howard ordered the meager line to act as a barrier to keep the fleeing men from passing, forcing them into line. For a few moments, the thin line of rallied men and officers kept the mass of retreating men back, as other officers reinforced it with sabers drawn. However, the crowd of men who'd had enough was too great, and the barricade finally gave way, sweeping the brave souls that manned it toward the rear, carrying General Howard and his staff with it. "Pharaoh and his chariots could have held back the walls of the Red Sea as easily as those officers could resist the retreat," Collins wrote later. At this point there was nothing left to do but order a general retreat, which Howard did with the intent of rallying what was left of the corps in the woods near Chancellorsville.[52]

---

[51] Collins, Turned our Right, *B&L*, vol.3, p.183.

[52] Collins, Turned our Right, *B&L*, vol.3, p.184; Howard, Oliver O., The Eleventh Corps at Chancellorsville, *B&L*, vol.3, pp.200-201.

The sheer volume of Eleventh Corps soldiers flooding rearward was not lost on their commander.

> "I could see numbers of our men... not the few stragglers that always fly like chaff at the first breeze, but scores of them... rushing into the opening, some with arms and some without, running or falling before they got behind the cover of Devens's reserves, and before General Schurz's waiting masses could deploy or charge. ...the masses of the right brigade struck the second line... and, more quickly then it could be told, with all the fury of the wildest hailstorm, everything, every sort of organization that lay in the path of the mad current of panic-stricken men, had to give way and be broken into fragments."[53]

Nine years later, Howard would admit his mind-set at that horrible moment. "I felt... I wanted to die. It was the only time I ever weakened that way in my life, before or since," he recalled, "but that night I did all in my power to remedy the mistake, and I sought death everywhere I could find in excuse to go on the field."[54]

Jackson had done it once again. He had performed the miracle Lee needed. After a ten-hour march across the front of the enemy, he had launched one of the most successful surprise assaults in the history of warfare. By the time the Confederate assault lost steam, it had been rolling forward for about two hours, pushing the Federals approximately two miles back toward Chancellorsville. As the battle progressed Jackson made many trips to the battlefront, imploring his men to, "Press on, press on!" His eyes were on fire with the urgency of battle, but he never failed to provide thanks to the Almighty for the great success his corps was experiencing. On numerous occasions during the advance, he would come across men from his command that had been shot down and killed. After reining Little Sorrel to a stop, he would lift his arms to the heavens and pray for their departed souls and bless their courage. "I have never seen him so well pleased with the progress and results of a fight," wrote an aide. As the attack began to lose momentum, it was approaching 8:00 p.m. A full moon, made red as its light was filtered by battlefield smoke, was rising, its color symbolic of the bloody work completed and the work yet to be done. Jackson would not be fully satisfied until Joe Hooker's Army of the Potomac was destroyed or captured. If he could drive on to the river, he could cut the Union army off from their only escape route. Lane and McGowan's brigades had not seen action. They were still in the road behind the shattered line. If they could be placed in line and pressed forward the victory achieved late that afternoon could be made complete.[55]

---

[53] Howard, The Eleventh Corps at Chancellorsville, **B&L**, vol.3, p.198.

[54] Furgurson, Ernest B., ***Chancellorsville 1863: The Souls of the Brave***, p.181.

[55] Freeman. ***Lee's Lieutenants***, vol.2, pp.560-561.

"Press on to the United States Ford."

Brigadier General James H. Lane led the vanguard of A. P. Hill's division. Lane's brigade of North Carolinians was tramping as quickly as possible down the Plank Road toward the sound of the fighting. As the Tar Heels were passing Dowdall's Tavern, Captain Moorman wheeled a rifled Parrott and two Napoleon guns off the road and into an area a half-mile east of the tavern. Moorman unlimbered his guns and began a long range duel with a Union artillery battery containing six guns at a range of 1,200 yards. Unfortunately for the captain of artillery, he was outgunned. Before long, the road, which Lane's boys were marching on, was raked with a heavy fire. "I ordered my command to lie down on the side of the road," Lane later recalled. The Yankee guns were incredibly accurate and the incoming rounds sent the Confederates on the road scattering in all directions, running for the cover of the nearby trees. The fire was appalling. Lieutenant Octavius Wiggins of Company D, 37th North Carolina, called it "the most unmerciful artillery fire I was ever under during the entire war." Wiggins spent most of the barrage laying face down on the ground.[56]

Shortly after the artillery had opened up, Major William H. Palmer of A. P. Hill's staff rode up to where Lane's men were seeking shelter and wanted to know why the men were not advancing. Lane informed Palmer, who was Hill's acting assistant adjutant general, that he was unwilling to form his men into line of battle "in the dark, under such a fire and in such a woods." An irritated Lane informed Palmer that the Confederate guns were drawing so much fire and it was not safe to use the road. He suggested that if Hill would order the guns east of the tavern to stop firing then the Federal guns might stop as well. Palmer contacted Hill with the request and the division commander ordered the guns to cease-fire. After a short period, the Federal guns stopped as well. As the barrage ended, Lane's brigade began emerging from the woods as Hill ordered the Carolinians to "push forward vigorously."[57]

A few of Lane's men found time to look over the abandoned Federal encampments. Lieutenant Wiggins, who would be wounded before the battle subsided, took the opportunity to scour the abandon camps of Howard's corps. "Fires were burning in every direction over which were pots filled with fresh beef," Wiggins wrote. "The Yankees were cooking supper for Jackson's men," he continued in jest, "and there is where Lane's men had the advantage of the line of battle. It was an easy thing to slip out of ranks and charge these pots and many was the old "reb" who brought his supper from the bottom of them on the point of his bayonet." Company I's Sergeant John Tally described the appearance of the deserted fires. "They left nearly everything on the battlefield, Knapsacks, havre sacks. Cantines [sic], Overcoats, Blankets, beef just in the act of being skinned. And pickled also. Crackers – in fact Everything that belongs to the army ... guns

---

[56] Robertson, *Stonewall Jackson*, pp.724-725; *OR* vol.25, pt.1, p.999; Moorman, Narrative of Events, *SHSP*, vol.30, p.112.

[57] Robertson, *Stonewall Jackson*, pp.724-725; Robertson, James I., *General A. P. Hill: The Story of a Confederate Warrior*, p.185; Moorman, Narrative of Events, *SHSP*, vol.30, p.112.

was more plenty than Sticks … [they] left their coffee pots on the fire making coffee but they never came back to get it. I think there must have been thousands of gallons of coffee making."[58]

Lane gathered his command, got it back on the road and finished his march to the position chosen for his push forward. It was dark when Hill ordered Lane to deploy his regiments in line of battle across the Plank Road. As he arrayed his soldiers, Lane realized that he was to make a nighttime attack. The four-hundred or so men of the 33rd North Carolina were pushed forward to form a skirmish line about five to six-hundred yards in front of the main battle line. The remaining four regiments of the brigade were arrayed with the 28th on the left and the 18th placed between it and the Plank Road. On the extreme right was the 7th with the 37th positioned between it and the road.[59]

To Lane's front were the woods of The Wilderness. Made up of large oaks with scant undergrowth, there were numerous thickets of smaller oaks and pine scattered about. One of these dense thickets was positioned to the left of the turnpike in front of the 18th and 28th. Lane made sure that all his officers understood that the brigade was in position on the front line and in the gathering darkness they would have to be vigilant. He warned them to "watch closely the front" expressing great concern over another cavalry charge.[60]

To support the coming advance, Major Robert F. Beckham, commander of the Horse Artillery, planned to leave Captain Moorman's guns forward with the forming battle line. Moorman unlimbered them between Lane's deployed regiments and the skirmish line fifty yards in front of the battle line near the Plank Road. Moorman's guns had not been fired, other than the short dual with the Federal battery back at Dowdall's Tavern, and were in better shape than the rest of his command. Beckham ordered the remainder of his guns, which had been engaged during the initial assault, to the rear. A few moments later, Colonel Stapleton Crutchfield, commander of the Second Corps Artillery Reserve arrived on the scene. He rode to Moorman's guns and reined his horse to a halt. "Captain, you can limber up and mount your men," he said. "As soon as my guns arrive, which I have ordered in, you can retire and join your command." Crutchfield's guns were bigger and had greater range. Moorman turned to his men and at once began limbering up his guns, preparing them to be taken to the rear to unite with Beckham.[61]

---

[58] Hardy, Michael C., *The Thirty-seventh North Carolina Troops*, p.129; Jordon, Weymouth T., *North Carolina Troops 1861-1865 A Roster* (hereafter *NCT*), vol.IX, pp.524, 950.

[59] Robertson, *Stonewall Jackson*, p.725; *OR* 25, pt.1, p.915; Lane, James H., History of Lane's North Carolina Brigade, *SHSP*, vol.8, pp.489-490.

[60] Lane, North Carolina Brigade, *SHPS*, vol.8, p.494.

[61] *OR* vol.25, pt.1, p.1050; Moorman, Narrative of Events, *SHSP*, vol.30, p.113. Moorman's account must be scrutinized due to its lack of mentioning Major Beckham as being present or ordering him forward.

It was now approaching 9:00 p.m. Jackson was slowly watching his chance to achieve total victory slip away. Riding forward along the Plank Road, he approached the right of the 18th North Carolina. He heard General Lane's voice in the darkness calling for A. P. Hill. Jackson rode up and asked what he wanted with General Hill. "My Carolinians are in line. I am looking for General Hill to ascertain if I should begin the advance," he said. "Push right ahead, Lane," Jackson said, pointing in the direction of the Union lines. Then, prompting Little Sorrel, the general slowly moved out to the east along the Turnpike.[62]

Jackson had not gone far when A. P. Hill rode up with his staff. Hill, clad only in shirtsleeves, reined his horse to a stop next to his commander.

"How long before you will be ready to advance?" inquired Jackson.

"In a few minutes," responded Hill, "as soon as I can finish relieving General Rodes."

"Do you know the road from Chancellorsville to the United States Ford?"

Hill thought for a moment, "I have not traveled over it for many years, he said."

Jackson's plan for continuing the battle had not changed. Hill's men would drive toward the fords, pushing through the gap between the Union force and the river. Doing so would cut Hooker off from the fords he used to get into position and effectively trap his army south of the waterway. But his plan could not come to fruition if Hill could not find the road to the river in the darkness. Jackson turned to his young engineering officer Captain Boswell. Boswell, who had joined Jackson's staff in February 1862, had knowledge of the roads and would make a good guide for Hill. "Captain Boswell report to General Hill," Jackson instructed. Turning back to Hill, Jackson said to him sternly, "General Hill, when you reach Chancellorsville, allow nothing to stop you! Press on to the United States Ford!" With that Jackson rode out in advance of Hill eastward, down the Plank Road.[63]

A number of aides and staff members accompanied Jackson as he moved beyond Lane's line. At hand were signal officer Captain Richard Eggleston Wilbourn and Privates William T. Wynn and William E. Cunliffe of the Signal Corps. Jackson's chief of couriers Captain William Fitzhugh Randolph, a member of the 39th Battalion Virginia Cavalry, was nearby. Privates Joshua O. Johns and Lloyd T. Smith, also of the 39th, were with Randolph to provide the service. Jackson's brother-in-law Lieutenant Joseph G. Morrison rounded out the staff members close at hand. Captain Wilbourn believed the whole party contained about a dozen horsemen. Morrison believed there were eight.[64]

The final member of Jackson's party arrived a short time earlier. Private Kyle, after leaving Stuart's cavalcade near Ely's Ford, headed southwest. Shortly thereafter he turned back to the southeast and exited the woods near the intersection

---

[62] Robertson, *Stonewall Jackson*, p.726.

[63] *Ibid*; Mitchell, Adele, Jackson's Engineer, *Civil War Times Illustrated* (hereafter *CWTI*), vol.7, no.3, p.12; McGuire, Dr. Hunter, Death of Stonewall Jackson, *SHSP*, vol.14, p.159.

[64] Kyle, David J., Jackson's Guide when Shot, *CV*, vol.4, p.308; Krick, *Smoothbore*, p.9.

of the Plank Road and the Old Turnpike. There, near the Wilderness Church the young man located a group of Confederate officers. When Kyle inquired as to where he might find Jackson, the officers acted confused. Finally they pointed him to the west. Kyle had gone a short distance when he came upon another group who had better information. Heading back to the east, he bumped into Melzi Chancellor. Chancellor lived in the vicinity and knew where Jackson was. Kyle was moving in the right direction. As he approached, the front a group of horsemen exited the woods onto the road and turn toward the west. Rushing forward, Kyle inquired as to where Jackson was. "There he is to the right in front," he was told.[65]

Riding up to Jackson and saluting, Kyle handed him the envelope. The General opened it and read its contents. As Jackson scanned the missive, Kyle looked around the scene. Remnants of the 8th Pennsylvania's cavalry charge could be seen in heaps of dead horses. Finishing the note, Jackson looked up at Kyle. "Do you know all this country?" Jackson asked tersely. Kyle answered in the affirmative. "Keep along with me," the General responded as he turned his horse to the east.[66]

Now, as Jackson moved out in front of Hill down the Orange Turnpike, Private Kyle was with his party. Seeing the value of a young man who spent most of his youth wandering around the woods near Chancellorsville, Jackson commandeered his services and began to utilize him as a guide. In the darkness, he would be a necessity. Kyle was nearby when Jackson approached the rear of the 18th North Carolina.

General Hill's party, including Captain Boswell, was not intermixed with Jackson's. As Jackson started east down the pike, Hill kept his party well to the rear. There were ten riders in the group. Major Palmer was with the party, as well as Captain Conway Robinson Howard, Hill's engineering officer. Hill had two aide-de-camps with him, Captain Benjamin Watkins Leigh and Lieutenant Murray Forbes Taylor. James Fitzgerald Forbes was along as a volunteer aide. The responsibility for couriering messages fell to Sergeant George W. Tucker, Hill's chief courier. Tucker had two couriers present, Privates Richard J. Muse and Eugene L. Saunders. The group did not follow Jackson's party down the road. Hill instead kept his group back, following military etiquette, allowing Jackson to put a little distance between the two groups which allowed the Second Corps commander to disappear into the gathering darkness.[67]

Jackson Reconnoiters the Front

Jackson, moving down the Plank Road to the east, noticed a pair of minor roads departing the left side of the main road. The two side roads were around two-hundred yards apart and Jackson veered of the north side of the road, pulling his horse to a stop near the right rear of the deployed 18th North Carolina. The General inquired of Kyle where the side roads led. The road furthest to the west was the Mountain Road. Kyle informed Jackson that after the Mountain Road left the Plank

---

[65] Kyle, Jackson's Guide when Shot, *CV*, vol.4, p.308.

[66] *Ibid.*

[67] Krick, *Smoothbore*, p.8.

Road, it quickly turned and ran parallel to the main thoroughfare about sixty yards to the north. The Mountain Road was sometimes used when spring rains turned the main road to a quagmire. The second road was called the Bullock Road, which ran, northeast about a mile to his sister Catharine's home. Kyle's siblings home, where he was currently a resident, was a mile or so north of Chancellorsville. One hundred yards down the Bullock Road, the Mountain Road crossed it running east and west.[68]

Now, sitting near the right of the 18th, Jackson had a decision to make. He wanted to determine what the enemy was up to in the darkness, and he had some options to choose from. He could reconnoiter down the Plank Road to get close to the Federals or he could take the alternate path of the Mountain Road. During the fighting, the main road had been a favorite target of the enemy's artillery and at any moment it could become a very hot place to be. The Mountain Road however was concealed and possibly unknown to Yankee guns. Determining the Mountain Road was his best chance at discovering what the enemy was doing with the least risk, he would reconnoiter along its path. Perhaps because he was leery of Kyle's youth or his knowledge of the area, Jackson's party, with the General placing Kyle in the lead, headed down the Bullock Road and turned east onto the Mountain Road.

After Jackson's party had traveled 200 yards, and Jackson was satisfied that the road was safe, he rode up next to Kyle and the two men moved forward slowly. Approaching the rear of the 33rd North Carolina's skirmish line, Jackson halted his assemblage. The sounds of men working in the darkness could be heard. Axes striking trees and logs were the sounds of breastworks being quickly erected. The voices of officers could be heard shouting orders to the workers. The Federals were digging in. Kyle thought the enemy soldiers were two to three hundred yards off, and their officers were trying to get their men into line in the darkness. After listening for a few minutes, Jackson turned Little Sorrel around and started back toward the Confederate line. Kyle recorded later that on the return trip he followed Jackson very closely until "we got in some fifty or seventy-five yards of where Gen. Jackson started to turn out of the road we were in." At that point, Kyle reined in his horse a little and four or five men got between the young private and Jackson.[69]

Meanwhile, A. P. Hill had lost his commander in the shadow of the moonlit night, and was unaware Jackson had turned off the Plank Road. Moving forward past the location where Jackson left the main road, Hill and his party ventured past Captain Moorman's guns and advanced out in front of the right flank of the 18th North Carolina. The 18th was a veteran regiment, but darkness, a nearby enemy, and the threat of another cavalry charge had made their ranks skittish. Hill's party congregated in the area of the Van Wert house, sixty or so yards in front of the battle line, astride or north of the road. Jackson's group on the Mountain Road was about 100 yards to the northeast of Hill's group. As Hill's party milled about near the main road, Jackson worked his way westward in the darkness. Deciding to leave the Mountain Road, Jackson turned to the left and departed the road heading south across the front of the 18th North Carolina. His party followed. Private Kyle

---

[68]   Kyle, Jackson's Guide when Shot, *CV*, vol.4, p.308; Krick, **Smoothbore**, p.10.

[69]   Kyle, David J., Jackson's Guide when Shot, *CV*, vol.4, p.308.

reported that as Jackson's horse was negotiating the bank along the edge of the road, a lone shot rang out at the far left of the battle line.[70]

Nervous Men and Twitchy Fingers

Prior to his short communication with Jackson, Jim Lane, on the left side of the pike, had pushed the 18th and 28th North Carolina forward a short distance to close the distance between the battle line and the skirmish line. Now he was riding to the right of the brigade to prepare it for forward movement. Upon arriving, General Lane discovered a great deal of confusion in the moonlight. The enemy, a portion of the 128th Pennsylvania, had somehow become trapped between the front of the 7th North Carolina and the back of the skirmish line. Union soldiers called out in the darkness to determine who was who. "Confederates," someone answered. "Come in, Confederates," was the Federal response. The Union troops asked whose brigade they were with. "General Lane's," was the reply. "Tell General Lane to come in," the Yankees repeated. Captain N. A. Pool of the 7th North Carolina was about ready to fire off a volley into the darkness toward the voices when a strange incident occurred.[71]

In an effort to get his bearings in the darkness, Lieutenant Colonel Levi H. Smith of the Pennsylvania regiment prepared a white flag and began wandering about communicating with whoever he bumped into as to who they were and for what side they fought. Smith, who had become separated from his unit and disoriented in the confusion at the front, walked up to the Southern lines carrying his white handkerchief attached to a stick, inquiring about the loyalty of soldiers. Now, finding himself lost between lines and confused, Smith attempted to determine if Lane's boys were friend or foe. After being informed he was in the presents of the enemy, Smith expressed a desire to return to his command. Since Smith made the point that it was not his intention to surrender, General Lane decided the utilization

---

[70] *Ibid*, Krick, **Smoothbore**, pp.8, 12-16; Robertson, **Stonewall Jackson**, p.727-728. Numerous accounts of the wounding of Jackson have been written over the years since the event. Kyle's account places Jackson's party just off the Mountain Road when the first shots were fired. This seems to be the most plausible record of the event since his retelling places him in the presence of Jackson up to and shortly after the shooting. Wilbourn's account, while very detailed after the shooting, seems to confuse the Plank Road with the Mountain Road. Wilbourn and Lieutenant Morrison who gave the most detailed accounts had not been to the location prior to that evening and it is safe to assume that they were never there during daylight hours. Kyle was a resident of Culpeper after the war, made numerous trips to the area to hunt wild game and purchase cattle. During these trips, he would have had numerous occasions to visit the area and could have authenticated his details. Since it was dark, it is plausible that both Morrison and Wilbourn did not know of the existence of the Bullock and Mountain Roads. Kyle's conversation with Jackson regarding the two roads may not have been within earshot of Wilbourn and Morrison and in the dark it seems possible that the two aides may not have realized they were off of the main road, or they may have simply forgotten. Since Kyle knew the area, he would have firsthand knowledge of the two roads. The issue is more complicated due to no second party verification of Kyle's account. Most contemporary authors have chosen to take Kyle's version of events up to and shortly after the wounding as the best account to that point.

[71] **OR** vol.25, pt.1, pp.916, 919; Lane, North Carolina Brigade, **SHSP**, vol.8, p.494.

of a white flag in this instance was improper. Lane dispatched his brother Lieutenant Oscar Lane to find A. P. Hill to help determine how to handle the situation. Smith was quite shocked that the General detained him and would not let him walk off into the darkness after his inquiry showed he was in the midst of the enemy. The incident prompted one Tar Heel to comment, "[t]he simpleton imagined that General Lane would allow him to return." Another incident occurred shortly thereafter when Lieutenant James W. Emack, with four of his men, gathered up around two hundred members of the 128th Pennsylvania. As the prisoners were lead to the rear, the jovial Carolinians confiscated muskets and swords as trophies.[72]

Company A of the 33rd North Carolina had been charged with holding the extreme right of the skirmish line. The company's commander, Captain Robert V. Saunders had recently left the line, accompanied by Lieutenant Colonel Robert V. Cowen. The two men, intent on determining what their final instructions would be, headed back toward the Plank Road to find whoever was in charge. After arriving at the road, the two were informed by a lieutenant from Company F that a Federal soldier had presented a flag of truce on the right. They started back immediately, but had only traversed half the distance when events were set in motion that would deprive the Confederate Army of its best corps commander.

Confederates were jittery up and down the line on the right of the pike. Although the moon was casting some illumination, the trees let little of it reach the ground. In the darkness it was nearly impossible to tell who was who. Shortly after the prisoners from the 128th were brought in, a Federal officer rode to within close proximity of the skirmish line's right. With Cowen and Saunders gone it became the responsibility of nineteen-year-old Sergeant Thomas A. Cowen to confront the Federal officer approaching the line. The younger Cowen advanced to face the stranger in the darkness. The visitor responded telling Cowen he was a "friend."

"To which side," Cowen asked.

"To the Union," came the response.

Cowen quickly returned to his skirmish line and ordered his men to fire in the direction of the Federal. A single shot rang out. Who fired it is not known. What is known is that fire from Company A picked up and rolled down the skirmish line and quickly involved men from neighboring companies. Soon members of the main line were firing as well, without orders to do so, directly into the backs of the men in the skirmish line. The 33rd was receiving fire from all sides. The enemy and their own men were peppering them with rounds. Lieutenant Colonel Cowen was wounded in the right arm as he and Captain Saunders worked their way back to the right. The sporadic fire rolled northward down the line toward the pike. The ground between the Confederate battle line and the skirmishers of the 33rd was no place for a living thing to be.[73]

---

[72] *OR* vol.25, pt.1, p.916; Lane, North Carolina Brigade, ***SHSP***, vol.8, pp.490, 494; Krick, ***Smoothbore*** p.16; Krick, Robert E. L., ***Staff Officers in Gray***, p.197.

[73] *OR* vol.25, pt. 1, p.916, 922; Lane, North Carolina Brigade, ***SHSP***, vol.8, p.495; Krick, ***Smoothbore***, p.17; *OR* vol.25, pt.1, p.922; The Federal officer was probably Brigadier General Joseph F. Knipe. Knipe had ridden forward not believing that the enemy was so close. He returned at a quicker pace than he departed minus his hat, which he lost in his rush to get out of the area.

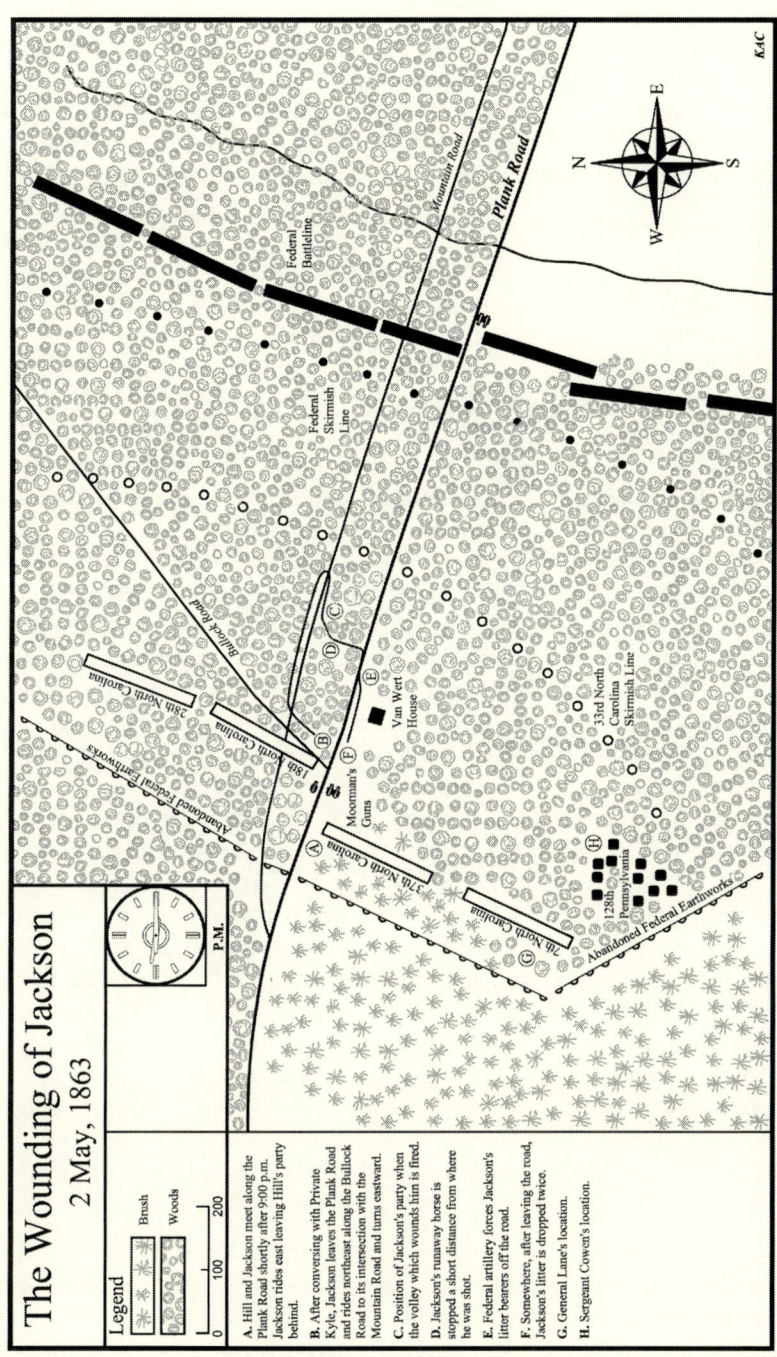

The Wonding of Jackson

Darkness and Chaos

Back near the Mountain Road, Jackson's party paused as the lone sound of the single musket discharging cut the darkness. Captain Wilbourn correctly determined that the shot came from the right, but thought it was in the rear of the line. Jackson believed it had come from the right front, and Lieutenant Morrison had no idea where it had originated. Kyle supposed it had come from the area to the right or the Van Wert house, just to the south of the Turnpike near the location of Hill's party. The effect was a tightening of nerves and a few additional shots were fired. More guns went off as the fire traveled northward along the line toward Hill and Jackson's parties. "Suddenly a large volley as if from a regiment was fired," penned Kyle. The volley came from the south side of the road, probably from the vicinity of the 37th and 7th North Carolina. A number of horses and men in Hill's party were hit. Jackson remained unscathed by the initial volley.[74]

Little Sorrel twisted away from the sounds of the fire and headed toward the 18th North Carolina's battle line. The remainder of the General's party followed, heading for the woods in an effort to hide from the fire. Wilbourn was at Jackson's side. He noted the party was approaching the Confederate line at an angle with the line of infantry off to their right.[75]

Near the Plank Road, Captain Moorman had limbered up his guns and was waiting for Colonel Crutchfield to arrive when the first shot was discharged and the fire rolled down the line. The two regiments on the right "opened one sheet of fire into the faces of my horses as they stood fronting the line," he wrote after the war. His horses reared up and with his guns limbered, the frightened animals jostled them about. As the horses thrashed about, a number of Moorman's caissons and gun carriages were damaged. Running up to the battle line, a dangerous move in the darkness, the Captain tried desperately to get the line to cease-fire. "What are you firing at?" he yelled. "Are you trying to kill all my men in front of you? There are no Yankees here." Private Thomas Yeatman recorded the incident. "Very quickly this discharge was followed by another, when the bullets rained around us, several striking the limber chest and gun-carriage." According to Moorman, an officer in their ranks instructed the men to stop shooting. Feeling he had managed to halt the firing, he turned to his guns to assess the damage.[76]

One round from the initial volley struck Lieutenant Morrison's mount. The animal went down dead. The aid fell from the steed, striking his head, briefly losing his senses. Quickly regaining his wits, Morrison also tried to arrest the gun fire, yelled at the Tarheels, "Cease fire! You are firing into your own men!" Another aide tried in vain to identify the targets as Confederate. Major John D. Berry of the 18th North Carolina heard the shouts to cease-fire. Having no idea that

---

[74] Sears, ***Chancellorsville***, p.294; Robertson, ***Stonewall Jackson***, p.728; Krick, ***Smoothbore***, p.17; Kyle, Jackson's Guide when Shot, *CV*, vol.4, p.308.

[75] Wilbourn, Richard E., Letter to General J. E. Early, ***SHSP***, vol.6, p.267.

[76] Moorman, Narrative of Events, ***SHSP***, vol.30, pp.113-114; Moore Robert H., ***Chew's Ashby, Shoemaker's Lynchburg and the Newtown Artillery***, p.75.

any friendly men were to the front of his line, and remembering General Lane's earlier warning regarding Federal cavalry, he chose to ignore the request. The perceived threat directly to his front was not Federal cavalry but A. P. Hill's party. "Who gave that order?" Berry inquired. "It's a lie! Pour it into them boys!" The battle line exploded lighting up the darkness with the muzzle flashes of hundreds of weapons. In an instant, the remnants of Jackson and Hill's parties crumbled in a hail of bullets.[77]

The horses and men of Hill's cavalcade who were not hit by the bullets scattered. Captain Boswell, who was near Hill's party, was killed instantly when two rounds hit him full in the chest, one piercing his heart. One of the balls tore through the young engineer's notebook before it entered. A third struck his leg. Boswell's body however, did not fall from his horse. The frightened animal spun, and bolted toward the enemy's works carrying the unlucky captain into the darkness. Captain Howard's horse also carried him into the Federal lines; however, unlike Boswell, he was not hit. His horse ran through the Federal lines taking the captain all the way to the clearing near Chancellorsville before the animal halted and Howard was taken captive. As Howard's horse ran through the Yankee lines, enemy soldiers who could identify him in the dark, fired at him. Federal bullets cut his reins and stirrups but he remained uninjured. Sergeant Tucker, experiencing the same events as Howard, also surviving the ride. After Tucker was capture he had the unusual experience of being interrogate by none other than Joe Hooker himself. Courier Eugene Saunders was killed. His partner, Richard Muse survived but he took two rounds in the face and his horse was killed. Captain James Forbes was severely wounded. He was born to Melzi Chancellor's home where he died later that night. Murray Forbes Taylor and Benjamin W. Leigh were not hit but their horses were not so lucky. Both steeds were killed.[78]

Major Palmer was severely wounded as well but not by a bullet. Palmer's horse was shot and during the subsequent melee the Major broke his shoulder. "My right arm was torn from the socket," he commented later, "…for some time, I lay insensible." Hill leaped from his horse and hit the ground to avoid being hit and he lay face down in the dirt. Captain Leigh, whose first thought was they were all going to die, tried to get off his horse as well, but his animal was rearing so wildly that he could not get down. Suddenly his horse rose into the air and he assumed that his steed had been shot. Whether the beast threw him or he managed to get to the ground himself he did not recall, but Leigh soon found himself on the forest floor. As he fell, he struck his head. Thinking he was wounded, he felt for blood but found none. He stayed down, low to the ground until the fire ended and then rose. Men and horses were lying all around. Some were wounded, and some were

---

[77] Robertson, *Stonewall Jackson*, pp.728-729.

[78] Sears, *Chancellorsville*, p.294; Robertson, *Stonewall Jackson*, p.728; Boswell, James K., Jackson's Boswell: The Diary of a Confederate Staff Officer, *CWTI*, vol.15, no.1, p.37; Wilbourn, Richard E., Extract from the Printed Narrative Marked and Endorsed by Captain Wilbourn, as on his Authority, *SHSP*, vol.6, p.268.

obviously dead. A rider less mount was near Leigh, and after climbing aboard, he began looking for Hill.[79]

The second volley was as lethal to Jackson's party as Hill's. The commanding general's group was about fifty yards further to the north. Wilbourn specifically remembered seeing a line of men kneeling on their right knees, only a few yards away, illuminated by the discharge of their weapons. William Cunliffe who was just a "few feet" from Jackson was killed while courier Joshua Johns was wounded. Johns' horse bolted and carried the young man into the lines of the enemy. Lloyd Smith's horse, like Morrison's during the initial volley, was killed outright. Four men, Kyle, Richard Wilbourn, Private Wynn and William Randolph all escaped unscathed. Of the five bullets that struck men in Jackson's group, one hit Cunliffe, another struck Johns, and the other three all struck the general. While Jackson seemed to be a magnet for bullets, the remainder of the party, both riders and mounts, escaped with only minor injuries. Wilbourn attributed this to the dense brush and woods between the group and the 18th North Carolina. He wrote later that he remembered hearing "General Hill calling at the top of his voice to his troops to cease fire."[80]

Jackson may or may not have heard Major Barry's command to fire. If he did, it may explain why the General raised his right hand. The act could have been a feeble effort to shield himself from the fire he knew was coming, or possibly a move to protect himself from the limbs of trees. Little Sorrel's reins were firm in his left hand when the three balls hit him. The first struck his upraised right hand in the palm, just above the base of his thumb. It passed through his gauntlet and entered his hand, shattering two of the bones. It lodged just under the skin on the back of his hand. The second ball entered the outside of Jackson's left arm just below his elbow. It passing down the length of his arm, spiraled around to the inside of his arm and exited just above the wrist, boring a hole in his left gauntlet as it departed into the darkness. The third ball caused the most severe damage and would cost Jackson an arm. It entered his upper left arm two or three inches below the shoulder. Punching a hole in the General's rubber coat, it struck the bone and shattered it.

When the rounds struck, Jackson's left arm went limp and fell to his side. The bullet damaged it so badly he lost all control over it. Little Sorrel's reins fell from the General's hand. Then, the faithful horse did something he had never done on all the battlefields Jackson had managed; he bolted. Spinning away from the barrage, the frightened animal headed for the Federal lines, carrying the wounded General with him. Wilbourn, seeing the animal heading in the wrong direction, gave chase. As he ran, Little Sorrel cut between two trees, one of which had a low hanging branch. The horse was low enough to pass under the limb, but

---

[79] Robertson, *Hill*, p.187; Leigh, Benjamin W., The Wounding of Stonewall Jackson-Extracts from a Letter, **SHSP**, vol.6, p.232; Krick, ***Smoothbore***, p.29.

[80] Wilbourn, Letter to General J. E. Early, **SHSP**, vol.6, p.267; Krick, ***Smoothbore***, p.30. Wilbourn's thirty yards seems a bit of an under estimate since most accounts have Jackson's party about 100 yards to the front of the line.

Jackson, still upright in the saddle, was not. The branch struck him violently in the face and forced him back, laying him across the rear of the horse. The blow almost knocked him from the saddle and his hat, ripped from his head, fell to the ground and was lost. The general managed to regain his seat on the terrified horse, and using his broken and bleeding right hand managed to grab the bridle. Pulling the bit tight, Jackson tried to get Little Sorrel pointed in a direction that would not take him into the enemy's works. By this time, he was so weak from loss of blood and shock that if Captain Wilbourn had not managed to grasp the horse's reins and check the animal Jackson would have most likely fallen from the saddle.[81]

After the gunfire died, Hill gathered himself and remounted his horse. Miraculously, Hill's horse had avoided being hit or was hit so slightly the steed was still capable. He quickly rode toward Lane's North Carolinians shouting, "You have shot my friends! You have destroyed my staff!" Captain Leigh rode up to Hill and together they approached the Plank Road. Shortly they came upon Lieutenant Taylor who was struggling to extricate himself from under his dead horse. The animal had pinned him to the ground as it fell. Hill dismounted and began to help the young man of nineteen get out of his predicament. As the general began to work, a courier suddenly appeared and with a shaky voice informed the group that General Jackson was laying wounded a short distance away. Hill jumped to his feet leaving Taylor partially freed. "Help yourself," Hill said, "I must go to General Jackson." As he began to leave, he turned to Taylor and informed the trapped man not to tell anyone the general had been wounded. With that, Hill turned and went in search of Jackson, Captain Leigh on his heels.[82]

With Private Wynn holding the reins of Jackson's horse, Captain Wilbourn tried to assist the wounded general. Jackson could not understand how his own troops could have fired upon him. Would they fire again if he approached the battle line once more? He continued to look in the direction of the fire, amazed that his own men could do such a thing. The round, which struck Jackson in the upper left arm, had not only broken the bone, but also torn the flesh. It seemed however, not to have damaged the artery. While the wound was bleeding steadily it was not hemorrhaging as if a main vessel had been severed. Blood was running the length of Jackson's now limp arm, pooling in his gauntlets. Wilbourn asked the general if

---

[81] Wilbourn, Extract from the Printed Narrative, *SHSP*, vol.6, p.268; Robertson, ***Stonewall Jackson***, p.729; Krick, ***Smoothbore***, p.31; McGuire, Death of Stonewall Jackson, *SHSP*, vol.14, p.157. Private Kyle presented a slightly different versions of the events immediately after the shooting. He wrote that Jackson's horse "wheeled to the right" and ran back across the Mountain Road for about twenty-five yards before the general got control of his horse. He noted that the branch which nearly unhorsed Jackson was that of an oak tree which hung low across the road. According to Kyle, Jackson brought Little Sorrel back toward the Mountain Road some ten yards before he was taken down from the frightened animal "by some officers." Kyle, David J., Jackson's Guide when Shot, *CV*, vol.4, p.308.

[82] Robertson, ***Hill***, p.187.

he could move his fingers. Jackson looked down and tried to make his digits move. Finally, giving up, he informing Wilbourn his arm was broken.[83]

"General, what can I do for you?" a concerned Wilbourn inquired.

Jackson wanted to know if his wounds were bleeding. Wilbourn dismounted and with Private Wynn still holding the horse, he began to examine the arm. Taking the limb in both hands he asked Jackson "Is it painful? Are you hurt anywhere else?" Responding in the affirmative, Jackson noted the wound to his right hand. Reaching up under Jackson coat, Wilbourn could feel the blood running down the arm. Finally, high up he felt the bump of a fractured bone. The captain came to the conclusion that he needed to remove Jackson's jacket and shirtsleeve if he was going to help him further. "Well, you had better take me down too," the general responded, in obvious pain.

Moonlight filtered through the trees as Wilbourn positioned himself for the task. Although it was now totally dark, the minimal illumination gave him enough light to work by. His position required Jackson to lean forward and to the left toward him. This placed the General's wounded arm between his torso and Wilbourn who was still recovering from a wound he had received to his left arm a year earlier. The circumstances caused both men to be cognizant of the wounded arm, making the attempt at dismounting awkward. Painfully Jackson responded, "Captain, you had better take me on the other side." Righting Jackson in the saddle, Wilbourn moved to the other side of the horse and Jackson, again, leaned forward. Catching him, Wilbourn held him up but the General was too weak to get his feet out of the stirrups. Wynn, who by this time had dismounted as well, worked feverishly to get Jackson's boots free. Finally the two men managed to extricate the general's feet and got him to the ground. In doing so Wynn had to let go of Little Sorrel's reins. The frightened horse turned and headed off into the darkness.[84]

Suddenly Wilbourn realized the party was not alone. In the woods to his left he noticed a lone figure of a man astride a horse. His dress was dark, signifying a Federal officer of some kind. The figure was motionless and still, appearing to watch the scene before him. If it was a Union soldier, how could he have make it past the skirmish line? The Captain did not have time to depart from his current task of caring for Jackson. Indicating the direction the crippling volley had been fired from, Wilbourn instructed the shadowy figure to "ride up there and see what troops those were." Without a word, the lone rider departed in the direction indicated. The rider was never seen or heard from again.

---

[83] Robertson, ***Stonewall Jackson***, p.729; Wilbourn, Extract from the Printed Narrative, ***SHSP***, vol.6, p.269. Robertson cites a letter from Captain Wilbourn to Robert L. Dabney written on 12 December, 1863.

[84] Robertson, ***Stonewall Jackson***, pp.729-730. Thomas Yeatman noted Second Sergeant John W. Webb, of Moorman's Battery came to be in possession of Little Sorrel. Webb kept the horse and rode him for a few days until Jeb Stuart, after becoming aware the horse was in possession of the battery, ordered Moorman to turn the horse over. Webb did so, but managed to keep the yellow nose band off the bridle. Moore, ***Chew's Ashby, Shoemaker's Lynchburg and the Newtown Artillery***, pp.75-76.

The mystery rider gone, the two men carried Jackson toward the Plank Road. Placing him under a small tree, Wilbourn sat, propping the general's head up in his lap. Private Wynn was sent to obtain help, preferably Jackson's personal surgeon, Dr. Hunter McGuire and an ambulance. Before he departed, the private was instructed not to inform anyone of the general's wounding. Once Wynn was gone, Wilbourn set about making Jackson as comfortable as possible and to do a more thorough examination of the wounds. He positioned himself in order to elevate Jackson's head slightly, and then began removing Jackson's personal affects, which consisted of his haversack, field glasses, two spiritual pamphlets, a few envelopes, and some papers. Wilbourn took the articles and kept them in his position for safekeeping. Next, he took out his pen-knife and carefully cut the sleeve of Jackson's raincoat, and then through the general's dress coat which covered two layers of shirtsleeves. Jackson was wearing four layers of clothing on a day when two or at the most three would have been enough to keep him warm.[85]

As Wilbourn cut the sleeves of Jackson's garments, the noise of riders on the Plank Road caught his attention. Looking in the direction of the disturbance, Wilbourn noticed A. P. Hill astride his horse. With him was Captain Leigh. Wilbourn called to Hill and "Little Powell" quickly dismounted. In an instant he was at his commander's side. Hill and Jackson had not seen eye to eye on a number of occasions, including a instance when Jackson had placed Hill under arrest. A softening of emotions had taken place recently, but now all the animosity which was so prominent between two clashing personalities was swept away. "I have been trying to make them cease firing," he said as he knelt next to Jackson. After telling Jackson he was sorry to see him wounded, Hill expressed his hope that the general was not seriously wounded. "My arm is broken," replied Jackson.

"Is it painful?" Hill inquired.

"Very painful," answered Jackson.

"Are you hurt anywhere else?"

"Yes, a slight wound in the right hand," added Jackson.[86]

Hill slowly pulled Jackson's gauntlets off. Both gloves were soaked or full of blood. Then Hill removed the general's saber and belt. After the remaining accoutrements were detached Hill held Jackson's shattered arm up, holding the elbow still as Wilbourn continued to cut away the shirt sleeves. As if asking permission, the captain informed Jackson that he would have to cut away all the sleeves to fully expose his wounded limb. "That is right, cut away everything," Jackson agreed. Once the arm was exposed Wilbourn noted the wound "had apparently ceased bleeding and we indulged the hope that the artery was not cut." Hill offered Jackson some whiskey, which Jackson refused. Wilbourn pushed the issue saying the beverage would help to revive him for the trip rearward.

---

[85] *Ibid*, p.730; Wilbourn, Extract from the Printed Narrative, **SHSP**, vol.6, p.269. There has been speculation over the years as to who the lone rider noticed by Wilbourn was. His identity remains a mystery.

[86] Krick, ***Smoothbore***, p.33; Robertson, ***Stonewall Jackson***, p.731; Wilbourn, Extract from the Printed Narrative, **SHSP**, vol.6, p.271.

Reluctantly Jackson accepted and drank the liquid which seemed to somewhat invigorate him. Hill assisted Wilbourn in tying crude bandages above and below the wound, and the useless limb was put in a sling for support. With the first aid work complete, Hill sat down under the tree and cradled Jackson's head and shoulders in his lap.[87]

While the bandages were being applied two Yankee soldiers strolled out of the underbrush and into the midst of the group. Hill calmly ordered them arrested. Once the wayward Federals where detained, Hill ordered Captain Leigh to go to the rear and search for medical help and an ambulance to bear Jackson out of danger. The appearance of the two enemy soldiers was proof enough that the area was not safe. "General Hill directed me to go for a surgeon and an ambulance for the General, and I hastened off for the purpose," Leigh recalled.[88]

Captain Leigh had not gone far when he met General Pender's brigade marching up the Plank Road. Finding General Pender near his brigade, Leigh inquired as to the location of a surgeon and an ambulance. He surly informed Pender that Jackson had been wounded and General Hill had sent him on a mission to find assistance and transport for Jackson. Pender told Leigh that assistant surgeon, Dr. Richard S. Barr was nearby. "He [Pender] called for Dr. Barr and that gentleman speedily appeared," wrote Leigh. The captain inquired as to the location of an ambulance. Barr informed him that there was not an ambulance "within a mile of the place," but that he did have a litter. Leigh didn't have time to wait; a litter would have to do. After procuring the litter and some men to act as bearers, Leigh and Dr. Barr began the return trip to the injured general.[89]

Captain Smith's Charter

Captain James P. Smith had made his bed the previous evening on the ground near his horse. Using his saddle as a pillow and his saddle blanket to keep him warm, Stonewall Jackson's aide-de-camp dosed through the early morning hours. The cool morning air moving through the trees stirred the slumbering captain awake. Rolling over and opening his eyes, he noticed a small fire flickering up the slope. His curiosity peaked; Smith sat up to get a better look. Two figures looked to be seated next to the fire warming their hands in an effort to shake off the morning cold. Rubbing his eyes to bring things into focus, he noticed the two men were the supreme chieftains of the army. Lee and Jackson huddled next to the small campfire sitting on two old hardtack boxes. The men who would direct the coming battle were finalizing their plans while the men who would deal in the bloody work during the coming day slept. No record of the discussion was made. What was discussed is left to conjecture. The conversation probably centered on

---

[87] Krick, *Smoothbore*, p.34; Wilbourn, Extract from the Printed Narrative, *SHSP*, vol.6, pp.269, 272-273; Robertson, *Stonewall Jackson*, p.731. Jackson's gloves were eventually given to his widow Anna.

[88] Leigh, The Wounding of Stonewall, *SHSP*, vol.6, p.232; Robertson, *Stonewall Jackson*, p.731.

[89] Leigh, The Wounding of Stonewall, *SHSP*, vol.6, p.232.

the movement against Hooker's right. After watching the two commanders for a moment, Smith rolled over, pulled his blanket around him to battle the cold and went back to sleep.

Smith slept the remainder of the night uninterrupted by the war. He was awoken by a rude kick to this foot and a voice saying "Get up Smith, the general wants you!" Startled to consciousness, he sat up. The sun was already above the horizon and beams of light filtered their way through the trees to the ground. The sound of clanking canteens and tramping feet told him the army was already on the move. Gathering his things and saddling his horse, he was soon mounted and off in search of Jackson. He found his general sitting on Little Sorrel just off the road watching the long column of Southern soldiers tramping by. Jackson, his hat pulled down low to shield his eyes watched in silence as Smith rode up. Shells from Federal cannon had already begun to fly as the men approached the furnace. Jackson now made the decision to traverse the corps' wagon train by a different route. Reconnaissance had shown another, more protected route which angled southwest toward Todd's Tavern, was available through the woods to the southeast. The side road turned west and returned to the main road about one and a half miles south of the furnace. Turning to Smith, the general gave orders to have the wagons and ambulances traverse the interior road. Smith quickly rode off to deliver Jackson's orders to the officers in charge of the trains. Completing his task, Smith returned to find Jackson gone. Determining Jackson had followed the column, Smith pointed his horse down the road toward the furnace.[90]

Smith spent the greater portion of the day chasing Jackson down. After a ride of nearly ten miles, Smith found him seated on the stump along the Brock Road writing his dispatch to Lee. He followed the vanguard of the column to its jump off point where he was ordered to remain behind acting as a communication center between the assaulting force and the cavalry grading its flanks.[91]

At 8 p.m., with the sounds of battle fading in the gathering twilight, Smith collected his couriers and started forward down the Plank Road. As darkness settled, the faint sounds gave way to stillness. His party moved east along the road, passing by the residue of battle. Scattered about, Smith saw wounded men, concentrations of prisoners and Confederate soldiers looking for their regiments. A mile west of Chancellorsville Smith noticed a group of riders near an old structure. Riding over, he found General Rodes and his staff trying to round up his scattered

---

[90] Smith, Jackson's Last Battle, **B&L**, vol.3, p.205; Krick, **Staff Officers**, p.269; Freeman, **Lee's Lieutenants**, vol.2, pp.548-550. Smith seems to imply that Jackson gave him orders to divert the wagons prior to the shelling at Lewis' Creek. This seems unlikely since the route was not reconnoitered during daylight hours prior to the beginning of the march. Jackson may have been aware of possible exposure of the column and been prepared for it. It is possible that the general planned in advance to traverse the wagons by a different route but most sources indicate the decision was made after the shelling began.

[91] Smith, Jackson's Last Battle, **B&L**, vol.3, pp.205-206.

troops. Smith asked where Jackson was. "Just ahead in the road," Rodes told him. "[T]ell him I will be here at this cabin if I am wanted."[92]

Returning to the road, Smith had not gone more than a hundred yards when a shot rang out. He heard a few more shots, followed by a heavy volley from the right side of the road and an even heavier one from the left side. A short distance further, Smith met Captain Taylor who had managed to extricate himself from under his horse. Smith remained seated on his horse as Taylor told the sad tale. Jackson had been wounded and a number of his party as well as Hill's group had been killed or wounded by fire from their own men. Smith spurred his horse forward into a gallop down the road and quickly came upon Captain Leigh, and Dr. Barr with his litter and bearers. Leigh, Smith and the doctor rode on leaving the litter bearers to catch up. Together they went and found Jackson just where Leigh had left him.[93]

While Hill continued to cradle Jackson's head and shoulders, Doctor Barr looked at the wounds. After making a quick assessment, Barr hastened off to obtain some supplies. After Barr departed, Jackson questioned Hill regarding the surgeon's capabilities. "Is that a skillful surgeon?" he asked. "He stands very high with his brigade," replied Hill. Noticing the wounded general still showed apprehension regarding Barr, Hill tried to reassure him, telling Jackson he would not do anything until Doctor McGuire arrived. Soon Barr returned with a tourniquet, but after noticing the current dressings were performing reasonably well, he chose not to apply the instrument. With medical attention near, it was time for Hill to resume his role as general. He was now in command of the Second Corps. He slowly removed his leg from under Jackson and eased the injured man's head and torso to the ground. As he got to his feet, Hill told Jackson he would try to keep his wounding from the troops. "Thank you," was all Jackson managed. Hill mounted his horse and rode off.[94]

The lull in the firing which allowed Jackson's various attendants to care for him was coming to an end. Joe Morrison noticed in the moonlight along the road a Federal artillery battery unlimbering a short distance away. He returned to the group near Jackson exclaiming, "We must get away from here!" The decision was made to pick Jackson up and carry him to the rear, but the General intervened. "No," Jackson said, "if you can help me up I can walk." Jackson was helped to his feet, and supported by two or three men began to walk slowly to the rear. Just as the party began moving west, Federal artillery opened up, peppering the group

---

[92] *Ibid*, p.209. The structure was probably the old schoolhouse near Hazel Grove.

[93] *Ibid*, p.210; Leigh, The Wounding of Stonewall, **SHSP**, vol.6, p.233. Smith notes Taylor as informing him that Hill was also wounded. Hill was not wounded until Jackson had departed the scene. In fact, Smith notes later in his narrative that Hill was "holding the head and shoulders of the wounded chief" when he arrived at the scene.

[94] Robertson, **Stonewall Jackson**, pp.731-732; According to the service record of surgeon Benjamin P. Wright from the 55th Virginia he was the first Doctor to treat Jackson. Wright claimed that Hill sent for him to attend the General. Wright claims this in his reminiscences but no officers or men in the area around Jackson mention him in any of the narratives of the event.

and the road with shrapnel. Captain Leigh, who was still mounted, had his horse killed from underneath him. Jumping from the dying animal, Leigh found himself near Jackson and took up supporting the wounded general on his right side. As he assisted Jackson, the general's blood stained his uniform and soaked his clothing. In an effort to keep the troops on the road from seeing and identifying their wounded leader, Captain Wilbourn lead three of the remaining horses, keeping them between Jackson and the soldiers. Federal infantry fire began to increase and artillery rounds commenced landing near the group as the trek to get Jackson out of harm's way began.[95]

The going was indeed slow, and Wilbourn's effort to keep the horses between the road and his wounded commander could not keep Hill's troops, who were now advancing on the road, from noticing the group. The men correctly deduced by the number in the party that the man being helped must be an officer and went out of their way to get around the horses for a glimpse. Inquires became so numerous that Jackson instructed his bearers to inform the men that it was only a "confederate officer." Passing through a beam of moonlight the bare headed general became visible for a moment. "Great God, that's General Jackson!" exclaimed a soldier. An evasive response was given and nothing more was heard from the man, but the cat was out of the bag. The questions from inquisitive soldiers had all taken place within twenty yards. By that time Jackson was exhausted. As luck would have it, the men carrying the litter arrived just in time. It was placed on the ground and Jackson was helped down to it. Four men grasped the corners, lifted the general up, and continued the trudge toward the rear.[96]

Captains Smith and Leigh took two corners while the other two were taken by Private John James Johnson from Company H of the 22nd Virginia Cavalry and another unnamed soldier. Shortly after Jackson was placed on the litter, the Federal artillery fire increased to the point where it became a serious hazard. "…great broadsides thundered over the woods," Smith recalled, "hissing shells searched the dark thickets through, and shrapnels [sic] swept the road along which we moved." At the left front corner of the litter, Private Johnson, was hit by fragments in both arms, causing him to lose his grip. Jackson was being carried at a height of about three feet when Johnson went down. The litter pitched downward, and forced Jackson to land hard on his broken arm. To go on would be suicide. The litter, with the groaning Jackson was set down in the road as the men scattered to seek shelter in the trees. Johnson's wounds would cost him one arm while the other was so damaged it would be useless the rest of his life. Wilbourn lost his grip on the horses and they broke under the screeching fire, bolting off into the night. Smith lay in the road along one side of the litter while Leigh lay next to Jackson on the other side. The road, which had been packed with men only a few moments ago, was now empty. "I could see no man or beast or thing upon it but ourselves," Leigh later

---

[95] *Ibid*, p.732; Wilbourn, Extract from the Printed Narrative, ***SHSP***, vol.6, p.270. The artillery battery which Morrison observed was probably a section of Major Thomas W. Osborn's 1st United States Artillery, Battery H.

[96] Wilbourn, Extract from the Printed Narrative, ***SHSP***, vol.6, p.270.

recalled. The two captains and the wounded general were its sole occupants. Shell fragments raked the road throwing stones and dirty in all directions. Jackson tried to rise, but Smith, fearing he would be struck again, put his arm over the general's chest to hold him down on the litter.[97]

The bleeding from Jackson's wounded arm had stopped or slowed significantly prior to the tumble from the litter. The impact upon the ground however, caused additional damage that drove the course of events to their ultimate conclusion. The jagged ends of the broken bone had evidently come in contact with the artery and caused the wounded arm to begin bleeding again.[98]

After a short period, the artillery fire began to slacken. Jackson once again rose and made an effort to walk. Smith assisted him to his feet, and after placing his arm around him, and with the General's weight "heavily upon" him, Smith helped Jackson off the road. The group made for the woods to escape the hail of fire, which still was severe. Thinking ahead, Captain Leigh, gathered up the litter and brought it along. It was the correct decision, for after a few steps Jackson again became weak. With his arm bleeding again he was placed on the litter. Once again, Leigh made an effort to secure bearers for the litter but he had no takers. Finally, in desperation, he informed the passing infantrymen that the wounded man was Jackson. Once it was known who the injured man was, Leigh had more volunteers than he needed. He was reluctant to use Jackson's name freely, wanting to keep his wounding a secret so as to not dampen the spirits of the men.[99]

With enough men now available to handle the litter, the group raised it and once again worked to bear Jackson to the rear. They stuck to the woods for protection should a resumption of the heavy shelling commence. Leigh estimated the group had proceeded about a half mile when the second significant event during the trek occurred. One of the lead bearers foot tangled in "a grape vine" and he went down hard. The litter pitched and once again Jackson landed on his wounded arm. "For the first time he groaned piteously," wrote Leigh. "He must have suffered agonies." The second fall, while not as violent as the first, probably sealed the fate of the general. The jagged ends of the broken bone finished their work on the artery and the wounded arm began to bleed again. Smith rushed to Jackson and in the moonlight lifted his head. The general weakly opened his eyes and recognized Smith. "Never mind me, Captain, never mind me," was all he was capable of uttering.[100]

---

[97] Kyle, David J., Jackson's Guide when Shot, *CV*, vol.4, pp.308-309; Krick, *Smoothbore* pp.35-37; Leigh, The Wounding of Stonewall, *SHSP*, vol.6, p.233; Smith, Jackson's Last Battle, *B&L*, vol.3, p.212; Wilbourn, Extract from the Printed Narrative, *SHSP*, vol.6, p.272, Private Johnson took up residence in Fluvanna or Louisa county after the war. His disability prompted the local citizens to take up a collection and construct the veteran a new home.

[98] Krick, *Smoothbore*, pp.35-37

[99] Leigh, The Wounding of Stonewall, *SHSP*, vol.6, p.233.

[100] Smith, Jackson's Last Battle, *B&L*, vol.3, p.212; Leigh, The Wounding of Stonewall, *SHSP*, vol.6, p.233.

Once again, Smith helped Jackson to his feet. As the group contemplated their next action, General William Dorsey Pender approached them. Pender's North Carolinians, who had trailed Lane's during the march, had arrived with his brigade. The men of his command had been scattered by darkness and enemy fire. "Oh, General," exclaimed Pender, "I hope you are not seriously wounded. I will have to retire my troops to reform them[.] [T]hey are so much broken by this fire." The mere mention of withdrawal summoned all the strength that remained in Jackson. Raising his head, his eyes burning, he spoke firmly to Pender. "You must hold your ground, General Pender; you must hold your ground, sir!" It is quite fitting these were the final orders uttered by Stonewall Jackson on a battlefield. His strength ebbed and he slumped back into Smith's arms. Placing Jackson once again on the litter, the party bore it up and made their way through the brush back to the road to avoid another fall.[101]

Sometime during the journey Captain Wilbourn left the party. He had gone in search of whiskey. The events of the evening would no doubt drive a man to search out lavations, but he was not seeking the liquid for himself. At one point, while Jackson was on the ground after his litter was dropped, he asked Wilbourn for some. Jackson was not a drinking man, but he must have thought the good Lord would permit it under the circumstances. Determined to find alcohol, Wilbourn first tried Melzi Chancellor's place, which was within a distance that could be covered on foot. A field hospital had been set up there and Wilbourn thought he could get some whiskey from the Yankee doctors there. When he asked the doctors if they had any spirits, they all admitted they did not. Whether he thought the response was a lie to conceal the booty, Wilbourn never mentioned. After inquiring, the captain decided that he needed to find Doctor McGuire. Commandeering a stray horse, he mounted and rode off into the darkness to the west.[102]

After what Wilbourn determined was a "short ride," he found Doctor McGuire, Brigadier General Pendleton and Jedediah Hotchkiss. Wilbourn relayed the sad story of Jackson's wounding to them. As the group rode back toward the point where Wilbourn left Jackson, Pendleton, evidently distraught at the thought of Jackson's wounding, began to feel lightheaded. He asked for a moment and dismounted. As his feet hit the ground he fainted, collapsing in a heap by the road. Just as Pendleton fell to the ground, an ambulance came up. The driver and team were instructed to go on ahead while Doctor McGuire dismounted and provided Pendleton some whiskey. After a few moments, the general was coherent once again and the group proceeded down the road toward the front.[103]

---

[101] Smith, Jackson's Last Battle, **B&L**, vol.3, p.212. Smith placed the incident with Pender occurring after the second fall from the litter. Douglas Southall Freeman in Lee's Lieutenants places it at the instant when Smith helped Jackson to his feet after the second fall. The wording of the exchange is somewhat different in various accounts. Captain's Leigh and Wilbourn do not mention the incident. Since Captain Smith was there, the author has chosen to rely on his account.

[102] Wilbourn, Extract from the Printed Narrative, **SHSP**, vol.6, p.272.

[103] Ibid, pp.272-273.

Captain Moorman Finds an Ambulance

After the firing along the Confederate line had ceased, Captain Moorman began the task of repairing his battery. After replacing his poles and righting his guns, he noticed through the darkness, Colonel Crutchfield's guns coming forward. With his replacements at hand, Moorman retired to the rear taking as much of his damaged battery with him as possible. Stopping after a short distance, he made arrangements to send men back to retrieve some horses and a broken down caisson. Near his position was an ambulance. Moorman did not say whether the wagon was present when he stopped or if it came up after he had halted.

As Moorman halted, a wounded man rode up. It was Major Arthur L. Rogers from the Loudoun Artillery. Rogers was serving on Colonel Crutchfield's staff as a volunteer aid. Moorman helped the hurt man off his horse and into the ambulance. Then another wounded man rode up. This time Moorman recognized his old classmate, Colonel Crutchfield. The colonel was in severe pain. "Captain, please assist me to dismount," Crutchfield said. "How are you wounded Colonel," Moorman asked. "My thigh is broken," was the response. Moorman helped Crutchfield off his horse and placed him in the wagon next to Rogers.[104]

As the colonel was positioned in the ambulance, Moorman turned and noticed a group of men bringing a litter forward bearing an injured man. Knowing that Jackson had been wounded, he inquired as to the identity of the stricken soldier. Once identified, Jackson was placed in the ambulance with Crutchfield. Rogers gave up his seat to make room for the general's litter. Morrison clamored into the wagon and made an effort to support Jackson's damaged arm as the wagon began its trip to the rear. Walking ahead of the wagon, Captain Leigh pointed out the rough spots in the road so the driver could avoid them. As the wagon rolled along Jackson continually asked for whiskey.[105]

A short time later, the wagon arrived at Dowdall's Tavern. Jackson's litter was removed from the ambulance and set on the side of the road. Two soldiers marked its location with torches as others in the party went in search of alcohol to soothe Jackson's pain. It was here that Doctor McGuire and his party found the general. "I hope you are not badly hurt, General," McGuire said, kneeling next to the litter. Jackson looked up, no doubt pleased to see his surgeon. "I am badly injured, Doctor; I fear I am dying," Jackson managed weakly. After taking a moment to gather additional strength the general continued. "I am glad you have come. I think the wound in my shoulder is still bleeding." McGuire noted that the general's clothing was drenched with blood and the arm was indeed bleeding. Sticking a finger into the wound he managed to arrest the hemorrhaging from the artery. After waiting for light to be brought near, McGuire noticed the handkerchief

---

[104] Freeman, ***Lee's Lieutenants***, vol.2, pp.576; Robertson, ***Stonewall Jackson***, p.734; Moorman, Narrative of Events, ***SHSP***, vol.30, pp.113-114; Freeman identified the man as possibly being Captain H. A. Rogers of the 13th North Carolina but did not confirm his identity. Robertson identified him as Arthur Rogers.

[105] Moorman, Narrative of Events, ***SHSP***, vol.30, pp.114-115; Freeman, ***Lee's Lieutenants***, vol.2, p.577.

that Wilbourn had applied during his first aid session had slipped. He adjusted it and the bleeding subsided. If not for McGuire's actions, Jackson most likely would have bled to death before he reached the hospital. McGuire believed the general would have lasted another ten minutes.[106]

McGuire could tell Jackson was in great pain. "His suffering at this time was intense," he later wrote. "…his hands were cold, his skin clammy, his face pale, and his lips compressed and bloodless; not a groan escaped him--not a sign of suffering except the slight corrugation of his brow, the fixed, ridged face, and the thin lips so tightly compressed that the impression of the teeth could be seen through them." Whiskey and morphine were procured and quickly administered which relieved Jackson's pain somewhat. The litter was then placed back in the wagon and with torches lighting the way, the ambulance slowly began to move toward the Second Corps field infirmary near the Wilderness Tavern. McGuire sat in the back of the wagon with his finger firmly on the upper portion of the artery in case the tourniquet should fail again. Wilbourn, having been with Jackson since the wounding, stayed behind. With Doctor McGuire taking charge he was no longer needed. He slowly watched the wagon and torches disappear into the night.[107]

As the wagon bounced down the road, it became obvious that Jackson was not the only passenger in pain. Colonel Crutchfield groaned constantly and when the wagon hit a rough spot he expressed his agony. Once, after a particularly hard bump, Crutchfield groaned openly. Jackson asked that the ambulance be stop and requested McGuire to check if something could be done about the man's suffering. At one point, Jackson grasped the Doctor by the back of the head with his wounded right hand and pulled him close inquiring as to the severity of the Colonel's wounds. "No, only painfully hurt," McGuire responded. "I am glad it is no worse," Jackson said as the ambulance bounced along.[108]

Early Morning Surgery

After what must have seemed like an eternity to the wounded passengers, the ambulance finally arrived at the hospital shortly after 11 p.m. Jackson was taken inside and placed in a bed, covered with a few blankets and provided another sip of whiskey. Doctor Harvey Black, the lead surgeon at the hospital, had been provided advanced notice that the wounded Jackson was being brought in. When he heard the news, he went to work converting his own tent to a makeshift hospital room. The bed was soft and a stove warmed the room and added a little ambiance, not that the atmosphere would make any difference to Jackson. Some of Jackson's strength returned after he was given whiskey. The wounded man's pulse was so shallow that McGuire could not examine him for fear the general would expire during the

---

[106] Freeman, *Lee's Lieutenants*, vol.2, pp.576; Robertson, *Stonewall Jackson*, p.735; McGuire, Death of Stonewall Jackson, *SHSP*, vol.14, pp.155-156,

[107] McGuire, Death of Stonewall Jackson, *SHSP*, vol.14, p.156.

[108] *Ibid*, p.156; Robertson, *Stonewall Jackson*, p.735.

investigation. For the next three hours James Smith, who had made the trip in the ambulance, and Doctor McGuire watched the Jackson closely.[109]

Close to 2:00 a.m., McGuire returned to the tent. Three other surgeons followed him. At the age of twenty-seven McGuire was extremely young for an army surgeon. He had received his degree from the University of Pennsylvania seven years earlier. He would now be called upon to perform the most important operation of his young career.[110]

Jackson heard his surgeon's voice as McGuire entered. The doctor told his patient that his pulse was now stronger and that it was time to examine his wounds. Even though Jackson had no doubt reached the limits of human endurance, McGuire felt waiting any longer would not be wise. He informed the general that chloroform would be administered so he would feel no pain. Then the more difficult question was asked. "I told him that amputation would probably be required, and asked if it was found necessary whether it should be done at once," McGuire wrote later. Jackson quickly answered. "Yes, certainly, Doctor McGuire. Do for me whatever you think right." With that, a cloth was formed into the shape of a cup, the proper amount of chloroform poured in, and the anesthetizing administered. As Jackson slid into a state of insensibility, he gave thanks for the removal of the pain. "What an infinite blessing," he uttered.[111]

Once Jackson slipped from consciousness, McGuire began his investigation. He turned first to the slightly wounded right hand. A round, smoothbore musket ball was removed from under the skin on the back of the hand. Surely the ball was from a Confederate weapon. Next, McGuire turned to the badly damaged left arm. The ball inflicting the slighter wound had entered the outside of the forearm an inch from the elbow. Although it had spiraled around the arm and exited just above the wrist, the bone had not been damaged.[112]

The third and final wound was life threatening. According to McGuire the round entered "about three inches below the shoulder-joint, the ball dividing the main artery and fracturing the bone." McGuire made no mention of the arterial damage occurring after the wounding. Jackson's left arm could not be repaired by mid-nineteenth century medicine. The arm would have to come off. Captain Smith was charged with holding the light above the table. With one surgeon monitoring the chloroform, another standing by to control any bleeding, and Doctor Black monitoring Jackson's pulse, McGuire went to work. The young surgeon quickly cleared the damaged flesh from the severed bone. Using a bone saw the jagged ends were trimmed and cleaned. Then the arm was lifted away before the exposed blood vessels where sealed. The arm was wrapped in a cloth and placed on the

---

[109] McGuire, Death of Stonewall Jackson, *SHSP*, vol.14, p.156; Robertson, *Stonewall Jackson*, p.736.

[110] Robertson, *Stonewall Jackson*, p.737.

[111] Robertson, *Stonewall Jackson*, p.736; McGuire, Death of Stonewall Jackson, *SHSP*, vol.14, p.156.

[112] McGuire, Death of Stonewall Jackson, *SHSP*, vol.14, p.157.

ground just outside the tent. Later that day, Reverend Lacy would find the arm still in the dirt outside the tent. Gathering it up, he took it to the nearby estate of J. Horace Lacy. He buried it in the family cemetery there. The surgery was over by 3 a.m. McGuire then charged Captain Smith with watching Jackson for the remainder of the night.[113]

An Army Commander's Grief

After the ambulance bearing Jackson departed Dowdall's Tavern, "Sandie" Pendleton approached Wilbourn with orders to report to General Lee and relay the sad news. Since he had been with Jackson when he was hit, he seemed a likely candidate to communicate the message. Wilbourn started at once for Lee's headquarters taking Private Wynn with him. They arrived early in the morning to find Lee still sleeping. The commanding general was awakened and Wilbourn stepped into his tent, which was actually a makeshift lean-to. As he entered, Lee remained in his bed, but elevated himself on his elbows. Wilbourn set on the edge of the cot and told the story. Lee was visibly shaken by the news. "When I told him that the wounding was by our own troops, he seemed ready to burst into tears, and gave a moan," Wilbourn later recalled. The tale told, Lee paused for a moment and said, "[A]h! Captain, don't let us say anything more about it, it is too painful to talk about." "It was the saddest night I ever passed in my life," Wilbourn wrote. "…when I saw this great man so much moved, and look as if he could weep, my cup of sadness was filled to overflowing." Lee could not speak of Jackson without weeping. Jackson's value to Lee would be sorely missed over the next few weeks.[114]

Exiting Lee's lean-to, Wilbourn was summoned by Lieutenant Colonel Walter Herron Taylor. As the remainder of Lee's staff gathered around, the story was told again. Tears began to flow long before the retelling was completed. As the story ended, General Lee appeared dressed and ready for the day. He asked for his horse and informed his staff to be ready to ride as soon as possible. Then, calling Wilbourn to him, the two men sat down and had breakfast, which Lee spread out before them himself. A woman in the area had prepared the food and Lee instructed him to sit and make a hearty meal of it with him. After breakfast was complete, Lee told the captain to lie down and sleep for a while. His night had been long and

---

[113] Robertson, ***Stonewall Jackson***, p.736, 918; McGuire, Death of Stonewall Jackson, ***SHSP***, vol.14, p.157. Robertson attributes the disposal of the arm to Charles W. Dabney whose papers are housed in the Southern Historical Society Collection at the University of North Carolina.

[114] Krick, ***Staff Officers***, p.240; Wilbourn, Extract from the Printed Narrative, ***SHSP***, vol.6, p.273; Robertson, ***Stonewall Jackson***, p.754. In 2002, two wooden trunks were discovered at Burke & Herbert Bank and Trust Company in Alexandria, Virginia. Inside the trunks were numerous papers and notes, a number of which were written in Lee's own hand. The contents had been collected and stored by Lee's eldest daughter, Mary Custis Lee. Among the documents was Lee's original hand written copy of General Order No. 61 announcing the death of Jackson to the army. While Jackson and Lee were never close friends, the fact that Lee kept his original letter speaks volumes regarding its importance to him, his respect for, and his relationship with Jackson.

he needed the rest. However, when Lee mounted his horse Traveller and prepared to depart, Wilbourn attempted to go with him. Lee shooed him away and forced him to lie down. "So I rested until the battle began," he noted, "and then joined my command again."[115]

The Dream Fades

Jackson's condition improved for the first few days of his convalescence. News of the battle arrived in bits and pieces as Jackson slowly began to regain his strength. At one point he dictated a note to General Lee congratulating him on the victory of the previous evening. He was awake Sunday morning, 3 May, when a courier arrived with a note from Lee.

>   HEADQUARTERS,
>   May 3, 1863
> General Thomas J. Jackson,
>   Commanding Corps:
> GENERAL: I have just received your note, informing me that you were wounded. I cannot express my regret at the occurrence. Could I have directed events, I should have chosen for the good of the country to be disabled in your stead.
> I congratulate you upon the victory, which is due to your skill and energy.
>   Very respectfully, your obedient servant
>   R.E. LEE
>   General.

Jackson responded saying Lee was quite gracious but he "should give the praise to God."[116]

Jackson appeared to be recovering quickly but other signs foretold the ultimate outcome. During the mid morning hours of 3 May, Jackson complained to McGuire of pain in his right side. He attributed the pain to one of the falls from the litter the previous night, believing he had struck a stump during one of the tumbles. McGuire examined Jackson's side. "No evidence of injury could be discovered by examination. The skin was not broken or bruised, and the lung performed, as far as I could tell, its proper function," noted McGuire. The first indicator of pneumonia, which would ultimately take Jackson's life, had shown itself.

The same morning, McGuire received a communication from General Lee. According to Lee, the Federals were pressing toward Ely's Ford and there was some danger to Jackson's location. Troops had been sent to the hospital to provide some protection, but they would not be able to hold off a determined Yankee effort. Jackson expressed a desire not to be moved citing his kind treatment of Union wounded. He felt the enemy would treat him with the same compassion if they

---

[115] *Ibid*, pp.273-274

[116] Robertson, ***Stonewall Jackson***, p.739; ***OR*** vol.25, pt.2, p.769.

were to capture him. A second message arrived from Lee later in the afternoon, and, thinking Jackson was well enough to move, preparations began to transfer him to Guiney's Station. McGuire was instructed to accompany Jackson and he turned his medical duties with the Second Corps over to the ranking officer.[117]

The next day would dawn clear and warm. Jackson woke invigorated and refreshed. He would need all his strength for the twenty-seven mile trip. McGuire had a mattress loaded into the back of an ambulance, and Jackson along with Colonel Crutchfield, who would also make the trip, were placed comfortably on it. McGuire took a seat next to the driver while Chaplin Lacy and Captain Smith rode in the ambulance. Bringing up the rear would be Jackson servant, Jim Lewis, who was in charge of the general's personal effects, headquarters supplies, and the remaining horses. In front of the procession would be Hotchkiss who had a group of engineers to remove debris and large rocks from the road which would smooth out the ride. The going was slow. At one point the procession used Jackson's name to disperse some obstinate teamsters from the road so they could pass. During the trip, Jackson complained of some nausea and a wet towel was placed over his stomach. Finally, after the long hot journey, the group pulled up to Guiney's Station. The trip completely drained Jackson's strength. He was placed in a downstairs office which had been converted to a bedroom, and made comfortable. After eating a little bread and drinking some tea Jackson fell asleep and slumbered the remainder of the night.[118]

A modern view of Guiney's Station. The window at the right rear looks into the room in which Jackson died. *KAC*

---

[117] McGuire, Death of Stonewall Jackson, ***SHSP***, vol.14, p.158-159.

[118] *Ibid*, p.159, Robertson, ***Stonewall Jackson***, pp.743-744.

The following day Jackson felt better. The day was cooler owing to rain the previous evening. McGuire thought his patient was doing "remarkably well." His wounds were beginning to show signs of healing and he "ate heartily for one in his condition." When Jackson was told his wounds were beginning to heal he "expressed great satisfaction" and quizzed McGuire as to how long the doctor thought he would be away from his command. McGuire however provided no specifics. On Thursday morning, everything changed.

At 1 a.m., Jackson awoke and complained of nausea again. He wanted to know if a wet towel could be applied. Jim Lewis asked permission to wake McGuire who was sleeping in another room. Jackson told his servant to leave the doctor alone and demanded the towel. As the sun rose McGuire woke to find Jackson "suffering great pain." After an examination he determined that the general was suffering from "pleuro-pneumonia of the right side." Jackson believed it was caused by one of his falls from the litter. McGuire wasn't so sure. "I think the disease came on too soon after the application of the wet cloths to admit to the supposition, once believed, that it was induced by" the falls from the litter. Had the wait in the rain for his wife and baby a few weeks earlier, and the resulting chest cold manifested itself into pneumonia due to his weakened state? Of course, McGuire knew nothing of the chest cold, and if he did, he left no record of it. Now there would be a battle for his life and McGuire administered all the currently accepted methods for treating the then deadly affliction.

Over the next three days Jackson weakened quickly. His wife, arriving with his daughter, brought some joy to him. He spent time playing with the child stroking the infants cheek lovingly. By Sunday, the situation was hopeless. McGuire tried all the trusted remedies of the day, but he was unable to arrest the progress of the affliction. Jackson's wounds were healing quite well, but the remainder of Jackson's body was dying. His wife informed him that he would not last the day. Seeing she was afraid, the general tried to reassure her. "Oh, no; you are frightened, my child," he comforted her. "[D]eath is not so near; I may yet get well." McGuire then informed him that his wife was correct. "Very good, very good," he responded. "[I]t is alright." Jackson had always wished to die on a Sunday. His wish would be fulfilled.

Toward the end, he became delirious recounting moments vivid in his memory. "Order A. P. Hill to prepare for action! Pass the infantry to the front rapidly!" His face was pale, his expression calm. Then as if relieving himself of his earthly burdens he uttered, "Let us cross over the river and rest under the shade of the trees." He died at 3:15 p.m. on 10 May 1863. Stonewall Jackson had gone to meet his God.[119]

The Price of Victory

Jedediah Hotchkiss was looking for his friend. After making his way to army headquarters to report the death of Jackson, he had returned to the scene of the catastrophe to look for James Boswell. He had not seen or heard of him since

---

[119] McGuire, Death of Stonewall Jackson, ***SHSP***, vol.14, p.160-163.

the shooting, and it was noon before he could get back to the area. He had feared the worst and after a short rest, his worries were confirmed. Hotchkiss found the captain lying dead along the Plank Road "some 20 steps in advance" of where Jackson had been. Boswell's body had fallen from his horse as it ran through the darkness toward the Federal line. Even though he was sure the result of his search would not bring happiness, Hotchkiss was overwhelmed at the sight of his friend lying dead along the road.[120]

Boswell's face looked content and calm in death. Although it was unknown to Hotchkiss, it looked much like the young Federal soldier which Talcott and Boswell had stumbled upon during their reconnaissance mission two nights earlier. His body had already been stripped of its personal belongings by scourging soldiers. A few days earlier Boswell had informed Hotchkiss that he fully expected to be killed in the upcoming battle, a premonition which turned out to be true although the bullets were not fired by the enemy.

Hotchkiss sadly procured an ambulance and loaded his friend's body. He took it to the field hospital where General Jackson was recuperating from his surgery. Taking Boswell to the family cemetery of J. Horace Lacy and digging a grave, Hotchkiss laid his friend to rest next to Jackson's amputated arm. The moon was rising as he placed the body in the hole and covered it. Chaplain Lacy said a few words. Only three others were present. The two men who helped dig the grave and a man named Brown. "I wept for him as for a brother," Hotchkiss wrote in his diary. "He was kind and gentle and with as few faults as most men. Peace to his memory."[121]

Sadness spread throughout the Confederacy as news of Jackson death quickly passed from town to town. Merit Seay form the Fluvanna Artillery, just happened to be at Guiney's Station on 11 May. He was on an errand for the battery when he observed one of the saddest sights he witnessed during the war. On the station platform General Jackson's coffin was being loaded onboard a waiting train.

> "They were putting him on the train just as I got there. He was in a very fine coffin and two large wreaths of flowers laying on it. He did [died] in a home about a quarter mile from the station. His wife and a good many of his relations were there. Everything looked very solemn and it is a solemn thing to lose such a man as he was."[122]

Lee and his Army of Northern Virginia would never be the same. While morale remained high their chieftain who had brought them great victories was

---

[120] Wilbourn, Extract from the Printed Narrative, **SHSP**, vol.6, p.273; Hotchkiss, Jedediah, **Make Me a Map of the Valley**, pp.139-140; Mitchell, Jackson's Engineer, **CWTI**, vol.7, no.3, p.17. Hotchkiss arrived after Captain Wilbourn and was shunned by Lee who had already heard the story and had no desire for it to be retold.

[121] Hotchkiss, **Make Me a Map**, pp.139-140; Mitchell, Jackson's Engineer, **CWTI**, vol.7, no. 3, p.17.

[122] Martin, David G., **The Fluvanna Artillery**, p.73.

lost. Indeed, Lee himself would never quite be the same. The day after Jackson's death he wrote to his son Custis, "It is a terrible loss. I do not know how to replace him." On the same day Lee announced the death of Jackson to the army. He used the notification to inspire his junior officers.

> "The daring, skill, and energy of this great and good soldier, by the decree of an all-wise Providence, are now lost to us. But while we mourn his death, we feel that his spirit still lives, and will inspire the whole army with his indomitable courage and unshaken confidence in God as our hope and our strength. Let his name be a watchword to his corps, who have followed him to victory on so many fields. Let officers and soldiers emulate his invincible determination to do everything in the defense of our beloved country."

With these words Lee began the process of finding a replacement for Jackson. It was a void which, by the end of the war, would never be adequately filled.[123]

Lee had the utmost confidence in Jackson and felt that if his Second Corps commander had been with him at Gettysburg the outcome would have been different. After the war Lee avoided taking high profile jobs and accepted a position as president of Washington College (later Washington and Lee University). Although he was paid the paltry sum of $1,500 a year he was still rather well off. While in his office one day, two friends, Reverend J. William Jones and Professor James J. White, stopped to pay a visit. As they arrived, Lee was reading a letter inquiring about the Battle of Gettysburg. According to Jones, partway through the correspondence, Lee slammed his hand down on the desk. In a stern voice, uncommon to his mild mannerisms, the general expressed his opinion of Jackson's worth. "If I had had Stonewall Jackson at Gettysburg, I would have won that fight, and a complete victory there would have given us Washington and Baltimore, if not Philadelphia, and would have established the independence of the Confederacy." Lee felt the Jackson he would have had in Pennsylvania would have been the same man who had performed the miracle of Chancellorsville.[124]

---

[123] *OR* vol.25, pt.2, p.793; Dowdey & Manarin, ***The Wartime Papers***, p.484.

[124] Faust, ***Encyclopedia***, p.430; Gordon, John B., ***Reminiscences of the Civil War***, p.154. Washington College was later known as Washington and Lee University. It should be noted that Reverend Jones spent a great deal of time and effort after the war defending Lee's reputation while attempting to level the blame for the Confederate defeat at Gettysburg on others. Gordon's account is second hand, as told to him by Jones. While there is little reason to doubt Gordon's account of the incident as told to him, it's quite possible that Jones embellished the incident to accent its impact and meaning.

Chapter II
Joe Hooker Gets an Army

> "go forward and give us victories." [1]
> *President Lincoln to Major General*
> *Joe Hooker the day after placing him*
> *in command of the Army of the Potomac,*
> *26 January 1863.*

As the end of January 1863 neared Abraham Lincoln had a problem. His mighty Army of the Potomac, under Major General Ambrose E. Burnside, occupied the area northeast of the Rappahannock River opposite Fredericksburg, Virginia. Since his appointment replacing General George McClellan on 5 November, he had made numerous attempts to dislodge the Confederates facing him from their position across the river. One effort resulted in the Federal bloodbath that was the battle of Fredericksburg on 13 December. After the beating, Burnside's army slunk back across the river to its previous position because he determined Lee's legions "would not come out of their strongholds and fight us with his infantry." Then came the infamous "Mud March," an effort to execute a plan based on General in Chief Henry Wager Halleck's suggestions put to Burnside on 7 January. The effort failed miserably due to uncooperative weather and roads which became nothing short of quagmires. Frustrated by bickering subordinates and Washington's meddling, Burnside requested he be relieved of command. Lincoln was eager to comply, but a suitable successor was not easily identified. Finding a man who could bring victories to an army that had become accustomed to failure would be a tall order.

The list of possible successors, while substantial, was unremarkable. The search began outside the ranks of the eastern army, when Halleck and Secretary of War Edwin M. Stanton showed favoritism toward Major General William S. Rosecrans, who was currently commanding the Army of the Cumberland in Tennessee. Being a westerner, Rosecrans would have received a favorable word from deposed General McClellan. After some consideration, the administration decided an outsider would not be the best choice. Rosecrans' selection could create friction between the new commander and the eastern army's current corps commanders. Other names were considered. Left Grand Division commander

---

[1] *OR* vol.25, pt.2, p.4.

William B. Franklin was measured but rejected due to questionable performance. General Edwin V. Sumner, commander of Burnside's Right Grand Division was qualified but at sixty-six years of age, he was considered too old. General Darius Nash Couch, who had been relieved from command of the Second Corps back in December, was a possibility, but he was rejected when the list was narrowed to Major General's Reynolds, Meade and Hooker.[2]

John Reynolds was eliminated from the list after Halleck inquired in confidence whether the commander of the First Corps would be interested in commanding the army. Reynolds responded by stating he would take command of the army if so ordered, but he would do so under duress if Washington did not grant a higher degree of flexibility regarding command decision than was currently allowed. Halleck was not willing to grant additional latitude, and Reynolds lost his opportunity. Of the remaining two, George Meade was the strongest candidate because Secretary Stanton was convinced Joe Hooker was the wrong man. Stanton believed that with Hooker there were two sides to the coin. One side displayed a man who was energetic, and clever, with a strong mental attitude. On the other however, was a man who greatly concerned Stanton. Hooker was incredibly opinionated, and he had never been slow to criticize a superior. This trait caused Ulysses S. Grant to write, "He was not subordinate to his superiors." However, Hooker did have some supporters, including Treasury Secretary Salmon P. Chase. The Joint House-Senate Committee on the Conduct of the War also thought Hooker the better choice.[3]

Personally Lincoln liked Hooker, and thought he would be more comfortable dealing with him than the caustic John Pope or the egotistical McClellan. He believed the lines of communication with Fighting Joe would be more open than those which he had struggled through with his previous generals. Lincoln also appreciated Hooker's aggressive nature and the general's seemingly unlimited confidence in himself. However, the president was leery of Hookers boastful assurances of his abilities which reminded Lincoln of the braggadocios attitudes of so many other generals who had been giving command of his mighty eastern army only to depart in shame.[4]

Meade, on the other hand, was supported by Halleck and Stanton, but he had little support from other individuals. Lincoln, wise to the political environment, did not wish to make an appointment that would split his support. Even though the president knew Hooker's shortcomings, Lincoln had made his decision. Joseph Hooker was named the new commander, much to the chagrin of Stanton and

---

[2] Benjamin, Charles F., Hooker's Appointment and Removal, *B&L*, vol.3, p.239; *OR* vol.21, pp.2, 67, 953.

[3] Benjamin, Hooker's Appointment and Removal, *B&L*, vol.3, p.240; Cleaves, Freeman, *Meade of Gettysburg*, pp.100-101; Grant, Ulysses S., *Personal Memoirs of U. S. Grant*, pp.581-582.

[4] LaFantasie, Glenn W., How Lincoln Won and Lost at Gettysburg, *Papers of the Ninth Annual Gettysburg National Military Park Seminar* (hereafter *9th AGNMPS*) p.201.

Halleck. Hooker displaced Burnside near the end of January, but Burnside would not go quietly.[5]

Burnside was not a Hooker supporter. In fact, he detested Hooker vehemently, and felt he was a traitor. The day before he was replaced, Burnside wrote a scathing order recommending to Lincoln that a number of subordinate officers be dismissed from the army. Prominent in the order was its first salvo aimed directly at Hooker.

> "General Joseph Hooker, major-general of volunteers and brigadier-general U.S. Army, having been guilty of unjust and unnecessary criticism of the actions of his superior officers, and of the authorities, and having by the general tone of his conversation endeavored to create distrust in the minds of officers who have associated with him, and having, by omissions and otherwise, made reports and statements which were calculated to create incorrect impressions, and for habitually speaking in disparaging terms of other officers, is hereby dismissed the service of the United States as a man unfit to hold an important commission during a crisis like the present, when so much patience, charity, confidence, consideration, and patriotism are due from every soldier in the field. This order is issued subject to the approval of the President of the United States."[6]

Additional officers who, in Burnside's mind, had proven themselves incompetent were summarily sacked within the remainder of the order. Needless to say, Lincoln did not accept the document and on 25 January, the War Department issued orders replacing Burnside with Hooker. Lincoln personally notified Hooker the following day, and he immediately assumed command.[7]

After spewing his venom to Lincoln and his administration, Burnside toned down his rant in his final order to the army. He was very pleasant to the troops, but stopped short of throwing his support to Hooker. "[G]ive to the brave and skilful [sic] general who has so long been identified with your organization," were the only good words he would bestow upon his successor. According to Burnside, if the troops provided Hooker with their "full and cordial support and cooperation," they would "deserve success." This statement in itself revealed Burnside's opinion of Hooker. Noting the army would merit victory if it supported the new commander without commenting on his trust and belief in the man is indicative of his ire toward Hooker.[8]

---

[5] Cleaves, *Meade*, p.101.

[6] *OR* vol.21, pp.998.

[7] *Ibid*, pp.998-999; Bigelow, *Chancellorsville*, p.7-8.

[8] *OR* vol.25, pt.2, pp.4-5.

In his first general order to the army, Hooker made no attempt to express thanks to Burnside for his past efforts. Instead, he bestowed upon the outgoing General "cordial good wishes for his future." It was obvious to all associated with the two men that Hooker probably did wish Burnside success in the future, but only if it was a long way from his army. In early February, after showing a copy of Burnside's letter to a member of his staff, Hooker commented, "Burnside shall eat it, or he [Hooker] will have his ears, as soon as the war is over." On 3 February, Hooker even tried to get Burnside, who was back in command of the Ninth Corps, removed. "…[P]ermit me to recommend that General [William F.] Smith be assigned by the President to command it [Ninth Corps]," he wrote to Halleck. The next day Halleck responded writing "[M]ajor General Burnside is the permanent commander of the Ninth Corps."

Later, in March, Burnside was transferred and given command of the Department of Ohio. After defending Knoxville, he would find his way back to the Eastern Theater and resume command of his beloved Ninth Corps. By the time he returned, Hooker would be long gone, a victim of his past and present.[9]

In Hooker, Lincoln knew he did not have the perfect general. This was confirmed when Hooker arrived in Washington the morning of 27 January to meet with the president and Secretary Stanton. During the conversation, Hooker informed the president that he could be victorious if Lincoln would act as a mediator between himself and Halleck. Hooker wanted to work directly with the commander in chief and be screened from direct association with the general in chief. He considered Halleck a westerner who seemed to regard the Army of the Potomac as an afterthought. In reality, Hooker's animosity toward Halleck was the product of numerous confrontations over the years, particularly those which occurred between the two while they were both in California before the war. "His animosity rises from another source," Halleck wrote to William T. Sherman a year later. "He is aware that I know some things about his character and conduct in California and, fearing that I may use that information about him, he seeks to ward off its effect by making it appear that I am his personal enemy." How Lincoln responded to Hooker's request is not known, but the new commanding general seemed to be satisfied as he departed.[10]

By the time Hooker arrived back at army headquarters, there was a letter waiting for him. It had been written the day before he met with Lincoln, so the president had already determined and documented his opinions before Hooker spoke out against Halleck. This was the true genius of Lincoln. He always seemed to be a step ahead.

---

[9] ***OR*** vol.25, pt.2, p.5; Faust, ***Encyclopedia***, p.97; Sparks, David S., Editor, ***Inside Lincoln's Army: The Diary of General Marsena Rudolph Patrick Provost Marshall General, Army of the Potomac***, p.212; ***OR*** vol.25, pt.2, p.44.

[10] Bigelow, ***Chancellorsville***, pp.9-10; Halleck to Sherman, 16 September 1864, William T. Sherman Papers, Manuscript Division, LOC.

Executive Mansion, Washington D.C.,

January 26, 1863.

MAJOR-GENERAL HOOKER

General:

I have placed you at the head of the Army of the Potomac. Of course I have done this upon what appears to me to be sufficient reasons, and yet I think it best for you to know that there are some things in regard to which I am not quite satisfied with you. I believe you to be a brave and skilful [sic] soldier, which, of course, I like. I also believe you do not mix politics with your profession, in which you are right. You have confidence in yourself, which is a valuable, if not an indispensable, quality. You are ambitious, which within reasonable bounds, does good rather than harm; but I think that during General Burnside's command of the army you have taken counsel of your ambitions, and thwarted him as much as you could, in which you did a great wrong to the country and to a most meritorious and honorable brother officer. I have heard, in such a way as to believe it, of your recently saying that both the Army and the Government needed a dictator. Of course it is not for this, but in spite of it, that I have given you the command. Only those generals who gain successes can set up dictators. What I now ask of you is military success, and I will risk the dictatorship. The government will support you to the utmost of its ability, which is neither more nor less than it has done and will do for all commanders. I much fear that the spirit which you have aided to infuse into the army, of criticizing their commander and withholding confidence from him, will now turn upon you. I shall assist you as far as I can to put it down. Neither you nor Napoleon, if he were alive again, could get any good out of an army while such a spirit prevails in it. And now beware of rashness. Beware of rashness, but with energy and sleepless vigilance, go forward and give us victories.

Yours very truly,
A. Lincoln.[11]

Lincoln was obviously well aware of Hooker's shortcomings, and Hooker, for his part, received the letter well. He outwardly expressed no animosity to the tone of the document. The general thought it rang with the tone of a father speaking to his son. "I shall not answer this letter until I have won him a great victory," he commented to a group of fellow officers. His positive reception of the letter however, was completely out of character. How he felt about the tone of the letter was not recorded. Unfortunately for Hooker he would not provide a great victory and the letter would go unanswered.[12]

---

[11] *OR* vol.25, pt.2, p.4.

[12] *Ibid*, p.10; *OR* vol.25, pt.2, p.4; Sears, **Chancellorsville**, p.503.

The Handsome Soldier

    Joseph Hooker was born on 13 November 1814 in Hadley, Massachusetts. His first home was a spacious structure located on West Street, the town's main thoroughfare. He was the fourth child and first son born to his parents Joe and Mary, and was promptly christened Joseph. Born into a prominent line of local officials and landowners, young Joseph was the fifth of his bloodline. It was not until Joe Hooker the third, the boy's grandfather, took part in the French and Indian War that a military tradition was established. Joe the third expanded the custom during the revolution, fighting with the Continental Army for his freedom against England. After the war, he became a land owner, and managed to acquire a great deal of property.

    Young Joe's father, the third son born to his grandfather, was not as prosperous as his namesake. When his first wife died, he packed his belongings and moved west to Hadley where he met and married Mary Seymour, bought property along West Street and started a family. There, under the shade of Hadley's great elm trees the future general would spend his first years.

    While Mary worked to maintain the household, Joe's father strove to make a success of his business dealings. Prosperity however, eluded him again, with most of the difficulties brought on by the War of 1812. Three years after Joe was born the family was forced to sell the grand house on West Street. The family moved to a smaller dwelling on Hadley's less posh Middle Street. The business failure broke Joe's father, and he never managed to provide the riches that his ancestors had managed to bring to their families. Mary showed her resilience by taking charge of the family and kept the clan pressing forward. Joe and his sisters helped with the financial situation by taking small jobs to provide addition income.

    As a young boy, Joe was extremely competitive and showed his spirited side on many occasions. When time permitted he would play games in the streets with the neighborhood children. One favorite game was Old Cat. Old Cat was a forerunner of baseball, and Joe proved to be an excellent catcher. His tendency to move in close behind the batter and snatch the ball seemingly before the batter had a chance to swing was a dangerous practice because the bat was usually an old axe or shovel handle. When it was his turn to take his swings, he had a propensity to stand close to the plate and risk getting hit with the ball. His aggressive tendencies, on display during the games of youth would become part of his personality, and Joe Hooker would carry them with him to the battlefields of the Civil War.[13]

    Desiring a quality education her children, Mary enrolled Joe in Hopkins Academy in Hadley. The school administrator, Reverend Daniel Huntington, originally provided a free education for his students. However, the school lost its

---

[13]   Hebert, Walter H., **Fighting Joe Hooker**, pp.17-18. Old Cat was the basic version of the game, with a pitcher or "giver"; a batter or "striker"; a catcher, and sometimes another fielder or two. The striker, upon hitting the ball thrown by the giver, attempted to run to a single base (often the giver's position) and back again. The fielders tried to "sting" the striker-runner with a thrown ball while he was not touching the base. The striker would also be put out if the struck ball were caught in the air, or if he swung three times at the giver's deliveries and missed. Old cat could be played with a variable number of bases. The four base version was the forerunner of modern baseball.

endowment, and Huntington had to implement a twelve dollar annual tuition fee. Joe paid the fee from his own savings which he earned from constructing parts for home wool spinning machines. He was not an exceptional student, but he did have a gift for public speaking. Money was even tighter when it came time to further Joe's education beyond Reverend Huntington's academy. Evidence indicates that Mary wished him to enter the ministry, but it seemed a career in the military was preordained. Besides his grandfather, two uncles had gained prominence fighting for the fledgling country during the Revolutionary War. At the suggestion of one of his instructors, the family decided to attempt to garner an appointment into West Point. The teacher, with the assistance of a lawyer friend convinced Massachusetts congressman George Grinnell to request the appointment. With the assistance of his instructor, Joe managed to pass the entrance exam. His application was accepted and at the age of eighteen Joseph Hooker headed to the Military Academy.[14]

Unlike his younger days, Joe applied himself at the academy and did well. He was a quick study and learned to apply new concepts in unique ways. Unfortunately, Hooker's standing in his class was not solely determined by academic performance. His above average grades were offset by a large number of demerits which quickly dropped him to the middle of his class. No doubt his personality traits, attributed to his fall. Hooker was an independent thinker and easily offended, which prompted him to be candid to the point of abrasiveness. His commanders and instructors would not have been impressed by these qualities. After four years of study, he graduated in the bottom half of his class, twenty-ninth out of fifty. Notables in his class were future Union generals John Sedgwick in the twenty-fourth position and William H. French at twenty-two. Classmates who would cast their lot with the Southern cause were Robert E. Lee's future chief of staff, Robert H. Chilton and generals Jubal A. Early, John C. Pemberton, and Braxton Bragg. It was however, the acquaintance of underclassmen, Henry Halleck that would have the greatest effect on his future military career.[15]

After graduation in 1837, Hooker, commissioned a second lieutenant, was assigned to the 1st U. S. Artillery and went to Florida to serve in the second Seminole War. After spending nearly year in Florida, he was transferred a short distance north to deal with marauding Cherokee Indians. Another assignment took Hooker further north, where he served along the Canadian border. The Treaty of Paris in 1783 had not established a definitive boundary between Maine and New Brunswick, causing a border dispute, which erupted when loggers began arguing over timber in the territory. The local militia was called out, and eventually eight companies of the 1st Artillery were sent to keep the peace until a solution to the quarrel could be found. It was here that Hooker received his first promotion, becoming a first lieutenant on 1 November 1838. With the advancement came a raise in pay that pushed his salary to $546 a year.

---

[14] *Ibid*, pp.18-21.

[15] Shanks, William F. G., ***Personal Recollections of Distinguished Generals***, p.166; Boatner, Mark M., ***The Civil War Dictionary***, p.154; Hebert, ***Hooker***, p.21.

During his time on the border, Hooker was recalled to West Point for three months to act as adjutant of the Military Academy. His first four years of service had earned him only one promotion and he was eager to get ahead. The position at West Point would provide him the opportunity to develop skills in handling administrative affairs and would expose him to influential members of the service who could help further his career. Being chosen for the position was telling in that many capable officers already had experience in the position. After fulfilling his duties at the academy, Hooker returned to the 1st Artillery, where he put his administrative skills to work as adjutant for the regiment.

Hooker's time on the northern border came to an end in mid-1845 when another border dispute began brewing in the southwest. Transferred to the Western Division, the 1st Artillery arrived at its new post along the Gulf Coast in September, and the regiment's headquarters where established in Pensacola Harbor. In addition to the execution of his adjutant duties, Hooker also took on the responsibilities of assistant adjutant general for all the troops in Pensacola. A year later word began to circulate that a dispute with Mexico was heating up. The Rio Grande River seemed to be the place for a young officer looking for advancement. Hooker quickly applied for a leave of absence from his regiment, but he had not yet left Pensacola when war broke out. While the politicians in his native state went so far as to call the war an attempt to reinforce slavery, Hooker saw it as an opportunity to further his career. As hostilities got underway, and news of the first battles arrived, he continued to wait for his leave to be approved. Finally the need for officers prompted an appointment, placing him on the staff of General Persifor F. Smith. Joe Hooker could now pack his belongings and search for glory and promotion in Mexico.

Before Hooker arrived in Texas, General Zachary Taylor's invasion of northern Mexico had begun. The Mexican army made its stand at Monterrey and after a hard fight, Taylor's force was successful in defeating the enemy. Hooker executed his duties during the engagement with great energy and helped lead Brigadier General Thomas Hamer's brigade in battle. Taylor's army, after two days of bloody fighting, drove the enemy out, occupied the town, and forced General Pedro de Ampudia to accept terms for an armistice. Hooker's efforts did not go unnoticed. General Hamer applauded his performance. "I am under particular obligation to the chief of staff, Lieutenant J. Hooker," Hamer noted. "…his coolness and self-possession in battle set an example to both officers and men that exerted a most happy influence."

As Taylor began to reform his tired army, the men made their way freely around Monterrey. It was a beautiful town with trees and green foliage, making it a virtual oasis in the heart of northern Mexico's arid region. Hooker enjoyed his time in the city, lounging about and participating in the social activities of the culture. The young ladies made no effort to distance themselves from the conquering soldiers, and according to Hooker the two months that followed the fighting were well worth the hardships of battle. Affection from local females was not the only reward he received for his work in Mexico. Hooker also obtained a promoted to captain. However, there was sadness in Monterrey as well. General Hamer, who had been in poor health since coming to Mexico contracted a severe case of dysentery and died late in the year. Hooker took the death of his chieftain hard for he had grown fond of his commander.

Despite a good deal of animosity toward him, Lincoln placed Joseph "Fighting Joe" Hooker in command of the army in January. *LOC*

Hooker's performance at Monterrey had also been observed by Major General William Orlando Butler, who commanded the volunteers in Taylor's army. When the general requested that Hooker be assigned to his command as aide-de-camp, a transfer was approved. Assuming his new post, Hooker marched with Butler to Buena Vista where Taylor won another victory in February 1847. As Taylor moved on Buena Vista, General Winfield Scott landed his force at Vera Cruz along the Mexican gulf coast, capturing the seaport. By this time, the authorities had determined an assault on Mexico City would be needed to bring the Mexican government to its knees. Not until Scott's force had moved inland toward Puebla did Hooker get his chance to join the advance upon the capital. He was transferred to the staff of Brigadier General George Cadwallader and took on the duties of the general's chief of staff. By June, Hooker was in Mexico advancing with Cadwallader up the Nation Road to join Scott. Cadwallader's force, comprised of 1,000 men, supply wagons and pack mules, was attacked and halted by Mexican soldiers 40 miles from Vera Cruz at the National Bridge. The enemy force was positioned on a bluff overlooking the bridge and a barricade had been constructed across the span. After the roadblock was removed, Hooker led two companies of the 9th Infantry against the enemy on the bluff. Fire was heavy as the young captain moved his men up the hillside carrying the heights. Hooker was brevetted major for his work that day.[16]

---

[16] Hebert, *Hooker*, pp.22-27. In the UK and US military, brevet referred to a warrant authorizing a commissioned officer to hold a higher rank temporarily, but usually without receiving the pay of that higher rank. An officer so promoted may be referred to as being brevetted.

By the time Cadwallader's men reached Scott's main force the army had defeated the Mexicans at Cerro Gordo and established itself in Puebla. It was here, for whatever reason, Hooker changed his affiliation when he was appointed assistant adjutant for General Gideon Johnson Pillow. Pillow was a less than average commander who had no head for military matters. In fact, Pillow allowed his new adjutant to issue orders without consultation. If Hooker's intention was to advance his career, as time passed his transfer to Pillow's command would prove to be a poor choice.

Leaving Puebla on 7 August 1847, Scott's army continued down the Nation Road toward the capital. As the road neared the city, it veered to the right to avoid a large lava bed. The lava was assumed to be impassable by the enemy and the main road had been barricaded. After a reconnaissance around the lava to the left showed a path through the rocks, Scott sent out two divisions, one of which was Pillow's to clear a way to the route. Riding to the top of a hill, Pillow could see off in the distance a substantial enemy force blocking them. Hooker rode back with the news informing Scott the enemy was blocking Pillow's line of march. Scott, not ready to bring on a general engagement, advised caution; however, by the time Hooker returned, Pillow had already arrayed his troops to attack the Mexicans. The attack went forward, but failed to drive off the enemy. Scott was justifiably irritated at the turn of events precipitated by Pillow's poor decision. The commanding general had sent Pillow out to "make a road." Now a general engagement was in process and Scott was not a happy man.

The situation was made worse when Pillow and Hooker, returning for a meeting with Scott, lost their way in the lava field. The weather was poor and by midnight the two men decided they should wait out the darkness. As daylight approached, Hooker discovered that his horse had wandered off, and Pillow went on as his adjutant searched for the animal. Meanwhile, in Pillow's absence, Persifor Smith had taken command and had guided Pillow's command to victory. The following morning an irritated Scott personally took command of Pillow's division. Pillow, who would eventually be wounded in the foot later in the campaign at Chapultepec, had opened a chasm between himself and Scott that would never close.

Hooker went on to further glory during his time in Mexico. His performance at Chapultepec earned him a third brevet and the rank of lieutenant colonel. Both Pillow and Scott praised him for his performance, but the two general's relationship continued to be frosty. The young lieutenant colonel learned much during the fighting in Mexico, which would later be of great benefit during the Civil War. Ample opportunities arose which placed Hooker in positions to observe the habits and traits of men who would be both above him and below him in the Army of the Potomac's command structure. He also learned the same about the men who would command the enemy during the coming conflict. Most importantly however, he became aware of logistic and supply problems encountered when handling a brigade size body of troops in combat.[17]

---

[17] *Ibid*, pp.27-31, 33.

Although the fighting was at an end, the war of words was about to begin. During the campaign, Generals Pillow and William J. Worth, whether to protect their own interests or to damage Scott's reputation, filed battle reports which were derogatory in their tone toward the commanding general. Scott had always believed the administration in Washington was unsupportive of him. He now became convinced that the two generals had contacted the administration and demanded that he be sacked. Whether true or not, Scott believed it, placed them under arrest, and filed formal charges. In February 1848 a court of inquiry was organized. President Polk demonstrated his treachery against Scott by summarily relieved him of command, promoting Worth, and releasing both of the accused from custody. In reality, the inquiry, which began in March, was not an inquiry of the charges against the accused, but an interrogation of both Scott and his enemies. In April, Lieutenant Colonel Hooker was called as a witness to defend Pillow. Hooker's testimony was not damaging to Scott, but it did not endear him to the deposed commanding general.[18]

After the Mexican conflict, Hooker was appointed adjutant general of the 6th Military Department, a position he did not want. The region included a number of Midwestern states which held very little excitement for a soldier fresh out of a major clash. It was not long before Hooker began to investigate moving to a new post. Thinking the west coast offered a more exciting future, he began to work toward a posting there. While gold fever had gripped almost everyone who had migrated to California, it was all about excitement and advancement for Joe Hooker. Before the end of the year, he received word of a transfer to the west and an assignment to the position of adjutant general of the Pacific Division. The division contained two departments, Oregon and California. On 1 February 1849, after a trip to Panama City, which included the trek across the isthmus, he boarded the Pacific Mail Steamship Company's *California* and began the voyage north. Traveling with Hooker was his old commander Persifor Smith. Arriving in San Diego, he spent four months working to realign the California, Mexican border, before boarded the *S.S. Panama* for the remainder of the trip. Arriving in San Francisco on 4 June, Hooker procured transport and traveled on to his new post at Sonoma.

Over the next few months, Hooker visited various regions within the department. His excursions included an 840 mile horseback ride from San Diego northward to visit critical points between the southern border and Sonoma, identifying potential sites for future military outposts. After the initial inspections, the novelty of the situation quickly wore off and Hooker found himself in another uneventful position that was too boring for his tastes. Additionally, the discrepancy between the levels of pay for military members, and pay scales available in the private sector began to concern him. To battle his boredom and discussed with his pay, Hooker, who was now a colonel, began spending a great deal of time at the local drinking establishments, building a reputation which he would carry with him for the rest of his life. Toward the end of 1851 he applied for, and received a two year leave of absence.

---

[18]   *Ibid*, p.34-35; Grant, **Memoirs**, pp.86-87.

Free of his military duties, Hooker took up farming. He purchased 550 acres northwest of Sonoma, and joined the local militia. Farming was not a profitable venture for him, and he soon began to put up for sale the natural resources on his land, securing a contract to sell timber. The work was contracted out and men were brought in to do the cutting, allowing Hooker plenty of time to spend at the local taverns and walking his land hunting game. On one excursion, he came face to face with a bear and after an errant round failed to drop his prey, the bear attacked. The two combatants wrestled and tumbled down the side of a canyon. Hooker was severely mauled, but he managed to extricate himself and climb a tree where he was later found and rescued.

As Hooker's physical wounds healed, his business ventures and gambling produced self-inflicted financial wounds. His poor judgment landed him in legal trouble but none of the problems did any permanent harm. Determining not to return to the army, when his leave ran out, Hooker resigned his commission. He remained a full time civilian for only a short period of time, as he ran for and was elected to the position of Sonoma County Road Overseer. Following up on his initial success, during the summer of 1853, Hooker ran for the position of state assemblyman, but was defeated by thirteen votes in a runoff election. Both he and running mate, Lindsay Carson complained that the election was rigged and that his opponent had brought in people to vote illegally, but nothing ever came of the complaint.[19]

It was during his time out west that Joe Hooker and his future boss and antagonist Henry Halleck, ran afoul of each other. Halleck, a prominent businessman in San Francisco, had joined a law firm which focused on land claim cases. It is possible that some of the individuals hurt by Halleck's legal activities were acquaintances of Hooker's. Hooker believed Halleck was guilty of concocting "schemes" and preying on vulnerable people. Never one to withhold his opinions, he let Halleck know his feelings using language, which he later thought had "never... been forgotten." Another story explaining the animosity between the two men stems from Hooker borrowing money from Halleck and William T. Sherman which he never repaid. Apparently Hooker went to Halleck's law office to repay the debt on a Saturday and found the office closed. The next day, the money he intended to pay back was gone, possibly lost in a poker game or spent on other recreational activities. Whatever the truth of the matter was, Halleck and Hooker were never able to see eye to eye again.[20]

One of Hooker's greatest character flaws was his tendency to speak his mind when discretion would have been a better and more obvious course. When dealing with his peers, he seemed to have little or no humility. George McClellan believed Hooker's character to be "of the worst" kind and accused him of being a heavy drinker and gambler. Other officials also accused Hooker of being a drinker, but there is a great amount of hearsay and vagueness as to Hooker's sobriety

---

[19] Hebert, *Hooker*, pp.35-40. Lindsay Carson was the brother of the famous frontiersman Kit Carson who was John Fremont's guide for both of his western expeditions.

[20] *Ibid*, p.41; Faust, *Encyclopedia*, pp.369-370; Sears, *Chancellorsville*, p.55.

or lack thereof. Lincoln's secretary John Hay had an opportunity to dine with Hooker during the war in Washington, and he made some interesting observations regarding the general's susceptibility to alcohol. "Hooker drank very little," Hay noted in his diary, "not more than the rest who were all abstemious, yet what little he drank made his cheek hot and red & his eye brighter. I can easily understand how the stories of his drunkenness have grown," Hay continued, "if so little affects him as I have seen …red florid cheeks and bright blue eyes…" Hooker, while he drank no more than the others at the party, in Hay's eyes, seemed to exhibit signs of heavy inebriation. There is no hard evidence that he was intoxicated during the fight at Chancellorsville, but there is little doubt that he drank from time to time. Hooker's morality was also of a questionable nature. He was particularly fond of the ladies, and he would build himself quite a reputation in the years to come.[21]

While Hooker's character was well known to the commanders who worked with him and for him, the foot soldiers saw him as a hard fighter and a good field commander. He was a natural communicator, even if the message was a bit hostile. Hooker's combat record in Mexico was notable, with high marks and multiple brevets and his organizational skills where first rate. A confident man, Hooker's mannerisms projected his self-assurance to those who met him and his outward personality was pleasant.[22]

The best physical description of Hooker was penned early in his career by Captain Richard L. Ogden when Hooker made an inspection trip to Fort Adams at Newport Rhode Island.

> "What a handsome fellow he was! [T]all, straight wavy light hair, blue eyes and a complexion a woman would envy, polished in manner, the perfection of grace in every movement, and with all, the courtesy of manner we attribute to the old time gentleman. He was somewhat effeminate in freshness of complexion and color perhaps, but his figure was robust, and of good muscular development. He was simply elegant and certainly one of the handsomest men the Army ever produced…"[23]

"Fighting Joe"

The moniker "Fighting Joe" Hooker came about as a mistake. A typesetter made the error when setting the headline of a newspaper article. Instead of simply putting the word "Fighting" as the heading, with the first two words of the article being Joe Hooker, he added the general's name to the title thus creating the label. Other papers picked up the nickname and before long it took hold. While the

---

[21] Sears, ***Chancellorsville***, p.55; Sifakis, Stewart ***Who was Who in the Civil War***, p.317; Burlingame, Michael & Ettlinger, John R. Turner, ***Inside Lincoln's White House: The Complete Civil War Diary of John Hay***, p.80.

[22] Coddington, Edwin, B., ***The Gettysburg Campaign: A study in Command***, p.26.

[23] Hebert, ***Hooker***, pp.23-24.

name was accurate regarding his battlefield behavior, Hooker actually disliked the label. He was a fighting man and had already proven it on a number of battlefields during the first half of the war. Once engaged, he fought his men hard, but he felt the nickname made him seem rash and willing to rush into a fight. In reality the designation was deadly accurate in describing Hooker when he felt he or his men were being needlessly sacrificed or when he felt he was being personally mistreated.[24]

When Fort Sumter was fired on, Hooker was still out west. When he finally arrived in Washington, the North and South had been sparring for two months. In order to secure a commission, he began contacting congressional friends made when he dabbled in Oregon politics while building roads for the state in the late 1850s. First, he contacted Senator J. W. Nesmith and asked for his support in securing an appointment. He then traveled to New York to meet with Oregon's other senator, Edward D. Baker. Baker was a good friend of Lincoln's and a few supportive words from him would be of great help. On 16 June, Baker obliged Hooker and wrote to the president a supportive letter. To garner support from his home state, Hooker spoke with Senator Charles Sumner. He supposedly informed the senator that if given a colonelcy of a regiment he would one day ascend to command the army and capture Richmond. The letters and testimonials eventually found their way to Lincoln's desk and, following protocol, the new president sent them on to General Joseph K. F. Mansfield, commander of the Department of Washington.[25]

With Winfield Scott still at the top of the Federal command structure, Lincoln requested that Mansfield "please consult with General Scott" on the subject. While Scott's body may have been failing him, his mind was still sharp. He had not forgotten or forgiven Hooker for testifying during the Pillow incident. There would be no position for Joe Hooker in the expanding Union Army. Undeterred, Hooker waited for another opportunity. One arose with the army's initial defeat at Bull Run. After the fighting was over, Hooker visited the battlefield. Approaching his old friend and commander from Mexico, George Cadwallader, he secured an audience with Lincoln where he informed the president "it is neither vanity or boasting in me to declare that I am a damned sight better general than, you Sir, had on that field." Lincoln asked Hooker to sit down and the two men had a candid conversation regarding military matters. The self-promotion worked. Lincoln stood, and placing his hand on Hooker's shoulder, called him "Colonel-not Lieutenant Colonel," and informed him that he had a regimental command for him. On 30 July Lincoln sent a letter to his secretary of war, Simon Cameron, requesting brigadier general commissions for a number of men. Included in the letter, along with others, were the names of Ulysses S. Grant, Edward Baker and Joseph Hooker. The Senate confirmed the commission on 3 August 1861. In two weeks Joe Hooker had talked

---

[24] Sears, *Chancellorsville*, pp.56-57.

[25] Hebert, *Hooker*, pp.47-48.

his way from a retired lieutenant colonel to a brigadier general of volunteers in the Union Army.[26]

A short time later, Hooker was assigned to command of a division at Budd's Ferry in lower Maryland. His task, on the eastern bank of the Potomac River, as outlined by McClellan, was to keep Confederates from crossing the river, to protect any Federal ships which may be navigating the waterway, to disrupt Rebel mail service and to arrest traitors he may find and search them for weapons. Hooker was not pleased with his restricted activities and suggested to McClellan that he be allowed to cross the river and do his disrupting from the Virginia side. McClellan squelched all his requests and Hooker settled down for a winter of boredom in which he took to drinking.[27]

Hooker's division was assigned to the Army of the Potomac's new Third Corps as its Second Division on 13 March 1862. Four days later, General McClellan began shifted the army's base of operations to the Virginia Peninsula. Hooker's division boarded a transfer vessel and sailed south. As the Confederates retreated up the peninsula, Hooker boldly pushed his men forward in pursuit and finally caught up with James Longstreet's rear guard at Williamsburg. The engagement resulted in a sound thrashing for the Yankees and Hooker's men were severely cut up but both the general and his soldiers had shown their willingness and ability to fight. McClellan was not pleased with Hooker's exploits and noted so in his report. The two men never had seen eye to eye and the commanding general's report regarding the Williamsburg clash fueled the fire. Afterward, Hooker began to show his malevolence by working against McClellan behind the scenes, trying to injure him in the same manner as he believed the report had scarred him.[28]

Out of the defeat came the newspaper report which gave him his moniker and the reminder of the Peninsular Campaign found Hooker's men at the heart of the fighting. A promotion to major general of volunteers was bestowed upon Hooker on 5 May 1862. The following September he was placed in command of the army's First Corps and fought it well at South Mountain and Antietam. At Antietam Hooker's men attacked Confederate positions on the north end of the battlefield. During the fighting he was wounded in the foot. The fighting swayed, first in the Yankee's favor and then the Rebel's and as the fighting came to an end, nothing had been decided. The carnage was incredible on both sides with no advantage being obtained by either. Three days after the battle, Hooker was promoted to brigadier general in the Regular Army. He recovered in time to participate in Burnsides

---

[26] *Ibid*, p.49; Sears, ***Chancellorsville***, p.56-57; Hassler, William W., 'Fighting Joe' Hooker, ***CWTI***, vol.14, no.5, p.6. Lincoln to Cameron, 31 July, 1861. A facsimile of this letter appears in Kenneth P. Williams' *Grant Rises in the West: The First Year, 1861-1862* which is a 1997 reprint of his original work *Lincoln Finds a General: A Military Study of the Civil War, Grant's First Year in the West*. The letter appears on page xxvi. Cameron served as Lincoln's Secretary of War until 20 January 1862. Edwin M. Stanton assumed the role on the same date.

[27] Hassler, Hooker, ***CWTI***, vol.14, no.5, p.6.

[28] *Ibid*, p.8. The Third Corps was organized on 13 March, 1862.

debacle at Fredericksburg and following the battle joined the slew of officers speaking out against their army commander.[29]

Shortly after Hooker took command of the army, General Sherman noted how he felt about Hooker's abilities. In a letter to his wife Ellen from his camp near Vicksburg on 17 April 1863, Sherman laid it out quite succinctly. "I know Hooker well," he wrote, "and tremble to think of his handling 100,000 men in the presence of Lee." Commenting on the situation along the Rappahannock River, Sherman prophetically continued. "I don't think Lee will attack Hooker in position because he will doubt if it will pay, but Let [sic] Hooker once advance or move laterally and I fear the result."[30]

Though Joe Hooker was not the perfect choice, in the president's mind, there were no other acceptable options. The man who had been dubbed "Fighting Joe" in the papers would now be tested at the next command level. Unfortunately, his fighting tag could be applied to the new commander's uncanny knack for alienating everyone who could have helped him. The man who would shape the Army of the Potomac for five months prior to the battle of Gettysburg entered the office under a cloud of suspicion held not only by his commander in chief but also by a number of subordinates. He would be relieved of his duties three days before the carnage in southern Pennsylvania began but now it was his job to reinvigorate a dispirited army. The organizational changes and operational decisions made during Hooker's tenure were still in place when the battle commenced later that summer.

Hooker Assembles a Staff

On 29 January Hooker issued General Order No.2 establishing his headquarters staff. To his chief of staff position he installed his friend Daniel Butterfield. Butterfield, compared to Hooker was quite short, only reaching Hooker's shoulder. "Little Dan" seemed very fragile when compared to the solidly built and robust Hooker. Born on 31 October 1831 in Utica New York, Dan was the son of Overland Mail Company founder John Butterfield. Not trained or educated in the military arts, he completed his schooling early, graduating from Union College at the age of eighteen. Butterfield went to work as a businessman and set up shop in his native state. He was employed in that capacity when the war broke out. Shortly after Fort Sumter was attacked, Butterfield, willing to do his part, stepped up and joined the Clay Guards in Washington, DC. By May, he had joined the 12th New York Militia as its colonel. Less than two weeks later, he was a lieutenant colonel in the 12th U. S. Infantry. Despite his lack of military training, he rose quickly through the ranks, serving first in the Valley then fighting on the Peninsula. Through political connections, he ascended to command the Fifth Corps. His inability to effectively command a corps became glaringly apparent at Fredericksburg. After the battle,

---

[29] Faust, Patricia L., ***Encyclopedia***, p.370; Eicher, John H., and Eicher, David J., ***Civil War High Commands***, p.304.

[30] William T. Sherman to Ellen Ewing Sherman, 14 April, 1863, Simpson, Brooks D. & Berlin, Jean V., Editors, ***Sherman's Civil War: Selected Correspondence of William T. Sherman 1860-1865***, p.452.

he was replaced and demoted to divisional command. Unwilling or incapable of looking inward, Butterfield believed his downfall was due to Stanton's dislike of him. With his head for business and ability to promote ideas, he showed brilliance in creating organization from chaos. However, due to his lack of military training, he lacked skills which would have made him a good chief of staff. Butterfield also possessed a volatile temper which he occasionally lost control of, earning him the nickname "Little Napoleon." During the early months of the war, he managed to forge a strong personal and political relationship with Hooker, much to the exasperation of many of his fellow officers. It remained to be seen if they could reinvigorate a dejected army.[31]

To fill the provost marshal position, Hooker chose to retain the services of another New Yorker, Brigadier General Marsena R. Patrick. Patrick, who held the position under Burnside was a West Pointer who had graduated toward the bottom of his class. Born in Watertown he had run away from home early in life and held a number of odd jobs before securing his appointment through an association with General Stephen van Rensselaer. Assigned to the 2nd Infantry, Patrick served five years in Florida fighting the Seminoles and another two combating the Mexicans before resigning to become a farmer. He was no ordinary farmer however, engaging in the development of sciences and technologies to improve production. He worked to promote the New York State Agriculture Society and the State Agricultural College. When the war began, Patrick became the inspector general for the state of New York. A year later he entered the army and was made a brigadier general. Installed as a brigade commander, Patrick led his men during most of the battles fought in the east until October 1862 when at McClellan's request he was selected as the army's provost marshal.[32]

The job of a provost marshal was to be the army's head policeman. The man occupying the position had to be a tough disciplinarian in order to deal with the dregs of the army. He also had to be a man of integrity and character. A provost marshal had to be willing to deal out punishment swiftly and be confident that the administration of any penalty was impartial. Discretion was also a requirement of the position. General Patrick possessed all these qualities and more. Many of his associates considered him to be courageous and honest, but his personality was anything but cordial. He lacked the friendliness that many other better known generals possessed. He was quick to chastise his fellow soldiers when he felt it was justified, and he had no fondness for Butterfield. "I have been annoyed very much by Butterfield being in command," Patrick wrote in his diary on 11 March 1863. Hooker was away at the time and Butterfield was in charge. "He thinks himself very smart, but is in reality nearly a fool about some things… I am utterly disgusted with him… He would keep me doing nothing but answering his follies…"[33]

---

[31] *OR* vol.25, pt.2, p.6; Hebert, ***Hooker***, p.172; Faust, ***Encyclopedia***, p.101; Eicher, & Eicher, ***Civil War High Commands***, p.157; Warner, Ezra J., ***Generals in Blue***, p.62.

[32] Warner, ***Generals in Blue***, pp.361-362.

[33] Sparks, ***Inside Lincoln's Army***, pp.11, 221.

Patrick was well-suited for his role as provost marshal but did not appear to look the part, as he was one of the oddest looking generals in the Union Army. Most of the oddity was created by the way he kept his hair. Bald on top, his hair around the bare spot from the top of his ears around the back of his head was thick and bushy giving his head the look of a life preserver. A large bushy white beard covered his face which was accented by a large darker colored mustache. Taken together all his facial attributes gave him the look of a young, balding Santa Claus.

Doctor Jonathan Letterman would stay on Hooker's staff as the army's medical director. Born in 1825, he was the son of a surgeon from Canonsburg in Washington County Pennsylvania. He spent time in Florida during the Seminole Indian War, after which he saw service in Minnesota, New Mexico and Virginia. Letterman was initially appointed to the position in July, 1862, but his duty with the Army of the Potomac dated back to 1861. He was a graduate of Philadelphia's Jefferson College in 1848 and of Jefferson Medical College in 1849. Shortly after commencement, he joined the Regular Army as a captain, and was appointed an assistant surgeon.[34]

As medical director, Letterman oversaw all aspects of treating the wounded. He also had overall responsibility for the Ambulance Corps, as ordered by General McClellan in August of 1862. Previous to Letterman's administrative attention, the Ambulance Corps had been the responsibility of the Quartermasters Corps. As a result, many ambulances were converted to supply wagons, assuring they would be in short supply when needed. Letterman rectified this situation in the Army of the Potomac. By spring of 1864, Congress noticed the improvements and passed legislation creating the Uniform System of Ambulance Service, patterned after Letterman's changes. He also made improvements in the treatment of wounded, developing a system of field hospitals and a method for supplying brigades with much needed medical supplies. He implemented the idea of forward aid stations, and he was the first to put into operation the concept of triage on a battlefield. It is no wonder that Hooker kept him on his staff since the general was always concerned about the welfare of his men. For his efforts, history would remember Letterman as "The Father of Modern Battlefield Medicine."[35]

In addition to Butterfield, Patrick and Letterman, Hooker's 29 January order included four men to perform aide-de-camp duties, two assistant adjutant generals, a chief quartermaster, deputy chief quartermaster, a chief commissary officer, and a judge advocate general. All these men would be kept busy over the coming months as Hooker implemented major changes which he felt would improve the operational side of the army and the welfare of his men.[36]

---

[34] Coddington, *Gettysburg*, p.27; Musto, R.J., The Treatment of the Wounded at Gettysburg: Jonathan Letterman: The Father of Modern Battlefield Medicine, *Gettysburg Magazine* (hereafter *GM*) Issue 37, p.120; Sifakis, *Who was Who*, p.384.

[35] Musto, Letterman, *GM*, Issue 37, p.120; *Electronic Source:* http://en.wikipedia.org/wiki/Jonathan_Letterman, Last accessed 4/27/2012.

[36] *OR* vol.25, pt.2, p.6.

Two days after establishing his staff, Hooker received his first set of detailed instructions from Halleck. While Lincoln was direct and to the point, Halleck, simply reiterated directions he had given Burnside three weeks earlier. In fact Halleck merely included a copy of a 7 January letter written to Hooker's predecessor with his communication. According to Halleck, the main objective of the Federal army was not the capture of Richmond, but the "defeat or scattering of Lee's army." Doing so would keep the Confederates from menacing Washington and threatening the upper reaches of the Potomac River. Halleck instructed Hooker through the Burnside letter to "cross by the fords above Fredericksburg rather than to fall down to that place," in order to confront Lee. The general in chief also wanted the army to "keep the enemy occupied" until a favorable circumstance revealed itself which would allow Hooker to "strike a decisive blow." He instructed Hooker to "use your cavalry and light artillery upon his communications, and attempt to cut off his supplies, and engage him at an advantage." Halleck's words, even though initially written for Burnside, were taken to heart by Hooker. During the spring of 1863, as his plans for the campaign against Lee slowly came together, all the elements outlined by Halleck were considered and implemented. Unfortunately for Hooker, while the fundamentals of the plan he developed met the desires of Halleck, he would be held responsible for the outcome while the general in chief remained safely in Washington to criticize the results of a plan he demanded Hooker execute.[37]

Deconstructing Burnside

Hooker wasted little time making major changes to Burnside's organizational structure. On 5 February orders were issued to disband the Grand Division configuration installed by his predecessor in favor of smaller, individual corps. General Order No.6 gave specifics as to why the new commander discarded the previous arrangement.

> The division of the army into grand divisions, impeding rather than facilitating the dispatch of its current business, and the character of the service it is liable to be called upon to perform being adverse to the movement and operation of heavy columns, it is discontinued, and the corps organization is adopted in its stead.

In short, the current grand divisions, in Hooker's mind, were too large and did not allow then too conform to the future responsibilities they would be required to shoulder. Typically a military unit is organized with two main responsibilities, logistics (administrative) and tactics (strategy). Reading between the lines of Hooker's order, it is easy to determine the underlying reason for his actions. While there were some commanders he trusted, he evidently did not trust enough of the upper echelon to justify turning over one third of the army to them. He

---

[37] *Ibid*, pp.12-13.

neither trusted nor considered any of his commanders capable of handling the responsibility of controlling such a large organization. Hooker used the "character" of the army's future tasks to justify the conversion. If he believed he possessed competent commanders, the character of future business would not have been a concern. Each corps of a grand division had their own commander, who had been placed in that capacity because he had shown himself capable of making critical decisions. While some of the decisions were questionable, all had shown they could obey orders. Hooker needed to look no further than across the river to his adversary's organizational structure to understand that larger bodies of men could be effective. General Lee had his army divided into two corps which were both approximately the size of Burnside's grand divisions. While Lee did believe that his corps' were too large, their size had not hampered them from being used to advantage. When Lee needed smaller originations to accomplish tasks he simply divided his army into units and sent them on their way. Lee and his corps commanders had proven that, when properly led and utilized, a larger organization could simply be divided as a situation might dictate. If smaller organizations made the "movement and operations" of the army easier, then it also allowed for smaller columns. This was evident during the later stages of the march to Gettysburg as Hooker searched for Lee's army, by spreading out his own army to hunt for the Confederates. However the argument that a larger organization would not have been able to conduct the operation effectively is only justifiable if the larger organization is not properly utilized. The simple fact is that evidence points to Hooker believing he had no one capable of commanding a group larger than the current Federal corps.[38]

Whatever failings Hooker may have possessed regarding his ability to work with his commanders, there is no doubt he was an excellent administrator, which was exactly what the army needed. Over the coming months, he would take it from the brink of disaster and mold it into an effective fighting force. Its numbers would increase and morale would slowly climb to a respectable level. It would be ready to face the challenges encountered as spring broke over war ravaged Virginia.

The Man from Pennsylvania

One problem Hooker faced with the abolition of the Grand Division structure was an overabundance of command grade generals. Four Grand Divisions populated by eight corps required twelve major generals within its configuration. With the corps being the largest operational command, Hooker would have more commanders than openings to fill. Orders issued by General Halleck on 31 January, sent General Burnside's old Ninth Corps to Fort Monroe, leaving Hooker with seven corps to distribute among his commanders. When the changes were complete there would be happy generals and irritated ones.

One of the content generals was John Fulton Reynolds who, after turning down Halleck's inquiry regarding command of the army, retained his position as commander of the First Corps. Born in Lancaster, Pennsylvania on 20

---

[38] ***OR*** vol.25, pt.2, pp.51; Bigelow, ***Chancellorsville***, pp. 39-40.

September 1820, Reynolds, the son of a newspaper man, was a good friend of former President James Buchanan. Reynolds, forty-two years of age in the spring of 1863, was one of the promising younger commanders in the army. He had stood twenty-sixth in a class of fifty-two cadets who graduated from West Point in 1841. After graduation he was brevetted a second lieutenant and spent five years in Texas and served during the Mexican War, exiting the conflict with a major brevet. On 8 September 1860, while the storm clouds of war hung over the land, Reynolds accepted the position of commandant of cadets at West Point where he taught tactics. He was one of the few high level commanders in the army who had managed to earn the respect of the fighting man. Possessing excellent tactical skills, Reynolds was bold, gutsy, and best of all, reliable. He was also skilled at expressing himself, including the use of most common curse words.[39]

When the fighting started, Reynolds was promoted to lieutenant colonel of the 14th U. S. Infantry. A few months later, on 20 August 1861, he was promoted to brigadier general of volunteers. He was placed in command of a brigade in Brigadier General George A. McCall's division of Pennsylvania Reserves. Reynolds' brigade spent the following winter and summer as a member of Major General Irwin McDowell's corps, and he did not participated in the initial fighting of the Peninsular Campaign. By mid-June of 1862, McClellan had managed to convince Lincoln that McCall's division should be sent to assist in the capture of Richmond. Reynolds directed his brigade during The Seven Days battles and his men performed well, but Reynolds himself received a large black mark upon his record. Two day of continuous fighting had taken its toll on him. Tired and worn out, he fell asleep under a tree after the battle of Gaines' Mill. Soon orders came for the army to fall back, and the general was accidently left behind as he slumbered. The following morning, he was rousted by Rebel pickets and taken captive. For the next six weeks Reynolds was a resident of the infamous Libby Prison in Richmond. Being captured in such an embarrassing manner did not set well with the Pennsylvanian. Luck was on his side however, as he was exchanged on 13 August, and returning to the Reserves, was placed in command of the division, ironically due to General McCall being captured.[40]

During the second fight at Bull Run later that summer, Reynolds conducted the delaying action as Major General John Pope's shattered Army of Virginia ran for the safety of the Washington defenses. After James Longstreet's hammer blow had crushed the Federal left and the army was in full retreat, Reynolds directed his Reserves in a counter attack that managed to slow the onrushing Rebels. After the initial attack, he reformed his lines and, grabbing the flag of the 6th Reserves, the staff of which had been splintered and broken by bullets, raised it aloft and

---

[39] Faust, *Encyclopedia*, pp.625-626; Eicher& Eicher, *High Commands*, p.450.

[40] *OR* vol.11, pt.2, p.32; Faust, *Encyclopedia*, p.625; Tagg, Larry, *The Generals of Gettysburg*, p.10; Eicher & Eicher, *High Commands*, pp.450-451.

galloped up and down the line urging his brave men to stand their ground. It could be argued that Reynolds' actions may have saved a large part of Pope's army.[41]

As Lee's army moved north into Maryland in September, an apprehensive Governor Andrew Curtin of Pennsylvania, fearing the invasion of his state, inquired as to whether Lincoln could detach Reynolds from his command to drill and lead the state's local militia units. Ignoring protests from Hooker and McClellan, Lincoln consented and Reynolds missed the battles of South Mountain and Antietam where the Reserves were heavily engaged. As his Reserves were fighting and dying in D. R. Miller's cornfield north of Sharpsburg, Reynolds was busy training men who were either too old to volunteer or boys who were too young, the art of marching, maneuver and fighting.[42]

Lincoln relieved McClellan of command shortly after Antietam and installed Burnside, who promptly reorganized the army onto his Grand Divisions. Returning from his militia assignment on 29 September, Reynolds took over the First Corps, which had been under the command of a junior officer since Hooker had been wounded. A promotion to major general came on 29 November 1862 and Reynolds retained command of the First Corps when Burnside placed Hooker in command of the Center Grand Division. As corps commander, Reynolds produced the only positive results that were to come out of the ill-fated Federal attempt to defeat Lee at Fredericksburg. His old division managed to punch a hole in General A. P. Hill's line on the Confederate right flank, but a failure to support the success with elements of Reynolds' other two divisions squandered the advantage. The lack of assistance was as much Burnside's fault as anyone's due to the somewhat vague instructions he supplied Reynolds.[43]

Reynolds was firm in his belief that the Army of the Potomac was hampered by a lack of leeway from the Lincoln administration and was effectively an army without a commander. He was of the impression that Halleck and Stanton's constant meddling from Washington restricted its commander from conducting successful military operations. So adverse was the interference that Reynolds thought the army would not be successful until the activity ceased, allowing the commander to manage the army as he saw fit. Burnside, who was also aware of the problem, at one point may have called for Halleck and Stanton to be relieved of their duties. Halleck was informed of the request second hand by General William Franklin, commander of Burnside's Left Grand Division at Fredericksburg. According to Franklin, after the battle Burnside "urged the President" to sack both men. While a number of generals, including Hooker, all mentioned to General Franklin that Burnside suggested the removal of Halleck and Stanton, Lincoln informed his general in chief when questioned about the request that General Burnside had never made such a demand. Whether or not Burnside actually asked Lincoln to

---

[41] Tagg, *Generals*, p.10.

[42] *Ibid*; *OR* vol.19, pt.1, pp.266-271; Eicher& Eicher, *High Commands*, p.451.

[43] Tagg, *Generals*, p.11. The officer whom Reynolds took over for was George G. Meade.

remove Halleck and Stanton was never confirmed by Burnside, but it was never refuted by him.[44]

Reynolds relayed his opinion of Washington's meddling in army business in a letter to his sisters after the army had returned from the "Mud March."

> [W]e are now "stuck in the mud," unable to get up our artillery or supplies and Burnside goes to Washington to know what to do!! If we do not get some one [sic] soon who can command an Army without consulting "Stanton and Halleck" at Washington I do not know what will become of this Army. No gen'l officer that I can find approved of the move [the Mud March] and yet it was made… I do not know how it is that the gen'l in command here is obliged to consult Washington every day, and yet there is no one there responsible for failure of operations here…[45]

Reynolds had concluded, somewhat correctly, that the army's failure in the field was more a part of Washington's refusal to allow the army to fight the war on the front lines and not from behind a desk. In his mind, the man at the head of the army was just a whipping boy to lay blame. The administration demanded specific actions, and when those actions brought demoralizing defeat, the army commander lost the confidence of his troops and the government. From the trenches of Washington, Lincoln and Halleck were devoid of any blame and seldom if ever acknowledged their part in the orchestration of the play. Lincoln, for all his wisdom, failed to see the problem until 1864 when Grant was brought

---

[44] *OR* vol.21, p.1006, 1009, 1011; Nichols, Edward, J., ***Toward Gettysburg: A Biography of General John Reynolds***, p.159. In a letter to his wife, George Meade relayed a conversation with Burnside regarding the issue. According to Meade, Burnside told him that Lincoln informed him [Burnside] that some of his generals had protested any further attempt to cross the river at Fredericksburg. Burnside requested the names of the generals in order to have them relieved, but Lincoln refused to comply. Burnside then submitted his resignation which was also refused. Meade wrote that Burnside then told him that "He [Burnside] then made a written protest against Stanton and Halleck, which he read to the President in their presence, stating that neither had the confidence of the people nor the army, and calling on him to remove them and himself." Meade is quite clear in his letter of the details, had no reason to stretch the truth and Burnside had no reason to fabricate the story. Obviously it would not be necessary for Lincoln to deny Burnside's request was ever made to Halleck, if, as Meade states, Burnside read the letter in Halleck's presence. The whole episode seems to be clouded in misstatement, but there is little doubt that Burnside made a request of some type centered around his displeasure with Halleck and Stanton. Meade, George G., ***The Life and Letters of General George Gordon Meade***, p.344.

[45] Nichols, ***Toward Gettysburg***, pp.158-159.

from the West, made supreme commander of the Union forces and Halleck was reduced to nothing more than a chief of staff.[46]

John Fulton Reynolds when he was Commandant of Cadets at West Point. *West Point Album 1861, USAHEC*

Though he had no love for it, Reynolds very seldom publicly spoke out against the administration. Rarely did he have an ill word for any of his fellow officers either, even though a number of them deserved it. He seldom spoke of or discussed his politics in public. Being a conservative Democrat endeared him to his fellow officers, but the radical Washington establishment thought little of him. It was probably Reynolds' refusal to get involved in the mudslinging that kept him from being drug into political wrangling and injured by more powerful men. Doing so kept his enemies from assembling any political ammunition to use against him. George McClellan, a man who knew the sting of political skullduggery, considered him one of the three best general officers with the Army of the Potomac. "He was remarkably brave and intelligent, an honest, true gentleman," McClellan wrote after the war.

Reynolds demanded no more from his men and subordinates than he was willing to contribute himself. Colonel Charles Wainwright, the First Corps' chief of artillery noted Reynolds followed his orders "literally" and "expected all under him to do the same." He was a soldier's general and one of the few commanders who had the complete confidence of his men. His straight and solid physical stature produced a figure which fit his personality and mannerisms. At six feet tall with a slim build he looked the picture of health. His features were chiseled and his skin

---

[46] *Ibid.* p.159; Boatner, **Dictionary**, p.367.

deeply tanned from years of soldiering. A full beard and mustache covered his face, but it was always neat and trimmed, even after weeks of hard campaigning. One of the best horsemen in the army, Reynolds was envied and respected by many of his peers.[47]

While held in high regard, Reynolds had surprisingly few battlefield accomplishments. Now, Burnside was gone and Reynolds' old commander was in charge. He was justifiably troubled when Hooker selected a junior officer to fill the vacancy at the head of the Center Grand Division. Reynolds would have been in his right to be discouraged but the situation was corrected a short time later. Within a week, Hooker dissolved the Grand Divisions and he retained command of the First Corps. Reynolds displayed some confidence in Hooker and he considered a number of the changes made by his new commander as positive. Writing to his sister, Reynolds informed her that under Hooker the army would "achieve success."

To Hooker it was clear that Reynolds should retain his command of the First Corps and, wanting to make sure the Pennsylvanian did not get discouraged, wrote a personal note to him in early April. In it Hooker made certain that Reynolds understood he valued his abilities.

> Do not fear that I undervalue the services of your corps. At the proper time full justice will be done yourself and them. No words of mine can express the appreciation I feel for your services. It will be right at the proper time. I can say no more now.[48]

It was quite clear that General Hooker knew who his friends were and John Reynolds, the man who some in Washington wanted at the head of the army instead of the caustic Fighting Joe, would remain subordinate and loyal, at least for the moment, to his old chief.

To command the Second Corps, Hooker chose to retain the services of Major General Darius N. Couch. Couch, born in Putnam City, New York on 23 July 1822, attended West Point and graduated thirteenth out of fifty-nine cadets in the infamous class of 1846, which included such notables as Thomas J. Jackson, George McClellan and George E. Pickett. He fought in the Mexican War and received a first lieutenant brevet for his work at Buena Vista. Couch had been a civilian for a number of years before the war, having resigned his commission in 1855 to enter the copper manufacturing business. Of slight build and frail, Couch's, performance in Mexico was hampered by his physical limitations. He began the Civil War as colonel of the 7th Massachusetts, and quickly rose to brigadier general and his outstanding performance during the Peninsular Campaign earned him a promotion to major general. He commanded a division at Second

---

[47] Tagg, *Generals*, p.9; McClellan, George B., *McClellan's Own Story*, p.140.

[48] Nichols, *Toward Gettysburg*, p.162. The original note was written personally by General Hooker. The man who commanded the First Corps after Antietam and commanded the Center Grand Division for the first few days of Hooker's command was George Meade.

Bull Run and during the Antietam Campaign and handled his men well enough to earn his current position as Second Corps commander. While an excellent soldier Couch was intolerant of what he defined as incompetence. His opinion of Hooker, while not rosy, was tolerable, but it quickly deteriorated over the next few months. Eventually he would run afoul of Hooker when his commander's actions degenerated to a point which fit Couch's definition of ineptitude. A frank, no nonsense man, Couch could be sarcastic and extremely caustic at times. He had commanded the corps at Fredericksburg and for the present, Hooker saw no need to make a change and determined to keep the New Yorker in that capacity.[49]

A Scoundrel of the First Order

Command of Hooker's Third Corps fell to Brigadier General Daniel Edgar Sickles. Sickles held the distinction of being one of the most controversial generals of the war. Born in New York City on 20 October 1819, he was not a military man but a politician and lawyer. Sickles was ambitions to a fault and at any early age showed that he would not let something or anyone stand in the way of anything he wanted. Studying law at New York University, he displayed his drive when, at the tender age of twenty-four, he was admitted to the New York Bar. Three short years later he was elected to the New York State Assembly. A hard drinker and womanizer, Dan Sickles seemed to be a magnet for controversy and scandal, which in most instances he brought upon himself. During his time in the assembly, he was known to have brought prostitutes into the legislative chambers. He created another controversy in 1852 when he married a young girl, Teresa Bagioli, who at sixteen was half his age.[50]

Like Hooker, Sickles loved the attention of women and sought comfort in the arms of prostitutes. However, while Hooker seemed to look at his association with "working girls" as a recreational activity, Sickles treated it as a lifestyle. A way of life which began as a young man in New York, and he seemed not to care who knew he was visiting the seedy side of the city. His job at a print shop near the Five Points area allowed him easy access to the seventeen nearby brothels and the numerous street girls working there. He frequented the Broadway Theater where many of the cleaner and higher priced women would await business propositions in the gallery while below men with wives and families watch the performance.[51]

In spite of his indiscretions, Dan's political star began to rise and he was selected to perform the duties of secretary to the Minister of Great Britain. Like Reynolds, Sickles was a friend of James Buchanan. In 1853 the future president was serving as the minister and chose to have Sickles accompany him on a trip overseas to visit the island nation. Sickles' wife had just given birth to their first

---

[49] *OR* vol.25, pt.2, p.51; Faust, **Encyclopedia**, p.187.

[50] Hessler, James A., **Sickles At Gettysburg**, p.1; Tagg, **Generals**, p.61. There is a great deal of debate as to Sickles' actual birth year. For a detailed summery see Hessler.

[51] Keneally, Thomas, **American Scoundrel: The Life of the Notorious Civil War General Dan Sickles**, p.5.

child and the infant was too young to withstand the crossing. Mother and child would have to remain behind. This presented a problem for Dan. He would be alone in a new country with no guarantee of female companionship. To solve this dilemma he solicited the assistance of a young prostitute acquaintance, Fanny White, to accompany him and to no doubt warm his bed. Once in Britain, Dan would provide Fanny a place to stay apart from his, and he would visit her from time to time. He even promised to take her sightseeing and would allow her to accompany him during some social activities.

In early 1854 New York papers reported that Dan had been bold enough to take Fanny to meet the Queen. According to the account, Fanny wanted to meet her and Dan was daring enough to allow her to go along. So it was that during a reception held at Buckingham Palace, future Civil War general, Dan Sickles, managed to introduce to Queen Victoria a bordello manager and prostitute from New York. He told the queen that she was Miss Julia Bennett and Fanny took the Queen's hand and executed a customary curtsy. Whether true or not, it was a story which defined Dan Sickles, bold, confident and unconcerned about any repercussions due to his actions. Sickles however, was not done thumbing his nose at the British Monarchy. At one point during his visit he refused to toast the health of the Queen.[52]

Returning to America, Sickles political career took a step up when he was elected to a state senator position in 1855. The following year he was elected to Congress. His political loyalties were to the Democratic Party where he promoted states' rights. Once in the national spotlight he quickly went about educating the Washington elites as to the kind of man he was. He even entertained thoughts of making a run for the presidency had it not been for a single event that would ruin any chance he had of attaining loftier political goals.

Philip Barton Key was a typical man about town in Washington. The son of Francis Scott Key, author of "The Star Spangled Banner", Philip was a fledgling political figure, a captain in the militia, and one of the best looking men in the capital. Legal business brought Key into contact with Sickles and subsequently Sickles' wife. Key became enamored with the woman and the two began secretly meeting for romantic rendezvous. The two tried to keep their meetings a secret, but after a short period Sickles became aware of the relationship. Evidently it was permissible for Dan to covet prostitutes, but not for his wife to engage in a relationship with a rising Washington elite. Seeing Key loitering outside his home, Sickles grabbed a pistol and tracked him down in Lafayette Park across the street from the White House, where his friend James Buchanan was now a resident. Catching up with Key, Sickles confronted him and then shot him twice. The first shot, which may have been a poorly aimed attempt at depriving Key of his manhood, struck the young man in the upper thigh. Falling to the ground, Key begged Sickles not to murder him. Dan, hovering over Key, took deliberate aim once again and fired a second round into Key's chest. The second wound was sufficient to take the young man's life, but Sickles was not yet done. Leveling the pistol at Key again, Sickles' took point blank aim at his head and pulled the trigger.

---

[52] *Ibid*, pp.2-3; Tagg, ***Generals***, p.61.

This time the gun misfired and Sickles finally gave up the assault, as he was pulled away from Key by an onlooker. Key was carried to a nearby restaurant and bar, where he quickly expired, drowning in his own blood as it flowed into his chest.[53]

After shooting Key, Sickles coolly walked down the street and turned himself in at the United States attorney general's office. He was put on trial for murder, defended by a plethora of attorneys, including Edwin Stanton. The argument his lawyers concocted in defending their client was "temporary insanity." For the first time in history a murderer, guilty of the crime, was acquitted using the insanity defense, opening the way for future judicial shenanigans. A short time later Sickles, completed the destruction of his political career when he publicly displayed his hypocrisy by forgiving his wife for her indiscretions. After the trial, congressmen and senators wanted nothing to do with him. Watching Sickles from the House gallery one day, Civil War diarist Mary Chesnut, noted lawmakers avoided him as if he had "smallpox."[54]

Dan's problems really began when he returned to New York and moved in with a friend, who lived not far from his old residence. Word soon began to circulate that Dan and Teresa had discussed the issue of divorce with their families and determined reconciliation would be the best course of action. It was reported that Teresa was the stumbling block to divorce and she would bring forth proof of Sickles' own adultery if forced into a legal separation. Obviously the citizenry would enjoy the scandalous nature of a very public divorce as opposed to settlement. The first hint of a reconciliation appeared in the New York *Herald* when the paper reported the families had decided the whole episode needed to be buried in "the past in a grave of oblivion." When word of the reunion filtered into the papers, the press and the public began to question the validity of the "not guilty" verdict. The quandary discussed was rather simplistic; if Teresa could be forgiven now that Sickles was off the hook for murder, why could Key not have been forgiven a few months earlier? Many questioned how quickly Sickles' sanity returned after he was no longer facing the hangman's noose. The Philadelphia *Press* struck the nail on its proverbial head when it noted, "[i]f Mrs. Sickles was herself guilty before the death of Key she is guilty still, and if one can be forgiven now Key ought to have been forgiven in February…" Returning to his wife also delivered a slap to the face of those who stood by him during the ordeal and placed a black eye firmly upon the face of the country's political elite. Once again the *Herald* accurately represented the mood of the population and their attitude toward Washington. The paper framed Dan and Teresa as "representatives of a bad state of society, wherein political success and power are to be had at any sacrifice of personal honor and private morality." The turnabout was total and intense. Many who had belittled the late Key now turned on Dan and questioned the need for him to avenge his honor by shooting the young man. The whole episode may have been driven by the simple fact that Dan did not want his own infidelity aired in

---

[53] Tagg, ***Generals***, pp.61-62; Sauers, Richard A., ***Gettysburg: The Meade-Sickles Controversy***, p.5; Keneally, ***American Scoundrel***, p.5.

[54] Tagg, ***Generals***, pp.61-62; Sauers, ***Controversy***, p.5.

the arena of public opinion. Either way, Dan's political career in Washington was over, and he had no one to blame but himself. Desperate for a chance to redeem himself in the public's eye, Dan needed an avenue to do so. As luck would have it, along came the Civil War.[55]

Sickles, leaving his Washington political career in shambles, returned to his New York law practice. He was working in this capacity when war broke out. Looking at the war as an opportunity to salvage his reputation, he quickly began to raise a unit of volunteers. Not stopping with just a regiment, he worked hard and eventually organized an entire brigade. With his usual arrogance, Sickles refused to turn control of his new brigade over to the Governor. Contacting his old cronies in Washington, he made efforts to have the regiments mustered in as United States volunteers, which enraged New York Governor Edwin Morgan. It took an order from the secretary of war to make Sickles release control and the units were mustered in as New York volunteers during the summer and fall of 1861. His support for Lincoln's war policies, and his zeal when raising the brigade earned him a star in September 1861, when he was commissioned a brigadier general of volunteers. Then something happened that would ensure Dan Sickles his place in military history. His unit was attached to Joe Hooker's division and transferred to the Virginia Peninsula for the campaign against Richmond in 1862. Realizing Hooker was a bit of a scoundrel himself, had a military background, and seemed to be moving upward quickly, Sickles latched onto Hooker's coattails and using his political skills as a crutch went along for the ride. As Hooker rose in the ranks, Sickles followed.

Sickles was often absent from his command, even during combat. He was missing from his brigade during the battle of Williamsburg. While his men were in the thick of the fighting, he chose to spend the time in Washington currying favor with his cronies. Again, at the second battle of Bull Run he was absent. While on his excursions to Washington he made significant efforts to develop a relationship with the president and Mrs. Lincoln. When Hooker was given command of the First Corps, Sickles succeeded him as commander of Hooker's old Third Corps division. His association with Hooker and his political connections garnered him a nomination for a major general's commission to date from 29 November 1862. Fifteen days later, during the Battle of Fredericksburg, his division was held in reserve and saw little combat. While Sickles had participated sparingly in actual fighting, Burnside may have made an error in keeping him idle during the battle for in the coming weeks the New Yorker would prove that he was as aggressive a fighter as he was a politician.

Once again, when Hooker ascended to command of the army, he rewarded Sickles' loyalty, giving him command of the Third Corps. While the position was initially intended to be a temporary one, Sickles would retain the post for the duration of Hooker's command and beyond. He was the only corps commander within the army that was not trained at West Point, a fact that left a sour taste in the other commander's mouths. Most of his peers had low opinions of him, were appalled at his private lifestyle, and distrusted his military instincts. His lack of

---

[55] Brandt, Nat, *The Congressman Who Got Away with Murder*, pp.190-191; Hessler, James A., *Sickles At Gettysburg*, pp.18-19.

military training, while deemed a handicap by most of his fellow officers, had not diminished his ability to maneuver his way to the upper echelons of the army.[56]

It is amazing that with his lack of morality and questionable abilities, Sickles rose as far as he did in the Federal command hierarchy. Even with the baggage he carried around, he seemed to be immune to the repercussions that most men with such a checkered past are subjected. It is likely that his skills as a lawyer and politician allowed him to gloss over the issues when confronted or questioned. It's also quite possible that few questioned him due to their desire not to be drawn into a malicious confrontation. Thoughts of confronting Sickles were no doubt quickly squelched with the memory of the Key incident only four years removed. No one ever questioned Sickles' tremendous personal courage. Philippe de Trobriand, one of his brigade commanders at Gettysburg, called attention to the qualities that made him a good general. Writing in his memoirs, de Trobriand noted Sickles possessed "a quick perception, an active temperament." De Trobriand also noted that the general had a "clear view" of his ambitions, possessed a "deep knowledge of political tactics," and "practical judgment." In addition, even though Sickles had not been present for much of the fighting in 1862 he would soon prove that while controversial, he was a fighter which was something Lincoln needed in his army.[57]

Daniel Edgar Sickles' questionable character made him a murderer before the war. For him the conflict would be a vehicle to recapture his notoriety. *LOC*

---

[56] ***OR*** vol.25, pt.2, p.51; Faust, ***Encyclopedia***, p.688; Tagg, ***Generals***, pp.61-62. Although nominated on 29 November 1862, his promotion would not be confirmed by the Senate until 9 March 1863.

[57] Tagg, ***Generals***, p.61.

Sickles was considered a handsome man. Tall and erect, his mannerisms displayed a confidence which many would say bordered on arrogance. Once Dan determined what he wanted or what in his mind needed to be done, it was difficult to persuade him to change his plans. Barton Key found this out first hand. When Joe Hooker gave him command of the Third Corps the winter of 1863 he was forty-three years old. The signs of middle age were beginning to display themselves. Sickles' hair line was beginning to slide backward, calling attention to his high forehead. His brown hair was offset by piercing blue eyes and he wore facial hair in the form of a large bushy mustache with a small patch covering the cleft of his chin. It was obvious to all associated with him that he was not a man to be crossed and a powerful associate if he was on your side. His fellow corps commanders however knew he was a loose cannon that could discharge at any time.

"Uncle John"

John Sedgwick was not the typical Army of the Potomac corps commander. In an army where many generals worked their way up through the ranks by befriending influential people and politicians, Sedgwick believed in advancement the old fashioned way, by deeds and ability. He preferred to let his record speak for him, and he made no effort to lead a crusade to obtain promotions. It was thought by some that he would have been a better choice to succeed Burnside, but he received scant consideration. Being passed over was obviously due to other more boisterous men like Hooker, Franklin, and Couch. It may also have been that Sedgwick, being a supporter of George McClellan, received little though due to the animosity which existed between Lincoln and the army's former commander.

Sedgwick was a soldier's general. During battle, he would walk the firing line in the dress of a common infantryman, usually wearing a blue coat with no insignia of rank upon his sleeve. Sometimes it was difficult to tell him from a common foot soldier, since on many occasions he chose to wear the trappings of a simple private. His boots seemed to always be muddy and a black hat shielded him from the sun and the rain. Frank Haskell, noted Gettysburg diarist, commenting on Sedgwick wrote that he dressed "carelessly." He very seldom carried himself like a general and his actions fell short of those expected from a corps commander. An easygoing bachelor, he was addicted to solitaire and would spend large amounts of time relaxing with a deck of cards.

Sedgwick understood that his success as a commander hinged upon the performance of his men, and he made every effort to see to their needs and take care of them. The men rewarded his effort with devotion and respect and took to affectionately calling him "Uncle John," although they never called by his first name when he was within earshot. He had a presence about him that reassured his men, even when facing trying events of battle. In his chest beat a gentle heart. Some noted it seemed to be that of a boy, and it was not unusual to be fooled by a practical joke precipitated by him. From the top down there seemed to be no one in the army who had any ill feelings for John Sedgwick, from the grimiest private to the commander of the army. He exuded the image of a fatherly figure but never let the discipline of his men relax. The soldiers always knew where they stood with

John Sedgwick, and it was usually at his shoulder when the firing was the hottest, as he showed his men by example how to be oblivious to bullets.

Haskell wrote one of the best descriptions of Sedgwick noting that the general was "short, thick-set" but "muscular." He also noted Sedgwick had a "florid complexion, dark, calm, straight looking eyes, with full heavyish [sic] features, which with his eyes, have plenty of ammunition when he is aroused," and that "he has a magnificent profile, …well cut, with the nose and forehead forming almost a straight line, curly short chestnut hair and full beard, cut short, with a little gray in it." On the occasions when he wore his dress uniform, Haskell observe Sedgwick appeared magnificent and that he looked "honest and modest."[58]

Born on a farm, 13 September 1813 in Cromwell Hollow, Connecticut, John Sedgwick was the grandson of Revolutionary War veteran General John Sedgwick, who served with George Washington at Valley Forge and the battle of Brandywine. Even as a boy, he demonstrated a strong will and the leadership qualities that would later be on display so prominently during the war. He attended Sharon Academy and taught school for two years before he entered West Point. At the academy, young John was an average student who graduated twenty-fourth in a class of fifty cadets.

Of all the generals with the Army of the Potomac, Sedgwick may have been the most experienced regarding actual combat. After graduation, he became a bit of an Indian fighter, participating in the Seminole War. He also fought the Comanche, Cheyenne, and Kiowa. In 1838, Sedgwick helped move the Cherokee Indians west; the last relocation of the southeastern Indian tribes along the "Trail of Tears" to reservations in what would eventually become the state of Oklahoma. When war broke out with Mexico, he was assigned to General Scott's command and earned distinction at Vera Cruz, Cerro Gordo, Churubusco and Chapultepec. For his bravery he was promoted three times, returning home with the brevet rank of major. Back home, Sedgwick kept himself busy with various military duties until the mid-1850s when the Kansas border war erupted. The conflict was precipitated by the passage of the Kansas-Nebraska Act of 1854 which promoted the concept of "popular sovereignty." The idea was nothing more than the Federal Government's attempt to use States' Rights as a crutch to avoid making a decision regarding the expansion of slavery. The act left the decision as to whether a state would enter the Union as free or slave up to the citizens of the territory, precipitating violence between abolitionists and pro-slavery factions. For Sedgwick however, it was another military assignment, providing additional experience under fire.

By the time the Civil War was looming on the horizon, Sedgwick had received a promotion to lieutenant colonel of the 2nd Cavalry. Nine days later, on 25 March 1861, he was elevated to colonel of the 1st Cavalry. By the end of August he had been made a brigadier general serving as acting inspector general in Washington. He missed the first Battle of Bull Run, but by early 1862 he was in command of the Second Division of the Second Corps. He replaced Brigadier General Charles Stone who had been unfortunate enough to participate in the Federal disaster at

---

[58] *Ibid*, pp.103-104; Byrne, Frank L., Weaver, Andrew T., Editors, **Haskell of Gettysburg**, pp.132-133.

Ball's Bluff. Stone, blamed for the debacle, was arrested, held captive, but never charged, opening the door of opportunity for Sedgwick.[59]

Sedgwick's division was assigned to the Army of the Potomac and when McClellan transferred his command to the Virginia Peninsula, Sedgwick's troops went along. His division participated in the siege of Yorktown and the fighting at Seven Pines, but was only lightly engaged. Sedgwick led his men during the early battles, but during The Seven Days fighting was so ill with camp fever that he could not sit in his saddle. Finally on 29 June he was well enough to take the field and led his men during the battle of Glendale. During the battle, Sedgwick paid the price for being so close to the front. He was hit by two bullets; one grazed his leg while the other struck him in the arm. Neither wound was serious, but it was a sign of things to come.

John Sedgwick was a competent commander who cared deeply for the welfare of his men. *LOC*

A promotion to major general was given on 4 July while Sedgwick convalesced. He returned to his division in time to march north with McClellan to engage Lee's army at Antietam. The battle turned out to be a low point in Sedgwick's career. The morning fight swirled around the West Woods, forcing General Edwin Sumner to send his Second Division, commanded by Sedgwick into the woods to clear out the Rebels. Shortly after Sedgwick's command entered the trees; it was savagely attacked on its left flank by a horde of Confederates and completely routed, being nearly destroyed. It was one of the most horrible poundings endured by any division during the war. Sedgwick, true to his nature, was leading his command from the front when his left flank was hit and gave way. During the ensuing melee, he was

---

[59]   Tagg, ***Generals***, p.103; Faust, ***Encyclopedia***, p.665; Boatner, ***Dictionary***, p.730.

hit by two bullets. One struck his wrist, fracturing the bone while the other passed through his leg. Unable to control his horse with his wounded wrist, he nonetheless remained in the saddle trying to rally his fleeing men. Finally, a third bullet struck him in the shoulder and forced him from the animal. Losing consciousness, he was carried to the rear by some of his men as the Rebels took possession of the woods.

Sedgwick, as he recuperated from his injuries made it known that he was tired of being wounded. "I want no more wounds," he commented, wishing that if he were ever hit again "it would settle me at once." Three months later he was ready to return to duty, though not in the field. He spent another two weeks recovering in Washington before returning to the army, but he was not restored to command of his division until after Fredericksburg.

Hooker had serious reservations about Sedgwick's abilities as a commander, feeling that Sedgwick was a poor judge of terrain and had "great distrust in exercising on the field important commands." The assessment was essentially correct since Sedgwick did have a tendency to pause and falter when he was giving discretionary orders which required him to read the situation on the field and apply orders based on his assessment. When Burnside was relived however, Hooker appointed him to command of the Sixth Corps, the largest corps in the army, in spite of his concerns.

While some of the top level commanders questioned Sedgwick's fitness for corps command, none of the men who fought for him questioned his concern for their wellbeing. His men genuinely cared for him, and their "Uncle John" was one of the most loved commanders in the army. He was a man who held a deep desire to return home to his native Connecticut and the peace of retirement, but that relaxing life would have to wait. His services where needed by his country, and John Sedgwick was ready to do his part.[60]

An "Officer of Uncommon Merit"

Oliver O. Howard was not a happy man. He had expected to receive a high-level command appointment, one that was due a man of his tenure and rank of major general. When it came time to pass out appointments for new corps commanders, Joe Hooker did not turn Howard's way. Even though he had commanded a corps in the grand division structure, he was denied a like command within the new organization, a victim of the overpopulation of command grade officers. Instead of Howard, the new commander appointed his old crony, Dan Sickles to the command of the Third Corp. Sickles' appointment did not set well with the grumbling Howard. Even though Sickles' command was specified as temporary, Howard still believed he had been passed over. Hoping to obtain the post he felt he was due, Howard wrote to Hooker requesting an appointment to a post worthy of his standing. Both Sickles and Howard had been commissioned major generals on the same day. Howard promptly accepted his promotion. Sickles, on the other hand, delayed his acceptance. Because of the "lag", Howard was of the opinion that his appointment predated Sickles' and therefore he should have been awarded command of a corps prior to the politician.[61]

---

[60] Tagg, *Generals*, pp.104-105.

[61] Bigelow, *Chancellorsville*, pp.40-41; Sears, *Chancellorsville*, p.65; *OR* vol.25, pt.2, p.17

Howard was not the only general complaining about his situation. When the grand divisions were abolished, Major General Franz Sigel found himself back in command of his old corps. Sigel had been in charge of the Reserve Grand Division, which had consisted of the Eleventh and Twelfth Corps. Now he was back in command of the Eleventh which contained a large number of first and second generation German immigrants. Sigel had fled Germany after the attempted revolution in 1848 had floundered. He was well liked by not only the German element of the corps but also by all German Americans in general. The troops where feverishly loyal to him and could often be heard audaciously calling, "I fights mit Sigel." Attempting to increase the size of his corps, Franz called for additional troops to be assigned to it. After the attempt failed, Sigel had enough. He wrote a request to be relieved from command on 12 February. "The reduction of my command.... makes it exceedingly unpleasant and dispiriting for me to remain longer in my present command," he commented. Hooker forwarded Sigel's request to Washington along with his endorsement. The administration responded saying of Hooker, "He has given General Sigel as good a command as he can, and desires him to do the best he can with it." Unsatisfied, Sigel departed on leave and never returned.[62]

With Sigel gone, command of Eleventh Corps fell to Brigadier General Julius Stahel, who had commanded the corps when it was a component of the now defunct Reserve Grand Division. Hooker could easily have reestablished the connection between the men and a well-loved commander by placing Major General Carl Schurz in command. Schurz was equally liked and could have very easily filled the void left by Sigel's departure. However, Hooker had no use for Schurz. "I would consider the services of an entire corps as entirely lost to this army were it to fall into the hands of Maj. Gen. Schurz," he informed Edwin Stanton. Instead, Hooker did nothing, choosing to wait out the protocol initiated with the submittal of Sigel's request. As he waited for Washington to act, the appointment of Sickles occurred, prompting Howard to level his complaint. Not wanting to remove his friend from command of the Third Corps, Hooker looked to the now vacant spot with the Eleventh. "Has the resignation of Major General Sigel been accepted," he telegraphed the secretary of war on 20 March, "or is that officer to be removed from command of the XI Corps? I desire to ascertain in order that, if so, Major General Howard....may be assigned to it." Hooker included in his message a note to the effect that Howard was the highest-ranking member of the commander pool, he was an "officer of uncommon merit," and should be assigned to the command. After waiting eleven days, and receiving no response, Hooker appointed Howard to "temporary" command of the corps on 31 March, but the complaining was not over. Schurz entered the fray by contacting Lincoln and arguing that the Germans joined because they believed they "would remain in the hands of one of their own." Griping had no effect, and Howard assumed command of the Eleventh Corps which he would hold three months later as its men marched toward Gettysburg.[63]

---

[62] *OR* vol.25, pt.2, p.70-71; Bigelow, ***Chancellorsville***, pp.40-41; Sears, ***Chancellorsville***, pp.64-65.

[63] Bigelow, ***Chancellorsville***, pp.41-42; Sears, ***Chancellorsville***, pp.64-65.

In the spring of 1863 Howard was only thirty two years old. His age made him the youngest corps commander in the Army of the Potomac. Born on 8 November 1830 in Leeds Maine, young Oliver was raised on the family farm, but tragically his father passed away when he was only nine. While short on years, Howard was not short on education. He attended a local school and later enrolled in schools in the towns of Monmouth and Yarmouth Maine. Money was scarce in the Howard family and Oliver paid for most of his schooling with his own money which he earned teaching school himself. Entering Bowdoin College, Oliver continued to show he was a good student by graduating with a Masters of Art. After leaving Bowdoin, he accepted an appointment to West Point which was arraigned by his uncle, a congressman. He continued to be an excellent student, even after an accidental tumble in which he landed hard on his head. Howard's commitment to his studies elevated him to the upper echelon of his class, graduating fourth in a class of forty-six in 1854. Seven months after graduation, Howard married Elizabeth Anne Waite from Portland Maine. Elizabeth would eventually bear him five boys and two girls over the next sixteen years. After commencement he was commissioned a second lieutenant. His first duty assignment was at the Watervliet Arsenal in New York. After a short time there, he was transferred to the Kennebec Arsenal in Maine. His duties at Kennebec were evidently minimal for soon after his arrival he was transferred back to Watervliet. After spending some time in Florida, from 1857 to the opening of the war, he taught mathematics at West Point and even considered entering the ministry.[64]

While Oliver Otis Howard had and would perform admirably on other Civil War battlefields; his lack of vigilance at Chancellorsville would give his corps a black eye. *LOC*

---

[64] Tagg, *Generals*, p.121; Carleton, Hiram, **Genealogical and Family History of the State of Vermont**, p.36, 39.

When Fort Sumter was fired upon, Howard was only a lieutenant. Putting his life plans on hold, he entered into the support of the Union, becoming the colonel of 3rd Maine Volunteers. Shortly before arriving in Washington, the accident prone Howard once again suffered a fall. This time he tumbling from an artillery limber at the arsenal in New York and crushed his toe. The injury evidently did not incapacitate him for long. Shortly after the regiment arrived in Washington, Howard found himself in the role of a brigade commander even though he had not been promoted to the rank of general. Showing their appreciation for his service, some of the brigade members presented him with a sword which he carried throughout the war. He led his brigade at First Bull Run and it was one of the last to evacuate its position. He was rewarded with a brigadier general's star on 3 September for his efforts. When the Army of the Potomac was organized, his brigade was assigned to the Second Corps and he led it during the Peninsular Campaign. On 1 June, as he guided his ranks forward in a charge against the enemy, he was hit in the right arm by two bullets. The first only damaged tissue, but the second one struck bone and shattering it just above his elbow. The wound resulted in the loss of his arm. Howard's arm wound and amputation was the first event in one of the most unlucky careers on record.[65]

During his recovery, he was visited by General Philip Kearny who had previously lost his left arm. As the two spoke, Kearny quipped that from now on the two would have to shop for gloves together. During his convalescence, Howard assisted in the recruitment of additional volunteers from Maine. Two short months later he returned to duty and was assigned command of the Philadelphia Brigade, part of John Sedgwick's Second Division of the Second Corps. Howard was at the head of the brigade when, with the remainder of Sedgwick's men they advanced to clear the West Woods at Antietam. After the division was overrun and Sedgwick wounded, Howard took command of the tattered remains, but he could do little more than preside over the residual men as they limped to the rear. Promoted to major general on 29 November 1862, he remained in command of the division and was unlucky enough to be selected to participate in the assault on Marye's Heights. The slaughter before the stone wall at Fredericksburg was possibly the worst moment for the Army of the Potomac during the entire war. The carnage was unfathomable and Howard's boys were butchered along with the other men who tried in vain to take the heights from the well-protected Confederates. By the spring of 1863, the Second Division had been a participant in arguably the two bloodiest events of the war in the east. Howard's luck would not improve in the near future.[66]

Slight of build and only five feet nine inches tall, Howard was not the dominating presence that one would expect in a General. Frank Haskell noted that Howard was "medium in size..." and that there was "nothing marked about him..." He was not capable of extracting a rousing cheer from the troops as he rode along the lines. Because of his missing arm, he typically wore the right sleeve of his coat

---

[65] Carleton, *Genealogical*, p.37; Eicher& Eicher, **High Commands**, p.306.

[66] Tagg, **Generals**, p.121; Boatner, **Dictionary**" p.413; Eicher& Eicher, **High Commands**, p.306; Carleton, **Genealogical**, p.37.

or jacket pinned to his side. His chief of artillery, Thomas Osborn noted that the general did not possess any natural abilities when it came to military matters and did not regard him as a great thinker. Haskell, however, noted some good points, calling Howard "a very pleasant, affable, well dressed little gentleman."[67]

No one questioned Howard's integrity, just his abilities as a general. After the war, he would spend a good deal of time defending his actions on the battlefield. His opinions and words would be challenged by others, but for now he was looked upon as a man of bravery and character. Unfortunately, many felt he lacked the spunk to lead men effectively. Colonel Charles Wainwright wrote of Howard that he was a "Christian as well as a man of ability, but there is some doubt as to his having snap enough to manage the Germans [of the Eleventh Corps] who require to be ruled with a rod of iron." Wainwright believed Howard to be a brave soldier and a gentleman. "He is the only religious man of high rank that I know of in the army and, in the little intercourse I have had with him, showed himself the most polished gentleman I have ever met."[68]

Howard's pale facial features were covered with a large bushy brown mustache and full beard. His most distinguished facial feature was his straight nose which gave his face rigidity. His blue eyes were unremarkable and a little soft. His youth was reflected in a full head of straight hair which was contrary to a number of other generals whose hair had begun to migrate backward. It was straight except for a bit of a wave at the front. Unfortunately for Howard, his look and name would become associated with some of the most recognized failures of the army.[69]

The Frugal General

To command the Twelfth Corps, Hooker chose to retain the services of Henry W. Slocum. Slocum owed the spelling of his last name to a clerical error when his ancestor Anthony Slocumbe arrived at New Plymouth (now Massachusetts) in 1637. The clerk who recorded his name in the register wrote it like it sounded and changed the spelling to Slocum. The error was never corrected and Anthony's name became truncated.

Henry was born in the small town of Delphi in upstate New York's Onondaga County on 24 September 1827. He was the eighth generation of Anthony's siblings and the fifth son and sixth child born to Matthew Barnard Slocum and his wife Mary, a union which would eventually produce eleven children. As a youth, Henry attended Delphi Public School, which provided year round instruction. For young Henry the regiment soon became boring. To fight the monotony, he went to work with his father to earn his own money to buy clothing and other necessities. Dealing with his own finances at a young age allowed him to develop a frugal attitude toward money. He bought sheep which he took care of himself, and supplemented

---

[67] Tagg, **Generals**, p.122; Byrne & Weaver, Editors, **Haskell**, p.133.

[68] Tagg, **Generals**, p.122.

[69] Byrne, & Weaver, Editors, **Haskell**, p.133.

the family's income with the wool he produced, and his self-sufficiency helped his large family make ends meet.

A new teacher began to see potential in Henry, as he displayed a solid understanding of mathematics by doing well in arithmetic, geometry and algebra. His progress allowed him to move on and attend the Cazenovia Seminary in neighboring Madison County. The seminary provided academic and theological instruction and was associated with the Methodist Episcopal Church. By the age of sixteen, his peers thought so highly of him that he was issued a public school teacher's certificate. For the next five years he taught school when time permitted. When his father could spare him he attended the State Normal School in Albany.[70]

In 1848 Henry applied for admittance to West Point. It was a happy day when he received his appointment. On 1 July he arrived at the academy and was admitted into the class of 1852. In his first year he ranked fourteenth in a class of sixty, showing high marks in mathematics and English, while only being assessed twenty-three demerits. During his second year, he gained a rank in standing by moving to thirteenth while not being assessed a single demerit. His third year produced an even bigger improvement to third in his class, which by then numbered fifty-three. A decline to seventh during his final year was not enough to harm his outstanding record and all individuals associated with Henry Slocum knew he had been a model student who did well with all his studies. One of his classmates, Philip Sheridan, wrote in his memoirs that it was his good fortune to have Henry as a roommate. Sheridan noted that Slocum's "education was more advanced than mine and, who's studious habits and willingness to aid others benefited me immensely."[71]

Graduating on 1 July 1852, Henry was assigned to duty in Florida fighting the Seminoles like many graduates before him. Commissioned a second lieutenant in the 1st U. S. Artillery, he spent slightly more than a year with it before he was transferred to Fort Moultrie on the north shore of Charleston Harbor, South Carolina. In 1854 Henry married Clara Rice, whom he had originally met during his school days at Cazenovia. He was on furlough at the time and when his leave ended, Clara accompanied him back to his post. While in South Carolina, the Slocum's had numerous opportunities to partake in society events and outdoor activities. Leisure time activities and military duties kept Henry busy for short periods, but the boredom of garrison duty drove him to other pursuits, particularly the study of law. Henry became serious about learning the practice and secured a local specialist from Charleston to teach him. As his studies continued, he began to consider resigning from the army.

In the spring of 1855, Slocum earned a promotion to first lieutenant which prompted him to remain in the service. The summer that year was unusually warm and the heat took its toll on the men of the garrison and their families,

---

[70] Tagg, *Generals*, p.143; Faust, **Encyclopedia**, p.692; Slocum, Charles E., *The Life and Service of Major-General Henry Warner Slocum*, pp.4, 6-8; *Electronic Source*: http://en.wikipedia.org/wiki/Cazenovia_Seminary, Last accessed 4/27/2012.

[71] Slocum, *Henry Warner Slocum*, pp.9, 10.

affecting their comfort and health. By that summer, Henry's family had grown by one member, a daughter, Caroline. Little Caroline was particularly susceptible to the heat and living conditions of garrison life. By the following summer Slocum decided he had sufficiently worked off his obligation for his military education through his service and decided to resign his commission. Before he could turn in his letter of resignation, tragedy struck as little Caroline succumbed to the harsh conditions and died on 20 October 1856. Eleven days later Henry resigned from the army. One can only speculate if he second guessed his decision to resign, wondering if he had left the army sooner and went back to New York, his daughter may have survived.

Returning to Onondaga County, Henry passed the bar exam and set up a law office in Syracuse. He soon had a thriving, profitable business which allowed him to generate a sizable amount of wealth. As his fortune grew, Slocum remained thrifty. Adding to his profits from the law office was the money he had managed to save during his time in the military. Because of his financial wellbeing he was able to assist his father monetarily when the elder Slocum's business ventures fell on hard times and his health began to deteriorate. In addition, Henry was able to purchase a home for his family in Syracuse. He also entered the real estate market, purchasing a group of vacant lots which he constructed homes on a few years later. The city authorities were so pleased with his efforts to improve the town that the street the homes were constructed on was renamed Slocum Avenue. [72]

Slocum next decided to try his hand at politics and was elected to an assemblyman position in the lower house of the New York state legislature in November 1858. Henry joined the newly organized Republican Party and became meticulous when examining any legislation he was required to vote upon. Two years later he was elected to the office of treasurer for his native county. Unfortunately his fledgling political career ended with the beginning of hostilities.

Slocum traveled to Albany and met with the governor to offer his services. He proposed raising a battery of light artillery, reverting to his previous military training, but the governor was not receptive. In a moment of incredible shortsightedness, the governor informed Henry that no artillery would be needed to put down the rebellion. Returning home, Slocum discovered that a regiment of infantry was being raised. His name was presented as a possible colonel for the new organization, but Henry lost out to another volunteer who had been a man of high standing in the local militia.

Just when it seemed he would not be joining the volunteers, another opportunity presented itself. The 27th New York Volunteer Infantry was being organized in Elmira. As the regiment assembled, it was suggested that a West Point man be found to lead it. While most of the men in the regiment were not personally acquainted with Slocum, he was still chosen to be their colonel. Slocum believed that since he owed his education to his country, it was time to repay the debt and help his country in its hour of need. He accepted the post and was commissioned colonel of the regiment on 21 May 1861. He quickly began drilling his new

---

[72]   *Ibid*, pp.11-12.

command and within a short period Slocum had his men well prepared for their upcoming trials.⁷³

While Henry Warner Slocum was a competent commander he had a tendency to get bogged down in military protocol. *LOC*

Less than two months later, the regiment traveled to Washington and took its place in the ranks of General McDowell's army. The regiment was in camp only a few days before it marched west to Manassas. Slocum and the regiment received their baptism of fire at Bull Run. The men crossed the run at Sudley's Ford as part of General David Hunter's Second Division. They formed in line of battle near the Robinson House. The 27th did well in its first action and gave a good accounting. As the tide of battle turned on Henry House Hill, the 27th, along with the rest of the Federal force began its retreat from the field. As he led his men toward the rear, Slocum was hit by a musket ball in the right thigh. Unable to continue, Henry turned his command over to Major Joseph J. Bartlett and retired to get medical attention.⁷⁴

When he became well enough to travel, Slocum returned home to recover from his injuries. While in New York he was the recipient of a brigadier general commission dated 9 August. He reported for duty a month later and was assigned command of the Second Brigade in Franklin's Division of the First Corps. He had been absent only fifty days. Slocum showed that he was a no nonsense brigade commander when he requested a court of inquiry be formed to investigate what he

---

⁷³   *Ibid*, pp.12-13; Phisterer, Frederick, ***New York in the War of the Rebellion*** (hereafter ***NYWR***), vol.3, p.2039.

⁷⁴   *Ibid*, p.14; ***OR*** vol.2, p.389.

considered blatant disregard for his direct orders during an expedition to capture a group of enemy cavalry. He also placed eighteen officers under arrest for lodging a formal complaint stating his orders regarding the property of the local residence were too strong. The men were eventually released, but the message sent to the officers and men of his brigade was that Henry Slocum would not tolerate insubordination.[75]

Slocum performed well during the Peninsular Campaign and was rewarded for his efforts, being assigned command of Franklin's Division when Franklin was promoted to corps command. On 4 July 1862, Slocum earned a promotion to major general of volunteers. Returning from the Peninsula, Slocum, who's division was now a member of the Sixth Corps, was ordered to move up and join General John Pope's army near Manassas. As evening approached, Slocum's division, marching toward the battlefield, met a mass of men in headlong flight toward Washington. The division was formed across the Warrenton Turnpike just beyond Centerville to arrest the stampede. After a great deal of effort, about three thousand men were formed in line. The skittish soldiers were spooked by some enemy cavalry and the rout began again. Slocum kept his division in position for the remainder of the night and in the morning fell back to Centerville, covering the retreat of Pope's shattered army.[76]

Slocum lead his command in action again at Crampton's Gap during the Antietam Campaign and once again showed his abilities as a division commander. After securing the pass, he marched his men on the morning of 17 September to the sound of battle along Antietam Creek. Once on the field, his men helped shore up the beleaguered Union defenses in the vicinity of the Dunker Church. During the battle General Joseph Mansfield, one of the oldest commanders in the army, was killed leading his Twelfth Corps into action. A month after the battle, Slocum was elevated to corps command and took over Mansfield's old command. Two months later, at Fredericksburg, Burnside chose to keep the Twelfth Corps in reserve and Slocum's boys saw no significant action during the debacle.[77]

Henry Slocum did not cut a very imposing figure. He was small in stature, a trait described by Frank Haskell as "rather spare." His hair was straight and black and on occasions he displayed a few days growth of facial hair when he was not sporting a full beard which had a tendency to be a bit sparse. A large bushy mustache accented his thin face. He had wide cheek bones which were all the more noticeable because his cheeks were hollow and depressed. His nose was slender and sharp and his completion was white and fair. Haskell also noted that Slocum had a tendency to be quick and choppy in his body movements which corresponded to his eyes, which, while actually brown, Haskell noted were "quick and black." Add to his physical features the fact that he exhibited a great degree of elegance in his dress and Slocum was, except for possibly George Meade, perhaps the oddest looking general in the Army of the Potomac.

---

[75] Slocum, *Henry Warner Slocum*, pp.16, 18.

[76] Faust, *Encyclopedia*, p.692; *OR* vol.12, pt.2, p.389; Slocum, *Henry Warner Slocum*, pp.40-41.

[77] *OR* vol.19, pt.1, pp.2, 380-382.

Slocum's men were confident in his abilities, mainly due to his record regarding the treatment of his soldiers. When the medical organizations within the army were suspect early in the war, Slocum took steps to make sure his men were well cared for. His effort showed in lower rates of sickness among his men than in other organizations. A soldier noted that his glowing brown eyes seemed to exhibit a "magnetic power over his troops." Slocum however, had a bad habit of getting bogged down in details and military protocol. Occasionally careful to the point of slowness, he demonstrated a somewhat vigilant personality. He very seldom displayed emotion, was independent, and loved the order and regiment of military life.[78]

Joe Hooker's decision to retain Slocum at the head of the Twelfth Corps would prove to be the correct one. The frugal man who owed the spelling of his last name to a clerical error had worked his way upward through the ranks and now was in a position of great responsibility. In the coming months, few would find reason to doubt his ability and resolve on the battlefield.

And, so it was that Joe Hooker reorganized the command structure of the Army of the Potomac. None of the players involved in the command shuffling could have known its effect on the opus to play itself out during the following months across the rolling hills of southern Pennsylvania. All the corps commanders, whether new or retained, had flaws and positive attributes. Some, such as the Third and Eleventh Corps commanders would become embroiled in controversies which would emerge after the great battle. Unknown to Hooker however, at the center of those controversies would be a Pennsylvanian who had spent his entire military career being simply a good soldier. His name was George Meade.

---

[78] Tagg, **Generals**, p.143; Byrne & Weaver, Editors, **Haskell**, p.133.

Chapter III

An Unremarkable Pennsylvanian

> "...here it was that Meade did this and there Meade did that..."[1]
> *Meade to his wife relaying McClellan's comments to Lincoln as they toured the battlefield at Antietam, 5 October 1862.*

George Gordon Meade was selected by Hooker to command the Fifth Corps. Meade, born in Cádiz Spain on 31 December 1815, was a year and a half old when he returned with his mother to the family's native Pennsylvania. His father Richard, however, was not allowed to accompany them. A player in the international mercantile trade, Richard had not endeared himself to the Spanish government. The elder Meade was imprisoned when the monarchy took exception to his handling of financial affairs. He had been jailed twice. His second stay behind bars had lasted for a year and it was beginning to look as if he would remain there for quite some time. As a last resort, he turned to some influential friends in Philadelphia to secure his release, but prospects did not look promising. Congressman John Sergeant of Pennsylvania brought the matter before the legislature but to no avail. It was not until the issues regarding Florida, which the Spanish controlled, came to a head that the government became serious regarding Meade's case. On 4 April 1818 the Senate finally forced the issue. "Any United States citizen who demeans himself as becomes a character is entitled to the protection of his Government, and... whatever intentional injury may be done him should be retaliated against by the employment, if necessary, of the whole force of this nation." The House of Representatives issued a comparable statement and King Ferdinand, not interested in another war, opened the gates of Castillo de Santa Catalina. Richard Meade was a free man.[2]

With his family back together, George's father began the task of rising his son. George began his formal education by attended elementary school in Philadelphia. He then entered a military school for youngsters in Germantown. He showing an aptitude for math, and his father began talking of sending young George to West Point. However, it was only talk, as his father passed away when George was

---

[1] Meade, *Meade*, vol.1, p.317.

[2] Cleaves, *Meade*, pp.3-7.

twelve. While the estate of Richard Meade was substantial and contained a large amount of property, it contained little disposable cash. With a large family to support, his mother could not afford to continue his schooling in Germantown, so George returned home. After a short stay at a small school presided over by Salmon P. Chase, George entered Mount Hope Institution in Baltimore.

Following through regarding her late husband's talk about West Point, Mrs. Meade began entertaining thoughts of sending her son to the academy. Concerned only in getting the best education possible for her son, she did not intend to place George's feet on the path of a military career. She would later regret her decision to send him there, but for now it seemed the best way to provide a good education for her boy. On 13 March 1830, she sent George's application to the secretary of war. "I offer my son, George Meade, as a candidate for the appointment of Cadet in the Military Academy," she wrote as if she was never going to see him again. The application was rejected, possibly because George was just fifteen at the time. While George went back to school in Baltimore, his mother began a crusade to procure testimonials for her son. It took her a number of months to gather the additional documents. Once again, supported by paperwork from George's instructors and acquaintances, she submitted a second application. After a five month wait, in July of 1831, President Andrew Jackson signed the appointment documents. George Meade was a cadet.[3]

At West Point, George was incredibly average and stood nineteenth in a class of fifty-six. He even had difficulty in mathematics, ranking twenty-first in the subject. He stood twenty-seventh in chemistry, twenty-second in engineering, and performed below average in artillery, infantry tactics, drawing and overall conduct. George Meade was a cadet who did not live up to his potential. Typically, top cadets were assigned to the Engineering Corps, but Meade was so far down in standing that it is likely his name was never considered for such a distinguished post. He had no notable classmates except for future Confederate General John C. Pemberton. A member of Meade's class described him as being tall and slender, but produced graceful movements. He was not uncoordinated as so many lanky youths seemed to be. When he graduated in 1835, he had established an unremarkable record.[4]

After graduation, Meade was brevetted a second lieutenant and assigned to Company C, 3rd Artillery. After visiting his mother and sisters, he reported for duty at Governors Island in the upper bay of New York Harbor. It was not long before Meade's regiment was ordered to Florida to help deal with the problematic Seminoles Indians. There seemed to have been no reason for Meade to hurry to his new assignment since he asked for and received permission to travel with his brother-in-law, Commodore James Dallas. He departed Hampton Roads on 8 October 1835, and after a leisurely three and a half month trip, he arrived at Tampa Bay on 22 January. Meade spent most of his military service in Florida and in the southeast. Evidently he became disheartened with the dull routine of

---

[3] *Ibid*, pp.9-10.

[4] *Ibid*, p.11.

military life, for after his year of field service was up, he resigned from the army on 28 October, 1836.[5]

With his military service over, Meade entered the private sector as a surveyor on a new rail line connecting the Florida town of Pensacola to Columbus, Georgia. The project was supported and run by the military which was authorized to pay Meade $1,000 a year plus travel expenses and food. When work on the railroad came to an end, Meade found it difficult to find employment. Being a civilian, it was much harder to find work than if he had remained in the service. Traveling west, he found work surveying the Texas-Louisiana boundary and helped ascertain depths of sand bars while establishing the channel of the Sabine River. He labored for six weeks to complete the measurements of the water depths. After making his report to the secretary of war, he was once again out of work. For the next year, Meade remained unemployed, while his friends in the military always seemed to have work. While they were busy building and establishing forts and keeping civilians safe from marauding Indians, Meade struggled to make ends meet.[6]

During this period, Meade caught the eye of a young women and she returned the interest. Her name was Margaretta Sergeant, the oldest daughter of his late father's friend John Sergeant. John was a widower, and when he entertained, which was often due to his political stature, Margaretta, typically acted as hostess. No descriptive information of her has survived. Known as Margaret within the family, she was an accomplished piano player and could read and write in multiple languages. She was a cultured woman whose sisters were married to prosperous men. Compared to her sister's spouses, George Meade was a step or two down the ladder of success. Her father, in the beginning, was not impressed with her choice of a suitor, but John soon warmed to the young man from a good family. The elder Sergeant developed a liking for George and would, in time, give his consent for him to marry his daughter.

During his courtship of Margaret, George found work once again along the Sabine River, extending the boundary of Texas and Louisiana to the Red River. Additional surveying assignments from the Topographic Bureau held promise for extended employment. Meade accepted a job to help survey the northern border of Maine and Canada. The project was intended to put an end to the border disputed which had been raging there. It would be difficult running lines through the dense forests and work could not be done during the winter months, but Meade felt he was up to the task. Feeling confident in his future Meade gathered his courage and asked for his sweetheart's hand in marriage. George and Margaret exchanged vows on his birthday, 31 December 1840, at Congressman Sergeant's home. After the wedding, Meade went to work in the office of the Topographic Bureau until the

---

[5]   *Ibid*, pp.13-15.

[6]   *Ibid*, pp.15-16; Eicher& Eicher, **High Commands**, p.384.

weather warmed sufficiently to begin work on the boundary survey. When spring began, he left his new bride behind and traveled north to his new assignment.[7]

As work progressed on the border, Meade began to contemplate a return to the army. A congressional measure limiting all government surveying work to the Topographical Engineers had forced him to rethink his situation. If the measure became law, he could soon be out of work. With a growing family to worry about, Meade decided to attempt reinstatement. After soliciting the assistance of his brother-in-law, Virginia congressman Henry A. Wise, he received an appointment with the rank of second lieutenant, and was assigned to the Topographic Engineers.[8]

Work was finally completed on the Maine boundary in 1842, allowing the treaty of Webster-Ashburton to be signed, putting an end to the dispute. Meade, however, did not return home, as he remaining in Maine to chart the Aroostock River. Finally, on 17 November 1843, he was transferred back to Philadelphia and a reunion with his family, which, by this time, had grown by two sons. The family moved its place of residence from Washington to Philadelphia and purchased a home within walking distance of Topographic Bureau headquarters. Meade, for possibly the first time since he married Margaret, was happy with his situation and was able to spend his days working to support his family and the evenings with them.

The first major project Meade tackled was the design and construction of a lighthouse to be built on Brandywine Shoal in Delaware Bay. The shoal, which was notorious and dangerous to ships, was in desperate need of a lighthouse to guide them to safety on misty nights and mornings when the waters were rough. Meade and Major Hartman Bache, who was in charge of the project, decided to try a new technique to support the structure in the soft mud. The method required the use of "screw-piles" which consisted of a long pile with what looked to be a fan blade on the end. The pile was sunk by turning the shaft which drove the pile downward into the mud. The idea seemed well-suited for the shoal, and Meade went to work, traveling to the site by boat and returning home in the evening. While working on the lighthouse, Meade became a father again. His wife gave birth to their first daughter, Margaret. Unfortunately, the happy times did not last long.

---

[7] Cleaves, *Meade*, pp.12-17. George and Margaretta had seven children. John Sergeant Meade, born 4 November 1841. He died 21 February 1863 at the age of twenty-one. Sources differ on the year of John's birth. Some even place his birth a month before the marriage of his parents. Cleaves places John's birth on the date noted above. George Meade, born 2 November 1843 in Philadelphia. He married Elizabeth Morris Lewis and served on his father's staff during the war. Margaret Butler Meade, born 26 February 1845. She died on 15 September 1905 at age sixty. She never married and was buried at Laurel Hill Cemetery, Philadelphia. Spencer Meade, born 19 January 1850. Married Fanny C. Florance. Sarah Wise Meade, born 26 September 1851 in Philadelphia. She married John Baldwin Large. Henrietta Meade, born 3 August 1853 in Philadelphia. She died on 20 March 1944 in Philadelphia at age ninety. She never married. She was buried at Laurel Hill Cemetery. William Meade, born 13 March 1855. He died 22 March 1891 at age thirty-six. He never married and was buried at Laurel Hill Cemetery.

[8] *Ibid*, p.18.

Joe Hooker was not the only future commander of the Army of the Potomac to serve under Zachary Taylor in Mexico. One day, while working on the lighthouse, Major Bache broke the news to Meade that Mexico was causing trouble down on the Rio Grande. Congress was trying to make Texas a state and the Mexican government was not pleased. Before his new daughter was six months old, Meade would be off again, taken away from his family by military duties. This time it would be to the Texas frontier. On 12 August 1845, he received orders to report to Aransas Bay, Texas. Tears were shed as he parted from his family. Meade wrote that it was a "terrible agony" to be torn away from them once again.[9]

"soldiering is no play"

Meade arrived at St. Joseph Island near Corpus Christi Texas on 12 September and made his way to army headquarters where he met General Zachary Taylor. Taylor was not convinced war with Mexico was at hand and thought that even though the two sides had occasionally traded shots, the situation could still be peacefully rectified. Meade was introduced to his superior officer Captain T. J. Cram, the senior topographical officer and Thomas J. Wood, a lieutenant under Cram. Meade was then officially assigned to Taylor's merger staff to assist with topographic duties.

George went to work scouting the area, creating maps based on his findings and performing various engineering duties. By October cold weather had set in and fever entered the camps. Both Cram and Wood became sick and were admitted to the hospital. The captain suffered from a severe attack of dysentery and Wood from a high fever. Meade, while not feeling completely healthy himself, continued his duties but noted to his wife that if he took sick he would "try to get out of the country." One day, while leading a survey detail along an inner waterway, storm clouds gathered and heavy rains pounded Meade and his men. Twice soaked to the skin when his tent was blown down, by the time George returned to camp he was down with a fever and took to his bed. He became sick with jaundice but continued to do his work. The doctors tried to send him away to recover, but Meade evidently changed his mind or forgot his previous words for he paid the doctors no heed. Sitting in bed with a lap board, he showed commitment to his responsibilities by working on maps and reports, between which he penned a number of letters home to Margaret. Cram and Wood became so sick they were both sent home and it looked as if Meade would follow them, but he resisted the temptation determined to recover. Eventually his health improved, and he was able to resume his duties, doing his best until a replacement for Captain Cram arrived.[10]

Spring and good weather did not come soon enough for Meade. Taylor transferred his command from St. Joseph Island to the Rio Grande early in March 1846. Along the river marauding Mexican militia made it known they were willing to cut down any American military party they felt could be bested. Ventures outside of camp became very dangerous. The post's quartermaster general, Colonel

---

[9] Cleaves, *Meade*, pp.18-19.

[10] Meade, *Meade*, vol.1, pp.25, 32-34, 36-38, 49.

Trueman Cross, left one day and never returned. The belief in camp was he had been captured and assassinated. A few days later Cross' remains were found and suspicions confirmed. Later, a dozen men, on a scouting mission, were ambushed when a drenching rain rendered their powder useless and them defenseless when the Mexicans attacked. Lieutenant Theodoric H. Porter, who led the expedition, was cut down along with another man. Nine men managed to scramble back to camp. The situation came to a head on 25 April when a sixty-four man scouting expedition was slaughtered by a horde of Mexicans. Taylor, preparing for the worst, called for five thousand volunteers but was not keen on the additional troops. He felt a large number of volunteers would draw attention and credit away from his trained and hard fighting Regulars. In order to provide his men an opportunity to prove themselves before the volunteers arrived, Taylor began looking for a chance to hit back at the Mexicans.

Seizing a chance to draw the Mexicans out, Taylor marched twenty two hundred of his men out to gather supplies, leaving five hundred and fifty in his garrison along the river. There were questions as to Taylor's actual need for supplies. Meade noted in a letter to his wife that the garrison was never *"in want of supplies"* and that Taylor "was anxious to try our strength before the volunteers" arrived. Taylor and his men got their chance at a place called Palo Alto near Brownsville, Texas, when a Mexican force of 3,400 infantry and cavalry confronted the general's smaller force. On 8 May 1846, the two forces engaged each other and the first battle of the Mexican War was fought. The Mexican cavalry tried to capture the numerous supply wagons but were turned away. Meade work feverishly, riding back and forth along the line urging the Regulars on while bullets whizzed by and artillery shells dug up the earth. As the battle ebbed and flowed, the dry grass caught fire and blanketed the field in heavy smoke. Eventually, after the Regulars had parried a number of thrusts, the Mexicans fell back leaving the field to Taylor and his outnumbered Regulars.[11]

Meade performed well during the engagement, spending most of his time at Taylor's side sharing the danger. In a letter to Margaret the following evening, he noted he was "in the action during the whole time…" One of Taylor's staff officer's horse was shot within a few feet of Meade, and a number of men and horses were killed close by, but Meade exited the battle unscathed.

The following day, after negotiating a nearly impassable chaparral, Taylor's army engaged the Mexicans again at Resaca de la Palma. The enemy had taken a strong position along a dry riverbed and after attacking the Americans twice, were driven from their location and routed from the field. The defeat was complete and losses among the Regulars light. A number of trophies fell into the hands of the Americans, including seven pieces of artillery and 150 Mexican prisoners. Several hundred stands of arms and most of the enemy's ammunition were also left behind and rounded up by Taylor's men. A few hundred pack mules, baggage, and wagons

---

[11] *Ibid*, pp.51, 62, 66-68, 93; Cleaves, **Meade**, pp.24-25. *Electronic Source:* http://en.wikipedia.org/wiki/Battle_of_Palo_Alto, Last accessed 4/27/2012. The italics are Meade's.

were captured as well. General Mariano Arista's private stationary, which Meade used to write some letters home, was also commandeered.[12]

After Resaca de la Palma, the action in northern Mexico receded and Meade spent the next few months executing military duties and trying to remain comfortable during the hot Mexico summer. As the warm weather wore on, many of the called for volunteers began to arrive. Meade quickly formed an opinion regarding the qualities of volunteer fighting men. They would discharge their weapons in camp even after orders prohibiting the activity were issued. Other times they would gather at a nearby river and would waste precious ammunition by firing wildly into the air. Meade called them a "disorderly mass" and "ignorant of discipline." With all the unnecessary firing, Meade considered it safer on a battlefield than inside his own tent. He was correct in his assessment of the unruly mob, for after three days of soldiering, the volunteers were ready to mutiny. "Gentlemen from Louisiana," Meade wrote, "owning plantations and negroes, came here as common soldiers, and then revolt at the idea of drawing their own water and cutting their own fire wood, and in fact, they expect the regulars, who have to care for themselves, to play waiter to them…soldiering is no play…" Drinking was uncontrolled and a number of Mexican citizens were killed in the streets for nothing more than shear entertainment value. The volunteers stole from the locals without repercussions. Gambling establishments and saloons sprung up almost overnight. Meade noted that even the volunteer officers could not keep them under control and Taylor had given up on discipline "in despair."[13]

For most of the summer Taylor maintained his army Regulars and rowdy volunteers in and around Matamoros. By 5 August it was time to move again, and Taylor put his army in motion toward Monterrey. On 12 September the army was within twenty-five miles of the town. Mexican forces had been busy constructing heavy fortifications, strong earthworks and rooftop sharpshooter positions. In addition, numerous forts and outposts guarded the approaches to the main defenses. To make matters worse, the town lay in a valley, protected on both sides by high mountains, some of which rose to 1,000 feet. It would not be an easy task driving the Mexicans from their stronghold.

In order to address the multiple strongholds, Taylor divided his force, sending General William Worth and 2,000 men to deal with some of the isolated outposts. Meade accompanied Worth as the general's troops engaged and drove the enemy from a number of their advanced positions in the valley and on the heights. On 19 September Worth's men arrived in front of Monterrey where they would be confronted with the greatest task of the advance. It was decided a storming party would ascend the slopes of the Loma de Independencia, one of the high rocky crags guarding the approach to the town. A scouting expedition revealed the top of the

---

[12] Meade, *Meade*, vol.1, pp.80-81.

[13] *Ibid*, pp.91, 94; Cleaves, *Meade*, pp.29-30.

crag to be heavily fortified. The position would have to be taken if the advance was to continue.[14]

Meade had been a member of the reconnoitering party which scouted the Independencia. Now, he and Captain John Sanders of the Engineers would assist a party of men to the mountain's summit to confront the enemy positioned on the heights. The force, consisting of 500 men, contained an assortment of Texas volunteers and Regulars. At 3 a.m., so darkness would conceal the effort, the men moved toward and started up the base of the hill. As they began the ascension, it started to rain. Meade urged the men to stay close to each other so they could "[t]ouch elbows with the next man." The ground was composed of loose dirt and gravel, making the footing difficult. Each step forward seemed accompanied by a half step backward. Larger rocks had to be negotiated as well, for if one broke loose not only could it take down a man, but it could also alert the enemy. The rain was cold and took a toll on the men as they worked their way up the slope. By dawn the force had moved within one hundred yards of the top of the rocky ridge with the enemy positioned just ahead. Rising up, Meade's force fired a few shots. Suddenly a volley from the attackers split the early morning silence. Rushing the stronghold, the Texans and Regulars poured over the walls only to find the position vacant and all the artillery removed. A dismantled twelve pounder, which had been hauled up the slope, was quickly assembled and positioned to lob rounds against the enemy positions below. Amidst the cheers of the men, the Mexican flag was quickly torn down and replaced with the red white and blue of the stars and stripes. Fire from the twelve pounder forced the Mexicans to make a feeble effort with infantry and cavalry to retake the position, but they were driven back and the position belonged to the Americans.[15]

A few days later the Mexicans terminated their token resistance and a white flag was hoisted above their position in the town. They requested an armistice even though they still occupied the area in and around the town with 5,000 men. Taylor was hesitant to demand strict terms. His campaign had taken him far from his base of supply and now with a chance to discontinue the fighting, Taylor took it. Lenient terms, intended to persuade the Mexican defenders to accept them, permitted the retention of their arms and gave them seven days to evacuate the town. Meade noted the terms were very merciful, writing that the enemy's strongest positions had not been assailed and there were still "three thousand men and twenty pieces of artillery" in the town alone. "[O]ur old general was desirous of playing a liberal and generous part by them, and thought it impolite to push them too hard." The truce, written on 27 September, halted fighting on the battlefield, but it would still need to be approved in Washington.[16]

During the campaign in northern Mexico, Meade established a bit of a reputation for being bad luck. It seemed all the senior topographical officers that

---

[14] Meade, *Meade*, vol.1, pp.118, 130, 132, 135.

[15] Cleaves, *Meade*, pp.34-35; Meade, *Meade*, vol.1, pp.135-136.

[16] Cleaves, *Meade*, pp.36; Meade, *Meade*, vol.1, pp.137-138.

had been sent had either fallen victim to bullets or disease. Captain Cram and Lieutenant Wood had both been forced home due to their illnesses before the campaign had even begun. Cram's replacement accidently shot himself in the leg at Resaca de la Palma. The next man was fatally wounded in battle, and the most recent replacement took ill and had been indisposed for weeks. The difficulties in keeping a senior topographical engineer with the army forced Meade to deal with the major portion of the group's command duties. This exposed him to both General Taylor and Worth, and each was impressed with his contribution. Worth noted the tall lanky Meade was full of "intelligent zeal and gallantry." Meade, a bit humbled by the praise thought Worth gave him more credit than he deserved.[17]

Though he performed well in Mexico, Meade was unable to garner a promotion. He harbored no illusions as to what was needed to advance in the army. Writing to Margaret shortly before the battle of Monterrey, he discussed his beliefs as to how men in the army advanced. "…I was always aware that the nomination of the commanding general was one thing, and the nomination by the president another, the one requiring hard service, the other political influence, the curse of our country." Not having any influential friends in Washington, Meade resigned himself to the understanding that it would be nearly impossible for him to be noticed and rewarded for his service. "If I had…strong friends at Washington," he continued, "to back the nomination of General Taylor, I might have hoped to have been rewarded; but on its absence my claims will meet with no attention." This would be a recurring theme for Meade during his military career. He believed that he possessed no friends in Washington and as such would be left to languish at the bottom of the command chain. During his time in Mexico, this was essentially true. Hard work and good soldiering would eventually allow Meade to establish contacts within the highest levels of Washington, though he continued to believe throughout his career he had no political support.[18]

Far away in Washington, the administration was not receptive to the terms of the armistice Taylor had demanded, and the politicians rejected the agreement. According to Meade, Taylor had been lenient in the dictation of terms to avoided animosity in an effort to prompt the Mexican government to listen to negotiations and proposals from Washington. Unfortunately the politicians saw it differently and thought the terms too compassionate. Taylor was no friend of the current administration, and after the government rejected the truce, they essentially ignored Taylor and his accomplishments. General Robert Patterson, who had complained of not being included in Taylor's advance southward, was ordered to Tampico along the coast, and instructed to transfer a portion of Taylor's force to his. The seat of war was about to be shifted, and Taylor, after all his efforts, would be denied any glory associated with his accomplishments. Meade, deeply disappointed with the developments thought the injustice done to Taylor, was

---

[17] Cleaves, **Meade**, p.37.

[18] Meade, **Meade**, vol.1, pp.128.

outrageous. The situation however, was a fine example of the backbiting between field armies and Washington that would bleed over into the Civil War.[19]

A frustrated Taylor set out with his army for Tampico, but after two days of marching he received word that Santa Anna was moving north. Taking the Regulars with him, he returned to Monterrey to discover that the report was only a rumor. Meade however, remained with the volunteers and continued the march to Tampico. It saddened Taylor to lose Meade and the young officer expressed disappointment as well. "[T]he old man was very kind to me on parting," he noted. One consolation for Meade was that he would be the only topographic officer in Patterson's command, a fact which might provide an opportunity to be notice.[20]

His time in Mexico with Taylor now behind him, Meade entered upon a new experience. General Winfield Scott, America's most noteworthy military man, had been ordered by Washington to lead an expedition by sea to conquer Mexico, and had ordered all of the Regulars and most of the volunteers to join his assembling armada at Tampico. Scott felt Taylor's effort in Mexico's interior had been inconsequential. His opinion irritated Meade greatly. Scott, who seemed to be oblivious to the battles fought by Taylor, thought the movements unimportant to victory. When quizzed about Taylor and his men, Scott called them "men of straw," implying they were poor soldiers. The truth of the situation however, was there would be a new front in the war with Mexico, and Scott would be in charge of it. Although Meade may not have been pleased with his new assignment, he determined to try and make the best of it.

Meade saw Taylor for a final time when they met by chance in Victoria shortly before he departed for Tampico. The meeting was cordial and mutual respect was relayed. Meade's longing for his old commander would swell over the next few weeks as he prepared for his new role within Scott's command.[21]

Scott's force boarded a fleet of ships for the journey south to the port of Veracruz. Shortly after his arrival, on 6 March 1847, Scott and his entourage boarded the steamer *Petrita* to reconnoiter the defenses around the coastal city. Commanding the naval elements of the action was Commodore David Conner. Conner, the commander of the naval squadron operating in the Gulf of Mexico, would be in charge of the amphibious portion of the operation. As he and Scott stood on the deck of the *Petrita* and discussed the situation with Worth, Patterson and General David E. Twiggs, Meade stood in the mists of a number of junior officers who would in a few short years become well known during the Civil War. Among the group of officers was an engineer from Virginia named Robert E. Lee. Neither man could have imagined that within sixteen short years they would be facing each other across the southern Pennsylvania countryside in command of

---

[19]   *Ibid*, pp.151-152.

[20]   *Ibid*, p.151; Cleaves, ***Meade***, pp.38-39.

[21]   Cleaves, ***Meade***, pp.38-39.

nearly two hundred thousand men. Until then, they would be associates ready to help Scott achieve victory over a common enemy.[22]

As Scott prepared to assault the port, most of the engineering duties were assigned to the engineers of his command. Few tasks fell to the topographic corps. In a letter to Margaret, Meade sarcastically commented that Colonel Totten of the Corps of Engineers wanted to "make as much capital for his own corps, and give us as little, as possible." When Meade complained about his lack of involvement, he was informed that his presence had not been anticipated and as such there were too many engineering officers with Scott's command for the duties required. Meade's disenchantment was dealt with by Scott when the general, deciding he had enough engineering officers, had orders written to send Meade back to army headquarters in Washington.

On 31 March, Meade ended his year and a half of service in Mexico as he said goodbye to friends and boarded a steamer for New Orleans. Although it meant a reunion with his family, Meade was less than thrilled with the thought of going home. He had hoped to be of some use, but now felt he was being pushed aside and would miss the culmination of what had been started by Taylor in northern Mexico. However, the prospect of being reunited with Margaret and his three children was reassuring. The only accolade for his service with Taylor was a hearty pat on the back and a brevet for bravery, which advanced him to the rank of first lieutenant. Even though he would miss the fighting during the campaign to capture Mexico City, Meade had proven himself to be a good and loyal soldier.[23]

Molding the Reserves

Returning to Washington, Meade reported for duty at the Topographic Bureau and received a bit of a shock. His efforts in Mexico had not gone unnoticed after all, and in many ways he was credited with proving the value of the Topographic Corps. A quick reassignment found him once again in Philadelphia under Major Bache. The lighthouse at Brandywine Shoal was still incomplete, so Meade and Bache went to work making arrangements to finish the construction. A few years later, another assignment took him away from his family again, sending him to Florida. Being away from his growing clan, which now included seven children, tugged at his heart. After returning from Florida, he determined to take them along if he ever received another distant assignment. In 1856 a new task, one that would take him to the Great Lakes, provided an opportunity for extended work. A great deal of survey work needed to be completed in the area. True to his convictions, Meade gathered up Margaret and the children and relocated his family to Detroit. By the spring of 1857, he was in charge of the entire project, bringing additional responsibilities and a promotion to captain. The job proved to be a large one and

---

[22] *Ibid*, pp.40-41.

[23] Meade, ***Meade***, vol.1 pp.192-194; Faust, ***Encyclopedia***, p.482.

by 1859 he was adding personnel and approaching Congress for additional funding to continue the work.[24]

Meade was still working on and around the lakes as the clouds of war began to cover the nation in 1861. In a letter to a friend, Meade expressed his feelings on the matter of civil war by writing "that a merciful Providence would so guide the hearts of the rulers on both sides as to terminate this unnatural contest. But, as for myself," he continued, "I have ever held it to be my duty to uphold and maintain the constitution and resist the disruption of this Government. With this opinion, I hold the other side responsible for the existing condition of affairs. Besides, as a soldier, holding a commission, it has always been my judgment that duty required I should disregard all political questions, and obey orders." There was never any question where George Meade stood on the approaching conflict. Duty, honor, and his oath were important to him. His devotion required him to fight to maintain the Union.[25]

While Meade was ready to commit his service to the Union, the Union was not ready for him. As hostilities began, Meade languished at his assignment in Detroit. His repeated requests of Washington to assign him to active duty were ignored. Finally, in June, he traveled to the capital and personally requested an assignment and promotion. While informed he would be utilized, Meade returned to Detroit with neither request being granted. Evidently there was some objection to conferring higher rank on him. Frustrated, Meade decided to take drastic action. He would resign his commission and accept the colonelcy of a volunteer regiment from Michigan. His plans changed quickly after 21 July when the upstart Rebel army routed the Federals at Bull Run. Later that month he received a notification appointing him to brigadier general of volunteers and was ordered to report to General McClellan in Washington. Having already sent his family back to Philadelphia, George Meade gathered his belongings and headed off to war.[26]

Arriving in Washington, the forty-six years old Meade was placed in command of a brigade of men from the Keystone State known as the Pennsylvania Reserves. The reserves were formed when Pennsylvania's turnout exceeded President Lincoln's original call for troops. The overflow had been organized and used to form a home guard. After the disaster at Bull Run, the reserves were hurried forward and used to form a division. The division was placed under the command of Brigadier General George McCall who had assisted in its organization. Meade was to command the Second Brigade while the First Brigade was commanded by fellow Pennsylvanian, John Reynolds. Command of the third Brigade went to Otho C. Ord.[27]

After spending a few months in and around Washington, McCall's command found itself scheduled to be transferred to the Virginia Peninsula as part of General McDowell's First Corps. Shortly thereafter, it was once again transferred, this time

---

[24] Cleaves, *Meade*, pp.45-51.

[25] Meade, *Meade*, vol.1, p.218.

[26] *Ibid*, pp.215-216.

[27] *OR* vol.5 p.21; Meade, *Meade*, vol.1 p.217; Cleaves, *Meade*, p.51; Boatner, *Dictionary*, p.154.

to General Fitz-John Porter's Fifth Corps. Before McClellan could launch his final drive on Richmond, General Lee, who was now in command of the Confederate forces, fell upon the Federal right flank. Porter had posted McCall's division on the right flank of the army along Beaver Dam Creek. Reynolds' brigade was on the right, Brigadier General Truman Seymour, who had supplanted Ord, was on the left, while Meade's brigade formed a reserve. The fighting was bloody and Reynolds brigade was forced back. Meade moved up from his position in the rear and stabilized the line. Seymour, in his report, noted that Meade "came up with his brigade, and by his advice, as well as by the presence and aid of his command, was of most valuable service." At the end of the day, nothing had been gained by either side, but McClellan decided to retire.

The following morning, 27 June, Porter ordered his men to fall back. As they departed, the Confederates pursued. For the next six days the Rebel and Yankee forces participated in a series of running battles known as The Seven Days. During the fighting, McCall and Reynolds were captured, and Meade suffered two wounds. When the smoke cleared, Seymour was in command of the division.[28]

Meade's wounds where serious. He had been hit in the side and arm. Initially, it was thought the wound to his arm was the more serious of the two. "I am badly wounded in the arm," he told a nearby lieutenant, "and must leave the field. Fight your guns to the last and save them if possible." After a few final instructions, Meade rode from the field. It was not long before his injuries debilitated him as he struggled toward the rear. Dismounting at a field hospital, he sought medical help. As the fighting continued, the battle line shifted, and it became apparent Meade needed to put more distance between himself and the front. Remounting his horse was not an option. His injuries would not allow him to make the effort. As luck would have it, Meade's own mess cart happened to come by. The cooking tools were discarded, and the general helped into the cart. After a long, dark, bumpy ride Meade arrived at McClellan's headquarters. He was helped aboard a ship and taken north to his home to recuperate.[29]

After spending forty two days recovering, Meade returned to the division to discover Reynolds, who had been exchanged after his capture, was now in command. Seymour had the Second Brigade; newcomer Brigadier General Conrad F. Jackson had the Third while Meade was given command of Reynolds' old First Brigade. He arrived just as the campaign which resulted in the second battle of Bull Run was unfolding. During the battle, Meade was with his brigade when Reynolds led the division in the charge to cover the army's retreat. He recorded the assault in his report. "…the brigade, in conjunction with the division, was deployed in line of battle and charged down the slope of the Henry House ridge toward the Sudley Springs road, driving before it such of the enemy as had advanced across this road…" Taking possession of the road, Meade's men, and the remainder of the

---

[28] Cleaves, *Meade*, pp.61, 64-67; *OR* vol.11, pt.2, p.400.

[29] Meade, *Meade*, vol.1, pp.298-299.

division held the position against "heavy infantry fire" until it was relieved. The action allowed for the timely escape of General John Pope's defeated legions.[30]

After Bull Run, Pope and McDowell were shown the door, and McClellan was reinstated to overall command of the reunited army. The restructuring saw the Reserves assigned to Joe Hooker's First Corps.

Instead of establishing a position in front of Washington, Lee took his legions north of the Potomac and McClellan followed, inaugurating the Maryland Campaign. As the armies maneuvered, Meade suddenly found himself in command of the division when Reynolds was ordered to Pennsylvania to train the state's militia. Initially, Meade seemed to get along well with the self-obsessed Hooker, and both men appeared to respect each other's abilities. While they were never close friends, they developed a solid professional relationship.[31]

McClellan, pressing Lee's rear guard at South Mountain, sent Hooker into Turner's Gap to clear the way over the ridge. As Meade's men moved forward, he surveyed the situation, noting that the terrain was much like that he had seen years earlier at Monterrey. An abundance of natural cover sheltered the steep slope of the ridge. As in Mexico, enemy artillery would have a difficult time causing any damage to the Reserves if they worked their way up slowly, using the foliage for cover. Gaining the heights, Meade's boys fought a tough engagement with stubborn Rebels and managing to push them off the mountain as the day drew to a close.[32]

Three days later Meade's division deployed on the north end of the Union line as the battle of Antietam unfolded. After a night of sporadic fire from pickets on both sides, the battle erupted at dawn on 17 September. Before the close of the day, more men would become casualties than on any other single day of fighting during the war. Seymour's brigade, along with Brigadier General James B. Ricketts' division opened the fighting, but both were soon hard pressed. As the struggle for possession of the cornfield on David R. Miller's farm intensified, Hooker called on Meade to send his other brigades forward in support. The fighting raged for almost three hours before the slaughter subsided. Neither side was capable of claiming victory.[33]

As his command moved forward, Meade could be seen stoically sitting on his horse, Old Baldy, peacefully observing the situation. According to one witness, Meade "calmly surveyed the prospect through his spectacles while rebel bullets were scarring the ground at his feet and...singing about his ears." However, Meade would not come out of the fight unscathed. As the battle raged, he was hit by a "spent grape-shot" which caused a "severe contusion" on his right thigh. Fortunately the shrapnel did not break the skin. Old Baldy was not as lucky. The horse was hit in the neck and became incapacitated. With no time to tend to Baldy, he was left to his own discretion. The horse would survive, but a new mount was

---

[30] *Ibid*, p.305; **OR** vol.12, pt.2, p.398.

[31] Cleaves, *Meade*, p.75.

[32] *Ibid*, pp.75-76.

[33] *Ibid*, p.79.

needed. Meade, commandeering a nearby cavalry horse, quickly got back into the action. His new horse was soon hit as well but was able to continue, as the wound was a minor one to its flank. Meade, who probably never expected to see Old Baldy again, was surely pleased when the horse was found a few days later quietly grazing in a field.[34]

During the battle, Meade showed his displeasure with men who chose to shirk their duties by trying to avoid the fighting. Observing a man cowering behind a tree, Meade called out to a nearby sergeant and ordered him to "[g]et that man in line." The sergeant tried, but the skulker would not move from the safety of the tree. Riding over, Meade struck the fearful man on the backside with the flat of his sword and moved on. Early in his career Meade felt such acts cruel and harsh, but after becoming an officer he acknowledged the need for them. He also despised straggling, but felt the worst kind of soldier was an uninjured man who would put down his weapon to help a wounded friend to the rear. "Three days after the battle," Meade wrote to his wife, "this corps numbered twelve thousand officers and men, though on the evening of the battle we could only muster seven thousand." He attributed most of the problems to the volunteer nature of the army. Meade noted that "the cowards, skulkers, men who leave the ground with the wounded and do not return for days, the stragglers on the march, and all such characters, which are to be found in every army, but never in so great a ratio as in the volunteer force of ours."[35]

Meade was so convinced that the reductions were due to healthy men abandoning their post that the day after the battle, he wrote an official communication to McClellan. "I enclose a field return of the corps made this afternoon, which I desire you to lay before the commanding general. I am satisfied the great reduction in the corps since the recent engagements [South Mountain and Antietam] is not due solely to the casualties of battle, and that a considerable number of men are still in the rear, some having dropped out on the march, and many dispersing and leaving yesterday during the fight." Meade's poor opinion of volunteers had not changed much since his days in Mexico.[36]

When Hooker was wounded and taken from the field, command of the First Corps fell to Meade. The stars aligned for him when Lincoln visited McClellan shortly after the battle. The two leaders toured the recent battlefield and Meade accompanied the entourage. McClellan pointed out to the president the scene of Meade's work. Writing to his wife in early October, George proudly relayed the event. "…McClellan pointed out to him [Lincoln] the various phases of the day, saying here it was that Meade did this and there Meade did that; which was all very gratifying to me. He [Lincoln] seemed very much interested in all the movements of Hooker's corps." Meade however, was of the opinion that the commander in chief had not come to the field to view the latest scene of battle. The president's

---

[34] *Ibid*, pp.78, 82; Meade, **Meade**, vol.1, pp.310-311, 314.

[35] Cleaves, **Meade**, p.79, Meade, **Meade**, vol.1, p.318.

[36] **OR** vol.19, pt.1, p.66.

purpose was to push McClellan to follow up his so called victory with a forward movement to catch Lee's wounded army and crush it.[37]

While Meade was singled out in the presence of Lincoln, it was different in the newspapers. "I am afraid I shall not get the credit for these last battles that I did for those near Richmond," he wrote Margaret. The reason in Meade's mind was his wounding during The Seven Days brought more attention. He was also disappointed with the coverage of his Reserves. "I find the papers barely mention the Pennsylvania Reserves…," Meade wrote. The reporters were continuing to call the Reserves "McCall's troops," which also irritated him. Unfortunately, it would be a few months before he would have another opportunity at corps command. Reynolds returned shortly after the battle and assumed command once more, sending Meade back to his division. For George Meade however, his ten days in command of the corps provided an opportunity to be noticed by the administration.[38]

No amount of pushing and prodding by Washington could get McClellan to move until the general was ready. The Lincoln Administration seemed to know or care little about the logistics of resupplying an army which had just fought a major battle. As Lee's army departed and crossed the river, Halleck and the War Department failed to understand that Lee was marching toward his base of supply, while the Federal army would be marching away from there's if it were to immediately pursue. Federal resupply efforts after the battle were so poor that Meade, after complaining to McClellan he could not get shoes for his men or his horses, spent his own money to have 1,200 mules and horses shod. It was not until the end of October that McClellan felt he could advance. Meade's division moved with the remainder of the army, but did not cross the Potomac and follow Lee until the twenty-ninth. Finally, on 5 November, Lincoln had enough and relieved McClellan from command of the army and replaced him with Burnside.[39]

Meade displayed no animosity toward Little Mac, but he was well aware of McClellan's failings as an army commander. Writing to his wife early in 1863 Meade summed up McClellan's faults quite plainly. "McClellan's vice…was always waiting to have everything just as he wanted before he would attack, and before he could get things arranged as he wanted them, the enemy pounced on him and thwarted all his plans." Meade knew there was risk in war. Knowing when the magnitude of the result justified taking the risk was a quality every good commander possessed. Weighing risk against reward was a capability Meade, with his average West Point performance, was able to grasp, while McClellan, with his top of the class stature, could not. While McClellan had the ability to rally a defeated and dejected army with his mere presence and organizational skills, he was one of the shoddier field generals of the war. He seemed so concerned about not losing a battle that he would not risk winning one. Meade, on the other hand,

---

[37] Meade, *Meade*, vol.1, pp.313, 317.

[38] *Ibid*, p.312; Cleaves, *Meade*, p.82.

[39] Cleaves, *Meade*, p.82;

knew the risks of command and did his best to take those risks when a favorable outcome was worth the effort.[40]

Still, the change in command came as a shock to Meade. "I must confess I was surprised at this," he informed Margaret, "as I thought the storm had blown over." Meade was also convinced that the politicians were once again playing their game. "This removal now proves conclusively that the cause is political, and the date of the order, November 5th confirms it." The midterm election of 1862 saw voters cast their ballots the previous day. Had the Lincoln Administration waited to make the command change until after the results of the election were known? Meade believed it to be so, whether it was true or not. George told his wife that Burnside "wept like a child" when he learned of his appointment. He wrote Burnside was "…the most distressed man in the army, [and] openly says he is not fit for the position…" Whether or not Burnside actually uttered the words, they would prove to be prophetic.[41]

George Gordon Meade was a steady and capable military man. *LOC*

When Burnside took command, he instituted his new organizational structure, assembling his four Grand Divisions. Doing so created vacancies at the corps command level. Meade was not promoted into any of the openings and remained in command of his First Corps division. Disappointed, he relayed his irritation

---

[40] *Ibid*, p.86.

[41] Meade, *Meade*, vol.1, p.325.

at being passed over to Margaret. The principal issue was that General Dan Butterfield, who was assigned to the command of the Fifth Corps, was junior to Meade. George had a right to complain about the situation. After airing his grievance to some fellow officers, who then took his complaint to Burnside, he was informed that the commanding general did not see how he could arrange the commands any other way. Meade, once again, was passed over when his time for advancement had come.[42]

On 12 December, Meade, as part of Reynolds' First Corps and William Franklin's Left Grand Division, moved his command across the Rappahannock south of Fredericksburg and took position between the divisions of Brigadier Generals Abner Doubleday and John Gibbon. The next day Meade's force was selected to make the initial attack on the southern end of the field while General Gibbon was placed in support distance. Doubleday's division would be held in reserve. As morning fog began to lift, Meade's men stepped off. Confederate guns opened up on the advancing Yankees and the assault ground to a halt. Meade ordered his guns to work and after an hour of firing, the Confederate guns had quieted enough for the assault to resume. The Confederate guns opened again, but this time the Pennsylvania Reserves would not be denied. Meade's cannons opened fire again and cleared out the Confederate guns allowing his First Brigade, under Colonel William Sinclair to gain a foothold in a patch of woods. After negotiating the trees, the Keystone Staters emerged to discover they had completely penetrated the enemy lines. A number of prisoners were taken while Meade paused to assess the situation. Turning Sinclair to the left and Colonel Albert Magilton's brigade to the right, Meade sought to widen the hole. Unfortunately, contact with General Gibbon and Doubleday had been lost and neither moved forward to support Meade. Tattered and worn out, the men were not able to hold their position without help and they were forced to fall back. Meade was justifiably proud of his boys. "[M]y men went in *beautifully*, carried everything before them, and drove the enemy for nearly half a mile, but finding themselves unsupported on either right or left, and encountering an overwhelming force of the enemy, they were checked and finally driven back." Three brigades of enemy troops counterattacked and drove the Reserves back through the woods. Meade tried to rally them in a hollow just in front of his gun batteries but was unsuccessful. Finally, the division was reformed along the Bowling Green road where Meade was able to assess the damage.[43]

Meade was irritated with the lack of support. During the fighting he sent two messengers to General David B. Birney with urgent requests for assistance. Birney responded by remaining in position arguing the request did not come from a higher authority. Riding back to confront Birney, Meade displayed his temper. "General, I assume the authority of ordering you to the relief of my men." Finally getting the message, Birney moved two brigades forward to provide support, but it was too late. The men were falling back from overpowering numbers and they could not be halted. Meade initially felt Burnside was to blame for the lack of assistance, having

---

[42] *Ibid*, p.329.

[43] *Ibid*, p.337; ***OR*** vol.19, pp. 509-512; Cleaves, **Meade**, pp.91-92.

not been more specific with his orders to Franklin. Later, he learned that Burnside had ordered Franklin to advance with his "whole force" which tempered Meade's opinion somewhat. Either way, he was understandably disappointed. Their hard fighting had been a waste of good soldiers.[44]

Another difficulty Meade encountered during the battle was both his brigade commanders who delivered the attack were killed or wounded. This left the men for a time leaderless in the midst of heavy woods with poor visibility. Without guidance, and overcome with excitement, the men pressed on until they encountered heavy Confederate reinforcements being rushed forward. Not in position to receive an attack, the Pennsylvanians were driven back and were unable to hold the ground they had gained. The ultimate failure could be attributed to a lack of timely support and over-exuberant soldiers. Meade's breakthrough however, while it was not exploited, was the lone bright spot in an otherwise depressing day for the Army of the Potomac.[45]

Shortly after the battle, Meade went to Burnside and requested leave to spend some time with his family. Burnside displayed no concerns over Meade departing for a few days, but informed George he was planning to assign him to the command of the Fifth Corps, currently under Butterfield. With the change looming, Meade decided to stay. Orders were written on 23 December and George Meade was finally rewarded with the corps command he had earned with his performance in the field and his seniority demanded. Joe Hooker however, was not pleased.

Hooker's concern was not that Meade was a bad choice to command a corps in his Grand Division. He was opposed to changing commanders during active campaigning. He felt Butterfield had performed his duty well enough to deserve retention. Meade accepted the appointment and reported to Hooker for duty the next day. When he arrived, Butterfield was closeted with Hooker. Meade was informed that the outgoing commander had just been notified of the change. Butterfield, in Meade's opinion, took it all in stride, and even invited George to have Christmas dinner with him. Later, Butterfield informed Meade that when first assigned to command the corps; Burnside had informed him that the post was a permanent one. "Little Dan" was disappointed and Meade felt his discontent. However, Butterfield would not be out of a job for long. Hooker would make him his chief of staff a few days later as Burnside departed.[46]

Corps Command

As the smoke of Fredericksburg cleared, Meade once again relayed his opinion of Washington bureaucrats in a letter to his wife on 2 January 1863. His thoughts regarding the constant meddling of Lincoln and his administration were consistent with his fellow Pennsylvanian John Reynolds. "No one in Washington has the courage to say or do anything beyond hampering and obstructing us," he

---

[44] Meade, *Meade*, vol.1, pp.359, 362; Cleaves, *Meade*, pp.91-92.

[45] Meade, *Meade*, p.340;

[46] *OR* vol.21, p.879; Meade, *Meade*, vol.1, pp.339, 341-342.

complained. "God only knows what will become of us and what will be done." As the end of January approached, pressure from the pen pushers forced Burnside's hand, and he ordered his army to march to his right in an effort to maneuver around Lee's flank. The winter weather however, did not cooperate and stymied the Federals. Heavy rains turned the roads to quagmires and put an exclamation point on Burnsides career as commander. The roads became so terrible that Meade, in order to get his corps back to its starting point, ordered his men to cut down trees to "corduroy" the road. Frustrated, Burnside finally issued orders instructing the army to return to their camps on 23 January. "I have never felt so disappointed and sorry for any one in my life," Meade wrote of Burnside. The hammer fell two days later as Burnside and two of his commanders, Franklin and Edwin V. Sumner, were relieved and ordered to Washington.[47]

On the afternoon of the following day, Meade went out for a ride to possibly get his mind off of the current situation. Upon his return, he found an order waiting for him. It had arrived earlier that morning and had been delivered by Burnside. It announced the installment of "Fighting Joe" as the army's new commander and the placement of Meade at the head of the Center Grand Division. He had missed the departure of Burnside and his staff by a few minutes. Meade quickly surmised that the command was a temporary one since he was of the mind that the Grand Divisions would be broken up. Burnside, while a poor commander had been good to Meade, and George appreciated the kind treatment his former commander had bestowed upon him. But, he knew Burnside had been in over his head. "I cannot shut my eyes to the fact that he was not equal to the command of so large an army."

Meade's opinion of his new commander would prove to align with the historical evaluations to come. "I believe my opinion is more favorable," he wrote, "than any other of the old regular officers, most of whom are decided in their hostility to him. I believe Hooker is a good soldier; the danger he runs is of subjecting himself to bad influences, such as Dan Butterfield and Dan Sickles, who, being intellectually more clever than Hooker, and leading him to believe they are very influential, will obtain an injurious ascendancy over him and insensibly affect his conduct. I may, however, in this be wrong; time will prove." The next six months would prove Meade quite prophetic.[48]

Shortly after Hooker returned from Washington on 27 January, Meade rode three miles in a blinding snow storm to meet with his new chief. Hooker was in good spirits when George arrived. According to the new commander, he had been treated well in Washington and had been told by the administration that "he had only to ask and he should have what he wanted." He did not inform Meade of any plans he may have had at the time. Indeed, it may have been too soon for Hooker to have formulated any plans, but he did indicate he intended to move as soon as the weather would permit. Meade had no preconceived notions about Hooker being capable of satisfying the Washington crowed. "[He] will find in time his fate in the fate of his predecessor," he wrote to Margaret the following day, noting that

---

[47]   Meade, *Meade*, vol.1, pp.344, 348.

[48]   *Ibid*, pp.350-351.

when replaced, Hooker would be supplanted by someone outside the ranks of the Army of the Potomac.[49]

That spring, as Hooker prepared his army, it was safe to say that Meade was one of the oddest looking generals in his command. His most notable facial features were his deep set eyes and large hook nose. Beneath his eyes were heavy bags that gave him a constant look of drowsiness. His nose was large and bulbous with neither a straight nor recessed bridge but rather a slight bump. A high forehead and receding hair line made him look a little older than his forty-seven years and gave the impression of an aging schoolmaster. His brown hair had become sprinkled with gray which gave him a distinguished look. Completing Meade's unusual appearance was his smallish head, narrow face, rapid eye movements and his need for spectacles. Taken together, all his features created one of the most unusual looking generals in the history of the United States military.

Meade's stature was tall, slender and straight. When sitting a horse, he was not one who projected a military persona. Unlike McClellan, he had little presence and when riding by his legions, would not receive the adulation and cheers of his men. He seemed to have a total lack of personality which was supplemented by a tendency to become quickly agitated, revealing his quick temper. Others thought him a bit standoffish and never thought him to be overconfident. He was not one to brag about himself or his accomplishments even when he may have had the right to do so. George also believed that he would not advance in the army much beyond where he was because he did not possess friends in Washington who would support a promotion. Like John Sedgwick, Meade seldom dressed the part of a general and sometimes it was hard to tell his rank if one did not look closely. Though he look odd, Meade had one quality which he was always able to rely on. He was a devoted family man who adored his wife and children, and they returned the admiration in kind.[50]

The abolition of the Grand Divisions, as outlined in General Order No.6, reassigned Meade back to the command of the Fifth Corps. He had expected the assignment and there is little doubt he was pleased when the orders were finally cut. "Fighting Joe" remembered the officer who had taken over his command at Antietam and rewarded him. This time it would not be for ten days. In the coming weeks, Hooker would project great confidence in his army and his own ability to lead it to success. George Meade would begin to believe in Hooker as well. Observing his commander's energy and effort at revitalizing the army would make Meade an advocate. Unfortunately, it all would come crashing down a few weeks later at the crossroads of Chancellorsville.[51]

---

[49] *Ibid*, pp.352-353.

[50] Tagg, **Generals**, pp.1-3; Byrne & Weaver, Editors, **Haskell**, p.132.

[51] Meade, **Meade**, vol.1, p.353.

Chapter IV
"The Best Soldier I Ever Saw"

> "[T]he greatest soldier now living."[1]
> General Winfield Scott to a
> close friend prior to the
> war regarding Robert E. Lee.

The stunning victory at Chancellorsville reinforced Lee's confidence in his army and was the crowning achievement of a man who seemed to have been born to be a soldier. Robert Edward Lee came into the world on 19 January 1807. He was born at Stratford Hall in Westmoreland County, not far from the birthplace of George Washington. He was the fourth child of five born to Anne Hill Carter Lee and Henry "Light Horse Harry" Lee. Harry had been married previously, but his first wife passed away around 1790. Three years later he married Anne. Harry was a Revolutionary War hero whom Washington thought highly of and classified as "an excellent" military commander. Washington also believed Harry was a cerebral officer saying he had "great reserves of genius." After the war Harry was elected to Congress and then to three terms as governor of Virginia. When it came time for the new country to determine its first president, Harry enthusiastically supported Washington. When the first president died, Harry was asked by Congress to deliver the eulogy. In it Harry, wrote and spoke the words "First in war, first in peace, and first in the hearts of his countrymen."[2]

Unfortunately for Harry, he was not as astute with business affairs as he was with military or political issues. After a number of financial schemes, he found himself and his family burdened with overwhelming debt. For the purpose of educating his children, and possibly to escape his creditors, Harry packed up his family and moved north to Alexandria, Virginia when Robert was four. A year later he accepted a major general's commission to fight the English once again during the War of 1812. Two years later, while in Baltimore visiting Alexander C. Hansen,

---

[1] Jones, J. Williams, The Friendship between Lee and Scott, *SHSP*, vol.11, p.425.

[2] [2] Bowden, Scott & Ward, Bill., **Last Chance for Victory, Robert E. Lee and the Gettysburg Campaign**, p.62; Lee, Fitzhugh, *General Lee: A Biography of Robert E. Lee*, pp.9-10; Long, *Memoirs of Robert E. Lee*, p.21. While Long's biography of Lee paints the Confederate commander as infallible, there are aspects, which are relevant. Long was close to Lee and had the opportunity to observe him as well as his subordinates during the planning and execution of the Gettysburg Campaign.

the editor of the *Baltimore Federal Republican,* a mob surrounded Hansen's home. Hansen, who had published articles in opposition to the war, was now having his life threatened by the mob. During the confrontation, Harry was severely wounded and after a period of time went to the West Indies to expedite his recovery, leaving his family and his creditors behind. Robert was six when Harry left. He never saw his father again. After spending a few years in the West Indies, Harry decided to return home. He had traveled as far as Cumberland Island, Georgia when his injuries and health finally got the better of him. He died there on 25 March 1818.[3]

With his father gone, one brother off to college, another in the navy and a sister in ill health, Robert found himself in a situation that required him to grow up faster than an energetic young boy should. He was asked to be responsible for and perform household chores beyond those that should be required of an eleven year old. He took care of the family's horses, chopped firewood, maintained the home, and took care of the shopping duties as well as other family related tasks. His mother, now burdened with being both nurturer and disciplinarian, taught him self-control and to put others before himself. In the wake of his father's business failings, she taught him fiscal responsibility. Anne also showed deep affection for Robert and the boy returned the warmth. Unlike other children his age, he would hurry home from school to make sure she would not miss her daily carriage ride. On some occasions, as he got older and his strength grew to that of a young man, he would carry her to the carriage, positioning the cushions just right, so she would be comfortable. The lessons matured the boy beyond his years and instilled in him the values he would be known for in manhood.[4]

Lee's early schooling took place at the Alexander Academy where he earned strong marks in mathematics and Latin. He was just as diligent in his schoolwork as he was with chores at home, and at the age of seventeen, Lee applied for an appointment to the United States Military Academy. In order to give himself the best possible chance of receiving the appointment, Lee attended a preparatory school during the winter of 1824-25 and was instructed in mathematics by Benjamin Hallowell. Hallowell noted, "He was never behind-time at his studies; never failed in a single recitation: was perfectly observant of the rules and regulations of the institution: was gentlemanly, unobtrusive, and respectful in all his deportment to teachers and his fellow-students." After refining his skills, Lee received his appointment and entered West Point in 1825.[5]

There is little doubt that Hallowell's instruction had a significant influence in the development of the Lee's personality and work ethic. During his time at the school, Lee demonstrated a knack for exactness that bordered on the ridiculous. Hallowell noticed that many of Lee's slate tablet drawings were of little use but were so exacting that they could have been engraved and printed. Even Lee's lettering was precise. Hallowell was a calming influence and instilled the quality of patience and composure in the young man, character traits that Lee would have

---

[3] Bowden & Ward, *Last Chance,* p.62; Long, *Memoirs,* pp.22, 24.

[4] Long, *Memoirs,* pp.24-26.

[5] *Ibid,* pp.27-28.

never learned from his irresponsible father. By the time he was ready to leave for West Point, Lee was well prepared. In fact he may have been too prepared. Lee did so well at West Point that other students began enrolling at Hallowell's school in order to ready themselves for the difficult academy curriculum. This was a distinction which Hallowell did not appreciate.[6]

Lee continued his exceptional academic record at West Point. In his second year, he served as staff sergeant, a position usually reserved for a third year student. Lee's strong aptitude in mathematics led to an appointment as acting assistant professor of the curriculum. During his last year he was appointed corps adjutant, the most coveted rank a cadet can receive. The post's superintendent chose the cadet to occupy the position from the students that displayed a good head for drill, military matters and academics. Lee proved during his time at West Point that his study habits developed earlier in life were deeply ingrained and for four years he was a model.[7]

Not only did Lee show his scholarly abilities, he also displayed integrity and established an excellent conduct record. The conduct of a cadet at West Point was monitored through a system of demerits. Demerits were given for a large number of offenses, such as being absent or tardy to drill, roll calls, inspections, and meals, as determined by the school's administration. If a student's equipment or his sleeping quarters were dirty, he could receive a demerit as well. Smoking in the barracks and disturbances or activities after taps were also an offence punishable by demerit. The rules were so strict that even the well behaved Lee could manage no better than fifth in conduct upon graduation.[8]

Lee's excellent record allowed him to graduate second in his class. He was brevetted second lieutenant in the Engineers on 1 July 1829. After graduation, his interest in the Napoleonic Wars prompted Lee to undertake an energetic, self-study regiment. He showed specific interest in Baron Antoine Henri Jomini, a military theorist from Switzerland. Robert also expressed great interest in military history and the theories of combat.[9]

Lee's personal habits served him well his entire life. He never partook in any of the popular vices of the day. He did not drink, except for an occasional glass of wine during special events or the holidays. He avoided whiskey and brandy and did his best to instill in his associates the same self-control. His association with Jackson was

---

[6] Tucker, Glenn, *Lee and Longstreet at Gettysburg*, pp.77-78.

[7] Bowden & Ward, *Last Chance*, p.62.

[8] Tagg, *Generals*, pp.193-194; Krick, Robert K., 'A Stupid Old Useless Fool', *CWTI*, vol.47, no.3, pp.48-49. The retelling of a story in which Lee did not receive a single demerit at West Point has appeared in many works over the years. It seems rather unrealistic that anyone attending the academy could manage the four year curriculum in place during the early 1800 without at least one minor incident. The extent which demerits were handed out was unfathomable and the simple fact that a cadet left his bunk in the morning put him at risk. Krick's monograph in *CWTI* is the first mention of Lee not finishing his education at the top of the conduct ladder that this author has seen, and seems more credible than the story of no demerits.

[9] Bowden & Ward, *Last Chance*, p.63.

strengthened because Jackson accepted the same philosophy. When Lee departed for the Mexican War, he took with him a bottle of brandy intended for medicinal purposes. When he returned, the unopened bottle returned as well. When Lee became aware that a subordinate or associate was under the influence of spirits, he typical refrained from chastising them. He did however, quietly, as a loving father would, rebuke the behavior in an effort to place guilt in the mind of the impaired. Lee also refused to offer a subordinate's name for promotion if the officer showed a fondness for drink. He never used tobacco and seldom, if at all used the mildest of profanities.[10]

The young lieutenant's first assignment was along the seacoast in Georgia. He worked industriously to help design and construct Fort Pulaski on Cockspur Island at the mouth of the Savannah River. Lee worked in the area until the mid-1830s. During the summer, Georgia heat, accented by elevated humidity, created a breeding ground for disease carrying mosquitoes. Work on the fort had to ceased until the risk waned in the fall. During one summer's work stoppage, Lee returned north to visit friends in the Washington area. It was during this time that Lee became enamored with a young woman named Mary Randolph Custis. Mary's father, George Washington Parke Custis was the step-grandson of the first president. Mary was still living with her parents in the family mansion at Arlington and as an only child, was heiress to the estate.[11]

The two had met years earlier, when they were both children, during one of Lee's visits to Arlington. Over the years a playful child's attraction grew into affection for one another. While the women of each family approved of the courtship, Mary's father was not as supportive. He felt Lee, being a military man, was not high enough up the social ladder for his classically educated daughter. In addition, Mary's father may have also understood that a military career would keep Lee, if he were to become Mary's husband, away from her for long periods of time. Lee however, was persistent, and managed to sufficiently impress Mary. He was her first love as she was his. The young suitor's efforts paid off and the two were married on the last day of June, 1831 at Arlington.[12]

---

[10] Long, *Memoirs*, p.29, 31.

[11] Bowden & Ward, *Last Chance*, p.63. Long, *Memoirs*, p.31.

[12] Bowden & Ward, *Last Chance*, p.63. Long, *Memoirs*, pp.31-33. Robert and Mary had seven children. George Washington Custis Lee, who was known as Custis or by the nickname Boo, was born 16 September 1832. He served as a major general in the Confederate Army and aide-de-camp to President Jefferson Davis. He never married, and died 18 February 1913. Mary Custis Lee, who was simply called Daughter, was born in 1835. She never married and died in 1918. William Henry Fitzhugh Lee was born 31 May 1837. Known as Rooney, he served as a major general in the Confederate Army. He married twice and died on 15 October 1891. Anne Carter Lee, known as Annie, was born 18 June 1839. She never married and died at the age of twenty-two of typhoid fever on October 20 1862. Eleanor Agnes Lee, born 1841. Known as Agnes, she never married and died of tuberculosis on 15 October 1873. Robert Edward Lee, Jr., born 27 October 1843. Known as Rob, he served as a captain in the Confederate Army with the Rockbridge Artillery. He married twice and died on 19 October 1914. Mildred Childe Lee, born in 1846. Known as Milly or Precious Life, she never married and died in 1905. All the children are buried with their parents in the crypt of the Lee Chapel at Washington and Lee University in Lexington, Virginia.

Lee was indeed a lucky man. Not only did his marriage bring him into, arguably, the most influential family in the history of the young country, it also changed his place of residence to the large, majestic Arlington estate. Mary however, felt that the greatest benefit of the marriage was hers. While she was the heiress of the estate, she had few skills in administrating such a large enterprise. Lee brought his organization, managerial and administrative proficiency to the operation of the manor. If Mary's father had indeed raised Robert's profession as a drawback to the union, he was proven correct for shortly after the wedding, Lee left his new bride and returned to Georgia and his military duties.[13]

The Forging of a Warrior

Lee returned to his military responsibilities, continuing work as an engineer at various locations. His work consisted mainly of the rechanneling of rivers and the repair and construction of coastal fortifications. In Baltimore harbor, he helped design and build Fort Carroll and along the Mississippi River, he worked to protect the port of St. Louis from floodwaters. 1844 was an important year for Lee, as it saw two significant events which greatly advanced his military career. The first was an appointment to the board of engineers for the coastal defenses along the Atlantic seaboard. The second was a trip back to West Point for the final exams of the current graduating class. It was during his time at West Point that Lee first met General Winfield Scott. Scott was impressed with the young officer and the two began a relationship which would provide the final piece of Lee's training. He had received an excellent military education and possessed a good head for technical matters and details. Now, Winfield Scott would make him a soldier.[14]

Two years later when war erupted in Mexico, Lee's first assignment was in Texas, where he worked to build bridges and roads for General John C. Wool's march south. The work lacked romanticism and Lee saw no combat. The following year Lee was assigned to General Scott's staff and worked with the General to plan the seaborne assault on Vera Cruz. The maneuver, the first large amphibious operation in the history of the United States military, was a resounding success. The plan consisted of a landing south of the city, a march northward and laying siege to the town. On 9 March 1847, Scott came ashore with 12,000 men, marched the short distance north and cordoned off the town. After two days of bombardment, it was over. Scott praised Lee in his report of the engagement. Lee, then forty years old and a captain, had seen his first combat.[15]

After defeating the Mexicans at Vera Cruz, Scott assembled 8,500 men and began marching inland toward Mexico City. During the march, Lee was asked to perform reconnaissance work for the general. Many of his excursions to gather intelligence were filled with danger but he always returned with valuable information. At Cerro Gordo, Scott was faced with the possibility of assailing a

---

[13]   Long, *Memoirs*, pp.32-33.

[14]   Bowden & Ward, *Last Chance*, p.65.

[15]   *Ibid*; Long, *Memoirs*, pp.31-33.

strongly defended position. Being outnumbered, the general could not afford to waste his troops against such a position. Lee was sent forward to scout for possible flanking routes and found a path through an area that allowed Scott's force to turn the entrenched Mexicans. Lee participated in the movement, assault, and pursuit of the retreating Mexican force, which netted 3,000 prisoners.[16]

Later, Scott was presented with a similar situation near Churubusco. A strong enemy force was in a fortified position at San Antonio (Mexico). Lee was once again sent out to scout for a path to turn the position. To the south was a vast lava field, which was undefended because it was considered to rugged for the Americans to pass through. Lee however, found a path through the jagged rocks and convinced Scott it could be successfully negotiated. Scott gave the orders and the army bypassed the fortification, forcing the Mexicans from their location.[17]

Lee showed his determination on many of his scouting missions and on numerous occasions, risked detection and capture. One particular instance, on 15 April 1847, Lee found himself too far from the American lines and in the heart of an enemy position. Lee, and his guide John Fitzwalter, were standing near a spring when suddenly they heard footsteps approaching, and voices speaking Spanish. Fitzwalter bolted, but Lee was unable to escape as he was more exposed. He quickly ducked under a log, hiding to avoided detection. Unfortunately, the log was near the spring, which the Mexicans were using as a source of water. He remained hidden for a number of hours as the enemy drew water from the spring and loitered nearby. Some of the Mexicans even sat on and passed over the downed tree and carried on conversations, never the wiser as to Lee's presence. He remained calm and still until darkness made it possible for him to sneak away without detection.[18]

Lee's exploits in Mexico earned him brevet promotions and he finished the war with the rank of colonel. Scott had high praise for him. In his report on the battle of Cerro Gordo Scott wrote the following regarding Lee's performance.

> "I am compelled to make special mention of Captain R. E. Lee, Engineer. This officer was again indefatigable during these operations in reconnoissances [sic] as daring as laborious, and of the utmost value. Nor was he less conspicuous in planting batteries and in conducting columns to their stations under the heavy fire of the enemy."[19]

After the war with Mexico ended, during a public reception in Richmond, Scott commented on the value of Lee in Mexico. "You seek to honor the wrong

---

[16] Bowden & Ward, *Last Chance*, pp.66-67.

[17] *Ibid*, p.67.

[18] Long, *Memoirs*, p.53; Thomas, Emory M., *Robert E. Lee: A Biography*, p.125.

[19] *Ibid*, p.53.

man," Scott said. "Captain R. E. Lee is the Virginian who deserves the credit for that brilliant campaign."[20]

Shortly before the Civil War began, Scott complimented Lee once again.

> "I tell you that if I were on my death bed to-morrow, and the President of the United States should tell me that a great battle was to be fought for the liberty or slavery of the country, and asked my judgment as to the ability of a commander, I would say with my dying breath, let it be Robert E. Lee."[21]

General Scott was not the only man in Mexico who saw Lee's promise. Richard S. Ewell, who would also make a name for himself in the coming war, saw the attributes Lee possessed. Writing home to his brother, Ewell singled out Lee. "I really think one of the most talented men connected with this army is Captain Lee, of the Engineers. By his daring reconnaisances [sic] pushed up to the cannon's mouth, he has enabled General Scott to fight his battles almost without leaving his tent."[22]

Lessons

During his time with Scott in Mexico, Lee learned many valuable lessons which would serve him well during the coming Civil War. Scott's force had been consistently outnumbered as it marched across Mexico. With Lee's help, the general was able to outmaneuver his enemy, who constantly took refuge in fortified positions in an effort to halt Scott's advance. Lee witnessed firsthand the defeat of a numerically superior force with the use of good reconnaissance and the art of maneuver.

Another philosophy which Lee learned was that a commanding general must have the courage to make decisions and act on them quickly. Lee understood this as an inherent requirement which was absolutely necessary for a campaign of maneuver to be successful. When subordinate commanders disagreed or provided options, Lee, as an army commander had to be willing to listen and evaluate any suggestion and if necessary modify his own plan. Once a decision was made however, quick action was required. Long delay between decision and execution could be disastrous. Lee recognize that conditions on a battlefield where in constant flux and delaying a plan whose design was based on fresh intelligence provided time for conditions on the battlefield to change and the chance of a plan succeeding would be reduced.

---

[20] Jones, Lee and Scott, *SHSP*, vol.11, p.424.

[21] *Ibid*.

[22] Hamlin, Percy Gatling, *The Making of a Soldier: Letters of General R. S. Ewell*, Richard S. Ewell to Benjamin S. Ewell, 25 November 1847, p.68-69. Ewell wrote his brother from Vera Cruz.

A further critical perspective Lee learned in Mexico regarding a numerically inferior force was that its commander had to be willing to take risks. However, while taking risks was a necessity for the smaller force, any hazards had to be weighed against the benefits to be gained. If great risk was required to gain very little, a plan should not be attempted. The best scenarios always contained low risk with high reward. Lee became very adept during the Civil War of evaluating the risks of a proposed operation and making quick and generally correct decisions.

In order to make the correct decisions, the commander of a numerically inferior force had to have good intelligence. Information about the enemy and the topography within the area of operations was required. This was another critical lesson Lee learned from General Scott. Lee's information gathering reconnaissance missions for the general allowed his commander to assess the risks and make decisions quickly. While at the head of the Army of Northern Virginia, Lee utilized all his available resources, allowing him to be as knowledgeable as possible regarding the enemy's position, intentions, and the political situations he faced. Lee's well-developed ability to reason allowed him to take known facts and weigh them against "indications of the enemy's intentions" to formulate his course of action.

Lee also learned that whenever possible a numerically inferior force had to dictate the action within the area of operations. Seizing the initiative was one characteristic of Lee's military skills, which he executed very well for the first half of the Civil War. It was critical for Lee's smaller force to determine, as much as possible, when, how, and where engagements were fought. Doing so meant that the enemy had to fight at a constant disadvantage. Lee took the initiative away from McClellan on the Virginia Peninsula during The Seven Days and held it until the fight at Sharpsburg where he was forced to give up the field the day after the battle. He regained it at Fredericksburg, held onto it at Chancellorsville, and still had it in his grasp as he prepared for the summer campaign of 1863. Only after the arrival of General Ulysses S. Grant in the east, did Lee fail to regain the initiative once he had lost it.

The concept of constant pressure also became clear to Lee during the Mexican War. Whenever Scott's army paused during the advance inland, the enemy used the time to reorganize and strengthen the next position on their line of retreat. Driving a defeated and demoralized enemy cost the army significantly less in effort, equipment and blood than driving them from an established position.[23]

While at the head of the Army of Northern Virginia, Lee would remember these lessons and utilize them with great effectiveness. There would be few instances when he swayed from these philosophies. Unfortunately for the upstart country, one of those times would be during the summer of 1863 in southern Pennsylvania.

Lee's experiences in Mexico made him a better soldier, but there were a few negative aspects as well. He had achieved much during the forty plus years of his life. Most had been through hard work. As the Mexican War came to a close,

---

[23] Bowden & Ward, *Last Chance*, pp.70-73; Dowdey, Clifford, ***Lee's Last Campaign: The Story of Lee and His Men Against Grant-1864***, p.8.

nothing had occurred during the conflict to cause Lee's confidence in himself to waver. He knew that he was a fine engineer and his duties prior to the war had borne that out. Now, under Scott's leadership he gained confidence in himself as a military officer. Lee never publicly displayed this confidence, because he was a person of morals, and self-control. He was not accustomed to self-promotion or boastfulness, and his deep respect for others and his own humility would not allow him to display confidence. However, Lee seemed to have an inability to adjust his plans after he had made a decision. Although he welcomed the opinions of others, there were few subordinates who had the ability to alter or influence Lee's decision making process.

Lee took from the Mexican War another lesson which would prove to be a detriment to his success. Scott's great achievement instilled in Lee the belief that offensive operations were superior to a defensive stance. This belief would have great impact on the shaping of events leading up to and during the battle at Gettysburg. General Scott continually delivered offensive operations against enemy occupied defensive positions during his drive on Mexico City. He did so by maneuvering his forces into positions which forced the enemy to abandon theirs or be defeated. Lee, participating in these maneuvers and battles, experienced only success and developed faith in the concept of offensive operations.[24]

Lee grasped the concept of offensive operations providing greater benefits if successful than taking a defensive stance very well. His early success as commander of the Army of Northern Virginia came during The Seven Days in which he delivered numerous offensive blows, forcing the enemy, in McClellan words, to "change his base" of operations. Turning north, Lee took the offensive again, confronting John Pope's Army of Virginia at Second Manassas. The result was another crushing victory, which drove the Federals back to the safety of Washington. Embolden by success, Lee moved his army north again and invaded Maryland. The result of the movement was the single bloodiest day of the war. Lee fought the battle of Sharpsburg from a defensive posture and it was the only engagement prior to the summer of 1863 in which he did not achieve victory. The two armies fought each other to a standstill and the battle was technically a draw. Both armies stared each other down from roughly the same positions for another day. Heavily outnumbered, and with McClellan possessing a large number of fresh troops, Lee withdrew across the Potomac. Three months later Lee fought another defensive battle at Fredericksburg, where he secured another triumph. The victory however, as with the tactical masterpiece of Chancellorsville, was hollow for nothing was gained in either engagement except the depletion of Confederate men and resources.

During the fighting at Fredericksburg, Lee's defensive position on the south side of the Rappahannock River had been a strong one. As the battle progressed, it was assailed by large numbers of Union troops. All the attacks were beaten off with the Federals suffering great slaughter. Lee's left was held by General James Longstreet's Corps positioned behind a stonewall on Marye's Heights. At the

---

[24] Bowden & Ward, *Last Chance*, p.72.

height of the Union effort, Lee expressed concern that Longstreet's line was in danger of being broken by massed assaults. Longstreet confidently replied that if he were supplied with enough ammunition he would "kill them all." Longstreet was correct, for no organized body of men got within one hundred yards of the wall. Knowing when to assume a defensive posture and when to take the offensive was a concept, which Longstreet may have understood to a greater degree than Lee. There is no doubt however, that General Scott's campaign across Mexico can be attributed to Lee's strong belief in offensive tactics and the formation of many aspects of Lee's philosophies on how to conduct military operations.[25]

Peaceful Pursuits and War Clouds

After the war with Mexico, Lee returned to his engineering duties. At Soller's Point in the Baltimore area, he oversaw construction of defensive positions from 1849 to 1852. On 1 September 1852, he returned to his alma mater when he was appointed Superintendent of West Point. Under Lee's stewardship the curriculum was revitalized and extended to a five-year course of study. Improvements in discipline and proficiency were also achieved. Physical enhancements were added under Lee's leadership, including a large, new riding hall and a new wharf. Unfortunately, it was during his time at West Point that Mary's health began to deteriorate. Concerns for her wellbeing and management of the estate began to encroach upon his career.[26]

Lee's tenure at West Point ended in 1855. During the fall of that year, he was assigned to the newly created 2nd U. S. Cavalry. The regiment was placed under the command of Colonel Albert Sidney Johnston with Lee being appointed as the unit's lieutenant colonel. Sent to newly acquired west Texas, the regiment's responsibility would be to protected the flood of new settlers from marauding Indians. Lee worked to organize and train the regiment, but he was not with it when it departed, having taken a leave of absence to attend to personal matters. After putting his private affairs in order, he left Alexandria on 12 February 1856. He arrived at Fort Mason, Texas on 25 March. Lee occupied his post for a year and a half before he received word on 21 October 1857, of Mary's father's death. Again, Lee returned to Virginia, attending to a number of personal matters and worked through the disposition of his father-in-law's estate, before traveling back to his duties in Texas.[27]

Nearly two years to the day of being informed of his father-in-law's death, Lee was once again on leave. Near midday, he was relaxing at Arlington when a messenger arrived with a note summoning him to the War Department in Washington. With the messenger accompanying him, he left immediately, without taking time to change into his uniform. During the ride the messenger relayed to Lee everything he knew about the reason Lee had been called upon. The

---

[25] Longstreet, James, The Battle of Fredericksburg, ***B&L***, vol..3, p.81.

[26] Long, ***Memoirs***, pp.73-74; Faust, ***Encyclopedia***, p. 430.

[27] Long, ***Memoirs***, pp.75, 78-80.

abolitionist John Brown had seized the United States Armory at Harpers Ferry. Brown had proven in the past that he was not opposed to spilling the blood of pro slavery civilians and was not one to be taken lightly. Brown, two of his son's and nineteen other men where now pinned down in the establishments engine house. Intending to insight support for a slave rebellion, Brown's effort was doomed from the beginning and it failed to accomplish its intended goal. The local militia and a marine unit had been called out and the building surrounded. Brown, who believed himself an instrument of God, was hemmed in with no chance of escape.[28]

Time was not being lost at the War Department. No army troops were available so ninety marines were dispatched by rail while Lee met with President Buchanan and Secretary of War John B. Floyd. The president signed a proclamation declaring martial law and gave Lee command of all the forces at Harpers Ferry. Discovering no train car was available for him to ride in, a single locomotive was commandeered and Lee rode to Harpers Ferry in the cab of the engine. As the engine arrived at its destination, Lieutenant Israel Green, commander of the marines, met Lee.[29]

By the time Lee arrived at the besieged arsenal, eight of Brown's men, including one of his son's had been killed. Lee quickly sized up the situation and formulated a plan to carry the building. Then, in turn, he asked the commanders of the militia if they would like the honor of assaulting the engine house. All the officers declined to accept the responsibility. Lee then turned to Lieutenant

---

[28] Davis, Burke, *Jeb Stuart: The Last Cavalier*, pp.8-9; Boatner, *Dictionary*, p.91. A number of events helped to shape John Brown's position on slavery but two seemed to have a profound effect. The sacking of Lawrence Kansas was the first. Second, there was the brutal beating of anti-slavery senator Charles Sumner by Preston Brooks in retaliation for Sumner's derogative and insulting speech to the United States Senate.

On 23 May 1856, Brown and a party of seven others, four of whom were his sons, set out on a killing spree. The next night, after camping in a ravine, the party left their place of hiding and proceeded on their "secret expedition." Around 10 o'clock they called at the house of James P. Doyle and ordered him and his two adult sons, William and Drury, to go with them as prisoners. They left Doyle's other son and his wife behind because they were not members of a pro-slavery political organization. The three men followed their captors out into the darkness, where Brown had his sons Owen and Salmon hack them to death with broadswords. John Brown did not swing a sword, but he fired a shot into the head of the elder Doyle to make sure he was dead.

Next, the murderers went to the home of Allen Wilkinson. Wilkinson, another pro-slavery man, was led from his home where he was slashed, stabbed, and killed by two other members of the group. Not finished with their spree, the group continued on and sometime after midnight forced their way into the cabin of James Harris at sword-point. Harris had three house guests. All were questioned by the vigilantes as to their loyalties in regard to supporting slavery. Three men gave satisfactory answers but evidently William Sherman did not. He was led to the edge of a creek and hacked to death with swords by Brown's sons, Winer and Thompson.

Five of the men accompanying Brown to Harpers Ferry were Blacks.

The modern spelling of Harpers Ferry is without an apostrophe. Except for quoted passages its modern spelling will be utilized.

[29] Davis, *Jeb Stuart*, p.9.

Green, who gladly accepted and executed the plan. By 6:30 a.m. the marines were in position and Lee's surrender demands were read. Brown promptly refused to accept them. After being informed the terms had been rejected, Lee raised his arm and the assault began. The thick doors of the engine house were pounded with sledgehammers but they did not give. Using a nearby ladder as a battering ram the door was soon forced open and the marines entered. Brown was wounded in the ensuing melee. The final tally saw ten of Brown's party killed, seven were captured, and five escaped.[30]

After order was restored, Brown was questioned by a number of high-ranking Virginia officials and for hours the abolitionist was interrogated. After the inquires ended, the bodies of the dead were removed and buried in a pit dug next to the Shenandoah River. Lee, still dressed in his civilian clothing, never held a weapon during the incident. He lingered for another night and then boarded a train to return to Washington. He probably did not realize that the incident at Harpers Ferry was a small opening act in a grand play that was about to erupt across the Virginia countryside. With his leave soon expiring, Lee returned to his post out west, the incident involving Old John Brown no longer a concern.[31]

During the affair at Harpers Ferry, Lee displayed one of his core beliefs instilled in him during his time with Scott. He worked swiftly to determine the situation and once the characteristics of the confrontation were known, he formulated a plan to deal with the insurgents. Once the plan was designed, he wasted no time in its execution. This same propensity for swift decision-making would follow Lee into the war and become one of the reasons why he was able to out-soldier many of the Union commanders in the east.

After the Harpers Ferry incident, the political situation in the east worsened. During this time, Lee, who had returned to his duties in Texas, experienced a health event which may have been the first indication of the heart disease which would eventually claim his life. In a letter to his wife, Lee noted he was still feeling the "rheumatic effects" of a cold. More alarming however, was the condition of his arm. "[M]y right arm seems stationary," he informed Mary. "It is not very bad, yet enough to add to my complaining mood & make me satisfied with myself." Two months later he was still experiencing pain in the arm. The pain could have been the result of an unknown cardiovascular event. By July he was sick once more, but this time with a fever. The illness kept him from performing his duties. Although not feeling well, Lee actually appreciated his illness since the summer had brought on the unbearable heat of the Texas frontier.[32]

While Lee performed his duties in Texas, at the seat of government, war became eminent. Political wrangling had failed to rectify the fissure which had developed between the North and South. The election of Lincoln was the final straw. South Carolina was the first state to sever its ties with the old Union. Many

---

[30]   *Ibid*, pp.9-13; Long, **Memoirs**, p.86.

[31]   *Ibid*, pp.9-13, 15-16.

[32]   Thomas, **Lee**, pp.184-185.

of the state's officials had warned that if a Republican were elected president they would proclaim their independence. True to their word the state seceded on 20 December 1860. On 9 January Mississippi followed the Carolinians. The following day Florida departed. Then, on the eleventh, Alabama cast their lot with the renegades. Within three weeks the country had lost four states. On 19 January, after some orations by representatives of the seceding states, Georgia departed, followed by Louisiana a week later.[33]

As chaos erupted in the east, loyalties within the army were tested. General Twiggs, a strong Southern sympathizer, was in command of the Department of Texas. He had campaigned in Mexico with Scott and held numerous positions within the army after the Mexican War. He tried to communicate with Washington regarding the disposition of his command and government property if the state should secede, but had not received a response to his inquires. Without any direction from the government it was clear to Twiggs what had to be done. On 1 February, Texas authorities voted to join the secession movement. On the eighteenth, five days before the citizens of Texas voted to approve the state's Ordnance of Secession, Twiggs officially turned all the property, money, forts, outposts, supplies and troops over to the secessionists.[34]

Lee was in Texas when the officials voted to follow the other states. A month earlier, with the possibility of the Union dissolving, Lee expressed his feelings on the subject to one of his sons. "…a Union that can only be maintained by swords and bayonets, and in which strife and civil war are to take the place of brotherly love and kindness, has no charm for me. I shall mourn for my country and for the welfare and progress of mankind. If the Union is dissolved and the Government disrupted, I shall return to my native State and share the miseries of my people, and save in defense will draw my sword on none."[35]

Lee, ordered to report to Scott in Washington, arrived in San Antonio on 16 February at 2 p.m., to find confusion. As luck would have it, he entered town as the fever over confiscating the government's property was at its height. As the ambulance he was riding in halted, he was surrounded by a group of Texas Rangers. "Who are those men?" Lee asked a local citizen. Once told who the men were, he was informed of the situation. "General Twiggs surrendered everything to the State this morning, and we are all prisoners of war." Lee's face tightened, his lips trembled and tears came to his eyes. "Has it come so soon as this?" After registering at the Road House Hotel and changing into civilian dress, possibly to avoid drawing attention to himself, he made his way to the outpost's headquarters. Late in the day he returned to his room and spent a restless night pacing about the room and praying.[36]

---

[33] Faust, *Encyclopedia*, pp. 3, 264, 303, 449, 500, 703.

[34] Ibid, p.767.

[35] Long, *Memoirs*, pp.88-89.

[36] Lee, *General Lee*, p.77; Darrow, Caroline Baldwin, Recollections of the Twiggs Surrender, *B&L*, vol.1, p.36. Thomas, *Lee*, pp.186-187.

Lee stayed in San Antonio a week. As he prepared to leave on the journey to Washington, Captain R. M. Potter noted that he had "seldom seen a more distressed man." Lee told Potter, "When I get to Virginia I think the world will have one soldier less. I shall resign and go to planting corn." Colonel Charles Anderson also spoke with Lee as he prepared to depart. "...my loyalty to Virginia ought to take precedence over that which is due to the Federal Government," Lee told Anderson. Lee did not believe that secession was a constitutional right, but he could not take up arms against his beloved Virginia. "If Virginia stands by the old Union, so will I. But if she secedes, then I will still follow my native State with my sword, and if need be, with my life." Lee thought the possibility of civil war deplorable, but if it were to erupt, he would stay true to his principles and defend family, property, and state.[37]

Decision of a Lifetime

Lee arrived at Arlington before the evening meal was served on 1 March. After spending a few days relaxing after his long journey, he mounted his horse and rode across the bridge into Washington to see his old friend General Scott. At the age of seventy-five, Scott's robust and solid 6-5 frame had deteriorated. His dash and bearing had vanished into an overweight mass that at times could barely move. He could no longer ride a horse and even walking without assistance was difficult. He was plagued with gout and vertigo, spent most of his time sitting on the couch in his office or in an enormous wing chair. There was not much left of the young country's most celebrated soldier. With the prospects of war hanging over the nation, Scott was surely pleased to see Lee.[38]

Lee and Scott spent three hours together that day. No records have ever been found of what topics the two old friends discussed. The issues obviously ranged from good memories of times gone by and an unsure future. Scott probably informed Lee of his pending promotion to full Colonel and command of the First Cavalry. The two men must have communicated concerns over the prospect of their native state seceding and what they would do if such an event took place. Each man's course of action must surely have been declared should Virginia leave the Union. Scott would have been disappointed in hearing Lee's decision to remain loyal to his state, but the old soldier also understood that Lee was a man who could not be untrue to his core values.[39]

Lee returned home and spent the next month and a half watching events unfold. The Southern government, working to organize itself, elected Jefferson Davis as its president. As he watched and waited, an offer of a brigadier general's commission in the forming Confederate Army was made to him. He seems to have

---

[37] Editors Notes, *B&L*, vol.1, p.36. Charles Anderson was the brother of Major Robert Anderson, the commander of the garrison in Fort Sumter when secessionists fired on the fort in Charleston Harbor.

[38] Thomas, *Lee*, p.187; Grimsley, Mark, Overthrown, *CWTI*, vol.19, no.7, p.20.

[39] Thomas, *Lee*, p.187.

allowed this offer to go unanswered while accepting his promotion to Colonel in the United States Army. As the confrontation over Fort Sumter in South Carolina's Charleston Harbor became heated, Lee continued to observe events. Lincoln, deciding to re-supply the fort, sent an expedition south on 8 April. On 12 April, with the resupply ships sitting offshore, Pierre Gustave Toutant Beauregard opened fire on the fort. The die was cast. Lincoln and Davis both called for volunteers. War had come.

Five days later, Lee received two requests; one was from his old friend General Scott, and the other from Francis P. Blair, a friend of Lincoln and father of the president's postmaster general. The following day, 18 April, Lee set out again for Washington. He called on the elder Blair who made plain the purpose of the summons. Blair, at the bidding of Lincoln, offered Lee command of the Union Army being assembled to put down the rebellion.[40]

"I never intimated to any one that I desired the command of the United States army," Lee wrote after the war, "nor did I ever have a conversation but with one gentleman, Mr. Francis Preston Blair, on the subject, which was at his invitation, and, as I understood, at the instance of President Lincoln."

"After listening to his remarks," Lee continued, "I declined the offer he made me to take command of the army that was to be brought into the field, stating, as candidly and as courteously as I could, that, though opposed to secession and deprecating war, I could take no part in an invasion of the southern States."[41]

Evidently Blair would not take no for an answer and raised the slavery issue. He implied Lee did not wish to part with his Negros, which, according to Blair, was the determining factor in Lee's desire to remain with his state. According to Mary, Lee flatly denied the slanderous accusation telling Blair that if he owned all the Negros in the South he would gladly free them if it would bring to an end the discourse between the two parties.[42]

After the meeting with Blair ended, Lee went directly to General Scott and told him of the offer and of his decision to decline. Scott was assuredly disappointed, for the aged general's loyalties lay with the Union, yet he surely must have understood Lee's decision. Scott had previously instructed the government to do everything possible to keep Lee with the North, feeling he was worth fifty thousand men to the Northern cause. Deep down, he may have actually been proud of his subordinate for honoring the core values, which made up the man known as Robert E. Lee.[43]

That night Lee returned home and after some time spent in reflection made his decision in the early morning hours of 20 April. Sitting down, he wrote two letters, one was to General Scott the other to Simon Cameron, Lincoln's secretary of war.

---

[40] *Ibid*, pp.187-188.

[41] Long, ***Memoirs***, p.93. Quoted from a letter from Lee to Reverend Johnson, 25 February 1868.

[42] Long, ***Memoirs***, p.92.

[43] Thomas, ***Lee***, p.188; Long, ***Memoirs***, p.92.

>Arlington, Washington City P.O.
>April 20, 1861

General:

    Since my interview with you on the 18th instant I have felt that I ought not longer to retain my commission in the Army. I therefore tender my resignation, which I request you will recommend for acceptance.

    It would have been presented at once, but for the struggle it has cost me to separate myself from a service to which I have devoted all the best years of my life & all the ability I possessed.

    During the whole of that time, more than 30 years, I have experienced nothing but kindness from my superiors, & the most cordial friendship from my companions. To no one Genl have I been as much indebted as to yourself for uniform kindness & consideration, & it has always been my ardent desire to merit your approbation.

    I shall carry with me to the grave the most grateful recollections of your kind consideration, & your name & fame will always be dear to me. Save in the defense of my native State, I never desire again to draw my sword.

    Be pleased to accept my most earnest wishes for the continuance of your happiness & prosperity & believe me most truly yours.

>R. E. Lee[44]

Then Lee wrote a simple, one sentence letter to Cameron.

>Arlington, Washington City P.O.
>20 April 1861

Honorable Simon Cameron
    Sect. of War
Sir:

    I have the honour to tender the resignation of my Commission as Colonel of the 1st Regt. of Cavalry.

>Very resply your obt servt
>R. E. Lee
>Col. 1st Cavalry [45]

    The day after Lee resigned he received another request to meet with government officials. This time it was with a representative of the governor of Virginia, John Letcher. After attending church with one of his daughters on Sunday, 21 April, Lee boarded a train the following day and traveled to Richmond where he met

---

[44] Dowdey & Manarin, **Wartime Papers**, pp.8-9.

[45] *Ibid*, p.9

with Letcher. The governor was direct and to the point. The state assembly voted to secede on 17 April and now Letcher needed someone to take command of the state's forces. The governor wasted little time in offering Lee the position, which he accepted. Within a span of five days, Lee had been offered command of the assembling Union forces, declined the position, resigned from the United States Army and cast his fortunes with the upstart Confederacy.[46]

Upon first meeting Lee, one of his staff members noted the general was an impressive human being. "I... was at once attracted and greatly impressed by his appearance. He was then at the zenith of his physical beauty. Admirably proportioned, of graceful and dignified carriage, with strikingly handsome features, bright and penetrating eyes, his iron-gray hair closely cut, his face cleanly shaved except a moustache, he appeared every inch a soldier and a man born to command." Another future Lee staff member described his first audience with the general as extremely cordial with Lee displaying the humility he would become known for. The staffer was impressed with "the ease and grace of his [Lee's] bearing and his courteous and mild but decided manner; and the high opinion... formed of him was fully sustained in the intimate relations which afterward existed... Though at the time he had attained the age of fifty-four years, his erect and muscular frame, firm step, and the animated expression of his eye made him appear much younger. He exhibited no external signs of his rank, as his dress being a plain suit of gray. His office was simply furnished with plain desks and chairs. There were no handsomely-dressed aides-de-camp or staff officers filling the anteroom. There was not even a sentinel to mark the military headquarters." The meeting was not unlike other first encounters with Lee. Many had heard of the man and seemed to expect something other than the simplicity and humbleness which arrived with him.[47]

Shortly before the war, Lee's old mentor, General Scott was asked who he believed to be the "greatest living soldier." Once again, the aging general responded in his typical, matter of fact way.

> "Colonel Robert E. Lee is not only the greatest soldier of America, but the greatest soldier now living in the world. This is my deliberate conviction, from all full knowledge of his extraordinary abilities, and if the occasion ever arises Lee will win his place in the estimation of the whole world."

After completing an exhaustive summery of Lee's service record, Scott concluded with a rather prophetic statement.

---

[46] Thomas, *Lee*, p.188; Long, *Memoirs*, p.92.

[47] Taylor, Walter H., **General Lee: His Campaigns in Virginia, 1861-1865**, pp.21-22; Long, *Memoirs*, p.112.

"I tell you, sir, that Robert E. Lee is the greatest soldier now living, and if he ever gets the opportunity, he will prove himself the greatest captain of history."[48]

It remained to be seen if history would provide Lee his "opportunity."

"Granny Lee"

One week after the stunning Confederate victory at Manassas, Lee was ordered to western Virginia to oversee operations in the region west of the Shenandoah Valley. He set up his headquarters at Valley Mountain and in short order began to assess the situation. The weather during the month of August was anything but conducive to military operations. It rained constantly and was incredibly cold. In a letter to his daughters, Annie and Agnes, Lee complained about the weather. "It is raining now. I have on all my winter clothes & am writing in my overcoat." As Lee grumbled about the weather, there was another storm brewing that would mark his three months in western Virginia as an utter failure.[49]

The situation in western Virginia was anything but stable. William W. Loring, a political general with no military instruction, had been sent to the region to take over the area after Robert S. Garnett had been killed conducting a delaying action after the battle at Rich Mountain. Although not militarily trained, Loring had been fighting all his life. As a boy of fourteen, he enlisted and fought in the Seminole Indian War. Later, he fought against Mexico, where he lost his left arm to a wound received before Mexico City. With his men located in the vicinity of Valley Mountain, Loring focused his attention on Cheat Mountain, a key position in central western Virginia. Atop the ridge was a Federal stronghold which had been made even more formidable with earthworks and fortification.[50]

Southwest of Cheat Mountain was another body of Confederates commanded by two more political generals, former Secretary of War John B. Floyd and George Meade's brother in law, Henry A. Wise. Floyd, while a talented politician and former governor of Virginia, was no leader of men. Toward the end of his service in the Buchanan Administration, he spent a good deal of time trying to transferring weapons from northern arsenals to those in the south. A staunch secessionist, Floyd raised a brigade when the war broke out and was rewarded with a field command. His other personal failing as a military commander was his deep seated determination to have his own way. He was accustomed to dealing with situations from a position of power, and he had no understanding of military protocol or the purpose of a chain of command. George Meade's brother in law was from the same mold as Floyd. Like the former secretary, Wise, after his congressional service, was

---

[48] Jones, Lee and Scott, ***SHSP***, vol.11, p.425.

[49] Dowdey & Manarin, ***Wartime Papers***, p.67. Lieutenant Walter H. Taylor and Colonel John A. Washington accompanied Lee to western Virginia.

[50] Faust, ***Encyclopedia***, p. 447; Thomas, ***Lee***, p.202.

elected governor of Virginia. His zeal for the Confederacy rivaled Floyd's, and he retained that spirit until the very end.[51]

Lee's first problem with his new command was that it was no command at all. President Davis sent him to act as an advisor, and, while a brigadier general, he was not the senior commander in the region. Loring, who was appointed a brigadier generalship on 20 May actually ranked Lee. Lee's instructions were to act more as a coordinator, therefore he never actually took active command of the forces in the area. Davis himself was feeling a bit apprehensive with Lee away from Richmond. "He [Davis] has not ceased to feel an anxious desire for your return to this city," wrote Davis' adjutant Samuel Cooper. "Whenever, in your judgment, circumstances will justify it, you will consider yourself authorized to return."[52]

Another problem Lee faced was a serious lack of military discipline and adherence to the chain of command by the three commanding officers in the region. The problem would be accented by Lee's roll of being a manager and not a commander. In addition, Lee's command style of providing discretionary orders or suggestions, which became so effective with men like Jackson and Longstreet, failed miserably with Loring, Wise and Floyd. This exposes one of Lee's flaws as a commander. Issuing discretionary orders or making suggestions relies on the receiver to understand the insight contained in Lee's instructions. When interacting with men who have an understanding of military operations, this method works on many levels. When dealing with untrained men who do not evaluate opinions based on military experience or training, it is extremely problematic.[53]

Lee's initial target for the campaign would be Cheat Mountain. A plan was agreed upon to move Loring's men down the Tygart River Valley. In conjunction with men from Colonel Albert Rust's command, they would move on the mountain from the east. Rust had discovered a concealed route to the rear of the Federal works that would allow the Confederates to seal off the fortifications on the mountain and starve out the Yankee's. The assault would consist of five separate columns and would require a great deal of coordination and depended on Rust to instigate the battle. After the movement began, rains came and Rust, another politician, faltered. After interrogating some prisoners, the colonel determined that there were 5,000 troops on Cheat Mountain, a number that was much larger than the actual garrison. This was more than he felt his 1,500 men could handle. After reconnoitering the position and meeting with his subordinates, Rust called off the attack and the effort to take Cheat Mountain failed. Loring retreated and the Confederates, after developing a good plan, were victimized by indecision and poor leadership.[54]

Completely frustrated with the results at Cheat Mountain, Lee watched as Federal General William S. Rosecrans moved his men into a position to attack

---

[51] Faust, *Encyclopedia*, pp.265, 839; Thomas, *Lee*, p.203.

[52] *OR* vol.5, pp.828, 829; Thomas, *Lee*, p.204.

[53] Thomas, *Lee*, p.204.

[54] Faust, *Encyclopedia*, p.135; Thomas, *Lee*, p.206.

Floyd at Carnifax Ferry. Requiring help to deal with Rosecrans, Floyd ordered Wise to march to his assistance. Wise refused to move. Floyd fought his men well but retreated because he thought he was confronted by more Federals than he actually was. Once again, Floyd ordered Wise to come to his assistance and again Wise did not budge. Wise constantly expressed some excuse for not moving or he simply ignored Floyd's pleas for help. For approximately a month, the two corresponded with each other, both finding fault in the other's opinions and neither making any effort to help the other or work together.

Finally, Lee had enough and on 21 September, he rode the seventy miles out to Floyd's position and discovered that Wise still had not moved. Three days later he rode on to Wise's command at Sewell Mountain. When he arrived Wise was still in his position, refusing to move. The stubborn Wise informed Lee his position was a better one than the one Floyd held. As Lee reviewed the location, he had to admit that Wise was correct, but the strength of a position was no excuse for ignoring direct orders from a superior. He also discovered Wise's command in such a state of confusion and disorder that a young lieutenant, obviously oblivious too who Lee was, asked him if he knew where the ordinance officer was because the young man needed ammunition. Lee, against his quiet peaceful nature, vehemently chastised the soldier. He was upset and he had every right to be.[55]

The feud between Wise and Floyd grew to epic proportions as Wise sent letters to Lee complaining about Floyd. Floyd in turn sent letters to Davis complaining about Wise. Neither man had an understanding of military protocol, nor paid any attention to the chain of command. Lee was presented with a dilemma not of his making. No matter what decision he made, in the eyes of one of his subordinates, he was going to be detested. Wise's position was strong so if he suggested that Floyd join Wise then the advantage of position could be obtained against Rosecrans; however, if he ordered Wise to move to Floyd's support Wise would be disappointed and no doubt upset with Lee. He decided to try and convince Floyd to join Wise in order to take advantage of the better position. The bickering came to an end when Wise received a letter from Secretary of War Judah P. Benjamin, ordering him to transfer his command to Floyd and report to Richmond. Wise, in a stunning act of insubordination, had the audacity to treat Benjamin's orders as a suggestion until Lee convinced him that he had better obey the order or he would forfeit any opportunity to obtain another command.[56]

With Wise out of the picture, Lee was able to unite all three of the western Virginia commands and form an integrated defense. Rosecrans however, refused to give battle and toward the end of October Lee returned to Richmond. Davis never blamed Lee for the failure in western Virginia but unfortunately for Lee the press did. Wise's son Obediah was editor of the *Richmond Examiner* and Lee's reputation took a beating in the papers. They took to calling him "Granny Lee," and argued he lacked nerve for the work of battle and shied away from conflict. To some extent, they were correct because Lee sought to soften confrontational situations between officers, a command trait that showed itself in western Virginia.

---

[55] Thomas, *Lee*, p.207.

[56] *Ibid*, p.208

A shrewd and crafty politician, John B. Floyd, along with William Loring, became a thorn in Lee's side in western Virginia. *LOC*

While Lee's reputation may have taken a serious hit, he managed to make at least one new friend. While at Sewell Mountain, Lee became acquainted with a majestic, four year old gray stallion, named Jeff Davis. Lee liked the horse and the animal seemed to take an interest in him as well. He spoke to the owner about purchasing the horse but at that time he did not acquire the animal. Later that fall, when Lee was in South Carolina, he was able to attain the horse, who was now called Greenbrier, for the sum of two hundred dollars. Because of the animal's ability to travel long distances with ease, Lee began calling the stallion Traveller. Lee would form a unique and strong bond with the animal, and he would ride him for the remainder of his life. Like Lee, his gray stallion would become an icon associated with the Southern cause.[57]

Lee, returning to Richmond, was anxious to see his wife. He had not seen Mary since he left Arlington on 22 April, but he would not have a chance to spend any time with her. On 1 November, Benjamin became concerned over a Federal expedition which he was convinced was headed for Port Royal, South Carolina. In a communication to South Carolina's governor, Francis Pickens, he wrote, "I have just received information, which I consider entirely reliable that the enemy's expedition is intended for Port Royal." To meet the threat he quickly organized a new military department which contained South Carolina, Georgia and the east coast of Florida. He assigned Lee to command of the new department and the general departed for South Carolina on 6 November. Lee did not arrive before

---

[57] *Ibid*, pp.209-210.

the Federal expedition had entered Port Royal Harbor, taking command on 8 November.[58]

Lee was less impressed with the circumstances in South Carolina than he had been in western Virginia. On 15 November, writing to his daughter Mildred he noted the situation was, "[W]orse than western Virginia" and that the assignment was a "forlorn hope." Lee set up his headquarters at Coosawhatchie South Carolina. It did not take long before his observations regarding the situation became evident. He tried to organize a force to resist the invaders but "the people do not seem to realize that there is war," he wrote his daughter Annie. "[T]he numerous deep estuaries all accessible to their ships, expose the multitude of islands to their predatory excursions…" The difficulties arose from a lack of resources. Lee did not have enough guns to defend all the areas that allowed access for the Federals. He would have to select his defensive positions carefully which unfortunately did not include many of the barrier islands. His lack of guns however, was not as important as the lack of soldiers. In a letter to Governor Pickens, Lee reiterated the need for troops. "I beg leave again to submit to Your Excellency the great need of troops to defend this line." The situation was dire enough to reduce Lee to begging Pickens for more troops.[59]

On 20 December, the Federals moved their "stone fleet" into the main shipping channel in Charleston Harbor and sunk it, effectively blocking the channel. Somewhere between thirteen and seventeen ships, laden with large rocks, were sent to the bottom by the Federals. Lee thought the act quite dastardly and termed it "unworthy of any nation." The grounding of the fleet indicated to Lee, however, that the Federals had no intention of attempting to capture the city.[60]

On 8 February, an old nemesis from western Virginia came back to haunt Lee. Federal General Ambrose Burnside landed on Roanoke Island off the North Carolina coast with 10,000 troops. Commanding the small group of Confederate defenders was none other than Henry A. Wise. Wise had been assigned command of the forces on the island on 22 January and was looking forward to leading them in battle. Unfortunately, he never got the chance. On the day the Federal assault took place, Wise was in bed at Nags Head suffering from an attack of pleurisy. The Rebels put up token resistance and then left the island to the Yankees. While

---

[58] *Ibid*, p.211; ***OR*** vol.6, pp.306, 309, 312; Dowdey & Manarin, ***Wartime Papers***, p.86. As with his assignment in western Virginia, Walter H. Taylor accompanied Lee to South Carolina. Taylor assumed the assistant adjutant general post while T. A Washington occupied the adjutant general position.

[59] Dowdey & Manarin, ***Wartime Papers***, p.86, 91, 99; Thomas, ***Lee***, p.212-213.

[60] Dowdey & Manarin, ***Wartime Papers***, pp.86, 91; A stone fleet was a series of small sailing ships which were loaded with stones and sunk in the main shipping channels of southern ports in an effort to restrict commerce. Typically the action was not effective since marine bores and microbes soon destroyed the integrity of the wood and the stones sunk into the mud. The activity had a greater effect on morale than it did on shipping.

Roanoke Island was not in Lee's department, it was another sign of the forlorn hope he had expressed to Mildred.[61]

Fortunately for Lee, he was not in South Carolina long. On 13 March 1862, he was ordered back to Richmond to assume duties as advisor to the president. "General Robert E. Lee..." the order read, "is assigned to duty at the seat of government; and, under the direction of the President, is charged with the conduct of military operations in the armies of the Confederacy." While he was glad to be in Richmond to assist the president, he did not think his new position would do much to support the Southern cause. "...I do not see either advantage or pleasure in my duties," he wrote to Mary, but he refused to openly complain about the situation as he had just been rescued from western Virginia and South Carolina.[62]

The days Lee spent in Richmond during the spring and early summer of 1862 were some of the Confederacy's darkest times. Much of the southern coast was under assault from aggressive Yankee forces and western Virginia was all but lost. In the east, Fort Henry, on the Tennessee River and Fort Donelson along the Cumberland River had been lost to Ulysses S. Grant. Grant then marched south to Pittsburg Landing where he won a victory for the Union in the bloodbath at Shiloh. During the fight, Albert Sidney Johnston, one of the South's top commanders had been killed. Nashville had been lost and the South's invasion of Kentucky had been turned back. To make matters worse, McClellan's mighty Army of the Potomac had transferred its base of operations to the Virginia Peninsula and was marching on the Confederate capital. The lone bright spot was Stonewall Jackson's campaign in the Shenandoah Valley. The outlook was bleak indeed, and many were of the opinion that the war for Southern Independence had already been lost.

Lee did everything he could to bolster Confederate defenses and took an active part, by way of correspondence; to provide support to the commanders in the field. On 26 March, he wrote to General John B. Magruder on the Virginia Peninsula.

> "It will no doubt be the policy of the enemy to disguise his intention by threatening one point while preparing to attack the other, and the utmost care and judgment should be exercised to ascertain his real design. You will use every means in your power to obtain information on this point, and communicate every material fact tending in your opinion to throw light on the subject, with your own inference from such facts."

Lee went on to outline strategy to Magruder, suggesting he be mindful of any Federal attempt to flank his position on the Peninsula by transferring troops by boat to the Pamunkey and Chickahominy River's and informed him to fall back to the line of the Chickahominy if necessary.[63]

---

[61] *OR* vol.9, p.72; Thomas, ***Lee***, p.204; Barrett, John G., ***The Civil War in North Carolina***, p.74.

[62] Dowdey & Manarin, ***Wartime Papers***, pp. 127-128.

[63] *OR* vol.11, pt.3, p.398.

On 25 March, Lee wrote to General Joseph E. Johnston, who was in command of the Confederate troops north of Richmond. Johnston's force was positioned in the Culpeper area to confront a possible threat from Washington if one developed. Lee called on him to send "nothing less than twenty to thirty thousand men" to reinforce the units already in front of Richmond. Johnston however, believed that there would be no effort made on his position, and with the majority of the Federal force now on the Peninsula, he responded to Lee on the same day suggesting that his whole force could be better used in front of Richmond. Lee agreed and at 1 a.m., on the morning on 28 March, informed Johnston to move south with his entire command.[64]

Lee understood it was not possible to defend every square mile of the Confederacy and began to call troops from other, less threatened regions. On 20 April he wrote John C. Pemberton, who had replaced him in South Carolina. After outlining the situation near Richmond, Lee asked Pemberton to send forth all the troops he could spare.

> "I fear therefore to be obliged to draw further detachments from your department & desire you to consider where they can best be spared, & to make every exertion to arm the new regiments still remaining in Georgia and South Carolina."

Lee also asked if Pemberton could send a brigade to Johnston north of Richmond on the Rappahannock line.[65]

Unfortunately for Lee, Joe Johnston was now showing the tendencies which would eventually lead to his downfall as a respected commander in the Confederate Army. While Lee informed him that his entire force would be needed, Johnston was slow to react and at times purposely delayed his movement. When he finally arrived in front of Richmond, he complained about the position his army was assigned, and Lee promised to discuss the issue with Davis. Friction between Davis and Johnston was in its infancy and Lee was caught in the middle, trying to act as a mediator between a general in the field who had one idea about how the city's defense should be conducted and the president, who had another. On the evening of 3 May, Johnston began pulling the army back toward Richmond. On 5 May, a rear guard engagement was fought at Williamsburg, delaying McClellan's move up the Peninsula, but the evacuation of the Warwick Line gave the Federal commander an open road to the gates of Richmond.

Once again, as in western Virginia, Johnston seemed to treat Lee's discretionary orders as suggestions and not instructions to act upon, making it difficult for Lee to communicate his intentions. But while Johnson presented a challenge, the same could not be said of Thomas Jackson in the Shenandoah Valley. During his time in Richmond, Lee issued many discretionary orders to Jackson and the latter used them as guidelines to develop his campaign in the Valley. With a little instruction and encouragement from Lee, Jackson waged one of the most

---

[64] *OR* vol.11, pt.3, p.397.

[65] Dowdey & Manarin, ***Wartime Papers***, p.150.

successful campaigns of the war. It was the first interaction between two men who would bring so many positive results over the next year.⁶⁶

Perhaps the most recognized and published wartime photo of Lee. It was taken in March 1864, nine months after the Battle of Gettysburg. *LOC*

The battle of Fair Oaks on 31 May, left both armies bloody with no tangible advantage gained by either side. During the battle however, an event occurred that would change the course of the war in the east. Johnston had chosen to observe the battle from a knoll that was well within range of enemy artillery. One of Johnston's couriers, Drury L. Armistead, recorded the scene. Most of Johnston's staff had been sent on errands leaving Drury and an unnamed colonel with the general. "...the air seeming to be alive with whizzing bullets and bursting shells," Armistead recalled. As the colonel made efforts to dodge the projectiles, Johnston turned and grinned. "Colonel," he said, "there is no use of dodging; when you hear them they have passed." A moment later, Johnston was reeling in his saddle, a victim of a Federal bullet to the right shoulder. An instant later a shell struck the ground immediately in front of his horse. A fragment from the exploding projectile hit Johnston in the chest, throwing the general from his mount. Armistead jumped from his horse and, taking Johnston up in his arms, carried him out of harm's way. Joined by others, he was able to facilitate the removal of the general to a place of safety a quarter mile to the rear, but the army was without a commander.⁶⁷

The next day, Jefferson Davis, turned to Lee to wrestle victory from what appeared to be certain defeat and save the capital.

---

⁶⁶ Thomas, *Lee*, pp.222, 224.

⁶⁷ Armistead, Drury L., The Battle in Which General Johnston was Wounded, ***SHSP***, vol.18, p.187; Sears, Stephen W., ***To the Gates of Richmond: The Peninsula Campaign***, p.138.

Richmond, Va., June 1, 1862

General R. E. LEE:

Sir: The unfortunate casualty which has deprived the army in front of Richmond of its immediate commander, General Johnston, renders it necessary to interfere temporarily with the duties to which you were assigned in connection with the general service, but only so far as to make you available for command in the field of a particular army. You will assume command of the armies in Eastern Virginia and in North Carolina, and give such orders as may be needful and proper.

Very respectfully,
JEFFERSON DAVIS[68]

It would be a temporary assignment that would last for the remainder of the war.

A Different Man

A few months earlier, while stationed in South Carolina, Lee took time to travel to Cumberland Island to visit the grave of his father. Perhaps curiosity drove Lee to seek out his father's final resting place. He had taken a much different track in life than his father, and he had developed into a man who was nothing like his famous but flawed parent, spending much of his life trying to outdistance the reputation of Harry. One thing was certain, Lee was his own man. He had been raised by his mother, schooled by Hallowell, and developed a persona of civility and responsibility that was nothing like his father's. Now he was in command of the most important military organization in the upstart Confederacy. The "chance" spoken of by old General Scott had come to pass. Over the next three years, he would become the most recognizable icon of the lost cause, and there is no doubt Harry would have been proud.

Some flowers were growing near his father's resting place. Bending down, Lee picked one. He lingered near the grave only a short time, then left as if spending another moment would develop a connection with his late father which he wished to avoid. He would not return until well after the war was over and his health was failing him. Between the two visits there would be a great deal of work to do.[69]

---

[68] *OR* vol.11, pt.3, p.568.

[69] Thomas, *Lee*, p.215. There is some evidence that Lee may have paid a visit to his father's grave while a young lieutenant stationed on Cockspur Island when he was fresh out of West Point. There is some question as to whether this visit actually occurred.

Chapter V
Confederate Players

> "Nothing preventing my proposing to you to
> reduce their size and increase their number but
> my inability to recommend commanders."[1]
> *Lee to Davis regarding the dividing of his
> army into three corps 20 May 1863*

    Lee used Jackson's departure to move forward with a major reorganization of his army. He had been concerned for some time that the two corps structure created organizations too large for one man to effectively control. Both Jackson and Longstreet had shown great ability to successfully direct a corps which numbered nearly 40,000 muskets but Lee continued to believe through the spring of 1863 that smaller corps would make their jobs easier. The January 1863 returns illustrate Lee's concern. The strength numbers recorded before Longstreet ventured south, showed his corps with a strength of over 37,000 present while Jackson documented nearly 39,000. Jackson and Lee had formed the backbone of the Confederate Army in the east. Lee with his audacious plans and Jackson with the determination to make them a reality had been the one-two punch that had brought the laurels of success. Lee was not confident he could find another corps commander who could step into a position of such weighty responsibility and display the tenacity of Jackson. In Lee's mind, the lack of a qualified corps commander had been a sticking point that kept him from proposing the addition of a third corps in the first place. The death of Jackson had now forced his hand. Writing to Davis on 20 May, Lee outlined his concerns regarding his desire to reorganize the current command structure. In the missive he proposed restructuring his army to consist of three corps, each smaller in size than the current two. Each of the new corps would be assembled from three divisions.

> "I have for the past year felt that the corps of this army were too large for one commander. Nothing prevented my proposing to you to reduce their size and increase their number but my inability to recommend commanders. Each corps contains, when in fighting condition, about 30,000 men. These are more than

---

[1] *OR*, vol.25, pt.2, pp.810.

one man can handle and keep under his eye in battle in the country that we have to operate in. They are always beyond the range of his vision and frequently beyond his reach. The loss of Jackson from command of one-half the army seems to me a good opportunity to remedy this evil. If, therefore, you think Ewell is able to do field duty, I submit to your better judgment whether the most advantageous arrangement would not be to put him in command of three divisions of Jackson's corps, to take one of Longstreet's divisions, A. P. Hill's division, and form a division of Ransom's, Cooke's and Pettigrew's brigades, and give the corps thus formed to A. P. Hill. *This would make three corps of three divisions each, under Longstreet, Ewell and A. P. Hill.* In this event I also submit to you whether it would not be well to promote Ewell and A. P. Hill. The former is an honest, brave soldier, who has always done his duty well. The latter, I think upon the whole, is the best soldier of his grade with me."

Lee then took the opportunity to lobby for the promotions for Ewell and Hill using the argument that the fighting prowess of his army would be improved if the Second and new Third Corps remained under the command of men the soldiers knew and trusted.

"Inasmuch as this army has done hard work, and there is still harder before it, I wish to take advantage of every circumstance to inspire and encourage them, and induce in the officers and men to believe that their labors are appreciated, and when vacancies occur that they will receive the advantages of promotion if they deserve it. I believe the efficiency of the corps would be promoted by being commanded by lieutenant generals, and I do not know where to get better men than those I have named."[2]

Lee's comment was a blatantly obvious effort to keep outsiders from other commands from being brought into his army. Davis agreed with the proposal and quickly approved Lee's suggestions. Seven days later, on 30 May, Lee's assistant adjutant general, Walter H. Taylor, finalized Special Order No.146 which completed the reorganization. Section VIII of the order gave the details.

VIII. The following changes are made in the organization of corps and division of this army:

---

[2] ***OR***, vol.25, pt.2, pp.601-602, 810; Dowdey & Manarin, ***Wartime Papers***, pp.488-489. The passage in italics is not included in the copy of Lee's letter in the ***OR*** but is present in Dowdey and Manarin.

1. The Brigades of Heth and [Brigadier General James J.] Archer, of A. P. Hill's division, with [Brigadier General James J.] Pettigrew's and Cooke's will constitute a division, and be under the command of Maj. Gen. Harry Heth.

2. The brigades of [Major General William D.] Pender, [Brigadier General James H.] Lane, [Brigadier General Edward L.] Thomas and McGowan, will constitute a division, and be under the command of Maj. Gen. W. D. Pender.

3. The divisions of Major-Generals Early, [Edward] Johnson, and Rodes will constitute the Second Corps, and be under the command of Lieut. Gen. R. S. Ewell.

4. The division of Maj. Gen. R. H. Anderson is detached from the First Corps, and, together with the divisions of Major-Generals Heth and Pender, will constitute the Third Corps, and be under the command of Lieut. Gen. A. P. Hill.

While a number of the brigades Lee initially desired to incorporate into the Third Corps were unavailable to him for various reasons, the changes accomplished his three corps of three division organization structure. Each corps now contained approximately 25,000 men which were of a size Lee felt one commander could effectively direct.[3]

Headquarter Staffing

One of, if not the most conspicuous shortcoming of Lee's army during the spring of 1863 was the miniscule size of his staff, and Lee supported keeping the number of staff personnel as small as possible. When both the Federal and Confederate armies were organized, they were assembled based on existing military practices and techniques. Many new capabilities and technologies had become available since the termination of the Mexican War. The sheer size of the army, for example, was an element which no one from either side had previously experienced. Another technical advancement was even more prominent. For the first time in history, railroads could be used to transport troops, wounded men and move large quantities of supplies quickly and efficiently. The logistics of waging war had change in a rather short period and the Federal and Confederate armies would have to experience those changes first hand before they would begin to adapt their philosophies and methods for dealing with the differences. However, throughout the war, neither side came to grips with the deficiencies of small staff

---

[3]   *OR*, vol.25, pt.2, p.840. Cooke's Brigade would not be sent north. Joseph R. Davis' Brigade would eventually replace Cooke. Colonel Daniel H. Hamilton was in command of McGowan's Brigade when the reorganization took place, but as the march north commenced a few days later, Hamilton became sick and left camp leaving the brigade in the charge of Colonel Abner M. Perrin. When Pender took command of the division Colonel Alfred M. Scales was placed in charge of his old brigade. (Caldwell, J. F. J., ***The History of a Brigade of South Carolinians First Known as Gregg's and Subsequently as McGowan's Brigade***, p.128.)

levels. They failed to understand how to structure and organized their headquarters as it related to the massive size of a Civil War army.[4]

Lee's concern over the size of a corps and a general's ability to handle it in combat, while never officially stated as such, could have been linked to the minimal staff personnel available to its commander. With the Confederate Army employing small headquarter staffs at the corps, division and even brigade level; control of a large body of men was increasingly difficult. The situation had been relevant in Joe Johnston's army prior to Lee taking command. When Lee took over for Johnston he inherited a crisis. With McClellan at Richmond's doorstep, there was no time to evaluate the merits, size or quality of the personnel Johnston left behind. Lee graciously offered to allow Johnston's staff to remain but only one member of his predecessor's group chose to stay. This may have been a blessing because Johnston's old staff had shown little, if any, ability to coordinate the efforts of his divisions and brigades, not to mention his artillery, cavalry and supply chain.

Compounding the problem of size was blatant preferential treatment shown by some early war generals in assembling what few staff members they employed. Most militarily trained men assigned to command took intense interest in the members they selected for their organizations. Personal traits such as character, professionalism and the understanding of military protocol were critical elements to the selection process. A prospective staff member's ability to work inside the system was critical. Staffs assembled with these traits in mind generally performed well since the men understood their roles and executed them within the structure of the entire organization. However, many men in high ranking positions who were businessmen, lawyers or from the political arena, and did not understand military protocol and function, selected their staffs differently. Many of these officers looked to their friends, relatives and neighbors to perform such duties. Whether the intent was to keep family members and friends out of the line of fire, or just to show favoritism, many of the choices made were unwise. An officer's lack of understanding the difficulties encountered in military organizations, and the requirements to run such an association effectively were prominently displayed in their selection of staff members. Exacerbating the problem was a war which many of them assumed would be a lark, simply providing chances for glory and fame. The romantic side of the adventure soon wore off but many continued, by their selection of unqualified individuals, to allow poor staff performance.[5]

By the spring of 1863, little had been done to increase the size and duties of Confederate headquarter staffs. This was perfectly acceptable to Lee who continued to believe that the army functioned at a higher level with minimal staff members. In addition, Lee was still smarting from the mishandling of Special Order 191 during the Sharpsburg Campaign. A copy of the document, which contained written marching orders for his entire army, had been misplaced and fell into the hands of the Federals. The misplaced order forced Lee's hand and brought his first attempt to invade Northern territory to a premature termination. After the

---

[4] Dowdey, Clifford, *The Seven Days: The Emergence of Lee*, p.142.

[5] *Ibid*, p.143.

episode, Lee took to personally delivering some critical orders verbally to avoid a repeat. While he still trusted his own staff, he took steps to make sure that his desires for the army did not have to be pass into the hands of unfamiliar couriers for delivery and execution.

In March of 1863, while camped in the vicinity of Fredericksburg, Lee's input was solicited regarding legislation under consideration in Richmond concerning the structure and size of headquarter staffs. Edward Sparrow, chairman of the Senate Committee on Military Affairs, asked Lee to provide opinions and express his views on the contents of Senate Bill No.73, which was intended to define the size of an army's staff. "[I]t may be proper for me to state," Lee noted before he reviewed the document, "that the more simple the organization of our army the more suitable in my opinion will it be to our service, and that every possible reduction in its expense should be made."[6]

The American continent had never seen armies the size of those assembled during the Civil War. Lee was keenly aware of this but for some reason failed to promote an expansion of his staff to better deal with the army's bulk, choosing instead to limit its size. Writing to Davis the day after he responded to Senator Sparrow, Lee acknowledged the size discrepancies, noting "[o]ur armies are necessarily very large in comparison with those we have heretofore had to manage." Returning to his Mexican War experience Lee continued. "Some of our divisions exceed the army General Scott entered the City of Mexico with, and our brigades are larger than his divisions." It seemed as though Lee, while recognizing that his army was much greater in size than those he had fought with previously, refused to use it as justification for instantly making a comparable increase in the size of his staff. Lee chose instead to keep his staff at minimal levels, believing it easier to make his organization larger than to reduce it. Lee addressed this issue in his letter to Davis. "Although the staff of the French army is larger than that proposed by Senate bill, I am in favor of keeping ours down, as it is so much easier to build up than to deduce, if experience renders it necessary." Another reason Lee retained a strong desire to keep staff levels low was his feeling that qualified commanders needed to be in the field directing men along the battle line not tending to administrative duties. It should also be noted that Lee's opinions regarding the Senate's proposed legislation came after the loss of Special Order 191. The misplacement of the order was obviously fresh in his mind as he responded to Senator Sparrow's request. By the spring of 1863, the reduction of field grade commanders had been keenly felt and Lee continued to keep his staff small to make sure as many command grade offices as possible were available for field duty.[7]

Lee continued his letter to the president by outlined his requirements regarding elements he felt were critical to a general's staff. Perhaps this was done in an effort to manipulate Davis into withholding his signature on any staffing bill which did not contain the stipulations Lee desired.

---

[6] *OR*, Series IV, vol.2, pp.446-447.

[7] *Ibid*, p.448; Taylor, Walter H., ***Four Years with General Lee***, p.2.

"I would… assign one general officer to a general commanding an army in the field, and give to his inspector-general, quartermaster-general, commissary-general, chief of ordnance, and medical director the provisional grade of colonel of cavalry. I would reduce his aides and give to his chief of staff and inspector-general assistants, or they will never be able to properly attend to their outdoor and indoor work, which from the condition of our Army, as before stated, is very heavy. I would apply the same principals to the division and brigade staff, placing their chiefs on an equal footing and giving each a complete organization in itself, so that it can maneuver independently of the corps or division to which it is habitually attached and be detached with promptness and facility when required. Each, therefore, in addition to its general staff, should have a surgeon, quartermaster, commissary, and ordnance officer."

Whether Davis heeded Lee's advice or not was probably irrelevant to the general for throughout the war he continued to maintain a reduced level of staffing. Even if the Confederate government passed legislation to increase or reduce the levels even further, Lee would have probably ignored the legislative requirements and continued to utilize a staff of the size he felt his army required. In addition, any mandates from the government would have been difficult if not impossible to enforce in an army which was actively engaged in field operations.[8]

The small size of Lee's staff was also keenly obvious to the men who populated the organization. One of the general's staffers observed the differences between a typical European headquarters encampment and Lee's minuscule one. "In visiting the headquarters of the Confederate generals, and particularly those of General Lee, anyone accustomed to seeing European armies in the field cannot fail to be struck with the great absence of all the pomp and circumstance of war in and around their encampments. Lee's headquarters consisted of about seven or eight pole tents, pitched with their backs to a stake fence, upon a piece of ground so rocky that it was unpleasant to ride over it, it's only recommendation being a little stream of good water which flowed close by the general's tent. In front of the tents were some three or four wagons, drawn up without any regularity, and a number of horses roamed loose about the field." Lee also refused to impose on local residents, often pitching his tents near homes and farmhouses, the occupants of which would have gladly opened their home to the general. It was Lee's policy for his army not to take liberties with anyone's personal property whether Northern or Southern, and on many instances he refused to occupy private homes for his headquarters, choosing to set the example for the entire army.[9]

---

[8] *Ibid*, p.448. The French army under Napoleon at the Battle of Austerlitz numbered nearly 75,000 men. The general himself utilized a headquarter staff which numbered almost 200 men, all of which were utilized during the fighting. Bowden & Ward, ***Last Chance***, p.22.

[9] Marshall, Charles, ***Lee's Aide-De-Camp***, p.xxxii.

Lee's Charges

The man who signed the order reorganizing the army was no stranger to important and critical communications within the upper echelons of the Army of Northern Virginia. Of all the men who became acquainted with, and served Lee during the war, the man who developed the most personal relationship with him was Walter Herron Taylor. As the war began, a number of high placed connections, including an advisor to Virginia Governor John Letcher, thought Taylor exceptional, and felt he would make a good administrator. On 2 May 1861, Taylor received orders to report to Richmond and assume the duties as an aide to Lee. For the next four years, Taylor would be at Lee's side. The two would see and converse with each other on a daily basis and their relationship would become both professional and personal. The only definitive event which Taylor would be absent from would be when Lee rode to meet Grant to surrender his army at Appomattox. An emotional Taylor could not bring himself to observe the scene of his great chieftain humbled before the victorious Federal general.

Early on, Taylor began dealing with the minutiae of his commander's daily operations and when Lee was assigned to duty in western Virginia, Taylor accompanied him. He was well suited for staff work. Staff members were the worker bees of army headquarters and Taylor quickly showed that he was adept at attending to every detail. He was hardworking, diligent and his highly developed intellect allowed him to attend to details effectively and completely. He wrote the majority of Lee's correspondence with his clear, easy to read, sweeping script. He also acted as a courier, distributing communications to many of Lee's subordinates. In addition, Taylor seemed to have a somewhat photographic memory for names, numbers and faces of the hundreds of men who sought an audience with Lee. He also screened all those interested in meeting his commander. If a request was made which Taylor thought low on the priority list, the requesting party was seldom allowed to enter Lee's tent. As the war progressed, Taylor became so adept at understanding Lee that on many occasions he made decisions, which in reality should have been left to his commander, on his own. Lee quickly grew to rely heavily on his aide's abilities and unreservedly trusted him. Taylor was also responsible for organizing and submitting the army's monthly returns, which put him in a position to be the most knowledgeable person in the army as to the true strength of Lee's force. The young man turned out to be a true blessing to Lee. With the general's desire to keep his headquarter staff size small, a man like Taylor was worth his weight in gold. His abilities and professionalism kept things running smoothly in an organization that would have suffered an increase in embarrassing moments if he had not been on the job.[10]

Taylor was born in Norfolk, Virginia on 13 June 1838, into a well-known family whose roots extended back to England. Walter showed himself to be a good student and when he was old enough to leave home, he enrolled in the Norfolk Military Academy. His studies at the academy allowed him to display his abilities

---

[10] Taylor, *Four Years*, pp.2-5. Taylor's biographical information is taken from the introduction by James I. Robertson of the 1996 Indiana University Press edition.

and while there, he won an award for his outstanding effort. At the age of sixteen, Taylor entered the Virginia Military Institute. Fifty-eight students entered the class of 1857 and less than half of them would graduate. Taylor unfortunately would be one of those who failed to complete the curriculum. He was forced to withdraw and return home after news of his father death. Taylor father had contracted yellow fever during one of the all too frequent southern epidemics that were prevalent during the 1800s. However, not all was sadness in Taylor's life. Shortly before he left for VMI, he fell in love with a young woman by the name of Elizabeth Selden "Bettie" Saunders. Bettie and Walter continued their relationship for a number of years, even when Walter was off fighting Yankees. Shortly before the war ended, Taylor took a few hours of leave and married Bettie. Keeping with his faith, the two recited their vows at St. Paul's Episcopal Church in Richmond as Lee's army was withdrawing from Petersburg and heading west. Taylor kissed his new bride goodbye and swiftly rode to catch up with Lee's departing legions.[11]

After leaving VMI, Taylor was pushed to continue his father's business but chose a more stable means of employment, obtaining a job working at the Norfolk branch of the Bank of Virginia. His father had been a commission merchant and the professions stability varied to a point where Taylor balked at taking the chance. He later became an administrator for the upstart Norfolk and Petersburg Railroad, but a promotion at the bank brought him back to the lending institution, in whose capacity he was working when the war began.[12]

Being true to his military education, in December 1859, Taylor joined a militia organization known by a number of names, the most prominent being simply "Company F." The organization was the largest company in the Norfolk area, containing roughly 125 to 130 men, who distinguished themselves from other militia units by dressing in black pants and red flannel shirts. On 19 April 1861, Walter, and his brothers, Richard and Robertson, enlisted in the 6th Virginia Infantry and were mustered in on 1 May, joining the regiment's Company G. Walter's infantry service however, ended before it began when on the following day he received a communication from Richmond ordering him to report there for duty. Early the next day, he boarded a train in Norfolk and arrived in the capital just in time for breakfast. While he was eating his meal at the Spotswood Hotel, Lee walked in and the two met for the first time. Taylor, commissioned a first lieutenant on the same day he met the general, was quickly assigned to Lee's headquarters. He was a quick study, and learned the duties of his new position under the tutelage of the adjutant general for Virginia's state forces under Colonel Robert S. Garnett. Taylor was impressed with the Colonel, noting that he was the best equipped man to deal with the military details of headquarter operations, and Taylor credited Garnett with outstanding tutelage during the young lieutenant's initial instruction.[13]

---

[11] Tower, R. Lockwood, *Lee's Adjutant: The Wartime Letters of Colonel Walter Herron Taylor, 1862-1865*, p.2; Taylor, *Four Years*, p.4.

[12] Tower, *Lee's Adjutant*, pp.3-4.

[13] Cavanaugh, Michael A., *6th Virginia Infantry*, pp.5, 128; Taylor, *General Lee*, pp.21-22.

Unfortunately for Taylor, his time with Garnett was limited and quickly came to an end when Garnett was sent to western Virginia to take control of the forces in the area. Promoted to general on 6 June, Garnett was lost to the cause on 13 July when he became the first general officer to be killed during the war He was shot in the back near Corrick's Ford on the Cheat River during a rear guard action.

Two weeks later, Lee, Taylor, Colonel John A. Washington, a body servant and a cook, left for the western Virginia mountains. Taylor thoroughly enjoyed his time with Lee as the party made their way to the remote location. The final segment of the journey was on horseback through the mountains, and Taylor relished the fresh air and undoubtedly spent a good deal of time becoming acquainted with his new chief. Tragedy struck the little band quickly when shortly after their arrival Colonel Washington was killed while on patrol with a detachment of cavalry. The loss of Washington was deeply felt by Taylor. With the colonel gone, Taylor and Lee's relationship grew even closer. They soon began to share a tent, which introduced each of them to the others personal habits. After the war Taylor recalled the camp with its single structure.[14]

> "One solitary tent was constituted his headquarters camp; this serving for the general and his aide; and when visitors were entertained, as actually occurred, the general shared his blankets with his aide, turning over those of the latter to his guest. His dinner service was of tin - tin plates, tin cups, tin bowls, everything of tin - and consequently indestructible; and to the annoyance and disgust of the subordinates, who sighed for porcelain, could not or would not be lost; indeed, with the help of occasional addition, this tin furniture continued to do service for several campaigns…"[15]

Taylor would be at Lee's side from their time spent in the mountains to the spring of 1863. His successful completion of his duties and the immense responsibility of his position earned him quick promotion. By that spring he had reach the rank of lieutenant colonel and was functioning as Lee's assistant adjutant general while also performing aide-de-camp duties. Lee would continue to rely on him heavily through the summer campaign, to Gettysburg and beyond.[16]

In addition to Taylor, Lee employed a number of other critical staff members who were instrumental in the smooth function of his headquarters.

Performing the duties of Lee's military secretary was Colonel Armistead L. Long. Long first served under Lee as his chief of artillery when Lee was stationed in South Carolina. At the time, Long was a major. Early in their association, he

---

[14] Eicher& Eicher, **High Commands**, p.250; Tower, **Lee's Adjutant**, p.7-8.

[15] Taylor, **Four Years**, p.35-36.

[16] Krick, Robert E. L., **Staff Officers**, p.283.

impressed Lee with his skills and the general rewarded him with a permanent position on his team.

Born in Campbell County, Virginia, on 3 September 1825, Long entered West Point on 1 July 1847, and four years later graduated seventeenth in a class of thirty-eight. Brevetted a second lieutenant, he was initially assigned to the 2nd Artillery. By February 1851, he had been transferred to the 3rd Artillery, but an additional transfer placed him back with the 2nd by the end of June. Long saw service in the garrison at Fort Moultrie in Charleston Harbor and in 1852 a transfer west lead to two years of frontier duty. He returned east for a year of service at Fort McHenry and Barrancas Barracks before going west again for a second tour, spending time in the Indian Territory, Kansas and Nebraska. When the emerging crisis began to develop in 1860, Long was stationed at the Augusta Arsenal in Georgia. He returned to Washington and served as an aide-de-camp to his father-in-law Edwin V. Sumner until he resigned his commission on 10 June 1861.

After traveling to Richmond, Long was commissioned a major in the Confederate service and assigned to General Loring as his chief of artillery. When Loring was assigned to duty in western Virginia, Long went with him. When Lee transferred to South Carolina, Long was ordered to report to the general. He would remain a member of Lee's staff until September, 1863. After joining Lee, Long began performing some of the functions a chief of artillery would typically execute. When the general returned to Richmond to be installed as President Davis' advisor, Long was promoted to colonel and took over duties as Lee's military secretary. His experience with the artillery expanded his role, requiring him to provide administrative support for the guns, and he performed valuable service during the Fredericksburg and Chancellorsville fights. While he was not quite as close to Lee as Taylor, Long would develop a relationship with his commander which would be both cordial and on occasions affectionate.[17]

Lee also maintained a number of staff members to perform aide-de-camp duties. A key member of Lee's clerical team and affiliate of his inner circle that spring along the Rappahannock was Charles Marshall. Marshall joined Lee on 22 March 1862, as an aide-de-camp when the latter was serving in Richmond. Less than a month later, he was promoted to major. Marshall, like Long and Taylor, was another Virginian, and would do service with his chief up to the bitter end.

Born in Warrenton on 3 October 1830, just a short thirty miles northwest of Fredericksburg, Marshall boasted a famous family lineage. His grandfather Thomas Marshall was awarded a sword by the Virginia House of Burgesses for his gallantry at the battles of Brandywine and Germantown during the Revolution. His most renowned relative however, was his great uncle John Marshall who served as the young nation's fourth Chief Justice. Charles received his formal schooling at his hometown's Warren Green Academy and in 1846 enrolled at the University of Virginia. Two years later he left the university with a master's degree and traveled

---

[17] Eicher & Eicher, **High Commands**, p.352; **Confederate Military History** (hereafter **CMH**), vol.3, part.2 pp.630-631. Most sources indicate that Long was born on 3 September but volume 3 of Confederate Military History notes the date as the thirteenth.

west to take a position teaching mathematics at the University of Indiana. After three years of teaching, Marshall retuned east to study law and after learning the trade, opened a practice in Baltimore. His education in the exacting art of mathematics and the organizational skills required to practice law would serve him well in his aide-de-camp position in Lee's entourage.

While Marshall's education reiterated his scholarly abilities, he also looked the part of an intellectual due to his need for spectacles. He would also prove over time that he was a brave and competent soldier. He shared the hazards of the battlefield and gained the respect of all who came to know him. His duties at headquarters consisted of drafting official reports, orders and other official documents. Like Taylor, Marshall was also responsible for administrating the mountains of official correspondence which departed and arrived at Lee's headquarters. Typically multiple copies of official documents had to be generated and all had to be written by hand. It was a laborious task which Marshall took seriously. He loathed incompetence, possibly due to his intellectual stature and skills, and seldom displayed a lack of proficiency. He had a fiery temper that presented itself regularly when confronting with what he perceived as ineptitude.[18]

Lee's relationship with a number of his staff members was one which a loving and concerned father would have for his offspring. One particular incident involving Marshall was relayed after the war by Edward P. Alexander, one of Lee's artillery battalion commanders.

> "I was visiting it [Lee's headquarters] one night & got into conversation with Col. Talcott on some mathematical problem, & we went to his tent to work it on paper. Col. Marshall was there, who cared little for mathematics; & after a while he produced a demijohn & proposed a drink. We told him to go ahead, & we would join him presently. He took a glass in his left hand & the demijohn by the handle in his right, raising it up so as to rest it behind his right shoulder. Then, raising his elbow, the neck of the demijohn came down over his shoulder, & the whiskey poured into the glass. Altogether, I don't think there can be any possible attitude of a man with a demijohn & a glass so utterly reckless & dissipated; so suggestive that the man proposes to drink all there [is] in the demijohn, by goblets full at a time, as that adopted by Marshall to pour out his drink. And as he poured a pretty stiff one, & looked the very quintessence of toughness, Gen. Lee opened the tent front & looked in; I can't at all recall now for what purpose. But I remember well how worried Marshall was over the incident, & how Talcott & I teased him, telling him how he had looked, & what Gen. Lee would likely do about it. And next day Talcott told me the sequel. At breakfast in the morning Marshall complained of a

---

[18] Marshall, *Lee's Aide-De-Camp*, pp.ix-x.

head ache, & Gen. Lee remarked that, 'Too much application to mathematical problems at night, with the unknown quantities x & y represented by a demijohn & tumbler, was very apt to have for a result a head ache next morning.'"[19]

Although Marshall's punishment for his escapade with the jug and glass was a good natured ribbing from his chief, it served as a reminder that Lee did not look kindly upon the consumption of alcohol. The chastising was simply Lee's way of gently reminding Marshall, and anyone else on his staff, that he did not condone but would put up with drink as long as it was not done to excess and affected performance. Marshall's concern over being caught with the demijohn reinforces the family type environment that was prevalent among Lee's diminutive staff. Everyone in the clan knew where they stood, and they respected the family elders so greatly that all strove to keep from being a disappointment.

Before the war, when Lee was serving in the west, he met a major performing the duties of paymaster in the San Antonio Area. The man, Robert Hall Chilton, was a fellow Virginian from Loudoun County. Chilton, who was just a few years younger than Lee, had transplanted his family to his duty station and Lee soon became acquainted with the major's clan, developing a fondness to his two young daughters, Emmie and Laura. Chilton impressed Lee with his administrative skills and when General Garnett was lost, Lee turned to Chilton to fill the void.[20]

Chilton, a West Pointer, had entered the academy when he was eighteen. His record at the institution was significantly below average and he graduated only two positions from the bottom of the class of 1837 which contained fifty cadets. Assigned the rank of second lieutenant, Chilton served at various posts in the west including Texas, the Indian Territory and Kansas. He served during the Mexican War and received a major brevet for his performance at Buena Vista when he carried a wounded colonel from a regiment of Mississippi volunteers to safety. The effect of Chilton's deed on history would become known later for the wounded volunteer colonel's name was Jefferson Davis. Returning from Mexico, Chilton began work as a paymaster at various locations, including Texas, where he met Lee. Shortly after the bombardment of Fort Sumter, Chilton, on 29 April, resigned his commission and joined the Confederate Regular Army as a lieutenant colonel. A month later he was promoted to full colonel and assigned to the cavalry of the Virginia Provisional Army as his native state left the Federal Union. He eventually ended up at Lee's side in western Virginia and when the general ascended to the command of the Army of Northern Virginia, Chilton's administrative skills were rewarded with a posting as the army's chief of staff.[21]

---

[19] Alexander, *Fighting*, pp.156-157.

[20] Freeman, Douglas S., *Robert E. Lee*, vol.1, p.377, 530; Taylor, *General Lee*, p.27.

[21] Eicher & Eicher, *High Commands*, p.171; Faust, *Encyclopedia*, p.139. Some sources list the number of cadets in the class of 1837 as being fifty-seven.

Chilton would serve as Lee's chief of staff during the first two years of the general's command. He would be with Lee as the general built not only his reputation but also the Army of Northern Virginia's status as the South's unwavering and unbeatable military force. Chilton spent those two years overseeing the operational aspect of Lee's headquarters staff and performing assistant adjutant general duties. One black mark on his record was his authorship of the lost order during the Sharpsburg Campaign. Although he was not responsible for its loss, his name appeared on the bottom of the document and as such, some assumed guilt by association. The accusations may have been brought on by Chilton's lack of self-defense and that he never offered an opinion on who actually misplaced the document.[22]

Promotion had been slow for Chilton and his first application for a brigadier generalship had been rejected in Richmond. In the spring of 1863, he was at the top of Lee's headquarters staff, directing the activities of the general's well oiled, but small machine. He would eventually ask to be relieved from his post and on 1 April 1864, shortly before General Ulysses S. Grant began his Overland Campaign he would depart Lee's army. Chilton would eventually take a desk job in Richmond, performing inspector general duties for Lee's army, but as the Gettysburg Campaign opened he was still Lee's number one staffer.

In addition to Taylor and Marshall, Lee kept two others on his staff for the purpose of performed aide-de-camp duties. Major Talcott's nighttime reconnaissance at Chancellorsville had highlighted only part of his skill set. Since joining Lee's staff on 21 April 1862, he had also proven he was a fine military aide. Talcott's father was a good friend of Lee's and while their relationship may have played a part in the major receiving his position, young Talcott had proven the appointment was deserved by his excellent work. Lee was also acquainted with Talcott's mother. She was a stunningly beautiful woman who Lee took to calling "The Beautiful Talcott." The major was one of the few non-Virginians on Lee's staff. Born in Philadelphia on 27 March 1838, he had turned just twenty-five years of age the previous spring, making him one of the youngest members of Lee's staff.[23]

If Colonel Taylor was one of the most intelligent men on Lee's staff, Colonel Charles S. Venable was the genius. Venable, another Virginian, was born in Prince Edward County on 19 April 1827. At the tender age of fifteen, he graduated from Hampden-Sidney College and during the years that followed tutored other students in mathematics. Choosing to advance his education, Venable entered the University of Virginia. He later traveled to Germany where he furthered his education in Bonn and Berlin. After returning to America, he moved between a number of teaching positions in Virginia and South Carolina and became an amateur astronomer. When the war began, Venable was serving as a lieutenant in South Carolina and assisted in the firing on Fort Sumter. When the firing in the harbor was over, he volunteered for service with Company A of the 2nd South Carolina, which he joined

---

[22] *CWR*, vol.5 no.3, p.17.

[23] Krick, *Staff Officers*, p.279; Alexander, *Fighting*, p.565, n.6.

as a private. Lee evidently saw Venable's potential when the general was fulfilling his duties as military advisor to Davis. When he took command of the army, Lee placed Venable on his staff as an aide-de-camp and he joined Lee's team the same day Talcott began his service. Charles would remain with the general for the rest of the war and would share in the grief of Appomattox.[24]

Although Taylor had been with Lee for some months before Lee took command, the remainder of the general's staff had little to no experience in the operational aspects of an army's headquarters when they began working for the general. They would be placed in situation which would force them to learn their traded while on the job. All however, were good men, equipped with a good deal of common sense, education and respect for Lee, which prompted them to execute their duties at a high level. All would be expected to pass on Lee's instructions, deliver orders, perform reconnaissance work and carry out general camp duties. These tasks would have been difficult under normal circumstances, but Lee possessed another habit which made their mission more difficult. The general had a tendency to climb aboard Traveller and ride around a battlefield with little or no escort. It was not uncommon to see Lee, alone, observing a battle from a distance. This made it difficult for his aides and staff to get answers to pressing questions. All things considered, Lee's staff performance was extraordinary considering its small size and lack of formal training in the art of staff work.[25]

Lee's "War Horse"

Retaining command of Lee's First Corps through the army's reorganization was one of the few high level commanders in Lee's structure who was not a Virginian. The corps that would be least affected by the changes would retain its old commander, James Longstreet. Longstreet was born in the Edgefield District of South Carolina on 8 January 1821. His father, James senior, was from New Jersey while his mother Mary hailed from Maryland. Longstreet was also a distant relative of Lee's staffer, Charles Marshall. James' Grandfather William was the first to utilize steam as a method of propelling boats, implementing his idea along the Savannah River in 1787. Unfortunately, William did not possess the funding to promote his invention and the technology passed into the hands of a group of New Yorkers who had the financial backing to develop the idea. "Grandfather William" lost out on any benefits the invention could have provided the family. Young James spent his early childhood near the border of Georgia and South Carolina along the river. While born north of it, James' earliest recollections were of the south side. His father, a farmer, owned a cotton plantation near the waterway in Georgia. The

---

[24] Sifakis, ***Who was Who***, p.675; Krick, ***Staff Officers***, pp.292-293. After the war Venable joined the staff of the University of Virginia and for the next thirty-one years worked as a math professor and became instrumental in the post war development of the universities Math department. He was also instrumental in the procurement of a large telescope for the Leander McCormick Observatory. ***Electronic Source:*** http://www.astro.virginia.edu/research/observatories/26inch/history/venable.php, Last Accessed: 4/29/2012.

[25] Adkin, Mark, ***The Gettysburg Companion***, p.278.

elder James always intended to provide a military education for his son, but he did not live to see it happen, as he died of cholera in Augusta when James was twelve. After his father's passing, his mother, for reasons unknown, packed up the family's belongings and moved to northern Alabama. During school months, James would returned to continue his education at the Richmond Academy, where his father had previously enrolled him. His mother slowly passed out of his life and his Uncle Augustus and Aunt Frances did most of the child rearing through his teenage years.[26]

James was a poor student and had no use for schooling. His lack of interest in education showed itself in his marks. He entered the academy in Westover on 7 October 1830 and from the start he despised attending. The school day lasted for eight and one half hours, and in the spring and summer as the weather warmed and daylight hours expanded, the school day was extended another two hours. A seven week vacation between late August and early October provided little time for fun. An exacting regiment of coursework, which included an intense study of mathematics, Latin, Greek, sentence structure, composition and strict discipline, wore James down and turned him against the rigors required to achieve a good education. In addition, the discipline, which James railed against, assisted in breaking him of any desire to work hard. He was more interested in the outdoors and spent much of his free time bounding about his uncle's property. As he turned into a young man, his excursions around the farm developed him into a daunting physical specimen. By the time he entered West Point in 1838, he had grown tall, almost reaching his adult height of six foot two inches. He was not lanky by any means but solid, strong and possessed a barrel chest, which seemed to provide him with a greater level of stamina than an ordinary man.[27]

In 1837, Longstreet's uncle, in an effort to fulfill his brother's wishes, made attempts to secure an appointment for his nephew to the Military Academy. With Georgia's regional appointment already awarded, Augustus made inquiries of a relative, Congressman Reuben Chapman, from the Alabama Congressional District in which James' mother was a resident. In December, Chapman recommended to Secretary of War Joel Poinsett that James be considered. Eventually an appointment was offered and in March 1838, James Longstreet accepted the nomination and became a West Point cadet. His time at the academy was uneventful and his dislike for school continued. After four years, he graduated fifty-fourth in a class of fifty-six. He did well when presented with training required to be a soldier, but poorly in general subjects. He also piled up demerits at an almost record pace. During his first two years he earned fifty-eight but during his final two years he was tagged with an astronomical two hundred and sixty six. While at the academy, Longstreet was given the epithet "Old Pete" by his classmates, a moniker that was a variation of his family nickname. The designation stuck and throughout his military career it was used regularly. His sense of humor and ability to pull off a good prank

---

[26] *OR*, vol.25, pt.2, p.840; Longstreet, James, ***From Manassas to Appomattox*** (hereafter ***MtoA***), pp.13, 15; Wert, Jeffry D. ***General James Longstreet***, pp.25-26.

[27] Wert, ***Longstreet***, pp.23-24.

endeared him to his classmates, but it was obvious James Longstreet did not care a lick for academia.[28]

Longstreet's class of 1842 contained a large number of notable graduates who would climb in rank during the war, including Confederates Daniel Harvey Hill and Lafayette McLaws. The class of 1843 however, supplied Longstreet with his best friend, a young cadet from Ohio, who wrote in his memoirs that he had "no charms" for the military, became Longstreet's most trusted companion. Ulysses Grant was the complete opposite of Longstreet in physical stature and usually did not display the same propensity for fun as James, but the two became good friends and remained so for the rest of their lives. Only the war interrupted an otherwise cordial relationship.[29]

Longstreet graduated when he was twenty-one years of age. Brevetted second lieutenant, his low class standing precipitated an assignment to the 4th Infantry and he was sent to Missouri. A year later his friend Sam Grant arrived at the post, when he was assigned there after his graduation. The two renewed their friendship and began to attend social events together. Times were good and as luck would have it, during 1844 both men became acquainted with their future wives. In February, Grant met the seventeen year old Julia Dent. A few months later James met and pursued Maria Louise Garland. Maria came from a military family. Her grandfather, Hudson Garland, a captain during the War of 1812, had been a member of the Virginia Legislature. Her father, Colonel John Garland, was currently Longstreet's regimental commander. Maria's family, who referred to her as Louise, was prominent in the Lynchburg Virginia area. She was a black haired beauty, petite, with high cheek bones. She was and was considered quite striking by all who met her and Longstreet was no exception. The young lieutenant took an immediate liking to Maria, but the courting and pleasantries of a new relationship did not last long.[30]

As May arrived, Longstreet's regiment was ordered to Fort Jessup Louisiana and formed part of what he called the "Army of Observation" under Zachary Taylor. Just short of a year later, he was transferred to the 8th Infantry Regiment and went to Florida where "those of active aspiration" were disappointed with the opportunities for advancement. However, things began to look up for Longstreet, as Texas began to seek annexation and war with Mexico seemed likely. When war became a reality, Longstreet packed his bags and left Florida, joining the troops assembling in Corpus Christi. He fought under Taylor along the Rio Grande and in the battles in the north before joining General Scott's campaign to conquer Mexico

---

[28] *Ibid*, pp.26, 30-31. Wert notes Longstreet's West Point academic record as that presented in the manuscript. Longstreet in *MtoA* says he was sixtieth in a class of sixty-two. p.16.

[29] Grant, **Memoirs**, p.14.

[30] Longstreet, *MtoA*, p.16; Wert, **Longstreet**, p.34. Information on Longstreet's first wife is very sparse. In fact he did not mention her in his memoirs published years later. This may be due to a fire, which destroyed his home, and no doubt many of his personal papers, in Gainesville Georgia in 1889.

City. He was wounded in the thigh at Chapultepec while carrying the flag of the 8th Infantry. Ironically, as he slumped to the ground, he handed the flag to Lieutenant George Pickett who then carried it into the fortress. The Mexicans were forced to retreat and the day was won. Longstreet, recovered fully and by the end of the war had received two brevets, one to captain for his performance at Contreras and Churubusco and one to major for Molino del Rey.[31]

1848 was an eventful year for Longstreet. During his time in Mexico, he kept a daguerreotype of his sweetheart Louise. At the battle of Resaca de la Palma, as he was about to leap from the protection of a river bank, he pulled the photo from his pocket. "I drew her daguerreotype from my breast-pocket, had a glint of her charming smile, and with quickened spirit mounted the bank..." Unknown to Longstreet, while he was away fighting, Maria's family watched as she matured into a young woman. Finally, after Longstreet's return, they agreed to her marriage to her twenty-seven year old suitor. The couple wed on 8 March, but the honeymoon was short. Most of it occurred as Longstreet traveled to his next military assignment, which involved recruiting duties in Poughkeepsie, New York. In August, Louise, who was pregnant with the couple's first child, accompanied her husband to Missouri to attend Sam Grant's wedding to Julia. Four months later, on the day after Christmas, Louise gave birth to their first child, John Garland. John, called Garland by the family, was the first of ten children born to James and Louise.[32]

The following twelve years found Longstreet traveling the country to a number of assignments, many of which his wife accompanied him. The greatest portion of the period was spent at Fort Bliss Texas, a few miles from El Paso on the Rio Grande River. The years spent along the Texas frontier were generally happy ones for Longstreet's family. There were many social activities courtesy of the citizens of El Paso. The folks from town were cordial and Louise was active in much of the social discourse with soldiers and citizens alike, participating in dances and other activities. Supplies were plentiful, with the soldiers hunting the abundant wild game and local farmers providing the outpost with fruits and vegetables. The social pleasantries of the local population however, were not the only benefit of Longstreet's posting at Fort Bliss. Louise's parents were living in Santa Fe. Their proximity allowed her to visit frequently and her father's business required him to travel to the fort quite often. On 7 December 1852, Longstreet was promoted to full captain in the Regular Army and by the end of July 1854, Captain Longstreet had been assigned command of Company K of the 8th Infantry, relieving his friend First Lieutenant George Pickett. Longstreet had grown to appreciate Pickett and their friendship became stronger during the year they spent together at Fort Bliss.[33]

---

[31] Faust, *Encyclopedia*, p.445; Wert, *Longstreet*, p.45; Longstreet, *MtoA*, pp.18-19; Eicher, & Eicher, *High Commands*, p.353.

[32] Wert, *Longstreet*, pp.46-47; Longstreet, *MtoA*, pp.18-19.

[33] Wert, *Longstreet*, pp.48-49; Eicher, & Eicher, *High Commands*, p.353.

Longstreet's life before the war was not without tragedy and grief. During the early spring of 1854, he was ordered to the east coast and while there his third son William, who was just over a year old, became sick and died in Washington on 19 July. The anguished parents buried their child and left immediately for Texas, arriving back at Fort Bliss on the last day of the month. In March 1856, Louise gave birth to their fourth child, a girl, Harriet Margaret. Harriet, like her brother William, took sick and five months later died on 30 August. James and Louise had lost two of their first four children within a span of two years. The couple was crushed, but the departure of the babies did not hinder their ability to procreate for on 8 July 1857, while in Santa Fe, Louise bore James a fifth child, a boy, which they named after his father.

As baby James and the remaining children grew older, Longstreet began to express concerns over his ability to provide a proper education for them on the Texas frontier. He requested and was granted a leave of absence and returned east to explore educational opportunities for his children. While in New Jersey Longstreet learned that as of 19 July 1858 he had been commissioned a major. After making arrangements to place his oldest child in a boy's school in Yonkers, New York, he received orders to report to Fort Leavenworth, Kansas. Stopping over in St. Louis, Longstreet discovered a few old comrades, including Sam Grant, and spent an evening reminiscing of days gone by. The next morning, as he was preparing to leave, Grant appeared and presented his friend with a five-dollar gold piece. Years earlier, while at West Point, Grant had borrowed five dollars from Longstreet. At first he refused to take the money but Grant insisted and Longstreet finally accepted payment for the old debt. It would be the last time the two friends would see each other until after the war.[34]

Longstreet spent little time at Fort Leavenworth. In October 1859, he received orders transferring him to Albuquerque. James was happy with his new assignment, telling his uncle Augustus the family was "tolerably pleasantly situated out here and indeed quite comfortable." The move put the family closer to Louise's parents but the happy times were short lived once again. Harriet Garland, Louise's mother took ill. After traveling to Saratoga, New York, she collapsed on a sidewalk and died. Less than a year later Louise lost her father who also died in New York, and was buried in a plot next to his wife. It seemed the shadow of death followed the Longstreet's wherever they went.

During the fall and winter of 1860-61, as war clouds gathered in the east, Longstreet agonized over his ignorance of events. Inconsistent mail service usually brought information that was at best a month old. When word of Lincoln's election arrived, a decision had to be made. He was a Southerner and his family was from the south. The choice was difficult, but it seemed to be inevitable; Longstreet would side with the Southern cause. A number of fellow officers in Albuquerque tried in vain to retain him in the service of the Union. Most of the discussions were cordial, with Longstreet using the argument of a necessity to follow his state. He soon began a string of correspondence, which ended with the submittal of his

---

[34] Wert, **Longstreet**, p.50; Eicher, & Eicher, **High Commands**, p.353.

resignation from the old army. "I have the honor to tender my resignation as Major and Paymaster in the Army of the United States," he wrote. On 1 June 1861, it was accepted. James Longstreet was out of the United States Army.[35]

When word of the acceptance of his resignation reached him, Longstreet was in the midst of his journey eastward. A number of other officers and enlisted men were traveling with him. During the journey Longstreet was asked how long he expected the war to last. "At least three years, and if it holds for five you may begin to look for a dictator," he answer. A lieutenant in a group from the 7th Infantry responded by expressing his desire that Longstreet be the dictator if it came to that. The following day the group of travelers crossed into Texas. Upon entering El Paso, evidence of the state's Southern sentiments were on display. People were gleefully dancing in the streets and expressing their excitement. The activities of one young Texas girl became so engrained in Longstreet's mind that years later he was able to vividly recall her excitement. "[T]he Texas girl did not ascend to a state of incandescent charm until the sound of the first note of 'The Bonny Blue Flag' reached her ear. Then her feet rose in gleeful springs, her limbs danced, her hands patted, her eyes glowed, her lips moved, though she did not care to speak, or listen to any one. She seemed lifted in the air, thrilled and afloat, holding to the 'Single Star' in joyful hope of Southern rights." The unthreatening atmosphere in El Paso persuaded Longstreet to leave his family there and continue his journey by train with the reminder of the group. The train however would not leave for a few days and Longstreet could not wait. Saying goodbye to his family, he boarded a stage and traveled to Galveston where he embarked on a small sailing ship bound for New Orleans. It was on this small vessel that Longstreet first met Thomas J. Goree. Goree would spend the entire war at Longstreet's side performing aide-de-camp duties for the future general.[36]

Friendships and loyalties were now severed. It was a time of sadness but duty called within an upstart nation. A month after resigning his commission, Longstreet reported to the War Department in Richmond. He never wanted a field command. "I had giving up [sic] all aspirations of military honor, and thought to settle down into more peaceful pursuits," he wrote after the war. James asked for a post in the pay department since his most recent duties had been in such a position, but his desire was not fulfilled. On 1 July he received an appointment to brigadier general. His first orders were to report to General Beauregard at Manassas Junction for assignment to duty with the Confederate Army of the Potomac. He arrived the next day and was given command of a brigade consisting of the 1st, 11th and 17th Virginia Volunteers. For James Longstreet it was the first step on a path that would lead to glory, defeat and controversy.[37]

---

[35] Wert, **Longstreet**, pp.51-53; Longstreet, *MtoA*, pp.29-30; Eicher, & Eicher, **High Commands**, p.353.

[36] Longstreet, *MtoA*, pp.30-32.

[37] Longstreet, *MtoA*, pp.32-33.

During the early portion of the war, while many men of lesser abilities struggled to make a name for themselves, Longstreet performed well enough to garner some recognition. He commanded troops at First Manassas and Williamsburg, but a misunderstanding of orders from Joe Johnston resulted in him faltering at Fair Oaks. He possessed a willingness to fight when asked, and great courage, two qualities that Lee was looking for as he took command of the army. Perhaps Ulysses Grant summed up Longstreet best when he wrote of him in his memoirs. Grant noted that Longstreet was "brave, honest, intelligent, a very capable soldier, a subordinate to his superiors, just and kind to his subordinates, but jealous of his own rights, which he had the courage of a mountain. He was never on the lookout to detect a slight, but saw one as soon as anybody when intentionally given."[38]

James Longstreet was Lee's "War Horse." He was the thunder to Stonewall Jackson's lightning. *B&L*

During The Seven Days, Jackson was uncharacteristically slow in his movements, while Longstreet moved quickly when ordered, adding to his growing reputation. Lee took notice of Longstreet's qualities during the fighting and afterward gave him command of a large portion of the army. In a dispatch to Davis, Lee informed the president, "Longstreet is a Capital soldier. His recommendation hitherto have been good, & I have confidence in him." Lee gave Longstreet much of the credit for the victories during The Seven Days. By the time of the Second Manassas Campaign, Longstreet was in command of half of Lee's army. In his new position he performed well, quickly earning the reputation of being the thunder to

---

[38] Piston, William Garrett, *Lee's Tarnished Lieutenant: James Longstreet and his place in Southern History*, p.21; Grant, *Memoirs*, p.344.

Jackson's lightning. Later he would be accused of being slow to move, particularly if he was asked to take the offensive; however, once committed to battle he was a bulldog when defending and tenacious when delivering a blow. Lee affectionately dubbed him "My Old War Horse," but to his men he remained simply "Old Pete."[39]

Although the popular notion is that Lee and Jackson were close, they never formed a binding friendship. The necessities of war frequently saw Jackson's command operating in a disconnected fashion from Lee's main body. His corps often formed the vanguard of the army while Longstreet's brought up the rear. In addition, Jackson spent the early months of the conflict conducting operations in the Shenandoah Valley, far away from Lee. His death midway through the conflict put a premature end to any deep friendship which may have been developing between the two.

By contrast, Longstreet and Lee forged a congenial relationship that grew stronger as the war progressed, and lasted until Lee's death in 1870. Unlike Jackson, Longstreet often established his headquarters near Lee's camp and they often dined together. They saw each other almost daily for the majority of the war and had ample opportunity to socialize. Lee spent much of his time in the company of Longstreet and his headquarters perhaps because of the lighter atmosphere of the camp. The relaxed environment may have reminded Lee of his youth when he was less burdened by the responsibilities of command.[40]

While the level of jocularity at Longstreet's headquarters was high, it took a serious downturn in January 1862. With the army encamped near Centerville, Longstreet received an urgent message from Richmond. All his children were sick, including the newest family member, Mary Anne, who was but a year old. Making his way quickly to his family, he found that Scarlet Fever had them all bedridden. Louise was doing her best to care for them. On 25 January, shortly after he arrived, the two concerned parents watched their youngest die, a victim of the fever. With Mary gone, attention was turned toward the three boys. Every effort was made to save them but four-year-old James died the day after his sister. The two older boys fought bravely but on 1 February Augustus died. Garland was the only child to survive, probably due to him being thirteen and stronger than the others. Louise had born six children since their marriage, now five where dead. The depth of the couple's grief could only be imagined.

Longstreet's good friend George Pickett and George's teenage lady friend, Sallie Corbell helped the Longstreet's through their ordeal. Sallie and Louise were good friends and had spent a great deal of time together. The loss of the children crushed her as well. George and Sallie made the funeral arrangements and attended to the details. Whether too grief stricken, or simply fighting to save their last child, the Longstreet's did not attend the services. When Garland's condition began to improve his father returned to the army, but he was not the same man. Gilbert Moxley Sorrel, an aide-de-camp to Longstreet, summed up the general's mood after he returned from Richmond, noting Longstreet came back a "changed man."

---

[39] Piston, *Tarnished Lieutenant*, pp.21-22; Faust, *Encyclopedia*, p.445.

[40] Piston, *Tarnished Lieutenant*, p.22.

Continuing, Sorrel explained Longstreet "had become very serious and reserved and a consistent member of the Episcopal Church. His grief was very deep and he had all our sympathies." While much of the old, fun loving Longstreet would return in time, he would never be quite the same.[41]

Longstreet's record was a testament to his abilities as a corps commander and he had proven he deserved to be in the position. Lee would rely upon his "Old War Horse" heavily in the coming campaign. His abilities were well known to Sorrel, who credited his own capabilities as aide-de-camp to his chief. Sorrel also saw firsthand the warrior in Longstreet and knew his skills as a field commander. "He was like a rock in steadiness when sometimes in battle the world seemed flying to pieces." There was no one better to command the army's First Corps, and Lee knew it. There was never any doubt he would retain his post, but his command would lose one division to the new Third Corps. Longstreet also had great trust in his division commanders and would rely heavily on those who remained. Like Longstreet, they would all prove their grit over the coming weeks.[42]

"Old Bald Head"

Lee, left with finding commanders for the revamped Second and new Third Corps, possessed a number of division commanders who had proven their ability to handle a body of men at that size. He now had to determine if any of them possessed the qualities required for corps command, and if they could successfully lead a group three times the size of their division. After evaluating his options, Lee chose to submit for Davis' consideration to lead the Second Corps, one of Jackson's old subordinates, Richard Stoddert Ewell. Lee informing the president of his desire to install Ewell in his 20 May letter. Lee believed him to be "an honest, brave soldier, who has always done his duty well." Ten days after Jackson's death, Lee made his choice, and Davis approved.[43]

Ewell was an experienced commander who had shown great promise fighting under Jackson as a division commander in the Shenandoah Valley during the 1862 Valley Campaign. Wounded at Brawner Farm, Ewell had spent the previous nine months convalescing from the loss if his left leg. He had been hit in the knee as he knelt to look under some low hanging tree limbs as the battle opened and had not commanded men in the field since. The bullet hit him squarely in the patella, shattering it before it destroyed the end of his tibia. The missile then exited the bone and lodged in his calf muscle. Some soldiers, seeing he had been hit, made an effort to take him to the rear, but Ewell refused to be removed from the field. "Put me down, and give them hell!" he growled. When a litter finally arrived to take the general to safety, two other wounded soldiers lay nearby. Feeling he was too badly injured to be moved, Ewell refused help, instructing the litter bearers to help

---

[41] Wert, **Longstreet**, pp.96-97; Sorrel, Gilbert M., **Recollections of a Confederate Staff Officer**, pp.37-38.

[42] Sorrel, **Recollections**, pp.37-38; Boatner, **Dictionary**, p.490.

[43] **OR**, vol.25, pt.2, p.810.

the other men and have a surgeon sent forward to work on his leg. There was no questioning Ewell's toughness, but it remained to be seen if his skill as a division commander would make him a successful leader of a corps, or if the loss of his leg had in any way taken the fire out of the man everyone called "Old Bald Head."[44]

Dick Ewell was born in the Georgetown area of the District of Columbia on 8 February 1817. His father, Thomas, married Elizabeth Stoddert in 1807 and over the following ten years the couple had four children with a fifth dying during birth. Their sixth child, Richard, came into the world in a large brick home overlooking the Potomac River, which had been built by Elizabeth's father. By the time Richard was a year old, his father had moved the family to Philadelphia. Thomas Ewell studied medicine at the University of Pennsylvania and became a skilled surgeon in the United States Navy. He supplemented his education by attending a number of medical lectures at the university. A brilliant man, the elder Ewell always enjoyed the challenge of a tough medical case. Burying himself in strange and misunderstood medical situations, he would work to discover the true causes and develop new methods of treating his patients. His work often pushed beyond the scope of acceptable medical practice, which precipitated trouble for him from time to time. He published a number of books containing his medical discoveries, and many of his progressive ideologies where shunned by the populace.[45]

By 1819, the family had moved back to the Washington area. Thomas did not return to the District of Columbia proper, but chose to purchase land across the Potomac River in Prince William County, Virginia. His health had become fragile due to alcoholism and depression, and he chose to relocate the family to the fresh air of a countryside farm known as "Belleville." Richard was three when the family moved into their new home. The land, due to its rocky nature was quickly tagged by the family as "Stone Lonesome" and it was there, on the 1,300-acre plot, that Elizabeth bore four more children of which three survived.

Continuing his medical vocation to support the family, Thomas published additional works on various subjects. His fondness for alcohol became well known and possibly cost him a faculty position at the University of Virginia. Unable to control his drinking, his health continued to decline, along with the considerable wealth he had accumulated from his medical work. Finally, in 1826, at the age of forty, Thomas Ewell died, leaving behind a family of eight children and a wife in poverty.

Richard was closer to his mother than his father, which proved to be a benefit because Elizabeth's linage was more prominent than her husband's. Her father, Benjamin Stoddert was the first Secretary of the Navy under John Adams and many more distant ancestors were prominently displayed within Maryland's history.

---

[44] *Ibid*, Boatner, ***Dictionary***, p.269; Pfanz, Donald C., ***Richard S. Ewell, A Soldier's Life***, p. 257. The fight at Brawner Farm was also known as the Battle of Groveton. The fighting was a prelude to Second Manassas.

[45] Pfanz, *A Soldier's Life*, pp.4-5. Ewell's siblings were as follows, Rebecca Lowndes, Benjamin Stoddert, Paul Hamilton, Elizabeth Stoddert, girl (died before first birthday), Charlotte (died at age one), Virginia, Thomas, William.

She continually made the children aware of their heritage and asserted that the current financial situation was just a bump in the road. She had been the oldest child growing up and it showed in her tough exterior, high moral character and deep devotion to her offspring. She worked hard to support her brood and the older children did their best to help out.

At the age of fourteen, another family tragedy forced Richard to become the man of the house. His oldest brother was off at West Point leaving Paul, the next male in line as the senior sibling. Sadly, Paul contracted a liver infection and died, making Richard the oldest male in the household. His elevated stature required him to take on additional responsibility, one of which was working the family farm. Administering the operation was a huge opportunity for Richard. He learned a number of life lessons including humility, integrity and honesty. As he grew to a young man, his family began to notice the traits that would define him as an adult. From his alcoholic father he inherited a greater than average intellect and a jittery quality, which he displayed during times of stress. Unfortunately, his father also passed on his love of alcohol, a violent temper and his eccentricity. His mother provided a sharp tongue, while his grandfather Benjamin supplied common sense and an exacting mind. Good or bad, all the elements and experiences of Richard's early existence were critical in grooming him for the next phase of his life.

Richard's older brother Benjamin had gone to West Point and graduated third in his class. Elizabeth, thinking Richard would do well at the same institution, began making inquiries into whether her younger son could attend as well. An appointment to the academy would be of great help financially to the family. Initial inquires bore no fruit and family members began to wonder if Richard would become a cadet. Their concerns prompted other options to be contemplated. His oldest sister, Elizabeth, express a desire to see her brother study and enter the ministry but a career with the church did not seem too likely for the swearing and drinking Richard. As a secondary plan, Richard's mother took steps to send him west to study law if the appointment did not come through. Determined to succeed in securing the selection, she decided to try a different course. She contacted her brother, William Stoddert and her brother-in-law George W. Campbell. Campbell's assistance was critical for he had held a number of positions in the government. He had been a former member of congress, a senator from Tennessee, secretary of the treasury and ambassador to Russia. While in congress and the senate, Campbell served on a number of influential committees and established a number of connections. After soliciting George and William's assistance, Elizabeth tried again to secure the appointment. Campbell even went so far as to escort Richard to visit President Andrew Jackson. After a short conversation, Jackson wrote a letter of recommendation to Secretary of War Lewis Cass. All the discussions and interviews paid off and after a year of waiting a confirmation letter arrived in March 1836. It was replied to promptly and a military career for Dick Ewell was secured. In June Richard packed up his belongings and left behind Stone Lonesome and his former existence, bound for the strict regiment of academy life.[46]

---

[46] *Ibid*, pp.6-14.

On 1 July 1836 Richard Ewell entered West Point. He initially did well in his studies, but as time passed and the course work increased in difficulty, he began to struggle. In the early nineteenth century most West Pointers entered their first year having gone to preparatory schools to groom them for the rigorous course work. Ewell did not have this advantage and was not as well equipped as most of his classmates. He tried to make up for his deficiencies by staying up into the early morning hours studying his lessons. On 6 November, Richard wrote his brother Ben about his late night study habits. "I have gotten along pretty well so far in my studies," he wrote, "the knowledge I had of algebra being of considerable service to me. At least I have not found it necessary to study hard, until within the last week or two. But during the last week I have found it no joke. I was obliged to sit up more than half the night several times, or go to the Section room without knowing anything of my lesson." Eventually the hard work paid off and he began to improve his standing. Finally, on 1 July 1840 Dick Ewell graduated, standing thirteenth in a class containing forty-two members. Other notables from Ewell's class where George H. Thomas and William Tecumseh Sherman, the latter becoming a good friend. Ewell enjoyed spending leisure time fishing while at West Point and it is said he never went unless Sherman came along.[47]

Richard's mother not only helped secure his appointment to the military academy but she also made efforts to secure companionship for her son. But Ewell, for whatever reason had determined he would remain a bachelor and he was not of marrying stock. "I am very much obliged to you for your information and advice," Ewell wrote to his mother after she had relayed information about a female acquaintance. "[U]nfortunately I made a vow many years ago that I would never marry, and my resolutions have been confirmed by my mature deliberations. You know there are two kinds of persons who never get married; one kind includes those who never 'fall in love,' and the other (to which I belong) those whose hearts are very susceptible, yet owing to this quality are too tender to retain an impression long enough for it to lead to any dangerous consequences." For now the young cadet would remain enamored with his studies and not the favors of any young lady.[48]

After graduation, Ewell was brevetted a second lieutenant and assigned to the 1st Dragoons. He spent his summer on leave before reporting to his first posting at the Carlisle Barracks in southeastern Pennsylvania. Carlisle was a sleepy little town thirty miles north of another small Pennsylvania town called Gettysburg. The army used the barracks as a training center for dragoon officers and the commander at the outpost, Captain Edwin V. Sumner, was a stern and ridged officer. Sumner demanded discipline and hard work from his men, even when harsh winter weather made the execution of duties difficult. However, there was time for the social graces of the post and Ewell became acquainted with a number of local citizens.[49]

---

[47] *Ibid*, pp.15-16; Hamlin, ***The Making of a Soldier***, Richard S. Ewell to Benjamin S. Ewell, 6 November, 1836, p.21; Eicher, & Eicher, ***High Commands***, p.229.

[48] Hamlin, ***Making of a Soldier***, Richard S. Ewell to Elizabeth S. Ewell, 3 October 1839, pp.26-27.

[49] Pfanz, *A Soldier's Life*, pp.28-29.

Ewell's time at Carlisle was short. On 20 November he was ordered west to Fort Gibson, located in what would eventually become the state of Oklahoma. After spending a few days there, he was transferred to nearby Fort Wayne. The fort itself was under construction and in reality was no more than an outpost. The garrison was desolate, and as Ewell put it, nothing more than "a collection of huts." There was little to do but attend to military duties. No social activities were available and any members of the fairer sex which may have resided nearby were not fair at all. Ewell, although attracted to pretty girls was still in no hurry to find permanent companionship, especially from the pickings near Fort Wayne. He remained on the frontier for the next few years, his time spent performing mundane duties required to keep things running smoothly and on occasions, was called upon to accompany expeditions westward. A year after he arrived at Fort Wayne, Ewell's Company A, was transferred to Fort Scott, another outpost about 100 miles to the north. Three long years later, in September 1845, Ewell was promoted to first lieutenant and transferred to Company G. Things were so uninteresting at Fort Scott that Ewell began investigating other opportunities, desiring to be moved to a more agreeable post. While on leave, he applied for and received an appointment to the Coast Survey but just as he arrived to begin his new duties, war erupted with Mexico.[50]

Eager to get into the fray, Ewell made efforts to be assigned to a command heading south but all his attempts were in vain. It was 5 October before his regiment was ordered to Point Isabel, Texas to join General Taylor. After a brief stop in New Orleans, Ewell finally arrived at his destination near the mouth of the Rio Grande River. Too late to participate in any serious fighting in northern Mexico, Ewell found himself assigned to scouting and reconnaissance missions. It was not long before he was bound for Vera Cruz with General Scott's flotilla. Like so many Civil War generals, Ewell gained much of his initial combat experience during the war with Mexico. His performance was good enough to earn him a brevet captaincy, but his adventure in Mexico was not without tragedy.[51]

Richard was not the only Ewell family member to serve in Mexico. His younger brother Thomas fought as well. On the morning of 18 April 1847, General Twiggs determined to capture the Mexican stronghold of Telegraph Hill. Tom's company was chosen as part of the assault team and he led his men forward during the effort to take the critical objective. Tom bounded over the wall of the earthworks guarding the position and was the first member of his company inside the fortifications. Drawing his sword, he found himself among a host of Mexican soldiers and was overwhelmed. Later, as he lay wounded, Tom described the event to his brother. "I there found about two hundred men lying down ready to fire. I found myself on the flank, and passed my sword through the first man, the next was aiming at me. I struck the musket, but the fellow fired and struck me." The ball entered Tom's abdomen about one inch from his navel and level with the top of his hip bone. It tore its way through Tom's intestines and lodged just under the skin on

---

[50] *Ibid*, pp.30-31, 34, 48-49; Hamlin, **Making of a Soldier**, Richard S. Ewell to Benjamin S. Ewell, 2 February 1836, p.39.

[51] Pfanz, *A Soldier's Life*, p.50; Faust, **Encyclopedia**, p.249.

his back next to his spine. It was evident the ball had not damaged his vertebrae since all his extremities were still functioning, but the damage it had done inside of him no man could survive.

When word of his brother's wounding reached Dick, he rushed to his side and tried to comfort him. "I found Tom with several officers of his regiment around him," he wrote to their mother, "...suffering much from his wound." Although he did not note as such, it must have been plain to him that his brother could not survive. Tom asked Dick to write home and relay the sad news and told him that he had already given another officer some of his personal effects. Although he was in pain, Tom still had his senses about him and knew his wound was mortal, telling Dick that he would rather die than continue to suffer. Unfortunately Richard could not stay at his brother's side. The Dragoons were moving out and he had to depart. With his emotions tearing up his heart, he mounted his horse and rode away, not knowing if he would see his brother again and if he did would he still be alive?

Dick did manage to return and found Tom still clinging to life and resting comfortably. Upon seeing his brother Tom, brightened slightly and informed him that General Scott had visited him. With Dick at his side, Tom recounted the story. "Mr. Ewell," the great chieftain had told him, "you are an honor to your name, an honor to the service to which you belong." Tom then told his brother of the attack on Telegraph Hill and how he managed to be wounded. Dick stayed at his brother side for the remainder of the night. Tom expressed hope that his intense suffering was God's way of exorcising his sins. Shortly after midnight, as if foreshadowing the inevitable, Tom informed his brother that his legs had gone numb. Finally, just after 1:00 a.m., his older brother Richard by his side, Thomas Ewell exhaled one final time and died.

The following morning, procuring some planks of wood, Dick built his brother an irregular coffin. With the help of some officers, he carried his brother's body to the location where he had been wounded. The hillside was covered with the corpses of slain soldiers who were not lucky enough to have a caring relative close by to tend to their remains. The bodies would soon be baking under the Mexican sun, covering the hillside with flies and the stench of rotting flesh. The scene would not be suitable for the living but Tom Ewell would not have cared since it had been his wish to be laid to rest where he fell. Finding a suitable spot, a grave was dug and Dick buried his brother in the Mexican earth. In less than twenty-four hours Richard Ewell had discovered how real war could be.[52]

Ewell's company of dragoons spent the majority of their time in Mexico as escorts for General Scott. Their duties included scouting parties and accompanying Scott's engineers on reconnaissance missions. On 18 August, Ewell and the Dragoons were sent out to escort Captain Lee on his investigation of the Pedregal. While Lee was out scouting for a way through the crags of lava, the Dragoons, under Captain Philip Kearny, encountered a group of approximately two hundred Mexican soldiers hiding among the rocky fissures. The enemy began a spirited

---

[52] Hamlin, *Making of a Soldier*, Richard S. Ewell to Elizabeth S. Ewell, 22 April 1847, pp.64-68.

fire, and Ewell, slow to react to the shooting, having never had rounds directed his way before, finally got down to the business of war. A horse in the column, having been shot through its heart, toppled and fell among the jagged rocks. Ewell noted in a letter to Ben that he "hear[d] bullets striking the ground around us and singing over our heads." To dislodge the Mexicans, Kearny sent Ewell and a number of other riders down a path which led them to the enemy's flank and rear. Finally, a group of infantry arrived on the scene and the Mexicans fled, pulling back to leave the area to the Dragoons.

On the following day, as fighting continued, Ewell found himself alone with Captain Kearny in the midst of a group of Mexican soldiers. Confusion during the battle had prompted men positioned in the rear to fall back leaving both Kearny and Ewell to fend for themselves. According to Ewell "[o]nly a miracle saved Captain Kearny and myself." Kearny, for his part took a grape shot in his arm. The wound eventually cost him the limb. Ewell had two horses shot from under him, one by a musket ball, the other by a piece of canister. Later, he was able to slowly ride to safety. He would receive his captain's brevet for the effort. Dick Ewell's introduction to war had been filled with adventure, hardships, glory and personal tragedy but it was just a preamble of the coming storm.[53]

Ewell returned to the eastern United States shortly after the war ended. He performed a number of military duties and tried his hand at farming, before heading west again in 1850. He spent the next five years attending to administrative tasks and protecting the local population from marauding Indians. Finally in 1855 Ewell took the first furlough of his military career. On his journey eastward, he stopped in Tennessee to visit a troubled family member.[54]

Ewell had held true to the statements he made to his mother years earlier and had not since his time at West Point actively courted a woman. While he had generally lived up to his beliefs, there was one young lady he became enamored with, his cousin Lizinka Campbell Brown. He had known her prior to leaving for West Point and had, at one point, intended to marry the young woman. Unfortunately for Dick, if he informed her of his intentions she paid him no mind and as Ewell entered his last year at the academy Lizinka married James Percy Brown and moved to Tennessee. James proved to be an abusive husband and Lizinka's marriage was unhappy from the beginning. By the age of twenty-four, she had given birth to three children, been severely mistreated and become a widow when James took his own life. The only positive outcome of the relationship was James leaving behind a substantial estate. Lizinka would not be short of funds to raise her children as her husband's death made her one of the wealthiest single women in the country.[55]

---

[53]   Hamlin, *Making of a Soldier*, Richard S. Ewell to Benjamin S. Ewell, 25 November, 1847, pp.70-71; Eicher, & Eicher, *High Commands*, p.229.

[54]   Martin, Samuel J., The Complex Confederate, *CWTI*, vol.25 no.2, p.27.

[55]   *Ibid*; Pfanz, *A Soldier's Life*, p.86.

As Jackson's replacement at the head of Second Corps, Richard Stoddert Ewell would never achieve the lofty heights of his lamented predecessor. *LOC*

While Lizinka had the land and the money to operate the properties, she did not have the expertise. Ewell however, always being interested in farming, possessed the skills to manage her holdings. After visiting the estate on his way east, he was offered the opportunity to managing the plantation. Here was the chance of a lifetime for Dick Ewell, the opportunity to run a plantation and be close to the only woman who had been able to capture his heart. Lizinka pleaded with Ewell to resign his commission and come to work for her, but Ewell did not accept her offer. Lizinka restructured the proposal, urging Dick to look at it from a purely business venture point of view, but he was not persuaded as he considered himself a lowly soldier who was not good enough for the fine, young, rich widow. Opportunity had knocked on Dick Ewell's door and he refused to let it in. It would not be the last time he refused to take a risk in order to achieve success.[56]

After completing his business, Ewell returned west and continued his army career. In addition to his military duties, he began to work a silver mine; possibly an effort to qualify himself in his own mind, to court Lizinka. Nothing ever came of the excavation and the work there along with controlling the Indians wore Ewell out. Contributing to his exhaustion was his wounding in 1859 while involved in a skirmish with a party of Apache Indians. The wound was not serious and he soon recovered but his physical wellbeing was still questionable. The eventful year of 1861 began in January with Ewell applying for sick leave. Inflicted with dyspepsia and malaria a tired and worn Dick Ewell saw his request granted and he returned east. Looming clouds of war greeted him there.[57]

---

[56]   Pfanz, *A Soldier's Life*, pp.86-87.

[57]   Martin, The Complex Confederate, ***CWTI***, vol.25 no.2, p.28; Eicher, & Eicher, ***High Commands***, p.229.

There was never any question as to which side Ewell would support. Though born in Washington, he considered himself a Virginian. His family and friends were from the South, and like so many others, could not side against his state. It was a hard decision but an obvious one. On 24 April 1861 he resigned his commission. "By taking up the side of the South I forfeited a handsome position, fine pay and the earnings of twenty years hard service," he later wrote to Lizinka. Immediately riding to Richmond, he learned his name had been placed in nomination as colonel of cavalry in the Virginia Provisional Army. He initially served on a committee organized by Governor John Letcher to identify Virginia residents currently in the service of the U. S. Army who should be contacted and invited to serve with the growing Southern force.[58]

Eventually Ewell would be promoted to brigadier general based on his performance during the war's initial engagements. He led a brigade at First Manassas and spent the winter of 1861-62 commanding a division under Stonewall in the Shenandoah Valley where he constantly complained about being in the dark as to Jackson's plans. After Lee took command of the forces in the Richmond area, Ewell came south with Jackson to fight during The Seven Days and at Cedar Mountain before being wounded at Brawner Farm.[59]

Lizinka attended to the general during his recovery. While convalescing, a marriage to the widow Brown was again contemplated. Seeking advice, Dick turned to his brother Ben. Ewell's association with the deeply religious Jackson had softened him somewhat regarding his language and drinking habits but he was still unsure of his worthiness. Lizinka seemed ready to take the next step, but should he wait until the end of the war? On 23 May 1863 Dick Ewell received his promotion to lieutenant general. Two days later orders arrived instructing him to return to Fredericksburg "without delay" to his new assignment at the head of the Second Corps. There was one thing to attend to before he could go. Ben had finally convinced him that further procrastination served no purpose. With Jefferson Davis in attendance, Richard Ewell and Lizinka Brown were married on 26 May. A few hours later he would be on a train headed north. Dick Ewell, new husband and commander of the Second Corps, Army of Northern Virginia, was back in the war.[60]

While he was headed back to the fighting, Ewell had never been a fire eating proponent of the war. Even before his wounding, he had written of his disgust to his niece Elizabeth. "I fully condole with you over the gloomy prospect in regard to the war. Some 100,000 human beings have been massacred in every conceivable form of horror, with three times as many wounded, all because of a set of fanatical abolitionists and unprincipled politicians backed by women in petticoats and pants and children. The chivalry that you were running after in such frantic style in Richmond have played themselves out pretty completely, refusing in some instances to get out of the state and fight. Such horrors as war brings about are not

---

[58] Pfanz, *A Soldier's Life*, pp.120-122.

[59] Sifakis, *Who was Who*, pp.208-209.

[60] Pfanz, *A Soldier's Life*, pp.275-276; *OR*, vol.25, pt.2, p.824.

to be stopped when people want to get home. It opens a series of events that no one can see to the end." It would remain to be seen if Dick Ewell was the same fiery commander or whether the loss of a leg and the responsibility of marriage would temper his stomach for the shock of war.[61]

The outpost soldier from the west now a general did not look the part. Although tall in stature at five foot ten inches Ewell was slender and tipped the scales at only 130 pounds. His deep-set, beady eyes and large nose gave him the look of a predatory bird. The hair upon his bald head had migrated to his face in the form of a large bushy beard. His voice was high and squeaky, and he spoke with a lisp. When excited or irritated Ewell's language became laced with profanities and he became known as one of the best cursers in the army. Not only were single swear words spoken when extremely agitated, but many times his tirades where so full of expletives that the greatest portion of the sentence structure were swear words. The simple fact was Ewell did not resemble, and at times, act the part of a general.[62]

The Sensitive General

Ambrose Powell Hill was a capable commander but his selection to command Lee's new Third Corps may have been a bit of a surprise to some. According to Longstreet, Lee was partial to selecting corps commanders from Virginia, and while Ewell had not been born there, he may as well have been, residing there since he was a young boy. True to Longstreet's claim, Lee selected Hill, another Virginian, to head his new corps. Doing so however, would require Hill to leap over the next two men in the Confederate command hierarchy. In line after Ewell was Daniel Harvey Hill. D. H. Hill, a North Carolinian, had proven himself on the battlefield but recently had become an immense thorn in Lee's side, two facts which may have prompted Lee to pass him over. Next in line was Lafayette McLaws, Longstreet's proven division commander. McLaws however, was a Georgian who fought his division well and was of great value to Longstreet.[63]

---

[61] Hamlin, *Making of a Soldier*, Richard S. Ewell to Elizabeth Ewell (niece) p.114.

[62] Martin, The Complex Confederate, *CWTI*, vol.25 no.2, p.28.

[63] Longstreet, James, Lee's Invasion of Pennsylvania, ***B&L***, vol.3, p.245. A copy of Special Order 191 addressed to D. H. Hill, which contained the marching orders for the entire army, was lost during the Maryland Campaign nine months earlier. Hill received a copy of the order from Jackson, whom he considered his immediate supervisor during the campaign. Hill kept the copy from Jackson to prove he received the orders. He always claimed he never received the original orders from Lee and assumed that Lee would not have sent a copy to him because in Hill's mind he was reporting to Jackson. The lost copy fell into McClellan's hands, bringing on a premature confrontation between the two armies. It is unlikely that Hill actually lost the order. A more plausible scenario is that the courier charged with delivering it lost the valuable document. Hill's name however was attached to it and he spent the remainder of this life defending his reputation. It is most certain that Lee was aware the order had been lost as he reorganized his army and may have been an additional reason for passing over D. H. Hill. For a full treatment of the lost order see *Civil War Regiments*, vol.5, no.3.

Lee settled on A. P. Hill and informed President Davis of his desire to install him in his 20 May recommendation. He managed to get around the seniority issue by implying that Hill was the best commander he had with his army after Ewell. A hard marcher and fighter, Hill seemed to spend an inordinate amount of time under the weather. This was undoubtedly due to his contraction of venereal disease while on furlough from West Point in 1844. While returning to the academy, Hill passed through New York City. The indiscretions of youth evidently got the better of him, and it was probably there that he contracted his affliction. At the time a treatment for his particular problem did not exist and the illness was allowed to progress unchecked. It would affect him for the rest of his life and his health would waver seemingly at the most inopportune times.[64]

Powell Hill was the fourth of seven children born to Thomas and Fannie Hill, providing Ambrose with three older brothers and three younger sisters. Tom was a successful businessman, politician and farmer. He was tall straight and well-formed and those who met him instantly determined he was a fine looking man. Fannie however, wore bifocals, was small, fragile and a bit shy. She was an introvert who preferred the quite surroundings of her home, often sitting next to a window while she puttered away at her knitting. Fannie was also quite an emotional woman and often had difficulty controlling her mood swings. She would often be observed standing quietly gazing out over the landscape seemingly lost in a daydream. She proved to be quite the opposite of Tom, seeking to spend time alone while her husband was hobnobbing with Virginia's elite. The outgoing Thomas and withdrawn Fannie lived on a large estate ten miles west of Culpeper Court House. It was there that Ambrose was born shortly after sun up on 9 November 1825. The youngster was provided a Jr. suffix since his father's older brother was known by the same name.

As a boy, Hill spent his time exploring the outdoors. He tramped through the fields, meadows and woods of the countryside on and around the family estate. As the youngest son, Ambrose naturally grew closer to his mother than his brothers and he was understanding and more liberal regarding her isolationism. He also spent a great deal of time with his father, who took him outdoors to hunt and fish. His father taught him to ride a horse almost before the boy had learned to walk. His early exposure to the equestrian arts would serve him well later in life and resulted in Hill being known as one of the best horsemen in the army. Extensive riding practice and outdoor activities no doubt decreased when Thomas, before young Ambrose had reached age ten, packed up his family and moved to Culpeper Court House. Thomas felt the move was necessary because his growing mercantile business required him to be in closer proximity to the operation. The family moved into a large three-story brick home on Main Street and Ambrose was enrolled in a one-room schoolhouse where he proved to be a good student. One of his boyhood friends, James Kemper, noted that Ambrose was unusually "bright."

While school was easy for Hill, religion was not. As he grew older, and became exposed to his family's religious beliefs, he showed scant interest in

---

[64] *OR*, vol.25, pt.2, p.810; Robertson, ***Confederate Warrior***, pp.11-12.

practicing them. Sitting in church held less charm than adventures outdoors. Things became worse when his mother became a Baptist. Suddenly all the vices typically enjoyed by the men of the house became taboo. The new restrictions put the boy off and he developed a deep disdain for Bible thumpers. While Thomas must have suffered more with his wife's conversion, young Ambrose seemed to take it all in stride. His leisure time interests lay more in reading military history, in particular the campaigns of Napoleon. He would often organize the neighborhood boys into competing armies and play war in the streets or the open areas of town. By the time he was in his mid-teens it was obvious that a military career was in his future. After garnering recommendations from a number of prominent Virginians, Ambrose received an appointment to West Point on 19 April 1842. Writing the secretary of war a week later, he accepted the appointment and became a cadet. One of his old schoolmasters reminded the young man as he departed, "It is pleasant and fitting to die for one's country." Before the war was over, Ambrose would do just that.

Hill became a member of the infamous West Point class of 1846, entering the institution on 1 July 1842. Its alumni list was littered with young men who would make a name for themselves during the rebellion. Among them were George Pickett, George Stoneman, Jesse Reno, Samuel Sturgis and a young Pennsylvanian named George McClellan, who was a superior student. McClellan and Hill became good friends, which helped Hill dealt with the difficult curriculum. His academic record improved because of his association with the gifted McClellan. Academically, his performance during the first year was average but his discipline was poor. The fun loving Hill piled up demerits by the dozen during the first half of the year. His behavior improved during the latter half, but he still finished his freshman campaign thirty-ninth in his class.[65]

Hill got along with most of his classmates and made friends easily. There was one classmate however whom he never seemed to be able to develop a cordial rapport. The lack of a professional working relationship between the two would haunt Hill for most of his military career. The cadet's name was Thomas J. Jackson. Jackson was the polar opposite of Hill and the two were never able to tolerate each other. Hill came from a well to do Virginia family. Jackson however, was dirt poor. Jackson practiced religion to the extreme while Hill ostracized it. Hill was prone to moments of jocularity. Jackson was serious and seldom appreciated levity. Hill made friends easily while Jackson felt it was undesirable to have a large number of acquaintances. Jackson neither drank nor swore but Hill was known to partake in both activities. Personal habits and lifestyles built a rift between the two that began at West Point and would widen until that chaotic evening in the moonlight near Chancellorsville.[66]

Hill was on track to graduate with his class, but his misadventure while on furlough, cost him so much time due to illness he was forced to repeat his third year. On 9 September 1844 he was admitted to the hospital with "Gonorrhea

---

[65] Robertson, ***Confederate Warrior***, pp.5-10. Hill's siblings were James, Theophilus, E. Baptist, Margaret, Evelyn, and Lucy.

[66] *Ibid*, p.9.

contracted on furlough." In some individuals the disease ran its course and the patient would achieve a full recovery. In others, more serious symptoms occurred and unfortunately, Hill fell into this category. He experienced difficulty urinating, severe pelvic pain and a high fever. Finally in November, he went home to recover but the process was slow. The disease had entered his prostrate and he continued to be incapacitated. Multiple extensions to his leave were requested and granted. Hill would eventually return and repeat the missed year. While the rest of his friends moved on, a disappointed Hill went back to his studies. After completing the year again, he was forced to deal with another major disappointment. War had broken out with Mexico and all the friends made during his time at the academy were graduating and going off to fight. Powell Hill would have to wait another year before he could join the fray.

Once again, Hill went back to class. He made new friends in Harry Heth, Ambrose Burnside and a Georgian named Julian McAllister. The four would become close and they spent a great deal of time together during Hill's remaining year. Finally, on 1 July 1847, Ambrose Powell Hill graduated from West Point. He stood fifteenth in a class of thirty-eighth, ahead of his friends Burnside and Heth, the latter finishing dead last. After packing his belongings, he returned home to wait for orders which finally came on 11 August. Hill was assigned to the artillery, and eventually ending up a second lieutenant in the 1st Regiment, U.S. Artillery. In a strange twist of fate, he was ordered to Mexico to replace First Lieutenant Tom Jackson. Hill boarded a train and journeyed from Richmond to Wilmington, North Carolina. He then traveled by sea to Charleston and from there, over land to New Orleans. Finally, he arrived in Vera Cruz, where he was assigned to a company of horse artillery which shortly set out for the interior.

By the time Hill arrived in Mexico the war was all but over and he saw limited action before the termination of hostilities on 2 February 1848. Although assigned to a combat unit, the opportunity for glory had passed and no occasion to advance his military career presented itself. His friends, who had graduated on time, were given ample chances to achieve glory in battle and promotion, but Hill, once again, missed out. Being the only member of the 1847 West Point class to spend time in Mexico, Hill made sure all who met him would remember him. He did so by sporting a somewhat unique uniform consisting of a bright red flannel shirt, blue pants, and boots with red accents. To this he added a myriad of weapons including horse pistols, revolvers, a large artillery sword and a rather hefty butcher knife. However, with the war at its end, Hill had few opportunities to don his flamboyant attire. Of all the accoutrements, the red flannel shirt would become Hill's trademark. The other articles would disappear over time but the red shirt would remain throughout his military career and when battle loomed he would outfit himself in the shirt. Everyone knew that if General Hill rode by wearing his red shirt a hot time on the firing line could not be far behind.[67]

Returning from Mexico, Hill spent the reminder of the 1840s and 1850s at various posts and his first assignment was a joyous one. He had always been

---

[67] *Ibid*, pp.11-15, 17.

fond of his youngest sister, Lucy, and his new posting at Fort McHenry was close to the Patapsco Female Academy where she was a student. His duty at the fort lasted for a year and an half and he saw Lucy often. It all ended in August of 1849 when he was sent to Florida to tie up loose ends from the Seminole Indian War. While his time at Fort McHenry was joyous, his time in Florida was not. He complained constantly about the insects, rain and the local population. "My God," Hill grumbled in his diary, "will these mosquitoes never satiate their vampirean [sic] appetite for blood?" His health suffered more than usual and by November of 1850 he requested a transfer. The request was granted and he went west to the dryer climate of Camp Ricketts in southern Texas. After two years on the frontier, he returned to the rain and bugs of Florida where he assisted in building forts and bridges. His second Florida tour was worse than the first and he became so sick that he decided to return home to recover. Hill was not sure whether he was suffering from another attack of prostatitis or yellow fever. By the time he reached Fort Capron he was dealing with a full bout of the fever. Slowly his health recovered and when he returned to duty Hill received an assignment to the post he would occupy until the war erupted. The work involved assisting the Navy in the Coast Survey office, performed various duties, all of which he seemed to collect praise for.[68]

During his time with the Coast Survey, love knocked on Ambrose Hill's door twice. The first instance was with a young woman named Ellen Marcy, whose father, Major Randolph B. Marcy, would become renowned for his exploration of the West. Ellen was a beautiful young blue eyed blonde and during the winter of 1855-56 she was living with her mother at the Willard Hotel in Washington while her father was away in Texas. Mother and daughter were popular in Washington social circles and Ellen's beauty brought many suitors. Unfortunately for Hill, Ellen's parents had already decided she was to be the wife of Hill's good friend George McClellan. George was away with Major Marcy and Ellen, whether actually smitten with Hill or just longing for the company of the opposite sex, accepted a marriage proposal from the Virginian. When the Major received the news, he was not at all pleased and berated his daughter for a "breach of confidence." The major also did all he could to degrade Hill in an effort to keep his daughter for McClellan. Finally, Ellen's desperate mother went so far as to dig up Hill's contraction of gonorrhea years earlier as leverage against him. How she managed to discover the truth is not known but eventually Hill withdrew and a few years later Ellen married McClellan. George retained no animosity toward his friend, whom he asked to be a groomsman at his wedding and Hill was glad to perform the duty.[69]

The second time Hill fell in love the results were more to his liking. At a Washington party he met a twenty-three year old widow named Kitty Grosh Morgan McClung. He was immediately attracted to the young lady, who as a girl had been given the nickname Dolly. While Hill had been busy chasing Ellen, Dolly met and married a prosperous merchant in St. Louis named Calvin McClung, who happened to be her cousin. McClung died suddenly a year later leaving Dolly a

---

[68] *Ibid*, pp.19-20, 23-26.

[69] *Ibid*, pp.27-28, 33.

young, attractive widow. She met Hill while in Washington visiting friends and the two were instantly attracted to one another. The romance progressed and after two years of courting they were married on 18 July 1859. Dolly adored her new husband and whenever possible she accompanied him as he moved from assignment to assignment. During the war, Dolly would develop a reputation for lingering too long with the army and on occasions ventured too close to the front lines. In some instances a direct order from the commanding general was required to encourage her to depart.[70]

One and a half years of happiness followed Hill's marriage, but the election of Abraham Lincoln made civil war seem inevitable. His loyalty to family, state and Culpeper would force him to side with the South. While some chose to wait until Virginia made its choice, Hill wasted no time. He had declared years earlier that the defense of his home state was the only event that would force him to make a decision regarding his allegiance. In his mind, that situation now existed and on 26 February 1861, he submitted his resignation. The institution of slavery was not agreeable to him and neither was the idea of secession, but more importantly he knew he could not stand against Virginia and his kin. Powell Hill would fight for the South.[71]

The young boy who had wandered the woods near Culpeper in pursuit of game with his father had grown into a capable soldier. His five foot ten inch frame was of slight build, and weighed just 160 pounds, prompting friends to call him "Little Powell." His features were sculptured, with his straight Roman nose and hazel eyes being framed by long flowing hair that contained a slight wave. His face was accented with a bristly red beard and according to a Confederate general he moved with a military bearing and looked every bit a soldier. During normal conversation his voice was soft and low but when he became excited and energetic it rose to a high pitched metallic whine. He was a cordial man and was generally easy to get along with but to his enemies, whether fellow Confederate officers or Federals, he was anything but pleasant. He would build a reputation for tenacity on the march and the battlefield that would make him well known to his adversaries. Unfortunately for Hill, he also possessed two other traits what would cause him great difficulties. He was an immensely proud man and overly sensitive to criticism. His arrogance and sensitivity would manifest itself as severe friction between himself and his superiors.[72]

On 9 May, Hill was made a colonel and given command of the 13th Virginia Infantry. Three weeks later, on 1 June, the regiment was given its numerical designation and a month later it entered into Confederate service. Colonel Hill immediately told his company commanders to begin training their men, instructing

---

[70] *Ibid*, pp.30, 32-33; Tagg, **Generals**, p.10. Dolly was the sister of the notorious Confederate cavalryman John Hunt Morgan.

[71] Robertson, **Confederate Warrior**, p.34.

[72] Hassler, William W., A. P. Hill: Mystery Man of the Confederacy, **CWTI**, vol.16 no.6, p.6; Hassler, William W., The Hill-Jackson Feud, **CWTI**, vol.4 no.2, p.36; Riggs, David F., **13th Virginia Infantry**, pp.2-3.

his officers to show attention to drill in order to keep the men interested in it as well. Hill's orders initiated constant training and the regiment, companies and even squads drilled from six to eight hours a day. As the war began, Hill and his men began to get noticed. His training schedule molded the 13th into a tough fighting unit and Hill was rewarded for his efforts with a promotion on 26 February 1862 to brigadier general. On 24 March he began putting his new rank to use, being assigned command of a brigade in the Confederate Army of the Potomac. Exactly three months later, Hill received a promotion to major general and assignment to division command. His ninety day, meteoric rise from regimental command to the head of a division was unprecedented, but his efforts at confronting his old friend McClellan's army on the Peninsula justified the elevation. It was during this time that Hill had his first run in with a superior officer, and such confrontations would become commonplace for the headstrong Virginian.[73]

Hill's abrasive attitude brought about a confrontation with his immediate superior, James Longstreet. It all began innocently enough when a reporter from the *Richmond Examiner,* who was a Hill supporter, began writing of Hill's accomplishments in glowing terms, stretching the truth. When Longstreet read the reporter's account of a recent engagement, he immediately became disgruntled. He quickly wrote a rebuttal to the story which was direct and scathing in its tone. Longstreet's chief of staff, who was also upset, signed the letter and sent it to the *Examiner's* rival, the *Richmond Whig*. Now it was Hill's turn. When he read Longstreet's refutation, he became incensed. The ugly side of A. P. Hill now came into view as his sensitivity to criticism reared its head. Perhaps if the criticism had come from someone other than Longstreet cooler heads would have prevailed; however, Hill would not let it rest. On 12 July, Hill wrote to Lee requesting that he be relieved of his duties. Since Hill was Longstreet's subordinate the message had to pass through Longstreet's headquarters as it worked its way up the ladder of command. Longstreet sent Hill's note on but before doing so wrote his own curt message. "If it is convenient to exchange the troops," He wrote, "or to exchange the commanders, I see no particular reason why Maj. Gen. A. P. Hill should not be gratified."[74]

Later the same day, when Longstreet's staff officer, Major Moxley Sorrel, was sent to Hill's headquarters to pick up a report, he was informed that "General Hill declined to hold further communications with Major Sorrel." Sorrel was surprised by the response and knew that serious trouble was at hand. Returning to Longstreet, he reported the incident and was instructed by the general to "[w]rite him again and say that note was written by my command, and must be answered satisfactorily." Once again, Sorrel sent a communication which was summarily refused. Longstreet then took up his pen and personally began writing to Hill. A number of messages were delivered back and forth between the two stubborn generals.

Finally Longstreet had enough and told Sorrel, "you will be good enough to put on your sword and sash, mount, and place Major General Hill in arrest, with orders

---

[73] Riggs, *13th Virginia Infantry*, p.3. Robertson, *Confederate Warrior*, p.34; Eicher, & Eicher, *High Commands*, p.296.

[74] Robertson, *Confederate Warrior,* pp.96-97; *OR*, vol.11, pt.3, pp.639-640.

to confine himself to the limits of his camp and vicinity." Sorrel did as he was told, riding to Hill's headquarters. When he entered Hill's tent, he managed a smart salute. Hill rose from his chair and returned the salute after which Sorrel read the arrest order. After he was finished, Sorrel bowed to Hill and the general saluted him after which Sorrel wasted little time. "[I] was quickly on the road to my own friendly camp," he recalled. The whole thing came to a head when the two generals prepared to fight a duel, at which time General Lee intervened, sending Hill's Division northward with Jackson on the end run which inaugurated the Second Manassas Campaign.[75]

Turning north, Hill saved the day for Stonewall Jackson at Cedar Mountain and put up a stubborn defense at Second Manassas. He performed well at Fredericksburg and was with Jackson on his march to Hooker's rear at Chancellorsville, but perhaps Hill's greatest moment was during the Sharpsburg Campaign. Lee's army, in a defensive position with its back to the Potomac River, was pounded by George McClellan's numerically superior force for an entire day. With his reserves committed, Lee had no force to counter any additional Federal assaults. Late in the afternoon, Hill's friend Ambrose Burnside managed to capture the southern bridge over Antietam Creek and transferred his Ninth Corps across the creek to the southern end of the battlefield. Disaster loomed for the Confederates as Lee had no troops remaining to confront Burnside's threat to his flank. Suddenly, in the distance the flags of Hill's Division could be seen, marching from Harpers Ferry to the sound of the guns. Hill arrived in the nick of time to save Lee's right. So engrained in Lee's mind was the sight of Hill's marching column that years later, as he lay in delirium near death, he uttered the words "Tell Hill he must come up!"[76]

While Hill was performing well on the battlefield under Jackson, it would soon become apparent that the personality clashes from their West Point days would resurface. Hill's character combined with Jackson's communication style and failure to follow the chain of command lead to intense friction. During the march north after The Seven Days, Jackson issued orders to Hill's Division, and then changed them without informing Hill. Hill, confused about his place in the column, and while waiting for some troops to pass, was confronted by Jackson. His response was not to Jackson's liking. In his report Jackson noted Hill "fail[ed] to move in obedience to said order..." The feud came to a head during the Maryland Campaign when Hill ignored Jackson's imposed rest periods during marches. For a second time, Hill was placed under arrest. He was forced to march at the rear of his division, a situation which humiliated him. As tensions mounted, and battle approached, Jackson released Hill from confinement. His performance at Harpers Ferry and Sharpsburg softened Jackson and he seemed satisfied, not placing Hill under arrest again after the battle. Hill however, would not let the issue drop, demanding to see the charges against him and have his day in court. When Jackson

---

[75] Sorrel, ***Recollections***, pp.88-89.

[76] Hassler, Mystery Man, ***CWTI***, vol.16, no.6, p.6; Lee, ***General Lee***, p.412. Lee, uttering Hill's name as he lay dying at first may seem to be a bit romantic, however, there has never been any hard evidence presented to contradict the event. Hill had remained at Harpers Ferry to deal with Union prisoners and to mop up the area after Jackson had left to rejoin Lee.

failed to provide a list of charges, Hill went directly to Lee with his grievances against his commander. Only Jackson's untimely death saved Lee from being forced to deal with the volatile situation.[77]

Although Ambrose Powell Hill was an effective division level commander. It remained to be seen if he could handle a corps in Lee's army. *MOLLUS Collection, USAHEC*

During the reorganization of his army, Lee intended to give Hill one, six brigade division from Jackson's old corps, Anderson's Division from Longstreet's Corps, which contained five brigades and Ransom's Division, which contained four or five brigades. Augmenting these units would be the untested brigades of James J. Pettigrew and Joseph Davis. With the brigades in place, Hill's Corps would be the largest in the army and would contain mostly battle-tested men. The corps however, did not come together as Lee envisioned due to Ransom's Division being retained in North Carolina. Anderson's Division would remain whole but the second and third divisions would be created from Hill's old division and the brigades of Davis and Pettigrew.[78]

A Preacher and His Guns

Reorganizing the army into three infantry corps required significant changes in the artillery branch. The current organization consisted of three divisional battalions within each corps and a corps reserve of two battalions. A general reserve of two battalions was also part of the structure which Lee's artillery had incorporated at

---

[77]   Hassler, Hill-Jackson, ***CWTI***, vol.4, no.2, pp.36-42.

[78]   Bowden & Ward, ***Last Chance***, p.43; ***OR***, vol. 25, pt. 1, pp.790-791; ***OR***, vol. 27, pt. 2, pp.288-290.

Chancellorsville. With a third corps now requiring artillery battalions, it became necessary to dissolve the general reserve and utilize its battalions to help assemble an artillery group for A. P. Hill's new command. On 2 June, Brigadier General William N. Pendleton, chief of artillery for the Army of Northern Virginia wrote orders defining each of Lee's artillery organization. Two days later, Lee issued General Order No.69 which dissolved the army's Artillery Reserve in order to free up the officers and battalions to be assigned within the new structure.[79]

Pendleton was one of the true enigmas of the Army of Northern Virginia. Although he was West Point educated, he seemed to possess limited military abilities but managed to retain a position with the army much longer than some believed he should have. Born in Richmond the day after Christmas, 1809, his early childhood was spent on the plantation of his parents, Edmund and Lucy. Young William could trace his bloodlines not only to the Pendleton's of Virginia but also to the famous Nelson family, as his mother Lucy hailed from that clan. His education was achieved through a combination of private tutors and structured classes at John Nelson's School in Richmond. William entered West Point on 1 July 1826. He was allowed to do so because his brother Francis decided not to accept the appointment his well-placed family had secured for him.[80]

Pendleton was a fairly good student. After his freshman year, he stood seventh in his class. He moved up in the rankings to third after his sophomore and junior years but slid backward slightly as a senior. When it came time to graduate, he found himself positioned fifth in a class of forty-two. He showed an aptitude for numbers, and after graduation, spent two years performing field duties, before he returned to the academy as an assistant professor of mathematics. On 31 October 1833, Pendleton decided to resign his commission and accepted a position on the faculty of Bristol College in Pennsylvania teaching the same topic. His strong Christian faith drove him to become an ordained minister in the Episcopal Church in 1838. He would remain with the church until the war began. Prone to severe periods of long windedness, Pendleton seemed well suited for his new profession. When hostilities commenced, he was preaching at the Grace Episcopal Church in Lexington.[81]

While at the academy, Pendleton, being a year behind Lee, became friends with his fellow Virginian. The association would continue over the years and serve him well later during the war. When many were calling for Pendleton to be removed from his position, Lee balked and kept him in place. It is difficult to understand why Lee would put up with Pendleton's continued mishandling of what seemed to be the simplest of assignments. Jefferson Davis was also at West Point with Pendleton. The future preacher's association with both Davis and Lee would cement his position

---

[79] ***OR***, vol.25, pt.2, p.850; ***OR***, vol.51, pt.2, pp.720-721.

[80] Wert, Jeffry D., Old Artillery: William Nelson Pendleton, ***CWTI***, vol.13, no.3, p.11; Wakelyn, Jon L., ***Biographical Dictionary of the Confederacy***, p.341; Krick, 'A Stupid Old Useless Fool', ***CWTI***, vol.47, no.3, p.48.

[81] Wert, Old Artillery, ***CWTI***, vol.13, no.3, p.11; Eicher, & Eicher, ***High Commands***, p.424.

within the army. While other men with greater abilities were removed for poor performance, Pendleton seemed to be immune to the penalties of incompetence.

When war came to the South, Pendleton had only three years of military experience under his belt and those years were a distant memory. He had spent even less time commanding troops in the field and had seen no combat. He had been completely disconnected from any military organizations or activities for almost thirty years. Shortly after Fort Sumter was attacked, Pendleton was asked to help drill a fledgling artillery battery. The Rockbridge Artillery, a Lexington area volunteer unit, was looking for a man to assist with training and contacted Pendleton. The former second lieutenant of artillery was more than willing to teach the young men of the battery what he knew. The men appreciated him and took to calling him "Old Penn," requesting he be installed as captain of the battery. On 1 May 1861 two representatives called on Pendleton insisting he assume the duties of the unit's commander. Initially, he declined noting that others would be better suited for the post, but when the members of the battery persisted, expressing the men would accept no other, Pendleton accepted.[82]

After the battery drilled for a few additional days under Pendleton's tutelage, it was ordered to Harper's Ferry to join then Colonel Thomas Jackson's command. Arriving at Staunton in the upper Shenandoah Valley on 11 May, the battery was sworn into Confederate service the following day. It marched to Winchester and boarded a train for the remainder of the trip. Pendleton, however, did not make the journey with the battery, having left for Richmond earlier to procure additional guns to compliment the two weapons which had been provided by the Virginia Military Institute. His efforts were successful and two additional weapons were garnered. Keeping with the mentality of his profession, Pendleton, and the men of the battery named their four guns "Matthew," "Mark," "Luke," and "John." Numbering seventy-six men, the only thing the battery was lacking was an adequate number of horses which Pendleton managed to acquire a few days later. The early days of the Rockbridge Artillery provided Pendleton the opportunity to showcase his organizational and administrative skills. There was no questioning his ability to manage logistics, but his poor head for tactical elements would be a drag on all who depended on him to make good military decisions.[83]

Although many questioned his tactical skills, no one ever questioned Pendleton's bravery. Shortly after being promoted to colonel on 13 July, he and the Rockbridge Artillery traveled over the mountains with Jackson to Manassas. As Jackson was making his celebrated stand atop Henry House Hill, Pendleton hurried his battery forward to assist the hard pressed infantry. With the battle raging around him, Pendleton, his sword drawn, rode in front of his guns, directing the activities of the battery. A man on a horse was a target for enemy fire and Pendleton drew his fair share. During the battle he was grazed across the back by one bullet while another clipped his ear. Eventually his horse was shot from under him. After the battle, General Joe Johnston named Pendleton in his report as having

---

[82] Krick, 'A Stupid Old Useless Fool', ***CWTI***, vol.47, no.3, pp.48-49; Driver, Robert, J. Jr., ***The 1st and 2nd Rockbridge Artillery***, p.1.

[83] Driver, ***Rockbridge Artillery***, p.2.

"distinguished" himself. "We had but one educated artillerist," Johnston noted, "Colonel Pendleton, that model of a Christian soldier, yet they exhibited as much superiority to the enemy in skill as in courage."[84]

Johnston was so impressed with Pendleton that he appointed him chief of ordnance and sent him on a mission to procure supplies for the artillery. The minister traveled extensively throughout Virginia working to locate the materials necessary to supply and support the army's guns. Pendleton's work during his pilgrimage did nothing to display his abilities as a field commander but it did reinforce his aptitude as an organizer and administrator. By the time he returned to the army, he had so impressed Johnston that the general appointed him chief of artillery. During the winter of 1861-62, Pendleton went to work organizing the army's guns. In addition to the needs of the men, he took steps to improve the well-being of the hundreds of horses needed to make the artillery mobile. He worked to acquire additional cannons and to renovate the existing weapons. To make sure quality men were in charge of the guns, he reviewed and promoted soldiers of whom he thought worthy of advancement. As Johnston's chief of ordnance he had been responsible for the administrative and material aspects of the artillery, but as chief of artillery he would be responsible for those elements as well as tactical decisions. Pendleton had yet to, and would never demonstrate, that tactics were a part of his repertoire. Why, at some point, he was not relieved from his duties with his strategic abilities in handling artillery being so poor was difficult to understand. Although quite capable of bringing order out of chaos, he lacked a dynamic personality and did not exhibit any leadership qualities that would have made him an effective field commander.[85]

Pendleton saw no active combat during the Battle of Fair Oaks. When Johnston was wounded and Lee took over, he reported to his new commander and was asked to remain with the army. Three days later Pendleton submitted a set of regulations to reorganize the army's artillery and presented his plan to Lee for approval. Shortly before the inauguration of The Seven Days fighting, orders were issued to put Pendleton's plan in place. The structure created a general Artillery Reserve which Pendleton himself commanded but before the reorganization could be completed the fighting began. Early in the contest, Pendleton was not actively engaged but as the campaign came to a close at Malvern Hill, Federal artillery began pounding Confederate positions. The Rebels needed artillery support to engage the Federals but Pendleton failed to bring his guns into action. The extensive swamps on the Virginia Peninsula bogged down the guns of the reserve. In his report, Pendleton blamed his tardiness on a lack of orders from Lee and his own negligence in failing to reconnoiter a path to the fighting. Lee's infantry suffered dearly for Pendleton's lack of initiative.[86]

Pendleton provided his greatest disappointment during the Maryland Campaign. On 14 September, three days before the Battle of Sharpsburg, Lee sent him across the Potomac River to protect the ford at Shepherdstown in case Lee

---

[84] *OR*, vol.2, pp.476-477; Wert, Old Artillery, *CWTI*, vol.13, no.3, pp.12-13; Tagg, *Generals*, p.371.

[85] Wert, Old Artillery, *CWTI*, vol.13, no.3, pp.11, 13.

[86] *Ibid*, p.14; *OR*, vol.11, pt.3, pp.612-613; *OR*, vol.11, pt.2, p.536.

was forced to withdraw and cross the river. When Lee pulled his army from the battlefield during the early morning hours of 19 September, he ordered two brigades of infantry to report to Pendleton, who he tasked with defending the ford against Federal incursions after the Rebel's had crossed. Pendleton placed his guns on a line of high bluffs overlooking the river and posted the infantry along the road. Late in the afternoon Federal artillery began pounding the bluffs. Federal infantry followed as darkness began to fall, crossing the river and driving the Confederates from their position. Informed of the catastrophe and assuming that all his men and guns would be captured, Pendleton rode away from the fighting to seek help. Unable to convince anyone to come to his assistance, he sought out Lee, telling his commander that all of his guns had been captured. Lee was stunned at the report and ordered a counterattack at daylight. Unfortunately for Pendleton, and luckily for the Confederates, after he had departed, one of his subordinates took control of the situation and managed to extract all but four of the guns. The episode destroyed any reputation Pendleton may have retained as a field commander. Lee avoided chastising him but the writing was on the wall. Through the fall and winter of 1862-63, Pendleton continued to show his abilities as an organizer but he would never be regarded as having any aptitude whatsoever for leading men or artillery in combat.[87]

The attitude of the men toward "Old Penn" can be best demonstrated by an incident which occurred later in the war, after the Confederates had been defeated at Gettysburg. Lee, riding past his marching columns was roundly cheered by the men. As Lee's entourage passed by someone in the ranks noticed Pendleton riding toward the rear of the group. A soldier shouted out calling for three cheers for General Pendleton. As the soldier's request died away a deathly silence settled over the column. Not a single man chose to raise a cheer. Then, to add to the insult the entire column broke into a tremendous round of laugher. It was not only the command structure but the common foot soldier who knew of Pendleton's deficiencies.[88]

Pendleton seemed to take it all in stride. His deep religious faith provided him enough strength to overcome the sarcastic talk and insults. Writing to his daughter on 26 May he relayed his feelings about his job and the lack of acceptance and approval by the men.

> ...I have been exceedingly busy trying to distribute justly, and according to the necessities of the service, the captured guns; also equalizing, as far as practicable, the armaments of the several artillery battalions of this army, and securing to the utmost from our means the complete fitness for duty – in the most efficient manner – of all the artillery. It is much the most complex branch of service, and requires ceaseless care and untiring labor. Few men have worked these two years as I have. And yet poor were the reward if the applause of men were my motive! Of this, however, no matter. I am trying to serve God

---

[87] Wert, *Old Artillery*, **CWTI**, vol.13, no.3, pp.15-16.

[88] Krick, 'A Stupid Old Useless Fool', **CWTI**, vol.47, no.3, p.46.

in manifold ways and through some trials. He gives me a large measure of peace of mind, and will enable me, I trust, to do some good to the country, and promote His glory in the upholding of His cause and in the salvation of souls."[89]

Although William Pendleton was shorter than Lee, he was often mistaken for the great chieftain. The most confusing element of the blunder was Pendleton's beard which held the same grayish white tint as Lee's. A resemblance of facial features made confusion of the two understandable but anyone who had met both men would have instantly known the difference between them. While Lee possessed a physical bearing that none could forget, Pendleton was the opposite, lacking any force of being whatsoever.[90]

Flamboyant Cavalier

A move northward would also require a major restructuring of the army's cavalry force. The early months of the war saw great success and accolades for Confederate horsemen. Guarding the flanks of Lee's army, foraging for food and supplies, harassing the Federals at every turn and keeping the enemy cavalry at bay provided Lee with the opportunity to be audacious and successful. As the summer campaign began to unfolded, a large and well-outfitted cavalry would be needed to screen the movements of the army in enemy territory, keep a watchful eye on the enemy's position and movements, perform scouting expeditions and forage for provisions in the fertile valleys north of the Potomac. In short, adequate cavalry would be critical to the safety and welfare of the army. During the previous battle at Chancellorsville, Lee had only two brigades of cavalry available to him. He would need many more troopers to protect the army from marauding militia and Federal horsemen as it moved through enemy country.

Lee's trusted cavalry commander; James Ewell Brown Stuart, continued to lead Lee's Cavalry Division. The flamboyant Stuart had been the messenger who arrived at Colonel Lee's door when he was needed by the War Department to visit Harpers Ferry and deal with old John Brown. Stuart was born 6 February 1833, in a small unassuming farmhouse on Laurel Hill plantation in Patrick County Virginia near the North Carolina border. James was the eighth child and fourth boy in a family of eleven children born to Archibald Stuart and his wife Elizabeth. His father was a country lawyer and politician who had fought in the War of 1812. The elder Stuart, a strong speaker and an avid socialite, possessed a keen wit and was charismatic in his actions. His famous son would inherit or develop all of these traits to an even greater degree than his father.[91]

---

[89] Lee, Susan P., *Memoirs of William Nelson Pendleton, D.D*, p.272.

[90] Wert, *Old Artillery, CWTI*, vol.13, no.3, pp.13-14.

[91] Perry, Thomas D., *Laurel Hill's Teachers Guide*, pp.25-26; Davis, *JEB Stuart*, p.17. The two brigades were those of Fitzhugh Lee and William H. F. "Rooney" Lee. However, Rooney was off chasing Stoneman which further reduced General Lee's available horsemen.

James spent his boyhood days bounding about the Virginia countryside near Laurel Hill. He loved the old plantation and wished nothing more than to return after the war, content to spend his remaining days in quiet solitude. The love for his boyhood home was expressed to his mother shortly before the war began. Writing her from Leavenworth, Kansas he relayed his desire to obtain a portion of the property. "What will you take for the south half of your plantation? I wish to buy it." During the war, he mentioned to one of his brothers how he longed to return to the old place and "quietly to spend the rest of my days there."[92]

Though sentimental about his boyhood home, Stuart was anything but soft. As he grew it became apparent he was a strong willed boy who seemed to be unafraid, if not unaware of danger. One day as he and his brother William, along with other local boys where doing the things boys do, they came upon a nest of hornets. With the insects swarming around, James ascended the tree where the nest was perched to confront his antagonists. While his brother and the other boys sought shelter, James, ignoring the stings of the mad hornets, destroyed the nest, and climbed down.[93]

After receiving his initial education at a school in Wytheville, James enrolled in Emory & Henry College where he received most of his formal education. Two years later he was appointed a cadet at West Point based on the recommendation of a prominent Virginia congressman. He worked hard and did well in a number of subjects including mathematics, English and French. His discipline was excellent and by the end of his first year he had received only forty-three demerits which ranked him eighty-second among the 229 cadets at the academy. His excellent performance continued through the remainder of his four years and in 1854 he graduated thirteenth in a class of forty-six.[94]

At the academy Stuart had the opportunity to become acquainted with some of the cadets who he would serve with during the war. Ironically the superintendent during his time there was Major Robert E. Lee. One of Stuart's acquaintances, Fitzhugh Lee, who entered West Point two years after Stuart, fondly remembered his friend's academy days after the war. Although Fitz Lee would not see Stuart again until the war began, his memory of him during their time at West Point was vivid. "I recall his distinguished characteristics," Lee commented in 1875, "which were a strict attention to his military duties, an erect, soldierly bearing, and immediate and almost thankful acceptance of a challenge from any cadet to fight, who might in any way feel himself aggrieved, and a clear, metallic, ringing voice."[95]

Upon graduation, James was brevetted a second lieutenant and assigned to the Mounted Riflemen then serving in Texas. Delayed by a yellow fever epidemic in

---

[92] McClellan, Henry B., *I rode with Jeb Stuart*, pp.5-6.

[93] Davis, *Jeb Stuart*, p.18.

[94] McClellan, *I rode with Jeb Stuart*, pp.6-7; Davis, *Jeb Stuart*, p.19; Boatner, *Dictionary*, p.812.

[95] Lee, Fitzhugh, Speech before, A.N.V. Association Banquet, October 28th, 1875, *SHSP*, vol.1, p.100.

New Orleans, he finally boarded a steamer to begin the journey across the gulf to the coast of Texas. The trip was anything but relaxing for a heavy storm tossed the boat and forced Stuart to remain in his cabin for the majority of the trip, suffering through a severe case of seasickness. After arriving in Galveston, a journey of nearly 800 miles across parched country was required before Stuart could catch up with the Mounted Rifles and his job as a soldier finally began. Highlights of his early career included encounters with Indians and a prairie fire which damaged his newly grown large flowing beard.[96]

In 1855 Stuart was transferred to the newly organized 1st Regiment, U. S. Cavalry and relocated to Fort Leavenworth, Kansas. During this time two significant events occurred, the first of which was the death of his father. Stuart took the loss hard and his correspondence regarding the event shows a great deal of affection and sadness. The other event was his marriage to Flora Cooke, the daughter of Colonel Philip St. George Cooke of the 2nd Dragoons. The wedding was held at Fort Riley where Flora's father was stationed with his command. Shortly before his father's death, James had informed him of his intention to marry Flora and Archibald gave his consent willingly. James' life had been changed forever with the departure of his father and the arrival of a wife and husbandly responsibilities. For the next two years he spent the bulk of his time balancing his duties as a soldier and his responsibility as a husband.[97]

James Ewell Brown "Jeb" Stuart's actions during the campaign would spark controversies which persist today. *MOLLUS Collection, USAHEC*

---

[96]   Davis, ***Jeb Stuart***, pp.29-33.

[97]   McClellan, ***I rode with Jeb Stuart***, pp.19-20.

During 1857 the 1st Cavalry spent the majority of its time fighting off marauding Indians and defending settlers near the north fork of the Solomon River in northwest Kansas. During one such engagement Stuart rode to the defense of a fellow soldier who would surely have been killed by an Indian armed with a revolver. As Stuart brought his saber down upon the head of his opponent, the revolver discharged no more than a couple feet away. The bullet struck Stuart in the center of his chest, hit bone, and lodged near his left nipple. Managing to dismount, he laid down as the remainder of the Indian's were driven off. A quick shelter was constructed from a blanket and sabers stuck in the ground. His wound was not considered mortal but the round had lodged "so far inside that it [could not] be felt." He would eventually recover from the wound and resume his duties, but the incident was a testament to Stuart's courage which he would display often as the colorful cavalier of the Confederacy.[98]

From late 1857 to the middle months of 1860, Stuart was stationed at Fort Riley with six companies of the 1st Cavalry. It was during this time, while on a six month leave of absence he was called from Virginia to Washington and was in the latter, when John Brown occupied the arsenal at Harper Ferry. After riding out to Arlington to fetch Lee, Stuart volunteered to act as the colonel's aid. Permission was given and he boarded the locomotive with Lee. As the affair came to a head, Stuart was given the task of reading Lee's surrender demands to Brown and his men. According to Stuart, two thousand spectators watched as he approached the door of the engine house and read the terms to Brown. The old abolitionist, who told James his name was Smith, but who Stuart recognized as Brown, refused the terms. The refusal was anticipated and as instructed, Stuart stepped aside and waved his cap, a predetermined signal to inaugurate the assault. It was all over quickly, with Stuart managing to commandeer Brown's "bowie-knife" as a souvenir.[99]

In 1861, as the clouds of war loomed in the east, Stuart asked for a two month leave of absence and returned to Virginia. He determined to cast his lot with his native state and on 7 May submitted his resignation which was promptly accepted by the War Department. Traveling to Richmond he offered his services and on 10 May was commissioned a lieutenant colonel of infantry and, like William Pendleton, was ordered to report to Jackson at Harpers Ferry. A month later he was in command of the 1st Virginia Cavalry within Joe Johnston's Army of the Shenandoah. At the time Stuart's command consisted of only three hundred and thirteen men and twenty one officers. In July he received his commission as colonel of cavalry and led the regiment at First Manassas. His performance during the battle merited a promotion and by September he was a brigadier general. On 22 October he was assigned command of a brigade and by the end of the year had molded his troopers into an effective fighting force.[100]

---

[98] *Ibid*, p.21.

[99] *Ibid*, pp.29-30. The details of Stuart's part in the John Brown affair are contained in a letter he wrote to his mother after returning to Fort Riley in 1860, part of which is published in McClellan.

[100] **OR**, vol. 2, p.187; **OR**, vol. 5, p.913; McClellan, *I rode with Jeb Stuart*, p.32.

Stuart came to prominence during the Peninsular Campaign when he was assigned the task of riding with his troopers north of Richmond to determine if there was any Union infantry in the area. After performing his task, and finding no resistance, Stuart led his 1,200 troopers on one of the most audacious adventures of the war. Instead of returning to Richmond, he guided his horsemen on a ride which completely circled McClellan's mighty army. Outfoxing his pursuers, after four days of riding he returned with much needed intelligence regarding the disposition of McClellan's entire force and its flanks. Remarkably, only one trooper was lost during the trip. Lee had his information, the South had a new hero and Stuart instantly became the darling of the Richmond papers and a champion of the cause. It was the first of many ostentatious cavalry adventures conducted by Stuart's troopers during the first half of the war.

By the spring of 1863, Jeb Stuart was at the height of his fame. He was in command of some of the best horsemen in the Confederacy, and his performance under Lee's supervision had been stellar. Lee had come to rely on Stuart and his horsemen to be the eyes and ears of the army, and Stuart's cavalry had given Lee everything the commanding general needed for the army to be successful. There was no sign that he would get any less from him as the active campaign season of 1863 opened. One must wonder however, now much of Stuart's success was due to his skill as a cavalry commander or the early war ineptness of the Federal horsemen.

Chapter VI
The Federals Come Full Circle

> "It is doubtful what the enemy are going to do,
> but many believe they are evacuating."[1]
> *George Meade to his wife*
> *the afternoon of 2 May 1863*
> *near Chancellorsville.*

The battle of Fredericksburg left the Army of the Potomac defeated, dejected and demoralized. For one and a half years the Federal army had fought the Confederates and had nothing to show for it. After the battle, the morale of the army plummeted to one of its lowest points in its history, and the soldiers knew who to blame. Writing in his journal, W. P. Cutler of the 6th Wisconsin summed it up well. "Our Potomuc [sic] army is so far a failure, and seems to be demoralized by the political influences that have been brought to bear upon it. All is confusion and doubt." Cutler believed Lincoln was being "tripped up" by his generals. "God alone can guide us through this terrible time of doubt, uncertainty, treachery, imbecility and infidelity," he concluded.[2]

Officers knew who to blame as well. General Marsena Patrick, writing in his diary on 16 December, expressed the same sentiments when he summarized the mood of the entire army. "There is a feeling of deep and painful anxiety as to the future. No confidence is felt in anyone." Joseph Elliot of the 71st Pennsylvanian was even more demonstrative. "Defeated-Discussed-Disheartened" he wrote shortly after the battle.[3]

The Cowardly and the Homesick

The dejected state within the army led to severe desertion problems. While the hardships of active campaigning and a military life were present from the first day the volunteer army entered the field, many men had underestimated the level of adversity they would face. With the army now mired in an existence which seemed

---

[1] Meade, *Meade*, vol.1, p.370.

[2] Dawes, Rufus R., *Service with the Sixth Wisconsin*, p.118.

[3] Sparks, *Inside Lincoln's Army*, p.192; Lash, Gary G., *A Duty Well Done" The History of Edward Baker's California Regiment*, p.297.

to hold little hope for victory, many men found the resolve to leave the suffering behind. The growing lack of faith in the ability of the army's leadership only fueled the problem. It took but a short time for Hooker to understand that if something was not done quickly the army might cease to be a legitimate fighting force.[4]

In order to stem the tide of desertion, Hooker tried to restructure the regulations regarding leaves of absence. Existing regulations had been established in the War Department's General Order No.62 on 7 June 1862. It stated that "the commander of an army, a department, or a district" could grant leaves and furloughs in the field to men or officers only to prevent death or permanent disability. Only the secretary of war could approve a leave of absence to anyone not meeting the medical conditions. Citing the order had never been strictly enforced, on 30 January, Hooker issued General Order No.3 which outlined extensive changes to the leave and furlough rules, changes which he "believed by it much desertion will be stopped."[5]

The new orders outlined a number of significant changes over the previous regulations, including a maximum limit of fifteen days for any leave of absence. Officers in command of corps', divisions or cavalry brigades were to have their leaves approved by army headquarters. At the regiment level, only one field officer could be absent at a time and then only when the regiment contained its full complement of officers. For line officers two could be absent and from artillery batteries only one could be on leave at a time. All leaves would be limited to ten days unless the man was from Maine, Vermont, New Hampshire, Ohio, Michigan or states further west, then the period of time was lengthened to the fifteen days maximum. Only two enlisted men could be on furlough at a time for every 100 men on duty with a regiment or artillery battery. In addition, only men who had exhibited exemplary performance of their duties could receive a pass. To make sure that men receiving leaves would return, no other men could be given leaves of absence until the men currently on leave were back with the regiment.

The order also included detailed requirements for documenting men who were absent, including descriptions of those currently away from their units. Officers were given eight days to fill out their returns and turn them into headquarters. For any enlisted men who were absent a full description was to be documented in the roster, including the missing man's height, age and a description of his physical features. If there was cause for dismissal of an absent officer, information regarding the officer's situation was to be presented so action, if necessary, could be taken.[6]

Listing all those absent was quite an undertaking in some regiments. In a letter to his sister Lucy, James Thomas, adjutant of the 107th Pennsylvania explained the extent of the task. "Genl Hooker issued a general order for all regmts to make and forward a report of the names, residence, full descriptive list, where supposed to be, when & where left the regmt, &c &c of all men on detached service, absent,

---

[4] McPherson, James M., *For Cause & Comrades: Why Men Fought in the Civil War*, pp.156-157.

[5] *OR* Series III, vol.2, p.112; *OR*, vol.25, pt.2, pp.10-11.

[6] *OR*, vol.25, pt.2, p.11.

sick in hospitals, and of all deserters since the regmt has been organized. It took myself & sergt. major 2 days to make ours and was 5 1/2 foot long written full both sides when finished."[7]

Hooker felt the changes were more lenient than the current regulations and would allow his men the freedom to take some much needed time away from the hardships of army life. He included a copy of the order in his 30 January correspondence with Halleck, who was quick to note that General Order No.62 was still in effect and had never been rescinded by the War Department. Halleck must have discussed Hooker's leave order with Secretary of War Stanton because in his response, he noted that Stanton had approved his orders even though Order No.62 was still in place. Halleck then proceeded to complain about the number of leaves being granted by grand division and corps commanders. According to Halleck, the flood of men infesting Washington due to the granting of so many leaves, was unacceptable. He informed Hooker that all leaves granted to officers to visit Washington that were not approved by the War Department were void and anyone caught who was not simply passing through or who spent more than twenty-four hours in town would be arrested.[8]

To assist in dealing with the rampant desertion problem, Hooker turned to Provost Marshal Patrick. Patrick quickly went to work hunting down missing men. Gathering up all the descriptions provided by the regiments, he sent the massive stack of paperwork to Washington, where General Halleck put a dozen war department clerks to work scouring the information. The descriptions were organized and sent off to draft authorities in each state to help in rounding up any of the men who may have been foolish enough to go home.

Patrick also communicated directly with civil authorities. In the city of New York a five dollar reward for the detention of deserters resulted in the arrest of men who were legally in the city on furlough or on military business. Men on picket lines were instructed that anyone not responding properly to inquiries regarding the reason they were away from the army were to be shot. Assistance from the flotilla on the Potomac River was solicited to cut off the river as a pathway north. Any soldiers trying to pass a picket line in a northerly direction were to be detained. In addition, men sent out to repair downed telegraph lines were required to carry identification papers in order to make it difficult for deserters to masquerade as line workers.

During the clamp down, one of the major contributors to the desertion problem was uncovered. Many men were receiving through the mail civilian clothing which made it easier to disguise themselves as a resident. To combat this, Hooker and Patrick took control of the mail service and began inspecting all incoming packages for material and items which could assist soldiers in escaping the camps. In a

---

[7] Thomas, Mary W., Sauers, Richard A, Editors, *The Civil War Letters of First Lieutenant James B. Thomas*, p.147.

[8] *OR* vol.25, pt.2, p.44

communication to the Adams Express Company, Assistant Adjutant General Seth Williams outlined Hooker's intentions.[9]

> "The commanding general directs me to inform you that in the future no packages will be permitted to be brought to this army for soldiers except under the following restrictions:
>
> First. Securely fastened to the outside of the package must be an invoice of the contents. This invoice must be certified to by the agent who receives the packages that the contents have been examined by him and are truly set forth.
>
> Packages containing citizens' clothing and intoxicating liquors will not be allowed to be brought to the army for soldiers' use. Packages for officers will only be subject to the restrictions that have heretofore been imposed upon them. It is not intended to class under the head of citizens' clothing anything but outer garments that facilitate desertion. There is no objection to underclothing, mittens, or other little articles that may be desired being forwarded. This course has become necessary by the pernicious practice of treasonable persons sending citizens' clothing to soldiers here to encourage and facilitate desertion.
>
> The commanding general desires to know what length of time it will take you to enter upon a full compliance with this order."[10]

Patrick sent men to both Belle Plains and Aquia Creek to appraise all incoming and outgoing supplies. All of the additional measures did produce results. Before the review of the description lists was completed in Washington, Patrick had manages to round up 467 missing men and return them to their units.

Not all of Patrick's efforts to deal with the desertion problem were met with enthusiasm. In Washington, Lafayette Baker, special provost marshal from the War Department, had been doing some detective work of his own. A rift between Baker and Patrick developed due to Baker's heavy handed methods in dealing with Patrick's officers as they went about their work. Writing to Butterfield, Patrick, under no uncertain terms, made his feelings known. "I believe him [Baker] to be capable of making any statement however false, & of committing any act, however criminal and of damaging the Public Service to gratify his own Passions [sic]." While Patrick had to later retract the comments regarding criminal acts, he continued to express animosity toward Baker, particularly when the reason for Baker's actions became known to him. Evidently Baker was of the opinion that Patrick was transferring supplies to the South. He formed his judgment when large amounts of salt were discovered in Richmond with paperwork pointing to Patrick as the instigator of the shipment. Baker seemed incapable of construing the possibility

---

[9] Fishel, Edwin C., ***The Secret War for the Union***, pp.283-284.

[10] ***OR*** vol.25, pt.2, p.73.

a shipment could have been captured and taken south by the Confederates. To Baker the facts were simple, Federal salt was seen in Richmond with Patrick's name on it, so therefore Patrick must be guilty. Baker also charged that Patrick had sent plunder from Fredericksburg northward. Patrick detested plunder of any kind and to be accused of that which he worked hard to bring to a halt irritated him further. "Baker swears hostility eternal against [Chief Quartermaster Colonel Rufus] Ingalls & myself," Patrick wrote in his diary. The dispute eventually got very nasty, but Patrick managed to keep his post and continued to work toward gathering up as many deserters as possible.[11]

On 7 February Hooker issued General Order No.10, which contained a great deal of additional detail regarding leave policies. The order expanded on Hooker's original limitations, and was more descriptive regarding the regulations. It specifically dealt with limiting the number of passes which could be issued. No passes would be valid unless they were signed by Hooker himself, Chief of Staff Butterfield, Assistant Adjutant General Williams or Provost Marshal Patrick. It was permissible for corps commanders or their assistant adjutant generals to issue passes to their officers or soldiers but only for travel between Washington and the army and only if it was determined that the man issued the pass could be spared from his duties. The order also put restrictions on civilians who were camped near or traveling with the army. All sutlers, the army's version of a street vendor, where required to be listed in a registry. The listings were also required to include anyone in their employ and all the wagons, horses and other draft animals that may be part of their entourage.[12]

Sutlers typically entered the camps, set up a tent or a hut and sold common items to the soldiers. They dealt in books, tobacco, food, newspapers and many other everyday items soldiers could not readily obtain because of their restrictions to camp. Many sutlers also sold contraband as well including alcohol. Typically, there was one sutler for each regiment in camp. While the concept of bringing these items to the troops was in the best interests of the men, many sutlers took advantage of the situation. They charged exorbitant prices for many necessities and extended credit to soldiers who could not afford it. The soldiers often complained that they were being cheated and on some occasions, raided the sutler's tents, taking what they felt they rightly deserved.[13]

Along with sutlers, all civilians in the employ of any officer would be listed in the register along with the officer they were employed by. News correspondents, newsboys and messengers traveling with the army and writing for the Northern press would also be included. Once completed, the registry was to be provided to General Patrick. The provost marshal would be responsible for issuing the proper passes and documentation for all those listed. Regarding sutlers, permits would be written to manage the transport of their goods.

---

[11] Fishel, *Secret War*, p.284; Sparks, *Inside Lincoln's Army*, p.217.

[12] *OR* vol.25, pt.2, pp.57-58.

[13] Faust, *Encyclopedia*, p.738.

Within the context of General Order No.10, Hooker also addressed the use and treatment of animals in the possession of the army. The use of any animal would be restricted to military business and the "[c]ruel or careless treatment of animals" would now be a punishable offense.[14]

A few days later Hooker strengthened his position regarding peddlers trading with soldiers when he issued orders to Patrick to only allow registered sutlers inside the lines of the army. "The commanding general directs," General Williams wrote, "that all trading establishments, peddlers, &c., within the lines of this army, except regularly authorized and appointed sutlers, be broken up, and the parties, with their goods, be sent outside our lines to the rear by to-morrow night…" Unregister vendors had twenty-four hours to pack their wares and depart or their goods along with their horses and wagons would be commandeered and distributed among the or to army hospitals. This left only approved sutlers, whose wares were no doubt strictly monitored to provide goods to the soldiers.[15]

On 3 March General Williams wrote lengthy General Order No.18. The document contained sixteen individual sections in which Hooker refined, expanded or tightened previous instructions. The order stated that any civilian was now required to obtain a permit to be within the lines of the army. In addition, reviews of inspection reports had shown some commands delinquent in discipline and efficiency. The worst offending regiments and batteries were identified by name, their officers recalled if they were on leave or furlough and no others issued until the command met headquarters' expectations. While poor performance was punished, excellent performance did not go unnoticed. Commands identified as being exceptional in their discipline and effectiveness were rewarded with an increase by one of the number of men who could be on furlough. As with poor performers, the names of outstanding commands were called out within the order. Criteria for issuing leaves and furloughs where also modified. Men "whose [sic] behaviors, appearance and character make them proper representatives of their command and the army" would be placed at the head of the furlough line. Rules regarding sutlers also received refinement. Any peddler using the name of an officer to supply themselves with transportation or to buy and sell contraband to the troops would be summarily dismissed from the army's lines and their inventory confiscated.[16]

By establishing tight controls on incoming packages and implementing stringent regulations as to who could sell goods to the men, Hooker shut off the distribution of contraband which could assist the men in deserting their posts. Supplies from home could no longer be relied upon and the sutlers where now under strict observation and would not be allowed to sell any articles which could assist a cowardly or homesick soldier to make the long trek home.

---

[14] *OR* vol.25, pt.2, pp.58-59.

[15] *Ibid*, p.74.

[16] *Ibid*, pp.119-121.

Little Patches, Mules and Food

The twelfth item included in General Order No.10 contained descriptive information regarding the design and makeup of flags intended to designate corps headquarters. The banners were to be blue and of the swallow-tail type. In the center of the flag would be a Maltase cross which contained the corps' number in red. The concept of a swallow-tail flag was a superior one considering its unique properties. While fluttering in a breeze it could be easily identified from a rectangular flag from a distance. While Hooker's idea and intentions were noble, and the chief quartermaster of the army was charged with supplying the flags, the orders were not universally carried out. An additional idea, intended to provide quick identification, was implemented with the exuberance of the men. Members of each corps would now be recognized with the use of a corps identification badge.[17]

During the Peninsula Campaign, Brigadier General Philip Kearny, having trouble identifying men from his division, came up with a method for distinguishing them from other troops. Kearny ordered his men to wear red flannel patches which were cut in the shape of a diamond. This made it easy to pick his men out in a crowd. Initially Kearny intended the patches to identify his men in order to keep them closed up when on the march. No man wanted to be caught and identified by the general when he was straggling behind the division. The men however, soon looked upon the patch as a badge of honor and while wearing the patches morale grew. Although, Kearny was killed at the battle of Chantilly on 1 September 1862, his men continued to wear the patches as a matter of pride.[18]

With morale at a low point, Hooker was desperate to find ways of improving the élan of his men. He also recalled instances when confronting stragglers in which the soldier in question provided false information regarding his membership in a specific command. The solution to both problems came in a suggestion by Butterfield to incorporate general Kearny's idea throughout the entire army. On 21 March a circular was issued directing the use of corps badges. "For the purpose of ready recognition of corps and divisions in this army, and to prevent injustice by reports of straggling and misconduct through mistake as to its organization, the chief quartermaster will furnish without delay... badges, to be worn by the officers and enlisted men of all the regiments of the various corps mentioned." Each corps would have its own uniquely shaped badge which would be attached to the center of a soldier's cap. The First Corps would utilize a circle as its identifying shape. The second would have a trefoil as its designation while the Third Corps would utilize a diamond. A Maltese cross was used for the Fifth Corps with a typical cross for the Sixth Corps. The Eleventh Corps would utilize a crescent with the twelfth using a star. In addition, each badge would be of a specific color to distinguish men from each division. The first division of each corps would be red, with the second and third divisions being white and blue respectively.[19]

---

[17] *Ibid*, p.59.

[18] Sears, ***Chancellorsville***, p. 72; Faust, ***Encyclopedia***, p.409.

[19] ***OR*** vol.25, pt.2, p.152.

While Hooker initially intended the badges to provide identification, the implementation of the little pieces of cloth had a profound effect on the morale of the army. Men now had a symbol in which to hang their pride on. Additional satisfaction was instilled when Hooker allowed each regiment to have stitched into their regimental colors the names of the engagements they had fought in. As the names Bull Run, Seven Pines and Antietam, began to be displayed so to was the pride of the men. Fighting Joe was slowly gaining the confidence of his boys by providing them vehicles to exhibit their pride and satisfaction with their earlier bloody labors.[20]

Not all of Hooker's efforts improved the physical condition of his army. Whether done to boost morale or to justify his own activities, the general opened the army camps up to prostitutes. His men no doubt appreciated the company and while acceptable to them, the activity was probably not received as well by Washington or any of the soldier's wives or girlfriends who may have become aware of the frivolity. The women who visited the camps soon garnered nicknames becoming known as Hooker's troops, Hooker's girls or just simply hookers. Hooker himself displayed a fondness for the girls as well. His first assignment of the war, during the fall and winter of 1861, was as a brigadier general in charge of a detachment of United States Volunteers in Washington. His command was stationed in the suburbs near a neighborhood known for its seedy saloons and houses of ill repute. Hooker spent much of his free time visiting the district. In fact he spent so much time there that the area became known as "Hooker's Division."[21]

In possibly one of the worst logistical moves in the history of nineteenth century warfare, Hooker established the use of pack saddles to transport supplies. On 19 March orders were issued distributing some 2,000 pack saddles at Aquia Creek among his seven corps. Two mules were provided to each regiment to carry officer's tents and gear, while the remainder would be loaded with ammunition. Small animals would carry two ammunition boxes, average size animals would carry two and one half and larger ones would carry three. All the ammunition was to be transported in waterproof pouches to keep it dry. The men would be drilled in the packing and unpacking of pack saddles to make preparations for marching and setting up camp second nature. Hooker would be the only commander in the history of the Army of the Potomac to incorporate pack saddles in exchange for wagons to move his supplies. The reason other commanders did not would become quite plain.[22]

There were many problems with utilizing pack saddles. More animals were needed to transport the same amount of ammunition which could be placed in a

---

[20] Sears, *Chancellorsville*, p.72.

[21] Lowery, Thomas, P., M.D., *The Story the Soldiers Wouldn't Tell*, pp.146-147. While it seems plausible that Joseph Hooker was the inspiration for the derogatory term now used to describe prostitutes, the term "hooker" had actually been in use for that purpose some time before Hooker lent his namesake to the brothels of Washington.

[22] *OR* vol.25, pt.2, pp.148-149; Bigelow, *Chancellorsville*, p.44.

wagon drawn by the same animals. The mules also took up more room on the thoroughfare being traversed by marching troops. In many instances the animals wandered, requiring a handler to keep them under control, moving in the correct direction and from blocking traffic. Every time a halt was called, the animals had to be unpacked to remove their burdens in order for them to be given a respite. When hitched to a wagon, the same animal could rest without being unhitched. It was soon discovered that it required approximately one hour for the unpacking and repacking of a mule. When the army was on the move, rest stops were seldom more than ten minutes. It was harder on the animals to stop than it was to keep moving. It was also discovered that a pack-train could actually travel faster than loaded wagons. In order to accomplish this however, the pack animals had to move at their own pace, which was typically not fast enough for most officers.

The pack trains were so slow and labor intensive that the army would be required to adapt to their pace during the march preceding the Chancellorsville battle. Problems would be encountered with straying animals in the wooded countryside and dense undergrowth. If a mule wandered off the road, it had a tendency to rub the pack against trees and brush which damaged its contents. To combat this, the men learned to tie the animals together to keep an individual mule from straying; however, the average soldier was not smart enough to fool a mule. The animals simply rubbed against each other and damaged the cargo anyway. Samuel Gracey, chaplain of the 6th Pennsylvania Cavalry noted after the war that the one thing the pack mules succeeded in doing was provide "a source of great amusement to the troops, and aggravation to the drivers." The animals were "not at all practicable for the active campaign."

The folly of establishing pack mules as a method for supplying an army on the march can be seen by simple comparison. A six mule wagon team could transport twenty five boxes of ammunition and eight days forage for the mules. While it was suggested that a mule could possible carry up to three boxes of ammunition, in reality most pack mules could carry only two boxes along with forage for itself for six days. The math should have been simple enough. Six mules pulling a wagon could transport twice the ammunition as the same number of mules fitted with pack saddles, without all the difficulties of dealing with wandering animals and unpacking the mules at every rest stop. A wagon was capable of hauling an average of 2,700 pounds of supplies while six mules could carry only 1,200 pounds. In addition, wagons could carry rations which could not be transported by pack mule for fear of hungry mules, without close supervision, eating a soldier's sustenance. Instead of ordering the use of the pack saddles Hooker would have been better off to requisition all the wagons he could get his hands on and use the mules to pull twice the supplies that the mules could carry individually.[23]

Another problem Hooker faced was the lack of sufficient nourishment for his men. In reality, many men had more than they cared to eat, but while the quantity of food was plentiful the volume of fresh food, fruits and vegetables was significantly

---

[23] *OR* vol.25, pt.2, pp.545, 547; Gracey, Samuel L., **Annals of the Sixth Pennsylvania Cavalry**, p.156.

low and the assortment was poor. The problem was that fresh food being delivered to the commissary was simply not getting to the men. The supply chain was being interrupted by greedy commissary officers who were selling the food for cash and pocketing the profits. In addition, any fresh food available, in many instances, was not being drawn by the corps commissary. Medical Director Letterman began to observe in late January an increase in attacks of diarrhea and fever throughout the camps. The beginnings of a scurvy epidemic also became apparent and sick men were not recovering and returning to their units as quickly as one would have thought they could. Letterman attributed this to the lack of fresh vegetables.[24]

With the army on the verge of severe nutritional problems, Hooker took action. On 7 February he issued orders requiring the distribution of fresh vegetables. Fresh potatoes or onions would be issued to the men twice a week while assorted mixed vegetables would be issued once during the same period. Even closer to the hearts of the men was the distribution of bread. "Flour or soft bread will be issued at the depots to commissaries for at least four issues per week to the troops." Then, Hooker put some teeth into the order in an effort to stop the hording and sale of supplies by crooked commissary officers.

> "Commanders of army corps', divisions, brigades and separate commands will require any commissary under their orders who fails to issue the above-named stores to the command to which he is attached, and as often as stated, to produce the written statement of the officer in charge of the depot from which he regularly draws his supplies to the effect that they were not on hand at the depot for issue to him, or otherwise to satisfactorily account for his failure."[25]

Bakeries were established in a number of brigades and steps were taken to make sure every company had a cook on their rolls. "My men shall be fed before I am fed, and before any of my officers are fed," Hooker declared. The Army of the Potomac would not go hungry while Joe Hooker was in command, unless of course your daily ration was being carried by and confiscated by a hungry pack mule.[26]

Unlike their Southern antagonist, the Northern solders did not have as severe a problem with food and forage during the winter of 1862. On 17 November the Union army took possession of the rail line running south from Aquia Creek to the army at Falmouth. A week later trains were running. Rail cars were transported down the Potomac on special barges then off loaded onto the tracks with the use of a rebuilt railroad platform that was over 1,000 feet long. By 1 March 1863, nearly 9,000 rail cars loaded with supplies, had made the trip south to the army. A staggering one hundred and forty cars made the trip each day carrying

---

[24] Bigelow, *Chancellorsville*, p.35.

[25] *OR* vol.25, pt.2, p.57

[26] Sears, *Chancellorsville*, p.73.

approximately eight hundred tons of supplies. Second only to forage, which required 4,663 cars to transport, were commissary stores which were shipped with the use 2,346 cars. One hundred and thirty two cars were used to transport ammunition and ordnance with another six hundred and forty four for mail delivery and passengers.[27]

With all the abundant food stores and forage it's hard to fathom any instance of a shortage, but some did exist. Most shortages were caused by poor roads and transportation which kept some forage from being distributed to horses and mules. Regimental surgeon Nathan Haywood of the 20th Massachusetts noted the condition of the roads and their effect on forage distribution. "The roads are in so bad a condition that hay can not [sic] be provided." The mules," Haywood continued, "are suffering badly. They will eat the hair off each other, and devour paper and rags."[28]

Hygiene

Sanitation was also a significant problem in the early days of 1863. Many regimental officers who were ignorant of good hygiene practices allowed their commands to develop poor habits regarding cleanliness. In a communication to Hooker on 9 March, Dr. Letterman called the commanding general's attention to a common camp practice that was a serious detriment to the health of the men.

> "I have the honor to invite the attention of the Commanding General to a practice quite prevalent in this army; that of excavating the earth, building a hut over the hole and covering it over with brush and dirt or canvas. This system is exceedingly pernicious and must have a deleterious effect upon the health of the troops occupying these abominable habitations. They are hotbeds for low forms of fever, and when not productive of such diseases, the health of the men is undermined, even if they are not compelled to report sick. I strongly recommend that all troops that are using such huts be directed at once to discontinue their use, and that they be moved to new huts or live in tents. I also recommend that, in huts covered by canvas, the covering be removed at least twice a week, if the weather will permit, and that the men throughout the Army [sic] be compelled to hang their bedding in the open air every clear day."[29]

Hooker's men were in generally poor physical condition when he issued his orders for improving food distribution. Coupled with the shoddy sanitary situation, a breeding ground for sickness and poor health had been created. Letterman's

---

[27] *OR* Series III, vol.3, pp.119-120.

[28] Bigelow, *Chancellorsville*, p.35, note 4.

[29] *Ibid*, p.48, note.2.

efforts to address the hygiene issues and the improvements in nutrition began the task of improving the overall wellbeing of the army. Monthly sick reports for January and February showed a significant reduction in the illnesses "which depend upon neglect of sanitary precautions and bad diet…" In March, Letterman noted that sick rolls "have decreased in a marked degree during the month of February." The rates of typhoid fever and diarrhea decreased twenty eight and thirty two percent respectively and Letterman felt that the improvements would continue through March.

Efforts to improve nutrition and sanitation benefited not only the sick but the entire army. According to Letterman, he received a number of reports from other officers that regular food distribution improved the "general… health, tone, and vigor of those who were not reported sick… This favorable state of the health of the army, and the decrease in the severity of the cases of disease," Letterman continued, "is in a great measure to be attributed to the improvement in the diet of the men, commenced about the 1st of February by the issue of fresh bread and fresh vegetables, which has caused the disappearance of the symptoms of scurvy that in January began to assume a serious aspect throughout the army…" Letterman also attributed "increased attention to sanitary regulations" in both hospitals and camps, and increased consideration to cooking and preparation of food in regimental encampments to the general improvement. He gave much of the credit to corps medical directors and the medical officers of the army for implementing and requiring adherence to the regulations. When taken together, all the improvements brought about a significant change in the wellbeing of the solders on the front lines.[30]

As the changes began to improve the condition of the army, the morale of the soldiers and officers began to show improvement as well. The disaster of Fredericksburg and the miserable winter conditions slowly ebbed from the immediate memory of the troops. On 18 February, Captain William Folwell of the 50th New York engineers wrote home commenting Hooker "seems to be gaining the confidence of the army completely…" noting the general's "soft beard" order was directed at the soldier's "tender spot." Slowly the men of the Army of the Potomac were reviving themselves, gaining confidence in their new commander and each other.[31]

Horses and Guns

Another major change Hooker made was to completely restructure the organization of his cavalry. Since the war's beginning, Confederate horsemen had ridden circles around their Federal counterparts and had never been seriously challenged. This was partially due to the failure of the War Department to adequately recognize the value and uses of a mounted force. Although the use of cavalry had changed significantly within the Federal service, more needed to be accomplished to bring the Yankees up to par with the Southern raiders.

---

[30] *OR* vol.25, pt.2, pp.239-240.

[31] Sears, ***Chancellorsville***, p.73.

To improve his horsemen's chances of dealing with their nemesis, Hooker decided to consolidate his cavalry into a single corps. Previously, the largest unit of organization had been a division with other smaller detachments spread throughout the army. The old structure had the cavalry sprinkled about each corps under the direction of the various corps or grand division commanders. The enemy had unified its cavalry early in the war and the results were obvious to anyone who had been paying attention. The Federal organization hindered the horsemen and limited their ability to counter the huge cavalry raids and scouting operations their counterparts were superior at conducting. The Southerner's success against Northern cavalry formations could be directly related to the Federal trooper's inability to array like numbers against General Jeb Stuart. Hooker believed, and rightly so, that as a unified corps the Federal cavalry would be better able to deal with Stuart's marauding bands. Now it would be possible to pitch a force of equal or greater strength against the Rebels and see just how capable Southern men were when evenly matched in numbers. Within the same order used to abolish the Grand Divisions, Hooker issued a very simple instruction. "The cavalry of the army will be consolidated into one corps, under the command of Brigadier-General George Stoneman, who will make the necessary assignments for detached duty." West Pointer George Stoneman took command of his new corps of horsemen on 7 February. The unified cavalry structure was seen as positive and received high praise.[32]

George Stoneman was a career military man born on his family's farm on 22 August 1822 near the small town of Busti in western New York. His schooling began at Jamestown Academy and ended at West Point where he shared a room with Thomas Jackson. He entered the academy on 1 July 1842, and after completing the four year curriculum he stood thirty-third of fifty-nine in the infamous class of 1846. Brevetted a second lieutenant, Stoneman was assigned to the 1st Dragoons and served during the Mexican War. Following the war, he fought Indians on the western frontier and helped surveying parties responsible for finding railroad passages through the Sierra Nevada Mountains. He was promoted to captain on 3 March 1855, followed by service with the 2nd Cavalry prior to and during the initial stages of the rebellion. When the war began, Stoneman was stationed at Fort Brown Texas. He refused to surrender his command to the Southern sympathizer General David Twiggs, opting to take his men out of reach of the upstart Confederate authorities.[33]

Stoneman was promoted to major on 9 May 1861 and served briefly with the 1st Cavalry before being transferred to the 4th Cavalry on 3 August. During the early stages of the war, he served on fellow West Point classmate George McClellan's staff in western Virginia and came to Washington when his superior was summoned to reform the defeated army after First Bull Run. Ten days after he was transferred to the 4th Cavalry, Stoneman was commissioned a brigadier general of volunteers

---

[32] Coddington, *Gettysburg*, p.30; *OR* vol.25, pt. 2, p.59; Sifakis, *Who was Who*, p.627.

[33] Boatner, *Dictionary*, p.801; Sifakis, *Who was Who*, p.627; *Electronic Source*: http://en.wikipedia.org/wiki/George_Stoneman, Last accessed 5/1/2012.

and placed in command of the reserve Cavalry Division of the fledgling Army of the Potomac. He led his new command on several reconnaissance missions in Virginia. During the fighting on the Peninsula, Stoneman took part in the engagements at Yorktown, Williamsburg and the fighting during The Seven Days.[34]

George Stoneman's cautious nature would eventually be his undoing. *LOC*

Transferred to command of the First Division of the Second Corps on 17 July 1862, Stoneman began a stint as a commander of infantry. He would later be transferred to command of the First Division of the Third Corps. A promotion to Major General followed on 29 November before he was given command of the Third Corps, which he led during the battle of Fredericksburg. Hooker thought enough of Stoneman's skill as a cavalry commander to place him in command of the largest Union cavalry force of the war. Time would tell if he was up to the task.[35]

Stoneman's major command weakness was his tendency to be too careful. He was conservative in both his actions and his orders. He was at times slow and meticulous which, on occasion kept him from being able to see and seize opportunities. He was exhaustive when it came to drilling his men and they respected his professionalism, compassion and his consideration for their welfare and the wellbeing of their mounts. Another drawback to Stoneman's efficiency as a cavalry commander were questions regarding his ability to endure long hard cavalry rides and sustained campaigning. This was due to an acute physical ailment

---

[34] Longacre, Edward G., ***Lincoln's Cavalrymen***, p.55; Boatner, ***Dictionary***, p.801; Eicher, & Eicher, ***High Commands***, p.514.

[35] Boatner, ***Dictionary***, p.801.

which made it difficult for him to sit on a horse for extended periods of time. Eight years earlier Stoneman had developed hemorrhoids. He had undergone surgery to help alleviate the problem, but the procedure was not entirely successful. When he experienced a flare up it was difficult for him to remain in the saddle for extended periods.[36]

Unlike their Confederate counterparts, during the early months of the war, Federal cavalrymen were subjected to a substandard quality of horse flesh. While many horses suitable for riding were available in the South, in the North the situation was reversed. The North's industrial economy provided the Yankees with an abundance of work horses but not many sleek mounts suitable for cavalry use. In addition, few good horsemen resided in the North and even fewer men who could handle weapons while in the saddle. Many of the men ushered into Federal cavalry service had never been on a horse. Shortly before Hooker took command, quartermaster Rufus Ingalls noted "[F]irst-class horses have never yet found their way into this army." As conditions in the South deteriorated the quality of horse flesh in each army become more equal, but as Stoneman took over his new Cavalry Corps the Federals were still lagging behind their enemies.[37]

When Hooker took command, Brigadier General Henry J. Hunt was manning the army's chief of artillery position. Hunt, a graduate of West Point in 1839, was a holdover from the Burnside regime. He was born into a military family in Michigan at the Detroit Barracks on 4 September 1819. As a boy, Henry traveled with his father, an officer in the infantry, on the expedition which would eventually establish Fort Leavenworth. Within two years of the trip, his parents had passed away making him an orphan. Carrying on family tradition, he entered West Point and graduating nineteenth in a class of thirty-one cadets at the age of twenty. While at the academy, he became interested in light artillery and joined the artillery upon graduation. During the Mexican War, he was wounded twice and became known for his grit, determination and bravery. One specific instance found Hunt's guns heavily engaged with those of the enemy. Acting quickly he ordered the gunners of one piece to run their weapon up point blank to an enemy gun. The gunners did so, setting up a muzzle to muzzle exchange that saw Hunt's gun victorious, destroying the Mexican piece. After the war, in 1856, he served on a commission which revised the tactics used by the light arm of the artillery.

As the Civil War began, Hunt was arguably the best Federal artilleryman in the service. It was obvious to all that he was from the "Old Army" and his traditional ways were not popular with his men. However, there was little doubt that Henry Hunt was the man to turn to when it came to artillery. He was a firm believer in concentrating on one enemy battery at a time when called upon to provide counter battery fire. Hunt would direct his guns to mass on a single enemy emplacement until it was silenced and then move their guns on to the next battery. He detested gunners who worked their pieces too quickly in order to expend their ammunition so they could be withdrawn. As punishment for such cowardly behavior, Hunt often

---

[36] Longacre, ***Lincoln's Cavalrymen***, pp.55-56.

[37] ***OR*** vol.21, p.983.

required the battery to remain in position and sent only the caissons to the rear to replenish ammunition. The gunners were forced to endured enemy fire which came their way, unable to respond. He preached to his men that every shot should be deliberately aimed and fired at a rate that provided the greatest accuracy.

During the early portion of the war, Hunt demonstrated his skill with light guns on a number of occasions. He successfully helped cover the retreat from First Bull Run. For his efforts, McClellan, whom Hunt had performed aide-de-camp duties for, placed him in charge of the Army of the Potomac's Artillery Reserve and promoted him to colonel. Hunt provided exemplary service during the Peninsula Campaign, and remained loyal to McClellan even after the general fell out of favor in Washington. By the Antietam campaign, Hunt had performed so well that McClellan made him a brigadier general and assigned him to the post of chief of artillery. During the battle, the guns were so well served that the enemy termed the fight "Artillery Hell." At Fredericksburg, Hunt arrayed his guns along Stafford Heights on the Union side of the Rappahannock River. It was the bristling hillside above the town which helped deter Lee from counterattacking after the Federals gave up the attempt to take Marye's Heights. Initially Hunt retained his position when Hooker was installed as army commander, but friction would later develop between the two men. Although Hunt had justified his position with deeds in battle, he was about to be reminded that the label "Fighting Joe" was not simply because of Hooker's work on the battlefield.[38]

While Hooker improved his cavalry by consolidating it, he damaged the artillery organization by removing Hunt from his position as chief of artillery in late March. Hunt's role was reduced to nothing more than administrative. This development did not sit well with the experienced artilleryman. Hooker justified the move by blaming Hunt for wanting the artillery organized into a corps in the same manner as the cavalry. "In this he [Hunt] showed so much ill feeling that I was unwilling to place my artillery in his charge at Chancellorsville…" Hooker no longer trusted Hunt to effectively command the batteries because of Hunt's dissention with him and the decision not to do as Hunt thought best. This reasoning was, at best, questionable. One thing Hunt had proven over the years was that he was a soldier first. Hooker should have known, based on Hunt's reputation, that no matter what position the gunner was placed, he would do his duty. In April, Hunt wrote to deposed General Burnside commenting that his duties had been diminished to those of a mere staff officer which any major or lieutenant could execute.[39]

Years later, Hooker tried to justify the move by citing loyalty between the fighting troops and the artillery batteries. "…I found that my men had learned to regard their batteries," he wrote, "with a feeling of devotion which I considered contributed greatly to our success…" During the flanking movement prior to Chancellorsville, a number of batteries were left behind at river crossings. Hunt

---

[38] Tagg, Larry, **Generals**, pp.187-188.

[39] Sears, **Chancellorsville**, p.68; Longacre, Edward G., The Soul of Our Artillery, **CWTI**, vol.12, no.3, p.4.

reported receiving numerous requests from corps commanders for additional batteries to be brought up during the fight. Because he was no longer in control, he could not help. Following the dismal performance, Hunt received somewhat of a reprieve when the artillery was returned to his control the evening of May 3, but it was to late to turn the tide of battle. "I doubt if the history of modern armies can exhibit parallel instance of such palpable crippling of a great arm of the service in the very presence of a powerful enemy," Hunt wrote in his report. Hooker no doubt realized later what he had done was not in the best interest of the army, but he was unwilling to admit that he had made a mistake, and he continued to defend his decision long after the war had closed.[40]

Hooker Established an Intelligence Team

Neither the Federals nor the Confederates had in place any type of intelligence gathering apparatus when the war began. Through the early part of the conflict individual commanders worked within the context of their own organizations to gather and disseminate intelligence information. While efforts were made to establish a national organization to collect and systematize military intelligence, the information was of little use to organizations in the field. In fact, a number of Federal defeats could be directly associated with poor or misread information.

The Army of the Potomac's first commander, George McClellan, understood the value of good intelligence, but failed miserably in his efforts to build a competent organization to gather information. Realizing the need for an organization, "Little Mac" brought in an old friend from his previous occupation as a railroad administrator, Allan Pinkerton. Pinkerton, who was from Glasgow Scotland, had organized his own detective agency before the war and had been assigned the task of guarding Abraham Lincoln as the president elect journeyed to Washington. While Pinkerton may have been good at detective work and guard duty, he was a poor gatherer of military intelligence. His men were not effective at observing the enemy's military formations and he constantly overestimated troop strength. In fact many credit Pinkerton's inflated numbers during the Peninsular Campaign as the primary reason why McClellan was not successful. When McClellan was sacked by Lincoln after Antietam, Pinkerton packed up his organization and all the intelligence records he had accumulated and departed. Since he was working for McClellan and not the government, he returned to his detective agency and the Army of the Potomac was again devoid of any organized intelligence gathering device.

To his credit, Hooker understood the need for a vehicle to gather, organize and review military intelligence specific to enemy troop strengths, position and intentions. In February 1863 he established the Bureau of Military Intelligence (BMI) and placed it under the jurisdiction of Provost Marshal Patrick.[41]

---

[40] Sears, ***Chancellorsville***, p.68; ***OR*** vol.25, pt.1, p.252.

[41] Faust, ***Encyclopedia***, pp.561, 586; Ryan, Thomas, J., A Battle of Wits: Intelligence Operations during the Gettysburg Campaign, ***GM***, Issue 29, pp.8-9.

In order to maintain the charter of gathering information regarding the enemy and not to imply that the new organization was in charge of counterintelligence, its name was changed shortly after its formation to the Bureau of Military Information. To head the BMI, Patrick and Hooker chose thirty-five year old Colonel George Henry Sharpe of the 120th New York. Patrick recalled the appointment during testimony before the Committee on the Conduct of the War. "I called Colonel Sharpe, commanding a regiment of New York troops, to headquarters, and put him in charge of that bureau as a separate and special bureau." Sharpe was instructed to use all resources available to him to gather and organize intelligence information. His assets would include spies, scouts, cavalry reconnaissance, Southern newspapers, reports of other commanders and information from the Signal Corps. Along with the new position came an appointment to the duties of deputy provost marshal general, made official by the distribution of General Order No.32 on 30 March.[42]

Sharpe was well prepared for intelligence work. He was college educated had received his degree from Rutgers in 1847, graduating when he was only nineteen years old. He was chosen to deliver the salutary address at his commencement ceremony which he presented in Latin. Wishing to further his education, he enrolled at Yale to study law and, when just past the qualification age, took and passed the New York State bar exam in 1849. He was fluent in a number of languages and had traveled abroad, serving with the United States delegations in both Rome and Vienna before setting up his own law practice. When the war began, he left his upstate New York home in Kingston and joined the militia, serving first as a captain in the 20th New York. The 20th was a three month regiment and was mustered out shortly after Bull Run. Sharpe later answered Lincoln's call for an additional 300,000 troops in the summer of 1862 and helped organize the 120th New York, becoming its colonel on 14 July.[43]

General Patrick believed Sharpe was the ideal candidate to head up the BMI. He was of the opinion that Sharpe possessed the proper education and a good head for intelligence work. Sharpe however, was reluctant to accept the position. His ties to the 120th were strong and he cared greatly for the welfare of its men. In fact, his devotion to the men went so deep that, in an army where many officers were manipulative in their efforts to advance their careers, Sharpe turned down brigade command because his beloved 120th would not be a part of his new brigade. Finally, after some prodding, Sharpe accepted the post but his links to his old regiment remained strong, and he continued to follow its progress to make sure the men were looked after.[44]

---

[42] Ryan, A Battle of Wits, **GM**, Issue 29, p.9; ***Report of the Joint Committee on the Conduct of the War*** (hereafter ***CCW***), vol. IV, p.74; ***OR*** vol.25, pt.2, p.167; Fishel, ***Secret War***, p.294.

[43] Ryan, Battle of Wits, **GM**, Issue 29, p.10; Fishel, ***Secret War***, pp.288-289; Phisterer, ***NYWR***, vol.4, p.3411.

[44] Fishel, ***Secret War***, p.290.

Although his ties to the 120th New York were strong, George Henry Sharpe proved to be the right man to head the BMI. *LOC*

To staff his new department Sharp first selected John C. Babcock. Babcock, an architect before the war, had been recruited by McClellan from Pinkerton's organization to utilize his drawing skills as a cartographer for the army. Babcock conducted his own scouting expeditions to gather information about the surrounding countryside for inclusion on his maps. His work was exceptional and McClellan expressed praise for his drawings. On one occasion, a Babcock map was sent to Lincoln by Pinkerton, who seemed to take credit for its construction by naming one of Babcock's assistants as the chief cartographer of the work, which no doubt irritated Babcock. When he joined the BMI he arrived as a civilian having been mustered out of the service near the end of 1862. Sharpe installed him as the organizations second in command, and put him to work as the primary interrogator and assessor of information. Babcock was very adept at reviewing information from a number of sources and extracting pertinent data which he then organized into written reports. The information contained in his reports was of great value to the army. His talents allowed Sharpe to assign to him the task of the BMI's chief report writer.[45]

Sharpe also brought in John McEntee whom he had known before the war through a business relationship. Sharpe wanted McEntee to be responsible for directing his team of scouts and spies as they made their way to and from the field. In addition, McEntee would be required to perform additional interrogation duties, and support Babcock with his report writing tasks. To his team of three

---

[45] Ryan, Battle of Wits, *GM*, Issue 29, p.11; Fishel, *Secret War*, p.153.

administrators, Sharpe added approximately 20 field agents. The agents were carefully selected and Sharpe took care to not bring in so called "experts." His requirements were so strict that a man who had been in Pinkerton's employ and a detective from New York was rejected.[46]

Together the men who made up the new organization would have a profound effect on the events of the Gettysburg campaign. They would be provided with numerous opportunities to demonstrate their worth to Hooker and would do their best not to disappoint their commander. The quality of their information would surpass that of the previous Pinkerton regime. This was due to intelligence being gathered and generated from all sources, while Pinkerton only presented information gathered by his own operatives. The dividends would make themselves clear very quickly and would be essential to the overall execution of the coming summer campaign.[47]

Lincoln Visits the Troops

By early April, Hooker was ready for his commander in chief to pay a visit to the army. An invitation was sent to Washington, which was promptly accepted. A meager party was assembled consisting of Lincoln, his wife, their youngest son Tad, his attorney general, Edward Bates, a friend, Dr. A. G. Henry and a newspaperman with the *Sacramento Union*, Noah Brooks. Brooks, who had developed a long-term friendship with Lincoln, was on assignment for the paper, and had been in Washington for less than four months. The little party set out from the Washington Navy Yard aboard the steamer *Carrie Martin*. Just as the group was departing, it began to snow. In true newsman fashion, Brooks documented the trip. "So thick was the weather, and so difficult the navigation, that we were forced to anchor for the night in a little cove in the Potomac opposite Indian Head." The group waited out the worst of the storm and as the weather began to clear in the morning the steamer continued on. With snow still falling, the president's party put into Aquia Creek on 5 April, Easter Sunday.[48]

The *Carrie Martin* slipped in between the numerous boats and barges anchored at the wharf. A small hamlet, Aquia Creek was nothing more than a group of supply buildings and a waterfront occupied by numerous government vessels. The trains employed to move the huge quantities of material to the army at Fredericksburg were scattered across the nearby rail yard. Lincoln's group was herded into a regular freight car outfitted with a few benches for seating. A number of decorations, including flags, had been hung from the makeshift coach. As the train pulled away cheers were heard from a crowd, which had gathered to get a glimpse of the commander in chief. The country showed the ravages of war. Abandoned and destroyed buildings and tore up fences indicated the hardships of

---

[46] Ryan, Battle of Wits, *GM*, Issue 29, p.11; Fishel, *Secret War*, p.293.

[47] Fishel, *Secret War*, p.298.

[48] Bigelow, *Chancellorsville*, pp.127-128; Sifakis, *Who was Who*, p.76; Noah Brooks, *Washington D. C. in Lincoln's Time*, pp.51-52; Furguson, *Chancellorsville 1863*, p.60.

war the civilian populace had endured. After the short train ride, the president's petite party arrived at Falmouth Station. General Butterfield was there to receive them along with a group of mounted officers numbering around two-hundred. Lincoln, simple man that he was, may have been a bit embarrassed by the fanfare, particularly since his eastern army had not accomplished much during the two previous years of war.[49]

Upon their arrival at army headquarters the president's party was provided with the best accommodations available. "[T]hree large hospital tents," according to Brooks, were "floored, and furnished with camp bedsteads and such rude appliances for nightly occupation as were in reach." After settling in and spending their first night, Lincoln's party began the execution of General Hooker's itinerary. A majestic visit had been planned, with the first day's highlight being a grand review of his reorganized Cavalry Corps. General Stoneman would lead his troopers, 15,000 strong, at a walk, a trot and finally a gallop past the president's party.[50]

Brooks was impressed by the pomp of the scene as the party departed camp to make their way to the reviewing ground.

> "The cavalcade on the way from headquarters to the reviewing-field was a brilliant one. The President, wearing a high hat and riding like a veteran, with General Hooker by his side, headed the flying column; next came several major-generals, a host of brigadiers, staff-officers, and colonels, and lesser functionaries innumerable. The flank of this long train was decorated by the showy uniforms and accoutrements of the 'Philadelphia Lancers,' (6th Pennsylvania Cavalry) who acted as a guard of honor to the President during that visit to the Army of the Potomac."

The melting snow had turned the road into a muddy thoroughfare and as the horses trotted along, mud splattered in all directions and coated those toward the rear with a heavy layer. Brooks noted that "[o]n the skirts of this cloud of cavalry rode the president's little son 'Tad,' in charge of a mounted orderly, his gray cloak flying in the gusty wind like the plume of Henry of Navarre." Due to continuing poor weather, Mrs. Lincoln spent the majority of the proceedings watching from the confines of a six-horse carriage. Captain Charles A. Phillips of Battery E, 5th Massachusetts Artillery described the festivities.[51]

---

[49] Bigelow, *Chancellorsville*, p.128; Brooks, *Washington D. C.*, p.52; Furgurson, *Chancellorsville 1863*, p.60

[50] Bigelow, *Chancellorsville*, p. 128; Brooks, *Washington*, pp. 52-53.

[51] Brooks, *Washington*, p.53. Henry the IV of France

> "The cavalry were drawn up in a hollow square covering considerable ground, in fact, there was no one spot from which you could see them all.
>
> An American flag in the centre of the square marked the position of the reviewing officer, and thither we rode and soon found ourselves in a crowd of mounted officers of all grades, from general to lieutenants; major-generals were quite plenty, in fact, I do not think I ever saw so many before, and there were brigadiers without number.
>
> A guard was placed to keep a place clear for the reviewing officer, and they paid no regard to brigadiers, keeping them back with the rest.
>
> General Stoneman was quite conspicuous, wearing his sash across the shoulder 'Officer of the Day' style.
>
> A little after twelve the President arrived, announced by a salute of 21 guns, fired on poor style by the horse battery. General Hooker rode alongside of him, General Butterfield just behind, and then a numerous, nameless staff, and an escort of Rush's Lancers.
>
> Then the President, accompanied by Hooker and Stoneman, started off to review, and immense cavalcade clattered after them. Although they rode along the lines at a slow gallop, the process occupied an hour or two.
>
> By and by the President returned to his station, and the troops commenced to pass in review. This was a rather tedious process, but we sat it through. The 1st Mass. looked very well. After the Cavalry came the batteries of Horse Artillery attached to Stoneman's command, and they passed a second time at a trot.[52]

The festivities concluded when the 6th Pennsylvania "wheeled into line at a trot in front of the President," Phillips noted. Phillips also recognized a number of the generals accompanying the president, including Howard, Meade and one of Howard's division commanders, Carl Schurz. That evening a large dinner party was held to honor the chief executive's visit. All the corps commanders were invited to attend, including George Meade, who wrote of the occasion to his wife three days later. "I was invited on this day (Monday) to dine with General Hooker, to meet the President and Mrs. Lincoln. We had a very handsome and pleasant dinner," he told Margaretta.[53]

The visit's second day was to be spent in the attendance of a grand infantry review but the weather was so poor the day was instead spent touring encampments. The visitors made themselves present at a number of divisional camps and cheers

---

[52] Cowles, Luther, Editor, **History of the Fifth Massachusetts Battery**, pp.568-569.

[53] *Ibid*, p.596; Meade, **Meade**, vol.1, p.363; Brooks, **Washington**, pp. 52-53.

along with hearty handshakes had a deep effect on the commander in chief. Thousands of common men gathered around in an effort to hear their leader speak or to simply touch him or his horse as he rode by. "God bless you," was the most common phrase of the day. Meade noted that "the President did me the honor to visit my camps and inspect them, and I believe (leaving out the fatigue) passed a very pleasant day." The weather finally improved and on the last day of the visit the grand review of the army was held. The Second, Third, Fifth, and Sixth Corps participated in the extravaganza. It totaled 60,000 men, and was less than half of the army's strength. Lincoln watched the review dressed in his typical black, mounted upon a black horse. His height allowed his feet to dangle nearer the ground than any other reviewer.[54]

During the visit, newsman Brooks noted some aspects of General Hooker's demeanor that brought him apprehension. According to the writer, Hooker seemed to be very relaxed in his attitude toward his opponent. Comments like "When I get to Richmond," did not set well with Brooks, nor did they instill any positive feelings within the president. During the party's stay Hooker commented to Lincoln, "I have under my command the finest army on the planet." The general's attitude led the president to comment to Brooks, it "seems to me that he is overconfident." During another exchange, Lincoln remarked, "[i]f you get to Richmond," to which Hooker responded, "Excuse me, Mr. President, but there is no 'if' in the case. I am going straight to Richmond if I live." Others noticed Hooker's carefree attitude as well. An Ohio soldier from the Eleventh Corps observed the stark contrast between the leader of the country and the leader of the army. Lincoln "was kindly, yet firm and serious, even sad" while Hooker "beamed of satisfaction and pride."[55]

"My plans are perfect"

By late April, Hooker was ready to move his revitalized army. "My plans are perfect," quipped the general. "...[M]ay God have mercy on General Lee, for I will have none." The plan was broad in scope. Utilizing his superior numbers, Hooker decided to divide his army sending the right wing northwest up the Rappahannock River. This force consisted of the Fifth, Eleventh and Twelfth Corps. Once opposite Kelly's Ford, Hooker's right wing would cross to the south side of the river, move southeast, cross the Rapidan, and uncover United States and Banks' Ford. Once the lower fords were clear elements of Couch's Second Corps would cross to support the movement. Finally, if unhindered, the force would take a position in Lee's rear near Chancellorsville. The total strength of the column would be near 60,000 men, equaling the number of men contained in Lee's entire army.

The second component of Hooker's plan included the First, Third and Sixth Corps along with the remaining elements of the Second Corps. The left wing would demonstrate and cross the Rappahannock south of Fredericksburg. This

---

[54] Bigelow, *Chancellorsville*, pp. 128-129; Byrne, & Weaver, Editors, *Haskell of Gettysburg*, pp.57-58; Meade, *Meade*, vol.1, p.363.

[55] Bigelow, *Chancellorsville*, p.130; Furguson, *Chancellorsville 1863*, p.62; Sears, *Chancellorsville*, p.116.

holding force would work in conjunction with the turning movement to present a choice to Lee. Would the Confederate general stay and confront the holding force or would he turn and meet the flanking force to his rear? Either way, Hooker believed he could do significant damage to Lee. If Lee turned to meet the force at Chancellorsville, the Union troops south of Fredericksburg would cross and pursue the Southerners. If Lee remained arrayed against the holding force, the troops to his rear would close. Whatever choice Lee made, Hooker believed he would have the Confederates in a vice.[56]

The final element of Hooker's plan involved General Stoneman's mounted force. As the movement commenced, Stoneman would take all but one brigade of his Cavalry Corps "for the purpose of turning the enemy's position on his left, and of throwing your command between him and Richmond." The riders were to pass to the rear of the Confederates, disrupting communications and supply lines in an effort to divide Lee from his support structure. A second task assigned to Stoneman would be to confront Lee's army if it withdrew toward Richmond. Hooker instructed Stoneman to "keep them from Richmond." On 11 April, the commanding general wrote to Lincoln explaining how he was planning to utilize his Cavalry Corps. "I hope that when the cavalry have established themselves on the line between him [Lee] and Richmond," he wrote, "they will be able to hold him and check his retreat until I can fall on his rear."[57]

At first glance, the battle plan showed promise. As with all battle plans however, it required execution, time and a predictable opponent to be successful. The first two elements had succeeded in damaging hundreds of battle plans over the history of warfare. The third had destroyed them, and Lee was anything but predictable. In addition, there were a number of suspect elements of the plan. How the commanding general proposed a cavalry force of 10,000 mounted men keep the Army or Northern Virginia, 60,000 strong, from going wherever it wanted was not communicated to Stoneman. It would be conceivable for the Union horsemen to harass Lee, but in order to halt a marching column, they would have to engage it. Lee could simply deploy a division in line of battle and hold the dismounted trooper while the remainder of the army marched on, bypassing the clash. Along the same thought process, how was Stoneman to keep Lee from marching to Richmond if he chose to do so? Hooker seemed to forget that Lee possessed a very fine and capable cavalry arm as well. Infantry movements would be screened by Stuart's troops, a function which the Union commanders had yet to fully utilize. Stuart would simply engage Stoneman before the Federal cavalryman could get close enough to engage the main body of Lee's army.[58]

The second issue with Hooker's battle plan was its reliance on a "strong demonstration" by Sedgwick's force along the river south of Fredericksburg. Intending to keep Lee guessing, this attack was to prevent the Confederate

---

[56] Sears, *Chancellorsville*, p.120; Stackpole, *Chancellorsville*, pp.95-96.

[57] Bigelow, *Chancellorsville*, pp.142-144; *OR* vol.25, pt. 2, pp. 199.

[58] Bigelow, *Chancellorsville*, p.144

commander from correctly concluding where the main effort was focused. Hooker hoped Lee would continue to guess while he moved his forces into position to strike. Lesser generals may have been fooled, but a general with the intellect of Lee was not so easily persuaded. Perhaps if Hooker had launched a full-scale attack along the river Lee would have been captivated more easily. To be of the opinion Lee would sit tight along the river facing Sedgwick while three Federal Corps crossed the Rappahannock and Rapidan Rivers in an effort to turn his left was at best wishful thinking.[59]

The final flaw with Hooker's plan was the assumption that Lee, after finally realizing the intention of his enemy, would pull up his roots along the river and withdraw back toward Richmond. Here Hooker's overconfidence failed him. Instead of learning from the trials of his predecessors, he continued to believe he already knew the solutions. Hooker should have known that Lee would not fall back when threatened. In September of the previous year Lee, badly outnumbered, and with his force divided, hunkered down along Antietam Creek in Maryland and fought McClellan's numerically superior army to a standstill. Hooker, who had commanded the First Corps during the battle, should have known or at least anticipated that Lee would not run if cornered. He should also have known based on the fight outside Sharpsburg, that cornered Rebels fought like rabid dogs.[60]

Even with its faults, Hooker's plan was simple and daring at its core. With all the pieces in place, he issued marching orders to the elements of his right wing on the evening of 26 April. The Fifth, Eleventh and Twelfth Corps would move in the early morning hours of the following day. Two divisions of the Second Corps would take position near Banks' and United States Ford in an effort to impress upon the Confederates that he was trying to cross closer to Fredericksburg. By midnight on the 29th they would be in place to cross the Rapidan and take position behind Lee's force. Part of the plan, which did not go as Hooker had intended, was the cautious Stoneman being fourteen hours late. His cavalry was to proceed across the river in front of the infantry. By the time the horsemen arrived at Kelly's Ford, Howard's Eleventh Corps was already across, the Twelfth Corps was on the pontoon bridge and Meade's men were waiting their turn. Stoneman was forced to wait until all the infantry was across before he could begin his sweep to Lee's rear, putting him even further behind schedule.[61]

Using the cover of the early morning fog, engineers managed to lay four pontoon bridges across the river south of Fredericksburg at Franklin's Crossing. Two additional bridges had been erected at Fitzhugh's Crossing further south. The Federal left wing would be in position to utilize these bridges during the early morning hours of the 29th. Negotiating the river at Fitzhugh's Crossing would be the First Corps. The Sixth Corps would cross further up river at Franklin's Crossing. The Third Corps would be held in reserve. With the supply trains and

---

[59] Stackpole, Edward J., *Chancellorsville*, p.93.

[60] *Ibid*, p.94.

[61] Stackpole, Edward J., *Chancellorsville*, pp.117-123; Bigelow, *Chancellorsville*, pp.173-174.

ambulances bringing up the rear, Sedgwick and Reynolds moved their troops into position and began the advance, feeling little or no resistance. Sedgwick's task was simple. He needed to demonstrate along the river with his entire force to hold Lee's attention. If this was not successful, and Lee turned his attention to the right wing at Chancellorsville, Sedgwick was to attack. His goal would be the Confederate works above the river and the Telegraph Road, the loss of which would eliminate a route Lee could use to withdraw toward Richmond.[62]

As the left wing began its crossing, Hooker's vice began to pinch. His army now in position, all he needed was aggressive action to give Robert E. Lee the whipping the Federal commander felt he richly deserved. On 30 April, Hooker issued a general order congratulating his army on its "splendid achievement." "[T]he operations of the last three days have determined that our enemy must either ingloriously fly, or come out from behind his defenses and give us battle on our own ground, where certain destruction awaits him." Unlike Burnside, confidence was not something Hooker lacked, in fact it could be said he was incredibly arrogant. Just as his grandiose plans for the destruction of Lee seemed to be coming to fruition, something happened which changed the entire campaign; Lee divided his outnumbered army and marched to meet Hooker. When it became obvious Lee was not "ingloriously fly[ing]" Hooker paused, giving Lee the opportunity to pounce.[63]

Over the next few hours, many messages were transmitted between army headquarters, Fredericksburg and the Federal left wing south of town. During the flood of communication, Sedgwick received a confusing dispatch from Dan Butterfield.

> "The maneuvers now in progress, the general hopes, will compel the enemy to fight him on his, Hooker's, own ground. He has no desire to make the general engagement where you are, in front of Brooks or Wadsworth."

Previously Sedgwick had been instructed to provide a serious demonstration to hold the Rebels on the river. Now it seemed as though his commander desired to fight a defensive battle on his front at Chancellorsville. There were signs that a portion of Lee's army was moving west. Should Sedgwick now let Lee depart without harassment, contrary to his prior instruction? Had the commanding general changed the strategy of the campaign in mid execution? After all the choreography, was Hooker losing his nerve for offensive maneuvers? Did he believe that Lee would see his predicament, decide his position was untenable, and retire toward Richmond? If so, lessons from the failures of previous commanders had not been learned. At the most critical juncture of the campaign Hooker, for some reason, seemed to lose his nerve.[64]

---

[62] Stackpole, Edward J., ***Chancellorsville***, pp.126-127; Bigelow, ***Chancellorsville***, p.178.

[63] ***OR*** vol.25, pt.1, p.171.

[64] ***OR*** 25, pt. 2, p.292; Bigelow, ***Chancellorsville***, p.212.

Even as the movement stalled, it was apparent that Hooker had managed to accomplish something which his predecessors had failed to achive. His march upriver had gone undetected by Lee and his scouts. The turning movement had placed the Federal army in a position to crush the Army of Northern Virginia between the two elements of Hooker's force, Sedgwick's on the river, and the main body at Chancellorsville. Hooker's pause however, provided Lee two things. First, it allowed him time to counter Hooker's moves, and second, it passed the initiative to him, something Lee would not give back easily and then only after three days of bloodletting at Gettysburg. Robert E. Lee however, would need a miracle if his 60,000 men were going to be successful against Hooker's 120,000. Fortunately for Lee, Stonewall Jackson delivering the blow required to send the Federal's reeling which began the task of forcing the enemy back across the river and giving General Lee arguably his greatest victory. Jackson paid for delivering the triumph with his life, a life which was debatably more valuable to the Confederacy than the individual victory.

To add insult to injury, Hooker received a report from Secretary of War Stanton on 7 May that Stoneman's horsemen had cause significant problems in Richmond. "Richmond papers of Tuesday received at this Department are full of accounts of the panic and destruction accomplished by Stoneman," Stanton wrote. Unfortunately, Hooker had not received the same information and the Richmond papers greatly exaggerated Stoneman's effectiveness. "From the most reliable information I have been able to gather," Hooker wrote back three days later, "railroad communication between Fredericksburg and Richmond, by the direct route, was interrupted but for one day. The bridges of importance appear to have remained untouched. With the exception of Kilpatrick's operation, the raid does not appear to have amounted to much." Other than Hugh Judson Kilpatrick's brigade reaching the outskirts of Richmond and creating the panic which prompted the newspaper accounts, Stoneman's raid had been an abysmal, although not complete failure. The New Yorker would have some explaining to do when he returned to the safety of the Federal lines.[65]

Shortly after the battle, Hooker issued another general order which was an obvious attempt to bolster the army's morale, which was again sagging. "The major-general commanding tenders to this army his *congratulations* (emphasis added) on its achievements of the last seven days." Many may have wondered what Fighting Joe was referring to since they had just been soundly thrashed by an army half their number. "The events of the last week may swell with pride the heart of every officer and soldier of this army." The communication was an obvious attempt to put a positive spin on the disastrous outcome and keep the spirits of the army from falling too far. Most of the fighting men however, were not as proud as Hooker envisioned them to be. General John Gibbon noted after the battle that Hooker had lost the confidence of the men. Gibbon argued that the men would fight for a general they did not respect if they felt the man was going to lead them

---

[65]   *OR* vol.25, pt.1, pp.1083-1084, pt.2, pp.463, 439.

to victory. Before Chancellorsville, the men felt Hooker was that man. After the battle they were not so sure.[66]

Line soldiers weren't the only individuals disgruntled by the Federal defeat. Second Corps commander Darius Couch, who had never warmed to Joe Hooker, may have been the most irritated man in the army. Within a few days of the battle he took a leave of absence and traveled to Washington in order to deal with some physical problems. While in the capital he met at least two times and possibly more with the president. Couch expressed to Lincoln his disgust with Hooker, questioned his integrity as a soldier and his abilities as a leader of men. He went on to complain that Hooker had shown great incompetence and deserved to be sacked. Although blunt and direct, Couch argued that his attitude was necessary to instill in Lincoln the shear ineptness of Hooker and the intense hazard he was to the welfare of the army. Lincoln must have been stung a bit since he had personally placed Hooker in command although he was well aware of the general's shortcomings. When Couch was finished with his verbal assassination, Lincoln did something Couch did not expect. The president asked the general if he would be a good choice to replace Hooker. "[W]hat about you?" Lincoln candidly questioned. Couch, now with the tables turned resisted, arguing that he was not in the physical shape required and lacked the energy needed to effectively execute the tasks of an army commander. Couch's hesitation seems puzzling since he was arguably an effective corps commander which required many of the same abilities as army command. However, Couch had seen the constant meddling from Washington and how it affected the operations of the army and wanted no part of it. Either way, he had too much respect for Lincoln and was not about to subject the president to further anxiety by accepting an appointment to a position which he felt he would not able to satisfactorily fill. Although he personally felt he was not fit for command of the army, Couch did suggest to Lincoln that General Meade was the best available officer for the post. Although senior to Meade, Couch informed Lincoln that he would have no issues with serving under Meade if Lincoln chose to remove Hooker and install the Pennsylvanian.[67]

When word of Couch's meetings with Lincoln filtered back to army headquarters, Hooker was livid. Shortly thereafter, Stanton wired him regarding the possibility of assigning Couch to a position outside the Army of the Potomac. Hooker quickly responded, sarcastically replying "I can spare General Couch." Finally, after spending three weeks in the capital, Couch, determining that he could not return to his command and face Hooker's wrath, requested a transfer. His request would be honored and General Couch would soon be on his way to a new command far away from his adversary at the head of the Army of the Potomac. Unfortunately, Couch's new command would not be distant enough to keep him out of the path of Lee's army.[68]

---

[66] *OR* vol.25, pt.1, p.171; Gibbon, John, ***Personal Recollections of the Civil War***, p.122.

[67] Gambone, A. M., ***Major-General Darius Nash Couch: Enigmatic Valor***, p.137.

[68] *OR* vol.27, pt. 3, pp.54-55; Gambone, ***Enigmatic Valor***, p.138.

The Perfect Soldier

To replace Couch at the head of the Second Corps, Hooker selected Winfield Scott Hancock a man who through hard work and ability would become one of the most beloved and respected Civil War generals. Hancock was born 14 February 1824 in Montgomery Square, a small settlement three miles east of Lansdale, Pennsylvania, and a short horse ride northeast of Philadelphia. Winfield, named after the famous general, and his twin brother Hilary's early childhood was filled with family relocations. The boy's father, Benjamin moved his clan to a new, nearby house and began teaching school. Two years later the elder Hancock moved his family again, to nearby Norristown, and took another teaching job at a local school. Evidently teaching was not profitable enough to provide the level of security Benjamin desired for his family. In an effort to become a lawyer, he began reading law at a local office. His wife Elizabeth, in order to make ends meet, opened a milliner's shop within the family's home.

In 1828 Ben passed the bar and began working as a lawyer, but he struggled to gain a foothold in the profession. A devoted Baptist and deacon at a local church, he dabbled in local politics and was elected the town burgess in 1841. A lifelong Democrat, he believed in the concepts of limited Federal government and the rights of sovereign states. Ben instilled all these beliefs into his sons and Winfield took them to heart. Years later the general observed that his father was a great influence on his life and noted that there was no one he "respected" more. The family remained in Norristown and the boys, including a third brother John, who was born six years later, matured to young men.

Hilary and Winfield attended the Norristown Academy until Pennsylvania instituted a free school system, at which time their father removed them and enrolled them in a public school. To make sure he had a say in his boy's education, Benjamin served on the Norristown School Board, retaining the post for thirty years. On Sundays the boys attended services at the Baptist Church. Winfield remembered undisciplined boys sitting on a fence outside the church while he made his way to Sunday morning services. The upbringing his parents provided instilled in him maturity and respect for others, making Winfield one of the most admired and finest young men in Norristown.

It is said that Benjamin Hancock was reluctant to send Winfield to West Point because of his devout Christian beliefs. After being reassured by his pastor, Benjamin wrote to his local congressmen and submitted his son for admittance. Finally, on 31 March 1840, at the age of sixteen, Winfield S. Hancock wrote his acceptance letter. The simple act of writing the letter began a career that would earn him the admiration and respect of the entire nation, including the men he fought with and those he fought against. The military would become his profession and he would continue in it until the day he died.[69]

Arriving at West Point in June, at the end of the month Hancock took the first great test of his training; he managed to pass the entrance exam and became a

---

[69] Jordan, David M., ***Winfield Scott Hancock: A Soldier's Life***, pp.5-7; Eicher, & Eicher, ***High Commands***, p.277.

cadet on 1 July. Along with the remaining successful candidates, he marched off to the standard summer encampment attended by all new recruits. Fifty-four cadets participated in the encampment that year. Of those, only twenty five would finally graduate four years later. Only five would serve the Union cause during the Civil War while three would serve with the Confederacy. The class of 1844 was one of the least distinguished groups to graduate from the institution. The shining star of the class would prove to be Winfield Hancock. He graduated eighteenth in standing and was brevetted a second lieutenant. Unfortunately the size of the peacetime military was so limited that there were not enough commissions available and Hancock had to wait two years for his. In the meantime, he was assigned to the 6th Infantry Regiment.[70]

The uninspiring nature of his class and his pedestrian academic performance did not raise eyebrows and great things were not expected from him as he began his career. Initially he was assigned to duty at Fort Towson along the Red River before being transferred to Fort Washita in order to keep the local Indians in check. When the Mexican War began, Hancock struggled to obtain a transfer to the scene of the fighting. Finally on 13 July 1847, Hancock arrived in Vera Cruz; however, General Scott's army was already at Pueblo. The next day, his regiment marched inland with 2,500 reinforcements to join the general's army. On 6 August he arrived with the 6th Regiment at Scott's encampment. The next day Winfield marching from Pueblo toward the interior of Mexico.

During August and September, Hancock felt the excitement of battle for the first time. He performed well and did nothing to dampen the opinions of his contemporaries that he was a capable young officer. Hancock also learned that he enjoyed the sting of a good fight. He was brevetted a first lieutenant "for gallant and meritorious conduct" during the Battle of Churubusco. Unfortunately, he suffered from an illness which restricted him to his tent during the final push upon the fortress of Chapultepec. The sounds of the battle brought out the fighter in him, and struggling from his bed, he encased himself in a blanket and managed to negotiate his way to the roof of a nearby house. There he watched with pride as the Americans stormed the walls of the castle. Suddenly, as the Mexican's were pushed back, he watched the regimental colors of his beloved 6th Infantry raised over the works. His heart swelled with satisfaction at the sight.[71]

As the fighting ended many of the solders settled down for a term of garrison duty. During this period Hancock formed many friendships which would last for the remainder of his life. He became close to First Lieutenant Edward Johnson, his West Point classmate Simon Bolivar Buckner, and two other Virginians, Henry "Harry" Heth and Lewis A. Armistead. Heth, Hancock and Armistead became inseparable. Heth enjoyed tagging along with Hancock because he seemed to get an inordinate amount of attention from the Mexican senioritas. While Hancock became good friends with Heth, he and Armistead formed a brotherly bond

---

[70] Jordan, *A Soldier's Life*, pp. 8-9, 11; Boatner, **Dictionary**, p.372.

[71] Jordan, *A Soldiers Life*, pp.14-17.

that retained its affection throughout the Civil War until they were separated by Armistead's death.

Eventually, Hancock and the 6th Infantry left Mexico and its pretty girls behind bound for New Orleans. During the period immediately after the war, Heth and Hancock found themselves in St Louis, where they spent a great deal of time together. The coming weeks would see many of the old regiments broken apart and scattered throughout the western frontier on garrison duty. While preparing to depart St. Louis, Heth came up with the idea of take the regimental band into town to serenade the local ladies. Hancock went along and while in town they were informed that the "most beautiful girl in the west" had just returned after spending the summer in the east. The band marched to the young lady's home and played a tune. A white glove fluttered from a cracked shutter. Heth picked it up and handed it to his friend. The young lady from the east, and the owner of the glove was Almira Russell. Unfortunately, there was no time to get to know Almira for Hancock and the 6th Infantry were setting out for Fort Crawford in Wisconsin.

While at Fort Crawford, Heth began suffering from a reoccurrence of the dysentery he had contracted in Mexico. The doctors did not expect him to survive and agreed to send him home to be with his family when the end came. Hancock asked to accompany his friend and was granted permission to do so. As the two traveled to Cincinnati, Heth's health began to improve but by the time they reached Cleveland, he was near death again. Hancock vigilantly cared for his friend and nursed Heth back to health, and Henry gave his friend credit for saving his life. Finally, the two arrived in Washington and with Heth doing much better, the Virginian traveled on to Richmond by himself while Hancock returned to Fort Crawford.[72]

A few months later the regiment's headquarters returned to St. Louis and Hancock was in a position to make his acquaintance with the lovely Almira. One account of their first meeting notes that Hancock would make it a point to ride past the young lady's home each morning just to get a glimpse of the beauty. One morning as he rode by he noticed Almira and her father pulling away in a carriage. Mustering his courage, he followed them to their destination which happened to be the home of an acquaintance of Hancock's. Shamelessly he entered and demanded that his friend introduce him to the lovely young lady. The elder Russell must have been impressed with Hancock's manner for the result of the meeting was an invitation to visit the Russell home. It did not take Winfield long to realize that Almira would be a prize if he could sufficiently impress her. He began courting her and Hancock was pleased that she returned his affection. The relationship grew and Winfield soon asked for her hand. Almira and her family agreed and the two were married on 24 January 1850 at her father's house in St. Louis during the violence of an out of season lightning storm. The union would bring two children, a son, Russell, and later a daughter Ada. Both children would precede their parents in death.[73]

---

[72] *Ibid*, pp.20-21.

[73] Hancock, Almira Russell, ***Reminiscences Of Winfield Scott Hancock***, pp.1-3, 34; Gambone, A. M., ***Hancock at Gettysburg and Beyond***, p.viii.

Over the next few years Hancock would fight in Florida during the Second Seminole War against Chief Billy Bowlegs. After dealing with the uprisings, Hancock was ordered to Fort Leavenworth, Kansas. General William S. Harney had been ordered to assist in squelching the trouble brewing between abolitionists and proslavery groups. Harney specifically requested Hancock's presence in Kansas and Winfield was more than happy to leave behind his previous assignment in Florida. He went to work in the quartermaster department, spending nine months in the caldron of bitterness the slavery argument brought to the region.[74]

Early in the spring of 1858, a decision was made to send General Harney and a party of men to support General Albert S. Johnston's expedition to Utah. Out west the Mormons, led by Brigham Young, had began to cause problems. The Buchanan Administration had handled the installation of new governor Alfred Cummings poorly, and the Mormons had refused to acknowledge his authority as territorial governor. Buchanan dispatched Harney to assist Johnston on 31 March, 1858, the latter having been forced by the lateness of the season and bad weather to establish winter quarters at Fort Bridger. Hancock was ordered to join the expedition. His duties in the quartermaster's department required him to organize and outfit the group. Displaying his executive skills, Hancock assembled a rather large train for the journey. It consisted of 128 wagons and over 1,000 mules. The assignment however, would separate him from his wife and children, a prospect which saddened him.

The expedition entered Salt Lake City on 26 June and upon his arrival Hancock learned he would be away from Almira even longer. New orders were issued requiring him to travel to Fort Bridger northeast of Salt Lake. Once there, he found his beloved 6th Infantry waiting along with orders for the regiment to march to California. Again, Hancock went to work organizing the expedition, but this time the task was more difficult. Many of the animals available were malnourished and in poor condition. In addition, many of the wagons were broken down and in such a state of disrepair that they could not be utilized without being refurbished. In a testament to his determination, Hancock managed to gather together enough supplies, suitable draft animals and wagons to get the expedition underway and on 21 August the caravan departed. The lateness of the season was an ominous sign and before the expedition arrived at its destination, Benicia, California, it would have to brave early season snows in the Sierra Nevada Mountains and ruffians in the Carson River Valley. The 1,119 mile journey ended on 15 November.[75]

Upon his arrival in California, Hancock immediately applied for leave in order to return east and bring his family to the west coast. Almira traveled to Washington and met her husband. For a few days the couple rubbed elbows with a number of Washington elites. Colonel and Mrs. Joe Johnston, Harriet Lane, Mrs. Jefferson Davis and her Senator husband were among the dignitaries

---

[74] *Ibid*, pp.32-36; Jordan, *A Soldier's Life*, p.25.

[75] Hancock, **Reminiscences**, pp.39-40; Jordan, *A Soldier's Life*, p.26.

which Winfield and Almira associated with that winter. One man Mrs. Hancock remembered vividly was a colonel from Virginia named Robert Lee. Lee somehow became aware Almira was contemplating remaining behind with the children when Winfield's leave expired. Perhaps speaking from lessons learned from many years of being separated from his wife, Lee provided Almira insight on the secrets to the success of a military family. "I understand that you contemplate deserting your post," Lee began, "which is by your husband's side, and that you are not going to California with him. If you will pardon me," he continued, "I should like to give you a little advice. You must not think of doing this. As one considerably older than Hancock, and having greater experience, I consider it fatal to the future happiness of young married people, upon small provocation, to live apart, either for a short or long time. The result is invariably that they cease to be essential to each other. Now promise me that you will not permit him to sail without you." On 4 April 1859 Winfield Hancock sailed from New York bound for California. His wife and children went with him.[76]

The journey to the west coast was anything but comfortable. The steamer which the Hancock's booked passage on was overcrowded with little room for any privacy. After reaching Panama, the party began the transit of the isthmus under a blanket of peril. It was reported that an earlier party had been ambushed and slaughtered by local indigenous persons. To make matters worse the group was detained near the Chagres River for fourteen hours without water. After surviving the trek, a second ship was boarded which was as crowded as the first. During the voyage a large number of steerage passengers roamed the ship freely. Many were hooligans and on one occasion Hancock discovered a group pestering his eight-year-old son. Winfield gathered up his son, and ran the crowd off with nothing but his fists telling them if they bothered his son again, he would kill them all. Finally, after what must have seemed like the longest month and a half of his life, Hancock and his family arrived in San Francisco only to find orders transferring him to Los Angeles. Boarding a third ship, the steamer *Senator*, the short trip back down the coast proceeded an eighteen mile coach ride before the Hancock family finally arrived at Winfield Hancock's assigned post.

Hancock time in California was filled with concern for his family and his country. During the trip, Almira became ill with stress and fatigue and his young daughter Ada became sick and feverish. The child was not expected to survive, but after a six week battle, the little girl began to improve and slowly worked her way out of danger. Settled into his duties with the quartermaster's office, it was not long before Hancock received word from the east telling of storm clouds on the horizon. After Lincoln's election and the first wave of secession rolled through the South, the clouds darkened. Finally, on 24 April 1861 word of the firing on Fort Sumter arrived by Pony Express. Signs of upheaval were prevalent throughout the department, including the arrival of

---

[76] Hancock, **Reminiscences**, pp.45-47; Jordan, *A Soldier's Life*, p.27.

General Edwin Sumner with instructions to replace Albert S. Johnston. Sumner was sent under a cloak of secrecy in order to avoid the same situation which had developed in Texas when General Twiggs surrendered the government property there. Johnston, who had been in command of the troops in California, handed in his resignation when his home state of Texas seceded. Hancock, for his part, immediately requested a transfer east when word of the attack on Fort Sumter reached the west coast.[77]

Finally, the day came that all junior officers at the post had been dreading. The Southern men would depart to take up the cause of their brethren. Parting was difficult and sadness filled the outpost. Friendships were torn apart as songs were sung and those present shared what would be for some their last words to each other. Particularly emotional was Hancock's dear friend Lewis Armistead. With tears running down his cheeks, he put both hands on Hancock's shoulders and looked his friend straight in the eye. "Hancock," he said, "good-bye; you can never know what this has cost me, and I hope God will strike me dead if I am ever induced to leave my native soil, should worse come to worst." Turning to Almira, he handed her a satchel and instructed her that if he should be killed, she was free to open it. She also received from Armistead a prayer book in which the Virginian had written "Lewis A. Armistead. Trust in God and fear nothing." He tried to give Hancock his shiny new major's uniform, having no need for it, but Winfield refused to take it.[78]

Returning by the same course he traveled two years earlier, Hancock and his family arrived in Washington but his stay there was rather short. His previous work with the quartermaster's department precipitated an assignment which he neither wanted nor felt was the best use of his abilities. The posting was to a staff position serving General Robert Anderson at Louisville, Kentucky. Winfield Hancock was a solder and he knew it. He had proven his ability to lead men in Mexico and when it was time for a fight he was an officer who led men from the front. Between the wars he had used the time to educate himself on the soldier's trade. He had a good teacher in General Harney and Hancock had paid close attention to how the general ran his command. He read accounts of campaigns conducted by the great European commanders. He learned battles were won and lost by the slimiest of margins and usually because commanders failed to have their men in the right position at the right time. He deserved a field command of some kind instead of a staff position in faraway Kentucky.

---

[77] Hancock, *Reminiscences*, pp.47-54, 65-67; Jordan, *A Soldier's Life*, pp.27-28, 33.

[78] Hancock, *Reminiscences*, pp.69-70. There is little doubt that Hancock and Armistead were close friends. The extent of the friendship however seems to have been exaggerated by a number of written accounts and Hollywood. The romance of an almost brotherly bond between the two seems to be a bit farfetched. While the concept of close friends being torn apart plays to the "brother against brother" aspect of the war, it is more likely the two were simply good friends forced apart by events beyond their control.

Although he never attaining an independent command, Winfield Scott Hancock was possibly the best corps commander of the Civil War. *LOC*

As luck would have it, George McClellan had just arrived in Washington. With the task of building an army out of the rabble defeated at Bull Run planted squarely on his back, McClellan began to scour the army for competent officers. After learning Hancock was in the capital, and remembering his worth in Mexico, McClellan quickly went to work. It would be a shame to send such an excellent soldier to obscurity in Kentucky. Instructing Hancock to keep a low profile at the Willard Hotel, McClellan went about organizing a brigade for Hancock to command. During his first night at the hotel, Hancock was paid a visit by McClellan and the two had a lengthy discussion which lasted for several hours. Finally, on 23 September 1861, Hancock was promoted from captain to brigadier general, skipping two full ranks. Armistead's major uniform would have gone unused if it had been accepted. The promotion was not received well with a number of other officers, but McClellan knew Hancock's quality and did not want to lose his abilities because of bickering generals. Hancock accepted command of the brigade which was part of General William F. Smith's division. Smith, who graduated from West Point a year after Hancock, quickly came to know his new brigade commander's value.[79]

Hancock's first battle experience of the war came on the Virginia Peninsula. At Williamsburg he led his brigade in a flanking movement which Longstreet counterattacked with Jubal Early's brigade. Longstreet intended to drive Hancock from his position, but a counterattack against Early's men, which included the execution a bayonet charge, drove the Rebels from the field. With his flank

---

[79] Jordan, *A Soldier's Life*, pp.35-36; Gambone, **Gettysburg and Beyond**, p.xiii.

exposed, Longstreet was forced to abandon his position and leave the field and Williamsburg to the Federals. Hancock had proven McClellan's confidence had not been misplaced. Describing his performance at Williamsburg, McClellan used the word "superb."[80]

During the Battle of Antietam, General Israel Richardson, commanding a division of the Second Corps was hit in the side by a shell fragment. The wound was serious and he was carried from the field to McClellan's headquarters. After receiving personal direction from McClellan, Hancock took command of Richardson's division. When he arrived on the scene, Hancock found the division fighting in the Federal center toe to toe against D. H. Hill's Confederates near the Piper House along the battlefield's infamous Sunken Road. After assessing the situation, Hancock ordered the division to hold its ground while he quickly began shifting commands from point to point to shore up his defensive line. The fighting was vicious, and by the end of the day neither side had succeeded in driving the other from the field. Hancock had handled the division well and for his efforts he was rewarded with its command and a promotion to major general on 29 November 1862.[81]

The day after the battle Hancock displayed his respect for the fallen soldiers of both armies. The ground between the opposing lines was littered with Union and Confederate casualties. Many of the pickets from both sides had struck up temporary truces for the purpose of collecting the bodies of the dead and assisting the wounded. The truce however, soon turned into a plundering session when the pickets began pilfering from the dead. Men from both armies wandered around no man's land rummaging through the pockets of the fallen looking for anything that could be of used or removing articles of clothing or shoes which were superior to their own. As soon as he became aware of the pillaging, Hancock put a stop to it and blamed his own men for initiating the outrageous behavior. He then sent a message through the lines to the Confederates to establish control over the state of affairs. Writing in his after action report, Hancock explained his intent. "[Brigadier] General [Roger A.] Pryor was notified that as nearly all the wounded between the lines belonged to the enemy, any communication having for its objective their collection must proceed from them, expressing a desire, however, that the wounded, who had been lying on the ground for thirty hours, might be removed." Hancock then mounted his horse and, drawing his pistol, personally rode the lines, intent on shooting anyone, Confederate or Union, who saw fit to plunder the dead. No one from either side was going to disrespect the fallen soldiers of either army, at least not while Winfield Hancock was in command.[82]

At Fredericksburg Hancock's men were ordered to participate in the ill-conceived assault upon Marye's Heights. The brigades advanced in line of battle, one positioned behind the other. The fire was incredible and Hancock's men

---

[80] *OR* vol.11, pt.1, pp.535-539.

[81] *OR* vol.19, pt.1, pp.279-280; Boatner, ***Dictionary***, p.372.

[82] *Ibid*, p.280; Murfin, James V., ***The Gleam of Bayonets***, p.297.

suffered terribly. Leading his men toward the heights through what seemed to be a sheet of lead, Hancock was hit by a single bullet that went through his coat and grazed his abdomen. Fortune smiled on him for it was the only wound he received that day as his men fell by the score. According to Hancock, his men managed to advance further than any other that day but little consolation could be taken in regard to that fact. Official returns showed his command decimated. His division lost more than 2,000 killed, wounded or missing from the 5,000 who went into action.[83]

At Chancellorsville, as Hooker pulled his forces back toward the river, Hancock, fought a delaying action which bought the commanding general the precious time needed to withdraw from the vicinity of Chancellorsville and form his army a mile to the rear. When Couch departed after the battle, Hancock was arguably the best available general to take his place. Although he never attained command of an independent army, there could be no argument; Hancock was on a path to become one of the finest corps level commanders in either army.[84]

One of Hancock's most valuable attributes was his ability to read a situation, assess it, and quickly make a decision as to what action was required. He was one of the few generals in the Union Army who seemed to grasp the concept of quick decision making and action. History has shown that the best devised battle plans typically last until they are put into action. The uncertainty of the battlefield and unknown factors force battle plans to evolve. Hancock knew that hesitation was a recipe for disaster, which usually gave the enemy time to dictate the course of events. At Williamsburg, after assuming his position on the Union flank in some abandoned Confederate entrenchments, he noticed 1,200 yards to his front another line of abandoned positions. Quickly he moved his command forward and occupied the location. His speedy thinking and action may have won the day for the Federals by forcing the Confederate's hand and the evacuation of the town. One thing can be said for Winfield Hancock, he was not the kind of man who would ever hesitate.[85]

To be an effective field commander, a soldier had to possess a number of personality traits which would not have endeared him to those uninformed as to how military success was obtained. Hancock was a bit egotistical and possessed a self-confidence which allowed him to make quick and decisive judgments and not second guess himself. Adding to these qualities were solid convictions and elevated emotions. Another critical element was a commanders understanding that in order to obtain military success, one had to be willing to commit troops to battle and live with the loss of blood. Weighing the chance of success against the cost in men and equipment was something which Hancock seemed to grasp. He knew that in order to win a battle a commander had to be willing to kill enemy soldiers which

---

[83] *OR* vol.21, pp.227-228; Tucker, Glenn, Winfield S. Hancock, *CWTI*, vol.7, no. 5, p.8.

[84] Tucker, Hancock, *CWTI*, vol.7, No. 5, p.8.

[85] *OR* vol.11, pt.1, p.536.

unfortunately meant the demise of some of his own. Taken together, these traits portrayed a man who looked and acted at home on a battlefield.

However, Hancock's most dominant personality trait, which he exhibited frequently, was his ability to curse and swear. His colorful language became more prevalent when used to enforce discipline and keep order among the men. Whether Hancock was a natural or he learned to curse during his association with General Harney is not known. Harney, who was one of the best orchestrators of colorful speech of any pre-war general, may have unknowingly instructed Hancock in the fine art of the swear word. Years later when recounting their exploits, many of the soldiers who reminisced about Hancock had little difficulty in recalling his more colorful and profane rants.

Hancock was also a stickler for discipline. In the midst of an engagement there was no time to question orders. He knew lives hung in the balance and any falter, however slight, could cost the blood of hundreds if not thousands of men. Hancock trained his men relentlessly, providing instruction and direction at all times. He also saw to the welfare of his boys and did everything possible to make sure they were comfortable and well cared for. The soldier was the instrument used to conduct the work of an army, and Hancock was well aware that any successes achieved would be directly related to the abilities and strength of his men.[86]

Like Hooker, Hancock was considered one of the most handsome men in the army. Upon a horse he was majestic. Frank Haskell called him the "most magnificent looking general in the whole Army of the Potomac…" Continuing, Haskell noted Hancock was a big man, not rotund but "well-shaped" and that his dress, even on the battlefield always seemed to be stylish. It was easy to identify him as the one in charge and he looked to be the "monarch of all he surveyed." Adding to his majestic look was his seemingly endless supply of freshly starched white shirts which he always wore into battle. The shirt supply was the result of Hancock's English valet spending a good deal of time cleaning worn shirts with the use of a scrubbing board.

Hancock was physically the tallest corps commander with the Army of the Potomac. His light brown hair always looked neat and tidy and his beard, worn as a goatee and mustache, was trimmed and straight. According to Haskell, Hancock's "ruddy" complexion and facial features where "neither large nor small, but well cut, with a full jaw and chin, compressed mouth, straight nose, full deep blue eyes, and a very mobile, emotional countenance." Hancock's charisma was so evident that Haskell believed if the general had been in civilian dress issuing commands to the men in uniform they still would have obeyed orders so powerful was his presence. Haskell concluded his description by noting that Hancock was always dignified in his dress and always looked "gentlemanly and commanding."[87]

---

[86] Jordan, *A Soldier's Life*, p.37.

[87] Byrne, Weaver, Editors, **Haskell of Gettysburg**, p.101, 133; Tucker, Glenn, Hancock at Gettysburg, **Manuscript GNMP**, p.9. Historian A. M. Gambone has likened Hancock to a Civil War era John Wayne.

Hancock had been in charge of the corps since 22 May when General Couch departed for Washington. When it became clear that Couch would not return, he was forced into the position on a permanent basis. While official orders would not be issued in Washington until 24 June, Winfield Hancock was now a corps commander. There is little doubt he was the right man for the position. Fate and the confidence of his commanding officer would put him at the center of the fighting at Gettysburg. His entire career seemed to have been a training ground for the critical moments ahead. His men respected and trusted him. At Gettysburg he would ask them for all they had as soldiers and most would give it willingly.[88]

Perhaps the best testament to Hancock's abilities and persona was provided by General Grant. Near the end of his life, Grant wrote in his memoirs a single paragraph describing his subordinate.

> "Hancock stands the most conspicuous figure of all the general officers who did not exercise a separate command. He commanded a corps longer than any other one, and his name was never mentioned as having committed in battle a blunder for which he was responsible. He was a man of very conspicuous personal appearance. Tall, well formed and, at the time of which I now write, young and fresh looking, he presented an appearance that would attract the attention of an army as he passed. His genial disposition made him friends, and his personal courage and his presence with his command in the thickest of the fight won for him the confidence of troops serving under him. No matter how hard the fight, the 2d always felt that their commander was looking after them."

General Meade noted that "no commanding General ever had a better Lieutenant than Hancock, he was always faithful and reliable." Meade would count heavily on Hancock's devotion and reliability in a few weeks.[89]

A Second Visit

The extent of Hooker's setback would become relevant over the next few weeks as the exodus of manpower from the army began with expiring terms of enlistment for a large number of nine month units. Hooker had been forced to initiate operations in order to take advantage of their presence. The manpower benefit that had been enjoyed would soon be eliminated by their departure and Longstreet's return to Lee's army. By the time Lee began shifting his troops northward, the two opposing forces would be as close to equal in numbers as they had ever been. Lee's continual scouring of Northern newspapers made him well aware of the impending decrease in Federal manpower. Even though he struggled

---

[88] ***OR*** vol.27, pt.1, p.1; ***OR*** vol.27, pt.3, p.299.

[89] Grant, ***Memoirs***, p.582; Gambone, ***Gettysburg and Beyond***, p.xv.

to have reinforcements sent to his army, the odds would be better during the summer of 1863 than ever before.

The prism of history has not been kind to Joe Hooker. The Union loss at Chancellorsville began a downward spiral which eventually led to his departure from the Army of the Potomac. Unfortunately, he is remembered more for the lowest point of his career than for his excellent administrative skills or his outstanding performances as a lower level commander on a number of battlefields. At Antietam Hooker's combat performance was exceptional and only his wounding forced him to turn command over to Meade. His performance on this and other eastern battlefields prompted Lincoln to place him in command of the army, even though the president was well aware of Hooker's personal shortcomings.

When Hooker assumed command he took over an army at its lowest point since its forming in the fall of 1861 when McClellan had taken charge of the defeated remnants which fought at Bull Run. Perhaps Rufus Dawes, of the 6th Wisconsin summed up Hooker's worth to the men better than anyone.

> "...he [Hooker] received the Army of the Potomac, rent by internal jealousies, discontented, discouraged and humiliated under the stigma of defeat. With indefatigable zeal he addressed himself to the task of its re-organization and, if I may so express it, re-inspiration. It was for Hooker to arouse the drooping spirits of the grand army and he accomplished the task. He had the true Napoleonic idea of the power of an 'Esprit de Corps.' It was he who first devised the beautiful, and to the soldiers inspiring system of corps badges. Forever the trefoil of the second corps, the crosses of the fifth and sixth corps, the arrow, the cartridge box with forty rounds, and the other corps badges of the war, will be the almost worshipped symbols of the glorious service."[90]

Hooker's efforts to improve the sanitation and nutrition of his army inflated its declining morale and improved its health. The rule changes governing leave provided much needed time away from the stress of army life. Reigning in abuses suffered by the soldiers do to crooked sutlers also helped improve the mental wellbeing of his men. His understanding of the value of cavalry when massed under a single command set the stage for the ascension of the Federal Cavalry arm. Future engagements with the legendary Stuart would now be waged on a more equal footing and the Federals would soon show the Confederate horsemen that the days of riding circles around their Northern antagonist were over. Forward thinking also resulted in the establishment of the BMI which was the first organization of its kind in either army or for that matter, in the history of the American military.

While Hooker made great strides regarding the improvement of the morale of the army, after Chancellorsville, the mood in the camps and command structure quickly returned to the low point of the post Burnside era. Contained in a letter to

---

[90] Dawes, *Service*, p.132.

his daughter near the end of May, General Alpheus Williams succinctly relayed the mood of the army.

> "We have lost physically and numerically, but still more morally, not by being dispirited, but by a universal want of confidence in the commanding general, growing out of the recent operations. I have not met the first officer who does not feel this, from the highest to the lowest. Of course, with such a feeling offensive operations are out of the question..."
> "I am greatly dispirited and almost disposed to resign. That our government shows symptoms now, as in the past, of being prepared in this way, as the instruments of our natural destruction, seems to me clearly manifested. I could tell you most astounding things, but cannot write them."[91]

Regarding his artillery, Hooker made one of his most critical errors. While he did reinstate Hunt as the battle of Chancellorsville came to its conclusion, personally, he was never able to acknowledge his error. Such was the character of Fighting Joe. The fact that he restored Hunt to his position speaks to Hooker's acknowledgement that the move was an incorrect one.

In the final analysis, the army that staggered back across the Rapidan and Rappahannock River's in early May of 1863 was Joe Hooker's army. He had taken 150,000 dejected men and molded them into a well-trained, confident fighting force. His influence would be felt throughout the summer campaign of 1863 and on to the end of the war. The outcome of Chancellorsville dampened the army somewhat, but the armed force which followed Robert E. Lee north one month later and fought at Gettysburg was still Fighting Joe's, even though he did not lead it to victory on the rolling hills of southern Pennsylvania.

Two days after Hooker re-crossed the river word came that Lincoln was on his way to visit the army.

---

[91] Quaife, Milo M., Editor, *From the Cannon's Mouth: The Civil War Letters of General Alpheus S. Williams*, p.204.

Chapter VII
North to Victory

> "we should choose a strong position, and force the Federals to attack us"[1]
> *James Longstreet*

When the middle of May arrived, Lee traveled to Richmond to meet with Confederate President Davis and his cabinet. War clerk John B. Jones, had the opportunity to observe Lee while the general was in the capital and noted he "looked thinner, and a little pale." Lee's frail look was probably due to a reoccurrence of his physical problems which first began in Texas prior to the war. Toward the end of March and into early April, Lee had complained of a sore throat and that he had "taken a violent cold." A few days later, he once again experienced pain in his torso and extremities. "I have not been so very sick, though have suffered a good deal of pain in my chest, back and arms," he wrote to Mary. The pain was most likely caused by acute pericarditis but could have been angina pectoris, or a mild heart attack. Lee continued to feel the effects of the incident for a number of weeks and would notice a weakening of his physical abilities as the summer progressed.[2]

Events in the west were causing great concern within the upper echelon of the government, specifically in Vicksburg, where Federal troops under Ulysses S. Grant where preparing to invest the city. While no records of the meeting have been found, the issues discussed can be pieced together from correspondence between Lee, Davis, and his cabinet. Surely one of the topics debated was how to deal with the developing situation along the Mississippi. One option would be to transfer some of Lee's men westward to reinforce the troops under siege in the city. Lee argued against diverting troops, feeling it was not in the best interests of not only his command but also the overall military success of the Confederacy. Lee pleaded his case in opposition to such a move by making a number of convincing arguments.

Transferring troops, Lee pointed out, would significantly decrease his already minimal numbers. If pressured by the Federals, he would have no choice but to

---

[1] Longstreet, *MtoA*, p.331.

[2] Jones, John B., *A Rebel War Clerk's Diary*, vol.1, p.325; Dowdey & Manarin, **Wartime Papers**, pp.427-428; Freeman, Douglas S., *R. E. Lee*, vol.4, p.525. Acute pericarditis is an inflammation of the sac which surrounds the heart.

fall back toward Richmond, a course of action that would eventually force his army into the defenses surrounding the Confederate capital. The outcome of such a siege would be defeat. Lee could not secure the Rappahannock line in central Virginia forever. Food and forage were in short supply, affecting the physical condition of his men and livestock. The Federal army north of the river was in a well-supplied position close to its base of operations. After being severely mauled at both Fredericksburg and Chancellorsville, the Northern troops had simply retreated back to their side of the river to replenish their supplies, reinforce their defeated legions and regain their morale. Hooker had caught Lee off guard at Chancellorsville and had easily flanked him, but Lee chose to meet him. If Lee had elected to fall back, it would have been more difficult to arrest the Federal advance before the Confederates were bottled up in Richmond.[3]

In addition, remaining on defense behind the river put Lee in a reactionary position. If he remained stagnant, he would be forced to meet the enemy at a time and place of its choosing. One of the most significant benefits of the Chancellorsville victory was wrestling the initiative from Hooker. With two defeats under their belts, the Federals, if left undisturbed in their position could lick their wounds. With the experiences of both defeats fresh in their minds, they could develop a new strategy, and advance once again. If given time, the Federals might eventually come up with a battle plan that Lee would not be capable of countering.[4]

The biggest tactical problem facing the Confederate commander was the proximity of Washington's defenses. The Federal army had been defeated many times since Lee took command. Past victories had resulted in Union troops retreating toward stable Washington forts and defensive positions. There, in relative safety, they would reorganize and move out once again to do battle. The scenario created an environment of casualty exchange which Lee and the Southern army could not afford. The war would come to a quick end if the Confederates continued to trade the Federal army man for man. Lee needed a strategy to get the Union army out in the open where he could maneuver, divide or concentrate his forces into positions that would keep the enemy from retreating to safety. Once the enemy had been exposed, Lee could engage the Federals on his terms.

Lee knew in the spring of 1863 the only way to defeat his enemy, not just wound him, was to evacuate the Rappahannock line, and move his army north to threaten Washington, and other major cities. If battle came and he was successful, Lee could continue northward to invade enemy territory, or if no encounter developed, he could continue north unhindered, drawing the nervous Federals away from the security of their capital. If the enemy could be defeated in the north, the Confederate Army could then threaten any critical point or population center. Lee also knew that the Virginia countryside was in dire need of a respite from the cruelties of war. The region would not be capable of sustaining his army for much

---

[3] Bowden, Scott & Ward, Bill., *Last Chance for Victory, Robert E. Lee and the Gettysburg Campaign*, p.35; Bandy, Ken & Freeland, Florence, *The Gettysburg Papers*, pp.46-47.

[4] Bandy and Freeland, *The Gettysburg Papers*, p.47.

longer and shipments of supplies from the Deep South where few and far between thanks to a somewhat lackluster quartermaster department.

Lee understood that after two years of war the South could not win its independence by relying only on its ability to win battles. The price of victory in the field had simply been too high. Numerous times Federal troops had advanced to engage Lee's men and had been defeated. Each of these battles had slowly withered the South's resource pool of able-bodied men. At Chancellorsville, Lee lost nearly 10,000 men to wounds and death while Hooker lost just over 11,000. While the loses seem somewhat equal at first glance, once Hooker's overall strength, which was twice that of Lee's, is factored in as a percentage of each forces overall size, the South lost nearly twice the strength. Lee knew that in order to defeat the North all the leverage he could muster was needed, including political pressure.[5]

Lee held the opinion that in order for the Confederacy to win its independence, President Lincoln had to be injured politically. He harbored no preconceived notions of winning the war through force of arms. Attrition was the enemy of the Confederacy. The longer the war drug on, the more difficult it would be for the Confederates to achieve victory. The only way to gain independence, in Lee's mind, was to force the Lincoln administration to come to the table and talk peace. Lincoln's political stature was already diminishing due to the recent Federal defeats. A crushing victory on Northern soil, Lee believed, would be a big step along the path to independence.[6]

The pressure a northward movement would put on the administration in Washington was perhaps the most overlooked aspect of the campaign. Now that he had the initiative, which he wrestled from Fighting Joe at Chancellorsville, Lee intended to seize the opportunity. Moving north would force the Army of the Potomac to follow in order to cover Washington and Baltimore. This would relieve pressure on Richmond, transfer the seat of hostilities away from war ravaged central Virginia, and allow Lee's army to survive on the melting pot north of the Potomac. Lincoln and Halleck would be pushing Hooker to follow, demanding he give battle. If Lee could catch Hooker's army out in the open countryside, dispersed on multiple lines of march, and meet portions of it on fields of his choosing, a great victory could be won. A Confederate victory might force the Lincoln Administration to acknowledge anti-war factions and a war weary population in the North. In this manner Lincoln might be persuaded to consider negotiations and bring independence to the South.[7]

Lee was keenly aware of the political situation in the North. After the Federal defeats at Fredericksburg and Chancellorsville, advocates for a peaceful resolution to the conflict gained momentum. Lee made it a habit to read as many Northern newspapers as he could get his hands on, and those he could not, were generally read and their contents reported by spies. The war in the west, while reported

---

[5] *OR* vol.25, pt.1, pp.185, 191.

[6] Bowden & Ward, **Last Chance**, pp.4-5, 35.

[7] *Ibid*, p.32.

in the papers, was not waged on the North's doorstep. Lee's army was the only Southern military force in a position where its success or failure could have direct effect on the morale of the North's major political centers. A victory north of the Potomac, Lee believed, would embolden peace activists, embed a defeatist attitude, and forced the administration in Washington to make an effort to deal with the Confederacy from a political standpoint. He knew that defeating the Federals militarily would be nearly impossible for the South owing to manpower and resources limitation issues. The longer the war, the more difficult it would be to succeed. If the new nation were to survive, it would be with the stroke of a pen not the slash of a sword. Lee had outlined his beliefs in a letter to his wife on 19 April. "If successful this year [1863], next fall there will be a great change in public opinion at the North. The Republicans," Lee continued, "will be destroyed & I think the friends of peace will become so strong that the next administration will go in on that basis." Simply put, Lee felt success in the field equaled a change of administrations after the elections of 1864. He believed a new president would be acceptable to a peaceful resolution to the conflict.[8]

Lee would certainly have used these arguments during the Richmond conference, but they were not the only valid reasons against sending a segment of his force to reinforce the army in Mississippi. During early May, Grant had managed to transfer his Union force across the Mississippi River below Vicksburg and was now positioning it to pin Lieutenant General John C. Pemberton's Confederates down in the city. Overall command of the Confederate forces in the west was charged to General Joseph E. Johnston. Davis had little if any confidence in his abilities. As the Peninsula Campaign unfolded in the spring of 1862, Johnston's continual retreat up the Virginia Peninsula began raising questions about his ability to be successful as a field commander. The retreating came to an end at the Battle of Fair Oaks where Johnston was wounded. Davis took the opportunity to replace him with Lee, and after Johnston recovered, the president shipped him off to command the Department of the West.[9]

A year later, while critical event were unfolding along the river, Johnston chose to manage the defense of Vicksburg from Tullahoma, Tennessee, nearly 200 miles away. Finally, after the situation had deteriorated to a critical point, Confederate secretary of war, James Seddon, ordered Johnston to go to the area and "take chief command" of the troops there. Johnston arrived in Mississippi on 13 May as the attendees of the Richmond conference were preparing to gather. His first communications to Davis informed the president his "forces are very inadequate," and the enemy "continues to re-enforce heavily." Johnston complained that Grant had interposed his force between Pemberton and himself and that he was too late. Davis would have none of it, wiring back "we cannot hope for numerical equality and time will probably increase the disparity." It was clear Davis would no longer accept Johnston's excuses.[10]

---

[8] Bowden & Ward, *Last Chance*, p.32; Dowdey & Manarin, **Wartime Papers**, p.438.

[9] Bowden & Ward, *Last Chance*, p.26.

[10] Cooper, William J. Jr., ***Jefferson Davis, American***, p.472; *OR*, vol.24, pt.3, p.870.

Arriving in Jackson Mississippi, Johnston evaluated the situation, and contacted Pemberton urging him to work in concert with his force in an effort to join their commands. After laying out a plan to unite their forces, Johnston, being true to his nature, retreated to the northeast, moving his command away from Pemberton before any pressure had been brought to bear on his position. Inexcusably, Johnston formulated a plan, issued orders to execute it, and then simply abandon it when he determined the numbers were not in his favor, leaving Pemberton to his fate. Johnston retreated six miles the first day and ten more the next. Wiring Davis on 16 May he informed the president about the retreat and then told him his goal was to unite his force with Pemberton's. Davis, who was from Mississippi, was beside himself. Johnston, who was fourth in seniority within the Confederacy's command structure, had refused to fight, just as he had done on the Peninsula. In Davis' mind, Johnston had simply abandoned Pemberton's men to whatever disaster awaited them at the hands of Grant.

Johnston's telegram arrived while Davis, Lee, and the rest of the Confederate Cabinet were in conference. It was now obvious that Johnston was the wrong man and could not save Vicksburg. Whether or not Davis contemplated sending Lee himself to Mississippi to try and relieve the city is not known, but it was clear the Mississippi River town was in serious jeopardy. Reducing Lee's force in the face of a superior enemy was not the only drawback to the idea of dispatching troops from the Army of Northern Virginia. Johnston had proven he had no intention of fighting and any troops sent there would languish and serve no purpose other than to reduce Lee's ability to be successful. There was also an issue with how long it would take for any dispatched troops to get to Mississippi. By the time they arrived, the issue, if not already settled, could have only one outcome. Additionally, once the men reached their destination they needed to be supplied. Wagons, horses and food could not be taken with them, but would be needed for any new troops to allow them to maneuver and operate in the field. The only way soldiers could function for an extended period of time away from rail lines was to take their supplies with them.

The final decision not to send troops from Lee's army came down to one simple fact. The Army of Northern Virginia operated in the only theater of the war where the outcome of a battle had a direct effect on the Federal Government in Washington and the morale of the civilian population in the North. The largest population centers in the North were all within easy reach of Lee's army if he chose to march in their direction. Only by keeping a strong military force in Virginia could Lee hope to create the political situation needed in the North for the Confederacy to succeed. In Lee's mind the facts were extremely simple. The South could lose the war in the west, but they could not win it there. Only in the east could the military and political situation be influenced to a point in which the South could gain its independence.[11]

After listening to all the arguments, Davis made his decision and gave Lee approval to prepare a northward movement. Only Davis' cabinet member, Postmaster General John H. Reagen, disagreed with the decision. However, while

---

[11] Bowden & Ward, *Last Chance*, pp.28-31, 33.

the president gave his approval for Lee's campaign he never fully embraced it or understood its scope. The commander-in-chief would prove over the next few weeks as Lee prepared his army to move that it was not his top priority.

Meaningless Victories

The late spring days of 1863 presented a number of problems for the embattled Rebels. The most critical issue seemed to be a lack of manpower to deal with the Federal hordes. Although the just concluded fight near Chancellorsville had ended with a Confederates victory, the cost had been extraordinarily high. Lee's casualties, at just short of twenty percent of his engaged force, were enormous. With limited resources available, a rate of attrition as high as the one experienced at Chancellorsville would doom the South in short order. Lee brought this fact to Jefferson Davis' attention three days after the fighting had ceased. "The disparity between our infantry force and that of the enemy is too large to reasonably expect success," he wrote. He estimated the Federals had outnumbered his troops during the previous battle three to one. In reality the difference had been near two to one but Lee's argument could not be ignored. The disparity was made to seem larger than it really could have been since two of Lee's First Corps divisions under Longstreet were foraging near Suffolk for supplies. Longstreet's divisions had been ordered to return, but the general's point to Davis was still valid. Lee concluded, "I fear that our loss in killed and wounded will approximate 10,000 men in the different engagements."[12]

The price of victory had indeed been extraordinarily high, with the greatest loss being Lee's trusted Second Corps commander General Jackson. As news of Jackson's demise spread, waves of grief covered the entire South. Men who had seen the horrors of battle wept openly. Soldiers who had followed Jackson and thousands who had only heard of his deeds expressed grief and worried about the future of their new country. When the news arrived in Richmond, men stood in the streets in shock. Women wept on street corners. War clerk Jones summed up the public feeling in his diary. "A multitude of people, mostly women and children, are standing silently in the streets, awaiting the arrival of the hero, destined never again to defend their homes and honor." In Lexington, Jackson's hometown and place of final interment, a young girl wondered if God did not want them to win their freedom. John H. Worsham of the 21st Virginia summed it up well. "The South produced many generals of great ability, but for brilliancy and dash, the world never saw Stonewall Jackson's equal." Jefferson Davis called the loss of Jackson a "national calamity." During the funeral, while the general's body lay in state at the governor's mansion, Davis, while viewing it, allowed a tear to escape which fell upon Jackson's face. "I am still staggering from a dreadful blow. I cannot think," he would tell a fellow mourner.[13]

---

[12] Bigelow, ***Chancellorsville***, pp.473-475; ***OR***, vol.25, pt.2, pp.760, 782. Bigelow puts the Union forces at Chancellorsville at slightly more than 120,000 and Lee's between 60,000 and 61,000.

[13] Jones, ***Diary***, vol.1, p.319; Robertson, *Stonewall Jackson*, p.754-755; ***OR*** vol.25, pt.2, p.791; Worsham, John H., ***One of Jackson's Foot Cavalry***, p.166; Davis, William C., ***Jefferson Davis, The Man and His Hour***, p.501.

Even the enemy knew the value of Jackson. Writing shortly after the general's death, a Federal colonel of artillery summed up the loss.

> "Regrets for the man himself are as freely expressed by all who knew him personally in our army as they can be on the other side. Every one of his old acquaintances whom I have heard speak of him say that he was one of the purest, most religious, verging a little perhaps on the fanatic... It is impossible to look upon this class of men in our Southern states as actual traitors... To the rebels the loss of Stonewall Jackson is almost equal to a defeat. Full of energy, prompt, obedient and lightning quick in his obedience, he well deserved the name of 'Lee's right arm'; a 'right arm' which had never failed him whether the blow was to be struck near by [sic], or hundreds of miles away."[14]

The loss of Jackson was the sad coda to a string of meaningless victories which saw the Army of Northern Virginia sap its strength against a foe which, although it had been defeated in battle, would be back for more.

Many times the Federal army had been defeated and driven from the field, but Lee lacked the manpower to execute a proper pursuit and crush the demoralized Union troops. "More than once have most promising opportunities been lost for want of men to take advantage of them," he wrote to Secretary Seddon earlier in the year. "...[V]ictory itself has been made to put on the appearance of defeat, because our diminished and exhausted troops have been unable to renew a successful struggle against fresh numbers of the enemy. The lives of our soldiers are too precious to be sacrificed in the attainment of success that inflicts no loss upon the enemy beyond the actual loss in battle." Lee also expressed concern over the installation of compliancy within the Southern populace. Writing to Seddon, Lee noted that, "... success with which our efforts have been crowned, under the blessing of God, should not betray our people into the dangerous delusion that the armies now in the field as sufficient to bring this war to a successful and speedy termination." His concern was over men, who, for whatever reason had not initially answered the call, would be of the opinion that they were not needed and remain home for the duration of the conflict. Thinning ranks due to battle and disease required Lee to constantly meet the enemy with inferior numbers. His desire was to have these uncommitted men come forward and help carry the burden. "...[E]very man who remains out of service," Lee wrote to Seddon, "increases the dangers to which the brave men, who have so well borne the burden of the war, are exposed." Success could only be achieved if Lee possessed the numerical strength to follow up future triumphs. He could accomplish the strengthening by gathering units he had dispersed over the winter and have all idle troops, including those not yet in uniform, sent to his assistance. Unfortunately for Lee, his definition of idle differed

---

[14] Wainwright, Charles S., *A Diary of Battle: The Personal Journals of Colonel Charles S. Wainwright 1861-1865*, Editor: Allan Nevins, pp.206-207.

somewhat from that of the Davis Administration and commanders in other regions of the Confederacy.[15]

Although Lee spent a good deal of time during the early months of 1863 complaining about his troop levels, he seemed to have made few efforts over his time as commander to limit their exposure to unnecessary danger. There had been a number of opportunities for Lee to reduce his army's vulnerability to Yankee bullets and shells, but he had chosen to fight rather than maneuver his force into a more advantageous position. One example was the bloodbath at Sharpsburg a few months earlier. Lee chose to position his army with its back to the Potomac and fight McClellan instead of crossing the river and positioning his troops on the Virginia side to cover the Potomac's fords. Washington would have been on McClellan's back to push forward and attack him and Lee knew this. If "Little Mac" decided to risk a crossing to engage him, Lee may have been able to limit his exposure and confront the Federal army as it crossed the river piecemeal. Instead he chose to stand and fight a larger force and suffered 10,000 casualties, all of which were good men who he could use now. While there were a number of instances where Lee needed to take offensive action or stand and fight, he seemed too fond of the offensive and in many instances could have preserved his resources had he considered his need to conserve his strength.[16]

The Fight for Troops

Lee was repeatedly confronted with roadblocks as he worked to reorganize his army. He knew the importance of having as many veteran troops as possible for his planned movement. Over the previous months, many of his brigades had been dispersed for minor duties in surrounding areas or simply moved to a location where they could sustain themselves. In addition, some of Lee's veteran brigades had been removed from his army in order to shore up defenses in other areas of the South, particularly in the North Carolina coastal region. Lee now wanted and indeed needed these troops returned, and he began efforts to have the dispersed troops sent back to his army. He believed these units still belonged him and had simply been on loan. Based on intelligence he had received, Lee thought active campaigning in North Carolina would be light during the summer. He also thought that a campaign along and north of the Potomac by his army would draw enemy troops from those regions. In addition, Lee also believed through the reading of Northern newspapers that the Federal army in front of him was to be reinforced. However, within Jefferson Davis' defend every inch of the Confederacy by troop dispersal war strategy; possession of a fighting force was nine tenths of the law.[17]

---

[15] Dowdey & Manarin, **Wartime Papers**, p.389; **OR**, vol.21, p.1085.

[16] Carman, Ezra A., Pierro, Joseph, Editor, **The Maryland Campaign of September 1862: Ezra A. Carman's Definitive Study of the Union and Confederate Armies at Antietam** (hereafter **Carman**), p.481.

[17] **OR**, vol.25, pt.2, pp.790-791.

Sometime before Chancellorsville, Lee made it known he wished to have Robert R. Ransom's division, or what was left of it, returned to his army. The division was not whole since John R. Cooke's brigade, a battle tested group of North Carolinians, had been sent to South Carolina. On 29 April, Secretary of War Seddon instructed Adjutant General Samuel Cooper to send forward "all available troops" to Lee. Cooper then contacted General Daniel Harvey Hill and instructed him to send forward Ransom's Brigade. Hill responded saying he would send the troops forward and that they were projected to be in Richmond the evening of 1 May.[18]

Earlier in the year, Hill had submitted a letter of resignation. After citing his poor health as the primary reason, Hill noted he had "[m]any motives" for his decision. One motive was surely the urging of his wife Isabella who happened to be Stonewall Jackson's wife's sister. After the war, General Jubal Early commented that Hill desired to resign due to conflicts with his brother-in-law, but Hill himself noted to Isabella that Jackson had never treated him unkindly. Jackson delayed sending in Hill's request, possibly to give him time to think about his decision, When Hill requested feedback on his submittal, Jackson suggested they have a discussion on the matter. At the time, concerns over the security in Hill's home state of North Carolina, had been elevated. Lee, once he became aware of Hill's desire to resign, wrote to President Davis and Secretary Seddon of detaching a general from his command to assist in securing North Carolina. Lee felt Hill was a fine officer and the Confederacy would suffer if he was lost. "If you think any benefit will be derived by sending a officer to Raleigh to inspire or encourage the people," Lee wrote to Seddon on 5 January, "I will detach from this army Maj. Gen. D. H. Hill, a native of North Carolina, and a most valuable officer, for the purpose." Lee failed to mention that Hill had already submitted his resignation. He may have done so in the hope that Hill could be persuaded to remain with the army or for the simple fact that he was unaware Jackson had received it. Hill's resignation was eventually forwarded to Richmond. A week later, Hill was ordered to the capital where Davis and Seddon were successful in persuading him not to resign. Hill's reason for changing his mind has never been determined. In short order, Hill was assigned command of forces in North Carolina, as Lee had suggested, but it would be a posting which Lee would soon begin to regret.[19]

Hill evidently changed his mind regarding Ransom's troops or Cooper misunderstood him, for some time before 6 May, Lee learned that Hill had ordered up James J. Pettigrew's brigade instead. Lee was not pleased. "I particularly requested Ransom's division," Lee objected, "...half of it, Cooke's brigade, is

---

[18] *OR*, vol.25, pt.2, pp.758, 763, 779. Ransom's Brigade was part of Ransom's Division. At the time of the discussions, Ransom's Division contained three brigades, Ransom's, Cooke's and that of Nathan Evans. Evans' Brigade was in North Carolina, but Cooke was in South Carolina. Lee constantly referred to Ransom's Division in his correspondence. The War Department and Hill referenced Ransom's Brigade, implying one brigade not the division that Lee was trying to have returned to him.

[19] Bridges, Hal, *Lee's Maverick General: Daniel Harvey Hill*, pp.162-163; *OR*, vol.18, p.819.

in South Carolina, where it is not wanted. General D. H. Hill has ordered up Pettigrew's brigade. If it is sent up in place of Ransom's, I do not want it." Seddon, once again, gently nudged Hill on 6 May. "General Lee urges you to send him Ransom's division. Do so, if you can, with any safety." Seddon's last comment left the decision in Hill's hands and the General had no intension of parting with Ransom's men.[20]

In the meantime, Cooke's men returned from South Carolina. The division was now whole again. Seddon contacted Lee on the same day, informing him that Cooke had arrived, and Hill had been instructed to send the division to Lee "if he can." This was not what Lee wanted to hear. Seddon's position provided him the power to order Hill to send forward the troops Lee wanted, but the secretary deferred to Hill's judgment and Hill determined he needed the troops. Lee obviously thought Hill didn't need them, and Seddon refused to make a decision. Seddon and Davis may have been concerned that Hill would once again attempt to resign if he were forced to give up Ransom's men. Whether concerned over Hill's future or not, Seddon and Davis refused to issue direct instructions to return Lee's men.[21]

The next day Lee wrote a long letter to President Davis outlining his army's current strength, the strength of the enemy and how he thought his army could be reinforced. "…[Y]ou may take such means as in your judgment seem best to increase the strength of the army," Lee wrote. "This can be done, in my opinion, by bringing troops from the departments of South Carolina, Georgia, and Florida. No more can be needed there this summer than enough to maintain the water batteries. Nor do I think that more will be required at Wilmington than are sufficient for this purpose."[22]

Again, on 11 May, Lee wrote Davis attempting to get the president to intervene. "I propose, for your consideration, to place D. H. Hill in command of the department between the James River and Cape [Fear] River, and to draw from it Ransom's and [M.] Jenkins' brigades." Micah Jenkins' brigade of South Carolinians and Montgomery Corse's brigade of Virginians, which had been detached from George Pickett's division of Longstreet's Corps, were two additional, hard fighting units Lee wanted returned. Through the month of May, Davis showed his ignorance for Lee's overall strategy by continuing to support a movement north but refusing to support Lee with as many veteran troops as possible. Davis, sticking to his defend everything policy undermined Lee's efforts to make sure the coming campaign would be successful.[23]

During this time, Lee also found himself defending his possession of another veteran combat unit. The situation in the west was deteriorating fast and Vicksburg continued to be in serious danger of being lost. Seddon contacted Lee and suggested that George Pickett's division be sent to Mississippi to help check Grant. Lee

---

[20] *OR*, vol.25, pt.2, pp.779-780.

[21] Ibid, p.780.

[22] Ibid, p.782, 783.

[23] Ibid, p.791; Bowden & Ward, **Last Chance**, p.36.

argued against this stating that Pickett, if sent, could not arrive in time to be of any use. Lee also questioned that even if the reinforcements managed to get there in time, would they be used effectively? Joe Johnston had proven his propensity to show his back to the enemy. There was no indication that he would not do so again, and in fact, as the Confederate high command found out later, Johnston had fallen back. Lee successfully made his case during the conference in Richmond and Pickett remained where he was.[24]

Hill now began to propose exchanges. On 14 May Cooper wrote to Lee relaying a proposal from Hill to exchange Julius Daniel's brigade for one of Lee's weaker ones. Lee was in Richmond when Hill's original communication was received and he responded to Hill on 16 May. While he agreed with the exchange of Daniel's brigade, Lee was opposed to any additional bartering. "The plan you propose of exchanging your full for its [the army's] reduced brigade I fear will add but little to its real strength," Lee complained. "It would increase it numerically but weaken it intrinsically by taking away tried troops under experienced officers and replacing them with fresh men and uninstructed commanders. I should therefore have more to feed but less to depend on." While Lee no doubt appreciated the gesture, it did nothing to change his mind about the return of Ransom's Division and Pickett's two brigades, telling Hill he had always considered them "belonging to the Army of Northern Virginia and have relied on their return."[25]

Once again, four days later, Lee wrote the Seddon regarding his desire to have all the troops possible returned to his army. "I wish General Hill to make such disposition of his troops as to give me all the force that can be spared from North Carolina." Lee also restated his desire to have Pickett's division made whole again. "Jenkins' brigade, belonging to Pickett's division," he wrote, "is still on the Blackwater [River], and I do not like to order it up until I hear whether proper dispositions are made to relieve it. It is much wanted with its division." Lee could have very easily ordered Hill to send the troops to him. His patience had not been tried to a point which infringed on his tendencies to be a gentleman. Instead he continued allowing Hill the luxury of sending the troops when he was prepared to do so.[26]

Finally, on 25 May, with his army preparing to move, Lee had to act. After informing Hill of the situation in northern Virginia, he issued positive orders to him. "I therefore desire that you direct Brigadier-General Jenkins to join his division (Pickett's) at Hanover Junction, and Brigadier-General Ransom to repair to Richmond. Should it be necessary to move him farther he will receive orders from General Elzey, to whom he will report." Lee's strategy can clearly be seen. Sending Ransom to Richmond extracted the command from the control of Hill and placed it within Lee's grasp. In an effort to possibly easy Hill's concern about losing the troops, Lee informed him that addition troops for his command could be

---

[24] *OR*, vol.25, pt. 2, p.790.

[25] *Ibid*, p.798; *OR*, vol.18, p.1063.

[26] *OR*, vol.25, pt. 2, p.811.

gathered from points further south. Lee then contacted General Arnold Elzey, who was in command of Confederate forces in and around Richmond, and informed him that he had ordered the troops up. "I have ordered Ransom's brigade to report to you in Richmond, and await further orders. Jenkins' brigade I have ordered up to General Pickett, at Hanover Junction."[27]

Hill was not about to give up any troops he felt he needed. He contacted Richmond to complain about the disposition of the units he obviously believed he had to retain to keep the enemy from posing a serious threat south of the James. On 29 May President Davis wrote a short communication to Lee. According to Davis, Hill had informed him that Lee was well aware of the situation in North Carolina. Playing upon Davis' defend it all war strategy, Hill complained, according to Davis, that to "withdraw Ransom's, Cooke's and Jenkins' brigades is to abandon the country to the enemy, if last information is correct." In addition, Lee was informed that another brigade that had been relieved on the Blackwater by Jenkins had been ordered up to Pickett. To top off the disappointment, Lee was also told that Ransom had been promoted and would remain in North Carolina taking over for General Samuel G. French who had been sent west.[28]

Lee finally had enough. It all came to a head on 30 May. So frustrating had been the exchange that he asked Davis to relieve him of his command responsibilities from the James River south to Cape Fear.

> "When in Richmond, I gave Genl. D. H. Hill discretionary instructions, stating my belief that the contest of the summer would take place in Virginia, to apportion his force to the strength of the enemy, and send me every man he could spare. He declined to act under those instructions, and requested positive instruction. He now offers objections, which if previously presented, I should not have issued the latter. You will see that I am unable to operate under these circumstances, and request to be relieved from any control of the department from the James to Cape Fear River. I have for nearly a month been endeavoring to get this army in a condition to move-to anticipate an expected blow from the enemy. I fear I shall have to receive it here at a disadvantage or to retreat. If I was stronger, I think I could prevent either, and force him back."[29]

"This army has been diminished since last fall by the brigades of Jenkins, Ransom, Cooke and Evans," Lee reiterated. "It has been increased by Pettigrew's. I consider Colquitt's exchanged for Daniel's. General Hill has retained in North Carolina a regiment from Pettigrew and Daniel." On the same day, Lee followed up

---

[27] *OR*, vol.18, p.1071; *OR*, vol.25, pt. 2, p.831.

[28] *OR*, vol.25, pt. 2, p.831.

[29] *OR*, vol.25, pt. 2, p.832.

his message to Davis by sending a communication to Hill suspending his previous orders and stating "[t]he President will give you such orders as he may see fit." Lee washed his hands of the whole affair. Davis wrote a long letter to Hill but never issued direct orders to him to send forward the brigades Lee wanted.[30]

Both Hill and Davis were blind to the facts of their situation. While Lee was endeavoring to move his army into a position to win for the South their independence through military and political means, Davis continued to believe in his departmentalized defense of the country. Hill, commanding troops in one of the less critical regions, failed to see or understand Lee's grand strategy for success. Their failure to understand the total military situation doomed the resource starved Confederacy to sprout, grow, blossom and then wither to die on the vine as the resources required to sustain it were reduced to a fraction of those needed by time and attrition.

The final outcome of all the arguing and the president's inflexibility was the loss of five veteran brigades. The hard fighting commands under Micah Jenkins and Montgomery Corse from George Pickett's Virginia division would be sorely missed. The other three brigades left behind, would be those of Nathanial "Shanks" Evans, Robert Ransom Jr., and John R. Cooke. Lee would feel the absence of all five brigades, containing over 11,000 chiseled veterans a few weeks later. Davis however did allow the brigades of James Pettigrew and Joseph Davis, the president's nephew, sent forward. Lee may have traded both of the brigades that were provided for any one of the other five if given the opportunity. Both units, while not completely green, were untested in the caldron of intense battle and the younger Davis was a lawyer by trade who had never led troops in the field. Jefferson Davis, in his own mind, no doubt believed he was supporting Lee by sending forward the remainder of Pickett's Division (three brigades) and the two untested units. Lee however had a different point of view. To the general, all of Pickett's Division already belonged to his army and the brigades of Davis and Pettigrew would be of little use. Lee had lost what constituted a division of veterans and gained two green brigades. It hardly seemed like a fair trade.[31]

The irony of Lee's problem with missing troops can be focused directly upon the commanding general himself. His lessons regarding offensive actions against a numerically superior foe learned from General Scott in Mexico were coming home to roost. Lee had fought five major campaigns during his reign as commander of the Army of Northern Virginia. Except for Fredericksburg, each had been fought as part of an offensive action. Even the blood bath at Sharpsburg, while a defensive fight, was the result of an offensive invasion of the North. Lee was not prone to take up or look for opportunities to take a defensive stance since in his mind a defensive stand typically provided no tactical gain. It did however serve to save resources, mainly the lives of troops. It is possible that if Lee had stood on the defensive more often during his first year as commander he may have easily had 11,000 more men already in his command. Taking a defensive stance on a battlefield was not

---

[30] *Ibid*, pp.833-835.

[31] Dowdey & Manarin, **Wartime Papers**, p.476.

in Lee's nature. Longstreet probably best summarized Lee's battlefield persona when he wrote after the war his commander sometimes "seemed under a subdued excitement, which occasionally took possession of him when the hunt was up."[32]

Davis responded to Lee's 30 May letter, admitting he "never fairly comprehended your [Lee's] views and purposes until the receipt of your letter of yesterday, and now have to regret that I did not earlier know all that you had communicated to others. I could hardly have misunderstood you, and need not say would have been glad to second your wishes, confiding, as I always do, as well in your judgment as in your information." Davis' message was tantamount to admitting that he was wholly unaware of Lee's intentions and communications with others regarding the return of his troops and bolstering his command. However, the communication breakdown was now irrelevant. Lee was still short on troops and the time to move was at hand.[33]

Hill's command was not the only source which Lee tried to draw reinforcements from. In a letter to Davis early in May Lee suggested that General Beauregard's force be brought north to Lee's location, instead of leaving it posted in South Carolina during the summer where exposure to disease would be high. Lee thought it better to "order General Beauregard in with all the forces which can be spared, and to put him in command here, than to keep them there inactive..." Moving Beauregard north would provide for the capital a covering force while Lee was off conducting his summer campaign.

Even as his army was preparing to move Lee continued to send requests for reinforcements to Richmond. On 2 June he wrote to Davis "I think General Hill's troops could be brought up from North Carolina," in case there was a movement by the enemy toward Richmond. Five days later, with his army on the move, Lee sent another letter to Davis suggesting that if rumors of the Federal force in front of Beauregard being withdrawn were true that the general and his men should be sent to reinforce his army or sent to Johnston in Mississippi. Unfortunately for Lee, once again, none of these suggestions were acted upon by the president even though he had recently written that he trusted Lee's judgment. Once again Davis' desire to defend every inch of the Confederacy thwarted Lee's efforts to increase his force to a point that would assure success during the campaign.[34]

Two months later, after Lee's defeated army limped back across the Potomac River into Virginia, he received a letter from Micah Jenkins which must have made his heart sink.

---

[32] Longstreet, James, Lee in Pennsylvania, *Annuls of the War* (hereafter *AW*), p.421.

[33] *OR*, vol.25, pt.2, p.843. Many historians have equated Davis' "never fairly comprehended" statement to his misunderstanding Lee's intentions regarding the summer campaign. The letter is clearly a response to Lee's frustration induced letter of 30 May. If one follows the letter chain, this is obvious to even the most novice historian.

[34] *OR*, vol.25, pp.782-783, 848; *OR*, vol.27, pp.293-294.

General: In all the trials of your noble army my heart has been with you and my desire has been to be with and share your danger and hardships. *I made repeated applications to be sent to you, but although promised that my brigade should be next sent, yet circumstances have prevented.* I sincerely trust that it may be arranged in the future that I may retake my place under you. My brigade is pronounced by all officers in unsurpassed condition, and I myself think I have never seen troops in such condition for efficient service. Can you not send some shattered brigade to rest and recruit and get the President to allow me to join you with my brigade? *I am here temporarily to guard against raiders, but do not think the place in danger.* [Emphasis added]

I am, general, with sentiments of highest respect and esteem, your obedient servant.

M. JENKINS,
Brigadier-General, Commanding Division.

According to Jenkins, Lee had been correct in his thoughts regarding his detached veteran brigades. Unfortunately, Davis, Seddon and D. H. Hill did not see it his way. They were grossly unaware of the situation north of the James and handicapped Lee by pinning down his veterans in a region where a little creative thinking and troop repositioning could have provided Lee with what he wanted and needed to be successful. Jenkins, being closer to the units in the field was of the same opinion as Lee and thought his troops could be better used elsewhere. Jenkins' letter must have reinforced Lee's prior opinions regarding the detached troops and fueled his irritation with Richmond and Hill after the fact.[35]

Food and Forage

The forage problem facing Lee and his men during the winter and early spring of 1863 was indeed dire. The winter that year had been very severe. The weather, coupled with eighteen months of war, had robbed the normally rich Virginia countryside of its ability to sustain itself. It was well known that the Confederacy did not possess the industrial and agricultural resources to sustain a prolonged and difficult war effort. As winter ravaged his men, Lee was forced into a situation in which his small army could only survive if it was dispersed into smaller groups and sent to areas where they could find sustenance.[36]

Most critical was the issue of forage for the army's horses. Armies of the mid-nineteenth century were made mobile by horsepower. The advent of railroad transportation had just begun to show itself as a viable method for moving troops; however, inconsistencies in gauge and regional military control limited rail when moving men long distances. While the infantryman marched, beasts assisted in all other aspects of an army's ability to move. Officers were mounted to provide mobility during

---

[35] *OR*, vol.51, pt. 2, p.745.

[36] *Ibid*, pp.3-4.

battle and on the march. Artillery batteries were moved from place to place by horses as was cavalry. Finally, and most importantly, supply trains were moved by horses not suited for cavalry or artillery use, oxen, mules or whatever beast was available.

Virginia had been stripped of most natural resources due to army foraging, tramping troops and war ravaging the countryside. Additional supplies were available further south but the logistics of getting them to the army, while difficult, could have been overcome with hard work and manpower. This was not so with horses and mounts for cavalry. Gathering horses from a defeated enemy was one option, but typically when the Union army abandoned the field after a defeat, the one thing they took with them were their horses. Even if the Rebels had been lucky enough to capture a few animals, by law, the beasts were property of the Confederate government. As the war progressed, property rights regarding captured animals reverted to one of possession with the capturing cavalryman or artilleryman replacing his own worn out or dead animal with the one that legally belonged to Jefferson Davis. Because of the scarcity of animals, as Lee reorganized his army, many members of the Confederate cavalry were mounted on animals that in peacetime would have been relegated to pulling a plow.[37]

During the winter of 1863, the cavalry suffered greatly because of a lack of forage as hay, oats, corn and grass were in short supply. On 13 February, Lee wrote Jeb Stuart regarding a mission into the Shenandoah Valley. Throughout the communication, Lee reiterated to Stuart that he take into consideration the condition of his horses before executing any movements. "I desire you to select from Genl Fitz Lee's brigade of cavalry such men and horses as may be fit for the service… If you think it advisable, & the condition of his horses will permit…" Lee warned. "Your particular attention *must* be given to the comfort of your men and horses, & should circumstances now unforeseen render it inexpedient in your judgment with a due regard to their future usefulness & service, upon your reaching the Valley, to carry out the objective of the expedition, you are desired to limit or abandon it at your discretion." Sending part of Stuarts command to the Valley served two purposes, it relieved pressure on the Virginia countryside to sustain the animals and it put pressure on General Robert H. Milroy's Federal command stationed at Winchester.[38]

Three days after Lee sent instructions to Stuart, he sent a message to President Davis voicing his thoughts regarding the military situation. He also took the opportunity to let Davis know the status of the army's livestock. "…our horses and mules are in that reduced state that the labor and exposure incident to an attack would result in their destruction, and leaves us destitute of the means of transportation," Lee complained. As spring wore on and the grasses grew, the countryside became green again and the remaining horses slowly regained their strength. The dwindling numbers however, would still be an issue, which the

---

[37] Longacre, Edward G., *Lee's Cavalrymen*, p.42.

[38] *OR*, vol.25, pt.2, p.621. emphasis added.

Rebels could address by possibly replenishing their numbers during the invasion from stock found north of the Potomac.[39]

Another problem encountered by the cavalry was the Confederate policy that all members of the mounted service were to provide their own horse and tack. This meant that when a horseman lost his mount to bullets, shell fragments or disease, he had to procure another or risk being transferred to the artillery or infantry. Most cavalrymen detested the notion of being a foot soldier. This prompted many horseless men to follow the cavalry around on foot, carrying their saddle in the hopes that a stray horse could be found, procured, or even stolen. The policy led to a large absentee rate within Southern cavalry units and made sure that General Stuart's command was never at full strength. Each horseman was to be paid 40 cents a day for the use of his personal property, and if his animal was killed, he was to be reimbursed for its value. The worth of the animal was determined when the trooper was mustered into service or shortly thereafter by a board of inspectors; unfortunately for the troopers, the animal had to be killed in battle and even when this event occurred, few men saw the money.[40]

Some advantages did exist with each trooper providing his own animal. The policy allowed the Confederacy to put a large mobile mounted force in the field much sooner than the Federals. It also instilled in the horseman pride of ownership and the Confederate cavalryman took the extra steps to make sure his own property was well cared for. However, this led to some men being too careful and not taking appropriate risks in battle in an effort to keep their horse from being harmed.[41]

Forage for Lee's livestock was not the only serious substance issue for the army. Food for the troops was almost or just as serious. On 26 January, Lee sent commissary officer Archibald H. Cole to Richmond "with a view of ascertaining what supply of provisions can be relied on for the support of the troops." Rations had already been reduced, and according to Lee the army only had a week's supply remaining and even less of "fresh beef" and "salt meat." Writing to Secretary Seddon, Lee reinforced the dire straits which haunted the army that January. "The question of provisioning the army is becoming one of greater difficulty every day," Lee wrote. "The country north of us is pretty well drained of everything the people are willing to part with, except some grain and hay in Loudoun [County], nor can impressment be resorted to with advantage, inasmuch as any provisions retained for domestic use are concealed." Lee felt that any further pressure on the population to provide additional support would only result in the installation of ill feelings toward the army with no significant improvement in supply.[42]

The reduced rations were miniscule at best, consisting of four ounces of bacon which usually was of poor quality and four ounces of flour. The rations, when a soldier could get some, represented about eighteen hundred calories a day

---

[39] Ibid, p.627.

[40] Longacre, *Lee's Cavalrymen*, pp.42-43.

[41] Ibid.

[42] *OR*, vol.25, pt.2, p.597

which was not sufficient to keep physically active men from losing weight. Like the situation in the Federal army, symptoms of scurvy began to show themselves due to a lack of fresh fruits and vegetables. To help combat the problem each regiment was required to send daily details to scour the countryside for lamb's quarters, wild onions and sassafras buds. Years later Harry Heth noted Lee's concern for supplying sustenance to his army was his primary anxiety, even after the conclusion of the Gettysburg Campaign. During the spring of the following year, Lee told Heth, "The question of food for this army gives me more trouble and uneasiness than every thing [sic] else combined." Heth became well acquainted with the hardships incurred by the reductions in rations that spring. "It is very difficult for any one not connected with the Army of Northern Virginia to realize how straitened [sic] we were for supplies of all kind, especially food." Continuing Heth noted, "[t]he ration of a general officer was double that of a private, and so meager was that double supply that frequently to appease my hunger I robbed my horse of a handful of corn, which, parched in the fire, served to allay the cravings of nature. What must have been the condition of the private?"[43]

Not all of Lee's supply problems were caused by the lack of sustenance in Virginia. While ample supplies were available in the southern region of the Confederacy, many of the supplies were not getting to the army. There were two reasons for this. First, so many animals had been commandeered to support the war effort that regional transportation had suffered significantly. While the rail lines could transport large volumes of material, food and forage could not be transported to the rail heads in any volume because of the lack of work animals.

The second problem was the substandard performance of the Confederate commissary under Commissary General Lucius B. Northrop. An old crony of Davis' from the pre-war years, Northrop, even after being reprimanded, continued to remain in his position. Instead of looking for solutions to the problems of supply, Northrop spent his time complaining about his situation and blaming field commanders for his problems. To make matters worse, his organization was fraught with inefficiency and waste. According to Northrop, early in January 1863, a representative from his department was sent to meet with General Lee regarding food and supplies. Northrop reported that the general refused to meet with the man and he returned to Richmond. It seems highly unlikely that Lee would refuse to see a representative from Northrop's department while, during the same period, chronically bringing the problem of supply for his army to the attention of Seddon and Davis.[44]

Desertions and Command Style

Lee was dealing with another severe problem during the months leading up to his push northward. The hard winter had precipitated an increase in the number of desertions and the volume grew to an extreme level. While desertions from any unit were a problem the epidemic reached a critical point in units from North

---

[43] Nye, Wilber S., *Here Come the Rebels*, p.4; Heth, Henry, Letter from Major-General Henry Heth, of A. P. Hill's Corps, A.N.V., *SHSP*, vol.4, p.153.

[44] Nye, *Rebels*, pp.4-5; *OR*, vol.25, pt.2, p.688.

Carolina. In a letter to Seddon on 21 May, Lee expressed his concern. "The desertion of the North Carolina troops from this army is becoming so serious an evil that, unless it can be promptly arrested, I fear that troops from that state will become greatly reduced." He cited an incident from Jim Lane's brigade in which thirty-two members of the 37th North Carolina, just after being paid, deserted, taking with them all their accoutrements. Lee was not the only person concerned about the desertion problem with the North Carolinian troops. General William Pender relayed his concern over the desertions in a letter to his wife on 23 May. "We have lost [a] great many men by desertion since the fight [Chancellorsville], most from N./C. Regts."[45]

When the desertion issue became serious in late May, Lee took steps to stem the tide and bring the fugitives either back to the army or to the stockade. He notified General Stuart that orders had been given to General William E. "Grumble" Jones to dispatch two regiments of cavalry from his command in the upper reaches of the Shenandoah Valley to the Stanardsville, Brownsville area of Virginia to capture some 200 armed deserters reported to be in the area. Lee instructed Stuart to help Jones if he could. "If you can assist in the destruction of these miscreants, I desire you to do so," he told Stuart.[46]

While cowardice was one reason for desertion, there were other characteristics of the Confederate fighting man that precipitated the problem. The Southern soldier was a rather independent sort. He was often poor at accepting authority. Most were from small rural towns where their family's survival was directly related to their individuality. While he fought well and hard, when he became concerned over the welfare of his family or thought he was needed at home, he simply packed up and went there. The majority of soldiers in Lee's army were from Virginia and North Carolina, the two states in or closest to the Army of Northern Virginia's region of operation. Many of the men were extremely close to home and many Virginians were within walking distance. Some even passed through their hometown as the army marched from camp to camp. It was easy for a soldier to succumb to a desire to go home when home was so close.[47]

Making things worse, was North Carolina Governor Zebulon B. Vance, who unintentionally exacerbated the desertion problem. Vance, a politician by trade, who had served as the first Colonel of the 26th North Carolina, found public service irresistible. After a year in the army, he left the regiment and was elected to the governorship. Taking office, he worked to organize his state's militia, finding it difficult to attain order among the mass of inexperienced men. His intention was to organize local men in order to find and arrest deserters and those who harbored them. Once prepared, the militia went about the task of searching out fugitives and their collaborator. In one instance Vance's troops became engaged in a battle

---

[45] *Ibid*, p.814; Hassler, William W., Editor, ***One of Lee's Best Men: The Civil War Letters of General William Dorsey Pender***, p.239.

[46] Nye, ***Rebels***, p.14; ***OR***, vol.25, pt.2, p.828. At the time Lee ordered Jones to Brownsville, he was returning from participating in a cavalry raid into West Virginia with General John Imboden.

[47] Nye, ***Rebels***, p.14.

with deserters and two of the militia were killed. The deserters were imprisoned but managed to obtain a writ of habeas corpus and their case was brought before North Caroline Supreme Court Chief Justice Richmond M. Pearson. Pearson, after hearing the case, dismissed the charges stating that the governor had no authority to arrest the men because the state legislature had not specifically provided it. Vance had requested such legislation in addition to a law making it illegal to harbor fugitives, but the lawmakers refused to act. He also made a similar request of the Confederate Congress, but that body declined to act as well. Vance now had two dead militiamen and no one to hold accountable. To make matters worse, word of Pearson's ruling spread to the army. The North Carolinians in the ranks took it to mean that once home within the boundaries of their own state, the civil authorities would protect them from the consequences of their actions. Once this falsity was held, the North Carolinians began streaming home by the dozen.[48]

Virginia's wartime governor, Zebulon B. Vance. *LOC*

Ten days prior to Lee's 21 May note to Seddon, Vance issued a scathing proclamation in which he left no doubt as to his opinion regarding the stature of any individual who encouraged desertion of a friend or family member who did likewise. Vance had studied law at the University of North Carolina and his ability to express his views with a pen was first rate. Regarding inciters of desertion he pulled no punches, instructing, "all such evildisposed [sic] persons to desist from such base, cowardly, and treasonable conduct, and warning them that they will subject themselves to indictment and punishment in the civil courts of the Confederacy, as well as to the everlasting contempt and detestation of all good

---

[48] Faust, ***Encyclopedia***, p.570; ***OR***, vol.51, pt.2, pp.709.

and honorable men." The governor also sought to reduce the inciter of desertion by shaming them into eliminating the problem.

> "...Certainly no crime could be greater, no cowardice more abject, no treason more base, than for a citizen of the State, enjoying its privileges and protection without the sharing of the dangers, to persuade those who have had the courage to go forth in defense of their country vilely to desert the colors which they have sworn to uphold, when a miserable death or a vile and ignominious existence must be the inevitable consequence. No plea can excuse it. The father or the brother who does it should be shot instead of his deluded victim, for he deliberately destroys the soul and manhood of his own flesh and blood. And the same is done by him who harbors and conceals the deserter, for who can respect either the one or the other? What honest man will ever wish or permit his own brave sons or patriotic daughters, who bore their parts with credit in this great struggle for independence, to associate, even to the third and fourth generations, with the vile wretch who skulked in the woods, or the still viler coward who aided him, while his bleeding country was calling in vain for his help?"[49]

While Vance's proclamation left no doubt as to his stance on the subject of desertion and the citizens who harbored them, it had little effect on reducing the number of departures, and neither did Vance's continuing efforts to arrest those, who in his mind were criminals.

While desertions were an issue that spring, the volume was not enough to cast any shadows on the spirit and fighting talent of the Confederate legions. Lee had great confidence in his troops and his opinion of their abilities was reinforced by the victory at Chancellorsville. When he returned from Richmond, he discovered a letter from his friend General John B. Hood. In it Hood had expressed his confidence in the Confederate fighting man. Lee responded on 21 May, boasted of his own confidence in the men. "I agree with you in believing that our army would be invincible if it could be properly organized and officered. There never were such men in an army before. They will go anywhere and do anything if properly led." The élan of the Confederate fighting man was at its highest point of the war. Porter Alexander of Longstreet's reserve artillery also thought the army indestructible. "I am sure there can never have been an army with more supreme confidence in its commander than that army had in Gen. Lee," he wrote after the war. "We looked forward to victory under him as confidently as to successive sunrises." They were a ragtag group who often marched in bare feet and were ferocious when dealing with the enemy. They considered themselves better fighters than the Yankee hordes. Now Lee had plans to take them into the enemy's country. It remained to be seen if

---

[49] *OR*, vol.51, pt.2, pp.706-707.

they would fight as hard outside of their beloved Confederacy. The other unknown however, was how would the Yankee's fight defending their territory.[50]

Another challenge Lee faced in restructuring his army was a lack of qualified brigade level commanders. Previous battles had shrunk the resource pool significantly. Lee need to replace brigade commanders lost or wounded during those struggles, but attrition was beginning to seriously limit his options. Brigadiers were typically attained from the best and brightest of regimental commanders. During the Civil War, regimental commanders were normally required to be at the forefront of their commands during the heaviest of fighting, taking a grave toll on prospective brigade commanders. Heavy losses at the brigade and regimental level greatly limited the choices. The loss of line officers during the Chancellorsville campaign had been exceedingly heavy, and if Lee was going to wrestle the South's independence from the North, it would need to be soon before the Confederacy was bled dry of its best command level prospects.[51]

Lee's command style required corps, division and brigade level commanders who could act with little direction in an effort to achieve the goals he outlined. He generally issue discretionary orders, stating the overall objective and allowed his subordinate commanders to determine how best to accomplish the desired task. Lee needed commanders who could evaluate situations, determine a course of action and execute the plan, all while keeping the overall objective in mind. A fine example of this is Jackson's flanking march at Chancellorsville. Once the information about the enemy was gathered and the decision made to turn Hooker's flank, Lee stepped back and allowed Jackson to organize, plan and execute the details of the movement.[52]

A hands off type of command execution was critical for Napoleonic era armies to function if headquarter staff levels were as limited as they were in Lee's case. In order for Lee to take more direct control over the army he would have needed a much larger staff with many couriers dedicated to delivering messages. His small staff did not provide this luxury, nor did Lee wish to have it, making it essential for his commanders to have the ability to think on their feet. Lee faithfully utilized this type of command execution throughout the war, very seldom straying from it, even when the army was concentrated in battle and a more hands on approach could have improved his chances for success.[53]

A course of action blatantly obvious to one commander may not be as obvious to another. The issuing of discretionary orders to a subordinate by a commander who sees an opportunity which the subordinate does not picture in a similar manner may be problematic. The subordinate now has the responsibility to assess the situation and make the decision as to a course of action. Lee's hands off style and habit of issuing discretionary orders was in all probability not the manner in

---

[50] *Ibid*, p.490.

[51] Bowden & Ward, **Last Chance**, p.39.

[52] *Ibid*, p.4, 52.

[53] *Ibid*, pp.22-24.

which his new corps commanders should have been initially handled, at least for the first few weeks, until Hill and Ewell became accustomed to Lee's intentions when he issued orders.

Later in the war, as the shortage of commanders grew even worse, Lee would be required to take greater control of the army. For the present however, he would continue to issue discretionary order. Throughout the Gettysburg Campaign, even when a more direct order may have been appropriate to ensure his desires were carried out, Lee would persist in relying on his commanders, once prompted by discretionary instructions, to see the same opportunities he saw and act upon them.[54]

Southern Grand Strategy

In the spring of 1863, the concept of invading Northern territory was not a new one. As far back as June 1861, before the first Battle of Manassas, Isaac R. Trimble, then a colonel, proposed moving a force north to Hagerstown, Maryland. Trimble felt the defense of Virginia could be better handled if the army was anchored north of the Potomac. At the time, Harpers Ferry was the northern most anchorage, but while the river town was easily conquered, it was difficult to hold. Positioned at the junction of the Shenandoah and Potomac River's, the town was surrounded by high bluffs on all sides and could easily be invested. Trimble's plan was to take Hagerstown and then pursue the Northerners into Pennsylvania while spreading the word that the attack was a precursor to a westward movement. Then, an additional column would be sent to Baltimore or possibly Washington. Such a move Trimble believed, would force the abandonment of the Federal capital. Trimble was an aggressive commander and of the belief that taking a defensive posture was not the way to win the war. He was a good friend of Lee's and sent his proposal directly to the general. There is no evidence that Trimble's plan was ever given any consideration, but he was the first to put forth a documented proposal to take the war north.[55]

Another plan for conquering the Yankees with a movement north of the Potomac was the brainchild of General Beauregard. As with Trimble's plan, Beauregard made his proposal shortly before the first Battle of Manassas. He sent one of his aides, Colonel James Chesnut, to Richmond to present his plan for dealing with the Federal armies in and around Washington. Chesnut arrived during the afternoon of 14 July 1861 and was ushered into a meeting with Davis, Lee and Inspector General Samuel Cooper. The first phase of Beauregard's plan was to unite his force with that of Joe Johnston, who was currently watching General Robert Patterson's Federal troops in the Shenandoah Valley. The united force acting with Brigadier General T. H. Holmes' small force from Fredericksburg would drive General McDowell's army back to the entrenchments of Washington. With McDowell dealt with, Johnston would take a portion of Beauregard's army and drive Patterson from the Valley. Once the Valley was cleared of Federals, a

---

[54] Dowdey, Clifford, *Seven Days*, p.144.

[55] *OR*, vol.51, pt.2, pp.129-130.

portion of Johnston's men would head west to help Brigadier General Robert S. Garnett defeat George McClellan in western Virginia. With the three major Federal armies defeated, Garnett would unite with Johnston and cross the Potomac to assault Washington from the north while Beauregard attacked from across the Potomac from the south.

Cooper, Lee and Davis considered the plan, as Chesnut recalled, "brilliant and comprehensive." While the plan was well thought out, Davis and Lee both rejected it due to the small size of Johnston's force, believing sufficient troops could not be drawn from it to guarantee success and still hold Patterson in the Valley. Another drawback was the proximity of Washington. It was felt that the entrenchments around the Federal capital were too close and a retreating army would simply fall back and regroup or be reinforced quickly to venture forth once again to the Virginia countryside. Lee and Davis informed Chesnut that the idea might be better executed at some point in the future but for now the time was not right.[56]

Beauregard and Trimble were not the only men presenting plans outlining the best manner in which to invade the North. In October of the same year, Stonewall Jackson sought out his commander, Gustavus Woodson Smith and presented a plan for conquering the Federals. Jackson sought out Smith who was lying in his tent feeling ill. Sitting on the ground next to the general's cot, he presented his plan. The time was right, according to Jackson to move north. McClellan was new to command of the Federal army in Washington and moving now while the Union troops were raw and unorganized would provide an opportunity to fight them to advantage. Jackson thought the Confederates should invade the North now before McClellan could organize, train and advance with a strong, numerically superior force. His plan was very similar to that proposed by Beauregard. "Crossing the upper Potomac, occupying Baltimore, and taking possession of Maryland, we could cut off the communications of Washington," he told Smith. Jackson felt severing the capital would force the Federal government to abandon Washington and require McClellan to come out with his army to receive a sound thrashing. The plan however had a few significant additions beyond the plans proposed by Beauregard.

After McClellan had been dealt with, Jackson suggested moving the army further north into Pennsylvania and have it enter into a campaign that brought the war to the doorstep of the Northern populace. Continuing on, Jackson proposed to Smith that they "destroy industrial establishments wherever we found them, break up the lines of interior commercial intercourse, close the coal mines, seize and, if necessary, destroy the manufactories and commerce of Philadelphia, and of other large cities within our reach; take and hold the narrow neck of country between Pittsburg and Lake Erie; subsist mainly on the country we traverse, and making unrelenting war amidst their homes, force the people of the North to understand what it will cost them to hold the South in the Union at the bayonet's point." This was nothing short of a scorched earth policy and in reality it was the only way to make Northern citizens feel the effects of war.

---

[56] *OR*, vol.2, pp.485, 507. James Chesnut was the husband of famed diarist Mary Chesnut.

Jackson asked his commander to present his plan to Johnston and Beauregard, but Smith was reluctant to do so citing the recent negative reaction to Beauregard's proposal. Disappointed Jackson departed, but his thoughts regarding a northward movement continued to develop. A few days after his discussion with Smith he was transferred to the Shenandoah Valley. From his new assignment, he began thinking about how an invasion north of the Potomac could be accomplished.[57]

Once in the Valley, Jackson began contemplating how his concept of invasion could be modified and executed from his new position. A major adjustment to his previous plan was the inclusion of a second column, his command, marching north into western Pennsylvania. First he would dispose of the Union presence in northwestern Virginia, to be followed by a brief period of recruitment to swell the numbers in his command. Whether enough men sympathetic to the Southern cause and willing to fight for it could be found to grow his numbers to the 25,000 he hoped for was questionable. After increasing his numbers, Jackson would then move north into western Pennsylvania and assault Pittsburg and raid the United States arsenal there. Then, moving eastward his column would join another moving north from Virginia. Once joined, the entire force would take Harrisburg and spend the winter north of the Potomac. In the spring, as the weather improved, the army would organize and march out to harass the Pennsylvania countryside and move on Philadelphia. Like his first plan, the modified version was also rejected.[58]

Even after a second denial, Jackson never let the notion of a northward movement stray far from his mind. Once again, after the Valley Campaign was over in the spring of 1862, he tried to get his plan approved. This time he sent a representative to Richmond with instructions. "You may tell them," Jackson informed Alexander R. Boteler, "that if my command can be gotten up to 40,000 men a movement may be made beyond the Potomac, which will soon raise the siege of Richmond and transfer this campaign from the banks of the James to those of the Susquehanna." This time he received interest from Davis, but the president wished to consult Lee before he gave approval for Jackson to move. "I think if it was possible to reinforce Jackson strongly, it would change the character of the war," Lee responded, feeling that Jackson moving into Pennsylvania would draw Federal troops from their positions along the southern coast. Unfortunately for Jackson, a few days later he was ordered to leave the Valley and with the bulk of his army, move south and join Lee to push McClellan away from the doorstep of Richmond.[59]

A common misconception regarding the Army of Northern Virginia's campaigns is that each battle or movement was the product of an individual goal

---

[57] Henderson, ***Stonewall Jackson***, vol.1, pp.174-175.

[58] Cooke, John Esten, ***Stonewall Jackson: A Military Biography***, pp.86-88. Cooke was Jeb Stuart's ordnance office.

[59] Boteler, Alexander R., Stonewall Jackson In Campaign of 1862, ***SHSP***, vol.40, p.165; Dowdey & Manarin, ***Wartime Papers***, pp. 183-184; ***OR***, vol.12, pt. 3, p.910.

at any specific moment in time. In truth, the movements and battles were associated with an overall strategy to win the war. Charles Marshal, Lee's aide-de-camp, wrote after the war that the "...battles and strategic movements which attracted so much attention were not separate and distinct events, entirely independent one of the other, but formed parts of one plan of warfare, adopted by General Lee at the time he took command of the army, and steadily pursued until his means were exhausted." According to Marshal, the battles and movements in Virginia and north of the Potomac were all part of a single campaign intended to bring the war to a successful termination. The issue with Marshal's conclusion however is his use of the term defense. He imparted the strategy and campaigns were that of a defensive operation. There is no doubt that while Marshal considered the overall operation as a defensive action, Lee used offensive tactics to accomplish short-term goals. While Lee thought Jackson's proposal a valid one, he could not let him march north to annoy the Northern populace while McClellan prepared to invest Richmond. Any move into Pennsylvania would have to wait.[60]

Jackson's proposed invasion remained under consideration even as he helped Lee deal with McClellan. Now that he was a direct subordinate of Lee's, he had numerous opportunities to discuss a northward movement. After The Seven Days battles came to a successful conclusion, the planning for a thrust north resumed. Lee officially organized his command into the Army of Northern Virginia and through the months of July and August of 1862, pushed it northward with Jackson spending most of his time leading the advance. Unfortunate circumstances kept the army from advancing across the state line into Pennsylvania, and Lee had to fall back across the river to Virginia after Sharpsburg, but, the plan to invade remained foremost in both Lee and Jackson's minds.[61]

Conversations continued throughout the winter and spring of 1862 and 1863. One man in a position to be privy to the discussions was Jackson's cartographer Jedediah Hotchkiss. Hotchkiss noted some years later that while the army wintered in and around Fredericksburg, Lee meet with Jackson and Stuart on numerous occasions to discuss a movement northward once spring arrived. Stuart's presence was important having recently returned from a successful cavalry raid to the Chambersburg area of southern Pennsylvania. According to Hotchkiss, Jackson spent much of his time at his headquarters busying himself with "his favorite design for a campaign into Pennsylvania, to break up the mining operations in the anthracite coalfield…"

Northern industry was powered by coal. It was the energy source for manufacturing goods and shipping them by both rail and steamship. Now that war had come, coal was also used to move troops by rail, power the Northern navy, and produce materials of war. Coal production in the northeast corner of Pennsylvania could be a prime target for Confederate troops. Over three-quarters of the total coal production in the North came from there. More importantly however, was the production of anthracite, or hard coal, which burned much hotter and

---

[60] Marshall, *Lee's Aide-de-Camp*, pp.67-68.

[61] The unfortunate incident was the loss of Special Order No. 191.

more efficiently than bituminous coal. Greater than half of the total production of anthracite coal came from the area. Jackson believed that if the Confederates could advance into the region and disrupt the mining operations, the Northern war effort would be crippled, forcing the Federal government to reevaluate their stance towards a negotiated peace.[62]

During the winter, Jackson asked Hotchkiss to prepare a detailed map of the region to be traversed during the campaign. He recorded the request in his diary on 23 February. "I got secret orders from the General [Jackson] to prepare a map of the Valley of Va. extending to Harrisburg, Pa., and then on to Philadelphia; wishing the preparation to be kept a profound secret. So I went to reducing a map of Cumberland Co., Pa." When the work was close to completion, Hotchkiss requested additional maps from Captain William W. Blackford of Stuart's staff. Blackford had been with Stuart's column as it entered Pennsylvania during the Chambersburg raid and had constructed some maps of his own. Hotchkiss used these to complete his master map of the area. He worked on it almost daily until it was completed on 10 March. When it was done, he showed it to Jackson who was impressed enough to take it to his commander. Lee would rely on the map heavily as his men marched north later in the year.[63]

With the planning and preparation progressing, Lee set the start date for his movement for some time in the late spring when the roads and weather would permit. Hooker's advance and the subsequent battle of Chancellorsville forced him to delay his departure. The loss of Jackson also forced him to bring First Corps commander James Longstreet into the discussion. Longstreet had not been involved in previous planning meetings. Now Lee would have to bring him up to speed and get him onboard with the overall concept.

Lee and Longstreet Discuss the Plan

Longstreet and his corps were near Suffolk when, on 1 May, he received an urgent message from Lee. Hooker's army was stirring and his corps was needed to help better the odds. With his supply trains in an exposed position, he wired back, asking Lee if he should abandon them to the enemy to expedite his departure. He received no reply to his inquiry and chose to delay his departure until the trains could be brought in. Pulling his corps away from Suffolk, he crossed the Blackwater River the march northward. However, before reaching Richmond, he received another telegram announcing the victory at Chancellorsville and the sense of urgency departed.[64]

With the emergency averted, Longstreet had time to stop in Richmond and pay his respects to Secretary of War Seddon. During his visit, Seddon showed great concern over the situation at Vicksburg. He suggested to Longstreet that his corps might be needed in Mississippi, and he thought such a move would

---

[62] *CMH*, vol.3, part.1, pp.375-376; Kegel, James A., *North with Lee and Jackson*, pp.47-49.

[63] Hotchkiss, Jedediah, *Make Me a Map*, pp.116-119.

[64] Longstreet, Lee in Pennsylvania, *AW*, p.415; Longstreet, James, *MtoA*, p.326.

make Joe Johnston's army strong enough to push Grant away from the city. The secretary's plan for a direct assault on Grant did not appeal to Longstreet. Instead the general put forth a plan to take his corps and reinforce General Braxton Bragg's army in Tennessee and drive north into Ohio. This course of action appealed to Longstreet because once the Federal army in Tennessee was deal with the road into Ohio would be free of organized resistance. Longstreet thought moving into the state would force Grant to lift the siege of Vicksburg and dispatch part of his force to deal with the threat. Seddon remained unconvinced and continued to support his original plan. Shortly thereafter, Longstreet left Richmond to rejoin Lee.[65]

Longstreet arrived in time to have dinner with Lee on 9 May. His chieftain was still distraught over the wounding of Jackson, and Longstreet noticed his anguish. The next day, the day Jackson died, the two men began a series of meetings to discuss the army's next course of action. He no doubt presented his proposal to reinforce Bragg and they surely discussed the situation at Vicksburg, and any options which might alleviate pressure along the Mississippi. Lee listened quietly to the proposal and then, according to Longstreet, asked if a move northward by his own army would not accomplish the same ends. Longstreet did not believe so, but he soon learned that Lee had already made the decision to move his army north. Determining that no amount of discussion would persuade Lee to change his mind, Longstreet took a different approach.[66]

Longstreet suggested that the coming campaign be fought with offensive strategies but utilize defensive tactics. The campaign could be successful, he advocated, if the army used offensive maneuvers to position itself so that the Federal force had to attack them. "I suggested that, after piercing Pennsylvania and menacing Washington, we should choose a strong position, and force the Federals to attack us, observing that the popular clamor throughout the North would speedily force the Federal general to attempt to drive us out." He used the recent battle of Fredericksburg as an example of a superior force beaten by a well-established one in a good defensive position.[67]

According to Longstreet, Lee acquiesced to his suggestion and promised him the campaigned would be fought as he wished. To help maintain the mindset Longstreet suggested, "...that we should have all the details and purposes so well arranged and so impressed upon our minds that when the critical moment should come, we could refer to our calmer moments and know we were carrying out our original plans." This was his way of trying to control Lee during the excitement of battle. Longstreet was well aware of Lee's propensity to lose sight of a campaign's

---

[65] Longstreet, Lee in Pennsylvania, *AW*, p.416.

[66] *Ibid*. No record of Lee ever offering his opinion on whether dispatching troops to reinforce Bragg would draw Union troops from Vicksburg has been found. Lee never noted his opinion in any correspondence or official document.

[67] Longstreet, *MtoA*, p.331.

ultimate goal once engaged with the enemy and utilized all his energies to take offensive action against his foe even when it was not warranted or required.[68]

Whether Lee emphatically promised he would not engage in an offensive *battle* is irrelevant. There is no doubt that Longstreet discussed the issue with Lee and he may have taken an offhand comment by his commander as being a promise. Even so, Lee as much as said his plan was to fight a defensive battle if he became engaged. Walter Taylor confirmed this when he wrote after the war that if Lee were to encounter the enemy it would be "upon his [Lee's] own terms as to the time and place." Taylor noted that Lee intended to "receive the attack which the enemy would be compelled to make." This comment implies a defensive stance during any battle which may have developed.[69]

Lee, in truth, nether had to acquiesce or even agree with Longstreet and Longstreet's implication that Lee consented to his offensive campaign with defensive tactics concept was to imply that Lee was the subordinate. The implication that Lee submitted to Longstreet's desires angered many Lee supporters after the war. Lee supposedly reinforced this agreement with his subordinate after the conflict was over. During a conversation with William Allan on 15 April 1868, Lee commented that "his offensive movements against the North were never intended except as part of a defensive system." The critical word within this statement is "system." Most historians have correctly interpreted this as a statement in regard to the overall Confederate strategy for winning the war. Longstreet's concept of offensive movements and defensive battle strategy, if executed properly, would be consistent with this overall approach. Lee's overall defensive strategy could consist of many variable battle strategies. Once the two armies where locked in combat it was well known that defending a position was much easier and cost less blood than taking one. With resources beginning to wane in the South, a defensive battle strategy would have been the best strategy for achieving overall victory within a "defensive system." The important difference between Lee's and Longstreet's concepts was quite simple. Longstreet's concept was to implement defensive strategies during battle. Lee's was to defend the Confederacy with no distinction between defensive or offensive actions when engage.[70]

Lee also noted after the war that it was not his intention to fight a general battle in Pennsylvania "if he could avoid it." In his preliminary report on the battle, he wrote of his desire to "strike a blow" if a "fair opportunity" presented itself. In the context of Lee's report the term could be taken to mean almost any engagement with the enemy of size not just a pitched battle pitting both full strength armies against

---

[68] Longstreet, Lee in Pennsylvania, *AW*, p.417; Longstreet, Lee's Invasion of Pennsylvania, *B&L*, vol.3, p.247; Swinton, William, *Campaigns of the Army of the Potomac: A Critical History of Operations in Virginia Maryland and Pennsylvania from the Commencement to the Close of the War, 1861-1865*, p.340.

[69] Taylor, Walter H., Memorandum by Walter H. Taylor, of General Lee's Staff, *SHSP*, vol.4, p.82.

[70] Allan, William, *Memoranda of Conversation with General Robert E. Lee, 15 April 1868*, Reprinted in "Lee the Soldier" Gallagher, Gary W., Editor, p.13.

one another. Longstreet weighed in on the subject as well during a conversation with author William Swinton after the war. Swinton did not use Longstreet's exact words, but the point of the comment was not lost in translation. "General Lee," wrote Swinton, "expressly promised his corps commanders that *he would not assume a tactical offensive*, but force his antagonist to attack him." Historians have used Swinton's wording of Longstreet's statement as evidence of the First Corps commander's philosophical change after the war. In reality the two statements are not in regard to the same subject. Lee's was obviously, based on his comments after the war, not looking for a confrontation with the Army of the Potomac in Pennsylvania, but he would not pass up an opportunity to damage the Yankees. Longstreet's comment to Swinton was in regard to the prosecution of a fight if one developed. Neither of Lee's other two corps commanders weight in on the subject. A. P. Hill did not survive the war and never addressed the question during the conflict. Ewell never mentioned it after the war making Longstreet the only voice in the matter from the upper echelons of the Confederate high command.[71]

Allan, during a discussion with Lee regarding Longstreet's comments to Swinton noted that Lee did not believe that Longstreet would ever say such a thing and that no agreement existed in which Lee had promised not to fight a "general battle" in Pennsylvania. In this instance Lee and Longstreet are both correct because once again they were discussing two different issues. Longstreet told Swinton that the agreement between Lee and his commanders was not to assume a "tactical offensive." The context of Longstreet's conversation with Swinton was "reported" to Lee and if Lee was told the so called agreement was not to fight a battle, which is the way Allan's notes of the conversation read, then it makes sense that Lee would refute it. Is it possible that during the planning stages of the campaign Lee informed Longstreet of his desire not to fight a "general battle" if he was not forced into one and Longstreet mistook the comment as a promise?[72]

Longstreet made additional comments regarding his ideas on how to contain Lee's propensity for offensive action on the battlefield. In a letter to Lafayette McLaws, written on 25 July 1873, Longstreet, more eloquent in the presentation, wrote on the same topics which he addressed in later years. "I proposed then," he wrote, "as the ruling idea of our campaign, Napoleon's advice to Marmot at the head of an invading army." Longstreet was not sure if he used Napoleon's words, "[t]o make the enemy fight him in his own position," but he was sure he had the context of his comment correct. Lee, Longstreet noted, agreed with this position, that it was a good "maxim" and was applicable to the army. Longstreet even committed his corps to receive the attack and make the defensive stand, then as the Federals battered themselves against his line, the Second and Third Corps would be free to maneuver and fall upon the flanks of the enemy and destroy them. Longstreet called these concepts the "ruling ideas" of the campaign, and he was sure that he had Lee's commitment to adhere to the strategy.

---

[71] *Ibid*; Swinton, **Army of the Potomac**, p.340; **OR**, vol.27, pt. 2, p.305.

[72] Swinton, **Army of the Potomac**, p.340; Allan, **Memoranda**, Lee the Soldier, p.15.

Longstreet also informed McLaws that his early conversations with Lee were not the only time the two men discussed the ruling ideas. "I have intimated our condition was discussed in all of its bearing and almost every day from the 10th of May '63 – until the Battle [sic] and the ... policy as above indicated was firmly fixed in our minds." He also remembered commenting to Lee that all men become excited as battle looms and that if they would submit to their "calmer moments" they would be better able to keep to the original concept of the offensive movement and defensive position strategy.[73]

So it was Longstreet wrote of his mid-May conversations with Lee after the war when he defended himself against an onslaught of criticism for what others perceived as his contributions to the loss at Gettysburg. There is little doubt that in Longstreet's mind he had discussed with Lee all the issues documented in his writings. Time may have clouded the details, but the basic concepts and points were no doubt remembered. However, on 13 May, probably after Lee had left or was preparing to leave in order to meet with Davis and Seddon, Longstreet wrote to his good friend Senator Louis T. Wigfall. Wigfall, who had originally been commissioned a brigadier general in 1861, had proven to be a less than average commander and resigned his commission, trading it for a Senate seat. Wigfall was a supporter of transferring troops to the west, and Longstreet had evidently discussed sending troops that direction with him. However, since his conversation with Lee, it seemed his position regarding sending troops had changed. "…[W]e should make a grand effort against the Yankees this summer," Longstreet wrote, "every available man and means should be brought to bear against them. When I agreed with the Secy & yourself about sending troops west," Longstreet continued, "I was under the impression that we would be obliged to remain on the defensive here. I told him [Lee] that I thought that we could spare the troops unless there was a chance of a forward movement. If we could move of course we should want everything, that we had and all that we could get." Longstreet informed Wigfall that there was a "fair prospect" of a movement northward and that no troops could be spared from the army for a thrust in the west and that 150,000 men would be needed for the march. Longstreet, who had not been a participant in the conversations between Lee, Jackson and Stuart, was probably unaware of what Lee was planning as he spoke with Wigfall and Seddon before rejoining the army.[74]

Many historians have berated Longstreet and used his lack of discussion regarding his talks with Lee in the Wigfall letter as evidence that his opinion changed after the war as he defended his actions. Others have gone so far as to use the Wigfall letter as proof that Longstreet originally endorsed Lee's plan and then later chastised it as he defended his honor. While it seems Longstreet conveniently changed his opinion, in truth, he was simply promoting the decision and proposal Lee was on his way to Richmond to make. As a subordinate, it was Longstreet's

---

[73] James Longstreet to Lafayette McLaws, July 25 1873, Lafayette McLaws Papers, Southern Historical Collection, University of North Carolina.

[74] James Longstreet to Louis T. Wigfall, 13 May 1863, Louis T. Wigfall Papers, LOC; Wert, **Longstreet**, pp.244-245.

job to review his commander's plans and offer suggestions as to how a plan could be improved. If his ideas were accepted so much the better, if not, then it was his job to adopt the plan as Longstreet once wrote "as if it were my own." The letter to his friend was simply worded as an adoption of Lee's plan and a courteous explanation as to the change of heart because he was now required, by his own moral compass to adopt and promote Lee's plan. Longstreet had no responsibility or authority to relay any conversation he may have had with Lee in which strategies for the proposed campaign were discussed. In fact, Longstreet began the letter by informing Wigfall, in a poorly worded preamble that the letter was meant for his eyes only, writing, "[s]ome of these matters by me to anyone beyond Gen. Lee and yourself." Wigfall although he was a senator, was neither a member of the military nor a member of the Confederate high command. Additionally, Longstreet would have betrayed Lee's confidence if he would have discussed any issues which the two men had conferred about during any of their private conferences. Longstreet, after the discussions, had obviously determined in his own mind that Lee intended to take his army north. Such a move was not feasible if troops from the army were sent west. He simply used the "prospect" of a move north to cordially backtrack from his previous discussion with Wigfall. As far as endorsing Lee's proposal, Longstreet only said that no troops could be spared if there was a "chance of a forward" movement and that a "grand effort" should be made during the coming summer. This was nothing more than adopting and promoting Lee's views as his "own."[75]

Longstreet's writings seemed not so much to disapprove the concept of a northward movement but to criticize the way the campaign was waged after he had what he believed to be an agreement with Lee on how the campaign would be executed. "I was never persuaded to yield my argument against the Gettysburg campaign, except with the understanding that we were not to deliver an offensive battle, but to so maneuver that the enemy should be forced to attack us," Longstreet wrote. In short, Longstreet supported the campaign since he believed he had an agreement with Lee on how the campaign would be conducted. It was only after Lee deviated from the agreed upon plan that Longstreet begin to question the wisdom of the campaign and only as to its execution. So in writing to Wigfall, Longstreet did nothing more than inform him that success was possible to the north. He did not tell Wigfall how, and informed him that the move would not allow the army to send troops west and that as many troops as possible should be sent to Lee's army. At no time before the battle did Longstreet discuss or communicate the offensive campaign with defensive tactics to anyone or at least no one other than Longstreet came forward. By not doing so, he kept that portion of his discussions with Lee confidential but left himself open to criticism for changing his position on the campaign after the fact. If Longstreet had noted in his letter that he had an agreement with Lee as to the campaign's plan of execution, the ammunition fired at him after the war would have been easier to refute.[76]

---

[75] Longstreet to Wigfall, 13 May 1863; Longstreet, Lee in Pennsylvania, *AW*, p.414.

[76] Longstreet, Lee in Pennsylvania, *AW*, p.417.

There is little doubt that Longstreet discussed the subject of an offensive campaign with defensive tactics with Lee. He commented on the conversation many times after the war and while his wording may have changed, the basic context remained the same. Lee's comments after the war, while used as a contradiction to Longstreet's beliefs, were in reality made in regard to whether a general battle would be fought not as to how it should be fought. Longstreet knew it was his job to make suggestions, and he believed in this instance they had been. Whatever the truth of the matter was, Longstreet thought he had Lee's word on how the campaign would be conducted. Lee however, had the luxury of changing his mind based on the events encountered during the campaign and did not have to explain himself to his subordinates. Lee was the commander and whatever he believed to be the best course of action, would be how the campaign would be executed. The fact that the two generals may have misunderstood each other is difficult to understand. Longstreet was very close to Lee during the march north and they saw each other often. To think they did not discuss the execution of the offensive with defensive tactics on additional occasions or that the misinterpretation was so total that it was not corrected during the movement north is hard to fathom. The entire episode quite possible could be boiled down to a simple misunderstanding of each man's definition of the phrase "assume a tactical offensive."[77]

---

[77] *Ibid*, p.414.

Book II
Pawns

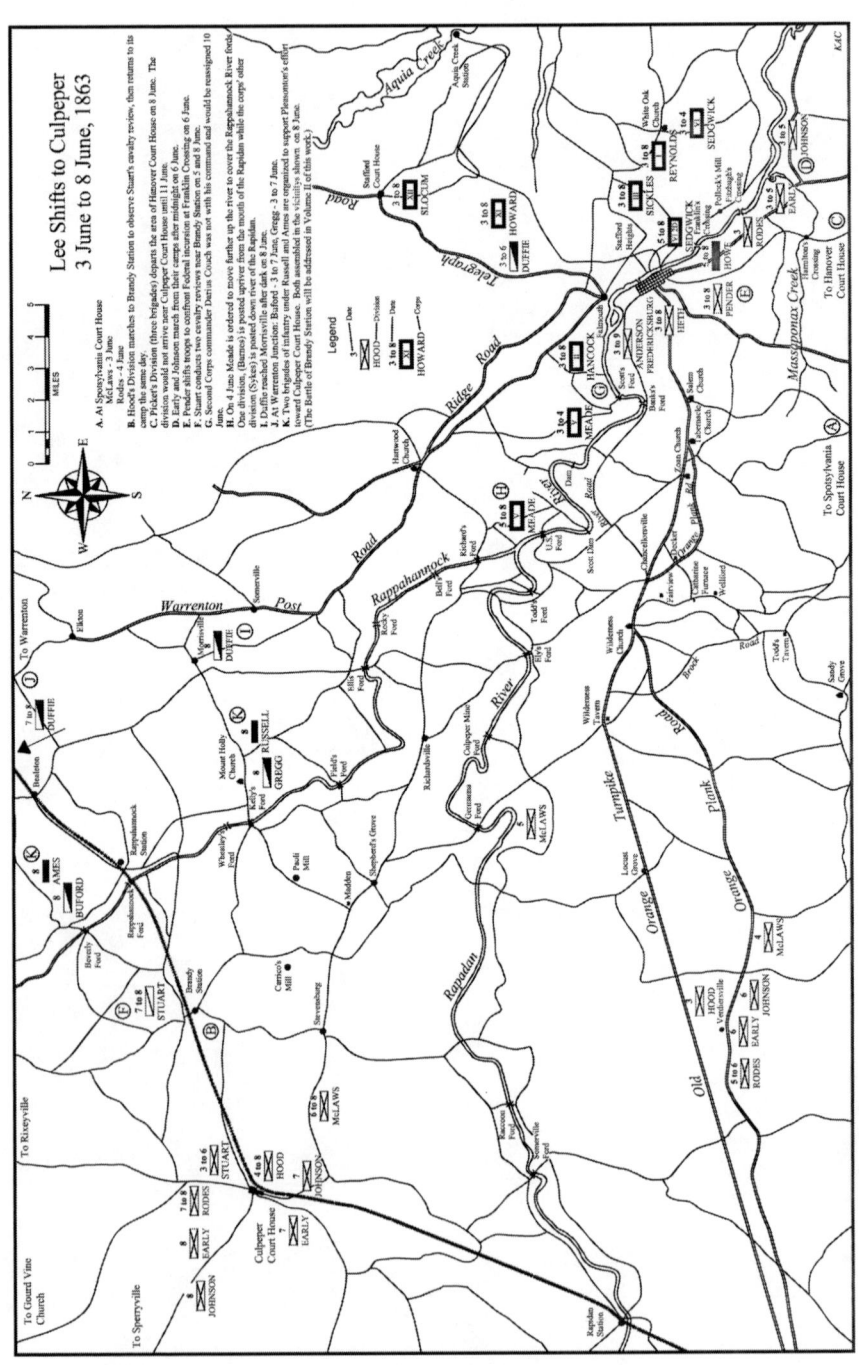

Lee Shifts to Culpeper

Chapter VIII
The Game Begins

> "I commenced to draw the army from the vicinity of Fredericksburg on Wednesday morning, June 3."
> *Robert E. Lee informing Jefferson Davis the summer campaign was underway.*
> *7 June 1863.* [1]

George Pickett was a bit perturbed. For some time he had been hearing rumors of another move northward by Robert E. Lee and was anxious to have his division participate. It was now late May and the bulk of Longstreet's soon to be smaller and revamped First Corps was positioned near Fredericksburg. Pickett however, was still twenty five miles south guarding the rail lines near Hanover Junction and the small town of Taylorsville. He had marched his men to Hanover, arriving on 18 May, without Jenkins' Brigade, which was still on the Blackwater River. Lee had done everything possible to dislodge Jenkins, short of riding to the Blackwater and taking command of the brigade himself to escort it north. The loss of Jenkins would be the beginning of a number of difficulties Pickett would face during the campaign. His disgust with the situation would eventually be directed toward Lee and any friendship the two men may have clung to prior to the campaign would wither and slowly die.[2]

While the loss of Jenkins was a severe blow, the worst was yet to come or so Pickett began to believe. With the army preparing for its push, word through the rumor mill came filtering in that he and his division would be left behind. Discussions concerning the deployment of his division to Mississippi to help Pemberton had taken place. Lee expressed concern over the transfer, and reinforcement by Davis, put an end to the idea. Local fears however, would play a larger role in detaining Pickett.[3]

---

[1] *OR* vol.27, pt.2, p.293.

[2] Wallace, Lee A. Jr., *1st Virginia Infantry*, p.40; *OR* vol.25, pt.2, pp.811, 826-827, 831, 833, 848-849; Longacre, Edward G., *Pickett: Leader of the Charge*, p.111.

[3] *OR* vol.25, pt.2, p.790.

On 2 June, in a letter to Davis, Lee conceded that Pickett's Division could be retained at Hanover Junction, but for how long he did not say. Lee's concession was an effort to calm Davis' fear of a Federal threat from the Potomac River. Earlier in May a Yankee force, which exceeded 5,000 men, had landed at West Point Virginia, only forty miles from where Pickett was stationed. The landing while short-lived, as the Federals departed almost as quickly as they came, increased the tension in Richmond. Lee, intending to extract his army slowly from the Fredericksburg area, planned to watch the actions of the Federals closely and to be in a position to recall troops if the enemy made a southward move toward the capital. It is probable that Lee intended all along to send for Pickett once on the march and the authorities in Richmond acknowledge the city's safety, which, in fact, is what he did.[4]

Before Pickett was allowed to march, Davis learned of a second Federal landing in approximately the same location. The new expedition was decidedly smaller than the initial Federal effort, being only around 400 men. Still stewing over the loss of Jenkins, Pickett's effort to deal with the invaders was anything but aggressive. When Lee became aware of Pickett's indifferent attitude he send a communication instructing him to advance and "drive" the invaders out. By the time the message was received, the raiding party had left the area, but Pickett, who always had a difficult time shaking off criticism, took offence to Lee's tone and instructions. The rift between the two was widening.[5]

By the time Pickett was ordered to leave Hanover Junction, it was well into June and Lee's army was already on the move. Hood's and McLaws' Divisions were already with Longstreet, and he was eager to join them. Once again however, as with Jenkins, he was instructed to leave one of his brigades behind. This time it was Montgomery Corse's brigade of battle-tested Virginians. While the brigade numbered less than 1,200 men, they would all have been welcome additions to Lee's force. Lee's intention was to eventually have Corse's brigade released and sought to have a replacement sent to the area and let Corse march north. On 9 June he suggested to Davis that Cooke's brigade of North Carolinians in the Richmond area be moved to Hanover Junction to liberate Corse, and Jenkins be brought to the Richmond area to cover for Cooke. Unfortunately Davis' administration once again failed Lee.[6]

In the same 9 June communication, Lee informed the president that he had already ordered Corse north to join Pickett, who had left Hanover the day before. As his division departed, he was under the impression that Corse would soon join him. Although Corse had been delayed slightly, Lee intended for him to reunite with his division after the march began. Again, Davis' narrow vision, his desire to defend every inch of the Confederacy, and his paranoia regarding the safety of the capital hampered Lee. The president seemed unable to recognize deep Federal concerns over the safety of the Northern capital by the Lincoln administration,

---

[4] *OR* vol.25, pt.2, p.848.

[5] Longacre, **Pickett**, pp.109-110.

[6] *OR* vol.27, pt.3, pp.874, 893; Manarin, Louis H., **15th Virginia Infantry**, p.43-44.

greatly reduced the vulnerability of Richmond. Washington had shown they would not take steps to develop a significant threat to Richmond with Lee's army on the loose in Northern Virginia. Political pressure and Lincoln himself would not allow such an effort. Instead of ordering Lee's wishes carried out, Davis simply forwarded the requests and allowed his subordinates, who had different ideas about defending their positions, to determine the course of action.[7]

"I was much pleased to hear that General Pickett had left at least a small brigade [Corse's] at the Junction," Davis responded to Lee, "for some force there, ...seems to be indispensable to render your communications tolerably safe." The following day, Adjutant General Cooper sent a communication to D. H. Hill relaying Lee's desires to have Corse's brigade turned loose. If Lee's plan to replace Corse with another brigade was carried out, Hill would lose Jenkins to Richmond. Cooper however, left the decision as to whether Jenkins would be released up to the North Carolinian. "With better knowledge of what is before you than is possessed here," Cooper wrote, "the matter is submitted to you with the hope that it may be practicable for you to send a brigade (Jenkins' or Colquitt's) to the Chickahominy." General Elzey had informed Hill earlier it would "require 100,000 men" to defend the capital and seemed to balk at releasing any troops to Lee. Hill continued to resist giving up troops and agreed with Elzey as to the Chickahominy line being too long to defend with a single brigade. Lee, not one to give in easily, offered another proposal to allow Corse to leave Hanover Junction. Writing to General Elzey, Lee suggested that a regiment from A. P. Hill's Corps, which was still in the Fredericksburg area, be sent to the junction to relieved Corse. Finally, Cooper put the question to rest when he wrote to Hill that Richmond and the Chickahominy would be defended as desired. The problem "has been obviated," Cooper wrote, "by the addition of Corse's brigade, drawn from General Lee's command at Culpeper." Corse would become part of Richmond's defenses.[8]

While Lee and Richmond haggled over his brigade, Corse, following Lee's orders, on 10 June gathered his dispersed regiments and began his march to catch up with his division. While the 15th Virginia was encamped near Taylorsville, the remainder of his regiments were scattered about guarding the course of the North and South Anna Rivers. The 15th marched the short distance to Hanover Junction where it was joined by the 17th and 29th Virginia. Together they marched north up the Telegraph Road past Mount Carmel. Turning off the main road the brigade marched to the small hamlet of Childsburg to meet the 30th Virginia, Corse's last regiment. Reunited, the brigade covered twenty hot and dusty miles up to Taylor's Mill where they were instructed to stop and wait for orders.[9]

Two days later, Lee wrote General Elzey from Culpeper that the previous order bringing Corse north had been reversed and the brigade would be on its way

---

[7] *OR* vol.27, pt.3, p.874; Manarin, *15th Virginia Infantry*, pp.43-44; Krick, Robert K., *30th Virginia Infantry*, p.38.

[8] *OR* vol.27, pt.3, pp.875, 880, 885, 887, 892.

[9] Manarin, *15th Virginia Infantry*, p.44.

back to Hanover Junction. Why Lee ordered the brigade north and then ordered it back is hard to decipher. One can only speculate that someone, possibly Davis, communicated with Lee and convinced him to reverse his decision. On 9 June, following Lee's suggestion, Davis requested Elzey to send Cooke's brigade to the vicinity of Hanover. It is possible that Lee assumed Cooke's arrival as a foregone conclusion and went forward with his plans to reunite Course with Pickett. In fact, Cooke's command never made it to Hanover, and continued to be relegated to the defenses of Richmond. After a couple of days rest orders were received and the brigade marched back to Taylorsville. Returning to its starting point, the regiments dispersed once again to guard the banks of the North and South Anna. While the remainder of Pickett's Division snaked its way north to Pennsylvania, the men of Corse's Brigade settled into the comforts of camp life. Women from Richmond would bring food and other luxuries from town while the men spent their off hours fishing and hunting for fresh meat, washing clothing in the river when they were not swimming in it, and relaxing in camp. The remainder of their comrades would not have the same luck and before the campaign was over could have dearly used Corse's assistance.[10]

Pickett was justifiably upset and seemed willing to lay the blame for Corse's loss directly on Lee's shoulders. If the loss of Jenkins had not been enough, now his division would be deprived of a second brigade. He left Hanover with three brigades when ordered to do so, and arrived at Culpeper Court House on 10 June, bivouacking his men roughly eight miles from town. He left Corse at the junction believing the brigade would be relieved and would follow him shortly. Before Corse and Jenkins were stripped from him, Pickett's command numbered 9,200 men. By the time his division reached Gettysburg, he would send less than 5,500 into battle. When he finally caught up with Lee, he vehemently protested the situation. "I have the honor to report," he wrote, "that in point of numerical strength this division has been very much weakened. I have now only three brigades," Pickett complained, "not more than 4,795 men, and unless these absent troops are certainly to rejoin me, I beg that another brigade be sent to this division ere we commence the campaign. I ask this in no spirit of complaint, but merely as an act of justice to my division and myself, for it is well known that a small division will be expected to do the same amount of hard service as a large one, and, as the army is now divided, my division will be, I think, decidedly the weakest." Lee responded to Pickett's letter by stating that he had "repeatedly requested that the two brigades be returned..." and that there were no other brigades available to bolster the strength of his division. Pickett would have to do without for the time being.[11]

Pickett's correspondence and attitude suggests that he was of the opinion that Corse would be marching north. If Lee did indeed tell Pickett that Corse would be joining them, Lee should have known better. His experience with Jenkins and

---

[10] *Ibid*, p.44; ***OR*** vol.27, pt.3, p.875; Jordon, ***NCT***, vol.V, p.499.

[11] Busey, John W. & Martin, David G., ***Regimental Strengths and Losses at Gettysburg*** (hereafter ***RSLG***), p.271; Bowden, & Ward, ***Last Chance***, p.38; ***OR*** vol.27, pt.3, pp.910, 944-945; Harrison, Kathy Georg, ***Nothing But Glory: Pickett's Division at Gettysburg***, p.2.

Ransom should have made him leery of such a statement. Lee however, never gave up his efforts to have Corse's command returned to the army, but a message received from Davis on 19 June must have been somewhat depressing. Davis had discussed the forwarding of Corse and replacing his small brigade with a "strong" regiment with General Elzey. Casualties and hard marching had diminished Corse's command to a size slightly larger than a full strength regiment. Could not a large regiment accomplish the same task so Corse could move north? Davis asked this of Elzey two days before and had not seen the general since. Could Davis not have sent a messenger to find Elzey and demand a response? It seemed as if Davis did not share the urgency of the situation, and once again he failed to do all possible to increase the size and strength of Lee's army.[12]

As late as 23 June, eight days before the Battle of Gettysburg, Lee was still trying to have Corse's brigade forwarded. In order to affect the release, Lee suggested that the 44th North Carolina of Brigadier General James Pettigrew's brigade which had been left behind to guard railroad bridges in the area of Hanover Junction, would be sufficient to garrison the area. Writing to Cooper, he once again argued for the brigade's liberation. "General Corse was subsequently ordered to remain at the [Hanover] Junction," Lee wrote, "and I have not heard whether he has yet been sent forward. If not, I think the regiment will suffice for a guard at that point, and wish Corse's brigade to be ordered to rejoin its division under General Pickett as soon as possible." Unfortunately, Lee had no more success than before and while the army marched onward, Corse remained on guard duty. Making matters worse was the additional retention of the 44th North Carolina, which ended up defending bridges and fords along the South Anna River.[13]

Pickett's note to Lee regarding a small division doing the work of a large one turned out to be quite ironic considering in a few short weeks his division would be asked to do more than mortal man could accomplish. His division, with the possible exception of Early's, entered upon the campaign as the weakest one of the nine Lee took to Pennsylvania.

Last in His Class

Longstreet's good friend George Edward Pickett was thirty-eight years old the spring of 1863. He was born in Richmond on 28 January 1825 to a prominent family who had developed a reputation for producing offspring who were active in the community and politics. George spent his early years roaming the meadows and woods of his grandfather's large estate, learning to hunt, fish and absorb the freshness of the outdoors. Although he bounced around the estate almost every day, George remained slight of build and somewhat short in stature. His features were somewhat feminine, his feet and hands quite small, his eyes gray. He often wore his brown hair long, accented by a slight natural wave. George's mother, who seemed to be plagued by ill health, may have transferred her susceptibility

---

[12] *OR* vol.27, pt.3, p.904.

[13] *Ibid*, p.926; Jordon, Weymouth T., *NCT*, vol.X, p.393; Hess, Earl J., *Lee's Tar Heels: The Pettigrew-Kirkland-MacRae Brigade*, p.107.

to health problems to her son. Throughout his life, George would have bouts with health related issues.

As a boy, George, possibly due to the freedom of his adolescence, developed a dislike for authority and began to defy instructions not to his liking. While his attitude allowed him to develop his independence, it became a serious detriment when his parents sent him off to school at the Richmond Academy. There, George seemed to be involved in an inordinate amount of youthful disagreements which often resulted in schoolyard fisticuffs. Being slight of build, he, although probably taking an excessive amount of punishment, earned the respect of his classmates. It was also at the Richmond Academy where George established a reputation for being a bit of a prankster, and his practical jokes made him popular with his contemporaries to the dismay of his instructors. All the levity and George's fierce independence restricted his abilities in the classroom and while at the academy he proved to be a rather poor student. He showed poor marks in English and mathematics and the school's code of conduct hindered him to a great extent. George did perform well in one subject however, showing somewhat higher marks in his study of the French language.

Although he was a substandard student, a military career seemed to be preordained by his family's heritage. During the Revolution, his relations offered up no less than fifteen men to fight for the country's independence, including George's great uncle and his grandfather. Many of the current generation of Pickett's were already in the army, but things looked bleak for George. His family took a severe blow during the financial panic of 1837, and the money needed to continue his education at the Richmond Academy disappeared. With funds tight, George's parents suggested that he look into studying law, but George would have none of it. Although he was uninterested in the profession, his parents pushed hard and sent him to Illinois to spend time studying with his uncle, Andrew Johnson. Johnson, the future president, took George under his wing and it was during this time that Pickett became acquainted with a tall slender lawyer from Illinois named Abraham Lincoln. Johnson introduced George to Lincoln in an effort to get the youth interested in the study of law, but George would not take the bait and soon returned home.[14]

George eventually received an appointment to West Point and entered the academy on 1 July 1842, becoming a cadet in the famous class of 1846. At the academy he continued his reputation as a prankster which made him one of the most likable cadets. Unfortunately his intellectual abilities came into serious question, and he carved out a scholastic record which placed him consistently at the bottom of his class. Pickett also struggled, as he did at Richmond, with West Point's strict and regulated code of conduct. Although his general performance was poor, he did excel in the subject of French where he ranked twelfth, just a few positions

---

[14] Longacre, *Pickett*, pp.3-5; Eicher, & Eicher, *High Commands*, p.428. Pickett's date of birth is a bit of a mystery. Military records indicate that he was born on 28 January. The memorial at his gravesite indicates 25 January and his baptismal records specify 16 January. For the purpose of this narrative the author has chosen to use Pickett's military record.

below the brains of the class, George McClellan. His performance in the classroom, coupled with his serious problem racking up demerits hampered his standing, and as his first year came to a close, he ranked fifty-fifth in a class of seventy-two. In fact, the rate in which Pickett piled up demerits had not been seen before. In his first year he amassed 165. During his second year he improved somewhat, being tagged with 140 marks on his record. The following year he was assessed another 155 demerits, while in his final year he was charged with a whopping 195. So poor was his conduct during his fourth year that as graduation approached he was close to being dismissed. Pickett's list of demerits was so extensive that it filled four legal sized sheets with two columns on each sheet. It is safe to say that George Pickett left a lasting mark within the record books of West Point. Academically he finished next to last or last in artillery tactics, engineering and ethics. When he graduated on 1 July 1846 he stood dead last in a class of fifty-nine.[15]

One reason why history has remembered so many of the graduates in 1846, was the commencement of the war with Mexico that same year. Brevetted a second lieutenant, Pickett returned home, but by the end of July, he was ready for the next phase of his career. Assigned to the 8th Infantry, he received orders to report to the unit's headquarters before the termination of his furlough in late September. The regiment was stationed in Mexico near the Monterrey battlefield. Departing on the morning of 3 September, it took him over two months to arrive at his destination. The journey was fraught with problems, including low water on the Mississippi River and a steamship out of New Orleans which had engine trouble and had to return to the Crescent City. Finally, on 9 November Pickett arrived at his unit's headquarters. Over a month late, he found himself listed as absent without leave. The regimental adjutant forced him to document his trip accounting for each problem and delay to explain his tardiness. It was not a very auspicious beginning to a military career.[16]

Pickett's time in northern Mexico was short. Within a few weeks he was sent to join General Scott's expedition. He fought at Contreras, Churubusco and Chapultepec, receiving a captain's brevet for the latter. The battle plan required the walls of the fortress to be scaled with the use of ladders. Lieutenant James Longstreet led Company H up the ladders in front of Pickett's Company A. When it came time to scale the wall, he led his men to the top of the escarpment in time to see Longstreet fall with his thigh wound. He took up the regimental colors from Longstreet, and, hoisting the flag, turned to face the enemy and struggled his way to the highest parapet. With bullets and shells flying, Pickett planted the flag on the wall. At least one Mexican tried to take him down, but the young Virginian leveled his weapon and shot his attacker. Reaching up, he hauled down

---

[15] Eicher, & Eicher, *High Commands*, p.428; Longacre, *Pickett*, pp.10-13; After the war it became almost common knowledge that Lincoln had been instrumental in garnering Pickett's appointment to West Point. The story is pure fiction, concocted by Pickett's widow. Lincoln could no more have secured an appointment for Pickett than his own mother since Lincoln had yet to amount to anything within either the Illinois or national political scene.

[16] Longacre, *Pickett*, pp.15-18.

the Mexican flag and working feverously managed to attach the banner of the 8th Infantry in place of the Mexican one. Quickly, he raised it high atop the wall. Soon others gathered around to support him, and the American flag was elevated next to the regimental colors. Picket had been first upon the parapet and soon a swarm of others followed. The Americans won the day and the outcome sealed the fate of Mexico City. Pickett's exploits did not go unnoticed and General Scott in his report singled him out for his conduct. While George Pickett may not have been one for the protocol and discipline of the armed forces, no one could doubt his courage and determination.[17]

Pickett's life between the wars was filled with garrison duty. Shortly after returning, he found himself at Camp Worth Texas just outside San Antonio protecting the local settlers from Indians. Taking an extended leave of absence, he returned to Richmond for the first time since his departure for Mexico. While there, he began to seriously court a young lady named Sally Minge. The two fell in love and were married on George's birthday in 1851. A short time later the happy couple was on their way to George's post. By the time they arrived, Sally was six months pregnant. Life on the frontier was hard and medical facilities were poor at best. Complications arose during the pregnancy and Sally along with the baby died during the birthing process. George was crushed and made arrangements to have her body sent back to Richmond for burial.[18]

George's grief deepened over the year following Sally's death. The more he talked and wrote about it, the worse his depression grew. His heartache would soon be lessened with the introduction of another young lady, who while not able to make George completely forget Sally, came very close to doing so. Her name was LaSalle Corbell and she had not yet turned four years old. Little Sallie was visiting her grandmother when she developed whooping-cough and found herself a bit of an outcast, having been shooed away from the healthy children. "I could not understand the change," the confused little girl noted later. She was relegated to pressing her little face up against the window panes to watch the festivities she had been participating in only a few days earlier. The little girl accompanied her grandmother to Old Point Comfort when the elderly woman went to visit a friend. It was during this trip that she first saw her dashing young soldier. "One morning, while playing alone on the beach," she wrote years later, "I saw a young officer lying on the sand reading, under the shelter of an umbrella. I had noticed him many times, always apart from the others and very sad. I could imagine but one reason for his desolation and in pity for him, I crept under his umbrella to ask him if he, too, had the whooping-cough. He smiled and answered no; but as I still persisted he drew me to him, telling me that he had lost someone who was dear to him and he was very lonely." Pickett evidently took a shine to the inquisitive little girl and bestowed upon her a small ring and a locket. "Child as I was," Sallie noted, "I believe I lost my heart to him on the spot."

---

[17] *Ibid*, pp.26-27.

[18] *Ibid*, pp.29-30.

Over the next few days Sallie visited George under his umbrella often. He sang to her while strumming on a guitar and taught her to spell her first words which were "Soldier" and "Sally." I remembered, too, the songs he used to sing me in the clear, rich voice of which his soldiers were so fond," she wrote. So striking was his image that it would be burned in her mind for the remainder of her life. "I particularly noticed his small hands and feet. He had beautiful gray eyes that looked at me through sunny lights – eyes that smiled with his lips. His mustache was gallantly curled. His hair was exactly the color of mine, dark brown, and wavy, in the fashion of the time." Sallie remembered the manner of Pickett's dress as well. He wore "the finest white linen" which exhibited "soft puffs and ruffles."

The rendezvous came to an end when the little girl and her grandmother departed. Pickett probably regarded the encounters with the little girl as a chance meeting and a cute reminiscence. However, George did not know who he was dealing with. LaSalle Corbell may have been a little girl, but she knew what she wanted. Years later, according to Sallie, she decided then and there that she would marry the handsome young soldier. Whether little Sallie was serious or her obsession was a child's passing fancy, before the age of four, she claimed to have chosen her man.[19]

With his heart on the mend, Pickett went back to his military duties and spent a good portion of his time on the frontier. He found himself at Fort Chadbourne, Texas, at Fort Clark, an outpost which guarded the road between El Paso and San Antonio, and the Ringgold Barracks on the Rio Grande. Early in 1854, Indian trouble grew along the Texas, New Mexico Territory border, and Pickett went with his regiment to Fort Bliss where he commanded Company E. He spent the next few years protecting the population from the marauders. On 3 March 1855 he received a promotion to full captain and was transferred to command the 9th Infantry's Company D.[20]

In 1856, Pickett received an assignment that would take him to the Pacific Northwest. The 9th, a new regiment, required training, and he was assigned the task of training the company's new recruits as they assembled at Fort Monroe. One visitor who arrived to see Pickett shortly before his regiment departed was little Sallie, now, all of seven-years-old. She had convinced her family to travel to Fort Monroe so she might be able to see him before he departed. The two managed to spend a little time on the beach where they had first met and LaSalle watched as Captain Pickett drilled and marched his company. The little girl returned home before he departed but when word came that he was to leave, Sallie returned to see him off. She later noting feeling "[t]he first real sorrow of... [her] life" as she watched him leave for an unknown future in a region ravaged by Indian wars. Unknown to Sallie however, her soldier was not on the ship she watched depart. Pickett would not accompany the regiment. He was headed for Florida where he

---

[19] Pickett, George E., *The Heart of a Soldier, Wartime Letters from General George E. Pickett, C.S.A. to His Wife*, Ed. La Salle Corbell Pickett, pp.1-3.

[20] Longacre, *Pickett*, pp.33-34; Eicher, & Eicher, *High Commands*, p.428.

was to spend four months performing court-martial duties. Whether Sallie actually thought he was on the ship or simply fell victim to a fading memory is not known.[21]

Arriving in the Washington Territory, Pickett was greeted by an ongoing Indian conflict. He spent his time dealing with the Indians and helping to lay out and construct Fort Bellingham at the mouth of the Nooksack River a few miles south of the British North American border. In 1859, Pickett became embroiled in a conflict with Great Britain known as the "Pig War." The conflict was precipitated by a swine belonging to the Hudson Bay Company which was shot by a local settler when the pig escaped and began eating the man's vegetables. The standoff came to a head when Pickett was sent to San Juan Island to contest the landing of one thousand British soldiers with a meager fifty-four men, two officers, two mountain howitzers and one six-pounder. Once on the island, he put the men to work constructing earthworks and fortification for his small command. He faced down the British for a few weeks until word of the confrontation reached Washington. President Buchanan, perturbed by the whole situation, sent aging General Scott on the long sea voyage to the Northwest to alleviate the situation. Cooler heads prevailed and the two sides agreed to joint occupation of San Juan Island, but Scott had few kind words for the stubborn Pickett in his official report. The possibility of armed conflict was warded off, with the only casualty being the vegetable eating pig.[22]

Pickett was still in the Northwest when Fort Sumter was attacked. Determining to support his native state, George submitted his resignation on 25 June 1861 but did not leave the Puget Sound area for three weeks. After dealing with some personal matters, he departed, taking the overland route east. His late departure and long trip kept him from participating in the First Battle of Manassas. Made a colonel in the Confederate Army on 23 July, he was assigned duty along the Rappahannock Line and served there until 22 October when he was transferred to the Aquia District. He continued to serve in Northern Virginia where he drew the attention of his superiors and was promoted to brigadier general on 14 January 1862. Pickett was given brigade command under a bit of controversy when he took command of Brigade General Philip Cocke's brigade after Cocke had shot himself in the head the day after Christmas. Cocke, evidently distraught and disappointed for being censure by General Beauregard returned home after Manassas, determine suicide was the solution to his problems, and took his own life, thus opening the door for Pickett.[23]

---

[21] Longacre, *Pickett*, pp.35-36; Pickett, George E., *The Heart of a Soldier,* p.4.

[22] Longacre, *Pickett*, pp.43-49.

[23] *Ibid*, pp.51-52; Eicher, & Eicher, *High Commands*, p.428; Tagg, *Generals*, pp.237. While in the Northwest, Pickett had taken a native wife and had fathered a boy who was four when he left. His second wife died not long after giving birth. George made arrangements to have a friend care for the youngster. While there are indications Pickett intended to return to either see or fetch the boy, he never did and the two never saw each other again. The boy, named James, made a name for himself as a newspaper artist during his short life. He died of tuberculosis at the age of thirty-two near Portland, Oregon.

George Edward Pickett entered the campaign already carrying animosity toward Lee. *LOC*

Pickett's first combat experience as a brigade commander took place on the Peninsula. His brigade, nicknamed the "Game Cock Brigade" fought at Williamsburg, Fair Oaks. During The Seven Days at the fighting near Gaines' Mill, Pickett, while in the saddle, was struck in the right shoulder by a bullet and unhorsed. There are various accounts regarding the severity of his wound. Standing next to his horse in a small vale, he evidently told a passerby that he had been mortally wounded and for the man should send for a litter. The man however, had no time and left without offering assistance. Others who saw him after his wounding noted that he was perfectly capable of taking care of himself, the wound being very slight. LaSalle noted years later that Pickett was urged by a surgeon to leave the field but the general refused to depart, commenting his men needed him. Sallie's statements however, are questionable since she spent a good portion of her later years defending and promoting the general. Most who saw him on the battlefield thought him quite capable of tending to himself and let him be, having other, more pressing things to attend to.[24]

No matter what the severity of his injuries, Pickett had been hit. His wound was severe enough to keep him out of action for three months. He made his way to Richmond by train and ambulance and took up residence at his sister's home to recover. Her husband, Blair Burwell, was an assistant surgeon with the 8th Virginia and George's shoulder and swollen right arm received good care. His recovery progressed steadily, although slower than Doctor Burwell had hoped. It was not until Sallie arrived, having left school early to come to the aide of her soldier, that Pickett's recovery began progressing at a faster pace. Sallie changed his bandages

---

[24] Tagg, *Generals*, p.237; Longacre, *Pickett*, pp.86-87.

regularly and made sure he was always at ease. She entertained him by reading out loud and singing and made sure that well-wishers were screened before they were allowed to see him. One of those well wishers was President Davis, who dropped by one day to check on his progress. After he was well enough to move about, Sallie assisted in helping him walk around the Burwell's property. She sat with him under the trees in the grass, and he spent the last days of his recovery talking with Sallie in the shade during the early fall of 1862. When it came time for him to return to duty, both George and Sallie were saddened by their parting. As he took his leave, Pickett may have begun to realize that the affection he felt for Sallie was becoming more than simply friendship.[25]

In September Pickett returned to duty and to the command of a division in Longstreet's First Corps. He was promoted to major general on 10 October 1862, but not without an undercurrent of controversy. He had not led men in battle except for the short stint on the Peninsula, and some thought him a poor choice for division command. He probably received the promotion based on a recommendation from his friend Longstreet. George and Sallie's assistance during the Longstreet's loss of their children may have endeared him to Longstreet enough to have the corps commander recommend he be assigned to a division. Lee, being short on command grade generals, may have had something to do with it as well.[26]

The division saw its first action under Pickett during the Fredericksburg Campaign but it was only lightly engaged. As Lee dispersed his army to battle the forage and food situation during the winter, he marched with Longstreet to Suffolk. During the campaign he once again had little opportunity to achieve any military glory. He did however have an opportunity to once again see Sallie, who was home from school. The siege had driven her from her hometown. Eventually she moved in with an aunt at Barber's Crossing which was only fifteen miles from Pickett's headquarters. George found himself on a nightly basis, unable to resist the thirty mile ride just to spend a few minutes with her. Initially he requested permission from Longstreet to make his visits, but when his friend began to balk at the continual trips, Pickett went to Colonel Sorrel, who also did not approve. "Pickett's visits were frequent," Sorrel wrote, "a long night ride and return for duty early next day. Perhaps he had wearied Longstreet by frequent applications to be absent, but once he came to me for authority."

"No, you must go to the Lieutenant-General." Sorrel told Pickett.

"But he is tired of it," he pleaded, "and will refuse; and I must go, I must see her." Pickett, at thirty-eight, was in love with a teenage girl young enough to be his daughter.[27]

---

[25] Longacre, *Pickett*, pp.88-90. Sallie noted years later that Stonewall Jackson also stopped to pay his respects to Pickett. Sallie probably overstated the story or possibly invented it. Jackson and Pickett, while they knew each other, were never close.

[26] *Ibid*, p.92; Eicher, & Eicher, **High Commands**, p.428

[27] *Ibid*, pp.105-106; Sorrel, **Recollections**, pp.155-156.

The nighttime encounters ended when Longstreet was recalled by Lee to Fredericksburg. Although Pickett had been in command of his division for approximately ten months, he was still untried as he moved north from Hanover Junction with his three remaining brigades. This may have been why Sorrel believed Longstreet paid special attention when issuing orders to him. Sorrel seemed to be plagued with making sure Pickett understood orders completely before sending him on his way. After Pickett's promotion to major general, Longstreet's aide noted he considered him a "good brigadier" but the comment was in jest, an indication he felt Pickett was in over his head regarding divisional command.[28]

Pickett's reputation as a dandy followed him into the Confederate service, and he continued to wear the white ruffles which young Sallie had so vividly noticed years earlier. Throughout his military career, Pickett would be known as an immaculate dresser, always kept his uniform in flawless condition and constantly wore gloves that covered its sleeves. He also wore a blue kepi, polished boots and golden spurs which always seemed to be glistening and bright. He carried a riding crop and rode a streamline black horse. It was easy to pick him out in a crowed of general officers.

Pickett's most recognizable feature however, was his flowing curly brown hair. Many officers and soldiers must have spent hours discussing his cascading locks which framed his somewhat round face. Longstreet remembered Pickett's hair as "dark. ...glossy" and "worn almost to his shoulders in curly waves." His mustache was large and turned up on the end he wore a goatee style beard which also contained some curl. Making him even more memorable was the perfume he constantly wore which on many occasions was so strong that, if the wind was right, announced his arrival even before he was close by. It is a foregone conclusion that Pickett received great amounts of good natured ribbing regarding his appearance and fragrance. Being a bit of a joker himself, he surely gave as well as he got.[29]

Pickett's Boys

With Corse's Brigade at Hanover Junction and Jenkins' South Carolinians still below the James River, Pickett's small three brigade division was wholly constructed of regiments from the Old Dominion. Forty-five year old Richard Brooke Garnett commanded Pickett's old Game Cock Brigade, which still contained its original regiments, the 8th, 18th, 19th, 28th and 56th Virginia. With Pickett convalescing, Garnett led the brigade at Sharpsburg and did well enough to receive praise from his superior.[30]

Dick Garnett was born 21 November 1817 in the tidewater region of Virginia at "Rose Hill" in Essex County. He came from a family where military service was prominent, and he was the cousin of Robert S. Garnett of Corrick's Ford fame. He grew up on his family's estate and after receiving his formal education began

---

[28] Tagg, **Generals**, p.238.

[29] Pickett, LaSalle Corbell, **Pickett and His Men**, p.ix; Tagg, **Generals**, pp.236-237.

[30] Longacre, **Pickett**, p.91; **OR** vol.27, pt.3, p.919.

efforts to enter West Point. After a number of attempts over three years, Dick finally managed to receive an appointment and entered the academy 1 September 1836, a year before his cousin. Unfortunately, it took Richard five years to complete the curriculum, and he graduated with Robert two positions behind him, twenty-ninth in a class of fifty-two. Commissioned a second lieutenant on 1 July 1841, he went to Florida to fight the Seminoles. His duty assignments would send him to all corners of the American frontier. After leaving Florida, he spent time in Texas, the Dakotas and traveled with the Mormon Expedition to Utah. Unlike many of his fellow graduates, he did not see action in Mexico, but did prove he was not afraid of confrontation, developing a substantial reputation as an Indian fighter. When the war began, Garnett was in California and attended Winfield and Almira Hancock's goodbye dinner party.[31]

Only a captain as hostilities opened, Garnett was quickly commissioned a major in the Confederate Army and given command of an artillery unit. On 14 November, he was promoted to brigadier general and took command of Stonewall Jackson's old brigade when Jackson was placed in command of the troops in the Shenandoah Valley. Garnett immediately gained the confidence of his command. Even Jackson, who remained interested in the workings of his old brigade, felt it was in capable hands. However, it was not long before Garnett and Jackson ran afoul of each other. Their confrontation began during the Romney Campaign when Garnett allowed his brigade to stop so his cold, hungry men could rest. Jackson was not pleased with the timing of the halt and informed Garnett that he must push his men onward. Later, during the Battle of Kernstown, after his men had run out of ammunition and were about to be flanked, Garnett ordered them to retreat. Once again Jackson was perturbed. This time he arrested Garnett and charged him with "neglect of duty." To make things worse, Jackson tried to restrict Garnett from being assigned to another duty station. Understandably irritated, Garnett demanded a court-martial to clear his name. No hearing was ever convened. Lee, who badly needed brigade commanders, place Garnett in command of Pickett's old brigade in Longstreet's corps while its commander recuperated from his shoulder wound. According to one of Garnett's regimental commanders, "he was one of the noblest and bravest men I ever knew."[32]

Whether out of pure veneration or an effort at closure, Richard Garnett made his way to Richmond to pay his respects to the fallen Jackson. Entering Governor Letcher's reception hall he walked to the casket and sobbed over Jackson's body. Turning to General Pendleton, who was standing nearby Garnett commented, "I believe that he did me a great injustice, but I believe also that he acted from the purest motives. He is dead. Who can fill his place?" The preacher-general Pendleton, asked Garnett to function as a pallbearer for the funeral procession and Garnett gladly accepted. He joined Pickett, James Longstreet, Montgomery Corse and a number of other high placed Confederates, who accompanied the hearse.

[31] Tagg, **Generals**, p.246; Warner, Ezra J., **Generals in Gray**, p.99; Eicher, & Eicher, **High Commands**, p.249.

[32] Tagg, **Generals**, p.247; Eicher, & Eicher, **High Commands**, p.249.

It seemed an odd place for a man who had felt humiliation at the hands of the departed chieftain, but Garnett was a soldier, and one of his contemporaries had been lost in battle. It was the least he could do.[33]

Commanding another of Pickett's brigades was Winfield Hancock's old friend Lewis A. Armistead. After putting his major's uniform away and saying goodbye to his friend, he headed east with Albert Sidney Johnston to cast his lot with his native state. Armistead was born on 18 February 1816 in New Bren, North Carolina. His father, General Walker K. Armistead, was a veteran of the War of 1812, and a military career for Lewis seemed to have been pre-ordained. Four of Armistead's uncles had also served during the second conflict with the British. One of then having commanded the garrison at Fort McHenry as Francis Scott Key wrote the Star Spangled Banner. After entering West Point on 1 July 1834, Lewis struggled academically. He had a tendency to be gruff and direct when addressing others which did not endear him to some. During an altercation with fellow cadet Jubal Early, Armistead broke a dinner plate over Early's head and was summarily expelled. The incident only hastened a departure which was inevitable due to his failing grades.[34]

Undaunted, Armistead managed to attain a second lieutenant's commission directly into the infantry on 10 July 1839. Humorously nicknamed Lothario, after the fictional seducer of women, the moniker was often shortened to simply Lo. The name was intended as a cruel joke since Armistead was a loner who normally acted a bit introverted around the ladies. The name would stick for the remainder of his life and he would continue to be unaccompanied by any members of the fairer sex.

Militarily Armistead's performance was satisfactory enough to garner a promotion to first lieutenant on 30 March 1844. When the Mexican War began, Lo Armistead was called to fight, and fight he did. He was brevetted captain for distinguished service at Contreras and Churubusco. Later, at Chapultepec, he was wounded, commended twice for bravery and brevetted major for his conduct at Molino del Rey. Armistead proved during his Mexican War experience that he possessed great personal courage and an almost insatiable desire to do his duty. After the war, he remained in the army and on 3 March 1855 he was promoted to a full captaincy. Following the promotion he was assigned to the frontier, ending up in Los Angeles.[35]

After resigning his commission on 26 May 1861, Armistead served for a brief time in the 57th Virginia Infantry as first a major and then colonel of the regiment. On 1 April 1862, before he had seen any action, he was promoted to brigadier general and assigned to command of a brigade in the Norfolk area. Armistead proved the promotion justified when he was cited for personal bravery while leading the brigade at Fair Oaks. He always fought his brigade well and

---

[33] Robertson, **Stonewall Jackson**, pp.756-757.

[34] Tagg, **Generals**, p.247; Eicher, & Eicher, **High Commands**, p.107; Wakelyn, **Biographical Dictionary**, p.77.

[35] Eicher, & Eicher, **High Commands**, p.107.

commanded them effectively from the battles on the Peninsula through most of the major campaigns in the Eastern Theater. Wounded in the foot at Sharpsburg, he was relegated to the defenses of Richmond until able to return to field duty, at which time his brigade was assigned to Pickett's Division when the Virginian was elevated to divisional command. Armistead, for a brief period, also executed the additional responsibilities of Provost Marshal General of Lee's army, being assigned the duty on 4 July 1862. He was a quality brigade commander and proved that fact over the months leading up to Lee's decision to invade the North. The men of his brigade regarded him as a quality commander. Armistead's Brigade consisted of five Virginia units, including his old 57th, the 9th, 14th, 38th, and 53rd regiments. All five were seasoned, admired and respected their commander.[36]

Pickett's remaining brigade was led by James L. Kemper. Born in Prospect Mountain in northern Virginia's Madison County on 11 June 1823, he was the youngest of Pickett's brigade commanders. Born to William and Maria Kemper, he was not a military man, although he had attended VMI. Graduating from Washington College in 1842, Kemper later studied law, opened a practice in his home county and used it as a springboard to get elected to the Virginia House of Delegates. He served three terms from 1848 to 1860. In 1853 he married Cremora Conway Cave and their marriage resulted in five children. Although he was not a stout secessionist, Kemper sided with the South when the war began.[37]

Although Kemper was not a military man, members of his family had served and distinguished themselves, including his grandfather who had served on George Washington's staff during the Revolution. Kemper also stepped forward to serve during the Mexican War, becoming a captain in the Virginia Volunteers, but he saw no action. His later election to political office provided an opportunity to develop fine oratory skill which he would demonstrate often during his military service. His pompous voice went well with his intense eyes which helped overcome his lack of training. Perhaps even more important to the Confederacy than his military service was his public service, for he spent time as chairman of the Military Affairs Committee. While chairman, he concentrated on the military preparedness of his state, which future Confederate government officials probably appreciated. Although the situation was anything but rosy when preparations for war commenced, conceivably it would have been worse had it not been for Kemper's efforts.[38]

Just before the war began, on 10 April 1861, Kemper was made a brigadier general in the Virginia militia. Seventeen days later he entered service with the Provisional Army of Virginia with the same rank. Although he was now serving his state as a member of its army, he still retained the speakership of the Virginia House of Delegates, a position he ascended too shortly before the war began.

---

[36] *Ibid*, pp.107; ***OR*** vol.27, pt.3, p.919; Wakelyn, ***Biographical Dictionary***, p.77.

[37] Wakelyn, ***Biographical Dictionary***, p.270.

[38] Tagg, ***Generals***, pp.240-241; Wakelyn, ***Biographical Dictionary***, p.270.

Kemper would retain his position at the head of the governing body until January 1863, even as he was off fighting Yankees.[39]

Kemper was one of the few political generals in Confederate service that built a solid reputation as a fighter. Being from the Virginia political arena, he found it easy to obtain a field command. His first assignment was Colonel of the 7th Virginia Infantry, which he assumed command of on 2 May 1861. The regiment fought with Longstreet's brigade at First Manassas and on the Peninsula at Williamsburg and Yorktown. Three days after A. P. Hill was promoted to division command, Kemper distinguished himself at Fair Oaks and was rewarded with command of the brigade and commissioned a brigadier general. He retained his position through the remainder of the battles on the Peninsula, at Second Manassas and Sharpsburg. Held in reserve at Fredericksburg, and away with Longstreet during Chancellorsville, in early June it had been nine months since Kemper's Virginias had seen serious combat.[40]

Kemper endeared himself to the men of his command, which consisted of his own 7th, the 1st, 3rd, 11th and 24th Virginia regiments. On many occasions, he looked as grimy as they did, as his large bushy beard often accented his grubby appearance. He shared their hardships, was cool under fire and paid specific attention to their comfort by going out of his way to make sure his wounded men were well cared for.[41]

On 8 June, after the bulk of Longstreet's Corps had already left the area, Pickett put his three brigades on the road to Culpeper Court House. The column, a little over half as long as it should have been, slowly snaked its way north. Taking an easy first day, it covered around ten miles to Hanover Court House arriving around midday. The following day saw a more difficult march of twenty miles to the New Market area, followed by the crossing of the Rapidan River the next day. By the end of the day on 10 June, Pickett had his men eight miles from their destination. The next day, the division moved a short five miles and went into bivouac south of Culpeper. Pickett was now back with his corps after a long odyssey which reduced his strength, and had placed seeds of doubt in his mind regarding Lee's intentions toward his division. There would be a few days of rest in their new encampment before the division moved into the Shenandoah Valley on the first leg of the campaign.[42]

The Spy

Shortly before Lee issued marching orders to Longstreet, the First Corps commander sent a requisition to Richmond for a sum of gold to be sent to him. The gold was not for him. Instead it would be used to buy information. The money

---

[39] Eicher, & Eicher, **High Commands**, p.329.

[40] Tagg, **Generals**, p.241.

[41] **OR** vol.27, pt.2, p.284; Riggs, David F., *7th Virginia Infantry*, p.2.

[42] Gregory, G. Howard, **53rd Virginia Infantry and 5th Battalion Virginia Infantry**, p.48.

was needed to compensate a spy in his employ. A man Longstreet simply called Harrison.

Henry Thomas Harrison was a Tennessean, reportedly born in Nashville in 1832. When the war began he joined the 12th Mississippi Infantry and was mustered during May 1861 but was discharged in September. After his release, he began a career as a scout and spy, initially working for Major General Earl van Dorn in the Manassas area. Later in February 1863, he was assigned to Longstreet by Secretary of War Seddon and began spying for General D. H. Hill.[43]

Harrison displayed his ability to extricate himself from tight situations when he was captured in North Carolina during the spring of 1863. After the Confederates fell back from New Bren, he was seized by a Federal patrol near the Neuse River. Harrison may have drawn attention to himself because he was riding a double branded horse which indicated it was not fit for military service. Although he held a valid pass, the colonel leading the Yankee detachment felt Harrison was up to some mischief. He was arrested and taken to New Bren to be interrogated.

Harrison informed his captors that he was from Yazoo County, Mississippi and that he had served in the 12th Mississippi for six months before he was discharged due to disability. When he was asked about his presence in the area, he informed his interrogators that his sister lived nearby in Pitt County and he had lived with her off and on. He also said he had a cousin living near Swift Creek. Harrison continued to spin his story by commenting he was a bit of a transient. He told his captors he moved around a lot since he was trying to stay clear of Confederate conscription because he did not want to fight anymore. He continued to fabricate his story by mentioning citizens he was acquainted with but were conveniently out of reach of his captors. The penalty for spying was death, and Harrison knew one mistake or a wrong word would probably result in his swift hanging. With no hard evidence of Harrison's espionage, the Federals made the decision not to hold him, and he was released on 13 April. How Harrison managed to negotiate his way through Union lines is not known. The whole episode indicated just how skilled at espionage he had become. [44]

Longstreet first met Harrison when he arrived unannounced at his headquarters while the general was at Suffolk. While the general was sitting in his tent one evening, Harrison arrived and presented himself. Longstreet invited him in, and the spy, who the general would constantly refer to as his "scout," handed the general a note from Seddon introducing him to Longstreet as a covert operative. Longstreet described Harrison as "a slender, wiry fellow about five feet eight, with hazel eyes, dark hair and complexion, and brown beard." He was dressed as a civilian in a dark suit, and Longstreet developed the impression that he was a man of "great activity" referring to Harrison's raged and worn appearance.

---

[43] ***Electronic Source:*** http://home.comcast.net/~site002/Harrison/index.htm, Last accessed 5/2/2012.

[44] Hall, James O., A Modern Hunt for a Fabled Agent: The Spy Harrison, ***CWTI*** vol.24, no.10, pp.22-23.

Seddon's message must have impressed Longstreet for the general provided Harrison with enough gold to allow him to "get along in Washington." Longstreet then sent him on his way, telling Harrison not to return until he had information that would be of great benefit to the army. The spy then asked where he would be able to find the general. Not wanting to provide any military information to a spy, Longstreet told the operative that "the head-quarters [sic] of the First Corps were large enough for any intelligent man to find." With that Harrison left, disappearing into the darkness. Longstreet would not see the man again until his corps was encamped at Chambersburg.

Harrison's unassuming appearance allowed him to negotiate his way into the heart of Union territory and Washington. He was so ordinary that he was capable of establishing dialogue with Northern officials, even eating and drinking with them. Longstreet understood he was an actor and believed Harrison's abilities as a thespian would work to his advantage. Whether he was indeed an actor or not has been disputed. The question was, would he be worth the gold Longstreet paid him. The spy would prove his worth in a few weeks.[45]

Longstreet Marches

When Pickett arrived in the vicinity of Culpeper, he found Longstreet's other two divisions already nearby. The divisions, those of Lafayette McLaws and John Bell Hood, had completed their march from the Fredericksburg area a few days prior. Unlike Pickett, Longstreet's other two division commanders had led their men during some of the hottest action in the Eastern Theater. McLaws, whose performance during the Chancellorsville Campaign had received little notice, was instrumental in the victory, but Lee had expected more from him. The neglect was to the highest degree due to Jackson's flamboyant flank attack. First, McLaws kept Hooker's attention concentrated on Lee while Jackson worked his magic. Then he marched his command back toward Fredericksburg to cut off Sedgwick's Sixth Corps and defend Lee's rear. Lee however was disappointed when Jubal Early and McLaws declined to significantly punish Sedgwick's isolated command. McLaws failed to make much of a case for himself. He had been the senior commander on the field but allowed Early to direct events. He seemed to be more comfortable taking orders than issuing them. His four brigade division broke camp south of Fredericksburg on 3 June and marched west into the region of Virginia known as the Wilderness. Three days later his men were encamped just west of Stevensburg a few miles from Culpeper Court House.[46]

---

[45] Longstreet, Lee's Invasion of Pennsylvania, **B&L**, vol.3, p.244; Longstreet, *MtoA*, p.333. The identity of the spy Harrison until the latter half of the 20th Century was believed to be that of James Harrison, who indeed was an actor. One of Longstreet's staff officers, Moxley Sorrel supposedly identified him in Richmond in September of 1863 when Sorrel attended a play that Harrison was cast in. Late in the 20th Century new information was discovered which indicates the man was actually Henry Thomas Harrison. See ***CWTI***, vol.24 no.10.

[46] Longstreet, Lee in Pennsylvania, *AW*, p.417; Bigelow, **Chancellorsville**, pp.232, 396-397; Gottfried, Bradley M., ***The Maps of Gettysburg***, pp.2-5; Tagg, ***Generals***, pp.210-211.

Lafayette McLaws was a classmate of Longstreet's at West Point and like Longstreet, was a Georgian. He was born in Augusta on 15 January 1821 and had the distinction of being related by marriage to former president, Zachary Taylor, and President Davis. McLaws owed his American residency to a shipwreck which occurred in 1783. His grandfather, Alexander McLaws, was returning with his family to Scotland from Santo Domingo when a heavy storm developed and wrecked the ship off the coast of Georgia. The region must have appealed to Alexander for instead of securing passage on another vessel, he moved his family inland and settled in the Augusta area. Lafayette's father, James was born seven years later. When he was in his mid-twenties, James married Elizabeth Huguenin, and six years later, little Lafayette was born.[47]

McLaws attended the Richmond Academy while Longstreet was a student there. Other than a few Ivy League schools, it was the oldest educational institution in the country. The school's difficult curriculums included mathematics ranging from simple arithmetic to calculus, chemistry, geology, astronomy and physiology. McLaws also spent some time during his informative years at the Georgia Male Academy, run by former West Pointer, Thomas S. Twiss. Twiss was an intellectual who, after exiting the military, spent a good deal of time as a Professor of Mathematics and Natural Philosophy. It may have been during his association with Twiss that McLaws began to seriously consider a military career. When Lafayette was sixteen, Georgia Senator John P. King, recommended he receive an appointment to West Point. At the time, no position from Georgia was available, so the application had to be deferred, allowing McLaws to complete a year of college at the University of Virginia. Finally, with a position available, on 1 July 1838, McLaws began his military career.[48]

Once again McLaws discovered Longstreet was a classmate. A few other cadets in McLaws' class would also be prominent during the war, including D. H. Hill and Abner Doubleday. He constantly struggled with the difficult academy curriculum. During his first year he was an average student but as the years progressed he consistently found himself in the bottom half of the standings. Demerits were also a problem for McLaws. Initially, he kept his number manageable but later, during his senior year, he amassed a rather large 147 which brought his four year total to 353, a quantity which placing him third from the bottom of the conduct rolls. Finally, in 1842, he graduated forty-eighth in his class, six positions above his future corps commander. His low standing forced him into the ranks of the foot soldier and upon graduation he was brevetted a second lieutenant and assigned to the 6th Infantry. Two years later he was transferred to the 7th Infantry. McLaws' career before the Mexican War saw him on frontier duty where he spent time in Texas. In 1845 a shooting accident damaged his left hand. It was disfigured so badly that he made efforts to hide the mangled hand anytime he sat

---

[47] Eicher, & Eicher, *High Commands*, p.381; Wakelyn, *Biographical Dictionary*, p.300; Oeffinger, John C., Editor, *A Soldier's General: The Civil War Letters of Major General Lafayette McLaws*, p.3. McLaws was married to Taylor's niece, Emily Allison Taylor.

[48] Oeffinger, *A Soldier's General*, pp.7-8.

for a photograph. McLaws' service in Mexico gained him little attention and no chance for promotion. Finally promoted to captain on 24 August 1851, McLaws participated in the Utah expedition seven years later, before assisted in escorting the Mormons to California. Another significant event in McLaws' life between the wars was his marriage to Emily Taylor. The couple exchanged vows on 9 August 1849, two days after they were legally married.[49]

When the Civil War erupted, McLaws returned to Georgia and resigned his commission on 23 March 1861. Initially he was assigned a major's commission, which was dated nine days before he actually resigned from Federal service. He worked at quartermaster duties before he began efforts to organize three companies of soldiers, who possessed no equipment, into a fighting unit. Promoted to colonel on 24 June, McLaws was ordered to Yorktown with instructions to report to General Magruder. At his new post, he worked to organize and train the 10th Georgia. Magruder, quick to recognize McLaws' skill at organization and attention to detail, put him to work constructing defenses. His hard work earned him a promotion to brigadier general on 25 September. His efforts on the Peninsula would assist in holding off George McClellan's massive Army of the Potomac, until Lee took command and drove the Yankees away from Richmond. On 23 May 1862, shortly before Fair Oaks, McLaws was promoted to major general and assigned to division command. After Richmond was saved, his division was assigned to his old schoolmate's First Corps. Unfortunately for McLaws, he would never manage to extricate himself from Longstreet's shadow and division command.[50]

McLaws missed the campaign and battle of Second Manassas but came north in time to be instrumental during the Maryland Campaign. He assisted Jackson in reducing the Federal garrison at Harpers Ferry and helped deliver the savage counter attack that all but destroyed John Sedgwick's division of General Sumner's Second Corps in the West Woods at Sharpsburg. At Fredericksburg McLaws was in position behind the stone wall at the top of Marye's Heights, and as the Federals marched toward him he did his best to "kill them all" as his corps commander had noted to Lee.

During the winter of 1862-63, McLaws became quite ill. Concern for his health prompted Lee to broach the subject of assigning him to less strenuous duties, and he requested that Longstreet discuss the possibility with him. When asked about the possibilities, McLaws reassured his superior that he was in good health and capable of enduring the hardships of the coming campaign. Lee's concern over his health may have been a factor in the army commander's failure to seriously consider McLaws for command of his new Third Corps.[51]

---

[49] Eicher, & Eicher, *High Commands*, p.381; Oeffinger, *A Soldier's General*, pp.10-9, 16; Wakelyn, *Biographical Dictionary*, p.300; Tagg, *Generals*, p.209. Eicher & Eicher note that McLaws was wounded in the chest in 1845, but no other references known to the author note such a wound.

[50] Oeffinger, *A Soldier's General*, pp.22-27; Eicher, & Eicher, *High Commands*, p.381.

[51] Longstreet to McLaws, 25 July 1873, McLaws Papers, UNC.

A few days later the subject of a transfer south to lighter duties arose again. Longstreet proposed that it might be possible for McLaws to exchange his division for an entire corps under the command of Beauregard. "This is for you to go there and let Beauregard come here with a corps," Longstreet wrote in a letter to McLaws on 3 June. Longstreet was of the opinion that Beauregard, who was in command of the coastal defenses in South Carolina, was "anxious" to come north. Whether Longstreet discussed the switch with Lee is not known. After the war, Longstreet wrote of the proposed Beauregard transfer, gathering Jenkins and Corse as he came. Then Beauregard would use his force to threaten Washington. Lee did try to persuade Richmond to bring the South Carolinian north to pressure Washington as the campaign unfolded. Fortunately for McLaws, he stayed with the army and Beauregard, to the possible detriment of the campaign, remained where he was.[52]

McLaws performance at the head of his division was good to average at times, but he never managed to distinguish himself or be flamboyant enough to achieve a higher level assignment. Later in the war, he was blamed for the disaster at Fort Sanders during the Knoxville Campaign and relieved by Longstreet. McLaws placed the blame for the failure at the feet of Longstreet and a war of words began between the two old friends. McLaws demanded a court-martial in order to clear his name and meticulously copied all the correspondence between himself and Longstreet's staff. He was eventually cleared of all charges, but the animosity between the two men spilled over into the post war years. As time went on, their disdain softened but never really dissipated completely. It seemed a sad way for a friendship to end since Longstreet had praised McLaws for his work early in the war. The turning point in the relationship was but a month away and would occur on the southern portion of the Gettysburg battlefield.[53]

McLaws was as rock solid in his physical appearance as he was on the battlefield. He was rather short and thick with large square shoulders which made his barrel chest seem even thicker. His conduct in a fight was steady and consistent, always giving Longstreet his best no matter what the situation. He was tenacious when bullets began to fly and his men took on the same attitude. When on defense, McLaws' boys developed a reputation for being impossible to drive from their position and when delivering an attack they hit as hard as any unit in either army. In fact, his failure to achieve higher command could possibly be attributed to the consistency of his performance, never providing his commander, until later in the war, a reason of chastise him. His jet black curly hair and massive beard and mustache formed a frame which seemed to miraculously part, allowing his rather round face, to project. His eyes were as dark as his hair, having been described as "coal black,"[54]

---

[52]   *Ibid*, Longstreet to McLaws, 3 June 1863, McLaws Papers, UNC; **OR** vol.27, pt.3, pp.924-925; Longstreet, *MtoA*, p.336.

[53]   Faust, *Encyclopedia*, p.464; Eicher, & Eicher, **High Commands**, p.381.

[54]   Tagg, **Generals**, p.209.

McLaws' Division contained some of the hardest fighting brigades in Lee's army. It had been together under McLaws' command since the Sharpsburg Campaign the previous fall and while some of the regiments had changed the fighting prowess of its brigade commanders was arguably the best in the army. Brigadier General Paul Jones Semmes, the brother of the Confederacy's most famous naval officer Captain Raphael Semmes, commanded one of two Georgian brigades in the division. Born on "Montford's Plantation" in Wilkes County, Georgia on 5 June 1815, Semmes attended the University of Virginia and became a plantation owner and banker before the war. He was not completely lacking in military training having served as an officer in the Georgia militia. His administrative skills also help him perform the duties of quartermaster general for his unit. When the war began, Semmes volunteered for service and was made colonel of the 2nd Georgia. He was a tall, gruff looking man who flaunted a large stately beard and mustache. A snappy dresser on the battlefield, it was hard to miss him in his stylish uniform with red accents. He wore a large red turban, a red sash across his shoulder and around his waist, and his boots were always polished. He fought his brigade and himself hard. During one particular incident on the Peninsula, Semmes became so intense during the fighting that when hostility slowed he had to be assisted from the field by some of his men due to exhaustion.[55]

Just prior to the Peninsula Campaign, Semmes was promoted to brigadier general and elevated to brigade command. He fought at Yorktown, Williamsburg and Fair Oaks as part of McLaws' Division in Magruder's command. Semmes fought the brigade well during The Seven Days, receiving congratulations from McLaws. "I beg leave to call attention..." his commander wrote in his report, "to the cool courage and knowledge of his duties exhibited by General Semmes." Missing the battle of Second Manassas, Semmes next action was during the Maryland Campaign. His brigade fought to delay the Yankees at Crampton's Gap and was in the thick of it at Sharpsburg, receiving another citation from McLaws. The brigade's next action came at Fredericksburg along Marye's Heights. During the Chancellorsville Campaign Semmes guided the brigade during the fight at Salem Church, where his men were severally mauled by the men of Sedgwick's Sixth Corps. Semmes, who was not opposed to exaggerating the effectiveness of his command, could not let a chance to prop up his boy's contribution pass by. Exaggerating in his report Semmes wrote "[o]f the 5,000 lost by Sedgwick, which is admitted by the enemy, after counting liberally for the losses at Fredericksburg and in his retreat across the river and elsewhere, not less than nearly one-half must have occurred in my front." Semmes appears to have forgotten that there were a number of other brigades shooting as well and his overstatement had no basis in truth.[56]

Semmes original brigade consisted of units from Georgia, Virginia and Louisiana but by early June 1863, the Virginia and Louisiana regiments were gone, replaced by additional Georgians. The 10th, 50th, 51st and 53rd Georgia regiments

---

[55] *Ibid*, p.216; Eicher, & Eicher, ***High Commands***, p.478.

[56] ***OR*** vol.11, pt.2, p.717; ***OR*** vol.25, pt.1, p.836; Tagg, ***Generals***, p.216.

were all tough outfits that had taken their share of battle casualties. Before the close of the summer campaign there would be many more.[57]

The other Georgia brigade in McLaws' Division was commanded by Brigadier General William T. Wofford. Wofford's brigade consisted of the 16th, 18th, and 24th regiments. Rounding out the brigade were two other commands, the Cobb's Legion and Phillips Legion infantries. Another lawyer general, Wofford was born in the mountains of northern Georgia's Habersham County on 28 June 1824. The boy's mother did most of the child rearing due to the untimely death of his father. Young William received his education at the area's local schools and the Gwinnett County Manual Labor School. Later, Wofford attended Franklin College where he studied law and graduated in 1844. The following year, he passed the bar and set up a practice in Cassville in 1846. His practice made him prosperous early in life, allowing him to become a plantation owner near Cassville. He was elected to the state legislature and served as clerk of the lower house from 1849 to 1853. In his spare time, Wofford busied himself editing a local newspaper. A Democrat, he was a staunch Unionist and as a delegate to the Georgia secession convention he voted against secession. When it became evident that there would be war, he volunteered for service, not wishing to turn his back on his state.[58]

Wofford had no formal training in the military arts. When the war with Mexico began, he stepped up and served as a captain in a company of Georgia mounted volunteers. The company saw action in 1847 when it fought at Vera Cruz. When civil war came, Wofford was installed as colonel of the 1st Georgia militia but when the unit was mustered into Confederate service it was designated the 18th Georgia. The 18th was initially stationed in North Carolina but soon found itself traveling north to take part in the battles around Richmond in 1862 as part of John Bell Hood's Texas Brigade. The regiment was "adopted" by the Texans and fought shoulder to shoulder with the Lone Star State volunteers at Yorktown, Eltham's Landing, and West Point, Virginia as well as during The Seven Days. At Gaines' Mill, Wofford's troops gained recognition when they managed to break through the Federal lines. The 18th also fought at Second Manassas, helping their Texas brothers deliver the initial blow against John Popes left, crushing it and driving the Federals from the field. When John Hood was promoted to division command, Wofford, still a colonel, took command of the Texas Brigade and lead it during the Maryland Campaign. In the thick of battle again at Sharpsburg, the brigade suffered over 500 casualties during the fighting in and around the Miller cornfield. After the battle, both Longstreet and Hood singled out Wofford for his service.[59]

After the Maryland Campaign, Wofford returned to the command of the 18th Georgia. On 26 November, the men of the 18th regiment said goodbye to their

---

[57] *OR* vol.27, pt.2, p.283.

[58] Eicher, & Eicher, *High Commands*, p.578; Wakelyn, *Biographical Dictionary*, p.445; Tagg, *Generals*, p.221. Franklin College would later become part of the University of Georgia.

[59] Warner, *Generals in Gray*, pp.343-344; Wakelyn, *Biographical Dictionary*, p.445; *OR* vol.19, pt.1, p.811; Tagg, *Generals*, p.221.

extended Texas family when they were transferred to the brigade of Brigade General Thomas R. R. Cobb, becoming part of McLaws Division. Wofford next directed the 18th on Marye's Heights at Fredericksburg. During the fight, Cobb fell mortally wounded, creating an opening for a new brigadier. A month later, on 17 January 1863, Wofford was promoted to fill the vacancy. Two days later, Special Order No.19 was issued from army headquarters. In it, Wofford's promotion was officially announced, followed by instructions requiring him to report to Longstreet for assignment to the command of Cobb's Brigade. The brigade's first action came at Chancellorsville, but Wofford, like McLaws' other brigade commanders, received no accolades from McLaws. Although McLaws was accused of lacking aggressiveness, the same could not be said of Wofford. In fact many though him too aggressive, often to the point of rashness. His peers knew he was one of the bravest men in the army and when the fighting became hot, Wofford always seemed to be pushing his men into the maelstrom. By early June he had seen plenty of action and his commander knew exactly what could be expected of him on a battlefield.[60]

McLaws' Division also included a fine brigade of Mississippians under the command of William Barksdale. Barksdale was not the typical Confederate brigade commander. Large and heavy he looked out of place on a horse and was one of, if not the most outspoken fire eater in the army. He had one burning desire; to kill as many Yankees as possible, and to all who knew him, it was obvious that the forty-two year old Barksdale enjoyed his work. When he rode into battle he seemed to lean forward on his horse in an effort to get at the hated Northerners as quickly as possible. In actuality, it was probably due more to his physical size than anything else. He was inspirational and charismatic but never displayed any understanding of tactics or military knowledge. What Barksdale lacked in military training he made up for with sheer determination, drive and ferocity. In addition to his size, he stood out on a battlefield due to his fair, almost white complexion which made him easy to single out in a crowd.[61]

Barksdale, another political general spent his informative years learning to be a lawyer and editing a pro-slavery newspaper. Born in Smyrna, Rutherford County, Tennessee on 21 August 1821, he was the older brother of Confederate Congressman Ethelbert Barksdale. After spending a year at the University of Nashville, he moved to Mississippi where he studied law at Columbia. Shortly after he began practicing his profession, he quite the trade and, at the tender age of twenty-one, became the editor of the *Columbus Democrat*. When the Mexican War began, he joined the 2nd Mississippi Regiment. Appointed captain, he was detailed to commissary duties and performed the task during 1847-48. While his responsibilities where those of a quartermaster, he could often be found at the front during heavy fighting, missing his coat and brandishing a large sword. After the war he returned to Mississippi, settling in Lowndes County. In 1853, as a Democrat, he was elected to congress and went off to Washington.

---

[60] *OR* vol.21, pt.1, pp.538, 1100; Tagg, **Generals**, pp.221-222.

[61] Tagg, **Generals**, p.218.

Evidently the scuffle with Mexico had not taken the fire out of Barksdale for when he arrived in Washington he quickly developed a reputation for being an adamant states' rights supporter. His opinions proved him to be radical, often producing confrontations with his fellow congressmen, sometimes to the point of violence. Shortly after his first term began Barksdale found himself disagreeing with fellow Mississippi Congressman Reuben Davis. Before the scuffle was over, Barksdale had been stabbed as many as eleven times with a pocket knife. All the wounds were superficial and, although he recovered, the incident failed to calm his confrontational attitude. Barksdale also may have stood by and watched as Preston S. Brooks beat abolitionist Charles Sumner within an inch of his life in the Senate Chamber with a cane. In one of his more mild confrontations, Barksdale lost his wig during a shoving match. Three days after Mississippi seceded, the confrontational Barksdale said goodbye to any friends he had left in Washington, withdrew from Congress and cast his fortunes with the South.[62]

Barksdale went back to Mississippi and signed up to support the cause in March 1861, becoming quartermaster general for the state militia. Once the Confederate military was organized, he was made a colonel and assigned to command of the 13th Mississippi on 14 May. At First Manassas, he guided his regiment into the flank of the Federals, helping turn the tide of the battle. Later that fall, Barksdale almost derailed his military career when he became so drunk that his superior, General Nathan Evans filed charges against him. Evans, who was somewhat of a drunk himself eventually withdrew the charges when Barksdale promised not to touch alcohol for the remainder of the war. After the incident, Barksdale straightened up, worked to train his men and led them during the Peninsula Campaign. Shortly before the close of the campaign Barksdale's brigade commander was killed. On 29 June the fiery Mississippian took charge of the brigade. Two days later he led it for the first time at Malvern Hill. With the shot and shell swirling around him, Barksdale grabbed a stand of regimental colors and personally led the men forward. Lee himself noted that Barksdale had exhibited "the highest qualities of a soldier." A short time after his escapade on the slopes of Malvern Hill, Barksdale was made a brigadier general, placed in permanent command of his Mississippians and transferred to McLaws' Division.[63]

During the Maryland Campaign, Barksdale's boys marched to Maryland Heights and cleared the ridge of the Federals garrisoned there; allowing Stonewall Jackson to occupy Harpers Ferry. A few days later he guided the brigade through the West Woods at Sharpsburg, helping to destroy "uncle" John Sedgwick's Division. At Fredericksburg, Barksdale was assigned the task of defending the town against the initial Federal assault from across the Rappahannock River. The Mississippian's defended the riverfront with a tenacity which gained them the respect of all. Barksdale's men conducted their defense first from rifle pits along the riverbank. When forced from the river's edge, entire companies snipped at the advancing Federals from cellars and from behind trees and building, conducting a

---

[62] *Ibid*, p.218; Wakelyn, ***Biographical Dictionary***, pp.86-87.

[63] Eicher, & Eicher, ***High Commands***, p.116; Tagg, ***Generals***, p.218.

guerrilla war through the streets. Many remained hidden, letting the Federals pass by, then emerging to assault the surprised Yankees from the rear. Stubbornly they held their position, even as a heavy artillery bombardment reduced a good portion of the town to nothing more than a pile of rubble. Finally, the Confederates were forced to pull back but not before making the Yankees pay dearly for their desire to claim the town. The fight marked the first time an American military force had established a bridgehead under enemy fire and technically, the fire had come from other Americans.[64]

Barksdale's finest hour however, came during the Chancellorsville Campaign when his brigade was detailed to form a portion of the defensive front at Fredericksburg to keep the Yankee's moving on Lee's rear in check. Once again, John Sedgwick's men encountered the stubborn Barksdale who put up a staunch defense with two regiments from behind the famous stone wall on Marye's Heights. Working together, the Mississippians fought off superior numbers until their position became untenable. Overrun by a good portion of the Federal Sixth Corps, undaunted, Barksdale pulled his men back, rallied them, and with the help of reinforcements, regained his footing. The following day, the Confederates dug in and halted the Federals at Salem Church. Afterword, Barksdale posted his brigade once again behind the wall on the heights. A few weeks later, at the end of May 1863, Barksdale's Mississippians could thump their chests and lay claim as one of the most battle hardened brigades in Lee's army. His regiments, the 13th, 17th, 18th and 21st Mississippi, while severely diminished in numbers, would march to Gettysburg and do their part. Many of them would remain there.[65]

Brigadier General Joseph B. Kershaw's brigade completed McLaws' division. Like Barksdale, Kershaw was a lawyer, and like the regiments under his command, he was from South Carolina. Kershaw was born to John and Harriet Kershaw in Camden, on 5 January 1822. There was past military experience in Joseph's family; his grandfather served during the Revolution, but lost most of his fortune in the effort. Orphaned at the age of seven, he was enrolled in a school taught by a strict disciplinarian who seemed to never spare the rod and enjoyed using it. At fifteen he entered the Cokesbury Conference School but did not stay long. Shortly thereafter, Joseph went to work for a dry goods merchant in Charleston but the business world held no charm for him. He soon returned to Camden and began studying law. In 1843, at the tender age of twenty-one, he took and passed the bar. Kershaw formed a law partnership and in 1844 married a young women named Lucretia Douglass. Young Joseph's life was beginning to take shape, but it was soon interrupted by war with Mexico.

Kershaw, along with his law partner, went to war as members of the DeKalb Rifle Guards, a local Camden militia company. Unfortunately things were not as rosy in Mexico as they had been in Camden. Before the war was over, Kershaw's

---

[64]   Tagg, ***Generals***, pp.218-219; Dinkins, James, Barksdale's Mississippi Brigade at Fredericksburg, ***SHSP***, vol.36, pp.21-22; O'Reilly, Francis Augustin, ***The Fredericksburg Campaign: Winter War on the Rappahannock***, p.101.

[65]   Sears, ***Chancellorsville***, pp.353-357.

business partner was dead and Joseph became so sick with fever that when he finally arrived home, he was so broken down physically that his wife had to nurse him until he was able to fend for himself. Once back on his feet, Joseph resumed his law practice. Political aspirations soon entered his mind and in 1852 he became a member of the South Carolina legislature, serving in the lower house. He served a number of terms and when the state began to take a stand against Northern tyranny, he became a member of the states' Secession Convention representing his district.[66]

When the war began, Kershaw assisted in raising a regiment constructed from volunteers from his and nearby congressional districts. He was elected colonel of the regiment shortly before South Carolina Governor Francis Pickens ordered it to Charleston. The regiment was sent to Morris Island near Fort Sumter, where it remained until after the South's second wave of secession. Eventually designated the 2nd South Carolina, the regiment was ordered north to Virginia. To keep him near her heart, when Joseph went off to war, Lucretia constructed for herself a bracelet and necklace from locks of the colonel's hair.

Kershaw and his regiment fought at First Manassas. After the battle, Beauregard called him a "military idiot" in reference to an article Kershaw had written for a South Carolina newspaper. After Beauregard left Virginia, Kershaw was elevated to brigade command when his brigade's preceding commander resigned because of a conflict over seniority. He led the brigade on the Peninsula and evidently impressed McLaws, who praised him in his official report. "I beg leave to call attention to the gallantry, cool, yet daring, courage and skill in the management of his gallant command exhibited by Brigadier General Kershaw," McLaws wrote. Kershaw took his brigade north into Maryland in August 1862. After helping Barksdale's Brigade drive the Yankees off of Maryland Heights, he helped Jackson occupy Harpers Ferry. He then marched his brigade north and gave a firm showing at Sharpsburg. Perhaps his most notable performance came at Fredericksburg. Along the stone wall atop Marye's Heights, Brigadier General Thomas Cobb's brigade met continuous massed Federal assaults. Kershaw's boys helped Cobb shore up the defenses and when Cobb fell; he took command of the fallen brigadier's section of the wall. Remaining mounted he rode his horse back and forth spurring on the men to keep up their fire. Kershaw and his brigade saw little action during the Chancellorsville Campaign. The respite was probably a welcome break from the hard marching and fighting of the previous year.

Kershaw was forty-one years of age in the spring of 1863. He had been at the head of his brigade for eighteen months. During that time he had gained the respect of his men. They knew that during the thickest fighting they could always find him leading his South Carolinians from the front of their ranks. He was intelligent, articulate and dignified in his mannerisms and the embodiment of what it meant to be a southern gentleman. His blond hair and blue eyes made it easy for his men to identify him during the heat of battle. His chiseled features were accented by a projecting chin and a mustache which hung below his mouth. In the midst of battle, Kershaw's voice seemed to carry over the chaos in clear ringing tones which the

---

[66] Dickert, Augustus D., *History of Kershaw's Brigade*, pp.86-87.

men of his six South Carolina units could easily identify. Although a six regiment brigade was uncommon, all had been reduced by hard work, making the brigade's size typical for the summer of 1863. Kershaw's original 2nd regiment along with the 3rd, 7th, 8th, 15th and the 3rd South Carolina Battalion populated the unit.[67]

McLaws' Division broke camp and headed for Culpeper on the morning of Wednesday 3 June. Colonel Edward Porter Alexander, commanding one of Longstreet's reserve artillery battalions recalled it being a "beautiful bright June day." The fair weather was a welcome sight since spring and early summer rains tended to turn the roads to mud. Dry roads caused other issues however, allowing great clouds of billowing dust to be churned up by the plodding feet of thousands of soldiers. Alexander noted that orders arrived around 11 a.m. and it took three hours to make arrangements. By 2 o'clock the division left the comforts of the Fredericksburg area for the hard road north. The first leg of the journey would be simple, requiring only a short three day march to Culpeper. The route initially took the division to the southwest through Spotsylvania Court House. Turning north McLaws' marching men tramped to Somerville Ford, where they crossed the Rapidan, arriving in the vicinity of the court house on 6 June.

Alexander remembered the day. "Although it was only to march to Culpeper C. H. we knew that it meant another great battle with the enemy's army, which was still confronting ours at Fredericksburg. I remember the hurried preparation, the parting with my wife & little daughter, & the looking back as long as even the tops of the locust trees & oaks about the house could be seen. And I can recall, too, the pride & confidence I felt in my splendid battalion, as it filed out of the fields into the road, with every chest & ammunition wagon filled, & every horse in fair order, & every detail fit for a campaign." Writing in his diary three days later Alexander recorded the battalion's arrival. "Jun. 6th, Sat. Arrived Culpeper C.H. 11 A.M. – 60 miles".

The same day McLaws' command broke camp, Hood's division, which was bivouacked further east near the Rapidan, received similar instructions to march to Culpeper. They were on the road later that day, arriving at their destination a day before McLaws.[68]

Longstreet's Shock Troops

John Bell Hood's father did not wish a military career for his son. Instead the elder Hood expressed a desire for his son to follow him into the medical profession, but the life of a doctor held no charm for the young Kentuckian. In an effort to persuade John to enter the field, his father offered to allow him to complete his studies in Europe. John however, stood by his convictions and his father put aside his desires. Hood was born in Owingsville, Kentucky, on 29 June 1831. He was a wild youth who seemed prone to fighting with other local youngsters. Little else is known about his childhood. His elementary education no doubt took place in local private schools but no records of where John received his initial schooling remains.

---

[67] *Ibid*, p.87; Tagg, **Generals**, pp.216-217, 221; ***OR*** vol.27, pt.2, p.283; ***OR*** vol.11, pt.2, p.717.

[68] Alexander, **Fighting**, p.221.

He undoubtedly learned all the trades of a youthful boy, which must have included hunting, fishing and the art of riding a horse. Later, as he matured, he fell in love with a local girl and only the intervention of the young woman's family kept the two from running off to elope.[69]

John's decision to follow a military path could have been influenced by his grandfather Lucas Hood, who most certainly described to the boy his exploits fighting Indians. As an impressionable teenager, John was enlightened with stories of daring deeds by soldiers fighting in Mexico. On 20 February 1849, Hood's uncle, Congressman Richard French, contacted the secretary of war and requested an appointment to West Point for his nephew. French must have been in the good graces of the secretary for six days later Hood was notified by the War Department that his request had been approved. Hood accepted the appointment on 9 March 1849. His father was probably a bit reluctant to sign the application, but John B. Hood became a cadet when he entered the academy on 1 July. Once enrolled, Hood proved that he was not a particularly good student and rebelled against the rigidity of a military existence. His performance was so poor that he was nearly expelled, but John managed to hang on to graduate forty-fourth in a class of fifty-two in 1853.[70]

His low class standing forced Hood into the infantry. Brevetted a second lieutenant, he was assigned to Company E of the 4th regiment. After spending some time in New York at Fort Columbus he ventured to his duty station at Fort Jones in northern California. With the organization of the new 2nd Cavalry, Hood found himself reassigned to mounted service in 1855 and transferred to Texas. The 2nd Cavalry contained a number of officers who would later make names for themselves. Second in command at the time was Robert E. Lee, and Hood formed a bond with the future Confederate commander. Hood knew Lee from his time at West Point for Lee had been the superintendant at the academy during Hood's final year.

Two years later, during a scrap with some local Indians along the Devil's River, Hood was shot in the hand with an arrow. Years later, he recalled the incident.

> "[T]he Indians charged desperately and forced our lines back a few paces in the centre. Having discharged my shot-gun, I rode at once with revolver in hand to that point, rallied the soldiers, who again drove them back, whilst our horses, in some instances, were beaten over the head with shields. The contest was at such close quarters that a warrior bore off a rifle which had been used and hung by one of the men upon his saddle. Meantime the Indians as quickly as they discharged their arms, handed them to their squaws, who ran to the rear, reloaded and

---

[69] Hood, John B., *Advance and Retreat: Personal Experiences in the United States and Confederate States Armies*, pp.v, 5; McMurry, Richard M., *John Bell Hood and the war for Southern Independence*, p.5.

[70] McMurry, *John Bell Hood*, p.6, Hood, *Advance and Retreat*, p.5. Hood's acceptance letter was misdated, the year being recorded as 1848.

returned them. At this juncture I was pierced in the left hand with an arrow which passed through the reins and the fourth finger, pinning my hand to the bridle. I instantly broke the spear head and threw it aside. Unmindful of the fact that the feathers could not pass through the wound, I pulled the arrow in the direction in which it had been shot, and was compelled finally in order to free myself of it to seize the feathered in lieu of the barbed end."

The wound would bother Hood for a couple of years as it healed. During the minor engagement he exhibited intense determination and aggressiveness, two traits which he would display again in a few years during much larger and more severe engagements.[71]

While his native state teetered on the edge of loyalty or rebellion, Hood cast his fortunes with the South. Even before resigning his commission, Hood entered Confederate service initially as a first lieutenant and then a captain commanding cavalry in March of 1861. A month later, on 16 April, he finally resigned his commission in the Old Army. Later that year, he was promoted to colonel, and assigned the task of organizing the 4th Texas Infantry. The new regiment was to be assembled with other regiments from Texas under politician turned brigadier general, Louis T. Wigfall. It took Wigfall little time to prove he was a poor general, and possibly to avoid embarrassment, he resigned from the army to join the Confederate Senate. The move opened the door for Hood, who took command of the brigade. His partnership with the Texans would be a good one, and during the first two years of the war, the brigade would earn hard won glory and establish itself as simply Hood's Texas Brigade.[72]

Hood and his brigade were on duty in the Fredericksburg area during the spring of 1862 when orders came instructing him to move with his brigade to the Virginia Peninsula. The brigade, which consisted of the 1st, 4th and 5th Texas along with Wofford's adopted 18th Georgia, arrived shortly before Johnston took command of the Confederate army near Richmond. Instead of allowing his men to loiter around, Hood began a regiment of drill and training. So well trained and prideful were the men that Hood harbored no concerns over their ability to perform on a battlefield.

In a short time, Johnston began his retreat up the Peninsula and Hood's Brigade fell back through Williamsburg. Soon information came that a force of Yankees had come ashore at Eltham's Landing. Hood was ordered to take his brigade and check the Federal's advance. This he did in fine style and was recognized for his performance. Hood's division commander, General G. W. Smith singled out the brigade in his official report, noting "[t]he brunt of the contest was borne by the Texans, and to them is due the largest share of the honors of the day at Eltham." Once again, at Gaines' Mill, Hood led his brigade in a charge which shattered the Federal defenses. General Jackson was quick to recognize the performance of the

---

[71] Hood, *Advance and Retreat*, pp.vi, 12. Early in the war the 2nd Cavalry would be re-designated the 5th U.S. Cavalry.

[72] *Ibid*; Eicher, & Eicher, **High Commands**, p.303

Texans. "In this charge," Jackson wrote in his report, "in which upward of 1,000 men fell killed and wounded before the fire of the enemy and in which fourteen pieces of artillery and nearly a regiment were captured, the 4th Texas, under the lead of General Hood, was the first to pierce these strongholds and seize the guns." By the time the Peninsula Campaign came to a conclusion, Hood's Brigade had established a reputation as one of the toughest and most gallant units in the army.[73]

Prior to Second Manassas, Hood's Texans lost their commander to promotion. That August Hood took command of the brigade's division, lending his name to his new command. As Longstreet's Corps arrived on the battlefield, Federal General John Pope was concentrating on pounding Jackson's Corps, which was already heavily engaged, into submission. Pope focused so intently on Jackson that he exposed his left flank, leaving it lightly defended. As Longstreet came onto the field, he pushed Hood's Division forward, the Texans, now under Wofford, leading the way. In the path of Hood's Division was a lone regiment, the 5th New York Infantry, known as Duryée Zouave's. Hood's entire division slammed into the lone, unsupported regiment, all but removing it from the face of the earth in ten minutes. One survivor, Private Andrew Coats, years later noted the ferocity of the attack. "I can assure you that where the regiment stood that day was the very vortex of Hell." Of all the men under Longstreet's command it was Hood's Brigade and then Division which built the First Corps' reputation as Lee's shock troops.[74]

Early in the fight at Sharpsburg, Hood's Division was rushed to the north end of the field to shore up the Confederate left near the Miller Cornfield. It was there that the division saw some of its most severe fighting of the war. Around 7:00 a.m., the Texans hit the cornfield and drove the Federals out, but a stiff counterattack forced the Texans back. By the time it was over, Hood's Division had suffered heavily, absorbing 1,002 killed, wounded and missing men. Hood reported that he tussled with two Federal corps. While there were two Federal corps on the northern portion of the field, Hood in reality, while still outnumbered, did not take on all the troops in both corps. Years later, he would note that the men were outnumbered ten to one but this also seems to be a bit of an exaggeration. In his report, he noted the savagery of the fighting. "It was here," he wrote, "that I witnessed the most terrible clash of arms, by far, that has occurred during the war. This most deadly combat raged till our last round of ammunition was expended." The bravery and tenacity of the division was acknowledged by Hood in his report when he reserved almost half the document for noting the gallantry of a large number of officers and men in his command.[75]

Hood's record in combat was exemplary. He possessed a fire which burned white hot when the prospect of combat loomed. Major Venable of Lee's staff noted that he had often heard of the fire which burns in a warrior's eyes when engaged in the hurricane of battle. Venable admitted he only saw that fire on a single instance

---

[73] Hood, *Advance and Retreat*, p.12; *OR* vol.11, pt.1, p.627; *OR* vol.11, pt.2, p.556.

[74] Hennessy, John, At the Vortex of Hell, *CWTI*, vol.24, no.9, p.17; Eicher, & Eicher, *High Commands*, p.303.

[75] Hood, *Advance and Retreat*, pp.43-44; *OR* vol.19, pt.1, pp.923-925.

during the war. Charged with carrying orders to General Hood, Venable found him deep in the whirlwind swirling about. He noted the general was transfixed by the events around him. "The fierce light in Hood's eyes I can never forget," Venable noted. General Jackson evidently saw the ferocity which burned in General Hood as well. In October, one month after Sharpsburg, Jackson recommended Hood for promotion to Major General. Lee evidently concurred for on 10 October Hood received his promotion.[76]

John Bell Hood was James Longstreet's hard hitting division commander. *MOLLUS Collection, USAHEC*

Heavy casualties forced the reinforcement of Hood's Division with two additional brigades shortly before Fredericksburg. The new brigades contained nine regiments of hard fighting Georgians. Although supplemented, his division saw little action during the battle and shortly thereafter, along with Pickett, went with Longstreet south to forage near Suffolk. Hood's blond hair and chiseled, intense look reminded all that he was a soldier. A bachelor, and only thirty-two years of age the spring of 1863, he drew the interest of the ladies. At over six feet in height, the lanky Hood could easily be found in a crowd. Many believed he had an intensely bright future in front of him. His potential however, would be marred by the horrors of armed conflict, the heaviness of command and the scares of battle.[77]

One of the two Georgia brigades added to Hood's command prior to Fredericksburg consisted of the 2nd, 15th, 17th and 20th regiments under the command of Brigadier General Henry Lewis Benning. A Georgina by birth, Benning was one

---

[76] Tagg, *Generals*, pp.224-225.

[77] Ibid, pp.223-224.

of the older Confederate brigade commanders having been born 2 April 1814. Prematurely gray for his age, he had a tough and gritty exterior accented by a heavy beard and wavy hair. Known as "Old Rock" or simply "Rock" by his men, due to his sturdily built frame, Benning had a rough and gravelly voice and a deliberate speech pattern that commanded attention when he spoke. He was a lawyer and graduate of Franklin College, a staunch supporter of secession, and a hard-line pro slavery man. A firm believer in the formation of an independent South, Benning promoted his opinions from a position on the bench of the Georgia Supreme Court. He believed that a strong centralized government of a Southern Republic comprised of states from the Deep South, would be able to place slavery "under the control of those most interested in it." When secession finally came he was in line for a position in Davis' cabinet but chose to be a soldier.[78]

After organizing the 17th Georgia, Benning was made its colonel. The regiment was mustered during August 1861 and Benning led it successfully during the early stages of the war. Assigned to Brigadier General Robert Toombs' brigade, Benning would find himself assuming Toombs' responsibility during most of its engagements due to Toombs' absence for extended periods. For the most part, Benning remained cool in battle, but he did lose his composure on a couple of occasions. One of those instances was during Second Manassas when Benning, after losing control of his brigade, for some reason determined it had been destroyed. Commandeering an artillery horse, he rode to find Longstreet and reported that all his men had been killed. Undaunted, Longstreet informed Benning that was "nonsense" and that if the Georgian would simply look around him he would see that his brigade was still somewhat intact. Longstreet then told Benning if he would bring what was left of his brigade forward, he would give them a place in line. The mild, if not firm chastising calmed Benning and he returned to the fight, rallied his men and got back into the battle.[79]

Benning's best performance prior to Gettysburg was possibly at Sharpsburg, where once again he was in command of Toombs' Brigade. On the southern end of the battlefield, on a bluff above the lower bridge over Antietam Creek, the 2nd and 20th Georgia snipped at Federals from General Burnside's Ninth Corps, while they attempted to cross the bridge. During the course of the battle, Lee pulled reinforcements from the southern reaches of his position to assist his battered troops in and around the Miller Cornfield and at the center of his defensive line at the Sunken Road. Lee had virtually no unused men to resist a Federal attack made against the southern part of the field. With grit and determination, the 2nd and 20th held the bluff throughout the morning and into the early afternoon against a number of Federal attempts to cross the bridge. With their ammunition almost exhausted, Union regiments managed to finally cross and drive the Georgians from the bluff, but it was too late. The delaying action bought the time needed for A. P. Hill to arrive from Harpers Ferry, saving Lee's right.[80]

---

[78] *Ibid*, pp.234-235; ***OR*** vol.27, pt.2, p.285. Franklin College is now the University of Georgia.

[79] Tagg, ***Generals***, p.235.

[80] Sears, ***Landscape Turned Red***, pp.260, 266-267.

With Toombs absent once again at Fredericksburg, Benning led the brigade during what little action it saw. A month later, on 17 January 1863, he received a promotion to brigadier general. Toombs expressed his displeasure, feeling he had been passed over. When the smoke cleared, Toombs, on 4 March, resigned and Benning took permanent command of the brigade in April. Toombs' departure placed the Georgians in the capable hands of the battle tested Benning. The men of the brigade showed great confidence in him. His leadership skills would be of great advantage in a few short weeks as the men arrived on the field at Gettysburg.[81]

Hood's other Georgia brigade consisted of the 7th, 8th, 9th, 11th and 59th regiments under the command of George Thomas Anderson, himself a Georgian. Born in Covington on 3 February 1824, Anderson attended Emory College, was a Methodist and prior to the war, married and became a family man. He was rather successful financially and before the war had amassed a sizable fortune. Although he had no formal military training, Anderson did have practical experience, serving as a second lieutenant in the Georgia mounted infantry during the Mexican War. Evidently military service held some charm for Anderson, for a few years after the Mexican War ended he received a commission in the Regular Army where he served as a captain in the 1st Cavalry. Three years later, on 11 June 1858, he resigned his commission and returned to civilian life. When the Civil War began his previous experience, stature as an influential land owner and his close friendship with Robert Toombs provided Anderson the opportunity to be installed as colonel of the 11th Georgia Infantry on 2 July 1861.[82]

Anderson's boys were mustered in too late to play an active role during First Manassas. Eventually the regiment was assigned to a brigade that had seen action during the engagement. The brigade's commander had been killed during the battle and Anderson, without seeing any serious combat, ended up commanding of the brigade for a short time until a new brigadier could be brought in. In May 1862, he ascended to brigade command once more and led his regiments at Yorktown on the Peninsula and during The Seven Days. He showed great personal courage and fought his men from the front. At Malvern Hill, Anderson was shocked to learn that his old 11th Georgia's colonel was missing. Dismounting from his horse, he also discovered a number of the 11th's men had also departed. Calling out to his former regiment, Anderson rallied the men, yelling that if he could not get the whole regiment to follow him at least he knew his old company would. Gathering as many men as he could find, he led the group up the slope of the hill into the teeth of the Federal fire. The minutes that followed saw seventy-two of the men who joined Anderson fall as casualties. The brigade itself lost 309 men over the final three days of the fighting. At Second Manassas, Anderson's brigade was at the head of Longstreet's Corps as it pushed its way through Thoroughfare Gap. Once across the Bull Run Mountains, it attacked with the remainder of the corps, caving in Pope's flank.

---

[81] Eicher, & Eicher, **High Commands**, pp.129, 532; Tagg, **Generals**, p.235.

[82] Eicher, & Eicher, **High Commands**, p.104; Wakelyn, **Biographical Dictionary**, p.73.

During the Maryland Campaign the brigade saw limited action, but its inactivity did not stop General Longstreet from noting Anderson in his report. A month later, Anderson and his brigade was transferred to Hood's Division and on 1 November he finally received a promotion to brigade general. The brigade saw little action at Fredericksburg and was preparing to march north to rejoin Lee when the Confederates engaged Hooker at Chancellorsville. It is fitting that Anderson's nickname was "Tige," a truncated version of tiger. The moniker exactly described how he conducted himself on a battlefield. His chiseled face and stern look projected a military bearing and his dark, wavy hair and beard always seemed to be neat and trimmed.[83]

Like General Hood, forty-eight year old Jerome B. Robertson was a Kentuckian in command of Texans. Born 14 March 1815 in Woodford County, he became an orphan at the age of twelve. Penniless with nowhere to turn, the boy began working as an apprentice hatter to earn enough money to feed himself and put a roof over his head. When his sponsor passed away, Jerome found himself relocated to St. Louis. Evidently making and selling hats was not a career that interested him. By the age of eighteen, he had saved enough money to purchase the final three years of his employment contract. Alone and uneducated, he became acquainted with a local physician who thought enough of him to employ the teenager as an office staffer. The doctor began tutoring Jerome and he eventually learned enough to enabled him to study medicine at Transylvania University. His education was cut short however, when revolution erupted in Texas. Wishing to get into the fight, Jerome helped raise a company of Kentuckians, of which he became captain. At the age of twenty he went south to join Sam Houston's army. Unfortunately, by the time he arrived, the Battle of San Jacinto was over and Santa Anna had been defeated.

Robertson remained in Texas, settled in Washington on the Brazos and began practicing medicine. It was there that he met and married a young woman named Mary Cummins and started a family. Mary proved to be a capable bearer of children and Jerome's brood quickly grew to include three youngsters, one of which, a boy named Felix, would also lead troops in the Confederate Army. Living out on the frontier afforded Robertson the opportunity to develop his fighting skills keeping the local Indians in check. From 1838 to 1844 he became well versed at putting down any marauding parties that threatened settlers. He also dabbled in politics and spent time in a few local elected positions. In 1848, his reputation as an Indian fighter helped get him elected to the Texas state House and to the Senate two years later. As the Civil War loomed, he served as a secession delegate to the Texas Convention in 1861.[84]

Once again Robertson raised a company of volunteers, this time from Texas, and marched them off to war. However, unlike his experience in Mexico, there would be plenty of bloodletting this time. His company was integrated into the 5th Texas, and brigaded with the other Texas regiments in Hood's Texas Brigade, forming the only Texas brigade to serve in the Eastern Theater. Through the promotion of his superiors and his own performance, Robertson was elevated to command of the

---

[83] Tagg, *Generals*, p.230; *OR* vol.11, pt.2, p.708.

[84] Tagg, *Generals*, pp.231-232; Wakelyn, ***Biographical Dictionary***, p.370; Eicher, & Eicher, ***High Commands***, p.457.

regiment and led it during the Peninsular Campaign where he was wounded in the shoulder at Gaines' Mill. While pushing his command forward at Second Manassas he was wounded once more, shot in the groin. Two weeks later he was back in the field and although weak from his wound, led his regiment until exhaustion overtook him at South Mountain. He was too feeble to guide the 5th through the bloodbath at Sharpsburg. A few days later, on 26 September, as he struggled to recover, he received a promotion to colonel. Just over a month later, on 1 November, he was promoted to brigadier general and elevated to brigade command. The famous Texas brigade, fell into the capable hands of Robertson when Hood was promoted to division command. His new brigade however, was not completely constructed from Texas regiments. Gone were the adopted men of the 18th Georgia. The men of the 1st, 4th and 5th Texas had been joined by the 3rd Arkansas. Robertson cared for the welfare of his men to such an extent that the Texans and Arkansas boys began to calling him "Aunt Polly" for his mothering attitude.[85]

Hood's two Georgia brigades and Robertson's Texans were not the only hard-hitting units under Hood's command. Brigadier General Evander M. Law could boast his brigade of Alabamans was just as tough under fire. All five of his regiments, the 4th, 15th, 44th, 47th and 48th had taken part in the thickest and most vicious fighting at Sharpsburg. His regiments had been spread around in various brigades until 19 January, 1863 when three North Carolina regiments were transferred out and the 47th, 48th and 15th were brought in.[86]

Evander was born to Ezekiel Augustus Law and Sarah Elizabeth McIver on 7 August 1836, in Darlington South Carolina. Known as Gus, Evander's father was a graduate of Yale Law School and had spent time in the state legislature. With his family residing on a plantation, young Evander participated in the typical outdoor pursuits of a boy, learning to ride a horse and hunt at an early age. He received much of his elementary education at local schools and St. John's Academy in his hometown.

Evander's family had been prominent during the Revolution. His grandfather and two of his great-grandfathers fought to established independence for the new nation. Holding to that tradition, on 1 January 1853, Evander, still a skinny teenager, entered the Arsenal Academy at Columbia. He remained only a year before moving his educational path to the South Carolina Military Institute. The training Law received at the academy prepared him well for his future role as a Confederate brigade commander. Twice a year the cadets were required to pack a knapsack with their belongings, handed a musket, and sent into the field to experience the existence of a soldier. The excursions gave Law an excellent perspective on what it was like to be an average soldier of the line. Upon graduation he ranked fourth in a class of fifteen, finishing with high marks in Constitutional Law and English Literature and average marks in Military Engineering and Tactics. He finished with poor marks for behavior, standing fourteenth in conduct.[87]

---

[85] *OR* vol.27, pt.2, p.284; Tagg, ***Generals***, p.232; Wakelyn, ***Biographical Dictionary***, p.370.

[86] *OR* vol.21, p.1099; *OR* vol.27, pt.2, p.284; Longstreet, ***WtoA***, p.337.

[87] Laine, J. Gary & Penny, Morris M., ***Law's Alabama Brigade in the War Between the Union and the Confederacy***, p.2. The South Carolina Military Institute is now known as The Citadel.

When the war began, Law, at the tender age of twenty-four, was young enough to vividly recall his military training. He felt it his responsibility, because of his training, to step up and defend his fledgling country; and he answered the call for volunteers to fill Alabama's rolls. After offering his services on 7 January 1861, Law was sent to Pensacola with his new company to assist in the capture of the forts in the area. Five days later he was commissioned a captain in Alabama's gathering force and assisted in the occupation of Fort Barrancas and the Naval Yard on the mainland; however, capturing the harbor's main facility, Fort Pickens proved to be more difficult. Its position on Santa Rosa Island on the outskirts of the harbor presented logistical issues with a direct assault. After a few weeks of inactivity, Law and his Alabamans went home, the big prize of Fort Pickens still in Federal hands.[88]

Late in April, ten companies of volunteers from Alabama, including Law's, traveled to Dalton Georgia. From this group of disjointed companies came the 4th Alabama volunteers. By 2 May all the companies had arrived and the election of field officers commenced. Law stood for lieutenant colonel and was elected on the first ballot. His regiment left for Virginia the next day and initially ended up in the Shenandoah Valley as part of Brigadier General Barnard Bee's brigade. However, they soon found themselves embroiled in the struggle at First Manassas. Law's initial battle experience was a disheartening episode. Seeing a group of gray clad soldiers he ordered the regiment to form in their rear. Unfortunately, when the color bearer of the 4th unfurled the regimental colors Law's boys soon discovered that the men in gray were not Confederates but a Yankee battle line. The 4th was hit with a heavy fire and fell back. Law tried to rally the regiment but was hit in the left arm, the ball shattering his elbow. Although he did not lose the arm, when it healed it became an almost useless appendage. As the battle raged, General Bee arrived and rallied the regiment, imploring them to march to Stonewall Jackson's aide, who was at that moment making his heroic stand on Henry House Hill. The Alabamians moved forward to assist the Virginian but were cut in half by artillery fire. Most of them ended up taking shelter in a wooded area.[89]

---

[88] *Ibid*, p.3.

[89] *Ibid*, pp.4-6, 8; Tagg, **Generals**, p.227. Bee is generally credited with providing Jackson his famous nickname. The story has been told by many over the years and the truth has no doubt been skewed somewhat. Possibly the most accurate version of the story is that told by James I. Robertson in his work *Stonewall Jackson*. Bee was with Jackson on Henry House Hill when it became apparent that the Federals were getting the best of the Rebels. Jackson, sternly told Bee that the Virginians, if necessary would give the Federals "the bayonet." Bee then rode to an area of the battlefield were a number of Confederates, including members of the 4th Alabama, were disorganized and milling around. Pulling his sword from its scabbard, Bee used it to point toward Jackson's battle line and supposedly said; "Look, men, there is Jackson standing like a stonewall! Let us determine to die here, and we will conquer! Follow me!" Thus Jackson garnered his famous nickname and the man who gave it to him would indeed die on the field. Some have noted that Bee may have been speaking of Jackson in a sarcastic tone because of Jackson's stubbornness to hold his line on Henry House Hill. While a plausible scenario, the romanticized version of the story seems more likely. Robertson, **Stonewall Jackson**, p.264.

Law's first stint at brigade command turned out to be a temporary affair when the previous commander was elevated, temporarily, to divisional command. Law accepted the post gladly since he was actively seeking advancement, having courted friendships with then brigade commander John Hood and General Wigfall. After Wigfall departed, Law's relationship with Hood grew. Their friendship was not surprising since Hood and Law were cut from the same fearless mold. Both had gained the trust of their soldiers quickly and each shared the same philosophical approach to war. To expedite his advancement, Law sent an application for a brigadier generalship to Senator Wigfall, and began a lobbying campaign with other influential Confederate officials. He even asked some of his contacts to petition President Davis on his behalf. Davis forwarded Law's petition to the Secretary of War, but Lee was not yet ready to promote Law and the Alabaman remained a colonel.[90]

Law led his brigade during The Seven Days battles, as part of Longstreet's hammer blow at Second Manassas and into the bloody struggle in the cornfield at Sharpsburg. Finally, on 3 October 1862, his battlefield performance and political lobbying paid off. At the age of twenty-six, Law was promoted to brigadier general, becoming one of the youngest brigadiers in Confederate service. Minimally engaged at Fredericksburg, Law's Brigade, like the rest of Hood's Division, missed the Battle of Chancellorsville, making the coming campaign Law's first major effort leading his brigade as a brigadier. Few men had bad things to say about Law. In fact, issues were so few that the only thing one of his regimental commanders could find to complain about was the general's negligence in writing reports. After action reports were critical in acquiring for the brigade its just due after an engagement. If reports were not produced, regimental commanders and their well-deserving men seldom acquired the attention of higher ups. Although his lack of report writing was a chronic problem, Law obviously retained the confidence and respect of his men.[91]

A handsome man, sporting a heavy black beard, Law carried himself upright and erect and looked the part of a soldier in uniform. Entering the campaign he would be the senior brigadier in Hood's Division. He was militarily trained, had experience, understood his men and their abilities, was daring, and would not back down from a fight. Although youthful, he handled his brigade like a seasoned veteran.[92]

Ewell Takes Command

Richard Ewell was a very busy man for someone who had to limp around on a wooden leg. Prior to his nuptials, he had seemed frail and weak, only capable of riding a horse for short distances. However, he knew the army would be moving any day and duty was calling him to his new command. After his wedding, he

---

[90] Laine, & Penny, *Law's Alabama Brigade*, pp.9-10.

[91] Wakelyn, *Biographical Dictionary*, p.277.

[92] Tagg, *Generals*, pp.227-228.

seemed to be invigorated and there was an additional spring to his step; at least a spring which a one legged man could achieve. The order promoting Ewell and A. P. Hill had been written with Ewell's name proceeded Hill's, placing him number three in the army's command structure behind Lee and Longstreet. After taking care of a few last minute details pertaining to his marriage, Ewell sent for his staff, included Lizinka's son George Campbell Brown. He then boarded a train on 29 May bound for Hamilton's Crossing with his new bride, step-daughter Hattie, and niece Lizzie.[93]

George Brown had served on Ewell's staff since 1 July 1861 as a first lieutenant working for the general as an aide-de-camp. Now a captain, he had been in Mississippi during the Battle of Chancellorsville. During his return, after arriving in Lynchburg, George learned two critical pieces of information. First, Ewell had already departed for Hamilton's Crossing and second, the general was now his stepfather. Brown had been aware of the engagement for some time and noted that word of the marriage brought him "great pleasure." After spending a couple of days in Richmond, George pushed on to take his place within his new father's staff.[94]

It was in the midst of a warm day when Ewell arrived, and a large portion of the command Jackson had led to the stunning victories in the Valley a short year ago, showed up at the station to welcome him. Three rousing cheers were heard as Ewell negotiated the steps down to the platform using his one good leg. Jedediah Hotchkiss noted that the welcome was "enthusiastic." Lee and Longstreet also attended the welcoming and along with Ewell reviewed the troops at the station before Ewell and his entourage made the trip to his headquarters, which he established at Yerby's. Lee, writing to his wife on 31 May, noted that Ewell "looks very well & is very stout of heart." Others however observed a change in Ewell. Gone was the high strung, swearing general. In his place was a calmer, more subdued man. Some attributed the change to his new wife who would not allow him to be vulgar in her presence. Possible due to his inability to accept his good fortune, Ewell continued to introduce Lizinka as "my wife, Mrs. Brown." The Yerby house was less than a mile from the station which was probably a benefit to Ewell, who obviously tired more easily than the man who had marched through the Valley with Jackson.[95]

With his headquarters established, Ewell went to work assembling a new staff for the Second Corps. At the suggestion of Lee, he worked to keep as many members of Jackson's old organization within his new group as possible. To that end, Jedediah Hotchkiss stayed on as topographical engineer, "Sandie" Pendleton remained as assistant adjutant general, and Captain Wilbourn kept his position as chief signal officer. Surgeon McGuire also stayed on as chief medical

---

[93] Pfanz, *A Soldier's Life*, pp.273-274, 276.

[94] Krick, *Staff Officers*, p.84.

[95] Pfanz, *A Soldier's Life*, p.276; Hotchkiss, Jedediah, *Make Me a Map*, p.146; Dowdey, & Manarin, *Wartime Papers*, p.499; Gordon, *Reminiscences*, p.158.

officer. To man Ewell's chief of staff position the general originally selected Lieutenant Colonel Charles J. Faulkner. Faulkner was another Jackson staffer, whose background as a lawyer and legislator made him a good candidate to handle the paperwork. Faulkner however would resign a few days later and the position would fall to Pendleton. Sandie would be assisted by Major Benjamin Greene, and Ewell's new step son whom he chose to occupy assistant adjutant general positions. Supplies would be handled by chief commissary officer Major Wells Hawks and Chief Quartermaster John Harman. William Allan was selected to deal with the duties of chief ordnance officer while engineering duties would be assigned to Captain Henry B. Richardson. The ranking member of Ewell's staff, Colonel Abner Smead, would assist with adjutant general duties and function as inspector general. Greene would be required to help out Smead when necessary. Reverend Lacy would also be retained as Second Corps chaplain.[96]

Under Lee's reorganization, each corps now had five artillery battalions assigned directly to them. For the position of chief of artillery, Ewell selected Colonel Crutchfield but his wounding at Chancellorsville would keep him sidelined during the campaign. As a replacement, Ewell tapped Colonel John Thompson Brown, who was in command of Ewell's two reserve artillery battalions, to act as his chief of artillery until Crutchfield was able to take the field once again.[97]

Few objected to Ewell replacing Jackson. Hotchkiss, while noting that Ewell looked "feebly" informed his wife that "[W]e have our wishes gratified here in having Gen. Ewell to command the old army of Gen. Jackson..." Sandie Pendleton saw Ewell's wellbeing a little differently. His "health is pretty good now," he wrote his future wife Catherine "Kate" Corbin, "& he seems quite pleased to get back into the field." Sandie was also impressed with Ewell's ability to get around on his wooden leg noting that he "manages his leg very well & walks only with a stick, & mounts his horse quite easily from the ground." Others thought the general had difficulty mounting his horse and did not seem to be the old Ewell they remembered from the Valley. "Ewell arrived in camp with his wife... a new acquisition... and with one leg less than when I saw him last," noted a Second Corps staff officer. "From a military point of view the addition of the wife did not compensate for the loss of the leg. We were of the opinion that Ewell was not the same soldier he had been when he was a whole man and a single one." Obviously Ewell's appearance and extent of his physical limitations were a matter of opinion.[98]

Shortly after Ewell's arrival, a great festival was held at Yerby's. A number of Virginia's most influential local families were in attendance. The women dressed in their finest ball gowns and the men sported their most impressive military uniforms. William Yerby spared no expense in seeing that his guests were well fed.

---

[96] Pfanz, *A Soldier's Life*, p.277.

[97] *Ibid*, pp.278-279.

[98] Hotchkiss, *Make Me a Map*, p.146; Pfanz, *A Soldier's Life*, p.277; Sandie Pendleton to Kate Corbin, 4 June, 1863, William Nelson Pendleton Papers, Southern Historical Collection, University of North Carolina; McKim, Randolph H., *A Soldiers Recollections*, p.134.

Spread out before them were huge trays of meats including ham, mutton, chicken, turkey and a roasted hog. Oysters were even brought in from Norfolk and great mounds of fruits and baked goods including cakes, pies and rolls were served. To drink, Yerby served coffee, wine, mint juleps and punch. The festivities included dancing which was typically an activity of the younger attendees as the older partygoers relaxed in quiet discussion. The gathering lasted throughout the night and terminated with breakfast which was served to anyone remaining at 9 a.m.[99]

Unfortunately for Sandie Pendleton he missed the ball, recovering from a bout with dysentery. General Pendleton saw his ill son on 31 May and wrote Sandie's sister regarding his condition. "…Sandie is quite sick with dysentery. I saw him yesterday flat on his back in his tent. Have tried to get him in a house near by [sic], but cannot. He may have to go away for a few days. I regret it as General Ewell has come, and needs Sandie in the position he has so long filled." The following day the general had a comfortable bed made in his tent for Sandie and the young aid came up by ambulance and tried to assume his duties but was too sick. Another ambulance ride to familiar Guiney Station saw him confined to the same room and bed which Jackson had expired in a few weeks earlier. Cautious nursing for the next few days brought Sandie out of his malaise and, though still very weak, he returned to the army on the evening of 3 June, traveling the distance, once again, in the back of an ambulance. Upon his arrival, word was received that the Second Corps would soon be on the move.[100]

With the festivities over, it was time to prepare for the commencement of the campaign. Ewell officially took command of his corps on 1 June. On the same day, at Ewell's headquarters, Lee disclosed his plans for the march north. Ewell was informed that Lee intended to march into Pennsylvania by way of Culpeper and the Shenandoah Valley. He learned that the army would first be shifted to Culpeper and then his corps would lead the advance through the valley. It is likely that Lee chose Ewell to act as the vanguard of the army due to his prior combat experience in the Valley and that the men in his command were experienced in leading the army, having done so previously under Jackson.[101]

The Norse God

Ewell's three divisions were all led by experienced commanders who fit Lee's rumored requirements of being a Virginia native. Robert Emmett Rodes, the most underrated of the three, was the third child born to David and Martha Rodes in Lynchburg, Virginia on 29 March 1829. David Rodes, a former court clerk who had made money speculating on real estate, was moderately successful in the venture and when Robert was four his father moved the family to a home overlooking the town. David evidently paid $900 for the large three-story house, taking advantage of a depressed market. The large home provided the family a wonderful view of

---

[99] Bead, W.G., *Stonewall's Man: Sandie Pendleton*, p.129; Pfanz, *A Soldier's Life*, p.276.

[100] Bead, *Stonewall's Man*, pp.129-130; Lee, *Pendleton*, pp.273-275.

[101] Pfanz, *A Soldier's Life*, p.279.

Lynchburg, which at the time was a thriving and affluent community. Nearly 5,000 inhabitants called the town home, with slightly over half the population being white and the remainder being a combination of slaves and free blacks. Like his father, seizing opportunities was a lesson Robert evidently learned. During his military career he would exhibit the same traits.[102]

Robert received his elementary education in the local schools of Lynchburg and attended a boys school located in the basement of a local Baptist church. Following in the footsteps of his older brother, Virginius, Robert, as a sixteen-year-old plebe, entered the Virginia Military Institute in 1845. Away from home for the first time, he experienced all the symptoms of a homesick young man, but his busy schedule provided no time for melancholy and longing for home. The regimented structure at the institute kept Robert engaged from before sun up to well after sundown. Codes of conduct and the struggle to adhere to them proved to be a difficult task. In addition, the cadets were required to cut and stack their own firewood, a necessity since the barracks were heated with wood stoves. During his second year, the winter and the coursework at the institute became harder. The extreme weather made the procurement of firewood more critical, but forced the cadets indoors, where Rodes could spend more time on his studies. The extra time however, did not enhance his standing and he finished the year sixteenth in a class of twenty-five. Rodes' final years were even more difficult, but he worked hard, improving his class standing to ten. He finished fourth in mathematics, English and engineering, sixth in French, third in physics, drawing and chemistry, and second in tactics. His tenth place standing was due more to his 159 demerits than his scholarly aptitude. Finally, on Independence Day, 1848, at the age of nineteen, the tall, handsome looking, blond haired, blue eyed Robert Rodes graduated from VMI.[103]

Unable to garner a commission in the Regular Army, which his father lobbied for, Rodes remained at VMI and accepted a position as an assistant professor. He spent the next three years teaching cadets at his alma-mater and generally enjoyed his work, but as time wore on, he began to seriously question his position's ability to provide financial stability. When a professor position opened, Rodes made his interest in the job known, but the institute's administration wanted a West Point graduate for the opening and Rodes lost out. Disappointed by his opportunities, he turned to another profession. During a semester break, Rodes accepted a position with the North River Navigation Company as an assistant engineer. The work may initially have been a vehicle for Rodes to gain practical engineering experience, but when he failed to secure the professor position at VMI, he chose to remain

---

[102] Collins, Darrell L., *Major General Robert E. Rodes of the Army of Northern Virginia*, pp.4-6. There is conflicting information regarding Rodes' date of birth. Documents indicate that he was born on 29 March but his headstone indicated his birth was on 30 March. Under scrutiny the 30 March date does not stand up and the 29 March date seems plausible.

Historian Douglas Southall Freeman wrote that Rodes was "a Norse God in Confederate Gray."

[103] *Ibid*, pp.7, 12-14.

at North River. When North River's chief engineer, who was also an instructor at VMI, left to return to the institute, Rodes was promoted and took his job. Later, he spent three and one-half years working in the engineering field as a civil engineer with the Southside Railroad. When his services were no longer needed, he traveled to Alabama and in 1855, took a job as chief engineer on the Alabama and Chattanooga Railroad.[104]

Rodes' duties took him to Tuscaloosa and a turning point in his life. Probably while attending the Presbyterian Church, he met a beautiful young lady named Virginia Hortense Woodruff. Going by her middle name, Hortense was a learned young woman who grew up exposed to culture, books and music. Rodes was instantly smitten with her, but Hortense showed little interest since she was still recovering from the loss of a previous suitor. Although Robert and Hortense's relationship started off a bit rocky, Robert persisted and a few years later, on 10 September 1857, the couple exchanged vows in the same church where it is believed they met. Although his employment situation was inconsistent, Rodes settled down and adapted to married life. In a few years the war would interrupt his peaceful existence.[105]

When war seemed inevitable, Rodes stepped up to do his part and joined a company of Alabama militia and, probably due to his VMI education, was made its captain. In May 1861, Rodes' company was assigned to duty with the 5th Alabama and his was commissioned colonel of the regiment. Promotion to brigadier general came a few months later on 21 October and Rodes experienced combat for the first time in his life during the Peninsular Campaign. At Fair Oaks he displayed his ability to lead a brigade and showed his grit by remaining with his brigade even after being hit in the arm. He turned over command at the end of the day but was back with his brigade in time to lead it at Gaines' Mill. However, his wound forced him to relinquish command once again before Malvern Hill. When the battles on the Peninsula terminated, Rodes was well on his way to developing a solid reputation as a hard fighting general. Justifiably so, he began attracting the attention of his superiors. At South Mountain, Rodes' Brigade became isolated and fought technically alone against an entire Union division for most of the afternoon. During the battle, he was ordered to occupy an open hillside, across a deep gorge, about three-quarters of a mile to the left of the Confederate line. The move left Rodes' Brigade dangerously exposed so the 12th Alabama was sent back to connect with the left of the battle line. Rodes directed his Alabamans well on the mountain and three days later at Sharpsburg, his brigade helped defend the Sunken Road against repeated Federal assaults. During the fighting, he received a minor wound to the thigh from shell fragments.[106]

Although his brigade was not actively engaged at Fredericksburg, Rodes had seen heavy action during the previous year. In January 1863, when D. H. Hill left

---

[104] *Ibid*, pp.17-18, 21, 27-28, 35, 37.

[105] *Ibid*, pp.38-39, 44-45.

[106] Tagg, **Generals**, p.284; **Carman**, pp.156, 277-278.

the Army of Northern Virginia for North Carolina, and with Major General Edward Johnston being unavailable, still recovering from a wound, Rodes was elevated to division command. At Chancellorsville, he proved that placing him in command of a division was not a mistake. On the morning of 2 May Rodes led his division at the head of Jackson's flanking column and late that afternoon he displayed great energy as he arrayed his brigades to crush Howard's right. Jackson was impressed with Rodes' performance that fateful day and while trying to recover from his injuries, recommended Rodes for a field promotion. The recommendation was well received for Rodes' promotion to major general was dated the day of his devastating attack.[107]

Later that evening, when A. P. Hill was wounded and taken from the field, command of Jackson's Corps fell to Rodes. He only held command for approximately two hours, relinquishing control to Jeb Stuart. Technically Rodes could have retained command since army regulations contained no previsions for turning over one branch of the service to a commander from another. Since Stuart was in command of Lee's cavalry, Rodes could have, based on regulations, retained command, but he respectfully turned command over to the cavalryman. Rodes recorded his reasoning for relegating command in his after action report.

> "I deem it proper to state that I yielded the command to General Stuart not because I thought him entitled to it, belonging as he does to a different arm of the service, nor because I was unwilling to assume the responsibility of carrying on the attack, as I had already made the necessary arrangements, and they remained unchanged, but because, from the manner in which I had been informed that he had been sent for, I inferred that General Jackson or General Hill had instructed Major Pendleton to place him in command, and for the still stronger reason that I feared that the information that the command had devolved on me, unknown except to my own immediate troops, would, in their shaken condition, be likely to increase the demonstration of the corps. General Stuart's name was well and very favorably known to the army, and would tend, I hoped, to re-establish confidence. I yielded because I was satisfied the good of the service demanded it."[108]

When Lee reorganized his army, Rodes was arguably his best division commander although he had only held the position for just over four months. Rodes had seen continuous campaigning since the Peninsula while Ewell had been on the sidelines for nine months. Questions regarding Ewell's stamina and physical ability to lead a corps were justified, but Lee rolled the dice with the once fiery Virginian. Rodes, for his part had shown he was of division command material,

---

[107] Tagg, **Generals**, pp.284-285.

[108] **OR**, vol.25, pt.1, pp.942-943.

met Lee's partiality for Virginians and had revealed great courage in the face of the enemy. Lee would have been justified and could have suggested Rodes be placed at the head of the Second Corps, but such a move would have been a much harder sell to Davis and his administration. In addition, Ewell was well known to the men of the Second Corps while Rodes was somewhat anonymous. Assuredly, based on past performance, he would have also been an adequate appointment to head the corps. Rodes however was not one to partake in the act of self-promotion and his humility, which he displayed in relinquishing command to Stuart, could have played a factor in his skills being passed over for Ewell's.

Robert E. Rodes simply looked like a soldier. His straight slender form and chiseled face projected confidence. His six foot figure looked regal upon a horse. He wore a large bushy, hanging mustache which sagged from the corners of his mouth. His narrow, dimpled chin was devoid of facial hair and he wore his wavy hair to the top of his ears. Although he cut a dashing figure, which accented his reputation, as the summer of 1863 opened, no one doubted his abilities. His division would consist of brigades composed of North Carolinians, Georgians and Alabamians.[109]

Robert Emmitt Rodes led Stonewall's flank assault at Chancellorsville. *MOLLUS Collection, USAHEC*

Rodes' command would be the first of Ewell's divisions to move. Marching orders were issued on 3 June and his troops had their feet on the road to Culpeper early the following morning. His men headed westward from Hamilton's Crossing, traveling sixteen miles before bivouacking for the night two miles north of Spotsylvania Court House. In order to limit straggling, strict orders were issued to

---

[109] *OR*, vol.27, pt.2, p.287; Boatner, *Dictionary*, p.706; Faust, *Encyclopedia*, p.640.

keep the men in ranks causing many to suffer due to lack of water. The next day's march covered twenty-one miles and included a turn northward toward the Rapidan River and Raccoon or Somerville Ford's, which had been designated as the division's crossing points. On 6 June Rodes had his men back on the road and had covered four miles when he received orders to halt and wait for further instructions.[110]

The reason for the delay was Federal activity along the Rappahannock River south of Fredericksburg. Hooker's intelligence team had determined that the Rebels had increased their activity. The Federal commander decided to make an effort to determine what the enemy was up to and pushed a small force across the river near Deep Run. Lee, concerned over the reason for the Federal movement, halted Ewell's corps until the intent of the activity could be discerned. Lee observed the situation for the reminder of the day and was able to conclude the Federals were doing nothing more than trying to establish the objective of his designs. By the end of the day, Lee felt confident enough to allow Ewell to continue his push toward Culpeper. The following morning, 7 June, Rodes resumed his march and crossed the Rapidan at Somerville Ford. His men traveled nineteen miles, passing through Culpeper and bivouacked four miles beyond the town.[111]

When Lee marched north, two divisions within his army contained five brigades. One of them was commanded by Rodes. It contained three brigades of North Carolinians, a brigade of Georgians and one of regiments from Alabama. One group from North Carolina was under the command of Brigadier General Junius Daniel. Born in Halifax North Carolina on 27 June 1828, Daniel became a West Point graduate in 1851. He ranked thirty-third in a class of forty-two. Exiting the academy, he was commissioned a second lieutenant and assigned to the 3rd Infantry. He served on outpost duty on the frontier and fought Indians for seven years until he resigned his commission in 1858. Daniel moved to Louisiana to run his family's plantation but was back in North Carolina by 1860 as the storm of war permeated the Deep South.[112]

Originally enlisting in Northampton County, Daniel was appointed colonel of the 14th North Carolina on 3 June 1861. He served with the 14th and was never absent from his post until he was made Colonel of the 45th North Carolina in April 1862. Less than a month later, with the situation around Richmond dire, the 45th was brigaded with the 43rd and 50th North Carolina and placed under Colonel Daniel's command. The brigade was sent to an area south of the city where it occupied Drewry's Bluff. During The Seven Days, Daniel's new brigade was positioned on the Confederate right flank and saw very little action. On 29 June, the brigade moved toward Malvern Hill and received fire from gunboats on the James River. They soon returned to their position on Drewry's Bluff and shortly thereafter two additional regiments, the 32nd and 53rd North Carolina were added to the brigade. On 1 September, Daniel was promoted to brigadier general and the brigade

---

[110]   *OR* vol.27, pt.2, pp.545-546; Jordon, *NCT*, vol. XIII, p.11.

[111]   *OR* vol.27, pt.2 p.293.

[112]   Tagg, *Generals*, p.292; Eicher, & Eicher, *High Commands*, p.199.

settled in for the winter. Later, toward the end of the month, the 2nd North Carolina Battalion was added to Daniel's force. Apart from a brief excursion to Suffolk, Daniel's North Carolinians spent time building fortifications and entrenchments to solidify their position on Drewry's Bluff.[113]

Daniel led his brigade south in December where it performed engineering work and participated in D. H. Hill's attempt to recapture New Bren. By May however, discussions began regarding the exchange of Daniel's men for one of Lee's current brigades. On 20 May, Adjutant General Taylor wrote out the order exchanging Daniel's Brigade for Colquitt's used up organization. Unfortunately for Daniel, the 50th was ordered to remain behind, as the reminder of the brigade headed north to join Lee's army at Fredericksburg. Now, assigned to Rodes' Division, Daniel's Brigade continued its northward move to Culpeper. Except for the departure of the 50th, his brigade remained intact. Most of the men in his five regiments had seen some action but had not been severely tested. Many would never see their home state again.[114]

The son of a congressman and United States senator, Alfred Iverson Jr. was born in Clinton Georgia on 14 February 1829. Alfred grew up in Columbus, having moved there with his father after his mother passed away from a prolonged illness a year after his birth. His father had done well in life and as a boy he enjoyed all the privileges accorded to one of the most prominent families in the area. Educated in the local schools of Columbus, he later studied law, although he did not particularly enjoy the subject. At some point Alfred Sr. decided his son would enter upon a military career, but his boy would not be a West Point man. To start the boy down the path, the elder Iverson enrolled his son in the Tuskegee Military Institute in Alabama. The core curriculum at the institute was comparable to that taught at West Point, with engineering and military subjects dominating the coursework.[115]

When the Mexican War began, the senator raised a regiment of volunteers. He gave young Alfred permission to quit school, and at the age of seventeen, the boy was commissioned a second lieutenant in a Georgia infantry battalion and sent off to war. Once in Mexico young Iverson quickly became aware of the hardships of soldiering. Sanitation almost instantly became an issue and over half of the battalion became ill, most suffering from diarrhea and fever. Alfred, being young and fit seemed to spend less time on the sick rolls and on a number of occasions commanded his company due his superiors being ill. When the battalion's commanding officer finally arrived, less than a dozen men from Iverson's company were fit for duty. Other than illness, his time in Mexico was rather uneventful and Iverson, along with the rest of the battalion was mustered out on 11 July 1848.[116]

Upon his return, Iverson became a lawyer and partnered in his father's business. He also spent time as a railroad contractor but the business world was

---

[113] Jordon, *NCT*, vol.V, p.393, vol.XI, pp.1, 7.

[114] Jordon, *NCT*, vol.XI, p.1, vol.XII, p.143; *OR*, vol. 25, pt. 2, pp.813, 798; *OR* vol.27, pt.2, p.287.

[115] Wynstra, Robert J., ***The Rashness of That Hour***, pp.1-5.

[116] *Ibid*, pp.6-8.

uninteresting, which showed in his lack of motivation. On 3 March 1855, Iverson's direction in life changed dramatically when he was commissioned in the Regular Army as a first lieutenant in the new 1st Cavalry. His father's political connections and lobbying played a role in his son's appointment. Alfred Sr. was blessed with deep connections into the Franklin Pierce administration, having established a significant political relationship with the secretary of war, Jefferson Davis. In order to ensure the passage of legislation creating the new regiment, half of the officers would be from the Regular Army while the other half would come from the civilian ranks. Davis took a personal interest in Iverson's case which undoubtedly helped in his appointment. No matter how it happened, Alfred Iverson was now an officer in the United States Army.[117]

Alfred soon found himself in Kansas and served there during the conflict between the abolitionists and the pro-slavery groups. The fighting between the factions provided him with his first real taste of the violence of war. Eventually, he was transferred to the Carlisle Barracks in Pennsylvania and took on recruitment duties. During his time in Pennsylvania he began a serious relationship with a young lady named Harriet Hutchins who happened to be his cousin. Harriet came from an affluent family and the couple eventually married. Following the wedding, Alfred and his new bride moved into the officer's quarters at Carlisle. The union produced two children, which Harriet would raise at a home that the couple purchased in Columbus, while Alfred continued his service. His final years in the Regular Army included duty with the Mormon Expedition, service at Fort Riley on the Kansas River, and at Fort Washita where he became embroiled in a few scrapes with local Indians. As the country slid toward civil war, young Alfred, whose father was a staunch states-rights supporter, chose to resign his commission on 21 March, 1861. After six years of duty, he turned his back on Federal service and cast his fortunes with the upstart southern nation.[118]

Using his father's connections with Jefferson Davis, Iverson initially received an appointment as a captain of infantry in the Confederate States Provisional Army before performing recruitment duties in North Carolina. He helped organize the 10th Regiment North Carolina Volunteers, which would eventually be designated the 20th North Carolina. Alfred would be commissioned colonel of the regiment to date from 19 July 1861. He led the regiment through the early months of the war when it was stationed in North Carolina. On 14 June, Iverson and his command were ordered north to Richmond where the 20th was brigaded with the 5th, 12th, 13th and 23rd North Carolina regiments under Brigadier General Samuel Garland. As The Seven Days fighting opened, Iverson lead his regiment forward at Gaines' Mill but shortly after the action began, he was critically wounded. General Garland singled him out in his report noting, "Colonel Iverson was seriously wounded at an early period while gallantly leading up his regiment to take the battery at the house on the left..." The regiment remained heavily engaged even after Iverson was hit, absorbed 380 casualties during the campaign, more than any other regiment in

---

[117] *Ibid*, pp.8-9.

[118] *Ibid*, pp.9-15.

Garland's Brigade. Of the five regiments sent forward, only Iverson's managed to reach and silence the Federal guns.[119]

Recovering from his wound, Iverson returned to his regiment in time to lead it during the Maryland Campaign. At South Mountain, after General Garland was mortally wounded, the entire brigade, including the 20th, broke and retreated. A few days later at Sharpsburg, the brigade, under new leadership, broke and ran as it tried to hold on to a portion in the West Woods. Although Iverson, to his credit, rallied his regiment, the brigade's reputation took a serious hit. It was obvious Garland's old brigade needed a new leader. On 1 November, Iverson was promoted to brigadier general and placed in charge. There is evidence indicating General Lee may have received political pressure and was forced into making the appointment.[120]

According to relatives, Iverson presented a soldierly bearing and looked the part of a proficient warrior. He was an average height man who possessed a high forehead and dark wavy hair and a straight, chiseled nose. He carried himself with a stately reserve which demonstrated his prosperous background. Alfred was an expert horseman; his skills no doubt a product of his affluent upbringing which allowed for training to be garnered from other experts. He was a Freemason who remained active in the order and detested being referred to as junior. He read Shakespeare, wrote poetry and possessed a tender side which accented his reputation as a hopeless romantic.[121]

While Iverson had shown that he was an adequate field commander, he possessed a vindictive nature, possibly the result of his association with an overbearing father and the political wrangling encountered as a youth in Washington. In a purely political move, when Iverson ascended to brigade command, he made an effort to install a personal friend from outside the regiment as its new colonel. The move brought outrage from inside the regiment and twenty-six of its officers signed a petition in protest. Iverson ignored the petition and refused to pass it up through channels, forcing the group of dissenters to go over his head, sending the petition to headquarters on their own. Iverson was furious and placed all the officers under arrest, which amounted to nothing more than blowing off steam. Eventually all the officers were released and Iverson's friend was not placed in command. He continued to refuse all efforts by the 20th's officers to have a man of their choosing installed as colonel. All those involved came away understanding their general possessed a nasty political characteristic. Although he led the brigade competently during Jackson's flank attack at Chancellorsville, the scuttlebutt in the army was favoritism had been a factor in his advancement. Gossip which many had little idea was actually true. Rumors and Iverson's volatile nature made him a target for scrutiny and someone who everyone kept an eye on. It was within this unstable

---

[119] *Ibid*, pp.15, 25; Tagg, **Generals**, p.295; Jordon, *NCT*, vol.VI, pp.425, 432; *OR* vol.11, pt.2, pp.644-645; *OR* vol.27, pt.2, p.287.

[120] Tagg, **Generals**, p.296.

[121] Wynstra, Robert J., ***The Rashness of That Hour***, p.13.

environment that the men of Iverson's old 20th, the 5th, 12th and 23rd North Caroline left their camps for Culpeper and points further north.[122]

Commanding Rodes' final brigade of North Carolinians was the sentimental but daring Stephen Dodson Ramseur. Born in Lincolnton, North Carolina on the last day of May, 1837, Ramseur spent the days of his childhood exploring the hills and valleys near his home. As a youth he attended the local schools of his hometown where his friends called him by his middle name. Ramseur later enrolled in North Carolina's Davidson College where he spent four years, from 1853 to 1855. While at Davidson, he became acquainted with Daniel Harvey Hill, who at the time was teaching mathematics. After a recommendation from Hill, Ramseur was accepted at West Point and entering the academy on 1 July 1855. Stephen's education at Davidson served him well, helping him deal with the difficult West Point curriculum. Graduating fourteenth in a class of forty-one, he was brevetted a second lieutenant and posted to the 3rd Artillery. Less than a year later, on 6 April 1861, he resigned to cast his lot with the Confederacy.[123]

Ramseur's first assignment was with the 10th North Carolina Militia where he was made captain of Company A on 16 March 1861, a position he held before he resigned from Federal service. Two months later, on 8 May, he was promoted to major. When the 10th was mustered into Confederate service, it was designated the 1st Regiment North Carolina Artillery and Ramseur settled in for a career in the artillery. His path however was almost derailed when on 25 July he was thrown from his horse while in Raleigh. The fall fractured his collarbone and the twenty-four year old Ramseur was sidelined until the following spring when he was made colonel of the freshly mustered 49th North Carolina Infantry. The regiment was organized on 12 April 1862, and was mustered into service on 2 May. In charge of a regiment for the first time, Ramseur went to work drilling and teaching the men the skills needed to be good soldiers. After a short time, the regiment was ordered north and assigned to the brigade of Brigadier General Ransom, going into camp north of Petersburg.[124]

The audacious Ramseur made a name for himself at Malvern Hill when he charged with his regiment into the teeth of the Federal artillery. The fire was of a strength which cut swaths through the men of the 49th. Ramseur was hit in the upper right arm but refused to leave the field. He was eventually forced to seek assistance at a nearby hospital. The wound was more severe than first thought, with not only the tissue damaged but also the nerves. Ramseur's arm would eventually heal but would be paralyzed and essentially useless. Based solely on his efforts at Malvern Hill, Lee personally sought out Ramseur, and after Sharpsburg, promoted the twenty-five year old North Carolinian to brigadier general on 1 November. At the

---

[122] Tagg, *Generals*, p.296.

[123] Eicher, & Eicher, *High Commands*, p.444; Tagg, *Generals*, p.290; Wakelyn, *Biographical Dictionary*, p.362.

[124] Manarin, *NCT*, vol.I, pp.40-41; Eicher, & Eicher, *High Commands*, p.444; Jordon, *NCT*, vol.I, p.1.

time of his promotion, Ramseur became the youngest general in the Confederate Army. He returned to the army in January 1863 to take command of his new brigade, although his wounded arm was in a sling and still giving him difficulty. His new command consisted of the 2nd, 4th 14th and 30th North Carolina regiments.[125]

Chancellorsville gave Ramseur his first solid opportunity to get back into the fight. As part of Jackson's column, he, from his position behind Colquitt on the right, led his brigade onward during the attack. On the following day, he pushed his brigade forward, ignoring the suggestions of other officers. Leading his men into a wall of enemy bullets, the brigade entered the Federal breastworks but found themselves isolated and alone. With retreat his only option, his men exhausted and their ammunition gone, he must have beamed with delighted when he saw the old Stonewall Brigade coming to his assistance. The Confederates managed to hold their position and Ramseur, who was wounded again, was lauded as a hero. During the effort he lost over 600 men, roughly half his command, to Federal bullets and shells. Rodes in his report noted Ramseur acted with "great gallantry and efficiency." General Stuart, acknowledging Ramseur's courage, called for cheers for him. Like Rodes, Ramseur had proven he was one of the most promising stars in Lee's army.[126]

Unlike Stuart, Ramseur was not interested in his name being splashed across the pages of Confederate newspapers. While he was extremely ambitions, he did not actively court the assistance of the press, but he was not opposed to finding his name in a paper if it was justified. He felt newspapers promoted the exploits of lesser men and gave credit where it was not due. He thought they endorsed those who did not earn praise but created it from falsehoods and exaggeration. Ramseur preferred to let his actions in the face of the enemy build his reputation. A general who led by example, earning the respect of his men, Ramseur chose to disarm skeptics with his actions and his youthful enthusiasm.

Of slender build Ramseur groomed himself with a somewhat unique appearance. To possibly hide his age, he chose to wear a large bushy black beard but for some reason chose to wear the hair on his head closely cropped to his scalp. His look was unique and for those who met him, it was difficult to forget his appearance. In battle Ramseur seemed to seek out danger and revel in the adrenalin of an intense fight. Expectations were high and he seemed to understand that his superiors were relying on him to lead by example and carry his brigade to victory. Although his damaged right arm was basically useless, the remainder of Stephen D. Ramseur was quite possibly the most useful brigade commander in Lee's army.[127]

General George Pierce Doles, after rolling up Howard's right flank during the onset of Jackson's devastating attack at Chancellorsville, realized that his brigade was spent, having taken 403 casualties. Although General Rodes tried to organize his men for a continuation of the attack, it was obvious that the

---

[125] Tagg, *Generals*, p.290.

[126] *Ibid*, pp.290-291; *OR* vol.25, pt.1, p.808.

[127] Tagg, *Generals*, pp.290-291.

Georgians of his brigade had worn themselves to exhaustion chasing the fleeing Federals. Doles, like the men in his brigade, was a Georgian who a few days after Chancellorsville would turn thirty-three years of age. The son of a tailor, Doles was born in Milledgeville and received his initial education at the town's school. An entrepreneur before the war, Doles made his living in the mercantile business in order to support his wife and daughter. He had no military experience or training prior to the war but it was not for lack of trying. When the Mexican War began Doles, then a teenager, ran away to join the army. He was located waiting for a stagecoach to take him off to war. His youthful dreams of glory were crushed when he was taken home. His only experience commanding troops was attained as a lieutenant and then a captain in the Georgia Militia.[128]

Doles and his militia company, known as the "Baldwin Blues," stepped up when the war began and volunteered their services. They soon found themselves members of the 4th Georgia. Two weeks after joining the regiment, Doles was made colonel and marched his new command off to war. Initially stationed near Norfolk, the 4th was transferred north to Richmond and brigaded with the 3rd and 22nd Georgia and the 1st Louisiana under Brigadier General Albert. G. Blanchard. Doles led it during the fighting at Fair Oaks but because of confusing orders, led it off away from the fighting. At Malvern Hill, he showed his mettle, leading his regiment into heavy action where it suffered serious losses, including Doles, when he was hit by a shell fragment. When the Maryland Campaign unfolded, Doles found his regiment reassigned to a new brigade under Brigadier General Roswell Ripley. Ripley however, possessed less than adequate abilities. After almost leaving the 4th stranded on South Mountain, Ripley was wounded at Sharpsburg and Doles ascended to brigade command. He was promoted to brigade general on 1 November 1862, and took permanent command of the brigade. After spending the Battle of Fredericksburg in reserve, Doles' Georgians found themselves at the center of the maelstrom on Howard's right at Chancellorsville. In his battle report, General Rodes listed Doles first among a group of officers who exhibiting "great gallantry and efficiency in this action." Even with his lack of a military education, Doles showed great talent for command and quickly developed a reputation as one of the best brigade level commanders in Lee's army. No one questioned the bravery and abilities of Doles, and like Ramseur, he was considered one of the rising stars of the Confederacy. Doles' brigade, as it marched toward Culpeper, consisted of his 4th, the 12th, 21st and the 44th Georgia regiments.[129]

Rodes' old brigade, the fifth of his division, was the group of hard fighting Alabamans he had led earlier in the war. The brigade was now under the command of Colonel Edward A. O'Neal. On 3 June, five regiments, the 3rd, 5th, 6th, 12th and the 26th called O'Neal's brigade home. Like Doles, O'Neal had no military experience before the war. His lack of training could have played a role in his promotion to brigadier general being held up by Lee and finally canceled by President Davis.

[128] *OR* vol.25, pt.1, p.808; Eicher, & Eicher, **High Commands**, p.212; Wakelyn, **Biographical Dictionary**, p.172; Tagg, **Generals**, p.287.

[129] Sears, **Richmond**, p.377; Tagg, **Generals**, p.298; *OR* vol.25, pt.1, p.946; *OR* vol.27, pt.2, p.287.

Born in Madison County Alabama on 20 September 1818, O'Neal was one of the elder statesmen of Lee's officer corps. When his father died, O'Neal's mother was forced to raise him on her own. A lawyer by trade, he attended LaGrange College from which he graduated with honors in 1836. While in school, O'Neal married and started a family that eventually became quite large. After spending a few years reading law, Edward took and passed the bar exam in 1840. He established a practice in Florence the same year. Like most lawyers of the period, O'Neal became politically active and entered the arena. A year after opening his law office, he was elected to the Alabama legislature as a Democrat.[130]

When talk of secession commenced, O'Neal became a staunch supporter of the idea. Deciding to become a soldier, at the age of forty-three, he enlisted in 1861 and entered service as a major in the 9th Alabama. He would later be promoted to lieutenant colonel, and on 2 April 1862, was elevated to colonel and transferred to the 26th Alabama without ever having led men in combat. His lack of experience however, did not deter O'Neal from executing his duties as colonel. During the Peninsular Campaign he led his men with a reckless abandon that not only put his men in danger but himself as well. He was wounded at Fair Oaks but was back in action during The Seven Days. His performance during combat was exemplary, garnering him accolades from General Rodes. Wounded once more at South Mountain, O'Neal went home to recover but continued to be the regiment's colonel through early 1863. When Rodes' was elevated to divisional command, O'Neal, while still a colonel, took command of the brigade. At Chancellorsville, on the day following Jackson's crushing attack, O'Neal was wounded for a third time. While Rodes may have been appreciative of O'Neal's exploits on the battlefield, he objected to him commanding his old brigade and voiced his opinions to Lee. Rodes' objections may have been another reason behind Lee's delay in submitting O'Neal's promotion to brigadier. Whatever the truth, Lee's shortage of brigade commanders allowed O'Neal, still a colonel, to depart for Culpeper in command of the Alabamans.[131]

"Old Jubal's Irish"

Perhaps the most outspoken and hotheaded division commander in Lee's army was Jubal Early. Of Irish descent, Jubal's great-great-grandfather immigrated from the old country in the 1600's. An old family tradition which required children to be christened with Biblical names beginning with *J*, provided Early with his first name. Jubal's irritability could possibly have been attributed to an internal conflict created by his father Joab's Irish ancestry, and his mother Ruth's Scottish heritage. Four years after Joab and Ruth married, Jubal was born. The family was residing in

---

[130] Wakelyn, *Biographical Dictionary*, p.334; Eicher, & Eicher, *High Commands*, p.606; *OR* vol.27, pt.2, p.287. Sources vary regarding the size of O'Neal's family. Some indicate six children while others specify as many as nine. The author also found multiple references to the year of O'Neal's marriage, including the years 1833, 1836 and 1838.

[131] Faust, *Encyclopedia*, p.545; Wakelyn, *Biographical Dictionary*, p.334; Tagg, *Generals*, pp.298-297.

Franklin County, Virginia at the time and Jubal came into the world on 3 November 1816. Joab was a loving father and his significant land holdings and wealth allowed him to shower his ten children with attention, gifts and affection. During summer the children were urged to invite their friends to the Early's for extended stays. Flower gardens were planted for the girls and the boys participated in racing the family's horses. Childhood was good to Jubal Early but as with all childhoods, they do not last nearly long enough.

Jubal was educated at a local one room school house before entering a school in Lynchburg. To further his education, he next entered the Danville Male Academy. At the age of sixteen, he began the application process to West Point and in April, 1833 he was accepted as a cadet. All prospective plebes admittance was contingent on successful completion of the entrance exam. Early's results were positive and on 1 July 1833, Jubal Early entered West Point.[132]

On 1 September, Early attended his first class, mathematics, which lasted three hours. After the semiannual exams were complete in January, he ranked tenth out of ninety-seven cadets in math and thirty-first in French. His overall ranking of eleventh was exceptional and placed him well within the upper half of his class. Unfortunately, Early's conduct was poor at best. Of the 242 cadets at the academy during Early's first year, he ranked 203rd after piling up 142 demerits. Most of his demerits came from his lack of attention or desire to execute the typical activities of a soldier. Early's disdain for the monotony of a soldier's life was clear when he noted he had no use for "scrubbing brass." With good marks academically, Early advanced to his second year and improved his standing three positions. He continued to hurt himself however, with an inflated demerit total of 189 which placed him seventh from the bottom in conduct among all 240 cadets. His third year was much like his second. Although he lost the three positions he had gained, his demerit total rose again to 196, precariously close to the 200 limit for automatic dismissal. His poor conduct placed him seventeenth from the bottom of all cadets at the academy. Consistency was the hallmark of Early's West Point career and in his final year the pattern did not change. He continued to do well in the classroom, but his conduct remained near the bottom of the cadet listing. His 189 demerits placed him 195th out of 211 cadets and gave Early a whopping four year total of 716. He was even arrested twice during his final year; hardly acceptable conduct for a final year cadet who was to set an example for new plebes. Finally, on 1 July 1837, Early graduated eighteenth in a class of fifty. One can only wonder where he would have stood in West Point lore if he were as diligent with his conduct as he had been in the classroom.[133]

Due to his class standing, freshly commissioned second lieutenant Jubal Early was able to select his branch of service and chose the artillery. He was assigned to the 3rd Artillery and quickly received a promoted to first lieutenant. His initial service during 1838 was in Florida dealing with the Seminoles. Evidently the regiment of military life continued to be difficult for Early and after his required

---

[132] Osborne, Charles C., ***Jubal: The Life and Times of General Jubal A. Early, CSA***, pp.5-7.

[133] *Ibid*, pp.12-14, 16-17.

term of service expired he resigned his commission. His contemporaries at the academy may have seen such an event coming based on Early's poor conduct record.

After leaving the military, Early began studying law at Rocky Mount, Virginia and in 1840 was admitted to the Franklin County bar. Once a member of the legal fraternity, he entered politics and was tapped to represent Franklin County in the Virginia House of Delegates for two years beginning in 1841. He also functioned as a commonwealth attorney from 1842 to 1852; but his time was interrupted by the Mexican War. He went south as a major of volunteers and served from 1847 to 1848. After the war, Early returned to his law practice. He conducted a failed bid for the state legislature in 1853, and served as a delegate to Virginia's secession convention.[134]

Jubal Anderson Early, Lee's sharp tongued "bad old man." *MOLLUS Collection, USAHEC*

While Early opposed secession, after his native state voted to leave the Union, he volunteered for service. Before Virginia departed, he was made brigadier general in the Virginia Militia. He was quickly appointed colonel in the Confederate Army and placed in command of the ten companies that would eventually become the 24th Virginia. Early began the task of transforming the inexperienced volunteers into fighting men, battling not only their lack of military training but a deficiency in equipment as well. It took almost a month to procure weaponry for the regiment and the guns made available were old smoothbore precession muskets. The wait was even longer for cartridge boxes, belts, bayonet scabbards, and the regiments first ammunition pouches were cloth instead of leather. Early led a brigade at First Manassas and shortly after the battle was promoted to brigadier general. He once

---

[134] Eicher, & Eicher, ***High Commands***, p.221; Wakelyn, ***Biographical Dictionary***, p.176.

again led a brigade at Williamsburg on the Peninsula where his command suffered 287 casualties, including Early, who was wounded in the shoulder. A few weeks later he was wounded again at Cold Harbor. His injuries were not serious and Early quickly returned to service, leading his brigade at Second Manassas. During the Maryland Campaign and at Fredericksburg, he led a division, and on 17 January 1863, he became a major general.[135]

At Chancellorsville, Early was left along the river to keep a watchful eye on the Union troops there. When the Federals threatened Lee's rear, he marched north to assist McLaws in boxing in Sedgwick. The aggressive Early lead his division against the flank of the Federal position along the Orange Plank Road near Salem Church. Working with McLaws, he helped to drive the numerically superior Federal force from the field and back across the Rappahannock River. General Lee recognized Early's efforts in his report on the campaign. "Major-General Early," Lee noted, "performed the important and responsible duty entrusted to him in a manner which reflected credit upon himself and his command."

Early had shown he could lead a division. During the first two years of the war, he displayed a personality and image which were anything but pristine. He was a heavy drinker and swore constantly. Nicknamed "Old Jubal' or simply "Jube," his sharp tongue was well known throughout the army, but it did not hinder his reputation as a rugged, tough commander. It remained to be seen if he would continue to live up to the confidence Lee entrusted in him.[136]

With Rodes' men on the path to Culpeper, Early prepared his own division to follow the same route. Most of his men departed on 4 June, but some did not get underway until the following day. Their shoes or bare feet, were on the road late morning or early afternoon. The division trudged past Spotsylvania Courthouse and went into camp. The next day Early marched along the same path as Rodes, crossing the Rappahannock at Somerville Ford and continuing on to Culpeper, passing through it and camp northeast of town on the road to Sperryville. Early's division was constructed from four brigades which contained some of the hardest fighters in Lee's army. Each was from a different state and included men from Georgia, Virginia, North Carolina and Louisiana.[137]

If Edward O'Neal was one of the older brigade commanders in Lee's army, Brigade General William Smith was the grandpa of the clan. Smith was born at Marengo in King George County, Virginia on 6 September 1797, and was in charge of Early's brigade of Virginians. At sixty-five years of age, he was by far the oldest brigadier in Lee's army. Born into a well-to-do family, William was educated in private schools in Virginia and later attended the Plainfield Academy in Connecticut. He studied law and set up a practice in 1818, passing the Virginia

---

[135] *OR*, vol.11, pt. 1, p.569; Gunn, Ralph W., *24th Virginia Infantry*, p.5.

[136] *OR*, vol.25, pt. 1, p.803; Faust, *Encyclopedia*, p.233; *OR*, vol.27, pt. 2, pp.285-286.

[137] *OR* vol.27, pt.2, pp.285-286, 459; Kleese, Richard B., *49th Virginia Infantry*, p.36;. Riggs, *13th Virginia Infantry*, p.34. Early notes that his division left Hamilton Crossing on 4 June, but Longstreet says in *MtoA* that Early departed on 5 June. Early's date seems more plausible.

bar the following year. He entered politics and served in the state Senate and as a Democrat in the U. S. House of Representatives before becoming the Governor of Virginia for three years in 1846. Smith moved to California in 1849 and served as president of the state's first Democratic convention in 1850. A year later he declined a seat in the U. S. Senate and returned to Virginia where he once again was elected to the U. S. House. Smith, known by all as "Extra Billy," attained his nicknamed before the war due to him receiving additional, shady payments, during his time as a mail coach operator.[138]

Smith did not immediately ride off to war, turning down a brigadier generalship claiming he was unfit for such a post. On 1 June, as the Federal's began inching their way across the Virginia countryside, a skirmish broke out at Fairfax Court House, a short distance from Smith's law practice in Warrington. When word came of the fighting, Smith mounted his horse and rode to the scene. Pulling his horse to a halt along the road to Germantown, he found a company of Rebels, the Warrenton Rifles, in full retreat, their captain, Quincy Marr having been killed. Smith rode into the midst of the fleeing men and rallied them. Reforming them across the road, he helped led them forward and drove the Federals back through Fairfax. Then Lieutenant Colonel Richard Ewell noted in his report that Marr's company was "receiving valuable aid from his excellency [sic] Ex-Governor Smith." Smith's actions brought attention to him, and as a result he was commissioned a colonel of Virginia Volunteers on 1 July 1862 by then Governor John Letcher.[139]

Placed in command of the 49th Virginia, Smith led it at First Manassas and did well commanding his new regiment. The following November, he was elected to the Confederate Congress and split time between the army and Richmond, attending congressional sessions between campaigns. He fought on the Peninsula where he received a minor wound to the thigh and again at Fair Oaks where the regiment lost 224 of the 424 men who went into action. In his after action report, Smith's brigade commander noted that the colonel "was conspicuous, as I can testify from my own observation, for coolness and courage." Smith commanded a brigade at Sharpsburg and while leading it was wounded three times. He remained with his brigade through the battle, but his injuries proved to be debilitating and he spent a number of months convalescing. Upon his return, Extra Billy's duel career continued when he received a promotion to brigadier general on 23 April 1863. A month later was elected to his states' governor's office. Over time, Smith developed disdain for West Pointers who he thought spent too much time reviewing and adhering to tactics as opposed to killing Yankees. With his political term beginning on 1 January 1864, Smith had time to continue his field service. He was assigned to command of Early's old brigade and marched north with it toward Culpeper.[140]

---

[138] Eicher, & Eicher, **High Commands**, p.499; Wakelyn, **Biographical Dictionary**, pp.392-393.

[139] **OR** vol.2, p.63; Kleese, **49th Virginia Infantry**, p.4.

[140] Faust, **Encyclopedia**, p.698; Wakelyn, **Biographical Dictionary**, p.393. Boatner, **Dictionary**, pp.774-775; **OR** vol.11, pt.1, p.953; Tagg, **Generals**, p.265.

Smith's new brigade had slowly been stripped of some of its regiments for duty assignments elsewhere. By the time it left for Culpeper only the 49th and 52nd Virginia were present. Both regiments left Hamilton's Crossing together, but the brigades other regiment, the 31st Virginia, was still on its way by rail and would not arrive in time to march with its sister regiments. According to James E. Hall's diary, the 31st did not leave their camp until 1 a.m. on 5 June. A few days later the men of the 31st finally caught up with their comrades at the brigade's encampment near Culpeper.[141]

The Army of Northern Virginia was home for some of the most colorful Louisiana regiments in Confederate service. Many of the units had reputations for being nothing more than groups of scalawags, drunkards and shysters. The men of Harry T. Hays' Louisiana brigade fit the reputation, but while some were of questionable moral character, when it came to fighting Yankees they were all business. Hays, himself was not a Louisianan, having been born in Tennessee on 14 April 1820 in Wilson County. Orphaned as a young boy, Harry was raised by an uncle in Mississippi. When he was old enough, he went to Baltimore to attend St. Mary's College. He studied law and in 1844 set up a practice in New Orleans, developing a reputation as a fine, tough attorney. Hays also became involved in politics and joined the Whig Party. Although he was never elected to public office, he was active in the organization. He served as a presidential elector in 1852, supporting General Winfield Scott. Hays also fought as a volunteer during the Mexican War, serving as a first lieutenant with the 5th Louisiana Infantry. He was honorably mustered out of service when the war ended. In 1854 Harry had met and fallen in love with a young woman named Elizabeth Cage. Called Bettie by her family, the couple exchanged vows on 13 July. The marriage would produce five children.[142]

When the war opened, Harry became colonel of the 7th Louisiana. Known as the "Pelican Regiment," he led it at First Manassas and proved he had the ability to lead soldiers, or at least a group of rag tag volunteers, in armed conflict. During the fighting, Hays, who would quickly become known as a passionate and impulsive commander, drew the attention of another fiery officer, Jubal Early. According to Early, Hays "displayed great coolness and gallantry in front of his regiment while they were being formed under a galling fire from [enemy] sharpshooters." Shortly after the battle, the 7th was brigaded with other Louisiana regiments under the command of Brigadier General Richard Taylor. The brigade fought with Jackson's command in the Valley, and at Port Republic on 9 June 1862, Hays took a bullet in the shoulder. While he was off recuperating, he was promoted to brigadier general.

---

[141] *OR* vol.27, pt.2, p.287; *OR* vol.25, pt.1, p.792; *OR* vol.21, p.543; Ashcroft, John M., *31st Virginia Infantry*, pp.49, 102; Kleese, *49th Virginia Infantry*, p.36.

[142] Wakelyn, **Biographical Dictionary**, p.222; Mingus, Scott L. Jr., **The Louisiana Tigers in the Gettysburg Campaign**, p.5. Wakelyn indicated Elizabeth Cage was a first cousin to Hays. Wakelyn also indicated Hays and Cage were married in 1858. Mingus notes the marriage took place in 1854.

Upon his return in the fall of 1862, he was placed in command of Taylor's old brigade since Taylor had been promoted and transferred to another military district.

The men of Harry's brigade, as well as his original 7th regiment, were a mixture of nationalities. Many had spent time in jail or were simply ruffians from the New Orleans docks and harbor district before they signed regimental rolls. While there was no doubt Harry's boys were a wild group of miscreants that caused trouble and stole indiscriminately, they all had one thing in common. They hated Yankees and cherished the thought of killing as many of the enemy as possible.[143]

Hays returned to his brigade, nicknamed the "Louisiana Tigers," the day Lee engaged George McClellan's Army of the Potomac at Sharpsburg. Charging into The Cornfield, the Louisianans ran head-long into the Federal's heavy battle line and fought viscously for a few minutes until they were overwhelmed and forced to retreat toward the Dunker Church. According to Hays, he took less than 550 men into the fight and suffered well over 300 casualties. Although lightly engaged at Fredericksburg, Hays' Tigers, as part of General Early's division, confronted General Sedgwick's Corps at Salem Church. As the battle progressed, Hays' men hammered the Federal lines, eventually breaking through their defenses. When General Early saw the Louisianans break open the line, he was heard to comment that the Tigers could continue to steal anything they liked. Helping to convince Sedgwick that his should take his Sixth Corps back across the river cost Hays another 369 men.[144]

Not being a professional soldier probably helped Hays control his Louisianans. He was quite possibly the only man in the army who could have led the renegades from New Orleans. A regimented West Pointer, who demanded strict adherence to army rules and protocol, would have been completely frustrated with the Louisianans. Hays, on the other hand, knew his men and while not as stringent as a Regular Army man, seemed to know just how far to let them go before pulling them back. It was a combination which provided General Early with solid results from his group of Louisianans. As the summer of 1863 opened, Hays' brigade consisted of his original 7th regiment and the 5th, 6th, 8th and 9th. In a few weeks the Louisianans would soon find themselves in the thick of the fighting once again.[145]

When Early's Division prepared to depart for Culpeper, the Georgia brigade under his command consisted of six regiments. The 13th, 26th, 31st, 38th, 60th and 61st were all veteran outfits that had seen action back as far as the Peninsula Campaign. Commanding the brigade was John Brown Gordon, himself a Georgian. Gordon was born on 6 February 1832 in Upson County and was educated in a private school before he entered Franklin College, a school which would eventually become the University of Georgia. Gordon would not graduate however, choosing to drop out and study law. After passing the bar, he opened a practice in Atlanta. Before the war, Gordon strongly supported secession and became a close friend of

---

[143] Tagg, ***Generals***, p.259-260; Mingus, ***Louisiana Tigers***, p.5; ***OR*** vol.2, p.558.

[144] Tagg, ***Generals***, p.260; ***OR*** vol.19, pt.1, pp.974, 978-979.

[145] ***OR*** vol.27, pt.2, p.285.

fire-eater William L. Yancey. When war finally came, he was working in a remote part of northwest Georgia. He quickly assembled a company of roughens called the Raccoon Roughs. When he arrived in Richmond, he was made colonel of the 6th Alabama. Gordon was a hard fighter and fought his men just as hard. His conduct at Sharpsburg was exemplary and while leading the 6th, he was hit five times in a short span while he led his regiment along the Bloody Lane. Years later Gordon recounted the experience.

> "The first volley from the Union lines in my front sent a ball...through the calf of my right leg. Both sides stood in the open at short range and without the semblance of breastworks, and the firing was doing a deadly work. Higher up in the same leg I was again shot; but still no bone was broken. I was able to walk along the line and give encouragement to my resolute riflemen, who were firing with the coolness and steadiness of peace soldiers in target practice. ...later in the day the third ball pieced my left arm, tearing asunder the tendons and mangling the flesh... A fourth ball ripped through my shoulder, leaving its base and a wad of clothing in its tracks. I could still stand and walk, although the shock and loss of blood had left but little of my normal strength..."[146]

Thinking the right of his regiment was starting to waver, Gordon sent a messenger to support the men there, but before the man went far, he was shot and killed by a bullet through the head. Gordon then decided to make the expedition himself. With great effort he began the journey but had not gone far when a fifth ball struck him in the face exiting out his neck. Unable to go on he fell forward, coming to rest face down with his bleeding face in his hat. The blood from his final wound, running into his hat might have pooled there and drowned him if not for a sixth Federal ball which had punched a hole in the hat, allowing his blood to drain. For his efforts Gordon was rewarded with a brigadier generalship on 1 November 1862, and placed in command of the Georgians in Early's Division. By Chancellorsville his wounds had healed adequately enough to allowing him to lead the brigade during the fighting. Although Gordon had a tendency to stretch the truth from time to time, his efforts at Sharpsburg proved beyond any doubt he was a tough and intense fighter. His self-serving writings after the war, although obviously designed for his own promotion, did little to damage his reputation on a battlefield since he had proven his tenacity in the face of the enemy. Although Gordon was an asset to the army's fighting ability, his wife was not. Mrs. Gordon, leaving their children with her husband's mother, accompanied him as the army

---

[146] Gordon, ***Reminiscences***, pp.89-90; Faust, ***Encyclopedia***, p.315; Boatner, ***Dictionary***, pp.348-349; Wakelyn, ***Biographical Dictionary***, pp.392-393; *OR* vol.27, pt.2, p.286.

marched from place to place. She was such a nuisance to the division that General Early once quipped he wished the Yankees would capture her.[147]

Early's final brigade, named after Brigadier General Robert F. Hoke, was populated by a group of five North Carolina regiments, the 6th, 21st, 54th 57th and the 1st North Carolina Battalion. Hoke's Brigade was under the command of Colonel Isaac Edwin Avery since General Hoke had been wounded at Marye's Heights while protecting Lee's rear during the fighting at Salem Church. Avery, born in Burke County on 20 December 1828, was a large powerful man weighting over 200 pounds. He attended the University of North Carolina but quit after his first year to perform administration duties on one of his family's farms. After a decade running the operation, Avery joined with other businessmen to begin construction of the Western North Carolina Railroad, but before the project was finished the war began.[148]

Leaving the railroad behind, Avery along with one of his business partners and his three brothers went off to war. When his partner was authorized to raise a regiment, Avery went to work organizing a company of volunteers. Canvassing Burke, Yancey, Mitchell and McDowell counties, he soon had enough volunteers assembled to accomplish his goal. He was made captain of the group on 16 May. Two weeks later Avery's boys became Company E of the 6th North Carolina. The regiment was engaged at First Manassas, where Avery was wounded and his business partner killed. They were two of the regiment's forty-six casualties. Avery returned to his company at Fair Oaks and after the battle, when the regiment's commander, Colonel William D. Pender was promoted, Avery was made colonel of the regiment. While leading his North Carolinians at Gaines' Mill, he was severely wounded in the thigh. His injury would keep him out of action for six months. He returned in January 1863 to find the 6th a member of General Hoke's brigade. The projectile that severely wounded Hoke struck his upper left arm, shattering the bone. Avery took over the brigade after Hoke went down and continued to lead it through the remainder of the battle. Recognized as a courageous commander who led his men by example, Avery would still be a colonel at the head of a brigade even though Generals Early, Pender and Hood had all recommended him for promotion.[149]

"Old Allegany"

General Rodes' good fortune in January 1863 when he ascended to division command had been caused by a Yankee bullet. At the battle of McDowell, as the sun descended below the horizon and twilight fell, Edward Johnson continued to encourage his Confederates to press the Yankees in front of them. The fighting had

---

[147] Gordon, **Reminiscences**, p.90; Faust, **Encyclopedia**, p.315; Boatner, **Dictionary**, pp.348-349; Wakelyn, **Biographical Dictionary**, pp.392-393.

[148] Tagg, **Gettysburg**, pp.267-268; **OR** vol.27, pt.2, pp.286, 439

[149] Tagg, **Gettysburg**, p.268; Jordon, **NCT**, vol.IV, pp.267, 317, 691; **OR** vol.2, p.570; Eicher, & Eicher, **High Commands**, p.300. Eicher & Eicher note that Hoke was hit in the "left shoulder."

lasted nearly all day and as the moon came out to light up the countryside, Johnson was hit in the ankle and carried from the mountainside. The wound itself was not life threatening but bled heavily and was very painful. Once off the mountain and at a makeshift hospital, the attending surgeon probed the ankle and determined the bones had not been seriously damaged and there would be no need to amputate Johnson's foot. The news was indeed good, for Johnson would be able to walk, ride and fight for the Confederacy once more. Unfortunately, when D. H. Hill was transferred to North Carolina, Johnson was still on the mend, to the good fortune of General Rodes.[150]

Jackson himself had requested Johnson command a division within his corps earlier that spring but Johnson's injured ankle would keep him out of action until 8 May 1863, when he returned as a major general to command some of Jackson's boys. Jedediah Hotchkiss noted in his journal on 9 May that "Major-General Ed. Johnson is expected here to take command of Jackson's old division." A few days later, during Reverend Lacy's Sunday religious services, Hotchkiss noted the absence of Jackson and the presence of Johnson. "General Ed. Johnson was there and looking very well indeed; he was very glad to see me."[151]

Edward Johnson was born to Edward senior and Caroline Johnson on 16 April 1816 at Salisbury, the estate of Caroline's father in Chesterfield County, Virginia. Young Edward joined his older brother Philip, becoming the couple's second child. Tradition demanded Edward take the name of his father, his older brother having been given the name of his grandfather. The boy's father, a practicing physician in both Chesterfield and Powhatan Counties, managed to earn a good living and supported his family adequately. He was also fortunate in marrying Caroline, whose family was also extremely well off. Doctor Johnson however, became disenfranchised with his practice and wished to move his family to Kentucky. Caroline, having to leave her family behind, was reluctant to relocate but evidently gave in and by the time Edward was four the family was living in Louisville. Unfortunately, a few years later, when Caroline's father passed away, she chose to return to Salisbury to take over management of her family's estate. While Philip elected to accompany his mother, Edward, and the family's newest addition, his sister Rosina, chose to stay in Louisville. It was in this environment that Edward began his formal schooling at Louisville's first schoolhouse.[152]

Possibly because of his late start, when Edward decided to attend Kenyon College in Gambier, Ohio, he discovered he lacked the minimum requirements for admittance. Enrolling in the college's grammar school, Ed began preparing himself for the institution's general curriculum. Kenyon, a prep school for students interested in joining the clergy, quickly fell out of favor with him. Even though he

---

[150] Clemmer, Gregg S., *Old Alleghany: The Life and Wars of General Ed Johnson*, pp.412, 415.

[151] Eicher, & Eicher, *High Commands*, p.321; Hotchkiss, *Make Me a Map*, pp.142, 144; Thomas J. Jackson to James Seddon, 10 February 1863, Jedediah Hotchkiss Papers, Manuscript Division, LOC.

[152] Clemmer, Gregg S., *Old Alleghany*, pp.11-12, 16-17, 20.

finished at the top of the grammar school class, a career with the church was not in the cards. His father had sent him to Kenyon to provide him the opportunity to receive a substantial education but the school had not solidified his path. Then, an opportunity to possibility attend the military academy at West Point sparked his interest. To Edward, a military education and a career as a professional soldier was more to his liking. He believed his time at Kenyon had prepared him for the exhaustive curriculum West Point would require him to complete. After receiving the customary support from influential individuals, Edward Johnson accepted his appointment and entered West Point on 1 July 1833.[153]

Johnson entered the academy with a bevy of future Confederate and Federal officers, including Robert Chilton, Joe Hooker, William French, John Sedgwick and the hot headed Jubal Early. He soon discovered that his Kenyon College experience had not prepared him to the extent he envisioned. Unlike Early, Edward proved to be a poor student. During his first year, he barely escaped dismissal after January testing revealed he ranked sixty-eighth. While he performed well in some subjects, such as French, he exhibited incredible ineptitude for mathematics, ranking eighty-eighth within the range of test scores, three places below the cut of point to be retained as a cadet. At the end of the year, French remained his strong subject but he showed no improvement in math. Out of a possible 200 points allotted to mathematics during June exams, 68.4 were all that Johnson could manage. Consistent with Early however, was his demerit total, which was dismal as well. Out of the 242 cadets at the academy, Johnson ranked 221st with a whopping 172. Ed Johnson's first year at West Point was less than anticipated and his failure to apply himself brought him dangerously close to dismissal.[154]

While demerits were a problem for Johnson, his continued poor performance in math during his second year threatened to derail him entirely. He ranked in the mid-seventies during the late winter and early spring months of 1835. As this second year came to an end, the news Johnson had feared came true. His marks in math were so poor that he would be required to repeat his sophomore year. Only fifty-seven of his fellow classmates advanced. Johnson, sixty-third on the list, would remain behind. Burying his emotions, Ed went on the customary furlough all second year cadets received the summer before their third year and upon his return, began repeating of his previous year's assignments. In reality, the extra year was of great benefit to Johnson. His familiarity with the coursework allowed him to make significant improvements in his standing and as the year ended he stood thirty-seventh in a class of forty-eight. Again, his demerits crept close to the magical two hundred mark, but he managed to slip by and complete the year. By the end of his fourth year, after completing the academy's third year curriculum, Johnson had shown marked improvement, raising his class standing to twenty-eighth out of fourth-six. His demerit total fell during his final year to a respectable amount and his studies remained at an acceptable level allowing him to graduate on 1 July 1838, thirty-second in a class of forty-five cadets. After five years of study,

---

[153] *Ibid*, pp.24, 31-32.

[154] *Ibid*, pp.48, 50.

bordering on the unacceptable, Edward Johnson finished the intense West Point curriculum. It can be said that some young men mature and become responsible at various points in their journey to manhood. Ed Johnson may not have been mature enough for West Point when he entered, but personal growth, hard work and determination guided him through the hardships. With his character firmly created by his adversity, Johnson would now be a soldier.[155]

Johnson's first assignment was to assist in the relocation of the final groups of Cherokee along the Trail of Tears to the Indian Territory in Oklahoma. Afterword, he traveled to Florida to help put down the Seminoles. He was promoted to first lieutenant on 9 October 1839, and fought in the Mexican War, where he was brevetted twice for gallantry during the conflict. A brevet of captain was issued for his performance at Molino del Ray on 8 September 1847. A major brevet was given for valor before the walls of Chapultepec Castle west of Mexico City five days later. After the war Johnson spent time on the frontier and was promoted to full captain on 15 April 1851.[156]

When the Civil War began, Johnson did not immediately resign his commission, choosing to wait until 3 June 1861 before submitting his resignation. The letter was endorsed and sent to Washington, where, on 10 June it was signed and sent on to Secretary of War Simon Cameron. Edward Johnson, who could trace is ancestry back to a point where it branched to included West Point founder Thomas Jefferson, had spent twenty-three years serving his country. Like his famous ancestor, he decided it was time to sever his bonds to join an upstart nation and help it achieve its own independence.[157]

Johnson went to war as the colonel of the 12th Georgia Infantry, a position he ascended to on 2 July 1861. Traveling to western Virginia, the regiment became part of Lee's ill-fated Cheat Mountain Campaign. During the winter of 1861-62, Johnson commanded the Army of the Northwest, which was little more than a brigade, along the crest of the Allegheny Mountains, prompting his christening with the nickname "Old Allegheny." Eventually, his small command was consolidated with Jackson's and as winter turned to spring he found himself in the Shenandoah Valley where he went down with his ankle wound. His ankle did not heal quickly or well and when he returned to duty, he exhibited a noticeable limp. Johnson, who did not carry a sword, began carrying a large cane before his wounding. Now he used it to assist himself while walking. The size of the cane prompted the men of his command to baptize him with another interesting nickname, "Old Clubby." While Clubby Johnson's abilities had been well known to Jackson, few members of his new command were aware of his quality and most in Jackson's old division considered him unproven.[158]

---

[155] *Ibid*, pp.52-53, 58-59.

[156] Eicher, & Eicher, ***High Commands***, p.320; Wakelyn, ***Biographical Dictionary***, pp.254-255.

[157] Clemmer, ***Old Alleghany***, pp.280-281.

[158] Eicher, & Eicher, ***High Commands***, p.320; Tagg, ***Generals***, p.269; Casler, John O., ***Four Years in the Stonewall Brigade***. p.74.

Although an intense fighter on the battlefield, Johnson had a warm and endearing, yet gruff personality, which made him a favorite of his superiors and subordinates alike. He was a notoriously bad dresser, and his poor attire made it easy to identify him in a crowd of mounted officers. He was also one of the most potent swearers in the army, not opposed to making his point with profanity laced statements that seemed to always produce results. Although thick through the shoulders as a youth, time had made Johnson a bit portly, but he was still well proportioned and sturdy. A bachelor at the age of fourth-seven, he had an eye for the ladies although the same affections seemed not to be returned. This could have been due to his loud voice and poor manners which he often exhibited in mixed company. Compounding the issue was a minor wound Johnson received while in Mexico, which resulted in the occasional uncontrolled winking of one eye. The affliction posed some difficulties when in the company of women and young belles of the South. He wore his facial hair in the form of a large thick goatee and a receding hairline brought notice to his high round forehead which Mary Chesnut wrote looked "like a cone or an old-fashioned beehive." Sagging eyelids completed his appearance and most thought Johnson not a very attractive man. But physical attractiveness mattered not on the field of battle and Johnson would prove that old Jackson had been correct in his assessment of the transplanted Virginian. "Old Allegheny's" men, who hailed from Virginia, Louisiana, North Carolina and Maryland, would come to understand Jackson's confidence was not misplaced.[159]

Johnson's Division was the last of Ewell's to depart its winter camp. The column took its placed in the road and began the march to Culpeper at 2 a.m., possibly in an attempt to mask its departure. The general noted in his report that his men left camp on 5 June. Whether he broke up his headquarters on that date or it was the date his division marched, he did not say. Private William Dunlap, in a letter to his sister, noted that the men were instructed to cook three days rations and be ready to move out. Dunlap had no idea where they were going, but he knew there would be "a hard fight in a few days." A segment of Johnson's command had departed a day earlier and, after spending a leisurely day encamped at Spotsylvania Court House, fell into line as the remainder of the division caught up. With the whole division assembled the transit continued around 2 p.m. on 6 June. The day's journey lasted well after dark and concluded with a cold, rainy night. The following day the men were up early and once again marching at 4:30 a.m. Cresting the hills above the Rapidan, the soldiers caught glimpses of the Blue Ridge on the distant horizon. In a few days they would be marching over that far-off ridge, descending into the valley of the Shenandoah. For now however, their descent was much shorter, down to ford the Rapidan, which proved to be a very wet crossing, its status a bit swollen on account of recent rain. After crossing the river, they continued to a point seven miles from Culpeper. Finally, on 8 June Johnson marched his legions through the town and camped eight miles to the northwest at 3 p.m.[160]

---

[159] Faust, *Encyclopedia*, p.397; *OR*, vol. 27, pt. 2, p.286; Tagg, *Generals*, pp.269-270;

[160] *OR* vol.27, pt.2, p.499; Murphy, Terrence V., *10th Virginia Infantry*, p.72; Wallace, Lee A. Jr., *5th Virginia Infantry*, p.48; McKim, *Recollections*, pp.138-139,141-142.

Johnson's division was populated by four experienced brigades from the Eastern Theater. Most of the men had seen hard service in the Valley with Jackson in 1862 and fought from the Peninsula to the recent victory at Chancellorsville. While commanders had changed, the results expected when the veterans of the Valley entered battle were not. The most recognizable brigade of the four was the old "Stonewall" Brigade. Originally led by the lamented Jackson at First Manassas, the members of the 2nd, 4th, 5th, 27th and 33rd Virginia regiments were now in the hands of Brigadier General James A. Walker. After Jackson's death, the Confederate War Department made the brigade's nickname its official designation. It was the only command of its size to have an authorized title. While it was at its apogee as the summer of 1863 unfolded, battlefield loses and attrition had decimated its command structure. The losses were so great that by the time battle was joined in Pennsylvania, the 33rd Virginia would be commanded by a captain.[161]

Walker, a Virginian himself, was only thirty years old as his brigade began it journey to Gettysburg. He had attended the Virginia Military Institute until his senior year when he had a disagreement with one of his professors. The difference of opinion centered on a classroom disturbance and the instructor, Thomas Jackson, and Walker entered into a verbal argument. Walker, an impetuous youngster challenged his future commander to a duel which fortunately for both never took place. James however, was court-martialed and expelled from the institute, and never completed his senior year. After a brief stint working for the Carrington and Ohio Railroad, Walker entered the University of Virginia and began studying law. This time he avoided confrontations with his instructors and finished his curriculum. He graduated in 1855, and was admitted to the Virginia bar in 1856. He set up a practice in the city of New Bren, in Pulaski County.[162]

When the war began, Walker left his practice and cast his lot with the Confederates. His first post was as captain of the Pulaski Guards, a position he assumed in April 1861. In June his command became Company C of the 4th Virginia. Walker however, left the 4th to take over the duties of lieutenant colonel of the 13th Virginia a month later. He fought with the 13th in the Valley, and after his brigade commander was wounded took over and led the brigade for the remainder of the Battle of Cross Keys. The next day, during fighting at Port Republic, his command got lost and was not a factor in the battle, raising the ire of division commander Ewell. On the Peninsula, Walker was back in command of the 13th, but once again, found himself commanding the brigade when his senior officer was wounded. He continued to lead the brigade for the remainder of the fighting and was nearly killed at Malvern Hill when a shell burrowed into the ground near him and exploded, blowing him off his feet. Returning to command of the 13th, he fought at Cedar Mountain and Second Manassas. He was injured at Sharpsburg, while once again commanding a brigade, when his horse was shot out from under

---

[161] *OR* vol.27, pt.2, p.286, 529; Tagg, **Generals**, p.278; *OR* vol.2, p.470.

[162] Riggs, *13th Virginia Infantry*, p.146.

him. He was recommended for promotion to brigadier general shortly after the battle but did not receive his star until 15 May 1863.[163]

Walker's return to the "Stonewall" brigade after its commander at Chancellorsville, Elisha Paxton, was killed would not be a smooth transition. Although he had at one time been a member of the brigade, many of the brigade's officers, objected to the appointment. For his part, Walker paid little attention to such complaints. A number of officers threatened to resign unless an officer from the brigade was selected to lead them. Lee averted the issue by simply refusing to accept the resignations and the outcry subsided.[164]

During the war, in a twist of irony, VMI officials sent Walker's diploma to him. Supposedly the document was sent at the request of his former antagonist Stonewall Jackson. It must have been quite a surprise to the hard fighting and hard drinking Virginian. Walker was an unbreakable man who liked his liquor and had no time for professionalism when it came to disagreements. Always ready to fight, he was tall, stoutly built and cared little for the pettiness of others. He had no time for it, normally being too busy enjoying life. His tough, jocular attitude soon won over the men and officers of his new command, so much so they began calling him "Stonewall Jim."[165]

Johnson's other brigade of Virginians was commanded at Chancellorsville by John R. Jones. During the heaviest fighting, Jones turned command over to his ranking subordinate. The reason for his departure was supposedly an "ulcerated leg" but many simply thought it a poor excuse for cowardice. Jones was summarily removed from command and he left the army. To replace John Jones another John Jones was selected in the form of West Point trained John M. Jones. If Lee indeed favored Virginians, Jones qualified, having been born in Charlottesville on 26 July 1820. He entered the Military Academy before his seventeenth birthday and showed he was not prepared to be a cadet. His poor classroom performance could have been attributed to his fondness for alcohol, a problem which would grow into a serious affliction in later years. After graduating thirty-ninth in a class of fifty-two, Jones chose to remain at West Point as an instructor. He taught there for seven years. Remaining at the academy kept him out of the fighting in Mexico, but provided little opportunity for advancement. Eventually leaving his teaching assignment behind, Jones traveled west and saw garrison duty in Texas, Michigan and Florida before he left the army on 27 May 1861 to join the Confederacy. At the time of his resignation, Jones was still just a captain in the 7th Infantry.

Jones joined the Confederate Army and was soon promoted to lieutenant colonel, but he did not receive a command. He spent the first two years of the conflict at various staff assignments, most of which were assistant adjutant general positions. He served under a number of commanders including Magruder, Early

---

[163] Ibid; Tagg, **Generals**, p. 279; Robertson, James I., *4th Virginia Infantry*, p.4, 78.

[164] Tagg, **Generals**, p.278.

[165] Ibid, pp.278-279.

and Ewell. In January 1862, he fell ill and traveled home to recuperate, but upon his return Jones found himself in a similar position, once again assigned to assistant adjutant general duties.

While Jones was a brave and excellent officer, he seemed destined to spend the war performing nothing more than administrative work. Ewell constantly praised him and many of his contemporaries talked in glowing terms of his abilities. Lee, though he continually complained about his lack of spirited brigade commanders seemed to ignore Jones and it took quite some time to get him out from behind a desk and into the field. The reason was quite simple; Jones' fondness for alcohol had not dissipated. He had been unable to control his drinking problem. At one point, after the battle of Cross Keys, he pulled a flask of whiskey out and proceeded to get inebriated. He was found a few days later in a hotel so intoxicated that he could not stand. Desperate for commanders, Jones was placed at the head of Johnson's second group of Virginians which included the 21st, 25th 42nd, 44th, 48th and 50th regiments. It would remain to be seen if Jones could stay away from the bottle long enough to effectively guide them through the coming campaign.[166]

Like Early's command, Johnson's Division also contained a brigade of Louisianans, which consisting of the 1st, 2nd, 10th 14th and 15th regiments. Brigadier General Frances T. Nicholls led the brigade during Jackson's flank attack at Chancellorsville. Unfortunately, he was wounded during the artillery barrage which raked the Plank Road as the wounded Jackson was carried to the rear. The wound was serious as Nicholls' foot was carried away by an artillery shell, forcing the amputation of the general's leg. After Nicholls' loss, command of the brigade fell to Jesse Milton Williams, colonel of the 2nd Louisiana. Williams leadership during the remainder of the fighting at Chancellorsville was suspect, resulting in a feeble performance from the brigade. After the battle a search was conducted for a brigadier general to command the Louisianans but the exploration bore no fruit and Williams remained in command as the brigade stepped off for Culpeper.[167]

Born on 11 January 1831, the thirty-two years old Williams hailed from a small town in northwestern Louisiana's Mansfield County and attended the University of Alabama prior to the war. When the war began he joined a company formed from men who resided in the northwest corner of the state. Eventually the company was mustered in as Company C of the 2nd Louisiana and Williams was chosen as its captain. The regiment fought on the Peninsula and at Malvern Hill. So many of the regiments line officers had been killed or wounded that Williams was promoted from captain to colonel to fill the gap. At Second Manassas, the regiment fought until their ammunition was gone and then proceeded to pick up rocks and hurl them at the oncoming Federals. During the Battle of Sharpsburg, Williams was hit in the chest by a minie-ball which passed completely through him. He survived his wound and was taken prisoner. After being exchanged, he spent the next seven

---

[166] Eicher, & Eicher, **High Commands**, p.324; Tagg, **Generals**, p.276; Warner, **Generals in Gray**, p.164; Faust, **Encyclopedia**, pp.402-403.

[167] Krick, Robert K., **Lee's Colonels**, p.403; **OR** vol.27, pt.3, p.922; **OR** vol.25, pt.1, p.1037; Tagg, **Generals**, p.281; Faust, **Encyclopedia**, p.533.

months recovering, returning in time to fight with the regiment at Chancellorsville and take over the brigade when Nicholls was wounded.[168]

The final and largest brigade in Johnson's Division was populated by men hailing from both North Carolina and Virginia. The 1st and 2nd North Carolina and three Virginia regiments, the 10th, 23rd and 37th were brigaded together under the command of Brigadier General George Hume Steuart. Steuart, a Marylander from Baltimore and son of a War of 1812 general was born on 24 August 1828. A military career seemed to be preordained for the youngster and at the tender age of fifteen he entered West Point on 1 July 1844. His youthfulness may have been a detriment to his study habits for after four years of work the best George could do was thirty-seventh in a class of thirty-eight. Assigned to the 2nd Dragoons, Steuart, spent his early days as a soldier on the frontier fighting Indians. His assignments took him to Texas, and the Utah, Kansas and Nebraska Territories. In 1856, he found himself involved in the Cheyenne expedition followed by the Utah expedition in 1858 and fighting against the Comanche in 1860. Steuart was one of the few Regular Army officers from Maryland who resigned and went south after the war began. He was welcomed with open arms by the Confederacy. His actions prompted the upstart Confederacy to market him in an effort to persuade more Marylanders to throw in with the Southern cause.[169]

After his resignation, Steuart was made a captain of cavalry but soon found himself promoted to lieutenant colonel and transferred to the 1st Maryland Infantry. He led the regiment at First Manassas. Before the day ended, Steuart would be promoted to colonel of the regiment. His old army discipline and routines molded the men of the 1st into a sharp fighting unit, and his abilities earned him a promotion to brigadier general and an assignment to brigade command. He was placed in charge of his own Maryland regiment and the 44th 52nd and 58th Virginia. Like a number of other Jackson subordinates, Steuart ran afoul of his general. A stickler for the chain of command, he refused to obey a direct order from Jackson because Ewell was his immediate superior. Nothing serious came of the disagreement and Steuart fought with Jackson until he was wounded Cross Keys. He was struck in the back of the shoulder by a canister ball which broke his collar bone. Unfortunately the bone did not heal correctly and it took a year away from the army to recover. He returned to duty after Chancellorsville, and took charge of Raleigh Colston's old brigade. Lee, had removed Colston due to poor performance and chose to replace him with Steuart. He was known as "Maryland" to avoid confusion with General Stuart who spelled his name different but pronounced it the same. Steuart had not spent a single day with the Army of Northern Virginia before his new brigade started north.[170]

---

[168] Krick, *Colonels*, p.403; Tagg, Larry, *Generals*, p.282.

[169] *OR* vol.27, pt.3, p.921; Tagg, Larry, *Generals*, p.272; Eicher, & Eicher, *High Commands*, p.506; Wakelyn, *Biographical Dictionary*, p.399. The 1st Maryland Battalion would be assigned to Steuart's Brigade on 13 June.

[170] Tagg, *Generals*, p.273; Faust, *Encyclopedia*, p.717; Boatner, *Dictionary*, p.796.

Ewell Takes a Ride

At 8:00 a.m. on 5 June Ewell broke up the Second Corps' winter camp and headquarters at Yerby's and began the trip to Culpeper. The season for active campaigning was at hand, and it was time to be on the move. Ewell however had one more personal issue to deal with before he departed. Now that he was married, the general needed to designate Lizinka as his beneficiary. With Dr. Hunter McGuire and aide-de-camp Turner as witnesses he took time on the evening of 4 June and drafted his will. Even though he possessed little property he could call his own, he left all he had to his new wife.[171]

Possibly due to his less than stellar stamina, Ewell's path was more direct than that taken by his corps. He would also spend part of the trip riding in a carriage rather than mounted on his horse. The general and his staff traveled directly west toward the old battlefield of Chancellorsville. As his party cross the area in which the fighting took place, Jed Hotchkiss, riding next to Ewell's carriage, provided the general with commentary, pointing out critical points of interest. "I gave General Ewell an account of the fight as we went along," he wrote in his diary. Hotchkiss noted he "pointed out to him [Ewell] the localities of incidents as we passed them." Hotchkiss recalled Ewell "was much interested and asked many questions." The general expressed surprise that Hooker had not made an effort to hold his position longer. Ewell thought the Federal position, with its entrenchments, was a strong one and was astonished that Hooker did not make a stand. Soon they passed the burnt remains of the Chancellor House which had been destroyed during the fighting. Its black timbers and exposed foundation was a lasting representation of the violence which had occurred there one month ago. While most of the bodies had been removed for burial, a great number of dead, decaying horses still littered the field. The smell of decomposing horseflesh penetrated the atmosphere. Eventually the old mansion would be rebuilt, but for now its rubble would serve as a reminder of the fighting and the men who died nearby. The excursion across the battlefield was a dusty one and the heat of the day took its toll on the party. That evening Hotchkiss noted in his diary, "[w]e are all quite weary tonight."[172]

The following day Ewell intended to move on at daylight, but the message arrived from Lee instructing him to halt until the intentions of the Federal's incursion at Deep Run could be discerned. Ewell and his staff settled down for a leisurely day in camp. Hotchkiss spent the time being constructive, continuing his work on a map of Culpeper County. During the afternoon it rained, dampening the dust and making the road slightly muddy. Finally at 4:00 p.m. word came that Ewell could move on and the party quickly departed, heading toward Raccoon Ford, halting within a mile of the crossing.

The next day was Sunday, and after morning services conducted by Reverend Lacy, the party left camp and crossed the Rapidan at the ford. After wading the river, Ewell's horsemen turned and traveled upriver to Somerville Ford where they found General Early's Division completing its crossing. Rodes' Division was already across

---

[171] Pfanz, *A Soldier's Life*, p.280; Hotchkiss, *Make Me a Map*, p.148.

[172] Hotchkiss, *Make Me a Map*, p.148; Nye, Wilber S., *Here Come the Rebels*, p.43.

and back on the road to Culpeper. As Ewell observed the men some recognized their new commander. Word spread through the ranks that the general was near. "The troops soon recognized General Ewell," Hotchkiss wrote, "and began to cheer him as had been their habit with General Jackson, thus transferring to him the ardor they felt for their old commander." Ewell, in recognition of the gesture, removed his hat, and riding up and down the line waved it in response to the cheering men.[173]

General Steuart's aid-de-camp, Randolph H. McKim, provided a detailed description of the transit within a letter to his mother.

> "...we turned off to the right and took the road to Somerville Ford, which is a few miles above Raccoon Ford on the Rapidan. This brought us through a beautiful country and we began to catch glimpses of the distant Blue Ridge. The view from the crest of the hills which extend along the south bank of the Rapidan was enchanting. The ground sinks almost precipitately within a hundred yards of the river. The river itself was swollen from the recent rain, and the water as red as Albemarle soil. The banks on either side were lined with willows which dipped their branches in the stream and made a beautiful feature in the landscape. Just above the ford there was a waterfall and an old mill in the last stages of decay. The north bank rises more gradually. Just upon the summit of a little knoll opposite the ford two tall chimneys mark the spot where once stood a large old-fashioned country house. From this point the ground ascends very gently and broad fertile fields lie on either side of the road, with here and there a pretty white cottage. Beyond rises the Piedmont Range and the dim blue mountains from the background. You can better imagine than I describe, how beautiful the aspect which was spread out beneath us for miles as we reached the crest of the hills I have described. Now cast your eyes down the road that leads to the ford and see that dense column of men stretching down to the river, across its swollen current up the farther bank, and extending for miles until lost where the road enters a thick grove of trees. Many of the men took off shoes and stockings, but some regiments marched straight through without breaking ranks. The water was nearly waist deep, but the men pushed on with shouts, in fine spirits. It was one of the most picturesque scenes I have ever witnessed, and the second of the kind in which I have borne a part since the war began."

McKim, being a reverend, noted that it was Sunday and the "air was fresh and cool" as the men negotiated the ford. He no doubt attributed the splendor of the sight to the hand of his Maker.[174]

---

[173] *Ibid*, pp.148-149.

[174] McKim, ***Recollections***, pp.141-142.

After rousing the spirits of the men, Ewell moved on to Culpeper, arriving there at 10:00 a.m. on the morning of 7 June. The trip was a quick one and many were impressed with his ability to travel the distance. Sandie Pendleton, writing to his mother praised the general for his efforts. "The more I see of Gen. Ewell the more I am pleased with him," he wrote. "He resembles Gen. Jackson very much in some points of his character, particularly his utter disregard of his own personal comforts and his inflexibility of purpose. Yesterday he rode some 20 miles on horse-back, often at full speed and exhibited no signs of fatigue last night. I look for great things from him," Pendleton continued, "and am glad to say that our troops have for him a good deal of the same feeling they had toward General Jackson, which must increase very much when they find on trail that he is so good a man." Although many still questioned his ability, Ewell's initial impression had been a good one. It remained to be seen if he would impress the army's command structure as well.[175]

Hill Watches the Backdoor

When Ewell and his party arrived at Culpeper they discovered General Hood's Division returning from a march toward Ellis Ford. According to Porter Alexander, Hood had been sent to the Rappahannock to cover the ford, which was on a direct line to the rear of Hooker's army near Fredericksburg. Alexander noted Hood was to bivouac with his division that night near the ford. In the morning Hood was to force in the Federal pickets guarding the crossing and transfer his division to the north side of the river. What Hood was to accomplish once across the river, Alexander, who had been sent along as an engineering officer to reconnoiter the ford, did not know. The matter was settled at midnight before the attack when Hood received orders to return to Culpeper and abandoned the endeavor.[176]

Hood's movement was a sign of uncertainty from Lee with respect to Hooker's intentions. Had the Union commander detected his movement? Was the fight at Franklin's Crossing a feint to disguise another movement to intercept his army? Lee's uncertainty about how Hooker would react to his departure required action on his part. He would have to leave a portion of his command in place to monitor Hooker and keep track of the enemy's disposition.

A second issue posed an even bigger problem. If the entire army was pulled away from Fredericksburg, the backdoor to Richmond would be wide open. Lee needed Hooker's army to follow him if his plans for getting the enemy out in the open and defeating him piecemeal were to come to fruition. If the Federals chose to remain near Fredericksburg and the authorities in Washington would allow it, Hooker would be free to march south to the Confederate capital and engage the troops guarding Richmond. In reality, Lee had nothing to fear since Lincoln's paranoia regarding the safety of Washington would keep Hooker between the Confederates and the Federal capital.

---

[175] *Ibid*, p.149; Sandie Pendleton to mother, 9 June 1863, William Nelson Pendleton Papers, UNC.

[176] Hotchkiss, **Make Me a Map**, p.149; Alexander, **Fighting**, pp.221-222.

With two corps headed for Culpeper, Lee chose to have A. P. Hill's new Third Corps remain and watch the Fredericksburg line. On 5 June he left instruction for Hill "to occupy the position of Fredericksburg with the troops under your command, making such disposition as will be best calculated to deceive the enemy, and keep him in ignorance of any change in the disposition of the army." Lee then left detailed instructions as to Hill's responsibilities if he were attacked and was unable to hold the enemy in check.

> "Should the enemy make an advance upon you, you will endeavor to repel him, and, if not able to do so, or hold him in check, you must fall back along the line of the Fredericksburg Railroad, protecting your communications, and offering such resistance as you can to his advance toward Richmond. If you find it necessary, you can call up Pickett and Pettigrew, now at Hanover Junction. Should you find that the enemy has evacuated his position opposite you, you will, after informing yourself of the fact by your scouts, & c[avalry]., if practicable and in your opinion advantages, cross the river and pursue him, inflicting all the damage you can upon his rear."

The wording was a bit out of character for Lee. Using words such as "you must" and "you will," Lee specifically outlined what he desired from Hill. The only discretionary part was the option to pursue Hooker across the river if Hill thought it would be advantageous. The order and its wording proved that Lee understood the ramifications of Hill being in command of a corps for the first time. He was specific in his instructions and definitive in what he wanted Hill's Corps to accomplish. With the stakes high, Lee knew he could not afford any errors or misunderstandings of what he required from his new Third Corps commander.

Lee went on to tell Hill to keep him "informed of everything material relative to yourself, position, and the enemy." A continuous line of couriers was established between Hill's headquarters and Lee's at Culpeper so that communications would be simple and swift. Lee was not going to take any chances with Hill. The task of monitoring the Federals was critical to guarantee the safety of both Richmond and the rear of the two corps now on the march for Culpeper and points north.[177]

To cover the withdrawal of Lee's other two corps, Hill arrayed his divisions with former First Corps division commander Richard H. Anderson north of Fredericksburg, Major General Henry "Harry" Heth's division fronted the town and Major General William D. Pender's controlled the area south to the town. When the affair at Deep Run began, Pender was forced to shift some of his troops further south to confront the Federals who had crossed the river. From these

---

[177] *OR* vol.27, pt.2, p.313; *OR* vol.27, pt.3, p.859. At the time, Hill had at his disposal the 15th and 4th Virginia cavalry. Both regiments were left at Fredericksburg, covering Hill's flanks. The 4th Virginia rode to Culpeper the morning of 8 June. Pickett and Pettigrew had yet to join their respective corps.

positions, Hill's Corps would spend the next ten days keeping a watchful eye on Joe Hooker's army as Lee strung his other corps' out along his line of march to Pennsylvania.[178]

A Promising North Carolinian

William Dorsey Pender was one of the most promising commanders in Confederate service. The son of wealthy North Carolina farmer James Pender and his wife Sarah, William was born in Edgecombe County, on 2 February 1834. His mother was affectionate, caring and patient, while his father was quick to forgive the indiscretions of youth. William, who liked to be called Dorsey, spent his early boyhood days tramping the bottomlands of the Tar River and performing chores on the farm. When he was of age, Sarah made sure he was enrolled in a local school. His education limited his outdoor adventures, which probably did not sit well with young Dorsey. In the nearby town of Tarboro, Dorsey's older brother Robert, fourteen years his senior, had set up a store and become a prominent merchant. At the age of fifteen, Dorsey entered the workforce when he was employed by his brother as a clerk in the store. It was not long before he discovered that while storekeeping may have been his brother's desire, it was not his. When the opportunity to attend West Point arose, the family used their contacts with a local congressman, Thomas H. Ruffin, to secure a recommendation for him. The effort was successful and on 24 June 1850, sixteen year old William Pender received an appointment to the Military Academy.[179]

Six days later, Pender became a cadet, entering West Point along with seventy other plebes. While Dorsey proved to be slightly above average at his studies, excelling in cavalry tactics and mathematics, it was his leadership qualities which drew the attention of his instructors. He worked his way upward through the ranks of the Battalion of Cadets, beginning at lance corporal and rising to lieutenant. Although his appointment to lieutenant was eventually withdrawn for disciplinary reasons, there was no doubt Dorsey Pender could lead a group of soldiers. After four years of coursework and military training, William D. Pender graduated. He stood nineteenth among the forty-six men who graduated in the class of 1854. Brevetted second lieutenant and assigned to the 2nd Artillery, Pender decided to go home for a bit of rest in North Carolina before reporting for duty.[180]

Accompanied by one of his classmates, Sam T. Sheppard, Dorsey stopped at Sam's home in Good Spring for a bit of relaxation. It was here that he met his future wife, Sam's younger sister, Mary Frances "Fanny" Sheppard. Although only fourteen at the time, Fanny caught Dorsey eye and he took a liking to her almost immediately. Unfortunately, he had little time to spend with her for Pender had to report for duty as the summer ended.

---

[178] Gottfried, *Maps*, pp.2-11.

[179] Wakelyn, *Biographical Dictionary*, p.341; Eicher, & Eicher, *High Commands*, p.424; Hassler, Editor, *One of Lee's Best Men*, p.3.

[180] Hassler, *One of Lee's Best*, p.4.

On 16 August Pender arrived at his duty station in Fort Meyer, Florida. After six months of service with the 2nd Artillery, he was transferred to the 1st Dragoons. His new assignment took him west where he saw service in New Mexico, Oregon, California and Washington. When Indians began threatening settlers, Pender sharpened his fighting and leadership skills against the renegades. He proved his grit during one engagement when, while on his horse, he was confronted by a mounted Indian. Reaching for his sword, he discovered the weapon had become entangled in its scabbard and could not be drawn. With the Indian bearing down on him, he reached up and grasped his assailants arm as the renegade attempted to deliver a blow. With his other hand, Pender took the Indian by the neck and pulled his attacker toward him. Thus engaged, with their horses side by side, he guided his animal into the midst of his men and, pulling the Indian toward him, unhorsed his assailant and pitched him into the throng of dragoons.[181]

In the spring of 1859, Pender returned to North Carolina and on 3 March, he and Fanny were married at Good Spring. The couple's honeymoon was short. They spent time in Washington and Tarboro, the latter visit probably to spend time with Dorsey's family before he took his new bride west to his duty station in the Washington Territory. Fanny's brother Samuel had died in 1855 at Fort Leavenworth, and the Pender's paid tribute by naming their first child after him. With Fanny and little Samuel established at Fort Vancouver, Dorsey rode out to continue the campaign against the high strung Indians in the region as a member of General William S. Harney's command. In addition to his fighting proficiency, Pender proved he was good with a pen as well. When he was transferred to San Francisco in November 1860, he used it to perform the duties of the regiment's adjutant. Fanny, who was not pleased with Dorsey's violent encounters with the Indians, probably appreciated her husband's new assignment to desk duty.

As the storm clouds of war floated over the land, Pender returned to the east coast where he began a short stint at Carlisle, Pennsylvania performing recruiting duties. Although he was not a supporter of war and secession, he chose to follow his native state and resigned his commission on 21 March 1861. Entering Confederate service, he was initially assigned to duty as a captain of artillery, but by 27 May he was serving as colonel of the 3rd North Carolina. A short time later, Pender received another transfer, taking over as colonel of the 6th North Carolina in August. His regiment saw no action until Fair Oaks, where, with President Davis watching in the distance, Pender advanced his regiment against the Federal position. Finding his command isolated and almost surrounded, he ordered his North Carolinians to charge the enemy, stunning their antagonists long enough for him to extricate his command. After the battle, the president rode up to Pender and, there on the battlefield, promoted him to brigadier general. During the fight at Malvern Hill, he was wounded in the arm, although not seriously. While recovering he received his official promotion when he was presented his star on 22 July 1862. Assigned to a brigade in A. P. Hill's Division, Pender marched north with Jackson's Corps.

---

[181] *Ibid*; Wakelyn, ***Biographical Dictionary***, p.341.

He was wounded once again, this time in the leg, when he was knocked down by an exploding shell at Second Manassas.[182]

His wound was slight and Pender was back on the battle line at Sharpsburg where he managed to emerge unscathed. Three months later, fighting on the left of Lee's line at Fredericksburg, he was again wounded in the arm. The damage was restricted to his flesh, allowing him to remain on the field, his arm dripping blood hanging at his side. At Chancellorsville, Pender found himself positioned in the middle of Jackson's savage flank attack. When Jackson and Hill were wounded, Pender ascended to divisional command for a short time. The following day, after taking a regimental flag in his hands, he rode forward, leading his men from horseback into the midst of a Federal storm of lead and into the enemy's entrenchments. Although not wounded in the charge, the next day, while in the entrenchments, a fellow officer standing next to him was hit and killed. The spent bullet exited the officer and struck Pender in the right arm. While only a bruise, the arm became rather sore and he was out of action until 13 May when he returned to his brigade.

When Hill was promoted to command of the new Third Corps, he wrote a glowing recommendation of Pender and lobbied to have him placed in command of his old division. "Gen. Pender has fought with the Division in every battle, has been four times wounded and never left the field, has risen by death and wounds from fifth brigadier to be its senior, has the best drilled and disciplined Brigade in the Division, and more than all, possesses the unbounded confidence of the Division." Lee noticed Pender's quality as well calling him "an excellent officer." On 27 May 1863, Pender received his promotion and ascended to the head of Hill's old division.[183]

At twenty-nine, William Pender was one of the younger division commanders in the Confederate Army. Although youthful, his clean cut hair and full beard gave him a distinguished look. At five foot ten, he cut a trim figure and carried himself as if to communicate to all that he was a soldier. He possessed a burning determination and a desire to succeed, which his performance on the battlefield reinforced. Later, Lee would pay Pender the ultimate compliment by using his name in conjunction with that of Jackson when identifying his "best men."[184]

Pender's Division contained four brigades, two from the Deep South and two from North Carolina. Once again the lack of brigade level commanders forced the brigade of South Carolinians in Pender's Division to be commanded by a colonel. Colonel Abner M. Perrin was born in South Carolina's Edgefield District on 2 February 1827. He was a lawyer by trade, but when the Mexican War began, he enlisted in the Regular Army, succumbing to the glory seeking fever which spread over the nation. While fighting Mexicans, Perrin served as a lieutenant in

---

[182] Hassler, *One of Lee's Best Men*, p.5; Wakelyn, *Biographical Dictionary*, p.341; Jordon, *NCT*, vol.V, p.283; vol.IV, p.267; Tagg, *Generals*, p.325.

[183] Tagg, *Generals*, pp.326.

[184] Hassler, *One of Lee's Best Men*, p.6; *OR* vol.29, pt.2, p.743.

an infantry regiment and when the war concluded he returned home and continued his law study. By 1854, he was proficient enough to pass the bar and practiced his craft until the war began.[185]

William Dorsey Pender may have been a better choice for corps command than either Hill or Ewell. *MOLLUS Collection, USAHEC*

Perrin enlisted on 10 August 1861, at the age of thirty-one. He joined The Edgefield Rifles, a company of men which would eventually become Company D of the 14th South Carolina. Perrin's prior military experience was sufficient enough to get him elected captain of the company. His regiment saw its first major action on 27 June at Gaines' Mill where eighteen were killed and 197 wounded. For the next year, Perrin and the 14th found themselves in the heat of battle, fighting in all the major engagements of the Eastern Theater. At Fredericksburg, his brigade commander, Brigadier General Maxey Gregg was shot in the spine and killed while riding at the front of the brigade. Command fell to the colonel of the 14th, Samuel McGowan which elevated Perrin to the command of the regiment. McGowan commanded the brigade for only a few months before he was disabled by a severe wound in the leg just below his knee at Chancellorsville. Perrin took command and led the brigade through the remainder of the battle. Evidently his performance was satisfactory for he retained command of the brigade after Lee's reorganization and directed its regiments as they patrolled the riverbank south of Fredericksburg. In addition to the 14th, the 1st, 12th and 13th South Carolina,

---

[185] Tagg, **Generals**, pp.330-331; Eicher, & Eicher, **High Commands**, pp.425-425.

along with the 1st South Carolina Rifles constituted the remainder of the brigade. Eventually McGowan would return to his command but Perrin, who had not led a brigade in battle until Chancellorsville, would command McGowan's Brigade as it fronted the Rappahannock River south of Fredericksburg. It would be up to the fighting prowess of the South Carolinians to carry themselves and the untried Perrin through the coming campaign.[186]

Like Perrin, shortly after he graduating from Emory College in 1846, Edward Lloyd Thomas joined the army to fight in Mexico. The son of a prominent Marylander, Thomas was born 23 March 1825 in Clarke County, Georgia. He entered the fighting as a private with a mounted unit known as the Newton County Independent Horse. He evidently proved he was a good soldier for he received a promotion to second lieutenant after his efforts at Vera Cruz. Once the fighting terminated, he was offered a commission in the Regularly Army but declined choosing instead to return to his family's Newton County plantation. Shortly thereafter, Thomas married and settled into a life of peace, remaining on his farm and administering the enterprise until Georgia left the Union.[187]

Thomas was initially appointed lieutenant colonel of the 4th Battalion Georgia Infantry on 14 October 1861, but only held the position for a day. His previous war experience and reputation in Georgia society prompted Jefferson Davis to grant him permission to raise a regiment of volunteers. His efforts resulted in the creation of the 35th Georgia, of which Thomas became colonel. The regiment saw action during the Peninsular Campaign at Yorktown and Fair Oaks. During the latter engagement, Thomas' commander, James J. Pettigrew was wounded and captured, forcing him to take over the brigade. The brigade however, was disbanded a few days later and Thomas reported back to the 35th. At Mechanicsville, the first engagement of The Seven Days, Thomas led his regiment in an attack against John Reynolds' Pennsylvania Reserves. The assault succeeded in establishing a position across heavily defended Beaver Dam Creek. His Georgians were the only Confederates to force a passage, and in their unsupported position, were obliged to retreat. During his withdrawal, he was wounded but ignored the injury and guided his regiment to safety. At Frayser's Farm, he took over command of his brigade once more after Brigadier General Joseph R. Anderson was wounded in the head. Anderson noted in his report that Thomas "evinced fearlessness and good judgment not only in this affair, but throughout the expedition."

Thomas remained in command of the brigade for a year, missing only the battle of Sharpsburg. His men stood toe to toe with the Federals at Second Manassas along the unfinished railroad and helped plug the hole George Meade's boys punched in Jackson's line at Fredericksburg. His Georgians always gave a good accounting when called on, but accolades for his performance were few and far between. The brigade was always praised in official reports, but Thomas

---

[186] Krick, Robert K., *The 14th South Carolina Infantry Regiment, of the Gregg-McGowan Brigade, Army of Northern Virginia*, pp.2, 7, 230-231; *OR* vol.11, pt.2, p.982; Caldwell, *McGowan's Brigade*, pp.93, 116; *OR* vol.27, pt.2, p.289.

[187] Wakelyn, *Biographical Dictionary*, p.408; Tagg, *Generals*, p.336.

was seldom singled out. The brigade was constructed from Thomas' original 35th Georgia, along with Georgia's 14th, 45th and 49th regiments, creating a solid brigade from a group of proven regiments.[188]

After accidently firing on A. P. Hill and Jackson in the darkness, and Lieutenant Emack had rounded up his prisoners from the 128th Pennsylvania, General James Henry Lane's boys prepared themselves for Jackson's planned night attack at Chancellorsville. Fortunately for the North Carolinians, A. P. Hill received his wound before the advance could be ordered and, in the wake of the Rodes, Stuart command confusion, the attack was canceled. The reprieve was short-lived however, for Lane's Brigade would be decimated during the remainder of the battle taking over 900 casualties, a number which eclipsed all other brigades.[189]

Jim Lane, like the general his men accidently wounded, taught at the Virginia Military Institute prior to the war. He was an extremely educated man and a Virginian by birth, having been born in Mathews Court House on 28 July 1833. As a boy he was instructed by private tutors, which thoroughly prepared him for the curriculum at VMI, from which he graduated with honors in 1854. Enrolling at the University of Virginia he received a science degree in 1857 before returning to VMI as an assistant professor of mathematics, where he taught until 1859. When war came, Lane was teaching Natural Philosophy at the North Carolina Military Institute. In order to support the Southern cause, he quickly organized the cadets into a regiment. He was offered a commission as major of the unit, which he accepted on 11 May 1861. The regiment, one of North Carolina's original six month units, was designated the 1st North Carolina. The young men led by then Colonel D. H. Hill, fought and won the first land battle of the war at Big Bethel. Through the early months of the war, Lane performed his duties efficiently enough to garner a promotion to lieutenant colonel. On 21 September, he was transferred to the 28th North Carolina and became colonel of his new regiment. Lane was wounded leading his new command at both Frayser's Farm and Malvern Hill but neither wound was serious enough to keep him out of action. He led his regiment once more at Cedar Mountain and defended the unfinished railroad at Second Manassas. When Lane's brigade commander, Brigadier General Lawrence Branch was killed at Sharpsburg, the men showed their respect for the Virginian by lobbying to have "Little Jim" Lane made their permanent commander. On 1 November 1862, Lane became a brigadier general and took command of his Carolinians.[190]

Lane's first effort at the head of the brigade nearly ended in disaster at Fredericksburg when Federal troops exploited a gap between Lane and the unit on his

---

[188] Henderson, Lillian, ***Roster of the Confederate Soldiers of Georgia 1861-1865*** (hereafter ***RCSG***), vol.3, p.843; ***OR*** vol.11, pt.2, pp.877-878.
Tagg, *Generals*, pp.336-337; *OR* vol.27, pt.2, p.290.

[189] Lane, ***SHPS***, vol.8, p.490; ***OR*** vol.25, pt.1, p.918. Lane's casualties in killed, wounded and missing were 161, 626, and 121 respectively.

[190] Eicher, & Eicher, ***High Commands***, p.338; Wakelyn, ***Biographical Dictionary***, p.276; Manarin, ***NCT***, vol.III, pp.2-3; Jordon, ***NCT***, vol.VIII, p.110.

right. He displayed his leadership skills, remaining calm during the ordeal, and averted catastrophe. As the brigade prepared for its march north, a depressing aura covered the men with the understanding they had been responsible for depriving the south of its second greatest hero. To make matters worse, a running belligerence existed between the North Carolinians and Virginians, which had been recently exaggerated by Jefferson Davis. The president appointed a Virginian as tax collector in North Carolina, drawing the ire of the Tar Heels. It would be a long gloomy journey when the brigade was finally released from their duty on the river, but Jim Lane's tough North Carolinian's would not shrink from responsibility or Federal lead.[191]

Pender's other brigade of North Carolinians, his old command, would march to Gettysburg under the direction of Alfred Moore Scales. Scales' brigade consisted of the 13th, 16th, 22nd, 34th and 38th regiments. When General Pender ascended to divisional command, Colonel Scales took the brigade, although he would not be promoted to brigadier general until 13 June. Like so many other Confederate brigadiers, Scales was a lawyer and politician by trade but, unlike many of his contemporaries, he did not lobby for a commission when the war began. Born in Reidsville, North Carolina on 26 November 1827, Scales was educated at Caldwell Institute in Greensborough and at the University of North Carolina where he studied law. After leaving the university, Scales opened a law practice in Madison and became the solicitor of Rockingham County. He was elected to the state legislature four times and served in the U. S. House of Representatives from 1857 to 1859. Scales also served as a presidential elector for John C. Breckinridge during the election of 1860.[192]

Scales enlisted as a private, but was elected to the captaincy of Company H in Pender's 3rd North Carolina which was later designated the 13th. When Pender was transferred to the 6th North Carolina, Scales was elevated to colonel and took command of the 13th. At Gaines' Mill, Scales was at the head of his regiment when a decisive moment of the engagement arrived. Taking hold of the regimental flag and advancing it to the front, he urged the men of the 13th to stand their ground. General Samuel Garland noted in his report that Scales "was conspicuous for his fine bearing". If ever a general gave his all on a battlefield it was Scales. After The Seven Days fighting was over, he collapsed from exhaustion and nearly died. He was absent during the Maryland Campaign, but returned to duty later that fall. When Pender was wounded at Fredericksburg, Scales took over the brigade and led it at Chancellorsville. He was shot through the thigh but remained on the field till weakness and blood loss forced him to relinquish command. A quick recovery allowed him to return to the army before the Gettysburg Campaign. Later, as Hill's corps was preparing to abandon the entrenchments at Fredericksburg, Scales was promoted to brigadier general and placed in command of his brigade due to Pender's elevation to the command of A. P. Hill's old division. Scales limited experience at brigade level command did not concern his superiors for he had

---

[191] Tagg, *Generals*, pp.333-334; Faust, **Encyclopedia**, p.424.

[192] Warner, **Generals in Gray**, pp.268-269; Eicher, & Eicher, **High Commands**, p.470; Jordon, *NCT*, vol.V, p.283.

displayed a style which always put him at the front of his troops. There was no reason to believe that would change.[193]

"Fighting Dick"

Richard H. "Fighting Dick" Anderson, a West Pointer from South Carolinia, as part of Lee's reorganization, brought his division from Longstreet's Corps to Hill's new Third Corps. Richard was born into a well to do family on Borough House Plantation in Stateburg, Sumter County, South Carolina. Richard, a grandson of the Revolutionary War hero of the same name, came into the world on 7 October 1821. It was obvious early in the boy's life that the military was in his blood. When he was old enough, efforts began to secure an appointment to West Point. The labors bore fruit and at the age of seventeen, Richard entered the academy. He joined his future corps commander James Longstreet, D. H. Hill, and Lafayette McLaws as a new plebe. Like Longstreet, Anderson was a rather poor student but managed to finish fourteen positions higher than the Georgian, fortieth out of fifty-six.

Exiting West Point in 1842, Anderson was brevetted a second lieutenant and assigned to the 1st Dragoons. He attended cavalry school at Carlisle prior to spending three years on the frontier before going to war in Mexico. Promoted to full second lieutenant before the fighting began, Anderson saw action at Vera Cruz, Contreras, and Churubusco, and was brevetted first lieutenant for his efforts at San Augustine. Returning from Mexico, he was honored by his native state for his conduct, and presented a sword for distinguished service. Anderson went back to cavalry school for a short period, before returning to the frontier, where he spent the major portion of the years between the wars. His service out west was interrupted for a brief time when Anderson when to Kansas during the period of violence between the abolitionists and pro-slavers. Promoted to captain on 3 March 1855, he participated in the expedition to Utah in 1858 and was stationed at Fort Kearny when his state succeeded.[194]

Anderson was thirty-nine years of age when he resigned his commission on 3 March 1861, more than a month before Fort Sumter surrendered. He entered Confederate service as a major of cavalry and saw his initial duty in the Department of South Carolina and Florida. When General Beauregard left South Carolina for Virginia, Anderson succeeded him as commander of the troops in the Charleston area. He was involved in the attack at Santa Rosa Island, Florida where he was wounded, although not seriously, in the left elbow. During the spring of 1862, Anderson was ordered to Virginia and placed in command of a South Carolina brigade, which he led during the Peninsula Campaign. He guided his Pimento State soldiers at Williamsburg and Fair Oaks and received accolades from Longstreet for his work. Longstreet credited Anderson with executing the decisive action of the battle. "[T]he

---

[193] Tagg, *Gettysburg*, pp.338-339; Jordon, *NCT*, vol.V, pp.275, 355; Faust, *Encyclopedia*, p.660; *OR* vol.11, pt.2, p.644. The 13th regiment was originally designated the 3rd Regiment N.C. Volunteers but was renamed the 13th Regiment North Carolina on 14 November, 1861.

[194] Wakelyn, *Biographical Dictionary*, p.75; Eicher, & Eicher, *High Commands*, p.105; Tagg, *Gettysburg*, p.306.

attack of two brigades under General R. H. Anderson" Longstreet wrote in his report, "was made with such spirit and regularity as to have driven back the most determined foe. This decided the day in our favor." During The Seven Days, at Frayser's Farm, Anderson took command of Longstreet's Division while "Old Pete" directed the battle. Once again Longstreet praised Anderson in his report, listing him first among a group of officers who received the general's approving words. Two weeks later, on 14 July, Anderson was promoted to major general and placed in command of a division in Longstreet's Right Wing of the Army of Northern Virginia.[195]

Anderson led his division admirably at Second Manassas, fighting on the right flank of Lee's army, helping to deliver Longstreet's crushing blow. Less than a month later, he found his division entangled in the bloody fighting along the sunken road at Sharpsburg. His troops dug in and put up a stubborn resistance against the hard-charging Federals. As the fighting intensified, Anderson, was hit in the thigh and knocked out of his saddle. After he left the field, his division, heavily pressed broke and retreated, exposing the center of the Confederate line. The loss of Anderson emphasized his value to the division and his worth to Longstreet and Lee as a division commander.[196]

Richard Heron "Fighting Dick" Anderson would join Hill's new corps and help anchor it with his experience. *MOLLUS Collection, USAHEC*

Anderson proved to be a quick healer and returned to his command in time to participate at Fredericksburg, but his division was lightly engaged. When Longstreet took part of his command south to winter near Suffolk, Anderson stayed behind

---

[195] *OR*, vol.11, pt.1, p.940; Wakelyn, ***Biographical Dictionary***, p.75; Eicher, & Eicher, ***High Commands***, p.105; *OR*, vol.11, pt.2, p.759.

[196] Tagg, ***Gettysburg***, p.307.

and found himself being called upon by Lee to confront and halt Hooker's advance toward Lee's rear as the Chancellorsville Campaign unfolded. His actions after being ordered to face Hooker and his effectiveness in containing the Federals until Lee could move more troops into position was exemplary. Anderson's Division also provided Lee with a significant portion of his holding force, allowing Jackson to move to Hooker's right. The following day, Anderson, in conjunction with the remainder of Lee's army, conducted a heavy attack against Hooker's position. On 4 May, with Hooker under control, he disengaged his division and marched back toward Fredericksburg to assist General Early in driving Sedgwick's Corps back across the Rappahannock. Anderson's value to Lee at Chancellorsville was immense and Lee praised the general in his official report. "Maj. General R. H. Anderson," Lee wrote a few months later, "was also distinguished for the promptness, courage, and skill with which he and his division executed every order..." It was obvious to Lee that Anderson was a valuable division commander.[197]

Anderson's personality was one of modesty. He was not bombastic or into self-promotion like many of his fellow officers. He was unselfish almost to a fault and never actively courted the press or political associations to gain advancement. "Fighting Dick" Anderson was a commander who let his fighting and courage on the field of battle talk for him. He was liked by all who met and knew him, and his competent leadership earned him the respect and admiration of his men. He was a professional soldier in every respect and understood well the necessity of chain of command. He was never insubordinate and always did his best to execute orders promptly and efficiently. Although he lacked the presence and inspirational personality that many of Lee's other high level commanders possessed, Anderson seemed capable of inspiring without fanfare. Unfortunately, his lack of endorsements often brought ill feelings from his subordinates. The problem was Anderson's failure to single out deserving individuals in his battle reports. The tall sturdy Anderson was one of Lee's best division commanders and he had proven it through deeds not self-promotion. If he approached his new assignment with the same vigor as his previous one, he would do well.[198]

With the transfer of Richard Anderson's division from Longstreet's Corps, Hill received a group of veteran soldiers that had proven themselves on a number of Eastern Theater battlefields. Anderson's command was another five brigade division and the origins of the men were as diverse as the number of brigades. Many of the regiments had fought on the Peninsula and had remained together within the same organizations. While attrition had changed many of the command level officers, the gritty men had shown they could defeat the hated Yankees no matter who was at the helm of their outfits.[199]

A brigade of Alabamans under Cadmus M. Wilcox represented the Deep South. Wilcox' regiments, the 8th, 9th, 10th 11th and 14th had all participated in the

---

[197] *Ibid*; **OR** vol.25, pt.1, p.803.

[198] Tagg, ***Gettysburg***, p.306.

[199] **OR** vol.27, pt.2, p.288.

battles around Richmond and Wilcox had led all but the 14th during the fighting. Heavily engaged, three of the regiment's lost over two hundred men while the 11th and 14th recorded losses in excess of three hundred, the heaviest casualties for any brigade during the campaign.[200]

Wilcox was born in North Carolina in 1824. He attended West Point and graduated fifty-fourth in the infamous class of 1846, five steps from the bottom. After commencement, Wilcox journeyed to Mexico and war. He arrived on 23 October 1846 and joined the 4th Infantry. When the war ended, Wilcox went west to various duties at frontier outposts and taught at his alma matter, where he wrote a book on rifle tactics. When war with the North came, he cut his ties with the old army and became a colonel in the Confederate service. By the time of the Peninsular Campaign he was a brigadier general commanding the Alabamians in Longstreet's Division. Through the remainder of 1862 and the early months of 1863, Wilcox capably led his men, garnering him approval from his superiors. However, promotion to divisional command eluded him. Many officers, who were junior to him, had moved ahead of him in the command structure. In addition, officers who had received their commissions solely due to political connections were also being moved past him. Although frustrated, he was too much of a gentleman to outwardly express his displeasure with his lack of advancement. Writing to Lee in November 1862, he finally expressed his frustration by informing Lee he intended to leave the army. Lee refused to accept the resignation telling Wilcox "I cannot consent to it for I require your services here." Wilcox would continue to let his performance on the battlefield present his case. During the Chancellorsville fight, he once again demonstrated his worth by possibly saving Lee's entire army.[201]

As the fighting unfolded, Wilcox' Brigade was positioned far from the action, guarding Banks' Ford along the Rappahannock above Fredericksburg. Although upset that he was far from the fighting, Wilcox continued to perform his duties, remaining vigilant and alert. His attention to detail paid off, for he soon discovered that the Federals in his area on picket duty were wearing haversacks. This was a sure sign they were preparing to march. Leaving some men to guard the ford, he quickly moved his brigade and placed them in a position to block Sedgwick's advance. Wilcox was the first of Anderson's brigades to confront Sedgwick's vanguard as it traversed the Plank Road in a westerly direction, straight toward Lee's rear. Intercepting Sedgwick's lead elements, Wilcox forced the Federals to go on line and wait for reinforcements. He placed his men across the road and fought a classic delaying action west of Salem Church which allowed Lee to defeat Hooker at Chancellorsville and then turn the remainder of Anderson's Division loose to help confront the Federals. The time Wilcox bought gave Anderson's other brigades the opportunity to arrive in time to help stop Sedgwick. Losses once again

---

[200] *OR* vol.11, pt.2, p.503.

[201] Faust, ***Encyclopedia***, pp.824-825; Patterson, Gerard A., ***From Blue to Gray: The Life of Confederate General Cadmus M. Wilcox***, p.1,51; Tagg, ***Generals***, p.310.

were heavy, but the stubborn Alabamans under Cadmus Wilcox had once again proven their tenacity and stubbornness.[202]

A group of regiments from Alabama's neighbor, Mississippi, constituted another brigade in Anderson's Division. The brigade was under the command of another lawyer turned general, Carnot Posey. Posey was a native Mississippian who had been educated in Louisiana and Virginia. Born near Woodville Mississippi on 5 August 1818, Posey studied law at the University of Virginia and became a partner in a law practice in 1844, but his fledgling career was interrupted by the Mexican War. Although unaware at the time, volunteering for service turned out to be a smart career move for Posey since he served under a young officer named Jefferson Davis. Returning home, he was appointed to a United States district attorney position which he retained until Mississippi left the Union. A member of the Democratic Party, his devotion to Mississippi and family, and his strong States' Rights stance, required he side with the upstart nation. He raised a company of volunteers which eventually was mustered as a company in the 16th Mississippi in June 1861. Following his election to colonel of the regiment Carnot Posey marched off to war with his fellow Mississippians.

Posey's boys saw their first combat at Ball's Bluff and fought with Jackson in the Valley, where Posey was wounded in the right arm and chest at Cross Keys. Returning to duty in August 1862, he participated in the fighting at Second Manassas and performed well enough to be elevated to command of his brigade for a short period at the end of the battle. At Sharpsburg, Posey commanded the brigade due to the illness of Brigade General Winfield Featherston. When Featherston returned to his brigade at Fredericksburg, Posey was relegated to command of his regiment. Featherston, a marginal commander at best, thought Posey handled the brigade adequately during the battle but was not completely pleased with Posey's overall abilities. After the battle, Featherston requested, and was granted a transfer west and Posey was placed in permanent command of the brigade. He got a chance to prove Featherston's judgment misplaced a few weeks later at Chancellorsville. He demonstrated his worth and intelligence when he took the initiative and marched his brigade from its position along the river back toward Chancellorsville. General Anderson was duly impressed; writing in his report the Posey's Mississippians "saved our army from great peril, while their chivalrous charge upon the trenches...contributed largely to the successes..." There was little doubt that Posey lead a confident brigade of Mississippians. His original regiment, along with the 12th, 19th and the 48th formed a stout group of Southern warriors. They would have ample opportunity in a few weeks to prove their worth once again.[203]

The state of Georgia was represented within Anderson's Division by the brigade of Ambrose Ransom Wright. Born in the town of Louisville in Jefferson County, Georgia on 26 April 1826, Wright turned twenty-seven on the day Hooker

---

[202] Patterson, *From Blue to Gray*, p.57.

[203] Tagg, *Generals*, pp.319-320; Eicher, & Eicher, *High Commands*, p.436; *OR* vol.25, pt.1, p.852; *OR* vol.27, pt.2, p.288.

began his march upriver, inaugurating the Chancellorsville Campaign. Another lawyer and politician, Ambrose had grown up destitute but through perseverance and hard work became a successful litigator in Augusta. Call "Rans" on account of his middle name Ransom, politically Wright did not fare as well. He was unsuccessful in bids to win seats in the Georgia legislature and the United States Congress. He did not support secession but when it came, he assisted in efforts of carve Maryland from the Union and acquire its support for the Southern cause. Commissioned colonel of the 3rd Georgia, he served in the south until June 1862, when he was promoted to brigadier general, given command of a brigade in General Benjamin Huger's division and transferred to the Army of Northern Virginia. At the time Wright's brigade contained regiments from his native Georgia, Alabama and Louisiana.

Wright fought his brigade hard during The Seven Days. During one engagement he found his command isolated on the slope of Malvern Hill. The brigade was decimated, taking almost 400 casualties. Eventually assigned to Anderson's Division, at Second Manassas, Wright's Brigade participated in Longstreet's crushing flank attack, taking 190 more casualties. During the Battle of Sharpsburg, after his horse had been shot from under him by a cannon ball, Wright, continuing forward on foot was hit in the leg and chest. His wounds were serious but seemed to heal quickly. Two months later he was back at the head of his brigade and led it at Fredericksburg, where his men saw no action. The story was different at Chancellorsville where Wright's men saw plenty of combat after their long march from their post on the river, but sustained rather low casualty numbers. By the end of May, Wright's Georgians were tried and tested and it was understood that the men of the 2nd Georgia Battalion, and the 3rd, 22nd and 48th Georgia regiments could be counted on when the fire was the hottest. The only negative afforded to Wright was his tendency to utilize colorful descriptions of his brigade's exploits in battle. Within his battle reports, he often exaggerated facts but never went so far as to write untruths.[204]

The only infantry regiment from Florida in Lee's army was also a component of Anderson's Division. Called Perry's Brigade after its commander, it consisting of only three regiments, the 2nd, 5th and 8th, and was the smallest brigade Lee would take to Pennsylvania. By the time it arrived at Gettysburg, it would number only 787 men which made it half the size of Anderson's next larger brigade. Brigadier General Edward A. Perry, who was recuperating from typhoid fever, had turned the brigade over to Colonel David Lang. Lang was not a Floridian, having been born in southern Georgia on 9 May 1838. A graduate of the Georgia Military Institute, Lang had been a surveyor in Suwannee County before the war. When the shooting started, he joined a company of volunteers which eventually became Company H of the 1st Florida. The 1st was organized as a one year unit and when it mustered out in April 1862, Lang had advanced to sergeant. Once out of the army, Lang

---

[204] Eicher, & Eicher, *High Commands*, p.582; Tagg, *Generals*, pp.316-317; Wakelyn, *Biographical Dictionary*, p.447; *OR* vol.12, pt.2, p.568; *OR* vol.11, pt.2, pp.487, 981; *OR* vol.27, pt.2, p.288.

immediately began working to organize another company which would become Company C of the 8th Florida.²⁰⁵

Lang's new regiment became part of a brigade under Brigadier General Roger Pryor, who was a poor commander at best. Lang, who had been made captain of his company, saw action at Sharpsburg when Pryor's men were given the task of supporting the fighting along the Sunken Road. After becoming jumbled and confused, Pryor's men fled the field, sustaining almost 400 casualties with a number of his men being shot in the back. Eventually removed from command, Pryor was replaced by General Perry. Lang evidently caught someone's eye during the Sharpsburg fracas, for shortly after the battle he was elevated two command levels, being made a colonel on 2 October and giving command of the 8th. He led the regiment competently at Fredericksburg until he was severely wounded in the head and had to be carried from the field. Lang missed Chancellorsville, but recovered from his wound sufficiently enough to rejoin the brigade prior to Lee's march when he took command due to Perry's poor health. His rise had been meteoric, having enlisted as a private two years earlier. Only twenty-five years of age, Lang, other than his education, possessed no significant military experience before the war. Now, he was in charge of a brigade in Lee's mighty army.²⁰⁶

Anderson's final brigade contained a group of regiments from the Old Dominion. The 6th, 12th, 16th, 41st and 61st Virginia regiments were under the leadership of the experienced brigade commander William "Little Billy" Mahone. Mahone owed his moniker to his small stature and most believed he weighed no more than 125 pounds. No one seemed to know how tall he was. Some believed he was no taller than five feet while others thought him as much as six inches taller. Most however, agreed with Mahone's service record, which listed him at five foot one. His inability to consume anything but bland food and milk due to digestive problems surely attributed to his small frame. Combative and irritable to a fault, he was not one to put up with any shenanigans and his temper brought on cussing fits which rivaled anyone in the army.

Born in Virginia's Southampton County on the first day of December, 1826, Mahone, the son of a tavern owner, probably picked up most of his colorful language from his father or tavern goers. After attending Littletown Academy, he enrolled in the Virginia Military Institute but lacked the formal education to excel. Only by hard work was he allowed to graduate, doing so in 1847. Afterward, he procured a teaching job at the Rappahannock Military Academy which he held until 1851. He next went to work as the chief engineer on the Norfolk and Petersburg Railroad. Once again, hard work bore fruit and Mahone rose to president of the line.²⁰⁷

---

[205] Krick, **Colonels**, p.231; Tagg, **Generals**, p.322; Busey, Martin, **RSLG**, p.234.

[206] Tagg, **Generals**, p.322; Krick, **Colonels**, p.231; **OR** vol.27, pt.2, p.288; Gottfried, Bradley M., **The Brigades of Gettysburg: The Union and Confederate Brigades at the Battle of Gettysburg**, p.584.

[207] Tagg, **Generals**, pp.313-314; Wakelyn, **Biographical Dictionary**, p.306; Eicher, & Eicher, **High Commands**, p.361.

When Virginia left the Union, Mahone, a staunch supporter of secession, offered his services and was appointed quartermaster general of Virginia's state troops on 4 April. Someone evidently determined Mahone was more valuable in the field than behind a desk for six days later he was appointed colonel of the 6th Virginia. With hostilities imminent, Governor Letcher, on 2 May 1861, sent Mahone and his 6th Virginia to Norfolk to seize the already smoldering Gosport Navy Yard. Shortly after supervising the construction of the defenses at Drewry's Bluff, Mahone was elevated to brigadier general. Assigned to brigade command with General Huger's Division, he participated in the fighting on the Virginia Peninsula. Enemy pressure forced Mahone to retreat from his position at Fair Oaks without orders which resulted in a confrontation with his new division commander D. H. Hill. The feisty Mahone contemplated challenging Hill to a duel, but cooler heads prevailed. After taking a bullet in the chest during Second Manassas, he missed the Maryland Campaign, but recovered in time to fight at Fredericksburg. During the Chancellorsville Campaign he once again showed his abilities when he marched from the river with General Posey. He directed his regiments well under fire and reinforced his superior's opinion of his abilities as a brigade level leader. Little Billy Mahone however, was not satisfied with being a brigade commander and had his eyes on a bigger job. Throughout the winter of 1862-63 he executed a campaign of his own to obtain a promotion to major general. While Lee believed Mahone capable, a command was not available. For now he would remained a brigadier. The irritable little Virginian would enter the Gettysburg Campaign still at the head of his brigade.[208]

On A First Name Basis with the Commanding General

Hill's final division commander was career military officer and Virginian Harry "Henry" Heth. Heth was born near Richmond in Chesterfield County on 16 December 1825. Harry's father John, served during the War of 1812 as a naval officer and was captured during the conflict. He was sent to prison in Bermuda where he summarily escaped from the island in an open boat upon the ocean. The boy's uncle, Colonel William Heth, served under General Richard Montgomery during the Revolution and fought with the general at Quebec. Harry's mother, Margaret, was a member of the Pickett clan, making Harry the cousin of then eleven-month old George. After completing his fundamental education, Harry decided not to follow his father's footsteps. He refused an appointment to the United States Naval Academy, opting to enroll in Georgetown College near Washington. It seemed Harry was destined to break with tradition and remain a civilian. However, he had a change of heart a year later when he accepted an appointment to West Point.[209]

Heth became a cadet on 1 July 1843, joining the class of 1847, a year behind his cousin George. Heth's class contained a few future Civil War notables, including Ambrose Burnside, John Gibbon and eventually, after his indiscretions during the

---

[208] *Ibid*; **OR** vol.27, pt.2, p.288; Cavanaugh, *6th Virginia Infantry*, p.111.

[209] Wakelyn, **Biographical Dictionary**, p.227; **CMH**, vol.3, part.2 p.601.

summer if 1844, Ambrose P. Hill. Like George, Harry proved to be an extremely poor student. He struggled with his studies and remained near the bottom of his class for his entire four years. In 1846, his education was almost derailed when he was accidentally stabbed in the leg with a bayonet. The wound was evidently not serious enough to keep him out of class for too long because he managed to graduate on schedule on 1 July 1847. Keeping poor academic performance in the family, he finished dead last within his class of thirty-eight cadets, matching his cousin's performance of the previous year.[210]

Brevetted a second lieutenant, Harry's low class standing required he be assigned to duty as a foot soldier. Joining the 1st Infantry, his initial service was during the war with Mexico. He fought at Matamoras and Galaxara and after the war, returned to the Jefferson Barracks near St. Louis. His next assignment at Fort Crawford was cut short by his bought with dysentery which his friend Winfield Hancock helped him through. After recovering, Heth received additional appointments to garrison duty and spent time at Fort Atkinson, Fort Kearny and Fort Laramie. During his time on the frontier, he participated in a number of encounters with renegade Indians, earning a promotion to first lieutenant on 9 June 1853. Harry's most serious injury during this period was not at the hands of an Indian but occurred when he was thrown from his horse, injuring his left arm. A promotion to captain and a transfer to the 10th Infantry were awarded to Heth on 3 March 1855. Later that year he accompanied General Harney on an expedition against the Sioux which resulted in a battle at Bluewater, which ending in a victory for Harney. In 1858, Harry's regiment was assigned to the Utah expedition which kept him busy until late 1860 when he returned to Virginia on a leave of absence. During his leave, Heth resigned his commission to join the rebellion. In addition to his normal duties during the later portion of the 1850s, he was assigned the task of developing a system of target practice for the army. The result was a small pamphlet called *A System of Target Practice*, which would become a staple for commissioned officers during the Civil War.[211]

Heth resigned his commission on 25 April, eight days after his native state departed the Union. He quickly volunteered for service with the Confederate Army. His initial duty was with the new Confederate Quartermaster's Department where he worked to bring structure and efficiency to the fledgling organization. A short time later he was commissioned major and shortly thereafter, promoted to colonel and given command of the 45th Virginia Infantry. Heth's regiment was assigned to politician turned soldier John Floyd's command. It did not take long for Harry to determine Floyd knew little about the organization and training of military personnel. To overcome Floyd's deficiencies, Heth took on additional responsibilities that should have been left to Floyd's staff. Writing in his memoirs Heth detailed his extra labors.

---

[210] Eicher, & Eicher, *High Commands*, p.361.

[211] *Ibid*; *CMH*, vol.3, part.2 p.601; Wakelyn, *Biographical Dictionary*, p.227.

"As companies reported for duty I mustered them into the service, taught them, or tried to teach them, how to make out their muster rolls, issued to them tents, knapsacks, etc. Night schools for the officers were organized, and tactics given them to study. But I found that some could not read, so schools were abandoned. When ten companies reported, a regiment was formed, and it received its number from Richmond. While this was going on, the commissary, quartermaster, ordnance and medical experts departments had to be organized. It will be readily seen that I had no time to play. I had no one to assist me."

Floyd, once again showed his ineptness later in August after he had marched his command to Carnifax Ferry where it was promptly confronted by a Federal regiment. Amazingly Floyd sought out Heth and asked the colonel what he should do. Dumfounded at such a question from a superior officer, Heth responded by telling Floyd to "[a]ttack them at daylight tomorrow." Floyd did so and routed the enemy regiment. Heth was eventually promoted to brigadier general and given his own command but his hard work and suggestions while under Floyd may have help mask the politician's inept military skills, allowing Floyd to remain in command longer than he should have.[212]

Heth took his new command to the Lewisburg area near the mouth of the Kanawha Valley and drilled it into a fine fighting unit. On 10 May 1862, near Giles Court House in western Virginia, Heth arrayed his brigade against a Federal force under future president Rutherford B. Hays, stopped it in its tracks and forced it to withdraw. Heth noted in his report that "with a determine shout, the force simultaneously charged, driving the enemy before them." The Yankees fell back beyond the town and tried to make a stand, but Heth's Rebels would have none of it and quickly drove them once again from their position. Taking refuge in the hills behind the town, the Federals made one more effort to hold off Heth's men, but once again they were driven out of their position and the Union force executed a general retreat. Eventually Heth had to withdraw his force from Lewisburg and the Federals quickly reestablished their position.[213]

On 25 June, Harry was transferred to the Department of East Tennessee where he joined the command of General Kirby Smith. He traveled to Knoxville and joined Smith prior to the general moving his command into Kentucky. Heth made his way to Lexington, where Smith was working to appease Kentucky politicians by assisting in the organization of a new state government. Heth urged Smith to move on Louisville and Cincinnati, but Smith declined citing political pressure. Heth then suggested that he be given a command and he would move in the direction of Cincinnati. This Smith thought acceptable and Heth was given a division and a brigade of cavalry. He marched his new command toward the river

---

[212] *CMH*, vol.3, part.2 p.601; Hassler, William W., Lee's Hard-Luck General, *CWTI*, vol.5, no.4, p.14.

[213] *OR* vol.12, pt.1, p.492; Hassler, Lee's Hard-Luck General, *CWTI*, vol.5, no.4, pp.14-15.

city, and by 6 September, had men in the vicinity of Covington. He positioned his 6,000 men for an assault but before he could launch the attack, he received an order from Smith countermanding the order to take the city. Smith informed Heth that once General Braxton Bragg defeated Federal General Don Carlos Buell, Cincinnati and Louisville would fall into the hands of the Rebels. There was only one problem with Smith's opinion; Bragg failed to defeat Buell and Cincinnati remained in the hands of the Federals. Heth's chance at glory had failed to materialize.[214]

One advantage Heth possessed was a high personal regard by both President Davis and General Lee. Smith was well aware of Heth's relationship with Davis and chose him to travel to Richmond to discuss with Davis the ineptitude of General Bragg. When Heth arrived in the capital, the Senate was deliberating his promotion to major general, which had been submitted on 10 October 1862. Unfortunately, the government was still stinging over the failure to capture Louisville and Heth, who was directly involved in the operation was denied his promotion. Lee, unlike the Confederate Senate, thought a bit more of Heth. "I think the interest of the service, as well as justice to individuals," Lee wrote to Jackson in February 1863, "requires the selection of the best men to fill vacant positions. It is on this principal that I applied for General Heth for one of your brigades…" Jackson responded the following day, obviously taking Lee's opinion as fact. "From what you have said respecting General Heth," Stonewall noted, "I have been desirous that he should report for duty." With Lee supporting the move, Heth soon found himself commanding a brigade of Virginians in A. P. Hill's division of Jackson's Corps.[215]

Heth's new brigade had been without a general since its previous commander had been wounded at Second Manassas. As a result, discipline among the men had suffered. Heth had two months to get the men of the 40th, 47th, 55th and 22nd Battalion Virginia Infantry in shape to fight before the Battle of Chancellorsville. His brigade marched near the rear of Jackson's flanking column and was deployed behind Jim Lane's North Carolinians preparing for Jackson's planned night attack when the general was shot. When Hill was later wounded, Heth, the senior brigadier on the field took command of Hill's Division until General Pender arrived. During the army's reorganization, Lee supported Heth for divisional command and on 24 May his promotion to major general finally came through. Lee's 30 May order reorganizing the army also assembled Heth's new division and placed him in command. The division was built from Heth's old brigade, Brigade General James Archer's, and the two brigades President Davis saw fit to release, James Johnston Pettigrew's and that of his nephew, Joseph Davis. Lee intended to have General John R. Cooke's brigade assigned to Heth's Division as well, but he was

---

[214] *CMH*, vol.3, part.2 p.602; Hassler, Lee's Hard-Luck General, *CWTI*, vol.5, no.4, pp.16-17.

[215] Hassler, Lee's Hard-Luck General, *CWTI*, vol.5, no.4, p.16; *OR* vol.25, pt.2, pp.644-645. Lee's note indicates that the rumors and opinions that he desired too place Virginians in high positions in his army may not have been entirely true. However, he was obviously to smart of an individual to place in writing any bias he may have had.

unsuccessful in convincing President Davis to release it and Heth marched north with four brigades under his command.[216]

When addressing Heth, Lee used Harry's first name, making him the only officer in the army to receive such an honor. This may have been due to Lee and Heth coming from much the same background. Heth was one of the few general in Confederate service that understood his weaknesses and yielded to the opinions of those who were strong in the areas he was not. He was extremely opinionated but also understood he was human. Understanding the frailties of his existence kept Heth from taking things too seriously. At thirty-seven years of age, he was a handsome man of average height. His chiseled chin, deep eyes and rather high cheekbones gave him a firm, distinctive look. His brown hair, which had receded slightly, was accented by a heavy mustache which somewhat concealed his mouth. It was easy to tell Heth was a military man, for he carried himself in a manner which made it apparent to all who came to know him. He would need all his military bearing and skill to lead his new division, which was the most inexperienced group of brigades in the army.[217]

Although a close friend of Lee's, Henry "Harry" Heth would prove to be an average division commander. *LOC*

The four brigades used to build Heth's Division contained regiments from five different states and a menagerie of Southern localities. The first brigade included the 800 man 26th North Carolina, by far the largest regiment in Lee's

---

[216] Hassler, Lee's Hard-Luck General, ***CWTI***, vol.5, no.4, p.17; ***OR*** vol.25, pt.1, p.791; ***OR*** vol.25, pt.2, p.840.

[217] Tagg, ***Generals***, p.340.

army. Rounding out the brigade were the 11th, 47th and 52nd North Carolina. The whole group was under the command of Brigadier General Pettigrew. While not totally green, the men of Pettigrew's Brigade had seen little of the hard fighting so common to the Army of Northern Virginia. Pettigrew, who generally went by his middle name, also hailed from North Carolina, having been born on a stately plantation in Tyrrell County on Independence Day, 1828. He was educated at the University of North Carolina, where he enrolled at the tender age of fifteen and graduated in 1847. He became an assistant professor at the Naval Observatory before traveling overseas to study law. Returning to the states, he found work as a lawyer, became a legislator and joined the militia. Present during the bombardment of Fort Sumter as colonel of the 1st South Carolina Rifles, the unit was eventually disbanded as the Confederate Army was organized. In order to get back in the war, Johnston joined the Hampton Legion but was transferred out of the famous unit after being elected colonel of the 12th Regiment North Carolina Volunteers on 11 July 1861. Eventually the 12th became the 22nd North Carolina.[218]

Pettigrew, when originally offered a promotion to brigadier general refused it on the grounds that he had no combat experience. A second offer was extended in February 1862 which Johnston accepted, evidently believing he now possessed adequate skill. Assigned a brigade, he led it at Fair Oaks, where he showed his toughness. While reconnoitering the enemy's position he was hit in the throat by a bullet. The round tore into his windpipe, travelled downward beneath his collar bone and destroyed the bones in his shoulder. The bullet also damaged an artery which nearly caused him to bleed to death. As if the bullet wound was not enough, while he lay unconscious he was hit in the left arm by another bullet and for some reason, bayoneted in the right leg. Left for dead, he was subsequently captured and regained consciousness as a prisoner of war. Eventually exchanged, he recovered from the horrific wounds and saw duty in Virginia and North Carolina, participating with his brigade in D. H. Hill's attempt to capture New Bren. When the brigade shuffling between Hill, Lee and Davis concluded, Pettigrew marched his men north to join Heth's command. Theoretical to a fault, he was a good commander, prompting one acquaintance to note "Pettigrew seemed to have every attribute of a great soldier." As the campaign unfolded, those who knew him were well aware that his courage would not need to be proven and his men understood and idolized him.[219]

The other brigade Davis sent north to bolster Lee's numbers was under the command of his nephew Joseph Robert Davis. Born on 12 January 1825 in Woodville, Mississippi, Davis went to school in Nashville, Tennessee before furthering his education by studying law at Miami University in Ohio. After completing his education, Joe began a law practice, which he quickly turned into a large and successful business. He also did some farming, and prior to the war, was elected to the Mississippi Senate in 1860, where he served as a secessionist Democrat. When war came, Joe joined the Confederate Army and become a

---

[218] Busey, Martin, **RSLG**, p.222; Tagg, **Generals**, pp.343-344; Sturkey, O. Lee, **Hampton Legion Infantry CSA**, pp.212, 636; Jordon, Weymouth T., **NCT** vol.VII, p.1

[219] Tagg, **Generals**, p.344; Sturkey, **Hampton Legion**, pp.212, 636; **OR** vol.18, pt.2, p.192.

captain in a company from Madison City. A short time later he was commissioned a lieutenant colonel in the 10th Mississippi Infantry. By the end of the war's first summer Davis was a colonel, working on his uncles staff in Richmond. He spent a year there, doing the government's bidding until he was nominated to receive a brigadier generalship. The recommendation was originally rejected on a vote of eleven to six. President Davis however, intervened, promising future political string-pulling if the Senators would reconsider. Two days later, Joe Davis was awarded his brigadier's star amidst charges of favoritism. There is no doubt that if not for his famous uncle's interference, Joe would have not been promoted. Davis had no combat experience and when he was placed at the head of a brigade destined for field duty, additional outcries erupted. No one had any issues with Davis personally. He was the image of a Southern Gentleman. It was advancement to a position that many felt he was unqualified to hold which put off the militarily trained and combat tested officers. Davis had been assigned to a command in which hundreds of men would be depending on him to see them through future combat. He was simply not prepared for the responsibility.[220]

Davis' Brigade, made up of the 2nd, 11th and 42nd Mississippi and the 55th North Carolina, like its commander, was handicapped by inexperience. While the 2nd and 11th Mississippi had seen their share of action, the 55th North Carolina had been lightly tested while the 42nd Mississippi had never been shot at in battle.[221]

Heth's brigade of Virginians was commanded by a farmer who also hailed from the Old Dominion, John Mercer Brockenbrough. Brockenbrough was born in Richmond County on 1 August 1830. He received his higher education at the Virginia Military Institute, from which he graduated in 1850. He married his cousin Austine in 1856, an event which was not that uncommon in nineteenth century America. Five years later he signed up to do his duty for the Confederacy and probably due to his education at VMI was elected colonel of the 40th Virginia on 25 May 1861. He led the regiment during the Peninsular Campaign and The Seven Days fighting, losing half his men in the latter engagements. During the fight at Second Manassas, after his immediate commander was wounded, Brockenbrough took over the brigade, and led it at Chantilly where it had the unfortunate experience of being driven from the field. Brockenbrough retained command of the brigade through the Maryland Campaign where his men help capture Harpers Ferry. After securing the town, they marched with Hill to save Lee's right at Sharpsburg but were not engaged. In December at Fredericksburg, Brockenbrough handled the brigade poorly at a critical point in the battle. Lee never considered him worthy of promotion to brigade command and prior to Chancellorsville assigned the brigade to outsider Harry Heth. Afterward, Brockenbrough returned to command the 40th; but was forced back to command of the brigade when Heth was elevated to divisional command. By 3 June, Brockenbrough was still a colonel as his

---

[220] Faust, *Encyclopedia*, p.209; Wakelyn, *Biographical Dictionary*, p.163; Martin, David G., *Gettysburg July 1*, pp.61-62; Eicher, & Eicher, *High Commands*, p.203.

[221] Martin, *July 1*, p.61; Winschel, Terrence J., Heavy was Their Loss: Joe Davis' Brigade at Gettysburg, *GM*, no.2, p.6-8.

Virginians from the 40th 47th, 55th and the 22nd Battalion patrolled the banks of the river covering Ewell and Longstreet's departure.[222]

Heth's final brigade, a group of Tennesseans and Alabamans, was under the command of Brigadier General James Jay Archer. Assigned to Archer were the 13th Alabama, the 5th Alabama Battalion, and the men of the 1st, 7th and 14th Tennessee. A Marylander born at Bel Air on 19 December 1817, Archer was a graduate of Princeton University, where he acquired the somewhat strange nickname "Sally." Some have asserted the name was coined due to Archer's slight build and smooth complexion. Others have implied that it was due to homosexual tendencies. The fact that he was unmarried and was not relaxed in the presence of single women was proof enough for some. Whatever the case, Archer managed to complete his schooling at Princeton before moving on to study law at the University of Maryland. After leaving school, he opened a law office and was practicing the profession when the Mexican War began [223]

Archer signed up for service and was made a captain of volunteers. He was brevetted for gallantry at Chapultepec and was never wounded in combat. However, he did not escape Mexico without being injured fighting a duel with a fellow officer. Archer's second during the duel was another young officer destined for greatness during the rebellion, Thomas J. Jackson. When the war ended, Archer returned home and to his profession as a lawyer. He either missed the army or became bored with his practice because in 1855 he once again joined the service. In early 1861 he was stationed in the Washington Territory as the first wave of secession swept over the South. Resigning in March 1861, Archer traveled overland instead of by ship and across Panama. After reaching Richmond, on 2 October he was placed in command of a number of Texas companies that had traveled to the capital to offer their services and had been organized into the 5th Texas Infantry.

Archer was not embraced by the Texans who thought him overbearing and tyrannical. Eventually he was removed from the regiment and given command of a group of Tennesseans who formed the same opinion of him. They considered him a strutting martinet and a poor communicator. When he did communicate, he lacked eloquence and persuasiveness. He was not passive and spoke his mind to both subordinate and superior. When agitated, his fierce temper showed itself and his men grew to detest him. However, no one questioned Archer's capabilities and courage as a leader of men in battle. As time progressed, he would gain the trust and admiration of the common soldier by his deeds and actions.

Assigned to A. P. Hill's famous Light Division, Archer lead his brigade during the Peninsular Campaign, guiding them to within a few paces of the Union lines at Mechanicsville before heavy enemy fire forced them to retire. As part of Jackson's corps at Cedar Mountain and Second Manassas, Archer led his men during some of the heaviest fighting. Although he was not injured, his horse was shot out from under him at the latter engagement. At Harpers Ferry in September, he became too

---

[222] Krick, Robert, E. L., *40th Virginia Infantry*, p.74; Tagg, Larry, *Generals*, p.347; *OR* vol.27, pt.2, p.289; Krick, *Colonels*, p.66.

[223] Tagg, *Generals*, p.349; *OR* vol.27, pt.2, p.289.

ill to accompany his brigade and traveled to the battle raging at Sharpsburg in an ambulance. Arriving on the southern part of the field, Archer pulled himself from the ambulance, struggle aboard his horse, which he could hardly remain upright on, and lead his brigade in a charge which checked the advancing Yankees.

Once again at Fredericksburg, Archer rose from his sickbed to lead his men in a counter attack which checked George Meade's breakthrough on the southern end of the Confederate line. While mounted and with the battle raging around him, Archer cut and hacked at enemy soldiers with his sword. Suddenly a Yankee reached up and grasped the general's horse by the bridle and a wild struggle ensued for control of the steed. Extricating his horse, Archer continued to fight to keep the enemy from exploiting the gap in Jackson's line, even after Yankees had flanked his position and gotten into his rear. General Early praised the effort in his report stating Archer was "due the credit of having held the enemy in check, with a small portion of his men, after his flank and rear had been gained, until reinforcements arrived…" Archer missed Jackson's flank attack at Chancellorsville because his brigade was at the end of the flanking column. He nonetheless provided great assistance by confronting Dan Sickles' attack on the rear of Jackson's marching legions.[224]

By 3 June, Archer boys would find themselves under a new division commander in Henry Heth. Archer, along with the rest of Hill's Corps, through the first two weeks of June would be entrusted with doing everything possible to keep "Fighting" Joe Hooker interested in what was going on across the river at Fredericksburg, while Lee shifted Longstreet and Ewell to Culpeper. Although Lee made every effort to deceive Hooker as two thirds of his army headed upriver, Hooker knew, almost immediately that something was amiss south of the waterway. The Union commander would spend the next few days working to piece together the puzzle. There was little doubt in the Union camps that the Rebels were on the move, but to where?

The Pieces are Set

When Ewell and his staff arrived at Culpeper, they trotted through town. Traveling a mile and a half northwest on the Rixeyville Road, they made their headquarters camp near the deserted home of a person Hotchkiss called "Mr. Cooper." After establishing their encampment, Ewell and his staff settled down and spent the rest of the day tending to the business of war or simply relaxing the day away during another fine Virginia early summer afternoon.

The following day, Ewell put Hotchkiss to work on a map which extended through Chester Gap in the Blue Ridge toward the town of Front Royal, informing the cartographer that they would soon be moving in that direction. Hotchkiss worked until around noon then ventured into Culpeper to obtain information regarding the roads in the area. Excitement was in the air. Hotchkiss noted that "[o]ur wagons were busy until late at night loading up commissary stores. We expect to start early tomorrow," he predicted.[225]

---

[224]   *Ibid*, p.349; **OR** vol.21, p.667; Eicher, & Eicher, **High Commands**, p.107.

[225]   Hotchkiss, **Make Me a Map**, p.149.

By the evening of 8 June, all three Second Corps divisions had marched through Culpeper and camped north or northwest of town, placing them in position to lead Lee's advance onto the Valley. Rodes' Division had bivouacked a couple miles beyond Ewell's headquarters northwest of town along the road to Rixeyville. Having been informed that the summer campaign was indeed underway and that a long march was ahead, Rodes took steps to prepare his men for the long march. He ordered all the baggage and tents which were not essential sent to the rear. The space freed up in the wagons by the removal of the equipment was used to store three days rations. The division's commissary trains also carried three days rations. With each man toting three days of food as well, Rodes could remain on the march for nine days before he would have to find additional sustenance for his division.[226]

Johnson and Early had camped south of town on 7 June. The following morning both marched through Culpeper and turned northwest. They headed out of town on the Sperryville Road which led directly toward the Valley. Johnson established his camp some six to eight miles from Culpeper, while Early marched out a distance of four miles and camped in back of Johnson. According to Hotchkiss, Lee gave Ewell the option of continuing his march north on the ninth, but Ewell chose to wait a day, giving his men a good rest. The men intended to put the extra day to good use, cooking rations and taking care of other personal issues. Unfortunately their relaxing afternoon would be interrupted by the sounds of battle to the south east as Stuart's Cavalry grappled with Federal horsemen near Brandy Station.[227]

Longstreet's two available divisions, McLaws and Hood, did not pass through town. Both divisions camped to the south and southeast of Culpeper. Longstreet established his headquarters to the southwest of town. Pickett and his delayed division would arrive in a couple of days.

Hill's new corps remained along the Rappahannock before Fredericksburg. He would linger in position for almost a week while the remainder of Lee's army conducted the initial phase of the invasion. Hill's men would, for the most part, spend the time preparing for the upcoming march, relaxing and executing the typical activities of an army in camp.

Once Longstreet and Ewell were on their way to Culpeper, Lee packed up his headquarters at Hamilton's Crossing and began his own journey to rendezvous with his army. Delaying his departure was the necessity of satisfying himself that the Federal incursion across the river at Deep Run was only a feint. Around midday on 6 June Lee left the vicinity of Fredericksburg, camping along the roadside that evening. The following day he joined Longstreet and Ewell at Culpeper. He set up his headquarters three-quarters of a mile east of Culpeper at East View.[228]

Like so many previous battles, the coming contests would provide the boys of '63 and their regiment and brigade commanders the opportunity for fame

---

[226] *OR* vol.27, pt.2, p.546.

[227] Hotchkiss, **Make Me a Map**, p.149; Pfanz, *A Soldier's Life*, p.281; Murphy, *10th Virginia Infantry*, p.72.

[228] *OR* vol.27, pt.2, p.347; Thomas, **Lee**, p.290; Nye, **Rebels**, p.45.

and glory. If all went as expected the Southern States would gain independence from their hated Northern antagonists and the criminal Lincoln Administration. Unfortunately, many of those young, smiling, confident Rebel faces patrolling the river's edge and setting up camp near Culpeper Courthouse during those early days of June would not return. Instead they would be left upon the clay of southern Pennsylvania. Many of them would be interned under it with the wind whipped grass and their fallen comrades their only company.

Chapter IX

Hooker Hunts for Lee

> "The movements of the enemy in our front do not indicate what their purpose or objective may be."[1]
> *Joseph Hooker to General Halleck.*
> *4 June 1863.*

Joe Hooker stole two marches on Robert E. Lee during the campaign resulting in the battle at Chancellorsville. The first put his army in position to defeat Lee. The second took place on the evening of 5 May and extracted his army from a strong position they had established a mile north of the intersection. Lee intended to attack Hooker's position the following morning but "Fighting" Joe had lost his desire to be accommodating. That evening he received a message from Hooker requesting that the Federals be permitted to send forth "a burial party." Lee quickly determined the request was an effort to stall for time. He summarily declined the request and moved forward with his plan to attack at daybreak. "Preparations were made to assail the enemy's works at daylight on the 6th," Lee wrote in his report, "but, on advancing our skirmishers, it was found that under cover of the storm and darkness of the night he had retreated over the river." In reality, Hooker did Lee a favor by withdrawing. An attack against the Federals would have inflated Lee's already heavy casualties, robbing the Confederacy of more assets. With Meade's Fifth Corps acting as rear guard, Hooker pulled his army back, leaving the field and the victory to Lee. A week later the men of the Army of the Potomac were back in their camps along the Rappahannock. The previous two weeks had gained them nothing but a reduction in the size of their fighting force, depression and confirmation of their inability to defeat Bobby Lee.[2]

When the telegram bearing the news of the Chancellorsville defeat filtered to Washington, newsman Noah Brooks saw firsthand its effect on the president. He would never forget the "picture of despair" on Lincoln's face. According to Brooks, his appearance, "usually sallow, was ashen in hue," which he noticed matched the "French gray," of the wallpaper. Lincoln handed the telegram to Brooks, instructing him to read it out loud which the newsman did. As he read the dispatch

---

[1] *OR* vol.27, pt.1, p.29.

[2] *OR* vol.25, pt.1, pp.508, 802; pt.2, p.432.

from Butterfield, Brooks thought Lincoln looked "to be so broken, so dispirited, and so ghostlike." With his hands entwined behind his back the president paced back and forth across the floor uttering "My God! My God! What will the country say!" Shortly thereafter, Lincoln left the office. Later, Brooks noticed a carriage pull up to the entrance to the White House. He watched as the president exited the residence and stepped into the carriage. The newsman noticed Halleck was already aboard. Inquiring as to the duo's destination, the Brooks was informed they were on their way to army headquarters.

Once it became known Lincoln was on his way to Falmouth, rumors began to fly. Some thought Hooker would be arrested while others believed Halleck would be put in command. Other, more unrealistic charges were leveled, including a story that Lee had destroyed Hooker and was at that moment marching toward Washington. Others had McClellan returning to take command for a third time. Generals who had been put out to pasture were rumored to be returning to take the fight to Lee. At the Willard Hotel, the crowd was so large it was difficult to enter the building. McClellan supporters were out in force, all with smiles and good spirits for their lamented champion.[3]

When Lincoln and Halleck arrived, they sat down with Hooker and received an update on the situation. The two bureaucrats had lunch and spent roughly two hours discussing the current state of the army. No conversations encompassing the disaster at Chancellorsville were conducted. Lincoln sought no opinions from any corps commanders and the president made it a point not to blame anyone for the setback. Keeping his opinions to himself was critical for he was well aware his judgment could spark additional dissension within the command structure. He believed that the effects of the defeat would be wide ranging and felt not only across the North and South but abroad as well.[4]

The purpose for the trip was to personally review and evaluate the condition of the army. George Meade agreed with the president and felt that once the true nature of the disaster was understood it would be difficult to maintain the morale of the army. Meade had opposed withdrawing, and he tried to convince Hooker to allow his command to enter the fray. Hooker would have none of it and pulled his army back across the river. Meade noted that he was chastised for ignoring orders and sending a brigade of Humphrey's Division into the fight. "General Hooker," Meade wrote to his wife, "has disappointed all his friends by failing to show his fighting qualities in the pinch." It was almost as if Hooker had taken on the McClellan mystique, so concerned with losing that he would not risk winning. "He was more cautious and took to digging quicker than even McClellan," Meade added. "[A] man may talk very big when he has no responsibility, but that it is quite a different thing, acting when you are responsible and talking when others are."[5]

---

[3] Hebert, *Hooker*, p.226; Brooks, *Washington*, pp.61-62.

[4] Meade, *Meade*, vol.1, p.372.

[5] *Ibid.*

After hearing Hooker's status report, Halleck informed the general no additional troops were available from Washington to bolster his army. Hooker was quick to inform his visitors he did not need any. Even with his losses at Chancellorsville and the departure of nine month and two year troops, he still had 100,000 men to confront the Rebels. Although he consistently inflated Lee's numbers, Hooker believed this would be plenty to deal with Lee, and his comments were evidently acceptable to Halleck and Lincoln. Halleck then offered additional troops from Major General John A. Dix's command who, at the current time, was responsible for the Department of Virginia at Fort Monroe. Prior to Chancellorsville the same offer had been made, and Hooker declined the assistance. Halleck proposed to move a portion of General Dix's force to any location Hooker thought would do him the most good. Hooker, once again, turn down the proposal. At the time he obviously felt that he did not need any additional assistance in dealing with Lee's victorious legions.[6]

As evening approached, Lincoln departed for Washington but instructed Halleck to stay behind and learn "everything." Halleck proceeded to discuss the past battle with Hooker's generals and staff officers. When he finally returned to the capital, he reported that the whole affair was inexcusable and concluded that Hooker was not fit to lead the army into another major battle. Hooker, for his part, offered his resignation in a letter hand carried by Halleck back to the president, but would only resign if he was allowed to return to his old command. Lincoln declined to accommodate him. "Fighting Joe" would retain his position even though almost everyone associated with the army had lost confidence in him.[7]

As his army returned to picket and camp duties, Hooker began to change his tune about the size of his army and his need for additional men. On 13 May, writing to Lincoln, he complained about his numbers being diminished by the departure of the two year and nine month regiments. Some intelligence reports had placed Longstreet's two missing divisions in Richmond while others indicated the divisions of Hood and Pickett had already rejoined Lee. According to Hooker, Longstreet's return would render his army at a disadvantage in overall numerical strength. He believed his effective numbers, which he now determined were closer to 80,000, would be less than the combined strength of Lee and Longstreet, and requested Lincoln make another 25,000 men available to him. Hooker should have been able to deduce, as the season for active campaigning arrived, that Longstreet would be returning to join Lee. His earlier comments to Halleck and Lincoln refusing reinforcements indicate his lack of understanding that Lee, with the loss of Jackson, required Longstreet's presence more than ever. Hooker's reversal on the necessity for reinforcements did nothing to endear him to Lincoln, not to mention Halleck.

Another self-inflicted wound Hooker gave himself was the systematic alienation of his subordinates. One particular instance was his disagreement with General Meade. Instead of extracting the army, Meade favored a general attack.

---

[6] *OR* vol.25, pt.2, pp.505-506; Faust, ***Encyclopedia***, p.222.

[7] Benjamin, Hooker's Appointment and Removal, ***B&L***, vol.III, p.241.

"I opposed the withdrawal with all my influence," Meade wrote his wife, "and I tried all I could... to be permitted to take my corps into action and to have a general battle with the whole army engaged, but I was overruled..." A few days later Hooker confronted Meade about the decision to retreat and displayed a logic which could only be described as bizarre. Hooker argued that Meade had "expressed the opinion that it was impractical to withdraw" and as such the Fifth Corps commander favored an advance. Hooker then said that since he knew it was "perfectly practicable to withdraw" he did not consider Meade's opinion of executing an advance as being in favor of an attack. Meade's head must have been spinning as he tried to defend his earlier conversation. Hooker's effort at mincing words can only be described as a creative attempt to lay blame for the withdrawal at the feet of others. Meade was justifiably irritated. "The fact is," he wrote in a second letter to Margaret, "he now finds he has committed a grave error, which at the time he was prepared to assume the responsibility of, but now desires to cast it off on to the shoulders of others..." The two men would retain a frosty relationship for the rest of the war.[8]

Colonel Sharpe Examines the Countryside

Hooker's request for additional men is easy to understand but difficult to justify since no Confederate strength numbers had been made available by BMI head Colonel Sharpe since fighting ended at Chancellorsville. Additionally, it had been a number of days since Sharpe's last report on Longstreet's whereabouts. Hooker either had additional information from another source, he was estimating Lee's strength, making a guess or possibly coming up with a number which he felt would prompt Lincoln to send forward more men.[9]

Sharpe employed three men who would have a significant effect on the quantity and accuracy of BMI information. One, who would spend the majority of May and early June working for John McEntee, was George S. Smith. Smith was a transplanted New Englander who had moved to Culpeper ten years earlier. The 1860 census of Culpeper County recorded Smith as owning the sum of $4,500, one slave and noted his occupation as a "gentleman." His political beliefs kept him loyal to the Union, but he had mixed sentiments regarding the Federal army. He had risked his life to provide information, being repaid for his efforts with the destruction of his personal property. In 1862 General John Pope's Army of Virginia had destroyed seventy-five acres of corn and confiscated one hundred and fifty tons of hay to feed their horses. Smith determined that he had suffered nearly twenty thousand dollars in damages but had received one hundred and fifty dollars in payment and some worthless receipts for the hay. McEntee had expressed concern

---

[8] Meade, *Meade*, pp.372, 377.

[9] *OR* vol.25, pt.2, p.477; Fishel, *Secret War*, p.414. On 13 May a deserter from the 3rd Alabama reported that the divisions of Pickett and Hood had "arrived." What was meant by arrived is not noted in the communications.

over Smith's loyalties but noted that "he [Smith] knows they [Rebels] are wrong and will do all in his power to thwart their purpose."[10]

General Pope evidently did not trust much, if any, of Smith's intelligence when the spy was working for his topographic engineers during the Second Bull Run campaign. Correspondence during the period does not imply a detailed knowledge of Lee's position and numbers even though Smith stated later he provided such information. According to Smith, he "passed through the whole rebel Army while they were in Culpepper [sic] Co... and told Pope what troops Lee had, and all about them." Pope placed no trust in Smith information. "I am told [he] is a damned rascal," Pope noted. "When you are done getting information from him, hand him over to the provost marshal." Pope, summarily defeated by Lee, was relieved and shipped off to the Department of the Northwest to spend the rest of the war in obscurity, leaving Smith free to continue his intelligence gathering efforts.[11]

When not with the army, Smith spent the majority of his time in Washington where he became acquainted with W. D. Wallach. Wallach was another transplanted Culpeper resident whose family included the mayor of the capital. The mayor was also the editor of the *Washington Star*, and Smith, when in the city sometimes received mail through the care of the paper. Provost Marshal Patrick and Colonel Sharpe, aware of Pope's concern over Smith, were evidently not ready to trust the man from Culpeper with Union sentiments. During the spring of 1863, after returning from Washington, Smith was assigned to work with the Cavalry Division of General Alfred Pleasanton. He would earn the sum of $5 a day; however, it would be a couple of months before Smith would earn Sharpe's confidence.[12]

Another man which Sharpe would rely on for information was John Howard Skinker. Skinker, another loyal Union man from Virginia had spent the early part of the war risking his own life, for no pay, spying for the Federals. By occupation he was a planter who owned slaves. He lived in the Fredericksburg area, just across the river in Stafford County and had developed a network of friends for infiltrating areas where he could not go himself. During some of the army's more active periods in Virginia, Skinker was just as active, providing reports that came in almost daily. His reputation for providing good intelligence while disregarding his own welfare was well known among the Northern high command. General Reynolds called him "the truest, boldest and most deserving Union man I have ever known..." Reynolds believed Skinker had proven he valued the Constitution more than even his own physical property.

In September of 1862, after Lee had driven the Federals away from Richmond and routed Pope back to Washington, Skinker was forced to take refuge in the capital. While there he received a sum of money for services rendered. Many of the generals milling about the city had benefited from Skinker's information and attested to his service. In November the War Department wrote the spy a check for

---

[10] Ryan, A Battle of Wits, *GM*, Issue 29, p.19; Fishel, **Secret War**, p.195.

[11] Fishel, **Secret War**, p.195.

[12] *Ibid*, pp.195 n.50, 292-294.

the sum of $1,107 for his service and expenses. The testimonials were a feather in Skinker's cap and pointed to the value of his information and the trust he had managed to build with the Army of the Potomac.

After the battle of Antietam, Lee returned to Virginia but Skinker did not. Possible concern over knowledge of his behavior may have prompted Skinker to decide it was time to take a sabbatical from his spying efforts. Confederate activity had picked up in the region, and Skinker was probably correct in taking a little time for things to quiet down. By March, either the threat of detection had slackened or Skinker simply became restless because he appeared at army headquarters ready to risk his life and property once more to save the Union.[13]

The last of the three spies Sharpe would rely on heavily was Ernest Yager. Yager had been in the espionage business since March 1862 and spent most of his early months in the Manassas area working for local commanders. He was a transplanted German who had difficulty writing the English language and spoke with a heavy German accent. He still wrote his name as *Jager*, which caused a great deal of confusion at headquarters and in the telegraph office. Yager did not help his situation by signing his name with an X on a number of occasions. To make matters worse, when others addressed him they called him Van Van which was a nickname not an alias.

On 7 February 1863, Yager arrived at army headquarters with a letter from General Samuel P. Heintzelman. The general, responding to a request from Butterfield to send forward from Washington his best scout and spy, had decided Yager was the man. "I can find a number of persons who will undertake the service you name, but few of them are worthy of confidence," Heintzelman told Butterfield.

Yager wasted little time getting to work. He left the army ten days later on an expedition, working his way to Culpeper along the Orange and Alexandria Railroad. After determining that Fitz Lee's horsemen had replaced General Wade Hampton's on the Confederate picket line, Yager was ready to return when another opportunity presented itself. Through an acquaintance he discovered a man and his wife had been issued a pass to travel to Philadelphia. The pass had been made out to include a second man who was not present within the party. Yager made arrangements to travel with the two and as they made their way north, he skillfully questioned them regarding any information they may have on the position and strength of the Confederate forces in the area. The two travelers informed Yager they had seen Longstreet's Corps passing through Richmond and that a body of 20,000 men under Jackson had been along the road. Leaving the man and his wife at Fairfax, Yager returned on 24 February and reported his findings. In many instances his information was incorrect, but the episode displayed Yager's desire and ability to gather information.[14]

On 14 May Sharpe received a report which put to rest the location of Longstreet. A few days earlier, he instructed Yager to travel to Culpeper and determine if Lee

---

[13] *Ibid*, pp.260, 292, n.82.

[14] *Ibid*, pp.292, 303-304.

had received reinforcements and what the position of the Confederate cavalry was. The day after Hooker complained to Lincoln about his lack of numbers, Yager determined "Longstreet's forces are guarding the Rapidan." He also reported that Longstreet would not be returning to Fredericksburg, the rumor being that his command would, in a few days, be moving toward Culpeper. To Sharpe this was telling information. Lee was not using his returning First Corps troops to bolstering the defenses at Fredericksburg. He was shifting a large portion of it to the northwest, posing a threat to Hooker's right. While Yager's data was in some instances erroneous, it did provide Sharpe with a glimpse of Lee's intention.[15]

As the month of May wore on, additional information began filtering in which provided Sharpe a clearer picture. All the signs indicated the Confederates were planning a general movement. It was a Rebel deserter however, who provided confirmation regarding Lee's intention to put his men on the road for a long strenuous march. On 21 May, a Confederate soldier, S. B. Flandreau, entered Federal lines and was quickly whisked away and questioned by BMI interrogators. Flandreau talked freely of attending a review a few days earlier in which an order was read that instructed the men to discard as much of their personal baggage as possible. This was a sure sign that Lee's army was about to move hard and fast. Initially Sharpe was leery of Flandreau's information, thinking the man could be a plant and that the evidence was designed to deceive. Additional evidence subsequently arrived which corroborated Flandreau's story and alleviated Sharpe's concerns. There was really no doubt remaining. Lee was planning a move, but the details still eluded Sharpe.

While Lee read Northern newspapers to gather intelligence, Sharpe's organization did likewise, using Southern publications for the same purpose. The *Richmond Examiner* provided Sharpe with additional information, which reinforced his belief that the Southerners were about to execute a general movement. "Within the next fortnight the campaign of 1863 will be pretty well decided," the *Examiner* brazenly projected. "The most important movement of the war will probably be made in that time." Sharpe thought the information, even though it came from a newspaper, was worthy of a communication to Assistant Adjutant General Seth Williams and General Butterfield.[16]

While Sharpe and his men did their best to determine the size, location and intention of Lee and his army, Hooker did what he could to discover the same information. On 25 May he sent a message to General Dix asking if enemy troops had been transferred from South Carolina to Richmond. Dix responded the same day noting Longstreet was in Richmond but his final destination was unknown. Dix' information was obviously old since Yager had earlier placed Longstreet on the Rapidan.[17]

---

[15]   Fishel, *Secret War*, pp.414-415; *OR* vol.25, pt.2, p.479.

[16]   Fishel, *Secret War*, pp.416, 673,n.13, 14.

[17]   *OR* 25, pt.2, p.523.

By 27 May, Sharpe was confident enough in the information he had gathered to develop a written report for submittal to army headquarters. The final document contained nine individual items and in most instances was quite accurate.

> PROVOST-MARSHAL-GENERAL'S OFFICE,
> ARMY OF THE POTOMAC,
> May 27, 1863.
>
> Brig. Gen. S. Williams, Assistant Adjutant General:
>
> Sir: By direction of the general commanding, I furnish the following memoranda of the positions of the enemy and other data obtained within the last few days:
>
> 1. The enemy's line in front of us is much more contracted than during the winter. It extends from Bank's Ford, on a line parallel with the river, to near Moss Neck. Anderson's division is on their left. McLaws' is next, and in rear of Fredericksburg. Early is massed about Hamilton Crossing, and Trimble's is directly in the rear of Early. Rodes' (D. H. Hill's old division) is further to the right, and back from the river, and A. P. Hill is the right of their line, resting nearly on Moss Neck. Each of these six divisions have five brigades.
> 2. Pickett's division, of six brigades, has come up from Suffolk, and is at Taylorsville, near Hanover Junction.
> 3. Hood's division, of four brigades, has also left from the front of Suffolk, and is between Louisa Court-House and Gordonsville.
> 4. Ten days ago there was in Richmond only the City Battalion, 2,700 strong, commanded by General Elzey.
> 5. There are three brigades of cavalry 3 miles from Culpeper Court House, toward Kelly's Ford. They can at present turn out only 4,700 men for duty, but have many dismounted men, and the horses are being constantly and rapidly recruited by the spring growth of grass. These are Fitz. Lee's, William H. Fitzhugh Lee's and Wade Hampton's brigades.
> 6. General Jones is still in the valley, near New Market, with about 1,400 cavalry and twelve pieces of light artillery.
> 7. Mosby is above Warrenton, with 200 men.
> 8. The Confederate army is under marching orders, and an order from General Lee was very lately read to the troops, announcing a campaign of long marches and hard fighting, in a part of the country where they would have no railroad transportation.
> 9. All the deserters say that the idea is very prevalent in the ranks that they are about to move forward upon or above our right flank.
>
> GEO. H. SHARPE,
> Colonel.[18]

---

[18] *OR* vol.25, pt.2, p.528.

Sharpe's surprisingly accurate write-up was a testament to the effectiveness of his organization. Other than the number of brigades with Pickett at Hanover, and that Trimble's division was now under the command of Edward Johnson the data was as accurate as could be expected. The critical elements of the document were the eighth and ninth items which defined the exact intentions of the Rebels. Sharpe's efforts had correctly predicted the intent of the Confederate army six days before the enemy began to extricate itself from the Rappahannock line. Sharpe and his spies had done their job. It was now up to Hooker to put the information to use.[19]

Hooker evidently did not understand the significance of Sharpe's conclusions, did not trust them or he simply assumed that Washington had come to the same revelations, for he chose not to forward the information by telegraph, opting instead to send a written copy of the document from army headquarters. It would be 8 June before the copy arrived in Washington. By that time the entire situation around Fredericksburg and Culpeper had change significantly and Sharpe's information was old and of little use to Washington, supplanted by fresher intelligence.[20]

Hooker informed Stanton that the information in the report was gleaned from Rebel deserters, but in reality it came from a number of sources. Many of Sharpe's spies had provided the information contained in the document. Data was also supplied by Signal Corps lookouts and observation balloons. The BMI was using all the resources at hand to provide as accurate information as possible, which is what Hooker intended even though he did not give credit to the men working for Sharpe.[21]

With his report made, Sharpe, on 29 May, set about trying to determine when the Rebels were going to move and exactly where they were headed. His wording "forward upon or above our right flank" could mean any number of destinations to the north or northwest. After hearing of Lee's intended move, Hooker sent additional cavalry twenty-five miles northwest of Fredericksburg near Bealeton to watch the fords on the Rappahannock and keep an eye out for the enemy. On orders to take advantage of the security offered by mounted troopers, Sharpe sent Captain McEntee along with five other scouts to the area. The spies were charged with attempting to discover Lee's position and intentions. Once settled in, McEntee sent two of his men downriver with orders to effect a crossing and determine if the intelligence regarding Confederate cavalry at Culpeper was accurate. He also sent two men upriver with the same instructions.[22]

Sharpe's Little Band of Scouts

Sharpe spent the spring of 1863 assembling an intricate group of scouts to probe the local area. Their task was to gather additional information regarding

---

[19] *Ibid*, p.787.

[20] *Ibid*, p.528.

[21] Fishel, ***Secret War***, pp.417-418.

[22] *Ibid*, pp.421-423; Ryan, A Battle of Wits, ***GM***, Issue 29, pp.16-17; ***OR*** vol.25, pt.2, p.518. The cavalry was the command under Colonel Alfred Duffié.

Lee's intentions and strength. Joining Skinker, Yager and Smith were three men who had originally signed the muster rolls of Company H, 1st Ohio Light Artillery. How these three men came to Sharpe is a bit of a mystery. It is possible that two of them wrote directly to Secretary of War Stanton requesting the duty assignment. Another possibility was that Sharpe, through a fellow classmate at Yale, was made aware of the three prospective scouts. Around mid-April, 1863, a member of Company H noted that three men had been detailed for scout work. They had been instructed to report to General Hooker and were to "leave the Battery in the morning." Working as a spy or scout must have been tempting for the three men for they would receive an additional $2.00 a day when they were in camp and extra compensation when they were out on scouting missions. Sharpe's new men, Privates Henry Wood Dodd, Benjamin F. McCord and Edwin P. Hopkins, would soon find themselves in the espionage business.[23]

Henry Dodd entered service for three years with Company H on 26 October 1861. The twenty-two year old private was born in Toledo, Ohio on 7 February 1839. His father, Brigadier General Ezra Squires Dodd of the Ohio Militia, died in 1845. Sometime before 1850, Dodd's mother, Sarah, relocated to Washington Township in Henry County where Henry lived with her and four brothers and sisters. He was back in Toledo by 1860 working as a clerk and was paying room and board to a local family. At five and a half feet tall, Dodd was slight of build with black hair and mustache.[24]

A group of Army of the Potomac scouts. Henry Dodd stands third from the left leaning on the chair back. *LOC*

---

[23] Browne, Edward C., Col. George H. Sharpe's "Soda Water" Scouts, *GM*, Issue 44, pp.29-32; ***Official Roster of the Soldiers of the State of Ohio In the War of the Rebellion, 1861-1865*** (hereafter ***OIWR***), vol.10, pp.412-413.

[24] Browne, Scouts, *GM*, Issue 44, p.31; ***OIWR***, vol.10, p.412.

Hopkins, who was also known as "Edward" or "Ned," like Dodd, volunteered for three years but signed the rolls five days earlier. Also from Ohio, Edwin was born at Zanesville in 1842. At the age of nineteen, he was the youngest of Sharpe's three Company H boys. Sometime after 1850, Edwin's parents, Thomas and Mary, relocated their family to Toledo. Company H documents list Edwin as having red hair. He was five foot eight inches tall and noted upon his enlistment that he was a student.[25]

Unlike Hopkins and Dodd, Private Benjamin McCord was not a native Ohioan. He was probably born in 1841, in Erie County, Pennsylvania, in the small town of North East, along the shores of Lake Erie. McCord most likely never remembered his mother, or if he did they were simply images, since she passed away sometime during 1842. Nine years later his father died, leaving the ten-year-old Benjamin an orphan. He must have been residing in the Toledo area in 1861 since the recruitment officer who enlisted Dodd and Hopkins, also recruited McCord. He signed up for three years on 28 October, and joined Hopkins and Dodd as a member of Company H. Records indicate the twenty year old McCord was five feet eight inches tall, had brown hair and, like Hopkins, was a student.[26]

In addition to these three men from Ohio, Sharpe recruited other soldiers from various regiments and organization to fill out his group. He made arrangements to have three men from the 3rd Indiana Cavalry, Private Daniel Plew and Sergeants Daniel Cole and Milton W. Cline, transferred to the BMI. Transferred from an Ohio Infantry regiment, was Sergeant Mordecai P. Hunnicutt. Another man, Ebenezer McGee, who had been a messenger during the final days of Burnside's command also joined Sharpe's little band of scouts. Joining Smith, Yager and Skinker as civilian scouts were Jackson Harding, another survivor of the Burnside administration, and Joseph M. Humphreys, a telegraph operator.[27]

These men, along with Hopkins, Dodd and McCord and the other men of Sharpe's organization, would play a significant role during the Gettysburg Campaign. On 15 April, the three new recruits from Ohio reported to army headquarters. It was nearly three weeks before they were sent on to report to Sharpe. Why such a delay occurred is unknown. It is possible Hooker, or other officers at headquarters wished to investigate the integrity of the three before sending them on. The new scouts did not have time to loiter around camp once they were assimilated into Sharpe's organization. By late May, they were on their way to the Bealeton area with McEntee and two other scouts, Arson Carney and another man who may have been Edward A. Carney.[28]

On 30 May, McEntee sent Henry Dodd and Arson Carney downriver. They tried to cross at Field's Ford but were turned back. Undeterred, they moved on to Ellis Ford but were also unsuccessful in conducting a crossing due to heavy pickets

---

[25]   *Ibid.* Edwin's mother's name may have been May.

[26]   Browne, Scouts, *GM*, Issue 44, p.31; ***OIWR***, vol.10, p.413.

[27]   Fishel, ***Secret War***, p.292.

[28]   Browne, Scouts, *GM*, Issue 44, p.33.

on the riverbank. Carney did manage to have a chat with a Confederate picket who informed the scout that he was a member of the 6th South Carolina Infantry. A neat trick, since the 6th was part of Micah Jenkins' command, still in southwest Virginia. The two also managed to capture a Confederate scout who, while trying to escape, Carney shot and killed. The man proved to be from the 4th Virginia Cavalry, part of Fitz Lee's brigade. On 31 May the two men returned to report that they had been unable to execute a crossing of the river due to the heavy enemy pickets and cavalry guarding the fords.

The two men, who traveled upriver, Benjamin McCord and Ed Hopkins, had an easier time of it and were successful in executing a crossing. The men were able to determine from local inhabitants that Wade Hampton's cavalry was in the area and that Stuart had moved his headquarters to Culpeper. Others corroborated the information stating the main body of Stuart's cavalry was in the same vicinity. While previous information provided by a deserter from the 1st North Carolina placed the bulk of the Rebel cavalry near Culpeper, this was hard evidence that the horsemen were indeed massed there.[29]

While his men were out gathering what information they could, an incredibly useful bit of evidence fell into McEntee's hands. A week earlier a slave owned by someone in Confederate General Raleigh E. Colston's Brigade managed to escape his bondage. The man came into a Federal camp, where McEntee had an opportunity to question him. Afterword McEntee managed to recruit the former slave as a spy. The man was evidently quite good at undercover work for a week later he returned, with information indicating no Rebel infantry was north of the river. He also informed McEntee that Lee's army was under marching orders and "the general rumor was that they [the Rebels] intend to march over to the valley [Shenandoah] and visit Maryland."

As the month of June arrived, McEntee began receiving additional reports which brought clarity to the cavalry situation. These reports now placed "Grumble" Jones' cavalry at Culpeper. In addition, a refugee entering a Federal camp spoke of two additional regiments of North Carolina cavalry, the brigade of General Beverly H. Robertson, had also arrived. It became obvious to Sharpe, when he received McEntee's report, that the Rebels were "about [to send] out a very heavy cavalry expedition."

Another piece of information that placed Brigadier General Albert G. Jenkins' Confederate cavalry in the Shenandoah Valley happened into McEntee's hands a few days later, when it was brought in by a Confederate deserter. The evidence was solid and indicated that Lee's direction was most assuredly the Valley of Virginia. George Smith had also learned from a reliable source that the cavalry at Culpeper was preparing to move. Horses were being re-shod and conditioned for a long journey. Smith also reported that large amounts of supplies were arriving daily. There could be no doubt that the Confederates were about to force the issue and put all or some of their army in motion. While all indications gave the general

---

[29] *Ibid*, pp.421-423; Ryan, A Battle of Wits, ***GM***, Issue 29, pp.16-17; ***OR*** vol.25, pt.2, p.518.

direction as north by the Shenandoah Valley, little information had been attained which provided a glimpse of timing and an ultimate destination.[30]

Small pieces of information and strange reports seemed to filter in on a daily basis. One of the oddest bits to arrive was from an infantry captain in Maryland. According to the captain, while he was somewhere between Frederick and Hagerstown a young boy was arrested and brought in for questioning. The boy reported he had previously been a servant of General Hill before escaping and making his way north. Remarkably the boy reported that General Lee was planning a major movement north. He had become privy to the information while performing his camp duties. The boy had evidently heard the information from Hill's own mouth as he discussed the operation with his officers.

The boy seemed unshaken by questioning and told the same story, time after time. Lee was intending the move north by shifting his army toward Romney and into the Cumberland Valley while Stuart's horse soldiers screened the march from the Shenandoah Valley. While the boy seemed confident in his information, the route he claimed Lee was to take was questionable. Marching to Romney would take Lee's men away from critical population centers and would make it easier for the Army of the Potomac to perform its task of protecting Washington. If it seemed the route of Lee's advance was questionable, the route the boy indicated for any retreat if disaster should occur was even more remarkable. Lee's route back to Virginia, the boy insisted, would be back through West Virginia, a direction even more unlikely than the pathway north.

Even stranger was the boy himself. Escaped slaves and servants were typically treated as deserters, Most were encountered trying to pass Federal pickets, not a two weeks march away. Was the boy a plant of some kind? Was his capture intended as an effort to deceive the Federals with false information, or was he simply a spy who had been careless enough to get caught? Was it hoped that a boy, who had also been a slave, be giving the benefit of the doubt if captured? All these questions made Sharpe suspicious when he became aware of the incident. He had no choice but to file the information away. If additional facts became available to support it, he could then act on it. For now however, it was just another piece of data.[31]

Lee Disappear, Hooker Probes

During the first days of June, the picket lines along the Rappahannock became more regular, exhibiting a higher degree of alertness. Many of McEntee's scouts and spies were turned back at the river's edge, or if they managed to cross could not return. The increased attentiveness could only point to one thing; the Rebels were either on the move or preparing to set their legions in motion.[32]

---

[30] Ryan, A Battle of Wits, **GM**, Issue 29, pp.16-18. Colston was relieved and replaced by Steuart on 28 May, probably sometime after the slave escaped.

[31] Fishel, **Secret War**, p.424.

[32] Ryan, A Battle of Wits, **GM**, Issue 29, p.18.

The application of tighter and deeper picketing suddenly put a damper on McEntee and Sharpe's ability to gather intelligence. As Lee's army was preparing to shift, Skinker, on 3 June, returned with a report which offered little new information. The additional security had kept him from getting across the river, but he had managed to solicit the help of a local resident who had managed to pass through the Confederate pickets. The man however, never reappeared and Skinker returned with only what he had been able to determine from his side of the river. As luck would have it, he intercepted a cavalryman from "Grumble" Jones command who had used the movement of his brigade to Culpeper as an opportunity to visit his home. Skinker questioned the man and determined that a large cavalry raid was in the offing, confirming Smith's report. Although Sharpe's report to Hooker of 27 May provided no creditable hint of a massive Rebel cavalry raid, for some reason the notion became a point of serious concern in Washington.[33]

Signs of Confederate activity supporting a general movement continued to be abundant. On 4 June it was reported that a number of pickets had been withdrawn and that the remaining guards seemed to be closer to the river and had little or no support. Another report indicated that pickets further down the river had been withdrawn completely and not replaced. It also seemed that the picket line was now more concentrated toward Fredericksburg with the men on the line closer together. This presented a problem for the Federals who had to determine if the changing status of the picket line was a sign of movement or simply one unit replacing the other. In reality the change in status was due to the withdrawal of Ewell's Corps and McLaws' Division. Lee's effort to keep his movement toward Culpeper a secret was succeeding on some levels, but it did not go completely undetected.

Signal officers reported that six regimental camps, where fires had burned the night before, were now vacant. Intelligence from observation balloons indicated infantry and artillery units moving about behind Fredericksburg. At Bank's Ford no infantry, other than that which was guarding the ford could be seen. A few miles away at Ely's Ford a small cloud of dust, determined to be that from two regiments of infantry, was also observed. Signal officers were instructed to keep their balloons aloft and to watch for additional clouds and reflections of the sun off bayonets and gun barrels. A few days later another report indicated that a four gun artillery battery near Falmouth had disappeared and was not replace. One particular artillery column was so long it took three quarters of an hour to pass by a specific point. Pickets reported hearing the rumble of wagons during quiet nighttime hours.[34]

On 5 June, McEntee sent the newly arrived Yager on a mission to cross the Rappahannock and travel to Culpeper to find out all he could. Two days later McEntee sent Smith out with a partner, a local Negro who seemed to have knowledge of the Confederates in the area. He hoped that if Smith could not cross the river, his colleague could. The following day Yager returned with information which confirmed prior reports that Lee was headed for the Shenandoah Valley with

---

[33]   Fishel, *Secret War*, p.425.

[34]   *Ibid*, p.424.

his infantry. McEntee however, questioned Yager's report, having been informed through another source that the spy had only been across the river for a half hour even though he had been gone for three days. When Yager told him that he had managed to cross the river and had gone all the way to Brandy Station, McEntee became irritated and send Yager away, back to headquarters.

McEntee would have been better off listening to Yager than to the report Smith returned with. Smith had not been able to negotiate the river but his companion had. His Negro partner told of a buildup of cavalry in the area but noted that there was very little infantry in the vicinity of the court house and that all the infantry shuffling around Fredericksburg was being done in an effort to improve sanitation. The information was totally off the mark since by the date of Smith's report, all of Lee's infantry, except for Hill's Corps was at Culpeper.[35]

Activity across the river prompted Hooker to shift a portion of his infantry force upriver to help picket the fords. On 28 May, a message was sent to General Meade delegating his corps for the duty. According to Meade's orders, if he needed additional artillery batteries, he was to take them from the Reserve Artillery.[36]

On the same day, a second set of instructions was sent to Meade. Hooker decided to put the remainder of the Pennsylvanian's corps on alert, instructing them to be prepared to move at a moment's notice. He wanted all commands to be awakened at daylight and one half hour later; all were to be at arms. All artillery batteries were to be harnessed and all was to be "in readiness for any movement that may be ordered." Was Hooker planning a general movement or perhaps preparing to fall upon Lee's rear guard?[37]

Two days later, at 11:30 a.m., Hooker evidently felt he had enough solid information to send a detailed note to Lincoln.

> "Yesterday morning appearances indicated that during the night the enemy had broken up a few of his camps and abandoned them. These changes were observed on the right of his line, in the vicinity of Hamilton's Crossing. So far as I was enabled to judge, from all my means of information, it was impossible for me to determine satisfactorily whether this movement had merely been a change of camps - the enemy had moved in the direction of Richmond or up the river – but, taken in connection with the fact that some deserters came in from the divisions of Hood and Pickett, I concluded that those divisions had been brought to the front from their late positions at Gordonsville and Taylorsville, and that this could be for no other purpose but to enable the enemy to move up the river, with a view to

---

[35] Fishel, *Secret War*, p.430.

[36] *OR* vol.25, pt.2, pp.535-535; *OR* vol.27, pt.3, pp.3-4; *Judson, Amos M., History of the Eighty-Third Regiment Pennsylvania Volunteers*, p.116.

[37] *OR* vol.27, pt.3, p.4.

the execution of a movement similar to that of Lee's last year. He must either have it in mind to cross the Upper Potomac, or to throw his army between mine and Washington, in case I am correct in my conjecture. To accomplish either, he must have been greatly re-enforced, and if making this movement, the fair presumption is that he has been by the troops from Charleston. Of this I have no evidence further than that furnished me by Major-General Dix, that they had come to Richmond."

Hooker went on to inform Lincoln that additional camps had been empty that morning. He then proposed to the president a plan to "pitch into his [Lee's] rear" before he turned his attention northward to deal with the remainder of Lee's army. If Lee moved as Hooker anticipated, the enemy would be spread out across a great distance. An opportunity to defeat Lee in detail may be at hand or at least Hooker seemed to think so.

In the final paragraph of his communication, Hooker lobbied Lincoln to install a single commander for all the Federal forces who could coordinate independent commands into one unified effort against Lee and the Rebels. The president effectively had this in Halleck, but the general in chief had done a poor job of synchronizing the war effort between departments. Hooker argued that he was ignorant of the movements of other commands and thus was unable to coordinate his efforts with others to wage a more effective grand strategy. So far the intent of the administration had been to utilize the Army of the Potomac to protect the capital, and while it was busy guarding Washington, find Lee and destroy his army. This requirement effectively handicapped whoever was in command.[38]

Lincoln replied in his usual cordial manner, telling Hooker that "professional military skill" was required to respond to his proposed actions. Instead the president offered suggestions on how Hooker should deal with the situation. Crossing to the south side of the river if Lee had moved north of it, in Lincoln's mind would be improper. "If he should leave a rear force at Fredericksburg, tempting you to fall upon it, it would fight in intrenchments [sic] and have you at disadvantage," Lincoln noted. The pain of Burnside's defeat the previous December was evidently still fresh in the president's mind. In addition, Lincoln argued that if Hooker were to move against a portion of Lee's army still on the Rappahannock the "main force would in some way be getting an advantage of you northward. I would not take the risk," Lincoln continued, "of being entangled upon the river, like an ox jumped half over a fence and liable to be torn by dogs front and rear, without a fair chance to gore one way or kick the other."

---

[38] *OR* vol.27, pt.1, p.30. The lack of coordination between departments and commands was never more evident than during the events which led to the defeat of the Eighth Corps' Second Division at Winchester a few days later. If intelligence from Hooker's team had been more thoroughly shared with Generals Robert Schenck and Robert Milroy, the division may have been saved from destruction at the hands Ewell's Corps.

Halleck responded forty minutes later and agreed with Lincoln. Fighting a portion of Lee's army, entrenched at Fredericksburg was problematic. Halleck expressed his opinion that Hooker's first goal should be to bring his force to bear upon Lee's advanced elements on the north side of the river. True to form the general in chief reiterated the army's responsibility for covering Washington. He also made sure that Hooker understood that the size of General Heintzelman's force was smaller than that recommended to defend the city. "[I]t seems to me," Halleck noted of Hooker's proposal, "that such an operation [Lee's] would give you great advantages upon his flank to cut him in two, and fight his divided force." Halleck thought it would be "perilous to permit Lee's main force to move upon the Potomac while your army is attacking an intrenched [sic] position on the other side of the Rappahannock."

Halleck also defended himself against Hooker's comments regarding the need for an overall commander. He, as general in chief, was technically in the role which Hooker defined and must have taken Hooker's observation as somewhat of a slight against him. "General Heintzelman and General Dix are instructed to telegraph directly to you all the movements which they may ascertain or make. Directions have also been given to forward military information which may be received from General Schenck's command." Halleck then made a prophetic if not obvious statement. "Lee will probably move light and rapidly. Your movable force should be prepared to do the same."[39]

Hooker's proposed attack across the river upon General Hill's corps, while not acceptable to Halleck and Lincoln, could have been a prudent move. A strong Federal force crossing the river to confront Hill would have had the same effect on Lee's intended move as a Federal shift northward for an attack on Lee's main body. Lee had shown in the past great concern for his line of communication. A serious assault on his rear guard, even if Hill managed to extricate himself and fall back toward Richmond as Lee had instructed, would have forced Lee, at a minimum, to halt the operation or possibly abandon it all together. Lee's movement was intended to get Hooker to follow him northward. If the bait was not taken, Lee would not have permitted the Federals to march unmolested into Richmond. The Confederate commander was counting on Northern paranoia to force "Fighting Joe" to chase him.

Denied the opportunity to confront Hill with his entire army, Hooker now set about trying to determine just what was in front of him along the river. Later that evening he sat down and wrote out a second note to Lincoln outlining a plan "to make a demonstration on the enemy by throwing a couple of brigades across the river at Franklin's Crossing, and to learn, if possible, what the enemy are about." Hooker however, failed to inform his commander in chief that the operation was already underway, it having begun earlier that day. Hooker sent the message at 9:15

---

[39] *Ibid*, pp.31-32. Schenck commanded the Middle Department and the Eighth Corps, which consisted of the area west of Baltimore. It included the Lower Shenandoah Valley, Maryland, Pennsylvanian and a good deal of West Virginia.

p.m., four hours after his troops had engaged Confederate pickets. The missive was received in Washington a half hour later.[40]

Hooker may have purposely neglected to inform Lincoln and Halleck of his intent to cross the river south of Fredericksburg earlier in the day. At 7:00 a.m. on the same day of his original message outlining the proposed attack on Hill, a note was sent to General Sedgwick, whose Sixth Corps was near the crossing. "The major-general commanding directs that you hold your command in readiness to march at short notice; that you furnish any assistance required… in throwing a bridge across the Rappahannock." Only Hooker knew if the pontoon bridge was intended for a general attack or a reconnaissance expedition. It must be left to conjecture as to whether or not the reconnaissance was an idea Hooker developed after the rebuke of a general attack. No serious objection to a reconnaissance effort was ever leveled from Washington.[41]

A Lack of Boats

In accordance with his instructions, Sedgwick had his men headed toward the river around 2:00 p.m. The road was familiar to them, having been traveled three previous times as they marched to meet the enemy. Their route took them past the old White Oak Church. If any of them entertained thoughts of stopping to have a short prayer or service, it would have been held outside the church. Built in 1789, the structure had fallen into a state of disrepair. Years of use and months of occupation by the Sixth Corps reduced the house of worship to what Private Wilber Fisk of the 2nd Vermont call "a miserable, insignificant structure, dilapidated and steepleless, [sic] and seem to have belonged to some former age." Much of the damage was surely due to the building's use as a hospital.[42]

The men were not enthusiastic about making the trek to the river, which they believed would culminate in another insignificant encounter with the enemy. "The boys were not in good spirits," Fisk wrote, "they hadn't even whiskey." If he wanted to tell a good story, Fisk noted, he could have written the men were enthusiastic to confront the Rebels again, but it would have been a lie. "[A]ll my experience goes to prove that to be nicely situated in camp with good tents and all the little conveniences which ingenuity can devise, where we can have clean, tidy quarters, with but little to do and plenty to eat, is decidedly preferable to fighting, marching, advancing or retreating." Fisk, like many of his comrades had grown to "deplore" the war and detested any order which required them to pack up their camps and move forward to meet the enemy. Hooker's latest order was no different. The men of the 2nd Vermont had grown to question their commander's decision making and had lost faith in his abilities. Many wished for the return of McClellan.[43]

---

[40] *Ibid*, pp.32-33.

[41] **OR** vol.27, pt.3, p.13.

[42] Rosenblatt, Emil & Ruth, Editors, **Hard Marching Every Day: The Civil War Letters of Private Wilber Fisk**, p.100.

[43] *Ibid*, pp.99, 107.

By 5:00 p.m. the five miles to the river had been covered. Brigadier General Albion P. Howe's Second Division was selected to make the initial effort. Sedgwick's remaining two divisions, those of Brigadier General Horatio G. Wright and Major General John Newton, were ordered to take positions on the north bank to provide support.[44]

General Howe, a Maine native, was born in Standish on 13 March 1818. As a boy, Albion proved to be an excellent student, catching the attention of his home state's governor. An appointment to West Point was procured and Howe did not disappoint, graduating eighth in a class of fifty-two cadets on 1 July 1841. His class standing prompted an assignment to the artillery which he joined with the typical West Point exist rank of second lieutenant. Assigned to the 4th Artillery, Howe spent time teaching mathematics at West Point before venturing off to war in Mexico. On 18 June 1846, he was promoted to first lieutenant, and distinguished himself at Contreras and Churubusco, actions for which he was brevetted captain. After the war Howe performed duties at various frontier outposts and spent time in Kansas during the fighting between the abolitionists and pro-slavery groups there. When John Brown raided Harpers Ferry, Howe and his battery were dispatched to the scene and, assisted in Lee's successful apprehension of Brown and his band of lawbreakers.[45]

Albion Parris Howe's command was chosen to probe the Rebel positions across the river south of Fredericksburg. *LOC*

---

[44] ***OR*** vol.27, pt.1, p.676.

[45] Eicher, & Eicher, ***High Commands***, p.306; Boatner, ***Dictionary***, p.414.

Howe served with McClellan during the summer of 1861 in western Virginia where he continued his duties with the artillery. Realizing the chance for advancement was greater in the volunteer force, he accepted a promotion to brigade general of volunteers and was assigned to brigade command in the Fourth Corps. He guided his brigade during The Seven Days battles. At Malvern Hill his men were positioned along an area of the line that was not heavily engaged. Shortly after the fighting, Howe's brigade traveled north and was attached, along with the remainder of the Fourth Corps, to the Sixth Corps prior to the Maryland Campaign. Once again, while the rest of the army grappled with Lee, Howe's men remained inactive, being held in reserve. Shortly after the battle, the Fourth Corps was officially transferred to the Sixth Corps and designated the corps' Third Division. Despite his meager battle record, Howe was elevated to division command on 16 November 1862 and given the assignment of leading the Sixth Corps' Second Division. Again, at Fredericksburg, Howe's command was not heavily engaged, losing about 144 men, most to artillery fire. His command was finally tested during the Chancellorsville Campaign when he was called upon to storm the heights above Fredericksburg. His men managed to wrestle the lightly defended summit from the Confederates posted there, but were heavily damaged by Rebel counter attacks. While singled out in Sedgwick's report, it was generally believed that the Sixth Corps had performed poorly, and Howe remained basically an unknown and unproven division commander.[46]

Howe's division contained only two brigades instead of the usual three. The Vermont Brigade, under the command of Colonel Lewis A. Grant, was chosen to be the first to attempt a crossing of the river. Grant was born in Winhall Vermont in 1828. He was, like so many volunteers who rose to brigade command, an average man thrown into an extraordinary situation who succeeded. He had no military training, but through the study of the military arts, made himself into a competent commander. A lawyer and school teacher before the war, at the age of thirty-one, he suffered through the death of his wife. Working at his law practice when the war broke out, Grant enlisted in the 5th Vermont, was designated the unit's major and in a short time was promoted to lieutenant colonel. His first opportunity to display his ability as a commander was when he skillfully led the regiment through the Peninsular Campaign. Fighting through sickness, he guided the regiment again at Savage Station during The Seven Days battles, where it fought hard and suffered over 200 casualties. Many of the men exhausted their ammunition before retiring. Grant was promoted to full colonel the day before the Battle of Antietam, but saw no action since McClellan chose to keep the Sixth Corps in reserve. At Fredericksburg, although only slightly engaged again, Grant was wound but stayed on the field.

Grant ascended to command of the Vermont Brigade and led it during the Chancellorsville Campaign. His brigade was chosen to assist in the storming of Marye's Heights, where so many boys in blue had met their maker the previous December during the fighting at Fredericksburg. Grant led his Vermonters up

---

[46] Tagg, **Generals**, pp.111-112; Boatner, **Dictionary**, p.414.

the slope to the crest of the ridge, capturing three Confederate battle flags. The following day a heavy Rebel counter attack drove Grant and his brigade off of the heights. The fight cost over 400 casualties, all proving to be wasted with the retreat of Hooker's force from the crossroads to the west. For his efforts, Grant would receive a Congressional Medal of Honor, although it would take thirty years for it to be presented.[47]

While the brigade was known as the Vermont Brigade it was not exclusively constructed of Vermont regiments. The bulk of the brigade was populated by the 2nd, 3rd, 4th, 5th and 6th Vermont. Supplementing the Vermonters was the 26th New Jersey, whose term of enlistment was about to expire. The 26th, commanded by Lieutenant Colonel Edward Martindale, where nine month volunteers whose term began when they were mustered into service on 18 September 1862. A number of the men, who may have thought their term of enlistment began when they signed up not when they were accepted into service, protested saying they had already done their duty and where going home. A few hot heads would refused to obey orders to cross the river, but most of the New Jerseymen eventually made the attack, which would be their final engagement of the war before they were mustered out four days before the armies met at Gettysburg.[48]

The 2nd Vermont was the first of the three year Vermont regiments to be mustered into service. It served longer than any other Vermont regiment save one. The 2nd was a handpicked unit. When it was formed, close to sixty companies of Vermonters had been assembled. The ten companies selected were the cream of the crop and represented a well-rounded sampling from nearly every region of the state. By early June 1863, command of the regiment was the responsibility of Colonel James H. Walbridge. Walbridge had an esteemed military background. His grandfather, General Ebenezer Walbridge was an officer with the Green Mountain Boys, fought in the battles around Quebec in 1776, and was later a general of militia during the War for Independence. James, following in his grandfather's footsteps, rushed to volunteer when the call for three year troops went out. He was elected captain of his company and had received the first commission issued to a three year unit officer. He was cool under fire and a deserving leader of the regiment.[49]

---

[47] *OR* vol.27, pt.1, p.676; Tagg, **Generals**, pp.112-113. Howe's Division carried no brigade with the designation of First Brigade. Grant's brigade was designated the second and Colonel Daniel D. Bidwell's brigade was designated the third.

[48] *OR* vol.25, pt.1, p.165; Parsons, George W., *Put the Vermonters Ahead*, p.57; Benedict, George Grenville, *Vermont in the Civil War: A History of the Part Taken by the Vermont Soldiers and Sailors in the War for the Union*, vol.1, p.380.

[49] Benedict, *Vermont in the Civil War*, vol.1, p.106

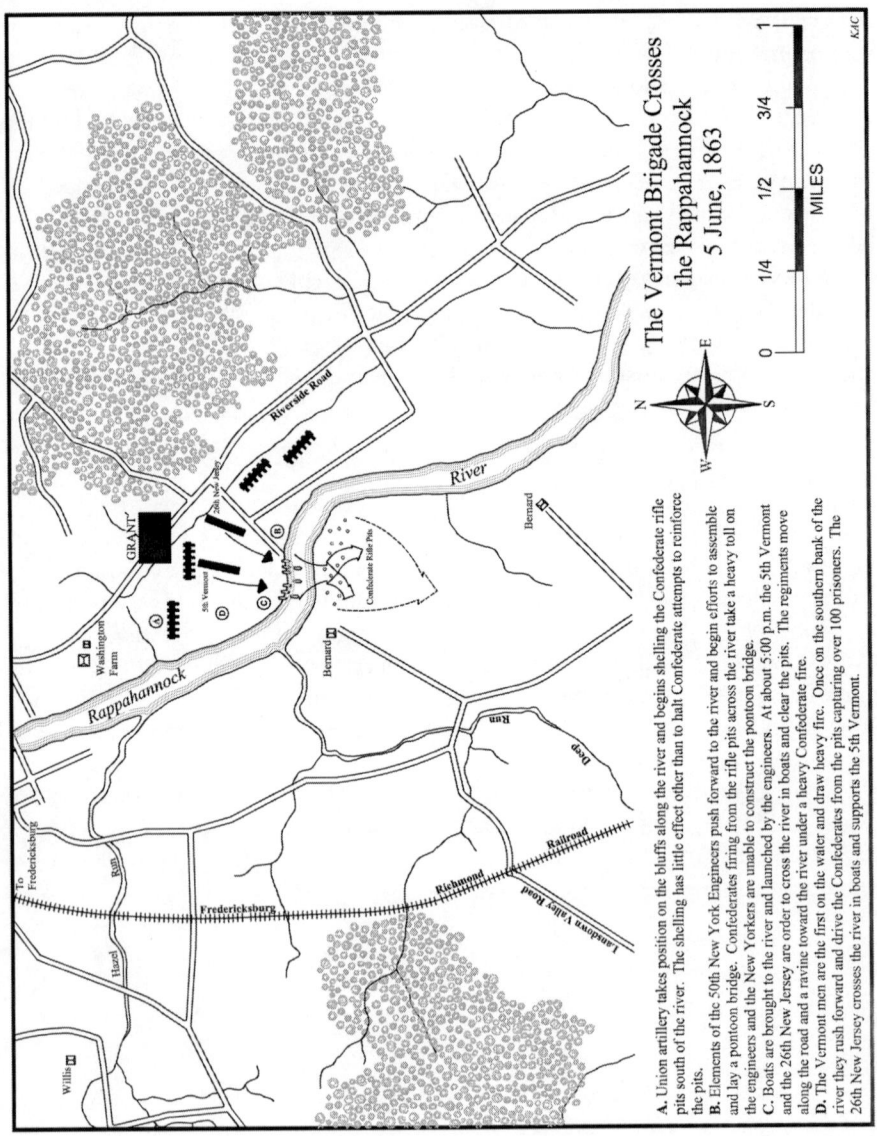

Vermont Brigade Crosses the Rappahannock

Like the 2nd, the 3rd regiment was formed during the first week of May, 1861. The 3rd Vermont was another of the initial three year units, and like the 2nd, it was formed by handpicking its members from the large group of organized companies. Companies from rural towns such as Coventry, Hartford, Guildhall, Charleston, St. Johnsbury and others gathered at the Caledonia County Agricultural Society. By 3 July all the companies were present and the regiment took quarters in the society's main building. After fighting off a measles epidemic which infected one in three men, the regiment was officially organized and marched off to war. Two years later, as they broke camp and marched toward the river, the regiment was led by their new colonel, Thomas O. Seaver. Seaver, who initially was the captain of Company F, had worked his way upward to the colonelcy. From the town of Pomfret, Seaver was twenty-seven years of age. Like Walbridge, he had enlisted when the call for three year troops was issued. He had shown coolness under fire and a level of bravery the men admired. His first test was during the Chancellorsville fight where he led the regiment against Marye's Heights. Now he would lead his men in another effort on the south side of the river to damage the Rebels.[50]

A Vermont man, Lewis Addison Grant proved to be a fine military man even thought he was self-taught in the military arts. *MOLLUS Collection, USAHEC*

The defeat at Bull Run on 21 July 1861 prompted Vermont Governor Erastus Fairbanks to make the call for an additional group of three year volunteers on 30 July. The call resulted in the formation of the 4th and 5th Vermont. The 4th regiment was constructed from companies that hailed from the southern portion of the state. It was formed at Brattleboro on 12 September and two days later all its companies

---

[50] *Ibid*, pp.126-127, 132, 143; *OR* vol.27, pt.1, p.676.

were in camp. Unlike the 2nd and 3rd regiments, who received gray uniforms from the state, the men of the 4th were outfitted with the dark blue of Federal Regulars and armed with Enfield rifles. The regiment's original muster included 1,042 men and officers. By early June 1863, command of the regiment had fallen to Colonel Charles B. Stoughton. Charles was the younger brother of the regiment's original colonel, an 1859 West Point graduate, Edwin H. Stoughton. The elder Stoughton had been absent during the Antietam Campaign and Charles lead the regiment at Crampton's Gap and during the fight along Antietam Creek. On 5 November 1862, Edwin received a promotion to brigadier general and was placed in command of the Second Vermont Brigade. Unfortunately he would suffer the distinction of being captured by the notorious John S. Mosby while in his bed one night. Although exchanged two months later, Edwin would never hold a field command again and resigned from the army. Charles, having proven himself a leader of men on the field of battle, was promoted to colonel, took over as regimental commander and replaced his disgraced brother.[51]

Commanding the 5th Vermont was Lieutenant Colonel John R. Lewis. Lewis, originally a captain in Company I, ascended to command of the regiment when Colonel Grant took command of the brigade the previous February. While probably not as popular with the men as Grant, Lewis nonetheless brought to the table a proven set of command skills. Lewis and the rest of his company had reported to the town of St. Albans in Franklin County on the northern border of the state sometime between 11 and 14 September 1861. When all the companies had gathered, the organization of the regiment began. Mustering started on 16 September, but it took an extra day to complete the task of signing up the regiment's 1,006 original members. By the spring of 1863, the three year volunteers of the 5th had seen significant action and like the other regiments of the brigade, were now bloodied veterans. Lewis would lead them through the summer, fall and into 1864 before he was forced to yield his command after receiving a ghastly arm wound at The Wilderness which would cost him the limb. Until then he would lead the 5th as it logged additional achievements into its stellar record.[52]

While the 5th Vermont was being mustered in, Governor Fairbanks, after receiving a request from the War Department to raise another regiment, appointed a group of men to act as recruitment officers for a sixth regiment. It took twelve days to solicit the enlistment of 900 men, and as additional men slowly filtered in, the rolls rose to nearly one thousand. Orders to assemble at Montpelier were given, and on 2 October the first company arrived. Four days later the remainder of the companies would be in camps arranged on the county fairgrounds. The men were provided uniforms as they arrived, and on 15 October they were issued Enfield rifles before they were mustered. The 971 men of the 6th Vermont, just thirty-three days after the Governor was asked for an additional regiment, were organized and marching off to war. Nineteen months later, the 6th left camp and headed toward

---

[51] Benedict, *Vermont in the Civil War*. pp.157, 159, 164; *OR* vol.27, pt.1, p.676; Warner, *Generals in Blue*, p.482.

[52] Benedict, *Vermont in the Civil War*, vol.1, pp.180-181, 190, 192, 196; *OR* vol.27, pt.1, p.676.

the river, under the command of Colonel Elisha L. Barney. Colonel Barney began the war as captain of the regiment's Company K and rose to the colonelcy, which he assumed on 18 March 1863. He had been wounded in the temple at Crampton's Gap and recently led the regiment at Chancellorsville. Eventually losing his life after being shot in the same temple at The Wilderness, Barney would earn the respect of his officers and men alike. His men would mourn him as a brother and 2,000 people would attend his wake. For now however, there was work to be done.[53]

When the ridge along the river was reached, the men of Howe's division settled in for a little rest. Few Rebels were in position on the south side of the Rappahannock as the Federals appeared in force. As the marching Yankees came into view, Confederates rushed forward from the tree line, across the broad open flats along the river and occupied a line of rifle pits along the bank. Although unaware at the time, Sedgwick's movement was against an area which had just been vacated by Ewell's Confederates during the previous forty-eight hours. The only Rebels in the area were pickets from the 2th Florida of Colonel David Lang's Brigade manning the rifle pits.[54]

To cover his movement to the river, General Howe deployed a number of artillery batteries along the ridge and opened fire on the rifle pits. The guns of the Massachusetts Light Artillery's 1st Battery, the New York Light Artillery's 1st Battery of, the 1st Rhode Island Light, Battery D, along with two additional batteries, unlimbered, sent their horses to the rear, and opened fire on the enemy's defenses. Federal shells pounded the pits for nearly half an hour and succeeded only in raising a great deal of dust. Private Fisk noted that "shot and shell from our batteries fell thick and fast among them, tearing up the ground on the flats and raising so much dust and smoke that the rebels could not see what was going on…" While very few of the enemy were wounded by the barrage, it did impair visibility providing a somewhat effective screen for the crossing attempt.[55]

To assist with the construction of a pontoon bridge, members of the 50th New York Volunteers, part of the army's engineering brigade, were instructed to proceed to the river. At 10:00 a.m. the members of the regiment gathered up enough bridging material to assemble a span 400 feet long and advanced with four companies to within a quarter mile of the river while the rest of the regiment remained further to the rear. There, in the hot June sun the regiment waited for the remainder of the afternoon. Finally, at 4:00 p.m., Major Wesley Brainerd,

---

[53] Benedict, *Vermont in the Civil War*, vol.1, pp.208-210, 216, 223-224.

[54] Toombs, Samuel, *New Jersey Troops in the Gettysburg Campaign*, p.21; Gottfried, *Maps*, p.4; Caldwell, *McGowan's Brigade*, p.129; Parsons, *Put the Vermonters Ahead*, p.57; Stevens, George Thomas, *Three Years in the Sixth Corps*, p.217; Waters, Zack C. & Edmonds, James C, *A Small but Spartan Band: The Florida Brigade in the Army of Northern Virginia*, p.58.

[55] Parsons, *Put the Vermonters Ahead*, p.57; Rosenblatt, *Hard Marching*, p.100; Stevens, *Three Years*, p.218; Brainerd, Wesley, *Bridge Building in Wartime: Memoir of the 50th New York Volunteer Engineers*, p.151.

commanding the detachment from the 50th looked to the rear to see Colonel Grant's brigade cresting the heights behind the river's edge a half mile away. "I saw a long line of steel, glistening and sparkling in the bright sun light," Brainerd noted, "and as they came nearer the blue uniforms of our men presented a striking contrast to the somber brown of the earth behind them."[56]

A pontoon bridge at Deep Run from a photo taken by Mathew Brady probably later in the war. The ravine in the right background could be the gully which the 5th Vermont and 26th New Jersey negotiated as they moved to the river. *NA*

Although the Federal artillery was making it hot for the Confederates, from the safety of their rifle pits at the water's edge they fired at the engineers as they tried to assemble the pontoons and decking of the bridge. Major Brainerd thought the situation eerily similar to the problems encountered a few months earlier as the Federals negotiated the river prior to Fredericksburg. "[T]he bullets came spitting and whizzing about in a manner that forcibly reminded me of the 11th of December," Brainerd recalled. The combined noise of flying bullets, booming artillery and shrieking shells made it so difficult to hear commands that officers had to communicate with their men by hand signals. "We worked liveley [sic] and yet the time seemed very long," Brainerd continued. "One after annother [sic] of my men dropped down and attempted to crawl away, some men hit in the arms, some in the body, others in the legs. I saw two hit in the knee within a minuiet [sic] of each other." In addition to the wounded some unhurt men went to the rear as well. A short distance in back of Brainerd's position was a small depression which contained a small amount of water. Into this shallow hole spilled wounded and unhurt men alike. Unfortunately for the unwounded men, they were observed

---

[56]   Brainerd, *Bridge Building*, pp.151; ***Annual Report of the Adjutant General of the State of New York***, (hereafter ***ARAGSNY***) vol.16, p.842.

by Lieutenant Colonel William H. Pettes. Pettes would have none of the cowardly skulking. Approaching the pit, he vehemently chastised the unwounded with a profanity-based tirade. Using a number of violent gestures to accent his irritation, Pettes screamed at them to "get out of here." His verbal outburst was so colorful that Major Brained noted it "sounded so strongly of sulphur [sic] as to put to shame the dense fumes of gunpowder."

It was not long before the Federals discovered that, due to the heavy Rebel fire, the engineers would not be able to construct the bridge. Before the bridge could be laid, the rifle pits on the far side would have to be cleared of the Floridians. Finally, a decision was made to attempt a crossing of the river in boats to directly assault the Rebels in the pits. The engineers halted their efforts and began unloading boats for an amphibious assault. Supervising the effort, from the Corps of Engineers, was Captain Charles E. Cross. Cross had graduated second in his class at West Point two years earlier and was considered one of the finest engineering officers in the army. Major Brainerd described Cross' efforts to get enough boats in the river to conduct the assault.

> "We had succeeded in getting 4 or 5 Pontons [sic] into the water and had them manned. I turned around to see how the Regulars were getting on. They had a few boats in the water but were evidently not making much progress. Captain Cross was in his shirt sleeves doing all in his power to urge his men up to their duty. I could see that this was a hard task to perform. Three of his men started to move away to the rear [but] he outflanked them and drove them back with vigorous blows with the flat side of his sword. A moment later his sword arm fell at his side, his head drooped and then his body seemed to wilt away. He fell dead, shot directley [sic] through the head, a portion of his body fell into the stream."

Brainerd noted that it took approximately a half hour to get enough boats into the water to accommodate at least a few of the assaulting force. During that time the 50th lost two officers and twenty two men to wounds or death.[57]

Shortly before 5:00 p.m., with ten boats in the water, Colonel Grant ordered his men up and the brigade moved forward across the ridge toward the river. As the Vermonters and Jerseymen crested the ridge, they came under fire from the Confederates on the far bank. Only after Grant and his men arrived at the river did they discover that the decision had been made to clear the pits and that a crossing under fire was the only way to accomplish the task. Colonel Grant selected his former regiment, the 5th Vermont, and the 26th New Jersey to make the assault. A few disgruntled men in the 26th objected to being ordered to make the risky assault, but most conformed to orders and fell in line. General Howe, attempting to lift their spirits, told the displeased Garden State veterans that in a short time they would

---

[57] Brainerd, ***Bridge Building***, pp.152-154, 376; *ARAGSNY*, vol.16, p.1089.

be home with their loved ones "with an untarnished reputation for gallantry and covered with glory."[58]

Lieutenant Colonels Lewis and Martindale formed their men in line of battle seventy-five yards from the riverbank. The 5th took position on the right near a ravine, while the 26th, deployed to the left along the road to the river. The Federal artillery fire was slackened as orders to advance were issued. The battle line lurched forward, the Vermont men moving quickly down the gulch, the New Jersey boys along the road. Advancing along the road placed the 26th in a more exposed position than those in the ravine. Sprinting across the flats to the edge of the river, the 26th arrived slightly in advance of the Vermonters. Once at the water's edge it was discovered that the ten boats the engineers had managed to drag to the bank and succeeded in launching were not enough to carry all the men across at once. To assist the engineers a detail from the 77th New York of General Howe's Third Brigade was assembled. The engineers and New Yorkers took heavy fire as they worked to unload more pontoon boats. Before the firing died down, the 77th would have one of their party killed by a shot through the head. The poor man had just returned from the hospital earlier in the day having recovered from an illness. A few additional New Yorkers would be wounded. The engineers counted additional casualties as well with close to a half dozen killed and a few more wounded.[59]

The situation on the bank now became critical. Fire from across the river had increased, and the mass of soldiers huddled together near the water was a tempting and easy target for Confederate bullets. Colonel Grant wrote in his report that the fire was "galling" and it was here that his first casualties were recorded. It quickly became obvious to all that remaining on the bank would result in slaughter. Martindale, working rapidly, directed a number of his officers to organize parties in order to manhandle additional boats to the river. Working with the assistance of the engineers, more boats were readied and men quickly clamored into them.

Captain Samuel Dodd, of Company H of the 26th, loaded as many men as would fit into one boat and soon the first boat was on its way. Dodd instructed his men to remain low and protect themselves with the gunwales of the boat. Dodd, who remained upright, managed to guide the vessel to the middle of the river before he was hit and mortally wounded. He was a large man and must have made a tempting target for the Floridians in the pits. Dodd would linger for another day before succumbing to his injuries. Close behind Dodd was another boat containing men from the 5th followed by three more boats loaded with men from the 26th. Some of the first men from Vermont to be upon the river were commanded by Captains Friend H. Barney and B. R. Jennie.[60]

---

[58] Toombs, *New Jersey Troops*, p.21; *OR* vol.27, pt.1, p.676; Stevens, *Three Years*, p.217; Brainerd, *Bridge Building*, p.153.

[59] Toombs, *New Jersey Troops*, pp.21-22; Stevens, *Three Years*, p.217-219. Toombs notes that only seven boats were in the water when the 5th and 26th arrived at the river's edge.

[60] Toombs, *New Jersey Troops*, p.22; *OR* vol.27, pt.1, p.677. Toombs does not indicate if the boat continued on or returned to the north bank after Dodd was disabled.

It was nearly 7:00 p.m. before men began to land on the south bank. A boat of men from New Jersey arrived first followed closely by a boat loaded with Vermonters. Once ashore the men huddled together along the bank and did their best to protect themselves from the heavy fire emanating from the pits. As a boat loaded with men from the 26th approached the riverbank, Captain Stephen C. Fordham, who Colonel Martindale singled out in his report for showing "conspicuous gallantry and spirited conduct," rose from the protection of the bank and called to Major William W. Morris, the officer in the approaching boat, asking what they were to do next. Morris called back to wait until he landed his boat. As Fordham waited for Morris, he noticed a number of men from the 5th Vermont had started toward the enemy in an effort to drive them from their position. Fordham had no time to wait for Morris. He was not about to let men from the 5th attain all the glory. Grabbing another man, Fordham pulled him along and the two of them rushed forward with the Vermonters. Additional men from the 26th noticed what was happening and joined in the dash toward the Rebels.[61]

Rising from the riverbank together, the Vermont and the New Jersey boys ran toward the enemy. The Rebels defended themselves, firing as rapidly as possible, but the Yankees were on top of them quickly. Major Morris led the 26th up to the enemy defenses while Major Charles P. Dudley urged on the men from the 5th. The artillery on the ridge north of the river covered the open ground behind the rifle pits with shot and shell, making it extremely hazardous place to be. As the Yankee's began pouring into the pits, the Rebels now had a choice to make, run for the trees or surrender. While some chanced an effort to escape and ran toward the woods, risking the Federal shelling, others decided that a Northern prison camp was a better choice and dropped their weapons.

Earlier, when the Federals opened with their artillery, Sergeant James Kirkpatrick and his fellow mess mates from the 16th Mississippi were cooking rations on the bluffs above the river. Writing in his diary, he noted "[w]e are immediately ordered to the trenches in our front." Kirkpatrick watched as the 2nd Florida boys were driven from the rifle pits, noting a number of them were captured.[62]

The quantity of prisoners taken varies between accounts of the engagement. Colonel Grant gave a broad range when he wrote in his after action report the number was between 100 to 200. Grant's numbers seem to be centered on the total number for the entire operation not just those prisoners taken near the rifle pits. Private Fisk noted that 150 prisoners were taken from the area of the pits. Another interpretation indicates the number was closer to ninty, which included "an entire" company of the 18th Mississippi. Yet another version submitted by a lieutenant from the 8th Florida indicated four officers and fifty-eight privates were captured from

---

[61] Toombs, *New Jersey Troops*, p.25, 28, 31.

[62] Winschel, Terrence J., The Gettysburg Experience of James J. Kirkpatrick, *GM*, Issue 8, p.113.

their sister regiment, the 2nd Florida. The exact number is no doubt lost to history, but the fact remains that a sizable body of Rebels were in now Federal hands.[63]

The chaotic nature of battle often produced more than one version of events within the historical record and the river crossing and capture of the enemy's rifle pits was no different. Colonel Grant wrote in his report that two companies under Captains Jennie and Barney from the 5th Vermont were the first to enter the enemy's works. The first man to leap into the pits, according to Grant, was a member of Company G, Private Henry Moren. The men of the 26th thought differently, taking credit for being the first to the pits. The confusion is possibly due to Major Morris pushing out a skirmish line from the 26th toward the tree line to pursue the fleeing Rebels while the 5th spent time rounding up prisoners. To get to the truth of the matter is impossible but realistically the two regiment's capture of the pits was probably a simultaneous event.[64]

The 5th Vermont organized the prisoners and a detail was assembled to march them back down to the riverbank while Captains Barney and Jennie sent skirmishers out to support the men from the 26th. The captured men were loaded into empty boats and ferried back across the river as additional troops arrived from the north bank. The next two regiments to negotiate the river were the 3rd and 4th Vermont. The 2nd Vermont was the last to cross in boats as the engineers, with the rifle pits cleared, had finally completed the construction of the pontoon bridge. The 6th Vermont, after crossing the bridge, completed the transfer of Grant's entire brigade to the south side of the Rappahannock.

As the rest of the brigade crossed, Colonel Martindale pursued the Rebels into the trees. Onward the men pushed until their advance put them astride the Bowling Green Road, nearly a half mile from the river. Martindale deployed the regiment along the road and advanced his skirmishers forward to keep an eye out for any Rebel counter attack. The hour was late and the colonel set his men about preparing to spend the night in their advanced position. The 2nd Vermont was advanced to the assistance of the Garden Staters and took position on an elevated area near the road before pushing their skirmishers beyond the thoroughfare. The 4th and 6th Vermont also advanced, taking position beyond the road with the 6th on the left and the 4th on the right, their right flank resting near Deep Run. As the brigade settled in for the night, its line formed a semicircle around the pontoon bridge with its flanks anchored on the river.[65]

As darkness fell, knapsacks were opened and blankets unrolled. The men, after a long day of marching and fighting, settled in to get some well-deserved rest. If orders came to fall in quickly some blankets may have to be left behind, but the men worried little and were soon asleep.

After dark, there was still activity out along the skirmish line. On the right near Deep Run, Captain George Davenport of the 5th Vermont was on the picket

---

[63] *OR* vol.27, pt.1, p.677; Rosenblatt, **Hard Marching**, pp.100-101; Benedict **Vermont in the Civil War**, vol.1, p.193; Waters, & Edmonds, *A Small but Spartan Band*, p.58.

[64] Toombs, **New Jersey Troops**, pp.25, 28, 31; *OR* vol.27, pt.1, p.677.

[65] Toombs, **New Jersey Troops**, p.27.

line, where men from his regiment and the 4th Vermont, under Captain Charles W. Boutin, were keeping lookout. In the darkness, a number of men from the 18th Mississippi were intercepted trying to cross the picket line. It was soon discovered the men were Southern soldiers who had simply had enough of the war and intended to surrender. Two officers and thirty-four enlisted men were captured and herded to the rear.[66]

Though the men who made the initial assault were under fire as they crossed the river and rushed over the south bank, casualties were surprisingly light. The 5th Vermont had only seven men wounded while the 26th New Jersey suffered two killed, including Captain Dodd, with another seventeen wounded.[67]

General Hill would react quickly to the threat, moving portions of Pender's Division to deal with the Federal probe. Scales' and Perrin's brigades were rousted around midnight and began a movement that would shift them to the threatened area. Daylight found them in roughly the same position which they had occupied during the Battle of Fredericksburg. Dawn also found the Federals still astride the road strengthening their position. As the South and North Carolinians arrived on the scene, they discovered the Vermonters and Garden Staters had begun to dig in, throwing up barricades and constructing earthworks. Not to be outdone, the Southerners began the construction of similar defenses and pushed out their own line of skirmishers. Both sides settled in and awaited orders.

Sergeant Kirkpatrick noted in his diary that his company "went forward this morning [6 June] as skirmishers. Halted in line on the R.R. Some of the Company voluntarily went forward and engaged in sharpshooting... The enemy that crossed, are lying close to the mouth of Deep Run, and don't seem to be at all hostile. They wish our pickets to stop the 'barbarous practice of sharpshooting'... A heavy battery across the river, on Bray's Hill, occasionally opens on us." Kirkpatrick's company would spend the day taking pot shots at the Federals before being withdrawn toward evening.[68]

Soon fire erupted on the left of the Federal line when Scales' skirmishers began a sharp engagement with the 6th Vermont's skirmish line. The Rebels charged forward and engaged the Federals near the road, and forced them back. Pushing on, Scales' boys succeeded in driving the left of the Northerner's line back toward the river. The fighting was spirited and the battle line rolled backward until the Federals where able to make a stand and stop the Southerners just before they reached the riverbank. The Vermonters fought hard despite being out numbered. The firing, while lasting most of the day, was initially brisk and continued as such for nearly three hours causing ammunition supplies to run low. Additional rounds had to be hurried forward. Casualties were not heavy with only four killed and 13 wounded, including a regimental officer. The road on the left of the line was now

---

[66] Rosenblatt, *Hard Marching*, p.100-101; *OR* 27, pt.1, p.677.

[67] *OR* vol.27, pt.1, p.677; Toombs, *New Jersey Troops*, p.25; Parsons, *Put the Vermonters Ahead*, p.57.

[68] Winschel, Gettysburg Experience, *GM*, Issue 8, p.113.

back in Rebel hands but the Federal line on the right was still solidly entrenched on the road, continuing around toward Deep Run to the north of the crossing point.[69]

As the fighting slowly died on the Federal left, the battle lines settled into positions which placed them quite near each other. The men on the firing line began to communicate and even exchanged newspapers. For the first twenty-four hours of the operation, the Vermont Brigade was the only group of Federal troops on the south side of the river. Other than those suffered by the 6th, no additional casualties were incurred by the New Englanders. Including those of the 26th New Jersey, combined casualties for the entire operation were rather light, at forty-three.[70]

As the afternoon wore on additional troops were ferried across the river to reinforce Grant's brigade. The newly arriving force pushed men forward and sent out a fresh line of skirmishers to relieve the tired and worn out Vermont boys. At the battle line, the reinforcements began digging additional defenses and erecting barricades to secure their foothold. Howe's men remained south of the river for the rest of the day and stayed on the battle line, supported by the new arrivals until the evening of Sunday, 7 June, when Wright's Division crossed and relieved them. The men of the 1st Vermont Brigade had been engaged or in the presence of the enemy for 50 hours. Packing up their weapons and accoutrements, they re-crossed the river. Finding a sheltered place to fall out, the men settled in for a much needed rest.[71]

As the firing died and darkness covered the field once again, General Lee was able to determine by the course of events that the operation was indeed a probe designed to discover his intentions. Having contained the bridgehead, he quickly sent word to his marching columns, and the advance toward Culpeper resumed. Lee was not about to let Joe Hooker dictate events. He was not going to let a simple recon expedition take away the initiative he, Stonewall Jackson and 10,000 Confederate lives had ripped from Hooker's grasp at Chancellorsville.

Early on 6 June, while the Vermont and New Jersey boys struggled to retain their foothold on the bank of the Rappahannock, Joe Hooker continued his information gathering efforts. Many of the enemy's pickets had been withdrawn from in front of the Second Corps north of Fredericksburg and information was still needed as to the extent of the extraction. Additional instructions were sent to Sedgwick to "make a reconnaissance in front of the bridges, and ascertain the position and strength of the enemy." Hooker gave Sedgwick permission to push his entire corps across the river if it was necessary to determine the disposition of the enemy.

Hooker also wrote instructions to Sedgwick to "[s]eize any citizens as prisoners who could give any information." The prisoners gathered by Colonel

---

[69] *OR* 27, pt.1, p.677; Caldwell, ***McGowan's Brigade***, p.129; Parsons, ***Put the Vermonters Ahead***, p.58; Benedict, ***Vermont in the Civil War***, vol.1, pp.220, 381. Confederate accounts of the fighting at Deep Run on 5 and 6 June is spotty at best.

[70] Caldwell, ***McGowan's Brigade***, p.129; *OR* vol.27, pt.1, p.677.

[71] *OR* vol.27, pt.1, p.677-678; Benedict, ***Vermont in the Civil War***, vol.1, p.382.

Grant had provided little intelligence, only stating the shifting troops were the result of the Southern Army's reorganization. Having been on the skirmish line, and part of Hill's Corps, it is plausible the captives new little if anything about a major shift toward Culpeper. As yet, no portion of Hill's Corps was headed that direction, and the men may have remained happily ignorant.

Later in the day, shortly before noon, Hooker sent a second communication to Sedgwick by telegraph resending permission to use his entire corps. According to headquarters, additional information had been gathered that indicated a single division would be sufficient to determine the intent and strength of the Rebels. The decision on how to proceed was left up to Sedgwick. Hooker then covered himself; making sure that if Sedgwick became careless and got embroiled in a serious fight, he had an excuse for any inquiries from Lincoln. "It is not intended or desired that you should jeopardize your command or bring on any general engagement, if the enemy is in such force as to make it probable." Hooker's message to Lincoln on 5 June implying his desire to confront Hill's Corps prior to turning on Lee necessitated the passage. At least he could now defend himself if Halleck or Lincoln questioned him, on allowing a general fight with Hill to erupt while Lee was roaming free to the northwest.

Sedgwick's difficulty once his men were south of the river was the result of a quick response from the Confederates. The reaction to his reconnaissance was so rapid that his men became hemmed in on the south back and had no avenue for determining the size and position of any Rebels, other than those in front of them. "Their picket line is stronger than last night," he responded to Hooker, "and has advanced on our pickets. I cannot move 200 yards without bringing on a general fight. Before bringing over the rest of my corps, I await orders. I am satisfied that it is not safe to mass the troops on this side." Sedgwick received the telegraphic message instructing against a general engagement after he determined on his own that a general engagement was not practical. Hooker's second message agreed with Sedgwick's argument against a general effort, and hints of an effort to satisfy Lincoln's desire not to become "entangled upon the river."[72]

The conclusion of the assault on the 6th Vermont skirmish line marked the end of serious fighting in the Franklin's Crossing area. While elements of Sedgwick's command remained across the river for as long as a week, the following days saw both sides spend most of their time sniping at one and other. Between random shots, the pickets partook in the typical activities of a skirmish line, including shouted conversations across "no man's land" and the exchange of various articles. Private Fisk, who in addition to his duties with the 2nd, was a war correspondent for *The Green Mountain Freeman* in Montpelier, summarized the events and mindset of the men. "We had [Rebel] batteries placed in position in front of us. All this

---

[72] *OR* vol.27, pt.1, pp.12-13. Sedgwick's response to Hooker's first message is time stamped at 10:30 a.m. on 6 June. Hooker's note to Sedgwick regarding a general engagement is time stamped at 11:15 a.m. Whether Hooker actually read Sedgwick's message within the 45 minute span is unknown but logic would dictate that Hooker's reinforcement of Sedgwick's thoughts dealt with his concern over his note to Lincoln in the same message.

time the rebels remained perfectly quiet, except now and then a random shot on picket. No doubt the rebels had batteries that could have annihilated us if they had seen fit to have opened on our men, but for some reason they remained quiet. It was a strange move. If we were going to attack, why wait? [I]f not, what were we going to do? The best solution we could get of 'the situation' was that we were only feeling to see if the rebel force was still there, and if not, pitch into them; if we found they were, we meant to keep them there to watch us. The Richmond *Sentinel* of day before yesterday, that we borrowed of a rebel picket, says that the whole affair is probably a *ruse*, but it says if we advance, we shall surely be driven back." Fisk's commentary shows that while the men on the battle line were not privy to the overall plan, they were extremely astute and deducing the purpose.[73]

Guarding the Fords

The message George Meade received On 28 May from Hooker instructing him to move one of his divisions up the Rappahannock River to relieve the cavalry pickets currently guarding the Rappahannock River fords. Meade quickly selected Brigadier General James Barnes' Division to march upriver and array itself at the crossing points beginning at Banks' Ford and ranging up the river to Kelly's Ford. Meade instructed Barnes to "assign that portion of the river between Banks' Ford and Richards' Ford to one brigade, posting at least a regiment at each ford, with detachments watching the dams and other crossing-places between, and posting the balance of the brigade at some suitable point in the center, so that either point, if threatened, can be re-enforced." Meade also instructed Barnes to post at least one artillery battery at both the fords.

Another of Barnes' brigades was posted to guard Ellis and Kelly's Fords and any of the other possible crossing points in between. Meade wanted two regiments at each of these fords and "strong detachments at the intermediate fords, ferries, dams and any other known crossing points." As with the lower fords, Meade wanted an artillery battery at each of the upper fords as well.

Barnes' third brigade was to act as a grand reserve. Meade instructed him to divide the brigade in half with each part posted within close support distance of the two brigades along the river. Meade suggested the road between Crittenden's Mills and Mount Holly Church be the location for the reserves for the upper fords. Meade wished the reserves for the lower fords be positioned along the Warrenton Road approximately halfway between Banks' and Richard's Fords near its junction with the road to Richard's Ferry. The position of Barnes' brigades, as outlined by Meade, formed a solid protective screen and would provide a more efficient early warning system.[74]

Barnes would remain in position for a week before the portion of his division below Richard's Ford was shifted up the river to make room for Meade's Second Division. At 10:00 p.m. on 3 June, Butterfield sent another set of instructions to Meade requiring him to move supplementary elements of his command upriver. At 3:00 a.m. the following morning, Meade began to shift his forces. Following his directions, he quickly made preparations to move his other division from the

---

[73] Rosenblatt, ***Hard Marching***, p.101.

[74] ***OR*** vol.25, pt.2, p.535.

vicinity of Falmouth. A second message from Butterfield warned of a possible attempt by the enemy to force a crossing in the morning. Hooker's chief of staff was leery of the information since it came from a Rebel deserter and it was unknown as to whether the data was an intended effort to deceive. Either way, Meade needed to be careful.[75]

Meade had every reason to believe that Banks' Ford would be well guarded since the additional division he designated was that of Major General George Sykes. By the following day, Sykes was personally supervising the posting of his First Brigade near Banks' Ford. Sykes was a career military man who, like McClellan, had the reputation for being a little slow when it came to military matters. It was said that he lacked drive but in truth his sluggishness was due more to his stringent adherence to military protocol than any need for personal ambition. Inside command circles he was known as a methodical, tireless man, who made sure all was in place before risking the lives of his men. Unlike McClellan however, who was constantly under the scrutiny and demands of Washington, Sykes' career did not seem to suffer. McClellan was well-liked within the army, and while Sykes never reached the lofty heights of a deity, like Little Mac, the military accepted Sykes for what he was. The fraternity that was the army saw benefit in officers who adhered to the traditional values and etiquette of the old army. Such values were even more important in the Army of the Potomac, which was assembled from far more volunteers than career military personnel. Sykes was a man who knew his roots and never strayed far from the tree. He was a strict disciplinarian who imposed it "like a machine" and was not swayed in his administration of it by any complaints or excuses. The summation of George Sykes was a simple formula. He was a product of all he had ever known. He was a soldier.[76]

George was born into a political family on 9 October 1822 in Dover, Delaware. His grandfather, James Sykes, served in the Continental Congress and his father, James junior, served as governor of the state. As a boy, George received his primary education at local schools and at a young age married into a prominent family from Maryland. His new family's connections may have been influential in gaining him an appointment to West Point. In 1838, George became a cadet and soon showed himself to be a poor student. He achieved lower than average marks, graduating in the allotted four years thirty-ninth in a class of fifty-six. Sykes' low standing may have been attributed to extensive social activities which interrupted his studies on a regular basis. His friend, roommate and future antagonist, Daniel Harvey Hill noted that Sykes was "a man admired by all for his honor, courage, and frankness, and peculiarly endeared to me by his social qualities." Hill no doubt appreciated Sykes for making the future Southern general's class ranking of twenty-eight look better than it was. Other notables in Sykes' class were James Longstreet, John Pope, Abner Doubleday and John Newton. His poor academic performance left

---

[75] ***OR*** vol.25, pt.2, pp.535-535; ***OR*** vol.27, pt.3, pp.3-4, 6; ***Judson, Amos M., History of the Eighty-Third Regiment Pennsylvania Volunteers***, p.116.

[76] *Ibid*, p.6; Tagg, ***Generals***, p.81.

no choice for him, and he received a posting to the infantry. Brevetted a second lieutenant, and assigned to the 3rd Infantry, he soon departed to fulfill his service commitment.[77]

Although his class standing at West Point was low, George Sykes proved to be a competent division commander. *LOC*

Sykes began his career in Florida fighting Seminoles. For his efforts he was promoted to first lieutenant and when the Mexican War came he fought at Monterrey before journeying to join General Scott's force, and assisted in conquering Vera Cruz. He was present at Cerro Gordo, Contreras, Churubusco, and finally when Scott's force captured Mexico City. Sykes was brevetted captain for Cerro Gordo and, after returning from Mexico, saw service in the southwest on outpost duty executing scouting missions and fighting Indians.[78]

With the loyalty of Maryland questionable when the war began, it became clear that a number of the state's military officers would side with the South. There was never any question about George Sykes. He was a man of the United States Army and he would remain so. If there was a fleeting thought about resigning and going south, it was quickly discarded. Promoted to major, Sykes was transferred to the 14th U. S. Infantry and during the fighting at First Bull Run he led a battalion of Regulars. As untested volunteers were routed from the field, Sykes' Regulars showed their experience and determination. Their efforts retarded the rout and

---

[77] *Ibid*, Powell, William H., ***The Fifth Army Corps***, pp.48-49.

[78] *Ibid*, Boatner, ***Dictionary***, p.825; Powell, ***Fifth Corps***, p.49.

division commander Colonel Andrew Porter called attention to Sykes' boys in his report. "Major Sykes and the officers of his command, three of whom were wounded, who by their discipline, steadiness and heroic fortitude, gave *éclat* to our attacks upon the enemy, and averted the dangers of a final overthrow." That September, Sykes' work at Bull Run earned him a promotion to brigadier general and shortly before McClellan's army departed to inaugurate the Peninsula Campaign, Sykes was given command of a brigade of Regular Army soldiers who, through hard fighting, would soon earn the name "Sykes' Regulars."[79]

Sykes was already known as a solid "Old Army" man when he led his new brigade toward the entrenchments of Yorktown during McClellan's initial movements on the Peninsula. By the time the Fifth Corps was organized in the middle of May, it was obvious Sykes was ready for more responsibility and he was placed in command of one of the new corps' divisions. Most of the regiments in his new command, like Sykes' brigade, were Regular Army. At Gaines' Mill he exhorted them to stand their ground, which they did until another section of the line gave way and they was forced to withdraw. Writing in his after action report, corps commander General Fitz John Porter was quick to mention Sykes' stubbornness. "Sykes, hard pressed on the right, maintaining his ground with all the obstinacy of the regulars and the spirit of the volunteers…" Porter made it a point to call McClellan's attention to the conduct of Sykes and his brigade commanders.[80]

A few weeks later, at Second Bull Run, some of Sykes' boys help General Reynolds fight the delaying action which allowed Pope's thrashed army to escape to the trenches of Washington. The Regulars were ushered into line by Pope himself who intercepted them as they were marching to the rear. Turning them around the bombastic Pope chastised the men when he discovered they were heading off to cook rations. The Regulars double-quicked across Henry House Hill, then broke into a full run until they were in position on Reynolds' left. As the Rebels broke from the woods, Sykes' men began a heavy fire fight which included not only Rebel bullets but a swarm of hornets which entered the fight when a member of the 11th U. S. accidently broke open a nest of the angry insects.[81]

With the Fifth Corps held in reserve at Antietam, Sykes' Regulars saw little action. Prior to Fredericksburg, on 29 November, Sykes received a promotion to major general and command of a division, but once again the Fifth Corps saw no serious combat during the battle. The story was much different at Chancellorsville. Sykes lead the vanguard of Hooker's flanking force toward the rear of Lee's army. On 1 May, after driving in Confederate skirmishers along the Old Orange Turnpike, a sharp fight with General McLaws' brigades ensued. Shortly thereafter, word was sent to Hooker relaying the state of affairs along Sykes' battle line. At this point, Hooker seemed to balk and lose his nerve. The messenger returned with orders

---

[79] Tagg, **Generals**, p.82; ***OR*** vol.2, pp.4, 386.

[80] Tagg, **Generals**, p.82; ***OR*** vol.11, pt.2, pp.225-226..

[81] Hennessy, John J., **Return to Bull Run: The Campaign and Battle of Second Manassas**, pp.409, 414.

for Sykes to pull his troops back toward Chancellorsville. For the remainder of the campaign Sykes' division loitered around unused.[82]

As the summer of 1863 opened, Sykes had seen little action at the head of his division. It had been ten months since the fighting at Second Bull Run and, while a competent officer, he had yet to prove himself at the head of his division in a serious fight. He had some experience conducting defensive operations but was still untried regarding offensive maneuvers. His lifelong commitment to a military career helped in his advancement and being Regular Army endeared him to many of his superiors. While his future held additional responsibilities, Sykes' priority in early June, 1863 was his division, and his corps commander General Meade knew it was in good hands.[83]

Slight of build, Sykes, at forty years of age, possessed a hair line which had begun to recede slightly. The best description of the general was possibly penned by Frank Haskell who thought Sykes "a small, rather thin man, well dressed and gentlemanly, brown hair and beard which he wears full, with a red, pinched, rough looking skin, feeble blue eyes, large nose, with the general air of one who is weary, and a little ill mannered." Sykes' look gave an impression of chronic fatigue and must have contributed somewhat to his reputation of being lethargic. Haskell failed to mention that Sykes' hair contained a bit of a wave and his large nose had some length to it. Awarded the nickname "Tardy George" at West Point, the designation followed him his entire career, and as the season of active campaigning began, the U. S. Regulars, and volunteers of General Meade's Second Division were under the command of a man they could depend on.[84]

Although Hooker thought he possessed credible information from a Rebel that an enemy incursion was eminent, the next morning dawned with no indication the Rebels intended to cross. A second note from Butterfield that morning informed Meade that an observation balloon, operating in the vicinity of Banks' Ford, would be a good source of information regarding the position and movements of the enemy, and suggested that Meade make efforts to communicate with the balloon's operators. Obviously Hooker was greatly concerned regarding the position and movement of Lee's army. Butterfield closed his second note with specific directions. "The general desires that you will use all exertions to keep yourself and him informed as to their movements."[85]

Passing on Hooker's desires, Meade sent a long detailed communication to Sykes instructing him of the commanding general's wishes. He also provided Sykes specifics on how he wanted his Second Division commander to deploy his brigades.

---

[82] *OR* vol.25, pt.1, pp.525; Boatner, **Dictionary**, p.825.

[83] Tagg, **Generals**, p.82.

[84] Byrne, & Weaver, Editors, **Haskell of Gettysburg**, p.133;

[85] *OR* vol.27, pt.3, pp.4-5.

HEADQUARTERS FIFTH ARMY CORP.
June 4, 1863.

Major-General SYKES,
   Commanding Second Division:

By direction of the major-general commanding you will without any delay move with your division and take position on the Rappahannock River, posting one brigade at Banks' Ford, one brigade at United States Ford, with a detachment from the latter to be sent to Richards' Ford and posted there for its protection. You will post the other brigade of your division in reserve at Benson's Mills, that being a central point from whence roads lead to Richards', United States, and Banks' Fords, and from which any portion of your line can be easily reenforced. The major general commanding directs me to enclose herewith copies of telegrams received from the commanding general; also a map of the section of the country to be occupied. The major-general commanding directs that you take with you the intrenching [sic] tools of the supply train, and direct your subordinate officers to immediately prepare defenses, such as rifle-pits, epaulements for batteries, and to make every disposition to check, retard, and prevent the crossing of the river at the points whose defense is intrusted [sic] to them. There are now two batteries of light 12s posted at Banks' and United States Fords. Two rifled batteries have been ordered to these points to report to you. The major-general commanding directs that you will instruct the several commanding officers at each of the places occupied to immediately make themselves acquainted with the woods, paths, &c., leading from their posts up and down the river and back into the country, to keep up communications with the posts on their right and left, and you will discuss and arrange with them a plan of operations in case the enemy should force a passage at any point, in which case you will concentrate all your command within striking distance as rapidly as possible, and hold the enemy in check the longest possible time, falling back, when pressed, on the main army at this place. You will be careful to see that you command takes with it a full supply of ammunition, and you will issue rations so as to have always two days' cooked on hand, being thus prepared for immediate movement. You will be particularly careful to require your commanders to keep all wagons well in rear, and caution them to consider themselves on advanced picket duty, requiring the utmost vigilance and activity. The major-general

commanding desires that you will give your personal attention to the posting of your troops in their respective position.
Very respectfully, your obedient servant,
FRED T. LOCKE,
Assistant Adjutant-General[86]

The extent of detail proved Meade was not taking any chances with the duty assigned Sykes. The men were rousted by blowing bugles at midnight. Camps were broken, coffee was made, and by 4:00 a.m. they were on the road toward the river. It was a cool dry morning and in a short time the division approached Banks' Ford. As the column passed the road to the ford one brigade departed while the remainder plodded on. By 9:00 a.m. elements of the Third Brigade under Colonel Patrick O'Rorke arrived at United States Ford. As directed, a detachment was sent the short distance to Richard's Ford. The elements of Meade's First Division which had been guarding the fords, packed up their belongings as their relief arrived, and the old guards departed, leaving the task to the new arrivals.[87]

The duty of guarding Banks' Ford fell to the division's First Brigade under Brigadier General Romeyn B. Ayres. Once in position, it took the Federals little time to determine that the Rebel cavalry, which had been picketing the ford, was withdrawn that morning and replaced with infantry. According to Ayers, an entire brigade of infantry was just across the river, but no other groups of organized enemy troops were in the area. Establishing communications with the officer in charge of the observation balloon, Ayers also discovered that infantry and artillery were moving about in the rear of Fredericksburg.

Shortly after Sykes began positioning his men, another messenger from Hooker's headquarters arrived with instructions to "report any movement of the enemy." These were similar to the instructions Sykes had received from Meade, and had been included in the dispatch from Hooker, which Meade had forwarded to him. "Old Army" Sykes probably did not concern himself with the additional communication since it reiterated the same information and requirements. Either way it should have been very apparent to him that Hooker was greatly interested in any information which could be obtained and passed on.[88]

As the men of the division's Third Brigade arrived at United States Ford, a squad of fifty men were pushed to the water's edge. One group, from the 140th New York, immediately began antagonizing the Rebels within earshot across the water. While it was all good natured and fun, it was well known by both sides that if either tried to cross in force all the pleasantries would be forgotten and serious fighting would begin.[89]

[86] *OR* vol.51, pt.1, p.1044.

[87] Bennett, Brian A, *Sons of Old Monroe: A Regimental History of Patrick O'Rorke's 140th New York Volunteer Infantry*, p.206.

[88] *OR* vol.27, pt.3, p.6.

[89] Bennett, *Sons of Old Monroe*, p..206-207.

The next morning, 5 June, Meade reported to Army Headquarters that another deserter had come into the Federal camps after swimming the river in the dark. The man was from the 10th Alabama, and fared poorly in impressing Meade with his intellect. "He does not seem very intelligent," and did not "know much beyond regimental matters." The deserter did however confirm Sykes' belief that there was a full brigade at the ford, commenting it was Wilcox's Alabamans. They were supported by artillery and their pickets extended upriver to connect with those of Longstreet's. Upriver, at United States Ford, according to the fugitive, there were both cavalry and infantry, but Sykes had seen no infantry in that area and there was scant indication of any camps in the vicinity.

Both Generals Meade and Sykes were of the opinion that if the enemy decided a crossing at Banks' Ford was necessary there would be little the Federals in the area could do to stop it. Confederate artillery in the vicinity of the ford commanded the ground on the north side of the river and could sweep the area with shot and shell. The artillery however, did not stop Sykes from digging in along the riverbank. Rifle-pits and abattis were constructed and advantageous locations selected for gun emplacements a short distance back from the waterway. By the end of the day Sykes had both fords covered and defended.[90]

The following day Hooker, being anxious about who and what was going on across the river began pushing Meade for intelligence. "Can you not feel the enemy, and cause him to develop his strength and position at various points along your front?" Butterfield asked. In an about face regarding Hooker's moratorium on Federal pickets conversing with the enemy, Butterfield gave Meade permission to let his picket line freely chat with the Rebels. Meade was puzzled. What was meant by "feel the enemy?" Butterfields' note was difficult to discern but it was well known that the picket line had proven to be one of the more prolific providers of information. To take advantage of the plethora of intelligence streaming forth, some of Meade's officers actually dressed as privates and manned the line themselves. These officers were the first to determine A. P. Hill was now commanding Lee's holding force at Fredericksburg.[91]

At 10:00 p.m., from his headquarters at Benson's Mills, General Sykes responded to Meade regarding Hooker's desire to "feel" the enemy. "I am opposed to any movement across the river with the forces I have at Banks' and United States Fords," Sykes wrote his chief. "At the former, the crossing is exceedingly difficult, and the ravines and woods on the south bank are of such a nature that a force such as I could send, once on the other side, could not get back if the enemy chose to prevent it." Sykes was unconvinced that any kind of demonstration or crossing of the river would yield the fruits Hooker desired. "I beg to say that the development of the enemy to meet such demonstrations as I would have in my power to make, would not determine a great deal about his strength," Sykes continued. Digging in his heals Sykes took a stand on principle. "To place the Rappahannock behind a small force would be extremely hazardous, and the inexpediency of it is so

---

[90]   *OR* vol.27, pt.3, p.9.

[91]   *OR* vol.27, pt.3, p.17; Fishel, **Secret War**, p.424.

apparent to me that I will not direct it unless more positive instructions are received from a higher authority." Sykes was not about to put his men in jeopardy unless Meade or Hooker so ordered.[92]

Meade must have inquired regarding an explanation for as it turned out, Butterfield's original and poorly worded communication was put right on 7 June. The intent was not as Sykes had suspected but rather the effort was to be one of espionage. "The idea was to find out, if possible, what troops the enemy have at Banks' Ford without bringing on a fight, by any stratagem or device that circumstances might make prudent," Butterfield responded to Meade. Butterfield also made it known that Hooker did not desire any effort or movement that would give the enemy any knowledge of the size or disposition of Meade's force at the fords. That day Sykes reported no Rebel activity at either of the fords entrusted to him.[93]

Upriver, Meade's First Division, under General Barnes, had been charged with guarding and picketing the fords beyond the confluence of the Rapidan and Rappahannock River's. On 6 June he reported to Meade the activity he had seen in his area. "Colonel [Strong] Vincent reports that at Kemper's Ford the pickets yesterday were weak and few appeared. This morning they are stronger and show themselves in considerable numbers. Last night two supports were heard to move nearer the river, being moved back at daylight. It was not possible to ascertain whether they were cavalry or infantry. At Ellis Ford the enemy makes no attempt to conceal his movements; has but small force, and there is apparently but little, if any, strengthening the line." Barnes' report showed that upriver, as with the lower fords there was not much activity beyond the coming and going of each side's pickets.[94]

Still in the Dark

While Colonel Sharpe was assembling his information into something that resembled a concise report, many facts still eluded the Federals and caused great confusion. None of the intelligence on shifting troops, the return of detached units or the clouds of dust and flashing bayonets indicated that Lee was indeed departing the Rappahannock. Even the prisoners taken at Franklin's Crossing did little more than confirm the bulk of the force before Fredericksburg was Hill's Corps. Hill, in command at Fredericksburg, protecting the roads and rail lines to Richmond, simply meant that Ewell or McLaws were not. Information on the location of Ewell's Corps and McLaws' Division was nonexistent. Information on the location of Pickett's and Hood's Divisions had been spotty at best and could not be relied on with any degree of certainty. Sharpe and his spies, while successful in detecting Stuart's concentration at Culpeper, had not been able to determine the location, movement or intentions of the missing Confederate foot soldiers.

---

[92] *OR* vol.27, pt.3, p.17.

[93] *Ibid*, pp.24, 26.

[94] *OR* vol.51, pt.1, p.1045.

General Sedgwick's reconnaissance across the Rappahannock, while aggressive and flamboyant, did little to enhance Hooker's knowledge of the position, number and intent of the Rebels. Sedgwick's predicament was simple. There was little to learn at the river's edge. In order to obtain any information, he would have to effort a movement into the countryside. To do so however, was to risk a general engagement. This was something which Hooker did not want and said so in his communications. After sorting through Butterfield's confusing notes, the same situation existed north of town along the river. Although he did not want a general engagement, Hooker pushed for as much information gathering as possible. With all the probing and inquisitiveness of the operations along the river in early June, it is surprising no serious confrontations occurred, other than the self-induced fight at Franklin's Crossing.

Even though much of the information gathered during that week was contradictory and incomplete, there was one fact that could not be ignored. Lee's cavalry was already on the move and it was a good bet that his army, if not already, would probably be on the move as well. Such was Lee's nature. He had learned his lessons well under General Scott's tutelage in Mexico. If Hooker was a competent general, he should have realized Lee's preferred method of routing an enemy from a strong position was to turn his flank. Lee had done so previously and there was no reason to believe he would change tactics which had proven to be successful. The general direction would no doubt be northward for Lee would not back away when challenged. Hooker had learned that lesson a month earlier at Chancellorsville. A great deal of evidence pointed toward the Rebel's destination as the Valley of Virginia but a point further to the east was still a possibility. Lee was also assembling his huge force of cavalry in the Culpeper area, but for what reason? Was this a precursor to a movement of the entire Confederate army or the beginning of a massive cavalry raid? Whatever the reason, Hooker felt the concentration of horsemen could not be allowed to take place unmolested. Something needed to be done.

Chapter X
Hooker's Command[1]

> "He must either have it in mind to cross the Upper Potomac, or to throw his army between mine and Washington..."[2]
> Joseph Hooker to President Lincoln.
> 5 June 1863.

The men sent across the river to come to the aide of Colonel Grant's Vermont boys were from the Third Brigade of General Howe's division. The brigade had been assembled earlier in the war from a group of regiments originating from the northeast. Three New York organizations, the 43rd, 49th, and 77th formed the brigade's core. Supplementing the New Yorkers were the 61st Pennsylvania, 21st New Jersey, and the 7th regiment from the state of Maine. Brigadier General Thomas H. Neill had been in command at Chancellorsville, but Neill's horse had been shot from under him. As the animal toppled, it fell on the general and injured him. He remained on the field, but after the fighting was over, turned command over to Colonel Daniel D. Bidewll of the 49th New York. Neill would return to his command before Gettysburg, but as May turned to June, Bidwell was in charge.[3]

Thomas Hewson Neill was a career military man and native Philadelphian. The son of a doctor, Thomas was born on 9 April 1826. His early education was obtained within the local public school system. As a young man he attended the

---

[1] The organization of the Army of the Potomac as it existed at the opening of the Gettysburg Campaign was not consistent with its structure as the battle began. Expiring terms of enlistment and numerical reductions in some regiments forced organizational changes. For the most part, this chapter presents the organization of the command structure as of the beginning of June, 1863. The officers portrayed may not have, at that time, been in command of the divisions and brigades they led at Gettysburg. It notes where possible, any internal organizational changes which affected them or the units they commanded. Additionally, some brigades and regiments which fought at Gettysburg were not with the army as Lee pulled his troops away from Fredericksburg. These changes to the army's organization will be addressed when they occur throughout this work. See Appendix A for the organizational structure of the Army of the Potomac as of 3 June 1863.

[2] *OR* vol.27, pt.1, p.30.

[3] *Ibid,* p.163; *OR* vol.25, pt.2, p.581.

University of Pennsylvania but dropped out after his second year to accept an appointment to West Point. He was a below average student and graduated in 1847 twenty-seventh in a class of thirty-eight. Unlike most of the young army officers in the late 1840s, Thomas did not serve in Mexico. Instead, possibly due to his low class standing, he spent the first three years of his military career as a second lieutenant on the frontier, assigned first to the 4th and then the 5th Infantry regiments. Three years after a promotion to first lieutenant in 1850, Neill returned to take a position at his alma mater teaching drawing. His tenure ended in 1856 when he went west with the Mormon Expedition. Promoted to captain on 1 April 1857, Neill returned to Philadelphia in 1861, as war clouds built in the east.[4]

When the war began, Neill took a position on fellow Philadelphian Major General George Cadwalader's staff, and held the position through the summer of 1861. His assignment, since Cadwalader was in command of the Department of Pennsylvania, allowed Neill to remain close to home. By February the following year, His abilities had been recognized and a promotion to colonel was awarded to him. With his advancement came command of the 23rd Pennsylvania Infantry. He led his new regiment during the Peninsula Campaign as part of General Couch's division of the Fourth Corps. Lightly engaged at Williamsburg, the regiment was in the heat of the fighting at Seven Pines where Neill led his Pennsylvanians in a counterattack which cost 129 men. Although the fighting was intense, and many deeds of valor were performed during the engagement, the brigade's commander, Brigadier General John Abercrombie felt it only necessary to single out members of his personal staff for courageous performance, leaving Neill's deeds unrecognized.

Neill's men were lightly engaged through the remainder of the campaign and did not see any serious action until Fredericksburg. By then, the 23rd along with the remainder of its division had been transferred to the Sixth Corps, becoming that organization's Third Division under the command of General John Newton. During the battle, Neill was forced to take command of the Third Brigade in Howe's Division when its commander, Brigadier General Francis L. Vinton was wounded shortly after the fighting began. Technically, Neill was a brigadier general during the battle. He was promoted on 29 November 1862 but the actual appointment would not be made until April of the following year.

Neill's first intense battle experience came during the Chancellorsville Campaign. On 3 May, his brigade, along with additional Sixth Corps forces, stormed and took Marye's Heights before pushing westward from Fredericksburg. The next day at Salem Church, the brigade was decimated by General Jubal Early's heavy counterattack. Neill was in the thick of the fighting when his horse was hit. The Confederates drove the Federal's back and eventually forced them to retire. The retreat was anything but orderly and the brigade reported 850 men killed, wounded, or captured. No other brigade reported a higher casualty number. Neill was praised by his superiors for his effort, but the severity of the fighting was no

---

[4] Eicher, & Eicher, **High Commands**, p.404; Tagg, **Generals**, pp.113-114.

doubt an eye opener for him. The violence of the war had finally made itself known to Thomas Neill.[5]

On the evening of 7 June, Brigadier General Horatio G Wright, marched his division across Major Brainerd's pontoon bridge and relieved General Howe's tired men. Wright was born 6 March 1829 in the small hamlet of Clinton, Connecticut. Like Thomas Neill, he was educated at the local schools before eventually receiving an appointment to the academy. An exceptional student, he graduated in 1841, second in a class of fifty-two. As with most high ranking graduates, Wright was appointed to the Corps of Engineers and spent his early military career constructing and improving fortifications and harbor garrisons. The prewar years also saw him teaching other West Point cadets engineering and French.

A captain since 1855, when war came, Wright acted as chief engineer for the expedition that destroyed the Norfolk Naval Yard. Unfortunately, he was captured during the operation on 20 April but was exchanged four days later. Promoted to major on 6 August 1861, Wright began a stint performing aide-de-camp duties for General Heintzelman. He was with the general's command when it crossed the Potomac River and took possession of Arlington. When the army marched out to confront the Confederates at Bull Run, Wright went with Heintzelman as his chief engineer. A short time later, on 16 September, with the prospect of a long war looming, Wright was promoted to brigadier general and assigned to the South Carolina expedition where he served as chief engineer during the effort resulting in the capture of Port Royal. Later, while leading a brigade at Secessionville, disaster ensued when the Federal's were bested by a Confederate force half their number. Wright argued against the assault which precipitated the defeat, but he was overruled. Luckily scant attention was paid to the whipping because the Peninsular Campaign was approaching its climax in Virginia.

A transfer and promotion came in July 1862 when Wright was given command of the Department of Ohio and a major generalship. Regrettably, he was forced to relinquish his command on 24 March 1863, when the Senate failed to confirm his promotion. A brief assignment in the Department of Western Kentucky followed. Then, on 23 May Wright was transferred to the Army of the Potomac and given command of Sedgwick's First Division after its previous commander showed poorly at Chancellorsville.

While no one questions Wright's intelligence, he was only an average division commander. Like George McClellan, Wright was deliberate and unhurried to a fault, but demonstrated he was very competent. He was a thinker not a doer, and while he possessed a brilliant mind, he was not a brilliant general. As his division crossed the Rappahannock to relieve General Howe's command, Wright would be facing the enemy for the first time as a member of the great eastern army. By 7

---

5   Eicher, & Eicher, **High Commands**, p.158; Warner, **Generals in Blue**, pp.342-343; Tagg, **Generals**, pp.113-114; Boatner, **Dictionary**, p.586; **OR** vol.11, pt.1, pp.897-898; **OR** vol.21, p.60; **OR** vol.25, pt.1, p.190.

June, he had only been in command of his division for fifteen days, and it would be a number of months before he would lead his new division in battle.[6]

Wright's new command, unlike General Howe's, had a typical compliment of three brigades, the first of which was the only brigade in the Army of the Potomac made entirely of regiments from New Jersey. Populating the "New Jersey Brigade" were the 1st, 2nd, 3rd, 4th, 15th and 23rd regiments. Commanding the Jerseymen was a twenty-nine year old career military officer from Delaware, Brigadier General Alfred Thomas Archimedes Torbert. Born 1 July 1833, Torbert was educated during his formative years at the public schools in Georgetown. In 1851 he received an appointment to the military academy and graduated in the bottom half of his class, twenty-first out of thirty-four. Exiting West Point, Torbert was assigned to frontier duty as a second lieutenant with the 5th Infantry and spent time in Texas, Florida, Missouri, and New Mexico. He helped to protect settlers from Indians and was part of the expedition to the Utah Territory when the disagreements between the Mormons and the Buchanan administration erupted.

Alfred possessed the unique distinction of being a commissioned officer in both the Northern and Southern armies. Evidently it was assumed that Torbert would side with the Southerners. According to Confederate congressional records, Torbert was commissioned a first lieutenant of artillery on 17 April 1861, ranking from 16 March. However, Torbert chose to remain with the North, working to organize a regiment of men from New Jersey. On 16 September 1861, he became colonel of the 1st New Jersey. He led the regiment during the Peninsular Campaign, earning an elevation to command of his division's first brigade. Wounded at Crampton's Gap on South Mountain, he remained on the field, a feat which earned him praise from his division commander General Henry Slocum. Rewarded for his battlefield accomplishments, Torbert was promoted to brigadier general on 29 November 1862.[7]

Although Alfred was a competent brigade commander, which he proved again at Fredericksburg and Chancellorsville, he had one habit which alienated many members of his support staff. He insisted that his staff share in all the hazards a brigade commander was required to endure. He would order members of his delegation and on occasion additional flag-bearers, escorts and orderlies to follow him as he exposed himself at the head of his brigade during battle. Many men who should not have been in the line of fire ended up being wounded or killed. On one occasion the brigade's medical director, who should have been nowhere near the fighting, was killed. No one doubted Torbert's bravery, just his judgment.[8]

General Wright's second brigade, as it prepared for the summer campaign season, was under the command of twenty-nine year old Brigadier General

---

[6] Warner, *Generals in Blue*, p.575; Tagg, *Generals*, p.106; Boatner, *Dictionary*, p.949; *OR* vol.11, pt.1, pp.897-898; *OR* vol.21, p.60; *OR* vol.27, pt.1, p.162; *OR* vol.25, pt.2, p.580.

[7] Warner, *Generals in Blue*, p.508; Eicher, & Eicher, *High Commands*, p.533; Boatner, *Dictionary*, p.842.

[8] Tagg, *Generals*, pp.107-108.

Joseph Jackson Bartlett. Born in Binghamton New York on 11 November 1834, Bartlett was a lawyer by trade, having been admitted to the New York bar in 1858. Throughout his life he showed a unique aptitude for military matters and seemed to possess talent for commanding soldiers. When the conflict began, Joseph left his law practice, signed the enlistment rolls in nearby Elmira, and went to war. With his leadership skills on display, Bartlett was elected captain of his company on 17 May 1861 but only held the rank for four days. When the company was mustered in as Company C of the 27th New York, Bartlett was promoted to major under then Colonel Henry Slocum. The regiment remained in New York for almost two months until it was transferred to Washington, arriving on 10 July.

When Slocum was wounded at First Bull Run, Bartlett took command of the regiment and skillfully led the defeated New Yorkers from the field. As other officers tried to rally fleeing men, Bartlett managed to form the 27th in line. His men were the first to rally and brigade commander, Colonel Andrew Porter, noted in his report "the other regiments engaged soon collected their scattered fragments." Bartlett's stock as a regimental commander rose that day. As luck would have it, when Slocum received his promotion, the regiment's lieutenant colonel resigned and Bartlett became colonel on 1 September. By the end of the year, he would be commanding a brigade but would not receive a promotion to brigadier general until 4 October 1862. By that time, Bartlett had already led the brigade with distinction on the Peninsula and during the Maryland Campaign. He missed the battle of Fredericksburg while on sick leave, but recovered to lead his command during the engagement at Salem Church.

Bartlett shared in the hard times and good times with the men. During leisure activities he could often be found playing camp games, and his participation went far in endearing him to the soldiers of his command. Three different states contributed soldiers to the regiments of Bartlett's brigade. Pennsylvania provided their 95th and 96th regiments while the state of Maine contributed its 5th Infantry. The final regiment, from Bartlett's native state, was the 121st New York. Many of the soldiers within the New York regiment were from the old 27th Infantry. Some men had signed three year papers while others signed two year rolls. The three year men transferred to the 121st when the two year men left the army to be mustered out.[9]

Like Bartlett's brigade, Wright's third brigade was constructed of men from Maine and Pennsylvania but instead of a New York Regiment, a group of Wisconsin boys rounded out the unit. The 5th Wisconsin, 6th Maine and the 49th and 119th Pennsylvanian formed the brigade which was under the command of Brigadier General David Allen Russell. Russell, born in Salem New York, near the Vermont border, on 10 December 1820, was the son of a New York congressman. His father, David Abel Russell, during his final year in Washington, secured for his son an appointment to West Point. Young David was not adequately prepared

---

[9] Warner, ***Generals in Blue***, pp.23-24; Tagg, ***Generals***, pp.108-109; Phisterer, ***NYWR***, vol.3, pp.2039-2040, 2043; ***OR*** vol.27, pt.1, p.162; ***OR*** vol.2, p.385. The 27th left the Army of the Potomac in May 1863 and mustered out at Elmira on 31 May.

for the rigors of academy life and the institution's tough curriculum. He stood third from the bottom among the forty-one cadets who graduated within his class. His low standing may have allowed him to more quickly identify his role within the army, for his assignment to the infantry seemed to bring out the best in him. Initially posted at Fort Scott, Kansas, Russell showed his nerve, making the journey to his new assignment across Indian Territory alone. The following year he proved himself a worthy leader of men during the Mexican War, as he received the brevet of first lieutenant. After the war, he was stationed at Fort Yamhill on garrison duty and fought the Yakima Indians in the Pacific Northwest. He was promoted to captain while serving with the 4th Infantry in 1854.

When the Civil War erupted, Russell was assigned to the defenses of Washington where he served until 31 January 1862, at which time he was made colonel of the 7th Massachusetts Volunteers. His regiment was assigned to McClellan's force and transferred to the Peninsula where he guided it with distinction at Williamsburg and Seven Pines. Russell was mentioned within a group of officers which brigade commander, Colonel John Henry Hobart Ward called out in his report. According to Ward, Russell was one "who conspicuously distinguished [himself]." At Oak Grove, he displayed a trademark of his command style that would earn him praise, reconnoitering in person the enemy's position from his advanced skirmish line. During the Maryland Campaign, Russell's regiment saw no action when it was designated part of the army's reserve force. The lack of combat however did not keep his name from being included within the mass of promotions on 29 November. Afterword, Russell found himself a new brigadier general and took command of his current Sixth Corps brigade. At Fredericksburg, his men were not seriously engaged but during the Chancellorsville Campaign the brigade participated in the storming of Marye's Heights. Before the fighting ended, Russell left behind nearly 360 dead, wounded, and captured. As the brigade prepared to enter upon the summer campaign of 1863, its regiments were reorganized. Two New York regiments whose terms of enlistment were about to end were removed from the brigade leaving Russell with only the two Pennsylvania regiments. To bolster his numbers, the boys from Maine and the Badgers were reassigned to his command.[10]

Sedgwick's Third Division commander, Major General John Newton, was a Southerner born in Norfolk, Virginia on 25 August 1822. Although Newton's family had called Norfolk home for nearly two hundred years, he chose to remain loyal to the Union cause. Having been born to twenty-nine year congressional veteran Thomas Newton, John probably found it fairly easy to garner an appointment to the Military Academy. Although his father had been out of Congress for six years, the elder Newton's associations with influential political figures must have played a role in his son being offered admission. With the proper paperwork filed and his appointment secured, John entered West Point, 1 July 1838. He gave his father no reason to regret sending him to the academy. His academic performance kept him near the top of his class for all four years of his schooling. He graduated second in

---

[10] Warner, *Generals in Blue*, pp.416-417; Tagg, *Generals*, p.110; *OR* vol.11, pt.1, p.856; *OR* vol.25, pt.1, p.165; Phisterer, *NYWR*, vol.3, pp.1946, 2103; *OR* vol.27, pt.1, p.163.

his class of fifty-six, putting Daniel Harvey Hill, George Sykes, John Pope, Abner Doubleday and James Longstreet to shame.[11]

Except for serving as chief engineer during the Mormon Expedition, and a period as an instructor at West Point, Newton spent his entire career prior to the war assigned to desk duty with the Corps of Engineers. Brevetted a second lieutenant, he performed the typical duties of an army engineer. He spent a majority of his time helping to improve coastal facilities including harbor installations, the building of fortifications, and the construction of lighthouses. When the war began, John ignored his Southern upbringings and sided with the Union. In late May 1861, he was assigned to engineering duties in the Department of Pennsylvania. Two months later he was transferred to the Department of the Susquehanna and after another month of engineering service he was promoted to major. On 23 September, after the disaster at Bull Run, Newton was promoted directly to brigadier general of volunteers. He went to Washington and used his refined engineering talents to improve and shore up the city's defenses. Prior to the Peninsular Campaign, Newton received his first field command when he was assigned to a brigade within Henry Slocum's division of the Sixth Corps. At Gaines' Mill, he encountered his first heavy combat and led his brigade with distinction. Again, at Malvern Hill, Newton guided his charges through the heaviest of fighting. According to Slocum, he was "entitled to the greatest praise, not only for [his] heroic conduct on the field, but for [his] untiring efforts after the close of the action in bringing off the wounded and in maintaining order and steadiness amid the prevalent confusion."[12]

Although elevated to major general, John Newton would see his promotion rescinded for his role in the Burnside affair. *LOC*

---

[11] Eicher, & Eicher, *High Commands*, pp.405-406. There is some confusion over Newton's actual day and year of birth. Some sources indicate 24 August 1823.

[12] Warner, *Generals in Blue*, p.345; Faust, *Encyclopedia*, p.530; *OR* vol.11, pt.2, p.433;

During the Maryland Campaign, Newton helped drive the Confederates from the crest of South Mountain, prompting his corps commander, General Franklin to recommend him for promotion to major general. When General Slocum departed to take command of the lamented General Mansfield's Twelfth Corps, Newton was elevated to divisional command. Fortunately for Newton, his division was not called upon to participate in the attack on Marye's Heights at Fredericksburg and after the battle he joined the chorus of generals speaking out against General Burnside. A week after the battle, Newton traveled to Washington to let his feelings be known. Accompanied by Brigadier General John Cochrane, Newton met with Lincoln and expressed to the president the army was in no condition to execute any movement Burnside may be contemplating. Shortly after the meeting, Lincoln informed Burnside that he had "good reason for saying [Burnside] must not make a general movement of the army without letting [him] know." This must have confused Burnside for during the same time period, Halleck was wiring with instructions to "press the enemy." Newton and Cochrane's efforts to halt the movement bordered on insubordination, and it is surprising that Newton was not dismissed. Perhaps he retained his command because his concerns were not intended to stop Burnside from making a bad decision but to prevent undue hardships being heaped upon the backs of a tired and bloody army. Newton, however, was unable to halt the effort which resulted in the infamous "Mud March" which sealed the fate of Burnside.[13]

As a result of his verbal degradation of Burnside, Newton ended up on the list of officers who Burnside wanted dismissed. Fortunately, Hooker was promoted and he remained with his division, but the expression of his views would not go unpunished. He was promoted to major general on 30 March 1863, but his appointment would be withdrawn almost a year later for his involvement in the revolt against Burnside. Whether his contemporaries approved or condemned his actions in the Burnside matter, no one could make a case that Newton was not a quality field commander. Perhaps his finest moment in battle came as he led his division in the storming of Marye's Heights during the Chancellorsville Campaign. He pushed the Confederates westward until they made their successful stand at Salem Church. The image of his success on that day would be fresh in the minds of his superiors a few weeks later at Gettysburg.[14]

John Newton was not a flamboyant man and lacked the flare of more notable generals, but his men respected his decision making. Some thought him lazy and fond of the comforts available to influential military commanders but all who came to know him considered him quite intelligent. Former 6th Wisconsin adjutant Frank Haskell penned a long winded description of Newton, noting he was "a well-sized, shapely, muscular, well dressed man, with brown hair, with a very ruddy, clean-shaved, full face, blue eyes, blunt, round features, walks very erect, curbs in his chin, and has somewhat of that smart sort of swagger, that people are apt to suppose

---

[13] Tagg, **Generals**, p.13; Sandburg, Carl, **Abraham Lincoln: The War Years**, vol.1, p.632; **OR** vol.21, pt.1, p.900.

[14] Warner, **Generals in Blue**, p.345; Eicher, & Eicher, **High Commands**, p.406.

characterizes soldiers." Like his West Point classmate, George Sykes, Newton was simply a soldier, nothing more, and certainly nothing less.[15]

Although Brigade General Alexander Shaler was not in command of his brigade as May turned to June, the Connecticut native would soon return to his position at the head of Newton's First Brigade. Born in Haddam on 19 March 1827, he moved to New York at the age of seven and received his formative education in his new home's public schools. As Shaler grew to adulthood, he became a man about town, joining and participating in many social clubs and activities. His gallivanting seems to have been bolstered by his independent wealth which he probably inherited. Without the need to provide himself income, Shaler enjoyed a great deal of spare time and chose to fill some of it by joining the "Washington Grays," a militia unit which eventually became the 8th New York Militia. Shaler would ultimately become a member of the 7th New York Militia, where he was mustered in with the rank of major. Five days after Fort Sumter was attacked, Shaler traveled to Washington with the 7th. He remained there for six weeks as the city cowered under the prospect of the Confederates marching into town.[16]

On 3 June, after its one month enlistment period expired, the 7th was mustered out. Eight days later, Shaler's volunteer career continued when he was commissioned lieutenant colonel of the 65th New York, becoming second in command behind John Newton's co-conspirator, then Colonel John Cochrane. His first action was at Seven Pines where he received high praise from Cochrane. Writing in his report, the colonel noted, "Lieutenant-Colonel Shaler evinced during the entire action that presence of mind and military abilities for which he is so highly reputed." At Malvern Hill, Shaler performed well enough to earn a promotion to colonel on 17 July. He took command of the regiment when Cochrane was promoted to brigadier general and led it through the Maryland Campaign. The brigade, as part of General Couch's tiny Fourth Corps, was held in reserve at Antietam and saw no action. Although the Fourth Corps was consolidated into the Sixth, the situation remained the same for the 65th at Fredericksburg, where it once again saw no action. In March 1863, Cochrane, for his part in the Burnside fiasco, was forced to resign his commission to avoided political repercussions, and Shaler took command of the brigade.[17]

Shaler's first opportunity to lead his brigade in combat came when Newton's Division, advancing from the streets of Fredericksburg, stormed and captured Marye's Heights on 3 May. Shaler's men, who were positioned behind the front line of assaults troops, supported the attack. The combined weight of the Federal

---

[15] Byrne & Weaver, Editors, **Haskell**, p.133.

[16] **OR** vol.25, pt.2, p.581; Warner, **Generals in Blue**, pp.434-435; Phisterer, **NYWR**, vol.1, p.555.

[17] Phisterer, **NYWR**, vol.1, pp.555, vol.3, pp.2630, 2645; **OR** vol.11, pt.1, p.900; Tagg, **Generals**, p.116. A number of sources indicate that Cochrane resigned his commission due to ill health. Although his health may have been an issue, many in the command structure of the army and Washington politicians knew the circumstances and correctly deduced that his outspoken attitude toward Burnside was the major reason for his departure.

effort was able to accomplish what had eluded Burnside's troops a few months earlier and the Confederates were driving off. While Shaler led his men with distinction during the engagement, he performed no extraordinary actions which would have caught attention or drawn praise. In two days of fighting, his brigade lost a total of seven men killed and eight-six wounded. Sixty-seven of the brigade's members were missing or captured. His total losses were far fewer than any other brigade in Newton's division. However, for some reason Shaler was awarded the Medal of Honor thirty years later for his role in the taking of the heights. Time and decaying memories, supported by exaggerations may have played a part.[18]

Although Shaler may not have deserved the honor, he had been recognized as one of the up and coming colonels in the army. On 26 May, he was made a brigadier general in a ceremony which saw none other than President Lincoln pin the star on his shoulder. Although there were still questions as to the former militia major's abilities as a brigade commander, Shaler was placed in permanent command of Cochrane's old unit. The men of his old regiment along with the 67th and 122nd New York, and the 23rd and 82nd Pennsylvania would march north under the command of a man who, in his spare time, as a member of the New York militia, learned how to be a soldier.[19]

Brevet Brigadier General Abraham Eustis, a veteran of the War of 1812 and the Black Hawk War, contributed to the Union war effort in the form of his son, Henry Lawrence Eustis. Abraham and his first wife, Rebecca Sprague, had seven children together, all of them boys, of which Henry was the last. Henry's father was stationed at Fort Independence in Boston harbor when Rebecca gave birth the first day of February, 1819. Unfortunately for the boy, he never really knew his mother for she died when he was sixteen months old.[20]

Henry, following his older brothers Horatio and Frederick, entered Harvard University from which he graduated in 1838. Optioning not to immediately utilize his education, he, once again chose to follow in the footsteps of a sibling and accepted an appointment to West Point, just as his oldest brother William had done a few years earlier. He entered the academy on 1 September 1838 and, obviously benefiting from his Harvard edification, instantly began to outdistance his classmate's academic skills and study habits. He quickly propelled himself to the number one position in the class of 1842. Even Henry's current division commander John Newton, who had shamed a number of his contemporaries and future antagonists finished behind the studious Eustis. Upon graduation, he joined the engineers as a second lieutenant and worked as an assistant to the Board of Engineers for a year. For the next four years, Eustis saw duty at Fort Warren, Lovell's Island and at Newport, Rhode Island, before returning to West Point to assume assistant professor of engineering responsibilities. After two years

---

[18] *OR* vol.25, pt.1, pp.189-190; Tagg, **Generals**, p.117.

[19] Tagg, **Generals**, p.117; *OR* vol.25, pt.2, p.581.

[20] Eustis, Henry Lawrence, **Genealogy of the Eustis Family**, pp.15, 22. There is no record of the cause of Rebecca's death in Eustis work.

of instructing the plebes at the academy, Henry resigned his commission on 30 November 1849, and returned to Harvard as a professor of engineering, a position he assumed the day following his departure from the army. Eustis held his teaching position at his alma mater until his death in 1885, his term interrupted only by his war service.[21]

When the war began, Eustis did not immediately rush to the defense of the Union. Shortly after the Peninsular Campaign concluded and although his health was questionable, Henry signed the volunteer rolls. Due to his military education, he was commissioned colonel of the 10th Massachusetts Infantry. The regiment had been without its colonel since Malvern Hill where a number of its commanding officers had been lost. For the next nine months Eustis would march his regiment north into Maryland and back to the banks of the Rappahannock but would see no action. Finally, during the Chancellorsville Campaign, Henry got a chance to lead the regiment in battle and the New Englander did not disappoint. At Salem Church, during some of the heaviest fighting, brigade commander William Browne fell wounded, forcing Eustis to assume command. Digging in and filled with resolve, Eustis led his men as they fought off a number of Confederate attacks and then skillfully guided them off the field after Sedgwick began his retreat to and across the river. Eustis left behind 342 killed, wounded, captured or missing and received a pat on the back from his old classmate Newton when the division commander told General Sedgwick that Eustis had provided "gallant service."[22]

Although Eustis proved himself under fire at Salem Church, he was basically untested at the head of a brigade. While the men of the 10th Massachusetts were well-acquainted with him and knew his skill, to the other regiments in the brigade, the 7th and 37th Massachusetts, the 36th New York and the 2nd Rhode Island, he was an unknown commodity.[23]

Newton's third brigade was built from a group of Pennsylvania regiments, the 93rd, 98th, 102nd, and 139th, all of which were supported by a fifth regiment, the 62nd New York. Commanded by Brigade General Frank Wheaton, all the regiments except the 139th had been brigaded together since the Peninsular Campaign as first, part of the defunct Fourth Corps and later, as part of the Sixth Corps. Wheaton, a Rhode Islander, born on 8 May 1833, was the son-in-law of the Confederacy's ranking general, Samuel Cooper. The son of a doctor and Brown University graduate, Frank entered his father's alma mater in 1850 but withdrew before graduation to take a position conducting surveying work with the Mexican-American Boundary Commission. Wheaton evidently made some connections during his time on the border for in 1855 he was commissioned directly into the 1th

---

[21]   Eustis, Henry L., ***Genealogy of the Eustis Family***, pp.15, 20-22; Eicher, & Eicher, ***High Commands***, p.228.

[22]   ***OR*** vol.25, pt.1, pp.190, 562; Tagg, ***Generals***, p.118.

[23]   ***OR*** vol.25, pt.1, pp.581.

U. S. Cavalry as a first Lieutenant on 3 March. For the next few years, Wheaton saw extensive service in the west and spent a good deal of his time fighting Indians.[24]

As the war loomed, Wheaton's family was torn apart by allegiance and political ideologies. Frank had been married to General Cooper's daughter for less than two years before she died, which may have provided the onus for him to forgo any connection with his late wife's family preference and remain with the Union. Joining the 2nd Rhode Island on 10 July 1861 as the regiments lieutenant colonel, he soon ascended to command of the regiment when, at First Bull Run, the unit's original colonel was killed. Wheaton fought the regiment as a member of the Fourth Corps on the Peninsula and was commended for his performance by his brigade commander who noted that Wheaton was "very efficient" in the execution of his duties.

On 29 November Wheaton was promoted to brigadier general but was not placed in permanent command of a brigade until he took over the Pennsylvanians and New Yorkers two days after Burnside's folly at Fredericksburg. During the Chancellorsville Campaign, he led his command across the river into Fredericksburg and up the slope against Marye's Heights, helping to dislodge the Confederates there. General Sedgwick noted in his report that Wheaton showed "skill and personal gallantry during the fighting." With one major engagement under his belt and having given his commander no ammunition for criticism, Wheaton would remain at the head of his brigade as it marched north in pursuit of Lee in the coming weeks.[25]

John Reynolds is Offered a Job, Again?

John Reynolds was on his way to a job interview. At 2:00 p.m. on 31 May, General Abner Doubleday issued a short communication indicating he was in temporary command of the corps while Reynolds was away at the inquest. Reynolds had heard through a friend that his name was under consideration by Lincoln to supplant Hooker. Not wanting to pass up an opportunity to take command of the Union's largest and arguably, best army in the field, Reynolds, on his own accord, left camp and made the trip up the Potomac to the capital. Reynolds however, was a principled man. His primary reason for declining the previous offer of command was the administration's meddling in army affairs. If things had not changed or Lincoln was not agreeable to negotiate a change in Washington's involvement, his answer to any offer made would still be no.[26]

Reynolds had every confidence in his abilities and qualifications. Although he had not been summoned by the administration, his intention was to meet with Lincoln and possibly Halleck to frankly discuss the situation and his interest in assuming command. When he arrived, he was given an audience with Lincoln

---

[24] Warner, ***Generals in Blue***, p.553; Eicher, & Eicher, ***High Commands***, p.563; ***Electronic Source:*** http://en.wikipedia.org/wiki/Frank_Wheaton. Last Accessed 5/5/2012.

[25] *Ibid*, ***OR*** vol.11, pt.1, p.522; ***OR*** vol.25, pt.1, p.562.

[26] ***OR*** vol.51, pt.1, p.1043; Meade, ***Meade***, p.385.

where the two men openly discussed the condition of the army. According to Reynolds, Lincoln then offered command of the army to him, and once again he declined. Evidently circumstances regarding the involvement of Washington would not change. Halleck and Lincoln would still require the army's commander to perform as instructed from the capital. This stipulation Reynolds could not accept and he rejected the offer. He evidently discussed Hooker's ability to command the army and must have spoke bluntly about his poor opinion of the commanding general. Lincoln listened intently and then informed Reynolds that he "was not disposed to throw away a gun because it misfired once" and "he would pick the lock and try again."[27]

Reynolds left no personal account of the visit with the president. After the meeting, he traveled to Baltimore to visit his sister Eleanor who was in town visiting family. Ellie recounted her brother's visit many years later in a letter to her nephew.

"We had been to a *"Union Concert"* that evening, and as we approached the house saw lights in the parlor, and found your Uncle John reading there. He told us he had been with the President that day, and that Mr. Lincoln had offered him the command of the Army of the Potomac, which he told the President he would accept if he was not interfered with from Washington. *This* the President would not promise him, therefore your Uncle declined the offer. I am positive as to the date being June 2nd because it was the *last* time I saw him, and because the next morning, before he left us, a telegram came from your father, announcing the birth of your youngest brother..."

There is little doubt as to Eleanor's recollection of the event, it being accompanied by other notable memories. The baby mentioned by Ellie was indeed born on 2 June and giving the name William Reynolds Landis and according to family sources her mind was alert and sharp although the event which she wrote of had occurred fifty years earlier, General Reynolds never documented his trip to see Lincoln in any letters or official correspondence, possibly because he took it upon his own accord to visit the president and some may have thought it inappropriate or a bit arrogant on his part. Additionally, if Hooker were to become aware of the communication, the crack which had developed between Reynolds and his chief after Chancellorsville would have turned into a chasm which would never close.[28]

There is one other piece of corroborating evidence regarding the general's meeting with the president. Reynolds' friend, General Meade, left an account of the meeting which Reynolds relayed to him ten days after the event. Stopping to see his friend as he passed Fifth Corps headquarters, Reynolds told his fellow Pennsylvanian that he had gone to Washington to talk with the president about taking command of the army. Meade wrote to his wife how Reynolds had traveled to the capital in response to being told by a friend he trusted that he was under consideration for command of the army. Meade's account differs from the Ellie Reynolds' letter in that, according to Meade, the general was going to Washington

---

[27] Nichols, *Toward Gettysburg*, pp.183-184; Meade, *Meade*, p.385.

[28] Nichols, *Toward Gettysburg*, pp.222-223.

to inform Lincoln he did not want the position and not to consider him. Meade then recorded that Reynolds had a candid conversation with Lincoln about Hooker and his abilities.[29]

While there is some doubt as to whether Reynolds was offered command of the army in January, the evidence that he was considered in early June is more substantial. Although, other than Ellie's letter and Meade's communication to his wife, no other evidence that Lincoln offered command of the army exists. There is no mention of it in correspondence or documents contained in Lincoln's extensive writings. The same can be said for the papers of Stanton and Halleck. Accounts of the event beyond the analysis of the two known records of the meeting are speculation or plain fiction.

The differences in the two accounts can be cleared up with the presentation of simple logic. According to Reynolds' sister, the president had offered command to her brother, but John declined citing continuing Washington involvement. Meade noted in his letter to Margaretta that Reynolds traveled to Washington to tell Lincoln he did not want the position even though it had yet to be offered. It is improbable that Reynolds would leave his command to travel to Washington to decline an offer, of which no details were known and had yet to be made. The more prudent action would have been to wait until an offer was made, if it indeed came, then inquire as to its conditions and then decline it if the extent of Washington's involvement had not changed. It is also likely that Reynolds went to Washington to head off any offer of command before it was made because once made he may have felt duty bound to accept. A more probable scenario however, is that Reynolds saw an opportunity to command the army under his terms. With Hooker's defeat at Chancellorsville fresh in the minds of Lincoln and Halleck, he may have thought himself in a position to dictate his terms for accepting any offer. After all the stipulations where laid out and an offer made, Reynolds declined the position because Lincoln was not ready to relinquish what he felt was necessary involvement from Washington. The two men then discussed Hooker remaining in command and its ramification. It is possible that Lincoln was patronizing Reynolds all along since Meade indicates that Lincoln was not yet ready to give up on Hooker. In the final analysis, only two absolute facts about the event are known; John Reynolds did go to Washington and turn down an offer to command the army and the actual content of the conversation between Lincoln and the general is lost to time and will never be known.

Some of the Toughest Men in the Army

The First Division of John Reynolds First Corps was particularly hard hit by expiring enlistments during late May and June of 1863. The First Brigade saw the 24th New York sent home for muster out at the end May. The 22nd and 30th New York followed, departing early in June. Only a single regiment, the 84th New York remained. The First Division was also reduced by the departure of an entire brigade of nine month New Jersey troops. After the mass exodus, the division was left with

---

[29] Meade, *Meade*, p.385.

only two full brigades and the depleted 84th New York. After absorbing the losses, the division was consolidated from four brigades to two, becoming a shadow of its former self. However, the group of regiments remaining had already proved they were some of the toughest men in the army.[30]

While Reynolds prepared to return to his corps, the men in the ranks spent the first week of June roasting under the hot Virginia sun. While the nights and mornings were cool, the afternoons indicated that summer had arrived. Their encampment near White Oak Church proved to be a good observation point from which to scrutinize the shifting Confederate forces across the river. The stirring Rebels caused orders to be issued to some First Corps troops to prepare to shift their position at daylight the following morning. Daylight brought great activity as tents were struck and preparations made. Unfortunately, no further orders were received until shortly before noon when the men were instructed to pitch tents and resume normal camp life. Again, on the evening of 5 June, orders were received to once again prepare to march at daylight. As the sun came up, men were rousted from their night's sleep and tents were struck. They filled canteens and loaded three days rations into their haversacks. As before, orders to move out were never issued and the men settled in for another night. Some elements of the corps however, did march but only for a short distance. One of the brigades was advanced to Franklin's Crossing and posted in line of battle to support Sedgwick's Corps. The hot weather drained the men as they took their new position and all longed for shade and rest. On one occasion, a man who had fallen asleep was roused when his fellow soldiers poured water in his ear.[31]

The men sent to support Sedgwick's boys were under the command of Brigadier General James Samuel Wadsworth. Wadsworth, a fifty-six year old white haired New Yorker, had studied law at Harvard and Yale although he never intended to practice the profession. Born on 30 October 1807 in Genesee County, western New York, James was the second of five children and the eldest boy. His father was one of the largest landowners in the state, and the family had determined early that James would follow in his parent's footsteps. The boy however, refused to cooperate spending his early years and his time at Harvard and Yale antagonizing his father and seemingly throwing a damper on the elder Wadsworth's plans. By the time the war began, James had joined the upstart Republican Party, become a philanthropist, and taken over his late father's large estate. The elder Wadsworth's fears of his son failing to amount to anything substantial ended up being nothing more than a father driving his son to become a man before the youngster was finished being a boy.[32]

Wadsworth had no training in military matters when the war opened but volunteered for service anyway. Although other men of his stature accepted

---

[30] Phisterer, *NYWR*, vol.3, pp.1982, 2002, 2078. The 24th was mustered out in Elmira on 29 May, the 22nd on 19 June and the 30th on 18 June in Albany.

[31] Curtis, Orson Blair, *History of the 24th Michigan of the Iron Brigade*, pp.142-143; Dawes, *Service*, pp.147-148.

[32] Mahood, Wayne, *General Wadsworth: The Life and times of Brevet Major General James S. Wadsworth*, pp.20-25, 44; Tagg, *Generals*, pp.14-15.

appointment to positions they were not qualified for, Wadsworth held no illusions as to his role in the coming conflict. He believed his administrative and organizational skills could be of best use working in Washington or with the army as a member of an officer's staff. To that end, he inquired of General McDowell if he might be allowed to serve on McDowell's staff as an aide-de-camp. McDowell was a bit puzzled by the query, as Wadsworth was ten years the general's senior, but McDowell arranged for Wadsworth to be appointed to the position. During the First Bull Run campaign Wadsworth showed great promise and after the battle McDowell put his aide in for a promotion. He bounded from his position as aide-de-camp to brigadier general on 9 August 1861, and was assigned command of the Second Brigade of McDowell's division on 3 October. Wadsworth held brigade command until 17 March 1862 when he was sent to the capital to fill the Department of Washington's military governor's position.[33]

Unfortunately for Wadsworth, the position required a level of administrative skill and responsibility he was not suited to handle. While in Washington, he also succeeded in making an enemy who would hinder his military career until the end of the year. When McClellan departed for the Peninsula with his mighty Army of the Potomac in 1862, it was Wadsworth who complained to Lincoln that the departure had left the capital too lightly defended. The president reacted by withholding McDowell's First Corps from Little Mac's invasion force. Wadsworth's actions put him on the bad side of McClellan which early in the war was not a good place to be if advancement was a goal. Later that year, he cast his hat into the ring for the governorship of his native state. Devotion to his military duties kept him from leaving the army and campaigning for the position which allowed his anti-war Democratic opponent to defeat him. McClellan did all he could to hurt Wadsworth's cause, spewing words which showed a deep and vile hatred for the New Yorker. "I [McClellan] must confess a double motive for desiring the defeat of Wadsworth. I have so thorough a contempt for the man & regard him as such a vile traitorous miscreant that I do not wish to see the great State of N. Y. disgraced by having such a thing at its head." By the beginning of 1863, McClellan had been removed for the last time, and Wadsworth was assigned a field command which he still held as the month of June opened.[34]

The men of Wadsworth's division soon learned that their new commander was a man of integrity who cared deeply for their welfare. They were impressed with the fact that he was serving his country for no pay and had given up his relaxing lifestyle on his New York estate. It did the men good to know that their commander was making sacrifices the same as any common foot soldier. Wadsworth was particularly interested in making sure his men were properly fed, clothed and had adequate shelter. It was not uncommon for him to be seen before sunrise wandering the camps inquiring as to whether the men were comfortable, warm and that their sleeping quarters were ventilated properly.

---

[33] Krumwiede, John F., *"Old Waddy's Coming" The Military Career of Brigadier General James S. Wadsworth*, pp.3-4, 8, 12; Eicher, & Eicher, *High Commands*, p.547.

[34] Krumwiede, *"Old Waddy's Coming"*, pp.12, 14, 17, 19.

After complaining to Lincoln that the capital was exposed, James Samuel Wadsworth found himself on the wrong side of George McClellan's ire. *LOC*

Though the men appreciated him greatly, Wadsworth displayed his inexperience as a field commander when his first engagement at the head of his division went afoul. Called on to cross the Rappahannock south of Fredericksburg; he procrastinated for a period of time. When he finally issued orders sending one of his brigades across the river in boats, Confederates on the far bank were ready and began harassing them with rifle fire. When the enemy began shooting, Wadsworth countermanded the order. Then after additional reflection he ordered the crossing to proceed. His hesitation was proof that he still had much to learn about leading combat troops in battle even though his casualties were light. No one questioned his abilities as an administrator but as his division waited for orders signaling the beginning of the summer campaign season, Wadsworth's skill as a division commander was still unknown.[35]

The First Division brigade, which Wadsworth had sent across the river, was the same body of men who would later march to support Sedgwick's crossing. They were known as the Iron Brigade and were distinguishable due to their tall black Hardee hats which the men wore as a badge of honor. When Rebel infantry saw the men in the black hats, they knew they were in for a fight. The Iron Brigade was the only all western brigade in the Army of the Potomac. The four original regiments, the 2nd, 6th and 7th Wisconsin and the 19th Indiana had been recently joined by the freshly mustered 24th Michigan. The brigade had suffered greatly in its previous engagements. On 9 October 1862, the 24th was added to boost the unit's numbers. While the Michigan men were also from the west, the remainder of the brigade

---

[35] Tagg, *Generals*, p.15.

would withhold judgment as to the 24th's fighting abilities until after they had shown their mettle in battle.[36]

Of the four original regiments only the 2nd Wisconsin had seen the "elephant" at First Bull Run. Its members had been some of the first to answer the call for volunteers and were present on the field when the first major battle of the war was fought. The other regiments could have been considered extremely raw when they were brigaded together in the winter of 1862 and placed under the command of Brigadier General Rufus King. A short time later, King went on to divisional command and the brigade was turned over to Brigadier General John Gibbon. Gibbon, who was responsible for outfitting the men with their famous black hats, led the brigade during their baptism of fire at Brawner Farm, the predecessor of Second Bull Run. General Ewell was well aware of the fighting talent of the brigade. It was quite likely a bullet from the weapon of a member of the Iron Brigade cost him his leg.[37]

Later, during the Maryland Campaign, the brigade fought on the wooded slopes of South Mountain where they met elements of General D. H. Hill's Division. Hill, acting as Lee's rear guard, was posted toward the summit of the ridge. The Iron Brigade ascended the slope and engaged the Rebels, eventually driving them from the mountain. During the fighting, General McClellan observed the brigade as it engaged the enemy and after learning the men where those of General Gibbon, proclaimed, "[T]hey must be made of iron." Whether truth or fabrication, as evidence cannot confirm McClellan's words, the name stuck and the men of the brigade began using the moniker and wore the designation as a badge of honor. Three days later the brigade suffered heavy casualties in and around the Miller Cornfield. It was shortly thereafter that attrition in the ranks precipitated the addition of the 24th Michigan.[38]

The winter and spring of 1863 saw limited action for the brigade, and it recuperated somewhat. Once again a change at the head of the unit took place as General Gibbon moved on to divisional command. The man appointed to lead the brigade was an unlikely military leader who had grown up poor in North Carolina. Solomon Meredith was born in Guilford County on 29 May 1810, and as a young man proved his grit and determination by walking to Indiana where once settled, he became a day laborer in order to pay for his education. Once out of school, he took up farming and entered the world of politics and at the age of twenty-four became a county sheriff. After serving two terms, Meredith was elected and served four terms in the state legislature where he displayed a talent for leading men. Governor Oliver P. Morton thought so highly of him that when the 19th Indiana was formed and sent off to war, Meredith, at the age of fifty-one, became its colonel.

---

[36] Curtis, *24th Michigan*, pp.65, 142-143; *OR* vol.27, pt.1, p.155.

[37] Warner, *Generals in Blue*, pp.269, 171; Nolan, Alan T., *The Iron Brigade: A Military History*, p.54. "Seeing the elephant" was a term used by Civil War soldiers to describe the experiences of war and soldiering.

[38] Nolan, *The Iron Brigade*, pp.335-336, n50.

Known as "Long Sol" due to his six foot seven inch frame, Meredith did not become the regimental commander Morton believed he would be. While the men of the regiment thought he meant well, they were not impressed with his leadership abilities. Sol was not a stickler for details, possibly an offshoot of his political career. Regimental inspection reports often showed the men in a poor state of military readiness. In addition, it was blatantly evident that Meredith had aspirations for high rank and did a number of things which were self-serving and designed to improve his visibility to the upper echelon. In fact, many of the men banded together in an effort to get Meredith promoted so that he would be assigned another command and leave the regiment.

At Brawner Farm, Meredith fell from his horse but recovered in time to march north into Maryland and lead the regiment at South Mountain. However, three days later, as the brigade deployed and fought at Antietam, he was absent. Using his fall as a crutch, Sol declared himself unfit for duty and went to Washington to recover. While in the capital, he did more lobbying for a promotion than he did recovering. General Gibbon, a professional soldier, was anything but pleased with the absence of one of his regimental commanders on the eve of one of the greatest battles of the war. Once recovered, Sol did not immediately return to his regiment but instead traveled to Indiana to try and organize an all Indiana brigade which he no doubt believed his political connections would appoint him as the new unit's brigadier. While in Indiana, word arrived of General Gibbon's promotion. Meredith now began a second campaign, lobbying for command of the Iron Brigade. His shenanigans paid off, and he took command of the westerners in time to lead them at Fredericksburg. During the battle, Sol failed to carry out an order from division commander, Brigadier General Abner Doubleday, and was relieved of his duties. By the time General Hooker inaugurated the movements which resulted in the fight at Chancellorsville, Meredith had been returned his command. The brigade suffered lightly during the campaign and as the army prepared to counter Lee's movements in early June, "Long Sol" Meredith had yet to prove to anyone associated with the army that he was up to the task of brigade command.[39]

The man who replaced Sol Meredith at the head of the Iron Brigade after the Indianan was relieved at Fredericksburg was Colonel Lysander Cutler. Cutler was a rugged looking old veteran of the Aroostook War, which took place along the Canadian Border in Maine during the 1830s. During the fighting, he commanded a regiment of state militia. Born 16 February 1807 in Royalston, Worcester County, Massachusetts, he was the son of a farmer whom Lysander disappointed when he chose to continue his education instead of helping the family work the land. Since farm life lacked appeal, Cutler, at the age of twenty-one, moved to Dexter, Maine and began teaching school. A no nonsense disciplinarian, he resorted to flogging his students if they did not behave. He later entered the business world, building a woolen mill which he ran for ten years. The enterprise was successful and generated a sizable amount of wealth, but a fire brought destruction to the mill and most of Cutler's fortune. Marshaling his determination, he built another mill and

---

[39] Warner, *Generals in Blue*, p.319; Tagg, *Generals*, pp.16-17.

was once again back on his feet. Other ventures followed including a grist mill, a foundry, a saw mill and some factories. His successful business ventures brought him notoriety and a seat in the Maine Senate, but the panic of 1856 reduced him to poverty once again. Packing his belongings, he left Maine and moved to Wisconsin and a fresh start. Once again, he began to rebuild his fortune, taking a position as a claims officer for a mining company. As the nation moved toward war, Lysander Cutler had seen both success and failure. He was well prepared for the elation of victory or the depression of defeat.[40]

Shortly after the war began, Cutler received a commission and was given the colonelcy of the 6th Wisconsin. As with his teaching experience, he quickly proved to be an overbearing officer who had no tolerance for any subordinate he deemed unfit. However, for all his supposed mistreatment of his men, there was no doubt whatsoever that Lysander Cutler was a fighter. He was tenacious on a battlefield and was looked upon by General Gibbon with favor. Cutler's tenacity was evident at Brawner Farm where he led the 6th Wisconsin with distinction before he was severely wounded in the right thigh. When Gibbon was promoted to division command, he recommended Cutler be elevated to head of the Iron Brigade, but the political wrangling of "Long Sol" Meredith, and the fact that Cutler was still recovering from his wound, kept him from the command and disappointed both Gibbon and himself. In October 1862, Cutler returned to his regiment even though he needed two canes to support himself and move around. His wound continued to improve and by early December he felt well enough to lead his regiment during the battle of Fredericksburg. As the fighting progressed, he ascended to command of the brigade when Meredith was relieved by General Doubleday. The promotion was only temporary and lasted for just a few hours as Meredith returned to command before the end of the day.[41]

Cutler was promoted to brigadier general in March of the following year and assigned command of the Second Brigade of the First Corps' First Division. His new brigade consisted of a group of New York regiments, the 76th, 95th and 147th, the 56th Pennsylvania and the 7th Indiana. He led his new command at Chancellorsville where it was lightly engaged. As the division reorganized to absorb the departing regiments, Cutler's brigade was augmented with a sixth unit, the 84th New York from the disbanded First Brigade. Cutler would be fifty-six years of age as the army made its way north. Everyone who knew him predicted he would preform well. He was already an able officer. In less than a month he would get his chance to prove he was as rugged a brigade commander as he had been a regimental one.[42]

Commanding the First Corps' Second Division was a crotchety old West Pointer who could lay claim to two unique characteristics. He possessed one of the most violent tempers in the army and he was considered the hairiest general.

---

[40] Dawes, *Service*, p.18; Warner, *Generals in Blue*, p.110; Tagg, *Generals*, pp.18-19.

[41] Tagg, *Generals*, p.19.

[42] *Ibid*; *OR* vol.25, pt.1, p.157; *OR* vol.27, pt.1, p.155.

He sported the most massive beard that the majority of men had ever seen. Such was the appearance and mannerisms of John C. Robinson. Born in New York on 10 April 1817, Robinson's time at the academy was cut short when he was summarily dismissed after a blatant violation of regulations during his second year. Not wishing to give up on a military career, he pursued a commission and managed to be assigned as a second lieutenant to the 5th Infantry in October 1839. He went to Mexico and served as a quartermaster during the war, seeing action at Palo Alto and Resaca de la Palma before marching inland to Mexico City. After the war, he was promoted to captain and spent time in Texas, Utah and Florida before the Civil War erupted.[43]

When Fort Sumter was fired upon, Captain Robinson was in command of the garrison at Fort McHenry in Baltimore Harbor. The state of Maryland and particularly the city had shown support for the South and many of the city's officials and riotous citizens had threatened aggression. On 19 April, as the 6th Massachusetts marched through the streets of the city while changing trains on their way to Washington, violence erupted and a number of citizens were killed.

As the situation in the city deteriorated, Robertson, a prudent commander for a captain, began preparing the fort to receive and hopefully repel any attack. A small brass field piece was place in position to cover the fort's main access road. An additioanl cannon was loaded with canister and positioned to cover the sally port. Eight inch shells were used to produce makeshift grenades. The shells were filled with gunpowder and set with short fuses so they could be lit and tossed from the top of the wall onto any force which my try to scale it. Finally, an old mortar was placed so it could lob shells into the heart of the city. The mortar was so old that Robinson could not be sure if it would fire or simply blow up when the lanyard was pulled.

The men of the garrison also ventured into town to purchase extra food stores to avoid being starved out of their stronghold. Robinson, dressed as a civilian, went into the city as well to determine the mood of the population and to purchase supplies. While there he met an acquaintance who informed him it was not safe to be out of the fort and that he should return to the protection of its walls. If anyone recognized him he would be detained or worse. The samaritan escorted Robinson back to the fort but the young captain had determined what he needed to know. He had few if any friends within the city of Baltimore.

One evening after dark a messenger from the police board arrived with a communication. It was suspected a group of plug-uglies might approach the walls of the fort sometime during the evening. The messenger proposed that he be permitted to have 200 armed men approach the fort to protect it and arrest any trouble makers. Robinson immediately saw through the man's falsehoods. The police board had done little if anything to calm the civil unrest in the city and Robinson had no reason to believe they were about to start. He calmly informed the man he would permit no one to come within three quarters of a mile of the fort. Pointing to the old mortar he told the messenger that if anyone did he would

---

[43] Tagg, ***Generals***, pp.20-21.

open fire on the city center. The man was taken by surprise and said he could not believe the captain would do such a thing. Robinson guaranteed him that he would. The messenger then displayed the true mood of the city.

"I assure you, Captain Robinson," the man stammered, "if there is a woman or child killed in that city there will be not one of you left alive."

Robinson never wavered and told the man he intended to carry out his threat if challenged. The messenger left, no doubt in a hurry. Luckily, Robinson never had to make the decision.

On the same night a steamship suddenly appeared with 800 Massachusetts volunteers aboard. The ship, bound for Fort Monroe had stopped to replenish its fuel supply. After a load of coal was on board the ship left for the Virginia Peninsula. Shortly thereafter, rumors began to spread that a large group of reinforcements had arrived at the fort. Robinson, seizing the opportunity, ordered a number of army tents pitched in plain sight of the city to give the illusion that the rumors where indeed true. The public did not discover their error for ten days and by then it was too late. Robinson's ingenuity and steadfastness was on display at Fort McHenry. He would show the same qualities two years later at Gettysburg.[44]

Leaving Baltimore, Robinson began the war on recruitment duty but by the spring of 1862 he was transferred to field command and made a brigadier general. At Seven Pines when another Federal brigadier fell ill Robinson was thrust into the limelight. He fought his new command well and led with distinction during The Seven Days. In his battle report Brigadier General Philip Kearny wrote glowingly of Robinson. "I have reserved General Robinson for the last. To him this day is due, above all others in the division, the honors of this battle… Everywhere present, by personal supervision and noble example he secured for us the honor of victory."

Robinson was uncharacteristically tentative at Second Bull Run and even when he committed his men late he failed to get his entire command into the fight. He missed the Maryland Campaign, remaining near Washington to help shore up the city's defenses. At Fredericksburg, his brigade was deployed late and never had a chance to show what it could accomplish. With only his work on the Peninsula as a solid basis, he was promoted to division command taking over the Second Division of the First Corps when General Gibbon was wounded. Robinson's division lost only fifty-five men during the Chancellorsville fight, being only lightly engaged. He would still be an unproven division commander as the Battle of Gettysburg unfolded a month later.[45]

On 3 June, Robinson's First Brigade commander was not with the division. Brigadier General Gabriel René Paul was still in command of the soon to depart brigade of Jerseymen in Wadsworth's Division. When the Garden Staters left for muster out, Paul was transferred to command of the brigade which had been under the commanded of the 13th Massachusetts' colonel, Samuel H. Leonard. Paul was the grandson of one of Napoleon's officers who immigrated to America and settled in St. Louis. He was born there on 22 March 1813. Some historical

---

[44] Detzer, David, **Dissonance: The Turbulent Days Between Fort Sumter and Bull Run**, pp.158-160.

[45] Tagg, **Generals**, p.21; **OR** vol.11, pt.2, p.164.

accounts indicate Paul's grandfather built the first house in St. Louis but this seems unlikely since the city was founded a generation before Napoleon gained fame in Europe. At fifty, His graying hair and neatly trimmed goatee made him appear much older. Paul was a Regular Army man who graduated eighteenth in the thirty-six cadet West Point class of 1834. He was promoted to first lieutenant in the 7th U. S. Infantry, 26 October 1836 and served in Florida during the Seminole Indian War, leading a surprised assault on an Indian encampment in 1842. He was commissioned a captain on 19 April 1846, and took part in the war with Mexico where he was wounded at Cerro Gordo. Gabriel received the brevet of major for his conduct at Chapultepec where he led a storming party, capturing an enemy flag.[46]

After returning from Mexico, the citizens of St. Louis presented Paul a sword as a reward for his service. In 1852, during an expedition to the Rio Grande River, Paul assisted in tracking down and apprehending a group of bandits. Two years later he was with a party which surprised and did away with a group of hostile Indians near Spanish Fork Utah. Shortly before the Civil War Paul was assigned to the 8th U. S. Infantry and promoted to major. When the war opened he left his position with the 8th and joined the 4th New Mexico volunteers, becoming the regiment's colonel.

The opening of the war found Paul fighting to keep the Confederates at bay in the southwest. He also took on the duties of inspector general for the Department of New Mexico until the end of 1861 and commanded the Southern Military District until 13 April 1862. When his regiment was mustered out in May of that year, and with no other assignments available, Paul lounged around with nothing to do. He was not prone to self-promotion, but his wife was not opposed to tooting her husband's horn for him. Mrs. Paul, attending to things herself, made a visit to the White House intent on meeting with the president on her husband's behalf. Somehow, she managed to secure an audience with Lincoln. After meeting with Mrs. Paul, Lincoln wrote a note to himself. "Today Mrs. Major Paul calls and urges appointment of her husband as a Brigadier. She is a saucy woman and will keep tormenting me until I may have to do it." Mrs. Paul was obviously of the opinion that her husband had been overlooked. The reason Paul was not yet performing service for the Union in the East was a simple matter. The term "out of sight out of mind" could have been applied. In short order Paul was a brigade general and in command of a brigade in the First Corps' First Division, replacing General Patrick who had recently received his assignment as the army's provost marshal.

Shortly after assuming command, the regiments of Paul's brigade where mustered out and replace with a group of new, nine month units from New Jersey that had yet to experience battle. The rawness of Paul's new recruits was placed on display at Chancellorsville. While the brigade was not engaged the men were so green they reacted to every sound and rifle shot. At one point some of them actually fired into a group of their fellow Jerseymen, inflicting seven casualties. Paul's boys ended up being a rather lucky group of soldiers for, as the end of their term of enlistment approached, they had seen no heavy action. Eventually, Paul would be placed at the head of one of Robinson's brigades. As of 3 June however, while his

---

[46] Warner, ***Generals in Blue***, p.363; Eicher, & Eicher, ***High Commands***, p.419.

New Jersey boys prepared to depart, he remained at the head of the retiring brigade. His future command would be comprised of the 94th and 104th New York, the 16th Maine, 13th Massachusetts and the 107th Pennsylvania. Like his future superior, General Paul was still unproven as a commander in battle. His experience on the field at Gettysburg would leave terrible physical scars.[47]

Henry Baxter, who had minimal military experience, found himself signing the muster roles of the 7th Michigan Infantry at the onset of the war. It was no wonder Henry stepped up and volunteered since both of his grandfather's where veterans of the Revolution. Born 8 September 1821, in Sidney Plains New York, Henry moved to Jonesville Michigan with his father when he was ten. In 1849 he caught gold fever and traveled to California with a group of men to strike it rich. Finding gold proved to be elusive for Baxter and three years later he returned to Michigan, taking employment as a storekeeper and miller. His soldiering knowledge was limited to the organization of a militia unit known as the Jonesville "Light Guards."[48]

Entering the war as a private, Henry soon found himself elected to the captaincy of Company C of his regiment. Throughout his military career, Baxter displayed a propensity for attract Rebel bullets. During The Seven Days he was hit in the abdomen. The wound was severe but Henry was not ready to let go of life. On the day the fighting ended, as he laid suffering, he was promoted to lieutenant colonel. His long convalescence ended in time for him to take his new position with the regiment shortly before the battle of Antietam. Once again, Baxter was severely wounded when Sedgwick's Division was crushed in the West Woods. This time hit in the thigh, the bullet ranged upward, lodging in Baxter's abdomen. He traveled to Michigan to recuperate, healed quickly, and was back with the regiment before Fredericksburg. By that time the 7th Michigan's commander, Colonel Norman Hall, had been promoted to brigade command and Baxter took over the regiment. During the battle His unit was selected to execute an amphibious operation which consisted of crossing the Rappahannock and rooting out Barksdale's Confederates dug in on the opposite shore. The fighting intensified as Barksdale's boy's, many of the them concealed in cellars and strong points, fought their urban battle with Baxter and the other Federal regiments charged with securing the town. While the crossing was ultimately a success, Baxter, had once again been shot. This time the bullet hit him in the upper body, passing completely through his left shoulder. Again, Henry proved hard to kill and he was once again laid up. When he returned to duty in the spring, he was promoted to brigadier general and given command of a brigade consisting of four regiments from the northeast. At Chancellorsville the brigade was only lightly engaged and suffered a minuscule twenty-two casualties. The amazing thing was Henry Baxter was not one of them.[49]

---

[47] Tagg, **Generals**, pp.22-23; **OR** vol.27, pt.1, p.156; Boatner, **Dictionary**, p.624; **Electronic Source:** http://www.arlingtoncemetery.net/grpaul.htm, Last accessed 5/5/2012; **OR** vol.27, pt.2, p.575.

[48] Tagg, **Generals**, pp.24;

[49] Warner, **Generals in Blue**, p.25; Eicher, & Eicher, **High Commands**, p.122.

Baxter's many wounds can be blamed on a leadership style which always placed him in the line of fire. He consistently led his command from the front, a trait which endeared him to his men and his superiors. He was still somewhat green regarding brigade command as the army prepared to follow Lee north but most had little doubt Henry Baxter would skillfully and nobly lead his men in the heaviest part of any fight. The regiments of his brigade, the 12th Massachusetts, 83rd and 97th New York and the 11th, 88th and 90th Pennsylvania would be in the thick of the fighting and Baxter would do them justice.[50]

Mister Baseball?
Commanding General Reynolds' Third Division was a man who history knows as famous for something his did not do as opposed to things he did accomplish. Abner Doubleday, who for years was erroneously credited with the creation of baseball, spent the Civil War years fighting for the Union. Born in upstate New York in the town of Ballston Spa near the Adirondacks on 26 June 1819, he was one of three sons to Ulysses F. Doubleday, a two term congressman. Abner went to school in Cooperstown and Auburn, intending to become a civil engineer. He practiced the trade for two years before an appointment to the Military Academy changed his path. Graduating twenty-fourth in the fifty-six member class of 1842, he was assigned as a second lieutenant to the 3rd Artillery.

Doubleday served in the Mexican and Seminole Wars and later, in 1852, on a commission organized to investigate a number of fraud allegations which had supposedly taken place during the war. Abner was promotion to first lieutenant in 1847 and eight years later was elevated to captain. He never used colorful language, was not a drinker and never saw the need to partake in the use of tobacco. The absence of vice in his life made Doubleday mild mannered and somewhat boring. A little portly, Abner, on occasions, could also be a bit ridged. He earned a reputation for being a little slow when quicker action would have been more prudent and often displayed a bit of a pompous attitude.[51]

Doubleday, still a captain at the time Fort Sumter fell, was a member of Major Robert Anderson's garrison charged with defending the forts in Charleston Harbor. He always portrayed himself as a hero for his part in the defense of the fort. Remembering the morning the bombardment began; Doubleday recounted how he was asleep in his bedroll when the initial round struck the outside wall of the fort near his head, the sound of the strike startling him from his slumber. Whether true or not, the incident as described by the captain seems to have been a bit overblown. Later, Doubleday sighted and fired the first Union cannon of the war. The shell from his gun however did no damage, flying completely over the targeted Confederate gun emplacement and landing in the marsh beyond.[52]

---

[50] Tagg, *Generals*, p.24; *OR* vol.27, pt.1, p.156.

[51] Eicher, & Eicher, *High Commands*, p.213; Warner, *Generals in Blue*, pp.129-130.

[52] Doubleday, Abner, From Moultrie to Sumter, *B&L*, vol.1, p.47; Chester, James, Inside Sumter in '61, *B&L*, vol.1, p.67.

Doubleday served with General Patterson in the Shenandoah Valley in July and August of 1861. He was promoted to brigadier general of volunteers on 3 February 1862, but was sidelined during the Peninsula Campaign as part of General McDowell's withheld corps. Doubleday's first real action came during the early stages of the second fight at Bull Run when he sent two regiments forward to assist General Gibbon's beleaguered Iron Brigade as they engaged Ewell's Division at Brawner Farm. Doubleday took the initiative when assisting Gibbon, sending the regiments into the fight without the approval of his commander General Rufus King who at the time was struggling through an epileptic seizure. During the next phase of the battle, Doubleday had the misfortune of running into General Longstreet's Corps as it arrived to support Jackson. Regaining their composure, Doubleday's men assisted in the final elements of the battle, covering the army's retreat toward Washington. After being elevated to division command he led the First Division of Hooker's Corps at Antietam. Abner guided his men as they plunged into the thick of the fighting on the north end of the battlefield, through the Miller Cornfield and the West Woods. He receiving accolades for his work that bloody day, being singled out as a "gallant officer" who was "remarkably cool and at the front of battle…" For his efforts Doubleday was promoted to major general on 29 November. A confusing order kept his division out of action through most of the fighting at Fredericksburg and his men were not seriously tested at Chancellorsville.[53]

Falsely given credit for inventing baseball, Abner Doubleday would play a critical role during the Battle of Gettysburg. *NA*

---

[53] Tagg, **Generals**, p.26; Eicher, & Eicher, **High Commands**, p.419;. Boatner, **Dictionary**, p.244.

It is difficult to comprehend how General Doubleday failed to gain the respect of his peers in the Army of the Potomac. He had shown above average abilities when at the head of his command. A number of generals, for some reason, did not think him worthy of his position. General Meade, after being made aware of Doubleday's placement at the head of his old division of Pennsylvania Reserves commented in a letter to his wife that it would be a "good thing for me, for now they will think a great deal more of me than before." Others thought Doubleday would be a poor person to depend upon in an emergency. It's possible his personality got in the way of his proven abilities on a battlefield. Either way, the man who was wrongly credited with inventing baseball would have his day. Unfortunately, the members of his generation would not acknowledge his efforts. It would take the efforts of historians, peeling back the layers placed by years of derision, to expose his work at Gettysburg. Eventually, Abner Doubleday would get credit for what he actually accomplished in life, not for what people believed his did.[54]

At Gettysburg, Doubleday's Division would consist of three brigades but only two would march north with the army. A third would be assigned to the division late in June and would march from Washington, catching up with the army after the battle had begun. The First Brigade, under Brigadier General Thomas Algeo Rowley consisted of the very green 121st, 142nd and 151st Pennsylvania. Rowley, whose military experience consisted of a captaincy in a company of volunteers known as the "Jackson Blues," had fought in the Mexican War with the unit. By trade, he was a cabinetmaker and county clerk from Pittsburg, being born there on 5 October 1808. Prior to the war, he also established a reputation as somewhat of a political operator. When hostilities began he used his clout to attain the colonelcy of the 13th Pennsylvania. The regiment was mustered on 25 April 1861, but, being only a three month outfit, it was disbanded in August before it saw any action. Most of the men, having not yet "seen the elephant", reenlisted to fill the rolls of the 102nd Pennsylvania and Rowley was retained as its colonel on 6 August.

Rowley first experienced combat on the Peninsula at Williamsburg and Seven Pines. He was hit in the back of the head by a bullet which severely stunned him and fractured his skull. Ignoring his injury, he stayed with the regiment for the remainder of the battle and earned a commendation for his efforts. He refused to leave the field, and led the regiment once again at Malvern Hill. Although he saw no action at Second Bull Run or Antietam, he was promoted to brigadier general on 29 November 1862. His new position came with command of the Third Brigade of the Sixth Corps' Third Division. He began the battle of Fredericksburg at the head of his brigade but was replaced as the battle progressed by Brigadier General Frank Wheaton for no other reason than Wheaton was ahead of Rowley on the promotion's list.

As spring broke, Rowley found himself with a new command, assigned to a fresh First Corps brigade that had been filled with green regiments from his native Pennsylvania. Chancellorsville brought no combat experience for the newcomers and when the two year regiments began departing, the 135th Pennsylvania left for

---

[54] Meade, *Meade*, p.349.

muster out. The Pennsylvanian's departure was actually a benefit to the brigade for it would eventually lead to the addition of the veteran 80th New York. In early June however, Rowley's brigade contain only the three remaining regiments of Keystone Staters. Fortunately for the green men of the brigade they would prove in a few weeks that although inexperienced, their conduct on the battlefield would be significantly better than their commander's.[55]

Roy Stone, a transplanted New Yorker, began the war as a volunteer from his adopted state of Pennsylvania. Born 16 October 1836 in Prattsburg, Stone attended Union College and graduating in 1856. When the state's quota of volunteers had been met, Stone had yet to be mustered in. Intent on serving, he eventually ended up as a major in the 13th Pennsylvania Reserves. The 13th was assembled from a group a hardy, rugged frontiersmen, most of whom were lumbermen from the northwest corner of the state. Most had learned to shoot at an early age and were extremely proficient at hitting what they took aim at. The regiment was soon tagged with the nicknamed "Bucktails," due to their custom of having each man wear, attached to his hat, the tail of a deer he had shot. The regiment became leaderless after its original colonel, Thomas L. Kane, stepped down due to inexperience. Kane's resignation forced Stone into the leadership role, and he guided the regiment through all their engagements early in the war.

The 13th was brigaded with other regiments of the Reserves under General Reynolds and fought with distinction during The Seven Days, proving they did indeed have the ability to shoot straight. The 13th lost 247 men during the fighting at Mechanicsville, most of them captured. Stone's Bucktails received the praise of their division commander, General McCall, for their performance. At Glendale, Stone was nearly captured himself as he and General McCall rode through a wooded swamp. McCall was apprehended, but Stone managed to escape, receiving a wound in his arm for the effort. With the capture of General's McCall and Reynolds, and the wounding of General Meade, General Seymour took command of the division. Seymour congratulated Stone's men noting "[M]ajor Stone deserves the highest praise on all occasions."[56]

Impressed by the performance of his regiment, the War Department detached Stone from his command and sent him on a mission to Pennsylvania with instructions to raise a brigade of men like the ones in the 13th. Unfortunately, Stone could only recruit enough men to form two new regiments. One, the 149th Pennsylvania, Stone would lead into battle. Bringing his new recruits to Washington, the regiment pined away in the capital until February 1863 when it

---

[55] Warner, **Generals in Blue**, pp.413-414; Boatner, **Dictionary**, p.711; **OR** vol.27, pt.1, p.156; **OR** 25, pt.1, p.158; Tagg, **Generals**, pp.27-28. The additional brigade assigned to Doubleday's Division was the Second Vermont Brigade under George J. Stannard.

[56] Eicher, & Eicher, **High Commands**, p.514; Tagg, **Generals**, pp.28-29; **OR** vol.11, pt.2, p.405. There is some question as to Stone's place of birth. Some sources specify Prattsburg which is located in central New York while others indicate Plattsburg(h), a town along Lake Champlain. Discrepancies also exist regarding his date of birth. Some note 16 October while others note the 17th.

was brigaded with two other Pennsylvania units, the 143rd and 150th and assigned to General Doubleday's Division. The men of the new "Bucktail Brigade" took to wearing the trademark deer tail on their hats which incensed the original bucktails, who began calling the new brigade the "Bogus Bucktails." Chancellorsville did not afford the new bucktails an opportunity to prove themselves worthy, as they were only lightly engaged with a Rebel picket line. Stone, who had not seen action since The Seven Days, was eager to prove the men equal to his original Bucktails. While he was an established regimental commander, he had yet to lead a brigade in battle. At Gettysburg he would get his chance, but before Colonel Stone could prove himself, a long march north awaited the three regiments of his brigade.[57]

On 8 June, the men of the First Corps welcomed back to camp their companions who had been sent to the aid of General Sedgwick. Fortunately, they had tramped their way to the river and back without being tested. They settled back into their old camp near White Oak Church with the remainder of the corps, where they hoped to be left out of anymore unnecessary marches. It would be a few days before the army began a serious movement to follow Robert E. Lee north, and they would need all the rest they could get.

Hancock's Boy's

The first week of June found General Winfield S. Hancock in command of the Second Corps. Technically the corps still belonged to General Couch, but Couch was away in Washington lobbying for Hooker's removal and would never return. The corps' encampment near Falmouth was in close proximity to Fredericksburg which required the men to spend a number of hours on the picket line. With General Sedgwick's corps now on the river to the south, many of the men were of the opinion that the Second Corps would soon be called upon once again to take the heights west of town. On 6 June, the idea must have gained popularity when the corps was ordered to pack three days rations and prepare their haversacks. Wagons were also loaded with small stores and made ready to move at a moment's notice. Pickets were not to be withdrawn but resupplied; their positions maintained. Orders were expected any moment, but as with many of the orders requiring preparations for active operations the first week of June, no follow up instructions were received and the men ate their three days rations in camp. The next day the Second Corps camps suffered through a blustery day which brought clouds of dust that made camp life miserable. Inspections were conducted to keep the soldiers in condition to move and orders to do so continued to be expected at any time.[58]

In Washington, General Couch was kept informed regarding conditions at the front by Captain James S. Hall of the Signal Corps. At 3:30 p.m., he received an update from Hall indicating seven regiments of Rebels had taken position in a line of rifle pits close to the Howison residents, along the rail line to Richmond

---

[57] Tagg, *Generals*, pp.28-29; *OR* vol.11, pt.2, pp.32, 357; Technically Doubleday commanded three brigades during the battle but the Second Vermont Brigade under General George Stannard was not assigned to the division until 23 June and did not arrive until after the battle had commenced.

[58] *OR* vol.27, pt.3, p.17; Lash, *"Duty Well Done"*, p.323.

below the house near the river. The Rebels, Hall reported, had occupied a position between the southern end of Marye's Heights and the men General Sedgwick had thrown across the river. Also sighted were a number of wagons and ambulances and a battery of artillery moving north on the Bowling Green Road. The following morning Hall noted the Rebel infantry was still in place, occupying the pits and railroad embankments from Fredericksburg to Hamilton's Crossing. Another battery was observed overlooking Sedgwick's men from a wooded ridge in back of the Bernard house. Later, he reported a four gun battery which he overlooked earlier, and additional field works under constructed in response to Sedgwick's bridgehead. Hall sent two more messages to General Couch, one that evening and one the following morning reiterating his earlier observations and called attention to various enemy works being repositioned and re-manned. He estimated the total reinforcements along the river amounted to three brigades or a division. What the signal officer was actually witnessing was the repositioning of troops to cover the withdrawal of others, although Hall seemed to be oblivious to that fact. The necessity to keep Couch informed of activity in front of the Second Corps came to an end a few days later when it became known the general would not be returning and General Hancock had taken over his command.[59]

Hancock's Second Corps was assembled from a group of battle tested brigades that had seen some of the fiercest fighting of the war. The veterans had fought on the Peninsula during The Seven Days and although only partially engaged at Second Bull Run, they had been tested in front of the Sunken Road at Antietam. Later that year the Second Corps was before Fredericksburg when General Burnside ordered the assault on Marye's Heights. The hopeless attack cost the corps 4,114 men and Burnside his reputation and ultimately his job. Again, at Chancellorsville, the corps was in the thick of it and lost nearly another 2,000 men. Now, gazing across the river at the dug in Rebels, the veterans of the Second Corps knew another hard fight was coming. Where and when the encounter would take place was still conjecture for the men on the front lines.[60]

Taking over for Hancock at the head of his old division was a Federal brigadier who had no military training or experience prior to the war. John Curtis Caldwell was only thirty years of age, yet despite his years he had shown some flashes of brilliance on the battlefield. At Glendale, he led his brigade in support of General Philip Kearny and had briefly commanded a division at Antietam after its commander; Major General Israel B. Richardson had been wounded. Unfortunately for Caldwell, before his wounding, Richardson, a fiery commander who his men called "Fighting Dick," received a report that Caldwell was cowering somewhere to the rear.

"Where's General Caldwell?" Richardson roared wanting to send Caldwell's brigade to the support of another besieged unit.

A lieutenant from the 5th New Hampshire informed Fighting Dick that his brigade commander was off behind a nearby haystack.

---

[59] ***OR*** vol.27, pt.3, pp.15, 25, 26, 29, 33.

[60] ***OR*** vol. 21, p.131; ***OR*** vol.25, pt.2, pp.171, 189.

"God damn the field officers!" the general bellowed. Turning, Richardson ordered the brigade forward, unwilling to delay any longer on Caldwell's account.

Holding his sword aloft, Richardson, on foot at the head of the men, his face blackened by powder, marched them toward the Sunken Road where he was severely wounded. He was carried from the field and taken to McClellan's Headquarters. Evidently Richardson informed his chieftain of Caldwell's alleged indiscretion for McClellan quickly replaced Caldwell with General Hancock after the fighting subsided. The fact that General Caldwell retained brigade command may invalidate the claim of the lieutenant. Or, he may have retained his position simply because shortly after the battle McClellan was removed and Richardson eventually died from his wound.[61]

Born in Vermont in 1833, Caldwell went to Amherst and became an educator in Maine. He worked as a teacher for the five years preceding the war. In November 1861 he entered volunteer service and was elected to the colonelcy of the 11th Maine. After being assigned to the Army of the Potomac, Caldwell was elevated to brigade command in June 1862. He took over the brigade of Oliver Howard after Seven Pines when Howard received the wound which cost him his arm. Caldwell led the brigade for the remainder of 1862 with marginal success. The largest scar on his record his tardiness at Antietam.

The Battle of Fredericksburg found Caldwell leading his brigade forward toward Marye's Heights. As his men struggled to gain a foothold on the bloody slope, Caldwell was hit in his left side but chose to remain with his command. A few moments later, with the caldron of battle swirling around him, Caldwell was hit again, this time in the left shoulder. Once again he chose to remain on the field, urging the men onward. Although little doubt remained as to his bravery, after the battle, additional bad news came Caldwell's way when it was discovered that during the fighting one of his regiments broke and ran. A few months later, Caldwell's men did fine work at Chancellorsville when they were required to reposition themselves to cover the retreat of the army from the crossroads near Chancellor House. Evidently General Hancock had a favorable opinion of Caldwell in spite of the school teacher's civilian background. When Hancock ascended to the head of the Second Corps he displayed no serious issues with Caldwell taking over the First Division. The men of Caldwell's brigade thought highly of him as well, and many men in the division considered him better than their own commander. Gettysburg would be General Caldwell's first challenge at the head of a division.[62]

Caldwell's division contained four brigades, the first of which, his old command, included the 5th New Hampshire, the 61st New York and the 81st and 148th Pennsylvania. When Caldwell took command of the division, his brigade was turned over to Colonel Edward Ephraim Cross. Cross, born in Lancaster, New Hampshire, was slightly older than Caldwell. At the age of fifteen he began working in the newspaper business. He spent time as a printer and, after moving to Cincinnati, a reporter. The news trade evidently held little excitement for Cross

---

[61] Sears, *Landscape*, pp.244-245; Tagg, *Generals*, pp.35-36; Warner, *Generals in Blue*, p.403.

[62] Tagg, *Generals*, p.36.

because he soon left his position and ventured west to the New Mexico Terretory where he tried his hand at trapping, mining and hunting buffalo between bouts with the local Indians. While out west he fought in and survived two duels, one being fought with swords and the other with rifles. By the time the war arrived, Cross was a chiseled looking, tough man who would not back down from a fight.

Cross returned to New Hampshire when war came. He quickly signed up to defend the Union and was made colonel of the state's 5th regiment. The men of the 5th soon learned that no one in Cross' command would be allowed to retreat. He drilled them hard and taught them to take the time to aim their weapons in battle. He also took good care of them making sure they knew how to take care of themselves in the field. He made sure they were always clothed, fed and had good ground to camp on. Although he looked after of his men, he was also critical of them and very outspoken toward both the army and prominent politicians who some believed had retarded his advancement. In combat he kept his promise of not allowing anyone to retreat and on at least one occasion pledged to shoot anyone who ran in the face of the enemy if his file closers did not shoot them first. Cross had a quick, nervous persona which resulted in him being observed on a number of occasions pacing back and forth with his hands locked firmly behind his back.

During the Battle of Seven Pines, Cross proved his toughness was not simply talk. Urging the men forward, he instructed them to "[c]harge them like hell" and show them that you are "damned Yankees." As the regiment advanced and engaged the enemy, Cross was hit and incapacitated. Coming to his aid, some of his men tried to assist the colonel, but Cross scolded them, instructing them to forget about him for the time being. He urged them to go forward and defeat the enemy before attending to him. The wound healed in time for him to return to the regiment before Antietam, where he was once again wounded. He recovered only to be hit a third time near the stone wall as the regiment struggled to capture Marye's Heights at Fredericksburg. There was little question as to the bravery and grit of Colonel Cross. One of his New Hampshire volunteers formed the impression that if the rest of the colonels in the army were made from the same mold as Cross, the army would have never lost a battle.[63]

Caldwell's second brigade was a hard fighting group of Irishmen known simply as the Irish Brigade. The brigade's regiments had been so decimated during the previous year it cast a shadow of its former self. Its first commander, Thomas F. Meagher, initially intended to recruit a brigade composed completely of Irish regiments. Meagher, a captain in Company K of the 69th New York, shortly after the first battle at Bull Run, requested that his regiment be utilized as the foundation of the new brigade. His desires were fulfilled when the 69th was joined by the 63rd and 88th New York but before two additional regiments could be raised, the brigade was called off to war. Joined by the 29th Massachusetts, the brigade fought during The Seven Days but missed Second Bull Run, remaining on the Peninsula with General McClellan. At Antietam the Irish Brigade fought at the Sunken Road where it lost 540 men. The losses were so heavy that before Fredericksburg the brigade had to

---

[63]   *Ibid*, pp.37-38; Sears, ***Richmond***, p.143.

be reorganized. Gone were the men of the 29th Massachusetts, replaced by the same state's 28th regiment. The 116th Pennsylvania was also added to offset the staggering losses. Again at Fredericksburg, the Irishmen were in the thick of the fighting and lost another 545 men. Meagher made multiple attempts to be allowed to leave the brigade and recruit additional volunteers. His first request was granted, but two subsequent inquiries were denied and in a fit of frustration he resigned and left the brigade. Command fell to Colonel Patrick Kelly, who like Meagher had been a captain in the old 69th.[64]

Patrick Kelly had been born in Ireland, where he worked as a farmer before crossing the ocean in 1849. Joining the 69th, initially a New York Militia unit, he was mustered in for only ninety days. When the regiment mustered out, many of its original members joined the reorganized 69th New York Volunteers and continued their service as members of the Irish Brigade. Kelly however did not return. Instead he joined one of the new Regular Army units, the 16th U. S. Infantry and accepted a commission as one of its captains. He fought at Shiloh where he won a brevet promotion before returning east to be commissioned a lieutenant colonel in the 88th New York, joining the Irish Brigade. Kelly commanded the 88th during the Peninsular Campaign, showing he was a competent leader of men. Unfortunately for Kelly, while General Meagher singled out the regiment for its efforts, he failed to mention Kelly by name. His next action came at Antietam where he received praise from General Hancock and a promotion to colonel on 20 October. Hancock paid tribute to Kelly again after Fredericksburg, noting in his report that the new colonel "was active and resolute, as he always is, and, with his regiment, performed their usual good service." Kelly's men were not heavily engaged at Chancellorsville, and shortly after the battle he was placed in command of the brigade when Meagher resigned. While he had never led a brigade before, the men of the Irish Brigade had confidence in him. Both Kelly and his brigade had already proven they could be very stubborn on a battlefield.[65]

Commanding another brigade in Caldwell's division was Pennsylvania born Samuel Kurtz Zook. Born on 27 March 1821 in Chester County, Zook spent very little of his childhood in the care of his parents. At a young age he was taken to live with his maternal grandparents near the site where General Washington bivouacked his troops at Valley Forge. The history of the area soon had the young man interested in the military. When old enough, he joined the local militia, and at the age of nineteen became the adjutant of the 100th Pennsylvania. In 1842 Zook went to work for the Washington and New York Telegraph Company which eventually forced his relocation to New York. He joined the 6th New York Militia and remained active in military affairs, eventually rising to the rank of lieutenant colonel. When the Civil War began, Zook traveled with the regiment to Annapolis where he took over duties as the city's military governor, holding the position during the first battle at Bull Run.

[64]   *OR* vol.21, p.129; *OR* vol.19, pt.1, p.192; Tagg, **Generals**, p.39; Phisterer, **NYWR**, vol.1, p.675.

[65]   Phisterer, **NYWR**, vol.1, p.674; Tagg, **Generals**, p.39; *OR* vol.21, p.229; Jorgensen, Jay, **Gettysburg's Bloody Wheatfield**, p.98.

The 6th was mustered into service for three months. Most of the men banded together to form the core of the 66th New York Volunteers when their term of service was up. Zook however, chose a different path, electing to form his own regiment. His efforts resulted in the creation of the 57th New York Volunteers. Zook was commissioned the units colonel and on 19 November 1861 the 57th left the state and marched off to war. [66]

Zook's men saw their first action on the Peninsula where the colonel showed initiative by riding in advance of his men to discover the Confederate ruse at Yorktown. General John Magruder was marching his men back and forth in the face of the Federals to make it appear his numbers were greater than they actually were. Zook reported the deception, but McClellan either never received the report or chose not to take action. The unit's first casualties came at Seven Pines where eighteen men were killed or wounded. During The Seven Days another forty-four were lost including twenty-seven men who were listed as missing. Zook was absent from Antietam, as he was away from the regiment on medical leave. He suffered from rheumatism which at times was quite severe. Unfortunately for Zook, the treatments of the day only increased an afflicted person's suffering. Finally, in October, He returned to his command and found himself, due to the previous commander being promoted, at the head of the regiment's brigade.

When the brigade arrived at Fredericksburg, the enemy had yet to congregate in numbers across the river. Zook wanted to cross and take the town, but a delay in the arrival of the army's pontoon bridges squelched the idea. By the time the bridges arrived, the Rebels were in Fredericksburg and dug in. Shortly before the battle, Zook wrote that only fifty men would have been lost taking the hills across the river if it could have been done when they arrived. Now, Zook noted, it would "cost at least ten thousand if not more." Three days later 527 of Zook's men become casualties trying to take the hills. The brigade was lightly engaged at Chancellorsville and suffered just 188 casualties as the bulk of the fighting took place to the west of Zook's position near the Chancellor House.

Zook, once again, was on medical leave as Hooker's army faced the Rebels before Fredericksburg in early June. At the time his brigade consisted of his own 57th New York, the 52nd and 66th New York and the 140th Pennsylvania. He loathed cowards and refused to put up with anyone in his command who failed to do their duty. He was a stickler for discipline and while tough dealing with the lack of obedience he was fare. The men of Zook's command also became aware early on that if monetary rewards were given for the mastery of profanity, Zook would be one of the richest officers in the army. At Chancellorsville he got into a shouting match with General Hancock which turned into the greatest cursing match some of the men ever saw. Zook, instead of trying to shout down Hancock, waited until the general was out of breath and when Hancock stopped to inhale, Zook showed he could give as good as he received. An enlisted man standing nearby noted "the air was very blue."[67]

---

[66] Phisterer, *NYWR*, vol.1, p.539; Warner, **Generals in Blue**, p.576.

[67] Tagg, **Generals**, pp.41-42; *OR* vol.21, p.130; *OR* vol.25, pt.1, p.176.

Caldwell's fourth and final brigade, which had just been added to the division in April, was constructed from regiments hailing from four different states. Representing Pennsylvania were the 53rd and 145th regiments. Three additional regiments, the 27th Connecticut, 2nd Delaware, and 64th New York rounded out the roster. Commanding the brigade was Colonel John Rutter Brooke. John R. Brooke was an ambitious young man of twenty-three when the war began. Answering the call for troops, he volunteered for service with a regiment from his native state and became a captain in the 4th Pennsylvania. The 4th was a ninety day regiment and its term of enlistment expired on 20 July 1861, the day before the battle at Bull Run. No amount of prodding could get the men to remain with the army a day longer, and before the battle began they marched back to Washington to be mustered out and sent home.[68]

Brooke must have been disappointed for he soon began efforts to raise his own regiment and on 7 November he was commissioned colonel of the 53rd Pennsylvania. He was at the head of his regiment when it encountered the enemy at Seven Pines. He led it well enough to receive praise for his efforts and remained with the regiment even after the end of his right index finger was taken off by a Rebel bullet. Brooke led his regiment into battle once again, at Savage Station, during The Seven Days. With General Zook away recovering from his rheumatism, Brooke commanded the regiment's brigade as it fought at the Sunken Road during the fighting at Antietam. He receiving accolades from General Hancock for his performance but when Zook returned, Brooke was relegated back to command of the 53rd. He led the regiment against the stone wall along Marye's Heights at Fredericksburg, where it suffered heavily taking 155 casualties.

When the fourth brigade of Caldwell's divisions was organized, the 53rd was taken from Zook's command and used to form the nucleus of the new unit. Brooke was tapped from the 53rd to command the brigade but would not be promoted to brigadier general for over a year. A few days later the brigade suffered 529 casualties at Chancellorsville as it fell back from the Chancellor House. Nearly half the casualties had been members of the 27th Connecticut, who were captured as the army pulled out. The indignity suffered due to the capture such a mass of men may have been the reason Brooke remained a colonel even though General Hancock singled him out in his report. He would still be somewhat untested as the army arrived at Gettysburg.[69]

The Artillery Man

General John Gibbon was born at 10:00 a.m. in the Holmesburg neighborhood of Philadelphia on 20 April 1827 but spent little time in the city of his birth. He was the third son of four boys and fifth of ten children born to Catherine Lardner and Dr. John Heysham Gibbon. There are some indications that his middle name was Hannum or Heysham, but John's younger brother noted in a letter that their

---

[68] Eicher, & Eicher, **High Commands**, p.145; **OR** vol.25, pt.2, p.577.

[69] Tagg, **Generals**, pp.42-43; Eicher, & Eicher, **High Commands**, p.145; **OR** vol.21, p.130; **OR** vol.25, pt.1, pp.176, 315.

father did not approve of middle names, so it is likely that he did not have one or it was simply never used. It is also possible that John's father dropped the "s" from his surname when he was a young man, making Gibbon the family name. In 1832, the elder Gibbon was elected to the Pennsylvania House of Representatives and served on a commission to construct railroads in the Philadelphia area. By 1837, when young John was eleven, his father, after returning from a surveying trip to Panama, packed up his family and moved to North Carolina, taking up residence in Mecklenburg County, where he went to work as the assayer for the Charlotte Mint.[70]

Four years after moving south, John received an appointment to West Point, but it was rumored he was held back a year because he could not correctly identify 4 July as Independence Day. He was not a good student or a model cadet when he finally entered the academy. He had difficulty mastering English and correct grammar. His performance was so poor that he was given the choice of repeating a year or being dismissed. Choosing the former, Gibbon finally graduated in 1847 in the bottom half of his class, standing twentieth of thirty-eight. On 1 July he became a second lieutenant and assigned to the 3rd Artillery.[71]

At the time, the 3rd Artillery was in Mexico, as part of General Scott's force, so Gibbon packed his bags and set out on the long journey to his new assignment. Accompanying him was his classmate, Second Lieutenant Ambrose Burnside, who was on his way to join the 2nd Artillery. Unfortunately the lieutenants were not able to join their units in time to participate in any fighting. Once in Mexico, Gibbon, instead of traveling to Mexico City, performed garrison duty at La Atalaya de la Concepcion, a fortification on a hill overlooking the road to the city. The location had been on the receiving end of almost daily attacks intended to cut General Scott's communications. Disappointed at the fall of the city, the renegades were relentless in trying to take out their frustration on the garrison. It was at La Atalaya (watchtower) where Gibbon got his first true taste of field duty and combat.

On 13 September Gibbon was transferred to the 4th Artillery and awarded the permanent rank of second lieutenant. One day, after joining his new unit, when there was evidently nothing better to do, Gibbon entered into a card game. Having only a few dollars to wager, he was inclined to put up his horse most of his equipment and his pistols. When the game finally ended, he had nothing left, having lost all his belongings to a string of bad hands and tough luck. The next day he was scheduled to enter upon detached service. In order to do so, he had to borrow money for expenses, a horse, saddle, bridle, and weapons. It is said that he never played cards again, at least not for money or tangible possessions.

---

[70] *Electronic Source:* http://www.shissem.com/Hissem_Heysham-Gibbon_Branch.html, Last accessed 5/6/2012. This site contains a large amount of genealogy information about the Gibbon family including Gibbon's brothers Lardner, who served in the Navy before casting his lot with the Confederacy, Robert, who, as a medical doctor, became a surgeon with the 28th North Carolina, and Nicholas who initially enlisted with the 1st North Carolina before joining the 28th as its assistant commissary of subsistence.

[71] *Ibid*; Eicher, & Eicher, **High Commands**, p.253.

After the war, Lieutenant Gibbon returned with the 4th Artillery to Fort Monroe, Virginia, but soon found himself in Florida helping to end the violence perpetrated by the Seminoles. During a visit home to North Carolina, John and his brother Lardner attended Daniel Harvey Hill's wedding. After marrying off Hill, John continued his service in Florida. He was promoted to first lieutenant and transferred west on 12 September 1850, where he participated in patrolling the border between Mexico and Texas. Stationed first at the Ringgold Barracks and then at Fort Brown, Gibbon served on the frontier until 1853 when he took an extended leave of absence and spent a period of time on court-martial duty.

Gibbon's career path took a turn on 25 September 1854, when he received orders to report to West Point where he began work as in instructor of artillery. He spent the next five years instructing cadets. It was during this time John Gibbon demonstrated his dive and will by authoring *The Artillerist Manual*. Based on his class notes and curriculum, the work was a detailed presentation of the science of artillery. It was heavy in mathematical theory and formulas and proved that John Gibbon, while he had not been a good student during his time as a cadet, had grown into an intelligent individual who could easily transfer his intellect to paper. The work was so well received it was adopted by the War Department as an official volume and was utilized by both Federal and Confederate artillerist during the war. Gibbon was evidently a hard worker for in addition to teaching responsibilities and authoring a book, he found time to perform the duties of post quartermaster for nearly three years. He also made time during his four years instructing artillery to court and exchange nuptials on 16 October 1855, with Frances "Frannie" North Moale, the daughter of a retired army officer. By 1858, Frannie had giving John two children, a boy Frank and a daughter Caroline.

In early November, 1859, Gibbon was promoted to captain and given command of Battery B in the old 4th Artillery. The battery was sent west to the Salt Lake area and stationed at Camp Floyd. The Mormon conflict, which had been more political than hostile, was winding down and Gibbon's unit, which spent much of the time policing the region, encountering no violence. As the disagreements waned many of the troops were removed. Shortly, only 488 men and twenty officers from the 4th Artillery, 10th Infantry and 2nd Dragoons remained at Camp Floyd. The men quickly transitioned to the tasks of protecting settlers from marauding Indians. Other than the occasional encounter with the renegades, life at Camp Floyd was rather boring and harsh. The camp was positioned in a valley which contained sagebrush, few trees and an abundance of dust. There was little for an army officer to do as there was no social life or recreation. The most anticipated event was the arrival of the Pony Express which typically brought old newspapers.

When Fort Sumter was fired upon, Captain Gibbon was forced to make a difficult decision. As rumors of war arrived at Camp Floyd, officers met to discuss their options. A level of distrust arose between the men in the battery. Worries over the Southern men's loyalties concerned the Northerners. Some men resigned immediately and headed home, while others, unsure of what to do, delayed their departure to see how events played out. Being from North Carolina, it would have seemed logical for Gibbon to side with the South. His family owned slaves and supported the cause, but to John it was always about principle. He was an honorable man and had taken an oath to his country. To him it was simply honoring his commitment. John Gibbon elected to remain with the army, choosing to fight against the rest of his kin. The decision would cause his family to disown him.[72]

After hostilities commenced, members of the 4th Artillery, including Captain Gibbon, received orders to transfer a portion of Camp Floyd's garrison to Fort Leavenworth Kansas. The camp, which had been renamed Camp Crittenden because its previous namesake, Secretary of War John B. Floyd, had sided with the South, was vacated by a large portion of the garrison. While in route Gibbon's entourage intercepted a Pony Express rider who carried word of the Federal defeat at Bull Run. Concern filtered through the procession over whether or not there was still an organized government in Washington. After arriving at Fort Leavenworth, Gibbon received a final communication from his family in which he discovered he was now an outcast. He was informed of the ill feelings toward him and that he was branded as a traitor by his relations. Boarding a train, the remainder of the journey was conducted by rail. If Captain Gibbon had any concern over Washington still being in Federal hands, his concerns were calmed when he arrived to find the government was indeed still functioning.[73]

Captain Gibbon began the war as chief of artillery for General McDowell's division during the fall and winter of 1861-62. He quickly discovered that opportunities for advancement were few and far between in the artillery. So, in the spring of 1862, Gibbon transferred from the branch of service he had spent his entire career in and joined the foot soldiers.[74]

On 2 May 1862, Gibbon was promoted from captain to brigadier general. The meteoric rise was not without challenge. After receiving an endorsement from General McDowell, his nomination was sent to the Senate with a number of other applicants. Since he was a native of North Carolina, his petition was passed over because the Senate questioned his loyalty. With no men from North Carolina present, he had no champions within the body of lawmakers. Another strike against him was the fissure which had opened between the prospective general and his family. The rejection stunned Gibbon. He had not anticipated any problems or questions regarding his devotion to his country. Gibbon solicited assistance from the politically connected General Wadsworth, who promptly communicated with the Senate and vouched for Gibbon's integrity. Wadsworth managed to sway the senators and Gibbon's commission was eventually approved. Any questions about his devotion would soon be crushed by his performance on the battlefield.[75]

General Gibbon's first assignment was to mold the yet to be famous Iron Brigade. Being a Regular Army man, Gibbon was surprised at the abilities of his group of volunteers. Strict discipline was not received well by most volunteer

---

[72] *Ibid*; Tagg, **Generals**, pp.44-45; Nolan, **The Iron Brigade**, p.39.

[73] **Electronic Source:** http://www.shissem.com/Hissem_Heysham-Gibbon_Branch.html.

[74] Tagg, **Generals**, p.45.

[75] Nolan, **The Iron Brigade**, pp.50-51.

regiments, but the western men seemed to understand the necessity and took to the rigors of army life rather easily. Gibbon also recognized the unique qualities of the westerners. They possessed originality and initiative. He also acknowledged that his Wisconsin and Indiana volunteers displayed a level of intelligence which many other brigadiers assumed did not exist in volunteers. Another epiphany which Gibbon had as he stepped into his new command was that volunteers needed to be led. It became obvious early on that, unlike regulars, who could from time to time be driven to accomplish goals, volunteers had to be guided through their trials. Chastisement and punishment could not be used as motivational tools. These men from the west, like most humans, responded more to encouragement and praise. Gibbon strove to tone down his typical rugged discipline and regulation adherence, replacing them with understanding and appreciation for their efforts. He tried to make them proud to be soldiers. In doing so, Gibbon was able to fashion one of the finest brigades of volunteers in Federal service.[76]

Gibbon however, was not a pushover. When discipline was required, he was not hesitant to dish it out. He instituted a schedule for drill which included activities before breakfast, before lunch, in the afternoon, the evening, and in some cases even at night. He instituted heavy drilling when he overheard some of his men suggest that being an artillery officer Gibbon knew nothing of infantry drill. The men soon found they were deeply mistaken regarding their commanding officer's ability to instruct foot soldiers. He also required men on guard duty to salute all officers. The first time a guard walking his post neglected to do so, the offending soldier was made to sit on a barrel outside the guard tent for the entire day. Additional rules were put in place to keep men from destroying public property. One particularly bad habit exercised by soldiers was the pilfering of fence rails for fire wood and building shelters. Gibbon put a stop to this activity with a rather unique rule. The regiment encamped closest to the destroyed fence had to rebuild the structure. The rebuilding of a fence, particularly if the regiment had not destroyed it, did not set well with the men, but it did inject a "self policing" of the activity and fence burglary ended. As a reward for soldiers who took time to stay sharp in their appearance, passes to go berry picking and perform other activities were awarded. The reward system had its desired effect, keeping the men and their attire looking good. All the rules and orders accomplished two things; they built pride and commitment within the ranks and established a high degree of respect between Gibbon and the men of his command. The respect was shared in both directions.[77]

Gibbon also proved he was a fighter with his performances at Brawner Farm and South Mountain. During the Battle of Antietam, he fought the Iron Brigade to their limit of endurance and then asked them for more. At one point in the battle for the Miller Cornfield, Gibbon ordered his tattered men to assemble at the brigade's artillery battery to defend the guns. Then Gibbon, the old artilleryman, his face black with powder and dressed in his brigadier general's uniform, leaped from

---

[76] Tagg, *Generals*, p.45.

[77] Nolan, Alan T., *The Iron Brigade: A Military History*, p.51.

his horse and entered the battery to help service one of the guns as the number three man for a few rounds until someone was found to take over the task. Gibbon remembered the incident after the war. "I jumped from my horse," he wrote, "and rapidly ran up the elevating screw until the nozzle pointed almost into the ground in front and then nodded to the gunner to pull his lanyard." The blast destroyed the fence in front of the gun and ripped apart the oncoming Rebels. The guns were saved and the enemy was held in check, at least for the time being. It would be Gibbon's last battle at the head of his beloved brigade for on 5 November he was promoted to divisional command, taking over the First Corps' Second Division.[78]

Gibbon led his new division into battle for the first time at Fredericksburg. As part of General Reynolds' First Corps, his command fought on Meade's right flank as the Pennsylvanian was breaking the Rebel line on the southern part of the field. As the fighting progressed, Gibbon rode to the left of his line to direct some artillery fire. As he returned, a Rebel gun near Meade's left flank opened fire. One of the rounds detonated near him and a piece of shell struck him in the right wrist. While the fragment broke the bone and caused great pain, the injury was not threatening, and he remained on the field until the division retired. The wound was dressed and Gibbon made his way to Baltimore for recovery. The injury healed slowly, and it was March before he was back with the army and a new command. Upon his arrival, he was placed at the head of the Second Division of the Second Corps. The division saw little action at Chancellorsville, as it was held in reserve on the north side of the Rappahannock. Now, at the end of May 1863, the men of General Gibbon's command as well as their commander wondered what was yet to come.[79]

While General Gibbon admitted privately that he was frightened by battle, he never showed it, remaining calm and reserved during the heaviest of fighting. He showed great composure during combat, and no one possessed any doubts about his courage. At thirty-six, he was remarkably restrained on a battlefield. Theodore Lyman, whose position as an aide for General Meade allowed him to observe Gibbon, noted after Gettysburg that Gibbon was "an off-hand, soldierly man of middle height." He was slender of build and straight, with a heavy chin, covered with a reddish brown beard and mustache. A sharp, straight nose and piercing eyes projected the seriousness in his intentions. He was blunt to the point of irritation and felt that the truth should always be told no matter how much it pained one to do so. He just looked like a soldier and everyone associated with him knew he was.[80]

General Gibbon's division contained three brigades. The first, shortly before Chancellorsville, had been commanded by Brigadier General Alfred Sully, but Sully was not in good standing with his commander. Gibbon, while an understanding general, did not tolerate some behavior. One such activity was a mutiny within

---

[78] Gibbon, **Recollections**, p.83.

[79] *Ibid*, pp.104, 106; Tagg, **Generals**, p.45.

[80] Tagg, **Generals**, p.44; Lowe, David W., Editor, **Meade's Army: The Private Notebooks of Lieutenant Colonel Theodore Lyman**, p.118.

one of his regiments which Gibbon chose to deal with by having the mutineers executed, and he ordered Sully to carry out the punishment. When Sully expressed reservations about fulfilling the order, Gibbon had him arrested. Sully was later exonerated, but he never returned to his brigade, being isolated to the command of the District of Dakota.[81]

With General Sully gone, command of the First Brigade was given to Brigadier General William Harrow. Harrow, a lawyer from Illinois, was born in Kentucky in the town of Winchester on 14 November 1822. He received his formal education in his hometown, before relocating to Lawrenceville, Illinois where he studied law prior to taking and passing the bar. He established a law practice in the Eighth Judicial Circuit where he associated with fellow lawyer Abraham Lincoln. By 1859, Harrow had relocated his practice to Indiana.[82]

Although nearing forty years of age when the war began, Harrow enlisted in the 14th Indiana and was installed as its major. The 14th fought in western Virginia before marching to the Shenandoah Valley to confront Stonewall Jackson's force in 1862. By the end of the year, Harrow had fallen ill and was considered too weak to remain in the field. His doctors felt he was suffering from tuberculosis since one of his symptoms was the coughing up of blood. After resigning from the army, Harrow's health improved and he was restored to regimental command in time to fight before the Sunken Road at Antietam. After the battle, more than half of his men were listed as casualties. His health failed again after the battle, and he spent the following six months fighting ailments which included bronchitis and neuralgia. Once again, his health improved and after receiving a promotion to brigadier general, he returned in April 1863 and took command of General Sully's old brigade.[83]

Harrow would never completely regain his health. His poor physical condition and lack of a military education hampered his ability to be an effective brigade commander. Although he was not with the brigade at the end of May and possibly early in June, he would return in time to travel with the army in pursuit of Lee. He was so new to the brigade that he could have walked through its regimental camps and many of the men would not have known he was their brigadier. The soldiers of the 19th Maine, 82nd New York, 1st Minnesota and 15th Massachusetts would eventually become acquainted with the unhealthy general who, this time, would not leave his command in the middle of a campaign, choosing instead to see it through to the end.[84]

The second brigade under Gibbon's command was the famous Philadelphia Brigade, originally mustered in as four regiments designated the 1st, 2nd, 3rd and 5th California. Senator James A. McDougall of California, fearing the war would be over before any California representation could be brought east, sought to have the

---

[81] *Ibid*, p.47; Warner, ***Generals in Blue***, p.489.

[82] Warner, ***Generals in Blue***, p.489; Eicher, & Eicher, ***High Commands***, p.284.

[83] Warner, ***Generals in Blue***, p.489; Tagg, ***Generals***, p.47.

[84] Tagg, ***Generals***, p.47; ***OR*** vol.27, pt.1, p.158.

regiments designated as Californian and even paid to outfit the 1st using his personal funds. Most of the men recruited to the brigade however, were common laborers of Irish descent from the Philadelphia area, whose occupations encompassed a wide range of specialties. Eventually the regiments would be designated as Pennsylvania organizations with the 1st California being renamed the 71st Pennsylvania, the 2nd as the 69th, the 3rd as the 72nd and the 5th as the 106th.[85]

In the spring of 1863, the brigade was on its fourth commander, Brigadier General Joshua Thomas Owen. Like the men of his brigade, Owen, who was born in Caermarthenshire, Wales, on 29 March 1821, was of Irish lineage. Joshua's father David, who had chosen the woolen industry as his trade, relocated his family to America in 1832. At the age of eleven, Joshua sailed across the ocean with his parents and ten siblings. Initially settling in Tioga County, Pennsylvania, David moved his family to Baltimore three years later and established a book publishing business. Joshua attended school there before moving to western Pennsylvania to attend Cannonsburg's Jefferson College in 1845. After graduating, he returned to Baltimore and his family's publishing business, but soon moved to Philadelphia to work with his brother. Joshua, who had been hampered by health issues, decided with the help of his brother, to open a boarding house for young men. After establishing the institution, known as the Chestnut Hill Academy, Owen went to work as an instructor, began practicing law, and entered the world of politics. He served in the state legislature for two years beginning in 1857 and was a private in the militia as a member of the 1st City Troop of Philadelphia. Owen's initial war service was with the ninety-day volunteers of the 24th Pennsylvania. When the unit mustered out, he began working to organize another regiment which would eventually become the 69th Pennsylvania. Owen, who had been labeled with the nicknamed "Paddy," would have a much troubled military career. He would experience the highs of gallant conduct, and a promotion to brigadier general on 29 November 1862, but would see his appointment expire due to lack of confirmation.[86]

While many thought he was a bighearted and gracious man, there were times when Owen could be violent and obnoxious. Those instances were usually precipitated by Owen's affection for the bottle. While still colonel of the 69th a particularly ugly incident occurred. Owen and his Lieutenant Colonel Dennis O'Kane had developed ill feelings and distrust toward one another. The animosity had been brewing for some time and eventually came to a head. Owen, who had accused O'Kane of being intoxicated and leaving his post, showed little professionalism one day as he accosted the lieutenant colonel while he, his wife and daughter rode in a carriage. Owen, evidently drunk himself, repeatedly rode his horse into the team pulling the carriage, impeding O'Kane's progress, all the while insulting his subordinate, calling him a son-of-a-bitch. O'Kane put up with the intoxicated Owen for a time but eventually had enough. Getting down off the

---

[85] Faust, *Encyclopedia*, p.580; *OR* vol.25, pt.2, p.577; *OR* vol.27, pt.1, p.158.

[86] Ernsberger, Donald, *Paddy Owen's Regulars: A History of the 69th Pennsylvania "Irish Volunteers"*, pp.13-15; Warner, *Generals in Blue*, pp.353-354.

carriage he pulled Owen off his horse and the two came to blows. O'Kane was brought up on charges, but he was exonerated by timely testimony from then brigade commander Oliver Howard. The incident, while not forgotten, was settled, and Owen eventually took command of the brigade while O'Kane became colonel of the 69th. As a testament to his troubled career, as June 1863 opened, Owen was at the head of the brigade. But, as the month closed, he would be placed under arrest by General Gibbon for an unknown charge. Some assumed it was due to his fondness for alcohol, and a few drinks at an inopportune time had forced the arrest. The result was that the Philadelphia Brigade, three days before the largest battle of the war, would be under a new brigadier.[87]

General Gibbon's Third Brigade was under commanded by Colonel Norman J. Hall. Hall, a Regular Army officer, like General Doubleday, saw the commencement of hostilities from inside Fort Sumter. After his graduation from West Point in 1858, he was assigned to Company H of the 1st U. S. Artillery. Second Lieutenant Hall acted as the garrison's assistant commissary of subsistence and assistant quartermaster. As the situation in Charleston Harbor deteriorated, and Major Anderson contemplated transferring his command from Fort Moultrie to Fort Sumter, he entrusted Hall to move the garrison's women and children to safety. Later, during the bombardment of Sumter, the fort's ten story flag staff, which was supported by four immense bracing poles, was taken down by a Confederate shell. The huge flag fluttered to the ground inside the fort, landing near a fire kindled by the shelling. Lieutenant Hall raced out and grabbed the flag before it caught fire. He managed to detach it from its halyards and with the help of a number of others began efforts to hoist the flag once more. Time was of the essence. With the flag down, the enemy could misconstrue its disappearance as a sign the fort had surrendered. Finding a pole of suitable length, Hall and his companions ventured to the parapet, the most exposed portion of the garrison. There, they quickly nailed the flag to the pole and fastened the staff to a heavy gun carriage. After restoring the banner, the group clambered back down into the fort to safety.

After the stronghold surrendered, Hall was placed in charge of a final salute as the colors were lowered. Ironically, the only men seriously injured during the entire siege were those manning one of the guns firing the salute. As a cartridge bag was rammed into the muzzle of one of the guns, it exploded, ripping the arm off of an unlucky gunner, killing him and injuring a number of others. Burning material landed in a stack of nearby cartridges causing additional explosions. It is believed that the private killed, Daniel Hough, had a history of mental instability. If his condition played a factor in the explosion, it evidently was not recorded. It can be said that the first Union man killed in the war was lost at Fort Sumter and was in the charge of Lieutenant Hall when he died.[88]

After his capture and release, Hall was promoted to first lieutenant and transferred to the 5th Artillery. He served as divisional chief of artillery for Joe Hooker and as adjutant general on the staff of Brigadier General John Barnard,

---

[87] Gottfried, Bradley M., *Stopping Picket: The History of the Philadelphia Brigade*, pp.124,151.

[88] Sifakis, *Who was Who*, p. 274; Detzer, *Dissonance*, pp.307-308.

the chief engineer for the Army of the Potomac during the Peninsular Campaign. In July 1862, Hall left the engineers to accept a promotion to colonel and the command of the 7th Michigan. At Antietam he was wounded as he led the 7th into the West Woods. Remaining on the field, he took command of the brigade when its commander was incapacitated.[89]

Hall's finest hour prior to the summer of 1863 came a few months later at Fredericksburg. Still at the head of the brigade, he personally volunteered it to cross the river and clear the town of William Barksdale's Mississippians entrenched in their rifle pits and cellars. After crossing under heavy fire, the Federals began the bloody process of rooting out the Mississippians. The brigade drove the Rebels from town before being summarily ordered to participate in the assault on Marye's Heights. The Hall's boys suffered 515 casualties for its efforts during the battle. The Battle of Chancellorsville was a bit of a respite for Hall's command as it was kept in reserve, a fate which they probably appreciated after the slaughter of Fredericksburg. As a result of their limited usage, the brigade suffered only 67 killed, wounded or missing.[90]

Known as "Old Blinky," William Henry French would command the men of his division during the early phases of the campaign. *LOC*

Hall, at the age of twenty-six, had been in command of the brigade since Antietam, but was still only a colonel. By Civil War standards this was a significant

---

[89] Sifakis, *Who was Who*, p. 274; Tagg, **Generals**, pp.51-52.

[90] O'Reilly, *The Fredericksburg Campaign*, p.79; Tagg, **Generals**, pp.51-52; *OR* vol.21, pt.2, p.130; *OR* vol.25, pt.1, p.188

period. Obviously his performance leading the brigade had been good enough for him to retain his command but had evidently eluded the attention of his superiors. The men of the 7th Michigan along with the 19th and 20th Massachusetts, the 42nd and 59th New York and the 127th Pennsylvania had been very effective under Hall's guidance. The 127th, whose term of enlistment would expire before the brigade arrived on the field at Gettysburg, would be sent home for muster out but the remaining regiments would continue to look to Hall for leadership. By the time the summer was over, his performance in the streets of Fredericksburg would no longer be his finest hour.[91]

Hancock's final division, which contained only two brigades since a number of its regiments had been sent home for muster out, was under the command of Major General William H. French. Born in Baltimore, Maryland on 13 January 1815, French entered the Military Academy as a teenager. Shortly after graduating twenty-second in a class of fifty with Joe Hooker and John Sedgwick in 1837, French received his second lieutenant brevet and was assigned to the 1st U. S. Artillery. He served in Florida, helping to subdue the Seminoles and during the Mexican War won two brevets while serving as an aide-de-camp on the staff of Brigadier General Franklin Pierce.[92]

When the fever of secession swept over Texas, French was stationed at a remote outpost near Eagle Pass on the Rio Grande River. Although from a state with a large contingency of Southern sympathizers, French refused to surrender his garrison to state authorities. He showed his determination by ordering his men to pack up their belongings. French then led his command on a sixteen day marched down the Rio Grande to the Gulf of Mexico. Once on the coast, he secured transport and sailed his men to Key West, where he remained until he was promoted to brigadier general of volunteers on 28 September 1861.[93]

French's initial service was as commander of a brigade within the defenses of Washington. He eventually found himself on his way to the Peninsula commanding a brigade in the Second Corps' First Division. After the fighting, French's division commander, General Israel Richardson, called attention to his subordinate's conduct in his report. "I cannot too much commend the admirable manner in which... French [has] done [his] duty with [his] brigade," Richardson noted. Afterword, French was elevated to divisional command and placed at the head of the corps' Third Division. He led the initial attack against the Confederates dug in along the Sunken Road at Antietam and for his labors was promoted to major general of volunteers on 29 November 1862. French once again led his command against an established position at Fredericksburg. This time however, success was not achievable, and his command suffered the same fate as the others which assaulted Marye's Heights. A few months later his role

---

[91] Tagg, **Generals**, pp.51-52; **OR** vol.27, pt.1, p.158; **OR** vol.25, pt.2, p.577.

[92] Warner, **Generals in Blue**, p.161; Eicher, & Eicher, **High Commands**, p.244.

[93] Warner, **Generals in Blue**, p.161; Faust, **Encyclopedia**, p.292; Boatner, **Dictionary**, p.316.

at Chancellorsville earned him another promotion, this time to brigadier general in the Regular Army.[94]

A touch portly with a ruddy look, photos of French show he sometimes wore a bushy salt and pepper beard which when in place covered a slight double chin. Earning the nickname "Old Blinky" due to a tendency to squint as he spoke, French's habit often spawned amusement from those who observed the routine. Since Old Blinky had a bit of temper, subordinates often came under his wrath for finding frivolity in his facial contortions. French also possessed a persistently red face which gave him the look of someone who was chronically upset, inebriated or gasping for air. While he would be reassigned five days before the armies arrived at Gettysburg, in early June General French was in charge and would lead his two brigades north through the Virginia countryside.[95]

French's brigades were commanded by colonels. The first was under Colonel Samuel Sprigg Carroll, who, like French, was a Marylander. Carroll was born 21 September 1832 in Takoma Park just outside Washington. Unlike French however, Carroll had little military experience beyond his graduation from West Point. He entered the academy in 1852 and after four years of study in which he displayed substandard performance, he graduated forty-fourth, five positions from the bottom of his class. A brevetted second lieutenant, Carroll performed routine duties on the frontier with the 9th and 10th Infantry before returning to the academy to assume quartermaster duties; a position he was in when the war began. Although the army had a need for competent field officers, he was not released from the academy for active duty until the fall of 1861.[96]

Coming from a well-placed Washington family, Carroll's father had performed clerk duties for the Supreme Court for many years. His relationships with Washington's elite may have helped with his son's appointment to West Point, but they did not help the youngster once he was a cadet. Samuel's poor academic performance had relegated him to the infantry, and his time out west lasted four years before he returning to assume his quartermaster duties. A connection which may have assisted in Carroll's advancement was his family's friendship with Oliver Howard. The two families had become acquainted with each other when they shared a duplex housing unit. The relationship grew even stronger when, in 1861, Howard became extremely ill and Carroll's mother took the future general into her home and nursed him back to health.[97]

Carroll's first field assignment was as colonel of the 8th Ohio, and he joined the regiment in the mountains of western Virginia near Romney in December 1861. The 8th was a member of General McClellan's command and after arriving; Carroll spent most of the early months of 1862 guarding the Baltimore and Ohio Railroad

---

[94] *OR* vol.11, pt.1, p.158; *OR* vol.11, pt.2, pp.24, 56; Sifakis, ***Who was Who***, p. 230; Boatner, ***Dictionary***, p.316.

[95] Catton, Bruce, ***Mr. Lincoln's Army***, pp.125,290; *OR* vol.27, pt.3, p.340.

[96] Eicher, & Eicher, ***High Commands***, p.165; Warner, ***Generals in Blue***, p.73.

[97] Eicher, & Eicher, ***High Commands***, p.165; Boatner, ***Dictionary***, p.129; Tagg, ***Generals***, p.55.

and the upper portion of the Chesapeake and Ohio Canal. In March, Carroll and his regiment were assigned to Brigadier General James Shields' division in the Shenandoah Valley. He led his Buckeyes at Kernstown where he exhibited his leadership abilities to the approval of his commander. Shields spoke highly of Carroll's aptitude and elevated him to permanent brigade command after the battle. However, Carroll remained on Shields' good side for only a short period time. Later during the campaign, Shields severely chastised Carroll for not burning the bridge at Port Republic. However, the responsibility for the bridge remaining was fully on Shields' shoulders. The general, on 4 June, ordered Carroll to "go forward at once with cavalry and guns to save the bridge at Port Republic." Shields attempted to shift blame by writing in his report that Carroll "neglected to burn the bridge at Port Republic." With this type of dishonesty exhibited by his commanding officer, Carroll must surely have been pleased when he was transferred to General John Pope's Army of Virginia.[98]

Carroll led his brigade at Cedar Mountain, but his command was only lightly engaged. His career path open up somewhat when after the battle General Pope placed his name on a short list of officers who distinguished themselves during the fighting. A few days after the battle, Carroll ventured forward to his picket line to determine its condition. Upon investigation there seemed to be no apparently danger in the area. Suddenly, a group of nearby Rebel cavalry began a sharp firefight with his skirmishers. During the encounter Carroll suffered a very painful flesh wound to his chest. The wound would keep him out of action for a couple of months, and he would be absent from the brigade during the fighting at Second Bull Run and Antietam. By late September, Carroll was well enough to return to duty. He spent a short period in the defenses of Washington before returning to field command to lead a brigade of the Third Corps at Fredericksburg in primarily a supporting role. Once again, after having been involved in a peripheral portion the battle, he was singled out by his commander.[99]

Early in 1863, Carroll was forced to go on sick leave, as his wound from the previous summer was still causing him trouble. The injury had begun to hemorrhage again and he developed an intermittent fever. To make things worse, Carroll had rheumatism in his left knee and hip. Before departing to recover, he requested a transfer back to the 8th Ohio which had been reassigned to a Second Corps brigade. The transfer was granted and after sufficiently recovering, he returned to command a brigade, of which his beloved 8th Ohio was a member. The brigade's previous commander had been wounded at Fredericksburg and Carroll took command, leading it at Chancellorsville. Once again praise was heaped upon Colonel Carroll in his commander's battle report. "I take great pleasure," General French wrote, "in calling the attention of the general commanding to

---

[98] Tagg, *Generals*, p.55; Christ, Elwood, *The Struggle for the Bliss Farm at Gettysburg July 2nd and 3rd 1863*, p.11; *OR* vol.12, pt.3, p.335; *OR* vol.12, pt.1, p.684.

[99] Tagg, *Generals*, pp.55-56.

the dashing and gallant manner in which Colonel Carroll carried his men into the fight."[100]

As June 1863 opened on the Rappahannock line, Colonel Carroll had proven himself to be a competent brigade commander and had caught the attention of his superiors. He was courageous in the face of the enemy and if an opportunity presented itself to damage the Rebels, Carroll would not hesitate to take it. If such an occasion was made available he would not wait for permission from a superior to seize the advantage. His men respected him and were proud to note that they belonged to his brigade while his commanders admired him for his daring and dash. One officer noted that the sound of his voice booming out orders was worth another regiment in battle. Unfortunately, the veteran of heavy fighting and brigade command was still laboring away as a colonel. He had accomplished more than lesser men who had achieved promotion. Although Carroll's red hair was beginning to thin somewhat, there was still enough upon his head to allow him to be nicknamed "Old Brick Top." The moniker may have been allowed to persist due to the fact that the missing hair on his head had migrated to his face in the form of two massive sideburns.[101]

As the month of June began, Carroll's brigade consisted of six regiments. By the time the brigade arrived at Gettysburg, it would contain only four. The six units hailed from two western states, an eastern state and one state which had just been admitted into the Union. Two regiments from Ohio, Carroll's own 8th and the 4th, the 14th Indiana, the 24th and 28th New Jersey and the 7th West Virginia, constituted the brigade. Over the next month, as the army marched to intercept Lee, the two New Jersey regiments would depart and be mustered out. At Gettysburg Carroll would still be a colonel and at the age of thirty he would show why his superiors thought so highly of him.[102]

General French's second brigade consisted of the 10th and 108th New York, the 12th New Jersey, the 14th Connecticut and, their brigade commander, Colonel Thomas Alfred Smyth's original 1st Delaware. Smyth had no military training prior to the war. Born on Christmas Day in the parish of Balleyhooly, county of Cork, Ireland, Smyth was educated in local schools and worked on his father's farm until he sailed to America in 1854. Settling in Philadelphia, he began a career working as a wood carver. Carving must not have been very exciting for in the mid-1850s he joined William Walker's revolutionary expedition to Nicaragua. Upon his return in 1858, Smyth took up residence in Wilmington, Delaware, where he began a career as a coach maker.[103]

When the war broke out Smyth raised a company of volunteers and offered them to the authorities in Delaware. The company ended up as part of the all Irish 24th Pennsylvania which was mustered into service for a period of three months.

---

[100] *OR* vol.21, p.51; Tagg, **Generals**, pp55-56; *OR* vol.25, pt.1, pp.160, 364.

[101] Tagg, **Generals**, pp.55-56.

[102] *OR* vol.25, pt.1, p.577; *OR* vol.27, pt.1, p.158.

[103] *OR* vol.25, pt.1, p.577; Warner, **Generals in Blue**, p.465.

Smyth served as captain of Company H and after being mustered out, he joined the 1st Delaware. His new regiment was mustered in as a three year unit and Smyth was appointed the regiment's major. In July 1862 the 1st was sent to Suffolk where the regiment and Major Smyth saw little activity. By September the regiment was back in Virginia and as part of the Army of the Potomac, marched into Maryland. Smyth and the regiment saw the "elephant" for the first time when they participated in the assault on the Sunken Road at Antietam. Of the 900 men who went into the fight, only half remained in the ranks after they were forced to withdraw.[104]

Their next battle found the men of the 1st once again participating in another charge upon a well-defended enemy position at the stone wall on Marye's Heights at Fredericksburg. Like the other units ordered up the slope toward the wall, the 1st lost its formation and gave way before the onslaught of Rebel lead. Taking any shelter they could upon the slope, the men, in an exposed position and unable to retreat, had to wait until nightfall for darkness to conceal them from the view of the Rebel riflemen. Singled out by his brigade commander for his work that bloody day, Smyth, on 30 December 1862 received a promotion to lieutenant colonel and on 7 February he became the regiment's commander.[105]

Colonel Smyth first led the men from Delaware during the battle of Chancellorsville. The regiment was lightly engaged during the fighting and shortly after its conclusion, two of the brigades three regiments left to be mustered out. The 1st Delaware, the only remaining regiment, was transferred to the Third Division's Second Brigade. Smyth, now his new brigade's ranking officer since its previous commander had been captured at Chancellorsville, was elevated to brigade command. His valor on the battlefield led to notoriety and promotion. Now the woodworker and carriage maker from Ireland would be tasked with leading a brigade of Hancock's boys.[106]

Old Dan's Boys[107]

Shortly after Chancellorsville, General Sickles was forced to take medical leave being diagnosed as suffering from "persistent enteritis" in camp. The condition, which was usually brought on by poor quality camp fare sent him packing for New York to recover. He would not return until three days before the battle in southern Pennsylvanian. In his place at the head of the Third Corps, which was encamped along the Rappahannock behind Fredericksburg in early June, was his senior division commander Major General David Bell Birney. Birney, the son of noted abolitionist James G. Birney, was born on 29 May 1825 in Huntsville, Alabama. James, a proven intellectual who owned a cotton plantation and slaves

---

[104] Warner, *Generals in Blue*, p.465; Priest, John Michael, *Antietam: The Soldiers Battle*, p.336.

[105] Tagg, *Generals*, p.57; *OR* vol.21, p.303; Boatner, *Dictionary*, p.777.

[106] Tagg, *Generals*, p.57; *OR* vol.25, pt.1, p.577.

[107] The organization of the Third Corps described in the narrative is reflective of the corps after it was reorganized in Mid June. For the organization of the corps at the time of Lee's shift to Culpeper Court House see Appendix A.

ran into trouble with its operation and moved to Huntsville two years before David was born. In Huntsville, James opened a law practice and spent much of his efforts defending blacks. In 1835 he moved his family back to Kentucky, the state of his birth, and then on to Cincinnati where he became a fiery spokesman for the abolitionist movement. While in Cincinnati, James began publishing a weekly abolitionist paper and ran for president twice on the Liberty Party ticket.[108]

David was born while his father was living in Huntsville on 29 May 1825. The boy quickly demonstrated he had inherited his father's intelligence and attended Phillips Andover Academy in Massachusetts. After graduation he joined his father in Ohio. He studied law in Cincinnati, entered the business world, and passed the bar. Moving to Philadelphia, Birney opened a law practice in 1856 which he operated until the war began. He also continued his business efforts, developing friendships with a number of influential citizens.[109]

David Birney was a man who would be hard to forget once one saw him. His complexion was pale and gray, giving him the look of a cadaver. One man believed Birney could have doubled as a bust of himself which could have adorned his own tomb. Theodore Lyman, of General Meade's staff, wrote that Birney "was a pale, Puritanical figure, with a demeanor of unmovable coldness; only he would smile politely when you spoke to him." Continuing on Lyman noted Birney "was spare in person, with a thin face, light blue eye, and sandy hair." His narrow face gave his cheeks a concave look which only added to his frigid appearance. Although his exterior and mannerisms were dull and a bit unnerving, as the war progressed he would prove himself to be one of the few political appointments who made a very capable commander.[110]

Birney evidently saw the war approaching, for in 1860 he began a concentrated study of military subjects. His self-education paid off when he was appointed lieutenant colonel of a regiment of Pennsylvania militia. Shortly after Fort Sumter surrendered, Birney, paying most of the expenses from his own pocket, recruited and organized the 23rd Pennsylvania Militia and was commissioned is lieutenant colonel. Initially mustered in as a three month regiment, Birney and his boys fought with General Robert Patterson's Army of the Shenandoah and took their first enemy fire at the Battle of Falling Waters. When the unit was mustered out, it was reorganized with Birney becoming its colonel on 31 August 1861. A few months later, on 17 February, he was promoted to brigadier general of volunteers.[111]

Birney's first combat action at the head of a brigade came at Seven Pines on the Peninsula. During the action some confusion precipitated his removal from command. Charged with disobedience for evidently halting short of the front, a court if inquiry was convened which found Birney innocent, and he was acquitted of the charges. As

---

[108] Keneally, **American Scoundrel**, p.273; **Electronic Source:** http://en.wikipedia.org/wiki/James_G._Birney, Last accessed 5/5/2012; Tagg, **Generals**, p.65.

[109] Warner, **Generals in Blue**, p.34.

[110] Tagg, **Generals**, p.65.

[111] Warner, **Generals in Blue**, p.34; Eicher, & Eicher, **High Commands**, p.132.

if to reinforcing his innocence, Birney was called out in division commander Philip Kearny's report as having performed his duty well. He was reinstated in time to lead his brigade during The Seven Days. Again, Birney was praised by Kearny who noted that "[I]n this engagement the coolness and judicious arrangement of General Birney influenced his whole command to feel invincible in a very weak position."[112]

Birney next led his brigade at Second Bull Run where it was engaged in some of the heaviest fighting. The intensity of the battle could be found in Birney's casualty list which contained 629 men. A few days later he found divisional command thrust upon him when General Kearny was killed on 1 September during the inconsequential engagement at Chantilly. Kearny accidently rode into the Confederate lines and as he turned his horse to gallop away he was killed instantly by a rifle ball. Birney and the division were assigned to duty in Washington and did not participate in the Maryland Campaign, but the division was back with the Army of the Potomac in time to fight at Fredericksburg. Birney may have cost the Federals a chance to prevail when he refused to support General Meade's breakthrough in a timely manner on the southern end of the battlefield. Chancellorsville provided Birney a chance at redemption and he led his division with distinction during the heaviest fighting in the Hazel Grove area taking over 1,600 casualties.[113]

Although he had no military background prior to the war, Birney had shown he possessed the abilities of a natural leader. At Fredericksburg he fixed himself too tightly to chain of command and by hesitating to support Meade made an error. But, he had proven himself on a battlefield and was a competent division level commander. A member of the corps since early 1862, he knew the command structure and the men in it well. As he prepared for the summer campaign, Birney would need all these skills to lead the corps north in Sickles' absence and the coming battle would be his greatest test.

The Third Corps had borne the brunt of the major fighting at Chancellorsville. It lost over 4,000 men killed, wounded or missing during the battle, a number which constituted over a third of the army's total casualties. Including casualties from Fredericksburg, the corps had lost well over 5,000 men in the two engagements. As June began the corps still contained three divisions. All had taken their share of casualties and been severely reduced in number. With a number of regiments scheduled to depart due to expiring terms of enlistments, its three divisions would be even more undermanned. In addition, the Third Division had lost its commander Major General Amiel W. Whipple, who was mortally wounded during the battle. As a result of all these issues, a decision was made in June to reorganize the Third Corps and reduce its number of divisions to two. The seven remaining regiments of the Third Division would be transferred to brigades in the first two, bolstering the strength of the remaining divisions.[114]

---

[112] Tagg, **Generals**, pp.65-66; Boatner, **Dictionary**, p.65; *OR* vol.11, pt.2, p.164.

[113] Warner, **Generals**, p.259; Cleaves, **Meade**, pp.91-92; *OR* vol.12, pt.2, p.257; *OR* vol.25, pt.1, p.178.

[114] *OR* vol.25, pt.1, pp.179; *OR* vol.25, pt.2, pp.578-579; *OR* vol.27, pt.1, pp.159-160.

David Bell Birney owed his position at the head of a division to the death of Philip Kearny. *LOC*

The shuffling of regiments resulted in a reduction in the number of division and brigade level command positions in the corps. The short end of the stick was given to Brigadier General Charles K. Graham. With his Third Division disbanded, he was relegated to command of the First Division's First Brigade. Born in the Ninth Ward of New York City on 3 June 1824, Graham joined the navy at the age of seventeen as a midshipman and spent seven years at sea, including duty in the Gulf of Mexico during the war with Mexico. Resigning in 1848, he began the study of engineering and law. Although he eventually began practicing law, it seemed Graham's love for engineering was stronger. He quit the lawyer business and took a position at the Brooklyn Naval Yard as a civil engineer working to construct landings and dry-docks. He also assisted in the planning and surveying of New York's Central Park.

Graham owed some of his success to an association he developed with Dan Sickles. The two had become acquainted within the halls of New York politics, and a friendship developed. Graham acquired his position at the shipyard when Sickles, displaying how much of a scoundrel he was, arranged the firing of the yard's engineer. When the displaced engineer discovered he had been ousted by Sickles, he became enraged and attacked him, but nothing came of the assault. Graham, evidently regarding the manner in which he attained his new position as typical New York politics, expressed little apprehension over the episode. He quickly settled in as the yard's new engineer and held the position until the war began. When hostilities broke out, he organized 400 men who were in his employ as dock workers. Taking the men with him, he volunteered for duty with the brigade Sickles was organizing. Graham and his men would become the core of the 74th New York Infantry and part of Sickles' Excelsior Brigade.[115]

Unfortunately for Graham, he saw little combat with the 74th due to his inability to stay healthy. The regiment traveled to the Peninsula with McClellan's army but almost immediately after arriving Graham was stricken with a fever and resigned on 10 April and went home to recover. A month and a half later, he re-enlisted and was back in command, leading the regiment at Seven Pines. Before Lee launched his initial attack inaugurated The Seven Days, Graham came down with dysentery. Choosing to stay with the regiment during the fighting, it was to Graham's good fortune that the 74th saw little action. After the battle, he determined he could not remain in the field. Being delirious and weak from his illness, he was assigned to recruiting duty in New York and once again left the army.[116]

While he struggled to recover, Graham began his recruiting duties and on 29 November received a promotion to brigadier general. The elevation was more for his association with Sickles than his work on the battlefield. Finally, nearly eight months after leaving the army, he returned and took command of John Robinson's old brigade when Robinson was promoted to divisional command. Leading the brigade at Chancellorsville, Graham directed his men with distinction in the whirlwind of fighting around the Chancellor House. General Birney was concerned about his new brigadier and expressed apprehension over Graham's abilities prior to the battle. Graham however met the challenge and Birney, in his report commented on his performance. "...[B]raver men never drew a trigger than those in the First Brigade, and Brigadier General Graham has gained by his fight, by his coolness, firmness, and enthusiasm, the entire confidence of myself and the division." On 4 May, when General Whipple fell, Graham took over command of the division. He would remain there until the corps was reorganized and he was placed in charge of a brigade in the First Division.[117]

Graham, armed with the confidence of his commander, would not take command of his new brigade until the corps reorganization in mid-June. The men of his future command, the 57th, 63rd, 68th, 105th, 114th and 141st Pennsylvania, would have no concerns over being able to recognize their new leader on a battlefield. The reason was not Graham's dominating presence or booming, distinct voice. It would also not be due to any type of unique uniform or identifying article of clothing. Graham was one of the few generals in the army that stood out in camp, on the march, and in battle due to his facial hair. He could be picked out in a crowd quite easily because he sported a huge curly brown beard. The beard's monstrous growth was obviously only achievable through the neglect of civilized grooming

---

[115] Tagg, **Generals**, pp.67-68; Phisterer, **NYWR**, vol.4, pp.2767, 2775; Graham Obituary, New York Times, 16 April, 1889.

[116] Tagg, **Generals**, p.68.

[117] *Ibid*; **OR** vol.25, pt.1, p.410.

habits. Active military operation probably helped Graham achieve such a manly growth and his distinct look.[118]

With Sickles away and General Birney in command of the corps, the First Division was left to the charge of eventual Second Brigade commander John Henry Hobart Ward. Ward, who would command the division until Sickles returned, would himself return to his brigade when the general came back from sick leave. Ward was born in New York City on 17 June 1823. A military career seemed to be in the cards for him since both his father and grandfather had fought for their country. His grandfather, John Ward, fought during the Revolution and suffered a debilitating wound that would eventually take his life. Ward's father, James, during the War of 1812 suffered the same fate but before succumbing to his injuries, was able to father John. After attending Trinity Collegiate School, John Henry continued the family's military tradition by enlisting in the Regular Army at the age of eighteen. Becoming a private in the 7th U. S. Infantry, Ward spent the next five years working his way up through the ranks and in 1847 was the regiment's sergeant major. He was present at Fort Texas (later Fort Brown) when the Mexicans bombarded the stronghold, inaugurating the Mexican War. He was wounded at Monterrey and was at Vera Cruz when General Scott captured the city.[119]

With the city in the hands of the Americans, Ward found time to partake in the pleasures of the culture, meeting and getting married to a local woman. Choosing to leave active service in 1851, Ward returned to New York and assumed the position of assistant commissary general for the state. He used his time in the commissary office to establish a number of political connections which came in handy as the war began. His associations would eventually assist him in securing the colonelcy of the 38th New York Volunteers. The regiment was mustered in for two years of service on 3 June 1861.[120]

Ward first led the regiment at Bull Run, but suddenly found himself in command of a brigade when his commanding officer was wounded. After the battle, he returned to the command the 38th and led it through some of the thickest fighting on the Peninsula. Afterward, he was soundly praised by division commander Kearny. "I report as conspicuously distinguished, imparting victory all around …J. H. Hobart Ward, of the Thirty-eighth New York," Kearny wrote in his report of operations at Williamsburg. In a follow up report four days later, Kearny noted that "Col. J. H. Hobart Ward has already been noticed as one of the 'bravest of the brave.'" During the battle, Kearny ordered Ward to "charge down the road and [take] the [rifle] pits and abates in flank." This Ward did to Kearny's approval, using his leadership skills to impart upon his men all the poise needed

---

[118] *OR* vol.27, pt.1, p.159; Eicher, & Eicher, **High Commands**, p.261.

[119] Ward Obituary, New York Times, 25 July 1903; Warner, **Generals in Blue**, p.537; Eicher, & Eicher, **High Commands**, p.553. The fort's name was change to Fort Brown in honor of its commanding officer Major Jacob Brown who was wounded during the bombardment and would later die.

[120] Warner, **Generals in Blue**, p.537; Phisterer, *NYWR*, vol.3, p.2173.

to perform the task. Although lightly engaged during The Seven Days, Ward once again found himself in temporary command of the brigade when his commander General Birney was relieved. Later, after General Kearny was killed at Chantilly, Ward was elevated to brigade command once again when General Birney was promoted to divisional command to replace Kearny. Ward received a promotion to brigadier general on 4 October 1862, after which he was placed in permanent command of the brigade.[121]

At Fredericksburg and Chancellorsville Ward's brigade, like the rest of the Third Corps, was in the thick of the action. During the former battle, Ward led his men in a counterattack against Stonewall Jackson's troops as General Birney belatedly moved his division to support General Meade's breach in the Rebel line. The latter battle saw Ward called upon to lead a night attack, ordering his battle line forward at 11:30 p.m. All went well until the shooting started. With bullits flying, the men, including Ward, became nervous and frightened in the darkness. Panic took hold, and the men began to seek whatever protection could be found. Ward, who was mounted on his horse during the attack, lost his composure as his command became uncontrollable. Galloping his horse toward the rear of his brigade, he accidently rode over two of his soldiers. The incident did not seem to stain his record, and as spring ended he was still the brigade's commander, although he was leading the division due to Sickles' absence.[122]

During the Third Corps' reorganization, Ward's brigade would be bolstered by the addition of regiments from the old Third Division. Gone would be Ward's original 38th New York, sent home after its two year enlistment expired on 8 June. The four remaining regiments, the 20th Indiana, the 3rd and 4th Maine and the 99th Pennsylvania would be joined by four more regiments from the first and third brigades of the carved up division. Eventually the 1st and 2nd U. S. Sharpshooters, along with the 86th and 124th New York would become part of Ward's command. After the shuffling was completed, his brigade contained eight regiments of veterans that had all seen hard fighting. For now, however, the brigade would retain its remaining four regiments until the reorganization was complete in two weeks. Ward, at the age of forty, had been associated with the military for over half his life and had proven to be a valuable brigadier. He would have another opportunity to prove his worth in a few weeks.[123]

The man who would eventually end up commanding the First Division's Third Brigade was already commanding a brigade within the division in early June. Colonel Philippe Régis Dénis de Keredern de Trobriand was at the head of the division's second brigade but as the corps was reorganized in mid-June, he would be transferred and placed in charge of its third. Colonel de Trobriand not only had the longest name of any brigade commander in the army but was also the son of a French baron whose ancestry included a general in Napoleon's army. He

---

[121] Warner, *Generals in Blue*, p.537; *OR* vol.11, pt.1, pp.493-494.

[122] Tagg, *Generals*, p.70; *OR* vol.21, p.133.

[123] *OR* vol.25, pt.2, pp.532, 578-579; *OR* vol.27, pt.1, p.159; Tagg, *Generals*, p.70.

was born in his father's Loire chateau near Tours, France on 4 June 1816. Philippe spent a goodly portion of his early life studying and writing poetry, learning law and, in 1840, he published a novel. He also seemed to have a confrontational streak, and fought a number of duels as a young man the old fashioned way, with swords. Traveling to America at the age of twenty-five, de Trobriand mingled with New York's elite and met a young heiress named Mary Jones. The two became enamored with each other and traveled to Paris where they were married. The couple lived in Venice for a short time but eventually returned to New York where de Trobriand earned a living editing and writing publications in French.[124]

In 1861, with the war underway, de Trobriand became a citizen of the United States, volunteered for service with the 55th New York Militia and was made its colonel. Known as the "De Garde Lafayette," the 55th was populated by mostly French immigrants from New York City. On 25 July, the War Department authorized de Trobriand to raise a regiment for Federal service. The members of the 55th Militia were used to form the core of the new regiment, which eventually became the 55th New York Volunteers. The regiment mustered in on 28 August with de Trobriand as its colonel and left the state three days later. Its first combat experience came on the Peninsula, where it performed well, but de Trobriand became incapacitated due to illness. Returning to the regiment in the fall, he found his command transferred to General Hobart Ward's brigade. At the Battle of Fredericksburg the regiment was held in reserve and saw little action. On 21 December the 55th was merged with Hobart Ward's 38th New York. The consolidated unit kept the designation of the latter and de Trobriand was made its colonel. Once again at Chancellorsville, he led his regiment in a major battle, but while the Third Corps was heavily engaged, de Trobriand's men saw minimal action.[125]

With General Sickles on leave and General Ward elevated to division command, at the beginning of June, de Trobriand found himself in command of Ward's brigade. When the reorganization of the corps took place, the 38th New York departed, but the Frenchman would remain with the army. One of the regiments of his future brigade, the 37th New York, would also be sent home for muster out. When the 37th departed so did its colonel, Samuel B. Hayman, who was also commanding the Third Brigade. To fill the void, de Trobriand was transferred to its command on 3 June. The remaining units, the 3rd and 5th Michigan, 17th Maine and the 40th New York would form the brigade's nucleus. Replacing the 37th would be the 110th Pennsylvanian from the purged Second Brigade of the carved up Third Division.[126]

Colonel de Trobriand was a refreshing departure from the typical Civil War commander. Unlike many of his fellow officers, he did not possess the stoic presence that so many of the militarily trained officers enjoyed. His lack of classical training in military protocol and pomp made him devoid of the ridged

---

[124] Tagg, *Generals*, p.71; Faust, *Encyclopedia*, p.217.

[125] Phisterer, *NYWR*, vol.3, pp.2463-2464; Tagg, *Generals*, p.71.

[126] *OR* vol.25, pt.2, pp.578-579; *OR* vol.27, pt.1, p.160; Phisterer, *NYWR*, vol.3, p.2159-2160.

persona portrayed by other officers. He was a romantic man of words and always seemed to be relaxed and easy going. Although he was an aristocratic Frenchman, he had little in common with the upper class, a demographic which had provided the majority of officers from New York. He would show himself to be a capable leader of men even though he had little combat experience before he arrived at Gettysburg.[127]

"Old Goggle Eyes"

Brigadier General Andrew A. Humphreys was a career military man and like General Meade spent a good deal of time before the war with the Topographical Engineers. Meade's aide Theodore Lyman described him later in the war as "a very neat, studious looking man, with a soft, gentlemanly way." Lyman noted Humphreys acted very boyish, was quick in his mannerisms and seemed to spend an inordinate amount of time on personal grooming. Some considered him an intellectual in both the military and scientific fields and a possessor of great personal courage and honor. He was not charismatic like so many Civil War generals, but a straight shooter who spoke his mind even when it may have been prudent to hold his tongue. Others considered him completely void of egotism. Based on the observations of his peers, these where the impressions left by General Humphreys. However, his soldiers had a somewhat different view of him.[128]

Humphreys' men considered him demanding and overbearing, calling him "Old Goggle Eyes" behind his back. The moniker was not intended as flattery but rather an affront to insult by means of the reading glasses he wore. They looked upon him as an unfeeling old man, an oppressor and authoritarian, whose discipline on many occasions was unnecessary and unjust. Thought of as incredibly demanding, when his men went into battle everyone was required to shoulder a gun. When accoutrements were dropped before a fight, no one was allowed to remain behind to guard the booty. If the equipment was missing when the survivors returned, appropriated by those who managed to avoid their duty, Humphreys' men would have to make do without. In addition, he was at the top of the list when it came to proficient swearing. He was "one of the loudest swearers" that Assistant Secretary of War Charles Dana had ever known and could rival General Hancock for his proficiency in the use of vulgarity.[129]

Humphreys was born on a sunny day in Philadelphia on 2 November 1810, into a reputable family. His father and grandfather had been engineers specializing in the field of naval architecture. His grandfather, Joshua, worked to build the upstart nations navy and was responsible for drawing the initial plans for the forty-four gun frigate *USS Constitution*, the thirty-six gun *Constellation* and other ships

---

[127] Tagg, ***Generals***, p.71.

[128] Lowe, ***Meade's Army***, p.27. Tagg, ***Generals***, p.73.

[129] Tagg, ***Generals***, p.73.

in the line. The design was unique to America being patterned after the famous French frigates which displayed an inward curve at the top of the hull.[130]

Young Andrew began his education at the hand of a private tutor, but showed little of the intellectual side of his personality. He was a poor student who spent much of his time during his informative years on truancy roles. His early instructors did little to help matters, resorting to the use of the rod more often than necessary to discipline the mischievous boy. One specific instance found Andrew blamed for something he was not responsible for, but one of his instructors punished him anyway. The teacher acknowledged his error, but the damage had been done. Andrew did not return to the school and the frequency of his absenteeism increased. The boy would often skip out on his lessons and travel by ferry with a friend to nearby Camden for activities which provided more stimulating entertainment.

When his father departed for Europe to further his shipbuilding career, Andrew's mother took over his rearing but was unable to control the youth. It was decided more structure was required and Nazareth Hall in Northampton County was selected as the place where Andrew would continue his education; if he could be kept in class. Arrangements were made to transport him to his new school, but on the morning the carriage arrived to pick him up, he could not be found. An extensive search found Andrew and his brother Clement, hiding in a chimney. The hiding place was so small that Clement could not adequately hide one of his feet and their location was compromised. The boys were dusted off and loaded into the carriage and taken to their new school. At the time he had no desire to leave, but later in life Humphreys credited the school with placing his feet on the straight and narrow. "If I have achieved any success in life," he noted later, "or have been able to render any service to my country or to my fellow men, I attribute all to the advantages which I received in this Institution." He later left the school to be instructed once again by a private tutor, but the structure of Nazareth let the boy see his potential.[131]

Humphreys entered the Military Academy on 1 July 1827, and graduated thirteenth in a class of thirty-three four years later. After commencement he was brevetted a second lieutenant and assigned to the artillery. His first posting was at Fort Moultrie, South Carolina, but like most graduates, he served in Florida during the Seminole War. Humphreys' engineering heritage may have prompted his resignation on 30 September 1836. After resigning, he became a civil engineer, taking a position with the government. However, two years later he was back with the army as a first lieutenant in the Corps of Topographical Engineers. He labored to construct bridges, conducted coastal and railroad surveys, and worked to construct harbor installations. Traveling south he toiled performing hydrological surveys along the Mississippi River and later published a report on the hydrology and physics of the river which was translation into various languages. The report was well received and went far in establishing Humphreys' reputation as an

---

[130] Humphreys, Henry H., *Andrew Atkinson Humphreys*, pp.17, 25.

[131] *Ibid*, pp.26-27. Nazareth Hall was the forerunner of Moravian College, a private liberal arts college and seminary located in Bethlehem, Pennsylvania.

intellectual. It served as a guide for navigation and flood control for years to come on the "Big Muddy."[132]

Humphreys was suffering ill health when the war began, and he was unable to begin serving his country until the latter half of 1861. A captain as hostilities erupted, by early August he received a promotion to major and by the end of the year was able to return to active duty. General McClellan placed Andrew on his staff on 1 December and Humphreys served until early March 1862, when he was made the Army of the Potomac's chief topographic engineer. He performed the duties of the position through the Peninsula Campaign and The Seven Days. Promoted to brigadier general of volunteers on 28 April 1862, Humphreys finally received a field command on 12 September when he took control of the newly created Third Division of the Fifth Corps. The division had been built from eight, nine-month regiments from Pennsylvania and was organized too late to participate in the battle of Antietam but did assist in the pursuit of Lee as the enemy general's legions returned southward.[133]

It wasn't until the battle of Fredericksburg that Humphreys was able to lead his men in combat. As his regiments formed for an assault, one of Humphreys' colonels detailed six of his regiment's youngest soldiers to guard their pile of haversacks. Humphreys, becoming aware of the detail, ordered the boys back in line. No one would be held back. Mounting his horse, Humphreys rode out ahead of his regiment, intent on leading them from the front. Federal troops had been battering Marye's Heights for some time and there were already thousands of men wounded, killed and unscathed on the field. Before riding out, Humphreys turned to his staff and without officially ordering them to do so, shammed them into going with him. "Young gentlemen," Humphreys lectured, "I intend to lead this assault; I presume, of course, you will wish to ride with me?" Seven of his staff officers mounted their horses and followed. During the assault the green Pennsylvanians advanced further toward the stone wall than any other unit that charged across the bloody slope. Like all other Federal troops who approached Longstreet's position that day, they were eventually forced to fall back. Humphreys remained mounted although by the end of the fight he was upon his third horse, the previous two, including his own horse, Charley, who had been hit twice, were shot out from under him. Although the maelstrom of battle flew all around him, Humphreys somehow managed to come through the episode unscathed. The haversack boys and his staff officers were not so lucky. Five of the officers were shot from their horses and two of the boys never saw their homes again. While the battle before the wall was lost, Humphreys went a long way toward gaining the respect of his Pennsylvanians. While he may have been an overbearing ogre in camp, he was not beyond sharing the dangers of battle with his men.[134]

---

[132] *Ibid*, pp.28,30; Tagg, **Generals**, p.73.

[133] *Ibid*; Boatner, **Dictionary**, p.417; Warner, **Generals in Blue**, pp.240-241.

[134] Tagg, **Generals**, p.73; Humphreys, **Humphreys**, pp.178-179.

Fredericksburg was the only major battle in which Humphreys' Pennsylvanians saw action. At Chancellorsville they were only lightly engaged and shortly afterward all but two of the regiment's enlistment terms expired. They were sent home for muster out leaving Humphreys a general without a command. However, the death of Major General Hiram G. Berry while leading members of his Third Corps division in a bayonet charge left an opening in the command structure. On 23 May, Humphreys was assigned to command Berry's old division. At the time he took command, he was the only classically trained military officer in the corps. Fellow Pennsylvanian George Meade thought highly of Humphreys, calling him "a most valuable officer, besides being an associate of the most agreeable character."[135]

General Humphreys' First Brigade consisted of three Massachusetts regiments, the 1st, 11th and 16th, the 11th New Jersey and the 26th Pennsylvania. Eventually the brigade would be bolstered by the last of the old Third Division regiments when the 12th New Hampshire and 84th Pennsylvania were transferred to it. Commanding the brigade was Brigadier General Joseph Bradford Carr. Carr was an Irishman whose parents immigrated from the Emerald Isle, settling in the Albany, New York area. Joseph was born there on 15 August 1828. His family had little money so Joe received his formal education at local public schools. After he grew to manhood, Carr moved to Troy where he began working as an apprentice in the tobacco industry. After learning the trade, he became a merchant, specializing in the manufacture of cigars.

From an early age, Carr displayed an interest in the military and eventually joined the Republican Guards, a New York militia unit from Troy. He entered at the bottom of the ranks, "and for a year carried a musket." He progressed slowly upward through the ranks, eventually attaining a second lieutenant's commission. On 10 July 1859, Carr became the commandant of the 24th State Militia and was in that capacity when Fort Sumter was fired upon. Two days after the fort surrendered, work began to organize a regiment from Troy. A month later the 2nd New York was mustered into the service of the United States for two years. Carr, after initially being installed as the regiment's lieutenant colonel, found himself at the head of the unit by the time it left the state. Command fell to him after the regiment's original colonel declined to serve.[136]

It did not take the men of the regiment long to discover Carr was a bit of a proper person. He was not a curser and some believed they never heard profanity pass his lips. It was also discovered that early in life, Carr had taught dancing and the men wasted little time using that fact as a tool to make light of their commander. Occasionaly, when Carr passed by, some of the men would craft derogatory comments using dance hall jargon to toss a few insults his way. Carr also had a tendency to keep himself well-groomed, and his appearance reinforced

---

[135] *Ibid*; Meade, **Meade**, vol.1, p.378.

[136] **OR** vol.27, pt.1, p.160; Carr Obituary, New York Times, 25 February 1895; Phisterer, **NYWR**, vol.2, pp.1707-08, 1718. Many sources note Carr was born on 16 August but his obituary indicates the date of his birth as the 15th.

the opinion that he as a bit of a dandy. Carr's large, bushy, and neatly trimmed sideburns and mustache were thick and full and seemed a bit out of place in an army where little time for personal grooming was available. His personality was never called into question and some noting "[H]is sturdy, upright character and manliness were everywhere recognized..."[137]

Carr's first field assignment was in southeastern Virginia when his regiment was stationed at Fort Monroe. After the regiment took part in the first engagement of the war at Big Bethel, Brigadier General Ebenezer W. Pierce, called Carr out in his report noting that the colonel "showed himself a good soldier..." By June of 1862, Carr and his regiment were on the Peninsula as part of the Third Corps. He would eventually end up leaving his regiment to command the division's Third Brigade. The brigade, made up mostly of New Jersey regiments, saw little action, and Carr had few opportunities to gain experience as a brigade commander. However, at Second Bull Run, Carr's experience, and that of his New Jersey Brigade was quite different. Division commander Joe Hooker ordered Carr's men forward and the brigade battered itself against Stonewall Jackson's stiff defensive line along an unfinished railroad line. The brigade suffered 393 casualties and Carr, in his first major battle, proved to be a stubborn commander and a fierce fighter. Hooker however, failed to acknowledge his efforts since he did not file a report. Afterword, Carr received a promotion to brigadier general on 7 September. Nine days later he was transferred to command the division's First Brigade, leaving his Jerseymen behind.[138]

At Fredericksburg, Carr's new brigade was lightly engaged. A few months later, at Chancellorsville, the brigade became embroiled in the heavy fighting in the vicinity of the Chancellor House. Battling along the Plank Road, Carr's boys took 534 casualties before Hooker made the decision to evacuate the position. After the battle, Carr took command of the division when General Berry was killed, and Sickles praised Carr for his handling of the situation. Unfortunately, shortly after the battle Carr's health began to deteriorate. He became extremely ill and had to leave his command for a time, as Hooker began to extract his army from the Rappahannock line to pursue Lee. Carr would begin to show signs of malaria, but in order to remain with his men, he resorted to large quantities of medicine and fought his way through the illness. During his sickness Carr proved he was as tough personally as he was on a battlefield.[139]

The second brigade of Humphreys' division contained Dan Sickles' old regiments from New York. Christened the Excelsior Brigade, its five units had been designated the 70th through 74th. On 6 September 1862 a sixth regiment, the 120th New York was added to the brigade making it the largest all New York brigade that would fight at Gettysburg. In command of the New Yorkers was a transplanted Connecticut native named William Root Brewster. Born in Goshen in July of 1828,

---

[137] *Ibid*; Tagg, **Generals**, pp.75-76.

[138] **OR** vol.2, p.86; **OR** vol.12, pt.2, p.258; Tagg, **Generals**, p.76; Boatner, **Dictionary**, p.128.

[139] Sears, **Chancellorsville**, p.345; **OR** vol.25, pt.1, p.178; Tagg, **Generals**, p.76.

Brewster had worked as a revenue agent before the war and had no military training prior to hostilities. After joining the 28th New York Militia he was made its major and served for three months. The unit, stationed in the Washington DC area, spent the majority of its term of enlistment guarding bridges along the Potomac River. It missed the Battle of Bull Run just before its muster out in early August 1861.[140]

In October, Brewster joined Sickles and assisted in recruit the brigade. For his efforts he was made colonel of the 73rd New York. The regiment was organized from men who were members of local fire departments and was initially designated the Second Fire Zouaves. It was mustered in on 8 October for three years service, and Brewster led it on the Peninsula at Williamsburg the following spring. For some reason, he was not with the regiment during the campaign which resulted in the second fight near Bull Run. He would not lead his boys again until Fredericksburg. His regiment however remained unengaged during the fighting and Brewster failed to gain any combat experience during the battle; an expertise he was sorely lacking.[141]

A few months later, Brewster was missing once again while the men of the 73rd bore the brunt of the fighting, taking 317 casualties during the struggle at Chancellorsville. Upon his return, he received an interesting surprise. The Excelsior Brigade's previous commander, Brigadier General Joseph Revere, grandson of the Revolution's famous message bearer, had taken command of the Second Division after General Berry fell. Revere had shown poor judgment during the remainder of the battle and was summarily court-martialed for incompetence and dismissed from the army. As the brigade's senior colonel, command was suddenly thrust upon Brewster. When elevated, he had no military skills and minimal combat experience, as he had only led men under fire once. He was the epitome of inexperience and a fine example of the inadequacies of a mostly volunteer force with politically connected organizers.[142]

Humphreys' Third Brigade, like the second, although for a different reason, found itself with a new commander as it prepared to begin its march north in pursuit of Lee. Contrasting Colonel Brewster was Colonel George Childs Burling, who had some military experience before he volunteered for his home state's 6th New Jersey regiment. Burling, a coal merchant, was born in Burlington on 17 February 1834. He had been a captain in the state's 4th Militia prior to the war. Unlike Brewster however, Burling had plenty of experience dealing with the violence and trials of battle and had been praised for his performance on a number of occasions. Recognition of his abilities came early and he rose from the captaincy of a company to the regiment's lieutenant colonel before McClellan's campaign

---

[140] *OR* vol.25, pt.2, p.578; Eicher, & Eicher, **High Commands**, p.144; Phisterer, *NYWR*, vol.4, p.3410.

[141] Phisterer, Frederick, *NYWR*, vol.4, p.2751; *OR* vol.12, pt.2, p.452; Some sources indicate that Brewster was captured during the Peninsula Campaign but no reliable accounts of him being taken into custody have been located.

[142] *OR* vol.25, pt.1, p.179; Warner, **Generals in Blue**, pp.365-396.

to take Richmond began. As part of Joe Hooker's division at Seven Pines, the 6th New Jersey found itself in the brigade of Colonel Carr. Burling fought his regiment well enough to be singled out by his division commander, who noted in his report that Burling performed "distinguished services on [the] field."[143]

At Second Bull Run, Burling took over command of the regiment when its colonel was wounded and incapacitated. The regiment contributed handily to the heavy casualties Carr piled up against Jackson's line along the railroad grade, racking up 105 killed wounded and captured, more than any regiment in the brigade. The high numbers could be attributed to the fact that when the brigade finally withdrew from its position, the 6th was left behind. A heavy Confederate assault soon slammed into Burling's position. With no support, he was forced to retreat, and did so while under heavy fire. Colonel Carr wrote in his report that Burling displayed "gallant and meritorious conduct."[144]

As part of the Third Corps, the 6th New Jersey missed the Maryland Campaign but was back with the Army of the Potomac at Fredericksburg. While not engaged during the battle, Burling and the 6th saw heavy action a few months later at Chancellorsville. The severity of the struggle was difficult on the brigades' command structure, both Brigadier General Gershom Mott and Burling were wounded. Burling's injuries were not serious and he was back with his regiment within a month. Upon his return, he, like Colonel Brewster, since he was the senior colonel in the ranks, found himself in command of a brigade. When Burling assumed command, the brigade, in addition to the 6th, was also home for three other regiments from New Jersey, the 5th, 7th and 8th. Two other regiments, the 115th Pennsylvania and Colonel Carr's original 2nd New York were also members. The New Yorkers however, would be sent home for muster out, their two year term having expired. By June the 2nd New Hampshire would be assigned to the brigade to strengthen its numbers. Although Burling had been with the brigade for a number of months and there was no question regarding his valor, he was untried as its commander. It remained to be seen if he could handle a brigade when bullets began to fly.[145]

The Men on the River

The majority of George Meade's Fifth Corps remained along the banks of the Rappahannock River during the first week of June. The corps' First Division under the command of General Barnes was further upstream on guard and picket duty near Ellis Ford. Barnes, one of the old men of the Army of the Potomac, was older than any other general except for Brigadier General George Greene. Born in Boston on 28 December 1801, James' received his formal education at the Boston Latin School. After graduation he entered the business world for a few years before

---

[143] *OR* vol.11, pt.1, pp.759, 819; Eicher, & Eicher, **High Commands**, p.154.

[144] *OR* vol.12, pt.2, pp.455-456; Tagg, **Generals**, p.79.

[145] Tagg, **Generals**, p.79; *OR* vol.25, pt.2, p.578; *OR* vol.27, pt.1, p.160; Toombs, **New Jersey Troops**, p.99.

receiving an appointment to West Point. He became a cadet at the age of twenty-four, on 1 July 1825. He managed to remain focused on his education during his four years of training, and graduated fifth in a class of forty-six cadets, three positions behind fellow classmate Robert E. Lee. Brevetted a second lieutenant in the 4th Artillery, Barnes did not immediately receive a field assignment. Academy administers evidently thought Barnes was more valuable as a teacher than as a field officer and bestowed upon him a position as an instructor of French and tactics which he quickly accepted.

His promoted to first lieutenant on 30 June 1836, was anticlimactic for Barnes had tired of the monotony of army life and the slow advancement opportunities of a peacetime military. Exactly one month later, he resigned his commission and began a career as a railroad man. Prospering in his new profession, by 1839 Barnes had advanced to the superintendence of the Western Railroad. In his position he oversaw construction as the railroad stretched out its fingers, extending lines and constructing new ones. He held the position for twenty-two years until the war began. Barnes then offered his services to his country, feeling it his duty to help bring to an end the rebellion.[146]

It had been twenty-five years since Barnes had been subjected to military discipline and its way of life. Undaunted, the professional railroad man volunteered for service and was elected colonel of the 18th Massachusetts on 26 July 1861. As part of the Third Corps the 18th traveled to the Virginia Peninsula but saw no action during McClellan's march up the isthmus toward Richmond. While before the Confederate capital, the regiment was transferred to the Fifth Corps, but Barnes' command once again saw no action during The Seven Days campaign due to his Bay Staters being assigned to help the cavalry guard the army's rear. While Barnes and his regiment spent the campaign away from rifle fire, the remainder of the brigade suffered terribly at the hands of the Rebels. At Malvern Hill the brigade's commander, Brigadier General John Martindale favored capitulation rather than a withdrawal from the hill. Martindale's commander was extremely displeased with his attitude and relieved him of his duties. As senior colonel, Barnes was suddenly entrusted with the additional duties of brigade command. On 10 July 1862, although he had yet to lead his regiment in battle, Barnes took his place at the head of the brigade.[147]

Barnes was not with his brigade at Second Bull Run and although he had returned by the time the armies clashed at Antietam, the Fifth Corps was held in reserve and Barnes once again saw no action. His first serious fight occurred three days after the battle as his brigade led the army's advance toward the Potomac River in pursuit of Lee. Receiving orders to cross the river and "report what [was] to be found there," Barnes traversed the river at Blackford's Ford and deployed his regiments along a bluff overlooking the road to Shepherdstown. It was not long before the Federals were hit by the Confederate rear guard. Outnumbered, Barnes was forced to pull back toward the river. While attempting to extract his regiments,

---

[146] Eicher, & Eicher, *High Commands*, p.116; Warner, *Generals in Blue*, pp.240-241.

[147] Tagg, *Generals*, p.84.

a Union battery on the north bank opened up on the advancing Rebels, but many of the battery's rounds found their way in to the ranks of Barnes' men. The 118th Pennsylvania was hit hard as it tried to extricate itself and suffered the majority of the casualties. Eventually the brigade managed to make its way back across the river but not before 326 were killed wounded, or missing, with some of the latter drowning in the river.[148]

Evidently some thought Barnes had conducted himself well in a bad situation, for that November he was promoted to brigade general. Two weeks later, sporting his new star, Barnes led his brigade during the attacks against Marye's Heights. Division commander, Brigadier General Charles Griffin, praised Barnes for his work that day, but his fate was the same as the others who attempted to conquer the heights. When Hooker failed to inject most of the Fifth Corps into the fighting at Chancellorsville, Barnes' brigade became distinguished for being the last unit to cross the Rappahannock during the retreat. Shortly after the battle, General Griffin became ill and left the army on sick leave. His departure thrust Barnes, one of the most inexperienced brigadiers in the army, to the head of the corps' First Division. It remained to be seen if he was capable of handling a body of men that size in battle.[149]

The fact that Barnes had little battle experience at the head of a brigade did not deter the men's appreciation and respect. On 21 May, respects were paid to Barnes with the presentation of a magnificent set of accoutrements. The articles included a four hundred dollar horse and a sword with two scabbards, one for dress and the other for battle, valued at three hundred dollars. The dress scabbard bore three medallions of silver one of which contained an inscription which read, "Presented to Gen. James Barnes by the officers of the First Brigade, First Division, Fifth Corps, Army of the Potomac, as a token of respect and esteem for their commander." In addition, two hundred dollars in horse accoutrements and tack were presented, including a fine saddle, a sash, spurs, and gloves. According to one attendee, the ceremony was "a brilliant affair, and all of us who could be spared from duty went." Invited guest were allowed inside while those who were not had to remain outdoors. One thing was certain; General Barnes would be well outfitted for the coming campaign.[150]

Taking Barnes' place at the head of the division's First Brigade was Colonel William Stowell Tilton. Tilton, former colonel of the 22nd Massachusetts, took command and then watched as a number of regiments from the brigade departed due to expiring enlistments. One of the units, the 2nd Maine, had some men in a peculiar situation. Most of the men had signed up for two years and were due to go home, but a number had signed three year papers and would not be allowed to depart, as they still had a year to serve. Under protest, the remaining men were

---

[148] *OR* vol.19, pt.1, pp.345-348.

[149] Tagg, ***Generals***, p.84.

[150] Parker, John L., ***History of the Twenty-Second Massachusetts Infantry the Second Company Sharpshooters and the Third Light Battery, in the War of the Rebellion***, pp.320-321.

marched off to bolster the ranks of another Maine regiment while they watched their comrades head home for muster out. The mood and morale of the remaining men could not have been high.[151]

Later, in June, Tilton's 13th and 25th New York had a number of men in the same predicament as the three year men of the 2nd Maine. Before it was sent home, two companies of three year men from the 13th were transferred to the 140th New York. The three year men in the 25th would eventually ended up in, the 44th New York. With three full regiments departing, Tilton was left with only four depleted units, his own 22nd Massachusetts, the 18th regiment from the same state, the 1st Michigan and the 118th Pennsylvania.[152]

Tilton began the war as a first lieutenant in the 22nd Massachusetts, a position he was placed in on 12 September 1861. Born in Newburyport, Massachusetts on 1 February, he was educated in local schools and became a businessman, manufacturer and merchant before the war. He spent his professional career in his native state until he volunteered to help put down the rebellion. He was promoted to major a month later, shortly before the regiment was placed in the Fifth Corps and transferred to the Peninsula where it saw action as McClellan pushed toward Richmond. During The Seven Days, Tilton fought at Gaines' Mill where he was shot through the shoulder and captured. While in captivity, on 27 May 1862, he was promoted to lieutenant colonel and on 15 August exchanged. As part of General Barnes' brigade, Tilton missed the action at Second Bull Run and Antietam but was with the general when the brigade crossed the Potomac and was assaulted by Lee's rear guard at Shepherdstown. A colonelcy came his way on 17 October, and at Fredericksburg he led the 22nd during the disaster in front of the stone wall. Missing Chancellorsville entirely, Tilton, like Barnes was untried at brigade command when he was elevated to take Barnes' place at the head of the division's First Brigade.[153]

Barnes' Second Brigade was also hit hard by departing regiments. The 14th New York left for their home state shortly after Chancellorsville where they were mustered out later in the month. Their departure left the brigade with four regiments, the 9th and 32nd Massachusetts, the 4th Michigan and the 62nd Pennsylvania, all under the command of Colonel Jacob Bowman Sweitzer. Born in Brownsville, Pennsylvania on Independence Day, 1821, Sweitzer studied law and graduated from Jefferson College in 1843 before becoming a lawyer. He had no military training or experience when he joined the 62nd Pennsylvania on his birthday in 1861. Initially installed as the regiments major, before the end of the year he would be promoted to lieutenant colonel.[154]

Sweitzer was with his regiment, whose designation had been changed to the 62nd, in front of Yorktown on the Peninsula. In June of 1862 the regiment and

---

[151] Pullen, John, J., *The Twentieth Maine*, pp.77, 79; *OR* vol.25, pt.1, p.163; *OR* vol.25, pt.2, p.579.

[152] Phisterer, *NYWR*, vol.3, pp.1887-1888, 2012; *OR* vol.25, pt.2, pp.579.

[153] Eicher, & Eicher, *High Commands*, p.531; Tagg, *Generals*, p.86.

[154] Eicher, & Eicher, *High Commands*, p.520; *OR* vol.25, pt.2, p.579.

Sweitzer were transferred to the newly formed Fifth Corps. At Gaines' Mill on 27 June, after the regiment's colonel had been killed, Sweitzer took command and was promoted to colonel the same day. As the battle raged, he led the regiment in a charge and was seriously wounded and captured. His brigadier praised him for his efforts that day and, two months later, after being exchanged, he quickly returned to duty. His regiment was not present at Antietam but was seriously beat up on the slopes of Marye's Heights at Fredericksburg, where it took 222 casualties. Although he had commanded his regiment's brigade during the battle, a few months later, at Chancellorsville, Sweitzer was forced to return to command of his regiment when the brigade's senior colonel returned. However, the colonel's return must have been premature, for during the battle he became ill and Sweitzer, once again, had to take charge. Like so many commanders that June, Sweitzer's abilities at the head of a brigade were still in question as the army lay along the river in Virginia.[155]

The division's Third Brigade, under the command of Colonel Strong Vincent, unlike the first two, retained all of its regiments during the exodus caused by expiring enlistments. The brigade consisted of Vincent's 83rd Pennsylvania, the 16th Michigan and the 44th New York with the three year men from the 25th and the 20th Maine with the leftovers from their states second regiment.[156]

Strong Vincent resembled his namesake, being of medium height but stoutly built. He was born in Waterford, Pennsylvania on 17 June 1837 into an affluent family. His formal schooling began at Erie Academy and by the time his education was complete, he had spent time at Trinity College in Hartford, Connecticut and Harvard before graduating in 1859. During his time at Harvard he had shown leadership skills on a number of occasions, was elected president of a student society and organized graduation day celebrations. After graduating, Vincent opted not to begin working for his father, who ran a local iron foundry. Instead, he studied law and within a year had passed the bar and began a practice in Erie. He had been practicing only a year when Fort Sumter was fired upon. At the time, Vincent, at the young age of twenty-three, had acquired no military experience. His lack of skill however, did not stop him from volunteering his services. He joined a regiment of Pennsylvania militia and for its three month term of service functioned as its first lieutenant. When the unit was disbanded, Vincent re-enlisted in the 83rd Pennsylvania and on 21 September, was commissioned its lieutenant colonel.[157]

Vincent possessed what can only be termed a forceful personality. But, while he owned a powerful individuality, he was personally quiet and when conversing could be quite merry. Although his experience in military matters was minimal, he was well aware of the need to drill and train the men in his regiment and the 83rd quickly became some of the best drilled and finest group of men in the volunteer

---

[155] *OR* vol.21, p.135; Tagg, **Generals**, p.86.

[156] *OR* vol.25, pt.2, pp.579.

[157] Warner, **Generals in Blue**, p.527.

service. He was an accomplished rider, as was his young wife, and when she visited the army, the two could be seen riding together displaying their skills.[158]

Vincent's first combat experience was gained before Yorktown. Unfortunately, shortly after the battle at Hanover Court House, he contracted malaria and was sent home to recover. While he was away, the regiment fought at Gaines' Mill, where the unit's colonel was killed. The men evidently thought Vincent a capable commander for while he was still at home convalescing he was elected colonel. His physical condition kept him from returning to the regiment before the battle of Fredericksburg. If there was any doubt about his personal courage it was abolished during the fighting there. At one point the 83rd was pinned down by artillery fire. To calm the men Vincent, oblivious to the danger, walk back and forth through the regiment as the men lay prone to avoid the shot and shell exploded all around. On 20 May, he rose to command the brigade to the extreme delight of the men. Others thought highly of Vincent as well. He was offered the position of judge advocate general of the army, but turned it down, noting that he had joined the army to fight Rebels not preside over court-martials. Although his time as a brigade commander had been limited, it was obvious to all he possessed exceptional leadership skills. Vincent's ability would be tested to the extreme at Gettysburg.[159]

The Second Division of Meade's Fifth Corps would remain under the command of General Sykes until shortly before the battle in Pennsylvania. Until then, future division commander, General Romeyn Beck Ayres would remain in command of the First Brigade of "Sykes' Regulars," as it guarded Banks' Ford and later marched north in pursuit of Lee. Early in June the division contained a disproportionate number of regiments between its First and Second Brigades. As the month progressed, their manpower would be evened out by the transfer of the five companies from the 6th U. S. Infantry from the Second Brigade to the First. The members of the 6th joined the 3rd, 4th, 12th and 14th U. S. Infantry, none of which contained a full complement of ten companies.[160]

General Ayres, a career military man, was born on 20 December 1825 in upstate New York in the small town of East Creek along the Mohawk River. His father, a small town doctor, pushed his children hard to be the best at anything they attempted. The elder Ayres worked with young Romeyn to teach him Latin at an early age, and he became so proficient that by the time he entered the Military Academy in 1843, he was fluent in the language and his fellow cadets considered him an authority. Ayres' ability to speak Latin however did not seem to assist him with the remainder of his studies, and he proved to be an average student graduating twenty-second in a class of thirty-eight in 1847. Brevetted a second lieutenant in the 4th Artillery, Ayers spent the early part of his military career on garrison duty in Mexico City after hostilities there had ended. Afterword, he was reassigned to the 3rd Artillery, spent the following years on outpost duty and was

---

[158] Tagg, **Generals**, p.90.

[159] *Ibid.*

[160] **OR** vol.25, pt.2, p.580; **OR** vol.27, pt.1, p.161.

promoted to first lieutenant on 16 March 1852. In 1859 his time on garrison duty ended with an assignment to the artillery school at Fort Monroe, a posting he retained until the war began.[161]

Romeyn was promoted to the captaincy of Battery E, 5th Artillery when the war began. His battery was engaged at First Bull Run where it distinguished itself by fighting during the rear guard action which helped save McDowell's beaten army. As the war progressed, Ayers' proficiency in commanding artillery came to the forefront, and he was installed as the chief of artillery for a division in the Sixth Corps. He performed the duties of his new position so well that after Antietam he was promoted to chief of artillery for the entire corps and functioned in that capacity at Fredericksburg. Accolades came fast and furious. Although he may not have taken his father's advice while at West Point, Ayers had obviously seen the light and taken to heart the belief that being the best was important. Excellence in the artillery however, did not necessarily mean promotion. Transferring to the infantry in April 1863, Ayers was placed in command of General Sykes' First Brigade of Regulars. The men of the brigade now had a Regular Army man at the helm and they were glad to get him.[162]

Ayers was a hard fighter on the battlefield and expected no less from his men. Although the brigade saw little action at Chancellorsville, it did not take long before the men realized that their new brigadier was a stickler for regulation and would not put up with any cowards in his outfit. On one particular instance, Romeyn discovered that a colonel in his command was shying away from enemy fire. When the opportunity arose, Ayers sent the colonel's regiment into an area where the fighting was heavy. It was soon reported that the colonel had been killed during the fight. In response Ayers simply noted that now his family could be proud of him.

Ayers, a big man at six feet tall, had become slightly plump over the years. The top of his head was beginning to bald, but the center still contained a bit of hair which resembled the topknot on a parrot. The remainder of his head however, contained an immense growth of hair including a massive beard that completely obscured his throat and a good portion of his upper chest. A large mustache covered his upper lip and if one did not look closely it was difficult to see his mouth and ears. His high forehead gave him an intellectual look and his size projected a certain authority that assisted him on the battlefield. Personally, his habits were painstakingly detailed and he was a bit of a socialite who could have fun with others while never compromising his own aura of authority.[163]

Although Ayers would command a brigade until shortly before the battle, he was more qualified for division command than most of the men who held such a position at Gettysburg. His experience at the head of the artillery had prepared him

---

[161] Eicher, & Eicher, *High Commands*, p.110; Warner, *Generals in Blue*, pp.14-15.

[162] Tagg, *Generals*, p.92.

[163] *Ibid.*

well, and his military training had honed his leadership skills. He would need to be on top of his game in southern Pennsylvania.

The Second Brigade of Sykes' Division was under the command of a career army officer who had spent the majority of the early months of the war without a field command. Sidney Burbank came from a military family. His father, who fought in the War of 1812, had been instrumental at the Battle of Niagara. Sidney, born in Lexington, Massachusetts in 1807, became a cadet at West Point in 1825. He graduated with Robert E. Lee, seventeenth in the class of 1829. Brevetted a second lieutenant in the 1st Infantry, Burbank began his career out west but soon became embroiled in the Black Hawk War. Afterward he participated in the Seminole War, and spent a period of time as an instructor at the academy. Burbank slowly worked his way up through the ranks until he was installed as a major in the 2nd Infantry on 8 December 1855. Leaving his teaching position, he took a post at Newport Barracks in the Department of Kentucky and was stationed there when the war began.

In 1861, Burbank's health began to fail him, but his condition did not keep him from being appointed lieutenant colonel of the 14th U. S. Infantry on 14 May 1861. A few months later he was elevated to colonel and transferred to command of the 2nd U. S. Infantry after Colonel Dixon S. Miles was mortally wounded before surrendering Harpers Ferry during the Maryland Campaign. In March 1863, Burbank was transferred again to command of the Second Brigade of Sykes' Regulars. Unfortunately, his vision was beginning to deteriorate, and his left eye began to wander. During the previous year, he had contracted hepatitis, an affliction which forced him to spend the majority of the winter of 1863 on bed rest. He was physically unable to take command of his brigade until April because of a setback in his recovery.

With his health in question, it was good that Burbank's first real combat would come at the head of a group of seasoned Regulars. It is doubtful Sidney Burbank could have gained the confidence of a group of volunteers, himself being untested and in such a dilapidated state. He led his brigade at Chancellorsville and participated in one of the first encounters of the battle on the morning of 1 May. The brigade formed astride the Old Orange Turnpike and along with General Ayers' command, confronted Confederates under Generals Mahone and Semmes, and took 147 casualties as they were forced back westward along the road toward Chancellorsville.

Eventually Burbank's command would consist of his own 2nd, the 6th, 7th, 10th, 11th and 17th U. S. Infantries. The 6th would ultimately be transferred to the First Brigade, but as May turned to June it was still part of Burbank's outfit. As with the First Brigade of Regulars, none of the regiments possessed their full complement of companies. The men would be called upon to display their fortitude in the coming battle to make up for their commanders ill health and age.[164]

---

[164] *OR* vol.25, pt.2, p.580; *OR* vol.27, pt.1, p.161; *OR* vol.25, pt.1, p.181; Eicher, & Eicher, **High Commands**, p.154; Tagg, *Generals*, p.95; Hunley, C. Russell, Editor, **The 14th U.S. Infantry Regiment in the American Civil War, John Young Letters**, p.52.

The men of Sykes' Third Brigade had just been through an extensive reorganization. The 5th New York, another two year regiment, was sent home to muster out leaving only two regiments in the brigade. Also hard hit by the expiration of enlistment terms was the Fifth Corps' Third Division. The division had been built from eight Pennsylvania regiments in two brigades and all but two would be leaving the army. The mass exodus included the 123rd, 126th, 129th 131st, 133rd, and 134th regiments from the Keystone State. The two remaining regiments, the 91st and the 155th were transferred to the Second Division's Third Brigade to replenish the manpower lost by the departure of the 5th New York. The result was a significant manpower reduction in the Fifth Corps since the Third Division was not promptly replaced.[165]

In early June the Third Brigade was under the command of Patrick O'Rorke, colonel of the 140th New York. However, before the brigade arrived at Gettysburg it would have a new commander in the form of West Point alumnus Stephen Hinsdale Weed. Born in Potsdam, New York on 17 November 1831, Weed entered the academy at the age of eighteen and graduated four years later, twenty-seventh in a class of forty-six. Prominent classmates included Oliver Howard, Jeb Stuart and Robert E. Lee's eldest son George who outdid his famous father by graduating at the classes' number one ranking.[166]

After graduation, Weed was brevetted a second lieutenant and assigned to the 2nd Artillery, but after receiving his commission he was reassigned to the 4th Artillery. He fought the Seminoles before being assigned to garrison duty out west and was present during the standoff with the Mormons in Utah. Two years later he was a first lieutenant and as the war began, Weed was promoted to captain and placed in command of Battery I of the 5th Artillery. He evidently showed promise for when the Fifth Corps was organized in June of 1862 his battery was assigned to the new corps' Second Division. During The Seven Days he was slightly wounded in the face by a shell fragment at Gaines' Mill. After the battle General Sykes commended Weed for the "superb manner" in which he conducted himself and handled his guns. Although he received accolades for his early war work, Weed remained a captain and fought in that capacity at Second Bull Run and Antietam. He had little chance to improve his stature since in both engagements the Fifth Corp was only slightly engaged. Although he saw little action during the latter half of 1862, Sykes evidently thought highly enough of Weed to install him as the Second Division's chief of artillery. He would function in that capacity a Fredericksburg and later at Chancellorsville.[167]

---

[165] *OR* vol.25, pt.1, p.164; *OR* vol.25, pt.2, p.580; *OR* vol.27, pt.1, p.162. A Third Division would be added to the Fifth Corps three days before the battle. The division would be led by Samuel Crawford and would contain two brigades of Pennsylvania Reserves.

[166] Eicher, & Eicher, *High Commands*, p.614; *Electronic Source:* http://en.wikipedia.org/wiki/Stephen_Weed, Last accessed 5/5/2012.

[167] Boatner, *Dictionary*, p.417; Eicher, & Eicher, *High Commands*, p.614; *OR* vol.11, pt.2, p.352; Tagg, *Generals*, p.96.

Weed, understanding promotions within the artillery were difficult to obtain, may have expressed a desire to exit that branch of the service for the infantry. Whether he specifically requested a transfer is not known, but on 6 June 1863, he was promoted from captain in the Regular Army to brigadier general of volunteers, jumping three ranks. Endorsements from both Generals Sykes and Henry Hunt no doubt expedited the process. A week later, on 13 June, he was placed in command of Sykes' Third Brigade, allowing O'Rorke to return to his regiment. Weed had no experience at the head of an infantry brigade and would have to rely on his training, natural abilities and the determination of his new command to succeed in his latest position.[168]

"Howards Cowards?"

The disaster which befell the soldiers of the Eleventh Corps at Chancellorsville was in no way the fault of anyone on the battle line. A great deal of the blame for the catastrophe can easily be laid at the feet of their corps commander, Oliver Howard. Howard spent a good deal of time defending himself during and after the war, but an examination of the record can place most of the blame directly on him. While it is true Hooker visited the Eleventh Corps after it was positioned on the army's right, it cannot be argued that Hooker did not try to warn Howard.

On 2 May, Hooker rode the lines of his army and eventually examined the position of the Eleventh Corps. He reviewed Howard's location and the breastworks his soldiers had erected. Howard noted later that his commander believed the position to be a good one when Hooker commented "How Strong!" Howard implied that the comment was in regard to the excellent strength of his line. The remark however was more likely a question as to whether the position was as good as it could have been. Shortly after Hooker's investigation, Captain Cyrus Comstock of the engineers quizzed Howard about gaps in his line.

"General, do close those spaces!" Comstock noted.

"The woods are thick and entangled," Howard responded, "will anybody come through there?"

"Oh, they may!" the engineer replied.

According to Howard he closed the gaps, but it was not the spaces in his line that allowed the disaster, but his failure to prepare after he was warned of the possibility of an attack.[169]

After Jackson's marching column had been detected and while confusion still swirled as to its destination, Hooker sent an urgent note to both Generals Howard and Slocum. Whether or not this note was written before or after he rode the lines is unclear. The tone of the message however implies that it came after Hooker reviewed Howard's position. Howard, for his part, claimed he never received it. His denial regarding the message sparked a controversy which still exists today.

---

[168] Bennett, **Sons of Old Monroe**, p.209; Eicher, & Eicher, ***High Commands***, p.614.

[169] Howard, The Eleventh Corps at Chancellorsville, ***B&L***, vol.3, p.195.

CHANCELLORSVILLE, VA.,
May 2, 1863-9:30 a. m.
Major-Generals HOWARD and SLOCUM:

I am directed by the major-general commanding to say that the disposition you have made of your corps has been with a view to a front attack by the enemy. If he should throw himself upon your flank, he wishes you to examine the ground and determine upon the positions you will take in that event, in order that you may be prepared for him in whatever direction he advances. He suggests that you have heavy reserves well in hand to meet this contingency. No artificial defenses worth naming have been thrown up, and there appears to be a scarcity of troops at that point, and not, in the general's opinion, as favorably posted as might be. *We have good reason to suppose that the enemy is moving to our right.* Please advance your pickets for the purpose of observation as far as may be safe, in order to obtain timely information of their approach.

J.H. VAN ALEN,
Brigadier-General and Aide-de-Camp[170]

Hooker, it seems, after visiting Howard and being informed that Jackson was on the move, instructed Howard to be prepared for an attack from his flank. The order was entered into Hooker's *Letters Sent* book with a notation in red ink that copies of the document where sent to both Howard and Slocum. Two months later and two days after Hooker was relieved, a copy of the order was entered into General Howard's *Letter's Received* book. The timing of the entry raises significant questions as to when the order was actually received, if Howard did indeed see it, why two months elapsed before it was entered and why only after Hooker had departed?[171]

Denial of reception of the order does not exonerate Howard. On numerous occasions he had opportunities to foresee the pending attack and did nothing. In fact, later that morning Howard informed Hooker that he was aware of the marching Confederate troops and was taking measures to resist a flank attack.

GENERAL:

From Gen. Devens' headquarters we can observe a column of infantry moving westward on a road parallel with this on a ridge about 1-1/2 to 2 miles south of this. *I am taking measures to resist an attack from the west.*[172]

---

[170] *OR* vol.25, pt.2, pp.360-361. Emphasis added. Another copy of the order appears in the Report of the Committee on the Conduct of the War. This copy differs only in the use of the word "circular" in the heading.

[171] Bigelow, *Chancellorsville*, p.277.

[172] Bates, Samuel P., Hooker's Comments on Chancellorsville, *B&L*, vol.3, p.219. Emphasis added.

Not only had Hooker informed Howard of the pending disaster, Howard had personally observed Jackson's column marching toward his right. If that was not enough, later in the day, along the skirmish line of the 153rd Pennsylvania, acting major Owen Rice saw something which terrified him. Quickly he wrote and sent a note to his brigade commander Colonel von Gilsa.

> On Skirmish Line, on Culpeper Road, 2:45 p. m.
> Colonel L. von Gilsa, Commanding 1st Brig., 1st Div., 11th Army Corps:
> A large body of the enemy is massing in my front. For God's sake, make disposition to receive him!
>
> Owen Rice
> Act. Maj. 153 P.V.

After receiving the note, Colonel von Gilsa personally carried a copy of the message to General Howard. Howard read the note and then shooed the colonel away commenting that the woods and thickets in the area were too dense for any attack to be made from that quarter. Colonel von Gilsa did not mention the message in his after action report but did indicate that shortly before his pickets were driven in by Jackson's attack a member of the 45th New York, who had been out on patrol, reported that there were "masses of the enemy in an open field opposite my line."[173]

Howard also received a warning from another of his brigade commanders, General Alexander Schimmelfennig. After it became apparent that Confederate troops were massing on their right, Major Gustav Schleiter of Schimmelfennig's staff, was quickly sent to report the event to Howard. Schleiter later recorded the swiftness with which he was dismissed from Howard's presence.

> "You will better understand my indignation when I inform you that, as Adjutant to General Schimmelfennig, I nearly killed my horse in riding to inform General Howard of the fact that the enemy was massing troops on our right flank, and that I was received with an incredulous smile, and directed to tell General Schimmelfennig to stop reconnoitering, and remain in the position assigned to him. This was two hours before the attack was made."[174]

After weighing the evidence, the assault which crushed the Eleventh Corps on the evening of 2 May 1863, was not the responsibility of the men on the battle line. Howard had ample opportunity to array his front to receive an attack launched

---

[173] Bigelow, *Chancellorsville*, p.288; *OR* vol.25, pt.1, p.636.

[174] Bates, Samuel P., *History of the Pennsylvania Volunteers* (hereafter *HPV*), vol.4, p.895. The volume designation used for Bates' HPV are based on Broadfoot Publishing Company's reprint edition.

from his right, but he failed to take appropriate action. While the men did flee after the attack began, there are numerous accounts of men making herculean efforts to stem the Confederate tide. The simple fact was once Jackson had his enemy on the run he was not in the habit of allowing them time to recuperate and make a stand. It is doubtful, even if properly deployed, the 11,000 men of the Eleventh Corps could have stopped Jackson's 30,000 screaming Confederates. However, the fact remains that Howard did little if anything to contain the onslaught before it began even after he was warned of the possibility.

Many of the men who would eventually populate Howard's Eleventh Corps began the war in western Virginia under the command of Major General John C. Fremont. Known as "The Pathfinder" for his early days of western exploration, Fremont ran afoul of Lincoln early in the war and was relieved of command. A few months later, he was placed in command of the Mountain Department and spent the early weeks of June, 1862 chasing Stonewall Jackson around the Shenandoah Valley. As the month ended, Fremont's command was assigned to General Pope's Army of Virginia, but Fremont refused to serve as its commander since he was senior to Pope. He went to New York instead and never returned to the army. Command of the new First Corps of the Army of Virginia fell to Major General Franz Sigel. When Sigel and his men joined Pope in Virginia, they were experienced fighters who had seen their share of early war combat. Immediately after Pope's defeat, Sigel's corps designation was changed from First to Eleventh.[175]

The German immigrants of the Eleventh Corps, even before the disaster at Chancellorsville, were looked upon as a bit odd. Although comprising approximately half the corps, the German's reputation had managed to infiltrate outside opinions of the entire organization. Most of the soldiers could not speak English and many of the corps' commanders could speak very little. Some viewed the Germans as poor fighters and displayed contempt toward them. Even though they had fought with distinction in previous battles, when they joined the ranks of the Army of the Potomac, they were looked upon as a foreign malignancy. The events on the extreme right at Chancellorsville, cemented the fallacy that the Germans were poor fighters and, even worse, cowards. Many incorrectly held the members of the Eleventh Corps responsible for the disaster, and the corps itself was a handy scapegoat. Terms like "The flying Dutchmen" and "Howard's Cowards" were unjustly awarded the unlucky Germans whose only crimes were to have been posted with their flank in the air and been led by a commander who refused to heed the warning signs and showed complete incompetence on the occasion.

No longer under the command of one of their own, the German's morale and discipline began to falter. The volunteers had believed from the start their fate would be left in the hands of a fellow countryman. No amount of gripping and complaining had any effect on Hooker's decision to place Howard in command. The growing lack of order and an ever increasing decline in confidence would be the primary reason the corps' performance began to suffer. Their poor showing at Chancellorsville had little to do with the ability or nationality of the soldiers but

---

[175] Fox, William F., ***Regimental Losses in the American Civil War***, p.86; *OR* vol.12, pt.3, p.435.

rather their lack of confidence in their commander and lagging discipline. Their concern over the quality of their leadership was shown to be justified.[176]

Commanders of a Disgraced Corps

The Eleventh Corps spent the fall and winter of 1862-63 encamped in northern Virginia fronting Washington. Most of the men took their turns performing guard duty in and around Centerville near the old Bull Run battlefield. In December it was ordered to the Fredericksburg area to join the Army of the Potomac, but it arrived too late to participate in Burnside's debacle. When it arrived, the corps went into camp near the rail line from Falmouth to Aquia Creek, south of Stafford Court House. After its thrashing at Chancellorsville, the men returned to their encampment, and as May turned to June, the Eleventh Corps lazily passed the time performing camp and garrison duties. From time to time picket duty would interrupt the otherwise easy camp existence of each regiment.[177]

The corps was not hit as hard by enlistment expiration as many of the others, losing only one regiment, the 29th New York. The New Yorkers departed shortly after 1 June and mustered out on 20 June in New York City. However, some shifting of regiments within the corps did take place with a few being moved from one brigade to another. The 134th New York was transferred from the Second Division's Second Brigade to its First Brigade. To replace the 134th the 55th Ohio was reassigned from the First Division's Second Brigade. A regiment swap also took place with the 68th New York moving from the Third Division's First Brigade to the First Division's First Brigade. The 68th was replaced with the 45th New York from its destination brigade. To bolster the strength of the Third Division's Second Brigade the 82nd Ohio was transferred in.[178]

The corps' First Division had taken the shock of Jackson's initial assault. Brigadier General Charles Devens, after initially refusing to act on Colonel John C. Lee's warning, finally realized the threat was substantial. Devens however, had been wounded during the fight and Howard, in order to try and reinvigorate the division, appointed twenty-eight year old Brigade General Frances C. Barlow to replace him. Barlow, who may have possessed the most impressive baby face in the army's command structure, was not part of the corps foreign contingency but rather the son of a minister. A New York City boy, Barlow was born in Brooklyn on 19 October 1834 but quickly moved to Brookline Massachusetts, his mother's hometown, where he spent his early years. While a young boy, his father, who suffered from alcoholism and possible mental problems, abandoned his wife Almira and the children. Francis' mother tried to raise him and his two brothers as best she could. She moved into her father's home but soon joined a farming commune where she and the three boys tried to construct a new life. Almira

---

[176] Hartwig, D. Scott., The 11th Corps on July 1, 1863, **GM**, Issue 2, p.35.

[177] Fox, **Regimental Losses**, p.86.

[178] Phisterer, **NYWR**, vol.3, p.2063; **OR** vol.25, pt.1, pp.166-167; **OR** vol.25, pt.2, p.582; **OR** vol.27, pt.1, p.164.

however soon fell out of favor with the commune's administrators and, in April, 1843, she was asked to remove herself and the boys. She moved with her sons to Concord, Massachusetts where she proceeded to fall into deep depression.[179]

Unlike his mother, Francis seemed to take pleasure during his time in Concord. He enjoyed the history of the town and attended lectures and debates at the Concord Lyceum, finding he cherished the intellectual conversation. It was during this time in his life that Barlow became aware of the abolitionist movement and met a friend of his fathers, Ralph Waldo Emerson. Barlow developed into an obstinate and independent youth who gained a reputation for charging headfirst into whatever confronted him. His self-centered and combative attitude earned him the nickname Crazy Barlow. At the age of seventeen, he entered Harvard and studied law. He quickly impressed both his fellow students and professors with his academic abilities. He would distinguish himself by graduating first in his class from the renowned school. Entering the private sector, the young lawyer returned to the city of his birth, passed the bar in May 1858 and opened a law practice. He also participated in the news business as a reporter and occasional editor for Horace Greeley's *New York Tribune*. He had no military experience before the war but did possess a number of personal qualities that would allow him to become an effective commander. He owned a head for fighting and an internal drive and vigor which would not go unnoticed by the men he commanded and the officers who directed him.[180]

Francis Channing Barlow had little experience in commanding large bodies of men when he was promoted to divisional command. *LOC*

---

[179] Samito, Christian G., *"Fear Was Not in Him" The Civil War Letters of Major General Francis C. Barlow*, pp.xiv-xvi.

[180] *Ibid*, pp.xvi-xix.

Determined to do his part, Barlow, when the war began, enlisted in the 12th New York Militia as a private on 19 April 1861. Evidently not wishing to go to war a single man, he married his sweetheart Arabella W. Griffith the following day. After three months of service, he was mustered out on 1 August, but the war was not over for him. He immediately signed up for additional service and became lieutenant colonel of the 61st New York on 9 November. The regiment was assigned to General Howard's Second Corps brigade, and Barlow saw his first action at Seven Pines where the regiment took 110 casualties, including those missing in action. Having been previously promoted to colonel, Barlow was singled out by Howard in the general's after action report. "I desire especially to notice the coolness and good conduct of Colonel Barlow," Howard wrote.[181]

Barlow showed his drive and willingness to fight when, at Glendale on the Peninsula, his regiment got separated from the remainder of the brigade. Hearing firing, on his own initiative, he directed his men toward the sound of battle, but his effort to reach the fighting was blocked when the regiment stumbled upon a portion of the Confederate battle line. Undaunted, Barlow aligned his men and ordered a bayonet charge across an open field. The Confederates had no stomach for the bayonet and broke and ran, leaving behind a battle flag which Barlow scooped up and sent to the rear. Pressing on, he and his soldiers encountered another Confederate battle line. The Rebel commander demanded that Barlow's men throw down their weapons and surrender. The New Yorker was not about to be accommodating and a heavy fire fight erupted which lasted until darkness ended the shooting. Later, at Malvern Hill, Barlow's boys stood their ground and repelled a number of Confederate assaults. As the fighting on the Peninsula came to an end, it was obvious to his superiors that Barlow was a fine regimental commander.[182]

At Antietam Barlow showed his abilities again, leading his regiment against the Confederate position at the Sunken Road. Luck had been with him and so far Barlow had escaped serious injury, but along the road his good fortune left him when he was hit by shell fragments in the face and groin. Prior to his wounding, Barlow had managed to impress his brigade commander General John Caldwell. Caldwell either left the safety of his haystack long enough to record Barlow's exploits or learned of the young colonel's activities second hand. Either way, Caldwell laid out Barlow's day in detail in his report. "After the enemy opposed to my left and center had broken and fled through the corn-field, Colonel Barlow, by a skillful change of front, partially enveloped the enemy on his right, and, after a destructive enfilading fire, compelled them to surrender. About 300 men and 8 commissioned officers… were here taken prisoner by Colonel Barlow, and conducted to the rear… Two stands of colors also were captured by Colonel Barlow at this place." Whether Caldwell personally observed Barlow or not, there was no doubt the colonel did his duty before being hit. His efforts were rewarded with a promotion to brigadier general two days after the battle.

---

[181] *Ibid*, p.xx; Eicher, & Eicher, **High Commands**, p.116; Tagg, **Generals**, p.125; **OR** vol.11, pt.1, p.769.

[182] Tagg, **Generals**, pp.125-126

The new general's wounds healed slowly. It would be April of the following year before he would return to the army. When he did come back, Barlow's injuries still had not completely mended. Adding to his suffering during his recovery was an abscess on his back, an illness which was thought to be malaria, and leg numbness from his wound. The winter of 1862-63 was a difficult one, but Barlow willed himself through his misery and upon his return he was placed in command of one of General Howard's brigades. His brigade managed to escape the stampede on the army's right, having been temporarily attached to Sickles' corps. On 24 May, he was elevated to division command, taking over for the wounded Devens. Barlow had advanced from regimental command to the head of a division without having seen significant combat at the brigade level. Gettysburg would be his first opportunity at the head of his new command.[183]

Lacking the gruff nature and facial hair of other Union generals, Barlow looked out of place issuing orders to chiseled veterans. He was small in stature, slender and frail looking, with a round pale face. He had a tendency to slouch which, with his pale complexion, made him look somewhat macabre. His voice was not that of a hardened field general who could boom orders above the din of battle but rather uninspiring and quiet. Offsetting his diminutive physical appearance and persona was the sword he chose to carry. Most Federal officers carried the typical regulation infantry officer's sword. Barlow however chose to tote around a regulation cavalry saber which was longer and heavier. Its purpose was to make certain when rounding up stragglers, a hardy whack on the backside with Barlow's sword to get a man's attention would be remembered.[184]

The unlucky group who had been responsible for holding Hooker's right at Chancellorsville constituted Barlow's First Brigade. Commanding them was the hard cussing Prussian, Leopold von Gilsa. Von Gilsa's mastery of German expletives was legendary, and his corps commander received a hefty dose of foul language when he found von Gilsa in the mists of the retreating Federal soldiers. The tirade of profanity that escaped the foreigner's lips, which was completely understandable given the circumstances, so shocked Howard that he assumed von Gilsa had lost hold of his sanity.

Leopold was born in Prussia, but the date of his birth is unidentified. As an officer in the Prussian military, he fought in the Schleswig-Holstien War in northern Germany during the late 1840s. Immigrating to America, he supported himself as an entertainer, and as the war began, he used his military experience in Europe to obtain a commission as colonel of the 41st New York on 6 June 1861. His regiment was held in reserve at First Bull Run and partook in no serious action. Later, during the campaign in the Shenandoah Valley, von Gilsa led the regiment against some of Stonewall Jackson's men at Cross Keys where he was gravely wounded. He spent the following nine months convalescing and performing minor duties in Washington. He returned to the army in time to struggle through the morass of Burnside's ill-fated Mud March.

---

[183] *Ibid*; **OR** vol.19, pt.1, p.285; Eicher, & Eicher, ***High Commands***, p.116.

[184] Tagg, ***Generals***, p.125

When Barlow took command of the division, von Gilsa immediately ran afoul of his new superior. Barlow promptly arrested the brigade commander for allowing too many men at one time to fall out to gather water. Von Gilsa was promptly taken into custody, a victim of Barlow's strict discipline. His confinement no doubt elicited a string of German profanity from the fiery von Gilsa and the Prussian would make the march north in the company of the provost marshal. His boys would be lead north by Colonel Gotthilf Bourry DeIvernois of the 68th New York while their leader cooled his heels in custody. The brigade was populated by DeIvernois' regiment, the 41st and 54th New York and the 153rd Pennsylvania.[185]

Brigadier General Adelbert Ames was completing his studies at West Point when the war began. He graduated fifth among the forty-five members of his class on 6 May 1861. Although initially commissioned a second lieutenant in the 2nd Artillery, with the war erupting, young officers were sorely needed. Eight days later, Ames became a first lieutenant and was transferred to the 5th Artillery. In just over two months, he found himself directing his battery at Bull Run. He was hit in the right hand, and, although the injury was serious, Ames refused to leave his battery. When he became too weak to stand, he was helped onto a caisson and directed his battery from the seat of his pants. Eventually the wound would take its toll. When he became too feeble to remain on the caisson, he was forced to make his way to the rear.

Brevetted a major for his work that day, Ames returned to duty in time to travel to the Peninsula to command his battery at Yorktown. During The Seven Days the battery fought at Gaines' Mill and Malvern Hill. Although Ames was once again brevetted for his performance and recognized for his work by then Colonel Henry Hunt, he realized that remaining in the artillery held few additional opportunities for promotion. Resigning his commission, he returned to his home state to join a volunteer organization.[186]

Ames was born in Rockland, Maine in 1835. He made his way early in life at sea aboard a clipper ship, but when an appointment to the academy came through, he gave up the seafaring life to become a plebe at West Point. After returning to Maine, he lobbied for a colonelship with one of the volunteer regiments. His efforts resulted in him being assigned command of the 20th Maine. When he arrived at the regiment's camp near Portland, he found a group of men with no discipline and little understanding of military protocol. One man was so devoid of military bearing while standing in rank, that Ames, already less than impressed, berated him by bellowing "For God's sake, draw up your bowels!" Although they looked pitiful, most of the men wished to be good soldiers and Ames went to work molding

---

[185] *Ibid*, pp.127-128; Phisterer, **NYWR**, vol.3, pp.2238, 2674; **OR** vol.25, pt.2, p.582.

[186] Eicher, & Eicher, **High Commands**, p.102; Tagg, **Generals**, p.129; **OR** vol.11, pt.2, p.240. Ames would eventually receive a Congressional Medal of Honor for his efforts at First Bull Run. One must wonder however, how much his public life as a Senator and Governor from Mississippi played in the awarding of the medal which was presented 32 years after the event.

them into a well-drilled, tight fighting unit. His efforts would bear fruit later in the war, but for now there was training to be done.[187]

Ames drilled and trained his unit hard and quickly molded his group of civilians into fine fighters. After leading the regiment during the Maryland Campaign and against Marye's Heights at Fredericksburg, Ames joined General Meade's headquarters staff and began performing aide-de-camp duties. If his intent was to garner a promotion by exposing himself to the general, his ruse worked for shortly after Chancellorsville he was promoted to brigadier general and placed in command of the Second Brigade of Howard's First Division, which consisted of the 25th, 75th and 107th Ohio and the 17th Connecticut. Like Barlow, Ames was brought in to instill discipline within the ranks of the depressed and irritated Eleventh Corps veterans. Ames, it was believed, had the background to be an effective leader and reestablish the confidence of the men. While inexperienced as a brigade commander, and unfamiliar with the men of his new command, it was believed Ames was just what they needed.[188]

Howard's Second Division was under the command of another Prussian, Brigadier General Adolph Wilhelm August Friedrich von Steinwehr. Steinwehr was born in the town of Blankenburg in the Duchy of Brunswick, Germany, on 25 September 1822. He came from a military family, his grandfather having served in the Prussian army, fighting against Napoleon. His father kept up the tradition by spending time in the service of the Duke. Adolph was educated at the Brunswick Military Academy, joining the family's tradition of military service. After completing school, von Steinwehr went on to become a lieutenant in the Duke of Brunswick's army but spent little time serving Germany. Taking a leave of absence, he traveled to the United States and fought with the American Army in Mexico. His ultimate goal was not met however, when he was unable to receive an officer's commission. After the war he remained with the army and worked as an engineer surveying the Mexican border. Later, Adolph was appointed to the coast survey and while assigned to Mobile Bay he met and married a woman from Alabama in 1849. After nuptials were exchanged, von Steinwehr took his new bride back to Germany but remained there only five years before the two returned and settled in Wallingford, Connecticut, where he tried his hand at farming. His effort at cultivating the earth evidently did not pan out, for in 1858 he relocated to Albany, New York where he worked as an architect and engineer designing the state arsenal.[189]

Von Steinwehr looked upon the outbreak of war as an opportunity to once again seek the elusive commission which he failed to acquire in Mexico. Using his military training as a springboard, he obtained the colonelcy of the 29th New York. The new regiment was a two year unit, raised mostly in New York City, with one

---

[187] Eicher, & Eicher, *High Commands*, p.102; Pullman, *The Twentieth Maine*, p.1.

[188] Tagg, *Generals*, p.130; Eicher, & Eicher, *High Commands*, p.102.

[189] Warner., *Generals in Blue*, p.530; Tagg, *Generals*, p.130; Eicher, & Eicher, *High Commands*, p.508.

company coming from the Philadelphia area. Like von Steinwehr, almost all the men mustered into the new regiment were German. Taking command on 6 June 1861, Adolph traveled with his regiment to Washington in time to march to Bull Run, where the 29th was held in reserve during the battle. What little action they saw consisted of performing rear guard duties while the remainder of the army sped toward the safety of the capital's defenses. Promoted to brigade general in October, von Steinwehr was assigned to brigade command in the Mountain Department under Fremont. He participated in the campaign against Jackson in the Valley during the spring of 1862 but was not present at the Battle of Cross Keys.[190]

Possibly because of his German connections and with General Sigel now in command of Pope's new First Corps, von Steinwehr was elevated to division command when the Army of Virginia was organized in June. Although technically a division commander, von Steinwehr had little more to do than he had in the Valley earlier in the year. This was due to his division being comprised of only three regiments from his old brigade. All three of the regiments were engaged in heavy fighting at Second Bull Run and lost over 400 men. Two additional brigades were later added to the division, but von Steinwehr's boys saw no more action until the disaster at Chancellorsville. Although the remainder of the corps fled the field during the fight, von Steinwehr was praised by Howard for his coolness under the pressure of the circumstance. Another officer noted that the Prussian was a very intellectual and pleasurable person. Although he had been associated with defeat for most of his career, there was no doubt that Adolph von Steinwehr was a capable general who had the confidence of his superiors.[191]

On 1 June, von Steinwehr's First Brigade was not under the command of the man who would lead it at Gettysburg. Charles R. Coster, who would eventually take command, was at the time colonel of the 134th New York. The transferred regiment would boost the brigade's allotment of regiments temporarily to five until von Steinwehr's original 29th New York went home to muster out. Sometime after the first of the month, brigade commander Colonel Adolphus Buschbeck, of the 27th Pennsylvania, took a leave of absence and Coster ascended to command of the brigade. In addition to the 134th, a second New York regiment, the 154th, Buschbeck's regiment and the 73rd Pennsylvanian would be under Coster's control.[192]

Coster was born in New York on 23 December 1839. After completing his formal education, he began a career in business, but the war interrupted his livelihood. Joining the 7th New York Militia he traveled to Washington and spent the first weeks of the war in the capital. For some reason however, Coster felt

---

[190] Phisterer, ***NYWR***, vol.3, pp.2062-2063; Warner, ***Generals in Blue***, p.530.

[191] ***OR*** vol.12, pt.2, p.250; Tagg, ***Generals***, pp.131-132.

[192] ***OR*** vol.25, pt.1, p.167; ***OR*** vol.25, pt.2, p.582; Bates, Samuel P., ***History of the Pennsylvania Volunteers*** (hereafter ***HPV***), vol.1, p.390. Bates spells Buschbeck's name as Bushbeck. Buschbeck was a German immigrant and the correct spelling in his native language was as shown in the ***OR***, which is how it is designated within the narrative.

it necessary to leave the militia. Returning home, he joined the 12th regiment of U. S. Regulars and, after being commissioned a first lieutenant, was assigned to General Sykes' Division of Regulars on the Peninsula. He fought at Gaines' Mill, receiving a severe wounded for his efforts. In his after action report, Colonel Robert Buchanan, who observed Coster's abilities first hand, made mention of his "gallant conduct." After recovering, Coster resigned his commission with the Regulars and returned home once again to accept the colonelcy of the 134th New York. The regiment was assigned to the Eleventh Corps spending the winter of 1862-63 in and around the defenses of Washington. The regiment's first combat was at Chancellorsville where it was spared the indignity of being routed while on detached duty with the Third Corps. When he was elevated to brigade command in June, Coster had no experience at that level, and his only action had been on the Peninsula. It remained to be seen if he would fulfill the promise his superiors saw in him.[193]

Colonel Orland Smith, another of von Steinwehr's brigade commanders, enlisted in November 1861 and was made lieutenant colonel of the 73rd Ohio on 26 November. A few weeks later, on 30 December, he became the unit's colonel. Smith, who was born in Lewiston Maine, was a railroad agent who relocated to Ohio in 1852, where he remained in the railroad business, going to work for the Marietta and Ohio. One of his first assignments was in western Virginia. His regiment, along with other Ohio units, was assigned to a brigade that moved into the Shenandoah Valley to do battle with Jackson. The regiment was not seriously tested and while it did taste some action at Cross Keys it suffered only seven casualties. Smith, for his part, was singled out by brigade commander Brigadier General Robert Schenck for his conduct during the fighting. When the Army of Virginia was created, Smith's regiment became part of the First Corps, and under a new commander fought at Second Bull Run. Smith's Buckeyes suffered greatly during the battle where the men saw intense fighting which inflicted 148 casualties, more than any other regiment in the brigade. In his report, brigade commander Colonel Nathaniel McLean singled out a number of officers including Smith who had conducted himself with "great coolness and Gallantry." [194]

Smith's regiment remained with the corps as its designation was changed to eleven. It ended up assigned to the same brigade as Colonel Coster's 134th and stayed the Washington area throughout the winter. The Buckeyes suffered only two casualties at Chancellorsville during their temporary assignment to Sickles' Corps. General Barlow commanded the brigade during the battle and when he departed to whip the men of the First Division into shape, and Coster's 134th New York was transferred to the First Brigade, Smith was elevated to brigade command. At the time, the brigade consisted of his own 73rd Ohio, the 136th New York, the 33rd Massachusetts and a second group of Buckeyes transferred in from

---

[193]   *OR* vol.11, pt.2, p.361; Coster Obituary, New York Times, 25 December, 1888; *OR* vol.27, pt.1, p.164.

[194]   *OR* vol.12, pt.1, p.668; Tagg, ***Generals***, p.134; *OR* vol.12, pt.2, pp.250, 287; Sifakis, ***Who was Who***, p.606.

the First Division's Second Brigade, the newly arrived 55th Ohio. While Smith was somewhat acquainted with the other regiments, the 55th was unfamiliar to him. As June opened he had no experience at brigade level command.[195]

Commanding General Howard's Third Division was a man who had seen a significant amount of upheaval and unrest in his thirty-four years of life. Carl Schurz, a German revolutionary and immigrant must have been one of the most frustrated men in the army. The Germans of the Eleventh Corps appreciated him and like the departed Sigel, would have followed him without question. However, Hooker's lack of confidence in him kept Schurz from attaining corps command, a fact which did not sit well with the German. Not even Schurz' lobbying of the president had any effect on his position. Adding to his frustration was Howard's negligence and failure during the Chancellorsville disaster. A more prudent move for Hooker may have been to place Schurz at the head of the corps, but Howard's chronic complaining over his lack of a corps command, was probably a factor in keeping Schurz from attaining, or at least being considered to head the Eleventh Corps.

Schurz was one of the most well rounded men in the army. Although he was born in a castle in the small village of Liblar, Prussia near Cologne on 2 March 1829, he was not of aristocratic ancestry. Carl's father was the schoolmaster of the village and when it came time to begin his education his father instructed him. As a boy, he remembered being able to read and write at an early age and credited his father, who provided home instruction, for the head start. Unfortunately, Carl only received instruction from his father for a year. A miniscule salary of $90 dollars a year forced the elder's resignation in order to search for a more lucrative occupation to provide for his expanding family. Schurz continued his formal education at the Jesuit Gymnasium in Cologne but had to leave a year before graduation due to continuing family financial problems. After the monetary issues were dealt with, Schurz finally managed to graduate after taking a special exam. He showed interest in the arts and learning to play the piano, utilizing a private tutor to learn the skill. Entering the University of Bonn, Schurz soon discovered that he possessed the gift of exceptional oration skills which allowed him to ascend to a leadership role within the German liberal movement at the tender age of nineteen. The experience would provide Schurz the opportunity to become acquainted with a number of men who he would once again become involved with during the American Civil War, including Franz Sigel and Alexander Schimmelfennig.[196]

The political movement, which promoted diplomatic efforts to improve human rights, establishment of a more democratic government and a unified Germany, became violent in 1848. During the hostilities Schurz served as a staff officer and received his first taste of fighting, of which he barely escaped from with his life.

---

[195] Tagg, *Generals*, pp.134-135; *OR* vol.25, pt.1, pp.166-167,183; *OR* vol.25, pt.2, p.582.

[196] Schurz, Carl, *The Reminiscences of Carl Schurz*, Vol.1, pp.5, 21; *Electronic Source:* http://en.wikipedia.org/wiki/Carl_Schurz, Last accessed 5/5/2012. The Jesuit or "Dreikönigsgymnasium" Gymnasium was founded in 1450 and still exists. It is the oldest school in Cologne and one of the oldest in Germany.

At one point he was forced to flee the Prussians by entering and escaping through a sewer. The upheaval however was not strong enough to achieve success and as the situation deteriorated, Schurz was forced to leave Germany and seek refuge in Switzerland. If there was any question about Schurz' determination, loyalty and bravery, it was put to rest when the young revolutionary returned to Germany. During his time at the University of Bonn, Schurz had become acquainted with and close to Professor Gottfried Kinkel. Kinkel had not been as lucky as Schurz and was captured and incarcerated by the authorities at Spandau Prison. Disguising himself to avoid detection, he successfully infiltrated the fortress at Spandau, freed Kinkel, and shepherded him out of the country.[197]

When the revolution failed, many of the participants, who were known as forty-eighters, were forced to depart Germany. Schurz himself went to France but eventually left the country when it became clear he was unwanted. He went to England, where he married the sister-in-law of a fellow revolutionary and, shortly thereafter, immigrated to the United States with his new wife in August 1852. The couple resided in Philadelphia for three years but eventually journeyed west in 1856, settling in Watertown, Wisconsin. Schurz' skill with language and the spoken word allowed him to learn English quickly. He became a much sought-after asset with his ability to translate and speak both his native tongue and the language of his new country. Taking an anti-slavery posture, Schurz used his speaking skills to campaign for political candidates who shared his opinions. He took an active role in John C. Fremont's campaign and helped get Lincoln elected four years later. In 1860 he led the delegation from Wisconsin during the Republican National Convention, although the delegation cast its lot with William Seward. After Lincoln was nominated, Schurz became a member of the committee which reported the news to the future president. Lincoln, was thankful for Schurz' efforts and rewarded the immigrant by appointing him Minister of Spain. His eagerness to help abolish the institution of slavery brought him back to America in January 1862, and he immediately began lobbying Lincoln to abolish the practice.[198]

Possibly in an effort to rid himself of a constant irritant, Lincoln, who at first had balked at a request from Schurz to be appointed a brigadier general, finally relented and approved the appointment to date from 15 April 1862. Schurz' nationality was an additional determining factor in Lincoln's decision to install the pushy German as a brigadier. Needing men to step up to extend the war effort and bolster the strength of his armies, Lincoln saw Schurz as a recruitment tool for soliciting volunteers from the heavy concentrations of forty-eighters who had settled in the Northeast and in the Cincinnati area. It was an obvious and blatant political move.

On 26 June the new general took command of the Third Division of General Pope's new First Corps. Schurz' first action began innocently enough on 22

---

[197] For a detailed account of Schurz' successful extraction of Kinkel see Schurz, vol.I, pages 253 to 314.

[198] Warner, ***Generals in Blue***, pp.426-427; Tagg, ***Generals***, p.136; ***Electronic Source:*** http://en.wikipedia.org/wiki/Carl_Schurz.

August during the Second Bull Run campaign. Sending a single regiment across the Rappahannock River at Freeman's Ford to scout for Confederates, the men, once across found what seemed to be an unguarded wagon train from Stonewall Jackson's command. The Federals considered the wagons an easy mark and after sending for two additional regiments, began preparations for capturing them. Jackson however, was too intelligent to have left his wagons vulnerable. Unknown to Schurz' men, trailing behind the wagons were the battle hardened veterans of Isaac Trimble's brigade. When the Federals burst from the woods to capture their easy mark, Trimble's men leapt forward and engaged the unsuspecting Yankees, and rolled them back upon themselves. To make matters worse, Hood's Division of Longstreet's command was also in the area and some of Hood's soldiers also entered the fight. After a short, furious brawl, the Federals were routed with one of the expedition's commanders killed. Try as he might, General Schurz was unable to rally the fleeing men. Although he redeemed himself later in the campaign, Schurz' first experience at the head of his division was a bit unnerving for he had no military training other than his time with the revolution in Germany.[199]

Schurz' questionable performance did not seem to hamper his ability to impress his superiors, for he was promoted to major general on 14 March 1863. The promotion triggered objections from other officers who considered themselves of better quality than the inexperienced Schurz. After Chancellorsville, using his position and political pull as a springboard, Schurz began to lobby Lincoln for the return of Franz Sigel to supplant Howard as corps commander. His political wrangling and assumption that he spoke for the men of the corps wore thin with the upper echelon of the Federal command structure. No amount of dialogue and rhetoric provided the results Schurz desired.

Schurz himself looked the part of a haggard collegiate academic, requiring a thick pair of glasses to supplement his vision. At thirty-four, his high forehead was made more prominent due to a receding hair line. His hair always seemed to be tossed about in an untidy manner, accented by a tuft in front, which in period pictures seemed to always be pointing toward the sky. He wore a heavy reddish beard and mustache which did more than make up for the lack of follicles on his forehead. In early June of 1863, only two other division commanders outranked him. No one questioned his courage only his ability on a battlefield, which after an inauspicious beginning seemed to be improving.[200]

Schurz' First Brigade commander, Alexander Schimmelfennig, could have passed for his division commander. Alexander's features and look were much like Schurz', and if his commander had not required thick spectacles to see effectively, the two could have easily been confused for one and other from a distance. Schimmelfennig, although lighter in color, also possessed the same heavy, bushy beard and mustache, the same receding hair line and a hair style matching his senior officer's messy look. A fellow forty-eighter described him as "short and lithe of stature..., aggressive, combative, a little haughty, but genial, and quite dashing, the

---

[199] Eicher, & Eicher, ***High Commands***, p.102; Hennessy, ***Return to Bull Run***, pp.68-70.

[200] Tagg, ***Generals***, p.137.

very picture and ideal of the typical sub-lieutenant of the Prussian army. His silky, cream-colored mustache was curled up defiantly at both ends, and he carried his dimpled chin high in the air like a boy with a chip on his shoulder." At the age of thirty-nine, Schimmelfennig had one thing Schurz did not, a military education. Born in Lithauen, Prussia on 20 July 1824, Schimmelfennig, as a teenager was a member of the Prussian army.[201]

Schimmelfennig fought in the Schleswig-Holstein War, but after becoming disheartened, resigned his commission and sided with the revolutionaries. When the uprising was squashed, he was charged with treason and fled to Switzerland to escape the authorities. There he became acquainted with other exiles, including Schurz and Kinkel. By 1853 he realized the revolution could not be sustained from outside the country and Schimmelfennig gave up the fight and immigrated to the United States. His military experience was put to good use when his adopted country put him to work in the War Department as an engineer and draftsman.

When the war began, Schimmelfennig was quick to step up and offer his services. He actively recruited other forty-eighters in the Philadelphia area and eventually became colonel of a German regiment from Pittsburg, the 74th Pennsylvania. Schimmelfennig however would not make it to Washington with the rest of the regiment. During the trip, while in Philadelphia, his horse fell on him, severely injuring his ankle. He was forced to remain behind and while nursing the extremity, he contracted small pox. Once recovered, he was finally able to join his regiment and work to build it into a cohesive fighting unit. But, before the task was complete, he reinjured his ankle and was forced to remain on the sidelines until shortly before the commencement of the campaign which culminated at Second Bull Run. During the fight at Freeman's Ford, General Schurz' First Brigade commander, Brigadier General Henry Bohlen, was killed, and Schimmelfennig took command of the brigade. That winter, while in Washington, he was promoted to brigadier general during the plethora of advancements which occurred on 29 November. When the corps took the field the following spring, he remained in command of Bohlen's old brigade.[202]

At Chancellorsville, Schimmelfennig and his brigade were fortunate enough to be posted near the Wilderness Church slightly to the west of the junction between the Orange Plank Road and the Old Orange Turnpike. The location was nearly a mile from Howard's right and as such, when the stampede began, Schimmelfennig had a short time to array his men in a manner so as to be able to meet the threat. In his after action report, he chastised both General Devens and Colonel McLean, and wrote he changed his front "in less than two minutes," which was probably a bit of an exaggeration. However, there is no doubt many of Schimmelfennig's

---

[201] *Electronic Source:* http://www.olypen.com/tinkers/74th%20Pennsylvania/Webpage, Last accessed 5/5/2012; Eicher, & Eicher, *High Commands*, p.472.

[202] Tagg, *Generals*, pp.138-139; Warner, *Generals in Blue*, pp.423-424; Eicher Eicher, & Eicher, *High Commands*, p.472. Being injured by a falling horse is another thing that Schurz and Schimmelfennig have in common. Schurz had been hurt in 1855 when his horse fell on him and injured his left leg.

men along with regiments from other brigades formed a token resistance which he noted lasted "for at least an hour." The proof of Schimmelfennig's stand lay within his casualties list, which shows well over 400 men from his command killed, wounded or captured. While he may not have been completely privy to the situation which befell General Devens' First Division, he knew in his own mind that his men were not cowards.

Schimmelfennig took on the purveyors of derogatory comments toward the corps and specifically his brigade in the final paragraph of his Chancellorsville report.

> "General [Schurz], I am an old soldier. To this hour I have been proud to command the brave men of this brigade; but I am sure that unless these infamous falsehoods be retracted and reparations made, their good-will and soldierly spirit will be broken, and I shall no longer be at the head of the same brave men whom I have had heretofore the honor to lead. In the name of the truth and common honesty; in the name of the good cause of our country, I ask, therefore, for satisfaction. If our superior officers be not sufficiently in possession of the facts, I demand an investigation; if they are, I demand that the miserable penny-a-liners who have slandered the division be excluded, by a public order, from our liners, and that the names of the originators of these slanders be made known to me and my brigade, that they may be held reasonable for their acts."[203]

For Schimmelfennig the indignation of the coward comments was a difficult pill to swallow. Regrettably, he received little if any satisfaction regarding the exoneration of his men before Hooker began shifting his army northward. The regiments of his disparaged brigade consisted of the 45th New York which had come over from Colonel von Gilsa's brigade to replace the transferred 68th New York. The remaining regiments were the 82nd Illinois, 157th New York, 61st Ohio and the 74th Pennsylvania.[204]

As the Gettysburg Campaign began to unfolded, Schurz' remaining brigade was under the command of the Polish immigrant Wladimir Krzyzanowski. Born 8 July 1824 in Raznova Prussia, Krzyzanowski, fled his country to escape the Revolution of 1846, and arrived in New York the same year. He adopted the ways of his new country, and unlike other European immigrants, learned to speak English rather well. Settling onto American society, he went to work as a civil engineer and continued to support himself within the trade until the war began. Intent on showing his patriotism to his new country, Krzyzanowski joined the Washington Militia on 22 April 1861, and was made a captain within its ranks.

---

[203] *OR* vol.25, pt.1, pp.182-183,662-663. General McLean's brigade actually suffered more killed, wounded, and captured than Schimmelfennig.

[204] *OR* 25, pt.2, p.582.

However, by the end of the summer he was working to organize his own regiment of volunteers. The War Department issued authority to raise the regiment on 20 August 1861, and a week later Krzyzanowski's men, along with men from other organizations, were combined into the 58th New York with Krzyzanowski installed as the new unit's colonel. The regiment was mustered in for three years of service in New York City, and left for Washington on 7 November.[205]

The 58th was assigned to General Fremont's command and went to the Valley where it fought at Cross Keys on 8 June losing twenty-nine men. The battle was poorly handled by Fremont, and Krzyzanowski was forced to retire when he was pressed by two Confederate regiments that emerged from a line of woods on the right of his position. The regiment conducted itself well, and brigade commander Bohlen recognized it in his report noting that under Krzyzanowski "the regiment behaved with great gallantry." Like the other members of Fremont's command, the 58th became part of the forces organized into Pope's Army of Virginia. During the restructuring, Colonel Krzyzanowski was elevated to brigade command. Once again during the fight at Second Bull Run, Krzyzanowski hammered it out with men from Stonewall Jackson's Confederates along the railroad embankment, taking 372 casualties. During the fighting, he was wounded, not by Confederate bullets or shrapnel, but by his own horse when the animal was felled.[206]

Like Schimmelfennig, Krzyzanowski spent the winter in Washington's trenches, during which time he was promoted to brigadier general. Unfortunately, Congress failed to approve the appointment and Krzyzanowski, after his confirmation period expired on 4 March 1863, was a colonel again. General Schurz, attempting to put some levity into the denial, quipped it was probably due to Congress' inability to pronounce Krzyzanowski name. Krzyzanowski and his men shared the same fate at Chancellorsville as Schimmelfennig as their men stood shoulder to shoulder trying to stem the Confederate tide near the Wilderness Tavern. Like Schimmelfennig, Krzyzanowski brigade took over 400 casualties.[207]

Wladimir's brigade contained five regiments from four different states. New York supplied its 58th and 119th regiments. The New Yorkers were joined by the 75th Pennsylvania, 26th Wisconsin and the 82nd Ohio. During the Battle of Chancellorsville, the boys from Ohio had been unattached, but shortly after the battle, the Buckeyes were assigned to Krzyzanowski's unit. An additional group of New Yorkers, a company from the 8th regiment, on 31 May, were reported as being assigned to the brigade on corps returns, but nether divisional nor brigade returns indicated the company was under Krzyzanowski's command. The company was

---

[205] Eicher, & Eicher, **High Commands**, pp.336-337; Phisterer, *NYWR*, vol.3, p.2502; Quaife, **Cannon's Mouth**, p.206.

[206] *OR* vol.12, pt.1, pp.664, 670, 673; *OR* vol.12, pt.2, pp.251, 311-312; *OR* vol.25, pt.1, p.183; Eicher, & Eicher, **High Commands**, p.337.

[207] Tagg, **Generals**, p.141; *OR* 25, pt.1, p.183.

assembled from a group of three year men which remained with the army as their regiment's two year men were mustered out.[208]

The heavy casualties suffered by Schurz' Division at Chancellorsville reinforced the fact that not all of Howard's Corps turned and ran at the first sign of trouble. Although the initial shock of the assault dislodged General Devens' men quickly, the remainder of the division tried desperately to organize and put up some sort of resistance. Some elements may have remained as long as an hour before eventually giving way to Jackson's weight in numbers. The stigma of "Howard's cowards" had been unjustly leveled against the corps through no fault of the men. The ultimate insult had been a refusal to acknowledge the verbal and visual warnings of the corps vulnerability. As preparations began for the summer campaign, the men of the Eleventh Corps were being blamed for the disaster. The soldiers however, knew the responsability should have been leveled squarely on the shoulders of General Howard. They also knew that if anyone or anything was going to salvage their reputation, it would not be squabbling officers but their own bravery and determination on the field of battle.

Henry Slocum Restores His Corps

Buried at the center of the fighting around the Chancellor House, Henry Slocum's Twelfth Corps had borne their fair share of the fighting taking nearly 3,000 casualties. When his battered command returned to the north side of the river, the men settled back into their old camps near Stafford Court House to lick their wounds. The court house, around eight miles from Hooker's Headquarters near Falmouth, isolated Slocum's boys a bit from the remainder of the army. Only some members of Meade's Corps were further away, up river guarding the fords. Once back in camp, the work of replenishing the ranks commenced. Daily life picked up in earnest as regimental camps were organized and picket details were sent out. Dress parades were conducted to help improve the morale of the men. Slocum personally went to work reviewing troops and took responsibility for the replenishment of supplies. The self-esteem and confidence of the men was rooted in their belief in their commander. Now was not the time to be invisible, and Slocum quickly began working through the details of getting his corps back into fighting shape.[209]

The decimation within the corps' First Division was so extensive that when combined with the expiring enlistment terms of the 28th New York and the 128th Pennsylvania of the First Brigade, it and the Second Brigade ceased to be effective fighting units. To remedy the situation, on 13 May, the six remaining regiments were combined into a single brigade. Although the assignment was intended to be temporary, by the time the two armies engaged each other at Gettysburg all six were still members of the division's First Brigade. The division's Third Brigade,

---

[208] *OR* vol.25, pt.2, p.582; Phisterer, *NYWR*, vol.3, p.1815. Phisterer indicated the company from the 8th New York was attached to Eleventh Corps headquarters as Provost Guard.

[209] Slocum, *The Life and Service of Major General Henry Warner Slocum*, p.93; *OR* vol.25, pt.1, p.185.

although suffering more casualties than either the first or second, remained intact, retaining all of its five regiments.[210]

Commanding Slocum's First Division was Brigadier General Alpheus Starkey Williams. Williams was the longest tenured division commander in the Army of the Potomac, having been placed at the head of the division on 13 March 1862 when the army had been reorganized under McClellan. Known as "Old Pap," "Pops," or simply "Pap," Williams possessed the same stubbornness for preparation as McClellan, and it is likely the two agreed on many of the preparatory activities which the army's commander believed necessary before it could move to meet the enemy the spring of 1862. McClellan expressed his approval of Williams by placing him at the head of a division in spite of Williams' lack of military training, although he did have some practical experience. His appointment however, had been months ago. McClellan was no longer a factor, and possibly due to his association with the relieved general, Williams saw slow advancement. In the spring of 1863, while other junior officers were advancing to fill vacancies, Williams remained a brigade general in charge of a division.[211]

An obvious political appointment, Old Paps was born in Saybrook, Connecticut on 20 September 1810. His parents died early in his life leaving him a substantial inheritance. Putting his money to good use, Williams attended Yale Law School, from which he graduated in 1831, after three years of study. After school, he spent a number of years traveling throughout the United States and overseas, no doubt spending a portion of his parent's money in the process. Finally settling in Detroit, he opened a law practice and became a probate judge. During his time in Michigan, Williams took a fancy to a young, well-to-do woman named Jane Larned. Jane, the daughter of Charles Larned, a prominent military figure and lawyer who had fought in both the Revolution and the War of 1812, evidently returned Williams affection and the two were married shortly before Jane's famous father died. In 1834 Williams entered the news business when he purchased an interest in the *Detroit Advertiser* where he worked as editor for five years promoting the political views of the Whig Party. He showed an interest in the military and military science, and he worked to improve the state's militia, where he took an ever expanding role, eventually joining the Brady Guards Militia Company. When the war with Mexico began, Williams became a lieutenant colonel in the 1st Michigan Infantry and went off to battle. Unfortunately, he arrived too late to participate in the fighting and was honorably mustered out of service as a major. He returned to his home and began a series of civilian pursuits, becoming the postmaster of Detroit, a banker, and returning to his duties as a judge.[212]

On 24 April 1861, Williams was made a brigadier general in the state militia. When the state contacted him and asked for assistance in training its first four volunteer regiments, Williams was more than happy to oblige. After completing

---

[210] *OR* vol.25, pt.1, p.184; *OR* vol.25, pt.2, p.583; *OR* vol.27, pt.1, p.165.

[211] Eicher, & Eicher, *High Commands*, p.571; Tagg, *Generals*, p.146.

[212] Williams Obituary, New York Times, 22 December, 1878; Tagg, *Generals*, p.147.

the training of the regiments, both Williams and the state's finest headed for Washington where he was promoted to brigadier general of volunteers on 17 August. He was assigned command of a brigade in Major General Nathanial Banks' division of McClellan's organizing Army of the Potomac. In the spring of 1862, when Banks ascended to command of the Fifth Corps, William's became a division commander and was transferred to the Department of the Shenandoah. He spent the spring of 1862 participating in the frustration of constant defeats at the hands of Jackson. That summer, as part of General Pope's Army of Virginia, William's led his division once again against Jackson at Cedar Mountain but managed to escape the embarrassment of Second Bull Run as he arrived too late to participate. As the Maryland Campaign unfolded, Williams' division was incorporated into the Twelfth Corps. During the march to catch the retreating Lee, he commanded the corps for a brief three days. Again, at the battle of Antietam, when corps commander Major General Joseph K. Mansfield was mortally wounded, Williams took command once more. He retained command for slightly over a month until General Slocum arrived to take over, relegating Williams back to his division. He missed the battle of Fredericksburg but was at the heart of the fighting at Chancellorsville, his division taking over 1,600 casualties.[213]

By May, 1863, Williams had become increasingly disappointed with his own lack of promotion. To make matters worse, he was forced to sit on the sidelines as brigadiers, who he considered lesser men, received promotions while his career languished. Williams' lack of military training hampered him somewhat while it was an obvious advantage to his contemporaries. He began to develop a genuine distaste for men from the Regular Army who, in Williams' mind, had not proven themselves in battle but seemed to be capable of working their way to the top of the command structure. In a letter to his daughter in early June of 1863, Williams vented his frustration. "Just think of the promotion of Birney over me for the battle of Chancellorsville!!" he vented. "An officer who has been once tried for misconduct or something else in the face of the enemy. I believe he was found not guilty and have no doubt he is patriotic and valiant enough, but he is my junior a year and a half and I have seen more service than he ever can." Williams did not plead his case like many of the advancement seekers, owing to the fact that he was not one to draw attention to himself. Unlike most other members of the army's hierarchy, he was not into self-promotion and did not utilize the media to document his accomplishments.[214]

However, there were those in the army who understood Williams' abilities and worth. One such officer was Williams new corps commander, General Slocum. On 5 June, in a letter to Lincoln, Slocum stepped up and lobbied the president on Williams behalf.

---

[213] Eicher, & Eicher, **High Commands**, p.571; Williams Obituary, New York Times, 22 December, 1878; Tagg, **Generals**, p.147. Williams' obituary indicates that he commanded the Twelfth Corps at Chancellorsville. He did command the corps for a time when Slocum was exercising command over the right wing of the army.

[214] Tagg, Larry, **Generals**, p.147; Quaife, **Cannon's Mouth**, p.206. General David Birney was promoted to major general on 20 May, 1863, eighteen days before Williams wrote to his daughter.

"Since I was assigned to the command of the corps, Gen. Williams has been in command of the 1st Division. I have found him in camp as well as on the field a most valuable and efficient officer. I cannot speak too highly of his conduct during our late movements [Chancellorsville] under Gen. Hooker. His division marched over sixty miles in three days, and forded the Rapidan during the time. In all our engagements with the enemy, his division did its full duty, as is attested by the loss sustained by it, which exceeded one-third of the number he took into the field. He, as its commander, was constantly at his proper post, both by night as well as day. I know of no officer in the service who has in my estimation so well earned promotion as Gen. Williams."

Slocum concluded his communication by inform Lincoln of Williams' refusal to utilize the press as a promotional tool to garner advancement. "I most earnestly hope he may be promoted," he informed the commander in chief.[215]

There is little doubt Williams owed much of his success to his early relationship with McClellan. Both men possessed the same devotion toward their men, were meticulous in their preparation, and were cautious to a fault. These traits in Williams would have been supported by McClellan. When his men failed to receive much needed accoutrements and clothing, Williams felt genuine empathy for their misery, but his concern over the welfare of his men was also a contributing factor when it came to being successful, or unsuccessful, on the battlefield. Like McClellan, Williams had a tendency to overestimate the strength of his opponent which restricted his activity and made him timid when he should have shown aggression. When he was chastised for inactivity, he returned the criticism to his accusers. He was also passive in his treatment of enemy civilians and failed to bring the harsh reality of war to the Southern populace when opportunities to do so presented themselves. He was inert to the point of praise by Southerners who thought him one of the more compassionate Yankees. Like McClellan Old Pap Williams seemed at times so concerned with losing a battle that he would not risk winning one. His love for the men was returned in kind. They surely appreciated his unwillingness to put them in too much danger.

Williams' other significant trait which singled him out was his appearance. At the age of fifty-three he had developed a rugged exterior which was enhanced by a large amount of scruffy facial hair, incorporating a large mustache which included not only the hair on his upper lip but also much of the growth on the forward portion of his cheeks. It was all gathered together and trimmed to a point where each side of the augmentation projected well beyond the extents of his face. He wore his curly hair rather long, hanging down to cover his ears. His hair line had begun to slip rearward, increasing the distance between it and his rugged looking eyes. Often seen at the head of his division chewing on an unlit cigar, he was one of the army's most recognized if not successful generals.[216]

---

[215] Quaife, ***Cannon's Mouth***, p.205.

[216] Tagg, Larry, ***Generals***, p.146.

Alpheus Starkey Williams could be identified on the field of battle by the unlit cigar which he typically chewed while directing his command. *LOC*

Colonel Archibald L. McDougall of the 123rd New York was in a unique situation in early June. When the First and Second Brigades of the Twelfth Corps' First Division were combined, McDougall and his regiment began reporting to Brigadier General Joseph F. Knipe. A few days later, Knipe left the army, a victim of reoccurring difficulties from previous wounds he had received at Cedar Mountain a year earlier and a bout with malaria. McDougall suddenly found himself thrust into the position of brigade commander, becoming responsible for the brigade's six regiments. A significant lack of field grade commanders plagued the regiments after the Battle of Chancellorsville. The lack of leadership would make it difficult for the forty-six year old McDougall. The returns of 31 May show the extent of McDougall's problem. Only two regiments were commanded by their colonel. The remaining four regiments were commanded by a lieutenant colonel, two majors and a captain.[217]

McDougall was not a militarily trained man. Born in 1817, he was a bit elderly to be a regimental field officer. Most men of his age were at least a brigadier, out of the army or assigned to desk duty. His balding head, gray hair and salt and pepper beard showed his age but provided a look of distinction. On 23 July 1862, McDougall was authorized to raise a regiment of volunteers from New York. The effort resulted in the creation of the 123rd New York, a group of men from

---

[217] Warner, *Generals in Blue*, p.272; Phisterer, *NYWR*, vol.4, p.3456; *OR* vol.25, pt.2, p.583. Knipe would spend the Gettysburg Campaign leading a brigade of New York militia.

Washington County in the upstate region near the Vermont border. McDougall became colonel of the regiment, and after it was mustered at Salem, the regiment traveled south to join the Army of the Potomac, where it was assigned to the Second Brigade in the Twelfth Corps' First Division.[218]

Joining the army shortly after Antietam, Colonel McDougall saw no action until Chancellorsville. As Jackson's flank attack drove Howard's command toward the crossroads, McDougall quickly positioned his men and awaited the arrival of the hard charging Rebels. With the enemy hot on their heels, the fleeing Federals of the Eleventh Corps entered, and passed through his line. When McDougall saw his command fidget as the regiment began taking fire, he jumped up onto a nearby log. Drawing his sword, he waved it over head and exhorted his men to make a stand. "For God's sake, boys, stand your ground! Don't let it be said the boys of Washington County ran!" Inspired by their colonel, the men did hold their ground, remaining engaged during some of the heaviest fighting. When the conflict finally subsided, the casualty list proved that McDougall's men refused to run. After the fighting, he was the only regimental commander in the division's first two brigades who remained unscathed. Brigade commander Colonel Samuel Ross noted in his report that McDougall acted with "coolness and bravery throughout" the battle.[219]

After the battle, McDougall spent two days guarding Banks' Ford while other units crossed the river to the safety of the northern bank. Although the battle had provided McDougall with combat experience, he was still untried at brigade level command. As the army picketed the Rappahannock and prepared for the coming summer's round of fighting, his brigade consisted of six units from four different states. Hailing from New York was McDougall's own 123rd and the 145th New York. Two regiments from Connecticut, the 5th and 20th, a Pennsylvania regiment, the 46th and the 3rd Maryland filled out the brigade.[220]

General Williams' other brigade consisted of a conglomeration of five regiments from a like number of states. Two of the regiments, the 27th Indiana and the 3rd Wisconsin, came from the west. The other three, the 2nd Massachusetts, 107th New York and the 13th New Jersey completed the brigade under Brigadier General Thomas Howard Ruger. Born in Lima, New York on 2 April 1833, Ruger relocated to Wisconsin when he was thirteen years old. Four years after settling in the town of Janesville, Ruger received an appointment to the Military Academy. Proving to be an exceptionally good student, Thomas, after completing his four year curriculum, graduated third in a class of forty-six. Other notables in his class were Robert Lee's son Custis at the head of the class, Oliver Howard, and Lee's cavalryman Jeb Stuart. His high standing attained for him a posting to the engineers, but Ruger

---

[218] Phisterer, *NYWR*, vol.4, pp.3454-3454, 4361; Pfanz, Harry W., **Gettysburg: Culp's Hill & Cemetery Hill**, p.445, n.65.

[219] *OR* vol.25, pt.1, pp.184, 688; Tagg, **Generals**, p.149.

[220] *OR* vol.25, pt.2, p.583.

decided to resigned his commission after spending less than a year at his post. He returned to Wisconsin and began a career as a lawyer.[221]

Shortly after the attack on Fort Sumter, Ruger was appointed chief engineer and aide to Wisconsin Governor Alexander W. Randall. A few months later, when the 3rd Wisconsin was organized in and around Fond du Lac, Ruger stepped up and joined the organizing Badgers and was mustered in as the regiment's lieutenant colonel on 29 June 1861. By 1 September, He was promoted to colonel when the regiment's original commander received his brigadier star. Assigned to General Bank's corps, Ruger marched the 3rd to the Valley of Virginia where it saw its first action during the spring of 1862. After returning from the Valley, Ruger saw more tough combat a Cedar Mountain, but his Badgers were not engaged at Second Bull Run. At Antietam, he lead his regiment until he was forced to take command of the brigade. He guided the brigade through some of the heaviest fighting, receiving a slight head wound.[222]

In November, Ruger was promoted to brigadier general. He spent the latter months of 1862 on the upper Potomac in the vicinity of Harpers Ferry with the remainder of the Twelfth Corps. The corps moved to Fredericksburg in December. Its late arrival spared it the horrors of the 13 December fight. Ruger and his 3rd Wisconsin went into camp near Stafford Court House and hunkered down for the winter. Two months later, his commander left the army, allowing him to take permanent position at the head of the brigade.[223]

He first led his new command at Chancellorsville. After marching his men through the water at Kelly's Ford on the Rappahannock, Ruger's boys encountered minor resistance at Germanna Ford. The Rebels were quickly dispatched and the brigade waded across the Rapidan River. Ruger marched onward to the Chancellor House where it spent 30 April building abattis west of the crossroads. The following day he led his command to a position along the Orange Plank Road where they met Jackson's advance. When Hooker pulled his forces back to Chancellorsville, Ruger fell back as well. On 2 May the brigade continued building earthworks until ordered to the left where they harassed the rear of Jackson's column until the assault on the Eleventh Corps began. Once the fighting commenced, Ruger, following orders, positioned his command across the road west of the Chancellor House where the brigade spent 3 May fighting for its survival against the screaming Rebels. After the battle, General Williams wrote of Ruger's conduct in his report. "I cannot let the opportunity pass without the especial mention of the valuable, faithful, and gallant conduct of Brigadier General Ruger… At all times and on all occasions [he was] prompt and zealous in the discharge of [his] duties, which were both arduous and constant night and day." The brigade's 614 casualties were

---

[221] Eicher, & Eicher, *High Commands*, p.464; *OR* vol.25, pt.2, p.583; Warner, *Generals in Blue*, p.415.

[222] Quiner, E.B., *The Military History of Wisconsin in the War for the Union* (hereafter *MHWU*), pp.59, 483-488, Eicher, & Eicher, *High Commands*, p.464.

[223] Eicher, & Eicher, *High Commands*, p.464; Fox, *Regimental Losses*, p.88.

a testament to the ferocity of the fighting and the stubbornness of Ruger and his men.[224]

Hard fighting had molded Ruger and the brigade into one of the most experienced and battle hardened unit in the army. He had proven himself, not only to his brigade, but also to his division commander, and Williams expressed nothing but praise for him. If anything, Ruger was a bit too modest. His humility was one of the reasons he had not garnered as much consideration for higher rank as other promotion seeking commanders. As Gettysburg approached, he would still be in command of his hodgepodge of regiments. Before the battle in Pennsylvania was over, many of the men in the brigade would no doubt be glad he was still in charge.[225]

"A Giant of a Man"

John White Geary, Slocum's Second Division commander was the epitome of a professional soldier although he was never educated in the military arts. Geary was one of the few Federal generals not educated at West Point that managed to acquire the respect and admiration of men trained at the Academy. Born in Mount Pleasant Pennsylvania near Pittsburg on 30 December 1819, Geary entered Jefferson College in Canonsburg at an early age. Unfortunately, young John's father died early in his life leaving a sizable amount of debt. To help with the family's obligations, John left school and began making his way in the world before he was entirely prepared. As the head of the family, he worked to settle his father's unpaid debt by performing various jobs. Traveling to Kentucky, he gained employment as a surveyor and became a land speculator. The ventures produced enough money to allow him to return to school where he study engineering and law. Early in his professional life Geary was a man of many trades. He worked as a teacher, a clerk, and with his education now complete, he went to work as an engineer, helping to construct the Allegheny Portage Railroad. He also began a legal career, taking and passing the bar.[226]

Geary embarked on his military career early in life as a member of the Pennsylvania Militia. By 1835 he was an officer holding the rank of captain. When the Mexican War began, he became captain of the 2nd Pennsylvania Volunteers and went off to war. Seventeen days later he was the regiment's lieutenant colonel. He participated in the attack against the fortress at Chapultepec where he showed his grit and determination, receiving no less than five wounds during the assault. His efforts were rewarded when he was made colonel of the regiment two months later. As the Mexican conflict came to a close, he was mustered out and returned home to continue civilian pursuits.[227]

---

[224] *OR* 25, pt.1, pp.682, 707-710.

[225] Tagg, *Generals*, p.153.

[226] Blair, William Alan, Editor, *A Politician Goes to War: The Civil War Letters of John White Geary*, p.xvii; Warner, *Generals in Blue*, p.169.

[227] Eicher, & Eicher, *High Commands*, p.251; Tagg, *Generals*, p.155.

As a Democrat, Geary supported James K. Polk during the election of 1844. He found himself out west in California in 1849, after Polk appointed him Postmaster of San Francisco. Geary quickly lost his position however, when the administration in Washington changed the same year. Out of work, he decided to remain in San Francisco and try his hand a politics. A successful campaign saw him elected as the city's first mayor in 1850. Unfortunately, his wife Margaret's health forced him to resign the position a year later, and he returned to Pennsylvania. The change of location did not help rectify Margaret's condition, and shortly after they arrived, she died leaving Geary a widower at a fairly young age. He was offered the governorship of the Utah Territory by the Pierce Administration but turned it down. Being a Northerner, he was opposed to the continuation of slavery and when giving the opportunity to assume the governorship of the Kansas Territory he accepted. He worked hard but his efforts were not sufficient to stem the tide of violence running rampant through the region. A year later he resigned the position after pro-slavery factions threatened his assassination and his health began to deteriorate. Traveling back to Pennsylvania, Geary, a wealthy, former mayor of San Francisco and governor of the Kansas Territory, settled down and removed himself from the public eye. He returned to his residence and became a simple farmer. During the years immediately preceding the war, he grew increasingly embittered regarding the institution of slavery.[228]

Margaret managed to bear John two children before her health failed her, both boys, Edward and Willie. In 1858, John met and married Mary Henderson, who had also lost her first spouse. Mary bore John two more children, both girls, Mary and Margaret. When the war began, he moved his brood from the Pittsburg area to New Cumberland, a small town across the Susquehanna from Harrisburg. It would be here that John's family would remain while he went off to war. Unfortunately for Mary and the children, New Cumberland would be squarely in Robert E. Lee's crosshairs during the latter half of June 1863.[229]

When the Civil War came, Geary left his family behind, intent on doing his part to save the Union. Traveling to Philadelphia, he worked to raise a regiment that eventually became the 28th Pennsylvania Volunteers. Using his own funds he outfitted the new unit, and led it through the early months of the war along the Potomac River in the Harpers Ferry area. Geary, wounded in the leg by a shell fragment on Bolivar Heights, was eventually captured in March at Leesburg. After being exchanged, he was promoted to brigadier general on 25 April, and given command of a brigade. Two months later when Pope's Army of Virginia was organized, Geary's brigade was assigned to the new army's First Division of its Second Corps. His initial action under Pope was at Cedar Mountain where he was once again wounded. He was struck twice in quick succession, first in the left ankle by a minié ball and again when a ball passed through his left arm. The injuries

---

[228] Blair, *A Politician Goes to War*, p.xvii; Tagg, **Generals**, p.155.

[229] Blair, *A Politician Goes to War*, p.xviii.

sidelined him until October. His arm was still bandaged when he returned to the army to find he had been promoted to division command in the Twelfth Corps.[230]

Like General Williams' Division, Geary's was heavily engaged at Chancellorsville. At one point during the battle Geary became annoyed with some of Hancock's men after they were ordered to concentrate near the Chancellor House. His irritation centered upon a portion of Hancock's men who began to depart before covering his retreat. Some of the men waved their bayonets in the direction of the demonstrative Geary, but calmer heads prevailed and nothing came of the incident. Later Geary was nearly killed when a Rebel cannon ball whizzed past his head so close that it knocked the general down and he lost consciousness. When he awoke, he was unable to speak above a whisper, and his voice remained quiet for a number of weeks. Slocum praised the Pennsylvanian in his report, noting that Geary's division "held its line until forced to retire by the appearance of the enemy in its rear."[231]

Geary may have survived his near miss with the cannonball due to his physical presence. He was a massive man standing six feet six and weighing well over 200 pounds, a size which placed him at considerable risk during combat, making him a very conspicuous target. He was not rotund, but firmly built and sturdy. His bulk and ruggedness projected an aura of invincibility, and simply stated, he seemed unbreakable. When mounted upon his horse, he projected a powerful presence which many men feared but all respected. It would make since that such a man would have a big heart and Geary possessed a large warm one. However, he also displayed a violent temper when he became irritated, which was unfortunate for any soldier on the receiving end of his angst. Combined with his size, when agitated, he displayed a persona which very few sought to challenge and most made sure they were not nearby when Geary became upset.

Geary, forty-four years of age during the spring of 1863, seemed a bit young for a man who was already displayed a receding hairline. His dark, deep set eyes and perpetual squint projected a constant look of annoyance. His face was accented by a straight, rugged, manly nose which was slightly bulbous at the end. A large, dark, heavy beard obscured his neckline, and a weighty mustache covered his upper lip all but obscured his mouth. Taken together, Geary's features made him look the part of a respected and admired general.[232]

Geary's First Brigade was populated by men who hailed from both the eastern and western parts of the country. While May and June saw numerous brigades have their numbers depleted by departing regiments, his First Brigade managed to retain its compliment. Four of the brigade's six units were from Ohio while the remaining

---

[230] Eicher, & Eicher, *High Commands*, pp.251-252; Warner, *Generals in Blue*, p.169; Blair, *A Politician Goes to War*, p.54. Bates, *HPV*, vol.1, pp.418, 424.

[231] Tagg, *Generals*, p.156; *OR* vol.25, pt.1, p.672. Some sources claim that Geary was struck in the chest by the cannonball. This is no doubt fiction since an airborne ball would have contained enough energy to cut a man in half.

[232] Tagg, *Generals*, p.155.

two called the Keystone State home. Geary's own 28th, and the 147th represented Pennsylvania, while the Ohioans were from the 5th, 7th, 29th and 66th regiments. All were veteran outfits with which Geary was well acquainted. Not only had he led the 28th as its colonel, but also all four of the Ohio regiments were under his command at Cedar Mountain. As June began however, control of the brigade had fallen to the former colonel of the 66th, Charles Candy.[233]

Candy, a Kentuckian, was born in Lexington on 7 August 1832. At the age of seventeen, he enlisted in the 1st Dragoons. He remained in the army for five years and advanced to the rank of first sergeant, but he must have encountered discipline problems for in July of 1854 he was listed as honorably discharged as a private. Candy either desired a military life or simply could not find any other ventures which appealed to him, for he was back in the army a few months later as a private in the 1st U. S. Infantry. Advancing once again through the enlisted ranks, he was functioning as a sergeant major when he was once again discharged on 1 January 1861. When the war began, Candy volunteered for service again, this time as a clerk in the Department of Ohio. By September he had been elevated to captain and assigned to the Second Brigade of General Charles P. Stone's division, working as an assistant adjutant general. He participated in the fighting during the Federal catastrophe at Ball's Bluff. Stone was propped up as the scapegoat for the disaster, and Candy resigned his post and returned to Ohio. Fourteen days later, he was back in the war after being commissioned a colonel and placed in command of the newly organized 66th Ohio.[234]

Candy's regiment was assigned to the brigade of Brigadier General James Shields and saw its first heavy action at Port Republic in the Valley on 9 June 1862. During the battle, Candy's boys were charged with defending an artillery battery on the left end of the Federal line. Hard fighting Rebels managed to wrestle three guns from Candy's position on three separate occasions but each time the guns were retaken before the Confederates could turn them on Candy's men. The battle however, did not go well for the other Federals and when a retreat was ordered Candy pulled his men from the field leaving 205 killed, wounded and missing in the wake of the fighting. A few months later, at Cedar Mountain, Colonel Candy ascended to brigade command when General Geary was wounded.[235]

Candy remained at the head of the brigade as Geary convalesced, but it was not engaged at Second Bull Run, and Candy himself was absent when the battle along Antietam Creek was waged. When General Geary returned it was to lead the division, and Candy found a permanent place at the head of the brigade. It was not until Chancellorsville that Candy saw his next action. His position at the center of

---

[233] *OR* 25, pt.1, p.168; *OR* 27, pt.1, p.165.

[234] Eicher, & Eicher, *High Commands*, p.162; Warner, *Generals in Blue*, p.480

[235] Reid, Whitelaw, *Ohio in the War: Her Statesman, Her Generals and Soldiers* (hereafter *OW*), vol.II, pp.387-388; *OR* vol.12, pt.1, p.690;

the firestorm around the Chancellor House late on the morning of 3 May earned him praises from General Geary and 521 casualties.[236]

By June of 1863, there was no question that Charles Candy was an accomplished brigade commander, but a promotion to brigadier general was not on the horizon. He lacked political connections, and his association with the unseated General Stone may have led to his difficulties in attaining higher rank. In addition, his early war experience as a private and clerk had not provided opportunities to develop associations with officers who could help him advance. As the army camped and patrolled the Fredericksburg area that spring, Candy may have been one of the most underappreciated brigade commanders in the army.

The man who would command Geary's Second Brigade at Gettysburg was not with the army as the month of June opened. Brigadier General Thomas Leiper Kane, had fallen into the Rapidan River on 28 April and drenched himself as the army marched upriver during the first phases of the Chancellorsville Campaign. Kane got up, shook himself off, got back on his horse and led his brigade during the fighting. However, by 7 May he left the army having become deathly ill. At the time of his spill, Kane was still trying to recover from a previous wound and time spent in a Confederate prison. He was soon diagnosed with pleurisy, and a short time later the affliction developed into pneumonia. He left the army for a sickbed in Philadelphia, turning command of his brigade over to its senior colonel, George Ashworth Cobham Jr.[237]

Cobham, not a natural born American, was from Liverpool, England. Born on 5 December 1825, he immigrated with his family to the United States when he was near the age of ten. Settling in Pennsylvania, Cobham furthered his education by attending Allegany College, and he later built a career as a bridge contractor. When the war began, he chose not to immediately join the effort to subdue the rebellion. Not until early 1862 did he signed up as a member of the 111th Pennsylvania. On 28 January, he became the regiment's lieutenant colonel.[238]

The 111th arrived in Baltimore on 1 March, and after spending time drilling, was pushed forward to Harpers Ferry to assist General Banks' Federals in the Valley. In late May the regiment boarded rail cars and headed for Winchester but was forced to return after traveling only five miles when word of Banks' defeat and retreat from the town intercepted the train. Cobham and his regiment spent a great portion of their early war experience in and around Harpers Ferry. Near the end of June, the regiment was transferred and rolled into the group of units that would make up General Pope's new army. As the regiment marched toward what would become the Battle of Cedar Mountain, many became ill and were hospitalized. Sickness had overtaken the regiment and a number of men were down with fever, including Cobham.[239]

---

[236] *OR* vol.25, pt.1, pp.723, 184.

[237] Tagg, *Generals*, p.160; Eicher, & Eicher, *High Commands*, pp.327, 178.

[238] Eicher, & Eicher, *High Commands*, p.178. Sifakis, *Who was Who*, p.130.

[239] Bates, *HPV*, vol.6, p.1014.

Although the 111th fought at Antietam as part of the newly organized Twelfth Corps, evidence indicates that Cobham, once again, was not with the regiment. Promoted to colonel on 7 November, he took command when the unit's previous colonel was discharged, but missed Fredericksburg along with the remainder of the corps. It is likely that Cobham's first heavy action at any command level came at Chancellorsville where the regiment fought with the other members of Kane's Brigade. When Kane left to recover from his illness, Cobham took command of the brigade which consisted of his 111th and two other Pennsylvania regiments, the 29th and the 109th. He would retain command until the brigade was on the field at Gettysburg.[240]

Brigadier General George Sears Greene, a relative of Revolutionary War hero Nathaniel Greene, was another old man of the army. Born on 6 May 1801, in the village of Apponaug in Warwick, Rhode Island, he was the second child born to Caleb Greene and his wife Sarah. Sarah bore Caleb a total of ten children, four of whom failed to reach adulthood. Caleb was a ship owner who built a successful merchant business and cloth factory on land his ancestors had purchased from the Native Americans in the area in 1640. His ships would transport cotton northward where his factory used it to produce clothing. On their return trips southward, the finished clothing would be transported to market. The business prospered and by the time George was born, Caleb Greene had a thriving enterprise which more than adequately provided for his large family. His land, which he planted with oats, corn, wheat and hay, provided additional revenue.[241]

Raised in a typical Quaker way of life, George was a particularly bright boy. He began school in Apponaug's one room school house and shortly thereafter entered the Old Warwick grammar school to complete his formal education. When he was sixteen, his parents sent him to a school in Wrentham, Massachusetts to continue his education and prepare him for college. A year later Greene returned to Rhode Island to attend the Latin Grammar School in Providence in preparation for entering Brown University. Unfortunately, all thoughts of attending the university vanished when President Jefferson installed a trade embargo with Europe which, according to family history, "ruined" Caleb's shipping merchant business, and placed the family's finances in jeopardy. Since Caleb's farming operation was not

---

[240] Eicher, & Eicher, ***High Commands***, p.178. Sifakis, ***Who was Who***, p.130; ***OR*** vol.25, pt.2, p.583. In the Official Records Cobham's name does not appear anywhere in the index of the volume containing reports or in the correspondence volume. The 111th was under the command of Major Thomas M. Walker during the Battle of Antietam. Walker wrote the units after action report. ***OR*** vol.19, pt.1, pp.179, 475, 512.

[241] ***Electronic Source:*** http://www.warwickhistory.com/index.php?option=com_content&view=article&id=103:apponaugs-george-sears-greene-&catid=43:apponaug-village&Itemid=96, Last Accessed: 7/8/2012; Clarke, Louise Brownell, ***The Greenes of Rhode Island: With Historical Records of English Ancestry 1534-1902***, p.x. The biography of George S. Greene, written by one of George's children, Frances Vinton Greene, indicates that Sarah bore Caleb nine children. Sarah actually bore ten children, one of which, Thomas Raymond Greene, survived only twenty-one days.

profitable enough to adequately provide support for his family and allow him to send George to Brown, all hopes of a college education for his son were dashed. To support himself, George traveled to New York and found employment working for a dry goods merchant.[242]

George showed great talent in mathematics and displayed signs of being a person of enormous intellect. Desiring more for George than a life as a merchant's apprentice, Caleb began to solicit assistance from his business associates to garner enough support to acquire an appointment to West Point. George's aptitude and abilities, once exposed to the administrators at the academy all but guaranteed a place for him. So special were Greene's talents that then Superintendent Sylvanus Thayer personally recommended George for the appointment, an honor which only a handful of cadets were able to boast. He entered the academy on 24 June 1819 and did not disappoint his supporters. So impressive were his scores in mathematics that as a senior, Thayer appointed him an acting professor on the subject. He remained near the top of his class in all subjects, and graduated 1 July 1823, second in a class of thirty-five.[243]

After graduation, Greene was allowed to remain at the academy to teach mathematics. After his post-graduation furlough, he taught for three years before he was finally sent to the field. During his time instructing cadets, he taught the North's future antagonist Robert E. Lee his numbers. Greens' class standing allowed him to select the branch of service he wished to enter. Most graduates at the upper end of the class tended to choose much sought-after engineering positions. George however chose the artillery and left the academy and his teaching position with the rank of second lieutenant in 1827. His first field assignment was with the 3rd U. S. Artillery stationed at Fort Monroe. A short time later, George was transferred to Fort Wolcott on Rhode Island's Goat Island. It was while on duty there that George met and married Elizabeth Vinton during the summer of 1828. Shortly afterward, Elizabeth decided to accompany George on his next duty assignment at Fort Sullivan, Maine. It was while in Maine that the tragedy of George Greene's life occurred.[244]

The living conditions at Fort Sullivan were anything but satisfactory, being deathly cold during the winter and cold and wet during the summer months. Although the circumstances were not optimum for starting and raising a family, George and Elizabeth decided to make the effort. Their first child, Mary Vinton, born 3 June 1829, survived the rigors of birth as did her brother George Jr., who was born in December of the following year. While Elizabeth was pregnant with the couple's third child, Mary became ill and died three days after her birthday in 1832. Frances Vinton, George and Elizabeth's second son, was born two months later. The happiness of a new family member was quickly overshadowed by additional

---

[242] Clarke, *The Greenes of Rhode Island*, p.xi.

[243] *Ibid*; Motts, Wayne E., To Gain a Second Star: The Forgotten George S. Greene, *GM*, Issue 3, p.65.

[244] *Ibid*, pp.xi-xii.

sorrow as George Jr. became sick and died two months later. Soon Elizabeth became ill as well. Whether she became sick due to a weakened state from giving birth to Frances or simply caught little George's illness is not known. She was unable to recover and died the day after Christmas, 1832. George, obviously distraught over recent events was forced to watch as his new son Frances become sick as well. The little boy, so new to the world and frail, succumb to his illness on 22 February 1833. Over a span of seven months George Greene watched all three of his young children and his wife of three years taken from him by disease. He was crushed emotionally and decided to resign his commission and return to Rhode Island. General Winfield Scott, understanding the depth of George's grief and not wanting to lose a valuable officer, suggested Greene take an extended leave of absence.[245]

Heartbroken, George determined to continue with his duties at Fort Sullivan. During his off hours he buried himself into the study of engineering, law, and medicine. For three years he read steadily, keeping up an intense regiment of self-improvment. In the fall of 1835, after twelve years of service, Greene, still only a first lieutenant, resigned his commission with the intent of becoming an engineer. George initially wavered somewhat, but eventually made up his mind and resigned leaving his military years behind. After turning down offers from his brothers to work in the family mill, George found employment at the Andover and Wilmington Railroad in Massachusetts as an assistant engineer. While employed with the railroad, he met the daughter of a Massachusetts congressman and state senator, Martha Barrett Dana. The two became enamored with each other and were soon married. Martha revitalized George's life, filled the void in his heart, and bore him six children. Unfortunately one child, the couple's fifth, died before it was a year old. The remaining five were no doubt a joy to Greene, and helped to ease the memory of Elizabeth and his three previously departed children.[246]

George continued his railroad work until 1846 when he became the chief civil engineer of the Croton Water Works for the City of New York. After relocating his growing family, he went to work trying to solve the city's serious drinking water situation. He devised a water supply system which consisted of large reservoirs in Central Park and methods for delivering water to the growing population. The plan included the installation of a ninety inch diameter wrought-iron pipe along the High Bridge across the Harlem River. Greene developed unique methods for supporting the pipe and preventing water loss due to leakage through the pipe joints. He also utilized half sleeves to join the pipes together. When the line was complete, the improvements alleviated many of the water supply problems the city had been experiencing. Greene also developed techniques for disposing of the city's sewage.[247]

---

[245] ***Electronic Source:*** http://www.warwickhistory.com/index.php?option=com_content&view=article&id=103:apponaugs-george-sears-greene-&catid=43:apponaug-village&Itemid=96, Last Accessed: 7/8/2012.

[246] *Ibid*; Motts, To Gain a Second Star, ***GM***, Issue 3, p.67.

[247] Palmer, David W., ***The Forgotten Hero of Gettysburg***, pp.47-48.

The tragedies of his pre-war existence helped make George Sears Green a gallant and determined commander. *LOC*

Although just short of his sixtieth birthday as the war was breaking, Old Man Greene, as his men would come to know him, was anything but feeble. He would prove to be a no nonsense commander who believed in the drill and training of his men. He neither sought nor won the affection of his men, but as his soldiers got to know him, they would come to respect his professionalism and skill as a commanding officer. Greene would also prove that his age was not a detriment to his leadership skills, spending extended stints in the saddle when the situation called for it. Although his age had little effect on his activity level, it could be seen in his appearance. Greene's white hair, huge mustache and beard made him easily recognizable both on and off the battlefield.[248]

Slow to step up and volunteer, Greene initially turned down offers of colonelcies in the Rhode Island, Massachusetts, and New York Militia. It's likely that his tardiness attributed to him still commanding a brigade during the spring of 1863. On 21 January 1862, Greene was made colonel of the 60th New York. The regiment had been mustered in on 30 October 1861 and when the unit's colonel was discharged, Greene stepped in and took over. An opportunity to lead the regiment in battle never arose before Greene was promoted to brigadier general on 28 April 1862 and assigned to brigade command. He first led his brigade at Cedar Mountain. As the battle progressed, Greene's division commander was wounded and his

---

[248] Tagg, ***Generals***, p.162.

replacement captured. Suddenly, he found himself in command of the division. After the battle, General Pope himself noted in his report that Greene "behaved with conspicuous gallantry." Although Pope used the same words to describe all his commanders' actions, Greene, in his first engagement had been recognized by the army's commanding general.[249]

Greene continued to lead the division through the remainder of the summer and early fall. Lightly engaged at Bull Run, the division was involved in the heavy fighting on the northern end of the field at Antietam. When the smoke cleared, Greene's command had left 1,746 casualties on the field, or in enemy hands. Shortly after the battle, General Geary, his wounds sufficiently healed, returned to the army and Greene, as Geary was his senior, returned to brigade command. Greene remained in command of his brigade until Chancellorsville when General Geary had his close encounter with the cannonball. Once again the Rhode Islander stepped up and took command of the division. His time at its head however was limited since Geary quickly returned. During the battle, Greene led his brigade in the thickest fighting, incurring more casualties than either of the divisions other two brigades.

The men of the 60th New York were probably pleased to see Greene back in command of the brigade. The entire brigade was built using five organizations from New York. In addition to the 60th, the 78th, 102nd, 137th and the 149th filled out the ranks making it a tough veteran group of Empire Staters. Greene's extended tenure at its head, and stints at the division level made him one of the few commanders in the army with whom his superiors were comfortable with at either position. Although he entered the summer at the head of a brigade, if an open spot at divisional command arose, Greene would be a serious candidate to fill the vacancy.[250]

Hooker's Command

The men of Fighting Joe Hooker's command structure had been born and raised within the shadow of the American Revolution. The sacrifice of their grandparents and in some cases their mothers, fathers, aunts and uncles were engrained in their minds. Whether or not the suffering portrayed in the story telling came bathed in blood on a battlefield, or from a rocking chair on a front porch as mothers strove to raise children in the absence of fathers, was irrelevant. Family patriarchs had reared their children on the stories of a fledgling nation struggling against a tyrannical and oppressive England to establish their great republic. These sons and grandsons were now grown men. Men who had risen to the challenge of determining whether the nation their forefathers struggled so mightily to establish could endure the ravages of civil war.

There is little doubt that life experiences had prepared General's Greene, Williams, Birney, Gibbon and other members of Joe Hooker's command structure for the work ahead. Each of Hooker's division and brigade commanders possessed

---

[249] *Ibid*; Phisterer, *NYWR*, vol.3, p.2548; *OR* vol.12, pt.2, p.134.

[250] *OR* vol.19, pt.1, p.199; *OR* vol.25, pt.2, p.583.

knowledge and skills which would help or hinder them on the field at Gettysburg. Most would show extraordinary courage and prove themselves worthy of their posts, some rising above even their own expectations. Others would demonstrate they were a liability to their men and the army.

Whether they were old West Pointers like James Barnes and "Old Pop," or youngsters such as Francis Barlow and Joseph Bartlett, all would be part of the story. Some, had reputations to establish or save and possessed the ambition to do so. Others simply thought it was the right thing to do. The pure irony of the situation was simple. The Federal armies were fighting, as Lincoln put it, to "save the Union." The president was fighting to restore the very thing their grandfathers or fathers had fought to dissolve. The Union was established when thirteen colonies separated from the English Monarchy. Now the tables were turned. Separatists were trying to break away from the Federal Union which had been built with the blood of their brethren. Complicating the issue was the scourge of slavery which hung about the neck of the country like a great albatross. The institution Old John Brown so prophetically noted moments before he was executed, would only be purged with blood.

As May turned to June, it is unlikely the men who would lead the elements of the Army of the Potomac into battle at Gettysburg had much time to contemplate the issues which precipitated the struggle. Most, like the soldiers in the ranks were more concerned with when and where they would meet Bobby Lee's army once again. Surely it would be soon. Of even greater concern however was whether the Federals would ever be able to defeat the Confederates in a pitched battle and would they be alive to celebrate the victory.

Chapter XI
Lee's Long Arm and Hooker's Superiority

> "...when you assumed command,
> ...my duties [were] made purely administrative..." [1]
> *Henry Hunt's Chancellorsville Report.*
> *1 August 1863*

A scrupulous discussion of the events leading to the Campaign and Battle of Gettysburg cannot be complete without a conversation regarding the development and state of both antagonists' artillery branches. When the Civil War began, few individuals in the North or South could have imagined the massive size of the armies which would confront one another. The image of a 100,000 plus member military organization marching, camping, scouring and fighting across the nineteenth century American landscape was unrecognizable to almost everyone, and few were aware of the enormity of events to come. Other than epic Napoleonic Campaigns, which most had only read about, the nearest point of reference was General Scott's campaign across Mexico. Scott's army was miniscule compared to a typical Civil War army as it numbered no more than 10,000 men at any time. In addition, the duration of the Mexican conflict was a meager eighteen months. The Civil War lasted for four years and saw more than one million men in uniform. Additionally, the war with Mexico was waged thousands of miles away and most Americans knew of its events weeks and sometimes months after they occurred. Comparatively, the rebellion was waged continually in almost every corner of the country; its events were conversation points for civilians, politicians and military personnel alike. For many residents of the eastern corridor between Washington and Richmond, the war came to their doorstep on a daily basis.[2]

---

[1] *OR*, vol.25, pt.1, p.252.

[2] Naisawald, L. VanLoan, *Grape & Canister: The Story of the Field Artillery of the Army of the Potomac, 1961-1865*, p.xv.

The state of readiness on both sides as hostilities began was incredibly poor. The North held a more advantageous position than the South, possessing a two to one advantage in population, and a peacetime Regular Army consisting of slightly more than 16,000 men. The South had no standing army and only state militia to rely on for immediate defense. The North however, experienced a significant setback when a great many general officers from the South resigned to cast their lot with the Southern cause. The North's resource pool of field grade officers was significantly depleted by the exodus. But, while reduced, the availability of capable officers still favored the North. Another Northern benefit was its industrialization, which allowed it to hold a significant advantage in skilled manpower. Mechanics, factory workers, and men who were good with their hands were abundant north of the Mason-Dixon Line. The Federal Army would hold a significant advantage regarding men who could produce, fix and repair the instruments of war.[3]

The Federal Gunners

The lack of preparation was even greater regarding each side's artillery organizations. Both adversaries were forced, early in the war, to deal with a deeply felt shortage of experienced artillery officers. Within the Federal service, only a few capable artillery men were available to train and develop additional officers and gunners; a problem attributed to the small size of the peacetime army and the flight of Southern born officers. Field artillery had never played an important role during previous conflicts; however, the small number of artillery units General Scott had transported to Mexico had performed yeoman service. The value placed on their effort induced a number of individual's to come to the conclusion that field artillery would indeed play a significant role during the Civil War.[4]

Initially, equipping the Federal artillery branch was not foremost in the mind of authorities. Both sides were devoid of sufficient firepower, and Northern officials saw quantity over quality as being the driving force behind the assembly of an adequate artillery wing. The issue of poor equipment was exacerbated by a number of volunteer artillery units which, with the best of intentions, brought substandard paraphernalia with them when they stepped up to help squash the rebellion. General McClellan's chief of artillery, Brigadier General William F. Barry, commented in September 1862 on the shoddy state of artillery units which arrived in Washington during the early stages of the war.[5]

---

[3] Population of the United States in 1860; Compiled from the Original Returns of the Eighth Census, p.iv; Cole, Philip M., *Civil War Artillery at Gettysburg*, p.18. According to the 1860 Census the states which chose to support the North had a population of 19,660,668 while those which formed the Confederacy possessed 10,812,232 inhabitants.

[4] Cole, *Artillery at Gettysburg*, p.19. Naisawald, *Grape & Canister*, p.xv.

[5] Cole, *Artillery at Gettysburg*, p.21.

"About one-quarter of all the volunteer batteries brought with them from their respective States a few guns and carriages, but they were nearly all of such peculiar caliber as to lack uniformity with the more modern and more serviceable ordnance with which I was arming the other batteries, and they therefore had to be withdrawn and replaced by more suitable material. While about one-sixth came supplied with horses and harness, less than one-tenth were apparently fully equipped for service when they reported to me, and every one of those required the supply of many deficiencies of material and very extensive instruction in the theory and practice of their special arm."[6]

Barry took over as McClellan's top artillery officer the day McClellan assumed command of the Military Division of the Potomac on 25 July 1861. Four days after the Federal disaster at Bull Run, Barry noted, "the whole field artillery of his [McClellan's] command consisted of no more than parts of nine batteries or thirty pieces of various and in some instances unusual and unserviceable calibers. Most of these batteries," the general continued, "were also of mixed calibers, and they were insufficiently equipped in officers and men, and in horses, harness and material generally."[7]

Going immediately to work, Barry began the herculean effort of building an effective Federal artillery force for McClellan's organizing army. He submitted to his commander a series of nine points to be followed in constructing the army's artillery which McClellan fully supported. Under the plan, Berry projected the as yet unnamed Army of the Potomac would require a minimum of two and one half guns for every 1,000 infantrymen. Every effort would be made to assemble every battery using six guns, but if batteries of fewer guns were organized, none would be allowed to contain less than four pieces. To the organization requirements was added the stipulation that all guns of a battery would be of the same caliber making ammunition easier to procure.

Barry believed that weapons and materials used to assemble the artillery should be limited to material which could currently be processed and supplied through the Ordnance Department. "That the proportion of rifled guns should be restricted to the system of the U. S. Ordnance Department," Barry suggested, "and of Parrott, and of smooth bore to be exclusively the 12-Pounder gun of the model of 1857, variously called the 'gun-howitzer,' the 'light 12-pounder,' or the 'Napoleon.'" Barry also noted that any smoothbore howitzers could be utilized for "special service."[8]

---

[6] *OR* vol.5, p.68.

[7] Cole, ***Artillery at Gettysburg***, p.21.

[8] *OR* vol.5, p.67.

Determining how many guns would be required to outfit a force the size of the Army of the Potomac was simple compared to how the batteries were dispersed and who would control them. A chain of command to provide optimum deployment and control of the artillery, although seemingly obvious, was not as straight forward as some believed. Civil War artillery fought in a rather distinct manner and finding the proper blend of infantry and artillery on the firing line would prove difficult. Infantry and cavalry organizations typically operated as large, cohesive groups and tended to remain intact as they fought. Artillery initially operated in a reverse manner, characteristically being spread around a battlefield. Batteries were, on many occasions, deployed in an arbitrary manner, often being sent to locations that were in jeopardy, causing loss of cohesiveness. In such an environment, it was impossible for any existing centralized artillery command structure to exercise control over the batteries. Additionally, it was nearly impossible to enforce regulations within the batteries. While on the march it was difficult for officers to control straggling. It was also difficult to inspect limbers and caissons for proper loading or manage the proper care and maintenance of equipment. The welfare of a battery's horses also suffered in such an environment. The dispersed nature bread lapses in discipline which the command structure was ineffective in regaining. Compounding the problem was the even greater dispersed nature of the resupply system. Once a battery had exhausted its ammunition, it had to be withdrawn from its position since resupply was seldom if at all quickly obtained. During the early months of the war, artillery ammunition and supplies were typically included in the army's general supply train of the infantry organization to which they were attached. The problems associated with this disjointed method of artillery supply were not corrected until shortly before the Battle of Gettysburg.[9]

General Barry thought the most effective placement for Federal artillery would be at the division level. Within his proposal to McClellan, he presented the concept of four batteries for each division with at least one of the batteries being associated with the Regular Army. Barry also placed the captain of the Regular battery in overall command of the four units. This was a prudent move which allowed inexperienced volunteers to associate with an experienced, militarily trained artillery commander. "[I]nstruction in the theory and practice of gunnery," Barry noted, "as well as in the tactics of the arm, was to be given to the officers and non-commissioned officer of the volunteer batteries by the study of suitable text-books and actual recitations in each division, under the direction of the regular officer commanding the divisional artillery." Barry also made allowances for providing artillery to an army corp. "In the event of several divisions constituting an army corps, at least one-half of the divisional artillery... [will] constitute the reserve artillery of the corps." A general Artillery Reserve was also provided for the "whole army ... [and] should consist of 100 guns, and should comprise, besides a sufficient number of light mounted batteries, all of the guns of position, and until the cavalry massed all the horse artillery." He also proposed a fifty piece siege

---

[9] Cole, *Civil War Artillery*, pp.32-33.

train which eventually expanded to 100 guns due to requirements precipitated by the siege of Yorktown.[10]

Although General Barry put together what seemed to be a solid artillery organizational structure, problems were discovered as the arrangement was implemented. One difficulty faced by battery commanders was their low rank. With experience came an understanding of how and where guns could be best placed on a field of battle to provide maximum effect; however, on many occasions officers from nearby infantry or cavalry commands overruled gunners and placed batteries in locations which limited their effectiveness. Because the batteries were placed within divisions and reported upward through the command structure, they often had little if any say in where their guns should be positioned. In addition, commanders were reluctant to send their guns away to threatened points along the battlefront, citing possible threats to their position.[11]

Compounding the problem was a severe lack of advancement opportunities. The small, peacetime Federal army could not keep pace with the demand for educated artillery officers needed to train and drill the influx of volunteer units. The situation was made worse by the elimination of field grade officers within the organizations. In 1862, the War Department issued orders which effectively eliminated any advancement opportunities in the Federal artillery. The orders were essentially an edict indicating that field officers were not needed in the artillery. Field officers, which were any command grade rank above captain were determined to be an unnecessary expense. Promotions to any rank above captain would no longer be confirmed. If an officer sought a higher grade, and most generally did, he was forced to transfer out of the artillery to the cavalry or infantry. The order resulted in a flood of capable officers requesting and receiving transfers, resulting in the artillery wing losing many good and capable men. Most notably was John Gibbon, the man who had literally written the book on artillery. To make things worse, no steps were taken to assure artillery units were properly manned. On many occasions, men from infantry regiments were temporarily assigned to the guns during battle, stripping many regiments already reduced through attrition of much needed manpower.[12]

---

[10] *OR* vol.5, p.67. Barry summarized his nine points in a report written at the request of General McClellan on 1 September 1862. The nine points Barry provided in his report differ slightly from the points Naisawald documents in ***Grape & Canister***. Although slight variances exist, the main points of the document are consistent and unaltered.

Barry's note regarding the massing of cavalry refers to the early war practice of distributing the army's cavalry to smaller units and utilizing it as a guarding force as opposed to a fighting force.

[11] Murray, R. L., ***Artillery Tactics of the Civil War: A Study of the Tactical Use of Artillery Based on the First Day's Battle at Gettysburg***, p.8.

[12] Hunt, Henry J., The First Day at Gettysburg, ***B&L***, vol.3, p.259.

By the summer of 1863, William Farquhar Barry had molded the Federal artillery into an effective and formidable arm of the Union war effort. *LOC*

With the prospects of advancement gone, many Federal artillery units evolved into tight-knit organizations. The men who remained sacrificed their own personal advancement for the good of the organization. Opportunities for glory and distinction remained, but any hope of upward mobility disappeared and eventually became an afterthought in the minds of dedicated gunners. The men learned their trade as they went and perfected their craft, often in the face of the enemy. New recruits gained insight from those who had been with the battery before they arrived. As the war progressed, slowly and methodically the artillery organizations became better at their occupation. Simply put, the men in the artillery wing of the Army of the Potomac did their jobs to the best of their abilities with little to no chance of promotion no matter how well they performed their duty. It is difficult to understand why advancement was squelched and the War Department did such an injustice to an extremely dedicated group of fighting men. The discrimination became even more preposterous when the qualifications required of an officer to command an artillery battery are considered.[13]

Graduates of the military academy were placed in one of three combat branches upon completing their education. All graduates were assigned to the infantry, cavalry or artillery, or within the noncombat branch of the engineers. Spots within the engineering ranks were coveted and reserved for graduates who had shown

---

[13]   Cole, *Civil War Artillery*, p.20.

great academic ability. A position near the top of his class and strong performances within the technical specialties of physics and mathematics normally placed a graduate on the road to the engineering corps. A cadet positioned at the other end of the spectrum, near the bottom of his class, was typically placed in the infantry. Infantry officers were not required to have technical expertise and the bottom of a graduating class was ripe with candidates. Next in line up the West Point placement hierarchy was the mounted branch. Those who graduated with a slightly higher class position than those destine for infantry service were usually given the option of joining the dragoons or the infantry. Above the cavalry and below the engineers was the artillery. Artillery officers were required to have performed well within the technical aspects of their education. They had to understand the physics of artillery and were required to have knowledge of mathematics. Short of qualifying for an engineer post, artillery officers were the most academically elite graduates of West Point. There is no question that, education wise, artillery officers were the cream of the crop within the combat branches of the Regular Army.

In addition to education, an artillery captain shouldered a greater responsibility than either of their corresponding officers in the cavalry or infantry. Within the infantry, a captain was typically responsible for a company of foot soldiers, an organization which under normal circumstances contained approximately 100 men. He was required to see to their physical needs regarding food, medical care, and comfort. He was also charged with keeping his company well equipped with the accoutrements of war, including clothing, shoes, haversacks, blankets, tents, cooking utensils or any other required articles. Finally, he had to be accountable for making sure his company had arms, ammunition and was trained to do war's bloody work. A captain of cavalry, while responsible for the requirements of a like number of men, was also responsible of equipping each man with a solid mount. Cavalry horses had to be equipped, fed, cared for and, like soldiers, had to be trained.[14]

By comparison, a Civil War artillery captain shouldered a great deal more responsibility. During war time a typical Federal artillery battery contained six guns and according to the army's own *Instruction for Field Artillery*, a battery commander was responsible for anywhere from 120 to 180 men.

> "The number of men required for the service of a battery, including non-commissioned officers and artificers, varies from *twenty* to *thirty* per piece, according to circumstances."

In addition to its captain, a battery's compliment of manpower included four lieutenants, twenty noncommissioned officers, two artificers, two buglers, fifty-two drivers and seventy cannoneers. On top of this was placed the requirements of the 110 horses needed to transport the battery. The large number of animals was necessary not only to draw the guns but also the additional wheeled articles required by the battery. Supporting the fielded pieces were twelve limbers, six caissons, two

---

[14] Kimmel, Ross M., Men and Material, *America's Civil War* (hereafter *ACW*) vol.14, no.3, p.12.

supply wagons, a battery wagon and a traveling forge. There was little doubt that a captain in command of an artillery battery shouldered more responsibility than a man of like rank commanding an infantry or even a cavalry company. But alas, the War Department saw it differently, and a captain of artillery, destined for hard work, hard fighting, and expanded responsibility, received little recognition.[15]

Members of cavalry and infantry companies all performed the same function when engaged with the enemy. Members of an artillery organization however, carried a great deal more responsibility and different responsibilities. Each gun within an artillery battery was serviced by a group of men typically called a platoon. Every man required to service a single gun or "piece," had a specific job to perform within each platoon. Commanding the men, and charged with servicing the weapon, was a corporal called a "gunner." The gunner was responsible for sighting the piece and issuing commands to the other seven members of the platoon. Two men were responsible for preparing rounds behind the gun at the platoon's limber. Four were needed to service the gun and one member transferred rounds from the men at the limber to the gun's loader. A platoon was controlled by a sergeant who was considered "chief of the piece" and responsible for overseeing the proper execution of the tasks necessary to service the gun during combat. Two platoons constituted a section which was generally under the command of a lieutenant who was responsible for the horses, caissons and limbers for both guns. Within Federal service, a battery typically contained three sections and was under the command of the battery's captain, although batteries of two to four sections were allowed.[16]

Artillerymen had to be hardy individuals and requirements were stringent and definitive. Recruitment standards outlined in the War Department's *Instruction for Field Artillery* indicated men "should be intelligent, active, muscular, well-developed, and not less than five feet seven inches high; a large proportion should be mechanics." During daily operation and combat, occasions arose when guns would need to be repositioned by hand and strong stout men were needed to perform the feat. A typical 6-Pounder was one of the lighter field weapons of the war and weighted in at almost 900 pounds, not including the weight of the carriage to which it was mounted. Within each gun's ammunition chest was nearly 400 pounds of ammunition, which also did not include the weight of the chest. As the war progressed, men of meager stature surely filtered into the ranks of depleted batteries, but physical strength and stamina would undoubtedly be a benefit to anyone attempting to shove a Civil War cannon around.[17]

---

[15] *Ibid*; French, William H., Barry, William F., and Hunt, Henry J., ***Instruction for Field Artillery***, pp.4-5.

[16] Typically a group of batteries was designated a battalion. With the definition of a battery being approximately equivalent to a company of infantry, in many instances groups of batteries were designated regiments of artillery (for example, the 1st Regiment Virginia Artillery). In most cases throughout the course of this work the terms regiment and battalion, when used in association with artillery are interchangeable except when associated with the proper name of an organization.

[17] ***Field Artillery Tactics***, pp.3, 13, 46; Kimmel, Men and Material, *ACW,* vol.14, no.3, p.12.

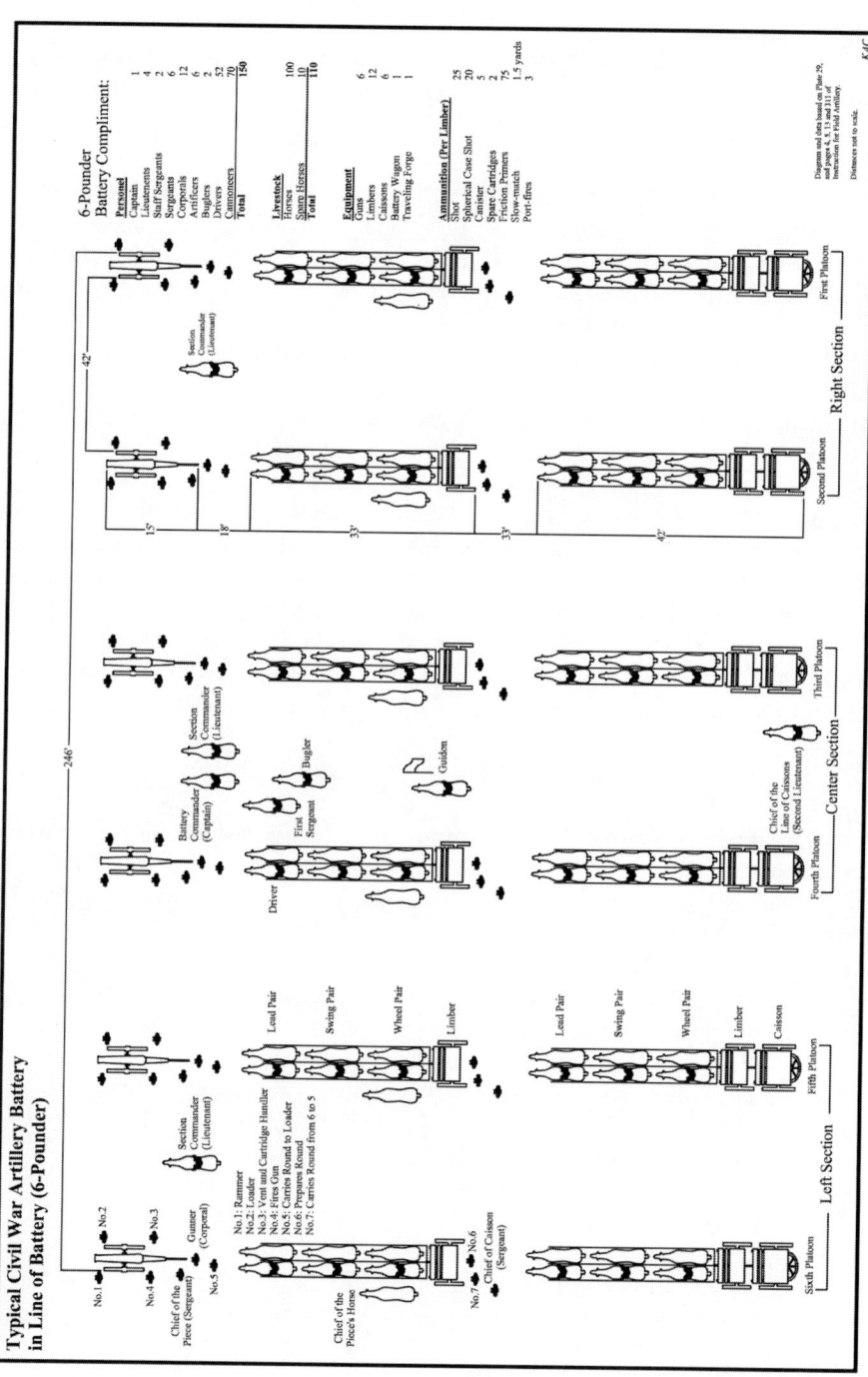

Artillery Battery

Organizational Realities

During the winter months of 1861-62, the industrial strength of the North was felt in the form of a steady influx of materials. Included in this was a consistent supply of provisions provided to the Ordnance Department which quickly transferred supplies to units in the field. When complaints of short supply were leveled, the department worked feverishly to rectify the problem and General Berry quickly saw his vision for an artillery wing grow within McClellan's army. The Washington Arsenal provided a quick transition of materials, and by the time McClellan's army left Washington for the Peninsula the artillery arm had grown significantly. The wing had expanded from its original thirty guns, 650 men and 400 horses to ninety-two batteries of 520 guns, 12,500 men and 11,000 horses. Thirty of the batteries were constructed from Regulars with the remainder being volunteers, exceeding Barry's original projections. When McClellan began the transfer of his army south, he chose to take with him an artillery force consisting of fifty-two batteries and 299 guns.[18]

While the Ordnance Department did an admirable job of supplying Barry's growing artillery requirements, they failed in the second portion of their charter. It was also the department's responsibility to investigate and develop new technology. The improvement of weapons, ammunition, and the testing of advancements for feasibility and functionality in the field, was also within their charge. This they failed at miserably for a number of reasons. The Joint Select Congressional Committee on Ordnance attributed the bulk of their failure to the department's narrow vision regarding innovation. The Ordnance Department spent seven million dollars during the war to develop advancements in weaponry. Internally, the department did little to put the money to good use. Externally, officers of the department closed their minds to ideas and innovations brought to their attention by sources which were not associated with the army or foreign militaries. Their closed minded attitude caused stagnation with regard to advancements. The Joint Committee excoriated the department's officers when, after the war, it issued its final report.

> "... These officers, educated to a specialty and proud of their positions, come to look upon themselves as possessing all the knowledge extant upon the subject of ordnance, and regard citizen inventors and mechanics who offer improvements in arms as ignorant and designing persons, and pretentious innovators, who have no claim to consideration. Instead of encouraging the inventive talent of the country, these officers seemed to have consistently discouraged it."

According to the committee, discrimination of the private sector was a serious contributor to Federal ineptness regarding any improvement to Northern ordnance during the war.[19]

---

[18]   *OR* vol.5, p.68.

[19]   Cole, *Civil War Artillery*, pp.26-27.

The first serious test of General Barry's artillery organization came on the Virginia Peninsula at Williamsburg. Three divisional artillery brigades and a battery of horse artillery participated in the action. Although the overall structure proved to be sound, the most glaring problem with the organization was quickly revealed. Divisional commanders took control of their batteries and through their ignorance of artillery, made poor decisions as to their gun's posting and use. The most egregious incident was that perpetrated by then Brigadier General Hooker. Through his own excitement and ignorance, Hooker pushed his artillery out into a swampy open area. The ground was poor and everywhere the men went with their guns, they sunk into the quagmire. Major Charles S. Wainwright, Hooker's chief of artillery, struggled mightily but was wholly unable to be effective with his guns. To Hookers credit, he took responsibility for the disaster, but the concept of division commanders in direct control of divisional batteries received its first major criticism.[20]

Issues with division command continued through the summer months of 1862. Later in the year, Henry Hunt identified a number of structural problems with the current organization. One was the lack of a supply train specifically intended to transport artillery ammunition. Hunt took steps to provide quick identification of artillery ammunition wagons after noticing that they tended to become intermixed with supply wagons while on the march. "I obtained orders from General McClellan," Hunt wrote later, "that the wagons should be covered with black water-proof covers, in order that they might be distinguished at a glance." Although the orders fell upon deaf ears at the Ordnance Department, Hunt had identified a serious resupply issue. Another difficulty encountered using general supply wagons to transport ammunition was the susceptibility of the wagons being commandeered for other purposes. On many occasions wagons were unloaded and used to transport other materials, often allowing the ammunition to be exposed to moisture, mud, or handling damage. Wagons were not waterproof and the weather often had access to cases of ammunition. Resupplying batteries from ammunition transported in wagons was also more difficult because the ammunition had to be removed from its crates and transferred to caissons before it could be transported to the batteries. A more acceptable scenario would have been to initially place all ammunition in caissons which provided better protection from the weather and could be taken directly to the batteries during battle. Most of the early war problems encountered with transportation of ammunition were rectified shortly after Chancellorsville. Special Order No.129 effectively created an independent ammunition train for each corps' artillery. "The artillery ammunition train of the batteries attached to corps will be organized and placed under the direction of the commander of artillery of the corps; the surplus will be transferred to the Artillery Reserve." However, by Gettysburg, many artillery batteries would still find their ammunition trains beyond their immediate reach, and many would be forced to pilfer rounds from the Artillery Reserve train.[21]

---

[20]   Naisawald, *Grape & Canister*, pp.37-38, 46.

[21]   *OR*, vol.19, pt.2, p.188; *OR*, vol.29, pt. 2, pp.237-238; *OR*, vol.25, pt.2, p.472.

Hooker's decentralization of the artillery prior to Chancellorsville is generally blamed, and rightly so, for its poor showing during the battle. The Federal artillery remained dispersed within the army with each division assigned a number of batteries, which continued to be under the control of the division's commander. This structure induced the treatment of artillery batteries as an afterthought, and on many occasions they were neglected or underutilized. Additionally, division commanders developed a tendency to hold their artillery as an insurance policy in case their infantry was pressed to the point of withdrawing. In such an instance, the artillery could be used to either cover a retreat or shore up a position. Divisional artillery often remained idle behind their assigned division when it could have been put to effective use elsewhere. Contained within Order 129 was a passage which rectified this situation. The artillery was reorganized into brigades with each corps assigned a brigade and a chief of artillery to direct it in battle and provide administrative oversight. The brigade's chief of artillery answered directly to the corps commander, effectively removing squabbling division commanders form dictating how, when and where artillery batteries would be positioned.[22]

When Hooker reinstated Hunt after Chancellorsville, the commanding general presented to his restored artilleryman an idea for reorganizing his batteries. Hooker's concept was, in Hunt's mind, unacceptable and appalling. "Fighting Joe" proposed each division be supplied one battery with all remaining batteries lumped into one massive Artillery Reserve. Hunt was aghast. Hooker was proposing all divisional control of any artillery be removed. This was a total and complete reversal of the system utilized at Chancellorsville, and Hunt knew if implemented it would present an even worse situation. The solution was not complete control by one entity, but rather a balance of responsibility in which all parties had well defined zones of control. Realizing Hooker's solution would create a dilemma worse than the current situation, Hunt proposed a system by which each corps would be provided a brigade of artillery with the remainder forming the reserve. Hooker, to his credit, approved the plan and Hunt began reorganizing his guns and Hooker issued Order No.129.[23]

The plan gathered the batteries of the army's seven corps and placed them in brigades with one brigade being assigned to each corps. This put them under the control of the corps' commander through his new chief of artillery. The army's cavalry received two brigades with the five remaining being consolidated into the Artillery Reserve. As previously outlined, each brigade generally consisted of five batteries with at least one of the batteries being from the Regular Army. It was probably not necessary to continue the old method of requiring a Regular battery for many of the volunteer batteries, through experience and drill, had become just as proficient or better at their craft than the Regulars. This would be the structure within the artillery wing of the Army of the Potomac when it arrived at Gettysburg.

---

[22] ***OR***, vol.25, pt.2, p.471.

[23] *Ibid*; Naisawald, ***Grape & Canister***, p.260-261.

Whether or not the organization provided a better system only time and battle would tell.[24]

Lee Grows an Arm

On 20 February 1861, the fledgling Confederate government, which then consisted of only those states seceding prior to the fall of Fort Sumter, approved an act which allowed the issuance of contracts to produce munitions of war. The act authorized the president or the secretary of war to:

> "...make contracts for the purchase and manufacture of heavy ordnance and small arms; and of machinery for the manufacture or alteration of small-arms; and munitions of war, and to employ the necessary agents and artisans for these purposes; and to make contracts for the establishment of powder mills and the manufacture of powder..."

The following day an additional act was approved establishing the Confederate War Department and created the position of secretary of war. The same day, Leroy P. Walker, a lawyer and legislator from Alabama, became the young country's first war secretary. Walker quickly went to work, taking over operations in the War Department.[25]

Seven days later, approval of an additional act provided the president power to conduct military operations within the current Confederacy's boundaries. The document also provided him the power to take charge of all military supplies and equipment which had been impounded from various Federal installations. The legislation moreover, allowed the chief executive to muster troops into Confederate service. Finally, on 6 March, an act was passed which officially established the Confederate States of America. The text included a description and outline for the creation of the young country's military. Section 5 of the legislation contained a description for a "corps of artillery" and established its manpower limits.

The corps as summarize was to consist of "...one colonel, one lieutenant-colonel, ten majors, and forty companies of artillerists and artificers." Each company or battery would be under the command of a captain and composed of two first-lieutenants, one second-lieutenant, four sergeants, four corporals, two musicians, and seventy privates. If completely filled, the manpower level specified would provide an artillery organization of 3,372 men. The limited number showed the early Confederate government's lack of understanding regarding the magnitude of the conflict. The limitations placed on rank effectively installed the same promotion restrictions upon Southern artillerist as existed in the Northern army. It was nearly impossible to promote anyone within the corps for any reason, including conspicuous service, if the ranks were full. Although an additional

---

[24] Naisawald, *Grape & Canister*, p.260-261.

[25] *OR*, Series IV, vol.1, p.106; Eicher, & Eicher, *High Commands*, p.549.

lieutenant and two majors were added on 21 August, the change did little to increase opportunities in the artillery.[26]

Unlike the Federals, the Confederates were able to identify some of the manpower issues early. In January 1862, legislation was approved to open up additional officer positions. The legislation provided the president the authority to appoint extra officers but placed limits on the number and congress was required to approve any appointments. The act allowed the president to "appoint... in the Provisional Army and in the volunteer corps, officers of the artillery above the rank of captain, without reference to the number of batteries under the actual command of the officers so appointed, not to exceed in number, however, one brigadier-general for every eighty guns, one colonel for every forty guns, one lieutenant-colonel for every twenty-four guns, and one major for every sixteen guns."[27]

The legislative work however, did little to provide organization and structure to the batteries. As such, the artillery branch of the Confederate Army went through many of the same organizational and supply difficulties as their opponent during the early stages of the war. It took failures in the field and in battle to call attention to the deficiencies of the Confederate's early war artillery. It would take a series of these difficulties and reorganizations before the Confederates, like the Federals put in place an artillery organization which allowed Lee's guns to become an effective and reliable branch of his army.

Like the Federal field artillery, Confederate light batteries would consist of six guns. Initially, the batteries were assigned to infantry brigades and received their orders from their brigade commanders. Any remaining batteries were organized into battalions or regiments and assembled into a reserve, which was placed under the command of a chief of artillery or division commander. This organization proved to be unproductive for a number of reasons. One of Longstreet's high profile artillerymen, Edward P. Alexander, commented on the incompetent nature of the organization after the war.

> "This organization was very inefficient, for the following reasons. The brigade-batteries depended for their rations, forage, and all supplies, upon the brigade-staff, and received from brigade-headquarters all orders, and thus acquired an independence of the division Chief of Artillery, which was often fostered by the Brigadier-Generals, resenting any interference with parts of their commands by junior officers, and took from the Chiefs of Artillery the feeling of entire responsibility which every officer should feel for the condition and action of his command. In action the Brigadier could not give proper supervision both to his infantry and artillery; and the Chief of Artillery with the best intentions could himself manage the batteries but inefficiently, as they were so scattered in position

---

[26] *OR*, Series IV, vol.1, pp.128, 580.

[27] *Ibid*, p.867.

along the line of battle. …under the above organization there could be but little concentration of batteries, except by bringing in the general reserve, which was commanded by the Chief of Artillery of the army. This body, however, not being in intimate relations with the infantry, who always develop the situation, and being invariably put on the march either behind the infantry commands or on some road to itself, was never promptly available on an emergency. [T]herefore that although the numerical strength of the Confederate artillery was as great in the first year of the war as ever afterwards, its weight in the scale of actual conflict is never seen to affect the result, until the second battle of Manassas."

Alexander also identified the "wretched character of the ammunition which filled its chests" as an additional culprit. However, he was quick to lay the majority of the culpability for the poor artillery performance at the feet of the organizational structure. "[A]n examination of the official reports of the battles will show," Alexander wrote, "that scattered and either uncommanded [sic] or too much commanded, as it was, there was an entire absence of that *ensemble* of action necessary to the efficiency of all arms, but peculiarly so to the artillery; and that when fought at all, it was put in only in inefficient driblets"[28]

While trial and error would eventually provide an understanding as to how batteries should be organize for maximum effect on a battlefield, outfitting Lee's gunners would be an even greater task considering the minimal industrial capabilities of the Confederacy. As the war began, the South was in dire straits regarding its ability to supply standing armies. With President James Buchanan's term in its final days, secretary of war and Southern sympathizer John B. Floyd embarked on his effort to covertly transfer as many munitions as possible to Federal arsenals and forts in the South. Floyd's intent was to allow easy access to war materials as renegade Southern states left the Union. His efforts however, would afford almost no tactical benefit as the war began. Anticipating hostilities, Federal authorities drew down many of the stores to minimal levels, limiting any booty the Southerners may have had an opportunity to seize. When the first shorts were fired, the Confederacy possessed no improved weaponry, no powder-mills, no armories, no modern cannon, and only the arsenals which the Rebels had managed to seize from Federal authorities. The only major supplier of Southern cannon was the Tredeger Iron Works in Richmond. Tredeger quickly transitioned its manufacturing from peaceful pursuits to the making of artillery pieces. The foundry's quick conversion and inability to procure quality iron caused performance problems with many of their early war gun tubes. Confederate Chief

---

[28] Alexander, Edward P., Confederate Artillery Service, **SHSP**, vol.11, pp.99-100; **OR**, Series IV, vol.1, p.128. Emphasis in original.

of Ordnance Josiah Gorgas was of the belief that poor quality iron was the culprit regarding Tredegar's quality.²⁹

The task of arming an unprepared Confederacy fell to West Point graduate Gorgas. Born 1 July 1818 in Running Pumps, Pennsylvania, he relocated to New York as a teenager and entered West Point on his birthday in 1837. Graduating four years later, sixth in a class of fifty-two, Josiah was brevetted a second lieutenant in the Ordinance Department, and served there four years until he traveled to Europe to further study his craft. Returning in 1846, Gorgas served in Mexico where he received accolades for his gallantry at the siege of Vera Cruz. After the war, he saw duty at various arsenals, married the daughter of former Alabama Governor John Gayle in 1853, and received a promotion to captain in 1855. Duty in Maine and South Carolina followed his promotion. As war became a distinct possibility, the authorities transferred Gorgas back to his native state, perhaps in an effort to retain his services for the North. However, Gorgas' roots were not sufficient enough to overshadow his southern wife's loyalties, and on 3 April 1861, he resigned his commission. Five days later, acknowledging his skills, Confederate authorities appointed him chief of the Bureau of Ordnance. At the time the bureau existed almost completely on paper.³⁰

Promoted to major, Gorgas immediately went about assembling a full and complete ordnance procurement operation. He sent a representative to Europe to develop and implement foreign supply lines. He took stock of all the Confederacy's internal supplies, whether seized or purchased, and took steps to properly account for and monitor them to make sure they were not wasted or dispersed. Gorgas worked to establish the South's own internal supply by identifying powder mills, investigating sources for copper and lead, and locating arsenals. He also developed a distribution system in order to transfer materials to processing locations, supply depots and finally to unit in the field. He fashioned the Mining and Niter Bureau and the Bureau of Foreign Supplies and took steps to establish a service for running the tight Federal blockade which had been placed along the coastline.³¹

Regarding field artillery, things were indeed bleak for the Confederates during the early months of the war. Of the material seized at Federal forts and arsenals, only thirty-five guns were found suitable for use as field artillery, although enough ammunition for sixty field guns was discovered at the Baton Rouge Arsenal. Of the pieces confiscated, none were assembled into functional batteries. Of the powder found within the boundaries of the Southern states, 60,000 pounds captured at Norfolk was of a modern composition. The remainder was left over from the Mexican War. Although a few volunteer batteries arrived with serviceable guns,

---

[29] Cole, *Civil War Artillery*, pp.22-23; Wise, Jennings Cropper, ***The Long Arm of Lee or The History of the Artillery of the Army of Northern Virginia***, p.36. The extent of Floyd's effort to move guns and munitions south can be found in a review of his correspondence from the months of November and December of 1860. *OR*, Series III, vol.1, pp.1-31.

[30] Wise, ***Long Arm of Lee***, pp.34-35; Eicher, & Eicher, ***High Commands***, p.260.

[31] Wise, ***Long Arm of Lee***, pp.35-36.

most of their tack, saddles, blankets and other artillery supplies were wholly inadequate. To make matters worse, as late as September 1861, the government controlled only one plant capable of manufacturing field gun carriages. Although plans were underway to increase its capacity, at the time it was only capable of producing one carriage a day, a production rate which would not be adequate.[32]

Although things looked bleak, Gorgas and his department worked feverishly to prepare the Southern Confederacy for war and, within what seemed too short a period for substantial accomplishments, managed to put the South on a footing to produce war materials. During the first year of conflict, rolling mills and foundries were established in Selma, Alabama, Richmond, Atlanta and Macon, Georgia. Arsenals and armories were established all across the South including depots in Richmond, Fayetteville, Charleston and Augusta with a number of cities having only arsenals established. In Savannah, Montgomery and Augusta, powder mills were established. By early 1862, Gorgas and his Ordnance Department had the Confederacy in a position to hold their own on the battlefield with the ordnance and supplies he was able to provide. After the war, Alexander expressed nothing but praise for Gorgas and the Confederate Ordnance Department's accomplishments.[33]

> "On assuming its duties at the commencement of the war, its admirable chief, ... J. Gorgas, might well have hesitated at the task before him. The emergencies and demands of the war were already upon him, and the immense supplies which it became his duty to provide were of a character which the South had neither the factories nor the skilled workmen to produce. With scarcely a single assistant instructed in the peculiar and technical details which are the first elements of an ordnance officer's attainments, and without even an office organization for the transaction of business, the whole machinery of a department was to be organized... With indefatigable energy... Gorgas formed and put in motion this whole machinery, selecting his important subordinates with such excellent judgment that the efficiency of the ordnance service was not only always equal to the demand upon it, but, in spite of continually increasing demands and decreasing resources, and in spite of serious interferences with the skilled labor of the arsenals and workshops by continued conscriptions, its efficiency continually increased, and all of its functions were faithfully performed as long as there was an army to need them. It is true that the Confederate armies were never in condition to use ammunition as lavishly as the enemy frequently did, but the supply never failed to be equal to the actual emergency, and no disaster was ever to be attributed to its scantiness. Wherever insufficiency was apprehended and

---

[32] *Ibid*, pp.37-38, 41.

[33] *Ibid*, pp.40-41;

economy imposed, in fact the scarcity arose far more from the lack of transportation to carry it with the army than from inability of the arsenals to furnish it."[34]

It can be safely said that if not for the efforts of Gorgas and his staff the Confederate war effort may well have floundered before it began. Gorgas can be given much of the credit for effectively putting the Confederacy on a war footing and arming its soldiers. After First Bull Run, as General McClellan labored through the winter to assemble and equip his army, Major Gorgas worked to arm the Southerners. During the late winter and early spring of 1862, while Lincoln pushed "Little Mac" to engage the enemy, Gorgas continued his work. Thanks to Gorgas' efforts, and McClellan's slowness in marching to meet his enemy, by the time the Federal commander moved, the Rebels were ready to meet him. His industrious efforts make him one of the Confederacy's unsung heroes of not only the Peninsular Campaign, but the entire war.

Pendleton's Trial and Error Process

With the Ordnance Department in Gorgas' capable hands, attention was turned toward the inefficient Confederate artillery's organization. A set of proposed regulations, which General Pendleton submitted to Lee were designed to improve the cohesiveness of the artillery. On 22 June 1862, Lee incorporated a number of these suggestions in General Order No.71.

> 4. The artillery of the army is necessarily so extensively diffused that it becomes essential for its due efficiency there should be in its administration rigid system.
>
> 5. The chief of artillery in each division will have charge of all the batteries thereto attached, whether acting with brigades or held in reserve. A battery duly assigned to a brigade will, until properly relieved, report to and be controlled by the brigade commander. It must also, however, report to and be inspected by the division chief of artillery, as he may require. When a brigade battery needs relief it will, when practicable, be made to change places with one of those belonging to the division reserve. Should this be impracticable, application, authorized by the division commander, must be made to the army chief of artillery for temporary relief from the general reserve.

Basically, the order placed all divisional batteries in both the artillery and the divisional reserve under the control of the division's chief of artillery. The army's Artillery Reserve was placed under the command of Pendleton, the army's chief of artillery. Pendleton also retained overall responsibility for all the army's guns. To his credit, he was quick to recognize the benefits of establishing not only a general

---

[34] Alexander, Confederate Artillery Service, *SHSP*, vol.11, pp.112-113.

reserve but also divisional artillery. At the time, this structure was essentially the same as the Federal system with the difference being the Federal's utilization of a corps reserve instead of a general reserve which the Confederates employed.[35]

With the artillery reorganized, Pendleton began the task of refitting for field service many of the batteries located in and around Richmond. A number of these batteries contained large, heavy guns which were not acceptable for service with a quick moving, mobile army. Pendleton mustered out some of the men, reducing each targeted battery's officer count, and refitted them with weapons better suited for field service. He also consolidated a number of substandard batteries and shored up experienced units. In a letter to his daughter Pendleton detailed his efforts and obligations.[36]

> "... The tedious duty to which I referred just now was inspecting a number of heavy-artillery companies in the different redoubts around Richmond, to ascertain which of them ought to be retained in commission and which broken up, their officers reduced to the ranks, and their man distributed among other companies. ...If I can break up four or five of these light-artillery companies, men enough will be distributable to fill up most of the veteran companies whose ranks have been thinned by the severities of long and arduous service..."[37]

Many inferior batteries were indeed broken up and the men were used to supplement batteries which Pendleton chose to retain. Unfortunately some of Pendleton's decisions were not well received by Lee's field commanders. For instance, he took three batteries from Longstreet's Division which Longstreet felt were in fine order, leaving him with five, two of which the general felt were not suitable for field duty. One was without horses and the other was fitted with guns "too heavy for the field."[38]

Within his new structure, Pendleton still allowed the retention of artillery batteries by brigades which continued to hinder the effectiveness of his guns. Of the fifty-one batteries assigned directly to infantry units, forty-five were dedicated to the support of brigades. The remaining six batteries were organized into a battalion attached to Longstreet's Division. Seventeen additional batteries were assembled into the General Reserve consisting of five battalions of which four contained three batteries while the fifth contained five. Since by this time most Confederate batteries contained only four guns, the typical strength of a battery

---

[35] *OR*, vol.11, pt.3, pp.612-613; Wise, **Long Arm of Lee**, pp.199-200.

[36] Wise, **Long Arm of Lee**, p.200.

[37] Lee, **Pendleton**, pp.190-191.

[38] *OR*, vol.11, pt.3, pp.686-688.

was approximately seventy-five men, providing a total of approximately 5,100 men manning the sixty-eight batteries.[39]

Shortly after the battle of Sharpsburg, Lee requested additional thoughts from Pendleton for once again restructuring of the army's artillery. Pendleton submitted a lengthy report on 2 October which once again proposed the elimination of some batteries and the distribution of their manpower compliment among the remaining ones. He prefaced his proposal with a preamble which outlined his thoughts and opinions.

> "It is clear that our service is now encumbered by too many artillery companies, of which some have never been strong enough, some are commanded by inadequate officers, and some, thought well officered and entitled to honor for excellent service, are so reduced in men and horses as scarcely to leave room for a hope of their restoration to efficiency. It becomes, therefore, an imperative duty to relieve the service and the Confederacy of this burden, so expensive every way, but especially in its enormous consumption of horses, if such relief can be legally and justly effected. The only practicable mode of accomplishing the object is to determine by the fairest standard that can be selected what companies should be dispensed with, to relieve from duty the officers of such, and to assign the men and equipments [sic] to other companies retained. In endeavoring to reach right conclusions in the premises, I have sought with great care the actual merit and condition of the several batteries connected with this army; and though it were vainly presumptuous to suppose that I had escaped error, I feel assured there is as little mistake as the complexity of the case and the limited time for investigation fairly admit."

Pendleton followed his justification with three pieces of criteria which he used "to determine right conclusions..." The first was the quality of the battery's previous service. "Laudable service undoubtedly entitles a company to honorable continuance," the general wrote, but only if the battery was not disqualified by either of Pendleton's other two conditions. The second criterion was based on the quality and abilities of the battery's officers. If the command structure was worth retaining, having proven themselves efficient in administration and combat leadership, they deserved retention. Thirdly, if the first two criterions were met, the battery should be retained; if both were not met the battery should be disbanded and merged with another. If either of the first two, but not both, were not met then the decision would be more difficult.[40]

---

[39] Wise, *Long Arm of Lee*, p.206. The numbers presented do not include three batteries assigned to General Magruder's command.

[40] *OR*, vol.19, pt.2, pp.646-647.

Using his three criteria, Pendleton proceeded to sequentially outline for Lee his recommendations. The general spared no one from his scrutiny. Not even the famous Washington Artillery, which Pendleton proposed reducing from four batteries to two, was exempt. The ten companies of the 1st Regiment Virginia Artillery were targeted for reduction to six. Pendleton's axing of batteries and officers continued throughout almost all areas of the artillery. All over the army battalions which were deemed undermanned and under equipped were reduced by one or two batteries, and their men and guns redistributed. The members of disbanded batteries were either reassigned within the battalion to bring the remaining batteries up to strength or to other battalions to accomplish the same goal. By the time Pendleton was finished, it seemed as if no one had been exempt from the restructuring.[41]

After Pendleton submitted his recommendations, Assistant Adjutant General Chilton wrote Special Order No.209 which, although it discarded Pendleton's minutia, contained the same basic language. Both documents were submitted to the secretary of war on 4 October and arrived in Richmond three days later.[42]

Officially, Lee was required to have the proposed changes reviewed and approved by the government. Unofficially however, he pushed forward with the changes, the only deviation being the retention of the four battery structure in the Washington Artillery. Hurt feelings and disappointed officers and men abounded. The ultimate goal was no doubt lost on the men who in their hearts believed they had performed good service but had become the victims of Pendleton's cutback. The purpose of creating a more efficient and effective artillery arm was secondary to the redistributed or dismissed men. When the changes were complete, the artillery wing of the army was nineteen batteries smaller, having been reduced from seventy-three to fifty-four.[43]

When the Richmond authorities reviewed Lee's submittal of Pendleton and Chilton's documents, they refused to sanction the changes. Replying to Lee on 8 October Secretary of War George W. Randolph noted that he had received Lee's communication. "[I]n reference to the reorganization of your artillery," Randolph wrote, "...feeling the imperative necessity of the measure, but doubting its strict conformity to law, I deem it best to refrain from any decision of the question." Lee assuredly understood the political nature of Randolph's refusal to sanction the changes. His greatest concern however, was the effectiveness of his army and not whether the Confederate government agreed with his handling of it. Lee, rightly so, moved forward with the changes, the result of which was an improvement in the functionality and effectiveness of his guns.[44]

Slowly, through attrition, poor performance, and reorganization, the concept of attaching artillery batteries to brigades gradually began to disappear from the Army

---

[41] *Ibid*, pp.647-648.

[42] *Ibid*, pp.652-654.

[43] Wise, ***Long Arm of Lee***, p.337-339.

[44] ***OR***, vol.19, pt.2, p.656.

of Northern Virginia. However, toward the end of 1862 or early the following year, Lee once more express to Pendleton his continued disappointment with the performance of the artillery, which he attributed to its brigade and divisional organization. Pendleton agreed, and sought input from other knowledgeable artillery men such as Alexander and Colonel Crutchfield. When his inquiries and thoughts were met with agreement, he developed another proposal to improve the artillery's functionality through its restructuring, which he submitted to Lee on 11 February.

"Burdened as are brigade and division commanders," Pendleton noted, "they can scarcely extend to batteries thus assigned that minute supervision which they require…" Pendleton also commented on supply issues writing, "supply officers, whose chief care lies with considerable bodies of infantry, cannot devote to one or more batteries the time and attention they imperatively need." He also observed the inability of batteries to be efficiently moved to where they were most needed because the possessive nature of brigade and division commanders, noting they felt a "vested right was violated."

"Toward remedying these evils," Pendleton suggested, "it is respectfully proposed that in each corps the artillery be arranged into battalions, to consist for the most part of four batteries each, a particular battalion ordinarily to attend a certain division, and to report to, and receive orders from, its commander, though liable to be divided, detached, &c., as to the commanding general or corps commanders may seem best…" Pendleton, in order to retain any camaraderie which had developed within current organizations, also proposed to retain the association of batteries, where practical, intending to keep batteries which had previously served together in a battalion. To command each new battalion, Pendleton proposed two field officers, an ordnance officer and a bond officer to deal with supply issues.

Within the document, Pendleton also presented a proposed organization consisting of one battalion for each division and a corps reserve to consist of two additional battalions. Divisional battalions would be designated using the initial of its commanding general, while reserve battalions would be designated utilizing the battalion commander's name. To provide overall direction, Pendleton chose to retain the corps level chief of artillery. The position would be charged with providing high level vision of artillery requirements and a vehicle to overrule obstinate division commanders who may make efforts to retain the services of their batteries when they were ordered away.[45]

Pendleton's proposed structure incorporated four divisional and two reserve battalions within Longstreet's First Corps. Longstreet's force was comprised of twenty-six batteries containing 112 guns. Within the Second Corps were a like number of divisional battalions with two in the corps reserve. Jackson's command would contain an additional battery within his battalions, pushing his gun total to 116. The General Reserve was assembled from two battalions with three batteries each containing a total of thirty-six pieces. When totaled, Lee's artillery wing,

---

[45] ***OR***, vol.25, pt.2, pp.614-619.

excluding the horse artillery, would contained 264 guns within Pendleton's new system.[46]

Four day after his proposal was submitted, Pendleton saw it implemented almost verbatim with only the naming convention for the battalions being neglected. The final two sentences of the order contained the critical element of the restructuring. "All the battalions of each corps will be under the command of, and will report to, the chief of artillery for the corps. The whole in both corps will be superintended by, and report to, the general chief of the artillery [Pendleton]." Lee waited until 2 March to submit Pendleton's promotion list in order to execute his own investigation of the officers tapped out for elevation before he provided the list to Richmond. It would be 16 April before the full organization, with the newly promoted officers, was in place. The organization would receive its first test at Chancellorsville.[47]

Lack of Horses and Dissimilar Guns

While the lack of horses and their poor condition was a problem for Lee during the winter of 1862-63, difficulties were even weightier within the artillery. The situation had shown itself in 1862 and continued to worsen as the year progressed. Providing mobility to an artillery battery required significantly more horses than a company of cavalry. Cavalry however, due to their system of resupply, garnered the cream of the crop regarding available livestock. Early in the war most Confederate artillery units were able to procure full compliments of horses, but as the war extended, it became more difficult to find worthy animals. Unlike Rebel cavalry, gunners were typically not allowed to leave their units to procure replacement horses. The supply of draft animals, which could be purchased or simply taken from local farms as the army moved about, began to dry up. With the local system deteriorating, the later months of 1862 found the lack of horses for artillery units growing to a serious issue. For example, late in September, shortly after Sharpsburg, one group of eight batteries was in need of 128 horses to make it serviceable with another 204 needed to effectively mount the batteries. Some batteries were only able to count 20 serviceable horses and many of these had defective harnesses and tack. By the spring of 1863, not only was it more difficult to procure enough animals to fill a battery's compliment, most new horses were of poor quality. As the war continued, and the supply dwindled, animals better suited to be put out to pasture were incorporated into the artillery. In some instances even mules or other draft animals were utilized.[48]

On 1 October, 1862, Lee took steps to provide for the general welfare of his army's artillery horses. Within Order No.115, Chilton wrote and distributed Lee's wishes for the treatment of the animals. "The general commanding," he noted, "desires to impress upon all officers in charge of horses of the army the urgent

---

[46] Wise, *Long Arm of Lee*, p.419.

[47] *OR*, vol.25, pt.2, pp.625-626, 651, 728-729; Wise, *Long Arm of Lee*, p.419.

[48] Wise, *Long Arm of Lee*, pp.111, 327-328.

necessity of energetic and unwearied care of their animals, and of preventing their neglect and abuse." Lee, chose to be extremely specific regarding the treatment of artillery horses.

> III. Artillery horses especially must be kept in good condition. To this end the chief of artillery will personally supervise all the reserve, and see that all instances of neglect are corrected, by penalty when deserved, and by suitable provisions when the evil has resulted from necessity. He will cause every practicable arrangement to be made for supplying the horses of his command with sufficient and suitable food, sparing no effort or reasonable expense.
>
> IV. Division commanders are reminded of their responsibility for the condition of their artillery, and especially their horses. On the march they will see that halting places are selected for their batteries where water and food can be obtained. They will charge their chiefs of artillery to secure, by ridged personal attention, adequate supply of forage from the quartermaster to whom that duty is committed. They will see that, when in the vicinity of the enemy, every possible opportunity is improved for resting, watering and feeding their horses. When the army is quiet, division artillery will be diligently cared for by division commanders and their chiefs of artillery. Their batteries must be kept under control, and not allowed to scatter at will. If scarcity of forage renders impracticable a full supply for the horses retained with divisions, and it becomes necessary to send batteries elsewhere for sufficient food, they must go together with proper officers to supply and supervise them, and report statedly to their division commander or they must be sent to the reserve camp to be there supplied, and report immediately to the general chief of artillery.
>
> V. Horses worn down, past recovery, will be turned into the chief quartermaster, who will send them off immediately, under proper regulations, to good pasturage, where they must be attended to and cared for under the supervision of responsible agents.
>
> VI. Battery horses will in no instance be ridden, except while in use by the usually mounted non-commissioned officers of the company, and by them only on duty. Their use, except with the battery, and them in battery service, is strictly prohibited, and chiefs of artillery will arrest and bring to trial all violating this order.[49]

---

[49] *OR*, vol.19, pt.2, pp.642-643.

Lee's concern for his animals throughout the winter can be seen within the tone of the order. He understood his horses moved the army and he was determined to make sure his officers understood their value as well. Lee also firmly believed that like his soldiers, his animals were God's creatures and deserved to be treated as such.

From a Confederate artilleryman's point of view, nothing was more coveted than the fine, sturdy horses use to draw Northern batteries. So desirable were the steeds that advanced teams, organized from a battery's drivers, were instructed to take proactive action regarding any opportunity which arose in battle, to capture elements of an opposing battery. Such teams could quickly take advantage of any situation and hopefully capture any high quality Federal horse which became available. The drivers would stay alert during any engagement and when a chance of capture enemy equipment and horses presented itself; they would rush forward into an enemy battery and extract the vulnerable horses and, if possible any guns. Drivers within Rebel batteries were no longer simply observers of a battle. They were now active participants. The concept proved successful on many occasions, but the deficiency of horses was so severe, the activity did little to alleviate the problem.[50]

Within the Federal service, most field artillery batteries contained six cannons and in almost all cases the guns were of the same make and model and used the same ammunition. This simplified ammunition resupply and servicing during battle. The Confederates however, on very few instances utilized batteries of six guns, with most containing only four. A further drawback was the continual mixture of uncommon gun models and calibers within batteries. By the fall of 1862, only three batteries contained guns of the same type and two of the three contained only two guns each. The mixed batteries, presented unique problems regarding ammunition resupply. Limbers and caissons which were not properly marked or placed during battle could cause delays in getting ammunition to guns capable of firing it.[51]

Alexander called attention to the severity of the mixed battery problem after the war.

> "[T]he variety of calibers comprised in the artillery was throughout the war a very great inconvenience, and materially affected the efficiency of the ordnance-service both in the quantity of ammunition carried and the facility with which it was supplied. At the commencement of the war this variety was often almost ludicrously illustrated by single batteries of four guns, of four different calibers, and it was only after the battalions were well organized in the winter of 1862 that anything was done to simplify this matter."

---

[50] Wise, *Long Arm of Lee*, p.111; *OR*, Series IV, vol.2, p.194.

[51] Wise, *Long Arm of Lee*, pp.284-285.

However, the practice must not have been a huge stumbling block for Pendleton. Even after the procurement or capture of guns in quantities which would have allowed the shuffling of guns to provide batteries with common weapons, the practice was allowed to continue.[52]

Preparations for Active Campaigning

Sometime during the spring, probably around the middle of May, Lee expressed to Pendleton a desire to have the artillery in top condition. On 19 May, Pendleton sent a message to Longstreet's chief of artillery, Colonel Ruben Lindsey Walker, indicative of others sent to officers commanding artillery. "He [Lee] wishes the artillery gotten in the best possible condition for service without an hour's delay, and ready to move at very short notice. The need of good grazing requires the battalions to be somewhat scattered," he continued, "but let not this prevent you keeping them all constantly within call and under regular inspection, so that you will know always the strength, &c., of each battery." Pendleton also requested reports on the condition of each command and for the commanding officers to pay specific attention to the wellbeing of their horseflesh.[53]

Although the organizational issues which plagued the artillery's performance had been rectified, some battalion commanders either failed to understand the implications of the command structure changes or simply chose to assume that the status quo would be maintained. Writing to one of his battalion commanders on 19 May, Pendleton reinforced the concept of centralized artillery. "I thought you clearly understood the views which I expressed in our conversation a few days ago, as the direction also of the commanding general, viz, that there no longer exists a fixed relation between any infantry division and any one artillery battalion. To prevent the continuation of the idea of any such relation, and to bring your battalion more into association with the others, so as to secure more thorough unity of administration in the artillery of the First Corps, and at the same time to get your horses into new pasturage,…" It was obvious that while the army's high command understood the intent of the reorganization, some battalion commanders were still beholden to their divisions. It would take the passage of time before the associations were adequately severed.[54]

Pendleton issued another order on 2 June abolishing the army's Artillery Reserve and distributing the battalions to the corps. The order effectively stripped him of any leadership responsibility. Previously the army's chief of artillery, he reverted back to that roll, although he had no command. It's quite possible Lee, understanding Pendleton's limitations, chose not to displace his old friend and used the restructuring to limit Pendleton's responsibilities. Keeping Pendleton as his chief allowed Lee to take advantage of his administrative skills. However, although stripped of his position, Pendleton still retained some authority. In General Order

---

[52] Alexander, Confederate Artillery Service, ***SHSP***, vol.11, p.109.

[53] ***OR***, vol.25, pt. 2, pp.808-809.

[54] *Ibid.*

No.69, Lee outlined two spheres of responsibility, one for his corps commanders and one for Pendleton. These two areas of accountability contradicted each other and placed the effectiveness of Lee's gun in jeopardy. "For harmony of movement on the march and in action on the battle-field, the artillery of each corps will be under the orders of corps commanders." Lee then gave Pendleton the power to override the desire of his corps commanders by allowing the chief of artillery to confiscate any gun or battery he thought necessary for another task. "The general chief of artillery, acting under the immediate orders of the commanding general may, in battle, command the artillery on any part of the line, and use it at such points as may be needed." If Pendleton determined guns were needed elsewhere Lee allowed him the latitude and authority to move them as he wished. The order placed the disposition of any artillery battery, during battle, under the final jurisdiction of Pendleton. It was an immense amount of responsibility for a man who had continuously proven he possessed no head for tactics. The statement would have profound consequences in a few weeks on the Gettysburg battlefield.[55]

Although Pendleton's performance in battle was anything but satisfactory, his efforts during 1862 and the first months of 1863 showed he understood the potential of artillery and his ideas about its organization helped improved the branch's capabilities. Without his administrating skills, Confederate artillery quite possibly could have remained stagnant and lagged even further behind its Federal counterpart regarding effective deployment. Instead, its tactical utilization rivaled that of its antagonist and while the quality and quantity of materials and ammunition may have been somewhat lacking, its tactical ability in the face of the enemy was, by the middle of 1863, up to par.

The Results

While a number of experts believe the Federal artillery at Gettysburg was superior to Rebel guns, the only explicit advantage it held was in regard to the number of guns it possessed. Due to the efforts of men like Union General William F. Barry and Confederate Captain Josiah Gorgas, both armies were never in the position of being devoid of adequate ammunition supplies as battle neared. Other claims include Federal superiority in ammunition, handling and mobility. While arguments can be made with respect to all three elements, only the debate regarding superior Federal ammunition could be won. Both sides had proven to each other that their guns were not to be taken lightly, and each organization had established and improved on its reputation. Defensively, massed artillery had demonstrated the ability to crush the spirit of an assaulting throng. While on offense, artillery from both sides had proven its ability to damage or weaken enemy positions prior to attack. Artillery also provided emotional support to the foot soldier. A hefty battle line supported by massed artillery had a tendency to encourage or dishearten infantry, depending on whether the infantry was supporting it or facing it.

---

[55] Wert, Old Artillery, *CWTI*, vol.13 No.3, p.11; Faust, **Encyclopedia**, p.570; *OR*, vol. 51, pt.2, p.721

The late spring of 1863 saw both antagonists well along a path to rectifying the command and control difficulties they experienced within their artillery branches throughout the first two years of war. The desire to control artillery on the battlefield had created internal struggles between commanders as to how the guns could be best used. Inexperience had prompted both antagonists to begin the conflict with artillery batteries scattered about and distributed among various infantry regiments. As the months progressed, batteries were slowly removed from the control of smaller units. Initially, some batteries remained detached, others were assigned to independent brigades while still others were placed in battalions and assigned to divisions. Although the Federals were somewhat swifter in identifying the value of artillery brigades, centralized command control, resupply and logistics, the Confederate authorities soon came to the same conclusions and followed a similar path.

Chapter XII
The Gunners

> "Burdened as are brigade and division commanders, they can scarcely extend to batteries thus assigned that minute supervision which they require..."[1]
>
> William Pendleton to R.E. Lee
> 11 February 1863

The ramifications of the 1862 War Department order restricting promotions could be seen in the organizational structure of the Army of the Potomac. Buy June 1863 only two of the army's artillery brigades were commanded by colonels. In fact, of the remaining eleven artillery brigades with the army, two were commanded by majors, eight by captains and two by lieutenants. With the exception of Chief of Artillery Hunt, Brigadier General Robert Ogden Tyler, at the head of the Regular Division of the Artillery Reserve, held the distinction of being the artillery's highest ranking field officer.[2]

Reductions in infantry manpower due to battle casualties and expiring enlistments prompted corresponding reductions in each corps divisional artillery. On 12 May, Hooker issued orders executing the reductions based on General Hunt's post Chancellorsville organizational recommendations. Charged with the supply, maintenance and administration of each artillery brigade would be each corps' chief of artillery. To bolster manpower within any battery which had been reduced, men would be transferred from the corps' infantry regiments. The number of men added would be based on the quantity required to effectively service a battery's current allotment of guns. To improve ammunition supply and availability, each brigade was provided its own ammunition train. The trains were also placed under each corps' head of artillery. Extra supplies or transportation equipment not required by the brigades would be transferred to the Artillery Reserve. The reserve would also be reinforced by any unassigned batteries.[3]

A native New Yorker, Tyler was born in Hunter on 22 December 1831. Relocating to Connecticut in 1839, he received an appointment to West Point from

---

[1] *OR*, vol.25, pt.2, p.614.

[2] *OR*, vol.25, pt. 2, p.575-586.

[3] *Ibid*, p.471-472.

his adopted state and entered the academy 1 July 1849. He graduated four years later, twenty-second in a class of fifty-two. Brevetted second lieutenant, Tyler spent the majority of his prewar service on the frontier and on the west coast fighting Indians. He was assigned to quartermaster duties as the war began but on 29 August 1861, he was made colonel of the 4th Connecticut Volunteer Infantry. Tyler had spent his career in the artillery, and once at the head of the 4th, he began a campaign to have it converted into an artillery organization. His efforts were rewarded when in the winter of 1862 the 1st Connecticut Artillery was organized from the old 4th Infantry.

By the time of the Gettysburg Campaign, Robert Ogden Tyler had proven to be an effective commander of artillery. *LOC*

Tyler went to the Peninsula, where he commanded siege artillery during the investment of Yorktown. When McClellan's campaign failed to capture Richmond and his army was being evacuated, Tyler worked hard to extract the siege artillery and managed to save all but one of the big guns. Afterward, he commanded artillery in the Department of the Potomac and was promoted to brigadier general on 29 November 1862. Later, he was placed in charge of the artillery in Burnside's Center Grand Division during the Battle of Fredericksburg. During the fighting, his big 10 and 20 pounders and 4.5-inch rifles persuaded Lee to think twice about transferring men from the flanks of his army across the open ground between Hazel Run and Deep Run. Directing the action from the relative safety of Stafford Heights, Tyler's guns did good service. After spending the early months of 1863 commanding artillery in the Washington area, he returned to the Army of the Potomac and at Chancellorsville, took command of the army's Reserve Artillery. He would retain command through the remainder of May and June and would direct them as the army met Lee in Pennsylvania.[4]

---

[4]   *Ibid*; Tyler Obituary, New York Times, 2 December 1874; Eicher, & Eicher, ***High Commands***, p.539; Sifakis, ***Who was Who***, p.666; Naisawald, ***Grape & Canister***, pp.186-187.

The bulk of Hooker's 12 May order consisted of an itemized listing of officers who were instructed to report to General Tyler to assume duties with the reserve guns. Tyler's reserve contained two divisions of artillery, one of Regular Army gunners and another composed of volunteers. Within the Regular Division were two brigades built from batteries associated with the 1st, 2nd, 3rd, 4th and 5th U. S. Artilleries. Commanding the First Brigade was Captain Dunbar R. Ransom. A member of the 3rd U. S. Artillery, Ransom had managed to gain an appointment to West Point in 1847 but for some reason left three years later before graduating. In 1855 he returned to the army and was appointed a second lieutenant. He had been with the Army of the Potomac since the fighting on the Peninsula, and was performing the duties of captain of Battery C of the 5th U. S. Artillery when he was saddled with responsibility for the brigade. His brigade contained six batteries including his own, Battery H of the 1st, Batteries F and K of the 3rd, and Batteries C and G of the 4th. Of the group all but Battery G of the 4th would be with Ransom at Gettysburg.[5]

Tyler's Second Brigade of Regulars contained five batteries under the command of Captain John Caldwell Tidball. Tidball's own 2nd U. S. Artillery, Battery A was joined by Batteries E, G, and K from the 1st U. S. and Battery C of the 3rd U. S. Artillery.[6]

John Tidball was born in a log cabin near Wheeling Creek in the hills of the western Virginia frontier on 25 January 1825. As a boy he relocated with his family a number of times. His resolve and determination was instilled in him early in life by events beyond his control, for tragedy was prevalent during his upbringing. On his ninth birthday, his mother passed away. She had been ill for some time and her condition had forced the family to reside with John's grandfather in New Castle, Pennsylvania. Six years later, John lost one of his two sisters when she was seventeen. The event must have touched him deeply for he evidently buried his heartbreak and never mentioned it in any of his future letters or communications. Four years later tragedy struck again when his youngest sister Maria died at the age of fifteen. Once again John remained quiet in commenting on her passing.[7]

John was educated in local schools, as the family's location limited his educational options. His father however, had served for a short period as a schoolmaster and John soon found himself devoting a great amount of time during the winter months on the family farm to home schooling. As spring blossomed, school work gave way to farm chores which John would perform until the weather forced him indoors again to take up his schoolbooks once more. At the age of seventeen, after reading a magazine article about the Military Academy, John send a letter of application to the secretary of war. Although he lacked the educational preparation for the rigors of the academy, if accepted John determined to do

---

[5]   ***OR***, vol.25, pt.2, p.585; ***OR***, vol.27, pt.1, p.167; Tidball, Eugene C., ***"No Disgrace to My Country": The Life of John C. Tidball***, p.528,n17; Naisawald, ***Grape & Canister***, pp.298-299.

[6]   ***OR***, vol.25, pt.2, p.585.

[7]   Tidball, ***"No Disgrace"***, pp.1, 3-5, 7.

whatever necessary to remain and finish his training. Unfortunately, his letter was returned with a note to the effect that appointments were made through the recommendation of his local congressman. Undeterred, he composed a second letter and sent it off to his congressman. Informed there were no openings for two years, John waited until his representative returned from Washington and traveled to see him. His tenacity eventually paid off with an appointment to the class of 1848. Four years of hard work followed, at the end of which John C. Tidball graduated from West Point eleventh in a class of thirty-eight cadets. His position was indeed remarkable considering he received none of the educational advantages which prominent, well-adjusted members of the country's elite class were provided.[8]

The tragedies of his upbringing and his father's strict discipline shaped Tidball's personal traits early in life. Quick to develop a grudge when he felt wronged, John was not opposed to holding his discontent for extended periods before extracting revenge upon those who he believed had wronged him. His vengeful attitude stemmed from an incident which occurred when he was a boy, which lingered for years before he was able to extract his retribution. Prone to periods of silence, Tidball tended to remain quiet and observant. He contained a stern streak which, combined with a dominating presence was a bit unnerving for any subordinate who was not acquainted with the demanding disposition. Beneath his exterior however, was an active sense of humor and among friends John would become more outgoing. Physically Tidball was a slender man, wiry and muscular. His physicality was quite helpful when dealing with the demanding regiment at the academy. John Tidball appeared a soldier and his physical presence, loyalty to duty and high level of personal integrity made him an exceptional one.[9]

After graduation, Tidball was brevetted a second lieutenant and assigned to the 2nd U. S. Artillery. On 31 March 1853, less than a year after graduating, he was promoted to first lieutenant. A month after the war commenced, he was once again promoted, receiving his captain's bars. He spent the first few months assigned to duty at Fort Pickens, but by the summer of 1861, he had been relocated northward. He commanded a battery of artillery during First Bull, but it saw no action during the fighting. He was later transferred to command the 3rd U. S. Artillery's Battery K, and led it during the fighting at Yorktown and Williamsburg on the Peninsula. Later, he returned once more to the 2nd Artillery and was placed in command of Battery A, which he guided with distinction during The Seven Days. After the fighting, General Sykes credited him with "frustrat[ing]" an attack made against the right of Sykes' brigade of Regulars, an act which helped the artilleryman gain a major brevet.[10]

---

[8] *Ibid*, pp.5-6, 10,-12; Eicher, & Eicher, **High Commands**, p.530.

[9] Tidball, *"No Disgrace"*, pp.5, 8.

[10] Eicher, & Eicher, **High Commands**, p.530; Sifakis, **Who was Who**, p.654; *OR*, vol.11, pt.2, pp.31, 352.

By Antietam, Captain Tidball's battery had been assigned to General Pleasonton's Cavalry Division in McClellan's mighty army. The added challenge of commanding horse artillery allowed Tidball to showcase his abilities and he flourished, proving himself an excellent horse artillerist. A classmate of cavalryman John Buford's at West Point, Tidball showed he was quite astute at shifting his guns to the support of the mounted wing of the army.

As the months leading to the Gettysburg Campaign came and went, Tidball would find his battery shifted from one organization to another on a regular basis. At Fredericksburg, his guns were part of General Hunt's Artillery Reserve. Chancellorsville found Battery A once again part of the horse artillery. Assigned to General William Averell's division, Tidball's cannons southward as part of Stoneman's Raid. However, by 24 May, the Cavalry Corps' artillery brigade had been dissolved. At the beginning of June, Tidball found himself at the head of a brigade of Regulars in Tyler's Reserve Division. The brigade, at the request of General Pleasonton, would soon be transferred once again to the horse artillery, the position it would occupy as the armies met at Gettysburg. For now however, as Tidball's boys prepared for the coming campaign, they remained with Tyler's Regulars.[11]

Captain John Caldwell Tidball stands second from the left in this photo taken near Fair Oaks, Virginia in June of 1862. *LOC*

Commanding General Tyler's Volunteer Division was Major John A. Tompkins. Tompkins, a former captain in the 1st Rhode Island Light Artillery's Battery A, had been given a much more demanding job than Tyler. The Volunteer

---

[11] ***OR***, vol.19, pt.1, p.180; ***OR***, vol.21, p.49; ***OR***, vol.25, pt.1, p.170; ***OR***, vol.25, pt.2, p.585; ***OR***, vol.27, pt.1, p.167; Tidball, *"No Disgrace"*, pp.298-300

Division was over twice as large as Tyler's group of Regulars with four brigades containing twenty-four batteries. Tompkins original service was as his former battery's second lieutenant, a position he assumed when the battery was organized. On 13 September 1861, he received his captain's commission and took command of the battery. He led it for over a year before he was commissioned major on 4 December 1862. On 26 March of the following year, he was installed as the chief of artillery for the Sixth Corps' First Division. He would retain responsibility for the corps' artillery until placed in charge of the volunteer gunners of the reserve.[12]

Like Tidball, Tompkins fought during the Peninsular Campaign. His battery was assigned to General Sedgwick's Division of General Sumner's Second Corps. He was called out by Sedgwick who noted John deserved "great credit for the able and efficient manner in which [he] handled [his battery]." At Antietam Tompkins was ordered to place his battery on a knoll near the burning Mumma Farm. After unlimbering his cannon, he opened fire on an enemy battery positioned west of the Hagerstown Road and on D. H. Hill's men along the Sunken Road. Tompkins fought his battery of Rhode Islanders to the point of exhaustion and after running out of ammunition he was relieved by the 1st Rhode Island's Battery G. According to Tompkins, the battery "expended 83 rounds of canister, 68 rounds of solid shot, 427 rounds [of] shell, and 454 rounds of case shot," for a total of 1,050 rounds. Through all the early battles, Tompkins proved himself a capable battery commander. Shortly after Chancellorsville, he took charge of General Tyler's Volunteer Division as directed by Special Order No.129. Although Tompkins would miss the great battle in Pennsylvania due to illness, as of 1 June he was using his expertise to directing the division.[13]

Tompkins' First Brigade was assembled from a group of batteries hailing from five different states. Representing New York were Batteries B and G from the state's 1st Artillery and the 10th New York Battery. The 6th Maine Battery and the 5th Massachusetts represented the New England area. From Ohio came the states 10th Artillery's Battery H. The brigade's final battery, from the Keystone State, was represented by the Pennsylvania Independent Artillery's Battery C.[14]

Commanding the brigade was a thirty-nine year old northeasterner from Maine named Freeman McGilvery. Born in Prospect, McGilvery loved the sea and spent his early days as a shipmaster and sailor. When the war broke out, he was in Brazil. Returning from Rio Janeiro, he began the process of organizing the 6th Battery of the 1st Maine Artillery. The battery saw its first action at Cedar Mountain and was again engaged at Sulfur Springs. During both engagements, McGilvery's gunners did their jobs well and praise was leveled on the battery. At Antietam, Captain

---

[12] Dyer, Elisha, *Annual Report of the Adjutant General of the State of Rhode Island and Providence Plantations for the Year 1865*, Corrected and Revised Edition (hereafter *ARAGSRI*), vol.2, p.735.

[13] *Ibid*; *OR*, vol.11, pt.2, pp.26,83; *OR*, vol.19, pt.1, pp.308-309; *OR*, vol.25, pt.2, pp.471-472; Pierro, *Carman*, p.255.

[14] *OR*, vol.25, pt.2, p.585.

McGilvery's guns where attached to the Twelfth Corps and performed excellent service supporting Mansfield's attack through the East Woods. He was promoted to major on 5 February 1863, and eventually found himself in command of his state's 1st Artillery. When the Volunteer Division's First Brigade was formed the following May, he took over as its commander, having never led more than a single battery in battle. McGilvery had shown himself to be a capable commander and would soon prove that when his efforts were needed most he would not shy away from the responsibilities.[15]

Tompkins Second Brigade was under the command of a New Yorker, Major Thomas Ward Osborn. Osborn had enrolled at Watertown for three years' service, joining the state's 1st Artillery Regiment. The twenty-six year old signed up on 10 August 1861, and was mustered in 6 September. On the day of his muster, he was made captain of the regiment's Battery D. The 1st however, was not officially organized until 16 October, in Elmira when the batteries were assembled into a single regiment. After spending the early months of its enlistment term near Washington, Battery D was assigned to Hooker's division of the Third Corps in March, 1862. Osborn's boys saw their first serious action at Williamsburg where the battery had one of its members killed and seven wounded. A few weeks later at Seven Pines, the battery was involved in the fighting but suffered no additional casualties. By June, Osborn and his gunners had been transferred to the corps' Second Division and later fought during The Seven Days, but once again suffered no casualties.[16]

Although elements of the Army of the Potomac's Third Corps saw action during General Pope's campaign in Virginia, Osborn's battery did not. It sat out the Maryland Campaign as well, spending the fall of 1862 in the Washington area with the remainder of the Third Corps. Not until December of 1862 were Osborn and his New Yorkers back in the war. Reassigned to the Ninth Corps' First Division, the battery, as part of General Sumner's Right Grand Division crossed the Rappahannock at the upper pontoon bridges and unlimbered in a position south of Fredericksburg near the riverbank. Osborn's location at the center of the Federal line helped keep his six 12 pounders out of the heavy action. He evidently caught the eye of his superiors for even though he had seen light action during the battle, on 6 March 1863, he was promoted to major. Leaving the boys of Battery D in the hands of the unit's lieutenant, Osborn ascended to the chief of artillery position within the soon to be lamented General Hiram Berry's Second Division of the Third Corps. It would be at the head of Berry's artillery where Osborn would make his mark on the progress, if not the outcome of the war, at Chancellorsville.[17]

[15] Sifakis, *Who was Who*, p.415; *Electronic Source:* http://en.wikipedia.org/wiki/Freeman_McGilvery, Last accessed 5/11/2012; Gottfried, Bradley M., *The Artillery of Gettysburg*, p.97. Wikipedia's information on McGilvery is derived from Wilson, James Grant and Fiske, John, editors, *Appleton's Cyclopedia of American Biography*.

[16] Phisterer, *NYWR*, vol.2, pp.1208-1209, 1211, 1228; *ARAGSNY*, vol.7, p.313; *OR*, vol.11, pt.1, pp.64, 450, 759; *OR*, vol.11, pt.2, p.27.

[17] *OR*, vol.21, p.183; Phisterer, *NYWR*, vol.2, pp.1213; *OR*, vol.25, pt.1, pp.162, 388.

As Stonewall Jackson's flank attack thundered down upon the Federal position near the crossroads, Osborn and his batteries were ordered forward. Working their way through the mass of fleeing Eleventh Corps soldiers, Osborn posted his batteries along a low ridge perpendicular to and on the south side of the Orange Plank Road near the Fairview House and cemetery. Shortly after the sun dipped below the horizon, a Rebel battery opened on Osborn's position from a distance of 1,200 yards. He ordered his gunners to return fire and a heavy barrage ensued. The Federal gunners were true to their mark and pounded the Plank Road, sending Jim Lane's North Carolinians scurrying to the woods. Osborn, thinking his guns had silenced the Rebels, had no idea the Southerners had simply ceased fire on their own, hoping the Federals would do likewise and Osborn accommodated the Rebel's by silencing his barrage.[18]

With his guns posted on the ridge, Osborn personally took a section of the 1st U. S. Battery H forward approximately 400 yards and established a position a few yards to the rear of the Federal battle line near the road. As darkness settled, he could clearly hear the Rebel infantry. Around 9:00 p.m., peering through the moonlight, Osborn noticed the enemy about 400 yards to his front. It was obvious the Rebels were massing their force, and the New Yorker could unmistakably hear shouted orders and swearing officers as the enemy prepared for a dangerous night attack. Suddenly Osborn saw through the moonlight what he "distinctly" believed to be the head of a marching column. "The column," Osborn wrote in his report, "seemed to cover the entire breadth of the road and moving very cautiously until within 150 yards of us, when it began to deploy in line of battle." Osborn was quick to give the order and his two cannons belched forth canister, which, according to the major, "clear[ed] the road almost instantly." The batteries to the rear opened as well and the Rebels scattered. The actions of Osborn that night, and for the remainder of the battle, would not go unnoticed. General Sickles, writing in his report, noted Osborn "sustained [his] reputation as [a] cool and reliable officer."[19]

Unknown to Osborn, his cannon fire forced the men bearing the litter containing the wounded Jackson to drop it and seek shelter as well. Osborn's fire drove the party off the road and into the trees as they once again tried to move the general to the rear through the flying debris from Osborn's guns. If the men would have remained on the road, it is likely they would have managed to ferry Jackson to the rear without the mishaps which allowed the general to plunge to the ground, instigating the additional hemorrhaging which may have cost the general his life. Osborn had no way of knowing his cannon fire that night in the darkness may have done more to assure ultimate victory for the North than the actions of any Federal general throughout the war.[20]

Unlike McGilvery's Brigade, Osborn's command was built with batteries from only two states, Connecticut and New York. From Connecticut were two

---

[18] *OR*, vol.25, pt.1, p.483. The guns Osborn targeted were those of Captain Marcellus N. Moorman.

[19] *Ibid*, pp.162, 388, 395, 483-484.

[20] Although this is total speculation, one cannot simply dismiss the possibility.

organizations, Companies B and M of the 1st Heavy Artillery. The New Yorkers were represented by gunners from five different independent batteries. The first of these was the 5th Light Artillery which had originally been part of Sickles' Excelsior Brigade. Of the remaining batteries, the 15th, 29th, 30th and 32nd, all but the 15th were veteran outfits and while they had undergone organizational and name changes, they had seen fighting during many of the war's early battles. The 15th, while it had been in a couple of minor engagements had yet to take any casualties. The 29th, 30th and 32nd would become victims of the journey north and would be reassigned before the army arrived at Gettysburg. The move would precipitate the breakup of his brigade, and Osborn would find himself with another command. For now however, as June opened, he would retain his position, and eventually lead his seven batteries on at least a portion of the march north.[21]

Commanding the Volunteer Division's Third Brigade was Rhode Islander, Captain Richard Waterman. Waterman, a resident of Providence, had received a first lieutenant's commission on 8 August 1861, and like division commander Tompkins, joined the 1st Rhode Island Light Artillery on 25 August. A member of Battery C, he fought with it during engagements on the Peninsula and first commanded it at Malvern Hill after the battery's captain had been promoted. Engaged in the thickest of the fighting, Waterman lost fifteen battery mates, a caisson and ten horses, two of which were shot from under him. Following the battle, on 25 July, He was promoted to captain of the battery, receiving his commission in the field. Leading the battery as its captain for the first time at Second Bull Run, Waterman directed the firing of approximately 600 rounds of case shot and shell before departing the field. In addition to four casualties, Waterman left behind six dead horses, two sets of tack and two caissons with broken axles. Although he had shown his stubbornness and tenacity during his first two engagements, Battery C was held in reserve at Antietam but fired close to 500 rounds at the retiring Rebel's from the bluffs overlooking Shepherdstown a few days later.[22]

Shortly before the battle at Fredericksburg, Waterman's guns were posted on a rise north of the river above the southern end of town. After firing close to 800 rounds throughout the two days preceding the battle, the battery was called upon to support the infantry attacks on Marye's Heights. At 10:00 a.m. Waterman received orders to commence firing in support of the attack, but he soon realized that as the blue lines approached the heights, his fire began falling dangerously close to the battle line, forcing him to halt his cannonade. To continue supporting the attack, Waterman was ordered across the river about 1:00 p.m. He rolled his guns, limbers and caissons through the streets and posted them at the northwest corner of town. From their new position the Rhode Islanders continued their fire until the attacks upon the heights were terminated. The battery remained in position until 7:00 p.m. the following day when it was ordered to re-cross the river, bivouacking near the Lacy house. Although his efforts had not provided enough assistance to help secure

---

[21]   *OR*, vol.25, pt.2, p.585; Phisterer, *NYWR*, vol.2, pp.1228, 1571, 1596, 1621, 1622, 1626.

[22]   *ARAGSRI*, vol.2, p.813; *OR*, vol.11, pt.2, p.31.

victory for the Federals, Waterman led his Rhode Islander's skillfully, showing he was capable of handling a battery under fire.[23]

Temporarily assigned to the Fifth Corps under its chief of artillery, Captain Stephen Weed, Waterman's Battery saw light action at Chancellorsville. Posted on the left flank of Hooker's position, his guns remained there throughout the major portion of the fighting. When General Hunt reorganized the artillery after the battle, Waterman was elevated to the command of the Volunteer Division's Third Brigade. His new brigade contained not only his Rhode Islander's but also the 1st New Hampshire Battery, Battery C of the 1st West Virginia Artillery and Batteries G and F of the 1st Pennsylvania Artillery. As Hunt continued to restructure his organization throughout June, Waterman would once again find a new home, but his journey to battle in Pennsylvania would begin as captain of one of Tompkins' brigades.[24]

Robert H. Fitzhugh decided to do his part for the war effort by joining the 1st New York Artillery. Signing up at Oswego as a spry twenty-one year old on 12 September 1861, Robert mustered into service two days later with the remainder of the regiment at Elmira. A few weeks later, on 21 October, Fitzhugh was installed as first lieutenant of Battery F. The battery saw its initial duty in the Washington area, but soon found itself on the Virginia Peninsula, where it became engaged at Mechanicsville on 24 May and later at White House during The Seven Days.[25]

If Fitzhugh craved the excitement of battle, he was about to receive some disappointing news, for after the termination of the campaign to capture the Rebel capital, Battery F remained behind in Virginia. Fortunately for Robert, he was allowed to return to the war with a transfer to the regiment's Battery K during the later portion of the summer of 1862. He fought with the battery at Beverly Ford on 22 August as part of General Pope's initial moments which terminated at Second Bull Run, and was wounded for his effort. He evidently displayed a high level of command skills for on 14 October, he was placed in charge of Battery K as its new captain.[26]

Fitzhugh and his battery would join the Twelfth Corps but remain in the vicinity of Harpers Ferry, not rejoining the army until after the battle of Fredericksburg. When Fitzhugh and his battery finally arrived on the banks of the Rappahannock, he was in command of General Alpheus William's divisional artillery, but he would return to command of his battery before the armies became entangled at Chancellorsville. During the afternoon of 2 May, Fitzhugh's guns helped form the line of artillery along the low ridge near Fairview, assisting Captain Osborn and the batteries gathered there in checking Jackson's planned night attack. He would

---

[23] *OR*, vol.21, pp.192, 195. Waterman notes that his battery re-crossed the river "[a]t 7 o'clock on Sunday evening, the 14th" of December. Tompkins notes that Waterman did not re-csross until "the morning of the 15th."

[24] *OR*, vol.25, pt.1, pp.523-524; *OR*, vol.25, pt.2, p.586.

[25] Phisterer, *NYWR*, vol.2, pp.1209, 1211, 1223.

[26] *Ibid*, pp.1209, 1223-1224; *OR*, vol.25, pt.2, p. 586.

retain his position and continue to perform the duties of a battery captain as General Hunt revised his artillery organization in May 1863.[27]

Hooker's 12 May order placed Fitzhugh in charge of Tompkins' fourth brigade. Including his own Battery K, the brigade contained four other outfits. An additional New York organization, the 11th Battery, Battery A from the Maryland Artillery, the Pennsylvania Artillery's Battery F and the 1st Rhode Island Artillery's Battery G. Like the other brigades in the Volunteer Division, some of Fitzhugh's guns would be transferred out while others would join the brigade to fill the vacancies; a sure sign that General Hunt's artillery organization was in a state of flux during June.[28]

The Corps Brigades

Chosen to command the artillery brigade assigned to the First Corps was Colonel Charles Shiels Wainwright, the thirty-six year old man General Hooker had entrusted his disorganized artillery with at Chancellorsville. Wainwright, a farmer from New York, was born on the last day of 1826 and entered the fight to preserve the Union as a major in the 1st New York Artillery Regiment. Charles was slightly tardy in stepping forward when the war initially began. His brother William had left the family farm, known as The Meadows, almost immediately, leaving Charles and his two sisters to help his eighty-five year old father manage day to day operations. Charles finally left to help crush the rebellion in early September, 1861, when the August harvest work was completed. After visiting his friend and fellow farmer Marsena Patrick, who suggested he raise an artillery regiment, Charles went to work recruiting men but was unable to assemble enough manpower. Patrick then suggested that Charles submit his name for consideration regarding a light artillery regiment he knew needed a major. Traveling to Elmira, Wainwright sought out Colonel Guilford D. Bailey of the 1st New York and inquired about the open position. Bailey was quick to take advantage of the situation, and Wainwright soon found himself a member of the regiment. He signed the rolls on 25 September 1861 in Elmira and was mustered on 17 October. He would eventually be promoted to lieutenant colonel before being assigned the colonelcy of the regiment.[29]

Charles saw action with General Pope's army in Virginia and after its defeat, spent the first two weeks of September 1862 in Washington. He was at the Willard Hotel on the 15th when a telegram arrived summoning him to General McClellan's Headquarters at Frederick, Maryland. It was 18 September before Wainwright could catch up with the army, missing the Battle of Antietam by a day. Shortly after General Reynolds returned from Pennsylvania to take command of the First Corps, Charles was assigned to the corps as its chief of artillery.[30]

Wainwright's first opportunity to show his skills as artillery chief came during the Battle of Fredericksburg where a number of his batteries supported Meade's

---

[27] *OR*, vol.21, p.937. *OR*, vol.25, pt.1, pp.720-721; *OR*, vol.25, pt.2, p.28.

[28] *OR*, vol.25, pt.2, p.586.

[29] Phisterer, *NYWR*, vol.2, pp.1213, 1231, 1233; Wainwright, *A Diary of Battle*, pp.xi-xii.

[30] Phisterer, *NYWR*, vol.2, pp.1213, 1231; Wainwright, *A Diary of Battle*, pp.98-102.

breaking of the Confederate line. After the battle, Reynolds felt it necessary to write in glowing terms of him in his after action report. "To Colonel Wainwright, First New York Artillery, chief of artillery" the general noted, "I am indebted for the excellent judgment he displayed in the management and disposition of the whole artillery of the corps, and for the admirable manner in which the damages it received were repaired on the field and the guns again brought into action under his supervision."[31]

After Reynolds' positive review, Wainwright entered the Chancellorsville Campaign on a high note, and although the corps was not seriously engaged during the battle, Wainwright still performed good service. Early in the campaign, he helped keep Reynolds informed as to the conditions along the river at Fredericksburg before the corps began its belated march to reinforce the Federal main effort at the crossroads. As the battle raged, Hooker quickly realized his error in severing control of the artillery from General Hunt. In an effort to perform damage control, Hooker took a dramatic step, placing Wainwright in charge of the army's batteries. He probably selected Wainwright because he was the senior officer on the field. Hunt had previously been sent to Banks' Ford, so Hooker turned to Wainwright to bring order to the chaos.[32]

Although Wainwright failed to note Hooker's order in his after action report, he did document the events of his weighty assignment in his journal. After posting some batteries, Reynolds sent him to Hooker's headquarters to report the state of the artillery. When he arrived, Wainwright found Hooker lying down in his tent trying to recover from the effects of an artillery shell near miss which had stunned the general. A solid shot had struck one of the wooden columns on the south porch of the Chancellor House which Hooker was leaning against at the time. The shot split the column and threw Hooker to the porch. The stunned general was now being denied visitors. Wainwright positioned himself near the opening of the general's tent in the hopes that as he delivered his report Hooker may see or hear him and invite him inside. Shortly after began his delivery to General Meade, who was nearby, Hooker did indeed call Wainwright into his tent. It was here that one of the most interesting conversations of the campaign took place. Wainwright, although not word for word, recalled the meeting "as near" as he could remember.[33]

"Well, Wainwright," Hooker inquired as the colonel entered his tent, "how is the artillery getting on?"

"As badly as it well can." Wainwright reported. "Batteries are being ordered in every direction, blocking up the roads; and no one seems to know where to go."

Then Wainwright asked a question Hooker may not have wished to hear or answer.

"Where is General Hunt?"

---

[31] *OR*, vol.21, p.456, 458-459.

[32] *OR*, vol.25, pt.1, pp.252, 255 ; *OR*, vol.25, pt.2, p.340; Naisawald, *Grape & Canister*, p.250. Both Hunt and Reynolds wrote in their reports that he had been detached from the First Corps.

[33] Sears, *Chancellorsville*, p.336-337; Wainwright, *A Diary of Battle*, p.193.

Hooker, still possibly suffering from the effects of the near miss or simply wishing not to respond, ignored Wainwright's inquiry.

"What is the matter?" Hooker questioned.

"As near as I can understand," Wainwright continued, "every division commander wants his own batteries, and battery commanders will obey no one else's orders. It is just the condition I told you of and wanted to provide against, by giving artillery officers of rank actual command, so that they could order any battery. The ammunition trains, too."

To Hooker the answer was simple. "Well," he said, "we have no time to talk now. You take hold and make it right."

Charles must have been a bit shocked at the comment. Was the commanding general placing him in charge of all the army's artillery? Once again Wainwright asked the question. "Where is General Hunt?"

"At Banks's [sic] Ford. You take his place."

Wainwright balked, suggesting other officers he felt more qualified for the weighty responsibility, but Hooker would have none of it.

"I know nothing of them as artillery officers," the commanding general responded. Hooker then committed to have orders drawn up so no one would question Wainwright's authority. "What do you want?" he asked.

"I must have power to put batteries with other divisions than their own," the colonel requested, "and to fill them from any ammunition train."

Hooker instructed orders be written so "[n]o officer whatsoever will give any order which may conflict with his [Wainwright's] arrangements."

"Will that do?" Hooker asked.

"Perfectly sir."

With that Wainwright stepped out of the tent. He had gone to Hooker's headquarters at the request of his corps commander to report on the status of the artillery and left in charge of it all. Although happy the guns would now be better handled, Wainwright now carried a heavy load. "I left the tent rejoicing," he wrote in his journal, "yet with a weight of responsibility on me such as I had never had before.[34]

Charles quickly went to work posting thirty guns to the left of the battle line, another forty-eight in the center and thirty-two on the right. All remaining guns, about 140, were retained in the rear and set up as a reserve. When General Hunt finally arrived on the field around 10:00 p.m. he took command, observed Wainwright's disposition and gave the New Yorker full approval of the placement.[35]

After the battle, Wainwright returned to his duties with the First Corps. When Hunt reorganized his guns, he placed Wainwright in charge of the corps' brigade of five independent batteries. Two of the units were the state of Maine's 2nd and 5th Batteries. The 1st New York Light Artillery contributed its Battery L, while the 1st Pennsylvania Light Artillery provided its Battery B. The final battery was a group of Regulars from Battery B of the 4th U. S. Artillery. Wainwright had proven

---

[34] Wainwright, *A Diary of Battle*, pp.193-194

[35] Naisawald, *Grape & Canister*, p.250.

through deeds that he was deserving of his position. In a few weeks at Gettysburg he would once again prove the trust placed in him was well earned.[36]

Charged with the direction of General Hancock's Second Corps artillery was Captain John G. Hazard of the 1st Rhode Island Light Artillery. Hazard had just ascended to chief of artillery for the corps, having begun his service as a first lieutenant in Battery C on 8 August 1861. His duties with the battery would have required him to take on a bit more responsibility than his first assignment, which was a short two day stint as the regiment's hospital steward. Hazard served with the regiment's Battery C only a short time before he was transferred on 17 September to Battery A, where he probably reported directly to battery captain John Tompkins. Taking charge of the battery's first section, Hazard lead his two guns effectively in the Washington DC, Harpers Ferry and Winchester region until the battery was transferred with the bulk of McClellan's army to the Virginia Peninsula.[37]

Early in his career, Hazard proved to his men that he was not one to put up with any insubordination. One particular episode began innocently enough with a disagreement between a sergeant and a man who had been detailed to care for Hazard's horse. The sergeant was in possession of a bridle which he claimed to be his; however, the man charged with caring for the horse said the bridle was one which had been used by Hazard's steed. When Hazard intervened in the discussion and ordered the sergeant to hand over the bridle, the man refused and a heated argument ensued. Calling the guard, Hazard had the disobedient sergeant reduced in rank and "buck[ed] and gag[ged]," a punishment which was more severe than those allowed by army regulations for such an offense. Although the sergeant was cleared of the charges it was apparent to the men that Lieutenant John Hazard was not to be taken lightly.[38]

Promoted to captain of the regiment's Battery B on 18 August 1862, Hazard showed his pleasure with his new assignment by arrived at his new post a few days early. After being introduced to his new battery by one of his lieutenants, Hazard gathered his officers and performed an inspection. The compliment of officers had been in a reduced state for some time, and Hazard's arrival along with a number of additional recruits brought the batteries manpower up to par.[39]

Perhaps Hazard's finest hour prior the summer of 1863, came at Fredericksburg. The day before the battle, orders were received instructing him to report to General Howard. The battery moved out and lumbered across the river at 6:00 a.m. John parked his guns an hour later along the riverbank in the northern end of town, where they remained until 10:00 a.m. the following morning. It was then that

---

[36] *OR*, vol.25, pt.2, p.576.

[37] Aldrich, Thomas M., ***The History of Battery A: First Regiment Rhode Island Light Artillery in the War to Preserve the Union 1861-1865***, pp.45-47, 68, 78 ; Rhodes, John H., ***The History of Battery B: First Regiment Rhode Island Light Artillery in the War to Preserve the Union 1861-1865***, pp.351; ***ARAGSRI***, vol.2, p.735.

[38] Aldrich, ***History of Battery A***, p.78.

[39] Rhodes, ***History of Battery B***, pp.118, 351; ***ARAGSRI***, vol.2, p.735.

Hazard received orders from Howard to form his battery in column on Caroline Street. There the battery loitered until 3:45 p.m. when it was ordered by the Second Corps' chief of artillery, Captain Charles H. Morgan to advance to the support of the beleaguered infantry on Marye's Heights. Morgan, when instructed where to place Hazard's battery, thought the location ludicrous due to its exposed nature, so he sought out General Couch to protest. "My God!" Morgan exclaimed, "General, you will lose your guns, a battery cannot live out there." Couch responded by noting he was willing to sacrifice a battery if it meant saving some of his infantry from the slaughter taking place on the slope.[40]

With the blue clad soldiers bogged down before the stone wall on the heights, Howard chose Hazard's battery to advance and provide close artillery support in an effort to break the Confederate line. It was nearly 4:00 p.m. before the battery got underway, being directed to advance to a small knoll, "some 150 to 200 yards in front of the enemy's rifle pits." Rumbling down Hanover Street, Hazard's guns approached a wooden bridge which spanned the canal at the base of the heights. As the guns approached their new position they passed by their fellow gunners of Battery A. As Hazard's boys thundered by, a member of their sister battery commented, "There goes Battery B to hell!" The man was right.[41]

As the battery crossed the bridge, a lieutenant guided the caissons off the road to the left and into a position in rear of the canal. The guns and their limbers continued across, and after a short distance Hazard ordered his left section off the road to the south where he placed it on the crest of the knoll. Between the road and the left section, he placed the center section before positioning the right section in the road some thirty yards in front of the four guns to the left. Once in position, Hazard, whose men were already taking heavy fire, ordered the guns left of the road to open fire with solid shot while the right section was instructed to open fire with shell.[42]

The battery's horses were conspicuous targets. Killing the animals would provide the Confederates with an opportunity to claim a valuable prize. Heavy blasts of musket fire slammed into the animals of the right section and dropped all the horses of one team. Undaunted, the men pushed the gun into position by hand. When the first round was taken to the muzzle, the man attempting to load it was hit. Another man stepped forward and tried to load the round, but he was shot down as well. A third stepped up and was likewise hit. Finally, a round was loaded and the gun fired. Serving the gun became less risky as smoke from the discharging weapons obscured the battery from Confederate view. Additional animals were shot as well including the wheel horses of a number of the guns. By the time an additional battery arrived to help, Hazard had lost twelve of his much needed animals.[43]

---

[40] Rhodes, *History of Battery B*, pp.139, 142; *OR*, vol.21, p.267.

[41] Rhodes, *History of Battery B*, p.139.

[42] Ibid.

[43] Walker, Francis A., *History of the Second Army Corps*, pp.177-178; Rhodes, *History of Battery B*, p.140.

Men fell quickly as the fighting became even hotter. Private Joseph Luther received a nasty wound in his hip. He would lose his life two months later in a Washington hospital. Corporal William Wells, who was hit in the foot, would eventually be discharged. Morris Carmichael took a spent ball to the groin and would be discharged for disability, as was Private Calvin Rathbone, after he was hit in the ankle. Another man was hit in the wrist while still others fell with additional slight or serious wounds. Through all the chaos, Hazard's men continued to service their guns, making it as hot as possible for the Confederates dug in behind the wall on the heights. As the limbers emptied, men from the rear quickly brought more ammunition forward from the caissons. One battery member described the location as "a perfect hornet's nest, with the hornets all stirred up. Minié balls were flying and singing about us," he continued, "with a zip… or a thud as they struck…"[44]

For forty-five minutes Hazard's battery kept up its fire through the hail of bullets until they were ordered to cease fire to let a body of infantry pass through the battery's position. The men from General Humphrey's command were pushing forward to make another effort against the wall. The battery however, would not fire another round from their forward position for as the last of Humphrey's men cleared the battery, Hazard was ordered to limber up his guns and withdraw. With the number of horses depleted, Hazard was forced to leave one limber on the knoll and the gun on his extreme left had to be brought off by hand. The battery's loss was high, with sixteen men and twelve battery horses as casualties. Additionally, three officers had their horses shot from under them, including Hazard. After departing the field, the battery took a position near its old location on Caroline Street and Hazard asked for volunteers to return to the knoll and retrieve the lost limber. Five men stepped forward and went back to the knoll. They managed to extract the limber, allowing Hazard to claim he had brought all his equipment off the field. The following day the battery returned to the North side of the river.[45]

Hazard's display of determination, bravery and ability to handle his battery during the fighting was recognized by his superiors. In his report General Hunt noted Hazard executed the order with "coolness and gallantry," and the guns were "handsomely served." General Couch wrote that the battery's "duty was bravely done," and after the war heaped additional praise on the battery noting "[m]en never fought more gallantly." General Howard commented in his report that "Captain Hazard's conduct was equal to anything I ever saw on a field of Battle." Colonel Joshua Owen of the 69th Pennsylvanian also appreciated Hazard's support. "Permit me to speak in the highest terms of the 1st Rhode Island Battery," Owen wrote, "and to thank Captain Hazard, his officers, and men to their timely, bold, and efficient services in my support." Captain John Hazard was making a name for himself. It seemed only a matter of time before he would receive additional responsibility.[46]

---

[44] Rhodes, *History of Battery B*, pp.140, 356, 362, 369.

[45] *Ibid*, pp.140-141; *OR*, vol.21, p.268.

[46] *OR*, vol.21, pp.185, 223, 263, 280; Couch, Darius N., Sumner's "Right Grand Division, *B&L*, vol.3, p.115.

In February 1863, Hazard took a short leave of absence. After returning to his command he fell ill and reported sick. He was absent from his battery until sometime in May. His illness kept him from participating in the Battle of Chancellorsville. Shortly after he returned, General Hunt reassigned Hazard to head the Second Corps' artillery brigade. His new brigade consisted of the two batteries from the 1st Rhode Island Light Artillery he had previously served with and two batteries of Regulars, the 1st U. S. Artillery, Battery I and the 4th U. S. Artillery's Battery A. The brigade would remain intact throughout the march north to Pennsylvania.[47]

Selected to perform the duties of the Third Corps' chief of artillery was Captain George E. Randolph of Battery E, 1st Rhode Island Light Artillery. Randolph's ancestral line could be traced back to some of the first settlers to arrive in the Virginia area. Early in the state's history, his kin were prominent in the political debates of the day. George's grandfather Richard was a nephew of William Henry Harrison, making George a third cousin of future president, Benjamin Harrison. Richard had been a wealthy tobacco farmer who cultivated his plantation along the James River a short six miles from Richmond. George's father John evidently had no stomach for planting and, being unsure of his path, initially chose a military education. He eventually received an appointment to West Point but remained only two years. After leaving the academy, he began to study law. Evidently John relocated his family to Quincy, Illinois for it was there his son George was born on 29 March 1840.[48]

When George was six, his father packed up his growing family, which would eventually include four boys and three girls, and relocated again to Newport, Rhode Island. Educated in the public school system, George, at the age of eleven, entered Providence High School. After completing his schooling, he went to work at a local shoe store and leather goods business. He proved to be a good worker and employee, managing to remain at his job until the outbreak of the war. When recruitment activities to organize a battery of artillery began, George stepped up and signed enlistment papers. Mustered in on 6 June 1861, he soon found himself the first sergeant of Battery A, in the 1st Rhode Island.

Randolph's baptism of fire came at Bull Run where the battery was attached to the 2nd Rhode Island Infantry. George was unable to come through the battle unscathed, being hit in both legs just above his ankles. The battery's historian noted George "showed the same self possession" that would become well known to men who would serve under him later in the war. Three weeks after the battle Randolph was promoted to second lieutenant. Within a month he was reassigned to the regiment's Battery C and promoted to first lieutenant. On 28 September, he was assigned to the captaincy of Battery E, assuming command of his new guns on 11 October. Within two months of his wounding at Bull Run, Randolph had advanced from first sergeant to the command of a battery. His quick promotion

---

[47]   *OR*, vol.25, pt.2, p.577; ***ARAGSRI***, vol.2, p.735.

[48]   Lewis, George, ***History of Battery E, First Regiment Rhode Island Light Artillery in the War of 1861 to 1865, to Preserve the Union***, pp.258-260.

was uncommon for a man of his youth, but all understood his advancement, for they agreed his performance in battle and ability to lead made him deserving of his new position.[49]

Transferred to the Peninsula, Randolph led his battery during the early battles of McClellan's effort to take Richmond but saw minimal action. Things changed however, during The Seven Days where Battery E saw significant fighting at Glendale and Malvern Hill. At Glendale, Randolph received a negative mark on his record, although it was of no fault of his own, and he was not directly involved. As the engagement progressed, one of Randolph's sections was ordered to remain with General Kearny's headquarters. The section, under Lieutenant Pardon S. Jastram, spent nearly a half hour loitering around Kearny's headquarters without orders. Finally, panicked directions were delivered by an orderly instructing Jastram to bring his guns forward or all was lost. The lieutenant quickly responded, but the hasty reaction demanded by the orderly resulted in a number of men being left behind, hurrying to catch up.[50]

As the gunners arrived on the field, Jastram dismounted and went forward to determine what was in front of him. Kearny's orderly had provided no specific information as to the disposition of any friendly or enemy troops in the area and seemed to indicate Kearny had no idea what the two guns were to do after they arrived. Returning to his section Pardon posted the guns as best he could and seeking further instructions was simply told to "fire toward the sun." Jastram, like his men were inexperienced in battle but did the best they could. One gun accidentally loaded with canister had to be fired in the air since the location of friendly troops was unknown. The smoke in the area was thick and heavy. Little could be seen beyond his guns in almost every direction. Later General Kearny would claim to have been in the area and that Jastram never sought him out for orders. The probable reason for the lieutenant not locating Kearny was simple. The orderly never told him Kearny's location and Jastram simply could not see him or the general's headquarter standards.[51]

Randolph's lieutenant was now confronted with another serious problem; retreating Federal soldiers suddenly began to stream through the section's position. Jastram continued to fire but was now forced to be extremely careful not to fire into the faces of the fleeing Federals. Pardon had no idea if his fire was having any effect, and became fearful of being captured by whatever or whoever was driving the soldiers back. Quickly, he decided it was time to go and gave the order to limber up and get out. At the same moment, a field officer who Jastram did not identify instructed the lieutenant to withdraw "as quick as possible." According to one of his gunners, the two weapons had fired a total of five rounds before they were ordered to leave. Unfortunately, the wheel horse of one piece had been hit and fallen over the pole, the harness having become so entangled that the gun

---

[49] *Ibid*, p.260.

[50] *Ibid*, p.62.

[51] *Ibid*, p.63; ***OR***, vol.11, prt.2, pp.167-168.

could not be withdrawn and Jastram gave orders to spike the piece. The remainder of the section managed to depart with minimal aggravation and after the battle Jastram complained that a lack of specific orders was the reason for his ineffective adventure to the front.[52]

Kearny was livid. The general, implying that his orderly was an intelligent man, would not have been at fault for Jastram's lack of effectiveness. Kearny also insisted none of his men retreated calling the withdrawing men "fugitives" and noted he was in the area and Jastram was negligent for not coming to him for orders. The general suggested a court of inquiry which was formed and did issue a finding, but it was after Kearny's death and nothing came of the incident. The whole episode is a fine example of the confusion associated with battle and speaks more to Kearny and his lack of abilities as a division commander than Jastram's ability to effectively lead his section. The black marks on Randolph and Jastram's records were insignificant and Kearny, who would be dead in two months, was not around to create a problem for the men of Battery E, some of whom had now "seen the elephant."[53]

Lieutenant Jastram returned to Randolph's battery at Malvern Hill where, with only five guns the battery performed good service. Positioning his cannons, the captain, for a time, engaged an enemy battery and afterward fired when targets presented themselves. As the attacking Rebels advanced, Battery E once again engaged enemy batteries and later turned its attention to Confederate reinforcements arriving in the area. Overall, when called on for service, Randolph and Battery E gave a good accounting of themselves on the Peninsula. The confusion during the fighting at Glendale would soon become a distant memory.

As the scene of the fighting shifted from the Peninsula to northern Virginia, Battery E found itself embroiled in the marching and fighting at Second Bull Run. Assigned to General Hooker division, General Kearny noted in his report that "Captain Randolph had powerfully contributed to General Hooker's success at Bristoe Station." The battery, its old Parrott guns having been condemned, was now equipped with a full complement of Napoleons and used them to good effect. Randolph claimed in his report to have driven three Rebel batteries from the field firing only 150 rounds while having two men killed.[54]

Randolph and his battery spent the months of September and October, 1862, in and around the defenses of Washington. As the weather turned cold, the men began to settle in for the winter, but orders came and the battery was soon on its way to Fredericksburg. The day before Burnside committed his troops to battle, Captain Randolph was installed as artillery chief for General David Birney's division. Randolph, with the battery now in the hands of Lieutenant Jastram, directed the division's guns in support of Meade's breakthrough. Third Corps commander George Stoneman called out Randolph in his report. "Captain Randolph and his

---

[52] *OR*, vol.11, pt.2, p.168.

[53] Ibid, p.167, 169.

[54] *OR*, vol.12, pt.2, pp.417,437; Lewis, ***History of Battery E***, p.80.

officers," Stoneman wrote, were to be praised "for the style in which they used their guns; all, while under the fire of the enemy, proving the value and efficiency of thorough drill and discipline."[55]

On the day Joe Hooker issued his marching orders inaugurating the Chancellorsville campaign, George Randolph ascended to chief of artillery for Sickles' Third Corps. A few days later, on the morning of 3 May, Randolph found a good portion of the Third Corps' batteries unlimbered along the Orange Plank Road fighting to hold off the determined assaults of Jeb Stuart, who was now in command of Jackson's Corps. The 152 casualties his batteries absorbed were greater than any other corps. At the end of his ten page report, General Sickles recommended Randolph for a brevet, a promotion which would remain a recommendation until after the Rhode Islander was mustered out of service.[56]

As the Gettysburg Campaign opened, Randolph was an experienced artillery man who had proven himself through nearly all the campaigns in the war's Eastern Theater. A Battery E historian noted Captain Randolph's "every movement showed the best qualities of a brave and reliable commander. His noble qualities as a man, and his high standing as an officer in the artillery service, had contributed largely to make the good reputation which his battery had won in the Third corps..." Randolph's humility was on display after the war when he implied that while Battery E was known as Randolph's Battery it had accomplished most of its "best work" under his successor, somewhat exonerating Jastram for the Glendale incident.[57]

In addition to his own battery, Randolph's responsibilities as the Federals pursued Lee north would be for the 1st New Jersey Artillery, Battery B, the 1st New York Artillery, Battery D, the 4th New York Battery, and the 4th U. S. Artillery, Battery K.[58]

In early June, George Meade's Fifth Corps artillery had been entrusted to future Massachusetts political personality and Boston Mayor, Augustus P. Martin. Martin was born in Abbot, Piscataquis County Maine on 23 November 1835. His family evidently relocated to the Boston area for his formal education was received through the city's school system. Augustus later attended Wesleyan Academy and private schools in Melrose. After completing his education, he entered the business world, first clerking in an office before performing the same duties for a boot and shoe company in Boston, a position he held when the war began.

Martin had earlier joined the Boston Light Artillery militia company in 1858 and when the unit was mustered for three month service, the shoe clerk

---

[55] Lewis, *History of Battery E*, p.127; *OR*, vol.21, p.361, 364.

[56] Lewis, *History of Battery E*, p.483; *OR*, vol.25, pt.1, pp.178-180, 383.

[57] Lewis, *History of Battery E*, p.69, 261. A suggestion from Randolph resulted in the inscription on the battery's monument at Gettysburg being appended. The original name for the battery inscribed on the monument read "Randolph's Battery." Eventually, added under the name was "Lieut. J. K. Bucklyn commanding."

[58] *OR*, vol.25, pt.2, p.579.

marched off to war as one of the battery's sergeants. His three months were rather uneventful, and upon his return, wishing to do more, he volunteered to serve with the 3rd Massachusetts Artillery. Martin was commissioned a first lieutenant when the battery was organized on 5 September 1861. Three months later he was the battery's captain.[59]

Captain Martin led his battery in its first serious action during the Siege of Yorktown where it suffered five casualties, two of whom were killed, and four dead horses. Later, at Hanover Court House, he lost two men to wounds, two horses killed and three wounded. During The Seven Days fighting at Malvern Hill, Martin and his battery found themselves in the thickest of the battle. After remaining in position the entire day, orders were finally received to retire, but suddenly a large force of enemy infantry appeared to Martin's front. Most of the troops in the area had already fallen back. Alone on the field, with only the 11th U. S. Infantry for support, Martin realized it would be difficult if not impossible to extricate his battery without incurring heavy losses. There was only one thing that could be done. Martin, deciding to stand his ground, ordered his gunners to load the cannons and to hold their fire. When the Rebels had approached to within 150 yards, Martin ordered the battery to open up, unloading double canister from their tubes. The fire tore huge holes in the Rebel lines and after discharging thirty-six rounds, Martin watch as the Confederates retired. According to the captain, the Confederates were driven to the rear in "utter confusion." With the enemy falling back, Martin took the opportunity to limber up and pull back his battery. He managing to get all his equipment off the field except three caissons whose horses were in such a state of disarray that even after two attempts they could not be retrieved.[60]

Martin led his battery through the fighting at Second Bull Run and Antietam and performed well, although during the latter battle, the Fifth Corps was held in reserve and the battery was not engaged. His performance had not gone unnoticed, for in the fall of 1862, he was elevated to chief of artillery for his division. With four batteries under his charge at Fredericksburg, once again, Martin's guns remained relatively safe on the bluffs above the north side of the Rappahannock. They spent the day shelling Rebel positions from a distance near Burnside's middle pontoon bridge. At Chancellorsville, once again Martin's batteries did a great deal of marching but spent the majority of the battle in a position on the left flank of the army near Scotts Mill. With the exception of Waterman's Battery, which at the time was detached under Captain Weed, Martin's guns never fired a shot. General Meade obviously believed in Martin's ability for after the battle the general installed him as the corps' chief of artillery. A position Martin would still hold at Gettysburg.[61]

---

[59] Rand, John C., *One of a Thousand: A Series of Biographical Sketches of One Thousand Representative Men Resident in the Commonwealth of Massachusetts*, p.397. The 3rd Massachusetts Artillery was also known as Battery C Massachusetts Light Artillery.

[60] *OR*, vol.11, pt.2, p.284.

[61] *OR*, vol.21, p.407; *OR*, vol.25. pt.1, pp.522-523; Rand, *One of a Thousand*, p.397.

Two batteries from the 5th U. S. Artillery, Batteries D and I, formed the core of Captain Martin's brigade. Supporting the Regulars was his own 3rd Massachusetts Artillery, the 1st New York Artillery's Battery C and Battery L from the 1st Ohio Artillery. Although it had been some time since Martin had seen heavy fighting, he had proven early in the war he was a quality field artillery captain and could handle himself under the pressure of combat.[62]

Colonel Charles Henry Tompkins, brother of Reserve Artillery Division commander John A. Tompkins, was a New York born Rhode Islander. As the summer campaigning season opened, Charles was in command of General Sedgwick's Sixth Corps artillery. Sedgwick was well acquainted with the colonel, having utilized Tompkins' services earlier in the war when the general commanded a division on the Peninsula. Two years earlier, Tompkins had been a driving force behind the organization and subsequent mustering for three months service of Rhode Island's 1st Battery Light Artillery. He guided the battery through its mostly uneventful term of service and on 2 August it was mustered out. Tompkins' service to his country however, was just beginning. The day before the battery's muster out, he was promoted to major and on 6 August he accepted a commission in the 1st Regiment Rhode Island Light Artillery. One battery of the regiment had previously been recruited and mustered. As additional batteries were organized and entered service they were placed under the command of the regiments new major. On 13 September, after the War Department granted permission to the governor, the final three batteries of the regiment were officially organized. With all eight of its batteries now assembled, the 1st Rhode Island Light Artillery contained a full complement. Tompkins was promoted to colonel on the same day the final three batteries were authorized and marched his artillery regiment off to war.[63]

Charles commanded Sedgwick's two divisional batteries on the Peninsula, but shortly after the fighting ended, he found himself relegated to a series of administrative positions and various field assignments. It was 26 February 1863, before Charles was once again commanding artillery with the Army of the Potomac. It was then that Sedgwick turned to Tompkins, installing him as his chief of artillery for the Sixth Corps.[64]

During the Chancellorsville Campaign, Tompkins directed his artillery well during Sedgwick's effort to take the heights west of Fredericksburg. As fighting commenced, he placed his batteries on the heights to support the corps as it crossed the river. After negotiating the waters themselves, Tompkins batteries shelled the heights on which so many blue clad soldiers had died the previous December. When the heights were captured, Charles moved his batteries west and supported the fighting at Salem Church before Sedgwick was driven from his position and

---

[62] *OR*, vol.25. pt.2, p.580.

[63] *OR*, vol.25. pt.2, p.581; Dyer, **CWR**, *vol.3, p.1633;* Sifakis, **Who was Who**, p.656; Rhodes, *History of Battery B*, pp.13, 77; *ARAGSRI*, vol.2, pp.717, 734. The battery which had already been mustered and sent to Washington was Battery A of which George E. Randolph was a member.

[64] Sifakis, **Who was Who**, p.656; *OR*, vol.25. pt.2, p.109.

forced to re-cross the river. In his report, the general called out a number of officers which he was "indebted" to "for prompt and efficient assistance rendered at all times..." Included in the list was Charles Tompkins.[65]

Hooker's 12 May order typically placed four to five batteries into each corps' artillery brigade. This was true for all the brigades except Colonel Tompkins' who found his command containing a total of nine. The enormous number would be difficult for a single commander to direct effectively, but Tompkins took on the challenge. Built with six volunteer batteries from four states and three batteries of Regulars, Tompkins' brigade would be the largest in the army, including those of the reserve. The 1st Battery of Massachusetts Light Artillery, Battery A of the 1st New Jersey Artillery, the 1st and 3rd independent batteries of New York Artillery, and Batteries C and D of the 1st Pennsylvania Artillery constituted the brigades volunteer contingent. The three remaining batteries were the 2nd U. S., Batteries D and G and the 5th U. S., Battery F. With so many batteries to tend to, Tompkins would have his hands full.[66]

Like Charles Wainwright, the late summer of 1861 found Captain Michael Wiedrich involved in the recruitment of an artillery battery. However, unlike Wainwright, Wiedrich was successful in his effort. The battery, having been approved by the War Department on 30 July, had its rolls filled by the end of August. A number of Wiedrich's men had come from the Buffalo area, and many were members from the 65th Militia. Wiedrick, also from Buffalo, would eventually be made the battery's captain at the ancient age of forty-nine. His battery was mustered into service on 1 October, joining Wainwright as part of the 1st New York Light Artillery Regiment. The battery departed for the nation's capital sixteen days later where it remained on duty until March 1862. Wiedrick and his boys saw their first campaign in the Shenandoah Valley as the Federals tried in vain to corral Stonewall Jackson during the late spring and early summer. At the Battle of Cross Keys, Wiedrick directed his battery as it shelled Confederate positions. However, after firing only a few rounds, he was ordered to retire against the wishes of his brigade commander, doing little to damage the enemy.[67]

Later that summer, as part of General Pope's Army of Virginia, Wiedrich's battery participated in the Second Bull Run Campaign but spent more time marching than fighting. After the battle, Wiedrich and the remainder of the newly named Eleventh Corps, spent the fall and early winter covering Washington before being transferred south, arriving too late to assist Burnside at Fredericksburg. Other than a small scrap in the Dumfries area on 2 March, Wiedrich saw no action until that fateful day when Stonewall turned Hooker's right at Chancellorsville. Wiedrich and his New Yorkers were caught in the chaos of the corps' retreat. The captain described the scenes and events in his report.[68]

---

[65] *OR*, vol.25. pt.1, p.562,-566.

[66] *OR*, vol.25. pt.2, p.581.

[67] Dyer, **CWR**, *vol.3, p.1391;* Phisterer, *NYWR*, vol.2, p.1210; Cozzens, Peter, **Shenandoah 1862**, pp.465-466; *OR*, vol.12, pt.2, p.670.

[68] Fox, **Regimental Losses**, p.86; Phisterer, *NYWR*, vol.2, p.1212.

When on the evening of May 2, the firing commenced on our right, we were for some time prevented from opening fire, first, on account of the thick woods some distance in front of the battery, which prevented us from getting sight of the enemy, and, secondly, when the enemy got in sight, our infantry, while retiring, rushed in such masses in front and past the battery that it prevented us for some time again to open fire. As soon as the infantry was out of the way, we opened with canister with good effect, and checked the advance of the enemy for a few minutes. Soon he advanced again in greater numbers, and, seeing that they were getting in our left flank, I gave the order to limber up and retire. In the act of limbering, all the cannoneers [sic] but 1 of one piece were wounded, and we were compelled to leave it on the field. On another one, after being limbered up and in the act of driving away, the 3 hand-horses and one saddle-horse were killed, and we had to leave this also. On another, 2 horses were killed, but, by the exertions and good behavior of the men, we succeeded in bringing it off with 2 horses.[69]

During the days that followed, while the battery licked its wounds, Wiedrich was informed of his new responsibilities as the commander of the Eleventh Corps' artillery brigade. Five batteries were assembled for the brigade. Captain Wiedrich's own Battery I of the 1st New York Light Artillery, and two independent batteries, the 2nd and 13th New York came from his home state. Rounding out the brigade were two western units, Battery's I and K from the 1st Ohio Artillery. Although he would not be in command of the brigade at Gettysburg, Wiedrich had been entrusted to the position as May turned to June while the enemy began to extract portions of its army from Fredericksburg.[70]

Commanding General Slocum's Twelfth Corps artillery brigade was Lieutenant Edward Duchman. Muhlenberg. Muhlenberg, a graduate of Yale University and a civil engineer had worked in the railroad industry most of his professional life. Born in Lancaster Pennsylvania on 15 May 1831, he graduated from the Ivy League school in 1850. He spent the first seven years of his career working on various railroad and canal projects in Pennsylvania. Taking his skills to Brazil with a number of other engineers, Muhlenberg helped construct a rail line running westward from Rio de Janeiro.[71]

Still in Brazil when the war broke out, Muhlenberg did not immediately return to the states. In October 1861, after arriving home, Edward enlisted in the United States Army in Philadelphia and was assigned as a second lieutenant in

---

[69] *OR*, vol.25. pt.1, p.647.

[70] *OR*, vol.25. pt.2, p.582.

[71] **Electronic Source:** http://en.wikipedia.org/wiki/Edward_D._Muhlenberg, Last accessed 5/11/2012.

the 4th U. S. Artillery. Promoted to first lieutenant before the end of the month, Muhlenberg fought with Battery F at the first Battle of Winchester. He next directed his battery at Cedar Mountain where Brigadier General Samuel Crawford noted that his "fire was most effective." At the battle of Antietam, Muhlenberg directed Battery F as part of the Twelfth Corps' artillery brigade but missed the Battle of Fredericksburg. After being attached to General Alpheus William's divisional artillery, at Chancellorsville, Muhlenberg's battery did most of its fighting under the watchful eye of General John Geary. Geary noted in his report that Muhlenberg deserved "great praise… for the courage, coolness, and indomitable bravery with which he contended against the fearful odds before him."[72]

When the artillery was reorganized, Lieutenant Muhlenberg was placed in charge of General Slocum's brigade of guns. The appointment was justified. His new command consisted of his own Battery F of the 4th U. S. and Battery K of the 5th U. S., Battery E of the Pennsylvania Artillery and Battery M of the 1st New York.[73]

For the Army of the Potomac, Special Order No.129 went a long way to curing the ills of Hooker's poor artillery decision. The new organization placed the batteries and ammunition of each corps within easy reach of corps and division commanders. Well established reserve divisions, now under the direction of their own commanding officer, could easily be concentrated to provide maximum effect at points on the battlefield where their services were needed. The batteries were now free of the meddling hands of division and brigade commanders. While the organization would remain in a state of flux, with new batteries arriving, and old ones departing, as the army marched north that June the organization would remain sound. At the battle of Gettysburg, the Army of the Potomac's artillery branch would arguably perform better than at any previous time.

Longstreet's Gunners

Perhaps the most renowned artillery organization in either the north or south prior to the war was Louisiana's Washington Artillery. Organized in New Orleans as a single battery in 1838, its ranks would grow to include four companies by the early months of the war and a fifth company would be mustered early in the second year of the conflict. As the unit's original commander, James Burdge Walton had a leg up on others who might be seeking an officer's commission in the upstart Confederacy.[74]

Walton, a native of New Jersey, was born in Newark on 18 November 1813. He attended college in Louisiana and by 1836 had graduated and married. He entered the business world by opening a wholesale grocery operation in the Crescent City. When the Washington Artillery was organized, he signed up and, possibly due to his education and business experience, became the battalion's adjutant. When the

---

[72] Ibid, **OR**, vol.12. pt.2, p.152; **OR**, vol.25. pt.1, pp.727, 732;

[73] **OR**, vol.25. pt.2, p.583.

[74] Sifakis, Stewart, **Compendium of the Confederacy Armies: Louisiana**, pp.33, 41.

Mexican War began, James put his business aspirations on hold and entered the conflict as colonel of the 1st Louisiana Regiment. He led the regiment through the campaign, gaining valuable military experience before returning to a somewhat normal life. As the Civil War broke, Walton, then a major, and the remainder of the Washington Artillery were mustered into Confederate service in May 1861. The Army of Northern Virginia's artillery historian Jennings C. Wise noted that "[a]t the outbreak of the Civil War there was not a finer organization of citizen soldiery [sic] in America."[75]

Walton guided his battalion through the early skirmishes outside of Washington and during the first Battle of Manassas. He continued to lead his gunners through the remainder of 1861 and early 1862 until he was made colonel on 26 May 1862 and chief of artillery for the Artillery Reserve of Lee's Right Wing on 20 June. At Antietam, Walton led the batteries of the Washington Artillery once again. He followed up the battle with a reliable performance at Fredericksburg where he directed his batteries along Marye's Heights until forced to withdraw having expended all its ammunition. When Longstreet packed up part of his corps and marched to Suffolk after the battle, his chief of artillery remained behind and defended the heights above Fredericksburg once again during the Chancellorsville Campaign.[76]

As Longstreet returned and the Gettysburg Campaign opened, Walton reestablished his official duties as the general's chief of artillery. Unfortunately, the man from Louisiana would find himself overshadowed by a West Point trained Virginian named Edward Porter Alexander.

The Finest Artilleryman in the Army

Some would argue the most prominent and most skilled individual within Lee's artillery organization during the spring and summer of 1863 was Colonel Edward Porter Alexander. Edward, within General Pendleton's new organizational structure, would be retained as commander of one of the First Corps' reserve battalions. His battalion contained six batteries, four of which were from Virginia, the other two hailing from South Carolina and Louisiana. His Virginians were those of the Ashland and Bedford Light Artillery and the Richmond and Bath batteries. The Madison Artillery's Louisianans and the Palmetto boys of the Brooks Artillery completed Alexander's allotment.[77]

---

[75] Krick, *Colonels*, p.390; Wise, **Long Arm of Lee**, p.94.

[76] Krick, *Colonels*, p.390; *OR*, vol.2, pp.465, 515; Wise, **Long Arm of Lee**, p.258; *OR*, vol.12. pt.2, pp.546, 548, 567, 570; *OR*, vol.21, pp.573-575; Owen, Allison, **Record of an Old Artillery Organization**, The Field Artillery Journal, vol.IV, no.1, p.11. Wise notes Walton as the Right Wing's chief of artillery but the *OR* does not note him as such in the organization published on 23 July. Walton noted his title under the signature on his report as "Colonel and Chief of Artillery, Right Wing." The Right Wing would become Longstreet's First Corps.

[77] Wise, **Long Arm of Lee, vol.2**, p.567; *OR*, vol.25. pt.2, p.850; Koleszar, Marilyn B., **Ashland, Bedford and Taylor Virginia Light Artillery**, pp.1-2, 5. The Bath Battery was more commonly known as Taylor's Battery after its captain, Osmond B. Taylor.

Porter, as his close friends called him, was the sixth of eight children born to Adam Leopold Alexander and his wife Sarah Hillhouse Gilbert. A well-known slaveholder, Adam owned two plantations and over fifty slaves in the Washington area of Georgia. By 1850, his real property holdings in the area were in excess of $25,000. Edward's father instructed young Alexander in the art of shooting, exposing and teaching the boy about weapons at an early age. When Adam's boys were old enough he "brought out several male teachers" to privately educate Edward and his brothers. Alexander's mother instructed their women servants how to make clothing and every Sunday taught the children the word of the Lord. The boys and men worked the plantation and together the group produced and put up all the supplies and rations required to be self-sustaining. During the winter, the main event was the butchering of hogs. It was not uncommon for thirty to forty of the animals to be slaughtered during the event. Cured meats, sausage, lard, ribs, jowls and hogshead cheese were put up. The proceeds of the butchering, which occurred two or three times a winter, must have kept the family and their servants well fed.[78]

From his earliest recollection, Edward expressed to his father a desire to attend West Point. His father however, would pay little heed to his son's persuasive measures. Pleading failed to sway his father's opinion. It was not until two of Edward's sisters managed to attract academy graduates as suitors, did his father's attitude soften. Finally, at the age of fourteen, Edward received consent from his Adam but only if he promised to study hard enough to graduate at the top of his class and receive an appointment to the engineers. Edward consented and his coursework at school was altered to concentrate on subjects he would need to be proficient in to succeed at the Academy. Adam contacted Robert Toombs, who at the time was representing Georgia's Eighth District in Washington, and tried to secure an appointment, but found the position already filled. Edward waited an additional two years, a period which proved to be a tremendous benefit to him. After spending the winter months of 1852-53 in Savannah studying drawing and French, he felt himself better prepared both in mind and maturity when he finally entered the Academy in 1853 at the age of eighteen. After four years of hard work, Edward Alexander graduated third in a class of thirty-eight cadets on 1 July 1857. He was brevetted a second lieutenant in the engineers, upholding his promise.[79]

After a three month furlough, Edward returned to West Point as an assistant instructor and spent the winter of 1857-58 at the academy. Later, he was selected as one of the sixty-four handpicked men to departed West Point for Fort Leavenworth to join Harney's expedition to support Johnston in Utah. He arrived in time to depart with General Harney's column on 31 March of the following year. The group's departure was delayed so spring grasses would be available to provide forage for the party's livestock. Ultimately, the expedition resulted in no armed conflict, as the disagreement was solved through negotiations. Alexander returned to West Point where he remained stationed until the summer of 1860 when he was ordered to the Pacific Northwest. The newly married Alexander traveled by ship

---

[78] Alexander, *Fighting*, pp.5-6, 556 n8. Edward had three brothers and four sisters.

[79] *Ibid*, pp.4-5, 7; Eicher, & Eicher, *High Commands*, p.101.

to Panama, across the isthmus and sailed up the west coast to Fort Steilacoom, near Puget Sound in the Washington Territory. While stationed there, the secession crisis exploded in the Deep South.[80]

Shortly after his native state seceded, Alexander admitted to himself that his path had been set. "I knew that I would finally have to resign from the U. S. Army," Edward wrote after the war, but admitted he "never realized the gravity of the situation. As soon as the *right to secede* was denied by the North I strongly approved of its assertion & maintenance by force if necessary. And being young & ambitious in my profession I was anxious to take my part in everything going on." Edward waited for orders to arrive calling the soldiers of his detachment home, not wishing to resign before he returned east. Finally, instructions came in April and the party started its journey, but in San Francisco he received additional orders assigning him to duty upon Alcatraz Island. His hand had been forced, and Edward could do nothing but resign. Unfortunately for the young lieutenant, he would now have to pay for his own passage home.[81]

Resigning his commission on 1 May, Alexander spent a month in transit and arrived in Washington, Georgia around midday on 30 May. A number of family members were present, and talk, as expected, centered on the prospects of war. Years later, Edward could not recall all the members of his family who were there but one thing was certain, hardships were coming. Alexander did remember his brother, James, being at hand. James had already volunteered for service in a company of men destined to become part of the 9th Georgia and was twelve days away from being mustered into service. Feeling responsible for getting to Richmond as soon as possible, Edward spent only one evening with his family. The morning was no doubt a tearful one, but, with the emotional partings out of the way, Alexander turned his back on his home and went to war.[82]

Arriving in Richmond the following day, Edward waited until Monday before reporting for duty. Initially a captain, he was assigned to the Engineering and Signal branch of the Confederate Army of the Potomac. A month later he received a promotion to major, the rank he would hold when the first Battle of Manassas was fought. Shortly before the fighting commenced near Bull Run, Edward joined the headquarters staff of General Beauregard where he implemented a new signaling system. "Capt. E. P. Alexander, Confederate States Engineer, fortunately joined my headquarters in time to introduce the system of new field signals," Beauregard recounted "[U]nder his skillful management rendered me the most important service preceding and during the engagement." The day after the battle Edward

---

[80] Alexander, *Fighting*, pp.9-10, 13-14, 16, 21; Wakelyn, **Biographical Dictionary**, p.70. General Harney was originally to be the leader of the expedition under Johnston, but he was delayed due to the difficulties in Kansas between pro-slavery factions and abolitionists.

[81] Alexander, *Fighting*, pp.21, 23.

[82] *Ibid*, p.36; Eicher, & Eicher, **High Commands**, p.101; Henderson, *RCSG*, vol.1, p.996. Porter admits he may be in error regarding the date of his arrival in Washington.

was transferred to the ordnance branch of General Beauregard's army and installed as chief of ordnance. Before the year was out, he would be a lieutenant colonel.[83]

The first year of the war saw Edward performing the duties of both chief of ordnance and chief signal officer for first Beauregard, then Joseph E. Johnston during the Peninsula Campaign. When Lee assumed command of the army, Alexander continued executing the same services for his new chieftain. As part of his responsibility with the signal corps, Edward coordinated intelligence activities, headed up reconnaissance operations and supervised the deployment and usage of balloon reconnaissance during The Seven Days. At the Battle of Gaines' Mill, he actually spent part of the engagement floating above the battlefield in his balloon. Ordnance duties also saw him laboring to keep the army supplied with ammunition and weaponry.[84]

Alexander's signal corps duties also required him to be proficient in the training and execution of signaling, and the men had to be instructed in his new, and somewhat unique method of signaling. As the skill sets of Alexander's signalers grew, so too did demand for their services. Shortly after his setback at Kernstown, Stonewall Jackson requested some men within his command be trained by an Alexander apprentice. Jackson felt Federal signalers were a serious disadvantage to his Confederates and needed to counter the enemy's proficiency. "If you can let me have a man who understands Alexander's system of signals I hope you will do so, in order that he may instruct others for me," Jackson requested of Longstreet. Three weeks later, Jackson made the same appeal to Lee. "Please send me part of Alexander's signal corps, if you can spare it; if not, please send me the system of signals, so that I may have persons instructed." Alexander was quickly developing a reputation as a fine ordnance officer and signalman. However, it would be in the artillery that he would make his most significant mark on the war.[85]

After taking command of the army in front of Richmond, Lee showed confidence in Alexander's skills when he requested Edward provide organization to his artillery. Shortly after the conclusion of The Seven Days, Lee, with Pendleton absent, contacted Alexander with instructions.

> Hdqrs. Department of Northern Virginia
> July 5, 1862 – 9 p.m.
> Lieut. Col. E. P. Alexander,
>   Chief of Ordnance:
> Colonel: General Lee directs me to say that General Pendleton is absent, and he [does] not know who is in charge of the Reserve Artillery; he therefore desires that you will go at once and ascertain the condition of the Reserve Artillery, and

---

[83] Alexander, *Fighting*, pp.37, 60; Eicher, & Eicher, *High Commands*, p.101; *OR*, vol.2, p.446.

[84] Alexander, Edward P., *Military Memoirs of a Confederate*, p.xx.

[85] *OR*, vol.12. pt.3, p.843, 872.

have it all put in condition to move to Malvern Hill early tomorrow morning.

The artillery will be held in readiness to move; everything ready for active service, but you will not move the artillery without further orders from these headquarters. You will also see that your ordnance train is ready to move at the same time, if necessary. If the artillery is ordered down the general desires that you go with it.

Yours, &c.,

A. P. Mason,
Assistant Adjutant General.[86]

Alexander took on his new responsibility with vigor and in a short time proved he was equally adept at the direction of artillery as he was at his other duties, which he also continued to perform. As the summer came to a close, Lee's army advanced into Maryland, inaugurating the campaign which led to the fight at Sharpsburg. On 14 September, while at Hagerstown, Lee received word of McClellan's increased activity. Taking steps to establish McClellan's intentions, Lee instructed some of his generals and Alexander "to keep out scouts and to use every means in their power to ascertain General McClellan's movements." After receiving word the Federals were advancing, Lee mounted Traveller and rode back toward the rear guard of his army. Alexander accompanied the general and as they approached the fighting on South Mountain, the colonel noticed what appeared to be a signal tower occupied by Federals. "[I]tching to have some personal part in a fight, I suggested to Gen. Lee that I might take a few men & go recapture it." Lee agreed and Alexander, along with eight men, struggled up the side of the mountain during the midday heat. Unfortunately, the party found the tower occupied by a group of curious civilians. While the exercise turned out to be no more than an exhausting hike, it demonstrated Alexander's desire and combative nature. Perhaps spending the first eighteen months of the war performing administrative duties had fuelled his fire.[87]

Alexander's impressive performance at all his assigned duties was rewarded shortly after Antietam. On 7 November, after Colonel Stephen D. Lee was transferred west, Alexander received orders to take the colonel's place at the head of Lee's former command in Longstreet's reserve artillery battalion. Colonel Lee, who had just been promoted to brigadier general, had recommended Alexander to General Lee to succeed him. Around 10 p.m. on a cold snowy night, Alexander was awake taking care of some paperwork when three men from the battalion arrived. The men had been sent to secure his commitment to assume command. Alexander informed the men that he was willing to "do whatever he [General Lee] thought

---

[86] *OR*, vol.11. pt.3, p.634.

[87] *OR*, vol.12. pt.3, p.931; Alexander, **Fighting**, pp.142-143, n.575. The signal tower was an old dilapidated stone tower built in the 1820s to pay tribute to George Washington. Forty years later, lack of maintenance had allowed the tower to fall into a state of disarray.

best for the good of the service." Soon after the men departed, a second visitor, Stephen Lee, arrived. The two were good friends from Alexander's academy days, Lee having been one of Edward's instructors. The new brigadier urged Alexander to accept the promotion noting the battalion was one of "the biggest & the best in the army."[88]

About midnight Alexander was summoned to General Lee's tent and a similar conversation took place. Once again, Alexander responded by telling the general he wished only to serve where the general thought he could do the most good. Lee's trust in Alexander was on display when the general questioned him regarding who should replace him as the army's chief of ordnance. Alexander suggested a man he was well acquainted with from the Ordnance Department in Richmond but had never met and had only dealt with through written correspondence. Lee immediately sent a telegram to Richmond to summon the man. The general's faith in Alexander's suggestion speaks to Lee's opinion of Edward's character and judgment. To appoint a man who Alexander had never officially met and Lee himself probably had little or no knowledge, so quickly to a critical position, cements the point of Lee's belief in Longstreet's new artillery battalion commander.[89]

Never having led artillery in battle, Alexander first saw action at Fredericksburg, where he was severely tested but showed his abilities with stern resolve and bravery. Near the southern end of the Confederate line along Marye's Heights, Colonel Walton's Washington Artillery, which had been in position since the Federal assault began, was dangerously close to expending all its ammunition. At approximately 3:30 p.m., Walton located Alexander and ordered him to relieve his beleaguered gunners with a like number of guns from his battalion. After selecting his guns, Alexander started forward but soon discovered a Confederate battery firing over his route to the front. Coolly, Edward sent a rider to halt the firing so his guns could pass unhindered, and when his path was clear, he led his command onward. Suddenly, Alexander noticed an incoming artillery shell screaming toward his position. The round struck 100 yards away, and ricocheted toward him, spinning end over end "like a stick." Expecting to be cut down by the shell, Alexander knew there was no sense in trying to dodge or move. His fate was no longer in his hands and he found himself for a split second wondering where the whizzing artillery shell would strike him. In what must have seemed like slow motion, the projectile lost elevation and took aim at his horse's legs. Luck was with Edward and his horse, for the deadly shot passed under his horse's abdomen and between the animals legs, doing no damage to rider or mount.[90]

Galloping his guns up to Walton's vacated position, Alexander quickly unlimbered and went into action, determined to stay for the remainder of the battle. The gun pits Walton evacuated were only empty for a few minutes, and it was not long before Alexander's gunners were cutting swaths through onrushing

---

[88] *OR*, vol.19, pt.2, pp.703-704; Alexander, ***Fighting***, p.159.

[89] Alexander, ***Fighting***, pp.159-160.

[90] Alexander, ***Fighting***, pp.177-178; ***OR***, vol.21, p.576.

Federals at close range. Ignoring counter battery fire, his guns continued with their bloody work until the battered Federals withdrew and darkness covered the battlefield. The cost in manpower and horses had been high. Alexander noted in his report that three quarter of his total losses were taken as the guns struggled to get into position. Of his eleven casualties, only one man was killed while the battery expending one thousand and eighty rounds. Critical for the battery however, was the loss of fifteen horses.[91]

Longstreet's artilleryman, Edward Porter Alexander. *LAL*

Like Walton, Alexander and his battalion remained in the Fredericksburg area when Longstreet transferred the majority of his corps to Suffolk. As the Confederates prepared to march west to confront Hooker near Chancellorsville, Alexander, at the direction of General Lee, posted some of his guns on Marye's Heights and took a position near the head of Jackson's column with the remainder of his guns as it marched toward Chancellorsville. Only two batteries would be in position to engage the enemy before the day came to an end. The following morning, the battalion, minus two batteries, fell in near the rear of Jackson's flanking column. Alexander's location in the column kept his guns from being in position to support the attack. As the assault commenced, his guns were held in reserve. During the night he took command of all the Confederate artillery on the field due to the wounding of Colonel Crutchfield. He spent the remainder of the night scouting and placing batteries, which must have been a bit nerve-racking

---

[91] Alexander, *Fighting*, p.178; *OR*, vol.21, p.576.

with both the Confederates and Federals possessing itchy trigger fingers. For the balance of the battle, he skillfully handled the Confederate guns, prompting Lee to note in his report that Edward was "deserving [of] especial commendation."[92]

Both Lee and Longstreet had great confidence in Alexander. Although his experience at the head of his battalion encompassed only two engagements, Edward's efforts had been conducted under the watchful eyes of both Lee and his First Corps commander. Longstreet later noted that Alexander had "particularly distinguished" himself at Fredericksburg. On 3 June, as the army began its shift to the Culpeper area, Alexander was perhaps the premier artillery commander within Lee's mighty army.[93]

Colonel Walton's famous Washington Artillery was designated as Longstreet's other reserve artillery battalion. Four companies from the infamous organization were used to populate the unit. With Walton performing duties as chief of artillery, command of the battalion had fallen to Captain Benjamin Franklin Eshleman. Although Walton remained involved in the command structure of the battalion; Eshleman had taken on more responsibility when the colonel began reporting to Longstreet. The original captain of the battalion's 4th Company, Eshleman had been designated its chief when the unit was mustered in on 26 May 1861 in New Orleans. Very little is known about Benjamin's early life. He was born in Lancaster County, Pennsylvania on 9 March 1830. He relocated to New Orleans, but the time period of his move is not known. Wounded at First Manassas, Eshleman sat out the fighting on the Virginia Peninsula and did not return to active duty until Second Manassas. While recuperating, he was promoted to major on 26 March 1862 and upon his return resumed command duties with the 4th company. Although Colonel Walton was officially the head of Longstreet's artillery, he still led the battalion at Second Manassas and Sharpsburg. Laboring at his duties through the winter and spring of 1862-63, Eshleman was finally rewarded in early June, when he was placed in command of all four of the Washington Artillery Battalion's batteries.[94]

Within Pendleton's new organizational structure, each of the divisions in Lee's three corps would have attached to them a battalion of artillery. The reorganization called for a group of four batteries under the command of Colonel Henry Coalter Cabell to remain assigned to Lafayette McLaws' Division as its battalion. Cabell, the son of Virginia's fourteenth Governor, William H. Cabell, was born in Richmond on 14 February 1820. Henry attended college at the University of Virginia studying first in the School of Academics and then the School of Law. After graduation, he partnered in a law firm in Richmond with Virginia attorney

---

[92]   *OR*, vol.25, pt.1, pp.799, 804, 820-822.

[93]   *OR*, vol.21, p.571.

[94]   *OR*, vol.2, p.443; Sifakis, **CCA**, **Louisiana**, pp.34, 39; Krick, **Colonels**, p.131. Within the Confederate command structure, an officer executing the duties of chief of artillery was not necessarily exempt from leading an artillery organization during battle.

general Sydney S. Baxter. In 1850 Cabell married Jane C. Alston, daughter of a wealthy South Carolina plantation owner.[95]

When the war began Cabell, on 25 April 1861, joined the Richmond Fayette Artillery and was appointed the battery's captain. Before the year was out, he received a promotion to lieutenant colonel and was placed in command of the 1st Virginia Artillery on 9 September. During the early stages of the Peninsular Campaign, Cabell performed the duties of General Magruder's chief of artillery and fought during the siege of Yorktown. Three days after the conclusion of The Seven Days fighting, Cabell was appointed chief of artillery for McLaws' Division and on 29 July 1862, was promoted to colonel. Henry accompanied the division on all its campaigns during the fall and winter of 1862 and into the spring of 1863. At Sharpsburg, Cabell rose from his sickbed to join his division commander on the field. In January 1863, he took a leave of absence but by Chancellorsville, was back with McLaws' command.[96]

Early June saw Cabell's Battalion possessing of the Pulaski and Troup Artillery batteries from Georgia, Battery A from the 1st North Carolina Artillery and the 1st Company of the Richmond Howitzers. For the men of the battalion, the coming campaign would be their most severe test since the war began.[97]

As artillery battalion commander for General George Pickett's Division, Major James G. Dearing and his batteries were spared the carnage of Chancellorsville. Dearing's command contained four batteries, all of which were from Virginia. One battery, the Hampden Artillery, was named after one of its organizer's father. Another battery, the Fauquier Artillery, originally raised as an infantry company, had actually fought as such at Manassas. The Richmond Fayette and Lynchburg Artillery constituted Dearing's final two batteries.[98]

Dearing was born in Campbell County Virginia on 25 April 1840. As a boy he attended Hanover Academy before accepting an appointment to represent Virginia's 5th District at West Point. James entered the academy at the age of eighteen on 1 July 1858, but the war would interrupt his education. Being a strong secessionist, he would, on 22 April 1861 resign his post. The day of his resignation, James joined the Virginia Militia as a captain of artillery, but when the famed Washington Artillery arrived in Richmond, Dearing joined it as a second lieutenant. Promoted to captain in April of 1862, he took command of the Lynchburg Artillery in spite of protests from a battery officer who objected to his placement. Eventually

---

[95] Brown, Alexander, *The Cabells and their Kin: A Memorial Volume of History, Biography and Genealogy*, pp.586, 588; Wise, *Long Arm of Lee*, p.567. Later in life Cabell would suffer an odd tragedy. His wife would lose her life when her clothing caught fire. Moore, Robert H., *The Richmond Fayette, Hampden, Thomas and Blount's Lynchburg Artillery*, p.147.

[96] *OR*, vol.11, pt.1, pp.411-415; *OR*, vol.19, pt.1, p.860; Brown, *The Cabells*, p.586.

[97] Wise, *Long Arm of Lee*, p.567.

[98] Ibid.

the protesting officer was released, and Dearing set about his new duties with enthusiasm.[99]

In November, Dearing was placed in command of a battalion, and assigned to the brigade of General Montgomery Corse. His new command contained three of the batteries he would eventually be charged with as part of General Pickett's battalion. Lightly engaged at Fredericksburg, Dearing's casualty list included only one wounded man and a disabled horse. Shortly after the battle, the batteries found themselves on a road leading south to their winter camps in the Suffolk area. Having proven himself a capable battalion leader, Dearing was promoted to major and during the middle of April assigned his fourth battery. His command now consisted of the four groups of guns he would lead into southern Pennsylvania.[100]

Longstreet's final artillery battalion, which was attached to Hood's Division, was under the direction of Kentuckian Mathis Winston Henry. Residing in Russellville, the twenty-five year old Henry was an 1860 graduate of West Point. After spending a brief period in the U. S. Army, Henry resigned his commission and cast his lot with the Confederacy. Initially joining the cavalry as a lieutenant, by March 1862, Henry had been elevated to the staff of Jeb Stuart. By August, he had been promoted to captain and placed in command of a battery within Stuart's horse artillery.[101]

Major John Pelham saw Henry's abilities early. Pelham had been well acquainted with Henry, the two having been classmates at the Academy. In his after action report on the campaign and battle of Second Manassas, Pelham noted Henry "displayed the greatest courage and daring during the engagement." However, it was during the Battle of Fredericksburg where Henry's determination was in full view, showing he was a capable artilleryman. During the early hours of 13 December, under the cover of early morning fog, Federal forces began crossing the river below town. To confront the threat, Pelham ran a section of his horse artillery up to engage the enemy. The guns unlimbered and began to roar, peppering the Federal soldiers with canister and driving them from their position. To counter the Confederates, the Federals rolled their own guns forward and an artillery duel began. For two hours the Confederate artillerymen spared with the Federal guns, holding the enemy infantry columns at bay and buying time for the Rebel army to prepare to meet the threat. The guns performing the remarkable feat were under the direction of Mathis Henry.[102]

After the battle, Henry left the horse artillery when he was reassigned to Longstreet's Corps and marched to the Suffolk area. Once again, he skillfully handled his guns through the winter and earned a promotion to major. Upon

---

[99] Moore, *The Richmond Fayette... Artillery*, pp.56, 65, 150-151.

[100] *Ibid*, p.65-66, 151; *OR*, vol.21, p.573; *OR*, vol.18, p.995.

[101] Krick, *Colonels*, p.189.

[102] *OR*, vol.12, pt.1, pp.754-755; *OR*, vol.21, pp.545, 547, 731, 742; Trout, Robert J., *With Pen & Saber: The Letters and Diaries of J.E.B. Stuart's Staff Officers*, p.119; Trout, Robert, J., *Galloping Thunder: The Stuart Horse Artillery Battalion*, pp.10, 144.

Longstreet's return, Mathis was awarded command of Hood's divisional artillery battalion. The battalion contained four batteries from both North and South Carolina. From the southern state came the German Artillery and the Palmetto Light Artillery while North Carolina contributed the Rowan and Branch Artillery.[103]

Ewell's Battalions

General Pendleton's early June reorganization placed Virginia native Lieutenant Colonel Thomas Hill Carter in command of the artillery battalion assigned to General Rodes' Division. A cousin of Robert E. Lee, Carter was born in King William County on 13 June 1831. Thomas received a military education at the Virginia Military Institute, and, after graduation in 1849, continued his schooling when he entered the University of Virginia Medical School. After finishing his education, Carter began a career as a physician. Noted Civil War diarist Mary Chesnut wrote Carter was "…a bluff Englishman to all seeming, a regular, red, big, strong John Bull – or the descendant of one." Carter could trace his lineage to some of the earliest settlers in Virginia. His younger half-brother, William Pleasants Page Carter, could follow his ancestry back to King Edward III of England, from whom William was a direct descendant. When the war began, Thomas undertook the work involved in recruiting a company of volunteers and by the end of May 1861, the organization's rolls were nearly full. The men were officially enrolled at Bond's Store in King William County on 1 June, with Thomas assuming its captaincy. By the end of June, enough additional men had been recruited to form a company of light artillery. The officers received their commissions on 2 July and exactly one month later, Carter's men were mustered into Confederate service, inaugurating Thomas Carter's career as an artillery officer.[104]

Known as the King William Artillery, Carter's battery spent the first months of its service in northern Virginia where it fought in its initial skirmish and suffered its first casualties. The opening of 1862 found the battery attached to Rodes' Brigade of General Beauregard's command. By 12 March the battery was in Fredericksburg, where it remained until early April when Carter's guns were summoned to the Peninsula. He directed the battery at Yorktown and during the muddy retreat up the isthmus toward Richmond. When General Johnston turned to face the Federals at Seven Pines, Carter's Battery, along with the remainder of Rodes' Brigade deployed near the extreme right of the Confederate line. It was not long before Carter had his guns engaged in a spirited duel with a number of Federal pieces positioned in a redoubt. According to Rodes, Captain Carter succeeded in silencing the Federals and driving them from their position. Rodes seemed greatly impressed with the performance of Carter's boys. "The conduct of the King William Artillery," wrote the general in his after action report, "has nowhere in the history of the war been equaled for daring, coolness, or efficiency."

---

[103] Wise, *Long Arm of Lee*, p.567.

[104] Krick, *Colonels*, p.83; Macaluso, Gregory J., *Morris, Orange and King William Artillery*, pp.19-20, 106.

The battery suffered heavily during the engagement with five men killed, including one officer, and twenty-five wounded.[105]

During The Seven Days, Carter's battery was engaged but was not severely tested. While a few men were lost, the conflict, at least for Carter's gunners, was not as intense as the fighting at Seven Pines. After the engagement concluded, D. H. Hill's command remained behind in the Richmond area as Lee transferred the bulk of his army north. It was not until shortly before the inauguration of the Maryland Campaign that Hill's Division and Carter battery caught up with Lee. After helping hold off the aggressive Federal attempt to force the South Mountain passes, Carter's guns became embroiled in the whirlwind of Sharpsburg. Posted along the ridge south of the Dunkard Church, Carter's guns, after exhausting all of its ammunition, where withdrawn to refill their caissons. Returning to the fight, the Virginian posted his battery to support the fighting northeast of town but was soon withdrawn and placed in a position to confront the Federal Ninth Corps on the southern end of the field. Although he was slightly wounded that day, luck was with Carter for the battery only suffered six casualties and as the month of September came to a close, he skillfully kept his battery in good condition in preparation for the next battle or skirmish.[106]

Early in October, Carter and his battery were brigaded with a number of other batteries into a divisional artillery battalion. Carter himself however, was destined for a different assignment. On 12 December he was promoted to major of artillery and assigned the role of chief of artillery for Hill's Division. After turning over command of the battery to his half brother, Thomas assumed his new post.[107]

At Fredericksburg, Hill's Division was posted on the extreme right of the Confederate line, and Carter performed his new tasks well, helping to keep Hill's guns well serviced and located where they could do the most damage to the enemy. His work did not go unnoticed by General Pendleton and when he issued his recommendations of 11 February 1863 to Lee, he tapped out Carter for battalion command.

> "Major Carter, some time since promoted to command the artillery of General D. H. Hill's division, was even then recommended for the rank of lieutenant-colonel, as fully earned by his distinguished service and eminent merit, and may well

---

[105] Macaluso, *Morris, Orange and King William Artillery*, pp.20-24; **OR**, vol.11, pt.1, pp.972-973, 975-976. D. H. Hill evidently did not see the intent of Rodes' comment. Obviously Rodes was very impressed with Carter's effort and used the strongest words he could find to express his opinion. Hill, always a realist, could not resist the opportunity to downplay Carter's work. "This is a strong statement," Hill wrote on Rodes report, "and argues that the writer was conversant with the conduct of artillery in all the various actions of the war."

[106] Macaluso, *Morris, Orange and King William Artillery*, pp.28-29.

[107] Ibid, p.30, 33.

be made lieutenant-colonel and given command of this [General Rodes' Division] battalion."

Carter's promotion to lieutenant colonel came through on 2 March, and he quickly began his duties as General Rodes' artillery battalion commander.[108]

During the Chancellorsville Campaign, Carter guided his guns as part of Jackson's flank march and deployed them in the rear of General Doles Brigade to the right of the Old Orange Turnpike. According to Carter, the battle line formed in "dense woods, which afforded no ground for artillery." When the attack began, Jackson's fast moving line soon outdistanced Carter's ability to be of assistance and his participation consisted of nothing more than pursuing the fight. The following day Carter pushed his guns forward, and along with Edward Alexander's command, deployed in Hazel Grove to shell the Federals near the Chancellor House. Even General Lee acknowledged his cousin's contribution to the fighting on 3 May. Writing in his report, the commanding general noted that "Lieutenant-Colonel Carter... being thrown forward to occupy favorable positions secured by the advance of the infantry, began to play with great precision and effect."[109]

As the month of June opened, Carter was looked upon as one of the finer artillerymen in the Army of Northern Virginia. The gunners within his four batteries had been through some of the fiercest fighting in the Eastern Theater. Three of Carter's batteries were from his home state, including his own King William Artillery and the Morris and Orange Artilleries. Rounding out the battalion, and hailing from the state of Alabama, his fourth battery, the Jeff Davis Artillery also brought the reputation of a fine artillery outfit.[110]

When the King William Artillery was first brigaded with other batteries in October 1862, the man placed in charge of the new organization was Lieutenant Colonel Hilary Pollard Jones. Jones, along with Lewis M. Coleman, a mathematics professor at the University of Virginia and former principal of the Hanover Academy, began working to recruit a company of light artillery in late July, 1861. Jones, a resident of Hanover County and a teacher in the town of Taylorsville, had just turned twenty-eight years of age when recruitment began. The battery mustered in mid-August and the officers, including Jones who was the battery's first lieutenant, received their commissions. When the infantry unit the battery was to be attached to, failed to organize, the battery was allowed to entered service as an independent company.[111]

Designated the Morris Artillery, the battery and Lieutenant Jones spent the early portion of the war defending the Virginia countryside and fighting McClellan's

---

[108] *OR*, vol.21, pp.638, 644; *OR*, vol.25, pt.2, p.616; Krick, *Colonels*, p.83; Rodes took command of D. H. Hill's Division when the North Carolinian threatened to resign and was transferred to command of the troops in his home state.

[109] *OR*, vol.25, pt.1, pp.800, 998-999.

[110] Wise, *Long Arm of Lee*, p.568.

[111] Macaluso, *Morris, Orange and King William Artillery*, p.1.

army on the Peninsula. Over the following months the officers, including Jones, developed a reputation for being tough and strict disciplinarians, traits which were not well received by the men of the battery and many began to despise the unit's officers. When the battery was reorganized on 14 May 1862, four of its officers, including Jones, were thrown out and new officers selected. Jones, who had been away from the battery most of the month of April, escaped the indignation of the rebuttal when he was placed in temporary command of the Jeff Davis Artillery.[112]

Although no longer associated with his old battery, the Confederate authorities had recognized Jones' abilities and promoted the Virginian to major two weeks after he was summarily tossed from the battery. General Pendleton, who had turned to Jones when the Jeff Davis Artillery needed a commanding officer, must surely have been instrumental in Jones' retention. As The Seven Days fighting opened, Jones found himself in command of an artillery battalion in General Pendleton's reserve. During the fighting, his battalion was assigned to support D. H. Hill's Division and Jones' unit suffered twenty-seven casualties during the week of fighting. He remained attached to Hill throughout the summer and early fall, and saw additional action at Sharpsburg.[113]

Pendleton's 2 October proposal to Lee suggested completely restructured Jones' Battalion. He wished to consolidate some batteries and have substandard officers removed from command. But, when the shuffling was complete, Jones' battalion retained five batteries and remained assigned to D. H. Hill's Division. Jones was free to guide his batteries, which included Carter's King William, and his old battery, the Morris Artillery. It must have been a bitter pill for the members of Jones' old battery to see one of the men they voted to remove from command now in charge of their battalion.[114]

Sometime after the Battle of Fredericksburg, Jones took command of the artillery brigade attached to General Jackson's old division, which was officially under the command of Brigade General William B. Taliaferro. When Pendleton proposed the promotion of Major Carter and his placement at the head of Hill's (now Rodes') artillery battalion, he also lobbied for Jones to be promoted and retain command of Taliaferro's guns.

> "Major Jones, now in command of the artillery of General Trimble's division, under special request from General Taliaferro, when in command of the division, has been recommended for promotion, and might worthily be made lieutenant-colonel and have command of this battalion. In addition to much gallant service, he is a very judicious and faithful officer."

---

[112] *Ibid*, pp.3-8.

[113] *Ibid*, p.7; Krick, ***Colonels***, p.215; ***OR***, vol.11, pt.2, p.630;

[114] ***OR***, vol.19, pt.2, p.648-649, 653; ***OR***, vol.21, p.541.

Taliaferro, who had been wounded at Fredericksburg, would not return to Lee's army and his division would be placed under the command by Raleigh E. Colston at Chancellorsville. Jones marched his battalion with Colston to the Union right but, like Carter's guns, was not in a position to assist in the attack. As the morning of 3 May dawned, Jones' battalion remained in the rear and although they did provide artillery support from a distance, they were never seriously tested during the battle.[115]

Ewell's third and final divisional artillery commander would earn a reputation for being not only a fine artilleryman but an accomplished antebellum architect. The son of an Irish immigrant, Richard Snowden Andrews was born in Washington on 29 October 1830. His formal education was courtesy of the private schools in the Washington and Georgetown area, and his boyhood years were filled with adventures in the Washington streets with his three cousins. During his formative years, Richard's father insisted that he spend time as a carpenter's apprentice in order to learn the proper use of the tools of the trade and develop his mechanical skills.

When he was nineteen, Richard's father relocated the family to Baltimore where Richard determined to make the practice of architecture his profession. Although he had found work with an architectural office, he would also continue with his studies. He completed his education while with the firm and remained in its employ until the beginning of the war. During his time with the firm, Richard help design a number of high profile structures, including the south wing of the Treasury Department in Washington, the governor's mansion in Annapolis, Maryland, and the United States Customs House in Baltimore.[116]

With rumors of war hanging over the nation, Andrews began to prepare himself for military service. He believed he was destined to serve in the artillery and began a rigid self-taught regiment to educate himself. When war finally came, he organized the 1st Maryland Light Artillery which would eventually become known as Andrews' Battery for its newly elected captain. Captain Andrews' architectural and engineering expertise came in handy when he took it upon himself to developed drawings and specification for his own guns, based on some captured twelve pound Napoleons. Richard's design would ultimately be cast in Richmond at the Tredegar Iron Works, but they would be returned when more effective guns were captured and supplied to the battery.[117]

Andrews' battery spent the early months of the war stationed along the Potomac River in northern Virginia trying to block the transit of supplies along the waterway. The winter of 1861-62 found the battery still in its position on the river at Shipping Point on the extreme right of General Joe Johnston's army. Andrews

---

[115] *OR*, vol.25, pt.2, pp.616-617; *OR*, vol.25, pt.1, p.793; Eicher, & Eicher, *High Commands*, p.521. General Trimble was away convalescing.

[116] Andrews, Richard S., *Richard Snowden Andrews, Lieutenant Colonel Commanding the First Maryland Confederate States Army: A Memoir*, pp.15, 25-26.

[117] *Ibid*, pp.27, 34, 39-40

showed his ability as a gunner when the schooner *Mary Washington* was observed by the battery being towed by a tug. The ship was carrying hay for McClellan's horses, and cement for the construction of fortification. Personally aiming one of his twelve pounders, Andrews fired a shot which cut the mast of the schooner. The tug quickly departed and the *Mary Washington* was guided into nearby Quantico Creek where the men of the battery unloaded its cargo to the joy of the battery's horses who feasted that evening on tasty Federal hay.[118]

The spring of 1862 found the 1st Maryland at Yorktown on the Virginia Peninsula confronting McClellan's advance on Richmond. The battery fought there, at West Point [Virginia], Fair Oaks and during The Seven Days fighting. Andrews' abilities were evidently recognized for he was quickly promoted to major. After receiving his promotion, his battery limbered up and marched north with Stonewall Jackson to confront John Pope's Army of Virginia.[119]

At Cedar Mountain, Major Andrews' military career nearly came to a tragic end, and indeed probably should have. While riding along a road behind his batteries directing their fire, a Federal shell exploded nearby. A shell fragment struck Andrews in the right side, tore through his jacket and sliced open his abdominal wall. The damage was so severe that if Andrews had not somehow maintained his composure and placed his hand and arm across the wound, his intestines would have surely fallen from his abdomen. Leaning forward, he wrapped his other arm around the neck of his horse and rolled off his mount, landing as gently as someone in his condition could, flat on his back. After managing to drag himself out of the road, Andrews lay down next to a fence to wait for assistance.

Unfortunately, his location was not well suited for a man with a nine to ten inch open gash in his abdomen. The road he lay near was rather dusty and the soldiers, wagons and horses which passed raised great clouds, making it impossible for Andrews' wound to remain free of debris. As luck would have it, Confederate troops were advancing on the far side of the fence under the cover of some nearby woods. The foot soldiers belonged to General A. P. Hill's division, and the General, who happened to be nearby, saw Andrews and ventured over to investigate. Before departing, Hill promised to send an ambulance for the injured major as soon as possible. While waiting for the ambulance to arrive, a surgeon happened by and stopped to see if he could be of assistance. After looking at Andrews wound, he told the major that the damage could not be repaired and that it was mortal. Andrews refused to give in to the reaper. Later, his wife, whom the major must have recounted the events to, recalled what happened next.

> "As he [the surgeon] was riding away my husband called to him to say that once while fox-hunting he had seen a valuable dog almost disemboweled in getting over a fence, that he had taken him home and cared for him, and the dog had lived to hunt again."

---

[118] *Ibid*, pp.42-43.

[119] *Ibid*, pp.44-45.

Finally, after lying along the road for some two to three hours, an ambulance arrived. Andrews was carefully gathered up and placed in the wagon to be transported to a nearby farmhouse. Once in the ambulance, his head was placed across the knees of a chaplain who began reciting verse as the wagon bounced along the rough road which no doubt caused Andrews great agony.[120]

When the ambulance arrived at its destination, the major was taken into the farmhouse and, placed on the floor. No surgeon was nearby so Andrews' attendants scoured the countryside and found a local doctor who happened to be passing by. Like the surgeon who had evaluated the wound alongside the road, the country doctor declared it mortal.

"Isn't there a chance in ten," Andrews asked, "or twenty or even a hundred?"

"Well," the local doctor replied, "since you are so plucky, I'll do the best I can for you."

The physician went to work cleaning the ghastly wound. He had no way to sterilize the gash so as best he could; he picked out pieces of clothing and debris which had lodged in the wound. Then the medical man took the only needle he could find, a rusty one, and sewed up the huge laceration. Once the wound was closed, Andrews was placed on a bed and made as comfortable as possible. Since he was not expected to recover and could not be moved, when Jackson marched away from the Cedar Mountain battlefield, Andrews was left behind and captured. Because of his condition, he was immediately paroled. He had a lot to live for. His wife had given birth to their fourth child a few months earlier and when she arrived, he laid his eyes on the baby for the first time. Like the hunting dog, Richard S. Andrews defied the odds and would eventually recover from what everyone believed was a mortal injury. On 3 March 1863, while still recuperating from his injuries, Andrews received a promotion to lieutenant colonel. By the time General Lee was ready to guide his army north that summer, he would be back with his command.[121]

Commanding the first of Ewell's reserve artillery battalions was the Virginian, Willis Jefferson Dance. Dance, a lawyer by trade, was born 20 June 1821 in Powhatan County. As a teenager he entered Hampden-Sydney College and later the University of Virginia. In 1861, Dance was practicing his profession in the

---

[120] Andrews, *Richard Snowden Andrews: A Memoir*, pp.55, 66

[121] *Ibid*, pp.57, 66-67, 77. Another version of Andrews' treatment was penned by Henry Kyd Douglas. Douglas indicated the doctor passing by while Andrews was lying next to the road was Hunter McGuire. McGuire supposedly told Andrews that the wound was mortal to which the major responded "Yes, that's what you fellows all say." McGuire then determined to do what he could. He washed out the wound, cleaned it, replaced the intestines and sewed up the gash. Andrews was then taken to a hospital. This author believes Mrs. Andrews' version is more credible. Both Mrs. Andrews and Douglas wrote their recollections of the events forty years later. Mrs. Andrews however, was more emotionally attached to the events and therefore more prone to have them engrained in her mind. Although she did not witness the events first hand, neither did Douglas, who reported the incident based on McGuire's telling of the story shortly after the event. It's quite possible, that the doctor who attended to Andrews along the road was indeed McGuire.

county of his birth when, assisted by a friend and fellow lawyer, he began the task of raising a company of volunteers to join the cause. The group would eventually become known as the Powhatan Artillery and on 16 July, at the age of forty, Dance would be selected as its captain. After its muster, the battery was assigned to Camp Magruder where it received instruction in the art of gunnery from a group of VMI cadets.[122]

On 3 October, Dance and his battery were ordered to Manassas Junction for duty with General Johnston. Although the order instructed the battery to "immediately proceed" to their new assignment, their departure was delayed until the seventeenth. The reason for the holdup was never adequately explained, but more than likely it was to obtain additional horses and equipment. After a three day trip which included a ride on the Virginia Central Railroad, Dance and his battery with their four smoothbore six-pounders arrived at their new duty station and were assigned to then Colonel Pendleton's Artillery Reserve.[123]

During the spring of 1862, as word of McClellan's move to the Peninsula became common knowledge, Pendleton's reserve, including Dance's battery, was shifted southward but Dance saw almost no action when the battery was placed in the defenses around Richmond. By July, with the city safe, Dance's Battery was made part of Colonel John Thompson Brown's 1st Regiment Virginia Artillery. The battery remained in the Richmond area and did not partake in the marching and fighting that culminated in the second Battle of Manassas. Toward the end of summer, Brown's command finally marched north and caught up with Lee's advancing army. However, if Dance was anticipating any action, he was about to be disappointed. On the morning of 17 September, Lee ordered Pendleton to move some artillery to the Potomac River to guard the fords and protect the army's ordnance train in case he was forced to withdraw. Once again, Dance missed out on any action during the campaign's major battle, but a panicked Pendleton probably assumed some of Dance's guns had been lost when he reported the demise of his command at Shepherdstown. Three months later, the day before the battle of Fredericksburg, Dance and his battery were south of town but marched north in time to take position on the extreme right of Lee's line. He directed his guns well during the fighting but became a victim of the poor organizational structure of Lee's artillery. During the battle, his guns were scattered about by orders from superior officers including General Stuart who took one gun for his own use.[124]

The changes to the artillery organization in February of 1863 saw Brown's Battalion and Dance's battery transferred to the reserve artillery of Jackson's Corps. When Jackson began his flanking march at Chancellorsville, he took Dance's single rifled gun with him leaving the captain with his two remaining howitzers.

---

[122] Nicholas, Richard L., & Servis, Joseph, *Powhatan, Salem and Courtney Henrico Artillery*, pp.6, 204; Krick, *Colonels*, p.109. Included in the group of cadets who trained Dance's battery was Joseph White Latimer who would be intricately involved in the Gettysburg fight.

[123] *OR*, vol.51, pt.2, p.333; Nicholas, & Servis, *Powhatan Artillery*, p.7.

[124] Nicholas, & Servis, *Powhatan Artillery*, pp.20-24, 28-30; *OR*, vol.19, pt.2, p.610.

When his immediate superior marched east with Anderson's Division to assist in confronting Sedgwick at Salem Church, Dance found himself in command of what remained of the 1st Virginia Regiment's batteries and guns along the Orange Plank Road. Commanding more than a single battery for the first time, Dance aggressively pushed his guns forward to a knoll 900 yards from the Federal rifle pits in front of Chancellorsville. From his new location he began pounding the entrenched Yankees. Dance held his position for the remainder of the battle and evidently drew the attention of his superiors. When Colonel Brown took over for the wounded Stapleton Crutchfield, and Major Robert Hardaway departed on sick leave, Dance took command of the battalion.[125]

Dance would retain his new assignment through Pendleton's reorganization in early June although some of the members of his command were not excited about his appointment. Dance would enter the Gettysburg Campaign at the head of the 1st Virginia Regiment and although experienced, it would remain to be seen if he could handle a battalion of artillery during a pitched battle. Five Virginia batteries, all of them experienced, comprised Dance's Battalion. The group was anchored by the well-schooled 2nd and 3rd Companies of the Richmond Howitzers. The 1st Rockbridge Artillery, the Salem Artillery and Dance's boys with the Powhatan Artillery completed the five battery roster.[126]

Commanding Ewell's final reserve battalion was Lieutenant Colonel William Nelson. Nelson, one of the old men of the army's artillery branch, was born 14 December 1808 at Yorktown. Before the war Nelson was a legislator from Hanover County and when fighting became eminent, he assisted in the organization of the Hanover Light Artillery. Most of the battery's original members were schoolboys from the Hanover Academy. Only after their muster and Nelson was installed as the battery's captain, did the youngsters from the academy discover that their new commanding officer was a hard-line taskmaster. Nelson drilled the battery continuously, keeping the boys busy from dawn until dusk. He drove his gunners so hard that the situation deteriorated to a point where the men petitioned for his dismissal. Nelson refused to depart and the bad blood continued to fester.[127]

During the opening salvos of the Peninsular Campaign, the Hanover Artillery was reorganized and Captain Nelson was summarily removed from his command, no doubt to the joy of the schoolboys. Evidently someone thought Nelson was worth retaining, for on 26 May 1862, he was promoted to major. Records show he retained command of a battery attached to D. H. Hill's Division until at least 23 July. On 5 September, General Pendleton, with one of his reserve artillery battalion commanders "assigned to other important duties," ordered Nelson to take command of the departed officer's batteries. When Lee instructed Pendleton

---

[125] *OR*, vol.25, pt.2, p.629; *OR*, vol.25, pt.1, p.878; Nicholas, & Servis, **Powhatan Artillery**, pp.35, 41.

[126] Wallace, Lee A. Jr., ***The Richmond Howitzers***, p.62; Wise, ***Long Arm of Lee***, vol.2, p.568.

[127] Krick, ***Colonels***, p.289; Moore, Robert H., ***Miscellaneous Disbanded Virginia Light Artillery***, pp.45-46.

to guard the Potomac fords in case of disaster at Sharpsburg, Nelson was forced to miss the battle. However, two days later, his guns were on the bluffs overlooking the river near Shepherdstown. At dawn, the morning of 19 September, he was up early and in the saddle. Riding with Pendleton, he helped secure and place forty-four guns along the heights. By 8:00 a.m. the Federals had appeared and a spirited artillery duel erupted. Although outnumbered Nelson worked his guns well and maintained his position, receiving accolades for his work. Writing in his report, Pendleton noted, "Nelson's cool courage and persistent vigor throughout the day, and in the trying hour at its close, deserves especial mention. His services were of great value." Pendleton's opinion of Nelson may have been enhanced by the simple fact that most of the major's guns were eventually retrieved after the general had reported to Lee that all was lost.[128]

After Fredericksburg, where Nelson was in direct control of only two of his batteries, Pendleton noted he was a "gallant and efficient…officer." He recommended to Lee that Nelson be promoted to lieutenant colonel and retain his command during the February 1863 reorganization. As the Chancellorsville fight neared, Nelson found himself in command of the three batteries he would lead to Gettysburg as part of Ewell's reserve. One group of guns, the Fluvanna Artillery from Virginia, had consisted of two batteries, but the previous October it had been consolidated into a single organization. Another Virginia battery, the Amherst Artillery, and the Georgia Battery, which hailed from its namesake state, completed Nelson Battalion. Shortly after the reorganization, on 3 March, Pendleton's recommendation was acted on and Nelson received his promotion.[129]

During the Chancellorsville Campaign, Nelson's command was utilized to confront Sedgwick's force along the Rappahannock River. The conflict however, did not provide him much of an opportunity to damage the Federals and his guns were lightly engaged. After the battle, his battalion returned to Fredericksburg, and by 12 May, they had settled back into their camps. Nelson, true to his nature, undoubtedly began the refit of his batteries and drill the men. His strict discipline may not have endeared him to his men, but it facilitated the creation of a sharp and capable artillery battalion.[130]

With Crutchfield out of action nursing his hip wound, Ewell turned to Colonel Brown, who originally been a member of the 2nd Company of the Richmond Howitzers, to perform the duties of his corps' chief of artillery. Brown, who had no military training other than any instruction received as part of his militia involvement in 1859, joined the rebellion on 21 April 1861. When the howitzers assembled its second company, Brown was elected its captain. He was promoted to major after guiding the battery through the initial engagement of the war at Big Bethel. The promotion came due to organizational changes necessitated by the

---

[128] Krick, ***Colonels***, p.289; ***OR***, vol.11, pt.3, p.650; ***OR***, vol.19, pt.1, pp.830-831, 834; Pierro, Editor, ***Carman***, p.433.

[129] ***OR***, vol.21, p.565-566; ***OR***, vol.25, pt.1, p.794; ***OR***, vol.25, pt.2, p.617; Krick, ***Colonels***, p.289.

[130] Martin, ***The Fluvanna Artillery***, p.73; ***OR***, vol.25, pt.1, pp.810, 812.

assembly of the 1st Regiment Virginia Artillery. Brown rose quickly through the ranks and on 2 June 1862, received a promotion to colonel and command of the regiment. When Lee inaugurated The Seven Days fighting on 25 June, Brown, and his group of guns were part of General Pendleton's reserve artillery.[131]

Remaining in Richmond after the fighting, Brown's batteries were not involved in the Second Manassas Campaign. After joining Lee on 3 September, the battalion marched north into Maryland but like Nelson's group, spent their time guarding the fords and missed the fighting at Sharpsburg. Brown directed his batteries through Fredericksburg, the ferocious winter of 1862-63 and the fighting at Chancellorsville. During the latter engagement, he displayed his skill as an artilleryman when he pulled a battery out of Jackson's flanking column and engaged the Federal batteries harassing the marching troops. When Crutchfield was wounded, control of the Second Corps' Artillery Reserve fell into Brown's hands.[132]

Brown was another lawyer turned soldier, having been educated at the University of Virginia. Born in Petersburg on 6 February 1835, the twenty-five year old was a practicing lawyer in the Virginia capital when the war began. He had been proven a capable commander of artillery, but as acting chief of artillery for his corps' reserve he would be in a new role at Gettysburg. It remained to be seen if he would rise to the challenges the campaign would present.[133]

A Bit of Disorganization

To provide artillery for A. P. Hill's new Third Corps, Pendleton would have to perform a bit of a juggling act. After pulling batteries from some existing organizations, he went about designating three battalions for the divisions and two for the corps' reserve. The first decision was rather simple. When General Richard Anderson's Division was transferred to Hill's command, he brought along his divisional artillery under the command Lieutenant Colonel John Jameson Garnett.

Garnett was born in May of 1839 in the same region of Virginia which produced Robert E. Lee. John was attending West Point and was scheduled to graduate the summer of 1861 when the war interrupted his education. Leaving the academy, he traveled south and joined the Provisional Army of the Confederate States on 16 March. He was appointed the rank of lieutenant, probably due to his incomplete military education. Three months later, he found himself a member of the 3rd Company of Louisiana's Washington Artillery. He remained with the battery until shortly after Lee took command of the army, but resigned his post on 16 June 1862 to accept the position of major of artillery for David R. Jones' Division. Later, on 14 November, Garnett was appointed inspector of ordnance

---

[131] Krick, *Colonels*, p.68; Sifakis, *Who was Who*, p.80; Wallace, *The Richmond Howitzers*, pp.53, 138.

[132] *OR*, vol.12, pt.2, p.551; Pierro, Editor, *Carman*, p.433; *OR*, vol.25, pt.2, pp.878, 924.

[133] Krick, *Colonels*, p.68; Wallace, *The Richmond Howitzers*, p.138.

and artillery for Longstreet's Corps. He retained the position until the spring of the following year.[134]

Pendleton evidently thought Garnett worthy of promotion because on 11 February he recommended him for battalion command based on Longstreet's approval. "Major Garnett is well known to General Longstreet," Pendleton wrote, "and highly appreciated by him as an efficient officer." Pendleton went on to recommend Garnett for promotion to lieutenant colonel and assignment to the battalion with General Anderson's command. Garnett's promotion came through on 4 April, and on 1 May, as the fighting at Chancellorsville was getting underway, he took command of the battalion. Only a few of Garnett's guns entered the fight and afterward his battalion was in possession of one captured cannon. His after action report consisted of two small paragraphs and was shorter than the reports of his subordinates, indicating a lack of personal participation and knowledge of what his batteries accomplished. Instead of writing his own version of events, he simply relied on the reports of his officers, which he submitted with his own short document. While it was customary for officers to submit the reports of their subordinates with their own, most wanted their version of events documented in case issues arose later. Whatever Longstreet thought of Garnett, the facts were plain. Although experienced in many of the logistical aspects of artillery, Garnett had little practical experience controlling a group of batteries in battle. His lack of experience would be a liability and would eventually lead to his downfall later in the war.[135]

While his battalion would eventually be reassigned to Heth's Division, as May turned to June, Garnett's guns remained somewhat unassigned. Although previously attached to Anderson's Division, information is sketchy as to when the transfer to Heth's Division actually took place. Four batteries populated Garnett's Battalion. Three Virginia batteries, the Huger and Lewis Artillery and the Norfolk Light Artillery Blues were joined by a battery from Louisiana, the Donaldsonville Artillery.[136]

Another divisional artillery battalion identified by Pendleton for assignment to Hill's new corps was that of Major David G. McIntosh. Like Garnett, McIntosh had four batteries in his battalion. From Alabama came the Hardaway Artillery. Virginia provided the remaining three in the form of the Danville Artillery, the 2nd Company of the Rockbridge Artillery and the Richmond Virginia Battery.[137]

McIntosh was born along the banks of the Pee Dee River on 16 March 1836 in Darlington County, South Carolina in the small hamlet of Society Hill. As a young man, David attended South Carolina College and after graduation began practicing

---

[134] Krick, *Colonels*, p.150; Sifakis, *Who was Who*, p.237.

[135] *OR*, vol.25, pt.2, p.615; Krick, *Colonels*, p.150; *OR*, vol.25, pt.1, pp.883-885.

[136] Crew, R. Thomas Jr., & Trask, Benjamin H., *Grimes' Battery, Grandy's Battery and Huger's Battery Virginia Artillery*, pp.59; Wise, *Long Arm of Lee*, p.569; *OR*, vol.27, pt.2, p.289.

[137] Wise, *Long Arm of Lee, vol.2*, p.569; *OR*, vol.27, pt.2, p.289; The Hardaway Artillery was also known as Hurt's Battery.

law in nearby Darlington. Shortly after his state left the Union, McIntosh, a former member of a disbanded local militia group, organized a company of volunteers which was built with the use of individuals from the dispersed group. The company, known as the Pee Dee Rifles, was assembled in January 1861 and mustered into service shortly thereafter. Designated Company B of the 1st South Carolina Regiment under Colonel Maxcy Gregg, the company was originally mustered for a term of six months. After its term expired, the company was reorganized and re-designated Company D of the likewise reorganized 1st Regiment. On 29 July, McIntosh was made captain of the company.[138]

McIntosh commanded his company through the winter and into the spring of 1862. In March, a decision to reduce the number of companies in the regiment resulted in the extraction of the Pee Dee Rifles and its conversion into a light artillery battery. The new battery, designated the Pee Dee Light Artillery, was assigned to A. P. Hills division and McIntosh went to work converting infantrymen into artillerymen. After a few weeks of drill, the men of the battery became proficient in the servicing of their guns and were soon embroiled in the fighting during the Peninsular Campaign. A short time later, during The Seven Days, McIntosh was riding in an exposed location when his horse was shot out from under him. Although it was a close call, he managed to escape serious injury. A few weeks later he directed his battery with good results at Second Manassas and helped capture Harpers Ferry prior to the battle of Sharpsburg. At the latter battle, the South Carolinian took his guns into action on the right of the Confederate line. After a spirited artillery duel, the Federals advanced infantry toward McIntosh's position. Holding his ground, the captain pounded the Yankee lines as quickly as his men could load their guns. As the enemy closed the distance, McIntosh ordered his guns loaded with double canister. The weapons belched forth a heavy dose of death as the rounds opened large gaps in the Federal line. Still, onward the enemy came. At a range of sixty yards, with almost all his horses down, McIntosh did the only thing he could. As the Federals began to enter the battery, he ordered the men to retreat and extricate as much of the battery's equipment as possible. Fortunately for McIntosh, Confederate infantry was nearby and after a spirited attack managed to drive the Yankees from the guns.[139]

For his part, McIntosh handled himself fairly well in a difficult situation. He continued to command the battery for the remainder of the year and into the spring of 1863. At Fredericksburg, the Pee Dee Artillery was located on the extreme right of Jackson's line and was positioned in a manner which allowed McIntosh to fire into the flank of Meade's breakthrough on the southern part of the field. Once again his guns took another pounding. By mid-afternoon almost all of their ammunition was gone and so many men had fallen that it was difficult to service all the guns. Replacements were ordered forward, and McIntosh was able to withdraw his guns from the field with another full day's work accomplished. The seven batteries

---

[138] Krick, *Colonels*, p.257; Caldwell, *McGowan's Brigade*, p.32.

[139] *OR*, vol.11, pt.2, p.858; Sears, *Landscape Turned Red*, p.287; *OR*, vol.19, pt.1, p.984.

from Hill Division engaged during the battle, suffered ninety-nine casualties that afternoon; a good portion of them belonged to McIntosh.[140]

McIntosh's abilities had not gone unnoticed. One of his most enthusiastic proponents was Colonel Crutchfield who noted that McIntosh was "an officer of rare qualification." On 16 February, at Crutchfield's request, Pendleton communicated to General Lee that McIntosh be promoted to major. Instead of another officer Pendleton had also recommended, it was decided to place McIntosh at the head of a battalion. On 2 March 1863, the South Carolinian was promoted to major and installed as the commander of a battalion within the Artillery Reserve of Jackson's Corps. The only down side was his battery, which had done a great deal of hard service, would be left behind.[141]

McIntosh first led his new battalion in battle at Chancellorsville, where it marched at the rear of Jackson's column and arrived too late to be of any use during the assault on Howard's Corps. The following day the battalion engaged the enemy, but McIntosh was away from his command on detached service. Fortunately, while he was away the battalion did nothing to damage his reputation. "He was a man of superior intellect, educated, dignified and rather reserve," wrote a subordinate. When the fighting ended and the armies returned to their old camps, McIntosh's batteries settled back into the typical routines of camp duty. It was not long before the reorganization of the army precipitated the battalion's reassignment to Hill's new command. Pendleton's original organization defined McIntosh's group as a divisional battalion but by the time the armies met at Gettysburg, it would be a member of Colonel Reuben L. Walker's Third Corps reserve. The battalion was probably moved to the reserves around the time Hill's Corps left the Fredericksburg area.[142]

Hill's final divisional artillery battalion commander, as designated by Pendleton, was another Virginia lawyer, Major William Thomas Poague. Born in Rockbridge County five days before Christmas in 1835, as a young man, Poague attended Brownsburg Academy. The school, a private Presbyterian institution for young men, was built with funds raised by the local citizenry. After a short time Thomas moved on to Washington College from which he graduated in 1857. After spending some time teaching school in Georgia, he studied law in Lexington until 1860 when he moved to Saint Joseph, Missouri and set up a law practice. When the war began, he returned to the state of his birth and offered his services, enlisting in the 1st Rockbridge Artillery on 4 April 1861.[143]

---

[140] *OR*, vol.12, p.858.

[141] *OR*, vol.25, pt.2, pp.628, 634, 655, 729. Crutchfield continued to lobby for McIntosh, noting to General Jackson on 5 March that he would "make a far better lieutenant colonel" than another officer.

[142] Wise, **Long Arm of Lee**, pp.467, 494, 508, 569; *OR*, vol.27, pt.2, p.290; Poague, William T., **Gunner with Stonewall**, p.63.

[143] Driver, **Rockbridge Artillery**, p.76.

Poague was elected second lieutenant on 29 April and promoted to first lieutenant four months later. He spent a good portion of the war's first year in Northern Virginia and the Shenandoah Valley where his battery campaigned with Stonewall Jackson. During the middle of April, 1862, while in camp, the company was reorganized into a battalion of three companies, but the Confederate government failed to recognize the new structure. The fallout of the failed attempt was a single battery, of which Poague was elected captain of on 22 April.[144]

Poague quickly earned a reputation as an excellent artilleryman. As chief of artillery in the Valley District, Colonel Crutchfield had ample opportunity to observe and receive reports of Captain Poague and his battery's exploits. "Considerable praise is due... his battery," Crutchfield wrote, "for the skill and perseverance manifested by them..." One of Jackson's brigade commanders, Charles S. Winder, also recognized Poague's talent for directing artillery. "Of Captain Poague..., and [his] officers and men I cannot speak too highly," Winder noted. "The skill, judgment, and bravery displayed by them at all times, under a heavy fire of artillery and infantry, reflect the greatest credit upon themselves."[145]

Poague marched with Jackson's command southward and fought during The Seven Days, then returned north to help drive Pope's Army of Virginia back to Washington, at Second Manassas. During the latter fight, he escaped serious injury when his horse was shot out from under him. The evening before the fighting at Sharpsburg erupted, Poague helped silence an enemy battery at a range of 500 to 600 yards. The next morning, from his previous night's position, his 1st Rockbridge became involved in the fighting during the early stages of the battle. After heavy action, Poague was forced to retire from his initial position, but his new location exposed his battery to a heavy enemy crossfire. Escaping the fire, he moved his guns into a position on a ridge which commanded the West Woods in order to cover that location in case the Confederates were forced to abandon their position in the trees. Later, moving back to a point near his original position, he discovered a 200 to 300 yard gap in the Confederate line which he proceeded to fill with the two guns he had with him. Battlefield smoke turned the sun blood red and by the time it dipped below the horizon the men of the 1st Rockbridge Artillery and their captain had done a full day's work.[146]

Three months later the 1st Rockbridge, having been transferred to Colonel John T. Brown's 1st Virginia Artillery, was encamped some distance from Fredericksburg as Burnside's army began crossing the Rappahannock. On the evening of 12 December, Captain Poague received word of the Federal activity and was instructed to return as quickly as possible. Swiftly he gave orders to pack up the battery and prepare to move. Using a local citizen as a guide the battery negotiated dark Virginia back roads and covered the sixteen miles to join the main body of Lee's army as daylight broke over the horizon. The battery arrived on the scene before

---

[144] Driver, *Rockbridge Artillery*, pp.18, 76;

[145] *OR*, vol.12, pt.1, pp.726, 737.

[146] Driver, *Rockbridge Artillery*, p.76; *OR*, vol.19, pt.1, pp.1009-1010.

any of Brown's other guns, although they all had shorter distances to travel. In fact, there was even time for Poague's gunners to grab a bit of shut eye after breakfast before leading the guns into action on the right of Jackson's line. Stonewall noted in his report that Poague deserved praise for "the promptitude with which he responded to the order by a fatiguing night's march is worthy of notice." Poague's reputation as a soldier and an artilleryman was on the rise.[147]

A few weeks after the battle, Pendleton recommended Poague for promotion to major. "Captain Poague," he wrote in his recommendation to Lee, "now commanding a battery in this battalion [Brown's], is a superior officer, whose services have been scarcely surpassed." The 1st Rockbridge was camped near Hamilton's Crossing when official word reached Poague of his promotion in early March. He also learned he would be assigned to Major McIntosh's command. He considered McIntosh a fine officer and had no issues with being the subordinate major in the battalion's command structure since McIntosh's promotion preceded his own. After putting his battery in order and biding his battery mates "heartfelt farewells and affectionate goodbyes," Poague reported to his new assignment.[148]

By Poague's own admission, Brown's guns "had very little to do" during the battle at Chancellorsville although the battalion did become involved in minor fighting on 3 May. A few weeks later, after the battalion had returned to its camps, Poague was summoned by Third Corps chief of artillery, Colonel Reuben Lindsey Walker who informed the Virginian that he had been selected to lead a battalion of artillery within the new corps.

Poague was assigned to Pender's Division, but it would be 10 June before all of his batteries were assembled. The last to arrive would be the Albemarle Artillery from Virginia. They would join their fellow Virginians of the Warrenton Artillery, the Charlotte Artillery from North Carolina, and the Madison Artillery from Mississippi. Although William was new to battalion command, he had spent the previous three months getting to know the duties of a battalion commander under McIntosh. Small in stature, he possessed a bearing which promoted authority and demanded respect. However, unlike most lawyers turned officers, Poague's greatest attribute was the fact the he possessed the heart of a warrior.[149]

When Hill's new corps was formed, Colonel Walker was identified to perform the tasks of its chief of artillery. Walker, who had been Hill's divisional chief, was undoubtedly left in place due to his performance and Hill's desire to retain him. Although he had done enough to justify Hill's retention of his services, others thought him unfit. A member of the Fredericksburg Artillery would note shortly after Gettysburg that "Walker (who by the way, is a perfect nincompoop) is a full colonel, chief of Artillery in A. P. Hill's Corps."[150]

---

[147] Poague, *Gunner with Stonewall*, pp.53-54; Driver, *Rockbridge Artillery*, p.34; *OR*, vol.21, p.633.

[148] *OR*, vol.25, pt.2, p.617;

[149] Poague, *Gunner with Stonewall*, p.67; Sherwood, W. Cullen & Nicholas, Richard L., *Amherst Artillery, Albemarle Artillery and Sturdivant's Battery*, p.126.

[150] Carmichael, Peter S., *The Purcell Crenshaw and Letcher Artillery*, p.57.

Perhaps Walker's reputation stemmed from his rigid discipline, which was on display early in his war career. Private John Worsham of the 21st Virginia remembered a definitive example of Walker's ridged standards. "I saw the first man of the war punished for disobedience of orders while we were in... camp; he was a member of Walker's battery and was strapped on one of the cannon wheels in such a manner as to keep him from moving." Generals Hill and Pendleton obviously thought more of Walker than the typical Confederate artilleryman.[151]

Walker was born in the crossroads hamlet of Logan in Albemarle County, Virginia on 27 May 1827. Reuben entered the Virginia Military Institute on 5 September 1842 and quickly proved he was a rather poor student. After four years of study, he managed to graduate on Independence Day, 1845, but only one position above the bottom of his class. Post-graduation, Walker began a career as a civil engineer and farmer in New Kent County, but as the war began he left his vocations behind and volunteered for service. His initial activities involved the raising of an artillery battery which would become known as the Purcell Artillery, of which he was elected the battery's first captain. When his initial term of service expired, he reenlisted for an additional two years in January 1862. By spring he had been promoted to major and placed in charge of A. P. Hill's divisional artillery. In July, he was made a lieutenant colonel, and by 14 March 1863, a full colonel. Walker would assume responsibility for all of the new Third Corps' artillery in early June.[152]

To direct Colonel Walker's old command, which would form one of Third Corps' reserve battalion, Pendleton suggested Major William Ransom Johnson Pegram. Affectionately known to his close friends and family as Willy, Pegram was one of the most resourceful and recognized artillerymen in Lee's army. Unlike many of his contemporaries, he became known for the use of his guns as offensive weapons. A somewhat mild mannered individual, the thought of battle and engaging the enemy transformed him into an intense and determined battlefield officer. But, the transformation failed to alter his attentive and composed character. While all around him was in chaos, Willy would remain calm and reserve, a characteristic which allowed him to be very effective. He never shied away from an opportunity to fight the enemy but never saw battle as an occasion for personal glory or advancement. William simply looked at battle as a method for displaying his devotion to God, community and family, three elements of his life which he had learned to treasure as a boy.[153]

---

[151] Worsham, *One of Jackson's Foot Cavalry*, p.21. The punishment was known as "strapping to the wheel" which was normally done by lashing the guilty party to the spare wheel of one of the battery's caissons. The punishment normally lasted for variable durations and could actually continue even if the battery was on the move, which would have been significantly more painful for the strapped individual.

[152] *Ibid*; **Electronic Source:** http://www.vmi.edu/archives.aspx?id=5673, Last Accessed: 5/11/2012.

[153] Carmichael, *Lee's Young Artillerist: William R. J. Pegram*, pp.1, 10. Various sources indicate two spellings of Pegram's nickname. For the purpose of this narrative the spelling "Willy" will be used as it seems to be how his immediate family spelled his moniker.

Pegram was born in Richmond on 29 June 1841 and spent his formative years in and around the city. As a young man Willy worked as a clerk for Richmond's circuit court and joined the city's elite militia unit, F Company. He was exposed to the equestrian arts early in life but never learned to be a good horseman, due to being terribly nearsighted. In fact the affliction was so severe that until he began correcting the problem with spectacles he could not tell his horse from another. His vision problem however, did not deter him from working toward an education and after a period of preparation, Pegram entered the University of Virginia during the fall of 1860. Attending the university's law school, he remained only a few months, departing the following spring to enlist in the Confederate Army. He initially joining the 21st Virginia Infantry, but transferred his services to Richmond's Purcell Artillery a month later. Like Walker, he reenlisted in January 1862 and when Walker was promoted to major, Pegram became the battery's captain.[154]

During The Seven Days, Pegram seized an opportunity to show the determination which would become typical of himself and his battery. At Malvern Hill on 1 July, rushing to the aide of another beleaguered Confederate battery, Pegram quickly unlimbered his guns and entered the fight. However, the battery he came to support, almost at the instant Pegram began firing, limbered up and withdrew, leaving the men of the Purcell Artillery isolated. The battery soon became the prime target of a number of Federal batteries which rained a destructive fire down on the Virginians. The half mile distance to the Federals allowed Pegram to watch intently as the enemy loaded their guns. Projectiles fell upon the battery in a continual hail of death, digging furrows into the earth as they dropped from the sky. Shrapnel flew into the air and battered Pegram's guns, equipment and men. As the men of the battery began to drop, the captain refused to flinch. One artilleryman, just a boy, at only nineteen years of age, was killed. The dead boy's sixteen year old brother picked up his body and carried it to the rear.[155]

Brigadier General Ambrose Wright, observing Pegram's actions documented what he saw in his report.

> "...Captain Pegram's battery was ordered up, and, taking a position 200 yards to the left of [Captain Marcellus N.] Moorman, opened a well-directed fire upon the enemy, which told of the fearful effect upon them. But this chivalric commander, by the retiring of Moorman's battery, was left alone to contend with the whole force of the enemy's artillery. Manfully these gallant men maintained the unequal conflict until their severe losses disabled them from using but a single piece; even then, with one single piece they firmly held their ground and continued to pour a deadly fire upon the enemy's line until, seeing the utter hopelessness of the contest, I ordered them to cease firing until I could get more guns in action."

---

[154] *Ibid*, pp.12, 21, 23; Carmichael, ***The Purcell Crenshaw and Letcher Artillery***, p.53.

[155] Carmichael, ***Lee's Young Artillerist: William R. J. Pegram***, pp.45-47.

Although General Wright possessed a reputation for glorifying his reports, and it is doubtful whether Pegram was able to single handedly "pour a deadly fire" into the Federals with only one serviceable piece, there is no question Pegram and the men of his battery did their duty that day. According to Lewis Armistead, Pegram and another battery were opposed by thirty or forty Federal guns "and only retired when entirely disabled."[156]

As if his exploits at Malvern Hill weren't enough to prove his daring, a few weeks later at Cedar Mountain, Pegram took his courage to the brink of foolishness. As the sun set after a day of fighting, it became impossible for Pegram to identify whether or not a group of soldiers to the front of his position were friend or foe. Turning to his Lieutenant Joseph McGraw, Pegram quipped, "I shall ride up close to these fellows; keep a sharp lookout, and if you see me wave my hat open all your guns." Placing a linen duster over his uniform and positioning a "Havelock" cap cover, Pegram, true to his word, rode across the open field up to the Federals and reined his horse to a stop. Remaining mounted, Pegram looked over the Federals in the moonlight. After a few moments Willy broke the ice.

"You look like Yankees," Pegram noted.

"And you must be a damn Rebel," replied one of the Northerners.

The linen duster ruse evidently fooled the blue clad infantrymen. Noting Pegram looked like a staff member of a Federal general, one of the soldiers told the cursing man to hold his tongue. Satisfied as to the composition and position of the Federals, Pegram quickly turned his horse and before the Yankees knew what was going on, rode back across the field waving his hat. Whether McGraw could not see in the darkness or simply chose to wait until Pegram returned is not known, but as the artilleryman rode into his guns, they opened fire on the now identified enemy. As his horse came to a stop, and knowing General Jackson was nearby watching the events, Pegram hollered; "Pitch in, men; General Jackson's looking at you."[157]

It is arguable whether Pegram's adventure was daring or foolhardy, but it was certainly audacious. He continued to display the same level of bravery through the Second Manassas Campaign, at Sharpsburg and at the end of the year at Fredericksburg. His body of work throughout 1862 prompted General Pendleton to recommend him for promotion to major in his 11 February proposal to Lee.

> "Captain Pegram, now commanding a battery in General A. P. Hill's division, has been recommended for promotion. He also has fully earned it by efficient service, and would no doubt, be highly approved by Lieutenant-Colonel Walker and by General Hill as the second field officer in this [Walker's] battalion."

Understanding the weight being from Virginia carried, Pendleton closed his argument in favor of Pegram by noting the young gunner was from the Old Dominion

---

[156] *OR*, vol.11, pt.2, pp.813, 819.

[157] Carmichael, ***Lee's Young Artillerist: William R. J. Pegram***, pp.55-56; Krick, Robert K., ***Stonewall Jackson at Cedar Mountain***, pp.304-306.

to make sure Lee was aware his protégé's roots. Within a few weeks, Pendleton's desires were fulfilled, and Pegram was promoted to major on 2 March 1863.[158]

On 29 April, Walker's Battalion received orders to march to Fredericksburg in response to Hooker's movement on Chancellorsville. A late start and intolerable road conditions prolonged the transit. It took the battalion sixteen hours to cover the twenty-five miles from their encampment to Hamilton's Crossing. No sleep, knee deep mud and played out horses kept the battalion from reaching its destination until 3:00 a.m. the following morning. During the march a great deal of cussing was prevalent throughout frequent halts to assist mired gun carriages, limbers and horses. Making matters worse was an intense stubbornness displayed by the battalion's horses. They seemed to spend a great deal of time refusing to move after each stop.[159]

There was little time for the battalion to rest at Hamilton's Crossing, for almost immediately it was marching westward toward Chancellorsville. On the morning of 2 May, as Jackson prepared his troops to march toward the Federal right, Pegram pushed his guns up the Orange Plank Road toward the crossroads to draw attention from Jackson's troops. After Jackson was away, Pegram worked to get Walker's Battalion limbered up and soon their guns were on the road, falling in at the rear of the column. By the time Pegram's guns arrived at the rear of Jackson's battle front, the fighting had long since moved to the east and as darkness descended, Pegram and the men fell out for some much needed rest.[160]

The wounding of Colonel Crutchfield placed the responsibility for the Second Corps' artillery upon Walker's shoulders, necessitating Pegram's elevation to command of the battalion. It was close to 5:00 a.m. on the morning of 3 May when Willy Pegram, for the first time in his life, took command of an artillery battalion. As dawn broke, his batteries were scattered in various locations near the Confederate front. Thick trees in the area forced the dispersion, but the distance did not keep Pegram's batteries from contributing to the ultimate success of the southerners. General Rodes, writing in his report noted Pegram's skillful handling of his guns. "Major Pegram," Rodes noted, "in getting several batteries in position in a field to the right, ...opened with such precision and rapidity on such of the enemy's batteries and troops as remained on the plain of Chancellorsville as finally to drive them back in utter confusion."[161]

Pegram did nothing at Chancellorsville to harm his reputation and when the army was reorganized, he retained his position as battalion commander of Walker's old group of batteries. When Walker took his place as General Hill's new chief of artillery, the battalion was transferred and assigned as one of the corps' two reserve artillery organization. In addition to Pegram's old Purcell Battery, now under the command of friend Joe McGraw, three other batteries from Virginia were members of the battalion. The Fredericksburg and Letcher Artillery and the

---

[158] *OR*, vol.25, pt.2, p.617; Krick, ***Colonels***, p.302.

[159] Carmichael, ***Lee's Young Artillerist: William R. J. Pegram***, p.83.

[160] *Ibid*, pp.85-86; *OR*, vol.25, pt.1, p.890.

[161] Carmichael, ***Lee's Young Artillerist: William R. J. Pegram***, p.87; *OR*, vol.25, pt.1, p.945.

Crenshaw Battery were all seasoned units and Pegram was well-acquainted with them. All four had been part of A. P. Hill's old division at Seven Pines before they were assembled into a battalion prior to The Seven Days. Major McIntosh's old South Carolina battery, the Pee Dee Artillery, was also a member of Pegram's command. The battery, like the four from Virginia, had been with Hill's Division even before the battalion was formed.[162]

Colonel Walker's second battalion of reserve artillery was comprised of Batteries A, B, and C of Georgia's Sumter Artillery. The Sumter Artillery Battalion, under the command of Captain Allen Cutts, had been created from a single battery when three additional batteries were assembled and added to it in mid-1861. Cutts was promoted from captain to major and then lieutenant colonel in quick succession and stepped into the role of battalion commander. A fifth battery was added to the battalion later in the year. The new battery was assembled from the infantrymen of the 9th Georgia's Company A after the men were transferred to artillery service on 12 December.[163]

Selected to command the fifth battery was former West Point cadet, Captain John Lane. Sometime before Company A was transferred to the artillery, Lane had joined the 9th Georgia and was with the company when its affiliation was altered. Prior military service ran in Lane's family. His father Joseph, a farmer turned politician from Indiana, had been a brigadier general during the Mexican War and served as the first and fourth governor of the Oregon Territory before running for vice-president as John C. Breckinridge's running mate in 1860.[164]

---

[162] Wise, *Long Arm of Lee*, p.569;

[163] Speicher, James L., The Sumter Artillery: The 11th Battalion, Georgia Light Artillery, *CWR*, vol.3 no.2, pp.1, 6.

[164] *Ibid*, p.6; *Electronic Source:* http://bioguide.congress.gov/scripts/biodisplay.pl?index=L000062, Last Accessed: 5/11/2012. The Biographical Directory of the United States Congress is a website which provides biographical information on all former and current members of the United States Senate and House of Representatives. It is an excellent source of information on Federal Government officials and provides references for all information presented.

Joseph Lane was one of the most prominent men in the early history of Oregon. Born in Buncombe County, North Carolina, on 14 December 1801, he moved with his parents to Henderson, Kentucky, in 1810. Educated in the local schools, he found work in a general store before moving to Vanderburg County Indiana in 1821. Taking up farming, he married and fathered ten children. He was elected to a number of terms in the Indiana State House and State Senate before going off to war in Mexico. Upon his return, Joseph was appointed by President James Polk to be the first governor of the Oregon Territory from 1849-1850. Joe threw his hat into the ring for the Democratic presidential nomination in 1852 but failed to be chosen. He was elected as a Delegate from the Oregon Territory to the Thirty-second Congress, and to the three succeeding Congresses serving from 21 June 1851, until 14 February 1859, when the Territory became a State. After Oregon was admitted to the Union, Joseph was elected as a Democrat to the United States Senate and served from 14 February 1859, to 3 March 1861. He did not run for reelection in 1860, since he ran with Breckinridge. He died in Roseburg, Oregon, 19 April 1881 and is buried there. Joseph's son La Fayette Lane, also a prominent Oregon politician remained loyal to the Union during the war and is also buried in Roseburg.

John was born in Evansville Indiana, 17 May 1837. He entered West Point on 1 July 1957 but was a very poor student and was ranked near the bottom of his class when he resigned on 16 February 1861. Perhaps it was his father's roots in North Carolina which prompted John, for shortly after his resignation he joined the Southern cause. A series of assignments lead him to Georgia's Fort Pulaski. He also performed duties as an aide to General Gustavus Smith in Northern Virginia, before becoming a member of the 9th Georgia. Once the infantrymen became gunners in Cutts Battalion, elections were held to determine the battery's officer corps. The results saw Lane being elected captain of the battery which, officially designated Battery E of the Sumter Artillery, would become known as Lane's Georgia Battery.[165]

Temporarily attached to Major John Garnett's artillery of David R. Jones Division, Lane's Battery saw its first action on the Peninsula during The Seven Days. During the late morning of 27 June, Lane unlimbered his guns in an open field to test the strength of some Union batteries entrenched behind some earthworks. A duel ensued which cost Lane two men killed and four wounded. In his report Garnett noted the contribution Lane made to the effort. "Captain Lane's battery distinguished itself for the accuracy of its fire and the coolness and courage of the officers and men." Shortly after the fighting, one of Cutts batteries was selected by General Pendleton to be disbanded, reducing the Sumter Artillery to four batteries. The elements of the disbanded battery were combined with the others in the battalion, creating four strong, well supplied units. Lane's battery was one of the retained outfits and was selected by Cutts to perform a reconnaissance expedition in late July. During the expedition, Lane and his battery assisted in the shelling of a Union position near Petersburg before returning to Richmond in mid-August. Shortly thereafter the battalion headed north but arrived too late to participate in the fighting at Second Manassas.[166]

Lane led his battery during the Maryland Campaign where it fought with distinction at South Mountain although General D. H. Hill thought the marksmanship of Cutts Battalion was "the worst I ever witnessed." A miscommunication found the battalion caught behind Union lines the following day, and Cutts, including Lane's Battery, had to fight a delaying action against Union cavalry in order to extract themselves. Eventually, Cutts managed to save almost all his gunners and equipment. The next day, late in the afternoon, Lane's Battery was brought up to support General Hood's Division but as the battle began the following morning Lane was held in reserve and saw no action during the fighting therefore suffering no casualties. Shortly after the battle another of Cutts' batteries was disbanded while Lane's remained active. The reorganization once again bolstered

---

[165] Speicher, The Sumter Artillery, *CWR*, vol.3 no.2, p.6. Krick in Lee's Colonels lists Lane's birth year as 1837. Speicher, who specifies 1838 as Lane's birth year, cites the Official Register of the Officers and Cadets of the U. S. Military Academy.

[166] *Ibid*, pp.7, 9, 11-12; *OR*, vol.11, pt.2, p.694.

Lane's command with twenty-nine men, raising his batteries membership to a full complement.[167]

While encamped at Culpeper Court House on 18 November, Lane received orders to report to General McLaws' Division which had already left the area for Fredericksburg. Two days later the battery arrived at its new position atop a hill north of town overlooking the Rappahannock River. Here the battery remained for nearly a month and was still in position as the battle raged during the second week of December. The major event of the period seems to have been the detachment of the battery's new 12-pound Whitworth cannon which was ordered to another part of the field. In his after action report, Pendleton noted that Lane's Battery contained the "best guns, were most in requisition, and rendered most service." The battery remained on the eminence north of Fredericksburg until it was ordered to accompany Longstreet south. Once near Suffolk, the prized Whitworth cannon was detached once more to General Pickett's Division. The gun would not be seen again as it was reported to have burst a short time later.[168]

In Pendleton's 11 February plan the general recommended Captain Lane for promotion. Lieutenant Colonel Cutts had been away from the battalion for an extended period of time and Pendleton sought to reward Lane's performance with an advancement in rank. "Captain Lane," Pendleton wrote, "commanding a battery in this battalion [Cutts], a trained officer, gallant and efficient, has been recommended for, and deserves, promotion. During a long furlough of Lieutenant Colonel Cutts," Pendleton maintain that, "he [Lane] has commanded the battalion, and would make a good major. The companies are large, the batteries have each six guns, and a second field officer would secure its greater efficiency." Pendleton's recommendation was acted on when Lane received a promotion to major on 2 March 1863.[169]

Lane's Battery returned to Cutts Battalion after Chancellorsville with Captain John T. Wingfield in command, Lane fulfilling his duties as major with the battalion. Although Lane had proven himself a capable commander, some in the battalion thought little of him. An officer once noted he was "so disgusting in his habits, and so prodigal and vagabondish [sic] in his principles that... the Battn. is much dissatisfied." Others however, thought Lane a fine officer and deserving of his position. Colonel Alexander's younger brother noted his pleasure when Lane returned after being away for some time. "Capt. Lane arrived this afternoon to the great joy of the camp." He recalled. Sometime later, after Lane returned from sick leave, young Alexander noted in his diary that "[w]e miss Capt. Lane very much here." Now, with Lieutenant Colonel Cutts away, Major Lane would be in command of the battalion as the month of May came to an end.[170]

---

[167] *OR*, vol.19, pt.1, pp.1020, 1022; *OR*, vol.19, pt.2, p.653.

[168] *OR*, vol.21, p.565-567; Speicher, The Sumter Artillery, *CWR*, vol.3 no.2, pp.26-27.

[169] *OR*, vol.25, pt.2, p.617;

[170] Krick, *Colonels*, p.230; Speicher, The Sumter Artillery, *CWR*, vol.3 no.2, p.39.

In early June, the Sumter Battalion was designated part of the Third Corps' Artillery Reserve when Pendleton reorganized his guns to accommodate three corps. However, sometime after the campaign began, the battalion was transferred to Anderson's Division while McIntosh's Battalion was moved to Colonel Walker's reserve. The shifting of these battalions within General Hill's artillery structure points to the state of flux within the Third Corps' artillery wing as the Gettysburg Campaign opened.[171]

Equality and Aptitude

As both armies gathered for the summer campaign, their assembled artillery organizations had advanced a great distance from the small, disorganized and under supplied branches of the war's early months. Within the Federal army, batteries were now organized in brigades assigned to a corps. All seven corps within the Army of the Potomac were supplied with a single brigade. All remaining brigades were organized into a strong, central reserve which contained a division of two Regular Army brigades and a division of four volunteer brigades. Although the Reserve Artillery would change its internal structure slightly before the battle, the organizational and command changes would remain in place throughout the campaign. The whole organization, under General Hunt could be controlled from the top down as opposed to the bottom up, reversing early war command and control problems.

Lee's army, on the other hand, contained a slightly different organization but was structured to provide the same command and control environment as the Federals. Each of his three corps would be supplied with five battalions, three of which were assigned to divisions, with two organized into a corps reserve. Each corps' artillery was then placed under a chief of artillery who reported directly to the corps' commander. With the corps commander in charge of his artillery and his chief responsible for all his guns, a top down control structure was achieved which significantly improved Confederate artillery performance. Unfortunately for Lee, he chose to retain Pendleton as his army's head of artillery. Although Pendleton technically maintained no command and control over the guns, he was provided with the power to control and move guns about in battle which would impair the Confederate batteries at Gettysburg during one of the most critical points of the engagement.

When comparing the men at the top of each army's artillery branch the differences are striking. The Federals possessed a superior artillery man in General Hunt, and his abilities and skill were acknowledged by practically everyone in the army. The Confederates however, would continue to be hampered by Pendleton's lack of tactical qualifications. Why Lee continued to place any trust in Pendleton is somewhat of a mystery. Their friendship seems to be the easiest and most accepted argument, but for the good of the army, common sense would have dictated his removal. Instead, Lee searched for ways to retain Pendleton and his administrative skills, much to the detriment of the army. Nearly every man in the

---

[171] See Appendix B.

Army of Northern Virginia regarded Pendleton as a liability. They would continue to deal with the burden through the coming campaign.

Both Federal and Confederate artillery organizations were reliable fighting forces, and although Union guns at Chancellorsville had generally performed poorly, the fault lay at the feet of the army's commander. Issues still existed for each, but the battalion and brigade structure established solid organizations at the corps and divisional levels and a reserve which served each army well for the remainder of the war. Although the organization greatly improved the artillery's functionality and performance in combat, it would not make the guns any less vulnerable to the horrors of battle. At Gettysburg both Federal and Confederate artillery would be put through some of the most extreme tests of the war.

Chapter XIII
The Boys of '63

> "In the cavity of one of these skulls was a nest with three speckled eggs of a field bird..." [1]
> Warren Goss
> Chancellorsville, May, 1864.

As the armies jockeyed for position and probed for each other around Fredericksburg and Culpeper, neither commander possessed a good understanding of the actual strength of his antagonist. While Lee's newspaper reading occasionally provided him a rough number, most were out of date or simply incorrect. Shortly after the Battle of Chancellorsville, a report provided to the War Department by Dr. Jonathan Letterman indicated the strength of Hooker's army in late April as 159,000 strong. For some reason the report ended up being published in the *Morning Chronicle*. Not only did all of Washington now know how large Hooker's army was, so did General Lee. Another report in the *New York Herald* indicated reinforcements were on their way to the Federal's. Lee assumed the additional troops were intended to make up for losses sustained at Chancellorsville. He presumed incorrectly however, for like much of the information Lee gleaned from newspapers, the report was simply incorrect.[2]

As Lee began to prepare for the campaign, he developed from what spotty information he had gleaned from various sources the strength of Hooker's force. Although he may have been aware that a few Federal regiments were preparing to muster out, he probably never understood that nearly 20,000 men would be leaving the Federal army during May and June. Lee, rightly so, maintained his belief that the Federals would continue to significantly outnumber his force; however, he never gave any indication that he knew the exact number of Federals arrayed against him. His official reports and volumes of correspondence do not provide any information which would lead one to believe he ever knew the exact size of Hooker's army. Using his available intelligence gathering tools, he became convinced that the Federal Army of the Potomac was, and consistently remained two to one against him, and possibly even greater. Although he had no idea at

---

[1] Goss, Warren Lee, **Recollections of a Private**, p.267.

[2] Coddington, ***Gettysburg***, pp.242-243.

the time, his antagonist's army would be at one of its lowest points regarding manpower during the coming campaign.[3]

Hooker incorrectly believed that Lee's army was roughly the size of his own and thought the difference could be no more than 2,000 men. He continued to give the size of Lee's command more credit than it was due. This may have been because he was still giving some credence to the extreme exaggerations leveled by the intelligence operation put in place by General McClellan during the early months of the war. McClellan's spies and agents had routinely overestimated Lee's numbers and on many instances doubled the size of the Confederate force. While Hooker's strength numbers were more credible than McClellan's, he still routinely overestimated the size of the enemy.[4]

The Armies by the Numbers

On 3 June Hooker's army consisted of fifty-one infantry brigades. At Chancellorsville, he had fifty-seven brigades available to him, but failed to utilize a sizable portion of them. Many of the brigades had suffered heavy battle losses and were significantly under strength. One had to look no further than the First Division of the First Corps to understand the severity of the situation. Although the division's casualties were extremely light at Chancellorsville, it would be half its strength as the army gathered its belongings and headed north in pursuit of Lee. Taking into account his under strength brigades and the regiments preparing to depart because their enlistments were expiring, Hooker's Army of the Potomac was a shadow of its former self. Measured against his mighty host of just a month prior the army would soon be reduced by nearly one third.[5]

Sickles' battered Third Corps, while it did not lose as may regiments to muster out, had lost almost a quarter of its strength to battle casualties. The Sixth Corps, the largest in the army, lost over 4,500 men killed, wounded, captured or missing. While many of the wounded and missing would return to active duty, a great number would be permanently lost to debilitating wounds and Southern prisons. Washington's inability to recognize the folly of a direct Confederate effort to physically capture the capital, kept a large military force entrenched in the city's fortifications and unavailable to Hooker. Although a few troops would be forwarded to him after the campaign commenced, his combat losses and departing regiments could have been bolstered from Washington. Government paranoia throughout the summer would keep the Army of the Potomac only a few thousand men larger than their antagonist.[6]

In addition to his infantry, Hooker, on 3 June, possessed thirteen artillery brigades spread among his corps and reserve. Within the brigades were seventy batteries. The largest brigade contained eight batteries while two brigades contained

---

[3] *Ibid*, Taylor, **Four Years**, p.89; **OR** vol.25, pt.2, p.532.

[4] Coddington, **Gettysburg**, p.243.

[5] **OR** vol.25, pt.1, pp.156-169; **OR** vol.25, pt.2, pp.523, 575.

[6] **OR** vol.25, pt.1, pp.180, 191; **OR** vol.25, pt.2, pp.320.

only four. Seven cavalry brigades and a brigade of horse artillery which contained five batteries, rounding out Hooker's early June force.

In comparison, the Confederate army contained thirty-eight brigades of infantry, including Montgomery Corse's Virginians. Although he had been victorious at Chancellorsville, the cost in manpower had been high. Sources differ regarding the actual numbers, but it is safe to say that between 10,000 and 11,000 Confederate soldiers were casualties of the fighting. The dwindling Confederate resource base made it difficult to replace the losses without striping soldiers from other locations. This, Lee believed could and should have been done, but others in the Confederate government and military districts resisted his efforts and believed it foolishness.[7]

Supporting Lee's brigades were fifteen divisional and corps reserve artillery battalions containing sixty-two batteries. At first glance, the eight battery disparity between the armies may seem to be minimal, however these numbers are deceiving. With the Federals utilizing six guns per battery to the Confederate's four, the Yankees possessed nearly a third more guns than the Rebels. Seven cavalry brigades, including the independent brigade of Brigade General John D. Imboden, constituted Lee's horsemen. Finally, one horse artillery battalion with six batteries completed his army.[8]

The Foot Soldier

The infantry regiment was the foundation of both armies. It was the basic combat unit for both North and South and each army contained hundreds of infantry, artillery and cavalry regiments. At assemblage, a typical Federal infantry regiment consisted of approximately 1,025 men while a Confederate regiment contained slightly more. The command structure of a Federal regiment consisted of a colonel, who commanded the unit, and as many as fifteen field and staff officers who performed administrative tasks.

Regimental Field and Staff:

Colonel	1	Adjutant	1
Lieutenant Colonel	1	Quartermaster	1
Major	1	Surgeon (Major)	1
Sergeant Major	1	Hospital Steward	1
Quartermaster's Sergeant	1	Principal Musicians	2
Commissary Sergeant	1	Assistant Surgeons	2
Chaplain	1		

---

[7] *OR* vol.27, pt.3, pp.919-922; *OR* vol.27, pt.2, pp.288-290. Information on the exact make up of A.P. Hill's Corps on 3 June is spotty. The corps; however, saw little if any changes in its composition from 3 June to the beginning of the battle.

[8] Wise, ***Long Arm of Lee, vol.2***, pp.567-569.

Regiments were typically broken into ten companies that usually consisted of 101 men each, including three officers, a number of sergeants, corporals and as many as eighty-two privates. Companies were designated A through K with the letter "J" being dropped from the sequence due to its resemblance to the letter "I."

Typical Company Composition:

Captain	1	Corporals	8
First Lieutenant	1	Musicians	2
Second Lieutenant	1	Wagoner	1
First Sergeant	1	Privates	82
Sergeant	4		

Most regiments however, were not assembled in a typical manner and frequently contained more or fewer man than an optimum organization. Confederate regiments characteristically contained more members than their Federal counterparts since they were authorized to contain forty-nine officers and 1,340 men. Unless they were newly organized, by the third summer of the war, neither army contained few regiments that were close to their original muster strength.[9]

A review of a typical muster role reveals a significant diversity regarding the vocations of the men who volunteered for service within both the Union and Confederate armies. The most common professions were farmer and laborer although laborer was a general catch all category for those who performed physical pursuits. Other categories were as diverse as the personalities of the men who joined. A review of the 5th Virginia muster roles indicated that seventy-one volunteers were carpenters, thirty-one were clerks, forty-one were shoemakers, and twenty-seven were blacksmiths. There were five machinists, seven lawyers, six painters, two plumbers, three millwrights and one man who listed his profession as a railroad superintendant. In many instances, men whose professions would come in handy also signed up. The 5th had a number of these men in its ranks, including three physicians, two dentists, a harness maker, one surgeon, nine butchers and even an undertaker. A region which volunteers hailed from also played a part regarding the vocational composition of a regiment. A review of the original muster roles for the field and staff, band, drum corps and the seven companies recruited in and around Richmond which became part of the 1st Virginia Infantry, showed 106 clerks and eighty laborers, but only thirteen farmers.[10]

From the Union standpoint about forty-eight percent of the volunteers listed their occupation as farmer. The next most prominent was mechanic at twenty-four percent while sixteen percent listed themselves as laborers. The composition of

---

[9] For example, the 26th North Carolina entered the campaign with somewhere between 800 and 900 men and was the largest regiment in Lee's army. Most Confederate regiments were between 300 and 500 men.

[10] Wallace, Lee A. Jr., *1st Virginia Infantry*, p.80; Wallace, Lee A. Jr., *5th Virginia Infantry*, p.73.

a Union regiment was similar to that of their counterparts and also contained a number of men whose vocations provided assistance with the daily functions of the unit.

Within the 140th New York, which seems to have been an average Federal regiment, there were 305 men listed who noted their occupation as farmer. Another 105 designated their livelihood as laborer with the third most popular trade being shoemaker of which fifty-two men were members. Forty-three men indicated they were boatmen while another forty-one said they were mechanics. Twenty-one of the volunteers failed to indicate an occupation which simply meant they did not have one, know what their trade was designated as, or wished it not be disclosed.

Many men, in both armies, listed occupations which seemed a bit out of the ordinary. A few of the more peculiar vocations were gambler, convict, rogue, loafer and even a few who considered themselves gentleman. The oddest occupation in the 140th seems to have been one man who designated himself a beer peddler although this may have been a simpler term for a bartender. Another man indicated he was a messenger while five men indicated they were, indeed, gentlemen.[11]

The ages of the men who joined the fight were almost as diverse as their occupations. On one end of the spectrum were the oldest, many of whom could have been grandfathers to the youngest. One man, known as E. Pollard, a private in Company D of the 5th North Carolina, signed the muster rolls at the age of sixty-two. Pollard listed his occupation as farmer and enlisted on 16 July 1862 for the duration of the war. Unfortunately, Pollard showed himself to be frailer than he may have imagined. Less than two months later, after arriving in Richmond, he was discharged due to rheumatism and old age. Although Pollard's discharge is dated 13 September, state rolls indicate that he died in August, and possibly never made it to Richmond. Another elder who signed up for Confederate service was Private Charles Michael, Company C of the 5th Virginia. Michael, at sixty years of age, was the oldest member of the regiment when he enlisted in April of 1861 as a member of the Staunton Rifles. The June 1861 muster roll shows he entered service on 22 May, but by November he had been discharged. His advanced age was no doubt a factor in his release. With Michael's departure, the honor of being the oldest man in the regiment fell to fifty-seven year old Company K private Joseph Kerczewsky. Kerczewsky, a shoemaker born in Poland in 1804, enlisted at Winchester on 18 April 1861. Before the end of the year, he too would be discharged. Unfortunately, a month after his release, Kerczewsky's wife died. Whether he was discharged due to his own physical limitations or to tend to his wife, who may have been ill at the time, is not known. However, he evidently possessed a great deal of vitality for slightly over a year later he married a woman who was only twenty years of age.[12]

The other extreme of the age spectrum was somewhat controlled by the fact that permission from a parent or guardian was required before anyone under the age of eighteen could volunteer. However, most prospective soldiers under the limitation simply lied about their age. While there is evidence that boys as young

---

[11] Bennett, *Sons of Old Monroe*, pp.683-686.

[12] Jordon, Weymouth T., *NCT*, vol.IV, p.180; Wallace, *5th Virginia Infantry*, pp.72, 135, 144.

as eight and nine volunteered, these instances were extremely rare. The age which seems to have been the cut off for most volunteer regiments was twelve or thirteen. In addition, most rolls contained an inordinate number of eighteen year olds, some of whom were no doubt under eighteen but were included in the listings because they deceived a recruitment officer. Generally the South recruited men who seemed to be slightly younger than the North but each had their share of soldiers on both ends of the age spectrum.[13]

To offset the aged Charles Michael and Joseph Kerczewsky of the 5th Virginia were a number of youngsters. The youngest of whom were Daniel Bush and Charlie W. H. Turner, who at the time of their enlistments were only fifteen. Bush, who enlisted on 30 June 1861, was sent home sometime in early July and was listed as being on sick furlough on the 23rd of the month. He would never return. Turner enlisted on 9 June as a private in the regiment's Company L. He would serve as an orderly for Stonewall Jackson before being discharged in 1862 to attend the Virginia Military Institute. In addition to Turner and Bush, four other men enlisted at the age of sixteen. A short time later these four were also sent home for various reasons. Only eight seventeen year olds were listed on the original muster roles, but a total of sixty-four eighteen year olds were present. The number was undoubtedly inflated due to a number of the seventeen year olds lying about their age.[14]

While the distinction of being the youngest soldier will probably never be substantiated, Charles Carter Hay, claimed to be the youngest to enter Confederate service. In a letter written after the war, Hay declare that at the tender age of eleven, he "helped to raise, drill, and organize the Glennville Guards" of the 15th Alabama Infantry. Hay also claimed to have voted for the regiment's first colonel and later helped to organize a company of the 45th Alabama of which he eventually became the unit's captain. Hay's story seems to contain some threads of fabrication and is a bit hard to believe, but it illustrates the extreme youth of some Civil War volunteers.[15]

Early in the war, little if anything was done to limit the age of the graybeards who wished to join or scrutinize the physical condition and limitations of the men who signed up. Few standards for examining men to determine whether or not they were in the condition required to participate in active campaigning were incorporated. The early months of the war saw many of the older men, and those with physical ailments or injuries spending an inordinate amount of time on the sick roles and in hospitals. Some regiments recorded as many as ten percent of their members admitted to infirmaries before their first fight. Many of these men never returned to their regiments. On 30 September 1862, the Federal War Department issued a series of instructions intended to provide guidelines for the mustering into service of all volunteers or militia. The document set forth a maximum age limit

---

[13] Coco, Gregory A., *The Civil War Infantryman, in Camp, on the March and in Battle*, p.7; Wiley, Bell Irvin, *The Life of Billy Yank*, p.299.

[14] Wallace, *5th Virginia Infantry*, pp.72, 102, 166.

[15] About Another "Youngest Soldier," *CV*, vol.9, no.8, p.352.

of forty-five and a minimum of eighteen. Exceptions could be made for those who were to fill commissioned officers positions, but a man had to be "Physically robust and active" in order to receive an exemption. Also outlined was a series of eight questions to be asked those who looked as if they may be outside the age range. An oath which volunteers could swear to was included, and physical requirements for prospective volunteers were also defined.

> 96. All officers and men must be sound and active, free from all malformations, defects of sight, hearing, ulcers, piles, rupture, fracture, dislocation, and disease of any kind. But the lack of or defect in the left eye, or slight injury of the left hand, will not reject the man. Stammerers must not be received. But all men who are enrolled and have performed duty in the organized militia will be received.

Evidently the War Department, based on the notations regarding a soldier's left hand and eye, was under the impression that everyone who wished to shoulder a musket fired it right handed.[16]

By the spring of 1863, most of the old-timers and youngsters had been weeded out in both armies. The men who remained were hard, chiseled and experienced in the bloody work of combat, but for many their greatest test had yet to be taken.

Disease and Death

By the third summer of the war, most regiments which had spent a significant amount of time marching and fighting were a shadow of their former selves. Although reinforcements were sometimes assigned to depleted regiments, the numbers supplied were nowhere near sufficient to make up for the effects of army life and active campaigning. Add to this the number of healthy men who managed to be someplace else when fighting erupted and by the summer of 1863, the average size of a regiment had fallen to around 340 enlisted men and officers.[17]

A number of factors contributed to the reduction. The greatest enemy of the common soldier was not a bullet but illness and disease. While the number of men on sick roles had fallen slightly over the first two years of the war, it was not uncommon for the infirmaries to contain four sick men for every able-bodied man on the firing line. From the Union standpoint, during the first summer of the war, for every 1,000 healthy men, 3,882 were ill. This number fell to 2,983 the following summer and to 2,273 by the summer of 1863. Summer seemed to be the season which saw the greatest elevation in the number of sick and new regiments seemed to be more susceptible to diseases than veteran outfits. Many of the sick men could blame their ailments on unsanitary conditions. A sad testament to the poor sanitation can be found in the simple fact that more men died during the war of dysentery and diarrhea than were killed outright in battle. In the final analysis,

---

[16]   *OR,* Series.III, vol.2, pp.236, 612

[17]   Coco, *The Civil War Infantryman,* p.9.

four men died of disease for every man who was killed while facing the enemy. Although the efforts of men like Dr. Letterman to improve sanitary conditions had reduced illness, the number of men out on sick leave at any one time was still terribly high.[18]

Other illnesses struck in epidemic form. Measles, malaria, and typhoid fever seemed to be the most prevalent with yellow fever and scarlet fever also being of concern. Although typhoid fever was less prevalent than malaria, it was far deadlier. Minor cases of all these ailments and common flu symptoms were typically termed "camp fever." Other less critical illnesses, which also placed men in the infirmaries, were rheumatism, scurvy, tuberculosis, and pneumonia.[19]

The Confederates were no less susceptible to the same health problems. As in the North, dysentery and diarrhea were the major maladies. In the Southern army however, medical records were not as diligently kept and it is difficult to determine the ratio of sick to healthy men. Through the first nine months of fighting, the Confederate army confronting Washington contained around 50,000 men. During that period, 36,572 cases of diarrhea and dysentery were reported. One of the South's largest military infirmaries was located in Richmond. During the war, 10,503 cases of dysentery and diarrhea were treated there. Of these cases, one out of every ten men died. Although the death rate from these ailments was light compared to a number of others, the weakening effect of their symptoms made patients more susceptible to other diseases. Once in the infirmary, where more serious diseases were prevalent, patients became infected with other, more deadly problems.[20]

A review of war time sources indicate the 9th Virginia Infantry absorbed 103 deaths due to sickness while only forty men were killed outright in battle. Of the 103, twenty-one lost their lives to dysentery and diarrhea. Nineteen were killed by typhoid fever while another sixteen were killed by pneumonia. Five men died of measles while a like number succumbed to small pox. Not all Southern regiments saw the same rate of dysentery. For example, the 11th Virginia Infantry lost only twelve men to the ailment but thirty-two men died from typhoid fever while another ten perished from pneumonia. The disparity could be attributed to a number of possibilities. Access to clean water, camp cleanliness and better quality food containing more fruits and vegetables could have lowered the rates of diarrhea and dysentery. The 11th Virginia however, was a bit of an anomaly, having nearly twice as many men killed in action than died of disease.[21]

Battle casualties and illness were the two largest culprits in reducing regimental manpower. Another offender although to a lesser extent was the fact that some men just disappeared. Whether actually a deserter, or missing in action, some soldiers simply vanished. Many of these men eventually returned, but a number were never

---

[18] Wiley, ***Billy Yank***, pp.124-125.

[19] *Ibid*, pp.133-135.

[20] Wiley, ***Johnny Reb***, p.252.

[21] Trask, Benjamin H., ***9th Virginia Infantry***, p.48.

seen again. A number of things could account for a soldier's missing status. The whirlwind of battle often separated men from their commands. Once detached from his regiment a number of things could happen to a soldier and most of them were bad. He could be captured, shot, or if wounded, crawl off into the woods and simply die. A soldier on his own also had another choice. Once away from the eyes of his companions, with no one sure as to his fate, he could simply leave. While desertion held a number of penalties, all of them bad, the horror of violent war prompted many to take the chance. At least their fate was now in their hands as opposed to those of an irresponsible or overzealous officer.

In addition to his own wellbeing, a soldier contemplating desertion had to weigh his decision not only against the hazards incurred upon himself but also his family. For unmarried men, the burden was less, but for those with a wife and children to consider, it was a troublesome decision. According to Private Wilber Fisk, while on picket duty one day, a Rebel soldier requested a letter he had written to his parents in Connecticut be shepherded northward by Fisk. "He said he would most gladly leave the rebel army and go home," Fisk recorded, "but he had a wife and child inside the rebel lines that he did not wish to leave to the tender mercies of such enemies as would surround them if he deserted the rebel cause." Fisk also noted that Rebel's chronically swam the river in an effort to desert to the Yankees but "through sheer timidity," Fisk and his fellow pickets, "refused them the privilege." While Fisk and his companions were sympathetic to the Rebel plight, they would not provide deserters sanctuary within Northern lines.[22]

An example of the toll taken on the number of men present for duty by combat, disease and desertion can be seen by examining the 13th Virginia Infantry's roster. At the First Battle of Manassas, A. P. Hill's original regiment contained approximately 550 men ready for duty. Approximately one year later at Gaines' Mill the regiment fielded only 250 men, of which 112 were killed or wounded. By the time the regiment fought at Sharpsburg it numbered less than 100 able-bodied men. The severe reductions cannot all be attributed to battle deaths. Between the years 1861 and 62, based on roster records, the regiment lost only fifty-eight men to death in battle. Disease claimed another forty-three while eighteen were transferred and another twenty resigned. Desertions accounted for the loss of 170 men. Some of these men were draftees who were assigned to the regiment in 1862 and took the first convenient opportunity to sneak away from the army. The regiment was obviously better off with these men missing since most probably did not wish to fight in the first place. By far the largest factor contributing to the reduction in the numbers in the 13th was the discharge of over 300 men. Discharges during the early portion of the war were usually for illness and physical disability. Inflating these numbers was the Confederate Conscription Act of 1862 which required that all men under the age of eighteen and over the age of thirty-five be dismissed from the service. Although poor recordkeeping was prevalent, the numbers for the 13th Virginia are fairly typical from the Southern point of view. By the end of the war, 1,537 men had served at one time or another in the 13th Virginia. When

---

[22] Rosenblatt, Editors, **Hard Marching Every Day**, p.104.

Lee surrendered his army at Appomattox, only sixty-three men were present to put down their arms. The toll taken on Northern numbers by combat and army life, while generally slightly more accurate, typically show the same tendencies.[23]

The sapping of regimental strength due to diseases, desertions, and combat, reduced both armies to shadows of their original strengths. Thinking of the manpower issue in a different light brings the effects of war to a frightening perspective. Assuming the Federal army had entered the Gettysburg Campaign with its compliment of regiments at full strength the Army of the Potomac would have contained close to 300,000 men of all arms. If the same standard were applied to Lee's force, the Confederates would have fielded around 225,000 men. The simple fact of the matter is that a large number of Civil War soldiers died during their military service without ever firing a shot at the enemy. Those who did manage to pull a trigger, were capable of doing so for only short periods between wounds, recovery and disease. Most would fight in only a few engagements before they were physically unable to continue.

Motivation

What motivated the common soldier has been the subject of debate since the termination of fighting. Sergeant-Major George Cary Eggleston of Virginia's Lamkin Artillery believed the motivating factors which kept both Union and Confederate volunteers true to the ideologies of the war were their pride and manhood.

> "The starvation and the excessive marching would have destroyed the morale of troops held together only by discipline. No historical criticism of our civil war [sic] can be otherwise than misleading if it omits to give a prominent place, as a factor, to the character of the volunteers on both sides, who, in acquiring the steadiness and order of regulars, never lost their personal interest in the contest or their personal pride of manhood as a sustaining force under trying conditions. If either side had lacked this element of personal heroism on the part of its men it would have been driven from the field long before the spring of 1865. ...[T]he most important duty of those who now furnish the materials out of which the ultimate history of our war will be constructed is to emphasize this aspect of the matter, and in every possible way to illustrate the part which the high personal character of the volunteers in the ranks played in determining the events of the contest."[24]

---

[23]　***OR*** vol.2, p.487; ***OR*** vol.11, pt.2, p.611; ***OR*** vol.19, pt., p.969; Riggs, David F., *13ᵗʰ Virginia Infantry*, pp.33, 143.

[24]　Eggleston, George Cary, Notes on Cold Harbor, ***B&L***, vol.4, p.232.

Initially, many men signed the rolls looking for adventure and excitement. Almost overnight Northern and Southern towns became filled with older and supposedly wiser men with great oration skills capable of working a younger crowd into a frenzy. In the North, these rallies produced unified mobs hell bent on putting down the rebellious Southerners. In the South the popular sentiment was to defend States' Rights, family, home, the right to self-government and their way of life which in most instances included slavery. Southerners displayed a more aggressive attitude while Northern rallies took on an air of seriousness and duty. However, the men who joined for the adventure soon discovered the novelty of war evaporated quickly when the realities of a vicious and horribly violent conflict became obvious.

While the sentiment of personal pride and masculinity was probably true to some degree, by the third summer of the war, a good portion of the volunteers had lost their romantic attitude toward the war. Civilian attitudes such as patriotism, the crushing of the institution of slavery, adventure, and glory, had given way to reality. Death, disease, poor food, bad weather, mud, dust, not to mention the belief that some commanders were extremely incompetent, all led to the erosion of a volunteer's motivation. Although these concepts remained within the minds of the soldiers, the simple facts were that by the third summer of the war the art of soldiering had collapsed into endurance and survival. The families which had seen them off with such fanfare and pride, while not forgotten, had been replaced by the members of their companies and regiments. These organizations became tight knit communities which tended to look after their own.[25]

While most men who signed up had no intention of disgracing their families by failing to do their duty, when bullets began to fly, some found the task of maintaining ones resolve in battle extremely difficult. They simply could not bring themselves to face the dangers of open combat and made great efforts to avoid fighting. It is believed that in some regiments as many as one half of the men in their ranks actively looked for ways to shun bullets. Known as sneaks, skulkers, stragglers, and coffee-coolers, these men always seemed to be missing when a fight was approaching. Shortly after the fighting was over, they seemed to magically reappear with some excuse as to why they happened to miss the action and expressed their displeasure with being absent during the brawl. Others actively sought duty which would keep them from the fighting. Tasks such as working in the hospitals, guarding wagon-trains or performing administrative tasks at headquarters were all cherished assignments. Even General Meade's despised task of assisting a wounded comrade to the rear was a welcome excuse to escape flying lead.[26]

Many men who did all they could to avoid fighting were those who would have seemed to seek it out. These men were the browbeaters of their towns and villages. They were the locals who always seemed to be in the mood to brawl in the streets over the most minor of issues. Quite simply they were the local bullies.

---

[25] Coco, *The Civil War Infantryman*, p.6.

[26] McPherson, James M., *For Cause and Comrades: Why Men Fought in the Civil War*, pp.6-7.

Many of them failed to join during the first wave of patriotism and only signed up later as substitutes and bounty men who took money from those who had been drafted and could afford to pay someone else to go. These men quickly showed that being tough in a street brawl was a poor measure of how effective they would be as a soldier. Veterans who watched their depleted ranks restocked with these men had very few positive words to say about them. The poor showing of paid men proved that money was not a significant motivator in developing a hard fighting Civil War soldier.

Conversely, many of the men who proved to be the toughest on the battle line were those who in civilian life were shy and timid. They joined because it was the right thing to do. Many of them no doubt looked upon the conflict as a chance to prove their worth to not only their families and friends but also to those who thought they were of lesser stock. It was an opportunity for those who were considered less manly to prove their mettle. Some of these men fought with a tenacity and determination which became legendary within their regiments and brigades. Although they assuredly understood the dangers of open combat, they were able to control their fear and showed little if any trepidation in battle. Most of these men spent a good deal of time complaining about the lowly life of a soldier, but always seemed to be in line when the shooting started, earning them the right to complain.[27]

An officer in the 3rd South Carolina observed the phenomenon of the meek becoming warriors first hand.

> "I have known men who at home were perfect cowards, whom a schoolboy could run away with a walking cane, become fearless and brave as lions in battle; while on the other hand men who were called 'game cocks' at home and great 'crossroads bullies,' were abject cowards in battle."[28]

These mild mannered warriors surely received inspiration that brought out their fortitude. There were three conventional methods used to inspire soldiers to march, fight, and endure life in the field. The first, leadership, was initially a weak area for both Confederate and Federal volunteer regiments. Many of the original volunteer units elected their officers, making the selection of their leaders nothing more than a popularity contest. Southern troops overcame leadership deficiency at a faster rate than their Northern counterparts. By the summer of 1863, most deficient regimental commanders had been discharged, assigned to other duties, or killed in battle due to their incompetence. While both armies still employed some officers who were poor to average, most were capable of leading their commands in battle and had experience doing so.

The second traditional method of motivating volunteer soldiers was training. At the beginning of the war, volunteers on both sides were woefully deficient in

---

[27] *Ibid*, pp.8-9.

[28] Dickert, D. Augustus, ***History of Kershaw's Brigade***, p.200.

military skills. Constant drilling educated the men in the art of marching, and loading and firing their weapons. Camp life brought to their attention the rigors of an army existence. While manuals provided documentation on the procedures and techniques required to be an efficient soldier, nothing could substitute for the constant practice of drill. Another element of training and drill, which was difficult for the men to stomach, was the establishment of who was in charge. In a land which was built upon rugged individualism, it was difficult for those who had not been subjected to a military lifestyle to understand that they were no longer the masters of their destiny. Many volunteers did not appreciate the ridged regulations or take kindly to the authority given their officers.[29]

Finally, motivation was rendered with the use of discipline. While training and leadership help to motivate men by providing them a sense of accomplishment and worth, discipline instilled motivation based on emotion, physical threats and punishment. Essentially, the Civil War was fought by armies commanded by small groups of professional soldiers. These leaders were required to manage the movements, supply and conduct in battle of massive bodies of military novices. Maintaining discipline in such a rabble of individualistic men was a difficult and sometimes impossible task. To make matters worse, officers of volunteer units were usually from the same local area as the men in their regiment. They were leery of implementing strict disciplinary action upon men who were acquaintances or even friends.

Civil War officers utilized both physical and verbal techniques to establish discipline and maintain control. Many officers became very adept at verbally motivating their soldiers and establishing and maintaining discipline with the spoken word. A soldier who prided himself in his duties and accepted a level of responsibility for his actions could be motivated in such a manner. If a soldier accepted his duty to country, reputation and the requirements of manhood as a badge of honor, then he was far easier to motivate verbally than one who did not. Within the Regular Army, officers and men had been exposed to the concepts of duty, honor and country, accepting them as a strong motivating force. Unfortunately for the volunteer armies of the Civil War, most of the men, including many early regimental officers, cared little about honor and duty when it came to standing in line of battle before a determined enemy. Verbally shaming these men into line and to maintain discipline in camp was impossible in many instances. When an officer's volunteers could not be effectively motivated through words, the second method of incentivizing his uniformed civilians had to be implemented.

When verbal motivation failed to establish control, physical punishment was enforced. While the level of rebelliousness within the volunteer force was high, most offences were minor and were taken care of with inconsequential penalties. Minor offences such as failing to perform camp duties, taking proper care of one's equipment or not maintaining a tidy camp were dealt with by requiring addition tasks around camp. Errands such as chopping wood, standing additional guard duty and digging latrines were often used to punish soldiers for minor infractions.

---

[29] McPherson, *For Cause and Comrades*, pp.46-47.

More severe offenses such as dereliction of duty, straggling, cowardice, drunkenness, fighting, desertion, insubordination, and theft, were dealt with utilizing harsh and sometimes severe punishments. Humiliating punishments such as carrying a heavy log while performing guard duty, being bucked and gagged, labeled with a placard identifying ones offence or carrying a knapsack loaded with heavy articles such as rocks, were a few of the more minor physical punishments. Some of the more severe were being strapped to the spare wheel of an artillery caisson, sitting on a wooden horse, being placed in a sweatbox or strapped to a stick. The duration of these punishments were based on the severity of the offense. Repeat offenders were often dealt harsher, lengthier punishments.[30]

The most severe form of discipline, which was practiced by both armies, was that of coercion. The threat of death was used often to force soldiers to stay in line during battle or influence them to resist the temptation to desert. During battle officers would stand behind the battle line with their sword in one hand and their revolver in the other and threaten to shoot anyone who failed to do their duty. At Seven Pines, a young captain named Oliver Wendell Holmes, used his sword to get a cowardly soldier back in line and swore he would shoot the first man who refused to do his duty. As the war progressed, officers began utilizing more stringent and heaver handed methods of coercion to maintain discipline. Some even threatened placing artillery in the rear of the line to keep the men in place. But, while a regiment's officer may threaten death to anyone who showed himself to be a coward, few had the intestinal fortitude to carry out their threats. Many officers feared the stigma that would follow them home after the war if they committed such an atrocity as to murder a man simply because his desire for self-preservation overpowered his ability to face the enemy.[31]

The most severe crimes, such as desertion, murder, treating with the enemy, and spying were offenses punishable with the most severe form of coercion, death. The Civil War contains a number of instances where soldiers convicted of such crimes were executed through hanging and firing squad. Some however, managed to get off easy and were simply branded on the face or hip or simply drummed out of the army. The suspect soldier typically stood before a court-marshal and if convicted would be informed of his fate. Typically, when an execution was carried out, the unlucky soldier's regiment or in some cases his entire brigade,

---

[30] Faust, *Encyclopedia*, p.220; Billings, John D., *Hard Tack and Coffee*, pp.144-154. When a man was bucked and gagged he was forced to sit on the ground and draw his knees up to his chest. A stick was then placed under his knees with the crooks of his elbows under the stick. His wrists were then tied together in front of his knees. A wooden gag was then placed in his mouth. When a soldier was strapped to the spare wheel of a caisson he was placed upon the wheel, straddling the wheel's hub. His wrists and ankles were then tied to the perimeter of the wheel. The position was incredibly uncomfortable and made more so by the fact that many who received this punishment were not taken down from the wheel when the army was on the march. Sitting on a wooden horse was simply being forced to sit upon an elevated log for an extended period of time. The log was elevated to a height which kept the man's feet from touching the ground.

[31] McPherson, *For Cause and Comrades*, pp.48-49.

was assembled to watch the event. The execution was used as a motivating tool to coerce the doomed man's friends and fellow soldiers to maintain their discipline and do their duty.[32]

Men

Literacy rates among Civil War soldiers were as varied as their occupations. Regiments typically contained men with educational backgrounds of the highest order while also containing some who had lacked educational opportunities and as such could not read or write. Regiments also contained members who possessed a great deal of common sense but also men who possessed an intrinsic stupidity. Within the Union army it was not uncommon for a company of foot soldiers to contain six to a dozen men who were totally illiterate. The Confederates had their share of illiterates as well. When Company A of the 11th North Carolina of General Pettigrew's brigade was mustered into service, twenty-seven of the 100 men mustered could not sign their name, making their mark instead. Typically a Confederate company had as many as twenty men who were functionally illiterate and could not sign their name.[33]

At the other end of the educational spectrum were the intellectual elite. Educated men had a tendency to single themselves out from the rabble rousers that made up the majority of the volunteers. Both Union and Confederate soldiers benefited from their educational status. One well educated member of the 3rd Indiana Cavalry, who entered service as a private, would later be commissioned a second lieutenant. In some instances entire companies were populated with educated men. Twenty members of the First Company of the Rockbridge Artillery were graduates of Washington College while another forty were students at the institution or at the University of Virginia. One company within the 11th Virginia Infantry, who's first captain was a professor at Lynchburg College, was populated by students from the institution.[34]

A common misconception is that the volunteer force within the Union army was assembled from mostly foreign born soldiers. This perception has its roots, to some extent, in the Southern fighting man's belief that Northern soldiers possessed an inherent inability to fight. Most Rebel's believed Northern men were cowards at heart and used their money to solicit and pay foreigners to fight for them. They assumed Northerners hired a mass of outsiders, who were itching for a fight, to march off to war for them while the cowardly Yankee's stayed home, using the war to expand their already swollen bank accounts. This opinion seems to have been formed based on the inordinate number of foreign accents they encountered when speaking with their antagonists.[35]

---

[32] Faust, ***Encyclopedia***, p.220.

[33] Wiley, Bell Irvin, ***Johnny Reb***, pp.336-337; Wiley, ***Billy Yank***, p.305.

[34] Wiley, ***Billy Yank***, pp.304-305; Wiley, ***Johnny Reb***, pp.335-336.

[35] Wiley, ***Billy Yank***, pp.306-307.

While it is true a large number of Union soldiers were foreign born, three-fourths of the volunteers were generational Americans. Of the remaining quarter, the most prominent foreign contingent within Joe Hooker's Army of the Potomac were the first and second generation German's of Howard's Eleventh Corps. In 1860 the Northern states contained approximately one million German immigrants. Of the approximately 814,000 people living in New York City, slightly over 380,000 were of foreign birth. Of these, 64,000 were males of German ancestry. The state of New York raised ten regiments which were assembled entirely from German immigrants and a large number of additional regiments which contained a sizable number. Some of these regiments found their way into the ranks of the Eleventh Corps. While the members of Howard's Corps, through no fault of their own, had established a reputation for being poor fighters, and indeed some of the German's were, the majority of them did their duty nobly. Regiments such as Leopold Von Gilsa's original 41st New York, which contained eight companies of Germans from New York City, and George von Amsberg's 45th New York, which was assembled almost entirely of German's, were determined to erase the stigma of failure which had been leveled upon them after Chancellorsville.[36]

Following the Germans in number were the Irish. During the first two years of combat, the sons of Erin had proven they were some of the most fanatic fighters in Hooker's army. Some 203,740 people of Irish descent called the city of New York home in 1860. Of these, 86,580 were males. Throughout its history, the Army of the Potomac would be the home of twelve regiments of Irish volunteers. As the army prepared for the summer campaign, seven Irish regiments were present in its ranks. A Yankee corporal once noted that the Irish "fight like tigers, & no regt. of Rebs can stand a charge from them." Although the Irish, like all other nationalities, had their share of cowards and ingrates, in general they fought hard and always seemed to be in the middle of the most vicious fighting. When circumstances were at their worst, commanders called on them to stabilize their lines and many soldiers admitted that they displayed courage bordering on madness. The most famous Irish organization in the Army of the Potomac was Colonel Patrick Kelly's Irish Brigade.[37]

Lee's Army of Northern Virginia possessed a number of foreign born soldiers as well. While their numbers were less than those of their Northern counterparts, Irishmen, Germans and Frenchmen were spread throughout Lee's legions. A hotbed for recruitment of foreign Confederates was Louisiana, and more specifically, New Orleans. In 1860 nearly eleven and one half percent of the population of the state was foreign. While most of the foreigners who came out of New Orleans were of Irish or German descent, there were a large number of other nationalities as well. The city was home for 10,715 German males, 11,494 men from Ireland and 6,197 men of French descent. The 1st Louisiana Infantry of Nicholls' Brigade contained men who hailed from thirty-seven different countries. One company in another of

---

[36] *Ibid*, pp.307-308; Phisterer, **NYWR**, vol.3, pp.2237, 2305; Population of the United States in 1860; Compiled from the Original Returns of the Eight Census (hereafter **Eight Census**), p.609.

[37] Wiley, **Billy Yank**, pp.308-309; Boyle, Frank A., *A Party of Mad Fellows: The Story of the Irish Regiments in the Army of the Potomac*, pp.16, 397-399; **Eight Census**, p.609.

Nicholl's regiments, the 10th Louisiana, marched off to war with men from fifteen different countries.[38]

The Louisianans gained a reputation for being nothing more than a group of ruffians. Many of the men forming the state's contingency in Lee's army were common laborers and wharf rats. Others had been employed to build levees in the area but when state funding ran dry, they were forced into military service to survive. They brought their dislike for authority to the units they joined, making it difficult for their officers to control them. During active campaigning, they were hard to manage and on numerous occasions ignored standing orders to leave civilian property undisturbed. While the Louisianans proved to be a rowdy and rough bunch who paid little attention to orders or army discipline, there was no doubt they were fighters and could be trusted to give a good accounting when engaged with the enemy. Their reputation for rowdiness and unwavering determination on the battle line would earn some of them the nickname Louisiana Tigers.[39]

By the summer of the 1863 both armies touted groups of foreign soldiers who had proven they could be counted as some of the toughest and most unruly men in the volunteer service. Some, such as Howard's Germans, had been tagged with a bad reputation. Others, like Lee's Tigers volunteered because they had nothing better to do and needed the money. Battle deaths and disease had reduced the ranks of each army's foreign contingent. Desertion and discharge had also thinned the ranks of all the regiments in both armies. Many men who volunteered during the original wave of patriotism had been mustered out and returned home when their enlistments expired. Having done their service, these men could have gone home and sat out the rest of the war. Instead, many volunteered once again and signed rolls in newly organizing regiments or reorganized versions of their old unit. Those who chose to return were typically the cream of the crop of each army's volunteers. These men knew the difficulties of army life but chose to return. They had seen the horrors of battle up close. They had watched men, many of them friends, die by their side. Many had visited field hospitals both as patients and observers and seen the misery and residue of conflict, yet, they chose to return and rejoin their comrades, even though they had already done their part. No one could think of them or call them cowards. What drove these men to return to the misery of a soldier's existence and the terror of open combat has been debated since the end of the war. One thing is certain, there was a task to finish, and they could not face the remainder of their lives without seeing it through to its conclusion.

Courage and Conviction

Both North and South possessed a number of common motives for fighting the war and during recruitment these common threads were used to stir the desire of prospective soldiers. Political ideologies, employment, adventure, a chance to

---

[38] Wiley, *Johnny Reb*, pp.322-323; Jones, Terry L., *Lee's Tigers: The Louisiana Infantry in the Army of Northern Virginia*, p.5; *Eight Census*, p.615.

[39] Jones, *Lee's Tigers*, pp.6-7.

become a man or simply doing what was right were all used to solicit volunteers. Above all others however, was a sense of duty to one's country. Loyalty to country, whether to the old Union or the new Confederacy proved to be a primary motivator.

However, the motivation and exhilaration of fighting the hated enemy of one's country quickly vanished after a volunteer's first battle. Although a soldier's devotion to country and his honor as a man were driving factors in his ability to continue fighting, each soldier had to deal with the fear that quickly entered his mind as fighting approached. Most men refused to acknowledge their dread of battle. To do so would confess to those around him his weakness and bring into question his masculinity. Divulging ones fear to both companions and family was difficult. Although many yearned for soft staff positions or work as hospital orderlies to escape the fighting, they would never admit such a thing to their fellow soldiers. Some acknowledged they became accustom to the whirlwind of battle and spoke of dying gloriously on the field. Everyone understood such comments were only a method of downplaying the danger. Obviously, everyone would have preferred the alternative of living.[40]

For most soldiers, the period shortly before battle was the most difficult. It was during this time that the courage of a soldier was put to the test. In reality, the bravery a soldier displayed during this interlude was nothing more than his ability to master his fear. The anxiety felt before battle overcame many. These men began actively looking for excuses to depart for safe locations. Those who remained were able to control their fear, fight the urge for self-preservation and deploy to face the enemy. Some told jokes and tried to calm their fears with merriment, but laughter was only a temporary means of relief. The aforementioned 3rd South Carolina officer also noted this phenomenon.[41]

> "Some men, on the eve of battle, the most trying time in a soldier's life, will stand calm and impassive, awaiting the command 'forward,' while his neighbor will tremble and shake, as with a great chill, praying, meditating, and almost in despair, awaiting the orders to advance. Then when in the heat of the contest both men seem metamorphosed. The former, almost frightened out of his wits, loses his head and is just as apt to fire backwards as forward; while the latter seems to have lost all fear, reckless of his life, and fights like a hero."[42]

Once fighting began, countless men noted they seemed to become oblivious to danger. Some equated the experience to hunting while others noted they had suffered greater levels of fear during other events in their lives. Some found themselves simply too busy with the business of killing, to mystified, or simply

---

[40] McPherson, *For Cause and Comrades*, p.36.

[41] *Ibid*, pp.36-37.

[42] Dickert, *History of Kershaw's Brigade*, p.200.

to resolute in their task to acknowledge the danger of their environment. While many of these comments no doubt contained a certain level of bravado due to hindsight, many men did indeed show less fear while fighting than they did during the anticipation of the event.[43]

One of the factors in a soldier's ability to control his fear was the level of internal pride he possessed. No combatant wished to give anyone, least of all his companions, any opportunity to call into question his manhood. Many looked to combat as a test of their integrity as a man. Simply stated, their fear of being thought a lesser man was more powerful than their fear of enemy bullets and cannon fire.

Other men found the courage to face the trials of battle in religion. Armed conflict tended to heighten an individual's adherence to his religious convictions. Men, who were deeply religious at the outset of the war, became more fanatical about their faith after their first battle. If a man had only a passing loyalty to his deity, he quickly developed a more intense connection to God during his experience as a soldier. His hope was that additional religious conviction would help to purify his soul so that if the war proved to be a fatal endeavor, his trip to meet his maker would be a positive experience. These men continued to expand their interest in religion and developed a much stronger passion for their faith as the war progressed. Even those who had never accepted religion into their lives, and spent their Sunday's lounging around camp, showed more interest in morning church services. Placing their destiny in the hands of God was a calming influence and gave some the additional strength of will to do their duty in the face of the enemy.[44]

The enduring question regarding the volunteers is why did they continue to fight after being exposed to the violence and horror of battle? Union volunteers cited a number of reasons, including their devotion to the legacy of the country's founders. If the Northern states simply let the Southerners go, the great experiment in a representative republic would have failed. The blood spilled by their fathers and grandfathers would have been in vain. Some felt their generation would have proven themselves unworthy of the freedoms and liberties provided by the founders and their brethren if they made no effort to maintain the Union. They believed the Union had to be sustained and if it should happen to be permanently divided, everyone, both North and South, would be ruined. A Northerner's sense of duty was also a strong influence for Union soldiers, particularly in convincing fathers and mothers to allow their sons to go on what a prospective volunteer perceived as the great adventure of his life.[45]

Few Northern soldiers spoke of the institution of slavery and its abolition as a driving factor in their desire to volunteer. While Northern abolitionists and political operatives used the issue to whip the population into a frenzy, only small numbers

---

[43] McPherson, ***For Cause and Comrades***, pp.36-37; Coco, ***The Civil War Infantryman***, p.93.

[44] McPherson, ***For Cause and Comrades***, pp.64-65.

[45] *Ibid*, pp.18-16, 22.

of volunteers expressed the liberation of slaves as a reason for their enlistment. Those who did were generally extremely vocal in their hatred for the institution, and those who practiced it and allowed it to continue. They believed it was a curse upon the land and if the war was to terminate without the practice being eradicated all the bloodshed would have been in vain. However, the simple fact remains that the chief goal of the majority of Union volunteers was the preservation of their country in the state their founding fathers had envisioned.[46]

Most Southern volunteers believed they were fighting for their own liberty, thought God was on their side, and were confident that what they were doing was right. They considered Northerners tyrants and believed it better to die in battle fighting an oppressive foe than to submit to the will of their enemy. They held an understanding that they were fighting in defense of their family, the virtue of their women, their homes and property, including their slaves, and their States Rights. Ironically, many Southerners felt they were fighting against the institution of slavery, as it was applied to the North's desire to enslave them with their rules and laws. They felt their only recourse was to fight against the subjection they were being forced to endure. While some Southern volunteers did cite the possible abolition of slavery as a reason to fight the Yankees, a far greater number felt they were fighting to defend their possessions and kin.[47]

The typical modern argument for why the South fought the war was to maintain the institution of slavery. While the South's upper class may have been motivated by a desire, rooted in economics to retain the institution, it is hard to imagine a typical Confederate soldier was so inclined. Most soldiers within Confederate service did not own or have the resources to purchase slaves, and would not have laid their lives on the line or endured the hardships of army life to retain the right for the political elites, plantation owners and lawyers. While the upper class Southerner who was supporting the war may have been striving to preserve the institution, the common fighting man was probably not so enthusiastic about the

---

[46] *Ibid*, p.19.

[47] *Ibid*, pp.19-21. While there can be no doubt the cause of the war was the issue of slavery, like most conflicts, individuals within the general populace tend to agree with or disagree with their leaders and elites. In reality there were five major causes for the war, which upon close examination, all had their roots in slavery. They are, in no specific order, social and economic conflicts, the election of Lincoln, States' Rights, conflict between pro-slavery factions and abolitionists and finally the expansion of the abolitionist's movement. If one looks deeply into these issues, it is easy to determine that the root cause was the country's inability to retain the values which brought it together. The core values of unity and nation had been circumvented by groups of extremists on both sides that refused to give ground on their ideologies. These extremists (abolitionists and pro-slavery), instead of reaching compromise, opted to see the nation destroyed if it meant accomplishing their goals. The issues had become so inflammatory by the beginning of the war that compromise was not only impossible but in the minds of the extremists, absurd. Even after the war was successfully conducted by the North, Southern extremists continued to rail against the Northern establishment. The most obvious example of this inability to compromise is the murder of Abraham Lincoln.

idea. There was something else driving him. Whether motivated by honor, duty, defending ones family, survival, the pursuit of glory or the simple idea of escaping what was considered an oppressive Federal Government, each man had his own reasons.

Every soldier was but a miniscule component of a gigantic machine called the army. When a majority of these small, insignificant elements were working in unison, the army performed well, and on a few occasions actually accomplished the intent of its commander. With proper leadership from the highest levels down, the soldiers of each army were capable of standing toe to toe with each other. A common misconception is that early in the war the Southern fighting man was more proficient at his craft than the ordinary Yankee. This belief is far from the truth. While it is true that the men of the Army of the Potomac were consistently whipped by Lee's army, the continual defeats were more the responsibility of incompetent officers than the fighting men's abilities. Incompetence was not only seen at the regimental level but ranged upward to the highest levels of the Federal army. As the war progressed, many of the inept officers were replaced with men who had achieved results at lower levels of the command structure. While there was still some ineptitude existing within the upper levels of the Army of the Potomac, by 1863, many of the lesser brigade and division commanders had been removed. As June began, the Army of the Potomac was well on its way to equalizing the disparity in officer quality between it and the Army of Northern Virginia.

Unfortunately for Lee's army, his dwindling resource base in both materials and manpower was depriving him of competent commanders. While the North was eliminating their incompetent officers, the South was losing their competent ones to combat. The summer of 1863 would see an equalization of each army's officer corps. The soldiers of both armies, for the most part, would be lead by experienced and capable men. Although there would be instances of poor leadership on both sides, the disparity regarding leadership quality had become relatively even. At Gettysburg, the fighting man would make the difference. This was all the Union infantryman had desired.

The American Civil War was an infantryman's war, fought for the most part, by a group of volunteers who were not soldiers but simple, ordinary citizens who managed to accomplish unbelievable tasks in the face of tremendous threats to their wellbeing. They brought to their regiments the good and the bad elements of mid-nineteenth century American society. They all had hopes, dreams and individuals who cared about them. Many had wives and children. Other had fiancées, some were courting their sweethearts. Most of these men were fighting for a cause which they believed was right and that God, if he was important to them, was on their side.

Men in Camp

Camp life for a Civil War soldier was a trying and grueling existence. It consisted of bad food, long periods of drill, sickness, drenching rain, snow in the winter, mud, cold, all of which were interspersed with extreme periods of boredom. In the summertime, heavy woolen uniform made every soldier extremely uncomfortable. Every man was encumbered with the accoutrements deemed necessary to make camp life as easy as possible. When in camp, firewood had to be gathered and food had to be cooked. In cavalry and artillery units, horses had to be cared for and guns had to be maintained. Harnesses had to be repaired. Wagons, caissons and artillery limbers also required maintenance. Latrines needed to be dug. During the winter, more permanent structures had to be built to protect soldiers from extreme weather. Men also had to take their turn performing guard duty. When in hostile country, guard duty meant walking in a straight line, back and forth for hours in all weather. It was a duty which would harden even the most cheerful infantryman. For the civilian soldiers of the Civil War, it was extremely difficult to accept the structure and demands of a life in the army. It was an existence made all the more difficult when he learned he was no longer in charge of his fate.

One of the most coveted and useful article in a soldier's possession was his blanket. Federal blankets were typically of wool and issued one per man. Confederate soldiers usually carried blankets brought from home until they found a superior one left behind or on a dead Yankee. Taking the new one he would leave his old one behind for the next desperate Federal or Rebel soldier. Gum blankets were also a prized position for the infantryman because of their multiple uses. A gum or rubber blanket was simply a blanket which had one side coated with a waterproof layer. Some of these blankets could actually be used as a poncho to keep solders dry, as a ground cloth or even as a shelter. It was approximately four feet by six feet six inches and contained brass grommets along its edges so it could be strung up if necessary. Like the Federals, Confederate soldiers coveted these waterproof versions, and since they were not manufactured in the South they had to be pilfered.[48]

In 1862 a new type of tent was issued to every Union soldier. It was a tiny two man tent which was so small they began calling it a dog tent because in their minds a dog was the only creature that could sleep inside it comfortably. Other names were used as well including fly tent, dog kennel, pup tent, dog shanty, and a number of other more colorful descriptions. A soldier from New York, writing after the war, described the typical pitching technique for the tiny shelter.

> "A shelter or dog tent is like a bargain – it takes two to make it. Each man is provided with an oblong piece of thick, unbleached muslin about the length of a man – say six feet – and two-thirds as wide, bordered all round with buttons and button-holes alternately matching respectively the button-holes and buttons of his comrade's piece. To set it up, cut two crotched stakes, each about four feet long, point them at the uncrotched end, and drive them into the ground about six feet apart; cut a slender pole to lie horizontally from one crotch to the other, button the two pieces of muslin together and throw the resulting

---

[48] Coco, *The Civil War Infantryman*, p.51.

piece over the pole, drawing out the corners tight and pinning them to the ground by means of little loops fastened to them. You will thus get a wedge-shaped structure – simply the two slopes of an ordinary roof – about three and a half feet high at its highest point, and open at both ends. This will accommodate two men, and in warm, pleasant weather is all that is needed. In rainy weather a third man is admitted. A piece of rope about four feet long is then tied to the top of one of the stakes and stretched out in the line of direction of the ridge pole, the free end being brought down to the ground and pinned there. The third man then buttons his piece of muslin to one slope of the roof, carries the other edge of the piece out around the tightened rope and brings it back to the edge of the other slope, to which it is buttoned. This third piece is shifted from one end of the tent to the other, according to the direction of the wind or storm. You thus get an extension to your tent in which knapsacks can be stored, leaving the rest of the space clear for sleeping purposes. This is large enough to accommodate three men lying side by side."[49]

Sometimes the tent was pitched by substituting two soldier's muskets for the "crotched sticks." On occasion the tents could be deploying as a lean-to when a rail fence was available. In this situation the tent would be pitched by attaching one edge to a fence rail while the other was attached to the ground. Confederate soldiers were not officially issued shelters but many were issued tarps or articles which could be set up as a lean-to. Touching the inside of the tent was taboo for in rainy weather if a finger, or the top of one's head came in contact with the fabric, water would pass through the material and drip inside. Like blankets, as the war progressed, most Confederate camps became littered with various Federal tenting paraphernalia.[50]

In addition to his heavy wool uniform, a Federal soldier typically carried all of the accoutrements required for his existence in a knapsack. His bed roll, blanket and tent were usually attached to the exterior. Early in the war men marched off to battle carrying almost everything they felt they would need as well as a few luxury items. It took little time for soldiers to realize that lugging around a thirty or forty pound knapsack was a task most did not enjoy. In short order, knapsacks became very streamlined and stored only the bare necessities. The number and weight of the trappings carried varied based on the size, strength and stamina of an individual man. Almost all carried a change of clothing, extra socks, razor, comb, a toothbrush and other personal items. Most soldiers, who were to some degree literate, carried ink, a pen, paper and envelopes in order to write their loved ones. A soldier quickly found that luxury items had no value in the army and were

---

[49] Thompson, David L., In the Ranks to the Antietam, **B&L**, vol.2, p.556.

[50] *Ibid*; Coco, ***The Civil War Infantryman***, pp.53-54.

quickly discarded to lighten his load. Due to the limited availability of supplies and accoutrements, the Southern soldier lived lighter than his Federal counterpart. Many Rebels possessing only a bed roll which they slung to their back.[51]

Other items a soldier carried outside his knapsack were a cartridge box, a percussion cap box and a scabbard to hold his bayonet. These items were typically carried attached to his belt. He also carried a haversack which was characteristically used to carry rations but on many occasions acted as a storage place for extra ammunition. Unlike the knapsack, a haversack was carried by almost every Civil War soldier. While the knapsack was missing from many soldier's paraphernalia, the haversack was considered a necessity. Next to his musket and canteen, no other article was coveted more by the infantryman. A haversack was a shoulder carried bag which was typically a foot square. Inside were his rations which normally consisted of salted meats and hardtack. There were a number of different versions of the bag, some of which contained separate pockets for food. Some contained draw string bags to carry salt, pepper, sugar, coffee and rice. Unfortunately for some soldiers in a hurry, the bag bounced around and the fine spices became mixed into a singular mass.[52]

By 1863, a Northern soldier's woolen uniform shirt was being issued in a dark blue color with lighter blue being used for the trousers. Both Northern and Southern soldiers were issued a frock coat. Frock coats were very heavy and cumbersome and were not appreciated much when the weather warmed. Most were either too large or too small since the coats came in a limited number of sizes. In both armies, undergarments were typically of cotton and usually sent from home. Northerners cherished the lighter cotton underwear and were quick to discard their itchy, woolen, government issued versions once they acquired the softer articles. Trading of clothing was prevalent since many soldiers were issued articles which were too large or too small. Mixing and matching with others often supplied an infantryman with a fine fitting uniform.

The images of Southern soldiers clothed with rags and outfitted as if they were a group of backwoodsmen is an enduring myth of the Civil War. Although early in the war it was not uncommon to see Southerners clothed in civilian dress, by the third summer of the war, most Rebel soldiers had been supplied with proper military attire by either the army or from home. A Southerner was typically clothed with a short jacket and pants which were made from a wool-cotton combination fabric which proved to be very durable. Dyed a variety of grays, tans and browns, very few regiments in Southern service were outfitted with like colors. Some Rebels also wore vests made of the same cotton, wool fabric.[53]

The undersupplied Confederate soldier traveled light. Very seldom was a Southern soldier found carrying an entire set of accoutrements. This was not due to him discarding items he did not care to pack, but because he seldom was issued

---

[51]   *Ibid*, pp.49-51.

[52]   *Ibid*, pp.55-56.

[53]   *Ibid*, pp.33-35.

an entire set of equipment. Many Southern soldiers carried only a haversack and blanket, usually made from wool, and their allotment of ammunition. Assuming a Southerner had shoes, he carried somewhere between twelve and fifteen pounds.[54]

The most severe uniform problem faced by infantrymen was the availability of adequate footwear. The number of men, who at some point in their Civil War career, were without shoes, is astounding. The shortage of footwear, which was exacerbated by a sizable portion of the country's shoemakers volunteering for service, was much more prevalent in Rebel ranks. Shortages began to be of concern to Southern officials before the war was a year old. When Lee marched his army north to commence the campaign which culminated at Sharpsburg, it was estimated that as many as 40,000 pairs of shoes were needed to re-shoe his army. Reporting on the battle, the *Richmond Examiner* noted that one-fourth of Lee's army was "entirely barefoot." After the battle a South Carolinian observed that a number of men marched the sixty miles from Winchester to Culpeper barefoot, enduring cold, frosty morning roads which gave way to cold caking mud. The authorities explored all avenues in an effort to provide footwear, even procuring some from European suppliers. Through the early months of 1863, the situation improved somewhat due to the government's extraordinary effort but throughout the winter months, many men would be required to survive the rigors of army life without satisfactory footwear. As Ewell and Longstreet's Corps' marched away from Fredericksburg to Culpeper, thousands of men were still without shoes.[55]

Many men had shoes which were either too big or too small. When faced with too loose or too tight footwear, soldiers actively tried to seek out better fitting ones. Scrounging a recent battlefield for better shoes was a common occurrence. Whether taken from a dead Yankee or a poor boy in gray, most Confederates made no effort to respect the dead of either side when it came to footwear. In the late spring of 1863, a sturdy pair of shoes which fit was a valuable commodity to a Rebel soldier. With their mismatched uniforms and bare feet, it's no wonder the image of the Confederate Army being nothing more than a group of vagabonds became prevalent.[56]

When not eating, sleeping, or trying to stay warm, the greatest portion of a soldier's life in camp was spent drilling. Regiments drilled constantly, working to perfect the art of being a soldier. Drilling consisted of learning the proper movements of the squad, company and regiment to specific commands as outlined in the United States Infantry Tactics Manual. Lessons on how to fall in and take proper position in rank, fixing a bayonet, shouldering arms, marching, changing direction while on the move, and loading and firing his weapon, were just a few of the skills taught during drill. Squads and companies drilled together in order to familiarize each soldier with the movements and characteristic of the men closest to him. Companies, after drilling for about an hour, typically rejoined their

---

[54] Coddington, *The Gettysburg Campaign*, p.22.

[55] Wiley, *Johnny Reb*, pp.120-121, 372,n53.

[56] Coddington, *The Gettysburg Campaign*, p.22.

regiment and drilled as a full unit. Loading and firing their weapons was repeated so often that old veterans in the twilight of their lives could still recite the steps ingrained in them years earlier regarding how to load, prime and fire their rifled-muskets. Artilleryman and cavalrymen drilled just as frequently and intensely as infantryman. Cavalrymen drilled mounted and un-mounted and practiced riding in formation, using their sabers, and firing their weapons. Artilleryman trained to limber and unlimber their cannons as well as marching in column, in battery and deploying their guns in line of battle.[57]

Ironically, marksmanship was not held in high regard on the rifle range. It was more important to regimental officers that their men were able to load and fire quickly and consistently in the face of the enemy. It was felt that when battle erupted each man would be capable of hitting his target at the range which bodies of infantry engaged each other. A lack of concern for accuracy also had an additional advantage. It saved precious ammunition. Occasionally, men would go out on their own with live ammunition and practice. Tempting targets were usually fence posts, a tree, stump, or perhaps, if lucky enough, wild game for supper.[58]

Drums were used to communicate with the infantryman while in camp. Throughout the day the beating of drums announced the beginning of group activities. At around 5:00 a.m. reveille was sounded to open the day. Regiments would fall out for morning role call followed by a short period of time allotted for breakfast. After breakfast was sick call followed by the assembly of men for guard duty. The remainder of the morning was allotted for drill or, if during active campaigning, to begin marching to their next destination. If the men remain stationary, the remainder of the day would be spent drilling and performing other camp duties and activities.

An advantage a Union soldier enjoyed over his Confederate counterpart was the quantity of food he received. Hooker's attention to improving the health of his soldiers with the distribution of fresh fruit, and the establishment of bakeries and fresh bread brought his army back from the brink of a medical disaster, without changing the amount of food distributed to each soldier. Based on army regulations, a Union soldier, although he was well feed by army standards, still received a rather meager daily ration. Regarding meat, he was to be provided twelve ounces of salt pork or bacon, or, one pound four ounces of salted or fresh beef. Bread rations were provided as either one pound six ounces of the soft variety or one pound of hard bread, typically in the form of hardtack. If soft bread was not available, a ration of one pound six ounces of flour could be substituted. If neither type of bread was available, one pound four ounces of corn meal could be substituted.[59]

The staple of the Federal soldier was hardtack. Hardtack was a water and flour biscuit about three inches square and, as the name indicates, so hard that it could

---

[57] Wiley, ***Billy Yank***, pp.50-52; U. S. Infantry Tactics for the Instruction, Exercise, and Maneuver of the United States Infantry, pp.17-18.

[58] Wiley, ***Billy Yank***, pp.50-51.

[59] Wiley, ***Billy Yank***, p.224.

not be chewed or crumbled and only broken with a hard blow. Federal soldiers nicknamed them "cast-iron biscuits", "tooth dullers", and "worm castles". The bread could be soaked soft and eaten. It was often crumbled into coffee to provide soldiers with both their morning drink and breakfast together. It could also be fried in meat drippings. Hardtack however, had a tendency to become moldy, possibly due to packing it for shipment too soon after baking. Another problem was the bread's tendency to become infested with weevils and maggots. When eaten in the dark, most men could not tell if the biscuits were infested and some soldiers preferred this instead of being able to see what they were eating. When hardtack was crumbled into coffee, the maggots or weevils could be skimmed off the top before the liquid was consumed.[60]

To supplement a Federal soldier's rations, additional items were issued in quantities intended to be consumed by a company of soldiers. Fifteen pounds of beans or peas along with ten pounds of rice or hominy were issued per one hundred men. Ten pounds of green coffee or eight pounds of roasted coffee or one pound eight ounces of tea was also issued in lots to sustain a like number. Regarding spices, fifteen pounds of sugar, three pounds twelve ounces of salt and four ounces of pepper were provided to company size groups. Thirty pounds of potatoes, four quarts of vinegar and a quart of molasses were also provided. On occasion, soldiers in Federal service would receive additional delicacies. Hooker's crack down on crooked commissary officers increased the quantity of these treats. Pickled cabbage, fresh and dried fruits, vegetables and pickles became more readily available. When fighting or marching was eminent, soldiers were often issued rations to sustain them for a period of time. On these occasions three days were typically issued with instructions to cook and prepare them for consumption. The rations were intended to sustain the men through any upcoming conflict, but in most instances the rations never lasted long enough. It was difficult for a hungry soldier to ignore freshly acquired sustenance in his haversack. Most of the rations lasted no longer than a day.[61]

While the type of rations available in the Southern army was basically consistent with those provided to Northern soldiers, the size of each ration was smaller. Early in the war, Rebel soldiers were well fed, but the abundance of sustenance quickly diminished in camps not within close proximity of regions which produced food. By January 1863, the Commissary Department had reduced the amount of meat in a daily ration. Later that spring, General Lee informed Secretary Seddon that his army was subsisting on a ration of eighteen ounces of flour and four ounces of bacon. When available, rice, sugar and molasses were provided. Many of the reductions were not prompted by a lack of available food, but the inability of the Confederacy to transport, or even pay for the provisions to supply Lee's army. The distribution problem was an issue the Confederacy never adequately corrected.

---

[60] Billings, *Hard Tack and Coffee*, pp.113-115.

[61] Wiley, *Billy Yank*, pp.224, 66-67; Coco, *The Civil War Infantryman*, p.24.

As early as the Peninsula Campaign, Confederate soldiers were already complaining of intense hunger pains. Many soldiers went for days without any food. If a garden was passed which contained available vegetables, by the time the hungry Southerners moved on not a speck of edible food remained. When McClellan was driven off the Peninsula, victorious Confederates scoured abandon Federal camps for any scraps the enemy may have left behind. Although some complained the defeated Federals only provided to the hungry hordes hardtack and poor quality meat, all accepted the plunder willingly. Bartering was also prominent and Southern soldiers openly negotiated with their fellow campmates to swap items. The lack of food in Rebel camps would not improve by the time the summer campaign of 1863 opened. The Confederate army would remain hungry during the Gettysburg Campaign.[62]

The Army Camp

During seasons of active campaigning, army camps resembled a vast mobile city of small white canvas tents positioned around hundreds of campfires. These camps could be assembled and disassembled with remarkable speed. During winter months, permanent camps were generally established. When winter quarters were erected, soldiers typically constructed some type of permanent shelter. Until the spring of 1863, many of the permanent structures built by the Federals were the subterranean log huts which Dr. Letterman wished to have condemned. The walls of these huts were built from logs which were laid out in a rectangle. A foundation of stone or brick was first laid with the logs then stacked on top. The joints between each log were packed with mud to keep wind and moisture from entering. At one end of the structure, stones were laid out in a manner which created a fireplace for cooking and warmth. At the opposing end was the entrance. The size of each hut determined the number of occupants. Bunks were typically built so men would not have to sleep on the floor. The methods used to construct a bunk were diverse. Some were built from boards while others were constructed from old hardtack boxes. Some were built with sapling branches and padded with hay or leaves. Some men made hammocks from grain sacks and poles. Each hut was generally covered with the canvas tents used during summer campaigning. Once completed, most soldiers gave their huts names either in jest or to make them feel more at home.[63]

Although it was against regulations, a number of men and regiments kept mascots and pets. Dogs seemed to be the most popular companion. They required little if any maintenance, existed upon table scraps, provided companionship and loyalty, and required no specific place to sleep. One of the biggest keeper of dogs within the Union Army was George Custer. Custer had a fondness for dogs and kept a number in and around his headquarters. In the 11th Pennsylvania, a small female bull terrier named Sallie accompanied the regiment through nearly all its campaigns. Although Sallie was the unofficial mascot of the regiment, the men adopted her and cared for her as if she was a man in the regiment. Confederates

---

[62] Wiley, ***Johnny Reb***, pp.90-93.

[63] Billings, ***Hard Tack and Coffee***, pp.73-75.

kept pets as well. The men of the 1st Maryland Infantry kept a number of dogs that traveled with the regiment. The most interesting pet however, did not belong to a soldier but to a general. Robert E. Lee reportedly kept a pet hen which he took with him on a number of campaigns. Each evening, Lee would leave his tent flap open, letting the chicken wander in. The hen would lay an egg under his cot each night, providing Lee his breakfast the following morning.

When in camp, soldiers spent their leisure time performing a number of personal tasks and entertaining themselves. Many became very adept at writing letters home. Most contained tales of their exploits in battle, the events and activities of camp life and the monotony of a long hard march. While they relayed hardships, most were quick to instruct their loved ones not to concern themselves with their welfare. Some soldiers sent portions of their pay home to assist in supporting their kin while they were away.

The arrival of mail within the camps was a celebrated event. Soldiers would often read letters from home over and over again, committing their contents to memory through repetition. Some read letters from home so many times they could recite them verbatim. The arrival of a package was even more coveted. After passing the inspections of the provost marshal's agents, many soldiers found fresh socks and under garments, towels, soap, toothbrushes and other necessities of life. Sometimes they would receive food items such as baked goods, canned fruit or other non-perishables. All of these things were cherished by the soldiers because it restricted the amount of hard earned pay that ended up in the pockets of crooked sutlers.

On occasion, celebrations were conducted, usually to commemorate a holiday or a significant birthday. Competitive activities such as horse racing, boxing, pitching horseshoes or a new game called baseball were played. Within Union camps, baseball quickly became a favorite and gained a devoted following. Rulebooks were written and organized games quickly became prominent. Soldiers also spent a great deal of time singing and playing music. Those in the ranks who could play were highly sought after and the instruments of choice were typically banjos, guitars, harmonicas and on occasion, flutes. Some industrious soldiers created instruments out of whatever they could find around camp. Pots and pans became drums. Some would invent string instruments out of the most unassuming articles. Makeshift bands would often entertain the regiments into the late evening hours. When the opposing armies were near enough to hear each other's bands, they would entertain each other with songs for their opponent.

One activity that kept the soldiers busy for an inordinate amount of time was gambling. Often activities used to keep themselves entertained would also have wagers placed upon them. The pervasiveness of gambling in some regiments was so appalling that some men took steps to shield themselves from the practice. Card games were the norm in many units. Games such as poker, twenty-one, and keno were prevalent. Unfortunately for the Confederates, as the war progressed, new decks of playing cards were hard to come by. Many became ragged and worn, allowing astute players to determine at least some of the cards their opponents possessed. Gambling became an addiction for some. A Federal soldier note that shortly after the Battle of Fredericksburg, he sat for twenty-four hours straight at a poker table. During the winter of 1862-1863, a gambling house was erected near the town by Confederate soldiers. For a number of weeks men came and went during their free time. Confederates and Federals alike also bet on horse racing. Betting on the horses sometimes reached astronomical heights. In at least one instance an officer was forced to issue orders prohibiting the activity.[64]

Liquor was another problem in camp, and its consumption caused serious safety issues. While commanders often took steps to restrict their soldier's access to spirits, others took no interest in curtailing its accessibility. But, no matter what the commanding officers opinion or desire, few were successful in checking their command's access to the liquid. In addition, many regimental and brigade commanders also possessed a fondness for drink. Regiments which came from metropolitan areas or large towns were typically more adept at building a reputation for drinking than those from rural areas. Regiments with heavy German or Irish enlistments also showed a fondness for alcohol. The drink of choice was typically whiskey, but brandy, wine and gin were also prevalent. German troops showed a significant fondness for beer.[65]

The effects of drinking depended on the personality of the drunken party. Guardhouses were filled with individuals who became quarrelsome and violent while others allowed the difficulties of their existence to move them to tears. Others became playful and laughed away their worries. Some gathered and broke into song. Try as they might, officers and chaplains were unable to curtail the activity and some admitted that there was little that could be done to stop it. A determined soldier was not about to let some high minded officer deprive him of the one activity which allowed him to put his situation out of his mind, even if for only a short time.[66]

In February 1862, General McClellan, while reviewing an insubordination issue which had arisen from the use of alcohol, summed up the effect drinking was having on his army. "No one evil agent so much obstructs this army... as the degrading vice of drunkenness. It is the cause of by far the greater part of the disorders which are examined by court-martial. It is impossible to estimate the benefits that would accrue to the service from the adoption of a resolution on the part of officers to set their men an example of total abstinence from intoxicating liquors." McClellan thought such a commitment by his officers "would be worth 50,000 men" to the Amy of the Potomac.[67]

Although drinking was also prevalent within the Confederate Army it was somewhat abridged from the levels seen in Federal camps. This could be attributed to a number of factors. The rural nature of the Confederate soldier bred more responsible individuals. The Southern soldier was also less affluent than his

---

[64] Wiley, *Billy Yank*, p.249; Wiley, *Johnny Reb*, pp.36-40.

[65] Wiley, *Billy Yank*, p.252.

[66] *Ibid*, pp.253-254.

[67] *Ibid*, p.252.

Northern counterpart and could not afford extravagant extras such as alcohol. Whiskey, on occasion, was actually issued to Federal soldiers through the supply system. Federals also spent more time near larger cities and had greater opportunity to procure liquor from the general population.

Some however, thought drunkenness within the Confederate service was a significant problem. According to a Rebel chaplain, drunkenness "became so common as to scarcely excite remark." In December 1861, a Confederate general observed that "[t]he evils resulting from the sale of intoxicating liquors... have become intolerable... We have lost more valuable lives at the hands of whiskey sellers than by the balls of our enemies." In June of 1862, the *Richmond Examiner* noted that "[w]hiskey – the sale of this popular but vitiating and deleterious beverage is lamentably on the increase in the alleys and purlieus of Richmond. Upwards of a dozen drunken soldiers were knocked down in the streets and robbed Saturday Night." The paper had earlier noted that it was not uncommon to see literally hundreds of soldiers "wearing the uniform of their country's service" drunk in the streets or littering the local taverns.[68]

Life in camp, drill, short rations infested with vermin, bare feet, poor living conditions, and other trying circumstances were still minor when weighed against open combat. The men of both armies would discover that difficulties encountered during passive times were minor when compared to the harsh reality of engaging the enemy.

The Realities of a Soldiers Existence

In early June, a Confederate soldier, when he reached Culpeper, hurried to the home of a friend who had cared for him during an illness. What he discovered devastated him. "I found the once happy home in ruins," the Rebel observed, "the family scattered and the proprietor crazed in his trouble, sitting idiot-like, mumbling over some faint recollection of his former affluence. My heart ached over old Culpeper," he continued, "...sad and sick, I wandered for a while gathering the flowers that grew in the wild neglected gardens, with that same luxury of color and perfume as when gentle hands planted, nurtured and culled them."[69]

Such was the existence of a Confederate soldier in central Virginia during the spring of 1863. Despite the devastation to the town and countryside, the land was still capable of providing some sustenance. Although Wade Hampton had complained a year earlier that the countryside's ability to sustain the army was "exhausted," the men could find food if one knew where to look for it. When food was found, soldiers complained about its exorbitant price. Others showed concern over the areas ability to provide the supplement to a soldier's meager rations necessary to strengthen him for active campaigning. Any food found was usually nothing special, consisting mostly of bread, sugar, butter, a few black-eyed peas and bacon. Unfortunately, after two years of providing for their soldiers, the citizens of Culpeper were tapped out. Most of the supplies which would fill Lee's

---

[68] Wiley, ***Johnny Reb***, pp.40-41.

[69] Styple, William B., Editor, ***Writing & Fighting from the Army of Northern Virginia***, p.226.

commissary wagons would not come from the local area but points further south. Trading remained an option for soldiers who had an abundance of something. They would seek out those who had more than their share of another item and make a deal to their mutual benefit. This occurred not only between soldiers but also between soldier and citizen. Trading even occurred between enemy soldiers on the picket lines.[70]

Lee's army would remain encamped in Culpeper for only a few days. During its time there, preparations were made to equip the men and each command for the long march northward. Hotchkiss noted in his journal that during a visit to Longstreet's headquarters he observed wagons being loaded for the trip. "Our wagons were busy until late at night loading up commissary stores." The number of wagons to keep Lee's army in fighting shape would be massive. According to historian Edwin Coddington, if strung end to end in a continuous line Lee's wagon train would have been sixty miles long. Livestock was required to keep the trains moving. The supply of animals was still short, even though spring weather had improved the health of the army's horsepower. Any animal with four sturdy legs was coveted. Lee even contemplated taking fewer cannons north in an effort to free animals to pull wagons. To make matters worse, the long winding snake would need to be guarded against marauding Federal cavalry that had become bolder during the previous months due to minor successes against their antagonists. While it was true that Lee's path north would take him into some of the most fertile land in Virginia and across the Potomac lay the bounty of Pennsylvania, to enter upon the campaign assuming that all the army's needs would be supplied by the countryside would be folly.[71]

The soldiers were well aware that a hard campaign was coming. Even before they left camp at Fredericksburg, many men were involved in procuring enough food for themselves and their regiments. They took opportunities whenever possible, to supplement their meager allotments by plundering anything they could get their hands on. A good example occurred within the Stonewall Brigade. The men received orders to acquire three days rations late in the afternoon the day before they were to depart for Culpeper. John Casler, of the 33rd Virginia, was among the twenty men detailed to go to the commissary and gather the provisions. Upon arrival the men went to work as quickly as possible so their detail could return in time to prepare the rations that night. As work commenced another man, Sam Nunnelly of the 21st Virginia noticed a pile of hams stacked up nearby. The meat, which was not intended for the soldiers of the Stonewall Brigade, was evidently ungraded. Nunnelly, after solicited the assistance of Casler, proceeded to the pile and pilfered two of the big juicy hunks of meat. The tasty bounty would no longer be issued to the officers it was intended for. Where the two thieves hid the hams, Casler did not say, but after returning to the work detail, they pointed out the booty to others and a total of nine were taken. "We never let an opportunity pass to get extra rations," wrote Casler after the war, "no matter if we had to steal

---

[70] Sutherland, Daniel E., *Seasons of War*, pp.193, 238.

[71] Hotchkiss, *Make Me a Map*, p.149; Coddington, *The Gettysburg Campaign*, pp.22-23.

them, never forgetting the motto that 'everything is fair in war.'" The extra meat would be greatly appreciated.[72]

While Rebel soldiers suffered hard times, most remained in good humor due to great success on the battlefield. The banter in camp was lighthearted and took place between men, regiments, various branches of service and even soldiers and officers. Infantrymen poked fun at cavalrymen asking if anyone had ever seen a dead man with spurs on or how long it took for spurs "to grow out of a man's heels." The horsemen responded with good natured threats regarding the safety of the foot soldier's wagon trains. One day, a soldier from the 9th Georgia, when passing General Hood's headquarters, spied the general nearby. Approaching Hood, the man asked if the general might not take a drink from his canteen with him. Hood accepted the soldier's offer and when the two were finished the bold infantryman informed the general that if he wanted a drink in the future "here's your mule." Hood, amused, thanked the man for his offer which seemed to embolden the canteen toting man. "General Hood," the man continued, "when you want fighting done, 'here's your mule.'" This prompted a good laugh from Hood who assured the soldier that when the fighting commenced he would surely seek him out.[73]

Men from both armies took the opportunity presented by the idle days to catch up on letters home or to read up on the latest war news from any newspapers they could find. Most papers were at least a few days old if not older but a soldier did not mind such delays since it was usually all fresh information to him. Some took time to wash their clothing, and clean themselves up. Others visited friends in the area. Some wandered through town and around the local countryside looking for anything they thought they needed and could pilfer without consequence. The numbers attending church services increased as well, indicating concerns over approaching battle which could be their last. On 3 June, shortly before breaking camp, aid-de-camp McKim, performed his duties as minister and held prayer services for fifteen men at a log house close to camp. The men prayed, read scripture, talked about their faith and discuss hardships to come. It was a typical gathering. Most men however spent their time relaxing, well aware that a long march was ahead.[74]

Life along the picket line in early June was an interesting time for soldiers of both sides. Sergeant Charles Bowen of the 12th U. S. Infantry left some accounts of his existence on the line. His regiment was a member of Ayers' brigade of Sykes' Division of Regulars. When Sykes was ordered up the Rappahannock River to picket the fords, Bowen took position along with the rest of Ayers' brigade near Banks' Ford. On 4 June, he entered into his diary that his regiment "[b]roke up camp & moved out to the right 12 miles to Banks ford [sic]. There the 1st Brigade

---

[72] Casler, John O., *Four Years in the Stonewall Brigade*, pp.164-165, 197. Casler called Nunnelly "the greatest of all in plundering."

[73] Casler, *Four Years*, p.164; Styple, *Army of Northern Virginia*, p.229.

[74] Sutherland, **Seasons of War**, p.238; McKim, *A Soldier's Recollections*, p.136.

relieved a force who [sic] were doing picket duty." Two nights later, Bowen and four companies of the 12th took their turn on the picket line near the river. While on the river, a number of Confederates came to the opposite bank and spent time conversing with Bowen and his companions. The men across the river were from the 8th Alabama of Cadmus M. Wilcox' brigade and Bowen discovered that the price of food in the South was astronomical.[75]

Although both armies frowned upon opposing soldiers communicating with each other along the picket line and issued orders to curtail contact with the enemy, a large portion of the men who manned the lines ignored the orders. A few days later, writing to his wife Kate, Bowen detailed his early June days on the picket line.

"We broke up camp on the 4th & after a tedious & hot march we arrived at our present position. It is some twelve miles up the river from the camp. The Rebs are on the other side & our boys hold conversations with them & visit them. I went in swimming yesterday & they invited me across. I swam over & sat on a rock at the edge & had quite a long chat. They belong to the 8th, 9th & 12th Alabama. They say they are heartily sick of the war & wish it was over. They think that they cant [sic] stand it more than another year anyhow. They offered me $15.00 worth of their money for $10.00 in greenbacks & say that one dollar of our money is worth one dollar and a half anywhere in the south of their ranks. Say they are only served out with one quarter of a pound of flour a day to a man, & have no sugar or coffee at all. I gave a Sergt. enough coffee & sugar to make two cups & he gave me about a pound of splendid Virginia leaf chewing tobacco, for which we should have to pay two dollars. These fellows are a fine lot of soldiers, look clean & healthy, although they are not very fat on their short rations. If the army here has to live on such short rations I wonder how they manage to live at all down at Vicksburg, where they are so completely cut off from their supplies. It is wonderful how man can be made to keep the field under such circumstances… I had to swim under some overhanging branches once & hide. One of their officers came around & they were afraid if he saw me he would make them capture me. After he went off I swam back to my own side again. In the afternoon the Sergt. to whom I gave the coffee came over & brought me a paper, the *Southern Christian Advocate*. I gave him a can of condensed milk, which was a great prize as well as a curiosity to him, for they dont [sic] have any. He brought over a canteen of whiskey, & two or three of us went into the woods

---

[75]   Cassedy, Edward K., Editor, ***Dear Friends at Home: The Civil War Letters and Diaries of Sergeant Charles T. Bowen***, p.280.

& and [had] a very social time out of sight & hearing of our officers. He said they paid $15.00 for a canteen of whiskey. Isn't it terrible to think that after being so friendly with each other, the very next day or week, we may be engaged in a deadly struggle. Oh how I wish this unnatural war would close."[76]

The time spent by a Civil War soldier fighting the enemy was miniscule compared to the time he spent in camp, on the march, on picket duty or in an infirmary due to illness. In many cases, being out of sight of the enemy was just as dangerous as a pitched battle. One of the most hazardous mishaps was an accidental discharge of a weapon. One incident, which occurred within the ranks of the 5th Texas, was typical of the danger. Dennis Rowe, in order to cross over a fence, placed his gun with its butt on the ground. Using it to steady himself, he put his right hand over the muzzle and as he cleared the fence the weapon discharged. The ball blew through his hand and removed his middle finger.[77]

Another incident, which did not occur within the ranks of the Army of the Potomac, was indicative of the absentmindedness of some soldiers. While guarding a railroad trestle, a Federal infantryman saw fit to place the butt of his weapon on a rail tie. Leaning over he placed his hands over the muzzle and then rested his chin on his hands. Rocking back and forth the soldier slowly worked the gun butt to the edge of the tie. The weapon slipped off the wooden member to the ground. As it struck the ground, the weapon discharged and shot the dim-witted soldier through the hands. The ball, ranging upward, hit him in the chin entered his head and exited out the top of his skull, killing him instantly.[78]

As one would expect, alcohol and guns did mot mix. There are many instances of the two in combination producing tragic results. One notorious episode within a Union regiment occurred late in the war when whiskey was issued. The men promptly became inebriated and began loading and firing their weapons randomly into the woods with no concern for who or what may be hidden in the trees. When control was finally restored, three men were dead and fifteen had been wounded. While this was probably an extreme case, the fact remains that drunken soldier's in possession of firearms was a deadly combination.[79]

Men on the March

While the modern infantryman moves about utilizing mechanized transportation, Civil War soldiers had no choice but to walk from one destination to another. Although locomotives and rail cars were available to a few lucky foot soldiers, most were utilized to transport supplies. Members of the armies in the east were seldom afforded the comforts of a ride on the rails. The Eastern

---

[76] Bowen, ***Dear Friends at Home***, pp.281-282.

[77] Coco, ***The Civil War Infantryman***, p.131.

[78] *Ibid*, pp.130-131.

[79] Coco, ***The Civil War Infantryman***, p.131.

Theater of war was the smallest region of the conflict. Both Lee and Hooker could relocate their armies from its upper reaches in the north to its southern extents near Richmond rather quickly, depending on how hard each chose to drive their army. On a comfortable day, while traversing good roads, a body of infantry could march from fifteen to twenty-five miles. Weather, the condition of the roads traversed, eminent battle or if any major rivers had to be crossed, could shorten this distance significantly. At a normal rate either army could transit the approximately 150 miles from Richmond to the southern Pennsylvania border in two or three weeks depending on the number of days spent resting in camp.

Somewhere between the terror of battle and the monotony of camp life was the rhythmic doldrums of the march. Marching soldiers dealt with a surprising number of issues which, on the surface seem rather elementary, but caused them extreme agony. Warm summer weather brought great clouds of dust which would rise and engulf a marching column with a thick blanket, covering everything and everyone. The Virginia clay would become pulverized by thousands of marching feet, wagon wheels and horse hooves, grinding it into a fine powder which covered the roads. It was often inches thick, and would cover everything it contacted. Faces would be coated with it and the furrows of a man's features became filled. Eyes became irritated and men had difficulty breathing. Sweat would solidify the dust which settled onto their faces into a disfiguring clay mask. In some instances, the dust was so thick it was impossible to see more than ten feet in any direction. It settled on the fences, trees, and grass and worked its way into equipment and rations.[80]

When a marching column was lucky enough to transit one of the few macadamized roads available other issues came to light. A macadamized road, in modern parlance, was nothing more than a gravel road. Constructed of stones pounded to a size which did not exceed two inches across, the road provided a stable base for wagons, horses and marching soldiers. Such roads also brought relief from the choking summertime dust. Unfortunately, for some men the roads created an issue even more severe than the billowing brown clouds. For those who had no shoes, the sharp edges of the stones turned the bottoms of their feet red, raw and bloody. Even men who wore shoes suffered. Many could be seen carrying their boots or shoes, wearing nothing on their feet but worn through socks, their poor fit having produced painful blistering.[81]

The other summertime enemy of the marching soldier was heat. Straggling became a severe problem for marching columns during long hard treks made during the heat of day. Men would fall out on their own, in small groups, or on occasion complete companies would vote to take a rest stop. Officers would halt their columns at regular intervals to provide some rest but they were often brief, for they knew the longer their men were allowed to rest, the more difficult it was

---

[80] Coco, *The Civil War Infantryman*, p.86.

[81] The Macadamized road was developed by John Loudon McAdam, a Scotsman, who first developed the method around 1820. The method simplified what had been considered state-of-the-art to that point. Single sized aggregate layers of stone with a coating of binder as a cementing agent were mixed and used to create a stable roadbed.

to return them to their feet and get them back on the road. Men who fell out on their own typically rejoined the column on their own schedule. Sun stroke also became a serious problem when temperatures ranged into the upper eighties and nineties. Loaded down with anywhere from thirty to fifty pounds of equipment and dressed in heavy woolen uniforms, marching men soon became overheated. Sweat poured from every pore and uniforms grew heavier as they became soaked. Men talked of physically ringing out their garments as if they had gone swimming fully clothed. In extremely hot weather it was not uncommon for half of a column to be collapsed along the line of march struggling to recover. Hundreds of men would seek the shade of trees and even fence rails to escape the heat. Others would simply march until they collapsed in the road and were taken out of the column by their comrades. Many lay down for the last time and expired from their affliction. Those who managed to recover would wait until the onset of cooler evening temperatures before resuming their trip, hoping to catch up to what remained of their regiment.

Opposite the heat and dust of summer was the cold rain, snow and mud of winter months. When forced to deal with the quagmires countryside roads became when under heavy rain, the distances a marching column could cover dropped significantly. Men, mules, horses, artillery pieces, wagons, would all become mired. Practically everything that moved would be hindered by the thick, deep, sticky muck. Wheels cut deep troughs, only to be quickly covered by the oozing mud which would bog down wagons and artillery pieces up to the axels. Men took off their shoes and socks, if they had any, and tied them to the barrels of their weapons. They would roll up their pants past their knees and trod barefoot through the morass. Anyone who chose to leave his shoes on ran the risk of having them pulled off when he extracted his foot from the knee deep mud. Mired wagons, artillery caissons and limbers often halted entire columns as gun crews struggled to extricate the hindrance.

However, not all the raindrops survived their fall long enough to reach the earth. Many fell upon soldiers who, with good reason, expressed great distaste for rain. Men would button up their coats and pull their hats down tight in an effort to keep as many of the drops off as possible. All efforts however were typically useless. Even with ponchos deployed, it was difficult to keep the water out. It would slowly find its way into a soldier's clothing and over a period of time, often drench him to the core. The worst element of a slow soaking from rain was the pending anticipation of the total discomfort and bone chilling cold that accompanied the drenching. Even more annoying was fresh snowfall which brought the same wet conditions but a much colder temperature, and the threat of frostbite.[82]

Perhaps the best description of a nineteenth century army on the march was recorded by Private David L. Thompson of the 9th New York Infantry. Shortly before his capture at the Battle of Antietam, he observed the Army of the Potomac as it pursued Lee across the Maryland countryside.

---

[82] Coco, *The Civil War Infantryman*, pp.86-89.

"The gathering of such a multitude is a swarm, its march a vast migration. It fills up every road leading in the same direction over a breadth of many miles, with long ammunition and supply trains disposed for safety along the inner roads, infantry and artillery next in order outwardly, feelers of cavalry all along its front and far out on its flanks; while behind, trailing along every road for miles, are the rabble of stragglers – laggards through sickness or exhaustion, squads of recruits, convalescents from the hospital, special duty men going up to rejoin their regiments. Each body has its route laid down for it each day, its time of starting set by watch, its place of bivouac or camp, appointed, together with the hour of reaching it. If two roads come together, the corps that reaches the junction first moves on, while the other files out into the fields, stacks arms, builds fires, and boils its coffee. Stand, now, by the roadside while a corps is filing past. They march 'route step,' as it is called, - that is, not keeping time, - and four abreast, as a country road seldom permits a greater breadth, allowing for the aides and orderlies that gallop in either direction continually along the column. If the march has just begun, you hear the sound of voices everywhere, with roars of laughter in spots, marking the place of the company wag – generally some Irishman, the action of whose tongue bears out his calling. Later on, when the weight of knapsack and musket begins to tell, these sounds die out; a sense of weariness and labor rises from the toiling masses streaming by, voiced only by the shuffle of a multitude of feet, the rubbing and straining of innumerable straps, and the flop of full canteens. So uniformly does the mass move on that it suggests a great machine, requiring only its directing mind. Yet such a mass, without experience in battle, would go to pieces before a moderately effective fire.

By the furthest road north… moved the baggage wagons, the line stretching from the bottom of the valley back to the top of the ridge, and beyond, only the canvas covers of the wagons revealing their character. …each dot… a heavily loaded army wagon, drawn by six mules and occupying forty feet of road at least. …they looked like white beads on a string. The constant swelling of the end of the line down in the valley, where the teams turned into the fields to park, gave evidence that, in this way, it was being slowly reeled along the way."[83]

Early in the war, while on the march, soldiers stepped in time. They were usually helped to keep in step by regimental drummers. As the war progressed, marching became less formal. After a trek was underway, the men were allowed to

---

[83] *ARAGSNY* vol.18, p.762; Thompson, ***B&L***, vol.2, p.557.

move in "route step." Route step was simply men walking along at the pace of the column with no effort to remain in time. This was usually done between population centers with the army isolated from the eyes of civilians. When entering a town, soldiers would again march in time, but once through the municipality, they returned to the easier gait of the route step. Officers allowed the route step more often because it was discovered that men could march greater distances at their own pace.[84]

In the Face of the Enemy

During the Civil War, infantry generally fought in lines of battle using tactics which had changed little since the American Revolution. While small unit skirmishing and sharpshooting occurred frequently, full scale infantry battles utilizing large formations of infantry took place less often. During such fighting, infantry usually stood in two ranks with the men side by side as they loaded and fired their muskets. These tactics were required to place soldiers in a position to damage the enemy with old obsolete smoothbore muskets. Unfortunately for the Civil War fighting man, by the time of the Gettysburg Campaign, the rifled musket had replaced a good portion of the old smoothbore weapons. Both the Union and Confederate armies incorporated these new weapons. The rifled musket however, was still loaded from the muzzle, which could explain why officers still labored under the false impression that their soldiers had to stand toe to toe with the enemy to be effective. Testing of a series of Civil War vintage muskets conducted around the middle of the twentieth century showed the effective range of a rifled musket to be significantly superior to the old smoothbore models. A British Enfield, Model 1853, when fired by an expert marksman, hit a target 400 yards away thirteen out of fifteen times. A smoothbore musket scored no hits on a like target at the same range. The effective range of a smoothbore weapon was fifty to seventy-five yards. One instance which proved this distance was a test conducted by a group of Illinois soldiers. These experienced soldiers fired 160 shots from their smoothbore weapons at a barrel 180 yards away and hit it four times. The use of rifled muskets with smoothbore tactics allowed opposing forces to decimate each other before they closed to a range officers believed was required to produce effective infantry fire.[85]

Another strike against the infantryman was the size and speed of a typical minié ball fired from a rifled weapon. Developed by Claude-Etienne Minié in the 1850s, a typical infantry weapon fired a minié ball with a diameter slightly greater the one half inch at rather slow speeds. The resulting impact had a tendency to be more explosive than piercing and created a great amount of damage to flesh and bone.

Because of its slow speed, a round fired from a rifled musket traveled in a more parabolic trajectory. In order to be effective with his weapon at range, a soldier had to understand his round's path. A weapon sighted to strike a target at 300 yards was deadly at ranges up to seventy-five yards and from 250 to 350 yards. The range

---

[84]   Coco, *The Civil War Infantryman*, p.83.

[85]   Coco, *The Civil War Infantryman*, p.65; Wiley, *Billy Yank*, pp.50-51.

between these two regions generally saw the minié ball sail above any prospective target. A soldier, who fired at targets within this range had to aim low in order for his bullet to sail upward into his target. Regimental officers tried to compensate for this problem by constantly reminding their men to fire at the legs of their targets when the range to their quarry was near the high point of the bullet's arc.[86]

A problem faced frequently by the Confederates, was the presence of numerous types of weapons within the same regiment. It was not uncommon for a Rebel regiment to contain three and sometimes four different makes and models of weapons, all of which required different ammunition. For example, one company in the 21st Virginia possessed Enfield muskets while another utilized Mississippi rifles while still another had been issued Springfield muskets. In an effort to correct this problem, Confederate ordnance officers were detailed to scour battlefields once the fighting had ceased and collect the weapons of the wounded and dead. Working weapons were used to replace those in mixed regiments in order to standardize them on one weapon type and caliber. Damaged guns were shipped off to Richmond to be refit and returned to the army to help correct the disparity.[87]

No matter what model weapon a soldier possessed, each received the same typical indications that the time for its use was approaching. One sure indicator of eminent battle was the issuing of ammunition. Ammunition was typically distributed in allotments of sixty rounds to Union men and from forty to sixty to Confederates. Rounds were usually stored in a cartridge box which could hold forty shots. Remaining rounds were stored in a soldier's haversack or on occasion he would place the extras in the pockets of his pants. A round was simply a paper cartridge with the bullet at one end and a twist at the other which contained the powder to propel the shot. The cartridge was cylindrical in shape to fit easily into the muzzle of the weapon. Percussion caps were also issued in like quantities. Percussion caps were required to create the spark needed to ignite the cartridge's powder. In wet weather, the issue of ammunition was delayed as long as possible in order to improve the chances of keeping it dry.

To load his weapon a soldier would pull a cartridge from his cartridge box, bite the twist off of the paper end, place the round, powder down in the muzzle of his weapon and place a piece of wadding on top of the round. Next, he took his rammer from his weapon and rammed the round down the barrel, tamped it down in place, extracted the rammer and replaced it on the weapon. Finally, a soldier would retract the hammer and place a percussion cap over the weapon's vent hole. His weapon was now ready to fire at any enemy foot soldier he felt was within range. If the weapon was already loaded, and it had been for some time, the existing load had to be extracted so it could be loaded with a fresh round. Often the powder of a round which had been loaded for some time would not ignite. This problem was more prevalent if the weapons had been exposed to high humidity, mist or rain. These rounds had to be removed before a new one could be loaded. Each regiment possessed special tools designed to accomplish this feat.

---

[86] Hess, Earl J., ***The Rifle Musket in Civil War Combat***, pp.92-93.

[87] Coco, ***The Civil War Infantryman***, pp.66-67.

With their ammunition safely stowed, soldiers settled in for the typical nervousness of the pre-battle period. After what would often seem like an eternity, the men would be rousted and assembled to march to the battlefield. After trudging part way, and as they approached the area of combat, all non-essential baggage would be discarded to be retrieved after the fighting was over. Knapsacks, tents, ponchos blankets and other articles not needed were stacked up in one location. A man or men from the quartermaster corps were left in charge of the safety of the regiment's material, and if it was stacked in one location, his job was pretty easy. Unfortunately, officers had difficulty keeping soldiers from simply discarding their belongings as they walked along.

During pre-battle moments, officers usually took time to inspire their men to do their duty. Often words of advice were given. Men were instructed to fire low so as not to overshoot their targets, stay in rank, remain as calm as possible and not to shoot until the enemy was within effective range. Huddling together was a bad habit and soldiers were taught to maintain a normal distance between each other. They were often coach to pick off the enemy's officers if the opportunity presented itself. Wounding a man was better than killing him outright, for if wounded, an able bodied man would often leave the fight to assist the injured to the rear. If ordered to fix bayonets and charge, they were trained not to hesitate and move forward as quickly as possible to take advantage of the shock an infantry charge delivered against the enemy's line. Stopping to plunder a fallen enemy while engaged was a bad habit and soldiers were told to resist the temptation. If a retreat was necessary, men were instructed to fall back slowly and deliberately, maintaining fire as they withdrew. More men were often lost during a disorderly retreat than a controlled one. They were instructed not to stop and help wounded friends as details had been assembled for that purpose. Straggling would result in extreme penalty. Cowards would be shot. Officers appealed to the integrity of their men and their duty to country and state. They reminded their men of their responsibilities to home, hearth and family. The invading enemy was a group of evil ruffians. They came to drive them from their homes, destroy the countryside and their property. They came to harm their women and children, their neighbors and friends. But, all the inspiring speeches and chatter could not prepare a green Civil War infantryman for what he was about to experience.[88]

With the inspiring words fresh in their ears, the regimental colors were waved, drums took up the beat and the men were marched toward their assigned place in the battle line. At this time the regiment was typically formed in two lines or ranks for battle. At the center of the first line the regimental colors and the color guard were positioned. At the extreme left was the front rank of Company A, which consisted of approximately half of the companies compliment. To the right of the color guard, forming the right end of the front rank was half of Company B. Each company's captain was positioned to the right of their formation. Positioned between the men of Company A and the color guard were, from left to right, the front rank of Companies, C, D, E and F. Positioned between the color guard and the left of Company B, were the front ranks of Companies G, H, I and K. The second

---

[88] Wiley, ***Billy Yank***, pp.66-67; Wiley, ***Johnny Reb***, pp.69-70, 360-361 n3.

rank was constructed from the second half of each company. The remainder of Company A was positioned behind their comrades on the left with Company C to their right and so on to Company B on the extreme right. In such a formation the regiment typically extended approximately 150 to 200 yards, but the length of the line depended on the number of men in rank.

Positioned in front of the regiment, between 300 to 500 yards distant, was the regiment's skirmish line. Typically members of each company were advanced to form the line, but occasionally an entire company would be pulled out of the standard formation and sent forward. A skirmish line was intended to protect the regiment form a sudden enemy attack and to provide advanced warning that the enemy was near and fighting was eminent. Behind the regiment's second rank was a group of file closers assembled from the sergeants and lieutenants of each company. File closers were responsible for keeping men in rank and to move any man who attempted to depart without a good reason back into line. Behind the file closers were the regiment's staff officers including the sergeant major, quartermaster sergeants, adjutant, major and lieutenant colonel. At the back of the regiment were the unit's musicians, and its commander, who was typically a colonel. The regimental quartermaster was to the rear in order to facilitate the distribution of additional ammunition and supplies if the regiment was lucky enough to receive any during the fighting. Although this was the official assembly for a regiment in battle, on numerous occasions the standard was not adhered to. The most common variance was the position of the regiment's commander, who often chose to lead from the front of his regiment instead of from behind.[89]

Once in line of battle, the men were advanced to their place along the brigade's battle front. Officer's continual shouts told their men to close up, dress their ranks and close any gaps which may have developed. The men at this point would begin to lose the anxiety of their pre-battle rituals. They could hear sounds of other regiments engaged on additional parts of the field. Occasionally a stray minié ball would whiz by causing some men to glance around. Some would falter slightly, but a stern word from a file closer would generally get them back in line.

Taking their place in line with the other regiments of their brigade, the soldiers would typically be told to hold their fire. Often the enemy would be out of sight when the regiment took its position, but screeching enemy shells and buzzing minié balls would signify their presence as their fire would began to intensify. When enemy soldiers finally appeared they may have been too distant to damage with infantry fire. This however, did not stop some soldiers from popping off a few rounds in their direction while being chastised by officers to once again hold their fire. With the enemy in sight, a sense of duty often took over the men. Fear and dread became grit and determination. As their adversary continued to close on their position, men began to be struck down by enemy rounds. Finally, after what must have seemed like an eternity, the command would be given and the regiment's line would erupt in a sheet of flame and smoke.

---

[89] Coco, ***The Civil War Infantryman***, p.97.

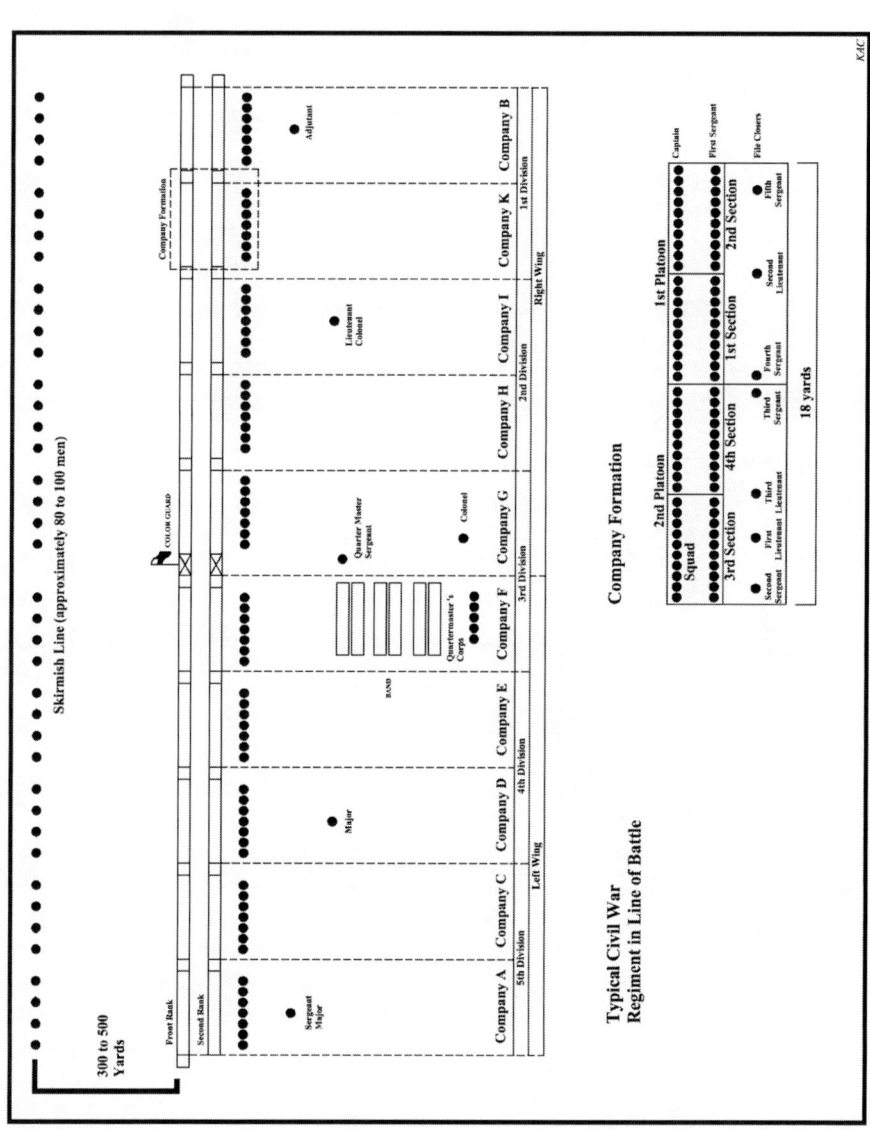

Regiment in line of battle

Once the first round was fired, each soldier got down to his deadly business. Those in the front rank would kneel or lay prone and fire. After firing many would roll onto their backs for protection as they reloaded their weapons. Many soldiers became very adept at loading their weapons while lying flat on their backs. Others, in the second rank, were required to remain upright to fire over the men in front of them, seeking the shelter of any trees, rocks or other natural cover they could find. The constant buzzing of minié balls passing by made some men believe they were fighting near the vicinity of a hornet's nest. Each ball seemed to sound different, some humming, others whizzing, some buzzing. Then came the inevitable thud of a bullet striking flesh. Some men would soon learn that the tale of never hearing the ball meant for you was true. Those struck down would be hit before the sound of the rounds flight was audible. Screaming artillery shells accented the minié balls. Those which sailed low over the battle line sounded more like a locomotive engine. Others, which landed in front of the line, would throw up dirt and debris making vision difficult or spray the men with soil and deadly shell fragments. Those which landed in the ranks would carry away appendages, or if a direct hit, cut whole men in half. As the fighting intensified men would began to fall in great numbers. The cries of the wounded could be heard above the din of battle. The acidic smell of smoke was inescapable. After a few minutes, there would be so much smoke covering the field in front of the regiment that it became difficult to find a target. Men, with their faces blackened by powder spilled as they bit the ends off of cartridges, would become almost machine-like in their movements. As the engagement progressed and additioanl men where wounded or killed, the ranks usually disintegrated into a mass of individuals feverishly loading and firing their weapons.[90]

Some men would become so anxious during the fighting they would fail to load and fire their weapon properly. Some would load their musket and be so bent on firing quickly that they would forget to pull the rammer out of the barrel. When the weapon was fired his rammer would sail through the air toward the enemy making his musket useless. Others would execute the actions required to load their weapon but fail to actually insert a cartridge in the muzzle. He would shoulder the weapon and fire it, then repeat the process, once again failing to put a cartridge in the weapon. Others would load the weapon but fail to place a percussion cap on the vent. The weapon would fail to discharge, after which he would load the weapon, believing it had fired. Again and again he would load his musket, each time failing to place a cap on the vent, raise it and squeeze the trigger. Six or seven rounds would be rammed up into the weapon before he realized he had failed to fire a shot.

Engagements were typically a series of surges and lulls. During surges the regiment's officer corps participated in the fighting, barked orders and generally tried to lead by example. Between surges they issued orders to reset the line and reorganize their mass of men into some sort of fighting formation. They also sought out reserves to shore up weakened points, directed the issue of additional ammunition and called out any other relevant directions required to meet the next

---

[90] Wiley, ***Billy Yank***, pp.71-73.

enemy push. The regimental commander directed these activities and relied on his subordinates to carry out his instructions and prepare the regiment to resuming combat.

Once fighting commenced, most men remained in line and did their duty. There were however, a few men who did all they could to get out of harm's way. One Confederate noted that he once saw an officer running as fast as he could away from the fighting. When he inquired as to where the officer was going in such a hurry, the answer somewhat shocked him. "[M]y leg is broken in two places," said the fleeing man. The puzzled Confederate was only able to identify a small flesh wound before the officer hurried away. Others were slightly more covert in their efforts, and because of the chaotic nature of combat, a soldier could usually manage to escape the danger if he tried hard enough. Some would concoct excuses for departing. Others expressed a desire to depart to acquire additional ammunition while others claimed their weapons had fouled. None of these excuses were satisfactory for additional ammunition and weapons were available from their wounded and dead comrades.[91]

Officers would urge their men on with inspiring words using whatever language they saw fit. Profanity often filled the air. Those well versed in the art of colorful speech seemed to elevate their skills to new levels. Those who swore very little elevated their usage. Pious men, who never swore under normal circumstances, used language that rivaled the professional cursers. Some spoke or yelled at the enemy as they fired telling them their shot was for Jefferson Davis or Bobby Lee. Some fought in anger. Sometimes their rage was expressed toward the enemy, other times it was toward comrades who had failed to do their duty. However, most men who fought angry did so as a response to a nearby friend falling to enemy fire.[92]

The chaos of battle usually failed to provide a soldier with a visual result of a fired round. Some men would fight the entire war and not know if they ever killed or wounded a member of the enemy. Others would pick a target and fire a number of shots with none of them hitting the mark, then return to firing at the mass in front of him, oblivious to whether his round had struck. Some would brag about killing a multitude of men. No one would actually be capable of proving such claims and each soldier's story became more embellished over time.[93]

Perhaps the most vivid account of a man in battle was penned by Oliver Norton of the 83rd Pennsylvania. In a letter home, which he wrote on Independence Day, 1862, Norton told of his adventures during the Peninsular Campaign.

> "Our brigade formed the left flank of the line and lay nearest the river. The Eighty-third was posted in a deep gully, wooded, and with the stream I mentioned running in front of us. We built a little breastwork of logs and had a good position. On

---

[91] Dickert, *History of Kershaw's Brigade*, p.200.

[92] *Ibid.*

[93] Coco, *The Civil War Infantryman*, pp.108-109.

the hill behind us... [other regiments] were posted. When the rebels made the first attack, we could not fire a shot, [a] hill concealing them from us, and so we lay still while the bullets of two opposing lines whistled over our heads. They were repulsed, but only to pour in new troops with greater vigor than before.

Suddenly I saw two men on the bank in front of us gesticulating violently and pointing to our rear, but the roar of battle drowned their voices. The order was given to face about. We did so and tried to form in line, but while the line was forming, a bullet laid low the head, the stay, the trust of our regiment – our brave colonel [John W. McLane], and before we knew what had happened the major [Louis H. Naghel] shared his fate. We were then without a field officer, but the boys bore up bravely. They rallied around the flag and we advanced up the hill to find ourselves alone. It appears [sic] that the enemy broke through our lines off on our right, and word was sent to us on the left to fall back. Those in the rear of us received the order but the aide sent to us was shot before he reached us and so we got no orders. Henry and Denison were shot about the same time as the colonel. I left them together under a tree.

I returned to the fight, and our boys were dropping on all sides of me. I was blazing away at the rascals not ten rods [fifty yards] off when a ball struck my gun just above the lower band as I was capping it, and cut it in two. The ball flew in pieces and part went by my head to the right and three pieces struck just below my left collar bone. The deepest one was not over half an inch, and stopping to open my coat I pulled them out and snatched a gun from Ames in Company H as he fell dead. Before I had fired this at all a ball clipped off a piece of the stock, and an instant after, another struck the seam of my canteen and entered my left groin. I pulled it out, and, more maddened than ever, I rushed in again. A few minutes after, another ball took six inches off the muzzle of this gun. I snatched another from a wounded man under a tree, and, as I was loading kneeling by the side of the road, a ball cut my rammer in two as I was turning it over my head. Another gun was easier got than a rammer so I threw that away and picked up a fourth one. Here in the road a buckshot struck me in the left eye-brow, making the third slight scratch I received in the action. It exceeded all I ever dreamed of, it was almost a miracle.

Then came the retreat across the river; rebels on three sides of us left no choice but to run or be killed or be taken prisoners. We left our all in the hollow by the creek and crossed the river to Smith's division. The bridge was torn up and when I came to the river I threw my cartridge box on my shoulder and waded through. It was a little more than waist deep."[94]

Norton admitted he "acted like a madman…" and "was stronger than [he] had been before in a month and a kind of desperation seized [him]… At other times," Norton continued, "I would have been horror-struck, and could not have moved, but then I jumped over dead men with as little feeling as I would over a log. The feeling that was uppermost in my mind was a desire to kill as many rebels as I could." The loss of his "comrades" had driven him mad with rage.[95]

On occasion, as fighting continued, officers would work to close the distance between their lines and the enemy. Once an appropriate position was reached, officers would call a halt to redress their lines. Then, while still under heavy fire, the command to fix bayonets would be given. The edged weapons were pulled from their scabbards and attached to the end of each musket. Then the order to charge was given and the regiment leapt forward. A great yell would escape from every man as he moved quickly toward the enemy's line in a desperate frontal assault. A hail of lead would greet them as the enemy desperately tried to cut them down before they reached their goal. Charging men often seemed to be leaning against a gale. A great desire to enter the enemy's lines existed since the achievement would terminate the wall of lead which barred their path. Gaps would open in the charging mass which officers would desperately try to close. As the charging throng neared the enemy, the pace would quicken, the last few yards covered at a full run. As the lines collide, the charge would deflect the enemy as they gave ground, their lines forced backward. Bayonets would be plunged into the enemy, muskets became clubs, fists thrown, rocks used as weapons, and combatants wrestled with each other, often falling to the ground. Muskets which were loaded at the time of collision would be discharged at point blank range, burning the target with the weapon's muzzle flash as the ball entered. Then, the musket would become a tool for bludgeoning since there was no time or space to reload it.

After a few minutes of intense struggle, the assaulting mass would either be successful in driving the enemy from the field or they themselves would be forced back. If the latter was true, officers would do their best to reorganize their men and, try once again to drive the enemy from their position or, reform a battle line and continue to try and destroy them with bullets. Often a position would be assaulted a number of times before success was achieved or denied. Battle lines would often close to ranges of less the 100 yards and pound away at each other until both lines were blown into oblivion. Frequently, when the fighting was over, the location of a regiment during the battle could be determined by the almost perfectly straight line of dead left upon the field.

---

[94] Commager, Henry Steele & Bruun, Erik, *Living History: The Civil War*, pp.126-127. Norton's account is from a letter original published in Norton's Army Letters 1861-1865, initially published in Chicago, 1903.

[95] Wiley, ***Billy Yank***, p.72. The quotations from Norton are from *Army Letters*, 1861-1865.

For the men who managed to survive the fighting, the indelible impression left upon their minds was the thrill and rush of adrenalin which accompanied open combat. They also remembered the sheer exhaustion felt after the fighting subsided. Most heavy campaigning occurred during the summer. Heat would quickly drain the energy of the heartiest soldier. Grubby faces accented by furrows scoured clean by running sweat would be everywhere. Men would walk hunched over, struggling to stay upright, at the edge of human endurance. For most of the men who fought, Civil War combat would be the most physically and mentally demanding activity of their entire lives.

When falling back from the field, unless pursued by the enemy, men left the scene of combat at a much slower pace than they arrived. When the fighting died and men began to slip toward the rear, many would walk backward, stopping to fire a final few shots at their antagonist if any were within range. There was nothing more damaging to a soldier's reputation than being shot in the back. Such a wound was interpreted as being received by a coward for a soldier could only be inflicted with such a wound if he had turned his back to the enemy.[96]

Debris

One of the most pressing matters encountered during fighting and post battle periods was the removed of as many wounded men from the vicinity of a battlefield as quickly as possible. The survival rate for a wounded soldier during the Civil War was directly related to the period of time he remained on the field, the time it took to receive medical attention, and of course, the severity of his wound. On average, seventy to seventy-five percent of all men injured in battle by a minie ball or a shell fragment would survive their wounds if they received prompt attention. Primitive medical practices and the atrocious nature of the wounds inflicted, made time precious. Men with serious injuries who remained exposed to the elements would quickly see their condition worsen. Their wounds could become gangrenous, infected or infested with maggots or other larva, deposited by the hordes of flies and other insects that flocked to a fresh battlefield.[97]

Men who could move under their own power, even as the battle continued, would make their way to a regimental aid station where a surgeon would dress their wounds if not serious enough to require surgery. When surgery was necessary, usually due to a broken bone or the need to remove a bullet or fragment, the soldier would be sent on to a field hospital. Hospitals were ordinarily set up in areas near farms, churches, or other large structures. When large buildings were not nearby, a grove of trees would be selected to provide shade and shelter to the wounded men. Hospitals were also typically established in less exposed positions and were usually selected prior to an engagement. Surgeons, orderlies, nurses, clerks, cooks and attendants staffed a hospital. Other than the surgeons, these men were usually those who were well enough to travel with the army but unfit for battle due to previous wounds or other ailments. If these men were in short supply, soldiers would be

---

[96] *Ibid*, pp.73-77.

[97] Coco, ***The Civil War Infantryman***, p.137.

detailed from their regiments to assist the surgeons. Unfortunately, assigning men to work in the hospitals, act as litter bearers, drive ambulances and perform other duties was a serious drain to the manpower on the battle line.

As Stonewall Jackson discovered, a trip to a hospital or aid station can be fraught with jeopardy. Men too injured to move on their own had to wait until the conflict was terminated before they could be moved by litter bearers. On many occasions litter bearers experienced the same dangers men in open combat endured. They were often required to ferry heavy, severely wounded men over dangerous ground, under the same infantry fire meant for those doing the shooting. It was not uncommon for stray bullet to strike these men while performing their merciful tasks. Once they had delivered their cargo to a secure aid station or an ambulance, litter bearers would return to the hazards of the fight to extract more wounded men.[98]

Sometimes wounded men would remain upon a battlefield for days before receiving any assistance. If a wounded soldier happened to be located in no man's land, he would have to suffer through the remainder of the battle. Only after the armies departed or permission and time was given for each side to scour the area for survivors would he be extracted and given aid. Many severely wounded men would expire during their wait. If the time period was exceedingly long, men who could have been saved with immediate attention would lose their life to gangrene, tetanus or other maladies. If he managed to survive the many hours he remained untreated, he could then be collected by litter bearers for his trip to a field hospital.

Often the worst part of a trip to the field hospital was the ambulance ride. A Civil War era ambulance was nothing more than a large wagon with a cover to provide injured men shade and protection from the elements. After the war, many soldiers who had been badly wounded seemed to possess vivid memories of their ambulance ride, and none of the remembrances were pleasant. Some men recalled the pain and shock of receiving their wound was minor compared to the agony of the ride. Typically, a wound became somewhat numb shortly after its occurrence. However, by the time a wounded man was loaded into an ambulance, the numbness was gone, replaced by the pain which accompanied movement. The condition of nineteenth century roads was the biggest culprit in providing agony. As an ambulance bounced along a rut filled and wash boarded road, the screams and groans of its cargo could be heard for hundreds of yards.[99]

While the battlefield was a place of violence, death and heroic endeavors, an army field hospital was a place of pure misery. The main hospital, where the treating of wounded men took place, was typically the largest open building on the chosen sight or a large open fly tent. If established on a local farm, the barn was typically the structure opened up to receive wounded. Inside were usually three or four large tables where surgeons performed their grisly work. Clothed in aprons which were no longer white but soaked in blood, they would quickly review the wounds of the soldier deposited on their table. If amputation was necessary,

---

[98] Coco, Gregory A., *A Strange and Blighted Land*, pp.156-157.

[99] Coco, *The Civil War Infantryman*, pp.140-141.

anesthesia was used to subdue the poor man so the limb could be removed easily. Unfortunately, chloroform often ran low or was not always available. In such instances, a wounded man had to be physically restrained; his leg or arm removed while his screams permeated the tent and spilled over to the exterior of the hospital. As each patient was moved to a table, more wounded would be brought in. They would be placed on the floor in the filth of the barn, and lined up at each table to wait their turn under the surgeon's knife and bone saw.

Bullet extraction was also a rather painful experience for a soldier. Surgeons would utilize probes to locate the projectile and often had to physically enlarge the wound to remove the bullet or in the case of a shrapnel wound, a jagged fragment. When the surgeon was finished, the patient was removed, the table splashed with water if available, and another poor soldier lifted and placed on it to receive treatment.

Sometimes an assembly line system would be used. Wounded men would be queued up in front of one table. When the table was empty the next man would be lifted up, anaesthetized, and his wounds exposed. He would then be moved to a second table where the surgeon would examine his wound or wounds, decide what needed to be done and treat the patient. Then the man would be moved to a third table where his wounds would be sewn and bandaged after which he would be resuscitated. The poor soldier would then be moved out of the hospital and deposited in an area where he could try to will his body onto the road to recovery.[100]

The mental state of a wounded man varied from total calm to complete paranoia. Some who were mortally injured would sit quietly, waiting for the inevitable visit from the reaper. Others who had received a simple scratch screamed out in pain. A member of Company H of the 3rd South Carolina remembered the extremes of the human nervous system.

> "A man in Company E…, having a minnie [sic] ball lodged between the two bones of his arm, made such a racket when the surgeons undertook to push it out, that they had to turn him loose; while a private in Company G, of the same regiment, being shot in the chest, when the surgeon was probing for the ball with his finger, looked on with unconcern, only remarking, 'Make the hole a little larger, doctor, and put your whole hand in it.' In a few days he was dead."[101]

It took little time for hospitals to become flooded with groaning men. Waiting men could be heard calling for a doctor to help them while others cried out to God to take away their misery. Some would fall asleep or lose conciseness, never to wake again. Others developed fever and infection. Flies would be thick upon them, landing upon their open wounds, as many of the injured were too weak to perform the constant motions required to keep them away. The stench of bile,

---

[100] *Ibid*, p.141.

[101] Dickert, ***History of Kershaw's Brigade***, p.200.

blood and filth was atrocious. While serious wounds received quicker treatment, the sheer volume of wounded men would require some with extreme injuries to go unattended for hours. Every nearby structure, shade tree or shelter was soon overflowing with men waiting for treatment and those who had already visited the surgeon. Outside the tent were piles of severed arms and legs sometimes as tall as a man, covered in blood and flies.[102]

Wounded men fought not only to survive their wounds but the lack of sanitation. Instruments used to cut the flesh away from a soldier's wound and trim back jagged bone so the remaining flesh could be closed around its stump would be dipped in water and rinsed off in preparation for use on the next man. If a sponge fell upon the floor, it would simply be washed out and used again. Blankets, towels or sheets were freely passed from one man to another. If a man perished, his blanket would be pulled off and as the body was being removed the covering would be laid over another suffering man. Silk used to sew up wounds was not sanitized. If the surgeon's assistant had difficulty threading it through the eye of a needle he would place it in his mouth to moisten it, roll it between his fingers and thread it before handing it to the surgeon. Under these conditions, even a minor wound could turn into a life threatening experience. It is a wonder any wounded men who visited a Civil War field hospital ever survived. A great many did not.[103]

After the fighting ended, exhausted and slightly wounded men would often return to the location their knapsacks had been left and gather up their belongings. Once the weary men finished claiming their personal things, many would gather up the knapsacks of their fallen comrades and rummage through their possessions. Often final letters would be discovered as well as mementos of loved ones. On occasion, men would ask friends to send home final letters or write their families if they were killed. Some men went so far as to write their name, regiment and company down on paper and place the document on their person. Doing so allowed their body to be identified and buried properly or sent home, if they should happen to be killed.

The residue of battle spent little time unattended. Both Confederate and Federal soldiers would rummage across ground fought upon in a ghoulish escapade of thievery and looting. While both armies discouraged such activity, if a soldier needed a specific article of clothing an unpicked battlefield was a ripe location to find needed items. As one would expect, great value was given to shoes and socks. Pockets were often rummaged through, with anything of value being kept. As burial details worked to clean up the debris of battle, many bodies were found with their pockets inside out. Officers were a particularly tempting target for scavengers. Most carried items of particular value such as swords, scabbards and revolvers. Pilferers also stole personal items, taking such things as pocket watches, pipes and tobacco, knives, decks of cards and any money a dead man way have possessed.[104]

---

[102]   Coco, *The Civil War Infantryman*, p.142.

[103]   Wiley, *Billy Yank*, p.148.

[104]   Coco, *The Civil War Infantryman*, p.115; Coco, *A Strange and Blighted Land*, p.157.

Bodies could not simply be left lying around, although some of them inevitably were. Few men who died in battle received a proper military internment. When a small number of bodies had to be buried, individual graves were dug. After a major battle however, the number of bodies to inter was so daunting that most were simply buried in large trenches. Men were detailed to dig while others wandered the field in search of the dead. Bodies would be carried to the location of the grave and arrayed side by side next to the trench. When digging was complete, the bodies were simply laid in the bottom of the trench with no effort to identify them. Men who may have crawled off to a secluded location were often not discovered and left to nature. Men buried in individual graves, on many occasions received some sort of marker while mass graves were often marked with a single board that indicated their loyalty and the number in the grave.

The treatment of the dead varied and was usually based on whether a burial detail was interring their comrades or the enemy. If burying their own, care was usually take to make sure a man's grave was dug deep enough to allow him to rest undisturbed. On the other hand, if the man had been a member of the opposing army, his body would often be covered with just enough dirt to place him out of view. In many instances enemy corpses were buried with hands and feet and even a portion of a head exposed. A visit to a battlefield during the months following an engagement often provided ghastly images of half buried bones and tatters of clothing.

But even in the midst of these appalling images, life seemed to continue. One soldier, when visiting the Chancellorsville battlefield a year after the fighting, noted that strung about were the bones and belongings of a number of men whose lives had vanished. As he wandered about, he came upon a human skull which, to his surprise was now the home for a bird's nest with three small speckled eggs nestled inside. "Life in embryo in the skull of death! ...singing the hopeful paeans of a nation redeemed by their death."[105]

America's Lifeblood

The young men who stepped up and volunteered to fight for their independence or subdue an insurrection were the future and lifeblood of a young country. Some had been Americans for a few generations while others were new to the freedom which America offered. Some were immigrants who were looking for something better or trying to escape persecution. Others had supported unsuccessful revolutions before and had been forced to leave their homelands because of their loyalties. Many had created prosperous lives and joined the cause to defend them while others, struggling to make their way in the world, needed the minuscule army pay to get by. Some were family men other rogues. Some were rich, others poor. They were farmers, educators, businessmen or simply men about town. They all would volunteer with generally good intentions.

Many would pass the test they had chosen to undertake. Others would simply survive. Some would find army life was not for them and simply drift away never

---

[105] Goss, ***Recollections of a Private***, p.267.

to be seen again. High minded men would struggle to relinquish authority over their lives to the officers of their regiments. Many would find army life just what they needed to restore discipline in their own lives and would be better men for the experience. Many would be recognized as heroes, others would be heroes but remain anonymous. Several who joined did not have the personality and stomach for combat and would show themselves unable to deal with their situation. Most however did their duty to the best of their ability, making those who they loved proud of them.

Tens of thousands would not return home. Some were interred in a grave in an everyday grove of trees and forgotten over time. Some of the men who buried their comrades also gave their lives for the cause, taking the location of their friends' resting place to their own grave. Others, who would lose their lives would be lucky enough to be identified and returned home to rest peacefully in family plots across the North and South where their kin could tend to their memory. A multitude would survive horrendous wounds and carry the scars of war for the reminder of their lives. Some would carry almost unbearable handicaps. Many would be captured and sentenced to an existence even worse than combat, spending the remainder of the war in a hellish prison, where many also died. Those who survived would also bear the scars of combat. And, while many had minor physical scars from bullets that nearly missed ending their life, they also possessed emotional scars which they buried deep in their souls. The horrors which had been observed would never be forgotten. In an age when emotional damage was not well known or acknowledged, most survivors bottled their emotions and pain inside their hearts and let it out on very few if any occasions.

Through it all, the friendships which had been formed were bound together by the trials they had faced together. Although many were torn from their companions by enemy bullets, the friendships would never be forgotten. Most had joined as boys or young men. They had borne previous dangers together, stood shoulder to shoulder, and fought together and in many cases died together. They had endured the hardships of forced marches in 100 degree heat and the bone chilling cold of harsh winters with seemingly endless snow. They had shared tents, blankets, food and even clothing. They had endured the agony of wounds and recovered only to march and stand in line of battle again. Their existence had instilled a companionship between them that could only have been created through such physical and mental extremes. Most would not have thought it possible for themselves to endure such cruelties, but, when placed in such a position, a sense of self-preservation filled them with a resolve; a resolve to do whatever necessary to survive their ordeal.

Such was the existence of the pawns of the American Civil War. By the third summer of the conflict almost every man in Joseph Hooker's Army of the Potomac and Robert E. Lee's Army of Northern Virginia had been exposed to the cruel realities of war. Most had already seen those horrors up close. The boys of 63' were about to embark upon what would arguably be the campaign to decide the outcome of the war. For many of them it would be their last. For those who survived, it would be a summer they would never forget.

Chapter XIV
The Federal Horsemen

> "Few bolder or more enterprising
> soldiers ever rode at the head of
> a column of horse..."[1]
> *Federal horse soldier regarding John Buford*

Unfortunately for Joe Hooker and more so for George Stoneman, the Confederates paid little or no attention to the raiding blue clad horsemen Hooker sent to harass Lee's rear during the Chancellorsville Campaign. Lee, concentrating on the major threat to his army, chose to remain and confront Hooker directly, leaving Stoneman to gallop about to the south causing little damage except to the fragile mental stability of the government and Richmond's populace. Lee's decision to keep the bulk of his cavalry nearby proved to be the correct one. Hooker, with the mass of his cavalry missing, had limited his resources and could not cover his flanks adequately, setting up a scenario for disaster which Stuart identified and Jackson exploited.

Stoneman had actually made two efforts to begin his raid. The first was forced to a halt by rainy weather, muddy roads, and an uncooperative Rappahannock River which rose several feet in depth at the ford he was to cross. The river was so high with so much water present that General John Buford was prompted to note in his report "[t]he country was at that hour like a sea." The situation compelled Stoneman to delay his raid, and he issued orders to his horsemen to pull back until the circumstances improved. One brigade, which had already crossed the river, was ordered to return. Swimming the swollen river caused the loss of some men and horses to the swift current. Twenty-five others were lost to enemy capture.[2]

Regrettably, Hooker had already sent word to Lincoln that the cavalry was in motion before he received notification that Stoneman had been delayed. "I am rejoiced that Stoneman had two good days to go up the river," Hooker informed Lincoln, "and was enabled [unable] to cross it before it had become too much swollen." Later the same day, as reports from Stoneman began to arrive, it became

---

[1] Starr, Stephen Z., *The Union Cavalry in the Civil War, Volume 1: From Fort Sumter to Gettysburg 1861-1863*, p.293.

[2] *OR*, vol.25, pt.1, p.1088; McKinney, Joseph W., *Brandy Station, Virginia, June 9,1863: The Largest Cavalry Battle of the Civil War*, pp.16, 267:n,50.

obvious that Hooker's plans were not unfolding as he had envisioned. He would suffer the indignity of retracting his previous communication. "Just heard from General Stoneman. His artillery has been brought to a halt by the mud, one division [brigade] only having crossed the river. If practicable, he will proceed without it." Hooker's embarrassment was made even more humiliating considering the general had previously told the president "the storm and mud will not damage our prospects." With the enemy now aware of Stoneman's effort, there was nothing left to do but bring his cavalry back to camp and try again.[3]

On 15 April, at 10:15 p.m., Lincoln wrote a short note to Hooker containing a tone all too typical of the early Federal war effort. He was justifiably disappointed although he expressed his displeasure with his characteristic logic.

> "An hour ago I received your letter of this morning, and a few moments later your dispatch of this evening. The latter gives me considerable uneasiness. The rain and mud, of course, were to be calculated upon. General S[toneman]. is not moving rapidly enough to make the expedition come to anything. He has now been out three days, two of which were unusually fair weather, and all three without hindrance from the enemy, and yet he is not 25 miles from where he started. To reach his point he still has 60 to go, another river to cross, and will be hindered by the enemy. By arithmetic, how many days will it take him to do it? I do not know that any better can be done, but I greatly fear it is another failure already."[4]

Both Lincoln and Hooker were not impressed with Stoneman's performance. The cavalryman would have a second chance to make amends but once again would fail to satisfy his chief. The day after Hooker put his legions in motion toward Chancellorsville, orders were issued to Stoneman to once again conduct his raid. Hooker specifically instructed him to have his command across the river no later than 8:00 a.m. on 29 April. The goals remained the same as the previous effort, which Hooker's assistant adjutant general had outlined prior to Stoneman's first excursion.[5]

> "If the enemy should retire by Culpeper and Gordonsville, you will endeavor to hold your force in his front, and harass him day and night on the march and in camp unceasingly. If you cannot cut off from his columns large slices, the general [Hooker] desires that you will not fail to take small ones. Let your watchword be fight, and let all your orders be fight, fight,

---

[3] *OR*, vol.25, pt.2, pp.213-214,

[4] *Ibid,* p.214.

[5] McKinney, **Brandy Station**, p.16.

fight, bearing in mind that time is as valuable to the general as the rebel carcasses. It is not in the power of the rebels to oppose you with more than 5,000 sabers, and those badly mounted, and, after they leave Culpeper, without forage or rations, keep them from Richmond, and, sooner or later, they must fall in our hands.

The general desires you to understand that he considers the primary object of your movement the cutting of the enemy's connections with Richmond by the Fredericksburg route, checking his retreat over those line, and he wishes to make everything subservient to that object…

It devolves upon you, general, to take the initiative in the forward movement of this grand army, and on you noble command must depend in a great measure the extent and brilliancy of our success."[6]

Once again Stoneman, even though under the pressure of his initial failure, began his second effort with another black mark on his record when he allowed his command to be late to the river. Finally, late in the afternoon, he got his riders across, hours behind Hooker's schedule. Once across, Stoneman marched his troopers only four miles before they went into camp for the night, having yet to make contact with the enemy. For the next two weeks, he rode around behind Confederate lines causing more panic than actual damage to enemy cavalry or Southern infrastructure.[7]

To make matters worse, Stoneman detached Brigadier General William Averell with a portion of his force to push toward Brandy Station and into Culpeper County. If he was relying on Averell's initiative for him to be successful in his assignment, Stoneman would be as disappointed as Hooker was with him. Although Stoneman had started south, Averell continued to send couriers requesting orders from him. After Averell advanced across the river, he became convinced that a superior Rebel force confronted him. Pushing south to the north bank of the Rapidan, he remained inactive near the river for two days. Unknown to Averell's troopers, as they camped along the river, a detail from Jeb Stuart's cavalry kept a watchful eye on them. Hooker, totally frustrated with Averell, ordered him back to the army, which at the time was fighting for its life around Chancellorsville. If Averell was not going to find a fight on his own, Hooker could provide him one. Even after being ordered back, for some reason Averell dallied for another two days until Hooker called him once more. The ineptness of Averell's expedition can be seen in his casualty list, which contained one officer killed and two wounded. In addition, only two enlisted men were killed and a few others wounded.[8]

---

[6] *OR*, vol.25, pt.1, p.1066-1067.

[7] McKinney, **Brandy Station**, p.16.

[8] *Ibid*, p.55; *OR*, vol.25, pt.1, pp.1059, 1079.

By the time Averell returned, the fighting was over, and Hooker was livid. The commanding general quickly relieved him and sent him packing to Washington. Averell complained that he was given conflicting orders by Stoneman and Hooker. His excuse however, did not satisfy Fighting Joe who had provided copies of his 12 April order for Stoneman to "fight, fight, fight" to Averell as well. On 9 May, Hooker wrote to the adjutant general of the army expressing his disgust with Averell and explained his decision. "It is no excuse or justification of his course that he received instructions from General Stoneman in conflict with my own," Hooker complained, "and it is his duty to know that neither of them afforded an excuse for his culpable indifference and inactivity. If he disregarded all instructions, it was his duty to do something. If the enemy did not come to him, he should have gone to the enemy." Hooker did not wish to charge Averell but did want him out of his army. "I could excuse General Averell in his disobedience if I could anywhere discover in his operations a desire to find and engage the enemy," Hooker continued. "I have no disposition to prefer charges against him, and in detaching him from this army my object has been to prevent an active and powerful column from being paralyzed in its future operations by his presence." Averell was not unemployed for long. On 23 May he was assigned command of the Fourth Independent Brigade of Major General Robert Cumming Schenck's command. The brigade was stationed in the western Virginia region, where Averell would become a bystander to the summer campaign.[9]

Although the initial reaction from Washington in response Stoneman's exploits were positive, they were based on newspaper reports out of Richmond which proved to be greatly exaggerated. Secretary of War Stanton, writing to Hooker on the evening of 7 May, informed the general that Southern papers were "full of accounts of the panic and destruction accomplished by Stoneman." Stanton went on to describe how Stoneman's boys rode within two miles of the Confederate capital and no Rebel troops were reported to be in the city to resist them. Reports had also been received indicating that railroad lines had been "torn up at various locations" and that Stoneman's force was "divided into detachments, operating in different directions, and producing great panic everywhere in the region." An hour later Hooker replied to Stanton, confirming many of the details. The general reported that the rail line between Fredericksburg and Richmond had been disrupted; a detachment had rode to the James River and destroyed a canal in the area while another had destroyed the railroad bridge across the Chickahominy River.[10]

---

[9] *OR*, vol.25, pt.1, pp.1072-1073; Eicher, & Eicher, **High Commands**, p.110. Averell's new brigade consisted of infantrymen and horsemen, most of whom were from the western Virginia area. He would perform credibly during the remainder of 1863. However, in 1864 when General Sheridan was placed in command of troops in the Shenandoah Valley he would become disenfranchised with Averell's lack of aggressiveness. In September Averell would be relieved of command once again for failing to pursue defeated Confederates after the battle of Fisher's Hill.

[10] *OR*, vol.25, pt.2, p.439.

Hooker next began his own investigation into the extent of the damage caused by Stoneman. The results of his inquires were less than adequate. Reporting to Stanton on 10 May Hooker noted the minimal extent of Stoneman's adventure.

> "From the most reliable information I have been able to gather, railroad communication between Fredericksburg and Richmond, by the direct route, was interrupted but for one day. The bridges of importance appear to have remained untouched. With the exception of [Colonel Judson] Kilpatrick's operation, the raid does not appear to have amounted to much... My instructions appear to have been entirely disregarded by General Stoneman. I shall know the particulars soon."[11]

Hooker began showing his disgust with Stoneman's performance even before communicating with Stanton. On 8 May Chief of Staff Butterfield wrote to Stoneman expressing Hooker's increased loathing with the cavalryman. The communication ended with Butterfield announcing to Stoneman that "General Averell, in consequence of his entire disregard of his instructions of April 28, has been relieved of his command..., and has been ordered to Washington." If Stoneman believed he had performed his duties to the letter of Hooker's orders he would soon find out the commanding general did not agree with him.[12]

Once again, on 12 May, Butterfield communicated with Stoneman informing him that Hooker "desires a full report of your operations." Butterfield then outlined a list of what Hooker wished to be included within the report. The commanding general's demand for specific information should have been a sign to Stoneman that his chieftain was not pleased. Demanding to know specifics within the context of a report was a unique request. Typically superiors allowed their subordinates to write reports without interference and only questioned their contents if a report was not consistent with supporting information. Hooker however, demanded specifics and Butterfield outlined the list which contained "...the condition of your [Stoneman's] command; its location and position, with all its detachments; the number fit for duty; a copy of any and all orders issued to Brigadier-General Averell from yourself subsequent to his crossing the river at Kelly's Ford; [and] the number and position of troops assigned to the duty of guarding the railroad from Rappahannock Station to Cedar Run."[13]

Butterfield followed up his 12 May message with a similar note the following day. Evidently the follow up note was sent before Stoneman had completed his response to the original request since both Butterfield's second note and Stoneman's response to the first possessed the same date. Stoneman informed Hooker's chief of staff that he was in the process of developing his official report on the expedition

---

[11] *Ibid*, pp.455, 463.

[12] *Ibid*, p.450.

[13] *Ibid*, pp.468-469.

and would forward it to Hooker as soon as it was complete. The hold up, according to Stoneman was the tardiness of the reports from his subordinates which he needed to complete his review. He then reported on the condition of his command noting that the horses were "used up," and needed shoes while the men were "pretty tired." As soon as inspections of his force could be conducted, he would provide Butterfield with the complete details Hooker required regarding the fitness of his command for further action. Stoneman then provide specific details regarding his instructions to Averell.

> "By direction of the commanding general, General Averell was furnished with copies of all the orders and instructions which I received from headquarters Army of the Potomac, and the only other orders I gave General Averell were to push the enemy in his front; that I turned the enemy over to him, as I had not time to bestow, and was going to push on to the execution of the duty assigned to me."[14]

The same day, 13 May, Stoneman submitted his length official report which contained details regarding the expedition but was lacking in particulars concerning the current status of his organization and its fitness for duty. Butterfield, once again, on 15 May, requested information on the cavalry's condition and Stoneman responded the same day. The request confused the cavalryman, who could not understand why he was being pressed for the information since he had previously promised information was forthcoming as soon as he had completed his inspections. "If you mean that I have failed to give the information required," Stoneman responded, "I beg to call your attention to my reply thereto in my letter to you of May 13, in which I say 'the force of those brought back with me which is fit for immediate duty in the field, I shall be able to say after inspections are made and reports furnished.'" Stoneman went on to point out that in his previous communication he had noted that 2,000 horses could be counted on for immediate operations if "little marching [was] required."[15]

The tone of the communications evidently led Stoneman to believe that he was being set up as the fall guy for the failed expedition. To make matters worse, the long ride had caused a significant flair up in Stoneman's hemorrhoids which probably also enflamed his temperament. Shortly after the 15 May confrontation with Butterfield, Stoneman requested a medical leave of absence which Hooker undoubtedly was happy to approve. Traveling to Washington, he underwent a surgical procedure to help alleviate his affliction which was wholly unsuccessful.

---

[14] *Ibid*, pp.474-475.

[15] *Ibid*, p.484.

Stoneman would remain in the cavalry service but would never return to the Army of the Potomac.[16]

At the time, General Hooker seemed so possessed with covering his tracks and his own responsibilities for the disappointment of Chancellorsville that he failed to evaluate Stoneman's raid from a common sense point of view. While it is true that a number of his tangible desires had not been accomplished, Hooker did not evaluate the raid from an intangible perspective. The raid marked the first time in which a Union cavalry force of significant size, operating as a unified unit and commanded by a single individual charged with directing the entire operation, had done any damage whatsoever to the enemy. Stoneman had also managed to pin down the two divisions of Longstreet's force, keeping them from supporting Lee during the battle. This was a fact that possibly saved Hooker from a worse beating than he received. Stoneman was also responsible for interposing himself between Lee and Richmond during the battle, successfully breaking up communications between the general and the government during the fighting. Finally, and possibly most notably, Stoneman lead a large cavalry force on an extensive raid behind enemy lines and returned it to safety with few losses. It was the first time in which the Union cavalry was able to conduct a raid of such magnitude. It mirrored operations which the Confederates had been carrying out since shortly after the war began.[17]

While Lincoln and Stanton were of the opinion that the raid was a success, Hooker remained disgruntled. Although Stoneman was singled out and reviled for what Hooker promoted as his part in the failure, Stoneman should have received at least some praise for his effort. Going forward from Chancellorsville, the Army of the Potomac's cavalry arm would become an integral part of its ultimate success. George Stoneman can be credited with being part of its renaissance.[18]

The "Knight of Romance"

Many within the army's high command were aware of the issues which arose between Hooker and Stoneman. Writing to his wife in late May, George Meade summed up the situation quite succinctly. "Stoneman is off on leave," he wrote, "and I don't think will return here again. He does not want to, and Hooker does not want him back. Hooker is very severe on him, and says his raid amounted to

---

[16] McKinney, ***Brandy Station***, p.57; Wittenberg, Eric J., ***The Union Cavalry Comes of Age: Hartwood Church to Brandy Station, 1863***, p.330. After Gettysburg, the War Department organized a Cavalry Bureau to oversee the refit of the cavalry for the entire army. On 28 July, Stoneman was made its first chief but accusations of corruption were leveled against the bureau and Stoneman soon tired of the position. Later, he was assigned to field command once again when he took over the cavalry in the Department of Ohio and later played a significant role in General Sherman's march to capture Atlanta.

[17] Wittenberg, ***The Union Cavalry***, p.330.

[18] *Ibid*, p.331.

nothing at all; that he was eight days going and only two coming back, and many other things of this kind tending to disparage Stoneman."[19]

Hooker wasted little time beginning his search for a replacement for the fired cavalryman. Initially he offered command of his horse soldiers to General Hancock, who at the time had not yet ascended to command of the Second Corps as General Couch was still officially in charge. Members of the corps' command structure and General Buford lobbied Hancock and urged him to take command. Second Corps chief of staff, Charles H. Morgan, noted that Hancock initially decided to accept the appointment although he had no desire to hold the position. "Circumstance, however, occurred," Morgan noted, "making an immediate change of commanders impracticable, and before the matter was revived the vacancy [Couch's departure] in the Second Corps occurred." Hooker would have to look elsewhere for Stoneman's successor.[20]

To temporarily fill the position, Hooker chose an officer from within his current cavalry organization, Brigadier General Alfred Pleasonton, who was the corps' senior commander. Although Pleasonton's appointment was to be temporary, with Stoneman's reassignment later that summer, Pleasonton would eventually take permanent command. Although he was not Hooker's first choice, Pleasonton was somewhat of a logical selection due to his familiarity with the cavalry organization, but the advantages of his expertise ended there.[21]

Pleasonton was born on 7 July 1824 in the nation's capital. At the age of sixteen he managed to gain an appointment to West Point where he proved to be an above average student. In 1844 he graduated seventh in a class of twenty-five and was assigned to the 1st Dragoons, receiving the typical second lieutenant commission. Transferred to the 2nd Dragoons on 3 November 1845, Pleasonton served during the Mexican War with his new unit. Two days of fighting at Palo Alto and Resaca de la Palma in 1846 earned him a first lieutenant brevet. Receiving his first lieutenant commission three years later, Pleasonton spent the remaining years before the war functioning as the regiment's adjutant. His duties ended when he was promoted to captain on 3 March 1855.[22]

Pleasonton saw limited field service during the years leading up to the war, but did campaign against the Sioux in the Dakota Territory with General Harney. Unfortunately, his position as the regiment's adjutant kept him out of action and behind a desk for the majority of his service, and he saw little opportunity for advancement. Perhaps it was this discouragement during his early years that fueled his desire for upward mobility later in his career. By the time the war began

---

[19] Meade, *Meade*, pp.381-382.

[20] Hancock, *Reminiscences*, pp.182-183.

[21] Wittenberg, *The Union Cavalry*, p.237.

[22] Eicher, & Eicher, *High Commands*, p.431. The 1st and 2nd Dragoons were re-designated the 1st and 2nd Cavalry on 3 August, 1861.

Pleasonton had given seventeen years to the military but was still toiling away as a captain.[23]

The war did not begin well for the attention seeking Pleasonton. Originally assigned to temporary recruitment duties in Delaware, he soon found himself back with his regiment, stationed far from the seat of war in the Utah Territory, keeping a watchful eye on the Mormons. As senior captain, he commanded the regiment and made a number of attempts to be reassigned to command of a volunteer regiment, but his inquires fell upon deaf ears. The disappointment was almost unbearable for a man who possessed an almost insatiable desire for fame. Finally, in the fall his regiment was ordered to Washington. He quickly packed up his command and immediately set out overland for the east coast.[24]

Once in Washington, Pleasonton spent a short time serving in the capital's defenses before receiving a promotion to major and assignment to field duty. It was during this time that he struck up and nursed a relationship with George McClellan, an association which would pay dividends. On 16 July 1862, Pleasonton, as a result of his rapport with Little Mac, was promoted to brigadier general and placed in command of a cavalry brigade. On 2 September, he was promoted to division commend due more to a lack of experienced cavalry officers than his own abilities. As the war progressed, he began to read and bask in his own press clippings which his vanity would not allow him to humbly acknowledge. During the Maryland Campaign, while he performed admirably in the face of Confederate Jeb Stuart's vaunted cavalry, he failed to accomplish his primary responsibility. McClellan needed intelligence information, but in gathering accurate and useful data Pleasonton failed. Not only did he fail to provide precise information, but the information he did supply was filled with fanciful speculation and gossip which was of no use to McClellan. Pleasonton failed again a few weeks later when Stuart launched his October 1862 raid into Pennsylvania. After moving his troopers into position to interdict Stuart before the Confederates could re-cross the Potomac, Pleasonton hesitated, allowing the enemy horsemen to escape to the safety of Virginia. By the spring of 1863, he had been provided ample opportunity to display his abilities as a cavalry commander and had squandered nearly all of them. The media however, portrayed him as a competent and brave cavalry officer.[25]

Outwardly, Pleasonton projected the persona of a professional soldier. An examination of his record would reveal few instances of incompetence or failure. The largest black mark was his showing on the Peninsula where he displayed less than adequate activity in pursuing Stuart's horsemen as the Confederate rode completely around McClellan's mighty army. Only the incompetence of McClellan saved the Federal cavalry from being made the scapegoat for Stuart's success.

---

[23] Longacre, Edward G., Alfred Pleasonton: "The Knight of Romance", *CWTI*, vol.13, no.8, pp.13-14.

[24] *Ibid*; Tagg, **Generals**, p.165.

[25] Longacre, Alfred Pleasonton, *CWTI*, vol.13, no.8, pp.14-15; Eicher, & Eicher, **High Commands**, p.431.

Pleasonton was incredibly self-assured, believed in his own abilities and was extremely vigorous when executing the duties of his position. He worked hard to inject his own confidence and charisma into his troopers. He wanted the members of his command to believe, as he did, that nothing was beyond the abilities of himself and his men. He wanted the men to accept the premise that he would lead them to greater glory and success, and together they would achieve great things and make a difference in the Federal war effort. Many considered him to be a pleasant, likable man, who only had the best interests of his men at heart. A young George Custer once noted that he did "not believe a father could love his son more than Genl. Pleasonton loves me."[26]

A rabid self-promoter, Alfred Pleasonton was not opposed to stretching the truth of his accomplishments to gain promotion and notoriety. *LOC*

But, while Pleasonton did possess a few endearing qualities required of an effective military leader, he also possessed and partook in some of the worst. These damaging traits created a legion of Pleasonton detractors which ranged from the upper ranks of the army to the lowliest private. Many who had direct contact with Pleasonton interpreted his outward confidence, and rightly so, as arrogance and camouflaged ambition. Many considered him interested only in further

---

[26] Longacre, Edward G., *The Cavalry at Gettysburg: A Tactical Study of Mounted Operations during the Civil War's Pivotal Campaign, 9 June-14 July 1863*, pp.48-49; Longacre, Alfred Pleasonton, *CWTI*, vol.13, no.8, p.11.

advancement and willing to do whatever it would take to accomplish his ultimate goal. An officer from the 1st Massachusetts noted that "[h]e [Pleasonton] does nothing save with a view to a newspaper paragraph." Still another officer noted that "it is the universal opinion that Pleasonton's own reputation, and Pleasonton's late promotions are bolstered up by systematic lying." Others thought him a tyrant and that soon someone would be pressing charges against him for some indiscretion or violation of military rule. Pleasonton, over the years, had cultivated strong ties with newspaper reporters and political operatives which he willingly and openly used to his advantage. In another sign of his desire for advancement, during the spring of 1863, he began sending some of his dispatches directly to Halleck and Stanton, bypassing channels in an obvious effort to impress Washington. Pleasonton even provided analysis of the information which he felt would fall in line with the administrations preconceived thought patterns. His arrogance and open courting of advancement created ill will for those who came to know him well.[27]

Pleasonton, through his adjutant duties before the war, had proven himself a capable administrator. However, as a military commander he was a demanding disciplinarian who through his strict adherence to regulation estranged a large portion of his troopers. Many thought him a tyrant and pulled no punches when relaying their opinions of their commander. One officer thought Pleasonton's methods a "tyrannical [sic] & illegal exercise of military authority." But, although a tough and rugged taskmaster, Pleasonton would never be a capable field commander. He was quite poor at one of the most critical aspects of the growing responsibilities of the Cavalry Corps, reconnaissance. Pleasonton's lack of scouting skills would be a serious detriment to the army during the coming campaign. Those who had opportunities to observe Pleasonton under fire felt he lacked bravery. His reports, communications and dispatches were filled with fluff and unnecessary jargon, designed to provide glowing reviews of himself and his command. His tendency to insert conjecture, gossip and rumor in his writings prompted post-war Confederate artillery expert Jennings Wise to label him the "Knight of Romance." All of Pleasonton's actions and his conduct pointed to one basic characteristic. He had quite simply an insatiable desire to achieve military fame, and there was no degree, including the sacrifice of integrity, he would not go to pursue notoriety.[28]

One example of Pleasonton's lack of integrity regarding personal promotion was a self-endorsement fashioned after the Battle of Chancellorsville. In his after action report, Pleasonton wrote that in order to buy time to place artillery, he "immediately ordered the Eighth Pennsylvania Cavalry to proceed at a gallop, attack the Rebels, and check them…" Pleasonton repeated the account later when testifying before the Joint Committee on the Conduct of the War. "I saw the moment was critical, and I called on Major Keenan of the Eighth Pennsylvania, and gave him his orders," Pleasonton told the panel. "'Major,'" he commented

---

[27] Longacre, *The Cavalry at Gettysburg*, pp.48-49; Nye, *Here Come the Rebels*, p.30.

[28] *Ibid*, p.49; Wise, *Long Arm of Lee, vol.2*, p.594.

quoting himself, "'you must charge in those woods with your regiment, and hold the Rebels until I get some of these guns into position.'"[29]

Unfortunately, the man who was actually in command of the 8th Pennsylvania Cavalry that fateful evening, Major Pennock Huey, noted the only order received from General Pleasonton by him was to report to General Howard at the Eleventh Corps commander's headquarters. According to Huey, Pleasonton never issued such an order to Major Keenan who was still playing cards when Huey arrived and order his men off to find General Howard. Keenan, at the time, had made no effort to prepare the 8th to mount up and ride toward Jackson's battle line. After the war Huey called out Pleasonton to set the record straight but the general declined to be accomidating. Huey went so far as to write a history of the charge and Pleasonton's subsequent testimony in an effort to set the record straight. While most historians acknowledge Huey's version of the events as fact, it must have been frustrating for the major to be denied the truth of the matter by a general who everyone knew was a blatant self-promoter.[30]

Although equally lauded and shunned by many of his contemporaries, there is no doubt Pleasonton was a flamboyant cavalryman. Although he was short in stature, he stood upright, taking advantage of every inch in height he possessed. His brown hair and beard gave him a rather distinguished look which he played to good effect. Like his counterpart Jeb Stuart, Pleasonton dressed the part, usually donning in camp and on the march all the trappings of a showy horseman. He wore elegant uniforms supplemented by polished boots, white gauntlets, a straw hat, which he typically cocked to one side, and a riding crop which hung from his wrist by a leather strap. When sitting upon his horse he presented a rather conspicuous image with his upright stature. Pleasonton's narcissism was not lost on others. George Meade thought Pleasonton's vanity overwhelming while Lieutenant Frank Haskell called him "a nice little dandy." He was cordial and capable of making polite conversation and would engage others in simple talk with little or no effort. Engaging superiors, political acquaintances, civilians or his troops in campfire chatter came naturally to Pleasonton.[31]

A purveyor of the finer things in life, it was not uncommon to find Pleasonton's headquarters abounding with all the comforts of home. During extended time in camp the general would have his mess lay out extensive fare which anyone who attended would vividly remember. On occasions, large meals, which sometimes consisted of six courses, would be served before being topped off by a fine wine. Unfortunately for the privileged citizens in the local area, much of the fare served by Pleasonton's mess was pilfered from their stocks of food and drink. He also had quite the eye for the ladies, exhibiting his charm whenever in the presence of the

---

[29] **OR**, vol.25, pt.1, p.775; Huey, *8th Pennsylvania Cavalry*, p.34.

[30] Huey, *8th Pennsylvania Cavalry*, pp.14-16. A detailed account of the 8th Pennsylvania's charge appears in earlier in this work.

[31] Byrne & Weaver, Editors, **Haskell**, pp.133-134; Longacre, Alfred Pleasonton, **CWTI**, vol.13, no.8, pp.11-12.

opposite sex. Although he would remain unattached for his entire life, his charisma attracted the attention of many fine ladies.[32]

During the coming summer campaign the personal promotion and arrogance of Pleasonton would be on display for all to see. He would go into the campaign with the reputations, both good and bad, he had fashioned for himself throughout his military career. During the summer he would do nothing to change anyones oppinion.

Pleasonton's Horsemen

One of Pleasonton's first priorities as commander of the Cavalry Corps was to provide to Hooker the status report which Stoneman's tardiness in submitting had borne a part in his removal. On 27 May, he presented a detailed review, including information on the number of serviceable horses and the condition of the corps.

From Pleasonton's old First Division, he reported 1,546 serviceable and 371 unserviceable mounts in its First Brigade, and 1,228 serviceable and 364 unserviceable in its second. Within the Second and Third Divisions, he noted that one half of the horses, around 3,000 mounts, were unfit for "active offensive operations." Within the Reserve Brigade the situation was even more calamitous. According to reports, 1,396 horses would be needed to mount the entire brigade. Based on the returns of the previous March, only 830 men in the brigade had serviceable mounts. Nearly one half of the entire corps was on foot. With Colonel Judson Kilpatrick's troopers still away Pleasonton could report approximately 4,700 mounted horsemen. The Army of the Potomac's returns of 31 March reported 594 officers and 11,811 troopers present and ready for duty. After Stoneman's Raid, Pleasonton could only muster a little over one third those numbers.

After reporting his available numbers, Pleasonton took the opportunity to drive the final nail in the coffin of General Stoneman's career in the Army of the Potomac. "In taking this command," Pleasonton wrote, "I cannot do myself such an injustice as to remain silent as to the unsatisfactory condition in which I find this corps. I shall use every exertion to bring it to a state of efficiency at the earliest possible moment, but the responsibility of its present state, it is proper the major-general commanding should know, does not belong to me." If Pleasonton had been truthful regarding the matter of responsibility for the corps' state, he would have silenced his pen. Hooker was more at fault than Stoneman since he ordered the grueling mission behind enemy lines. He should have understood such a mission would exhaust the horsemen. The condition of the corps, while dire, should have been expected after such a trying exercise. Pleasonton, obviously trying to expel any direct blame for the corps' condition, and knowing Stoneman was out of favor with Hooker, did nothing more than display his lack of leadership skills.[33]

---

[32] Longacre, Alfred Pleasonton, *CWTI*, vol.13, no.8, p.12.

[33] *OR*, vol.25, pt.2, pp.180, 533.

The Best Horse Soldier in the Army

Perhaps a better man for the job of commanding Hooker's horseman would have been Brigadier General John Buford. Buford, known as John junior by his family until his father passed in 1847, was every inch a cavalryman. Colonel Charles Wainwright wrote that Buford was "the best cavalry general we had" and that he possessed a "rough... exterior, never looked after his own comfort, untiring on the march and in the supervision of all the militia of his command, quiet and unassuming in his manners." Buford also possessed another trait which kept him from garnering the distinction he deserved. Unlike Pleasonton, he cared not for what the papers and tabloids had to say about him. He regarded newsmen as hacks and sycophants and would not allow them into his camps or to travel with his command. He was the epitome of his typical facial expression which was hard-bitten and stern. Although he possessed a light-hearted disposition all associated with him knew he was not one to be crossed or undermined. He always led his men from the front, seemingly unaware of any danger and made no efforts to disguise his rank while walking a skirmish line directing fire. He lacked the flamboyant qualities so many other self-serving officers possessed, but instead was quiet and reserved. He drove his men hard, but they seemed not to mind since Buford drove himself even harder. Many historians have identified him as possibly the best cavalryman ever to sit a horse in the history of the United States Army. Anyone knowledgeable of the subject would be hard pressed to make an argument otherwise.[34]

General Meade's staff officer, Colonel Theodore Lyman, writing of Buford after Gettysburg, may have penned the best, most honest physical description of him.

> "He is one of the best officers of that arm and is a singular-looking party, figurez-vous... a compactly built man of middle height, with a tawny moustache and a little, triangular gray eye, whose expression is determined, not to say sinister. His ancient corduroys are tucked into a pair of ordinary cowhide boots and his blue blouse is ornamented with holes; from one pocket thereof peeps a huge pipe, while the other is fat with a tobacco pouch. Notwithstanding this get-up, he is a very soldierly-looking man. He is of a good natured disposition but not to be trifled with."[35]

Buford came from a family with a deep military heritage. He could trace his lineage back to the year 1066 when his ancestors traveled as part of William the Conqueror's band to England. His family first settled in Virginia but after the British ransacked much of the family's property during the Revolution, they

---

[34] Longacre, Edward G., **General John Buford: A Military Biography**, pp.16-17, 86; Tagg, **Generals**, p.168; Starr, **Fort Sumter to Gettysburg**, p.293.

[35] Starr, **Fort Sumter to Gettysburg**, p.293.

packed what was left and moved west to put down roots in an area which would eventually become part of Kentucky. The elder John Buford along with his bride, relocated in 1801 to Woodford County and there the couple raised two children. A year after his wife died suddenly, John Sr. married Anne Bannister Howe Watson, the daughter of an army captain who had served during the Revolution under "Light Horse Harry" Lee. Approximately one year later, on 4 March 1826, Anne gave birth to the first of three sons, John Buford Jr. Although his mother died when he was still a youngster, her passing did not seem to affect John greatly. His lack of feelings may have been an early sign of his ability to focus on relevant issues and remain in the moment, forgoing concerns which were beyond his control.[36]

Young John was raised in the backwoods of Kentucky. He spent a good portion of his time outdoors and the activities of a youth spent tramping the countryside shaped him well. He developed a solid physique and his gallivanting kept him in good health. He grew up hunting, fishing and riding. By the time he was a young man he was a talented horseman and an expert in spotting the finest steeds. With his family's strong military background, John was exposed to martial philosophies and developed early in life an interest in all things military. John's older half-brother, Napoleon, who graduated from West Point a year before John was born, greatly influenced him. From the point in life where memories begin to remain, John's knew only the image of his brother as a soldier. Napoleon also instilled in his younger brother the need for a superior education and John, probably wanting to emulate his role model, worked hard to educate himself. By the time he was a teenager it looked as if John would be capable of handling the difficult curriculum at the academy, so a West Point education seemed possible.

Although John Sr. moved his family to Illinois when his son was twelve, young John continued to work in his new environment to prepare himself for the academy. Unfortunately, his first effort to gain admission did not achive results. Not even testimonials from congressman and high profile friends produced an acceptance letter. Undaunted, John continued with his studies and the pursuit of an appointment. He enrolled in Knox College in Galesburg, Illinois and studied there for one year. Relocating to Cincinnati, he took up residence with Napoleon and enrolled in another college to continue his education. Soliciting the assistance of his half brother, who wrote letters on John's behalf, positive results were finally obtained. At the age of eighteen, John accepted his appointment to the United States Military Academy on 20 April 1844. A few weeks later, he left his home, departing on the journey to become a soldier which began on 1 July when he officially entered the academy.[37]

---

[36] Longacre, *General John Buford*, pp.16-17.

[37] *Ibid*, pp.17-22; Wittenberg, Eric J., John Buford and the Gettysburg Campaign, *GM*, Issue 11, pp.21-22.

John Buford was perhaps the best cavalry commander of the war. *LOC*

John's class contained a few men who would obtain notoriety during the war, including South Carolinian, Nathan G. Evans, Marylander George H. Steuart and future Federal artilleryman John C. Tidball. Some upperclassmen that Buford became close friends with included Ambrose Burnside and, coincidently, George Stoneman.[38]

His first year of study began well, but as the semester wore on John slowly sank in the rankings, much to his dismay. The sheer volume of work seemed to be his downfall, but as the year ended, he was safely positioned within a range which shielded him from dismissal. John also earned forty-nine demerits; a total well within the acceptable amount. Slowly, as his four year curriculum progressed, he improved his standing while keeping his demerits in line. He continued to show slow but steady advancement in the core curriculum subjects of math and French, and proved to be exceptional at all the physical aspects of his training. During his third year he was exposed to the equestrian elements of his education and proved to be one of the finest students in his class. He displayed great enthusiasm for the course, and it became obvious to all that he would be an exceptional horseman.

In his final year, John continued his upward journey academically but from a discipline standpoint he slipped significantly. His downfall was the discovery that he enjoyed a good cigar or a pipe full of tobacco. His habit became so desirable that he risk disciplinary action to partake in it. He would spend the rest of his life, as Theodore Lyman noted, with a cigar or his pipe within easy reach. Due to his skill as a horseman, it became apparent that a spot in the cavalry was the most

---

[38]   Longacre, **General John Buford**, pp.24-25.

advantageous place for him. On 1 July 1848, John graduated sixteenth in a class of thirty-eight, was brevetted a second lieutenant and assigned to the 1st Dragoons.[39]

After spending less than six months at his initial assignment, Buford was promoted to full second lieutenant. However, within the 1st Dragoons there was no vacancy at that rank. There was however an open spot in the 2nd Dragoons and in the spring of 1849 he was transferred to fill the position. Although the regiment was stationed on the frontier and was charged with protecting settlers from marauding Indians, Buford spent part of his early career with the 2nd on detached service. Unfortunately he had few opportunities to see any action, which at the time was the best environment to achieve advancement. On 9 July 1853, an end to his inactivity seemed imminent when he received a promotion to first lieutenant.[40]

With his professional life moving forward John also found time to improve his personnel wellbeing. Sometime in 1851, John was introduced to a young woman named Martha McDowell Duke. Although he became smitten with the girl, his upbringing of country life and the outdoors certainly did not allow him to develop the social skills needed to actively and swiftly court a fine young woman. Although the two would eventually wed, it would take three years for the relationship to grow before the joyful day arrived. Evidence points to the simple fact that John Buford fell in love with his future wife over time. More than likely Martha simply would not go away and forced herself upon the romantically deficient Buford. Two children resulted from the union but unfortunately neither managed to reach adulthood.[41]

In early September 1855, Buford found himself embroiled in the Battle of Ash Hollow in the newly organized Nebraska Territory. It would be his only engagement against Native Americans. Although the fight was somewhat inconsequential, Buford took from it a lesson which would define his methods as a cavalry commander during the Civil War. He learned that superior numbers of mounted men were no match for well trained and dug in foot soldiers possessing accurate infantry weapons. He also learned that a saber was a demoralizing weapon when brandished against an enemy who was ready to take flight. Both lessons would serve Buford well as a cavalry commander in the Federal army a few short years later.[42]

The years leading up to the war were rather uneventful for Buford. Although from the border state of Kentucky, after a bit of deliberation and the rejection of a commission in the Confederate Army, he threw his hat into the ring with the North. After making the trek eastward, He found himself buried in the bureaucracy of Washington performing administrative duties. His refusal to participate in self-promotional activities was undoubtedly a big reason why he was relegated to managerial tasks. Another situation which Buford found hard to deal with was the

---

[39] *Ibid*, pp.26, 29-31.

[40] *Ibid*, p.37.

[41] *Ibid*, p.40.

[42] *Ibid*, p.50.

massive amount of untrained volunteers gathering to form the army which would fight to reestablish the Union. Now a captain, he would spend the first months of the war away from combat. It would be the summer of 1862 before he would see his first action.[43]

When General Pope's Army of Virginia was organized, the general snatched up Buford, liberating him from his Washington desk duty. Pope placed him in charge of his new army's reserve cavalry brigadier and promoted him to brigadier general. Once in the field, Buford proved he was much more adept at performing the vital task of reconnaissance than Alfred Pleasonton.[44]

As the second fight at Bull Run unfolded, Buford's command was on patrol along the Bull Run Mountains. About midmorning, while in the vicinity of Thoroughfare Gap, he detected seventeen regiments of infantry, an artillery battery and about 500 mounted cavalrymen of Longstreet's Corps, marching through the gap. Quickly Buford sent off a message to General McDowell before beginning a delaying action that would hold up the Confederates for a number of hours. Although his message got through, General Pope chose not to act on the intelligence and paid the price. Pope failed to treat Buford's report as a threat to his army. The cavalryman's reputation grew due to his scouting work and his determination in hold Longstreet in check as long as possible. Unfortunately for Buford, his first battle experience would be his last for some time.[45]

During the fighting, he ordered a charge against a group of enemy cavalry. It was one of the first instances during the war which involved cavalry from each side engaging each other in a direct confrontation. As the mêlée progressed, Buford was struck in the knee by a spent ball. While the injury was not serious it was very painful and restricted his ability to remain in the saddle. Although he would stay with his command, he was forced to leave the fight and spent the next few months nursing the injury.[46]

Buford spent less than three days allowing his sore knee to heal before he was back on the line. Unfortunately, he was left behind when McClellan marched north in pursuit of Lee. Three days later the commanding general sent word and Buford was quickly on his way to "Little Mac's" headquarters. McClellan, in need of an administrative man to support his cavalry, appointed him chief of cavalry for the Army of the Potomac. Although the position was not a field command, Buford was a soldier and he felt it his duty to accept the responsibility. He was put to work for the remainder of the Antietam Campaign, and when McClellan was replaced by Burnside, he stayed on to perform the same function for his old West Point friend.

---

[43] *Ibid*, pp.73-75; Tagg, ***Generals***, p.168; Wittenberg, John Buford, ***GM***, Issue 11, p.22.

[44] Tagg, ***Generals***, p.168.

[45] ***OR***, vol.12, pt.2 Supplement, p.1010

[46] Longacre, ***General John Buford***, pp.111-112; Tagg, ***Generals***, p.168-169. Tagg actually notes that Buford was so badly wounded that he was left on the field for dead. Other period accounts have him severely wounded as well but seem to confuse Buford with another, more seriously injured man.

By February 1863, Buford was ready to return to action, although his knee was still causing him some discomfort.[47]

Hooker's ascension to command of the army was a stroke of good luck for Buford. When the new commander decided to lump his cavalry into a cohesive corps, he went in search of the best cavalrymen available and, once again, pried Buford loose from desk duty. On 11 February 1863, Stoneman issued General Order No.4 which gave structure to his new corps. General's Pleasonton and Averell were placed in command of the first and second divisions respectively. The corps Third Division was placed in the hands of Brigadier General David McMurtrie Gregg. Stoneman singled out Buford to command the corps' Reserve Brigade which, at the time consisted of four regiments of U. S. Regulars and a battery of artillery. Another regiment, the 6th Pennsylvania Cavalry, although part of the reserve, was on detached duty and would join Buford's command during the weeks to come. His backlog of work, and his appearance as a witness during the Fitz John Porter court-martial trial, would keep him from his new command for almost a month. It would be 7 March before he would arrive and take command.[48]

As part of Stoneman's raiding party, Buford and his reserves crossed the receding Rappahannock River at Kelly's Ford on 29 April. In his after action report he complained about the weather noting throughout "the whole expedition the roads were in a worse condition than I could have supposed to be possible…" After crossing the Rapidan, Buford led his column south to Louisa Court House, on to the South Anna River, and through Gordonsville before turning back toward the Rappahannock. The reserves fought numerous engagements as they rode through Confederate territory, capturing supplies and destroying infrastructure, while struggling along the poor roads. On 8 May Buford returning to the north side of the Rappahannock, bringing an end to his part of Stoneman's incursion.

The hardships of the raid had been vast. Many of the men had gone hungry since the wet weather had destroyed their rations. Any rations which remained in a consumable state could not be cooked since no fires could be lit as they would draw the attention of the enemy. The Reserve Brigade was constructed from a group of experienced and tough Regulars who performed their duty with no complaints. They were accustomed to hardships and Buford himself set the example with his drive and professionalism under trying circumstances. "I have not heard of a complaint or murmur," he wrote in his 15 May report. The trying situation brought out the best in him. His first field command since the previous summer allowed him to display his leadership skills and abilities as a cavalry officer. It was a resounding success.[49]

Period and post war testimonials abound regarding Buford's professionalism and skill as a soldier. A member of the general's command once wrote the general "was the best cavalry officer ever produced on this continent." "Few bolder or more

---

[47] Longacre, **General John Buford**, pp.114-115, 119.

[48] **OR**, vol.25, pt.2, pp.71-72; Longacre, **Lincoln's Cavalrymen**, p.129.

[49] **OR**, vol.25, pt.1, pp.1087-1090.

enterprising soldiers ever rode at the head of a column of horse...," another man noted. John Buford was "tireless in the search for information and always eager to fight... the perfect cavalryman." There was little doubt that John Buford was on the path to success and, unlike Alfred Pleasonton, he would not need to court the press or fill his reports with falsehoods and stretch facts to achieve advancement.[50]

Due to Buford's stature as ranking officer, he received temporary command of the corps' First Division when General Stoneman departed on sick leave and Pleasonton ascended to command of the corps. Unfortunately for Buford, who had received his brigadier general commission on 27 July 1862, Pleasonton ranked him by eleven days. After the war, and assisted by hindsight, Hooker finally admitted that Buford would have been a better choice for command of the corps when Stoneman was relieved. However, it would have been difficult for him to promote Buford over Pleasonton, especially with Pleasonton's desire for advancement and his active courting of Washington bureaucrats. When it became known that Stoneman would not return and Pleasonton's elevation to command of the corps became permanent, a new First Division commander would be needed and Buford seemed the logical choice. Although Pleasonton would not officially give him command until 11 June, Buford would take over the First Division on 22 May, splitting time between divisional duties and his duties as commander of the Reserve Brigade. Eight days later, as Pleasonton tried to get a handle on his corps, Buford would be sent northward to the Bealeton area to take charge of operations for the Second and Third Divisions of Pleasonton's command.[51]

As May turned to June, the Federal cavalry had yet to officially organize its horse artillery onto a cohesive unit. The batteries assigned to the cavalry arm were still distributed among the various divisions. Buford' Reserve Brigade however, was in possession of its own group of guns, Battery E of the 4th U. S. Artillery. The battery supported five regiments of horsemen including the 6th Pennsylvanian. Buford's other four regiments were the 1st, 2nd, 5th and 6th U. S. Regulars.[52]

A Division in Waiting

In 1855, when an expansion of the army occurred, additional regiments of Regular Cavalry were added. Six years later, when the war began, most of the regiments were re-designated. During the late summer of 1861, the 1st and 2nd Dragoons, which had been in existence since 1833, were both changed to the 1st and 2nd U. S. Cavalry respectively. During the same period, other existing cavalry regiments received elevated numeric designation. The original 2nd U. S. Cavalry, which had been organized in 1855 was renamed the 5th U. S. Cavalry on 3 August

---

[50] Starr, *Fort Sumter to Gettysburg*, p.293; Tagg, *Generals*, p.168.

[51] Eicher, & Eicher, *High Commands*, pp.431, 153; *OR* vol.25, pt.2, pp.513, 584; *OR*, vol.27, pt.3, p.64; Coddington, *Gettysburg*, p.44.

[52] *OR* vol.25, pt.2, p. 585.

1861. Buford's final regiment, the 6th U. S. Cavalry was organized as a result of the war during the same period.[53]

Commanding Buford's Regulars while he was away on divisional command was senior regimental commander Major Charles Jarvis Whiting. Whiting had been born in Massachusetts, but relocated to Maine as a youngster. In 1830, he was accepted to West Point but when he underwent the physical examination it was discovered he was one-quarter inch short of the minimum height requirement. Undaunted, Whiting returned home to grow a little more. To assist in the effort he took to hanging from a tree branch with bricks tied to his feet to, in theory, stretch himself out. Whether successfully stretched or not, Whiting returned the following year and found himself tall enough to gain admittance to the class of 1835.[54]

Even though he graduated second in his class, evidently Whiting chose not to enter the army's elite engineering branch as his first commission was in the artillery. After serving briefly in Florida against the Seminoles, he resigned his commission and entered the private sector. Whiting must have possessed a desire to instruct others, for after returning to his home state, he opened the Military and Classical Academy in the town of Ellsworth. After six years of teaching, he evidently grew tired of the routine and structure. Leaving his school behind, he ventured west to work conducting the survey of the U. S. Mexican boundary. When completed, the survey was used to establish the Treaty of Guadalupe-Hidalgo.

Whiting remain out west. A short time later he was installed as the surveyor general of California. When a problem arose regarding an overpopulation of grasshoppers in the area, the authorities asked Whiting if he could formulate a solution to reduce or eliminate the pests. Whiting's solution to the problem was quite unique. He proposed putting the state in the poultry business, suggesting that the government bring in thousands of turkeys to consume the grasshoppers. As the birds ate the overabundance of insects, they would become plump with the sustenance. The state could them sell the birds at a huge profit to the local citizenry. Whiting included charts and graphs with his proposal to indicate exactly how many birds would be needed. As could have been predicted, the proposal fell on deaf ears at the legislature and the idea was never considered. Whether Whiting was serious about his odd suggestion was never determined.[55]

In 1855, when the cavalry increased it size, Whiting asked for a commission in one of the new regiments. He was accommodated by being given a captaincy in the newly created 2nd Cavalry on 3 March. He served with the unit for the years leading up to the war and through the conflict after the unit's designation was changed. He showed his skills as a leader during the fight at Gaines' Mill on the

---

[53] McKinney, **Brandy Station**, pp.63-64; Sifakis, **Who was Who**, p. 710. Unlike an infantry regiment, which typically contained ten companies, a cavalry regiment usually contained twelve which were often designated as troops. A squadron of cavalry typically consisted of two companies and a battalion was anywhere from three to five companies depending on their size.

[54] *Ibid*, pp.63, 275,n48.

[55] McKinney, **Brandy Station**, p.63.

Peninsula when he led the 5th Cavalry in a futile charge which resulted in the death of his horse. Left afoot on the battlefield he was eventually captured. However, luck was with Whiting that day for he was taken captive by members of John B. Hood's Brigade. Hood had been a member of Whiting's company before the war and the two were old friends. Hood took good care of his old comrade and Whiting soon found himself exchanged and back in the war.[56]

After being promoted to major on 17 July 1862, Whiting was transferred to the old 2nd Dragoons, now the 2nd U. S. Cavalry. Soon afterward, he was assigned command of the First Brigade of General Pleasonton's division but duty in the field did not last long. As winter approached Whiting was placed on detached service and sent to Annapolis to recruit new troopers. Later he traveled west to Indianapolis where he once again performed recruitment duties. By Chancellorsville, he was back with the army, once again in command of his 2nd Cavalry. With the elevation of Pleasonton and Buford's assignment to divisional command in late May, Whiting's responsibilities within the command structure of the Reserve Brigade would be increasing.[57]

When Buford was ordered to ride to Bealeton and take command of the cavalry in the area, command of the First Division fell to Colonel Benjamin Franklin "Grimes" Davis. Davis was a Southerner and West Point graduate from the class of 1854. When the war began his Southern roots were not deep enough to retain his loyalties. Originally commissioned in the infantry, he served with both the foot soldiers and dragoons in the southwest fighting Indians along the Gila River, receiving a wound for his efforts. He was a first lieutenant with the 1st Dragoons when the war began. Four days before the unit's designation was changed, he received a promotion to captain but just outside of two weeks later he resigned to take a lieutenant colonelcy with the 1st California Cavalry. In November 1861, Davis would once again resign his commission and return east when his Regular Army unit was sent to the seat of war. He fought at Yorktown and Williamsburg with his Regulars before he was transferred to the 8th New York Cavalry. He was mustered in as the regiment's colonel on 11 July 1862.[58]

Perhaps Davis' finest hour occurred during the Maryland Campaign the following September. The 8th New York was stationed at Harpers Ferry when Stonewall Jackson's force closed in to reduce the town. On the afternoon of the 13th, Colonel Davis and the commander of the 12th Illinois Cavalry proposed a daring escape for the cavalry wing of Colonel Dixon S. Miles' surrounded garrison. The cavalry officers wished to extract their horsemen from the hopeless situation by marching them across the Potomac under the cover of darkness using a currently erected pontoon bridge. After a conference to weigh their options, Miles and the cavalry commanders decided to attempt the audacious break out. They

---

[56] *Ibid*, Sifakis, ***Who was Who***, p. 710; Burton, Brian K., ***Extraordinary Circumstances: The Seven Days Battles***, p.133.

[57] Sifakis, ***Who was Who***, p. 710; McKinney, ***Brandy Station***, p.64.

[58] Sifakis, ***Who was Who***, p. 169; Phisterer, ***NYWR***, vol.1, p.885.

also discussed proposals to extract the artillery and infantry, but it was decided they would move too slowly in the darkness and become victims of the attempt. When the discussion turned to what route would be best, a heated disagreement arose. Miles drew the ire of the cavalryman when he mentioned that there was danger in any route taken. Davis almost certainly pointed out that there was no more danger on the roads out of Harpers Ferry than there would be remaining in town surrounded by Jackson. Miles finally gave permission and ordered the cavalry to depart, but cautioned them to secrecy, not wanting to cause a stampede of infantrymen attempting the same evacuation.

The following evening, the cavalry assembled and rode out of town across the bridge. Turning northward up the Maryland shore of the Potomac, the riders soon bore to the right and entered the woods. Riding toward Sharpsburg, the column discovered they were facing a new set of dangers. Lee had withdrawn his army from South Mountain and was assembling it near the town. Adjusting their route slightly, Davis and his horsemen rode throughout most of the night, resting off and on to give the horses and weary men a break. Shortly before daylight the column came upon a group of wagons which they quickly determined to be an enemy supply train. Swiftly, the Union horsemen went to work. Colonel Davis posted himself near the road. As it was still dark the Confederate wagon masters were unable to make "Grimes" Davis out as the enemy. As each wagon past his location the colonel guided it down a side road where each wagon was captured as it passed between elements of the Davis' cavalry. A few troopers rode along with each wagon and many of the Rebel teamsters were unaware they had been captured until the sun began to come up. The entire wagon train was taken in the same manner, and as the last wagon was detained, Davis and the remaining riders fell in behind the wagon to prevent their recapture. He was brevetted for his efforts during the escape and subsequent detainment of the enemy train.[59]

Two days later Davis was in command of a cavalry brigade at Antietam but would return to his regiment before the fighting in and around Fredericksburg in December. As the spring grasses began to sprout, he would once again be back in command of a brigade. During the Chancellorsville Campaign he rode south with Stoneman before his brigade returned to its position within the corps' First Division. As the summer campaign season opened, B. F. Davis, a Southerner by birth, was primed through experience and trial by fire to be a significant element within General Pleasonton's cavalry force.[60]

Records show that on 1 June, command of the First Division's Second Brigade had fallen to Colonel Josiah H. Kellogg of the 17th Pennsylvania Cavalry. Kellogg however, was only temporarily commanding the brigade. The unit's official commanding officer, Colonel Thomas Casimer Devin was away from his brigade. Devin's brigade, which was a fine, battle tested unit, would see the return of its

---

[59] Carman, *The Maryland Campaign*, Pierro, Editor, pp.122-124.

[60] Sifakis, *Who was Who*, p. 169.

chief within a few days. It consisted of Major Pennock Huey's 8th Pennsylvania, Major Kellogg's boys and Devin's own 6th New York Cavalry.[61]

Devin was a rugged faced Irishman with a receding hair line. He was also one of the few non-West Point trained horsemen in the Army of the Potomac. He had no prewar military experience other than his activities with the New York State Militia. However, once mustered into Federal service, he showed a significant knack for the art. Born 10 December 1822 in New York City, Devin received little formal education and ended up a partner in a paint company. His life in the army no doubt seemed a far cry from the painting jobs he worked to earn a living before the war. He gain experience handling a horse as his militia service was with a cavalry unit which he served in as a lieutenant colonel. Although rather old for a cavalry commander, when the war began Devin organized his militia company but was soon mustered out in order to accept the colonelcy of the 6th New York.[62]

Devin quickly displayed his skill as a cavalryman and proved he was no ordinary house painter. Early in the regiment's history a disagreement developed over the serving of what the men had determined to be rotten fish. Conditions at the regiment's initial encampment were poor and some of the men looked upon the bad fish as the last straw. They began a riot, which resulted in the burning down of the camp's cookhouse. As the plug-uglies continued the insurrection, Devin, wielding his pistol, waded into the mass of humanity. Confronted by an angry gun waving colonel, the men slowly calmed themselves. As the situation became tolerable again Devin rudely informed the men that they would be eating outdoors since the cookhouse was now a pile of embers. Although he possessed a rough and rugged exterior, Devin was well respected for his leadership.[63]

Discipline and leadership however, were not Thomas Devin's only strong points. He was also a surprisingly well trained cavalry officer for being a simple militia man. When an old Regular Army man from the War Department was sent out to train Devin the old expert returned as the student. "I can't teach Col. Devin anything about cavalry," the man quipped, "he knows more about the tactics than I do." Devin quickly drilled his men into a solid fighting unit and by the second year of the war, the troopers of the 6th New York were some of the best and hardest riding cavalrymen in the army.[64]

Devin led his regiment at South Mountain and Antietam before being elevated to brigade command. He first led a group of regiments in combat during the Battle of Fredericksburg when then Colonel David M. Gregg was transferred to a cavalry brigade in Burnside's Left Grand Division. Although Fredericksburg was rather uneventful for Devin, the next engagement at Chancellorsville was not. Selected as the only group of cavalry to remain with the main body of Hooker's army, Devin

---

[61] Bates, *HPV*, vol.8, p.1009; *OR* vol.25, pt.2, p.585;

[62] McKinney, **Brandy Station**, pp.61; Eicher, & Eicher, **High Commands**, p.208; Longacre, *The Cavalry at Gettysburg*, p.51.

[63] McKinney, **Brandy Station**, pp.61-62;

[64] Longacre, *The Cavalry at Gettysburg*, p.51.

was forced to disperse his brigade to screen the advance of three army corps as they marched toward Lee's flank. When the fighting erupted, Devin's boys were in the thick of the battle, including Major Huey's headlong gallop into Jackson's assaulting force. When the smoke cleared, Devin had lost over 141 horsemen but gained a reputation as the hardest fighting group of riders in the army. His peers would soon begin referring to him as "Buford's Hard-Hitter."[65]

The Fabricated Warrior

Perhaps the most interesting of all Pleasonton's cavalry officers was the man who replaced General Averell at the head of his Second Division. Colonel Alfred Napoléon Alexander Duffié was a Frenchman, who had been born in Paris on 1 May 1835. He was the son of an entrepreneur who operated a manufacturing plant which processed beets to make sugar. Alfred was seventeen when he chose a military career, enlisting in a regiment of French dragoons. Promotions to corporal and sergeant followed by fighting in the Crimean War lead to multiple citations for gallantry. Promoted to first sergeant in 1858, Duffié promptly volunteered for another seven years of service, but his tenure would be cut short by the affections of a woman.

Her name was Mary Ann Pelton, an American who was in Europe working as a nurse. Alfred became quite smitten with her and Mary must have returned his favors for he soon submitted his resignation from the military which was quickly refused. Undaunted, and obviously in love, Duffié gathered up everything he could pack with him and traveled with his lady to New York, leaving his military career behind. He was quickly convicted of desertion, dismissed from the French service with his previous citations stripped. Eventually he would be dishonorably discharged, but it mattered not to Duffié who would not return to Europe until well after the Civil War.[66]

When America's war began, the now married Duffié was twenty-six years old. Wishing to do his part, he used his military background to join the 2nd New York Cavalry on 9 August 1861, as the original captain of Company A. Six days later he was promoted to major. By July of the following year a colonelcy with the 1st Rhode Island Cavalry was available and Duffié resigned his commission with the New Yorkers to accept the position at the head of the Rhode Islanders. The following day he was commissioned colonel of his new regiment and officially mustered in two days later.[67]

Duffié spent a great deal of time and effort deflecting attention from his previous military record in Europe. Part of the ruse was his consistent references to his father as being a count and not a simple sugar refiner. He maintained that he had graduated from a military college at Saint-Cyr and had graced the Military Academy at Vincennes with his presence. Duffié also concocted an element of

---

[65] *OR*, vol.21, pp.53, 221; *OR* vol.25, pt.1, p.185; Longacre, *The Cavalry at Gettysburg*, p.51.

[66] Wittenberg, *The Union Cavalry*, pp.19-20.

[67] Phisterer, *NYWR*, vol.1, p.765; *ARAGSRI*, vol.2, p.52.

field service to his collection of stories, claiming to have been a lieutenant of cavalry who had served in Senegal and Algiers. He also alleged he had been badly wounded at the Battle of Solferino during the war for Italian independence. This would have been a significant trick since the 3rd Hussars, Duffié's unit, was not even present at Solferino. Another fabrication was Duffié's insistence that he had been wounded in battle a total of eight times. Unfortunately for the Frenchman, his service record fails to mention even a single wound. He also concocted a story about coming to America which explained his reason for relocation as being a desire to submerge himself in the mineral waters at Saratoga Springs. Evidently Duffié thought a concocted story would be better than the truth about his desertion and flight to America with a woman. To complete his new image, Duffié claimed that Queen Victoria had personally presented him with the Victoria Cross. The fact of the matter was quite simple. Alfred Napoléon Alexander Duffié was a liar.[68]

Fortunately for Duffié and unfortunately for the rest of the army, anyone who could speak to the truth about the Frenchman's qualifications and experience would never be encountered. The effort to construct the image of a superlative soldier evidently worked for when he ascended to command of the 1st Rhode Island the men, who initially were not fond of Duffié soon grew to like him. He was a decent tactician and was well versed in the drill of his horsemen. After being associated with Duffié for a short time, some of the troopers formed the opinion that he would soon be promoted to a higher position. In February 1863, the predictions came true when Duffié was elevated to command of the First Brigade in General Averell's Second Division. He first led his new brigade in action at the Battle of Kelly's Ford on 17 March. He fought with distinction against General Fitz Lee's Confederates and was seriously injured in a vicious fall when his horse was shot from under him.[69]

As part of General Averell's Division, Duffié's participation in Stoneman's Raid was limited. Shortly after the horseman returned and Stoneman was in the process of falling out of favor, Duffié, as a colonel, was promoted to command of the corps' Second Division. The promotion appeared to be based on nothing more than seniority for it seems as if Pleasonton was neither questioned nor consulted on the matter. It is highly unlikely that Pleasonton would have given approval to Duffié's elevation. First of all, he was only a colonel and there were many other men of the same rank that in Pleasonton's mind would have been much more deserving. In addition, Pleasonton, favored natural born Americans of high rank and had little if any use for foreign officers. He would later write to a friend that he had no faith in outsiders and that "in every instance foreigners have injured our cause." Duffié would have a difficult time impressing his new corps command even if his performance merited recognition.[70]

---

[68]   Wittenberg, *The Union Cavalry*, p.20.

[69]   *Ibid*, pp.20-21; Eicher, & Eicher, *High Commands*, p.217.

[70]   Longacre, *Lincoln's Cavalrymen*, p.150.

The most interesting and humorous aspect of Duffié's persona was his failure to master the English language. He spoke with a thick French accent and placed incorrect enunciations on various syllables when attempting to converse in the tongue of his adopted country. To make his verbal efforts even more interesting he had a tendency to interlace his words with expletives. On many occasions his swearing was so deprived of definition that the only portion which could be interpreted was the verbiage containing the cursing. No one to whom the tirade was directed knew what was said. To make matters worse, Duffié's grammar was nearly as bad as his syntax. On one occasion he informed his troopers that they all had to die sometime and that if they were killed today they would not have to die again later. It was very evident to all who spent time in the presence of Alfred Duffié that soldiering would not be boring and absent of humor.[71]

During Stoneman's Raid, Averell's First Brigade had been under the command of Colonel Horace Binney Sargent of the 1st Massachusetts. However, on 20 May, the brigade was taken over by another foreigner, Colonel Luigi Palma di Cesnola. Born in Italy in 1832, di Cesnola's father had also been a soldier, fighting with Napoleon's legions. Luigi was educated at the Royal Military Academy at Turin and as a teenager, enlisted in the infantry. He received a commission in the Sardinian Army and fought against the Austrians during his country's struggle for independence. In the late 1850s, he fought in the Crimean War alongside the British and would later claim to have met Captain George B. McClellan when the future general was functioning as a military observer for the United States Army. In 1860, di Cesnola immigrated to America and put down roots in New York. He quickly became infatuated with the daughter of an American naval officer. The two were married and the Italian began a career as the administrator of a New York military school.[72]

When the war began, di Cesnola joined the 11th New York Cavalry on 11 September 1861 to serve three years. In February of the following year he was promoted to lieutenant colonel but everything was not going well for him. With the regiment assigned to garrison duty in the Washington area, he became increasingly frustrated as he saw no combat. On 20 June he resigned his commission but foolishly encouraged a number of his troopers to leave the regiment to find more active units which were involved in the fighting. For his efforts he was arrested and

---

[71] Wittenberg, *The Union Cavalry*, p.21.

[72] Dyer, Frederick H., *A Compendium of the War of the Rebellion (hereafter CWR) vol.1, p.324;* McKinney, **Brandy Station**, pp.73-74, 277n10; Wittenberg, Eric J., ***The Battle of Brandy Station***, p.41; Adams, Charles Frances, Jr., *A Cycle of Adams Letters 1861-1865*, vol.1, p.24; Crowninshield, Benjamin W., *A History of the First Regiment of Massachusetts Cavalry Volunteers*, p.317. Although Sargent is listed in the *OR* as being in command of Duffié's First Brigade on 31 May, Dyer lists di Cesnola as taking command on 20 May. Sargent graduated from Harvard with honors but had no military experience prior to the war and some of his officers despised him. Captain Charles Adams of Company C, in a letter to his father called Sargent "an ass," noting the colonel was "[i]gnorant to the last degree of his supposed profession..." and that his "ignorance [was] only surpassed by his conceit and vanity and his love of display."

charged with promoting mutiny. Eventually the charges would be dropped, but it would not be the last time di Cesnola would be in the stockade.[73]

Once free of the authorities, the twenty-nine year old Italian was awarded a commission as lieutenant colonel of the 4th New York Cavalry. The resignation of the regiment's original colonel early in the fall of 1862, opened the way for di Cesnola, and he was promoted to the colonelcy of the regiment on 11 September. The regiment was a hodgepodge of various nationalities and was not a favorite of the army's upper command structure. The historian of the 1st Massachusetts provided the best description of di Cesnola renegades.

> "The 4th New York cavalry was a peculiar, and might have been called the polyglot regiment. The colonel, Di Cesnola, was an Italian. Other field officers were Americans and Germans, while the men included Americans, Germans, Frenchmen, Italians, Spaniards, Hungarians and perhaps men of other countries. Most of them could speak only their own language. A large proportion had been in cavalry service in their own country, and many were well set up, and fine looking. They were sad rogues, and the regiment lacked cohesion and unity, as might be expected from the elements. The officer of the day gave them a wide berth when coming to their pickets, as they could not understand him, nor he them. In some battles they fought very well, but generally they were not considered reliable, and there were scandals of frequent occurrence."[74]

Assuredly Luigi's native tongue came in handy when dealing with at least some of the men of his regiment. In many instances however, the regiment was slow to react to orders because most commands had to be repeated by translators in many different languages.

Di Cesnola himself also contributed to the regiment's scandalous reputation. During February 1863, he was dismissed from the army for stealing public property. The charges stemmed from an incident in which the provost marshal discovered six army revolvers in a package which the colonel was trying to mail home. According to di Cesnola he was sending the weapons home to provide arms to a group of men trying to protect the state depot. Luigi argued that he was merely using his home address because it was convenient. Why the Italian thought using his personal residence as a destination to send army property would be acceptable to the authorities is puzzling. For five weeks di Cesnola pleaded his case. Finally, he was reinstated, but the episode leveled more suspicion upon his already troubled regiment.

---

[73] Phisterer, *NYWR*, vol.2, p.945; McKinney, **Brandy Station**, p.73.

[74] Phisterer, *NYWR*, vol.1, p.806; ***ARAGSNY***, vol.1, p.1075; Crowninshield, **History of the First**, pp.307-308.

As the season for active campaigning approached, di Cesnola had been pushed around by the authorities, was leading a regiment of hooligans, been arrested once, and dismissed from the service. All his difficulties had not endeared him to his superiors, and he had formed a rather harsh opinion of their leadership. He must have been a bit surprised when he was placed in temporary command of Duffié's First Brigade. Comprising his new command were the men of his own 4th New York, eight companies of the 1st Massachusetts, ten companies of the 6th Ohio and the 1st Rhode Island Cavalry.[75]

At the head of Colonel Duffié's Second Brigade was Pennsylvanian, "Long John" Gregg. Colonel John Irvin Gregg was born at Bellefonte in the central portion of the state on 26 July 1826. Known as Long John due to his six foot four inch frame, Gregg's family had lived in the area for almost one hundred years. Politics was in his bloodline. His father, Andrew Gregg, had served two terms in the United States Senate during the late seventeen and early 1800s. John was the cousin of David M. Gregg and both Gregg's were cousin's to Pennsylvanian Governor Andrew Curtin. John was educated at the local schools within Centre and Union counties. When the Mexican War began he volunteered for service. Entering the army as a private, he was promoted to first lieutenant in the 11th U. S. Infantry after arriving near Jalapa in Mexico. He served throughout the remainder of the war, was promoted to captain during the conflict, and was mustered out when the fighting ended. Upon his return he went to work in the family's iron business and joined a local militia unit, the Centre Guards. He worked his way up through the organization's ranks until he achieved the position of lieutenant colonel. In November of 1857, John married a fine, attractive woman named Clarissa A. Everhart, but she would die at an early age and would bear him no children. He would eventually marry again, his second union resulting in two youngsters.[76]

When the war began, Gregg was installed as captain of Company E of the 5th Pennsylvania Reserves, but he soon resigned his position to accept a captaincy in the Regular Army. John's cousin, David, who was the colonel of the newly formed 6th U. S. Cavalry, was joined by John as one of his captains. John's first action was on the Peninsula at Williamsburg. Additional engagements followed in quick succession. He fought during The Seven Days, Second Bull Run, and the Antietam Campaign. As 1862 neared its conclusion, John's deeds on the battlefield had earned him his own command. On 14 November he was mustered in as the colonel of the newly organized 16th Pennsylvania Cavalry. By January the regiment was on the battle line, having been brigaded with the other regiments of General Averell's command. Gregg spent the remainder of the winter on outpost duty where he developed a reputation as an efficient and capable officer. He led his regiment in battle for the first time at the Battle of Kelly's Ford on 17 March. He earned a

---

[75] McKinney, **Brandy Station**, p.73; **OR** vol.25, pt.2, p.584.

[76] Bates, Samuel P., **Martial Deeds of Pennsylvania**, p.851; Wittenberg, **Brandy Station**, pp.42-43.

Regular Army major's brevet for his days' work near the ford, and on 13 May was given command of Duffié's Second Brigade.⁷⁷

John was considered a reliable and exceptional officer by his peers. They knew him to be a true soldier in every sense of the word and acknowledged his willingness to get into a scrap with the enemy and fight them hard wherever he met them. He was calm and collected under fire and cared not if confronted by greater numbers. His new command was the only group of cavalry regiments in the Army of the Potomac from the same state which were brigaded together. Gregg's own 16th Pennsylvania along with the 3rd and 4th regiments of cavalry from the Keystone State made up his group.⁷⁸

Old Reliable

John's cousin David commanded Pleasonton's Third Division. David was born on 10 April 1833 in the town of Huntingdon, Pennsylvania, just south of his older cousin's hometown. His early education was courtesy of a number of private schools. After his primary education was complete, he attended college at the University of Lewisburg, a school which would eventually become Bucknell University. In 1851 he was awarded an appointment to the Military Academy. Four years later he graduated eighth among the thirty-four members of the class of 1855. Upon graduation he was commissioned a second lieutenant and assigned to duty with the 2nd Dragoons. David spent the first two months of his service on the frontier before he was promoted to full first lieutenant and transferred to the 1st Dragoons on 4 September. During the years preceding the war, he saw duty in the Pacific Northwest fighting Indians in both the Washington and Oregon Territories. He was on duty at Fort Tejon in California when hostilities began.⁷⁹

Gregg was promoted to captain and assigned to the newly created 3rd U. S. Cavalry on 14 May 1861. His first wartime duty was commanding a company of Regulars in the defenses of Washington. He would be transferred to the newest regiment or Regular cavalry, the 6th U. S., on 3 August, but by January 1862 he had been reassigned to the 8th Pennsylvania Cavalry, made the regiment's colonel, and placed in command. By June he was in command of the Fourth Corps' cavalry but a month later was commanding a brigade of horsemen in the Army of the Potomac's Cavalry Division. Gregg gained enough notoriety by the end of the year that as the flood of promotions filtered through the army on 29 November, he was made a brigadier general of volunteers.⁸⁰

Gregg went with McClellan to the Peninsula where he spent a good deal of time battling Jeb Stuart's vaunted cavalryman. When General Lee launched his

---

77   Bates, *HPV*, vol.2, p.680, vol.8, p.956; Bates, *Martial Deeds*, pp.851-852; Wittenberg, *Brandy Station*, p.43; Eicher, & Eicher, *High Commands*, p.267.

78   Wittenberg, *Brandy Station*, p.43; *OR*, vol.25, pt.2, p.584.

79   Warner, *Generals in Blue*, pp.187-188; Wittenberg, *Brandy Station*, p.44; Bates, *Martial Deeds*, p.769.

80   Eicher, & Eicher, *High Commands*, p.267.

assaults inaugurating The Seven Days and McClellan was driven from the gates of Richmond, Gregg remained near the Chickahominy River, fighting a delaying action to cover a portion of McClellan's army. During the Maryland Campaign, he and his 8th Pennsylvania remained on the right flank of the army and saw only minor activity. On 1 November, after returning to Virginia, Gregg and his Pennsylvanians entered into a series of running engagements with the Rebel cavalry which lasted a number of days. The fighting took place in the vicinities of Philomont and Upperville and Gregg's boys gave a good accounting of themselves. "The daily successes of the brigade," wrote Gregg in his report, "in its engagements with Stuart's cavalry, inspired such feelings of enthusiastic soldierly confidence that the enemy had only to be pointed out to be defeated." Gregg's boys had proven they were willing to face Stuart wherever the flamboyant cavalryman's riders could be found. It was the beginning of the renaissance of the Federal cavalry which would come to fruition at Brandy Station.[81]

A tough West Point man, David McMurtrie Gregg was a reliable and steady commander of cavalry. *LOC*

Gregg's West Point training and his experience on the frontier fighting Indians prepared him for the difficulties of the war. He also gained valuable leadership experience which taught him how to discipline and train the men in his command while earning their respect. He was very accomplished at molding his horsemen into a cohesive fighting force. Many thought Gregg was a natural cavalry commander

---

[81] Bates, *Martial Deeds*, pp.769-770; *OR*, vol.19, pt.2, pp.129-131.

who possessed outstanding character but was also quite humble. During a fight he was courageous and possessed an intense resolve to succeed. Like John Buford, he did not care for newspaper reporters but for different reasons. While Buford saw them as a cancer on the army's clandestine operations, Gregg avoided them because he was modest and did not seek recognition. He was tall but slight with a heavy, massive beard which hung to his chest. His square straight nose, light colored eyes and high forehead gave him a stern, somber look which mimicked his solid persona. As of June 1863, Gregg was the longest tenured cavalry division commander in the Army of the Potomac. The men took to calling him "Old Reliable," which was an accurate description of the sturdy David Gregg.[82]

Commanding Gregg's First Brigade was one of the most recent West Point graduates in the army. Hugh Judson Kilpatrick, a flamboyant caviler, was also reckless, turbulent and on some occasions uncontrollable. He was often shameless in his actions and hovered near the extreme end of reason. His passion for his craft made him a number of friends within the army, but his occasional unreasonable stance and desire to be successful made enemies as well. Of those who became acquainted with Kilpatrick one of two opinions was generally formed. He was either a hero and a fine, driven soldier or a bragging self-promoter who had no common sense. In simpler terms, he possessed a thoughtless energy which made him seem to always be in a hurry, and his propensity for urgency made him reckless.

Physically Kilpatrick did not project an image which would lead one to believe he was an effective cavalryman. He was slight of build, slender and slight in stature. He had a square ridged jaw, deep inset eyes, a large hawkish nose and shaggy but sparse reddish sideburns. His vanity could be seen in his flashy dress. He wore a large black felt hat, knee high leather boots and customized uniforms which made him look slightly silly. A staff officer once wrote that it was difficult to look at him without breaking into a chuckle. Kilpatrick's nervous energy gave the impression of continuous activity and state of excitement. He was partial to speaking to his troops to inspire them and spent an inordinate amount of time trying to be noticed. He was a hard driver and often pushed his command to the brink. In fact, he was giving the nickname "Kil-cavalry" for disregarding the welfare of his men and horses in favor of his blatant self promotion and push for personal glory. Although many thought him devoid of integrity and one who partook in some vices, Kilpatrick was one of the few officers in the army who neither gambled nor drank alcohol.[83]

Hugh Kilpatrick was born near Deckertown, New Jersey on 14 January 1836. He was the son of a farmer but early in life decided that tilling the earth was not a life he wished to pursue. Instead, he became interested in government, and at an early age became politically active. After vigorously supporting a congressional candidate who happened to win election, he was rewarded with an appointment to West Point. Although Kilpatrick seems to have had no formal primary education;

---

[82] Bates, ***Martial Deeds***, p.769; Wittenberg, ***Brandy Station***, pp.44-45; McKinney, ***Brandy Station***, p.68.

[83] Longacre, Edward G., Judson Kilpatrick, ***CWTI***, vol.10, no.1, p.24.

he still received the appointment and became a cadet in July of 1856. During his time at the academy, for some reason, he determined to drop his first name. From his West Point days onward he would be known as Judson Kilpatrick. Academically he was slightly above average, graduating seventeenth in a class of forty-five in 1861.[84]

As Kilpatrick's West Point career neared its end, the succession crisis came to a head. Always in the mood for a fight, he seemed to continually court confrontations with his Southern classmates. Although slight of frame, he showed little concern with his ability to actually come out on top during an altercation, many of which resulted in fisticuffs. He also showed a great desire to support the Union war effort. When the war began, the class of 1861 was still a few months short of graduation. Kilpatrick, wishing to get into the fight as soon as possible, circulated a petition to allow his class to graduate early. After gathering enough signatures, he submitted the appeal which was granted. On 6 May, Judson graduated and went off to war.[85]

Realizing his chance for advancement was greater within the volunteer service, the ambitious Kilpatrick immediately turned away from the Regular Army. Three days after departing from West Point, Judson accepted a commission as the captain of the 5th New York Infantry's Company H. Not wanting to miss any fighting, he immediately left and traveled to the Virginia Peninsula to join his new regiment. Within a month, after working hard to shape his company into a viable fighting unit, Kilpatrick had earned the respect of his men. They had grown confident in their new captain and had shown friendliness toward him. Initially conducting foraging and intelligence gathering operations, Kilpatrick obtained his first taste of combat on 10 June at the Battle of Big Bethel. During the fighting he showed poise and bravery. He also became the first Regular Army officer to be wounded during the war when he was hit in the thigh by grapeshot. While he recuperated, Northern newspapers published glowing reports of his exploits. The young man from New Jersey was on his way to a high profile military career.[86]

While recovering from his injury, Kilpatrick was promoted to lieutenant colonel and joined a cavalry organization which would eventually be designated the 2nd New York Cavalry. Mustered into the regiment on 12 August 1861, Judson spent the next twelve months on scouting and reconnaissance missions. In July of 1862, he rode with the regiment as it struck at Stonewall Jackson's line of communication between Gordonsville, Virginia and Richmond. The horsemen rode southward from the Fredericksburg area and on the 20th were astride the Virginia Central Railroad near Beaver Dam Station. With quick precision Kilpatrick's men proceeded to destroy a great deal of infrastructure. The regiment tore up several miles of railroad lines, burned rail ties, burned the railroad depot at Beaver Dam and cut telegraph lines. Within the railroad depot were 100 barrels of flour and 40,000 rounds of ammunition which met the same fate as the structures. In addition

---

[84] *Ibid*, Eicher, & Eicher, ***High Commands***, p.332.

[85] Longacre, Judson Kilpatrick, ***CWTI***, vol.10, no.1, p.24.

[86] *Ibid*, p.24-25; Phisterer, ***NYWR***, vol.2, p.1763;

to all the destruction, the raiders also captured a Confederate captain of cavalry named John S. Mosby.[87]

Hugh Judson Kilpatrick's West Point graduation photograph. *West Point Album 1861, USAHEC*

Kilpatrick continued to ascend the ladder of rank and in early December was promoted to colonel and placed in command of the regiment. Two months later he was placed in command of a brigade which he led throughout the spring of 1863. During Stoneman's Raid, Kilpatrick, and the 2nd New York were detached from the main body of Stoneman's command. His exploits during the raid marked the high point of the excursion. With his command detached, Kilpatrick raided towns, frightening citizens and destroyed almost everything of military significant he could get his hands on. Once again he smashed rail lines, depots and equipment. His command ventured within two miles of the Confederate capital, raising additional panic, before veering southeast to pierce the Confederate lines before riding to Fort Monroe on the Virginia Peninsula.[88]

---

[87] *OR*, vol.12, pt.3, p.490; *OR*, vol.12, pt.2, p.119; Mosby, John S., ***Mosby's Memoirs***, pp.126-127. Captain Mosby would be taken to the Old Capital Prison in Washington but would be exchanged the day after he arrived. He would shortly be promoted to colonel and, as the leader of a band of partisan cavalrymen, would wreak havoc among the Federal forces in Virginia during the spring and summer of 1863 and would vehemently defend Stuart's actions during the coming campaign.

[88] Longacre, Judson Kilpatrick, ***CWTI***, vol.10, no.1, p.26.

On 3 June, as Ewell's Second Corps began to slip away from the Rappahannock River, Kilpatrick himself had not yet returned to the Army of the Potomac. Although a portion of his brigade had ridden north, the 2nd New York Cavalry was still on the Peninsula near Yorktown. It would be 7 June before the brigade and its commander were reunited. Until then Colonel Calvin S. Douty of the 1st Maine Cavalry would command the elements of the brigade with the army near Fredericksburg. The brigade contained Douty's regiment, Kilpatrick's 2nd New York, the 10th New York, and one Independent Company of the District of Columbia Volunteer Cavalry.[89]

Pleasonton's final brigade was under the command of self-proclaimed soldier of fortune, Colonel Percy Wyndham. Wyndham's life had been rather remarkable, beginning with his birth aboard a ship in the English Channel on 5 February 1833, during his parent's passage to Calcutta, India. Soldering was in Wyndham blood. His father Captain Charles Wyndham had been a member of the British 5th Light Cavalry. When he was fifteen, Percy entered the French navy and served during the French Revolution in 1848. He later joined the Austrian army and over an eight year career advanced to first lieutenant within the Austrian Lancers. In 1860 he joined the Italian army of liberation and fought with Giuseppe Garibaldi and his revolutionaries. His efforts during the fighting at the Battle of Milazzo, gained Wyndham a major brevet. His conduct during the engagement also earned him a knighthood from King Victor Emmanuel. As the fighting in Italy ended, Wyndham went in search of another conflict in which to exhibit his skills. As luck would have it, things were heating up across the Atlantic. He traveled to America in 1861 and by February, 1862, his past exploits had earned him the colonelcy of the 1st New Jersey Cavalry.[90]

Before his arrival the regiment had been a disorganized band of misfits commanded by a seventy year old lawyer who was not qualified to lead them. The men had shown a lack of discipline and training and the officers of the unit had been prone to squabbling and undermining the authority of others for the sake of swift advancement. Colonel Wyndham stepped in for the discharged senior citizen and quickly began to put the regiment in order. The soldiers were cynical at first but quickly warmed to the British Knight who began a rigid program to drill the men. He also secured pay for the men and made sure that it was distributed on a regular basis. Wyndham evaluated the regiment's officer corps, promoting men who showed promise and sending the ones who were detriments packing. Within two months he had his new regiment ready to take the field. At the end of April the men of the 1st New Jersey Cavalry and their English Lord leader packed up their camp and marched off to war.[91]

The regiment's first heavy action came in the Shenandoah Valley against Jackson's Confederate cavalry. In early June, 1862, Percy led his regiment into an ambush set by Turner Ashby and the colonel and a number of his men were

---

[89] *OR*, vol.25, pt.2, p.584; *OR*, vol.27, pt.3, p.32.

[90] McKinney, **Brandy Station**, p.70; Wittenberg, **Brandy Station**, pp.45-46.

[91] Longacre, Edward G., Sir Percy Wyndham, **CWTI**, vol.7, no.8, pp.12-14.

captured. After two months of captivity Wyndham was exchanged. He rejoined his regiment in time to participate in the campaign which resulted in the second battle near Bull Run. During the campaign, as Stonewall Jackson fought elements of Pope's army near the old Bull Run battlefield, Percy's regiment dropped trees across the road through Thoroughfare Gap in an effort to delay Longstreet's force. After blocking the road, his men took defensive position and when the Confederates arrived poured a heavy fire into the gray clad enemy. The sheer weight of numbers eventually forced Wyndham to fall back. During the remainder of the campaign, he led his regiment with distinction. A short time afterword, he left his now hardened New Jersey veterans behind for brigade command.[92]

Like Kilpatrick, Wyndham developed a reputation for running his horses into the ground to accomplish his mission. A fellow cavalryman once wrote that Wyndham seemed determined to kill as many horses as possible and had the same regard for his men. The cavalryman equated Wyndham's actions to a desire to get his exploits and name in the papers. Wyndham showed great enthusiasm in the execution of his assignments and was tireless in his efforts to achieve his goals. He was so zealous in his pursuits that the Confederate high command became focused on stopping him. In the spring of 1863, General Stuart, having become fixated on Wyndham, developed a desire to rid himself of the Brit. In the wake of Mosby's capture of General Edwin Stoughton on 9 March, Stuart all but demanded Mosby repeat the feat and capture the Englishman. Writing to the exchanged captain on 25 March, Stuart insisted, "[w]e must have that unprincipled scoundrel Wyndham. Can you catch him?" Unfortunately for Mosby, Wyndham had been ordered to the capital, and Mosby never was able to find and detain Sir Percy. A short time later, Wyndham was reassigned to the Army of the Potomac.[93]

Although Hooker considered the Stoneman raid a tactical failure, Wyndham actually performed well during the incursion. He exuded all the persona of a nineteenth century British warrior and in many respects looked the part. He wore a massive mustache which turning upward at its end and transitioned into his side whiskers. Taken altogether the impressive crop of facial hair, which at its height of growth, extended almost two feet from tip to tip. A long pointed goatee fit between the enormous mustache giving his growth a three pronged look. Although blessed with impressive facial hair, Wyndham possessed sparse wavy hair upon his head. His bright eyes projected an air of youthfulness. Percy was a brawny man, sturdy in his presence and confident in his actions. His personality, while appreciated by some was seen as braggadocios by other. One Federal officer called him "a big bag of wind," while others thought him vain for changing his dress a number of times each day. He wore tall polished boots and spurs when in the saddle, and he supplemented his outfit with a slouch hat which he complimented with a plume.[94]

---

[92] *Ibid*, p.15.

[93] McKinney, ***Brandy Station***, p.70; Wittenberg, ***Brandy Station***, p.47; ***OR***, vol.25, pt.2, p.858.

[94] Wittenberg, ***Brandy Station***, p.47; Longacre, Sir Percy Wyndham, ***CWTI***, vol.7, no.8, p.14.

Vain or not, Wyndham impressed enough superior officers to, at least in their eyes, justify his retention of brigade command. During the first days of June Wyndham's command consisted of four regiments from different states. In addition to his own 1st New Jersey, the brigade contained the 1st Maryland, and 1st Pennsylvania Cavalry. The brigade's final regiment, the 12th Illinois Cavalry, was still on duty at Yorktown and would not join Wyndham's command until later in the month.[95]

With Captain Tidball's Brigade of artillery assigned to the Artillery Reserve's Regular Division, the only collection of horse artillery with Pleasonton's Cavalry Corps was Captain James M. Robertson's group of five batteries. Robertson's set of batteries consisted of Batteries B, L, and M of the 2nd U. S. Artillery, Battery E of the 4th U. S. Artillery and the 6th New York Independent Battery. Typically, when in camp, the batteries were brigaded together but during active campaigning they were dispersed among the Cavalry Corps' Divisions.[96]

Robertson, a New Hampshire, native enlisted in the army in 1838. Assigned to the 2nd U. S. Artillery he spent time in both Batteries F and H. When the Mexican War began, Robertson served as a quartermaster sergeant and on 28 June 1848 he was promoted to second lieutenant. Four years later he was elevated to first lieutenant, before fighting the Seminoles in Florida from 1855 to 1858. As the Civil War was breaking out, Robertson received a promotion to captain and assignment to command of the 2nd U. S. Artillery's Battery B. Eventually, prior to the Peninsula Campaign, his battery would be combined with Battery L of the 2nd U. S. and he would lead them both until assigned to brigade command. Robertson was a rugged veteran artilleryman and was well versed in servicing and commanding his guns.[97]

Although the Federal Cavalry Corps had seen hard service during the spring of 1863, it had done a great deal to boost its confidence and élan. The early years of the war had seen Confederate cavalry out perform their Federal counterparts on an almost daily basis. Fighting during the spring of 1863 however, had seen the Union riders giving as good as they received. While Stoneman's expedition accomplished little in Hooker's eyes, it did have one positive outcome. Federal horse solders realized they enjoyed riding and raiding to a much greater degree than loitering around camp reading about the exploits of their Southern counterparts in Richmond newspapers. However, fighting had also reduced the number of available officers and rendered a large group of horses unserviceable. Although many of the regiments were under the command of lower grade officers, most were seasoned. It would not be long before the troopers of the Army of the Potomac's Cavalry Corps would meet the vaunted Confederate riders in battle again.

---

[95] ***OR***, vol.25, pt.2, p.584.

[96] ***OR***, vol.25, pt.2, p.584-585; Wittenberg, ***Brandy Station***, p.47.

[97] Sifakis, ***Who was Who***, p. 548; Wittenberg, ***Brandy Station***, pp.47-48.

Chapter XV
Stuart Concentrates

> "I request that you move into Culpeper, where you can better observe the enemy." [1]
> Robert E. Lee to
> Jeb Stuart, 11 May, 1863.

Late on the evening of 28 April 1863, marauding Confederates under the command of Brigadier General William E. "Grumble" Jones entered Morgantown West Virginia. Jones brigade of cavalry, and men of the Northwestern Brigade under Brigadier General John D. Imboden, had ridden into the area to do as much damage to the Federal war effort as possible. During the latter half of April, the two generals were ordered to gather their forces and moved into West Virginia to destroy elements of the Baltimore and Ohio Railroad line. The B & O's initial track was laid in the 1850s, and by the end of the decade it had become one of the busiest commercial lines in the country. When the war began the line was transformed into one of the North's busiest and most critical military arteries. The tracks provide a direct line between the Potomac River and the upper reaches of the Ohio River. Resources from the Ohio and western Virginia region could be transported directly to the Eastern Theater. Timber and coal were provided for use by the navy to maintain the Northern fleet's stranglehold on Southern ports. Men and supplies could also be transported quickly, and the line became a chief supply route for military operation in the Lower Shenandoah Valley and the Trans-Allegany region. The Confederates quickly realized the B & O Railroad was a great hindrance to the Southern war effort.[2]

In the spring of 1863, the Confederate's planned and executed a raid intended to render the B & O line unserviceable. The plan seemed simple on the surface. Imboden would go with his brigade, along with Jones' Virginians into the region. They would operate in a detached manner, destroying the rail lines, infrastructure and bridges, while rounding up as many horses, cattle and other supplies they could

---

[1] *OR* vol.25, pt.2, p.792.

[2] Collins, Darrell L., ***The Jones-Imboden Raid***, pp.3-4. President Lincoln signed the proclamation approving the admission of West Virginia as the thirty-fifth state on 20 April. Within the context of the narrative, references to the region prior to 20 April will be noted as western Virginia. References on or after 20 April will be noted as West Virginia.

transfer into the Shenandoah Valley and points further south. Prime targets along the rail line included the Cheat River Bridge and the Trey Run and Buckeye Run viaducts in the Rowelsburg area.³

After the raid was over, both Jones and Imboden praised their commands for their efforts. Imboden noted in a congratulatory order to the brigade that they managed to damage "millions of dollars" of enemy property and that great destruction had been done to the B & O line. Unfortunately for the Confederates, the dollar amount was somewhat high and the duration which the railroad was unserviceable was inconsequential. Federal work crews, who had spent time developing contingency plans for just such an incident, were prepared for the reconstruction work. With stockpiles of track and timbers nearby, and easy access to materials to rebuild bridges and trestles, the Federals quickly went to work. Most of the twenty-six bridges which had been destroyed or damaged were back in service almost before the raiders had returned to the safety of the Shenandoah Valley. On 13 May, the trains were running again. The high profile spans in the Rowelsburg area remained standing, much to the chagrin of General Lee and the Confederate authorities.⁴

A more successful aspect of the raid was the capture of a large number of cattle. Jones managed to herd 1,200 head into Confederate controlled areas while Imboden took into custody 3,100 more. While Lee wished to use some of the booty to feed his army's hungry men, he was talked into allowing the beeves to fatten on the summer grasses. He would use a great deal of the meat to feed his army during the winter of 1863-64.⁵

Regarding horses, Imboden took in around 1,350 head, while Jones reported the capture of 1,200 more. The numbers however were hardly sufficient to make up for the large number of animals which became victims of the hard riding required by the nature of the raid. Great numbers of horses gave out along the way. A colonel from one of the regiments noted in his report that he was able to replace seventy-two horses which had given out with horses he had bought, more than likely with worthless Confederate script. In addition, most of the horses which managed to return to the Shenandoah Valley intact were not in serviceable condition and would need to refresh themselves. Taking into consideration the wear and tear on the men and horses, the only positive outcome of the raid was the rounding up of the cattle. The effort seemed hardly worth the price.⁶

Lee Prepares His Cavalry

Shortly after his victory at Chancellorsville, while Imboden and Jones were off in West Virginia, Lee initiated an effort to place his cavalry in position to screen his coming advance. However, even before the effort began, Lee initiated

---

3   *Ibid*, p.3.

4   *Ibid*, pp.185, 188-189.

5   *Ibid*, p.186-187.

6   **OR** vol.25, pt.2, pp.120, 133; Collins, ***The Jones-Imboden Raid***, p.187.

conversations with the Confederate authorities in Richmond to bolster his mounted arm. On 20 April, Lee sent a communication to President Davis regarding the increase of his cavalry and requested that Brigadier General Albert Gallatin Jenkins' Brigade be sent to his army. The following day, Adjutant General Samuel Cooper responded noting three regiments of Jenkins' West Virginia cavalry brigade could be shipped off to Lee. Cooper immediately communicated with Major General Samuel Jones, commander of Confederate forces in West Virginia. Jones replied to Cooper indicating it would be possible to send two or three of Jenkins' regiments, but there were not enough horses available to outfit all the brigade's troopers. It would be some time until enough mounts were available to send the regiments to Lee. Cooper followed up with an additional communication on 23 April informing Jones that "General Lee is greatly in want of an increase of cavalry," and the president was in favor of Lee's request.[7]

Jones may have thought he was getting pressured. On the same day Cooper used the president's name as leverage, Jones reiterated his intent to send the regiments but only when the horses were ready. He explained that with the spring in West Virginia being late, the grasses required to reinvigorate the animals had been slow in their growth. He also noted that he was "reluctant" to send the troopers "and hoped they [would] be returned... as soon as General Lee [could] spare them." On 25 April, Jones went straight to Lee, communicating his desire to provide the regiments. He then added another reason for the delay, noting the horses were not "collected" from their winter foraging ground in North Carolina. Jones also noted the men of Jenkins' Brigade were from West Virginia, and suggested that Jenkins' troopers may be more comfortable serving closer to their homes and proposed the men be used to replace "Grumble" Jones' brigade in the Shenandoah Valley. A few days later, Lee became aware of Hooker's movement up the river and the task of reinforcing his cavalry was placed on hold as the Battle of Chancellorsville unfolded.[8]

Whether Lee determined to replace "Grumble" Jones' Brigade with Jenkins' on his own, or took Samuel Jones' suggestion as a logical one is a matter of speculation. Lee evidently assumed his desires would be fulfilled for he had previously informed Jeb Stuart on 20 April that he intended to have Jenkins' Brigade transferred to him. Only after the Battle of Chancellorsville did Lee began to refer to Jenkins replacing Jones' troopers once the later had returned from their raid. Finally, on 9 May, Lee once again communicated with Stuart regarding the reinforcement of his cavalry. "As regards [to] General W. E. Jones, I have had it in my mind to make a change in the Valley, and order him to report with his brigade to you, and place the cavalry from Western Virginia there."[9]

---

[7] *OR* vol.25, pt.2, pp.740-742.

[8] *OR* vol.25, pt.2, pp.747-748, 750-751. Jones was referring to the region of Virginia which had just been accepted as the Union's newest state.

[9] *Ibid*, pp.738, 747-748, 789;

Communicating with Jenkins, Lee instructing the brigadier to organize his command and transfer it to Staunton in the Valley. Lee then, in quick succession, sent off two communications to General Samuel Jones on 9 May. One relayed orders instructing Jones to transfer Jenkins and his cavalry to the town of Staunton or another "convenient point in the Valley." The second contained an inquiry as to how Jones believed Jenkins would feel if his brigade replaced Grumble Jones' brigade so the latter could ride to reinforce Stuart.[10]

Before receiving Lee's messages, Samuel Jones, on 12 May, sent a communication of his own to Lee complaining about his situation and suggested alternatives. Jones argued that his command was scattered, and if forced to send Jenkins to the Valley, he would not be able to sufficiently reinforce Imboden or adequately protect the approaches to the Kanawha Valley. Jones did not receive Lee's note of the 9th until 14 May. He responded the following day with a communication which certainly satisfied Lee.

Although Jones may not have agreed with Lee's intentions and orders, he was a good soldier and a West Point graduate who understood the chain of command. After he received instructions to move Jenkins, he made every effort to provide Lee with information he thought Lee needed as well as what he had requested. "Eight to ten [companies] of Jenkins' cavalry," Jones noted, "ought to be at Staunton now or further to the east, as they had moved from Rockbridge and Augusta several days since to join General Stuart, as ordered." According to Jones, two companies of the 16th Virginia Cavalry were near his location and would be started toward the Valley immediately. The remainder of the regiment had started its journey the previous day. The rest of Jenkins' command would be delayed since, as Jones had previously noted, he did not have horses to mount them since the animals had not yet returned from their wintering grounds. Another of Jenkins' units, the 37th Battalion Virginia Cavalry would also be delayed, having been assigned to Imboden's raiding party. Jones Informed Lee that as soon as Imboden returned he would order the 37th to the Valley.[11]

Lee also inquired of Jones regarding Jenkins' abilities as an officer. Lee knew Jenkins was a "gallant soldier" but was unsure of his administrative skills. Jones responded by heaping praise upon Jenkins for his capability as a soldier but noted his lack of confidence in Jenkins did indeed have to do with his clerical skills and principles.

> "Brigadier-General Jenkins is a bold and gallant soldier, but I do not think him a good administrative officer. I believe he is capable of becoming a fine officer in that respect, but unfortunately many of his men are his constituents, and he has been a politician, and, I believe, still has aspirations that way. I do not know enough of Brig. Gen. W. E. Jones to venture a

---

[10] *Ibid*, pp.789, 792, 804.

[11] *Ibid*, pp.795, 804. Rockbridge is located in the upper reaches of the Shenandoah Valley, Augusta is near Romney in West Virginia.

comparison between him and Jenkins. The latter will, I think, prove quite as daring as you can desire, and that, I think, is a very desirable quality, especially in a cavalry officer."[12]

Although his departure for the Valley had been delayed, by late May the regiments of Albert Jenkins' Brigade were either in the Shenandoah Valley or on their way. Jenkins himself, along with three regiments and one battalion were in the Staunton area. Sam Jones retained the 19th Virginia while two other regiments currently with Imboden were slated to be returned. The 34th Virginia Battalion which was currently with Grumble Jones was also intended to be returned but would not rejoin the brigade until after the Gettysburg Campaign had begun. By the time all the shuffling was completed, Jenkins would enter the campaign with the 14th, 16th and 17th Virginia Cavalry, the 34th and 36th Virginia Cavalry Battalions and Virginia's Charlottesville Artillery Battery.[13]

Jenkins was the son of a ship-owner. He was born in Cabell County, Virginia on 10 November 1830. His father moved to Cabell County in 1825 and established a residence for his family which would eventually became known as Green Bottom Plantation. Jenkins attended the Virginia Military Institute before entering Jefferson College in Pennsylvania. After graduating in 1848, he entered Harvard Law School, from which he graduated in 1850. He put his degree to use for only a short time before deciding to try his hand at farming. He never again practicing the profession he was trained for. He began his political career in 1858, serving as a congressman from Charleston, Virginia until he resigned in April of 1861 because of the war. He was a slave owner but prior to the war, like many western Virginia citizens, was a supporter of the Union. When the war erupted he could not bring himself to wage it against his state.[14]

The following month Jenkins helped assemble a company of volunteer infantrymen known as the Border Rangers. A few weeks earlier he had delivered a rousing speech at a town meeting and afterward, marched a number of men to Green Bottom to sign them up for service. The Rangers would eventually become Company E of the 8th Virginia Cavalry. Various dates exist as to when the company was organized and officers elected. Jenkins would be chosen as the company's first captain and would lead it for the first time during a small skirmish near Scary Creek. During the fighting, Jenkins was slightly wounded in the head. His injuries healed quickly and he was back with his company a month later. During a fight at Piggot's Mill, he was injured again. This time however, his wound was not from enemy fire but was acquired when his horse fell and injured Jenkins' arm.[15]

---

[12] *Ibid*, pp.789, 804.

[13] ***OR*** vol.25, pt.2, p.826; ***OR*** vol.27, pt.2, p.290; Longacre, Edward G., ***The Cavalry at Gettysburg***, p.18.

[14] Dickinson, Jack L., ***8th Virginia Cavalry***, pp.9-10; Wakelyn, ***Biographical Dictionary***, p.252. Green Bottom still stands today and as of this writing is being restored as a museum.

[15] Dickinson, ***8th Virginia Cavalry***, pp.15-16; Eicher, & Eicher, ***High Commands***, p.318. Some sources note Piggot as being spelled with an additional "t."

In quick succession Jenkins rose from captain to lieutenant colonel and then colonel of the regiment. His elevation to regimental command occurred in November 1861. By February the following year, Jenkins evidently felt his services could be used elsewhere and took on the added responsibility of a representative in the First Confederate Congress. However, on 5 August, he resigned his congressional post, having determined he enjoyed military duty to a greater degree than the political wrangling's of government. Upon returning to the army, he was promoted to brigadier general and assigned command of a cavalry brigade. Jenkins' first assignment as a brigadier was in the Department of Southwest Virginia. His brigade served there until 25 November when it was transferred to the Trans-Allegheny Department and came under the jurisdiction of Major General Samuel Jones.[16]

Jenkins was of average build, stood about five feet ten inches tall, and was of average shape. He possessed brown hair which had begun to recede slightly. Although the hair on his head was slowly disappearing, his facial hair was quite impressive. He sported a massively long, full beard which could rival any set of whiskers in the army. His long straight nose split soft blue eyes which accented Jenkins' agreeable mannerism. He was kind, pleasant and always seemed to present his opinion in a manner which could not be refuted or spur conflict. However, although pleasant during conversation, he could be direct and confrontational when a dispute happened to arise.[17]

Crusty William Jones

Lee's desire to move Jenkins to the Valley was spawned by his need to strengthen Stuart. His intention was to move Brigadier General William E. Jones' cavalry brigade to support his Cavalry Division near Culpeper when Jones' troopers returned from their effort against the B & O Railroad. When Jenkins arrived, Lee wanted Jones to bring his riders east. His first communication to Stuart regarding Jones' transfer seems to have occurred on 9 May. "I have had in mind to make a change in the Valley, and order him [Jones] to report with his brigade to you," Lee wrote to his cavalry chieftain. Again, on 11 May, Lee reiterated his wish for Jones' transfer. "I believe I told you," Lee reinforced, "of my desire to place Jenkins' cavalry in the Valley and draw Jones' to you." Continuing, Lee informed Stuart that orders had been issued and Jenkins would be on his way to Staunton, freeing Jones to ride southeast once his command was in condition to travel. Twelve days later, Lee informed Stuart that the move was underway and Jones would be joining him as soon as Jenkins was in position.[18]

When Jones returned from the B & O raid, his command entered the Valley and went into camp near Harrisonburg on 22 May. The following day General Lee issued his instructions to Jones to move to Culpeper and reinforce Stuart. "I

---

[16] Eicher, & Eicher, **High Commands**, p.318.

[17] Dickinson, **8th Virginia Cavalry**, p.16.

[18] **OR**, vol.25, pt.2, pp.789, 792, 820.

desire you to join General Stuart," Lee wrote, "by easy marches, as soon as you can, giving your men and horses proper rest and refreshment." Lee also informed Jones that General Jenkins would soon be in the Valley to relive his pickets so that Grumble's entire command could march to connect with Stuart. "Bring with you your transportation and equipment for service in the field for the summer's campaign on this side of the mountains, and pay particular attention to the thorough organization of your command." If Jones was unaware of his future responsibilities prior to receiving Lee's communication, it should have been obvious to him afterward. His brigade would be campaigning with the Army of Northern Virginia through the summer.[19]

Grumble Jones was truly one of the most loved and hated men in Confederate service. His attitude and personality generated heated and diverse opinions regarding his quality. Jeb Stuart despised him, but Lee thought him a fine cavalryman and appreciated his abilities. Confederate renegade John S. Mosby revered him. The late Thomas Jackson expressed complete trust in very few individuals. One man Stonewall had trusted fully was William Jones. Jones' men, although not fond of his strict discipline and constant demand for drill, respected and worshipped the grumpy old West Pointer. He possessed a piercing tongue and when irritated spoke in profane tirades which became legendary.[20]

In the fall of 1862, when Jones' name was put forth as deserving promotion, Stuart, writing to his wife, openly hoped Jones would be assigned to the infantry. On 24 October, he wrote to Adjutant General Cooper expressing his opinion saying Jones was not "deserving" of promotion. Stuart informed Cooper that he had been acquainted with Jones since early in the war and had been in a position to observe him for some time. He felt that any brigade under the command of Jones would soon lack discipline, be inefficient, and display an unacceptable amount of insubordination. Stuart also told Cooper that Jones would "ruin" any brigade he commanded. Earlier in the war he had praised Jones for his "courage and determination" and called Grumble "the best outpost officer in the army." Within a few short months, Stuart's opinion of Jones quickly deteriorated. By the spring of 1863, their relationship was dreadfully cold. When it became apparent Jones would be joining his division, Stuart, once again, tried to have him transferred to the infantry. Lee, however, would have none of it. In his 9 May message, he informed Stuart that Jones would not become a foot soldier. "I am perfectly willing to transfer him [Jones] to Paxton's brigade if he desires it," Lee wrote Stuart, "but if he does not, I know of no act of his to justify my doing so."[21]

Jones was evidently aware of Stuart's shenanigans and felt much the same regarding his proposed new commander. After becoming aware he was to be transferred, Jones, writing to Secretary Seddon on 24 May, tendered his resignation. "My reason for doing so is my conviction that where I am now ordered my services

---

[19] Frye, Dennis E., *12th Virginia Cavalry*, p.34; *OR*, vol.25, pt.2, p.820.

[20] *CWTI* Staff Members, 'Grumble' Jones: a Personal Profile, *CWTI*, vol.7, no.3, p.35.

[21] *OR*, vol.25, pt.2, p.789; Wittenberg, Eric J., ***Brandy Station***, pp.57-58.

cannot be serviceable to my country," Jones explained. Seddon however refused to accept the resignation and Jones soon found he had no choice but to report to Stuart.[22]

Grumble had not always been such a caustic individual. Born in Virginia's Washington County on 3 May 1824, as a young man, he attended Emory and Henry College before entering West Point. He graduated tenth in a class of thirty-eight and at the age of twenty-four, received the typical second lieutenant brevet upon exiting the academy. Assigned to the U. S. Mounted Rifles, Jones spent three years on the frontier at various outposts from the Midwest to the Pacific Northwest. He received his full second lieutenant's commission on 30 November 1850 and a promotion to first lieutenant four years later.[23]

Few men navigate life without tragedy, and the calamity of William Jones' occurred in 1852. Jones married a young woman named Eliza M. Dunn while on furlough visiting family in Virginia. When his furlough ended, the newlyweds boarded a ship to travel to Jones' new duty station. During the journey, while off the coast of Texas, a heavy storm developed. The vessel floundered in the rolling waters and the ship was ordered abandoned. Life boats were launched and the passengers and crew began clamoring into the boats. As the ship rolled, heavy waves crashed into the evacuees. Jones held his new wife tight but evidently not tight enough. As a wave crashed into them she was literally ripped from his grasp, tumbled overboard and drowned. Although Jones survived, his heart did not. Those who knew him believed not only did William Jones' new wife perish in the heavy waters off Texas but his spirit was lost as well. He became introverted, withdrawn, caustic, and turned his back on God. A few years later he left the army and after traveling in Europe, returned to the states, isolated himself and became a planter.[24]

When the war began, Jones put aside his planting and volunteered for service. A cavalry company was organized in Washington County and Jones, most likely due to his previous service, became its captain. Shortly thereafter he accepted a position in the 1st Virginia Cavalry as captain of Company D and was quickly promoted to major. At the time the regiment was under the command of Colonel Jeb Stuart. Jones and Stuart were polar opposites. Jones was direct, crusty, introverted, paid little attention to women and cared not for the pomp and circumstance of the military. Stuart, on the other hand was flamboyant, extroverted, loved to laugh, and although married, loved the attention of the ladies. Jones was also extremely sensitive and it disturbed him to be placed under a West Pointer who was ten years his junior. The animosity between the two would fester for two years and would be at its height as the cavalry prepared to ride north in early June 1863.[25]

When Stuart received his brigadier's star in the fall of 1861, Jones was promoted to colonel and placed in command of the regiment. General Joseph

---

[22] Wittenberg, ***Brandy Station***, p.57.

[23] Eicher, & Eicher, ***High Commands***, p.325.

[24] McKinney, ***Brandy Station***, p.49; ***CWTI*** Staff, 'Grumble' Jones, ***CWTI***, vol.7, no.3, p.35.

[25] 'Grumble' Jones, ***CWTI***, vol.7, no.3, p.36.

E. Johnston hardly endorsed Jones advancement. Johnston noted that Grumble "commands the strongest troop in the regiment and one which is not surpassed in discipline or spirit by any in the army…" Johnston also noted Jones was "skillful, brave, and zealous to a very high degree." Jones took his place at the head of the regiment on 28 September.[26]

Near the time of his promotion, an incident occurred which allowed Jones to display the qualities that endeared him to his men. One day a local farmer rolled into camp with a wagon loaded with fresh vegetables, meat and butter. Private George Eggleston of Company G captured the moment.

"His prices were exorbitant, but the troopers were hungry for fresh produce, meat, and butter," Eggleston wrote. "The cavalrymen complained, but neverless [sic], some of us were buying with the recklessness of men who do not know at what hour a bullet may draw a red line below all accounts."

"Just then old Jones came out in his yellow coat and his pot hat, looking greatly more like a farmer than the wagon man did. Speaking through his nose, and with that extraordinary deliberation which always made his conversation a caricature of human speech, he asked: 'What are you chargin' for turkeys? What are you chargin' for butter!' And so on through the list, receiving a reply to each query, and carefully noting it in [his] thoroughly organized mind."

After the list was complete Jones called for the regiment's commissary. When the commissary arrived Jones instructed him to "[t]ake these supplies and distribute them equitably among the different messes according to their numbers."

By this time the farmer had become nervous and inquired, "[w]ho's goin' to pay for this?"

"I am," said Jones, "in my own way."

"Well hold on." countered the concerned farmer.

"No, I reckon we won't hold on."

"But I'll send for the colonel of the regiment."

"I am the colonel of this regiment," responded Jones. "And I have ordered these food supplies distributed to men in the messes. The regimental commissary will obey my orders. And as soon as your wagon is emptied, you will get out of this camp in a considerable hurry, or I'll hang you in front of headquarters. There's no court of appeals in this camp. Now git [sic]!"

Private Eggleston believed Jones may have used a much shorter and sharper word than "considerable" to express his desire for the farmer to exit the camp when the contents of his wagon had been depleted. "We were all a little bit sorry that the poor farmer should lose his entire load. And yet we sympathized with old Jones's [sic] remark as he walked away."

"I'll teach these thieves that they can't loot a camp that I'm a runnin'," Jones unsympathetically exclaimed.[27]

In the spring of 1862, elections were held to reset the officers of Jones' regiment. Whether because of his caustic personality, his consistent adherence to

---

[26]   *Ibid*, p.37.

[27]   Driver, Robert J. Jr., *1st Virginia Cavalry*, pp.21-22, 171.

a ridged drill regiment or his politicking for re-election, Jones failed in his bid to retain his post. Being a capable regimental commander, he was not out of a job for long. In September he was placed in command of the 7th Virginia Cavalry. For the remainder of the year Jones proved to his detractors that returning him to command was the right move. His performance during the fall of 1862 was superb and even prompted positive comments from General Stuart. With Jackson's recommendation, Jones was placed in command of Stonewall's old cavalry brigade which had fought in the Valley during the spring of 1862. Jones' new command, known as the "Laurel Brigade," lacked discipline, but the rigid Jones quickly rounded the men into a well structured and drilled fighting unit.[28]

As the year came to a close, Stuart and Jones became more distant. At the recommendation of Jackson, Lee placed Jones in command of the Valley District and effectively separated the two in December. Jones soon found his new responsibilities were going to be difficult to uphold. He possessed a small command but was required to patrol a large area and quickly became frustrated at his inability to accomplish his goals. In addition, Jones struggled with limited supplies and equipment, and he seemed to posses the poorest quality ammunition in the Confederacy. His mood, if it were indeed possible, worsened.[29]

As if his logistical problems were not enough, the citizenry began to protest against Jones and complained to Richmond that he was not protecting them from the Yankees. On 24 December, Union troops under the command of Brigadier General Robert H. Milroy entered Winchester. Milroy arrived a week later and quickly declared his "will" as being "absolute law." The overbearing Milroy proceed to demand the citizens' bow to his every whim and the populace began voicing its complaints to anyone who would listen. Local newspapers criticized Jones for being ineffective. Members of the state legislature sent a petition to Secretary Seddon demanding Jones' replacement. "The well-ascertained sentiment of the people in the Valley of Virginia," wrote Seddon on 26 February, "concurring with the best judgment I can form in relation to the operations of General W. E. Jones in that region, constrains me to request that he may be relieved from his command there..." Lee, to his credit, stood behind Jones. The commanding general was well aware of the difficulties Jones faced and was unwilling to remove a good soldier simply because he possessed a force too small and ill-equipped to get the job done to the satisfaction of an uninformed populace.[30]

Lee responded to Seddon on 4 March, noting that he was ready to pull Jones from the Valley "as soon as circumstances will permit." Lee knew Jones' abilities and went on to defend his actions to Seddon. "I beg leave to say, in justice to General Jones, that I do not know that under the circumstances, with his force and that opposed to him, any one would have done better." Lee went on to explain that Jones' brigade had served with Jackson in the Valley, was organized with men

---

[28] *CWTI* Staff, 'Grumble' Jones, *CWTI*, vol.7, no.3, p.37.

[29] *Ibid*, pp.37-38.

[30] *Ibid*, p.38; Robert Milroy to Mary Milroy, *RHMC*, 18 January 1863; *OR*, vol.25, pt.2, p.641.

from the region, had not seen service outside the area, and it would be difficult to extract the brigade from the region. He proposed promoting a lesser commander to head the brigade and placing Jones at the head of an infantry brigade to satisfy the disgruntled citizenry. Lee's tone however, made it clear he was not in favor of such a move.[31]

When the raid on the B & O Railroad was complete, Lee issued the orders requiring Jones to join his nemesis at Culpeper. Lee had used Seddon's directive as a tool to provide reinforcements to his Cavalry Division while fulfilling the secretary's wish to have Jones extracted from the Valley. Taking Lee's suggestion for his march to be a leisurely stroll, Jones rested his command and remained static for nine days. After making arrangements for the 11th Virginia Cavalry to remain behind until General Jenkins arrived, Jones saddled up the Laurel Brigade and began the roughly fifty mile ride east over the Blue Ridge on 1 June. The 11th would depart two days later and rejoin the brigade near Culpeper on 7 June.[32]

As the summer opened, the men of the Laurel Brigade were well acquainted with the thirty-nine year old Jones. All of the regiments were from Jones' home state. In addition to the 11th, the brigade contained the 6th, 7th, and 12th Cavalry and the 35th Battalion Virginia Cavalry. The men had grown accustomed to Jones' high pitched voice which, during times of excitement became a loud screech. He was a somewhat petite man with a dark complexion and a receding hair line which seemed a bit premature for a man his age. A round robust beard and heavy mustache completely covered his face from the nose down. His eyes were sharp, and when agitated burned with a fire which made most men with any common sense avoid him. At times Jones could be a frightening man when his temper was combined with his tendency to practice the art of profanity. His propensity to disregard the pageantry of the military could be seen in his dress. He never dressed in a fine uniform, preferring to wear comfortable pants, tattered shirts and a common man's coat to which he tacked the insignia of his rank. Although the men saw him as a crusty, opinionated commander, he was respected for they knew he cared deeply about their welfare.[33]

Stuart's Troopers Assemble

Stuart's command, when it assembled at Culpeper Court House the third week of May, consisted of three brigades. The division's second brigade, under Fitzhugh Lee, was a strong group of veteran Virginia regiments which had performed well through the early months of the war. Stuart's third brigade was in the capable hands of Robert E. Lee's second eldest son, Brigadier General William H. F. "Rooney" Lee. Rooney was not a career military man, having graduated from Harvard but had proved himself to be a very capable cavalry officer. The core of William's brigade

---

[31] *Ibid*, p.654.

[32] Armstrong, Richard L., *11th Virginia Cavalry*, p.40; Frye, *12th Virginia Cavalry*, p.34; McDonald, William N., *A History of the Laurel Brigade*, p.130.

[33] *CWTI* Staff, 'Grumble' Jones, *CWTI*, vol.7, no.3, p.36; *OR* vol.25, pt.2, p.825.

was also built from veteran Virginia regiments, but it also contained a regiment of North Carolinians. The first brigade had recently returned from south of the James River. It had been on recruitment duty, attempting to enlist new troopers, during the Chancellorsville fight. The brigade was under the direction of Brigadier General Wade Hampton, a South Carolinian. Hampton a big, powerful man had shown great courage and resolve during the early days of the war, becoming one of Stuart's most trusted and dependable subordinates.[34]

Robert E. Lee had ordered Stuart to concentrate his troopers near Culpeper in a communication sent on 11 May. He wanted his cavalry chief in position and organized for his proposed northward movement which he was preparing to lay out to Davis in Richmond. When Ewell and Longstreet arrived at Culpeper in early June, they forced Stuart's Cavalry Division to shift their encampment to the east toward Brandy Station. Stuart, from his location near the station, would also be in a better position to keep an eye on any Federal cavalry or infantry that may try to move west across the river in an effort to flank his position as was the case during the Chancellorsville encounter.

Initially, only the two Lee's, Fitzhugh and Rooney, made the journey, Hampton remaining behind with his brigade to continue recruiting new troopers. The South Carolinian had also furloughed a number of dismounted men south to procure new mounts. He would follow Stuart and the Lees a few days later when his men had returned and his recruiting efforts had signed up as many new men as possible.[35]

Stuart himself arrived at Culpeper on 20 May and set up his headquarters just east of town in the front yard of Samuel Kellett Bradford's home on his estate of Afton. The general and his staff stayed at the main house, bringing with them Stuart's legendary frivolity. Parties and dancing seemed to be continuous and Stuart's banjo player picked numerous tunes as young ladies from the local area came and went. From time to time Stuart himself could be heard belting out a song before demanding his men join him.[36]

South Carolina's Finest

Wade Hampton III was born 28 March 1818 in the future heart of secession, Charleston, South Carolina. The memorable event of his childhood occurred when he was but three years old. His days took him into the family's yard to explore the world. Also in the yard was a mean goose which would, on occasion, chase the boy around the yard and fly right into the lad's face. Wade, would sometimes chase the bird himself, but most of the time he simply turned and ran to escape, frightened at the beasts approach. As his fourth birthday neared, he was asked what he wanted on his special day. Wishing to be presented with a sword, he was given a small, light, child sized model with a metal blade. Upon his next trip into

---

[34] Boatner, *Dictionary*, pp.370, 475, 477; *OR*, vol.25, pt.2, p.823.

[35] *OR* vol.25, pt.2, p.792; von Borcke, Heros, ***Memoirs of the Confederate War for Independence***, p.363.

[36] Scheel, Eugene M., ***Culpeper: A Virginia County's History Through 1920***, p.202.

the yard, the goose made its customary charge. Wade, standing his ground, thrust the blade straight out in front of him. The gander, none the wiser, failed to realize the danger and proceeded to impale itself upon the small sword. Wade Hampton had made his first kill in battle, at the tender age of four.[37]

If there were ever a royal family of South Carolina, the Hampton clan would have been a good candidate for the designation. Young Wade's grandfather fought in the Revolutionary War and quite possibly became the wealthiest planter and slaveholder in the state. Wade Hampton Senior had established his stake, along with his four brothers, during the late 1700s in the South Carolina backcountry. Through two wars, murdering Cherokee Indians, and hard times, the Hampton clan utilized initiative, optimization, and rugged inner strength to carve out their empire in the rugged wilderness of the unsettled state. Through a series of astute land deals, Wade Senior used his materialistic character to build the empire which he passed on to his family. Unlike a number of principal South Carolinians, he did not begin at the top of the state's nobility. He took his place within the upper echelons of wealth through hard work and drive.[38]

As a young boy, Wade III was entertained by his grandfather telling stories of his exploits during the Revolution. The boy showed signs of a deep and passionate courage and the spirit of a fighter. His grandfather saw the youngster's passion and catered to the boy's desires. One family story identifies Wade's grandfather as the one responsible for procuring the special sword which terminated the four-year-old's tormentor in the yard. The old man also showed the youngster a real man's sword, which he extracted from the possession of a British officer during the nations fight for independence. He showed his grandson how to hold it properly and use it effectively. Grandpa Hampton also gave the boy a pony and educated the lad on how to properly sit and ride the animal. According to family legend, by the age of four Wade III had mastered the pony. He was seventeen years of age when his grandfather passed away. The boy had learned his lessons well and before he passed the elder Hampton made arrangements for his prized Revolutionary War sword to be given to the teenager.[39]

Young Wade's formal education included class work at nearby Rice Creek Academy. When he was not in school, he could usually be found in the outdoors. His exposure to the woods and countryside, and possibly the death of the aggressive gander, sparked a passion for hunting. The stalking of wild game seemed to be an obsession, and he became quite astute at bagging his prey. His favorite game was bear. It seemed the more dangerous his prey the more he enjoyed the quest. Hampton would often go into the woods alone and emerge with the sought after game. When his family's property became inundated with unwanted creatures, they would often solicit the services of Wade to take care of the problem. Throughout his life, his reputation as a hunter grew to mythical proportions. Even future president

---

[37] Andrew, Rod, Jr., ***Wade Hampton: Confederate Warrior to Southern Redeemer***, p.23.

[38] *Ibid*, pp.3-13.

[39] *Ibid*, p.23.

Theodore Roosevelt became a victim, once writing Hampton had killed thirty to forty bear with only a hunting knife. In reality, Wade did subdue at least one bruin with a blade. While trying to protect a pack of hunting dogs, Hampton covertly approached a cornered bear from the rear. Jumping the animal, he quickly slit its throat, killing the beast.[40]

As Hampton matured, he grew into a large physical specimen, a trait which no doubt would assist him later in slaying the bear. His dominating physical presence and strength supplemented his great moral and political courage. His family's prominence in South Carolina society, his interest in weapons and hunting, and his grandfather's tutelage, made the teenager a prime candidate for West Point. However, there seems to have been little to no effort to procure an appointment. Instead, he continued his education at South Carolina College and graduated with a law degree. Wade never put his degree to much use, opting instead to administer the family's plantation which he managed to immense prosperity.

Hampton did not believe a state had the right to secede, arguing that it was not economically feasible for a state to do so. He also questioned the soundness of slavery from an economic point of view. The slavery argument became personal for Hampton when Senator Charles Sumner insulted South Carolina Senator Andrew Butler. Although Congressman Preston Brooks seemed to resolve the matter by his beating of Sumner, the die for Wade Hampton was cast. If it came to war, he would support his state.[41]

Hampton's experience as a businessman prepared him to be a leader, and when the war began, he determined to do his part. He was in Mississippi reviewing his land holdings there when news of Fort Sumter reached him. Returning to South Carolina, Hampton stopped in Montgomery, Alabama on 27 April 1861 to pay a visit to the forming Confederacy's new president. The topic of discussion between Hampton and Davis was the South Carolinian's request for approval to raise a legion of troops. The legion would consist of a six company infantry battalion, a battery of artillery and four companies of cavalry. Davis approved Hampton's request and upon his arrival in South Carolina he posted a call for volunteers on 30 April. He was concerned that turnout would be light since the state had already raised nine regiments of infantry. The response however was overwhelming and more volunteers stepped up than were needed. He soon began a tour of the state to inspect his volunteers and selected the men he thought best suited for immediate field service to form his new legion. On 7 May he reported to the secretary of war that his efforts to populate his command had been very fruitful.[42]

Although he had no military training, Hampton took on the role of the legion's colonel and spent the following weeks drilling and training his new soldiers. By July the men were ready to fight. They boarded a train northward, arriving at

---

[40] *Ibid*, pp.25-26.

[41] Faust, ***Encyclopedia***, p.334; Andrew, ***Wade Hampton***, p.51. South Carolina College would eventually become the University of South Carolina.

[42] Sturkey, ***Hampton Legion***, p.1; ***OR*** Series IV, vol.1, pt.2, p.296.

Manassas Junction before sunrise on 21 July. Before the day was over, the First Battle of Manassas would be history and Hampton along with a good portion of his command would be bloodied. The legion marched to the battlefield and fought during the holding action which allowed Jackson's Brigade to form its defensive line on Henry House Hill. During the fighting, Hampton's lieutenant colonel was killed, having been shot in the head. Hampton's horse was shot from under him before the colonel himself was hit. By his own admission Hampton believed the wound was "slight." He was struck in the face by a ball from a volley of canister fire. Eventually he was forced to turn command over to his only remaining senior officer.[43]

In his after action report, Hampton wrote his men showed "unflinching courage" during the fighting. Although his report noted his own wound as minor, it was more serious than he led people to believe. The ball had lodged itself near his eye and doctors insisted it could not be removed. The wound was painful, and Hampton could not return to his command for a number of days. He soon began to understand how incredibly lucky he was that he had not been killed. In a letter to a family member he wrote that if the ball had struck him a little higher it would have "gone through [his] head." He began to experience headaches and resigned himself to the fact that he would suffer from his injury for the remainder of his days.[44]

Through the winter months of 1861-62, the Hampton Legion remained on the Occoquan River in northeastern Virginia. Many of Hampton's boys were hopeful for active service or returning to South Carolina for the winter. Their desires however would go unfulfilled, as the legion remained on the Occoquan throughout the winter. Periodically, Hampton would receive reports of Yankee activity, but the legion saw no significant action and his command suffered no casualties. While spending the winter recovering from his wound, Hampton took the time to see to the needs of his command. He showed great concern for the wellbeing of the men and worked hard to make sure they had all the accoutrements they required. Some of the men were still equipped with old muskets, and he worked to replace them with new Enfield rifles. Additional rifles and artillery pieces which Hampton had requested months earlier also arrived. Constant pressure on the War Department had proven successful and Hampton managed to acquire almost all the equipment he needed to refit his command. In addition, he managed to procure supplies to keep his soldiers warm and cozy through the winter and took steps to make sure those who became ill were looked after. The quiet atmosphere quickly evaporated when the Federal army under General McClellan shifted its base of operations to the Peninsula during the spring.[45]

Hampton also put the winter months to good use when he struck up a friendship with General Joe Johnston. The two became quite close and Johnston

---

[43] Davis, William C., *Battle at Bull Run*, pp.194-195; Andrew, *Wade Hampton*, pp.77, 79; *OR* vol.2, p.567.

[44] *OR* vol.2, p.567; Andrew, *Wade Hampton*, p.80.

[45] Andrew, *Wade Hampton*, p.83; Sturkey, *Hampton Legion*, p.7.

saw that although Hampton was not trained militarily, he was a strong presence on the battlefield and in camp. Hampton was first placed in command of a brigade by Adjutant General Cooper on 22 October, but the brigade consisted only of his legion. Johnston, recognizing the South Carolinians leadership qualities, added three additional regiments to the brigade on 14 January, and recommended him for promotion. When winter broke, Hampton marched his brigade to the Peninsula where it fought in a few skirmishes. A week after receiving his brigadier's star, Hampton and his boys found themselves embroiled in the Battle of Fair Oaks.[46]

While leading his command in battle, Hampton was once again wounded. As he directed his brigade from atop his horse, he was struck in the foot by a bullet. As the projectile passed through his boot, it flipped over and drove its base into his flesh. The bullet then impacted the bone, breaking his foot. Hampton refusing to leave the field, choosing to remain on his horse as the fighting swirled around him. Ignoring the pain, he called to his surgeon, and as he remained mounted, instructed the doctor to remove the bullet. As the surgeon prepared to dismount, his horse was shot from under him. Gathering himself, the doctor managed to extract the missile from Hampton's foot before he was hit in the arm. The wound was much more serious than Hampton's and would cost the surgeon his limb.

Hampton's superior praised the new general, noting in his report that he "was remarkable for coolness, promptness, and decided practical ability as a leader of men in difficult and dangerous circumstances." Eight days after the battle Hampton's foot was so swollen that he could only wear a slipper. Although he could still ride a horse, and initially felt he should stay with the army, he eventually hobbled home on his crutches to South Carolina. He recovered quickly and was back in Richmond on 24 June, the day before The Seven Days erupted.[47]

Organizational realities made the continued utilization of legions in the Army of Northern Virginia difficult and in early June, while he was away, the Hampton Legion was disbanded, the various elements being dispersed to the artillery, cavalry and infantry. When Hampton returned, he no longer had a command. As the fighting raged, the South Carolinian volunteered for various duties until an opening arose at the head of one of Stonewall Jackson's brigades. The previous commander had been mortally wounded and Hampton stepped into the position on 28 June. None of the regiments in his new brigade, all of which were from Virginia, were familiar with him. The situation must have been a bit unnerving for both the soldiers and Hampton, with the command change taking place during a lull in the heavy fighting. The brigade however, was underutilized and took a miniscule fourteen casualties.[48]

When the fighting ended, Hampton was once more without a command. His skill as a military leader had been put to the test and he had proven he was up to the challenge. Although he was not a connoisseur of military text and literature, or

---

[46] *OR* vol.5, pp.913, 1030; Tagg, **Generals**, p.360.

[47] *OR* vol.11, pt.1, p.991; Andrew, **Wade Hampton**, pp.96, 98.

[48] Andrew, **Wade Hampton**, pp.100-101, 103; *OR* vol.11, pt.2, pp.484, 506.

a skilled map-reader, he had displayed a knack for reading terrain. His experiences as a hunter had provided him with an astute mind for assessing topography and how to utilize the features of the land to his advantage. The skills learned as a youth and young man would certainly come in handy while employed in his next command position. On 26 July, Hampton was transferred to the cavalry and given command of a brigade in Jeb Stuart's Cavalry Division. He initially expressed reservations about the move, but he accepted the post. Although in his mid-forties, the stout South Carolinian still possessed the endurance required to meet the rigors of cavalry operations.

Wade Hampton III was a mountain of a man with a reputation to match. *MOLLUS Collection, USAHEC*

Hampton's tenure would make him the division's senior brigade commander. His brigade rode with Lee's army as it advanced into Maryland in the fall of 1862 and fought near South Mountain as McClellan's army pressed Lee's rear. He participated in Stuart's Chambersburg Raid and conducted a series of his own cavalry raids during December. Hampton's reputation continued to grow and shortly after the Battle of Fredericksburg, he was once again considered for command of an infantry brigade. Although he had initially wished to stay with the infantry upon his transfer to the cavalry, he must have had a change of heart regarding mounted service. He declined the opportunity, choosing to remain with his horsemen.[49]

---

[49]   Tagg, ***Generals***, p.360.

Hampton acknowledged Stuart's abilities as a cavalry commander, but, like Grumble Jones, detested some of his division commander's habits and traits. He felt the Virginia regiments received preferential treatment, while his Carolinians were poorly treated and did not receive the same benefits as Stuart's home state boys. He also was not a supporter of Stuart's flamboyant attitude, his flashy social gatherings and the unnecessary cavalry reviews which Stuart seemed to take great pride in presenting and overseeing. His dislike of Stuart's activities grew his own deep desire to make sure the men of his command received the care they required. Hampton's troopers repaid him with a deep devotion that made them extremely effective on the battlefield. His coolness during a fight was legendary. His tone was the same, whether around the campfire or ordering his men into a thick fight.[50]

Hampton's brigade spent the spring of 1863 in Southern Virginia. Hard riding and raiding had worn the men and horses down, forcing the period of replenishment and refit south of the James River. General Lee's concern for the welfare of his cavalry horses prompted the dispersal. During the latter half of April, Lee began to urge the return of Hampton. On the 20 April he wrote Stuart that he "hope[d]" Hampton would bring his brigade back to the army as soon as it was ready. However, Lee expressed concern that if Hampton returned too soon Stuart might not be able to keep his cavalry concentrated "before the grazing season" opened. Lee, although he had cause to be concerned, Hampton did not begin his return trip until 3 May. By that time, the spring grasses were beginning to push their stalks upward.[51]

By 25 May, Hampton's 2,200 man brigade was in the Culpeper area and ready for duty. Of his six regiments, only five were present. The sixth, Georgia's Phillips Legion Cavalry, was on picket duty in the Fredericksburg area and would not join Hampton until after the campaign northward was underway. Ready for duty at Culpeper were the 1st and 2nd South Carolina, the 1st North Carolina, Cobb's Legion Cavalry from Georgia and the Jeff Davis Legion from Mississippi.[52]

The General's Nephew

By the time Hampton arrived with his brigade, Stuart's second brigade, which consisting of the 1st through 5th Virginia Cavalry, were already at Culpeper. Officially it was in the capable hands of the commanding general's nephew, Fitzhugh Lee. During the middle of May, the regiments were somewhat spread out. General Lee's communication of the 11th prompted Stuart to issue orders for them to concentrate at Culpeper. On 16 May, the 1st Virginia moved its camp. The 2nd Virginia was bivouacked along the Rapidan River on 13 May but by the 20th it was also camped near Culpeper. The 3rd Virginia also arrived in the Culpeper area during mid-May. The 4th regiment however was tardy. It remained on picket duty

---

[50] Sutherland, *Seasons of War*, p.234; Haines, Douglas Craig, Jeb Stuart's Advance to Gettysburg, *GM*, Issue 29, p.37.

[51] Jordon, Weymouth T., *NCT*, vol.II, p.3; *OR* vol.25, pt.2, pp.737-738.

[52] *OR* vol.25, pt.2, p.825.

along the lower Rappahannock to cover the left flank of Hill's Corps and would not receive orders to ride north until 7 June. The 5th regiment had been in the vicinity of Spotsylvania Court House on 7 May, but by 18 May, it was in Culpeper. A sixth regiment, the 1st Maryland Battalion, Also belonged to Lee's command. It was on detached service in the Shenandoah Valley and would not be ordered to join the remainder of the brigade. It would eventually ride north with the vanguard of Lee's infantry advance.[53]

Fitz Lee's identification of the Federal right at Chancellorsville may have been the biggest moment in his short military career. If he had been more experienced, he would have understood that Jackson's silent response was nothing more than a commanding officer responding to a subordinate doing his duty. The twenty-seven-year-old Lee had been a member of the military for almost eleven years, four of which had been spent training at West Point. Perhaps the best description of Lee was written by Heros von Borcke. Von Borcke, a big Prussian soldier of fortune who served on Stuart's staff noted Lee was "…a short, thick-set man, with a tendency toward stoutness, but still a first-rate horseman. He had a fresh, intelligent face with an extraordinary full, flowing beard. He was characterized by an especially jolly temperament and an irrepressible sense of humor…" Lee's propensity for humor would later earn him the nickname "laughing cavalier." He had "a merry eye" and was "overflowing with animal spirit." His merriment was so prominent that times of seriousness seemed abnormal for him. Physically he possessed "a square head and short neck" which was placed atop sturdy wide shoulders.[54]

Lee was born on 19 November 1835, on the family plantation of "Clermont" in Virginia's Fairfax County. His father, Sidney S. Lee, was a talented and respected naval officer. "Light-Horse Harry" was Fitzhugh's grandfather, which allowed him to claim some of his uncle's esteemed pedigree. Fitz's great-great-grandfather, George Mason, was the principle author of the Virginia Declaration of Rights; the document which formed the basis for the first ten amendments to the Constitution. While still a boy, young Fitz exhibited his reputation for fun and merriment. With his father away for a good portion of his youth, he came under the influence of the females of the family. His close ties with the womenfolk however, did not hamper

---

[53] Driver, *1st Virginia Cavalry*, p.60; Driver, Robert J. Jr., *2nd Virginia Cavalry*, p.80; Stiles, Kenneth L., *4th Virginia Cavalry*, pp.27-28; Driver, Robert J. Jr., *5th Virginia Cavalry*, p.51; *OR* vol.27, pt.3, p.859; *OR* vol.27, pt.2, p.290. The 1st Maryland Battalion was stationed in the Valley and during the winter and spring of 1863 conducted scouting missions and sorties against the Federals occupying Winchester and the surrounding areas of the Lower Valley. When Ewell moved his corps northward up the Valley during the first stage of the campaign, he took control of the battalion and it, except for Company A, conducted expeditions on the edges of the corps' line of march. Company A was attached to Ewell's headquarters to perform "special service on important occasions." Goldsborough, William W., *The Maryland Line in the Confederate Army: 1861-1865*, p.176.

[54] Driver, *1st Virginia Cavalry*, p.35; Tagg, **Generals**, p.362. Historian Douglas S. Freeman, if not the originator of the moniker, seems to be one of the first to utilize the nickname.

his manliness and he partook in manly activities including hunting, fishing and the equestrian arts. His favorite activity however, seemed to be wrestling with his five younger brothers.

Fitzhugh, like his famous uncle, was a West Point graduate but unlike Robert, he was not a stellar cadet. He graduated fourth from the bottom in a class of forty-nine and was nearly expelled by his uncle, who was the institution's superintendant at the time, for misconduct. While his preponderance for amusement won him a number of friends, it also interrupted his studies, and his performance suffered. He was particularly poor in mathematics which he had been ill prepared to deal with in the context of the rigorous curriculum of the academy. Although Lee could and did exhibit seriousness when required, he seemed to do just enough to get by. Upon graduation in 1856, he received his second lieutenant brevet and was assigned to the fledgling 2nd U. S. Cavalry.[55]

Posted to frontier duty in Texas, the foremost event of his pre-war service occurred during an encounter with a Comanche raiding party. During the fighting, Lee, when confronted by one of his antagonist, raised his pistol at the same moment the Comanche drew down on him with his bow. Both men fired in the same instant. Lee's ball entered the brave's skull, killing him instantly. The arrow struck Lee in the chest piercing his lung and impaling him on the shaft, the arrowhead projecting out his back. Lee slumped against a tree and sank to the ground. Those around him assumed he would not survive but Lee proved tougher than expected and was not ready to give up his life. The unit's surgeon extracted the arrow, placed salt on the wound and tried to make him comfortable. Slowly Lee improved. When he was strong enough, he was transferred east and began a stint as assistant instructor of tactics at West Point. He was teaching at his alma mater when the war began.[56]

Lee was actually appointed first lieutenant in the fledgling Confederate Army on 16 March 1861, over two months before he resigned his commission. In a possible effort to purchase his loyalty, he was promoted to first lieutenant in the Regular Army on 31 March. A few weeks later, following the lead of his native state, he resigned from the army. He initially served as assistant adjutant general on the staff of General Beauregard before serving as a captain on General Ewell's staff at Manassas. He was assigned to the 1st Virginia Cavalry when Jeb Stuart was made colonel of the regiment. Along with his new post came a promotion to lieutenant colonel on 27 September. When Stuart was elevated to brigade general and left the regiment, Grumble Jones took command, but when Jones was ousted in the spring of 1862, Lee took over the 7th Virginia and ascended to the colonelcy of the regiment. At the time he became colonel, the regiment was before Yorktown on the Peninsula preparing to confront McClellan's gathering army.[57]

---

[55] Faust, ***Encyclopedia***, p.429; Longacre, Edward G., ***Fitz Lee***, p.6; Eicher, & Eicher, ***High Commands***, p.347.

[56] Longacre, Edward G., ***Fitz Lee: A military Biography of Major General Fitzhugh Lee, C.S.A.***, pp.3-4.

[57] Eicher, & Eicher, ***High Commands***, p.347; Driver, ***1st Virginia Cavalry***, pp.17, 32, 198.

Lee showed that Stuart's trust in him was not misplaced as the Confederates delayed and then eventually halted McClellan before Richmond at Fair Oaks. When Stuart selected his horsemen for his famous ride around McClellan's army, Lee was the first unit on the general's list. The accomplishments of the expedition were quickly written into Confederate lore by the press and Lee was credited with much of its success by Stuart. In an addendum to his official report, Stuart recommended "Col. Fitzhugh Lee, First Virginia Cavalry, for promotion as brigadier-general of cavalry. In my estimation," Stuart continued, "no one in the Confederacy possesses more of the elements of what a brigadier of cavalry ought to be than he."[58]

Stuart's recommendation was acted on when Lee was awarded a brigadier generalship on 24 July. However, the good feelings did not last long. In August, Lee's command was late for the cavalry gathering as the Second Manassas Campaign got underway. The result was the capture of Stuart's cape and famous plumed hat. All was forgiven a few days later when Fitz raided Catlett's Station, taking a number of prisoners and capturing Federal General John Pope's headquarters' wagon. In the wagon were a number of prized articles including Pope's dress uniform and a Federal general's hat with a large plume. Lee wasted no time in outfitting himself in the uniform, much to the delight of his command. He presented the captured uniform and hat as partial payment for the previous loss of his commander's articles. Although all may not have been forgiven, the gesture made the situation tolerable and Lee regained a good portion of his reputation.[59]

During the Maryland Campaign, Fitz once again expanded his reputation. As General D. H. Hill pulled his battered division back from the battlefield at South Mountain, Fitz covered his withdrawal. He then imposed himself between his uncle's army and General McClellan's, helping to delay the Federal advance long enough to allow the Confederates to establish a strong defensive position near Sharpsburg. After the battle was over, and General Lee began extracting his army, Fitz relieved General Early's picket line sometime between 10 and 11 p.m. and performed a stubborn rear guard action. The sluggish Federal response to General Lee's withdrawal allowed the Confederates to successfully cross the river and make good their escape. Fitz' uncle typically refrained from praising family in his official documents. Fitz however, forced his uncle's hand and the general had to acknowledge his nephew's activities. Lee noted Fitz "efficiently and skillfully" covered the withdrawal from South Mountain. Of the extraction from the Sharpsburg area, General Lee wrote that Fitz "covered our movement with boldness and success."[60]

In the spring of 1863, Fitz became embroiled in a scrap with a numerically superior force of Federal cavalry near Kelly's Ford along the Rappahannock River. Federal General William Averell approached the ford before sunrise on the morning of 17 March, only to find it defended by Lee's pickets. After two hours

---

[58] *OR* vol.11, pt.1, pp.1036, 1041.

[59] Driver, *1st Virginia Cavalry*, p.44; Tagg, *Generals*, p.363.

[60] Tagg, *Generals*, p.363; *OR* vol.19, pt.1, pp.147, 151, 972.

of fighting, Lee's stubborn pickets were driven from their position. After crossing the river, the Federals engaged Fitz' brigade. The fighting lasted five hours, with a number of attacks and counterattacks being made. Lee's outnumbered riders were pushed back for a mile but counterattacked to stabilize their line with a classic cavalry charge. When the warring parties finally disengaged, neither side could claim a decisive victory. Even though the Federals had pulled back, for the first time since the war had begun, they gave as well as they received. Fitz, although roughed up, had fought hard, his own horse being shot out from under him. Two days after the battle, General Lee, in a letter to his wife, expressed pleasure with Fitz' work. "…[H]e has his brigade in hand & is prompt," the commanding general noted. "I trust he will make a good soldier & serve his country well."[61]

A timely report by Fitzhugh to Stuart at Chancellorsville set in motion the events which lead to the crushing of Hooker's flank and Lee's improbable victory. Fitz' identification of the Federal line to Jackson from the crest of the bare knoll provided Jackson with additional critical intelligence. The information had prompted Jackson to march his column to the Old Orange Turnpike before turning east; a decision which would make his attack a resounding success. When the fighting at Chancellorsville died away, Fitzhugh Lee, through deeds, had earned the trust of not only his cavalry commander but also the trust of his famous uncle. Unfortunately for Fitz, he would spend the early part of the Gettysburg Campaign confined to an ambulance, battling an attack of "inflammatory rheumatism." His pain would eventually sideline him until the latter half of June.[62]

While Lee's relationship with Stuart was warm and cordial, his attitude toward Wade Hampton was somewhat frosty. Lee was an opinionated individual and looked upon Hampton as an outsider who owed his position in the army to his relationship with President Davis. Fitz also despised Hampton's path to power and the fact that he had no military training. Hampton's satisfactory record seemed to carry little if any weight with Lee. The other issue which irritated Fitz was the fact that Hampton ranked him. Lee had earned his position through hard work and years of training and experience. In his mind, Hampton had used his influence and money to form an organization during the onset of the war and make himself its leader. Finally, Fitzhugh possessed a somewhat reserved opinion regarding slavery and may have developed a dislike for Hampton simply because the South Carolinian owned thousands of them.[63]

The Framer from Lynchburg

As Stuart's cavalry concentrated at Culpeper, Colonel Thomas Taylor Munford, was in command of the stricken Fitz Lee's regiments. Munford, the colonel of the 2nd Virginia, would remain in command until Lee was well enough to return.

---

[61] Faust, ***Encyclopedia***, p.411; Dowdey & Manarin, ***Wartime Papers***, pp.414-415.

[62] Tagg, ***Generals***, p.364. After the war Thomas T. Munford noted that Lee was incapacitated due to being kicked by a mule or a horse.

[63] Longacre, ***Fitz Lee***, pp.69-70.

Born on 29 March 1831, in Richmond, he was the son of Colonel George Wythe Munford, who, for twenty-five years served as secretary of the commonwealth. Thomas attended the Virginia Military Institute and graduated from the institution in 1852. He entered the business world shortly after leaving school, becoming a planter. He relocated for a brief time during 1857-58 to plant cotton in Carroll County, Mississippi, but returned to Virginia and was residing in Lynchburg when the war began.

With hostilities eminent, Munford joined a local company, the Radford Rangers which, on 8 May 1861, become Company G of the 2nd Virginia Cavalry. Originally a first lieutenant, when the regiment was later reorganized he was promoted to major. Munford fought with the regiment at Manassas and a few weeks later was promoted to lieutenant colonel. When the 2nd Virginia was reorganized in the spring of 1862, Munford was elected its colonel shortly before the regiment was assigned to Ewell's Division of Jackson's army in the Shenandoah Valley. He fought at Cross Keys and Port Republic before transferring with Jackson's command to the Peninsula.[64]

Munford's regiment spent the major portion of August 1862, picketing the Rappahannock near Waterloo Bridge. Late in the month, he received orders to report to General Jackson. Leaving one squadron behind, Munford's command formed the advance of Jackson's Corps as it moved toward what would become the Second Battle of Manassas. As the army advanced, he established pickets at the roads along Jackson's line of march which led toward Federal positions. During the battle, he deployed his regiment on Jackson's left, protecting the general's flank from the vicinity of Sudley Church. As the regiment took position, it encountered a group of enemy cavalry which Munford summarily charged. A severe hand to hand fight ensued and a number of Munford's officers and men were wounded. He himself, received a saber cut across the head and his horse was killed. Three days later he was ordered to Leesburg to deal with a Federal raiding party that was harassing the locals in the area. After dispatching the marauders, the 2nd Virginia rode along the Potomac collecting cattle.[65]

Munford had proven his abilities were more than adequate and was deserving of higher command. Late in the campaign, the regiment was assigned to the "Laurel Brigade," then under the command of Brigadier General Beverly Robertson. Stuart however, despised Robertson and shortly after the fighting was over, Robertson was relieved, assigned to recruitment duties and sent to North Carolina. Munford stepped in and took command of the brigade on 4 September, as the opening moves of the Maryland Campaign commenced.[66]

When the Federals increased the pace of their pursuit and pressed toward South Mountain, Munford found himself forced into a difficult situation. Ordered to hold Crampton's Gap "at all hazards," he watched as the Federals gathered in

---

[64] Driver, *2nd Virginia Cavalry*, pp.2, 252

[65] *Ibid*, pp.55-58; *OR* vol.12, pt.2, pp.747-749.

[66] Wittenberg, **Brandy Station**, p.56; Driver, *2nd Virginia Cavalry*, p.59; *OR* vol.19, pt.1, p.825.

the valley before him. At his disposal were only 300 men from the 16th and 41st Virginia Infantry regiments and 200 men form his own command. His brigade had been partitioned and dispersed for other duties and with the men available to him Munford took position behind a stone wall and waited for the Federals. When the slow moving Yankees finally pressed forward to the gap, Munford's meager force fought hard. From behind their naturally strong position, they did heavy damage to the Federal advance. During the fight, fortunately for Munford, he received about 300 additional men in the form of the 6th and 12th Virginia Infantry regiments. Together, under Munford's direction, the Confederates held the gap for over two hours. Timely reinforcements from two additional regiments of North Carolinians and Georgians, under Brigadier General Howell Cobb, helped Munford hold the position. Eventually the Confederates were forced from the mountain but not before Munford had done as asked, holding the pass at all costs. Only after command was turned over to Cobb were the Confederates driven from their position. Fourteen Federal regiments fought against the dug in Rebels, suffering 113 men killed and another 418 wounded. The stiff defense of Crampton's Gap bought Lee much needed time to concentrate his dispersed army and may have been Munford's finest hour.[67]

Munford's superior service record prompted Stuart to request his promotion to brigadier general. Writing on 25 October, Stuart painted a glowing picture of the Virginia planter.

> "Respectfully recommended that Colonel Thomas T. Munford be appointed brigadier-general, and assigned to command of the brigade now commanded by him as colonel. My reasons for this recommendation are that no colonel in the brigade has been as deserving. He is a gallant soldier, a daring and skilful [sic] officer, and is thoroughly identified with the brigade as its leader. As a partizan [sic] he has no superior. While others not in the brigade might command a higher tribute for ability and military genius, yet when I consider the claims of the Colonel for promotion, and the gallant service he has rendered, I am constrained to ask that he receive this merited reward."[68]

Unfortunately for Munford and Stuart, General Lee did not see the situation in the same light. Instead, he took the recommendation of General Jackson and placed Grumble Jones in command of the Laurel Brigade, a move which increased Stuart's animosity toward Jones, and Munford returned to command of the 2nd Virginia. On 10 November 1862, orders were issued transferring Munford's regiment to Fitz Lee's brigade. By 26 November, Munford's troopers had joined their new brigade and were camped five miles southwest of Fredericksburg. The fighting during

---

[67] *OR* vol.19, pt.1, p.183; Harsh, Joseph L., ***Taken at the Flood: Robert E. Lee and Confederate Strategy in the Maryland Campaign of 1862***, p.280-282.

[68] Driver, *2nd Virginia Cavalry*, p.62.

the Battle of Fredericksburg offered little opportunity for Munford to display his talents, and by the end of the year the regiment had settled into winter camp near Guiney's Station. The boredom of winter was interrupted periodically by scouting missions and picket duty along the Rappahannock.[69]

Munford missed another opportunity to showcase his abilities when General Averell crossed the river on 17 March. While the 2nd Virginia battled with the rest of Fitz Lee's brigade near Kelly's Ford, Munford was away in Culpeper. The colonel was presiding over court-martial proceedings, and by the time he became aware of the fighting, it was too late to join his command.[70]

A few weeks later as events unfolded near Chancellorsville, Munford and his regiment were detailed to accompany Jackson's column as it traversed its route to Hooker's flank. With the remainder of Fitz Lee's brigade picketing the roads leading to the flank and rear of Jackson's line of march, Munford rode at the head of the column with the general. He remembered Jackson being in good spirits and contemplating the fact that Hooker had more troops at his disposal than the Federal general could handle. "I wish I could see the time when I had as many as I wanted," Munford recalled Jackson saying. As the column negotiated the Brock Road, the 2nd ran into an enemy cavalry picket which the Virginians quickly dispatched. When the head of the column struck the Old Orange Turnpike, Munford turned the column east and immediately encountered another Federal cavalry picket which was also driven in. As the battle lines formed, he positioned his force on the left of General Rodes' Division, on the north end of the battle line.[71]

Munford's orders, which he received directly from Jackson, were to guard the left flank of the line and to seize and hold the road to Ely's Ford. When the advance began, Munford pushed forward and managed to find and capture General Howard's commissary, including as many prisoners as they had men to guard them, and six to eight freshly slaughtered cattle. As late evening began to settle over the battlefield, Munford turned his attention to the second part of his orders and rode out toward Ely's Ford. The Virginians quickly cleared the road of Federal cavalry pickets and drove the enemy back to the river.[72]

Throughout the war Munford had proven himself on the field of battle, had not shirked his duties within the midst of heavy fighting and was generally regarded as a fine leader of men. Although Stuart considered him brigadier material, and had once again recommended him for promotion in March, Munford would enter the Gettysburg Campaign as a colonel. At thirty-two years of age, his hair was turning prematurely gray, but his large, heavy mustache, remained dark and thick making him easy to spot in a crowd. It could be argued that Munford was a more talented brigade commander than two or three of the six men in charge of cavalry brigades

---

[69] *OR* vol.25, pt.2, pp.705, 712.

[70] *OR* vol.25, pt.1, p.62.

[71] Driver, *2nd Virginia Cavalry*, pp.79-80.

[72] *Ibid*, p.80.

during the campaign. Events during the coming crusade would prove that passing over him may have been a serious mistake.[73]

The General's Son

Stuart's remaining brigade at Culpeper was under the command of William Henry Fitzhugh Lee. William, the second son of the commanding general was born 31 May 1837 at his mother's grand estate of Arlington. For some reason, which is unknown, Robert began calling his son "Rooney." The name stuck and William, for the remainder of his life would be known within and outside the family by the nickname. Rooney was an energetic, outgoing child who always seemed to be romping around creating a ruckus. On one occasion, when he was quite small, Rooney's mother lost track of him for a moment. Before she realized it, the youngster had scaled his father's writing desk and was firmly planted on the desktop before his mother finally noticed him. The boy seemed to always treat his father or mother's writing tools as toys for his amusement. On one particular instance, while Mary was writing a letter, Rooney played with and pulled on her paper and pen, and when he tired of tormenting her, he began attempting to throw his father's hat out the window.[74]

Rooney's propensity for mischief got him into trouble on more than a few occasions. His most damaging adventure occurred when he was eight-years-old. After having been instructed to remain in the yard and play, the lure of a nearby horse stable got the best of the boy and he wandered over to see the animals. Inside the barn workers were putting up hay for the horses and Rooney became enthralled with the straw cutter. After watching how the machine worked, Rooney tried to cut some straw and ended up removing the ends of two fingers on his left hand. The cutter took the end of his index finger to the root of the nail, and the tip of his second finger at the first knuckle. An orderly carried the boy to a nearby hospital, but unfortunately the doctor was away and would not return for an hour and a half. During the wait, Rooney sat quietly, his fingers bleeding heavily. When the orderly, who sat with him, showed concern for his welfare, Rooney rebuke him for making a big deal of his plight. Others present were shocked at the youth's calm attitude. Although his fingers hurt, he refused to complain to anyone. Those present noted that grown men had come in with comparable injuries and babbled like children. Neither of his parents were home at the time of the accident. When Robert returned that evening he found his son sitting quietly by the fire, his hand heavily bandaged, waiting for his supper. It was not until the middle of the night, when Rooney awoke to see his concerned father next to his bed that he shed his

---

[73] Wittenberg, ***Brandy Station***, p.53; McKinney, ***Brandy Station***, p.41; Longacre, ***The Cavalry at Gettysburg***, p.18.

[74] Daughtry, Mary Bandy, ***Gray Cavalier: The Life and Wars of General W. H. F. "Rooney" Lee***, pp.1-3.

first tear over his wounded hand. The tears were not for the pain in his hand but the pain of his worried father.[75]

When Rooney's father returned to West Point as its superintendent in the fall of 1852, he began an investigation to find a suitable school for the fifteen-year-old teen. Although Lee was hesitant to place his son in any of the schools in New York City, William finally entered a boarding school run by a Mr. Peugnet within the city. The colonel was concerned over his mischievous son's possible exposure to the sins of the city. "All things being equal I prefer a school in the country," Lee wrote, "though for certain consideration I have placed Rooney in the city of New York and shall keep him there this year. Young men must not expect to escape contact with evil, but must learn not to be contaminated by it. That virtue is worth but little that requires constant watching and removal from temptation." By all accounts Rooney's performance at Mr. Peugnet's school was satisfactory. His father tried to keep him in line by relaying the stories of West Point cadets who had not adhered to their studies and had been released from the academy and sent home in shame. Whether the colonel's prompting influenced Rooney or not, the boy was aware of his parent's concern regarding his recklessness. Robert knew of Rooney's sensitivity to his parent's feelings and used it to steady the boy's course.[76]

Robert E. Lee's second son, William Henry Fitzhugh Lee, was not a West Pointer but became a solid officer none the less. *LOC*

---

[75] *Ibid*, pp.6-7.

[76] *Ibid*, pp.13-14.

The disappointment of Rooney's life occurred when he was unable to follow his father and older brother, Custis to West Point. His little sister Agnes recorded his disappointment in her journal. "I am sorry it is such a disappointment to him," she wrote. "He is so anxious to enter the army in some way." After finishing his second year at Mr. Peugnet's school, Rooney returned to Arlington. As the summer ended he embarked upon the next phase of his education when he entered Harvard University. Perhaps feeling somewhat responsible for his son not receiving an appointment to the academy, Robert traveled with him to Cambridge. The colonel helped his son get established in his new environment before departing, leaving his second born to the pursuit of his studies. Rooney's disciplinary and academic record was not stellar. By the spring of in 1857 he was firmly positioned in the bottom half of his class.[77]

William Lee's career path once again changed that spring, when he decided to return to the profession of his first love. After recommendations from two uncles, his father's boss, General Winfield Scott, offered Rooney a commission as a second lieutenant in the 6th U. S. Infantry. That spring, Rooney's father had complained his son was distant and uncommunicative, which may have been why the colonel was completely unaware of the appointment until it had been offered. Wishing to join his father's regiment, the 2nd Cavalry, Rooney initially hesitated to accept the appointment. He wrote to his mother and indicated his wish to leave the decision to his parents. "My only objection is your's [sic] and Pa's pleasure & happiness & will joyfully make any sacrifice that you wish." Respecting his parent's desires, Rooney accepted the appointment and entered upon a military career, leaving his studies at Harvard three weeks before the end of his third year.[78]

The next fall saw the passing of Rooney's grandfather, George Washington Parke Custis. Custis' large estate and land holdings were bequeathed to his family. Rooney, who his father had now begun to address as Fitzhugh, became the owner of White House Plantation along the Pamunkey River in New Kent County. The plantation, like the majority of George Custis' holdings, had fallen into disrepair and lacked operating capital. Rooney's father, as executor of the estate, worked to straighten out the mess for his children.

The other major event of Rooney Lee's antebellum life occurred in the spring of 1859. A few years earlier, he had met Charlotte Georgina Wickham and on 23 March, the two were married in a ceremony attended by a large number of guests. Rooney decided to settle down and raise a family. He resigned his commission on 31 May and the couple stayed at Arlington until the White House Plantation could be rendered habitable. Two years later, Charlotte gave birth to their first child, a boy, who they named Robert Edward Lee III. In two years White House had gone from a rundown dilapidated property to a prosperous farm. The capital expenditures for equipment, animals, and improvements to the structures had not been in vain for the property actually turned a profit for the year 1860. Life was

---

[77] *Ibid*, pp.17, 19.

[78] *Ibid*, pp.33-34.

good for Rooney Lee; however, things would quickly change as the war was just around the corner.[79]

Like his father, Rooney volunteered for service with his native state when it seceded and was initially commissioned a captain and later a major in the cavalry. First posted in western Virginia, on 18 January 1862, he was made lieutenant colonel of the 9th Virginia Cavalry. Three months later he was promoted to colonel and given command of the regiment. He guided his command through Stuart's ride around McClellan during the Peninsula Campaign where he performed his duties well enough to receive a recommendation for promotion from Stuart. Within the same addendum to his report which he praised Fitz Lee, Stuart noted that "Col. W. H. F. Lee, rivaling his cousin in the daring exploits of this expedition, established a like claim to promotion to the same grade." In a congratulatory order to the cavalry brigade, Stuart note that he would "certainly despair of no enterprise when he can hold such guarantees of success as Cols. Fitzhugh Lee [and] W. H. F. Lee… and their brave and devoted commands."[80]

Rooney always seemed be at the front of his command and during battle risked personal safety to inspire his troopers. One specific instance, which occurred during the Sharpsburg Campaign, took place just outside of Boonsboro, Maryland when William's horse was shot from under him. The animal fell on him, pinning him, to the ground. As the Rebels fell back, Yankee cavalry assembled in the area but did not notice Lee, who remained unconscious under his horse. Back and forth the cavalry charged, the Rebels taking the area, then the Yankees. Some of Lee's troopers were eventually able to extract him from under the horse, but were unable to get him off the field. Luck was on Rooney's side that day, for while enemy cavalry were nearby, he was not captured and managed to crawl to a nearby field where he was discovered by two Confederates who were disconnected from their unit. The two men helped the staggered Lee to a farm where they procured a horse and managed to return to the safety of the Confederate lines.[81]

William's promotion to brigadier general came through the same day as the horse incident near Boonsboro, 15 September 1862. Less than a month later, he was placed in command of Stuart's third brigade but saw little action during the winter of 1862-63. Other than a minor engagement along the Rappahannock River on 4 December and participation in a raid against Dumfries and Fairfax Station, the brigade remained inactive. During the Chancellorsville Campaign, Rooney spent time harassing General Averell before riding off to confront the main body of General Stoneman's raiding party. Stuart noted in his report that Lee showed "sagacity and good conduct throughout" the fighting and displayed "great

---

[79] *Ibid*, pp.41, 43, 48-49. The White House Plantation was the home of the widow Martha Dandridge Custis when she was courted by George Washington.

[80] Eicher, & Eicher, **High Commands**, p.345; **OR** vol.11, pt.1, p.1041.

[81] McClellan, Henry B., *I Rode with Jeb Stuart*, pp.125-126.

efficiency on the part of his command." As the month of June opened, Stuart's two most trusted subordinates were the two relatives of his commanding general[82]

William H. F. Lee was a large man, standing six feet four inches tall, a height which allowed him to tower above his famous father. He was large for a cavalryman with huge hands and feet. His size prompted a number of his troopers to express concern for the steed which bore him. Some wondered how it was possible to find a horse capable of effectively carrying his bulk. But, Lee was an excellent judge of horseflesh and seemed to be capable of picking mounts which allowed his large frame to work in unison with the animal. The fact that Rooney was a good horseman helped in projecting harmony with his mount. Although his physical presence projected an overbearing aura, his mannerisms and voice made it known that, like his father, he was a gentleman. He seemed to be uneasy in a crowd of strangers, but was warm and cordial to those who knew him. Like his father, he possessed a distinguished look with a high forehead, a square straight nose and full, bushy beard.[83]

Lee's brigade, as it joined Stuart's encampment near Culpeper, contained five regiments, but only four had ridden to Culpeper. The 2nd North Carolina and three other Virginia regiments, the 9th 10th and 13th would move to Culpeper. The 15th Virginia would remain behind and picket the Rappahannock near Fredericksburg.[84]

"...perfectly unreliable..."

Another addition to Stuart's division that June was Brigadier General Beverly Holcombe Robertson's brigade. However, Robertson's command, at the time it was transferred from North Carolina to Culpeper, was a shadow of its former self. D. H. Hill had stripped some of Robertson's regiments and assigned them to his infantry divisions leaving Robertson with only two active regiments in his brigade. Hill thought the troopers could be better used attached to infantry divisions and took them from Roberson, dispersing one to himself and two others to different commands. The 7th Confederate Cavalry and the 62nd Georgia remained in North Carolina while the 3rd North Carolina Cavalry patrolled the regions along the Blackwater River. Hill, who was not fond of Robertson, may have done the reorganizing because of his universal disdain for cavalry. In fact, Hill once offered a reward to anyone who could locate a dead man on a battlefield with spurs on. He had nothing good to say about Robertson, calling him "wonderfully inefficient." Hill once wrote Longstreet noting that his command needed a "better man." One of Stuart's aides pulled no punches when he called Robertson "perfectly unreliable." General Lee had wished to leave Robertson stationed in North Carolina. He also thought him a prime candidate to head up a training organization for cavalry.

---

[82]   *OR* vol.21, pp.37, 742; *OR* vol.25, pt.1, p.1047.

[83]   McKinney, ***Brandy Station***, pp.10-11; Longacre, ***The Cavalry at Gettysburg***, p.29.

[84]   *OR* vol.25, pt.2, p.290; McKinney, ***Brandy Station***, p.260.

Unfortunately, no training camp existed and since Robertson would "have but little to do," Lee brought his small, two regiment brigade north to join Stuart.[85]

Robertson was the outcast of the cavalry corps. No one wanted him and for good reason. His combat record was littered with lost opportunities and poor command decisions. He was overly cautious, undependable and seemed to take orders literally, which kept him from exercising any initiative to hit the enemy when opportunities arose. He was perhaps the poorest brigadier in the Eastern Theater of the war, and if not he was near the bottom of the list. Although he was outstanding with paperwork and training military units, on a battlefield he was a significant liability.[86]

Robertson was born on "The Oaks" Plantation in Amelia County, Virginia, on 5 June 1827. He entered the Military Academy in 1845 and graduated four years later, twenty-fifth in a class of forty-three. Brevetted a second lieutenant in the 2nd Dragoons, Robertson spent the first year of his military service at the cavalry school at Carlisle Barracks in Pennsylvania. Afterword, when he was a full second lieutenant, he was ordered to the western frontier. He served in the New Mexico, Kansas and Nebraska Terretories, fought the Apache at Jornado del Muerto and the Sioux at Blue Water River, earning a promotion to first lieutenant. In 1859, Robertson put his administrative skills to work when he was ordered to Utah to taking over assistant adjutant general duties for his regiment. On 3 March 1861, as the storm clouds of war grew in the east, Robertson was promoted to captain. Unlike most of his fellow Virginians, Robertson did not immediately resign his commission. Instead, he remained in the army but evidently his conduct was anything but acceptable. By 8 August, he had been dismissed for disloyalty. His unfaithfulness stemmed from his acceptance of a commission from his native state before he had resigned.[87]

Robertson volunteered for service and, on 19 September, was commissioned colonel of the 4th Virginia Cavalry. He fought with the regiment in the Valley as part of Jackson's force but was transferred to the Peninsula to support General Johnston after McClellan shifted his army to threaten Richmond. Although Robertson's regiment was present at the Battle of Williamsburg, Robinson himself was not. He had taken sick and was lying in a bed as the fighting raged. He was back at his post when his regiment became engaged in a series of minor skirmishes at New Bridge on 23 and 24 May. Evidently his efforts were looked upon with approval for two weeks later he was promoted to brigadier general and placed in command of the lamented Turner Ashby's Laurel Brigade.[88]

Ashby had been a favorite with the brigade and had not been particularly demanding regarding discipline and drill. Robertson however was the opposite. He

---

[85] *OR*, vol. 25, pt. 2, pp.820-821, 823; Barrett, ***The Civil War in North Carolina***, p.155.

[86] Wittenberg, ***Brandy Station***, p.56.

[87] Eicher, & Eicher, ***High Commands***, p.456; ***CMH***, vol.3, part.2 pp.656-657; McKinney, ***Brandy Station***, p.48.

[88] *OR* vol.11, pt.1, pp.445, 572.

entered upon his new responsibilities with all the regulation and discipline of a West Point graduate and quickly alienated his entire command. He became unpopular with the troopers almost immediately. Most of the men equated Robertson's strict discipline as a slap in the face and a reflection upon their ability to fight. In addition, they became convinced that Robertson was significantly better at drilling his men then he was at fighting. He led his strictly disciplined brigade through Second Manassas and into the opening moves of the Maryland Campaign. Evidently the complaining over Robertson's abilities reached Jeb Stuart, for shortly after the Confederates moved into Maryland, Robertson was relieved of command and sent south to command a brigade of cavalry in the Department of North Carolina.[89]

General Lee was not particularly pleased at the thought of Robertson returning to his army. On 23 May, in a communication to Stuart he let his feelings be known about the inept Robertson.

> "I wished to leave Robertson in North Carolina, but learned from the President that General Hill had attached each of the three regiments there to the divisions of Generals [Samuel G.] French, [William H. C.] Whiting, and himself, and consequently he had no command but the regiments he brought out. I shall endeavor, if possible, to get another regiment from North Carolina, but think it doubtful."[90]

Stuart received little comfort from Lee's words. He had no use for Robertson and would have preferred Lee leave him in North Carolina with "little to do." Robertson, minus the three regiments which D. H. Hill had commandeered, arrived and joined Stuart's command shortly before the end of May. His two regiments, the 4th and 5th North Carolina Cavalry, had both been raised during the middle of 1862 and neither had seen significant action. They had spent the majority of their service on picket and patrol duties in eastern North Carolina.[91]

On 30 May Lee suggested to Stuart that it would be prudent to try and bolster the size of Robertson's force and create a brigade of all North Carolina regiments. Lee proposed taking the 1st North Carolina from Hampton's Brigade and the 2nd North Carolina from Rooney Lee's command to supplement Robertson's two regiments. However, the creation of a strengthened, all North Carolina brigade did not come to fruition. Stuart was probably appreciative of the failure. If he was going to be saddled with Robertson, it was probably best for his division that the incompetent Virginian have command over as few regiments as possible. The two cavalrymen had been friends before the war but the trials of the conflict had soured

---

[89] McDonald, *A History of the Laurel Brigade*, p.74; Eicher, & Eicher, **High Commands**, p.456; McKinney, **Brandy Station**, p.49.

[90] *OR* vol.25, pt.2, pp.820-821.

[91] McKinney, **Brandy Station**, p.49.

their relationship. Stuart would have to determine a way to handle Robertson, whom he once called "the most troublesome man I have to deal with."[92]

The final element of Stuart's Cavalry Division was his famous group of horse artillery batteries under the command of Major Robert Franklin Beckham. The concentration of Stuart's horsemen near Culpeper allowed Beckham to return home. He had been born in the town on 6 May 1837. He was a West Pointer and had graduated sixth in his class in 1859. Shortly after the war began, he resigned his second lieutenant's commission with the topographic engineers. He accepted a lieutenant's commission in the Confederate artillery and at one point was elected to a captaincy in the Jeff Davis Artillery; a position he did not accept. On 30 August 1862, Beckham was promoted to major. Throughout most of his war service he had been a staff officer, but General Stuart thought enough of him to recommend Beckham for command of his horse artillery when the battalion's previous commander was killed in action. Writing to Adjutant General Cooper, Stuart pushed to have Beckham assigned to command his guns. Beckham himself had some misgivings about the position, but on 8 April 1863 he was placed in charge by an order from Stuart. His first major battle would be at Chancellorsville.[93]

Stuart's Staff

In a war touted as a brother against brother affair, Confederate Major Henry Brainerd McClellan was the epitome of the label. Born in 1840 in Pennsylvania, he was raised in Philadelphia, and trained in the ministry. After his graduation, he traveled to Cumberland County Virginia to become a private tutor in 1858. Although only a resident of the Old Dominion for two years when the war began, McClellan chose to take the path of States' Rights and supported the Southern cause. He enlisted in the 3rd Virginia Cavalry as a private on 14 June 1861. Henry had four brothers who served in the Union army, one of which would be an adjutant general to Brigadier General Andrew A. Humphreys. Henry's most famous relative however, was his first cousin, General George McClellan.

In October 1861, Henry was detailed to act as clerk for Company G of his regiment. Four months later he was serving as the regiment's adjutant. His paperwork skills must have been satisfactory for on 20 April 1863 he was promoted to Major and installed as adjutant general of Stuart's Cavalry Division. Stuart became acquainted with Henry early in the war and had the opportunity to observe his growth as a soldier. Although McClellan was not military trained and was a transplanted Northerner, Stuart turned to him and came to appreciate the Pennsylvanian's administrative skills. In a communication to Adjutant General Cooper, Stuart requested McClellan be assigned to his staff. "I deem it proper to state," Stuart wrote, "that I am influenced in this recommendation by the signal gallantry displayed by him in the field his efficiency and zealous devotion to duty as a staff officer." Although he was on Stuart's staff to do paperwork, in a few days

---

[92] *OR* vol.25, pt.2, pp. 836-837; Wert, Jeffry D., *Cavalryman of the Lost Cause*, p.69.

[93] Sifakis, *Who was Who*, pp.44-45; Krick, *Lee's Colonels*, p.48; Trout, Robert J., *Galloping Thunder*, pp.184-185; Trout, Robert J., *They Followed the Plume*, p.56.

he would prove to be the determining factor in fending off a serious setback for his commander's cavalry at Brandy Station.[94]

Another staffer which Stuart displayed great confidence in was Johann August Heinrich Heros von Borcke. Born in 1835, the twenty-eight year old von Borcke was a Prussian cavalry officer on leave from the 2nd Brandenburg Dragoons. In the spring of 1862, he secured passage on a Confederate blockade runner named *Hero*, and after a twenty day voyage, arrived in Nassau. To reach the seat of the American war, a second vessel was boarded and he entered the Confederacy through Charleston, South Carolina, barely escaping capture in the harbor. The final leg of the Prussian's journey to Richmond would be made by train. After being made a captain in the Provisional Army, von Borcke rode north and joined Stuart's staff as a volunteer aide.[95]

Von Borcke was a mountain of a man, standing six-feet four inches tall and weighing around 240 well-proportioned pounds. Of the foreigners who fought for the Confederacy, none received more accolades than von Borcke. Armed with a letter from the secretary of war, von Borcke met Stuart shortly before the Battle of Fair Oaks. After reading the message, Stuart informed the big Prussian that he would be pleased if his new staffer would remain by his side during the coming fight. In a few moments a cannon roar signaled the beginning of the battle, and von Borcke, along with the remainder of Stuart's entourage rode off to the front.[96]

Von Borcke was not the type of staff member who balked at an opportunity to fight. While some staffers adhered to their duties during battle, von Borcke actively sought combat. His size and strength allowed him to carry the largest saber in the Confederacy and only the huge Wade Hampton sported anything close to von Borcke's massive blade. His sword earned him the nickname's "Long Blade" and "Major Armstrong" but those who became close to him simply called him "Von."[97]

Although he was an experienced military officer von Borcke was not accustomed to the carnage of the American Civil War. After his first engagement, he was appalled by the scenes which confronted him. "Terrible was it to see on every side the wounded returning from the battle," von Borcke wrote later. "[T]he more severely wounded in the ambulances, groaning and wailing in a manner that made my heart shrink." Promoted to major in August 1862, the big Prussian fought with Stuart in all the major battles of the Eastern Theater, up to and including Chancellorsville. On a number of occasions he was reported killed in both the Southern and Northern newspapers. He was a tough fighter who, during his short time with the army, had grown to love his comrades and his adopted country.[98]

---

[94] McClellan, *I rode with Jeb Stuart*, pp.v-viii; Nanzig, Thomas P., *3rd Virginia Cavalry*, p.118.

[95] Freeman, *Lee's Lieutenants*, vol.1, p.279; von Borcke, *Memoirs*, pp.1, 8-9,449; Faust, *Encyclopedia*, pp.770-771.

[96] von Borcke, *Memoirs*, pp.12, 16.

[97] Faust, *Encyclopedia*, p.791.

[98] *Ibid*; von Borcke, *Memoirs*, p.19.

Performing the function of chief engineer for Stuart's Division was Captain William Willis Blackford. Blackford, a Virginian, was born in Fredericksburg on 23 March 1831. He was educated in a private school which his father opened and staffed to instruct his own children. Admission of students outside the family was limited to from eight to ten children so intimate instruction was available for all who attended. William chose the engineering profession and after spending three years as a rodman on various surveying crews, he had earned enough money to enter the University of Virginia. However, he stayed at the university only a short time before going to work for the Virginia and Tennessee Railroad for $1,800 a year. When the chief engineer of the line resigned, Blackford took on his duties. In 1856, he married a young woman named Mary Robertson. Mary's father, Wyndham Robertson, had been governor of Virginia and had served in the Virginia House of Delegates. The Robertson family summered in Washington County, where the former governor owned a plaster mine. After his railroad duties were complete, Blackford joined Mary's father as a partner in the mining business. He was working at the mine when the war began.[99]

William enlisted at Abingdon on 14 May 1861 and joined Jeb Stuart's 1st Virginia Cavalry as a first lieutenant. Two months later he was appointed adjutant of the regiment. He fought with the 1st during the battle at Manassas and performed his duties well enough to be mentioned in Stuart's report. "[M]y attention was particularly attracted to the adjutant," Stuart noted. That fall, when the regiment was reorganized, Blackford found himself a captain in command of Company D. It was not long after assuming his new post that Captain Blackford was placed under arrest at the hand of his former company commander, and short-tempered Grumble Jones.[100]

Like Stuart, Blackford had no use for his regimental commander. Blackford's animosity stemmed from an incident in which Colonel Jones' strict adherence to discipline precipitated a confrontation. As the winter months of 1861 opened, Stuart imposed a moratorium on fires along his picket lines. The restriction came about after a sentry was shot as he stood in the light of a warming fire. While fires on the picket line disappeared, fires to the rear of the line continued to be used for warmth. During one instance, when Blackford's company was posted on picket, Jones, patrolling the line, discovered one of the fires in the rear of the line. Before he was aware of the facts of the situation, Jones sent his adjutant in search of Blackford with a written order calling for the arrest of the captain. Blackford was placed under "close arrest" which meant he was confined to his tent. "I felt like doing a little murder," Blackford wrote later. "It would have been most grateful to me to have run him [Jones] through with my saber..." Stuart called on his former adjutant many times and, although sympathetic to Blackford's plight, military protocol would not allow him to extricate Blackford from his situation. After a number of weeks, a court martial was convened in which Blackford was acquitted of the charges. Upon returning to the regiment, he found that Jones had personally

---

[99] Blackford, William W., *War Years with Jeb Stuart*, pp.7-8.

[100] Blackford, *War Years*, p.53; *OR* vol.2, p.484; Driver, *1st Virginia Cavalry*, pp.23, 152.

taken charge of his company and discovered that many of the men had soured on Blackford's authority, preferring Jones' influence over his own.[101]

After spending a short time on recruitment duty, Blackford returned to his company. He failed to be reelected to its captaincy in April 1862, possibly due to Jones' influence. A month later he was appointed captain in the engineering corps and in a short time joined Stuart's staff as his chief engineering officer. Stuart was greatly appreciative of Blackford's efforts during the Second Manassas Campaign and called out the captain in his report. "Capt. W. W. Blackford, Corps of Engineers," Stuart wrote, "was quick and indefatigable in his efforts to detect the designs of the enemy and improve the positions within our reach." By the time Stuart's horsemen concentrated at Culpeper, Blackford had become one of the general's most trusted staffers.[102]

Another attribute which Blackford would effectively display while in Stuart's service were his ability's as a mapmaker. He would become Stuart's chief cartographer and on a few occasions, the captain's maps would accompany Stuart's official reports. Blackford would also prove his worth to Stuart during the latter's Chambersburg Raid in October, 1862. His engineering skills would be utilized in constructing additional maps of the area. The maps would not only be useful to Stuart but to Jedediah Hotchkiss as he secretly constructed his map of the invasion route which Lee and Jackson intended to take into the heart of Pennsylvania.[103]

Shortly after arriving at Culpeper, Blackford's mapmaking services were solicited once more. He received orders to make a reconnaissance of the Rappahannock River from south of Fredericksburg to Warrenton. He was to gather information regarding "the strategical [sic] strength of positions along the riverbanks with reference to forcing a crossing." Evidently General John Hood's Division was to be at the forefront of the crossing, for Blackford was to report all he discovered to the general.[104]

With an escort of twenty-five handpicked men and an additional officer, Blackford began his ride northward up the west bank of the river. The further north the group traveled, the fewer Federal outposts were observed on the opposite bank. The number of Yankees at each post also diminished significantly the further north Blackford and his small band rode. On most occasions, the Federals were seen well back from the river, posted on the hills or other prominent terrain features. [A]t one place," Blackford recalled. "where there was an important road crossing, they had built a fort right on the river bank at the toe of a horseshoe bend, with the concave of the bend on their side, and bold hills encircling it on ours, a most absurd location for a redoubt."[105]

---

[101] Blackford, *War Years*, pp.52-54.

[102] Driver, *1st Virginia Cavalry*, p.152; *OR* vol.12, pt.2, p.738.

[103] *OR* vol.12, pt.2, pp.728, 732, 738; Hotchkiss, *Make Me a Map*, p.117.

[104] Blackford, *War Years*, p.210.

[105] *Ibid.*

Near the fort, Blackford's band was forced exited a grove of trees along an extremely narrow section of the river, into an open field. The Confederates were shocked to discover "the opposite side [of the river] swarming with blue jackets." In order to determine the position and number of Federal troops near the river, Blackford would have to expose his riders to the watchful eyes of the enemy. He decided to try and move his group across the open field and hope that the Yankees would think them friendly and leave them alone. He spread the word to his command not to "fire nor to appear on their guard but to go on talking and laughing as usual..." Moving out into the open, Blackford's little band led their horses slowly; talking and showing no concern for the enemy only fifty yards away. The enemy acted just as Blackford had expected. The Federals, instead of being suspicious of the Rebels "exchanged good-humored jokes with the men of my party," he recalled. The mapmaker believed there was an entire regiment of the enemy in and near the fort "eight to ten hundred strong" and that if the charade had not been successful the little band of Confederates would have been easy prey. Blackford reported his findings to General Hood who shortly thereafter came down to the river late in the evening to take a look at the exposed fortress. Hood decided to attack the location with artillery the following morning, but before the movement could get organized, the general was ordered further up the river and the attack was called off.[106]

The officer who rode along with Blackford on his reconnaissance was Second Lieutenant Francis Smith Robertson. Known as Frank, the young lieutenant was probably chosen for the assignment because of his stature as Blackford's brother-in-law and his position as assistant engineer on Stuart's staff. Robertson became associated with Stuart shortly after the cavalry leader paid him a visit while he was attempting to recover from a bout of pericarditis. He must have impressed the cavalry leader for he soon received a letter from Stuart offering him the assistant engineer position. Robertson had been contemplating taking a sea voyage to help his recovery, but quickly put his travel plans on hold and accepted the position. A few months would pass before he would be able to join his new chieftain, but eventually Robertson would become a vital part of Stuart's inner circle during the summer of 1863.[107]

Robertson's early ancestors were some of the first settlers to homestead in the Virginia region. In fact, so early did his family arrive that Robertson could trace his lineage back to the Indian maiden Pocahontas. Born in Richmond, on 3 January 1841, Frank's father was ex-governor Wyndham Robertson. His mother, to whom he owed his connection to Pocahontas, was an heiress to a large fortune consisting mostly of sizable land holdings in Louisiana and Virginia. Early in life, Frank showed great interest in horses and became quite an accomplished rider. His education began at the Hanover Academy before he moved on to the

---

[106] *Ibid*, pp.210-211. Hood's decision to attack and subsequent reversal probably took place during the period of time between his division being ordered to the river and subsequently withdrawn shortly after it arrived at Culpeper.

[107] Trout, ***They Followed the Plume***, pp.232-233.

University of Virginia in September of 1859. In late 1860, Robertson and two of his classmates formed a military organization called "Sons of Liberty." When the war began, his company was deployed at Harpers Ferry, but after four days on duty there, the company was sent back the university's campus. A short time later, he was commissioned a second lieutenant in the state's force but soon joined the 48th Virginia Infantry out of fear that the war would be over before he had been given an opportunity to seek glory.[108]

Robertson was sent to western Virginia, but before seeing much action he became ill and had to leave the regiment. Eager to get into the war, he forced himself out of his sickbed sooner than he should have and suffered a relapse of his condition. He was slowly recovering from his setback when Jeb Stuart came calling. It would be March, 1863, before Robertson would be well enough to take his position on Stuart's staff. His first assignment was to color one of his brother-in-law's maps; a tedious project which took Frank a great deal of time. Later, he was assigned to a detail to construct a new bridge at Germanna Ford. The effort quickly became a struggle for survival when information arrived indicating a Federal column was approaching the ford. Unwilling to believe the report, the details captain crossed the river with a group of riders, included Robertson. The band was surprised and quickly taken captive. Robertson was the only member of the part to escape. After being fired at numerous times, he realized his only escape route was up over a hill within full view of the Federals. Somehow the lieutenant was able to make it over the knoll without being hit, although several rounds were fired in his direction.

The longer Robertson remained with Stuart's headquarters, the more his health improved. The life of a cavalryman seemed to appeal to his physicality. Soon, he would find himself embroiled in the fighting about to erupt around Brandy Station. He would continue to prove Stuart did not make a poor decision when offering him a staff position.[109]

Another member of Stuart's staff, Chiswell Dabney, was born on his father's plantation in Virginia's Campbell County on 25 July 1844. Chiswell, the last of nine children born to Reverend John Blair Dabney and Elizabeth Lewis Towles, joined Stuart's organization in early 1862. Dabney was educated at the New London Academy, and like Frank Robertson, entered the University of Virginia to further his education. When the war began, he set aside his studies for the quest of glory and adventure.[110]

At the age of seventeen, Dabney became a courier for Stuart, and performed well enough to earn a spot on Stuart's staff as an aide-de-camp. He was the youngest member of the cavalryman's inner circle but proved early on that he was quite capable. When his promotion to lieutenant was approved, Dabney was

---

[108] *Ibid*, pp.233-234.

[109] *Ibid*, pp.234-236.

[110] Trout, ***They Followed the Plume***, pp.95-96; ***Electronic Source***: http://worldconnect.rootsweb.ancestry.com/cgi-bin/igm.cgi?op=GET&db=adgedge&id=I32588&style=TABLE, Last accessed 11/11/13.

not with Stuart, having been sent on furlough to recover from a bout with typhoid fever. He returned to duty in the early spring of 1862, and served with Stuart throughout all the eastern campaigns during the remainder of 1862 and into the following year.[111]

Lee's Western Screen

Brigadier General John D. Imboden's weary command established its camp in the Churchville, Virginia area and remaining there during the first week of June. Throughout the past month, the men of the Northwestern Brigade had ridden over 400 miles. Over $100,000 dollars in wagons, arm, horses and mules had been captured. The 3,100 head of cattle Imboden's men had taken, had been rounded up and maneuvered south. Recruiting had been somewhat fruitful as well, with around 400 new men joining the ranks. All this had been accomplished with the help of Jones' Brigade and cost only sixteen of Imboden's troopers. Although the destruction of the B & O Railroad had not been accomplished, the raid had been somewhat of a success from Imboden's point of view.[112]

The men needed rest from their hard, demanding journey into West Virginia but their recuperation time would be short. As Stuart's Cavalry Division organized itself near Culpeper, Imboden received a communication from General Lee. Unlike the remainder of Lee's cavalry, the commanding general retained direct control of Imboden's command. He would utilize it for a critical element of his northward movement. The men of the Northwestern Brigade would be responsible for protecting Lee's drive north through the Shenandoah Valley from the west. After informing Imboden of the current situation, Lee issued very specific instructions to him. The brigadier had no way of knowing at the time, but the next six weeks would be the liveliest period of the war for him.[113]

> HEADQUARTERS ARMY OF NORTHERN VIRGINIA
> June 7, 1863.
>
> Brig. Gen. J. D. Imboden
> Commanding Northwestern Brigade, via Staunton:
> GENERAL: In view of operations in the Shenandoah Valley, I desire you to attract the enemy's attention in Hampshire County, and to proceed down to Romney, or such other point as you may consider best calculated for the purpose. After leaving a sufficient guard on the Shenandoah Mountain, you can use the rest of your command for the purpose specified. In attracting their attention and detaining whatever force they may have at New Creek, Cumberland, Cacapon, &c., you will, of course, do them all the injury in your power by striking them a damaging blow at any point

---

[111] Trout, ***They Followed the Plume***, p.96.

[112] Delauter, Roger, U. Jr., ***18th Virginia Cavalry***, p.6.

[113] *Ibid*; French, Steve, ***Imboden's Brigade in the Gettysburg Campaign***, p.9

where opportunity offers, and where you deem most practicable. It will be important, if you can accomplish it, to destroy some of the bridges, so as to prevent communication and the transfer of reinforcements to Martinsburg. After accomplishing what you can in Hampshire, should you find it practicable or advantageous, you can co-operate with any troops that you may find operating in the Valley. Forward to the commanding officer of the force there any information that you may deem important, and comply with any requisition on his part.

I desire you to move into Hampshire as soon as possible. Let me know the time of your departure and the time of your expected arrival. In connection with this purpose, it is important that you should obtain, for the use of the army, all the cattle that you can. Communicate with the agents of the Commissary Department you may find purchasing in the country west of Staunton, and let them make arrangements to assist you in the purchasing and taking care of the cattle. I hope you will also be able, while in that country, to collect recruits for your brigade, both cavalry and infantry, and bring them out with you.

I am, very respectfully, $c.,

R. E. LEE,

General.[114]

Lee's intention was to utilize Imboden's command on the left flank of his army as it marched northward, screening its advancing columns from threats emanating from West Virginia.

John Daniel Imboden was the first of eleven children born to his parents between 1823 and 1846. Born 16 February in Staunton, Virginia, John was a handsome boy and grew into a distinguished looking and intelligent young man. He was educated in the county schools and as a teenager showed an enthusiastic interest in reading and self-education. At the age of eighteen he enrolled in Washington College, where he studied mathematics, chemistry, French, rhetoric and ancient history. He also studied engineering at the Virginia Military Institute, which was located close to Washington College, although he was never formally enrolled at VMI. After completing his education, he returned to his home town where he began a short teaching career at the Virginia Institute for Education of the Deaf and the Dumb and of the Blind. However, he soon changed his thoughts on a career and began to study law. He loved to read, and the study of the profession seemed to be a natural fit. Imboden read for about a year before being admitted to the bar. He then formed a partnership, possibly with his mentor, and specialized in business related cases, debt collection and property law. After leaving his original partner behind, he became a junior partner in the firm of John Howard McCue in 1854. Imboden married Eliza McCue, the daughter of close friend Colonel Franklin McCue and first cousin to John Howard, on 16 June 1845.

---

[114] *OR* vol.27, pt.3, p.865.

He worked hard to help develop a successful practice which, like Imboden's first partnership, specialized in business cases. Eventually the partnership would dissolve, but not before both John McCue and John Imboden had made it a success. Imboden also began dabbling in politics. He joining the Whig Party and his political star quickly rose. In 1850 he was elected to the Virginia House of Delegates. However, it was his association with the McCue family that would inaugurate his military career and guide John Imboden toward his destiny.[115]

Imboden began his military career in 1846 when a relative by marriage, John Marshall McCue, a major in the 32nd Regiment of Virginia Militia, asked if Imboden would join the unit and become its adjutant. Imboden accepted, but by 1848 his desire to continue as the unit's administrator was waning. In a letter to the major in January, Imboden informed him that he had no military aspirations and intended to pursue an occupation away from the service. He remained quietly on the sidelines, showing no interest in reentering the military until November 1858, when he once again joined the militia. He was commissioned a captain on 22 May and entered service with the 160th Regiment, 13th Brigade, 5th Division of the Virginia Militia.[116]

In response to public uncertainty, which arose from John Brown's failed attempt to insight his slavery revolt at Harpers Ferry, Imboden initiated the organization of a local artillery battery which became known as the Staunton Artillery. Shortly before Brown was hung for his insurrection, Imboden secured a full complement of men for the battery. Although tasked with the duties of the battery's captaincy, he remained with his law practice, contemplated buying land in Florida and became involved in a number of business dealings in his native state. Although sentiments in the Valley and western Virginia were mixed, Imboden chose to remain with his state.[117]

Imboden trained his battery between its formation and the inauguration of the war. He led it at First Manassas as part of Brigadier General Barnard Bee's defense of Henry House Hill. During the fighting, he was wounded twice. Initially he was struck by a shell fragment which caused no permanent injury. The second wound, which was the fault of Imboden himself, caused some permanent damage. While directing the battery's fire, he moved forward slightly to see under the battery's smoke. When he commanded one of the guns to fire, the lateral muzzle blast struck him full in the side. "Heavens," he wrote later, "what a report. Finding myself full twenty feet away, I thought the gun had burst, but it was only the pent-up gas, that, escaping sideways as the shot cleared the muzzle, had struck my side and head with great violence." Blood began flowing from his left ear and in short order he would permanently lose his hearing in the ear, having suffered a perforated eardrum.[118]

---

[115] Tucker, Spencer C., ***Brigadier General John D. Imboden: Confederate Commander in the Shenandoah***, pp.2-7. In today's parlance the institute would no doubt have been referred to as for the hearing and learning disabled and the visually impaired.

[116] *Ibid*, pp.7, 13, 317.

[117] *Ibid*, pp.15, 17, 19.

[118] Driver, Robert J. Jr., ***The Staunton Artillery – McClanahan's Battery***, p.11.

John Daniel Imboden received his orders directly from Robert E. Lee. *LOC*

Imboden took charge of the artillery in the Valley District and remained in the position until March 1862 when he was given permission to raise a regiment of partisans to patrol northwest Virginia. Originally called the 1st Virginia Partisan Rangers, the unit was forced to reorganize itself in January 1863 and officially became part of Lee's Army of Northern Virginia. The regiment, which became the 62nd Virginia, was a mixture of cavalry and infantry. It was actually organized on 9 September 1962, but a number of companies would be transferred to the 18th Cavalry in December. Other companies would be distributed to other commands before the 62nd took its final shape. Imboden however, did not stay with the regiment long. On 28 January 1863, he was promoted to brigadier general but did not receive his commission until 13 April. Given independent brigade command, he spent the early months of 1863 roaming the mountains of the western Virginia region that in April became the state of West Virginia.[119]

Imboden had rested his command for a few days before he received Lee's instructions. His brigade had been reduced somewhat from the size it had been during the recently completed raid. It currently consisted of only three units, Imboden's old 62nd infantry, which had been mounted, the 18th Cavalry, under the command of the new general's brother, Colonel George W. Imboden, and the six gun battery of Captain John H. McClanahan's horse artillery. Two days after

---

[119] Eicher, & Eicher, ***High Commands***, p.313; Sifakis, Stewart, ***Compendium of the Confederacy Armies:*** *Virginia*, p.257.

receiving Lee's orders, Imboden had his 1,300 men on the road north toward Hampshire County.[120]

John Imboden was not the only brigadier general of cavalry who received direct instructions from Lee on 7 June. Lee also needed a cavalry command to cooperate with his infantry column as it traversed the Shenandoah Valley and points north. To provide his vanguard its eyes and ears, he chose Brigadier General Albert Jenkins' command.

> HEADQUARTERS ARMY OF NORTHERN VIRGINIA
> June 7, 1863.
> Brig. Gen. A.G. Jenkins, Commanding. &c., via Staunton:
> GENERAL: I desire you to have your command ready to be concentrated at Strasburg or Front Royal, or any point in front of either, by Wednesday, the 10th instant, with a view to co-operate with a force of infantry. Your pickets can be kept in advance as far as you deem best, toward Winchester. See to their arms, ammunition and equipment, and make arrangements for provisions and forage. Send me all the information you have about the position and strength of the enemy at Winchester, Martinsburg, Charleston, Berryville, and any other point where they may be.
> Keep your horses as fresh as you can, and have your whole command prepared for active service.
> I am, very respectfully, your obedient servant,
>
> R. E. LEE,
> General.[121]

Shortly after receiving his orders, Jenkins gathered his horsemen and placed them on the roads north toward the points Lee had instructed him to scout in advance of the army.

By the end of the first week of June 1863, Lee's entire cavalry force, except for Jenkins' Brigade and Imboden's command, was encamped in the Culpeper area. During the week Stuart would conduct numerous events intended to display the romantic elements of armed conflict. Little did he or anyone in his command know that just across the Rappahannock River plans were being made to test his newly expanded organization. In a few days, Stuart and his nearly 10,000 man force would be severely tested and in some instances embarrassed by a Union cavalry force both he and many of his contemporaries considered inferior to his. While General Imboden and the men of his command made their way toward the

---

[120] Collins, ***The Jones-Imboden Raid***, p.5; French, ***Imboden's Brigade***, pp.9-10. McClanahan's Battery was raised as part of the recruitment effort which led to the mustering of the 62nd Infantry. McClanahan, like George Imboden had been a member of the Staunton Artillery.

[121] ***OR*** vol.27, pt.3, p.865.

Potomac River and Jenkins' horsemen rode from their camp, Jeb Stuart's Cavalry Division would be fighting for its life just east of Culpeper Court House near a small railroad siding called Brandy Station. The first encounter of the Gettysburg Campaign would be fought within the boundaries of Stuart's camp.

Epilogue

Intentions

"I shall throw an overwhelming force on their advance"[1]
Robert E. Lee to Isaac Trimble
27 June 1863

Robert E. Lee did not leave a detailed summary of his overall plan and battle strategy for the campaign. A reading of his correspondence and reports however, can provide a glimpse at his intentions. As noted, he did not intend to seek a major fight during the movement and subsequent summer occupation of southern Pennsylvanian, but he was not opposed to hitting the Federals if an opportunity arose. He wanted the campaign to be one of offensive movements within the context of the South's overall defensive strategy.[2]

Only one corps would advance to and cross the Susquehanna River, assault Harrisburg and possibly move on to Philadelphia. The other two would keep a watchful eye on the Federals with the help of Stuart's cavalry. The threat posed by a force the size of Lee's to the Federal capital and Baltimore could not and would not be ignored by the administration in Washington.

The month of June was projected to be poor for grain supplies in the South. While his horses were slowly beginning to regain their health munching on the green spring grasses, a summer spent north in Pennsylvania would be even better for the wellbeing of the animals and men in his army. It would also circumvent the shortage of grain when spring forage turned dry and brown in the heat of summer. Lee knew that to stay in Virginia for the summer put his army at risk because if the horses were not replenished his force could become immobile. Once static his men would be in serious jeopardy and defeat would surely follow. Lee knew he had to get his animals across the Blue Ridge and into the Shenandoah Valley and then across the Potomac.[3]

With his army out of Virginia, Lee expected the Army of the Potomac to follow and give the Virginia countryside a much needed break. It was his intention to spend the entire summer in the north feeding his legions and livestock, gathering

---

[1] Trimble, Gettysburg, **SHSP**, vol.26, p.121.

[2] Allan, **Memoranda**, Lee the Soldier, p.13.

[3] Bowden & Ward, **Last Chance**, p.46.

supplies and moving around the countryside. Whether Lee intended to move toward the northeast corner of Pennsylvania and wreak havoc on the North's coal industry he never mentioned after the war.[4]

Once north of the river, Lee would encourage Northerners involved in peace movements to step up their protests and bring the Lincoln administration to the negotiation table. The South could not survive for long on dwindling resources and if a political solution was to be found it had to be soon. It would come about only by internal pressure on Lincoln and his government.[5]

Another benefit would be the clearing of the Shenandoah Valley of the occupying Federal troops positioned there. Major General Robert H. Milroy had moved his Second Division of the Federal Eighth Corps into the town of Winchester the previous December and had done little to endear himself to the local population. Milroy had built a reputation for being a pain in the side of his superiors. This was due to his belief that since he was not a West Pointer he was looked down upon by those who were graduates of the institution. Lee would have to rid the Valley of his presence if he was going to be able to use the Blue Ridge to shield his advance.[6]

Lee was not in the habit of revealing his plans, even to some of his most trusted subordinates. Seldom did he expose his intentions until shortly before their execution and then only to those who needed to know or to those whom he sought council. At the end of May, as Lee completed reorganizing his army, he invited Armistead L. Long into his tent. Long found Lee mulling over a large map, possibly the one drawn by Hotchkiss, spread across a table. Lee began to outline his operational plan for the coming campaign. The general traced the invasion route across the map to its destination in Pennsylvania while he calmly explained the plan to his military secretary. Long learned of Lee's intention to maneuver in such a manner as to draw Hooker's army away from the Rappahannock River. "The plan," Long noted, "…was already matured in his own mind, and the whole line of movement was laid down on the map." Listening intently, until Lee was done, Long then began to discuss the proposal. He wondered if it would be beneficial to engage Hooker in the vicinity of the old Manassas battlefields. To this Lee was not receptive explaining that if defeated, Hooker would once again retreat to the safety of Washington, recuperate, rearm and advance none the worse for wear.

Long noted that Lee's intention was to invade Pennsylvania in the vicinity of Chambersburg, Gettysburg or York. Lee indicated that if required to give battle he would prefer to do so in the vicinity of Gettysburg due to its proximity to the mountain passes which would allow him to keep his communication lines open. Gettysburg also held the advantage of being closer to the Potomac in case of disaster. The argument against fighting in the vicinity of York was the additional twenty-five miles from the mountains. How much of Long's writing was influenced

---

[4] Kegel, *Lee and Jackson*, p.219.

[5] *Ibid.*

[6] Maier, Larry A., *Gateway to Gettysburg: The Second Battle of Winchester*, p.14.

by hindsight is hard to say. If his notes are genuine, Lee had evidently developed a strategy in case the Federal army was encountered in the southeastern corner of the Keystone State. If Lee indeed was not taking his army to Pennsylvania to seek a battle with Hooker, at least, if one developed, he would be prepared to engage the enemy.

According to Long, Lee believed that if a battle was fought and the Federals were defeated, they would be forced to retreat across the Susquehanna River toward Philadelphia. A Federal retreat to the east from southern Pennsylvania would give Lee control of the state, Maryland and possibly West Virginia. This scenario would only occur however, if Lee was in a position to block a Federal retreat toward Baltimore or Washington, which would have been the route preferred by Hooker's force. His army or Stuart's cavalry would need to be prepared to keep itself between Hooker and the security of Washington.[7]

Another person Lee relayed his plans to sometime later, during the march north, was Isaac Trimble. Trimble was five years Lee's senior and like Lee, a West Point graduate. He was a native Virginian and after leaving the military in 1832, spent the next 29 years as chief engineer for a number of railroad systems. Trimble was not part of the inner command circle of the army but perhaps his engineering background and friendship with Lee provided him the opportunities to meet with the commanding general during the advance and learn what his commander had planned for the Army of the Potomac.[8]

Trimble accepted a commission as colonel of engineers in Virginia's state forces in May 1861. As the war gathered steam later that year, he was made a brigadier general in the Confederate Army. He was assigned to the command of a brigade in Ewell's Division of Jackson's army in the Shenandoah Valley in 1862 where he developed a reputation as a fiery, hard fighter, earning accolades from Jackson. He commanded his brigade during The Seven Days and fought with Jackson at Cedar Mountain. During the Second Battle of Manassas, Trimble was severely wounded, hit by an exploding bullet, which inflicted heavy damage and required almost a year to heal. His extended period of recuperation was lengthened by an attack of camp erysipelas. On 15 May, ready to return to field command even though his wounds had not completely healed, Trimble wrote to Lee from Shocco Springs, North Carolina requesting a command within the army.[9]

On 20 May, Lee responded to Trimble's request. "I hope you will soon recover your strength," Lee wished, "but you must not return to the field until able to endure fatigue." While Lee had no command for Trimble, he did have a post where he could be of use, proposing that he take command of troops in the

---

[7] Long, *Memoirs*, pp.268-269.

[8] Faust, *Encyclopedia*, p.763.

[9] *Ibid*; *OR* vol.25, pt.2, pp.801-802; Trimble, Gettysburg, *SHSP*, vol.26, p.118. Trimble notes the date of his initial letter to Lee as June 18th, which is in error. Trimble's narrative in the *SHSP* contains a number of errors regarding the dates of specific events. These are no doubt due to the extended period of time between the events and when they were recorded by Trimble.

Shenandoah Valley. The clear air of the countryside would be good for Trimble's health, or at least Lee thought it would be. Once at his new post Trimble would supervise operations, protect the left flank of the Army of Northern Virginia and if able, capture Union General Milroy or at least run him out of the Valley. Lee also charged Trimble, if he accepted the post, with organizing any local Southern sympathizers into some kind of fighting force. Lee believed there were a number of supporters in the Valley and Maryland who were ready to help the Confederate cause. So far however, no organization had materialized. He hoped Trimble could accomplish what he had not been able to during the Maryland Campaign the previous fall. When Trimble was ready to take command Lee would "issue the order."[10]

Trimble responded five days later, saying he was prepared. Walter Taylor made it official, communicating Lee's wish that Trimble be "assigned to the command of the Shenandoah Valley, and will proceed to Staunton, and assume command of all the troops in the Valley." It took Trimble a month to reach his new post on 22 June. By the time he arrived, Lee's army had already cleared the upper Valley of Union troops and pushed on northward. Finally on 24 June, Trimble overtook Lee's army near Berryville and spent the next three days loitering around army headquarters. On the afternoon of the 27th, with the army halted for the night, Trimble called on Lee at the commanding general's tent.[11]

Lee was seated in his tent when Trimble entered. Motioning him over to where he was seated, Lee pulled a map of southern Pennsylvania out and opened it up for viewing and asked Trimble to comment on the topography of the area east of South Mountain and Adams County. According to Trimble, Lee valued his opinion as a civil engineer. After Trimble's comments were complete, Lee outlined his plan for defeating the Union Army. While Trimble admits his recording of Lee's comments may not be exactly what his chief said, he is certain that the words he wrote are very close to being verbatim.

> "Our army is in good spirits, not over fatigued, and can be concentrated on any one point in twenty-four hours or less. I have not yet heard that the enemy have crossed the Potomac, and am waiting to hear from General Stuart. When they here where we are they will make forced marches to interpose their forces between us and Baltimore and Philadelphia. They will come up, probably through Frederick; broken down with hunger and hard marching, strung out on a long line and much demoralized, when they come into Pennsylvania. *I shall throw an overwhelming force on their advance, crush it, follow up the success, drive one*

---

[10] *OR* vol.25, pt.2, p.812. In September of 1862, Lee had issued a proclamation to the people of Maryland in an effort to solicit support for the Southern cause. The response was almost non-existent.

[11] *Ibid*, p.822, 830; Trimble, Gettysburg, **SHSP**, vol.26, pp.118, 120-121. Trimble says in **SHSP** that he received the order to take command on June 19th. This is obviously another date error.

corps back on another, and by successive repulses and surprise before they can concentrate; create a panic and virtually destroy the army."

The concept seemed sound. According to Trimble, Lee intended to bring his army together and isolate one or two of the Federal corps before the Federals could gather their army. If this scenario could be created then he could, in theory defeat the Federals in detail rather than face their entire army in one pitched battle.[12]

Whatever the truth was in planning, it was now time to move. Lee could wait no longer. To do so would be to risk another forward movement by Hooker. The battle at Chancellorsville had given Lee the opportunity to retool his army and complete his preparation for a summer campaign. Now it was time to take the fight north. A successful summer crusade could mean the establishment of a new independent Southern nation. Lee believed Confederate independence could not be won in the west, in Tennessee, or as the result of another pitched battle on some already bloodied field somewhere between Washington and Richmond. Independence, he believed, lay to the north, on an as yet to be determined battlefield somewhere beyond the Potomac.

---

[12] Trimble, Gettysburg, ***SHSP***, vol.26, p.121. Emphasis added.

Appendix A

Organization of the Army of The Potomac – 3 June 1863[1]

Major General Joseph Hooker, Commanding

GENERAL HEADQUARTERS

Major General Daniel Butterfield – Chief of Staff
Brigadier General Seth Williams - Assistant Adjutant General
Brigadier General Rufus Ingalls – Chief Quartermaster
Brigadier General Henry Jackson Hunt - Chief of Artillery
Jonathan Letterman – Medical Director
Brigadier General Gouverneur Kemble Warren – Chief Engineer

Provost Guard[2]
Brigadier General Marsena Rudolph Patrick – Provost Marshal
80th New York – Colonel Theodore B. Gates[3]
93rd New York – Colonel John Simpson Crocker[4]

---

[1] The organization shown here is based on a number of sources and is intended to portray the Federal Army's organization and unit commanders at the inauguration of the campaign. General source is: *OR* vol.25, pt.2, pp.575-585. Although most regimental commander names are taken from the *OR*, many names are shown within the *OR* having only first and, or middle initials with the surname. In addition, a great number of middle initials were completely omitted in the *OR*. Many first and middle names as well as full names, have been confirmed through additional sources. *Italics* indicate some doubt as to a commander's presents on 3 June.

[2] Some elements of the Provost Guard had recently left the army to be mustered out, including the 21st, 23rd and 35th New York Regiments. The 21st was mustered out in Buffalo on 18 May. The 23rd was mustered out in Elmira on 22 May. The 35th was mustered out in Elmira on 5 June. In addition the 12th Ohio Battery had been transferred to the Artillery Reserve. Phisterer, *NYWR*, vol.3, pp.1971, 1994, 2173.

[3] Phisterer, *NYWR*, vol.4, pp.2861, 2869.

[4] *Ibid*, pp.3043, 3050.

94th New York – Colonel Adrian R. Root[5]
6th Pennsylvania Cavalry (two companies, E & I) – Captain James H. Starr[6]
8th United States Infantry (six companies, A, B, C, D, F, G) – Captain Edwin W. H. Read[7]
Regular Cavalry Detachment – Lieutenant Tattnall Paulding[8]

Bureau of Military Information
Colonel George Henry Sharpe
Second Lieutenant Charles Stuart McEntee

Engineer Brigade
Brigadier General Henry Washington Benham
15th New York (three companies, A, B, C) – Colonel Clinton G. Colgate[9]
50th New York - Colonel Charles B. Stuart
(Lieutenant Colonel William H. Pettes)[10]
United States Engineer Battalion – Captain Charles N. Turnball[11]

---

[5] *Ibid*, pp.3060, 3075.

[6] Busey, John W. & Martin, David G., **RSLG**, p.18; Bates, **HPV**, vol.4, p.775; Whittenberg, **Rush's Lancers**, p.6. Starr was captain of Company I.

[7] Rodenbough, Theophilus F. & Haskin, William L., *The Army of the United States; Historical Sketches of Staff and Line with Portraits of Generals in Chief, 1789-1896*, pp.520-521. Rodenbough & Haskin indicate that only companies A, B, C, D, F, and G marched with army headquarters to Gettysburg. This is consistent with the organization of the Army of the Potomac on 31 May which indicates that only six companies were with the regiment at that time (*OR* vol.25, pt.2, p.575). Companies E and I were reorganized at Fort Columbus on Governors Island in New York Harbor on 22 May, 1863. Rodenbough & Haskin do not specifically indicate that the two companies joined the remaining companies with Army of the Potomac headquarters before the battle but sources indicate that eight companies were with the regiment during the battle including the *OR* (*OR* vol.27, pt.1, p.155).

[8] This group of cavalry contained elements of various cavalry regiments.

[9] Phisterer, *NYWR*, vol.2, pp.1650-1651, 1659. This regiment was made up of two year and three year volunteers. On 18 June the three year men were transferred to Companies A, B and C on the same day the term of service expired for the two year men. Colonel Colgate was a two year man. The two year men were mustered out in New York City on 25 June. Only companies A, B and C remained with the regiment.

[10] *Ibid*, pp.1671, 1685-1686. Colonel Stuart resigned his commission on 3 June and Lieutenant Colonel Pettes took command. Pettes would be commissioned a colonel on 13 June to rank from 3 June.

[11] Turnball would command the battalion through the majority of the month of June, but would be replaced shortly before the battle.

Guards & Orderlies
Oneida Cavalry (New York) – Captain Daniel P. Mann[12]

Signal Corps
Captain B. F. Fisher

Ordnance Detachment
Lieutenant John R. Edie

FIRST ARMY CORPS
Major General John Fulton Reynolds

FIRST DIVISION
Brigadier General James Samuel Wadsworth

First Brigade[13]
Colonel Edward Brush Fowler
84th New York (14th Militia) – Lieutenant Colonel Robert B. Jordon[14]

Second Brigade
Brigadier General Lysander Cutler
7th Indiana – Lieutenant Colonel Ira G. Grover[15]
76th New York – Colonel William P. Wainwright[16]
95th New York – Colonel George H. Biddle[17]
147th New York – Lieutenant Colonel Francis C. Miller[18]
56th Pennsylvania – Colonel J. William Hofmann[19]

---

[12] Phisterer, *NYWR*, vol.2, pp.1187-1188.

[13] Phisterer, *NYWR*, vol.3, pp.1982, 2002, 2078. The First Brigade was depleted by the loss of three New York regiments to expiring terms of enlistment, the 22nd, 24th and 30th. The 22nd was mustered out in Albany on 19 June, the 24th was mustered out in Elmira on 29 May and the 30th was mustered out in Albany on 18 June. The 22nd is still listed as with the brigade on 31 May but by 3 June it was likely preparing to depart or had already left.

[14] Phisterer, *NYWR*, vol.4, pp.2930-2931. The 84th was transferred to the Second Brigade sometime in June. Robert B. Jordon, in June 1863, was second in command of the regiment.

[15] *Report of the Adjutant General of the State of Indiana*, (hereafter *RAGSIN*) vol.2, p.40.

[16] Phisterer, *NYWR*, vol.4, pp.2797, 2812.

[17] *Ibid*, pp.3081, 3085.

[18] Phisterer, *NYWR*, vol.5, pp.3706, 3715.

[19] Bates, *HPV*, vol.3, pp.216, 225. Reliable sources, including Bates, do not indicate Hofmann's first name, only that his first initial was J. Some electronic sources indicate his first name was John.

Third Brigade[20]
Brigadier General Gabriel René Paul
22nd New Jersey – Colonel Abraham G. Demarest[21]
29th New Jersey – Colonel William R. Taylor[22]
30th New Jersey – Colonel John J. Cladek[23]
31st New Jersey – Lieutenant Colonel Robert R. Honeyman[24]

Fourth Brigade[25]
Brigadier General Solomon Meredith
19th Indiana – Colonel Samuel. J. Williams[26]
24th Michigan – Colonel Henry A. Morrow[27]
2nd Wisconsin – Colonel Lucius Fairchild[28]
6th Wisconsin – Colonel Edward Stuyvesant Bragg[29]
7th Wisconsin – Colonel William W. Robinson[30]

SECOND DIVISION[31]
Brigadier General John Cleveland Robinson

---

[20] *OR* vol.25, pt.2, pp.532, 575. Prior to the end May the 137th Pennsylvania was sent home for muster out. All four regiments in the brigade were 9 month units. During the month of June the entire brigade was released and sent home to muster out. The term of the 22nd expired on 22 June. The term of the 29th expired on 20 June. The terms of the 30th and 31st expired on 17 June.

[21] Stryker, *ROMNJ*, vol.1, p.761. The regiment was mustered out at Trenton on 25 June.

[22] *Ibid*, p.901. The regiment was mustered out at Freehold on 30 June.

[23] *Ibid*, p.920. The regiment was mustered out at Flemington on 27 June.

[24] *Ibid*, p.940. The regiment was mustered out at Flemington on 24 June.

[25] After the departure of the New Jersey Brigade and the remaining regiment of the First Brigade was transferred to the Second Division and the Fourth Brigade was re-designated as the First Brigade.

[26] Dunn, Craig L., *Iron Men, Iron Will: The Nineteenth Indiana Regiment of the Iron Brigade*, p.313.

[27] Curtis, O. B., *History of the 24th Michigan of the Iron brigade*, p.321.

[28] Chapman, *RWV*, vol.1, p.345.

[29] *Ibid*, p.494; Hardgrove, J. G., General Edward S. Bragg's Reminiscences, *Wisconsin Magazine of History* (hereafter *WMH*), vol.33, no.3, p.282.

[30] Chapman, *RWV*, vol.1, p.538.

[31] *OR* vol.25, pt.1, p.158; *OR* vol.25, pt.2, p.158; The Second Division was consolidated from three brigades to two after the loss of the 26th New York and 136th Pennsylvania in May to expiring enlistment terms.

First Brigade
Colonel Samuel H. Leonard[32]
16th Maine – Colonel Charles W. Tilden[33]
13th Massachusetts – Lieutenant Colonel N. Walter Batchelder[34]
94th New York[35] – Colonel Adrian R. Root[36]
104th New York – Colonel Gilbert G. Prey[37]
107th Pennsylvania – Colonel Thomas F. McCoy[38]

Second Brigade
Brigadier General Henry Baxter
12th Massachusetts – Colonel James L. Bates[39]
83rd New York – Lieutenant Colonel Joseph A. Moesch[40]
97th New York – Colonel Charles Wheelock[41]
11th Pennsylvania – Colonel Richard Coulter[42]
88th Pennsylvania – Major Benezet F. Foust[43]

---

[32] On 3 June the brigade was under the command of Colonel Leonard. In mid June, as the New Jersey brigade under General Paul left the army for muster out, Paul was placed in command of General Robinson's First Brigade. Colonel Leonard returned to his regiment, the 13th Massachusetts.

[33] *Annual Report of the Adjutant General of the State of Maine* (hereafter *AGSM*), 1863, Appendix D, p.465; *Maine at Gettysburg, Report of Maine Commissioners*, p.51.

[34] *MSSM*, vol.2, p.71. Batchelder is listed as in command of the regiment on 31 May. The organization of the army at Gettysburg list Colonel Samuel H. Leonard, who returned to the regiment sometime during the month of June. *OR* vol.27, pt.1, p.156.

[35] Phisterer, *NYWR*, vol.4, p.3059. On 30 May, the 94th New York was placed under the control of the Provost Marshal of the army and performed the duties of the Provost Guard, Army of the Potomac for a short period until sometime in June.

[36] *Ibid*, pp.3060, 3075.

[37] *Ibid*, pp.3220, 3229. Phisterer lists Colonel Prey as being in command on 3 June but the Army of the Potomac's 31 May organizational list notes Lieutenant Colonel Henry G. Tuthill in command. Prey was probably away from the regiment, placing Tuthill in command of the regiment when the listing was assembled.

[38] Bates, *HPV*, vol.6, p.866.

[39] *MSSM*, vol.2, p.3.

[40] Phisterer, *NYWR*, vol.4, pp.2914, 2923. The regiment's colonel, John Hendrickson had been wounded at Fredericksburg and had not returned to the regiment.

[41] *Ibid*, p.3112

[42] Bates, *HPV*, vol.1, p.267.

[43] Bates, *HPV*, vol.5, p.75.

90th Pennsylvania – Colonel Peter Lyle[44]

THIRD DIVISION
Major General Abner Doubleday

First Brigade[45]
Brigadier General Thomas Algeo Rowley
121st Pennsylvania – Colonel Chapman Biddle[46]
142nd Pennsylvania – Colonel Robert P. Cummins[47]
151st Pennsylvania – Colonel Harrison Allen[48]

Second Brigade
Colonel Roy Stone
143rd Pennsylvania – Colonel Edmund L. Dana[49]
149th Pennsylvania – Lieutenant Colonel Walton Dwight[50]
150th Pennsylvania – Colonel Langhorne Wister[51]

Artillery Brigade
Colonel Charles Shiels Wainwright
2nd Maine Battery – Captain James A. Hall[52]
5th Maine Battery – Lieutenant Greenlief T. Stevens[53]
1st New York Light Artillery, Battery L – Captain Gilbert H. Reynolds[54]
1st Pennsylvania Light Artillery, Battery B – Captain James H. Cooper[55]

---

[44] *Ibid*, p.158.

[45] *OR* vol.25, pt.2, p.576; Bates, *HPV*, vol.7, p.303. The 135th Pennsylvania's term of service expired in May. The regiment was mustered out in Harrisburg on 24 May.

[46] Bates, *HPV*, vol.7, p.37.

[47] *Ibid*, p.469.

[48] Bates, *HPV*, vol.8, p.681.

[49] Bates, *HPV*, vol.7, p.492.

[50] *Ibid*, p.617. On 3 June, the regiment's original colonel, Roy Stone, was in command of the brigade.

[51] Bates, *HPV*, vol.8, p.658.

[52] *AGSM*, 1863, Appendix D, p.83; *MGRMC*, p.35.

[53] *AGSM*, 1863, Appendix D, p.91; *MGRMC*, p.101.

[54] Phisterer, *NYWR*, vol.2, p.1217. The *OR* lists Captain John A. Reynolds as in command of Battery L on 3 June. However, John A. Reynolds' service record indicates that as of 3 March 1863 he was promoted to major. Gilbert H. Reynolds is listed in Phisterer as commanding the battery on 3 June.

[55] Bates, *HPV*, vol.2, p.976; *OR* vol.25, pt.2, p.576.

4th United States Artillery, Battery B – Lieutenant James Davison[56]

SECOND ARMY CORPS
Major General Winfield Scott Hancock[57]

FIRST DIVISION
Brigadier General John Curtis Caldwell

First Brigade
Colonel Edward Ephraim Cross
5th New Hampshire – Lieutenant Colonel Charles E. Hapgood[58]
61st New York – Lieutenant Colonel Knut Oscar Broady[59]
81st Pennsylvania –Colonel H. Boyd McKeen[60]
148th Pennsylvania – Lieutenant Colonel (Major) George A. Fairlamb[61]

Second Brigade
Colonel Patrick Kelly
28th Massachusetts – Colonel Richard Byrnes[62]
63rd New York – Lieutenant Colonel Richard C. Bentley[63]
69th New York – Captain James E. McGee[64]

---

[56] Rodenbough & Haskin, *The Army of the United States,* p.361. Powell, William H., *List of Officers of the Army of the United States from 1779 to 1900* (hereafter ***LOAUS***), p.276. According to Rodenbough & Haskin, Davison was an officer with the 5th U. S. Artillery whom had been attached to the 4th Artillery's Battery B. Captain James Stewart was the battery's ranking officer and would command the battery at Gettysburg.

[57] Technically General Darius Couch was still in command of the corps as of 3 June. He was away from the army at the time and would not return. Couch would be assigned command of the Department of the Susquehanna on 10 June.

[58] William, Child, *A History of the Fifth Regiment, New Hampshire Volunteers*, part 2, p.82.

[59] Phisterer, *NYWR*, vol.3, p.2556.

[60] Bates, *HPV*, vol.4, p.1173. McKeen had been wounded at Chancellorsville on 3 May but was back with his regiment as of 31 May.

[61] Bates, *HPV*, vol.7, pp.579, 583. Fairlamb had been wounded at Chancellorsville but was back with the regiment by 3 June. The *OR* lists him as a lieutenant colonel as of 31 May but Bates lists him as being promoted to the rank on 15 November 1863, after Lieutenant Colonel Robert McFarlane was honorably discharged. McFarlane would command the regiment at Gettysburg.

[62] *MSSM*, vol.3, p.190.

[63] Phisterer, *NYWR*, vol.3, p.2588.

[64] *Ibid*, pp.2695, 2697. McGee was captain of Company F on 3 June but was in command of the regiment, being the ranking officer present. On 12 June he was transferred to Company A where he was installed as its captain.

88th New York – Captain William B. Nagle[65]
116th Pennsylvania – Major St. Clair A. Mulholland[66]

Third Brigade
Colonel Orlando H. Morris[67]

52nd New York – Lieutenant Colonel Charles G. Freudenberg[68]
57th New York – Lieutenant Colonel Alfred B. Chapmen[69]
66th New York - Captain John F. Bartholf[70]
140th Pennsylvania – Lieutenant Colonel John Fraser[71]

Fourth Brigade
Colonel John Rutter Brooke

27th Connecticut (Companies D, F & Consolidated)
– Captain Joseph R. Bradley[72]
2nd Delaware – Colonel William P. Baily[73]

---

[65] Phisterer, *NYWR*, vol.4, pp.2977, 2981; *ARAGSNY*, vol. 31, p.122. The *OR* lists Nagle's middle initial as J. Phisterer lists it as B. Volume II of the New York Adjutant General's annual report for 1863 lists Nagle's middle initial as I (*Annual Report of the Adjutant General of the State of New York* (hereafter *NYAGR*) 1863, Volume II. p.172). Volume. 31 of the *ARAGSNY*, lists Nagle's middle initial as B. Nagle was mustered out on 13 June 1863 at Falmouth. The regiment was formed into a battalion of two companies in June 1863. Company A was formed from the original regiment's companies A, B, C, D, E and F. The new Company B was formed from the original companies G, H, I and K.

[66] Bates, *HPV*, vol.6, p.1235.

[67] Brigade commander, General Samuel Kurtz Zook, was on medical leave on 3 June. Colonel Morris, of the 66th New York, was in command of the brigade.

[68] Phisterer, *NYWR*, vol.3, p.2416.

[69] *Ibid*, p.2490.

[70] *Ibid*, p.2651. Bartholf was captain of Company F on 3 June but was in command of the regiment, being the ranking officer present.

[71] Bates, *HPV*, vol.7, p.413. Fraser was in command of the regiment at the beginning of June. The regiment's colonel, Richard P. Roberts would return sometime during the month.

[72] *Catalogue of Connecticut Volunteer Organizations* (here after *CCVO*), pp.859, 867; Busey, Travis W. and John W., *Union Casualties at Gettysburg*, p.41. Bradley was captain of Company F and on 31 May was listed as in command of the regiment. Most of the regiment had been captured at Chancellorsville. Only Companies D, F, and a company consolidated from the remnants of the regiment's another companies remained. By the time of the battle in Pennsylvania the regiment's lieutenant colonel, Henry C. Merwin would be in command.

[73] *Official Army Register of the Volunteer Force of the United States Army* (hereafter *OARVF*), vol.3, p.1050.

64th New York – Colonel Danial G. Bingham[74]
53rd Pennsylvania – Captain Archibald F. Jones[75]
145th Pennsylvania – Captain John W. Reynolds[76]

SECOND DIVISION
Brigadier General John Gibbon

First Brigade
Colonel Turner G. Morehead[77]
19th Maine – Colonel Francis E. Heath[78]
15th Massachusetts – Colonel George H. Ward[79]
1st Minnesota – Lieutenant Colonel William Colvill, Jr.
34th New York – Colonel Byron Laflin[80]
82nd New York (2nd Militia) – Lieutenant Colonel James Huston[81]

Second Brigade
Brigadier General Joshua Thomas Owen
69th Pennsylvania – Colonel Dennis O'Kane[82]
71st Pennsylvania – Major John H. Stover[83]
72nd Pennsylvania – Colonel DeWitt C. Baxter[84]

---

[74] Phisterer, *NYWR*, vol.3, p.2609.

[75] Bates, *HPV*, vol.3, p.119. Captain Jones of Company G was in command of the regiment as of 31 May. During June, Lieutenant Colonel Richards McMichael would return to the regiment.

[76] Bates, *HPV*, vol.7, p.527. As of 3 June, Captain Reynolds of Company A was the ranking officer in the regiment. Major John W. Patton was mortally wounded on 3 May at Chancellorsville and died 12 days later.

[77] Morehead is listed as in command of the brigade on 31 May. Brigadier General William Harrow most likely returned to the brigade sometime in early June but may still have been absent on 3 June.

[78] *AGSM*, 1863, Appendix D, p.536; *MGRMC*, p.297.

[79] *MSSM*, vol.2, p.133. Ward was promoted to colonel on 29 April 1863.

[80] Phisterer, *NYWR*, vol.3, pp.2125-2126. The 34th New York was a two year regiment whose term expired on 16 June. It was mustered out in Albany on 30 June.

[81] Phisterer, *NYWR*, vol.4, pp.2898, 2907.

[82] Bates, *HPV*, vol.4, p.707.

[83] Bates, *HPV*, vol.6, p.833. Major Stover was a member of the 106th Pennsylvania. Evidently he was transferred for a short time to command the regiment while its new colonel, Richard Penn Smith, who was promoted as the Chancellorsville Campaign was unfolding, returned to his regiment.

[84] Bates, *HPV*, vol.4, p.834.

106th Pennsylvania – Lieutenant Colonel William L. Curry[85]

Third Brigade[86]
Colonel Norman Jonathan Hall
19th Massachusetts – Major Edmond Rice[87]
20th Massachusetts – Colonel Paul J. Revere[88]
7th Michigan – Captain Amos E. Steele Jr.[89]
42nd New York – Colonel James. E. Mallon[90]
59th New York – Colonel Lieutenant Max A. Thoman[91]

THIRD DIVISION
Major General William Henry French[92]

First Brigade
Colonel Samuel Sprigg Carroll
14th Indiana – Lieutenant Colonel Elijah H. C. Cavins[93]
24th New Jersey – Colonel William B. Robertson[94]
28th New Jersey – Captain Horatio S. Disbrow[95]
4th Ohio – Major Gordon A. Stewart[96]

---

[85] Bates, *HPV*, vol.6, p.833.

[86] The 127th Pennsylvania, which had been with the brigade at Chancellorsville, saw its term of service expired on 14 May. It returned to Pennsylvania and was mustered out 29 May.

[87] *MSSM,* vol.2, p.454. Rice was originally mustered as captain of Company F.

[88] *Ibid*, p.494. Revere was commissioned colonel of the regiment on 14 April 1863. Colonel Revere was the grandson of Paul Revere of Lexington and Concord fame.

[89] *RSMV*, vol.7, p.97. Steele was promoted to lieutenant colonel on 17 May but was not mustered until 12 June.

[90] Phisterer, *NYWR*, vol.3, p.2255.

[91] *Ibid*, pp.2520, 2536.

[92] The Third Division at Chancellorsville contained three brigades but during the month of May the Third Brigade was disbanded due to expiring enlistments. The remaining Third Brigade regiments were consolidated into the Second Brigade.

[93] *RAGSIN* vol.2, p.112.

[94] Stryker, *ROMNJ*, vol.1, p.799. The 24th New Jersey's term of service would expire on 24 June. The unit was mustered out on 29 June in Beverly. *OR* vol.25, pt.2, p.532; *Dyer, CWR*, vol.3, p.1363.

[95] Stryker, *ROMNJ*, vol.1, pp.883. Disbrow was captain of Company B. The 28th New Jersey's term of service would expire on 22 June. The unit was mustered out on 6 July at Freehold. *OR* vol.25, pt.2, p.532; *Dyer, CWR,* vol.3, p.1364.

[96] *OIWR*, vol.2, p.89.

8th Ohio – Major Albert H. Winslow[97]
7th West Virginia – Lieutenant Colonel Jonathan H. Lockwood[98]

Second Brigade
Colonel Thomas Alfred Smyth
14th Connecticut – Colonel Dwight Morris[99]
1st Delaware – Lieutenant Colonel Edward P. Harris[100]
12th New Jersey – Colonel J. Howard Willets[101]
10th New York – Major George F. Hopper[102]
108th New York – Colonel Charles J. Powers[103]

Artillery Brigade
Captain John G. Hazard[104]
1st Rhode Island Light Artillery, Battery A – Captain William A. Arnold[105]
1st Rhode Island Light Artillery, Battery B – Lieutenant T. Frederick Brown[106]
1st United States Artillery, Battery I – Lieutenant George A. Woodruff[107]
4th United States Artillery, Battery A – Lieutenant Alonzo Hersford Cushing[108]

THIRD ARMY CORPS[109]

---

[97] *Ibid*, p.237.

[98] ***OARVF***, vol.4, p.1130.

[99] ***CCVO***, p.570.

[100] ***OARVF***, vol.3, p.1048. Transferred from the disbanded Third Brigade in late May.

[101] Stryker, ***ROMNJ***, vol.1, p.585.

[102] Phisterer, ***NYWR***, vol.3, p.1845.

[103] Phisterer, ***NYWR***, vol.4, p.3270

[104] ***OR*** vol.25, pt.2, p.577.

[105] ***ARAGSRI***, vol.2, p.742.

[106] *Ibid*, p.769.

[107] Ladd, David L. and Audrey J. Editors, ***John Bachelders's History of the Battle of Gettysburg***, p.794; ***LOAUS***, p.688.

[108] *Ibid*; Rodenbough & Haskin, ***The Army of the United States***, p.360; ***LOAUS***, p.269.

[109] The Third Corps was reorganized from three divisions to two during mid June. The reorganization was precipitated by severe casualties taken at Chancellorsville and the departure of a large number of regiments to expiring enlistment terms. The organizational structure for the Third Corps shown here has been developed to reflect the status of the corps as of 3 June when Robert E. Lee inaugurated the Gettysburg Campaign by shifting the bulk of his army to Culpeper Court House.

Major General Daniel Edgar Sickles (Major General David Bell Birney)[110]

FIRST DIVISION
Brigadier General John Henry Hobart Ward[111]

First Brigade
Colonel Andrew H. Tippin[112]
57th Pennsylvania – Colonel Peter Sides[113]
63rd Pennsylvania – Captain James F. Ryan[114]
68th Pennsylvania – Lieutenant Colonel Anthony H. Reynolds[115]
105th Pennsylvania – Colonel Calvin A. Craig[116]
114th Pennsylvania – Colonel Frederick F. Cavada[117]
141st Pennsylvania – Colonel Henry J. Madill[118]

Second Brigade
Colonel Philippe Régis Dénis de Keredern de Trobriand [119]
20th Indiana – Colonel John Wheeler[120]
3rd Maine – Captain William C. Morgan[121]

---

[110] General Sickles, shortly after Chancellorsville would depart on sick leave and turn the corps over to General Birney. Birney would remain in command of the corps until Sickles return on 28 June.

[111] When General Sickles left on sick leave shortly after Chancellorsville, and General Birney took over the corps, General Ward took command of the First Division. Upon Sickles return, Ward would return to command of the Second Brigade.

[112] Brigadier General Charles K. Graham, who was in command of the corps' Third Division on 3 June, would be transferred to command this brigade on 20 June when the Third Division was disbanded. Eicher, & Eicher, *High Commands*, p.261. Colonel Tippin would return to his regiment, the 68th Pennsylvania.

[113] Bates, *HPV*, vol.3, p.255.

[114] *Ibid*, p.497.

[115] Bates, *HPV*, vol.4, p.687.

[116] Bates, *HPV*, vol.6, p.789.

[117] *Ibid*, pp.1184, 1188.

[118] Bates, *HPV*, vol.7, p.442.

[119] On 3 June, de Trobriand was transferred to command of the Third Brigade upon the departure of Colonel Samuel B. Hayman and the 37th New York which left due to expiring enlistment.

[120] *RAGSIN* vol.2, p.178.

[121] *AGSM*, 1863, Appendix D, pp.125, 142. Captain Morgan was the commanding officer of the regiments Company F. Sometime in June, regimental commander Colonel Moses B. Lakeman returned to take command of the regiment.

4th Maine – Lieutenant Colonel Lorenzo D. Carver[122]
38th New York – Lieutenant Colonel Robert F. Allason[123]
99th Pennsylvania – Major John W. Moore[124]

Third Brigade
Colonel Samuel B. Hayman[125]
17th Maine – Lieutenant Colonel Charles B. Merrill[126]
3rd Michigan – Colonel Byron R. Pierce[127]
5th Michigan – Major John Pulford[128]
37th New York – Lieutenant Colonel Gilbert Riordan[129]
40th New York – Colonel Thomas W. Egan[130]

SECOND DIVISION
Brigadier General Andrew Atkinson Humphreys

First Brigade
Brigadier General Joseph Bradford Carr
1st Massachusetts – Major Gardner Walker[131]
11th Massachusetts – Colonel William Blaisdell[132]
16th Massachusetts – Lieutenant Colonel Waldo Merriam[133]
11th New Jersey – Colonel Robert McAllister[134]

---

[122] *Ibid*, p.157.

[123] Phisterer, ***NYWR***, vol.3, pp.2173-2174. The 38th New York's term of service expired on 8 June. It was mustered out in East New York on 22 June.

[124] Bates, ***HPV***, vol.5, p.514.

[125] Phisterer, ***NYWR***, vol.3, pp.2159-2160. Colonel Hayman departed with the 37th New York, leaving the brigade to Colonel de Trobriand on 3 June.

[126] ***AGSM***, 1863, Appendix D, p.503.

[127] ***RSMV***, vol.3, p.89.

[128] ***RSMV***, vol.5, p.100.

[129] Phisterer, ***NYWR***, vol.3, p.2159. The 37th New York's term of service expired on 7 June. It was mustered out in New York City on 22 June.

[130] *Ibid*, pp.2214-2215; ***ARAGSNY***, vol.23, p.405. Transferred from the Third Brigade, First Division during May 1863. Consolidated to five companies on 25 May. The three year men from the 38th New York were transferred into the 40th on 30 May and used to form three companies.

[131] ***MSSM***, vol.1, p.22. Major Walker was originally mustered in as captain of Company B.

[132] *Ibid*, p.737.

[133] ***MSSM***, vol.2, p.215.

[134] Stryker, ***ROMNJ***, vol.1, p.532.

26th Pennsylvania – Major Robert L. Bodine[135]

Second Brigade
Colonel William Root Brewster
70th New York – Colonel J. Egbert Farnum[136]
71st New York – Colonel Henry L. Potter
72nd New York – Colonel John S. Austin
73rd New York – Major Michael W. Burns[137]
74th New York – Lieutenant Colonel Thomas Holt
120th New York – Lieutenant Colonel Cornelius D. Westbrook[138]

Third Brigade[139]
Colonel William J. Sewell[140]
5th New Jersey – Captain Virgil M. Healy[141]
6th New Jersey – Lieutenant Colonel Stephen R. Gilkyson[142]
7th New Jersey – Colonel Louis R. Francine[143]
8th New Jersey – Captain John G. Langston[144]
115th Pennsylvania – Major John P. Dunne[145]

---

[135] Bates, *HPV*, vol.1, p.354.

[136] Phisterer, *NYWR*, vol.4, p.2710.

[137] *Ibid*, p.2753.

[138] *Ibid*, p.3411.

[139] *OR* vol.25, pt.2, p.592; Toombs, *New Jersey Troops*, p.99; Dyer, *CWR, vol.3, p.1347*. The 2nd New Hampshire, which would eventually join the brigade, was transferred to Washington DC on 23 May. The regiment arrived in Washington on 28 May and remained there until it was ordered to join the Army of the Potomac. It joined the brigade 11 June at Hartwood Church.

[140] Eicher, & Eicher, *High Commands*, p.261; Toombs, *New Jersey Troops*, p.99. Colonel George C. Burling of the 6th New Jersey, who was wounded at Chancellorsville, would resume command of the brigade sometime in June.

[141] Stryker, *ROMNJ*, vol.1, pp.228, 235. Healy was captain of Company B. Healy was listed as in command of the regiment on 31 May. The regiment's colonel, William J. Sewell, was in command of the brigade on 31 May. When Colonel George C. Burling would eventually return to command of his brigade and Sewell would return to his regiment.

[142] *Ibid*, p.267.

[143] *Ibid*, p.300.

[144] *Ibid*, p.421. Langston was captain of Company K. The regiment's colonel, John Ramsey, would return sometime in June.

[145] Bates, *HPV*, vol.6, p.1213.

THIRD DIVISION[146]
Brigadier General Charles Kinnaird Graham[147]

First Brigade[148]
Colonel Augustus Van Horne Ellis[149]
86th New York – Major Jacob H. Lansing[150]
124th New York – Lieutenant Colonel Francis M. Cummins[151]

Second Brigade
Colonel Samuel M. Bowman
12th New Hampshire – Captain Nathaniel Shackford[152]
84th Pennsylvania – Lieutenant Colonel Milton Opp[153]
110th Pennsylvania – Colonel James Crowther[154]

Third Brigade
Colonel Hiram G. Berdan[155]
1st United States Sharpshooters – Lieutenant Colonel Casper Trepp[156]

---

[146] In mid June the Third Division would be broken up and its remnants dispersed among the brigades of the First and Second Divisions.

[147] Graham was transferred to command of the First Division's First Brigade on 20 June.

[148] Bates, *HPV*, vol.7, p.55. Shortly after Chancellorsville, the 122nd Pennsylvania was sent home for muster out. It was mustered out on 16 May in Harrisburg.

[149] Phisterer, *NYWR*, vol.4, pp.3465-3466. Colonel Ellis returned to command of his regiment, the 124th New York, when the regiment was transferred to the Second Brigade of the corps' First Division in mid June.

[150] *OR* vol.27, pt.1, p.159; Phisterer, *NYWR*, vol.4, pp.2954-2955. The 86th New York was transferred to the Second Brigade of the corps' First Division in mid June.

[151] *OR* vol.27, pt.1, p.159; Phisterer, *NYWR*, vol.4, pp.3465-3466. The 124th New York was transferred to the Second Brigade of the corps' First Division in mid June. According to the Army of the Potomac's 31 May organization listing, Cummins was in command of the regiment but according to Captain Charles Weygant of Company A, Colonel A. Van Horne Ellis was in command when the regiment left camp on 6 June, bound for Brandy Station. Weygant, Charles H., *History of the 124th Regiment of New York State Volunteers: The Orange Blossom Regiment*, pp.142, 144.

[152] *OR* vol.25, pt.2, p.579. The regiment was transferred to the First Brigade of the corps' Second Division in mid June.

[153] *Ibid.*

[154] *Ibid.* Regiment was transferred to the Third Brigade of the corps' First Division in mid June.

[155] When the Third Brigade was dissolved, Colonel Berdan returned to command of his regiment, the 1st U.S. Sharpshooters.

[156] *OR* vol.27, pt.1, p.159. Regiment was transferred to the Second Brigade of the corps' First Division in mid June.

2nd United States Sharpshooters – Major Homer R. Stoughton[157]

Artillery Brigade
Captain George E. Randolph
1st New Jersey Artillery, Battery B – Captain A. Judson Clark[158]
1st New York Artillery, Battery D – Captain George B Winslow[159]
4th New York Battery – Lieutenant William T. McLean[160]
1st Rhode Island Artillery, Battery E – Lieutenant John K. Bucklyn[161]
4th United States Artillery, Battery K – Lieutenant Francis W. Seeley[162]

FIFTH ARMY CORPS[163]
Major General George G. Meade

FIRST DIVISION
Brigadier General James Barnes

First Brigade[164]
Colonel William Stowel Tilton
18th Massachusetts - Colonel Joseph Hayes[165]
22nd Massachusetts - Lieutenant Colonel Thomas Sherwin, Jr.[166]
1st Michigan - Colonel Ira C. Abbott[167]

---

[157] Ibid.

[158] Hanifen, Michael, *History of Battery B, First New Jersey Artillery*, p.151.

[159] Phisterer, *NYWR*, vol.2, p.1215.

[160] Ibid, p.1570.

[161] *ARAGSRI*, vol.2, p.851.

[162] *OR* vol.25, pt.1, p.490; Rodenbough & Haskin, *The Army of the United States*, p.369; *LOASU*, p.579. Lieutenant Isaac Arnold, who commanded the battery at Chancellorsville, was wounded during the battle. Lieutenant Francis W. Seeley was in command of the battery on 3 June.

[163] The corps Third Division was dissolved due to expiring enlistments. Six regiments, the 123rd, 126th, 129th 131st, 133rd, and 134th Pennsylvania all left the army and were mustered out. The two remaining regiments of Pennsylvanians were reassigned to other units in the corps. Throughout June the Fifth Corps contained two divisions. Three days before the battle the corps would be joined by a third division, sent from Washington.

[164] Dyer, *CWR, vol.3, p.1219*. The 2nd Maine was ordered home on 20 May. The regiment's three year men were transferred to the 20th Maine. Its two year men were mustered out on 9 June.

[165] *MSSM*, vol.2, p.351.

[166] Ibid, p.651.

[167] *RSMV*, vol.1, p.4.

13th New York Battalion (two companies) – Captain William Downey[168]
25th New York – Colonel Charles A. Johnson[169]
118th Pennsylvania – Lieutenant Colonel James Gwyn[170]

Second Brigade[171]
Colonel Jacob Bowman Sweitzer
9th Massachusetts – Colonel Patrick R. Guiney[172]
32nd Massachusetts – Colonel George L. Prescott[173]
4th Michigan – Colonel Harrison H. Jeffords[174]
62nd Pennsylvania – Lieutenant Colonel James C. Hull[175]

Third Brigade
Colonel Strong Vincent
20th Maine – Colonel Joshua L. Chamberlain
16th Michigan – Lieutenant Colonel Norval E. Welch[176]
44th New York – Colonel James C. Rice[177]
83rd Pennsylvania – Captain Orpheus S. Woodward[178]

SECOND DIVISION
Major General George Sykes

First Brigade
Brigadier General Romeyn Beck Ayres[179]

---

[168] Phisterer, *NYWR*, vol.3, p.1887-1889. The bulk of the regiment was mustered out shortly after Chancellorsville in Rochester. Two companies, H and K, of three year men remained with the brigade until late June when they were transferred to the 140th New York.

[169] *Ibid*, p.2013. The 25th New York would be ordered home for muster out in late June.

[170] Bates, *HPV*, vol.6, p.1316.

[171] Phisterer, *NYWR*, vol.3, p.1901. The 14th New York was sent home for muster out shortly after Chancellorsville. The regiment was mustered out in Utica on 22 thru 24 May.

[172] *MSSM*, vol.1, p.651.

[173] *MSSM*, vol.3, p.464.

[174] *RSMV*, vol.4, p.61.

[175] Bates, *HPV*, vol.3, p.460.

[176] *RSMV*, vol.16, p.169.

[177] Phisterer, *NYWR*, vol.3, p.2290.

[178] *OR* vol.25, pt.2, p.579; *OR* vol.27, pt.1, p.161.

[179] *OR* vol.25, pt.2, p.580.

3rd United States Infantry (Companies B, C, F, G, I
and K) – Captain Henry W. Freedly[180]
4th United States Infantry (Companies C, F, H and K) – Captain Hiram Dryer[181]
12th United States Infantry, 1st Battalion (Companies A, B, C, D and G)
12th United States Infantry, 2nd Battalion (Companies
A, C and D) - Captain Matthew M. Blunt[182]
14th United States Infantry, 1st Battalion (Companies A, B, D, E, F and G)
14th United States Infantry, 2nd Battalion (Companies
F and G) – Major Grotius R. Giddings[183]

Second Brigade
Colonel Sidney Burbank[184]

2nd United States Infantry (Companies B, C, F, I
and K) – Captain Samuel A. McKee[185]
6th United States Infantry (Companies D, F, G, H
and I) – Captain Levi C. Bootes[186]
7th United States Infantry (Companies A, B, E and I) – Captain James P. Martin[187]
10th United States Infantry (Companies D, G and H) – Captain William Clinton[188]
11th United States Infantry, 1st Battalion (Companies B, C,
D, E, F and G) – Major De Lancey Floyd-Jones[189]
17th United States Infantry, 1st Battalion (Companies A, C, D, G and H)

---

[180] Rodenbough & Haskin, *The Army of the United States*, p.447; *OR* vol.27, pt.1, p.161; *LOAUS*, p.317. Freedley was brevetted major for gallantry at Chancellorsville.

[181] *LOAUS*, p.289. Dryer was brevetted major for gallantry at Fredericksburg and lieutenant colonel got gallantry at Chancellorsville.

[182] Rodenbough & Haskin, *The Army of the United States*, p.560; *Official Army Register for January 1889*, p.156. *LOAUS*, p.199. Blunt was in command of the eight companies from both battalions. He was brevetted major for gallantry at Malvern Hill and lieutenant colonel for gallantry at Fredericksburg. Unsubstantiated sources note Blunt's middle name as Marsh.

[183] *OR* vol.25, pt.2, p.580. *LOAUS*, p.329. Giddings was in command of the eight companies from both battalions.

[184] *OR* vol.25, pt.2, p.580.

[185] Rodenbough & Haskin, *The Army of the United States*, p.428. *LOAUS*, p.470. Captain McKee was in command of the regiment in early June. Sometime during the month Major Arthur T. Lee took command.

[186] *OR* vol.27, pt.1, p.161; *LOAUS*, p.202. Bootes was brevetted major for gallantry at Malvern Hill and lieutenant colonel for gallantry at Fredericksburg.

[187] *LOAUS*, p.454.

[188] *LOAUS*, p.248.

[189] *OR* vol.27, pt.1, p.161; *LOAUS*, p.312. Floyd-Jones was brevetted lieutenant colonel for gallantry during the Peninsular Campaign.

17th United States Infantry, 2nd Battalion (Companies
A and B) – Major George L. Andrews[190]

Third Brigade
Colonel Patrick H. O'Rorke[191]
140th New York – Major Isaiah F. Force[192]
146th New York – Colonel Kenner Garrard[193]
91st Pennsylvania – Lieutenant Colonel Joseph H. Sinex[194]
155th Pennsylvania – Lieutenant Colonel John H. Cain[195]

Artillery Brigade
Captain Augustus P. Martin
Massachusetts Artillery, 3rd Battery (Battery C) – Captain Augustus P. Martin[196]
1st New York Artillery, Battery C – Captain Almont Barnes[197]
1st Ohio Artillery, Battery L – Captain Frank C. Gibbs[198]
5th United States Artillery, Battery D – Lieutenant Charles Edward Hazlett[199]
5th United States Artillery, Battery I – Lieutenant Malbone F. Watson[200]

SIXTH ARMY CORPS[201]

---

[190] *LOAUS*, p.163. Andrews was in command of the seven companies from both battalions. Andrews was brevetted lieutenant colonel for gallantry at the second battle at Bull Run and colonel for gallantry at the Battle of Chancellorsville.

[191] Bennett, ***Sons of Old Monroe***, p.209. Although the brigade was under the command of O'Rorke in early June, Colonel Stephen H. Weed would assume command on 13 June.

[192] Phisterer, *NYWR*, vol.4, p.3616.

[193] Phisterer, *NYWR*, vol.2, p.1751, vol.5, p.3688. The 5th New York's two year men left the brigade, their term of enlistment up on 14 May. They were mustered out in New York on same date. The regiment's three year men were transferred to the 146th New York.

[194] Bates, *HPV*, vol.5, p.193.

[195] Bates, *HPV*, vol.8, p.806.

[196] *MSSM*, vol.5, p.378.

[197] Phisterer, *NYWR*, vol.2, p.1214.

[198] *OR* vol.27, pt.1, p.162; Reid, *OW*, vol.II, p.889. Ohio in the War lists Frank C. Gibbs as T. C. Gibbs.

[199] *OR* vol.27, pt.1, p.162; *LOAUS*, p.366.

[200] *OR* vol.27, pt.1, p.162; *LOAUS*, p.658.

[201] *OR* vol.25, pt.2, p.466. At Chancellorsville the Sixth Corps contained a small organization known as the Light Division. The division was nothing more than a brigade size group of regiments under the command of Colonel Hiram Burnham. As two year regiments began departing, the division was broken up and its regiments distributed to various brigades in the Sixth Corps which had lost regiments. One regiment, the 31st New York, returned to its home state for muster out.

Major General John Sedgwick

FIRST DIVISION
Brigadier General Horatio Gouverneur Wright

First Brigade
Brigadier General Alfred Thomas Archimedes Torbert[202]
1st New Jersey – Lieutenant Colonel William Henry Jr.[203]
2nd New Jersey – Lieutenant Colonel Charles Wiebecke[204]
3rd New Jersey – Captain William E. Bryan[205]
4th New Jersey – Colonel William Birney[206]
15th New Jersey – Lieutenant Colonel Edward L. Campbell[207]
23rd New Jersey – Colonel Edward Burd Grubb[208]

Second Brigade[209]
Brigadier General Joseph Jackson Bartlett
5th Maine – Colonel Clark S. Edwards[210]
121st New York – Colonel Emory Upton[211]
95th Pennsylvania – Captain Edward Carroll[212]
96th Pennsylvania – Major William H. Lessig[213]

Third Brigade[214]
Brigadier General David Allen Russell

---

[202] Eicher, & Eicher, *High Commands*, p.533.

[203] Stryker, *ROMNJ*, vol.1, p.68.

[204] *Ibid*, p.102.

[205] *Ibid*, p.150.

[206] *Ibid*, p.182.

[207] *Ibid*, p.697.

[208] *Ibid*, p.779; Grubb Obituary, New York Times, 8 July 1913.

[209] The 16th and 21st New York regiments were sent home in May for muster out. The former was mustered out on 22 May, the latter on 18 May. The 95th Pennsylvania was transferred in from the Division's Third Brigade.

[210] *AGSM*, 1863, Appendix D, p.188; *MGRMC*, p.367.

[211] Phisterer, *NYWR*, vol.4, p.3424.

[212] Bates, *HPV*, vol.5, p.340. Captain Carroll was captain of Company F.

[213] *Ibid*, p.390.

[214] The 18th and 32nd New York regiments were sent home for muster out. The 18th was mustered out in Albany on 28 May. The 32nd had just departed, mustering out on 9 June in New York City.

6th Maine – Colonel Hiram Burnham[215]
5th Wisconsin – Colonel Thomas S. Allen[216]
119th Pennsylvania – Colonel Peter C. Ellmaker[217]
49th Pennsylvania – Lieutenant Colonel Thomas M. Hulings[218]

SECOND DIVISION
Brigadier General Albion Parris Howe

Second Brigade[219]
Colonel Lewis Addison Grant[220]
26th New Jersey – Colonel Andrew J. Morrison[221]
2nd Vermont – Major John S. Tyler (Colonel James H. Walbridge)[222]
3rd Vermont – Colonel Thomas O. Seaver[223]
4th Vermont – Colonel Charles B. Stoughton[224]
5th Vermont – Lieutenant Colonel John R. Lewis[225]
6th Vermont – Colonel Elisha L. Barney[226]

---

[215] *AGSM*, 1863, Appendix D, p.219; *MGRMC*, p.398. Transferred from the Light Division. Colonel Burnham commanded the corps' Light Division until it was broken up on 11 May, when he returned to command of the 6th.

[216] Chapman, *RWV*, p.437. Transferred from the Light Division.

[217] Bates, *HPV*, vol.7, p.6.

[218] Bates, *HPV*, vol.2, p.1244.

[219] The division did not contain a First Brigade.

[220] Peck, Theodore S., *Revised Roster of Vermont Volunteers and List of Vermonters Who Served in the Army and Navy of the United States During the War of the Rebellion 1861-66* (hereafter *VVWR*), p.144.

[221] Stryker, *ROMNJ*, vol.1, p.839.

[222] Peck, *VVWR*, p.30; Benedict, *Vermont in the Civil War*, vol.1, p.106-109. The 31 May organization of the Army of the Potomac list Major John S. Tyler in command of the regiment. Walbridge is listed as having led the regiment at both Chancellorsville and Gettysburg. Since Walbridge was not a casualty at Chancellorsville it must be assumed that he was away from the regiment when the army's 31 May organization table was compiled.

[223] Peck, *VVWR*, p.70.

[224] *Ibid*, p.108.

[225] *Ibid*, p.144.

[226] *Ibid*, p.181.

Third Brigade[227]
Colonel Daniel D. Bidwell[228]
7th Maine – Lieutenant Colonel Selden Connor[229]
21st New Jersey – Lieutenant Colonel Isaac S. Mettler[230]
43rd New York – Colonel Benjamin F. Baker[231]
49th New York (Detachment 33rd New York) –
Lieutenant Colonel George W. Johnson[232]
77th New York – Lieutenant Colonel Winsor B. French[233]
61st Pennsylvania – Lieutenant Colonel George F. Smith[234]

THIRD DIVISION
Major General John Newton

First Brigade
Brigadier General Alexander Shaler (Colonel Silas Titus)[235]
65th New York – Lieutenant Colonel Joseph E. Hamblin[236]
67th New York – Colonel Nelson Cross
122nd New York – Colonel Silas Titus (Lieutenant Colonel Augustus W. Dwight)[237]

---

[227] Phisterer, *NYWR*, vol.3, pp.1958, 2115. The 20th and 33rd New York regiments were sent home for muster out. The 20th mustered out on 1 June. The 33rd mustered out on 2 June.

[228] *Ibid*, p.2379. Bidwell was colonel of the 49th New York.

[229] *AGSM*, 1863, Appendix D, p.250.

[230] Stryker, *ROMNJ*, vol.1, p.742.

[231] Phisterer, *NYWR*, vol.3, p.2271. Transferred from the Light Division.

[232] *Ibid*, pp.2115, 2379. When the two year men of the 33rd New York were sent home for muster out, the three year men of the 33rd were attached to the 49th New York. The men of the 33rd were not officially transferred to the 49th until October 1863.

[233] Phisterer, *NYWR*, vol.4, p.2815.

[234] Bates, *HPV*, vol.3, p.416. Transferred from the Light Division.

[235] Brigadier General Alexander Shaler was the brigade's commander as the campaign began but was not listed as being in command on 31 May. Evidently he was absent when the brigade submitted its information. Colonel Silas Titus of the 122nd New York is shown as being in command on 31 May according to the organization document.

[236] Phisterer, *NYWR*, vol.3, p.2630. Hamblin took command of the regiment when Colonel Shaler was elevated to brigade command.

[237] Phisterer, *NYWR*, vol.4, p.3440. Colonel Titus was the regiment's commander as the campaign began but was listed as in command of the brigade due to General Shaler's absence on 31 May. When Shaler returned, Silas Titus returned to command of the 122nd New York.

23rd Pennsylvania – Colonel John Ely[238]
82nd Pennsylvania – Major Isaac C. Bassett[239]

Second Brigade
Colonel Henry L. Eustis
7th Massachusetts – Lieutenant Colonel Franklin P. Harlow[240]
10th Massachusetts – Lieutenant Colonel Joseph B. Parsons[241]
37th Massachusetts – Colonel Oliver Edwards[242]
36th New York – Lieutenant Colonel James J. Walsh[243]
2nd Rhode Island – Colonel Horatio Rogers, Jr.[244]

Third Brigade
Brigadier General Frank Wheaton
62nd New York –Colonel David J. Nevin[245]
93rd Pennsylvania – Colonel James M. McCarter[246]
98th Pennsylvania – Colonel John F. Ballier[247]
102nd Pennsylvania – Captain William McIlwaine[248]
139th Pennsylvania – Colonel Frederick H. Collier[249]

Artillery Brigade
Colonel Charles Henry Tompkins[250]
Massachusetts Artillery, 1st Battery (Battery A) – Lieutenant Jacob Federhen[251]

---

[238] Bates, *HPV*, vol.1, p.319.

[239] Bates, *HPV*, vol.4, p.1209.

[240] *MSSM*, vol.1, p.512.

[241] Ibid, p.698.

[242] *MSSM*, vol.3, p.771.

[243] Phisterer, *NYWR*, vol.3, p.2148. The regiment's colonel, William Henry Browne, was wounded at Salem Church and would not return to the regiment until it was mustered out on 15 July 1863. While the regiment was present with the brigade at the inauguration of the campaign, it left on its journey to New York for muster out before the brigade fought at Gettysburg.

[244] *ARAGSRI*, vol.1, p.193.

[245] Phisterer, *NYWR*, vol.3, p.2574.

[246] Bates, *HPV*, vol.5, p.294.

[247] Ibid, p.469.

[248] Ibid, p.653.

[249] Bates, *HPV*, vol.7, p.383.

[250] *OR* vol.27, pt.1, p.163.

[251] *MSSM*, vol.5, p.347.

1ˢᵗ New Jersey Artillery, Battery A – Lieutenant Augustine N. Parsons[252]
1ˢᵗ New York Battery – Captain Andrew Cowen[253]
3ʳᵈ New York Battery – Lieutenant Alexander S. Thomson[254]
1ˢᵗ Pennsylvania Artillery, Batteries C and D – Lieutenant William Munk[255]
2ⁿᵈ United States Artillery, Battery D – Lieutenant Edward D. Williston[256]
2ⁿᵈ United States Artillery, Battery G – Lieutenant John H. Butler[257]
5ᵗʰ United States Artillery, Battery F – Lieutenant Charles R. Hickox[258]

ELEVENTH ARMY CORPS
Major General Oliver O. Howard

FIRST DIVISION
Brigadier General Francis Channing Barlow

First Brigade
Colonel Gotthilf Bourry DeIvernois[259]
41ˢᵗ New York – Major Detleo von Einsiedel[260]
54ᵗʰ New York – Major Stephen Kovacs[261]
68ᵗʰ New York – Lieutenant Colonel Carl Vogel[262]
153ʳᵈ Pennsylvania – Major John F. Frueauff[263]

Second Brigade
Brigadier General Adelbert Ames

---

[252] Stryker, *ROMNJ*, vol.2, p.1369.

[253] Phisterer, *NYWR*, vol.2, pp.1560-1561.

[254] *Ibid*, pp.1566-1568. Captain William A. Harn, who took command of the battery on 13 April, was evidently absent from his command at the end of May.

[255] Bates, *HPV*, vol.2, p.956, 983, 986.. Captain Michael Hall of Battery D resigned his commission on 21 March. Captain Jeremiah McCarthy of Battery B, shortly after Chancellorsville, departed due to illness, placing Batteries C and D in the hands of Lieutenant Munk.

[256] *OR* vol.27, pt.1, p.163.

[257] *Ibid*; Rodenbough & Haskin, *The Army of the United States,* p.323.

[258] *OR* vol.27, pt.1, p.163. According to the *OR* Lieutenant Hickox was in command of the battery on 13 May. By the battle of Gettysburg, Lieutenant Leonard Martin was in charge of the battery.

[259] Phisterer, *NYWR*, vol.3, p.2674. DeIvernois was in command of the brigade due to the arrest of Colonel Leopold von Gilsa.

[260] *Ibid*, p.2238.

[261] *Ibid*, p.2446.

[262] *Ibid*, p.2674.

[263] Bates, *HPV*, vol.8, p.777.

17th Connecticut – Lieutenant Colonel Douglas Fowler[264]
25th Ohio – Lieutenant Colonel Jeremiah Williams[265]
75th Ohio – Captain Benjamin Morgan[266]
107th Ohio – Major George Arnold[267]

SECOND DIVISION
Brigadier General Adolph Wilhelm August Friedrich von Steinwehr

First Brigade
Colonel Adolphus Buschbeck[268]
29th New York – Colonel Louis Hartmann[269]
134th New York – Colonel Charles R. Coster[270]
154th New York – Colonel Patrick H. Jones[271]
27th Pennsylvania – Lieutenant Colonel Lorenz Cantador[272]
73rd Pennsylvania – Lieutenant Colonel William Moore[273]

Second Brigade
Colonel Orland Smith
33rd Massachusetts – Colonel Adin B. Underwood[274]
136th New York – Colonel James Wood Jr.[275]
55th Ohio – Lieutenant Colonel Charles B. Gambee[276]
73rd Ohio – Lieutenant Colonel Richard Long[277]

---

[264] *CCVO*, p.668.

[265] *OIWR*, vol.3, p.167.

[266] *OIWR*, vol.6, p.207.

[267] *OIWR*, vol.7, p.629.

[268] Bates, *HPV*, vol.1, p.394. Buschbeck left the brigade on a leave of absence in early June and turned the brigade over to Colonel Charles R. Coster.

[269] Phisterer, *NYWR*, vol.3, p.2063. The 29th left the army early in June and was mustered out in New York City on 20 June.

[270] Phisterer, *NYWR*, vol.4, p.3566.

[271] Phisterer, *NYWR*, vol.5, p.3792.

[272] Bates, *HPV*, vol.1, p.394.

[273] Bates, *HPV*, vol.4, p.869.

[274] *MSSM*, vol.3, p.538.

[275] Phisterer, *NYWR*, vol.4, p.3583.

[276] *OIWR*, vol.5, p.39. Transferred from First Division, Second Brigade.

[277] *OIWR*, vol.6, p.125.

THIRD DIVISION
Major General Carl Schurz

First Brigade
Colonel George von Amsberg[278]
82nd Illinois – Lieutenant Colonel Edward S. Salomon[279]
45th New York – Captain Charles Koch[280]
157th New York – Lieutenant Colonel George W. Arrowsmith[281]
61st Ohio – Colonel Stephen J. McGroarty[282]
74th Pennsylvania – Captain Henry Krauseneck[283]

Second Brigade
Colonel Wladimir Krzyzanowski
8th New York (one company) – Lieutenant Hermann Foerster[284]
58th New York – Lieutenant Colonel August Otto[285]
119th New York – Captain Otto von Borries[286]

---

[278] According to the 31 May organization of the army, brigade commander Alexander Schimmelfennig was not with the brigade at the beginning of June.

[279] *RAGSI*, vol.5, p.100

[280] Phisterer, *NYWR*, vol.3, pp.2306, 2315. As of 31 May, Koch was listed as a Captain but according to Phisterer he was promoted from Captain of Company E to Major on 19 May.

[281] Phisterer, *NYWR*, vol.5, p.3832.

[282] *OIWR*, vol.5, p.295.

[283] *Electronic Source:* http://www.digitalarchives.state.pa.us/archive.asp, Last accessed: 7/21/12. Bates does not list a Captain Henry Krauseneck within the 74th. No were in Bates' narrative is he listed as ever commanding the regiment. The master index for the Broadfoot addition of Bates does not list him as well. The *OR* lists him as in command of the regiment on 31 May. He is also listed as commanding the regiment at Gettysburg after three previous commanders were either wounded or captured. He evidently took command of the regiment sometime during or after the retreat through town. The Pennsylvania State Archives contains a copy of Krauseneck's service record in its veterans card file. According to his service record Krauseneck enrolled on 21 September 1861 at Allentown, Pennsylvania. He was mustered into Company I and promoted to captain on 23 September 1862.

[284] Phisterer, *NYWR*, vol.3, pp.1815, 1820. The two year men of the 8th New York was mustered out on 22 April 1863. The remaining three year men were organized into an independent company and attached to Eleventh Corps headquarters as Provost Guard. On 31 May the company was reported on corps returns as being assigned to the brigade, however, on brigade and divisional returns the company is unaccounted for.

[285] *Ibid*, p.2503.

[286] Phisterer, *NYWR*, vol.4, p.3398.

75th Pennsylvania – Major August Ledig[287]
82nd Ohio – Colonel James S. Robinson[288]
26th Wisconsin – Lieutenant Colonel Hans Boebel[289]

Artillery Brigade
Captain Michael Wiedrich
1st New York Artillery, Battery I – Captain Michael Wiedrich[290]
2nd New York Battery – Captain Hermann Jahn[291]
13th New York Battery – Lieutenant William Wheeler[292]
1st Ohio Artillery, Battery I – Captain Hubert Dilger[293]
1st Ohio Artillery, Battery K – Captain Lewis Heckman[294]

TWELFTH ARMY CORPS
Major General Henry Warner Slocum

FIRST DIVISION
Brigadier General Alpheus Starkey Williams

First/Second Brigade[295]
Colonel Archibald L. McDougall
5th Connecticut – Captain Henry W. Daboll[296]
20th Connecticut – Major Philo B. Buckingham[297]
3rd Maryland – Colonel Joseph M. Sudsburg[298]

---

[287] Bates, *HPV*, vol.4, p.922.

[288] *OIWR*, vol.6, p.509.

[289] Chapman, *RWV*, vol.2, p.312.

[290] Phisterer, *NYWR*, vol.2, pp.1210, 1217. Captain Wiedrich would return to his battery when Major Thomas Osborn took command of the Eleventh Corps Artillery Brigade later in June.

[291] *Ibid*, pp.1563.

[292] *Ibid*, pp.1591.

[293] Reid, *OW*, vol.II, p.889.

[294] *Ibid*.

[295] Phisterer, *NYWR*, vol.3, p.2052; *OR* vol.25, pt.2, p.583. The First and Second Brigades were consolidated on 13 May. The 28th New York of the First Brigade was sent home for muster out. It was mustered out on 2 June in Albany. The 128th Pennsylvania was relieved of duty with the First Brigade on 12 May and was mustered out in Harrisburg on 19 May.

[296] *CCVO*, p.271.

[297] *Ibid*, p.720.

[298] *HRMV*, vol.1, p.113.

123rd New York – Major James C. Rogers[299]
145th New York – Lieutenant Colonel Roswell L. Van Wegenen[300]
46th Pennsylvania – Colonel James L. Selfridge[301]

Third Brigade
Brigadier General Thomas Howard Ruger
27th Indiana – Lieutenant Colonel John Roush Fesler[302]
2nd Massachusetts – Major Charles R. Mudge[303]
13th New Jersey – Captain George A. Beardsley[304]
107th New York – Captain John M. Losie[305]
3rd Wisconsin – Colonel William Hawley[306]

SECOND DIVISION
Brigadier General John White Geary

First Brigade
Colonel Charles Candy
5nd Ohio – Colonel John H. Patrick[307]
7th Ohio – Colonel William R. Creighton[308]
29th Ohio – Lieutenant Colonel Thomas Clark[309]
66th Ohio – Lieutenant Colonel Eugene Powell[310]
28th Pennsylvania – Captain Conrad U. Meyer[311]
147th Pennsylvania – Lieutenant Colonel Ario Pardee, Jr.[312]

---

[299] Phisterer, *NYWR*, vol.4, p.3456.

[300] Phisterer, *NYWR*, vol.5, p.3680.

[301] Bates, *HPV*, vol.2, p.1117

[302] *RAGSIN*, vol.2, p.261.

[303] *MSSM*, vol.1, p.111. Major Mudge was promoted to Lieutenant Colonel on 6 June 1863.

[304] Stryker, *ROMNJ*, vol.1, p.628

[305] Phisterer, *NYWR*, vol.4, p.3258-3259. The regiments colonel, Nirom M. Crane was absent from the regiment on 3 June and would not return until 24 June.

[306] Chapman, *RWV*, vol.1, p.385.

[307] Reid, *OW*, vol.II, p.40.

[308] *Ibid*, p.54.

[309] *Ibid*, p.197. Clark would resign on 19 June.

[310] *Ibid*, p.385.

[311] Bates, *HPV*, vol.1, pp.437, 460. Meyer was captain of Company G. The regiment's colonel, Thomas J. Ahl was absent on 31 May and would not return before the Battle of Gettysburg.

[312] Bates, *HPV*, vol.7, p.557.

Second Brigade[313]
Colonel George Ashworth Cobham, Jr.
29th Pennsylvania – Lieutenant Colonel William Richards, Jr.[314]
109th Pennsylvania – Captain Frederick L. Gimber[315]
111th Pennsylvania – Lieutenant Colonel Thomas M. Walker[316]

Third Brigade
Brigade General George Sears Greene
60th New York – Lieutenant Colonel John C. O. Redington[317]
78th New York – Major Winslow. M. Thomas[318]
102nd New York – Captain Benjamin F. Clayton[319]
137th New York – Colonel David Ireland[320]
149th New York – Lieutenant Colonel Koert S. Van Voorhees[321]

Artillery Brigade
Lieutenant Edward Duchman Muhlenberg[322]
1st New York Artillery, Battery M – Lieutenant John D. Woodbury[323]

---

[313] *Ibid*, pp.92, 110. The 124th and 125th Pennsylvania were sent home and mustered out on 16 May and 18 May respectively.

[314] Bates, ***HPV***, vol.1, p.503.

[315] Bates, ***HPV***, vol.6, p.963. Gimber was captain of Company E. The regiment's colonel, Henry J. Stainrook was killed at Chancellorsville.

[316] *Ibid*, p.1022.

[317] Phisterer, ***NYWR***, vol.3, p.2540.

[318] Phisterer, ***NYWR***, vol.4, p.2831; ***OR*** vol.25, pt.2, p.583. The ***OR*** notes that on 3 June Winslow M. Thomas of the 60th New York was in command of the 78th New York. This seems plausible since according to Phisterer the highest ranking officer with the 78th was Major William H. Randall. Thomas' service record does not indicate he was ever in command of the 78th. On 16 June, Lieutenant Colonel Herbert von Hammerstein took command of the regiment.

[319] Phisterer, ***NYWR***, vol.4, p.3188.

[320] *Ibid*, p.3594.

[321] Phisterer, ***NYWR***, vol.5, p.3832. Van Voorhees was a lieutenant colonel in the 137th New York. He is listed in the ***OR*** as in command of the 149th at the beginning of June. Sometime during June, the regiment's colonel, Henry A. Barnum returned to the regiment and is listed as being in command of the 149th at Gettysburg. Van Voorhees' service record does not indicate he was in command of the 149th at the beginning of June. His name is misspelled in the ***OR*** as Van Voorhis.

[322] Rodenbough & Haskin, ***The Army of the United States,*** p.365. Muhlenberg commanded the battery at Chancellorsville. Most sources list his middle name as Dutchman. The ***OR*** lists Muhlenberg as commanding the Twelfth Corps' artillery brigade as well as Battery F in early June.

[323] Phisterer, ***NYWR***, vol.2, p.1218.

Pennsylvania Artillery, Battery E – Lieutenant James D. McGill[324]
4th United States Artillery, Battery F – Lieutenant Edward Duchman Muhlenberg
5th United States Artillery, Battery K – Lieutenant William E. Van Reed[325]

ARTILLERY RESERVE
Brigadier General Robert Ogden Tyler

REGULAR DIVISION

First Brigade
Captain Dunbar R. Ransom[326]
1st United States, Battery H – Lieutenant Philip D. Mason[327]
3rd United States, Battery F – Lieutenant George F. Barstow[328]
3rd United States, Battery K – Lieutenant John G. Turnbull[329]
4th United States, Battery C – Lieutenant Evan Thomas[330]
4th United States, Battery G – Lieutenant Bayard Wilkeson[331]
5th United States, Battery C – Captain Dunbar R. Ransom[332]

Second Brigade
Captain John Caldwell Tidball[333]

---

[324] Bates, *HPV*, vol.10, p.886.

[325] *OR* vol.27, pt.1, p.166. Van Reed is listed as being in command of the battery as of 31 May. By the Battle of Gettysburg the battery would be under the command of Lieutenant David H. Kinzie.

[326] Captain Ransom was in command of the 5th United States Battery C and the brigade in early June. By the Battle of Gettysburg he would command the brigade, a junior officer being place in charge of the battery.

[327] *OR* vol.27, pt.1, p.167; *LOASU*, p.456.

[328] *LOASU*, p.181.

[329] Rodenbough & Haskin, *The Army of the United States*, p.348; *OR* vol.27, pt.1, p.167; *LOAUS*, p.638. Turnbull was brevetted captain for gallantry at Chancellorsville.

[330] Rodenbough & Haskin, *The Army of the United States*, p.362; *OR* vol.27, pt.1, p.167; *LOAUS*, p.626. Thomas was brevetted captain for gallantry at Fredericksburg.

[331] Rodenbough & Haskin, *The Army of the United States*, p.366; *OR* vol.27, pt.1, p.165; *LOAUS*, p.674. Wilkeson was brevetted captain for gallantry at Fredericksburg.

[332] Rodenbough & Haskin, *The Army of the United States*, p.382, 384; *OR* vol.27, pt.1, p.167; *LOAUS*, p.545. Ransom was brevetted captain for gallantry at Fredericksburg.

[333] *OR* vol.27, pt.3, p.57; Tidball, *"No Disgrace"*, pp.1, 298-300. On 24 May the horse artillery was broken up. On 31 May Tidball's Brigade was listed as part of the army's Regular Artillery Division. Tidball's Brigade was not with the force which crossed the Rappahannock on 9 June, inaugurating the Battle of Brandy Station. On 11 June Tidball's Brigade was ordered to replace Robertson's Brigade of Horse Artillery which was then assigned to the Cavalry Corps.

1st United States, Battery E – Captain Alanson M. Randol[334]
1st United States, Battery G – Lieutenant Egbert W. Olcott[335]
1st United States, Battery K – Captain William M. Graham[336]
2nd United States, Battery A – Captain John Caldwell Tidball[337]
3rd United States, Battery C – Lieutenant James R. Kelly[338]

VOLUNTEER DIVISION[339]
Major John A. Tompkins

First Brigade
Major Freeman McGilvery

6th Maine Battery – Lieutenant Edwin B. Dow[340]
5th Massachusetts Battery – Captain Charles A. Phillips Jr.[341]
1st New York Artillery, Battery B – Lieutenant Albert S. Sheldon[342]
1st New York Artillery, Battery G – Captain Nelson Ames[343]
10th New York Battery – Lieutenant Samuel Lewis[344]
Pennsylvania Artillery, Independent Battery C (Thompson's Battery) – Captain James Thompson[345]

Second Brigade

---

[334] *OR* vol.27, pt.1, p.167; *LOAUS*, p.545. Randol was brevetted captain for gallantry at New Market.

[335] *LOASU*, p.512. Olcott was brevetted captain for gallantry at New Market.

[336] *OR* vol.27, pt.1, p.167; *LOAUS*, p.337. Graham was brevetted major for gallantry during the Peninsular Campaign and lieutenant colonel for gallantry at Antietam.

[337] *OR* vol.27, pt.1, p.167. In early June Tidball was in command of the brigade as well as his battery.

[338] *LOAUS*, pp.408-409; Whittenberg, *The Battle of Brandy Station*, pp.48, 212. This battery was attached to Colonel Wyndham's cavalry brigaded at Brandy Station. At Brandy Station it was under the command of First Lieutenant William D. Fuller. Sometime between 31 May and 9 June Fuller took command from Lieutenant Kelly. Kelly was brevetted captain for gallantry at Gaines' Mill and major for gallantry at Fredericksburg.

[339] The Volunteer Division was organized on 16 May 1863 as outlined on 12 May in Special Order, No.129.

[340] *MGRMC*, p.332.

[341] Cowles, *History of the Fifth Massachusetts Battery*, p.979.

[342] Phisterer, *NYWR*, vol.2, p.1214.

[343] *Ibid*, p.1216.

[344] *Ibid*, p.1584.

[345] Bates, *HPV*, vol.10, p.869.

Major Thomas Ward Osborn[346]
1st Connecticut Heavy Artillery, Company B – Captain Albert F. Brooker[347]
1st Connecticut Heavy Artillery, Company M – Captain Franklin A. Pratt
5th New York Battery – Captain Elijah D. Taft[348]
15th New York Battery – Captain Patrick Hart[349]
29th New York Battery – Lieutenant Bernhard Wever[350]
30th New York Battery – Captain Adolph Voegelee[351]
32nd New York Battery – Captain Charles Kusserow[352]

Third Brigade
Captain Richard Waterman
1st New Hampshire Battery – Captain Frederick M. Edgell[353]
1st Pennsylvania Artillery, Battery F – Captain Robert Bruce Ricketts[354]
1st Pennsylvania Artillery, Battery G – Lieutenant Beldin Spence[355]
1st Rhode Island Artillery, Battery C – Captain Richard Waterman[356]
1st West Virginia Artillery, Battery C – Captain Wallace Hill[357]

Fourth Brigade
Captain Robert H. Fitzhugh

---

[346] Major Osborn would be transferred from command of the Second Brigade of the Reserve Volunteer Artillery Division to command of the Eleventh Corps Artillery Brigade before Gettysburg and would command it during the battle.

[347] *CCVO*, p.174.

[348] Phisterer, *NYWR*, vol.2, p.1572.

[349] *Ibid*, p.1597.

[350] *Ibid*, p.1622.

[351] *Ibid*, p.1623.

[352] *Ibid*, p.1627.

[353] Ayling, Augustus D., ***Revised Register of the Soldiers and Sailors of New Hampshire in the War of the Rebellion***, (hereafter ***RRSSNH***) p.1246.

[354] Bates, ***HPV***, vol.2, p.995; Sauers, Richard A. & Tomasak, Peter, ***Ricketts' Battery: A History of Battery F, 1st Pennsylvania Light Artillery***, p.229.

[355] Bates, ***HPV***, vol.2, p.1000.

[356] ***ARAGSRI***, vol.2, p.813. Waterman, although Captain of the 1st Rhode Island Light Artillery Company C was also in command of the Third Brigade in the Volunteer Division. When the Army of the Potomac's artillery was reorganized shortly before Gettysburg, Waterman lost his brigade and return to command of his original company.

[357] ***OARVF***, vol.3, p.1118.

Maryland Artillery, Battery A – Captain James H. Rigby[358]
1st New York Artillery, Battery K – Captain Robert H. Fitzhugh[359]
11th New York Battery – Lieutenant John E. Burton[360]
Pennsylvania Artillery, Independent Battery F (Hampton's Battery) – Captain Nathaniel Irish[361]
1st Rhode Island Artillery, Battery G – Captain George W. Adams[362]

CAVALRY CORPS[363]
Brigadier General Alfred Pleasonton[364]

FIRST DIVISION
Brigadier General John Buford (Temporary)[365]

First Brigade
Colonel Benjamin Franklin Davis[366]
8th Illinois Cavalry – Colonel David R. Clendenin[367]
3rd Indiana Cavalry (6 Companies) – Colonel George H. Chapman[368]
8th New York Cavalry – Lieutenant Colonel William L. Markell[369]

---

[358] *HRMV*, vol.1, p.797.

[359] Phisterer, *NYWR*, vol.2, p.1217.

[360] *Ibid*, p.1586.

[361] Bates, *HPV*, vol.10, p.895.

[362] *ARAGSRI*, vol.2, p.907.

[363] See Appendix C for the strength and composition of the Federal forces engaged during the Battle of Brandy Station.

[364] *OR* vol.25, pt.2, pp.513. When General Stoneman departed on sick leave, General Pleasonton was elevated to command of the Cavalry Corps on 22 May.

[365] *Ibid*; *OR* vol.25, pt.2, pp.522. Due to him being ranking officer, Buford assumed temporary command of the corps' First Division when General Pleasonton ascended to command the corps although he still maintained control over the Reserve Brigade.

[366] Davis commanded the First Division while General Buford was on detached service in the Bealeton area.

[367] *RAGSI*, vol.8, p.105.

[368] *RAGSIN*, vol.2, p.440; *SOR*, Series.II, vol.15, pp.228-229, 233. Only Companies A to F were with the regiment. Companies G thru K were with the Army of the Cumberland while Companies L and M were in Indianapolis on provost guard duty.

[369] Phisterer, *NYWR*, vol.1, p.889.

9th New York Cavalry (5 Companies) – Colonel William Sackett[370]

Second Brigade
Colonel Thomas Casimer Devin[371]
6th New York Cavalry (7 Companies) – Captain William E. Beardsley[372]
8th Pennsylvania Cavalry – Major Pennock Huey[373]
17th Pennsylvania Cavalry (10 Companies) – Major Coe Durland[374]

Artillery
6th New York Battery, Lieutenant Joseph William Martin[375]

SECOND DIVISION
Colonel Alfred Napoléon Alexander Duffié

First Brigade
Colonel Luigi Palma di Cesnola[376]
1st Massachusetts Cavalry (8 Companies) –
Lieutenant Colonel Greely S. Curtis[377]

---

[370] Phisterer, *NYWR*, vol.2, pp.913-914, 916; *SOR*, Part.II, vol.41, pp.388, 424. Colonel William Sackett was absent from the regiment on 31 May. The *OR* lists Major George S. Nichols as in command on 31 May. Phisterer lists Nichols as promoted to lieutenant colonel on 30 May to date from 1 May. Evidently the *OR* is incorrect in listing Nichols as a major by one day, pointing to the organization information being submitted before anyone was aware that Nichols was a new lieutenant colonel. Companies D and L were detached as headquarter escort for the Twelfth Corps. Companies B, C, E, G, and I were detached at Stafford Court House.

[371] The *OR* lists Colonel Josiah H. Kellogg as in command of the brigade on 31 May.

[372] Phisterer, *NYWR*, vol.1, pp.847, 854; *SOR* Part.II, vol.41, pp.345; Dyer, *CWR*, vol.3, p.1375. See Appendix C.

[373] Bates, *HPV*, vol.5, pp.115, 118. On 14 May the 8th Pennsylvania was detached for picket duty in King George County. It remained on picket below Aquia Creek and Falmouth until the army evacuated the Fredericksburg area.

[374] Bates, *HPV*, vol.8, p.1009. *SOR* Part.II, vol.57, pp.485, 502. Two companies, D and H, were on detached duty with Fifth Corps headquarters.

[375] *ARAGSNY*, vol.15, p.407. On 1 May Martin's Battery was ordered to report to General Pleasonton. Although the Battery was part of the First Division on 31 May, on 6 June it was ordered to report to General David Gregg and at the Battle of Brandy Station the battery was part of the Third Division.

[376] Dyer, *CWR*, vol.1, p.324. Colonel Horace Binney Sargent is listed in the *OR* as being in command of Duffié's First Brigade on 31 May. Dyer lists di Cesnola as taking command on 20 May.

[377] Crowninshield, *History of the First*, pp.118, 317; *SOR*, Series.II, vol.27, pp.107, 110, 112, 113. Companies K and L were stationed at Beaufort, South Carolina while Companies I and M were on duty at Hilton Head.

4th New York Cavalry – Lieutenant Colonel Augustus Pruyn[378]
6th Ohio Cavalry (10 Companies) – Major William Stedman[379]
1st Rhode Island Cavalry – Lieutenant Colonel John L. Thompson[380]

Second Brigade
Colonel John Irvin Gregg

3rd Pennsylvania Cavalry – Colonel John B. McIntosh
(Lieutenant Colonel Edward S. Jones)[381]
4th Pennsylvania Cavalry – Lieutenant Colonel William E. Doster[382]
16th Pennsylvania Cavalry – Major William A. West[383]

THIRD DIVISION
Brigadier General David McMurtrie Gregg

First Brigade
Colonel Calvin S. Douty[384]

1st Maine Cavalry (11 Companies) – Lieutenant Colonel Charles H. Smith[385]
2nd New York Cavalry (Detachment) – Lieutenant Robert Loudon[386]
10th New York Cavalry – Lieutenant Colonel William Irvine[387]

---

[378] Phisterer, *NYWR*, vol.1, pp.806, 818. With di Cesnola's elevation to brigade command, Pruyn was the ranking officer of the regiment. The *OR* list di Cesnola as the commanding officer of the 4th as of 31 May.

[379] McKinney, *Brandy Station*, p.254. Companies F and M would not join the regiment until March of 1864.

[380] *ARAGSRI*, vol.2, p.142.

[381] Bates, *HPV*, vol.3, pp.363, 369. McIntosh is listed in the *OR* as being in command of the 3rd Pennsylvania on 31 May. During the first days of June, command of the regiment would fall to Lieutenant Colonel Edward S. Jones. McIntosh would not be in command at Brandy Station but would replace the wounded Percy Wyndham at the head of the Second Division's First Brigade when the Cavalry Corps was reorganized on 11 June.

[382] *Ibid*, pp.522, 531.

[383] Bates, *HPV*, vol.8, p.950. Major West is listed as commanding the regiment on 31 May but by Brandy Station the regiment was under the command of Major William H. Frye.

[384] This brigade would be commanded by Colonel Hugh Judson Kilpatrick at Brandy Station. As of the end of May, Kilpatrick had yet to return from the Peninsula to take command.

[385] *MGRMC*, p.471; *SOR*, Part.II, vol.25, p.6. Company L was on detached duty with the headquarters of the First Corps.

[386] Phisterer, *NYWR*, vol.1, p.771. As of 31 May a portion of the regiment was still in the Yorktown area. The portion of the regiment near Fredericksburg was under the command of Lieutenant Robert Loudon of Company E.

[387] Phisterer, *NYWR*, vol.2, p.933.

District of Columbia Volunteer Cavalry (1 Company) – Captain William H. Orton

Second Brigade
Colonel Percy Wyndham
1st Maryland Cavalry – Lieutenant Colonel James Monroe Deems[388]
1st New Jersey Cavalry (11 Companies) – Lieutenant Colonel Virgil Broderick (Brodrick)[389]
1st Pennsylvania Cavalry (11 Companies) – Colonel John P. Taylor[390]
12th Illinois Cavalry – Lieutenant Colonel Hasbrouck Davis (Colonel Arno Voss)[391]

Reserve Brigade[392]
Brigadier General John Buford[393]
Major Charles Jarvis Whiting[394]

---

[388] *HRMV*, vol.1, p.704.

[389] Toombs, *New Jersey Troops*, p.424. Company L was assigned as headquarter escort for the Sixth Corps. Sources exist indicating Broderick's name was also spelled Brodrick.

[390] Bates, *HPV*, vol.2, p.1025. Company H was assigned as headquarter escort for the Sixth Corps.

[391] Eicher, & Eicher, *High Commands*, p.387; McKinney, *Brandy Station*, p.101; *OR* vol.25, pt.2, pp.455, 457; *OR* vol.27, pt.3, p.33. The 12th Illinois was still on the Virginia Peninsula as of 31 May. During Stoneman's Raid, the regiment had been under the command of Lieutenant Colonel Davis. The regiment returned north with Kilpatrick the first week of June. About this time the regiment's colonel, Arno Voss, returned from sick leave and assumed command. Upon its return, the regiment was ordered to join its original brigade, Wyndham's. Kilpatrick's order allowed Voss to take his time reporting to his old commander. As a result the 12th loitered around Stafford Court House while its old brigade and its new division moved into a position from which to inaugurate the fighting at Brandy Station on 9 June. As such, the 12th missed the fighting. Only a portion of the regiment would march north with the remainder of the army. At Gettysburg four companies would be present in General Buford's command.

[392] Elements of the 1st, 2nd, 5th, and 6th U. S. Cavalry were on detached duty at Army Headquarters.

[393] *OR* vol.25, pt.2, pp.513, 537, 584; *OR* vol.27, pt.3, p.64. On 28 May Buford was ordered to Bealeton with instructions to take command of all the cavalry forces in the area. He commanded Pleasonton's Right Wing at Brandy Station and was assigned permanent command of the First Division on 11 June.

[394] *OR* vol.25, pt.2, p.585. Whiting was in command of the Reserve Brigade in Buford's absence. Although Buford, as of 3 June, was official still in command of the reserves he would never return to brigade command. On 11 June Buford was placed in permanent command of the First Division and Whiting would continue to command the Reserve Brigade. Before Gettysburg however, Whiting would depart the army for recruitment duties in Maine.

6th Pennsylvania Cavalry (10 Companies) – Major Robert Morris Jr.[395]
1st United States Cavalry (10 Companies) – Captain Richard S. C. Lord[396]
2nd United States Cavalry – Captain Wesley Merritt[397]
5th United States Cavalry – Captain James E. Harrison[398]
6th United States Cavalry – Captain George C. Cram (Captain James S. Brisbin)[399]

Artillery Brigade[400]
Captain James Madison Robertson (Robinson)[401]
2nd United States, Battery B - Lieutenant Albert Oliver Vincent[402]
2nd United States, Battery L - Lieutenant Leroy L. Janes[403]
2nd United States, Battery M - Lieutenant Alexander Cummings McWhorter Pennington Jr.[404]
4th United States Artillery, Battery E – Lieutenant Samuel Sherer Elder[405]

---

[395] Bates, *HPV*, vol.4, p.753. Two companies of the 6th Pennsylvania, E and I, were on duty with the provost marshal at Army Headquarters.

[396] Dyer, *CWR*, vol.3, p.1689; *OR* vol.27, pt.1, p.166; *LOAUS*, p.439. Companies D and G assigned to duty in New Mexico.

[397] Eicher, & Eicher, *High Commands*, p.387; McKinney, *Brandy Station*, p.64. Merritt took command of the 2nd U. S. Cavalry due to the units ranking officer, Captain Charles Norris being on recruitment duty in Annapolis.

[398] *LOAUS*, p.358.

[399] *LOAUS*, pp.211, 261. Captain George C. Cram would be in command of the 6th U. S. at Brandy Station. Sources indicate that Captain Cram's, command was camped in the vicinity of Hartwood Church on 12 May 1863. While returning from a trip to General Buford's headquarters, he was captured by a small band of John S. Mosby's men. After being relieved of their supplies and horses, Cram and his companions were paroled. Reports seem to indicate that he returned to command of his regiment on or around 2 June. Commanding the regiment in his absence was Captain James S. Brisbin. *Electronic Source:* http://crossedsabers.blogspot.com/2009/05/fiddlers-green-george-c-cram.html, Last Accessed: 7/21/2012.

[400] Only one artillery brigade was assigned to the Cavalry Corps as of 31 May. Tidball's Brigade had been reassigned to the Regular Artillery Division 24 May.

[401] *LOAUS*, p.558. During his period of service Robinson would change his name to Robertson. When he changed his name is not indicated in his service record in *LOAUS*.

[402] *LOAUS*, pp.646-647. Batteries B & L were consolidated prior to the Peninsular Campaign and were officially under the command of Lieutenant Vincent.

[403] *LOAUS*, p.397.

[404] Wittenberg, *Brandy Station*, p.43, 211; *LOAUS*, p.565.

[405] *LOAUS*, p.299.

Appendix B

Organization of the Army of Northern Virginia – 3 June 1863[1]

General Robert Edward Lee, Commanding

GENERAL HEADQUARTERS[2]
Colonel Robert Hall Chilton - Chief of Staff and Inspector General[3]
Brigadier General William Nelson Pendleton - Chief of Artillery
Doctor Lafayette Guild - Medical Director
Lieutenant Colonel Briscoe Gerard Baldwin - Chief of Ordnance[4]
Lieutenant Colonel Robert Granderson Cole - Chief of Commissary[5]
Lieutenant Colonel James Lawrence Corley - Chief Quartermaster[6]
Major Henry Edward Young - Judge Advocate General[7]
Colonel Armistead Lindsay Long – Military Secretary
& Acting Assistant Chief of Artillery

---

[1] The organization shown here is based on a number of sources and is intended to portray the Confederate Army's organization and unit commanders at the inauguration of the campaign. The Confederates were not as diligent, or as frequent in documenting their organizational structure. General sources are: *OR* vol.27, pt.3, pp.919-922.; *OR* vol.25, pt.2, pp.823, 825-826. Although most regimental commander names are taken from the *OR*, many names are shown within the *OR* having only first and, or middle initials with the surname. In addition, a great number of middle initials were completely omitted in the *OR*. Many first and middle names as well as full names, have been confirmed through additional sources. *Italics* indicate some doubt as to a commanders presents on 3 June.

[2] Laino, Philip, ***Gettysburg Campaign Atlas***, p.445. The basis for the listing of General Lee's staff is taken from Laino's Order of Battle.

[3] ***CMH***, vol.3, part.2 p.584.

[4] Krick, ***Staff Officers***, p.66.

[5] *Ibid*, p.100.

[6] *Ibid*, p.103.

[7] *Ibid*, p.311.

Lieutenant Colonel Walter Herron Taylor – aide-de-camp & Assistant Adjutant General
Major Charles Marshall – aide-de-camp & Assistant Military Secretary
Major Charles Scott Venable – aide-de-camp & Assistant Inspector General[8]
Captain Samuel Richard Johnson – Engineer Officer[9]
39th Virginia Cavalry Battalion Companies A & C – Headquarters Escort[10]

FIRST ARMY CORPS
Lieutenant General James Longstreet

PICKETT'S DIVISION[11]
Major General George Edward Pickett

Garnett's Brigade
Brigadier General Richard Brook Garnett
8th Virginia – Colonel Eppa Hunton
18th Virginia – Lieutenant Colonel Henry Alexander Carrington[12]
19th Virginia – Colonel Henry Gantt
28th Virginia – Colonel Robert Clotworthy Allen[13]
56th Virginia – Colonel William Dabney Stuart[14]

Armistead's Brigade
Brigadier General Lewis Addison Armistead
9th Virginia – Lieutenant Colonel James Skelton Gilliam[15]
14th Virginia – Colonel James Gregory Hodges[16]
38th Virginia – Colonel Edward Claxton Edmonds[17]

---

[8] *Ibid*, pp.292-293.

[9] Hyde, Bill, Did You Get There? Captain Samuel Johnston's Reconnaissance at Gettysburg, *GM*, Issue 29, p.86.

[10] Sifakis, *CCA*, Virginia, p.142.

[11] While the Federal Army typically numbered their divisions and brigades, Confederate divisions and brigades, on most occasions, were designated with the name of the unit's commander.

[12] Delauter, Roger U., *18th Virginia Infantry*, pp.44, 85; *SOR* Part.II, vol.71, p.529. Colonel Robert E. Withers had been wounded at Gaines' Mill and was permanently detached on duty at Danville.

[13] Fields, Frank E. Jr., *28th Virginia Infantry*, p.47; *SOR* Part.II, vol.72, p.76.

[14] Wallace, *A Guide to Virginia Military Organizations 1861-1865*, p.134; *SOR* Part.II, vol.72, p.601.

[15] Trask, Benjamin H., *9th Virginia Infantry*, pp.22, 66; *SOR* Part.II, vol.71, p.76. Early in June 1863, Gilliam would leave the regiment in the hands of Major John Crowder Owens due to what was termed "dropsy and debility."

[16] *SOR* Part.II, vol.71, p.346.

[17] Wallace, *Virginia Military Organizations*, p.120; *SOR* Part.II, vol.72, p.290.

53rd Virginia – Colonel William Roane Aylett[18]
57th Virginia – Colonel John Bowie Magruder[19]

Kempers's Brigade
Brigadier General James Lawson Kemper
1st Virginia – Colonel Lewis Burwell Williams Jr.[20]
3rd Virginia – Colonel Joseph Mayo, Jr.
7th Virginia – Colonel Waller Tazewell Patton[21]
11th Virginia – Major Kirkwood Otey[22]
24th Virginia – Colonel William Richard Terry[23]

Corse's Brigade[24]
Brigadier General Montgomery Dent Corse[25]
15st Virginia – Major Charles Hammett Clarke[26]
17th Virginia – Lieutenant Colonel Arthur Herbert[27]
29th Virginia – Lieutenant Colonel James Giles[28]
30th Virginia – Lieutenant Colonel Robert Stanard Chew[29]

---

[18] Gregory, G. Howard, *53rd Virginia Infantry and 5th Battalion Virginia Infantry*, p.143; *SOR* Part.II, vol.72, p.502.

[19] Wallace, *Virginia Military Organizations*, p.135.

[20] Wallace, *1st Virginia Infantry*, p.122; *SOR* Part.II, vol.70, p.579.

[21] Riggs, *7th Virginia Infantry*, p.88; *SOR* Part.II, vol.71, p.107. Waller Patton was the great uncle of General George S. Patton Jr.

[22] *OR* vol.27, pt.2, p.284; Bell, Robert T., *11th Virginia Infantry*, pp.24, 88, 75. Colonel David Funsten was wounded at Seven Pines on 5 May 1862 and was still listed as the regiment's colonel when General Lee inaugurated the campaign. Funsten would not resign until after Gettysburg.

[23] *SOR* Part.II, vol.71, p.778.

[24] When the campaign began, Corse's Brigade was left behind guarding the Hanover Junction area.

[25] *SOR* Part.II, vol.72, p.445.

[26] Manarin, *15th Virginia Infantry*, pp.88, 94; *SOR* Part.II, vol.71, p.408 The regiment's colonel, Thomas P. August was wounded at Malvern Hill on 1 July 1862 and never returned to the regiment. He was assigned to commandant duties at the Bureau of Conscription in Richmond. He is listed as "Permanently detached" in the 22 June commanding officer listings for Longstreet's Corps.

[27] Wallace, Lee A. Jr., *17th Virginia Infantry*, pp.118, 127; *SOR* Part.II, vol.71, p.445. The regiment's colonel, Morton Marye was wounded in the left leg at Second Manassas, forcing its amputation.

[28] Alderman, John Perry, *29th Virginia Infantry*, pp.80, 106; *SOR* Part.II, vol.72, p.112.

[29] Krick, Robert K., *30th Virginia Infantry*, p.88, 102; *SOR* Part.II, vol.72, p.128. The regiment's colonel, Archibald T. Harrison spent an inordinate amount of time absent from the regiment, supposable sick. By October 1864 he was assigned to temporary duty on the board of retirement of disabled and incompetent officers.

Divisional Artillery
Dearing's Battalion
Major James Griffin Dearing Jr.[30]
Fauquier (Virginia) Artillery – Captain Robert Mackey Stribling[31]
Hampden (Virginia) Artillery – Captain William H. Caskie[32]
Richmond Fayette Artillery – Captain Miles Cary Macon[33]
Lynchburg Artillery – Captain Joseph Gary Blount[34]

McLAWS' DIVISION
Major General Lafayette McLaws

Kershaw's Brigade
Brigadier General Joseph Brevard Kershaw
2nd South Carolina - Colonel John Doby Kennedy[35]
3rd South Carolina - Major Robert Clayton Maffett[36]
7th South Carolina - Colonel David Wyatt Aiken[37]
8th South Carolina - Colonel John Williford Henagan[38]
15th South Carolina – Colonel William Davie DeSaussure[39]
3rd South Carolina Battalion – Lieutenant Colonel William George Rice[40]

Semmes' Brigade
Brigadier General Paul Jones Semmes
10nd Georgia - Colonel John B. Weems[41]

---

[30] Wise, *Long Arm of Lee*, p.567.

[31] Andrus, Michael J., *The Brooke, Fauquier, Loudoun and Alexandria Artillery*, p.115; *SOR* Part. II, vol.70, p.356.

[32] Moore, *The Richmond Fayette… Artillery*, p.148; *SOR* Part.II, vol.70, p.357.

[33] Moore, *The Richmond Fayette… Artillery*, p.161; *SOR* Part.II, vol.70, p.264.

[34] Moore, *The Richmond Fayette… Artillery*, p.145.

[35] Wyckoff, Mac, *A History of the Second South Carolina Infantry 1861-65*, p.520.

[36] Wyckoff, Mac A., *A History of the 3rd South Carolina Regiment: Lee's Reliable*, p.412.

[37] Seigler, *South Carolina's Military Organizations Volume II*, p.157.

[38] Seigler, Robert S., *South Carolina's Military Organizations Volume I*, p.64; *SOR* Part.II, vol.64, p.748. Seigler lists Henagan's middle name as William. The *SOR* specifies the colonel's middle name as Williford.

[39] Clary, James B., *A History of the 15th South Carolina Volunteer Infantry Regiment 1861-1865*, p.375; *SOR* Part.II, vol.65, p.57.

[40] Davis, Sam B. *A History of the 3rd South Carolina Volunteer Infantry Battalion (James Battalion) 1861-1865*, p.442-443; *SOR* Part.II, vol.64, p.485.

[41] Henderson, *RCSG*, vol.2, pp. 1, 8.

50th Georgia – Colonel William R. Manning[42]
51st Georgia - Colonel Edward Ball[43]
53rd Georgia - Colonel James Phillip Simms[44]

Wofford's Brigade
Brigadier General William T. Wofford
3rd Battalion Georgia Sharpshooters – Lieutenant Colonel Nathan Louis Hutchins, Jr.[45]
16th Georgia – Colonel Goode Bryan[46]
18th Georgia – Lieutenant Colonel Solon Zackery Ruff[47]
24th Georgia - Colonel Robert McMillan[48]
Cobb's Legion – Lieutenant Colonel Luther Judson Glenn[49]
Phillips Legion – Lieutenant Colonel Elihu Stuart Barclay[50]

Barksdale's Brigade
Brigadier General William Barksdale
13th Mississippi – Colonel James W. Carter[51]
17th Mississippi – Colonel William Dunbar Holder[52]
18th Mississippi - Colonel Thomas M. Griffin[53]
21st Mississippi – Colonel Benjamin. Grubb Humphreys[54]

Divisional Artillery
Cabell's Battalion

---

[42] Henderson, *RCSG*, vol.5, p.289

[43] *Ibid*, pp.370, 420.

[44] *Ibid*, pp.532, 569; *SOR* Part.II, vol.7, p.65.

[45] Sifakis, *CCA*, South Carolina and Georgia, p.184; *SOR* Part.II, vol.6, p.185. The 3rd Battalion Georgia Sharpshooters were organized in May and June of 1863 and fought with Wofford's Brigade at Gettysburg. The unit was so new that it does not appear on nearly all published Gettysburg orders of battle.

[46] Henderson, *RCSG*, vol.2, p.480.

[47] *Ibid*, p.614; *SOR* Part.II, vol.6, p.444

[48] Henderson, *RCSG*, vol.3, p.1

[49] *SOR* Part.II, vol.7, p.223.

[50] *Ibid*, p.256.

[51] *SOR* Part.II, vol.33, p.271.

[52] *Ibid*, p.424.

[53] *Ibid*, p.476.

[54] *Ibid*, p.600.

Colonel Henry Coalter Cabell[55]
1st North Carolina Artillery, Battery A – Captain Basil C. Manly[56]
Pulaski (Georgia) Artillery – Captain John C. Fraser
1st Company Richmond Howitzers – Captain Edward Stephens McCarthy[57]
Troup (Georgia) Artillery – Captain Henry H. Carlton

HOOD'S DIVISION
Major General John Bell Hood

Benning's Brigade
Brigadier General Henry Lewis Benning[58]
2nd Georgia – Lieutenant Colonel William Terrell Harris (Colonel Edgar M. Butt)[59]
15th Georgia – Colonel Dudley McIver De Bose[60]
17th Georgia - Colonel Wesley C. Hodges[61]
20th Georgia - Colonel John Augustus Jones[62]

Anderson's Brigade
Brigadier General George Thomas Anderson
7th Georgia – Colonel William Wilkinson White[63]
8th Georgia – Colonel John R. Towers[64]
9th Georgia – Lieutenant Colonel John Clark Mounger[65]
11th Georgia - Colonel Francis Hamilton Little[66]

---

[55] Wise, *Long Arm of Lee*, p.567.

[56] Manarin, Louis H., *NCT* vol.I, p.41.

[57] Wallace, *The Richmond Howitzers*, p.129.

[58] *SOR* Part.II, vol.6, p.437.

[59] Henderson, *RCSG*, vol.1, p.373; *SOR* Part.II, vol.6, p.84. Gottfried, Bradley M., *Brigades of Gettysburg*, p.449. Colonel Edgar M. Butt had been away from the regiment since Malvern Hill, when a shell exploded nearby, blinding him.

[60] Henderson, *RCSG*, vol.2, p.408; *SOR* Part.II, vol.6, p.391.

[61] Henderson, *RCSG*, vol.2, p.558.

[62] *Ibid*, pp.766, 824.

[63] Henderson, *RCSG*, vol.1, p.833.

[64] *Ibid*, pp.912, 947.

[65] *OR* vol.27, pt.2, p.285; *SOR* Part.II, vol.6, p.289. Colonel B. Beck was wounded at Second Manassas and was still absent convalescing.

[66] Henderson, *RCSG*, vol.2, p.73; *SOR* Part.II, vol.6, p.339.

59th Georgia - Colonel Jack Brown[67]

Law's Brigade
Brigadier General Evander McIver Law
4th Alabama – Lieutenant Colonel Lawrence Houston Scruggs[68]
15th Alabama – Colonel William Calvin Oates[69]
44th Alabama – Colonel William Fake Perry[70]
47th Alabama - Colonel James W. Jackson[71]
48th Alabama - Colonel James Lawrence Sheffield[72]

Robertson's Brigade
Brigadier General Jerome Bonaparte Robertson
1st Texas – Lieutenant Colonel Phillip A. Work[73]
4th Texas – Colonel John Cotlett Garrett Key[74]
5th Texas – Colonel Robert Michael Powell[75]
3rd Arkansas - Colonel Vannoy Hartrog Manning[76]

Divisional Artillery
Henry's Battalion
Major Mathis Winston Henry[77]
Branch (North Carolina) Artillery – Captain Alexander C. Latham[78]

---

[67] Henderson, *RCSG*, vol.6, pp.1, 74.

[68] Krick, *Colonels*, pp.60, 339; Laine, & Penny, *Law's Alabama Brigade*, pp.76; *SOR* Part.II, vol.1, p.256. Sometime during the spring of 1863 the regiment's colonel, Pinckney D. Bowles was placed under arrest by General Law. Lieutenant Colonel Lawrence H. Scruggs was in charge of the regiment as the Confederates marched north.

[69] *SOR* Part.II, vol.1, p.465.

[70] *Ibid*, p.723.

[71] Krick, *Colonels*, p.207; Laine, & Penny, *Law's Alabama Brigade*, pp.28. Jackson had been in ill health since the beginning of the war.

[72] *SOR* Part.II, vol.1, p.767.

[73] *OR* vol.27, pt.2, p.284; Gottfried, *Brigades*, p.438; *SOR* Part.II, vol.68, p.500. Colonel Alexis T. Rainey was wounded at Gaines' Mill, 27 June 1862 and was still absent convalescing.

[74] Sifakis, *CCA*, South Carolina and Georgia, p.112; *SOR* Part.II, vol.68, p.583.

[75] Gottfried, *Brigades*, p.436; *SOR* Part.II, vol.69, p.610.

[76] *SOR* Part.II, vol.2, p.311.

[77] Krick, *Colonels*, p.189.

[78] Manarin, *NCT* vol.I, pp.464-465. This unit's official designation was changed to 1st Company H, 40th Regiment North Carolina Troops (3rd Regiment North Carolina Artillery). The designation first appeared on its October 1863 muster roll.

Rowan (North Carolina) Artillery – Captain James Reilly[79]
German (South Carolina) Artillery – Captain William K. Bachman[80]
Palmetto (South Carolina) Light Artillery – Captain Hugh Richardson Garden[81]

CORPS ARTILLEY RESERVE
Chief of Artillery Colonel James Burdge Walton[82]

Alexander's Battalion
Colonel Edward Porter Alexander
Ashland (Virginia) Light Artillery – Captain Pichegru Woolfolk, Jr.[83]
Bedford (Virginia) Light Artillery – Captain Tyler C. Jordon[84]
Brooks (South Carolina) Artillery – Captain S. Capers Gilbert[85]
Madison (Louisiana) Artillery – Captain George V. Moody[86]
Richmond (Virginia) Artillery – Captain William Watts Parker[87]
Bath (Virginia) Artillery – Captain Osmond B. Taylor[88]

Eshleman's Battalion
Major Benjamin Franklin Eshleman[89]
1st Company, Washington (Louisiana) Artillery
– Captain Charles Winder Squires[90]
2nd Company, Washington (Louisiana) Artillery – Captain John B. Richardson[91]
3rd Company, Washington (Louisiana) Artillery – Captain Merritt B. Miller[92]

---

[79] *Ibid*, p.75. Also known as Company D, 10th Regiment North Carolina State Troops (1st Regiment North Carolina Artillery).

[80] Seigler, *South Carolina's Military Organizations Volume I*, p.279.

[81] Seigler, *South Carolina's Military Organizations Volume II*, p.327; *SOR* Part.II, vol.64, p.260.

[82] Wise, *Long Arm of Lee*, p.567.

[83] Koleszar, *Ashland, Bedford and Taylor Virginia Light Artillery*, p.72.

[84] *Ibid*, p.84.

[85] *SOR* Part.II, vol.64, p.256.

[86] *SOR* Part.II, vol.23, p.600.

[87] Wallace, *Virginia Military Organizations*, p.28.

[88] Koleszar, *Ashland, Bedford and Taylor Virginia Light Artillery*, p.102. Battery was also know as Eubank's then Taylor's Battery but appears as the Bath Artillery in most Confederate accounts.

[89] *SOR* Part.II, vol.23, p.605.

[90] Krick, *Colonels*, p.359.

[91] Sifakis, *CCA,* Louisiana, p.36.

[92] *Ibid*, p.38.

4th Company, Washington (Louisiana) Artillery – Captain Joseph Norcom[93]

SECOND ARMY CORPS
Lieutenant General Richard Stoddert Ewell
Escort – 39th Virginia Cavalry, Randolph's Company[94]
Provost Guard – 1st Battalion North Carolina Sharpshooters
(2 companies-A & B) – Ruffus Watson Wharton[95]

RODES' DIVISION
Major General Robert Emmett. Rodes

Daniel's Brigade[96]
Brigadier General Junius Daniel
2nd North Carolina Battalion–Major Hezekiah L. Andrews[97]
32nd North Carolina – Colonel Edmund C. Brabble[98]
43rd North Carolina – Colonel Thomas S. Kenan[99]
45th North Carolina - Colonel John Henry Morehead[100]
53rd North Carolina - Colonel William Allison Owens[101]

Iverson's Brigade
Brigadier General Alfred Iverson Jr.

---

[93] *Ibid*, p.39.

[94] Sifakis, *CCA*, Virginia, p.142; Laino, ***Gettysburg Campaign Atlas***, p.449.

[95] Manarin, Louis H., *NCT*, vol.III, pp.66-67, 69. This battalion was formed from companies B and E of the 21st North Carolina which were transferred and organized in late April 1862. In most Orders of Battle, which happen to include the battalion, it is not designated as a sharpshooters battalion.

[96] Daniel's Brigade joined Lee's army on 20 May 1863, replacing Colquitt's Brigade.

[97] Manarin, *NCT*, vol.III, p.264. Andrews received a promotion to lieutenant colonel on 6 June.

[98] Jordan, Weymouth T., *NCT*, vol.IX, p.5.

[99] Jordan, Weymouth T., *NCT*, vol.X, p.293.

[100] Jordan, *NCT*, vol.XI, p.7. Morehead was in command of the regiment on 3 June and marched north with it as Ewell's Corps began the invasion. He is listed as still in command as of 22 June. During the march, or shortly before it began, Morehead became ill. He evidently became too sick to accompany the regiment across the Potomac River, and remained in Martinsburg, where he died of typhoid fever on or around 26 June.

[101] Jordan, Weymouth T., *NCT*, vol.XIII, p.64.

5th North Carolina – *Captain Speight Brockhurst West*[102]
12th North Carolina – Lieutenant Colonel William S. Davis[103]
20th North Carolina – Lieutenant Colonel Nelson Slough[104]
23rd North Carolina – Colonel Daniel Harvey Christie[105]

Ramseur's Brigade
Brigadier General Stephen Dodson Ramseur
2nd North Carolina – Major Daniel Washington Hurtt[106]
4th North Carolina –Colonel Bryan Grimes[107]
14th North Carolina – Colonel Risden Tyler Bennett[108]
30th North Carolina – Colonel Francis Marion Parker[109]

Doles' Brigade
Brigadier General George Pierce Doles
4th Georgia – Colonel Phillip Cook[110]
12th Georgia – Colonel Edward Willis[111]
21st Georgia – Colonel John Thomas Mercer[112]

---

[102] Jordan, Weymouth T., *NCT*, vol.IV, pp.127, 130, 185. The regiment's colonel, Thomas M, Garrett, had been wounded at Chancellorsville and would not return until after Gettysburg. The regiment's lieutenant colonel was also wounded during the battle and was on furlough on 3 June. Two days later he would be captured at Gatesville, North Carolina. According to the *OR* (*OR* vol.27, pt.3, p.922) Colonel Garrett was in command on 22 June. Manarin however, lists him as absent. The regiments ranking officer present on 3 June was probably West. West ranked Captain Benjamin Robinson of Company A by a single day (West's captaincy is dated 5 March 1862, Robinson's is the following day).

[103] Jordan, Weymouth T., *NCT*, vol.V, p.114. Davis was promoted to lieutenant colonel and took command of the regiment on 23 May.

[104] Jordan, Weymouth T., *NCT*, vol.VI, p.432.

[105] Jordan, Weymouth T., *NCT*, vol.VII, pp.142-143.

[106] Manarin, *NCT*, vol.III, p.379-380, 689. The regiments colonel, William Ruffin Cox is listed in the *OR* (*OR* vol.27, pt.3, p.922) as being in command of the regiment on 22 June. However, Cox had been wounded at Chancellorsville and did not return to command of the regiment until 1 August 1863. The regiment's lieutenant colonel, Walter S. Stallings, was also wounded at Chancellorsville and would return to the regiment the same day as Cox. These facts would place the regiment under the command of its ranking officer, Major Hurtt, on 3 June.

[107] Jordon, *NCT*, vol.IV, p.9. Grimes was slightly wounded at Chancellorsville.

[108] Jordan, *NCT*, vol.V, p.393.

[109] Jordan, *NCT*, vol.VIII, p.321.

[110] Henderson, *RCSG*, vol.1, p.551.

[111] Henderson, *RCSG*, vol.2, p.160.

[112] *Ibid*, p.838

44th Georgia – Lieutenant Colonel Samuel P. Lumpkin[113]

O'Neal's Brigade
Colonel Edward Asbury O'Neal[114]
3rd Alabama – Colonel Cullen Andrews Battle[115]
5th Alabama – Colonel Josephus Marion Hall[116]
6th Alabama – Colonel James Newell Lightfoot[117]
12th Alabama – Colonel Samuel Bonneau Pickens[118]
26th Alabama – Colonel Edward Asbury O'Neal[119]

Divisional Artillery
Carter's Battalion
Lieutenant Colonel Thomas Hill Carter[120]
Jeff Davis (Alabama) Artillery – Captain William J. Reese[121]
King William (Virginia) Artillery – Captain William Pleasants Page Carter[122]
Morris (Virginia) Artillery – Captain Richard Channing Moore Page[123]
Orange (Virginia) Artillery – Captain Charles William Fry[124]

EARLY'S' DIVISION
Major General Jubal Anderson Early

Smith's Brigade
Brigadier General William Smith

---

[113] Henderson, *RCSG*, vol.4, pp.726, 751.

[114] *SOR* Part.II, vol.1, p.573. Colonel O'Neal also commanded the brigade on 3 June.

[115] *Ibid*, p.234.

[116] *Ibid*, p.310.

[117] *Ibid*, p.342.

[118] *Ibid*, p.432.

[119] *OR* vol.27, pt.2, p.601. O'Neal would command the regiment and the brigade until 26 June when John Chapman Goodgame, lieutenant colonel of the 12th Alabama, would take command of the regiment until O'Neal lost command of the brigade and returned to the regiment.

[120] Macaluso, *Morris, Orange and King William Artillery*, p.106.

[121] Laboda, Lawrence R., *From Selma to Appomattox: The History of the Jeff Davis Artillery*, p.322.

[122] Macaluso, *Morris, Orange and King William Artillery*, p.106; *SOR* Part.II, vol.70, p.397.

[123] Macaluso, *Morris, Orange and King William Artillery*, p.89; *SOR* Part.II, vol.70, p.507.

[124] Macaluso, *Morris, Orange and King William Artillery*, p.97.

13th Virginia – Colonel James Barbour Terrill[125]
31st Virginia – Colonel John Stringer Hoffman[126]
49th Virginia – Lieutenant Colonel John Catlett Gibson[127]
52nd Virginia – Lieutenant Colonel James H. Skinner[128]
58th Virginia – Colonel Francis Howard Board[129]

Gordon's Brigade
Brigadier General John Brown Gordon
13th Georgia – Colonel James Milton Smith[130]
26th Georgia – Colonel Edmund N. Atkinson[131]
31st Georgia – Colonel Clement Anselm Evans[132]
38th Georgia - Captain William L. McLeod[133]
60th Georgia – Captain Waters Burrus Jones[134]

---

[125] Riggs, *13th Virginia Infantry*, pp.33, 35, 143; *SOR* Part.II, vol.71, p.299. Colonel Terrill assumed command of the regiment shortly after Chancellorsville and would guide it through the Gettysburg Campaign. The regiment however would miss the fighting in Pennsylvania, when it was left behind on garrison duty at Winchester.

[126] Ashcraft, John M., *31st Virginia Infantry*, pp.132. The 31st Virginia participated in the Jones-Imboden raid in April and May of 1863. Shortly after its return it was assigned to Smith's Brigade. The brigade arrived in the Hamilton's Crossing area on 3 June.

[127] Kleese, *49th Virginia Infantry*, p.98; *SOR* Part.II, vol.72, p.427.

[128] Driver, Robert J. Jr., *52nd Virginia Infantry*, p.150; *SOR* Part.II, vol.72, p.486.

[129] Driver, Robert J. Jr., *58th Virginia Infantry*, p. 92; *SOR* Part.II, vol.72, p.630. The *SOR* lists Board's middle name as Hoard, but this seems to be a typographical error in the list of regimental officers.

[130] Henderson, *RCSG*, vol.2, p.245; *SOR* Part.II, vol.6, p.367.

[131] Henderson, *RCSG*, vol.3, p.183.

[132] *Ibid*, pp.576, 613.

[133] Krick, *Colonels*, p.269; Henderson, *RCSG*, vol.4, p.839; *SOR* Part.II, vol.6, p.682. The regiments colonel, James D. Mathews, was wounded at Gaines' Mill and was absent from the regiment. He would eventually be retired to the Invalid Corps but on 3 June he was still listed as the regiment's colonel although Captain William L. McLeod of Company C was in command.

[134] Henderson, *RCSG*, vol.6, pp.105, 131. Jones is listed as being in command of the regiment in most orders of battle for the Battle of Sharpsburg, but is noted as having the rank of Major (Murfin, James V., *The Gleam of Bayonets*, p.366). Some sources designate Jones' first name as Walters while others list his name as Waters. Henderson designates his first name as Walters. Sifakis designates his first name as Waters (Sifakis, *CCA*, South Carolina and Georgia, p.274), as does Ezra A. Carman in his study of the Maryland Campaign. Carman's organizational information however, was created using some post battle information and seems to reflect the army's condition after the fighting. Carman also indicated Jones as holding the rank of major at Sharpsburg. Evidence indicates, the regiment's colonel, William H. Stiles Jr., was absent from his command on 3 June and would not return before the armies clashed at Gettysburg.

61st Georgia – Colonel John Hill Lamar[135]

Hays' Brigade
Brigadier General Harry Thompson Hays
5th Louisiana – Major Alexander Hart[136]
6th Louisiana – Colonel William Monaghan[137]
7th Louisiana – Colonel Davidson Bradfute Penn[138]
8th Louisiana – Colonel Trevanion D. Lewis[139]
9th Louisiana – Colonel Leroy A. Stafford[140]

Hoke's Brigade[141]
Colonel Isaac Erwin Avery
6th North Carolina – Lieutenant Colonel Robert F. Webb[142]
21st North Carolina – Colonel William Whedbee Kirkland[143]

---

[135] *Ibid*, p.201; *SOR* Part.II, vol.7, p.138. The 61st was originally designated 26th Regiment Georgia Infantry. Its designation was changed to 7th Battalion Georgia Infantry which eventually became the 61st.

[136] *SOR* Part.II, vol.24, p.3; Grunder, Charles S., Beck, Brandon H., *The Second Battle of Winchester: June 12-15, 1863*, p.21; *Records of Louisiana Confederate Soldiers and Louisiana Confederate Commands* (hereafter *RLCS*), Vol.2, part.1, p.898. According to the *RLCS*, the regiment's colonel, Henry Forno is listed as in command of the regiment as of 22 June but would depart the regiment for Mobile and recruitment duty on 25 June. Although he led the regiment at Second Winchester, Major Hart would take command after Forno departed. Hays indicated in his report of the Battle of Winchester that Forno was in command of the regiment on 14 June when his brigade stormed the works west of town. Jones however, implies that Forno left the regiment shortly after Lee reorganized his army and missed the Battle of Winchester. Jones, Terry L., *Lee's Tigers: The Louisiana Infantry in the Army of Northern Virginia*, p.156.

[137] *SOR* Part.II, vol.24, p.42. Colonel Monaghan was in command of the regiment on 3 June and would lead it north but would become ill during the fighting at Second Winchester and would be left behind. Mingus, *Louisiana Tigers*, p.56.

[138] *Ibid*, p.112.

[139] *Ibid*, p.165; *Records of Louisiana Confederate Soldiers and Louisiana Confederate Commands* (hereafter *RLCS*), Vol.3, book.1, part.2, p.753. Lewis' service record in *RLCS* lists him as a lieutenant colonel on 3 June. Most other primary and secondary sources list him as a colonel.

[140] *Ibid*, p.197.

[141] Hoke had been seriously wounded at Salem Church and was absent from the brigade. Colonel Isaac E. Avery was in command of the brigade.

[142] Jordon, *NCT*, vol.IV, p.267.

[143] Jordon, *NCT*, vol.VI, pp.534, 538; Manarin, *NCT*, vol.III, pp.66-67. The regiment possessed twelve companies, but after the Battle of Chancellorsville, two companies, B and E, were detached and used to form the 1st Battalion North Carolina Sharpshooters. The battalion was attached to General Ewell's Headquarters as provost guard.

54th North Carolina – Colonel Kenneth McKenzie Murchison[144]
57th North Carolina – Colonel Archibald Campbell Godwin[145]

Divisional Artillery
Jones's Battalion
Lieutenant Colonel Hilary P. Jones
Charlottesville (Virginia) Artillery – Captain James McDowell Carrington[146]
Courtney (Virginia) Artillery – Captain William A. Tanner[147]
Louisiana Guard Artillery – Captain Charles A. Green
Staunton (Virginia) Artillery – Captain Asher Waterman Garber[148]

JOHNSON'S DIVISION
Major General Edward Johnson

Steuart's Brigade[149]
Brigadier General George Hume Steuart
1st Maryland Battalion (2nd Maryland) – Lieutenant Colonel James R. Herbert[150]
10th Virginia – *Captain William Benjamin Yancey*[151]

---

[144] Jordon, *NCT*, vol.XIII, p.247. Murchison was promoted to colonel on 8 May after his colonel died of wounds received at Salem Church.

[145] Jordon, *NCT*, vol.XIV, p.97. Godwin was wounded in the knee a Chancellorsville but only absent from his command for seven days.

[146] Moore, Robert H., *The Charlottesville, Lee Lynchburg and Johnson's Bedford Artillery*, p.62.

[147] Nicholas, & Servis, *Powhatan, Salem and Courtney Henrico Artillery*, p.236.

[148] Driver, *The Staunton Artillery – McClanahan's Battery*, p.54.

[149] The 1st Maryland Battalion Infantry would be assigned to Steuart's Brigade on 15 June. *OR* vol.27, pt.2, pp.440, 450; William W. Goldsborough, *The Maryland Line in the Confederate Army: 1861-1865*, p.96.

[150] *SOR* Part.II, vol.27, p.35. This regiment was serving in the Shenandoah Valley and would join the brigade as Ewell's Corps cleared the lower Valley in mid June.

[151] Murphy, *10th Virginia Infantry*, p.68, 174, 178, 180; *OR* vol.25, pt.2, pp.1034-1036; *SOR* Part. II, vol.71, p.210 Colonel Edward T. H. Warren was wounded in the shoulder at Chancellorsville while in command of the brigade. The regiment's Lieutenant Colonel and Major were both killed during the battle. The regiment's after action report was written by Captain Adam H. Smals. Evidently Warren's wound was not serious for while he was absent from his command on 22 June he is listed as present at Gettysburg and wrote the regiments Gettysburg battle report. While there is some evidence that Warren returned to his command before 3 June, it is likely that the regiment was under the command of Captain Yancey as it marched away from Fredericksburg. Warren evidently returned, at least for a period of time during mid June, because General Steuart indicates in his report of the action his brigade took part in at Stephenson's Depot on 15 June that Warren was with the regiment. *OR* vol.27, pt.2, p.507.

23rd Virginia – Lieutenant Colonel Simeon Taylor Walton[152]
37th Virginia – Major Henry Clinton Wood[153]
1st North Carolina - Colonel John A. McDowell[154]
3rd North Carolina – Major William Murdock Parsley[155]

Stonewall Brigade
Brigadier General James Alexander Walker
2nd Virginia –Colonel John Quincy Adams Nadenbousch[156]
4th Virginia – Colonel Charles Andrew Ronald[157]
5th Virginia - Colonel John Henry Stover Funk[158]
27th Virginia - Colonel James Kerr Edmondson[159]
33rd Virginia – Colonel Frederick William Mackey Holliday[160]

Jones' Brigade
Brigadier General John Marshall Jones
21st Virginia – Captain William Addison Witcher[161]
25th Virginia – Lieutenant Colonel John Carlton Higginbotham[162]

---

[152] Rankin, Thomas M., *23rd Virginia Infantry*, pp.130, 134; *SOR* Part.II, vol.71, p.725. The regiment's colonel Alexander G. Taliaferro was absent on conscript duty.

[153] Rankin, Thomas M., *37th Virginia Infantry*, pp.146-147; *SOR* Part.II, vol.72, p.267. Colonel Titus V. Williams was absent from the regiment having been wounded at Chancellorsville.

[154] Manarin, *NCT*, vol.III, pp.141, 696. McDowell had been slightly wounded at Chancellorsville but there is no evidence he was away from the regiment due to his wounding.

[155] Manarin, *NCT*, vol.III, pp.487, 703. The regiment's colonel, William Lord DeRosset was severally wounded in the hip at Sharpsburg and never returned to the regiment. Major Parsley was wounded in the hand at Chancellorsville but probably did not leave the regiment for any extended period.

[156] Frye, Dennis E., *2nd Virginia Infantry*, p.121; *SOR* Part.II, vol.70, p.665.

[157] Robertson, James I., *4th Virginia Infantry*, p.71; *SOR* Part.II, vol.70, p.761.

[158] Wallace, *5th Virginia Infantry*, p.119; *SOR* Part.II, vol.71, p.15.

[159] Reidenbaugh, Lowell, *27th Virginia Infantry*, p.142; *SOR* Part.II, vol.72, p.44.

[160] Reidenbaugh, Lowell, *33rd Virginia Infantry*, p.125; *SOR* Part.II, vol.72, p.175.

[161] Riggs, Susan A., *21st Virginia Infantry*, p.97; *SOR* Part.II, vol.71, p.666.

[162] Armstrong, Richard L., *25th Virginia Infantry and 9th Battalion Virginia Infantry*, pp.59, 176, 225; *SOR* Part.II, vol.71, p.801. The 25th Virginia joined the brigade on 3 June. *OR* vol.27, pt.3, p.858; *OR* vol.27, pt.2, pp.286, 503. Higginbotham was promoted to colonel on 13 June. He was in command of the regiment on 15 June but by 22 June Lieutenant Colonel John Armstead Robinson was in command. Higginbotham however, was in command at Gettysburg.

42nd Virginia – Lieutenant Colonel Robert Woodson Withers[163]
44th Virginia – Major Norvell Cobb[164]
48th Virginia – Major Oscar White[165]
50th Virginia – Colonel Alexander Spottswood Vandeventer[166]

Nicholl's Brigade
Colonel Jesse Milton Williams[167]
1st Louisiana – Captain Edward D. Willett[168]
2nd Louisiana – Lieutenant Colonel Ross. E. Burke[169]
10th Louisiana – Major Thomas N. Powell[170]
14th Louisiana – Lieutenant Colonel David Zable[171]
15th Louisiana – Major Andrew Brady[172]

Divisional Artillery
Andrews' Battalion
Lieutenant Colonel Richard Snowden Andrews[173]
1st Maryland Battery – Captain William Findlay Dement[174]
Alleghany (Virginia) Artillery – Captain John C. Carpenter[175]

---

[163] Chapla, John, *42nd Virginia Infantry*, p.141; *SOR* Part.II, vol.72, p.351. Withers was present with the regiment up to 8 June and was present at Gettysburg. Whether he remained with the regiment continually until the battler is debatable.

[164] Ruffner, Kevin C., *44th Virginia Infantry*, p.79; *OR* vol.27, pt.3, p.922; *SOR* Part.II, vol.72, p.359. The regiment was commanded by Major Cobb, having no colonel and its lieutenant colonel having resigned. Cobb would be promoted to colonel on 16 June but the Second Corps organizational listing of 22 June still identifies him as being a major.

[165] Chapla, John D., *48th Virginia Infantry*, p.53, 124; *SOR* Part.II, vol.72, p.420. The regiment was commanded by Major White, its colonel, Thomas. S. Garnett having been mortally wounded in the throat at Chancellorsville and its lieutenant colonel having been previously wounded.

[166] Sifakis, *CCA*, Virginia, p.241; *SOR* Part.II, vol.72, p.442.

[167] Krick, *Colonels*, p.403.

[168] *SOR* Part.II, vol.23, p.632.

[169] *Ibid*, p.705.

[170] *SOR* Part.II, vol.24, p.219.

[171] *Ibid*, p.308.

[172] *Ibid*, p.334.

[173] Grunder & Beck, *The Second Battle of Winchester*, p. 22; Andrews, *Richard Snowden Andrews: A Memoir*, pp.94-96.

[174] *SOR* Part.II, vol.37, p.17.

[175] Bohannon, Keith S., *The Giles, Alleghany and Jackson Artillery*, p.103.

Chesapeake (Maryland) Artillery – Captain William Dawson Brown[176]
Lee (Virginia) Battery – Captain Charles I. Raine[177]

CORPS ARTILLEY RESERVE
Chief of Artillery – Colonel John Thompson Brown[178]

First Virginia Artillery Battalion[179]
Captain Willis Jefferson Dance[180]

2nd Richmond (Virginia) Howitzers – Captain David Watson[181]
3rd Richmond (Virginia) Howitzers – Captain Benjamin H. Smith Jr.[182]
Powhatan (Virginia) Artillery – Lieutenant John M. Cunningham[183]
1st Rockbridge (Virginia) Artillery – Captain Archibald A. Graham[184]
Salem (Virginia) Artillery – Captain Charles Beale Griffin[185]

Nelson's Battalion
Lieutenant Colonel William Nelson[186]

Amherst (Virginia) Artillery – Captain Thomas J. Kirkpatrick[187]
Fluvanna (Virginia) Artillery – Captain John L. Massie[188]
Georgia Regular Battery – Captain John Milledge Jr.

---

[176] *SOR* Part.II, vol.27, p.21.

[177] Moore, *The Charlottesville, Lee Lynchburg and Johnson's Bedford Artillery*, p.119.

[178] Wise, *Long Arm of Lee*, p.568.

[179] Nicholas, & Servis, *Powhatan Artillery*, p.41. Ewell's Reserve Artillery Brigade commander Colonel John Thompson Brown was acting as Ewell's chief of artillery in Crutchfield's absence.

[180] *Ibid*, p.204; *SOR* Part.II, vol.70, p.422.

[181] Wallace, *The Richmond Howitzers*, p.147.

[182] *Ibid*, p.157.

[183] Nicholas, & Servis, *Powhatan Artillery*, p.203.

[184] Driver, *The 1st and 2nd Rockbridge Artillery*, p.67.

[185] Nicholas, & Servis, *Powhatan Artillery*, pp.218-219. Griffin is listed as a lieutenant in most organization listings for the Army of Northern Virginia but his service record in Nicholas and Servis indicates he was promoted to captain of the battery on 2 September 1862. The battery's original captain, Abraham Hupp, was ill with cancer and absent from the battery. He would die on 2 September 1863.

[186] Moore, *Miscellaneous Disbanded Virginia Light Artillery*, p.120.

[187] Sherwood, & Nicholas, *Amherst Artillery, Albemarle Artillery and Sturdivant's Battery*, p.85.

[188] Martin, *The Fluvanna Artillery*, p.154.

THIRD ARMY CORPS[189]
Lieutenant General Ambrose Powell Hill

HETH'S DIVISION
Major General Henry Heth

First Brigade
Brigadier General James J. Pettigrew
11th North Carolina - Colonel Collett Leventhorpe[190]
26th North Carolina – Colonel Henry King Burgwyn Jr.[191]
47th North Carolina - Colonel George H. Faribault[192]
44th North Carolina – Colonel Thomas C. Singletary[193]
52nd North Carolina - Colonel James Keith Marshall[194]

Second Brigade
Colonel John Mercer Brockenbrough
40th Virginia – Captain Thomas Edwin Betts[195]
47th Virginia – Colonel Robert Murphy Mayo[196]
55th Virginia – Lieutenant Colonel William Steptoe Christian[197]
22nd Virginia Battalion – Major John Samuel Bowles[198]

Third Brigade
Brigadier General James Jay Archer

---

[189] The base organizational structure for Hill's Corps is taken from *OR* vol.27, pt.2, pp.288-290. No detailed organizational information exists for Hill's new corps between the time it was formed and the battle of Gettysburg. Determining who was in command of each of the corps' regiments on 3 June requires a great deal of investigative work, which on occasion leads to even more questions. The listings included for Hill's Corps, while probably correct in most cases should be viewed with some skepticism. Readers should review an entries footnote for specifics.

[190] Jordan, *NCT*, vol.V, p.6. Leventhorpe was previously colonel of the 34th North Carolina. He was transferred to the 11th around the end of March, 1862.

[191] Jordan, *NCT*, vol.VII, p.463.

[192] Jordan, *NCT*, vol.XI, p.244.

[193] Jordon, *NCT*, vol.X, pp.393, 396. Singletary's regiment was left in the vicinity of Hanover Junction when Lee's army began its march north.

[194] Jordon, *NCT*, vol.XII, pp.415.

[195] Krick, *40th Virginia Infantry*, p.73; *SOR* Part.II, vol.72, p.321.

[196] *SOR* Part.II, vol.72, p.406.

[197] O'Sullivan, Richard, *55th Virginia Infantry*, p.112; *SOR* Part.II, vol.72, p.578. Christian would be promoted to colonel on 23 June.

[198] Rankin, Thomas M., *22nd Battalion Virginia Infantry*, p.70; *SOR* Part.II, vol.71, p.707.

5th Alabama Battalion – Major Albert Sebastian Van de Graaff[199]
13th Alabama – Colonel Birkett Davenport Fry[200]
1st Tennessee (Provisional Army) - Major Felix Grundy Buchanan[201]
7th Tennessee – Lieutenant Colonel Samuel G Shepard[202]
14th Tennessee – Captain Bruce L. Phillips[203]

Fourth Brigade
Brigadier General Joseph Robert Davis
2nd Mississippi – Colonel John Marshall Stone[204]
11th Mississippi – Colonel Francis Marion Green[205]
42nd Mississippi - Colonel Hugh Reid Miller[206]
55th North Carolina – Colonel John Kerr Connally[207]

McIntosh's Battalion[208]
Major David Gregg McIntosh[209]
Danville (Virginia) Artillery – Captain Robert Sidney Price[210]
Hardaway (Alabama) Artillery – Captain William B. Hurt[211]
2nd Rockbridge (Virginia) Artillery – Lieutenant Samuel Wallace[212]
Richmond (Virginia) Battery – Captain Marmaduke Johnson[213]

---

[199] *SOR* Part.II, vol.1, p.330.

[200] *Ibid*, p.441.

[201] *SOR* Part.II, vol.66, p.401.

[202] *Ibid*, p.558.

[203] *Ibid*, p.657.

[204] *SOR* Part.II, vol.32, p.659.

[205] *SOR* Part.II, vol.33, p.219.

[206] *SOR* Part.II, vol.34, p.206.

[207] Jordan, *NCT*, vol.XIII, p.430.

[208] McIntosh's Battalion was designated a divisional artillery battalion within Pendleton's organization structure of early June. Sometime during the campaign McIntosh was transferred to the Artillery Reserve, Cutts' Battalion, under a new commander, was transferred from the Artillery Reserve to Anderson's Division and Garnett's Battalion was assigned to Heth's Division.

[209] Seigler, *South Carolina's Military Organizations Volume I*, p.304.

[210] Moore, Robert H., *The Danville, Eight Star New Market and Dixie Artillery*, p.54.

[211] *SOR* Part.II, vol.1, p.178.

[212] Driver, *The 1st and 2nd Rockbridge Artillery*, p.135.

[213] Sifakis, *CCA*, Virginia, p.76; Wallace, *Virginia Military Organizations*, pp.16-17.

PENDER'S DIVISION
Major General William Dorsey Pender

McGowan's (First) Brigade
Colonel Abner Monroe Perrin
1st South Carolina – Major Comillus Wycliffe McCreary[214]
1st South Carolina Rifles – Captain William M. Hadden[215]
12th South Carolina - Colonel John Lucas Miller[216]
13th South Carolina – Lieutenant Colonel Benjamin Thomas Brockman[217]
14th South Carolina – Lieutenant Colonel Joseph Newton Brown[218]

Second Brigade
Brigadier General James Henry Lane
7th North Carolina – Captain John McLeod Turner[219]
18th North Carolina – Colonel John Decatur Barry[220]
28th North Carolina - Colonel Samuel D. Lowe[221]
33rd North Carolina – *Colonel Clark Moulton Avery*[222]
37th North Carolina – *Colonel William M. Barbour*[223]

---

[214] *SOR* Part.II, vol.64, p.338.

[215] Seigler, *South Carolina's Military Organizations Volume III*, p.49; *SOR* Part.II, vol.64, p.356.

[216] Seigler, *South Carolina's Military Organizations Volume III*, p.146; *SOR* Part.II, vol.65, p.6. According to Seigler, Miller was promoted to lieutenant colonel on 7 November 1863 to date from 9 February 1863, the date the regiment's previous colonel, William H. McCorkle resigned. The Gettysburg OOB lists Miller as a Colonel but according to Seigler, Miller was not promoted to full colonel until 9 November, 1863.

[217] Wadsworth, Mike, *The 13th South Carolina Volunteer Infantry C.S.A.*, p.37; *SOR* Part.II, vol.65, p.27.

[218] Krick, *The 14th South Carolina Infantry*, p.72; *SOR* Part.II, vol.77, p.45. Brown is listed on regimental rolls as being in command of the regiment from June to October 1863.

[219] Jordan, *NCT*, vol.IV, p.405. Turner was appointed major of the regiment after the unit's colonel and lieutenant colonel were both wounded at Chancellorsville. As of 3 June, he officially remained a captain.

[220] Jordan, *NCT*, vol.VI, p.306. Berry was promoted to colonel on 27 May.

[221] Jordan, *NCT*, vol.VIII, p.110.

[222] Jordan, *NCT*, vol.IX, p.118. Jordon indicates that Avery, who was wounded at Chancellorsville, returned to duty prior to 1 November, 1863. The *OR* (*OR* vol.27, pt.2, p.290) indicates he was in command of the regiment at Gettysburg although he did not file a report, or at least one has not been found. Whether he was in command of the regiment on 3 June has not been determined conclusively by this author.

[223] *Ibid*, p.468. Barbour was wounded in the right arm at Chancellorsville. Jordon indicates he returned to duty prior to 1 September. However, Barbour was present at Gettysburg. When he returned to command is sketchy.

Third Brigade
Brigadier General Edward Lloyd Thomas
14th Georgia – Colonel Robert Warren Folsom[224]
35th Georgia – Colonel Bolling Hall Holt[225]
45th Georgia – Colonel Thomas Jefferson Simmons[226]
49th Georgia – *Lieutenant Colonel Samuel Thomas Player*[227]

Fourth Brigade
Colonel Alfred Moore Scales
13th North Carolina – Lieutenant Colonel Joseph H. Hyman[228]
16th North Carolina – *Captain Able S. Cloud*[229]

---

[224] Henderson, *RCSG*, vol.2, pp.339, 348; *SOR* Part.II, vol.6, p.379.

[225] Henderson, *RCSG*, vol.3, pp.843-844; *SOR* Part.II, vol.6, p.654.

[226] Henderson, *RCSG*, vol.4, p.839; *SOR* Part.II, vol.6, p.734.

[227] Henderson, *RCSG*, vol.5, pp.197, 199, 244; *SOR* Part.II, vol.7, p.26. Trudeau, Noah, Andre, *Gettysburg: A Test of Courage*, p.592; *OR* vol.27, pt.2, p.290. Who was actually in command of the regiment on 3 June is unclear. Trudeau lists Captain Cooke as being in command of the regiment at Gettysburg. If this was the case then no other officer the rank of major or above would have been with the regiment just prior to the battle. Henderson notes Samuel T. Player was promoted to lieutenant colonel on 8 May and colonel on 9 June. John T. Jordon is listed in Henderson as being promoted to lieutenant colonel on 23 February 1864, which implies that he held the rank of major or less during the Gettysburg campaign but his service record in Henderson lists no previous promotion to major. If Jordon or Player were not with the regiment on 3 June, it is possible that Cooke lead the regiment while it was encamped in the vicinity of Fredericksburg, but Player took command before the regiment marched north after Hooker abandoned his position to follow Lee. Henderson does not list any wounds or detached service for either Player or Jordon which would have kept them from duty with the regiment during the Gettysburg Campaign. The *OR* lists Player as in command of the regiment at Gettysburg. Simple logic puts Player in command of the regiment first as lieutenant colonel on 3 June and later as colonel after his promotion.

[228] Jordan, *NCT*, vol.V, p.283. Hyman had been elevated to command due to the promotions of William D. Pender and Alfred M. Scales. He would be promoted to colonel on 13 June.

[229] Jordan, *NCT*, vol.VI, pp.10, 46-47, 107. The regiment's colonel, John S. McElroy was wounded at Chancellorsville and would never return. According to Jordon, Captain Leroy W. Stowe was "absent wounded" from 1 September 1862 to 14 August 1863, at which time he submitted his resignation due to disability. Most Gettysburg orders of battle, including the one from the *OR*, list Leroy Stowe as being in command of the regiment. Captain Leroy Stowe is not mentioned in any of the Official Confederate Reports contained in the *OR*. He is also not mentioned in any Confederate correspondence in the *OR*. John Bachelder in his history of the battle lists Captain William A. Stowe as in command of the regiment at Gettysburg. Jordan however, indicates that William A. Stowe was a Lieutenant Colonel at the time of the battle and was wounded in the neck and head at Chancellorsville and was absent until January or February, 1864. This leaves Captain Able S. Cloud who was captured at the battle as the most likely commander of the regiment on 3 June.

22nd North Carolina – *Colonel James Conner*[230]
34th North Carolina – Colonel William Lee J. Lowrance[231]
38th North Carolina – Colonel William J. Hoke[232]

Poague's Battalion
Major William T. Poague[233]
Albemarle (Virginia) Artillery – Captain James W. Wyatt[234]
Charlotte (North Carolina) Artillery – Captain Joseph Graham[235]
Madison (Mississippi) Light Artillery – Captain George Ward[236]
Warrenton (Virginia) Battery – Captain James Vass Brooke[237]

ANDERSON'S DIVISION
Major General Richard Heron Anderson

Wilcox's Brigade
Brigade General Cadmus Marcellus Wilcox

---

[230] Jordan, *NCT*, vol.VII, p.10; Sturkley, ***Hampton Legion Infantry***, pp.161-162, 574; Conner's whereabouts on 3 June is difficult to determine. Originally a member of the Hampton Legion, Conner took command of the legion when Wade Hampton was wounded at First Manassas. Conner became colonel of the 22nd on 13 June 1862. His service record indicates thirteen days later he was severally wounded in the left leg at Mechanicsville. Records also indicate his leg was broken but there is no reference it was amputated. Afterword, Conner spent time on wound furlough and desk duty. Some sources indicate he returned to the regiment the winter of 1862-63, but did not return to active duty. At Chancellorsville the 22nd was under the command of its lieutenant colonel, Christopher Columbus Cole, who was killed. Conner is designated in the ***OR*** (*OR*, vol.27, pt.2, p.290) as being in command of the regiment at Gettysburg, However, Jordon indicates that he was absent due to his wound until he resigned from the regiment on 13 August 1863. Conner is not mentioned in any Gettysburg after action reports in the ***OR*** or in any correspondence of the period. When or if he returned to active command of the regiment before Gettysburg has not been determined beyond a reasonable doubt by this author.

[231] Jordan, *NCT*, vol.IX, p.251.

[232] Jordan, *NCT*, vol.X, p.8. Hoke, although wounded at Mechanicsville and returned to duty toward the end of 1862. Although he was the regiment's ranking officer, he is not listed in the ***OR*** (*OR*, vol.25, pt.1, p.791) as being in command at Chancellorsville.

[233] Driver, ***Rockbridge Artillery***, p.76.

[234] Sherwood, & Nicholas, ***Amherst Artillery, Albemarle Artillery and Sturdivant's Battery***, p.178. Wyatt's battery did not join Poague's Battalion until 10 June.

[235] Manarin, Louis H., *NCT*, vol.I, pp.61-62. The Charlotte Artillery joined Poague's Battalion on 21 June.

[236] ***SOR*** Part.II, vol.32, p.590.

[237] Andrus, ***The Brooke, Fauquier, Loudoun and Alexandria Artillery***, p.100.

8th Alabama – Lieutenant Colonel Hilary Abner Herbert[238]
9th Alabama – Captain Joseph Horace King[239]
10th Alabama – Colonel William Henry Forney[240]
11th Alabama – Colonel John Caldwell Calhoun Sanders[241]
14th Alabama – Colonel Lucius Pinckard[242]

Wright's Brigade
Brigadier General Ambrose Ransom Wright
3rd Georgia – Colonel Edward J. Walker[243]
22nd Georgia – Colonel Joseph Wasden[244]
48th Georgia - Colonel William Gibson[245]
2nd Georgia Battalion – Major George W. Ross[246]

Mahone's Brigade
Brigadier General William Mahone
6th Virginia – Colonel George Thomas Rogers[247]
12th Virginia – *Colonel David Addison Weisiger*[248]
16th Virginia – Colonel Joseph Hutchinson Ham[249]
41st Virginia –Colonel William Allen Parham[250]

---

[238] *SOR* Part.II, vol.1, p.364.

[239] *Ibid*, p.396.

[240] *Ibid*, p.414.

[241] *Ibid*, p.425.

[242] *Ibid*, p.454.

[243] Henderson, *RCSG*, vol.1, p.494.

[244] Henderson, *RCSG*, vol.2, p.934. Wasden took command of the regiment on 22 April 1863.

[245] Henderson, *RCSG*, vol.5, p.125. Gibson joined the regiment as a private on 4 March 1862 and was elected colonel the following day.

[246] Henderson, *RCSG*, vol.6, pp.771, 796.

[247] Cavanaugh, *6th Virginia Infantry,* p.121; *SOR* Part.II, vol.71, p.78.

[248] Henderson, William D., *12th Virginia Infantry*, pp.105, 134, 163; *SOR* Part.II, vol., p.259. Weisigner was wounded at Second Manassas and was away from the army until sometime in June 1863. Whether he returned to the regiment before it departed Fredericksburg on 14 June is unclear. If not the regiment was probably under the command of Major Richard W. Jones who had commanded the regiment previously.

[249] Trask, Benjamin H., *16th Virginia Infantry*, p.93; *SOR* Part.II, vol.71, p.429. Ham was wounded at Second Manassas and spent a good portion of 1863 on furlough. It is believed he was present when his regiment marched from Fredericksburg.

[250] Henderson, William D., *41th Virginia Infantry*, pp.128; *SOR* Part.II, vol.72, p.334.

61st Virginia – Lieutenant Colonel William Frederick Niemeyer[251]

Perry's Brigade
Brigadier General Edward A. Perry (Colonel David Lang) [252]
2nd Florida – Major Walter R. Moore[253]
5th Florida – Captain Richard N. Gardner[254]
8th Florida – *Lieutenant Colonel William Baya (Colonel David Lang)* [255]

Posey's Brigade
Brigadier General Carnot Posey
12th Mississippi – Colonel William H. Taylor[256]
16th Mississippi – Colonel Samuel E. Baker[257]
19th Mississippi – Colonel Nathaniel H. Harris[258]
48th Mississippi – Colonel Joseph McAfee Jayne[259]

Garnett's Battalion[260]

---

[251] Trask, Benjamin H., *61st Virginia Infantry*, p.65, 82; Wallace, *Virginia Military Organizations*, p.139; *SOR* Part.II, vol.72, p.717. The 61st's colonel, Virginius Despeaux Groner was wounded at Chancellorsville and on 3 June was listed as being hospitalized. Lieutenant Colonel Niemeyer, who actually had commanded the regiment prior to Groner's election as colonel on 1 October, 1862, being the senior commander with the regiment, would have been in command when Hill departed the Fredericksburg area. Groner's service record notes he was "trans. 6/24 to private quarters." All sources list Groner as being in command at Gettysburg which means sometime before 1 July he returned to the regiment.

[252] *SOR* Part.II, vol.5, p.332. Brigadier General Edward A. Perry led the brigade at Chancellorsville but was stricken with typhoid fever after the battle. Colonel David Lang of the 8th Florida took command of the brigade when General Perry went on leave to recuperate. When Lang took command is speculative.

[253] *Ibid*, p.205.

[254] *Ibid*, p.286.

[255] *Ibid*, p.333; Waters, & Edmonds, *A Small but Spartan Band*, p.67. Waters and Edmonds cite Colonel Lang's letter-books housed at the Florida State Archives as the source for information regarding Lieutenant Colonel Baya assuming command of the regiment when Colonel Lang took over the brigade. They do not indicate when Baya took command.

[256] *SOR* Part.II, vol.33, p.244.

[257] *Ibid*, p.391.

[258] *Ibid*, p.524.

[259] *SOR* Part.II, vol.34, p.336.

[260] *OR*, vol.25, pt.1, p.790; Wise, *Long Arm of Lee*, p.569; *OR*, vol.25, pt.2, p.850; *OR*, vol.27, pt.2, p.289; Crew, & Trask, *Grimes' Battery, Grandy's Battery and Huger's Battery Virginia Artillery*, pp.59, 109. At Chancellorsville Garnett's Battalion was attached to Anderson's Division. When Pendleton reorganized the artillery in early June the battalion was defined as a divisional artillery battalion. On or around 15 June, Garnett's Battalion was attached to General Heth's Division.

Lieutenant Colonel John Jameson Garnett
Donaldsonville (Louisiana) Artillery – Captain Victor Maurin[261]
Hugar (Norfolk Light) (Virginia) Artillery – Captain Joseph D. Moore[262]
Pittsylvania (Virginia) Artillery – Captain John W. Lewis[263]
Norfolk Light (Virginia) Artillery Blues – Captain Charles R. Grandy[264]

CORPS ARTILLEY RESERVE
Chief of Artillery - Colonel Reuben Lindsay Walker[265]

Pegram's Battalion
Major William Ransom Johnson Pegram
Crenshaw (Virginia) Battery – Captain William Graves Crenshaw[266]
Fredericksburg (Virginia) Artillery – Captain Edward Avenmore Marye[267]
Letcher (Virginia) Artillery – Captain Thomas Alexander Brander[268]
Purcell (Virginia) Artillery – Captain Joseph McGraw[269]
Pee Dee (South Carolina) Artillery – Lieutenant William E. Zimmerman[270]

Cutts' Battalion[271]
Major John Lane[272]

---

[261] *SOR* Part.II, vol.23, p.593.

[262] Crew, & Trask, *Grimes' Battery, Grandy's Battery and Huger's Battery Virginia Artillery*, p. 109.

[263] Sifakis, *CCA*, Virginia, p.63; Wise, *Long Arm of Lee*, p.569.

[264] Crew, & Trask, *Grimes' Battery, Grandy's Battery and Huger's Battery Virginia Artillery*, p. 90.

[265] Wise, *Long Arm of Lee*, p.569.

[266] Carmichael, *The Purcell, Crenshaw and Letcher Artillery*, p.113.

[267] Krick, Robert K., *The Fredericksburg Artillery*. p.106.

[268] Carmichael, *The Purcell, Crenshaw and Letcher Artillery*, p.160.

[269] *Ibid*, p.52.

[270] Seigler, *South Carolina's Military Organizations Volume I*, p.306.

[271] Wise, *Long Arm of Lee*, p.569; *OR*, vol.27, pt.2, p.288. Cutts' Battalion was designated as part of the Reserve Artillery of Hill's Corps by Pendleton in early June. By the time of the Battle of Gettysburg, Cutts' Battalion was assigned to Anderson's Division as its divisional artillery.

[272] Krick, *Colonels*, p.108, 230; Sifakis, *CCA*, South Carolina and Georgia, p.120. Speicher, James L., The Sumter Artillery: The 11th Battalion, Georgia Light Artillery, *CWR*, vol.3 no.2, p.39. Sometime before early June 1863, Cutts' departed on an extended leave of absence due to illness. When the battalion marched north on 14 June, Major John Lane was in command.

11th Artillery Battalion (Georgia) Battery A (Sumter Artillery) – Captain Hugh Madison Ross[273]
11th Artillery Battalion (Georgia) Battery B (Sumter Artillery) – Captain George M. Patterson[274]
11th Artillery Battalion (Georgia) Battery C (Sumter Artillery) – Captain John T. Wingfield[275]

CAVALRY DIVISION
General James Ewell Brown "Jeb" Stuart[276]

Major Heros von Borcke – Assistant Adjutant and Inspector General
Major Henry Brainerd McClellan – Assistant Adjutant General[277]
Major Andrew Reid Venable – Assistant Adjutant General[278]
Major Norman Richard Fitzhugh - Quartermaster[279]
Major William J. Johnson – Commissary of Substance
Captain William Willis Blackford – Engineering Officer[280]
Captain John Esten Cooke - Chief of Ordinance[281]
First Lieutenant Chiswell Dabney – Aide de-camp[282]
First Lieutenant Robert Henry Goldsborough – Aide de-camp[283]
Surgeon Talcott Eliason – Medical Director[284]
Captain William Downs Farley – Volunteer Aide[285]
Captain James Louis Clark – Volunteer Aide[286]

---

[273] Wise, *Long Arm of Lee*, p.569; Sifakis, *CCA,* South Carolina and Georgia, p.118; *SOR* Part.II, vol.5, p.695; Speicher, James L., *The Sumter Flying Artillery*, p.411.

[274] Wise, *Long Arm of Lee*, p.569; Sifakis, *CCA,* South Carolina and Georgia, p.119; *SOR* Part.II, vol.5, p.696.

[275] Wise, *Long Arm of Lee*, p.569; Speicher, James L., The Sumter Artillery, *CWR*, vol.3 no.2, p.39; *SOR* Part.II, vol.5, p.696.

[276] *OR*, vol.25, pt.2, p.862. Stuart's staff is based on General Order No.19 which was issued from Stuart's headquarters on 1 June 1863.

[277] Trout, *They Followed the Plume*, p.197.

[278] *Ibid*, p.268.

[279] *Ibid*, p.114.

[280] *Ibid*, p.63.

[281] *Ibid*, p.89.

[282] *Ibid*, p.95.

[283] *Ibid*, p.145.

[284] *Ibid*, p.99.

[285] *Ibid*, p.107.

[286] *Ibid*, p.86.

Hampton's Brigade
Brigade General Wade Hampton

Cobb's Legion Cavalry – Colonel Pierce Manning Butler Young[287]
1st South Carolina Cavalry – Colonel John Logan Black[288]
2nd South Carolina Cavalry – Colonel Matthew Calbraith Butler[289]
1st North Carolina Cavalry – Colonel Laurence Simmons Baker[290]
Jeff Davis Legion (Mississippi) Cavalry (6 Companies)
– Colonel Joseph Fred Waring[291]
Phillips Legion (Georgia) Cavalry (6 Companies) – Colonel W. W. Rich[292]

Fitzhugh Lee's Brigade
Brigadier General Fitzhugh Lee (Colonel Thomas T. Munford)[293]

1st Maryland Battalion – Major Harry Gilmor[294]
1st Virginia Cavalry – Colonel James Henry Drake[295]
2nd Virginia Cavalry – Lieutenant Colonel James Winston Watts[296]
3rd Virginia Cavalry – Colonel Thomas Howerton Owen[297]
4th Virginia Cavalry – Colonel Williams Carter Wickham[298]

---

[287] Mesic, Harriett Bey, *Cobb's Legion Cavalry: A History and Roster of the Ninth Georgia Volunteers in the Civil War*, p.177.

[288] *SOR* Part.II, vol.76, p.3.

[289] Seigler, *South Carolina's Military Organizations Volume II*, p.287; *SOR* Part.II, vol.64, p.42.

[290] Manarin, Louis H., *NCT*, vol.II, p.7.

[291] Hopkins, Donald A., *Horsemen of the Jeff Davis Legion*, pp.103, 145.

[292] McKinney, *Brandy Station*, p.260. The Phillips Legion Cavalry was on picket duty on the lower Rappahannock and would not join the brigade until after Brandy Station and the campaign was underway.

[293] Although he was battling "inflammatory rheumatism," brigade commander, Brigadier General Fitzhugh Lee, was still near his command. However, Colonel Munford was involved in much of the brigade's daily operations.

[294] Goldsborough, *The Maryland Line*, p.176. Gilmor's command of the battalion was temporary. As of 3 June, the 1st Maryland was serving in the Valley with the 1st Maryland Infantry. After the second battle at Winchester, the battalion, except for Company A, would ride north with the remainder of the army and conduct operations during the campaign in Pennsylvania. Company A was attached to Ewell's headquarters to perform "special service on important occasions."

[295] Driver, *1st Virginia Cavalry*, p.169.

[296] Driver, *2nd Virginia Cavalry*, p.282.

[297] Nanzig, *3rd Virginia Cavalry*, p.121.

[298] Stiles, *4th Virginia Cavalry*, p.143.

5th Virginia Cavalry – Colonel Thomas Lafayette Rosser[299]

William H. F. Lee's Brigade
Brigade General William Henry Fitzhugh Lee
2nd North Carolina Cavalry – Colonel Solomon Williams[300]
9th Virginia Cavalry – Colonel Richard Lee Turberville Beale[301]
10th Virginia Cavalry – Colonel James Lucius Davis[302]
13th Virginia Cavalry – Colonel John R. Chambliss Jr.[303]
15th Virginia Cavalry – Major Charles Read Collins[304]

Jones' Brigade
Brigade General William E. Jones
6th Virginia Cavalry – Major Cabell Edward Flournoy[305]
7th Virginia Cavalry – Lieutenant Colonel Thomas A. Marshall Jr.[306]
11th Virginia Cavalry – Colonel Lunsford Lindsay Lomax[307]
12th Virginia Cavalry – Colonel Asher Waterman Harman[308]
35th Battalion Virginia Cavalry – Lieutenant Colonel Elijah V. White[309]

Robertson's Brigade[310]
Brigade General Beverly Holcombe Robertson
7th Confederate Cavalry – *William C. Claiborne*[311]

---

[299] Driver, *5th Virginia Cavalry*, p.249.

[300] Manarin, Louis H., *NCT*, vol.II, p.104.

[301] Krick, Robert K., *9th Virginia Cavalry*, p.57.

[302] Driver, *10th Virginia Cavalry*, p.107. Company D was on detached duty and not with the regiment.

[303] Balfour, *13th Virginia Cavalry*, p.69.

[304] Fortier, John, *15th Virginia Cavalry*, p.127. The 15th Virginia was on picket duty along the Rappahannock River south of Fredericksburg.

[305] Musick, *6th Virginia Cavalry*, p.115.

[306] Armstrong, Richard L., *7th Virginia Cavalry*, p.191. Marshall's service record in Armstrong denotes his middle initial as A. Wittenberg in *The Battle of Brandy Station* notes Marshall's middle initial as C.

[307] Armstrong, *11th Virginia Cavalry*, p.160.

[308] Frye, *12th Virginia Cavalry*, p.134.

[309] Divine, John E., *35th Battalion Virginia Cavalry*, p.108.

[310] Only the 4th and 5th North Carolina Cavalry would come north with Robertson. The remaining regiments of his command had been detached for duty with D.H. Hill's command.

[311] *SOR*, Part.II, vol.73, p.250. On Detached service in North Carolina.

3rd North Carolina Cavalry – John A. Baker[312]
4th North Carolina Cavalry – Colonel Dennis Dozier Ferebee[313]
5th North Carolina Cavalry – Colonel Peter G. Evans[314]
62nd Georgia Cavalry – Joel R. Griffin[315]

Jenkins' Brigade[316]
Brigade General Albert Gallatin Jenkins
14th Virginia Cavalry – Colonel James Addison Cochran[317]
16th Virginia Cavalry – Colonel Milton J. Ferguson[318]
17th Virginia Cavalry – Colonel William Henderson French[319]
34th Battalion Virginia Cavalry – Lieutenant Colonel Vincent Addison Witcher[320]
36th Battalion Virginia Cavalry – Major James W. Sweeney[321]
Charlottesville (Virginia) Battery – Captain Thomas E. Jackson[322]

Northwestern Brigade[323]
Brigade General John Daniel Imboden[324]

---

[312] Manarin, Louis H., *NCT*, vol.II, p.180. The 3rd North Carolina was on detached duty along the Blackwater River in Southern Virginia.

[313] *Ibid*, p.266.

[314] *Ibid*, p.372.

[315] Henderson, *RCSG*, vol.6, p.276. The 62nd Georgia was on detached duty in North Carolina. On 25 October 1864, the unit's designation would be changed to the 8th Georgia Cavalry.

[316] Jenkins' Brigade was stationed in the Shenandoah Valley in early June and at the time of the fighting at Brandy Station.

[317] Driver, Robert J. Jr., *14th Virginia Cavalry*, p.110.

[318] Dickinson, Jack L., *16th Virginia Cavalry*, p.98.

[319] Harris, Nelson, *17th Virginia Cavalry*, p.70.

[320] Cole, Scott C., *34th Battalion Virginia Cavalry*, p.176. The 34th was attached to Brigadier General "Grumble" Jones' brigade and would not join Jenkins' Brigade until after the campaign had begun.

[321] Scott, J. L., *36th and 37th Battalions Virginia Cavalry*, p.40

[322] Sifakis, *CCA*, Virginia, p.29, 43; Wallace, *Virginia Military Organizations*, p.23. Jackson's battery was organized on 2 May from remnants of his previous command which had surrendered at Fort Donaldson. Jackson's battery did not march north with Jenkins' Brigade, but remained in Staunton. It needed to be refit and was not ready for field duty.

[323] The Northwestern Brigade operated in western Virginia and West Virginia when the region became a state in the Union in 1863. Imboden's command was not part of Stuart's command but reported directly to Lee.

[324] Driver, *The Staunton Artillery – McClanahan's Battery*, p.56.

18th Virginia Cavalry – Colonel George William Imboden[325]
62nd Virginia Infantry (mounted) – Colonel George Hugh Smith[326]
Virginia Partisan Rangers – Captain John Hanson. McNeill[327]
McClanahan's (Virginia) Battery – Captain John H. McClanahan[328]

Stuart Horse Artillery
Major Robert Franklin Beckham[329]
1st Stuart (Virginia) Horse Artillery – Captain James Breathed[330]
Ashby's (Virginia) Horse Artillery – Captain Roger Preston Chew[331]
2nd Baltimore (Maryland) Battery – Captain William Hunter Griffin[332]
Washington (South Carolina) Horse Artillery – Captain James F. Hart
2nd Stuart (Virginia) Horse Artillery – Captain William Morrell McGregor[333]
Lynchburg (Virginia) "Beauregard" Rifles – Captain
Marcellus Newton Moorman[334]

---

[325] Delauter, *18th Virginia Cavalry*, p.74.

[326] *SOR* Part.II, vol.72, p.790.

[327] Delauter, Roger, U. Jr., *McNeill's Rangers*, p.122. McNeill's Rangers were not present with Imboden's command when it was ordered north by Lee on 7 June. McNeill's command would not join Imboden's brigade until 14 June when Imboden arrived in Hampshire County.

[328] Driver, *The Staunton Artillery – McClanahan's Battery*, p.116.

[329] Trout, *They Followed the Plume*, p.56.

[330] Moore, *The 1st and 2nd Stuart Horse Artillery*, p.164.

[331] Moore, *Chew's Ashby, Lynchburg Newton Artillery*, p.102.

[332] *SOR* Part.II, vol.39, p.18.

[333] Moore, *The 1st and 2nd Stuart Horse Artillery*, p.174.

[334] Moore, *Chew's Ashby, Lynchburg Newton Artillery*, p.116.

Abbreviations

The following abbreviations are utilized within the footnotes and photo captions.

ACW: *America's Civil War*
ACWR: *A Compendium of the War of the Rebellion*
AGNMPS: *Annual Gettysburg National Military Park Seminar*
AGSM: *Annual Report of the Adjutant General of the State of Maine*
ARAGSNY: *Annual Report of the Adjutant General of the State of New York* (Rosters)
ARAGSRI: *Annual Report of the Adjutant General of the State of Rhode Island and Providence Plantations for the Year 1865*
AW: *The Annals of the War, Written by Leading Participants, North and South*
B&L: *Battles and Leaders of the Civil War*
Carman: *The Maryland Campaign of September 1862: Ezra A. Carman's Definitive Study of the Union and Confederate Armies at Antietam*
CCW: *Report of the Joint Committee on the Conduct of the War*
CCVO: *Catalogue of Connecticut Volunteer Organizations*
CMH: *Confederate Military History*
CWR: *Civil War Regiments*
CWTI: *Civil War Times Illustrated*
Eight Census: *Population of the United States in 1860; Compiled from the Original Returns of the Eight Census*
GM: *Gettysburg Magazine*
GNMP: *Gettysburg National Military Park*
HPV: *History of the Pennsylvania Volunteers*
HRL: *Handley Regional Library*
HRMV: *History and Roster of Maryland Volunteers, War of 1861-5*
HSRBNC: *Histories of the Several Regiments and Battalions from North Carolina in the Great War 1861-65*
LOC: *Library of Congress*
LOAUS: *List of Officers of the United States Army from 1779 to 1900*
MC: *Museum of the Confederacy*
MHWU: *The Military History of Wisconsin in the War for the Union*
MOLLUS: *Military Order of the Loyal Legions of the United States*
MSA: *Maine State Archives*
MSSM: *Massachusetts Soldiers, Sailors, and Marines in the Civil War*

MtoA: *From Manassas to Appomattox*
NA: *National Archives*
NCT: *North Carolina Troops 1861-1865 A Roster*
NYAGR: *Annual Report of the Adjutant General of the State of New York* (Reports)
NYT: *New York Times*
NYWR: *New York in the War of the Rebellion*
OARVF: *Official army register of the volunteer force of the United States army for the years 1861, '62, '63, '64, '65*
OIWR: *Official Roster of the Soldiers of the State of Ohio In the War of the Rebellion, 1861-1865*
OR: *The War of the Rebellion: A Compilation of the Official Records of the Union and Confederate Armies*
OW: *Ohio in the War: Her Statesman, Her Generals and Soldiers*
RAGSI: *Report of the Adjutant General of the State of Illinois*
RAGSIN: *Report of the Adjutant General of the State of Indiana*
RCSG: *Roster of the Confederate Soldiers of Georgia 1861-1865*
RHMC: *Robert H. Milroy Collection*
RLCS: *Records of Louisiana Confederate Soldiers and Louisiana Confederate Commands*
ROMNJ: *Record of Officers and Men of New Jersey in the Civil War 1861-1865*
RRSSNH: *Revised Register of the Soldiers and Sailors of New Hampshire in the War of the Rebellion 1861-1866*
RSLG: *Regimental Strengths and Losses at Gettysburg*
RSMV: *Record of Service of Michigan Volunteers in the Civil War*
RWV: *Roster of Wisconsin Volunteers, War of the Rebellion, 1861-1865*
SHSP: *Southern Historical Society Papers*
SOR: *Supplement to the Official Records of the Union and Confederate Armies*
USAHEC: *United States Army Heritage and Education Center*
UV: *University of Virginia*
VRS: *Virginia Regimental Series*
VVWR: *Revised Roster of Vermont Volunteers and List of Vermonters Who Served in the Army and Navy of the United States During the War of the Rebellion 1861- 66*
WMH: *Wisconsin Magazine of History*

Bibliography

Manuscripts and Collections

Gettysburg National Military Park Archives
    Winfield Scott Hancock Papers
        Glenn Tucker Hancock at Gettysburg, Unpublished Manuscript
    Flavius J. Bellamy Diary File
Jasper County Public Library, Rensselaer, Indiana
    Robert H. Milroy Collection
        Robert H. Milroy to Mary Milroy, 18 January 1863
Library of Congress, Washington DC
    David McMurtrie Gregg Papers
    Jedadiah Hotchkiss Papers
        Thomas J. Jackson to James Seddon, 10 February 1863
    Louis Trezevant Wigfall Papers
        James Longstreet to Louis T. Wigfall, 13 May 1863
    Richard Stoddert Ewell Papers
        Richard S. Ewell to Benjamin S. Ewell, 25 November 1847
    William Tecumseh Sherman Papers
        Henry W. Halleck to William T. Sherman, 16 September 1864
United States Army Heritage and Education Center, Carlisle Pennsylvania
    Civil War Photograph Collection
    MOLLUS- Massachusetts Photograph Collection
    Daughters of the US Army College
    M. F. Steele Collection
    West Point Album-1861
    Roger D. Hunt Collection
University of North Carolina, Southern Historical Collection, Wilson Library, Chapel Hill North Carolina
    Lafayette McLaws Papers
        James Longstreet to Lafayette McLaws, 3 June 1863
        James Longstreet to Lafayette McLaws, 25 July 1873
    William Nelson Pendleton Papers
        Sandie Pendleton to Kate Corbin, 4 June 1863
        Sandie Pendleton to mother, 9 June 1863
Virginia Historical Society, Richmond Virginia
    Henry Brainerd McClellan Papers

Official and Semi-Official Reports and Publications

History of the Pennsylvania Volunteers, 5 Volumes, Bates, Samuel P., B. Singerly, State Printers, Harrisburg, Pennsylvania, 1869-71; Reprint: Broadfoot Publishing Company, Wilmington, North Carolina, 10 Volumes plus 4 Volume Index, 1993-94. Bates' work is probably the best single publication for concise regimental histories and information on soldiers from Pennsylvania. Broadfoot's reprint breaks the five oversized volumes of the original work into ten less cumbersome volumes and adds a four volume index. The footnote listings contain references to the Broadfoot volumes.

List of Officers of the United States Army from 1779 to 1900. Colonel William H. Powell United States Army, L. R. Hamersly & Co., New York, 1900.

New York at Gettysburg: Final Report of the Battlefield of Gettysburg, New York Monuments Commission, 3 Volumes, J. B. Lyon Company, Albany New York 1902.

Official Army Register for September 1861, Adjutant General's Office, Washington DC, 1861.

Official Army Register for January 1889, Adjutant General's Office, Washington DC, 1889.

Official Army Register of the Volunteer Force of the United States army for the years 1861, '62, '63, '64, '65, 8 Volumes, Adjutant General's Office, Washington DC, 1865, 1867; Reprint: Olde Soldier Books Inc., Gaithersburg, Maryland, 1987. This publication contains officer listing for each volunteer regiment and an itemized listing of officers who were killed, discharged, promoted etc.

Pennsylvania at Gettysburg: Ceremonies at the Dedication of the Monuments Erected by the Commonwealth of Pennsylvania, 2 Volumes, William Stanley, State Printers, 1904.

Population, of The United States in 1860: Compiled from the Original Returns of the Eighth Census, Kennedy, Joseph C. G., Government Printing Office, Washington DC, 1864.

Report of the Joint Committee on the Conduct of the War, Government Printing Office, Washington DC, 1863 Report in 3 volumes, 1865 report in 3 volumes, 1863-1866 Supplemental Report in 2 volumes; Reprint: Broadfoot Publishing Company, Wilmington North Carolina, 8 Volumes plus Index, 1999. The Joint Committee on the Conduct of the War was created in December of 1861 in response to the large number of early war setbacks for the Union. While it is an excellent source of firsthand accounts regarding a number of pivotal events, researchers must be vigilant regarding its content due to a number of witnesses who made efforts to rewrite their records. The other issue with the committee centers on it being assembled from government officials who possessed no military training or background and as such tended to take a simplistic point of view toward the testimony of knowledgeable military men.

State of Connecticut:
Catalogue of Connecticut Volunteer Organizations, Brown and Gross, Hartford Connecticut, 1869. Contains listings of infantry, cavalry and artillery, and brief summaries noting the operations and service of the regiments and batteries. It was prepared from the records in the Adjutant-General's Office.

State of Georgia:
Roster of the Confederate Soldiers of Georgia 1861-1865, 6 Volumes, Henderson, Lillian, Longino and Porter Inc., Hapeville Georgia, 1955-64. Published in the mid 1900s, Henderson, the director of the Confederate Pension and Record Department, compiled this nearly complete listing of Georgia soldier's service records for the state government.

State of Illinois:
Report of the Adjutant General of the State of Illinois, 8 Volumes, Alexander H. Conner, W. R. Holloway, Samuel M Douglass, State Printers, Indianapolis, 1865-69. Contains short regimental histories which include information on the unit's formation and service before listing the service records of each man who served.

State of Indiana:
Report of the Adjutant General of the State of Indiana, 8 Volumes, Alexander H. Conner, W. R. Holloway, Samuel M. Douglas, State Printers, 1865-69. This publication also contains the Indiana Adjutant General's report *Indiana in the War of the Rebellion*. The 8 volume publication is one of the most detailed post war reports published by any state.

State of Louisiana:
Records of Louisiana Confederate Soldiers and Louisiana Confederate Commands, Booth, Andrew B., Commissioner of Military Records, New Orleans, 1920.

State of Maine:
Alphabetical Index of Maine Volunteers Mustered into the Service of the United States from the Commencement of the Rebellion to January 1, 1863, Stevens and Sayword, Printers to the State, Augusta, 1864.

Alphabetical Index of Maine Volunteers, Etc., Mustered into the Service of the United States During the War of 1861, Stevens and Sayword, Printers to the State, Augusta, 1867.

Annual Report of the Adjutant General of the State of Maine, for the Year Ending December 31, 1861, Stevens and Sayword, Printers to the State, Augusta, 1862.

Annual Report of the Adjutant General of the State of Maine, for the Year Ending December 31, 1862, Stevens and Sayword, Printers to the State, Augusta, 1863.

Annual Report of the Adjutant General of the State of Maine, for the Year Ending December 31, 1863, Stevens and Sayword, Printers to the State, Augusta, 1864.

Annual Report of the Adjutant General of the State of Maine for the Year Ending December 31, 1866, Stevens and Sayword, Printers to the State, Augusta, 1867.

Maine at Gettysburg, Report of Maine Commissioners, The Lakeside Press, Portland Maine, 1898; Reprint: Stan Clark Military Books, Gettysburg Pennsylvania, 1994.

Report of the Adjutant General of the State of Maine for the Years 1864 and 1865, Stevens and Sayword, Printers to the State, Augusta, 1866.

State of Maryland:

History and Roster of Maryland Volunteers, War of 1861-5, 2 Volumes, Wilmer, L. Allison, Jarrett, James H., Vernon, George W. F., Press of Guggenheimer Weil and Company, Baltimore Maryland, 1898.

State of Massachusetts:

Record of the Massachusetts Volunteers, 1861-1865, 2 Volumes, Wright and Potter, Printers to the State, 1868. This was the state's first effort at publishing a complete roster of its soldiers.

Massachusetts Soldiers, Sailors, and Marines in the Civil War, The Norwood Press, Norwood Massachusetts, 1931-37. Contains brief regimental histories and complete rosters with service records of each soldier. The eight volume publication is more complete and better organized than the states original effort.

State of Michigan:

Record of Service of Michigan Volunteers in the Civil War, 45 Volumes plus Index, Ihling Brothers and Everard, Kalamazoo Michigan, 190_. The state of Michigan published individual volumes for each of its 42 artillery, infantry and cavalry regiments as well as its engineers, and sharpshooters.

State of New Hampshire:

Revised Register of the Soldiers and Sailors of New Hampshire in the War of the Rebellion 1861-1866, Ayling, Augustus D., Ira C. Evans, Public Printer, Concord New Hampshire, 1895. The contents of his massive single volume work is broken down by regiment. Each listing includes a sketch of the regiment and a register of its members. A summary of the regiment's service and a listing of commissioned officers are also included.

State of New Jersey:

Record of Officers and Men of New Jersey in the Civil War 1861-1865, 2 Volumes, Stryker, William S., Steam Book and Job Printer, Trenton New Jersey, 1876. Capsule histories of each unit's organization and service as well as complete rosters.

State of New York:

Annual Report of the Adjutant General of the State of New York, 1860, Charles Van Benthuysen, Albany New York, 1861.

Annual Report of the Adjutant General of the State of New York, 1861, Charles Van Benthuysen, Albany New York, 1862.

Annual Report of the Adjutant General of the State of New York, 1862, Comstock and Cassidy, Albany New York, 1863.

Annual Report of the Adjutant General of the State of New York, 1863, 2 Volumes, Comstock and Cassidy, Albany New York, 1864.

Annual Report of the Adjutant General of the State of New York, 1864, Charles Van Benthuysen, Albany New York, 1865.

Annual Report of the Adjutant General of the State of New York, 1865, 2 Volumes, C. Wendell, Albany New York, 1866.

Annual Report of the Adjutant General of the State of New York, 1866, Charles Van Benthuysen and Sons, Steam Printing House, Albany New York, 1867.

Annual Report of the Adjutant General of the State of New York, 1867 with Register of Officers Commissioned in Volunteer Regiments from the State of New York, 1861-1865, 3 Volumes, Charles Van Benthuysen and Sons, Steam Printing House Albany New York, 1867.

Annual Report of the Adjutant General of the State of New York, 43 Volumes, James B. Lyon, State Printer; Wynkoop Hallenbeck Crawford Company; The Argus Company, Printers; Brandow Printing Company, Albany New York, 1893-1905. Each volume of this series contains four to eight regimental rosters which include the service records of each member of the regiment.

State of Ohio:
Official Roster of the Soldiers of the State of Ohio In the War of the Rebellion, 1861-1865, 12 Volumes, The Werner Company, Akron Ohio, 1886-95. Publication contains detailed rosters of each regiment, and artillery units.

State of Rhode Island:
Annual Report of the Adjutant General of the State of Rhode Island and Providence Plantations for the Year 1865, Corrected and Revised Edition, 2 Volumes, E. L. Freeman and Son, Providence Rhode Island, 1893 and 1895. Rhode Island's original 1865 publication of its soldier's service records was incomplete and contained numerous errors. In 1882 the state government took steps to correct these issues and preserve the state records. The result was this revised publication which contained expanded unit histories and extensive soldier records.

State of Vermont:
Revised Roster of Vermont Volunteers and List of Vermonters Who Served in the Army and Navy of the United States During the War of the Rebellion 1861-66, Peck, Theodore S., Press of the Watchman Publishing Company, Montpelier Vermont, 1892. Contains short histories and detailed service records for all Vermont soldiers, sailors and marines. Also includes an officers list and lists of colored troops from Vermont who served in the United States Army.

State of Wisconsin:
Roster of Wisconsin Volunteers, War of the Rebellion, 1861-1865, 2 Volumes, Chapman, Chandler P., Democrat Printing Company, State Printers, Madison Wisconsin, 1886. Contains full rosters of each Wisconsin unit with basic service records.

The Army of the United States; Historical Sketches of Staff and Line with Portraits of Generals in Chief, 1789-1896, Rodenbough, Theophilus F. & Haskin, William L., Maynard Merrill and Company, New York, 1896.

Supplement to the Official Records of the Union and Confederate Armies, 100 Volumes, Hewett, Janet B., Editor, Broadfoot Publishing Company, Wilmington North Carolina, 1994-98. This publication contains three parts plus a five volume index. Part I contains reports and pertinent documents which were not contained in the *Official Records*. Part II contains eighty volumes of transcribed unit itineraries from the microfilm rolls at the National Archives (225 Union rolls and 74 Confederate rolls). Part III contains three volumes of additional correspondence. Many of the Confederate itineraries contain compete listings of all regimental officers with full names.

United States War Department

Instruction for Field Artillery, French, William H., Barry, William F., and Hunt, Henry J., J. B. Lippincott and Company, Philadelphia Pennsylvania, 1861. *Instruction for Field Artillery* was written in 1861 by then Captains William H. French, William F. Barry and Henry J. Hunt. It was originally published by Philadelphia publisher J. B. Lippincott and Company for the United States War Department in 1861. It was republished in 1864 by D. van Nostrand.

United States Infantry Tactics for the Instruction, Exercise, and Maneuvers of the United States Army, 1861, Reprint: J. B. Lippincott and Company, 1863.

The War of the Rebellion: A Compilation of the Official Records of the Union and Confederate Armies, 128 volumes and index, United States Government Printing office, Washington DC, 1880-1901. This is the definitive primary source publication on the Civil War. Although it lacks some data (much of which has been published in the *Supplement to the Official Records of the Union and Confederate Armies*, it remains the one source for the majority of military correspondence and after action reports. James I. Robertson once noted that any serious military study of the Civil War must have its basis grounded in the *Official Records*.

Periodicals

Americas Civil War, Leesburg Virginia
Blue & Gray, Columbus Ohio
Confederate Veteran, Nashville Tennessee, Reprint: Broadfoot Publishing Company, Wilmington North Carolina
Civil War Times Illustrated, Harrisburg Pennsylvania
Gettysburg Magazine, Dayton Ohio
Indiana Magazine of History, University of Indiana, Bloomington Indiana
North & South, Tollhouse/Auberry California
Southern Historical Society Papers, Richmond Virginia
Civil War Regiments, San Jose/Campbell California, Mason City Iowa
The Field Artillery Journal, The United States Field Artillery Association, Washington DC

Newspapers

New York Times
Carr, Joseph Bradford, Obituary, 25 February 1895
Charles R. Coster, Obituary, 25 December 1888
Edward Burd Grubb Obituary, 8 July 1913
Graham, Charles Kinnaird, Obituary, 16 April 1889
Tyler, Robert Ogden, Obituary, 2 December 1874
Ward, John Henry Hobart, Obituary, 25 July 1903
Williams, Alpheus Starkey, Obituary, 22 December 1878
The Gettysburg Times
First Pennsylvanian Cavalry in the Gettysburg Campaign, Volume 6, 26 May 1880

State and Regional Histories

Confederate Military History, 12 Volumes, Confederate Publishing Company, Atlanta Georgia, 1899; Reprint: The Archive Society, Harrisburg, Pennsylvania, 1994. This publication contains first person accounts of the activities of each Confederate state. There are numerous accounts of battles, observational narratives and a number of biographical sketches.

Benedict, George Grenville, *Vermont in the Civil War: A History of the Part Taken by the Vermont Soldiers and Sailors in the War for the Union*, 2 Volumes, The Free Press Association, Burlington Vermont, 1886-88. Benedict's work contains a great deal of statistical data, maps and quite detailed histories of the regiments and brigades from Vermont.

Quiner, Edwin Bentlee, *The Military History of Wisconsin in the War for the Union*, Clarke and Company, Chicago Illinois, 1866. Quiner was a journalist and printer from Madison who, as the conflict began, started collecting as many newspaper articles he could find regarding Wisconsin's part in the war. The articles contained a hodge-podge of information including soldier's letters on conditions in camp to full battle narratives. His work was the first to be published for his state, beating a competitor's effort by only a few months. Quiner died less than two years after his work was completed.

Reid, Whitelaw, *Ohio in the War: Her Statesman, Her Generals and Soldiers*, 2 Volumes, Moore Wilstach and Baldwin, Cincinnati, Ohio, 1868. One of Ohio's best journalists, Whitelaw Reid wrote what is probably the most comprehensive state history of the war. Volume one contains the state's history during the war and biographical information of its generals. Volume two contains 249 capsule histories of every regiment from the state which had an active part in the war.

Primary & Secondary Regimental Histories and Rosters

North Carolina Troops 1861-1865 A Roster, 18 Volumes, North Carolina Office of Archives and History, Raleigh North Carolina, 2011. This publication is the definitive source for information on all of North Carolina's Civil War soldiers.

Since 1966 eighteen volumes have been published. The North Carolina Office of Archives and History indicates that additional volumes are to be published in the coming years. When completed the set is estimated to number twenty-four volumes including a comprehensive index. One to three volumes of addenda information are also projected.

Alderman, John Perry, *29th Virginia Infantry*, H. E. Howard Inc., Lynchburg Virginia, 1989. The Virginia Regimental Series, of which Alderman's work is a part, is a series of unit histories and soldier rosters for all Virginia military units which served during the war. The series was conceived by publisher Harold E. Howard in 1974. The first volume was published in 1982, the last in 2004. Each volume contains a unit history and annotated muster roll which includes every soldier known to have served with the unit. While the series is an excellent source of information, the body of each volume's text lacks footnotes making it difficult to utilize them as a reference tool without the ability of verifying data with its source. Each volume does contain a bibliography. Most of the rosters included contain quite detailed service records and a number of entries contain personal histories. Unfortunately a number of the volumes are out of print, are expensive and difficult to find. Publications which are from this series are identified with the abbreviation ***VRS*** after its entry.

Aldrich, Thomas M., *The History of Battery A: First Regiment Rhode Island Light Artillery in the War to Preserve the Union 1861-1865*, Snow and Farnham Providence, 1904.

Andrus, Michael J., *The Brooke, Fauquier, Loudoun and Alexandria Artillery*, H. E. Howard Inc., Lynchburg Virginia, 1990. ***VRS***

Armstrong, Richard L., *7th Virginia Cavalry*, H. E. Howard Inc., Lynchburg Virginia, 1992. ***VRS***

_____, *11th Virginia Cavalry*, H. E. Howard Inc., Lynchburg Virginia, 1989. ***VRS***

_____, *25th Virginia Infantry and 9th Battalion Virginia Infantry*, H. E. Howard Inc., Lynchburg Virginia, 1990. ***VRS***

Ashcroft, John M., *31st Virginia Infantry*, H. E. Howard Inc., Lynchburg Virginia, 1988. ***VRS***

Balfour, Daniel T., *13th Virginia Cavalry*, H. E. Howard Inc., Lynchburg Virginia, 1986. ***VRS***

Bell, Robert T., *11th Virginia Infantry*, H. E. Howard Inc., Lynchburg Virginia, 1985. ***VRS***

Bennett, Brian A, *Sons of Old Monroe: A Regimental History of Patrick O'Rorke's 140th New York Volunteer Infantry*, Morningside, Dayton Ohio, 1999.

Bohannon, Keith S., *The Giles, Alleghany and Jackson Artillery*, H. E. Howard Inc., Lynchburg Virginia, 1990. ***VRS***

Brainerd, Wesley, *Bridge Building in Wartime: Memoir of the 50th New York Volunteer Engineers*, The University of Tennessee Press, Knoxville Tennessee, 1997. Brainerd's memoir provides an inside glimpse of the workings of the engineering units within the Army of the Potomac. Initially intended for his family, Brainerd's work is more personal than most Civil War remembrances.

Carmichael, Peter S., *The Purcell Crenshaw and Letcher Artillery*, H. E. Howard Inc., Lynchburg Virginia, 1990. ***VRS***

Cavanaugh, Michael A., *6th Virginia Infantry*, H. E. Howard Inc., Lynchburg Virginia, 1988. ***VRS***

Chapla, John, D., *42nd Virginia Infantry*, H. E. Howard Inc., Lynchburg Virginia, 1983. ***VRS***

_____, *48th Virginia Infantry*, H. E. Howard Inc., Lynchburg Virginia, 1989. ***VRS***

Child, William, *A History of the Fifth Regiment, New Hampshire Volunteers in the American Civil War*, R. W. Musgrove Printers, Bristol New Hampshire, 1893. Child was a surgeon with the regiment and after the war was the historian of the veterans association for the regiment.

Clark, Walter, *Histories of the Several Regiments and Battalions from North Carolina in the Great War 1861-65*, E. M. Uzzell Printers and Binders, Raleigh, Nash Brothers Book and Job Printers, Goldsboro North Carolina, 1901: Reprint: Broadfoot Publishing Company, Wilmington North Carolina, 1996. Clark's work is a collection of regimental histories and monographs for each North Carolina regiment and military organization. When utilized in conjunction with *North Carolina Troops* (see above), a complete picture of the service and soldiers of each North Carolina military unit can be obtained.

Cole, Scott C., *34th Battalion Virginia Cavalry*, H. E. Howard Inc., Lynchburg Virginia, 1993. ***VRS***

Cowles, Luther, Editor, *History of the Fifth Massachusetts Battery*, Luther E. Cowles, Publisher, Boston, 1902; Reprint: Butternut and Blue, Baltimore Maryland, 1996. This is one of the most thorough unit histories written for any Civil War unit. It contains not only a narrative of the battery's service but numerous excerpts from diaries, recollections and soldier's letters.

Crew, R. Thomas Jr., & Trask, Benjamin H., *Grimes' Battery, Grandy's Battery and Huger's Battery Virginia Artillery*, H. E. Howard Inc., Lynchburg Virginia, 1995. ***VRS***

Curtis, Orson Blair, *History of the 24th Michigan of the Iron Brigade*, Winn and Hammond, Detroit Michigan, 1891; Reprint: Olde Soldier Books Inc., Gaithersburg Maryland, 1988. Curtis was an original member of the regiment but was discharged in March of 1863 due to wounds received at Fredericksburg.

Dawes, Rufus R., *Service with the Sixth Wisconsin*, E. R. Alderman & Sons Marietta Ohio, 1890; Reprint: Bison Books, 1999. Dawes joined the regiment as captain of Company K and was brevetted a brigadier general near the end of the war.

Delauter, Roger, U. Jr., *18th Virginia Cavalry*, H. E. Howard Inc., Lynchburg Virginia, 1985. ***VRS***

_____, U. Jr., *McNeill's Rangers*, H. E. Howard Inc., Lynchburg Virginia, 1986. ***VRS***

Devine, John E., *35th Battalion Virginia Cavalry*, H. E. Howard Inc., Lynchburg Virginia, 1985. ***VRS***

Dickinson, Jack L., *8th Virginia Cavalry*, H. E. Howard Inc., Lynchburg Virginia, 1986. *VRS*

_____, *16th Virginia Cavalry*, H. E. Howard Inc., Lynchburg Virginia, 1989. *VRS*

Driver, Robert J. Jr., *The 1st and 2nd Rockbridge Artillery*, H. E. Howard Inc., Lynchburg Virginia, 1987. *VRS*

_____, *1st Virginia Cavalry*, H. E. Howard Inc., Lynchburg Virginia, 1991. *VRS*

_____, *2nd Virginia Cavalry*, H. E. Howard Inc., Lynchburg Virginia, 1995. *VRS*

_____, *5th Virginia Cavalry*, H. E. Howard Inc., Lynchburg Virginia, 1997. *VRS*

_____, *10th Virginia Cavalry*, H. E. Howard Inc., Lynchburg Virginia, 1992. *VRS*

_____, *14th Virginia Cavalry*, H. E. Howard Inc., Lynchburg Virginia, 1988. *VRS*

_____, *52nd Virginia Infantry*, H. E. Howard Inc., Lynchburg Virginia, 1986. *VRS*

_____, *58th Virginia Infantry*, H. E. Howard Inc., Lynchburg Virginia, 1990. *VRS*

_____, *The Staunton Artillery – McClanahan's Battery*, H. E. Howard Inc., Lynchburg Virginia, 1988. *VRS*

Fields, Frank E. Jr., *28th Virginia Infantry*, H. E. Howard Inc., Lynchburg Virginia, 1985. *VRS*

Fortier, John, *15th Virginia Cavalry*, H. E. Howard Inc., Lynchburg Virginia, 1993. *VRS*

Frye, Dennis E., *2nd Virginia Infantry*, H. E. Howard Inc., Lynchburg Virginia, 1984. *VRS*

_____, *12th Virginia Cavalry*, H. E. Howard Inc., Lynchburg Virginia, 1988. *VRS*

Gracey, Samuel L., *Annals of the Sixth Pennsylvania Cavalry*, E. H. Butler and Company, 1868; Reprint: Vanberg Publishing, Lancaster Ohio, 1996. Gracey was the regiment's chaplain.

Gregory, G. Howard, *53rd Virginia Infantry and 5th Battalion Virginia Infantry*, H. E. Howard Inc., Lynchburg Virginia, 1999. *VRS*

Gunn, Ralph W., *24th Virginia Infantry*, H. E. Howard Inc., Lynchburg Virginia, 1987. *VRS*

Hanifen, Michael, *History of Battery B, First New Jersey Artillery*, Republican-Times Printers, Ottawa Illinois, 1905. Hanifen enlisted as a private in Battery B on 3 September 1861.

Hardy, Michael C., *The Thirty-seventh North Carolina Troops*, McFarland & Company Inc., 2003.

Harrell, Roger H., *The 2nd North Carolina Cavalry*, McFarland and Company Inc., Jefferson, North Carolina, London, 2004. Harrell tells not only the history of the regiment but he establishes the context of each event in which the regiment participated. Also included is a detailed listing of the battle casualties of the regiment broken down by each engagement the regiment fought.

Harris, Nelson, *17th Virginia Cavalry*, H. E. Howard Inc., Lynchburg Virginia, 1994. **VRS**

Henderson, William D., *12th Virginia Infantry*, H. E. Howard Inc., Lynchburg Virginia, 1984. **VRS**

_____, *41st Virginia Infantry*, H. E. Howard Inc., Lynchburg Virginia, 1986. **VRS**

Hopkins, Donald A., *Horsemen of the Jeff Davis Legion*, White Mane, Shippensburg Pennsylvania, 1999.

Judson, Amos M., *History of the Eighty-Third Regiment Pennsylvania Volunteers*, B. F. H. Lynn Publisher, Erie Pennsylvania, 1865; Reprint Morningside, Dayton Ohio, 1986.

Kleese, Richard B., *49th Virginia Infantry*, H. E. Howard, Inc., Lynchburg, Virginia, 2002. **VRS**

Koleszar, Marilyn B., *Ashland, Bedford and Taylor Virginia Light Artillery*, H. E. Howard Inc., Lynchburg Virginia, 1994. **VRS**

Krick, Robert, E. L., *40th Virginia Infantry*, H. E. Howard Inc., Lynchburg Virginia, 1985. **VRS**

Krick, Robert K., *9th Virginia Cavalry*, H. E. Howard Inc., Lynchburg Virginia, 1982. **VRS**

_____, *30th Virginia Infantry*, H. E. Howard Inc., Lynchburg Virginia, 1985. **VRS**

_____, *The 14th South Carolina Infantry Regiment, of the Gregg-McGowan Brigade, Army of Northern Virginia*, Broadfoot Publishing Company, Wilmington North Carolina, 2008. A volume in the publisher's series on South Carolina Regiments.

_____, *The Fredericksburg Artillery*, H. E. Howard Inc., Lynchburg Virginia, 1986. **VRS**

Laboda, Lawrence R., *From Selma to Appomattox: The History of the Jeff Davis Artillery*, White Mane Publishing Company Inc., Shippensburg Pennsylvania, 1994.

Lash, Gary G., *"A Duty Well Done" The History of Edward Baker's California Regiment*, Butternut and Blue, Baltimore Maryland, 2001. Lash's work is published in an oversized format which makes reading difficult but its contents are worth the inconvenience.

Lewis, George, *History of Battery E, First Regiment Rhode Island Light Artillery in the War of 1861 to 1865, to Preserve the Union*, Snow and Farnham, Providence Rhode Island 1892. Lewis' work is a first rate history of a battery which fought in almost every major and a number of minor engagements in the Eastern Theater.

Macaluso, Gregory J., *Morris, Orange and King William Artillery*, H. E. Howard Inc., Lynchburg Virginia, 1991. **VRS**

Manarin, Louis H., *15th Virginia Infantry*, H. E. Howard Inc., Lynchburg Virginia, 1990. **VRS**

Martin, David G., *The Fluvanna Artillery*, H. E. Howard Inc., Lynchburg Virginia, 1992. **VRS**

Mesic, Harriett Bey, *Cobb's Legion Cavalry: A History and Roster of the Ninth Georgia Volunteers in the Civil War*, McFarland and Company Inc., Jefferson North Carolina, London, 2009. The roster included in Mesic's work is first rate and provides extensive biographical information for most of the regiments members.

Moore Robert H., *Chew's Ashby, Shoemaker's Lynchburg and the Newtown Artillery*, H. E. Howard Inc., Lynchburg Virginia, 1995. **VRS**

_____, *Miscellaneous Disbanded Virginia Light Artillery*, H. E. Howard Inc., Lynchburg Virginia, 1997. **VRS**

_____, *The 1st and 2nd Stuart Horse Artillery*, H. E. Howard Inc., Lynchburg Virginia, 1985. **VRS**

_____, *The Charlottesville, Lee Lynchburg and Johnson's Bedford Artillery*, H. E. Howard Inc., Lynchburg Virginia, 1990. **VRS**

_____, *The Danville, Eight Star New Market and Dixie Artillery*, H. E. Howard Inc., Lynchburg Virginia, 1989. **VRS**

_____, *The Richmond Fayette, Hampden, Thomas and Blount's Lynchburg Artillery*, H. E. Howard Inc., Lynchburg Virginia, 1991. **VRS**

Murphy, Terrence V., *10th Virginia Infantry*, H. E. Howard Inc., Lynchburg Virginia, 1989. **VRS**

Musick, Michael P., *6th Virginia Cavalry*, H. E. Howard Inc., Lynchburg Virginia, 1990. **VRS**

Nanzig, Thomas P., *3rd Virginia Cavalry*, H. E. Howard Inc., Lynchburg Virginia, 1989. **VRS**

Nicholas, Richard L., & Servis, Joseph, *Powhatan, Salem and Courtney Henrico Artillery*, H. E. Howard Inc., Lynchburg Virginia, 1997. **VRS**

O'Sullivan, Richard, *55th Virginia Infantry*, H. E. Howard Inc., Lynchburg Virginia, 1989. **VRS**

Parker, John L., *History of the Twenty-Second Massachusetts Infantry the Second Company Sharpshooters and the Third Light Battery, in the War of the Rebellion*, Press of Rand Avery Company, Boston, 1887.

Phisterer, Frederick, *New York in the War of the Rebellion*, Third Edition, 5 Volumes and Index, J. B. Lyon Company, State Printers, 1912. Since its publication, Phisterer's work has been the definitive source for officer's service records and capsule histories of all the volunteer organizations from New York. When used in conjunction with the regimental rosters published by the state's adjutant general in the late 1800s and early 1900s, a researcher has available information on nearly every man from the Empire State that fought in the war.

Rankin, Thomas M., *22nd Battalion Virginia Infantry*, H. E. Howard Inc., Lynchburg Virginia, 1999. **VRS**

_____, *23rd Virginia Infantry*, H. E. Howard Inc., Lynchburg Virginia, 1985. **VRS**

_____, *37th Virginia Infantry*, H. E. Howard Inc., Lynchburg Virginia, 1987. **VRS**

Reidenbaugh, Lowell, *27th Virginia Infantry*, H. E. Howard Inc., Lynchburg Virginia, 1993. **VRS**

_____, *33rd Virginia Infantry*, H. E. Howard Inc., Lynchburg Virginia, 1987. **VRS**

Rhodes, John H., *The History of Battery B: First Regiment Rhode Island Light Artillery in the War to Preserve the Union 1861-1865*, Snow and Farnham, Providence, 1894. Rhodes, a sergeant in the battery, wrote his history based on his diary and a number of official documents.

Riggs, David F., *7th Virginia Infantry*, H. E. Howard Inc., Lynchburg Virginia, 1982. **VRS**

_____, *13th Virginia Infantry*, H. E. Howard Inc., Lynchburg Virginia, 1988. **VRS**

Riggs, Susan A., *21st Virginia Infantry*, H. E. Howard Inc., Lynchburg Virginia, 1991. **VRS**

Robertson, James I., *4th Virginia Infantry*, H. E. Howard Inc., Lynchburg Virginia, 1982. **VRS**

_____, *4th Virginia Infantry*, H. E. Howard Inc., Lynchburg Virginia, 1982. **VRS**

Rodenbough, Theophilus F., *From Everglade to Canyon with the Second United States Cavalry*, D. Van Nostrand, New York, 1875; Reprint: University of Oklahoma Press, Norman, 2000. This is a collection of articles written by members of the regiment which cover the entire history of the regiment up to 1875. It also contains the full military records of the regiment's commissioned officers, a listing of the battles and engagements the regiment participated in and a collection of pertinent correspondence.

Ruffner, Kevin C., *44th Virginia Infantry*, H. E. Howard Inc., Lynchburg Virginia, 1987. **VRS**

Sherwood, W. Cullen & Nicholas, Richard L., *Amherst Artillery, Albemarle Artillery and Sturdivant's Battery*, H. E. Howard Inc., Lynchburg Virginia, 1996. **VRS**

Sauers, Richard A. & Tomasak, Peter, *Ricketts' Battery: A History of Battery F, 1st Pennsylvania Light Artillery*, Luzerne National Bank, 2001.

Scott, J. L., *36th and 37th Battalions Virginia Cavalry*, H. E. Howard Inc., Lynchburg Virginia, 1986. **VRS**

Seigler, Robert S., *South Carolina's Military Organizations During the War Between the States,* 4 Volume, (The Lowcountry and Pee Dee, The Midlands, The Upstate and Statewide Units, Militia and Reserves) The History Press, Charleston South Carolina, London, 2008. This is probably the most complete and thoroughly researched publication presenting statistics for South Carolina's military organizations. Each listing contains a synopsis of its organization, a listing of field officers, a breakdown of each of the organizations companies and a short narrative of the major engagements in which each organization was involved.

Sifakis, Stewart, *Compendium of the Confederacy Armies*, 10 volumes, Facts On File Inc., New York, 1995. According to the author, the ten volume compendium is intended to be the Confederate companion set to Frederick H.

Dyer's *Compendium of the War of the Rebellion*. Its contents consist of information regarding nearly every Confederate regiment which saw service. Each group of regimental data is broken down into organizational information, the units first commander, its field officers, what departments or military organizations it was assigned to, and a listing of battles and skirmishes it participated in.

Speicher, James L., *The Sumter Flying Artillery*, Pelican Publishing Company Inc., Gretna Louisiana, 2009. Speichler's effort contains a plethora of portraits, photographs, illustrations and maps as well as a very detailed roster of the battalion based on the compiled service records housed in the National Archives.

Stiles, Kenneth L., *4th Virginia Cavalry*, H. E. Howard Inc., Lynchburg Virginia, 1985. ***VRS***

Sturkey, O. Lee, *Hampton Legion Infantry CSA*, Broadfoot Publishing Company, Wilmington North Carolina, 2008. A volume in the publisher's series on South Carolina Regiments.

Trask, Benjamin H., *9th Virginia Infantry*, H. E. Howard Inc., Lynchburg Virginia, 1984. ***VRS***

_____, *16th Virginia Infantry*, H. E. Howard Inc., Lynchburg Virginia, 1986. ***VRS***

_____, *61st Virginia Infantry*, H. E. Howard Inc., Lynchburg Virginia, 1988. ***VRS***

Wadsworth, Mike, *The 13th South Carolina Volunteer Infantry C.S.A.*, Broadfoot Publishing Company, Wilmington North Carolina, 2008. A volume in the publisher's series on South Carolina Regiments.

Wallace, Lee A. Jr., *A Guide to Virginia Military Organizations*, H. E. Howard Inc., Lynchburg Virginia, 1986. ***VRS***

_____, *1st Virginia Infantry*, H. E. Howard Inc., Lynchburg Virginia, 1985. ***VRS***

_____, *5th Virginia Infantry*, H. E. Howard Inc., Lynchburg Virginia, 1988. ***VRS***

_____, *17th Virginia Infantry*, H. E. Howard Inc., Lynchburg Virginia, 1990. ***VRS***

_____, *The Richmond Howitzers*, H. E. Howard Inc., Lynchburg Virginia, 1993. ***VRS***

Weygant, Charles H., *History of the 124th Regiment of New York State Volunteers: The Orange Blossom Regiment*, Charles H. Weygant, Newburgh New York, 1899. Weygant entered service as a captain with the regiment and was eventually promoted to lieutenant colonel. He served for nearly the entire war.

White, Gregory C., *'This Most Bloody and Cruel Drama' A History of the 31st Georgia Volunteer Infantry*, Butternut and Blue, Baltimore Maryland, 1997. This regiment fought in all the major battles in the Eastern Theater from The Seven Days to Appomattox. It contained over 1,200 men when organized. When it surrendered only 120 men were present for duty, sixty-six of them were armed. White has written a fine regimental of a unit which really did fight to the bitter end.

Wyckoff, Mac, *A History of the Second South Carolina Infantry 1861-65*, Broadfoot Publishing Company, Wilmington North Carolina, 2011. A volume in the publisher's series on South Carolina Regiments.

_____, *A History of the 3rd South Carolina Regiment: Lee's Reliables*, Broadfoot Publishing Company, Wilmington North Carolina, 2008. A volume in the publisher's series on South Carolina Regiments.

Primary Publications

The Annals of the War, Written by Leading Participants, North and South. Philadelphia, 1879. Reprint: The Blue and Grey Press: Edison New Jersey, 1996. A collection of articles from *The Philadelphia Weekly Times*, a weekly eight page publication which initially went to press in 1877.

Battles and Leaders of the Civil War, 4 volumes, The Century Co., New York, 1887-1888; Reprint: The Archive Society: Harrisburg Pennsylvania, 1991. One of the best collections of first person accounts ever published, the four volume set contains 388 articles which were originally published in *Century Magazine* between 1884 and 1887. Contributing to the work were 226 different authors. The articles are presented in chronological order and in most cases both Northern and Southern viewpoints are included. The monographs are supplemented with 197 maps and approximately 1500 engraved illustrations. Extensive editorial notes, statistics and orders of battle are also included.

Adams, Charles Frances, Jr., *A Cycle of Adams Letters 1861-1865*, 2 Volumes, Houghton Mifflin Company, Boston/New York, 1920. Charles Adams, a captain in the 1st Massachusetts, wrote an extensive number of letters during his time with the regiment. Most of his correspondence was to family members and contained a great amount of detail regarding army life and his involvement in a number of battles and skirmishes.

Alexander, Edward Porter, *Fighting for the Confederacy – The Personal Recollections of General Edward Porter Alexander*, Gallagher, Gary W., Editor, The University of North Carolina Press, Chapel Hill/London, 1989. Porter Alexander wrote to versions of his wartime experiences, one for his family and one for the consumption of the general public. *Fighting for the Confederacy* is the version which he wrote for his family and contains *his* wartime experiences. The manuscript lay dormant for nearly eighty years until Gallagher brought it to the light of day. The candor and descriptions of events within the work are refreshing and powerful and Alexander gives his true feelings regarding a number of controversial issues.

_____, *Military Memoirs of a Confederate: A Critical Narrative*, Charles Scribner's Sons, New York, 1907; Reprint: Da Capo Press, New York, 1993. This is the version of Alexander's memoirs which is really more of a general history of the Army of Northern Virginia. Generally devoid of his personal feelings, it is one of the seminal works on Lee's army and when it was released received praise from the general public.

Andrews, Richard S., *Richard Snowden Andrews, Lieutenant Colonel Commanding the First Maryland Confederate States Army: A Memoir*, The Sun Job Printing Office, 1910. Andrews wrote very little of his memoir, the bulk of the work being penned by his wife. It also.contains a large number of correspondence. It is however, a fine reference work and provides excellent detail of Andrews wounding at Cedar Mountain and his part in the second battle of Winchester.

Bandy, Ken and Freeland, Florence, *The Gettysburg Papers*, Morningside, Dayton Ohio, 1986. This is a collection Gettysburg related material first published within the MOLLUS volumes (*Military Order of the Loyal Legions of the United States*).

Beale, George W., *A Lieutenant of Cavalry in Lee's Army*, The Gorham Press, Boston, 1918. Beale was the son of Richard L. T. Beale, Colonel of the 9th Virginia Cavalry.

Billings, John D., *Hard Tack and Coffee*, George M. Smith and Company, Boston, 1887; Reprint: Time Life Books, New York, 1982. Billings' work is one of the finest accounts of what it was like to be a foot soldier in a Civil War army ever published. The text provides in vivid detail what it was like to an ordinary soldier in camp on the march and during the chaos of battle.

Blackford, William W., *War Years with Jeb Stuart*, Charles Scribner's Sons, New York, 1945. Blackford was a member of Stuart's staff and brother of Charles Minor Blackford. His memoir provides a vivid glimpse into the inner circle of Stuart's command.

Blair, William Alan, Editor, *A Politician Goes to War: The Civil War Letters of John White Geary*, The Pennsylvania State University Press, University Park Pennsylvania, 1995. A collection of John Geary's personal letters to his wife.

Brooks, Noah, *Washington D. C. in Lincoln's Time*, Quadrangle Books, Chicago, 1971. As the favorite Washington correspondent of Abraham Lincoln, Brooks had a ringside seat to the inner workings of the president's administration. Lincoln evidently explicitly trusted Brooks for he met privately with the newsman a number of times each week. Brooks acted as not only a war correspondent but as a mouthpiece for Lincoln and Washington in general.

Burlingame, Michael & Ettlinger, John R. Turner, *Inside Lincoln's White House: The Complete Civil War Diary of John Hay*, Southern Illinois University Press, 1997. John Hay was Lincoln's assistant presidential secretary. His diary provides possibly the most personal glimpse inside the Lincoln White House. His position allowed him to observe not only Lincoln but those in the president's cabinet, high profile military figures and those who sought an audience with the Commander in Chief.

Byrne, Frank L., Weaver, Andrew T., Editors, *Haskell of Gettysburg: His Life and Civil War Papers*, State Historical Society of Wisconsin, 1970; Reprint: Kent State University Press, Kent Ohio, London, 1989. Frank Haskell, who originally joined the 6th Wisconsin, served on General John Gibbon's staff during the Gettysburg Campaign. He left some of the most descriptive recollections of the battle and its participants ever committed to paper. His recollection of Gettysburg is considered one of the best accounts of the battle written.

Caldwell, J. F. J., *The History of a Brigade of South Carolinians First Known as Gregg's and Subsequently as McGowan's Brigade*, King and Baird, Philadelphia, 1866; Reprint: Morningside, Dayton Ohio, 1992. Possibly the best unit history of any South Carolina organization. Its contents are both personal in nature and descriptive of the engagements in which the unit participated.

Carman, Ezra A., Joseph Pierro, Editor, *The Maryland Campaign of September 1862: Ezra A. Carman's Definitive Study of the Union and Confederate Armies at Antietam*, Routledge, New York/London, 2008. Carman's manuscript lay dormant at the Library of Congress for nearly 100 years before being edited for publication by Pierro. Since its publication, the manuscript has received additional attention and has been edited by Thomas G. Clemens and published by Saves Beatie.

Casler, John O., *Four Years in the Stonewall Brigade*, Appeal Publishing Company, Girard Kansas, 1906; Reprint: University of South Carolina Press, Columbia South Carolina, 2005. Casler was a member of the 33rd Virginia and saw the activities and battles of the Stonewall Brigade from the inside. Although he writes about many events which he did and did not witness his presentation in many instances is both moving and exciting. His description of Jackson's funeral procession is both emotional and powerful.

Cassedy, Edward K., Editor, *Dear Friends at Home: The Civil War Letters and Diaries of Sergeant Charles T. Bowen*, Butternut and Blue, Baltimore Maryland, 2001. Bowen wrote extensively to his wife and family during his time with the 12th U. S. Infantry. He also kept a detailed diary of his activities. Combined the two make an excellent collection of first person accounts of life in the military.

Chesnut, Mary, *A Diary from Dixie*, D. Appleton and Company, New York, 1905. Mary Chesnut's diary is probably the most popular work on Southern life during the war ever published. It has appeared in many forms since it was first published.

Clarke, Louise Brownell, *The Greenes of Rhode Island: With Historical Records of English Ancestry 1534-1902*, The Knickerbocker Press, New York, 1903. Provides details of the Greene families lineage, including particulars of the life of George Sears Greene

Commager, Henry Steele & Bruun, Erik, *Living History: The Civil War*, Originally published as *The Blue and the Gray*, 2 Volumes, Bobbs Merrill Company Inc., Indianapolis, 1950; Reprint; Tess Press, New York, 2000. Originally published as *The Blue and the Gray*, the volume contains first person accounts of most of the major campaigns and events of the war. The Tess Press addition has been expanded and a number of additional accounts have been added. It is an excellent volume for anyone interested in the full scope of the war from a personal level.

Cooke, John Esten, *Stonewall Jackson: A Military Biography*, D. Appleton and Company, New York, 1866. Cooke wrote extensively after the war including numerous publications on Jackson, a biography of Lee and writings regarding other officers he had known.

Crowninshield, Benjamin W., *A History of the First Regiment of Massachusetts Cavalry Volunteers*, Houghton Mifflin and Company, Boston/New York, 1891; Reprint: Butternut and Blue, Baltimore Maryland, 1995. Crowninshield presents a fine regimental which contains not only his recollections but is augmented with letters, orders and reminiscences written by other members of the regiment.

Dickert, Augustus D., *History of Kershaw's Brigade*, Elbert H. Aull Company, Newberry, South Carolina, 1899; Reprint: Morningside, Dayton Ohio, 1973. Dickert's history is another fine work on the exploits of a Southern infantry brigade. It is considered possibly the finest work regarding a South Carolina volunteer organization.

Dowdey, Clifford & Manarin, Louis H., *The Wartime Papers of R. E. Lee*, Little, Brown, Boston, 1961, Reprint: Da Capo Press Inc., New York, 1987. While most of the military correspondence in Dowdey and Manarin's work is also found in the **OR**, the real treasure of the publication are the letters to Lee's wife and family. They provide a personal glimpse of the man the South grew to love and admire.

Dyer, Frederick H., *A Compendium of the War of the Rebellion,* 3 Volumes, Thomas Yoseloff, New York/London, 1959. Dyer, a veteran of the war, compiled his compendium from data contained in the **OR** as well as a number of other sources. His work is without doubt the most complete inventory of military organizations mustered into Federal service. Unfortunately with any work of its size, there are some inconstancies in the listings. In addition, the accuracy of some early records have been proven to be questionable. The discrepancies however, are few in number compared to the sheer volume of material Dyer included in his publication.

Eustis, Henry Lawrence, *Genealogy of the Eustis Family*, David, Clapp and Son Printers, Boston Massachusetts, 1878. Simply a genealogical listing of the members of the Eustis family.

Gibbon, John, *Personal Recollections of the Civil War*, G. P. Putnam's Sons, New York/London, 1928; Reprint: Morningside, Dayton Ohio, 1988. A no holds barred personal account that Allen Nevins called a "Reliable, straightforward memoirs by an officer who for a time commanded the Iron Brigade; particularly good for the Gettysburg campaign."

Goldsborough, William W., *The Maryland Line in the Confederate Army: 1861-1865*, The Board of Governors of the Association of the Maryland Line, 1900.

Gordon, John B., *Reminiscences of the Civil War*, Charles Scribner's Sons, New York, 1903; Reprint: Time-Life Books, 1981. Although some of Gordon's opinions and narratives of events have been called into question over the years, his reminiscences are still note worthy. His account covers the entire war from his efforts to raise a regiment in Alabama to the surrender at Appomattox.

Goss, Warren Lee, *Recollections of a Private*, Thomas Y. Crowell and Company, New York, 1890; Reprint: Time Life Books, New York, 1910. Goss's work is an absorbing look into the life of the common foot soldier in the army of the Potomac. He recounts the experiences of both himself and his companions as they grow from unrefined recruits to battle hardened veterans.

Grant, Ulysses S., *Personal Memoirs of U.S. Grant*, World Publishing Company, Cleveland Ohio, 1952; Reprint: Da Capo Press Inc., New York, 1982.

When Grant's term as president expired he had no plans to document the events of his life. By the time he was sixty, like just before the war, he was once again broke. In order to continue to hold off his creditors, and with the urging and support of Samuel Clemons, Grant began putting his experiences on paper. He wrote a paltry number of pages covering his life before and after the war, his troubled times between the Mexican and Civil Wars and nearly nothing on his time as president. The bulk of his work covers his war experiences which can easily be seen by the reader as having been the most memorable to the general. As the end of his work approached, he developed throat cancer and would complete his writings in a rambling state probably produced by the large doses of morphine he was administered for the pain. Shortly after completing his work, the general died. Unlike Lee, Grant managed to record his personal thoughts for a grateful nation. Ultimately the venture proved to be the financial boon which Grant had hoped. His wife Julia would see nearly half a million dollars in royalties.

Hamlin, Percy Gatling, *The Making of a Soldier: Letters of General R. S. Ewell*, Whittet and Shepperson, Richmond Virginia, 1935. The letters in this volume range from Ewell's time at West Point to his peaceful existence as a farmer after the war. They provide insight into the general's personality and his human side as well as his thoughts on war and personal integrity.

Hancock, Almira Russell, *Reminiscences of Winfield Scott Hancock*, Charles L. Webster and Company, New York, 1887. Written by Hancock's wife, and published a year after the general died.

Hassler, William W., Editor, *One of Lee's Best Men: The Civil War Letters of General William Dorsey Pender*, The University of North Carolina Press, Chapel Hill/London, 1965. A collection of Pender's wartime correspondence to his wife Fanny. Pender was one of Lee's lesser known generals but many believe he should have been elevated to Corps command instead of Ewell or Hill. His letters supply a vivid look into the relationship between the general and his wife as well as an inside and candid commentary on the state of Lee's army and Pender's opinion of a number of army officers.

Hood, John B., *Advance and Retreat: Personal Experiences in the United States and Confederate States Armies*, Hood Orphan Memorial Fund, New Orleans Louisiana, 1880; Reprint: University of Nebraska Press, Lincoln Nebraska, 1996. Although Hood's autobiography contains a great deal of pertinent information on his military career, the bulk of his work consists of an answer to the charges made against him by Joe Johnston. The book was originally published posthumously.

Hopkins, Luther W., *From Bull Run to Appomattox*, Fleet-McGinley, Baltimore Maryland, 1908. An excellent recollection of the experiences of a typical cavalryman. Hopkins was a mere boy of eighteen when he began his Civil War experiences and his youthfulness shows in his recollections. Although he was much older when he wrote of his experiences, his youthful exuberance was still present in his descriptions of events.

Hotchkiss, Jedediah, *Make Me a Map of the Valley*, Southern Methodist University Press, Dallas,1973. Hotchkiss' journal is a treasure trove of anecdotal information from the inner workings of first the command of Stonewall Jackson and then Ewell's Second Corps. It is one of the best and most engrossing reads ever produced by a Civil War veteran.

Howard, Wiley C., *Sketch of Cobb Legion Cavalry and Some Incidents and scenes Remembered*, 1901. A small, twenty page pamphlet, comprised of a speech which Wiley delivered before Atlanta Camp 159 of the United Confederate Veterans on 19 August 1901.

Huey, Pennock, *A True History of the Charge of the 8th Pennsylvania Cavalry at Chancellorsville*, Porter and Coates, Philadelphia, 1883. Huey wrote his short history of the 8th Pennsylvania's charge as a rebuttal to General Pleasonton's misrepresentation of the events which led to the regiments attack.

Humphreys, Henry H., *Andrew Atkinson Humphreys: A Biography*, The John C. Winston Company, Philadelphia, 1924: Reprint: Ron R. Van Sickle Military Books, Gaithersburg Maryland, 1988. Written by Humphrey's son, this work has become the generally accepted biography of Andrew Humphreys.

Hunley, C. Russell, Editor, *The 14th U.S. Infantry Regiment in the American Civil War, John Young Letters*, Burd Street Press, Shippensburg Pennsylvania, 2000. A collection of letters written primarily by Young to his wife, describing his exploits and life during the war.

Jones, John B., *A Rebel War Clerk's Diary*, 2 Volumes, J. B. Lippincott and Company, Philadelphia, 1866; Reprint: Time Life Books, New York, 1982-83. Jones' work is one of the seminal publications depicting the inner workings of the Confederate government and war effort. He wrote his diary entries from a candid point of view and according to the clerk, his president and secretary of war were aware he was documenting his experiences. From his position, Jones was able to observe at one time or another, nearly every key player within the Confederate government and military.

Jones, J. William, *Life and Letters of Robert Edward Lee, Soldier, and Man*, The Neale Publishing Company, New York/Washington, 1906. Jones was one of the most rabid Lee supporters after the war. His promotion, and in many cases, exaggeration of Lee's wartime record help to establish Lee as the champion of the Lost Cause and the infallible general that many Southerners came to believe him to be.

Lee, Fitzhugh, *General Lee: A Biography of Robert E. Lee*, D. Appleton and Company, New York, 1894; Reprint: Da Capo Press Inc., 1994. As a member of Stuart's Cavalry and the nephew of General Lee, Fitzhugh Lee had the opportunity to observe his uncle in both a military environment and in personal situations. His work is filled with a number of insights and anecdotal observation of not only Robert E. Lee's military methods but his human side as well. Unfortunately, like others who were personally close to their subject, Fitz failed to take an objective look at his uncle.

Long, Armistead L., *Memoirs of Robert E. Lee*, J. M. Stoddart & Company, New York, 1886; Reprint: The Blue and Gray Press, 1983. Another memoir of Lee written by a member of his inner circle. Long however, was, as historian A. M. Gambone put it, one of the Lee "myth-makers."

Longstreet, James, *From Manassas to Appomattox, Memoirs of the Civil War in America*, J. B. Lippincott Company, Philadelphia Pennsylvania, 1896; Reprint: Blue and Grey Press, 1984. After the war and Lee's death, Longstreet was assailed from all directions by those who painted Lee as an infallible commander who was defeated by the failures of others, most notably, his second in command. Longstreet wrote his memoirs as a portion of his defense. Although Longstreet did a decent job of defending himself, the sheer volume of attacks and his sometimes variable methods of defending his actions, kept him from attaining any credibility during his life. Toward the end of the 20th Century, a number of works which reevaluated Longstreet's contributions to the Confederate war effort have painted him in a more favorable light.

Lowe, David W., Editor, *Meade's Army: The Private Notebooks of Lieutenant Colonel Theodore Lyman*, Kent State University Press, Kent Ohio, 2007. Lyman recorded the events of his military service on nearly a daily basis. He noted events in his notebook and dispatch book as they happened, creating an almost instantaneous history of the events swirling around him. Lyman used his notes to assembly a historically accurate retelling of the events. Many of his notes included the exact time an event took place making his work a chronology of many historically significant events.

Marshall, Charles, *An aide-de camp of Lee*, Little Brown, Boston, 1927; Reprint: As *Lee's Aide-De-Camp*, Bison Books, 2000. A fine commentary on Lee and the events occurring in and around his headquarters. Marshall also offers an informative interpretation of his understanding of Lee's objectives during the Gettysburg Campaign.

McClellan, George B., *McClellan's Own Story*, Charles L. Webster & Company, New York, 1887; Reprint: The Easton Press, Norwalk, Connecticut, 1995. McClellan's work is the second version of his story due to the fact that his first draft was accidently destroyed by a fire. While it is a worthwhile read, it is often difficult to follow and seems disorganized at times. However, it is a valuable part of the overall documentation of the history of the Army of the Potomac.

McClellan, Henry B., *I rode with Jeb Stuart*, Indiana University Press, Bloomington Indiana, 1958; Reprint: Da Capo Press, New York, 1994. McClellan conducted a great deal of investigative work after the war and using his own experiences as a backdrop, penned one of the most vivid accounts of the Confederate cavalry in the Army of Northern Virginia. It is a very entertaining and unique read.

McDonald, William N., *A History of the Laurel Brigade*, Mrs. Kate S. McDonald, 1907; Reprint: Olde Soldiers Books Inc., Gaithersburg Maryland, 1987. Like Dickert's history of Kershaw's Brigade, McDonald's work is first rate and contains an in depth and often personal account of the exploits of Turner Ashby's Cavalry.

McKim, Randolph H., *A Soldiers Recollections*, Longman's Green and Company, New York/London, 1910. McKim wrote the majority of his work by relying on the diaries he kept during the war. He utilized his entries as they were written without changing the tone or the context of his previous comments. The result is a clear, and as McKim put it "unvarnished" view of the war.

Meade, George G., *The Life and Letters of General George Gordon Meade*, 2 Volumes, Charles Scribner's Sons, New York, 1913; Reprint: Butternut and Blue, Baltimore Maryland, 1994. Assembled and written by the general's son and aide-de-camp, not only does it contain a wide-ranging collection of correspondence, but also an extensive narrative on the battle of Gettysburg and a number of appendices which help bring light to Meade's version of events. Anyone interested in the general should not neglect his son's work.

Mosby, John S., *Mosby's Memoirs*, Little Brown and Company, 1917; Reprint: J. S. Sanders and Company, Nashville, 1995. John Singleton Mosby's guerrilla fighters operated in central Virginia and as such were an integral element of any military operation in the area. Mosby's men terrorized Federal operations from near Fredericksburg in the south to Leesburg in the north and from the Blue Ridge to the Potomac River in the east. His memoirs are a unique look at a number of lesser know operations in Virginia.

Nicolay, John G. & Hay, John editors, *Complete Works of Abraham Lincoln*, The Tandy-Thomas Co., New York, 1905; Reprint: The National Historical Society, 2008, 12 Volumes. Lincoln's speeches and writings have appeared in many formats over the years. One must keep in mind when reviewing Lincoln's writings that they only tell the president's side of the story.

Oeffinger, John C., Editor, *A Soldier's General: The Civil War Letters of Major General Lafayette McLaws*, The University of North Carolina Press, Chapel Hill/London, 2002. Most of the letters in Offinger's volume are to McLaws' wife. They paint a more human picture of the man who at the time of the Gettysburg Campaign was the senior major general in the Army of Northern Virginia.

Pickett, George E., *The Heart of a Soldier, Wartime Letters from General George E. Pickett, C.S.A. to His Wife*, Seth Moyle Inc., New York, 1913; Reprint: Stan Clark Military Books, Gettysburg Pennsylvania, 1995. A collection of letters from Pickett to his sweetheart beginning during the fall of 1861 and terminating after the war. Pickett's letters portray a man very much in love with his child sweetheart and his candor in explaining to her his feelings seem to be somewhat exaggerated.

Pickett, LaSalle Corbell, *Pickett and His Men*, J. B. Lippincott and Company, Philadelphia, 1913. Mrs. George E. Pickett spent much of her life after the death of her husband promoting his legacy and trying to damage the reputations of his critics. Although her comments should always be taken with a certain level of trepidation, there is relevant information within her remarks regarding her husband.

Poague, William T., *Gunner with Stonewall*, McCowat-Mercer Press, Jackson Tennessee, 1957; Reprint: University of Nebraska Press, Lincoln/London, 1998. A useful source of information regarding the campaigns of Stonewall Jackson and the operations of the artillery.

Powell, William H., *The Fifth Army Corps,* G.P. Putman's, 1896, Reprint: Morningside, Dayton Ohio 1995. A fine and extensive history of the Federal Fifth Corps written by a member of the 11th U. S Infantry.

Quaife, Milo M., Editor, *From the Cannon's Mouth: The Civil War Letters of General Alpheus S. Williams*, Wayne State University Press, Detroit Michigan,

1959; Reprint: University of Nebraska Press, Lincoln/London, 1995. Williams' private letters are full of candor and are refreshing in their content and opinions.

Rosenblatt, Emil & Ruth, Editors, *Hard Marching Every Day: The Civil War Letters of Private Wilber Fisk 1861-1865*, University Press of Kansas, Lawrence Kansas, 1983, 1992. Fisk, a school teacher by trade, acted as a war correspondent, writing about 100 letters to the *Montpelier Green Mountain Freeman*. Possibly one of the most well written collections of letters by any soldier during the war.

Samito, Christian G., *"Fear Was Not in Him": The Civil War Letters of Major General Francis C. Barlow*, Fordham University Press, New York, 2004. Barlow's letters provide unique insight to the evolving opinions on the war through the eyes of a Northern intellectual.

Schurz, Carl, *The Reminiscences of Carl Schurz*, 3 Volumes, The McClure Company, New York, 1907-09. Possibly the best and most complete reminiscences of any general who served with the army of the Potomac. Schurz retells the events of his life with an eloquence which keeps the reader interested in a story, which, if told by a lesser man, would be less appealing.

Simpson, Brooks D. & Berlin, Jean V., Editors, *Sherman's Civil War: Selected Correspondence of William T. Sherman 1860-1865*, University of North Carolina Press, Chapel Hill/London, 1999. A wonderful and extensive collection of Sherman's correspondence which will take readers into the mind of the second most influential Federal General of the war.

Sorrel, Gilbert M., *Recollections of a Confederate Staff Officer*, The Neale Publishing Co., New York, 1905; Reprint: Smithmark Publishers Inc, New York, 1994. An excellent reminiscence written by General Longstreet's chief of staff.

Sparks, David S., *Inside Lincoln's Army: The Diary of General Marsena Rudolph Patrick Provost Marshall General, Army of the Potomac*, Thomas Yoseliff, New York/London, 1964. Patrick's diary contains candid comments on the conflicts and workings of the upper echelons of the Army of the Potomac and the administration in Washington.

Stevens, George Thomas, *Three Years in the Sixth Corps*, S. R. Gray Publisher, Albany, New York, 1866. Stevens was the regimental surgeon for the 77th New York. He was dismissed from duty late in 1862 but was reinstated a few months later. His work is a very entertaining and telling recollection of his time in the Army of the Potomac.

Styple, William B., Editor, *Writing & Fighting from the Army of Northern Virginia*, Belle Grove Publishing Company, Kearny New Jersey, 2003. A collection of war correspondence published in the *New York Sunday Mercury*.

Taylor, Walter H., *Four Years with General Lee*, Indiana University Press, Bloomington and Indianapolis, 1962; Reprint: 1996. Taylor wrote two remembrances of his time with General Lee. The first, this publication, was originally published as *Four Years with General Lee: Being a Summary of the more Important Events Touching the Career of General Robert E. Lee, in the War Between the States, Together with an Authoritative Statement of the Strength of the Army which He Commanded in the Field*. According to Taylor, he intended the work to be a statistical look at the operations of the Army of Northern Virginia.

His second work, *General Lee: His Campaigns in Virginia, 1861-1865* (see below) was never intended to be published but after the urgings of friends Taylor allowed his second effort to be seen by all.

_____, *General Lee: His Campaigns in Virginia, 1861-1865*, Nusbaum Books, Norfolk Virginia; Reprint: Bison Books, 1994.

Taylor, Walter H., *Lee's Adjutant: The Wartime Letters of Colonel Walter Herron Taylor; 1862-1865*, Tower, R. Lockwood, Editor, University of South Carolina Press, Columbia South Carolina, 1995. Although Taylor wrote two volumes on the activities of Lee and his army after the war, the publication of his personal letters provide new insight into the opinions of Lee's loyal adjutant.

Thomas, Mary W., Sauers, Richard A, Editors, *The Civil War Letters of First Lieutenant James B. Thomas*, Butternut and Blue, Baltimore Maryland, 1995. A fine collection of letters from the adjutant of the 107th Pennsylvania Volunteers.

Toombs, Samuel, *New Jersey Troops in the Gettysburg Campaign*, The Evening Mail Publishing House, Orange New Jersey, 1888: Reprint: Longstreet House, Hightstown New Jersey, 1988. An excellent record of the active part New Jersey troops played in the campaign. The various regimental organizations provided Toombs with support and his work is augmented by the personal reminiscences of a number of survivors.

Trout, Robert J., Editor, *Memoirs of the Stuart Horse Artillery Volume 1: Moorman's and Hart's Batteries*, The University of Tennessee Press, Knoxville Tennessee, 2008. Additional recollections of members of Stuart's Horse Artillery Battalion.

Trout, Robert J., *With Pen & Saber: The Letters and Diaries of J.E.B. Stuart's Staff Officers*, Stackpole Books, Mechanicsburg Pennsylvania, 1995. This collection of correspondence and diary entries by Stuart's staff members is an excellent research tool which also is an entertaining read.

von Borcke, Heros, *Memoirs of the Confederate War for Independence*, W. Blackwood and Sons, Edinburgh, 1866; Reprint: J. S. Sanders and Company, Nashville Tennessee, 1999. Von Borcke published his memoir a year after the war had concluded. He no doubt wrote much of it while the war was still in progress and he was recovering from the wound which ended the war for him. While much of his work is interesting and relevant, von Borcke tended to stretch the truth somewhat but usually failed to reach the point of fantasy.

Wainwright, Charles S., *A Diary of Battle: The Personal Journals of Colonel Charles S. Wainwright 1861-1865*, Harcourt, Brace and World, Inc., New York, 1962; Reprint: Da Capo Press, New York, 1998. Wainwright kept probably one of the most detailed personal journal/diary of any officer with the Army of the Potomac. He offers insight on not only his personal experiences but also discusses the men who led the army and ventures into the political and social aspects of the war.

Walker, Francis A., *History of the Second Army Corps in the Army of the Potomac*, Charles Scribner's sons, New York, 1887; Reprint, Olde Soldier Books Inc., Gaithersburg Maryland, 1987. Like Powell's history of the Fifth Corps, Walker's work is quite lengthy. Walker solicited information for his history from a number of participants including some of the corps former commanders and prominent Confederate officers who fought against the corps. His work is probably if not the best and most complete single volume work of the Second Corps record during the war.

Worsham, John H., *One of Jackson's Foot Cavalry*, The Neale Publishing Company, New York, 1912; Reprint: Time Life Books, New York, 1982. Worsham participated in the fighting in the Valley in 1862 and fought with the army of Northern Virginia as a member of Company F of the 21st Virginia. Worsham relays his experiences in a well written narrative which is considered by many to be a classic work on the life of a soldier.

Secondary Publications

Andrew, Rod, Jr., *Wade Hampton: Confederate Warrior to Southern Redeemer*, The University of North Carolina Press, Chapel Hill, 2008. An excellent contemporary biography of the man who was possibly the South's second most prominent cavalryman.

Barrett, John G., *The Civil War in North Carolina*, The University of North Carolina Press, Chapel Hill, 1963. An excellent single volume treatment of the Civil War in North Carolina.

Bates, Samuel P., *Martial Deeds of Pennsylvania*, T. H. Davis and Company, Philadelphia, 1875. A military history of Pennsylvania during the war. Bates' work contains a number of biographical sketches and a good deal of information on Pennsylvania's role during the Gettysburg Campaign.

Bead, W.G., *Stonewall's Man: Sandie Pendleton*, The University of North Carolina Press, Chapel Hill London, 1959. A fine biography of one of the Second Corps most efficient staff members.

Bigelow, John, Jr., *The Campaign of Chancellorsville*, New Haven, 1910; Reprint: Morningside, Dayton Ohio, 1980. Bigelow's work continues to be the standard by which all other civil war battle studies are measured. It contains a plethora of charts, tables and maps. For those interested in an in-depth, purely military treatment of the Battle of Chancellorsville, Bigelow's work is the best offering.

Bowden, Scott & Ward, Bill., *Last Chance for Victory, Robert E. Lee and the Gettysburg Campaign*, Savas Publishing Company, 2001; Reprint: Da Capo Press, 2003. An outstanding work on the generalship of Lee during the campaign and his decisions which shaped the campaign and the battle.

Boyle, Frank A., *A Party of Mad Fellows: The Story of the Irish Regiments in the Army of the Potomac*, Morningside, Dayton Ohio, 1996.

Brandt, Nat, *The Congressman Who Got Away with Murder*, Syracuse University Press, 1991. An entertaining work detailing the Sickles' murder of Barton Key.

Brown, Alexander, *The Cabells and Their Kin: A Memorial Volume of History, Biography and Genealogy*, Houghton Mifflin and Company, Boston/New York, 1895. A detailed listing of the genealogical lines of the Cabell family.

Bridges, Hal, *Lee's Maverick General: Daniel Harvey Hill*, McGraw Hill Book Company, Inc., New York, 1961; Reprint: University of Nebraska Press, Lincoln/London, 1991. A fine and detailed biography of Major General Daniel Harvey Hill. Much of Bridges' work is based on Hill's papers held in a number of repositories.

Burton, Brian K., *Extraordinary Circumstances: The Seven Days Battles*, Indiana University Press, Bloomington/Indianapolis Indiana, 2001. A detailed battle study of the campaign which saved Richmond from McClellan's mighty Army of the Potomac.

Busey, John W. & Martin, David G., *Regimental Strengths and Losses at Gettysburg*, Longstreet House, Hightstown New Jersey, 2005. A seminal work on the strengths of every regiment which fought at Gettysburg. Includes breakdowns of strengths and losses based on a number of different metrics including percentage of losses and rankings among other regiments. Reference to Busey's work on the casualties at Gettysburg appears in nearly all prominent works on the battle.

Carleton, Hiram, *Genealogical and Family History of the State of Vermont*, The Lewis Publishing Company, New York/Chicago, 1903. A collection of Genealogical information regarding prominent families from Vermont.

Carmichael, Peter S., *Lee's Young Artillerist: William R. J. Pegram*, University Press of Virginia, Charlottesville/London, 1995. Drawn from mostly manuscript and primary sources, Carmichael's work is a concise and informative work on this well known Rebel gunner.

Carter, William Harding, *The Life of Lieutenant General Chaffee*, University of Chicago Press, Chicago Illinois, 1917.

Catton, Bruce, *Mr. Lincoln's Army*, Doubleday and Company Inc., Garden City New York, 1951, 1962. Probably the best known of the mid-20th Century Civil War historians, Catton was a journalist by trade and wrote extensively on the war. He wrote three trilogies, *The Army of the Potomac*, of which this volume is a member, *The Centennial History of the Civil War* and the *Ulysses S. Grant* trilogy, of which Catton penned the final two volumes. The first was written by historian and biographer Lloyd Lewis, who died in 1949. Mr. Catton won a Pulitzer Prize for his 1953 work, *A Stillness at Appomattox*. Catton was a storyteller, and while his writings are well researched and factual, he presented the story in a manner which gave life to the participants, a style which endeared him to his readers.

Christ, Elwood, *The Struggle for the Bliss Farm at Gettysburg July 2nd and 3rd 1863*, Butternut and Blue, Baltimore Maryland, 1994. A short, excellent monograph of one of the lesser known but critical actions at the battle of Gettysburg. The author would recommend Mr. Christ's work to anyone who would like to know more about the events leading up to the Confederate assault on the 3rd day.

Cleaves, Freeman, *Meade of Gettysburg*, University of Oklahoma Press, Norman/London, 1960. A well written and honest assessment of General Meade. Meade has not been treated well over the years. Cleaves' work gives Meade his due and portrays a man who was first and foremost an excellent and competent soldier.

Clemmer, Gregg S., *Old Alleghany: The Life and Wars of General Ed Johnson*, The Hearthside Publishing Company, Staunton, Virginia, 2004. When published,

General Johnson finally received his just due in regard to a complete and fair biography.

Coddington, Edwin B., *The Gettysburg Campaign: A Study in Command*, Charles Scribner's Sons: New York, 1968; Reprint: Morningside, Dayton Ohio, 1979. Simply the standard by which all other works on Gettysburg are judged. Coddington was the first to mine the huge stacks of correspondence between John B. Bachelder and the veterans of the battle housed unbeknownst to historians for years at the New Hampshire Historical Society. The author has been informed by a knowledgeable individual that many licenses Gettysburg battlefield guides reread Coddington on a regular basis.

Coco, Gregory A., *A Strange and Blighted Land*, Thomas Publications, Gettysburg Pennsylvania, 1995. The late Greg Coco wrote extensively regarding the plight of the common soldier during the Civil War. His works are excellent studies in the hardships and often horrific results of armed conflict.

_____, *The Civil War Infantryman, in Camp, on the March and in Battle*, Thomas Publications, Gettysburg Pennsylvania, 1996.

Cole, Philip M., *Civil War Artillery at Gettysburg*, Colecraft Industries, Orrtanna Pennsylvania, 2002.

Collins, Darrell L., *Major General Robert E. Rodes of the Army of Northern Virginia*, Savas Beatie, New York/California, 2008. A fine and long overdue study of the life of one of Lee's best generals. Many believe that Rodes would have been a better choice to succeed Jackson at the head of the Second Corps.

_____, *The Jones-Imboden Raid*, McFarland and Company Inc., Publishers, Jefferson North Carolina, 2007. A well written recounting of the operation which Lee and Davis hoped would incapacitate the B&O Railroad for a significant period.

Cooper, Willian J. Jr., *Jefferson Davis, American*, Alfred A. Knopf, New York, 2000. One of the two best single volume biographies of Jefferson Davis.

Cozzens, Peter, *Shenandoah 1862*, The University of North Carolina Press, Chapel Hill, 2008. Cozzen has written extensively of the Civil War and the Indian wars in the West. Shenandoah 1862 is his latest effort within the Civil War realm.

Daughtry, Mary B., *Gray Cavalier: The Life and Wars of General W. H. F. "Rooney" Lee*, Da Capo New York, 2002. A well written work which makes extensive use of manuscript collections to build a well rounded and fair assessment of Robert E. Lee's son.

Davis, Burke, *Jeb Stuart: The Last Cavalier*, Rinehart & Company, New York, 1957. Mr. Davis' biography of Jeb Stuart sets near the top of the mountain of work done on Stuart since the end of the war.

Davis, William C., *Battle at Bull Run*, Doubleday and Company Inc., Garden City New York, 1977; Reprint: Louisiana State University Press, Baton Rouge/London, 1985. Eminent historian Davis writes with a flare of a novelist and thus produces a well written and easy to read recounting of the first major battle of the war.

_____, *Jefferson Davis, The Man and His Hour*, Louisiana State University Press, Baton Rouge, 1991. The other superlative single volume account of Davis' life.

Detzer, David, *Dissonance: The Turbulent Days Between Fort Sumter and Bull Run*, Harcourt Inc., New York, 2006. A history professor at Connecticut State University, Detzer's work is a fine retelling of the period between the opening of the war and Bull Run when each antagonist was preparing for war.

Dowdey, Clifford, *The Seven Days: The Emergence of Lee*, Little Brown and Company, 1964; Reprint: Barnes and Noble Books as *Lee Takes Command*, 1994. Dowdey, another of what historian A. M. Gambone called "The Myth-Makers," wrote extensively of Lee approximately two decades after D. S. Freeman completed his second multi-volume work on Lee and his army. He continued the painting of Lee as an infallible commander who had been wronged by his lieutenants. Unlike Freeman however, Dowdey failed to footnote his work and although he does include a bibliography with each of his efforts, the context which his thoughts are presented cannot be traced back to their source for independent review.

_____, *Lee's Last Campaign: The Story of Lee and His Men Against Grant-1864*, Little Brown and Company, 1960; Reprint: Barnes and Noble Books as *Lee's Last Campaign*, 1994.

Dunn, Craig L., *Iron Men, Iron Will: The Nineteenth Indiana Regiment of the Iron Brigade*, Guild Press of Indiana Inc., Indianapolis, 1995. A fine regimental history of a famous Iron Brigade regiment.

Ernsberger, Donald, *Paddy Owen's Regulars: A History of the 69th Pennsylvania "Irish Volunteers"*, 2 Volumes, Xlibris Corporation, U.S.A., 2004. A micro-history of a regiment which defended the angle on the third day at Gettysburg. Ernsberger tells the story through first person accounts, personal letters and regimental orders. Unfortunately the narrative is a bit choppy and tends to bounce to new topics without much transition.

Fishel, Edwin C., *The Secret War for the Union*, Houghton Mifflin Company, Boston/New York, 1996. The title of Fishel's work can be somewhat misleading. While it touts the fact that the volume is a study of intelligence operations during the war, it is in actuality mostly told from the Union point of view and only covers the period from the outset of the war to the end of the Battle of Gettysburg. The work has tremendous value since Fishel tapped the previously ignored *Files of the Bureau of Military Information* located in the National Archives. Although some of the documents were stolen in 1962 and some remain unrecovered, Fishel made good use of the papers available to him.

Fox, William F., *Regimental Losses in the American Civil War*, Brandow Printing Company, Albany New York, 1898; Reprint: Morningside, Dayton Ohio, 1974. A standard work on regimental statistics.

Freeman, Douglas S., *Lee's Lieutenants, A Study in Command*, 3 volumes, Charles Scribner's Sons, New York, 1943. Freeman was, without doubt, the most influential biographer of Robert E. Lee. He won a Pulitzer Prize for his four volume life history of the general. But, Freeman was more than a simple biographer; he was also a dramatist who commanded the English language like no other Civil War historian. He used his way with words to promote Lee, elevating him to the stature of an unfailing defender of the Lost Cause who fell victim to lesser men.

_____, *Robert E. Lee*, 4 Volumes, Charles Scribner's Sons, New York/London, 1936.

French, Steve, *Imboden's Brigade in the Gettysburg Campaign*, The Morgan Messenger, Berkeley Springs West Virginia, 2008. A much ignored aspect of the Gettysburg Campaign finally gets its due with Mr. French's fine history.

Furgurson, Ernest B., *Chancellorsville 1863: The Souls of the Brave*, Alfred A. Knopf, New York, 1992. A fine, quick paced treatment of the Chancellorsville Campaign. Although it lacks the technical aspect of Bigelow's work, it still provides a general feel for the battle.

Gallagher, Gary W., Editor, *Lee the Soldier*, University of Nebraska Press, Lincoln/London, 1996. A collection of primary and secondary source information conveying character and military assessments of Lee.

Gambone, A. M., *Hancock at Gettysburg and Beyond*, Butternut and Blue, Baltimore Maryland, 1997. A valuable work on the life and generalship of Winfield Hancock. Gambone is a first rate historian and has produced probably the best volume on the activities of Hancock at Gettysburg. He provides the reader with a sense of just how critical Hancock's presence and activities during the battle were to the Federal victory.

_____, *Major-General Darius Nash Couch: Enigmatic Valor*, Butternut and Blue, Baltimore Maryland, 2000. Another excellent work by Gambone, providing extensive coverage of Couch's life a career.

Gottfried, Bradley M., *Stopping Picket: The History of the Philadelphia Brigade*, White Mane Publishing Company, Shippensburg Pennsylvania, 1999. This is a fine history of a brigade which saw heavy action throughout the war.

_____, *The Artillery of Gettysburg*, Cumberland House, Nashville Tennessee, 2008. An excellent supplement to Gottfried's *Brigades of Gettysburg*. Unlike Brigades, it is written in a narrative fashion rather than as capsule histories of each unit.

_____, *The Brigades of Gettysburg: The Union and Confederate Brigades at the Battle of Gettysburg*, Da Capo Press, Inc., New York, 2002. Probably the best brigade level review of the activities of each unit during the battle of Gettysburg. Gottfried provides a divisional overview before entering upon a three to four page review of the division's brigades. The work is extensively footnoted making it a valuable reference tool. Any Civil War library would be incomplete without a copy.

Grunder, Charles S., Beck, Brandon H., *The Second Battle of Winchester: June 12-15, 1863*, H. E. Howard Inc., Lynchburg Virginia, 1989. A short and concise battle history of Robert H. Milroy's efforts to defend Winchester in 1863.

Harrison, Kathy Georg and Busey, John W., *Nothing But Glory: Pickett's Division at Gettysburg*, Thomas Publications, Gettysburg Pennsylvania, 1987, 1993. This work contains a history of the charge and a full roster of the men from Pickets Division who participated in the charge.

Harsh, Joseph L., *Taken at the Flood: Robert E. Lee and Confederate Strategy in the Maryland Campaign of 1862*, The Kent State University Press, Kent Ohio, London, 1999. The late Joseph Harsh's volume is an excellent and extensive review of Confederate strategy during the Maryland Campaign. Although Harsh covers the military aspect of the campaign his attention to detail regarding the strategies adopted by Lee and the changes made to his original plans paint a vivid picture of how a military plan constantly evolves due to unforeseen events.

Hebert, Walter H., *Fighting Joe Hooker,* Bobbs-Merrill 1944, Reprint: Bison Books, 1999. The only full length work on Joe Hooker's life.

Henderson, George F. R., *Stonewall Jackson and the American Civil War*, Longmans, Green And Company, New York, 1898; Reprint: Smithmark, New York, 1994. A detailed study of Stonewall Jackson by British writer George Francis Robert Henderson. The work opens by covering Jackson's boyhood days, his time at West Point and the Mexican War. It terminates with the generals wounding and death after Chancellorsville.

Hennessy, John J., *Return to Bull Run: The Campaign and Battle of Second Manassas*, Simon and Schuster, New York/London, 1993. A comprehensive look at the Second Battle of Bull Run. Hennessy not only discusses the tactics of the campaign but the details of the battle and lays out the difficulties in maintaining and controlling the flow of a major battle once it has been inaugurated.

Hess, Earl J., *Lee's Tar Heels: The Pettigrew-Kirkland-MacRae Brigade*, The University of North Carolina Press, Chapel Hill/London, 2002. Pettigrew's brigade is one of the unsung heroes of the battle of Gettysburg. Hess chronicles the brigade's formation and its first major action in Pennsylvania on through to the end of the war. It also contains an extensive appendix which includes a great deal of statistical information.

_____, *The Rifle Musket in Civil War Combat*, University Press of Kansas, Lawrence, 2006. A revealing look at the use of the rifled musket in Civil War combat. Hess exposes the mythology and confirms the truth about the weapons effects on Civil War combat. Experts and novices will gain from examining this study.

Hessler, James A., *Sickles at Gettysburg*, Savas Beatie, New York/California, 2009. This work provides a glimpse of Sickles' early life and background before presenting a comprehensive look at the general's actions at Gettysburg and the fallout after the battle. Hessler's assessment does not pass judgment but lets the reader from their own opinion as to Sickles' actions during and after the war.

Jones, Terry L., *Lee's Tigers: The Louisiana Infantry in the Army of Northern Virginia*, Louisiana State University Press, Baton Rouge/London, 1987. A fine portrayal of the Louisianans covering their formation, composition and campaigns with the Army of Northern Virginia.

Jordan, David M., *Winfield Scott Hancock: A Soldier's Life* Indiana University Press, Bloomington/Indianapolis, 1988. Probably the best work on Hancock. It is comprehensive, well written and thoroughly documented.

Jorgensen, Jay, *Gettysburg's Bloody Wheatfield*, White Mane Publishing Company, Shippensburg Pennsylvania, 2002. A tactical study of the fighting in the Wheatfield. It places the confusing nature of the fighting in the Wheatfield in a new light. The course of the fighting is easy to follow and understand.

Kegel, James A., *North with Lee and Jackson*, Stackpole Books, Mechanicsburg Pennsylvania, 1996. Kegel's investigation into the reasons why Lee took his army north during the summer of 1863 and what the general hoped to accomplish provides an interesting read. He brings to light a number of little known facts regarding Lee's planning and makes the reader aware that a northern invasion was not a new idea in the spring of 1863. While Kegel's thoughts on a number of topics are somewhat suspect, his work does inspire thought regarding a number of preconceived notions about Lee and the campaign.

Keneally, Thomas, *American Scoundrel: The Life of the Notorious Civil War General Dan Sickles*, Doubleday/Random House, New York, 2002. Love him or hate him, no one can doubt that Dan Sickles was one of the most controversial generals of the Civil War and the post war period. While Keneally's work is a worthy read, there are other works more attune to Sickles Civil War career such as Hessler's work listed above.

Krick, Robert K., *Stonewall Jackson at Cedar Mountain*, The University of North Carolina Press, Chapel Hill/London, 1990. Robert K. Krick probably knows more about the Army of Northern Virginia, Lee and Jackson than any other modern historian. His work on Jackson at Cedar Mountain is the only battle study of the conflict known to this author. Krick however, leans toward traditional interpretations of his subjects which in today's dialog have been challenged by other historians.

_____, *The Smoothbore Volley That Doomed the Confederacy*, Louisiana State University Press, Baton Rouge, 2002. A collection of monographs by Krick concerning a number of aspects of the Army of Northern Virginia.

Krumwiede, John F., *"Old Waddy's Coming" The Military Career of Brigadier General James S. Wadsworth*, Butternut and Blue, Baltimore, Maryland, 2002. A short but concise examination of Wadsworth's military career.

Ladd, David L. and Audrey J. Editors, *John Bachelder's History of the Battle of Gettysburg*, 3 Volumes, Morningside, Dayton Ohio, 1997. For years the correspondence and papers of John Bachelder lay undisturbed at the New Hampshire Historical Society. Then, near the mid 20th Century, Professor Edwin Coddington used them as the centerpiece for his landmark work on the Gettysburg Campaign. Since then they have been utilized by hundreds of historians and buff alike. With Morningside's publication of the bulk of the New Hampshire holdings, his papers are now available to the masses.

Laine, J. Gary & Penny, Morris M., *Law's Alabama Brigade in the War Between the Union and the Confederacy*, White Mane Publishing Company Inc., Shippensburg Pennsylvania, 1996. An outstanding work on one of the most respected and hard fighting brigades in the Eastern Theater. Laine and Penny pay heavy attention to the brigades role at Gettysburg and examine the feud between Law and Longstreet which erupted later during the war.

Lee, Susan P., *Memoirs of William Nelson Pendleton, D.D*, J. B. Lippincott Company, Philadelphia, 1893; Reprint: Sprinkle Publications, Harrisonburg Virginia, 1991. Written by Pendleton's daughter, this work relies heavily on the writings of Pendleton and provides a look into General Pendleton's personality and his opinions.

Long, Armistead Lindsay. L., *Memories of Robert E. Lee: His Military and Personal History*, M. J. Stoddart, New York, 1886; Reprint: The Blue and Gray Press, 1983. Long's volume is a treasure trove of antidotal information on Lee, much of which must be taken as suspect. Like most post war recollections about Lee written shortly after the war, Long paints Lee as the faultless defender of the Lost Cause.

Longacre, Edward G., *Fitz Lee: A Military Biography of Major General Fitzhugh Lee, C.S.A.*, Da Capo Press, Cambridge Massachusetts, 2005. Longacre has written extensively on the cavalry and their activities in the Eastern Theater of the war. All his work is generally well footnoted with extensive bibliographies. He generally tells the story, refraining from overstated opinions, but not without cross-examining conventional wisdom. His work on Fitz Lee is a first rate biography on a significant member of Stuart's inner circle.

_____, *General John Buford: A Military Biography*, Combined Books Inc., Conshohocken Pennsylvania, 1995. Unfortunately for history's sake, John Buford did not survive the war and as such never got the change to write his memoirs. Longacre's work is a welcome treatment of Buford's life which concentrates mostly on his Civil War service.

_____, *Lee's Cavalrymen*, Stackpole Books, Mechanicsburg Pennsylvania, 2002. This volume, and its companion work, *Lincoln's Cavalrymen*, present concise and detailed reviews of cavalry operations in the Eastern Theater.

_____, *Lincoln's Cavalrymen*, Stackpole Books, Mechanicsburg Pennsylvania, 2000.

_____, *Pickett: Leader of the Charge*, White Mane Publishing Company, Shippensburg Pennsylvania, 1995. The first modern work on Pickett. It sheds new light on a number of aspects of Pickett's life.

_____, *The Cavalry at Gettysburg: A Tactical Study of Mounted Operations during the Civil War's Pivotal Campaign, 9 June-14 July 1863*, University of Nebraska Press, Lincoln/London, 1993. Probably the best single volume study of cavalry operations during the Gettysburg Campaign.

Lowry, Thomas P., *The Story the Soldiers Wouldn't Tell*, 1994, Stackpole Books, Mechanicsburg Pennsylvania, 1994. Lowry takes the reader through the seedy side of the Civil War. Anyone who believes that the war was fought by a group of brave, pious, and ethical men will have their eyes opened by Lowry's work.

Mahood, Wayne, *General Wadsworth: The Life and Times of Brevet Major General James S. Wadsworth*, Da Capo Press, New York, 2003. A well written and detailed account of Wadsworth's life. Simply an enjoyable read.

Maier, Larry A., *Gateway to Gettysburg: The Second Battle of Winchester*, Burd Street Press, Shippensburg Pennsylvania, 2002. A detailed account of the battle which cleared the Shenandoah Valley. Included is a thorough biography of Robert H. Milroy.

Martin, David G., *Gettysburg July 1*, Combined Books, Conshohocken, Pennsylvania, 1995-96. An incredibly detailed regimental level battle study of the first day's action at Gettysburg. Although the first day's battle has received scant attention over the years (General Sickles told the *CCW* that he did not consider the first day as part of the Battle of Gettysburg), it has been brought to the forefront by works such as Martin's.

McKinney, Joseph W., *Brandy Station, Virginia, June 9,1863: The Largest Cavalry Battle of the Civil War*, McFarland and Company Inc., Publishers, Jefferson, North Carolina, 2006. Although his time as president of the Brandy Station Foundation has been filed with controversy, McKinney has written a comprehensive and detailed history of the fighting which occurred there on 9 June 1863.

McMurry, Richard M., *John Bell Hood and the War for Southern Independence*, University Press of Kentucky Lexington, 1982. McMurry's work concentrates mostly on Hood as an individual and a general rather than his battlefield accomplishments and failures.

McPherson, James M., *For Cause & Comrades: Why Men Fought in the Civil War*, Oxford University Press, New York/Oxford, 1997. This is a fine and concise work on a subject which seems to elude not only the average citizen but the learned historian as well.

Mingus, Scott L. Jr., *The Louisiana Tigers in the Gettysburg Campaign*, Louisiana State University Press, Baton Rouge, 2009. In interesting and gripping account of the notorious Tigers during the campaign.

Murfin, James V., *The Gleam of Bayonets*, Thomas Yoseliff, New York/London, 1965; Reprint Louisiana State University Press, Baton Rouge/London, 1982. Although it has been supplanted by more recent works, and the publication of Ezra Carman's manuscript, Murfin's work was the first modern history of the campaign.

Murray, R. L., *Artillery Tactics of the Civil War: A Study of the Tactical Use of Artillery Based on the First Day's Battle at Gettysburg*, Benedum Books, Wolcott New York, 1998. A small pamphlet intended to provide a better understanding of the tactics utilized within Civil War artillery batteries. Murray, who has published a number of pamphlets keeps his topics focused and his writing concise.

Naisawald, L. VanLoan, *Grape & Canister: The Story of the Field Artillery of the Army of the Potomac, 1961-1865*, Oxford University Press, New York, 1960; Reprint: Stackpole Books, Mechanicsburg Pennsylvania, 1999. Naisawald's publication provides a detailed look at the operations of the artillery with the Army of the Potomac. Although somewhat lacking in detail regarding the Overland Campaign of 1864, the Siege of Petersburg and Appomattox, Naisawald does include additional technical data.

Nichols, Edward, J., *Toward Gettysburg: A Biography of General John Reynolds*, Pennsylvania State University Press, 1958. General, and then President Dwight Eisenhower once noted John F. Reynolds was "the best general" who served in the Federal army during the war. Reynolds, with the possible exception of John Buford, was more responsible for the great battle taking place at Gettysburg than anyone. Nichols work provides a balanced look at the general whom, had he survived the war, probably would have been elevated to the same stature as Hancock as a war hero.

Nolan, Alan T., *The Iron Brigade: A Military History*, Macmillan, New York, 1961; Reprint: Indiana University Press, Bloomington Indianapolis, 1994. Historian Bruce Catton once noted that he was "immensely impressed" with Nolan's work on the most recognized brigade in the Army of the Potomac. Although numerous works on the brigade have become available over the years since its first publication, it still remains the seminal work on the only all western brigade in the Army of the Potomac.

Nye, Wilber S., *Here Come the Rebels*, Louisiana State University Press, Baton Rouge, Louisiana, 1965; Reprint: Morningside, Dayton Ohio, 1988. The best single volume coverage of the Gettysburg Campaign which seems to go unnoticed among the multitude of Gettysburg literature. One reason may be that it treats only the movements of the Southerners from the time Lee left the Rappahannock to the commencement of the battle. Since it does not address the battle most may discard it as lacking interest. In reality it is one of the most well written volumes on any aspect of the campaign.

O'Reilly, Francis Augustín, *The Fredericksburg Campaign: Winter War on the Rappahannock*, Louisiana State University Press, Baton Rouge, 2003, 2006. This volume is probably the most comprehensive study of the Battle of Fredericksburg ever published. Well over half of O'Reilly's work deals directly with the regimental and battery level action. His writing ability places the reading directly into the action, providing an excellent read.

Osborne, Charles C., *Jubal: The Life and Times of General Jubal A. Early, CSA*, Algonquin Books, Chapel Hill North Carolina, 1992. Osborne's biography of the cantankerous Early addresses not only his early life and war participation but his post war days which were filled with controversy and accusations against his fellow soldiers.

Palmer, David W., *The Forgotten Hero of Gettysburg*, Xlibris Corporation, U.S.A., 2004. A wonderfully written and detailed biography of one of the unsung commanders who's efforts at Gettysburg contributed to Federal success.

Parsons, George W., *Put the Vermonters Ahead*, White Mane Publishing Company, Shippensburg Pennsylvania, 1996. A short and summarizing work on the activities of the 1st Vermont Brigade during the war. It presents a general overview of the brigade's campaigns, but lacks regimental detail.

Patterson, Gerard A., *From Blue to Gray: The Life of Confederate General Cadmus M. Wilcox*, Stackpole Books, Mechanicsburg Pennsylvania, 2001. Although this work is rather short, it is a well written volume about one of the lesser known members of the Army of northern Virginia's command structure.

Pfanz, Donald C., *Richard S. Ewell, A Soldier's Life*, The University of North Carolina Press, Chapel Hill/London, 1998. Pfanz's work is one of the most researched biographies of a Civil War General in recent years. More than a story of Ewell's war service, It also documents the generals life before and after the war in great detail.

Pfanz, Harry W., *Gettysburg: Culp's Hill & Cemetery Hill*, The University of North Carolina Press, Chapel Hill/London, 1993. Pfanz, a PhD in history and a ten year historian at the Gettysburg National Military Park, provides analysis and opinions on the events which swirled around the Northern end of the famous Gettysburg "fish hook."

Piston, William Garrett, *Lee's Tarnished Lieutenant: James Longstreet and his place in Southern History*, University of Georgia Press, Athens Georgia, 1987. Piston traces Longstreet's career and his controversial post war life, providing a fair analysis of his military record and his defense of his record.

Priest, John Michael, *Antietam: The Soldiers Battle*, White Mane Publishing Company, Shippensburg Pennsylvania, 1989; Reprint: Oxford University Press, Oxford/New York, 1993. Love or hate his writing style, Priest has produced an extremely detailed account of the fighting which raged in Maryland on 17 September 1862 from the point of view of the individual foot soldier. A high school teacher by trade, Priest makes no effort to analyze the battle but simply presents the brutal realities of the conflict that was the Civil War. While many of Priest's works have met with a great deal of controversy, this author enjoys them for their elaborate detail.

Pullen, John, J., *The Twentieth Maine*, J.B. Lippincott Company, Philadelphia Pennsylvania, 1957; Reprint: Morningside, Dayton Ohio, 1991. For nearly half a century Pullen's work stood as the decisive work on Chamberlain's 20th Maine. While additional efforts have been produced since then, none have ever surpassed his work.

Robertson, James I. Jr., *General A. P. Hill: The Story of a Confederate Warrior*, Random House, New York, 1987. An excellent biography of Hill by a learned scholar.

_____, *Stonewall Jackson-The Man, the Soldier, the Legend*, MacMillan, New York, 1997. Robertson's work on Jackson is the standard by which all future biographical work on Civil War figures should be measured. It won eight national awards and, in this author's opinion has supplanted all previous works on the Army of Northern Virginia's second most loved general.

Sandburg, Carl, *Abraham Lincoln: The War Years*, 4 Volumes, Harcourt Brace and Company, New York, 1939. Sandburg's biography of the president won him one of his three Pulitzer Prizes in 1940. Known primarily as a poet, He wrote a two volume treatment of Lincoln's prewar years (*Abraham Lincoln: The Prairie Years*) in 1926, before following it up with his 4 volume prize winning effort.

Sauers, Richard A., *Gettysburg: The Meade-Sickles Controversy*, Potomac Books, Inc., Washington DC, 2003. Sauers does a masterful job of presenting a full and fair review of the dispute which arose between Dan Sickles and George Meade after the battle of Gettysburg. Sickles, whether trying to defend his actions or simply trying to inflate his own status instigated a controversy which still rages today.

Scheel, Eugene M., *Culpeper: A Virginia County's History Through 1920*, The Culpeper Historical Society, Culpeper Virginia, 1982. An indispensable work for anyone conducting research on events which occurred during the Civil War in Culpeper County.

Sears, Stephen W., *Landscape Turned Red – The Battle of Antietam*, New York, 1983; Reprint: Houghton Mifflin Company: New York/Boston, 2003. Sears has written a number of well received volumes regarding the major battles and campaigns in the east. While all his works are interesting reads, he seems to be a writer first and a historian second which plays to the mass market more effectively. This author gladly sacrifices a little expertise in writing ability for a work which is obviously produced by a first rate historian.

_____, *To the Gates of Richmond: The Peninsula Campaign*, Ticknor and Fields, New York, 1992.

_____, *Chancellorsville*, Houghton Mifflin Company, New York/Boston, 1996.

Shanks, William Franklin Gore, *Personal Recollections of Distinguished Generals*, Harper and Brothers Publishers, New York, 1866. A work which provides antidotal information on a number of Northern Civil War generals.

Slocum, Charles E., *The Life and Service of Major General Henry Warner Slocum*, Slocum Publishing, Toledo Ohio, 1913. An excellent work which concentrated mostly upon the Civil War career of General Slocum.

Stackpole, Edward J., *Chancellorsville*, Harrisburg Pennsylvania, 1988.

Starr, Stephen Z., *The Union Cavalry in the Civil War*, 3 Volumes, Louisiana State University Press, Baton Rouge Louisiana, 1979, 1981, 1985. When originally published, Starr's work on the Federal cavalry was groundbreaking. Since then more focused works have been made available which highlight various aspects of Starr's subject but no other single work has covered the activities of Union mounted operations during the war as well.

Sutherland, Daniel E., *Seasons of War*, The Free Press, New York/London, 1995. An excellent work which presents the Southern point of view regarding the war from the prospective of the residents of Culpeper Court House. However, one of the photos facing page 281 is miss marked. The pontoon bridge shown in the upper photo is at Deep Run along the Rappahannock River south of Fredericksburg, not on the Rapidan at Germanna Ford. This however is probably due to it being miss-labeled at **USAHEC**. The same photo, labeled correctly, along with a second photo from another camera angle, is also in the **NA**.

Swinton, William, *Campaigns of the Army of the Potomac: A Critical History of Operations in Virginia Maryland and Pennsylvania from the Commencement to the Close of the War, 1861-1865*, Charles B. Richardson, New York, 1866. Swinton wrote the first history of the Army of the Potomac, and was able to interview a number of participants while the war was still fresh in their minds. Swinton's interview with Longstreet and his subsequent comments, planted the seeds for the conflict between Longstreet and a great many former Confederate officers regarding Gettysburg.

Thomas, Emory M., *Robert E. Lee, a Biography*, W. W. Norton & Company, Inc., New York London, 1995. Thomas's biography of Lee is well researched and written but does contain a couple of minor factual errors. He also provides the reader with his opinions which have a tendency to lean toward the negative aspects of the Lee.

Tidball, Eugene C., *"No Disgrace to My Country": The Life of John C. Tidball*, The Kent State University Press, Kent Ohio, 2002. Simply an amazing piece of scholarship on one of the lesser known members of the eastern army. During his life John Tidball wrote a great deal. Unfortunately, until ten years ago, no one had researched and told his story.

Trout, Robert J., *Galloping Thunder: The Stuart Horse Artillery Battalion*, Stackpole Books, Mechanicsburg Pennsylvania, 2002. Trout's encyclopedic knowledge of Stuart's Horse Artillery is present on nearly every page of this excellent work which draws on a number of primary and manuscript sources.

_____, *They Followed the Plume*, Stackpole Books, Mechanicsburg Pennsylvania, 2003. A multi-biographical work covering the men who served on Jeb Stuart's staff. Once again, Trout utilized a great deal of unpublished and primary sources to create a volume that is not only a great reference work but an interesting read.

Trudeau, Noah, Andre, *Gettysburg: A Test of Courage*, HarperCollins Publishers Inc., New York, 2002. Trudeau's treatment of the battle appeared a year before Stephen Sears' work, and in this authors opinion is the better of the two.

Tucker, Glenn, *Lee and Longstreet at Gettysburg*, Bobbs-Merrill Company, Indianapolis, 1968; Reprint: Morningside, Dayton Ohio, 1982. Tucker, a former newspaperman, wrote this volume as somewhat of a follow up to his masterful *High Tide at Gettysburg*. His investigative and research skills as a correspondent show in the depth of his detail. It is unfortunate that today's news correspondents are not as methodical at reporting the facts of a story as Tucker was. He was simply one of the best mid 20th Century historians.

Tucker, Spencer C., *Brigadier General John D. Imboden: Confederate Commander in the Shenandoah*, The University Press of Kentucky, Lexington Kentucky, 2003. A superb biography of a general who's contribution to the Gettysburg Campaign is generally overlooked or marginalized.

Waters, Zack C. & Edmonds, James C, *A Small but Spartan Band: The Florida Brigade in the Army of Northern Virginia*, The University of Alabama Press, Tuscaloosa Alabama, 2010. The first work of substance to present the story of the Florida units in the Army of Northern Virginia. During the mid 19th Century, Florida was a sparsely populated region which provided a small number of hardy frontiersmen who fought hard. It is an interesting read which fills a void in the history of the ward in the east.

Wert, Jeffry D., *Cavalryman of the Lost Cause*, Simon and Schuster, New York/London, 2008. Eminent historian Wert draws upon a plethora of unpublished sources to create a modern view of Stuart which is devoid of the romantic overtones present in so many previous works on the cavalryman.

_____, *General James Longstreet*, Simon and Schuster, New York, 1993. A fair and evenhanded assessment of Longstreet and his conduct at Gettysburg. For years after the war Longstreet was made the scapegoat of the Confederacy's downfall because he supposedly failed Lee at Gettysburg. Wert argues that had Lee paid more credence to his lieutenant's suggestions, the outcome may have been different in Pennsylvania.

Wiley, Bell Irvin, *The Life of Billy Yank*, Bobbs Merrill, Indianapolis, 1952; Reprint: Louisiana State University Press, Baton Rouge/London, 1978.

_____, *The Life of Johnny Reb*, Bobbs-Merrill, Indianapolis, 1943; Reprint: Louisiana State University Press, Baton Rouge/London, 1978. Wiley's two publications have become the standard work on the men who fought the battles. One of Americas most renouned Civil War historians; Wiley was professor emeritus of Emory University. It is rumored that before his death in 1980, he had read over 30,000 individual letters written by soldiers during the war. His two "Life of" volumes have been reprinted a number of times.

Williams, Kenneth P., *Lincoln Finds a General: A Military Study of the Civil War, Grant's First Year in the West*, MacMillan Company, New York, 1952; Reprint: *Grant Rises in the West: The First Year, 1861-1862*, Bison Books, 1997. This volume was originally the third volume of Williams' initial plan to write a seven volumes series. Originally intended to be a work depicting how Lincoln found Grant and brought him east, it turned into a command study of Union operations during the war. His death do to cancer in 1958 terminated the series at five volumes. Volume three has been reprinted as *Grant Rises in the West*.

Wise, Jennings Cropper, *The Long Arm of Lee or The History of the Artillery of the Army of Northern Virginia*, 2 Volumes, J. P. Bell Company, Lynchburg Virginia, 1915; Reprint: University of Nebraska Press, Lincoln/London, 1991. A masterful work published when Wise was commandant at VMI. No other publication has been able to supplant Wise's study as the preeminent work on the artillery in the Army of Northern Virginia. It contains not only a narrative of the artillery's operations but a great deal of statistical and organizational data.

Wittenberg, Eric J., *Rush's Lancers: The Sixth Pennsylvania Cavalry in the Civil War*, Westholme Publishing, Yardley Pennsylvania, 2007. Not since the publication of Chaplain Samuel L. Gracey's work in 1868 has the 6th Pennsylvania Cavalry been the sole subject of a book length treatment.

_____, *The Battle of Brandy Station*, The History Press, Charleston, South Carolina, 2010. Much of the material in this work is simply an expanded and illustrated version of the Brandy Station segment of Wittenberg's *The Union Cavalry Comes of Age*, reprinted as a volume in The History Press' Civil War Sesquicentennial Series. It, like his previous work is an interesting and easy read.

_____, *The Union Cavalry Comes of Age*, Potomac Books, Inc., Washington DC, 2003. There is no doubt the rise of the Union cavalry in the east helped turn the tide of the war in the summer of 1863. Wittenberg's work is one of the most refreshing treatments of the Federal horsemen in some time. His insightful analysis clears up how the Federals managed to convert their dysfunctional cavalry arm into an effective branch of the Army of the Potomac.

Wynstra, Robert J., *The Rashness of That Hour*, Savas Beatie, New York/California, 2010. Wynstra'a work is a significant biography of the ill-fated Iverson. It concentration on his participation and actions during the Gettysburg Campaign. It is built upon ten years of research and utilized a great deal of manuscript and primary sources.

Primary Source Articles

About Another "Youngest Soldier," *Confederate Veteran*, Volume 9, 1901.

Alexander, Edward P., "Confederate Artillery Service", *Southern Historical Society Papers*, Volume 11, 1883.

Allan, William, "Memoranda of Conversations with General Robert E. Lee, 15 April 1868," in Gallagher, *Lee the Soldier*.

Armistead, Drury L., "The Battle in Which General Johnston was Wounded", *Southern Historical Society Papers*, Volume 18, 1890.

Bates, Samuel P., "Hooker's Comments on Chancellorsville", *Battles and Leaders of the Civil War*, Volume 3.

Benjamin, Charles F., "Hooker's Appointment and Removal", *Battles and Leaders of the Civil War*, Volume 3.

Boswell, James K., "Jackson's Boswell: The Diary of a Confederate Staff Officer", *Civil War Times Illustrated*, Volume 15, No.1, 1976.

Boteler, Alexander R., "Stonewall Jackson in Campaign of 1862", *Southern Historical Society Papers*, Volume 40, 1915.

Chester, James, "Inside Sumter in '61", *Battles and Leaders of the Civil War*, Volume 1.

Collins, John L., "When Stonewall Jackson Turned our Right", *Battles and Leaders of the Civil War*, Volume 3.

Darrow, Caroline Baldwin, "Recollections of the Twiggs Surrender", *Battles and Leaders of the Civil War*, Volume 1.

Dinkins, James, "Barksdale's Mississippi Brigade at Fredericksburg", *Southern Historical Society Papers*, Volume 36, 1915.

Doubleday, Abner, "From Moultrie to Sumter", *Battles and Leaders of the Civil War*, Volume 1.

Eggleston, George Cary, "Notes on Cold Harbor", *Battles and Leaders of the Civil War*, Volume 1.

Hunt, Henry J., "The First Day at Gettysburg", *Battles and Leaders of the Civil War*, Volume 3.

Heth, Henry, "Letter from Major-General Henry Heth of A. P. Hill's Corps, A.N.V.", *Southern Historical Society Papers*, Volume 4, 1877.

Howard, Oliver O., "The Eleventh Corps at Chancellorsville", *Battles and Leaders of the Civil War*, Volume 3.

Jones, J. Williams, "The Friendship between Lee and Scott", *Southern Historical Society Papers*, Volume 11, 1883.

Kyle, David J., "Jackson's Guide when Shot", *Confederate Veteran*, Volume 4, 1896.

Lane, James H., "History of Lane's North Carolina Brigade", *Southern Historical Society Papers*, Volume 8, 1880.

_____, "How Stonewall Jackson met his Death", *Southern Historical Society Papers*, Volume 8, 1880.

Lee, Fitzhugh, "Chancellorsville-Address of General Fitzhugh Lee before the Virginia Division, A.N.V. Association, October 29th, 1879", *Southern Historical Society Papers*, Volume 7, 1879.

_____, "Speech before, A.N.V. Association Banquet, October 28th, 1875", *Southern Historical Society Papers*, Volume 1, 1876.

Leigh, Benjamin W., "The Wounding of Stonewall Jackson-Extracts from a Letter", *Southern Historical Society Papers*, Volume 6, 1878.

Longstreet, James, "Lee in Pennsylvania", *Annuls of the War*, Philadelphia, 1879. Reprint: The Blue and Grey Press: Edison, New Jersey, 1996.

_____, "Lee's Invasion of Pennsylvania", *Battles and Leaders of the Civil War*, Volume 3.

_____, "The Battle of Fredericksburg", *Battles and Leaders of the Civil War*, Volume 3.

Moorman, Marcellus N., "Narrative of Events and Observations Connected with the Wounding of General T. J. (Stonewall) Jackson", *Southern Historical Society Papers*, Volume 30, 1902.

McGuire, Dr. Hunter, "Death of Stonewall Jackson", *Southern Historical Society Papers*, Volume 14, 1886.

_____, "General T.J. ("Stonewall") Jackson, His Career and Character", *Southern Historical Society Papers*, Volume 25, 1897.

Moffet, George Henry, "Battle of Brandy Station", *Confederate Veteran*, Volume 14, 1906.

Pleasonton, Alfred, "The Campaign of Gettysburg", *Annuals of the War.*

Smith, James Power, "Stonewall Jackson's Last Battle", *Battles and Leaders of the Civil War*, Volume 3.

Talcott, Thomas M. R., "General Lee's Strategy at the Battle of Chancellorsville", *Southern Historical Society Papers,* Volume 34, 1906.

Taylor, Walter H., "Memorandum by Walter H. Taylor, of General Lee's Staff", *Southern Historical Society Papers,* Volume 4, 1877.

Thompson, David L., "In the Ranks to the Antietam", *Battles and Leaders of the Civil War*, Volume 2.

Trimble, Isaac R., "The Battle and Campaign of Gettysburg", *Southern Historical Society Papers,* Volume 26, 1898.

Wilbourn, Richard E., "Letter to General J. E. Early", *Southern Historical Society Papers*, Volume 6, 1878.

_____, "Extract from the Printed Narrative Marked and Endorsed by Captain Wilbourn, as on his Authority", *Southern Historical Society Papers*, Volume 6, 1878.

Young, T. J., "Battle of Brandy Station", *Confederate Veteran*, Volume 23, 1915.

Secondary Source Articles

Browne, Edward C., "Col. George H. Sharpe's "Soda Water" Scouts", *Gettysburg Magazine*, Issue 44, 2011.

CWTI Staff Members, "'Grumble' Jones: a Personal Profile", *Civil War Times Illustrated*, Volume 7, No.3, 1968.

Grimsley, Mark, "Overthrown", *Civil War Times Illustrated*, Volume 19, No.7, 1980.

Haines, Douglas Craig, "Jeb Stuart's Advance to Gettysburg", *Gettysburg Magazine*, Issue 29, 2004.

Hall, James O., "A Modern Hunt for a Fabled Agent: The Spy Harrison", *Civil War Times Illustrated*, Volume 24, No.10, 1986.

Hardgrove, J. G., General Edward S. "General Edward S. Bragg's Reminiscences", *Wisconsin Magazine of History*, Volume 33, No.3, 1950.

Hartwig, D. Scott., "The 11th Corps on July 1, 1863", *Gettysburg Magazine*, Issue 2, 1990.

Hassler, William W., "A. P. Hill: Mystery Man of the Confederacy", *Civil War Times Illustrated*, Volume 16, No.6, 1977.

_____, "'Fighting Joe' Hooker", *Civil War Times Illustrated*, Volume 14, No.5, 1975.

_____, "The Hill-Jackson Feud", *Civil War Times Illustrated*, Volume 4, No.2, 1965.

_____, Lee's Hard-Luck General, *Civil War Times Illustrated*, Volume 5, No.4, 1966.

Hennessy, John, "At the Vortex of Hell", *Civil War Times Illustrated*, Volume 24, No.9, 1986.

Hyde, Bill, "Did You Get There? Captain Samuel Johnston's Reconnaissance at Gettysburg", *Gettysburg Magazine*, Issue 29, 2004.

Jones, Wilber D. Jr., "Stonewall Jackson, his Courier, and Special Order No.191", *Civil War Regiments*, Volume 5 No.3, Savas Publishing Company, 1997.

Kimmel, Ross M., "Men and Material", *America's Civil War*, Volume 14, No.3, 2001.

Krick, Robert K., 'A Stupid Old Useless Fool', *Civil War Times Illustrated*, Volume 47, No..3, 2008.

LaFantasie, Glenn W., "How Lincoln Won and Lost at Gettysburg", *Papers of the Ninth Annual Gettysburg National Military Park Seminar*, National Park Service, 2002.

Longacre, Edward G., "Alfred Pleasonton: 'The Knight of Romance'", *Civil War Times Illustrated*, Volume 13, No.8, 1974.

_____, Judson Kilpatrick, *Civil War Times Illustrated*, Volume 10, No.1, 1971.

_____, "The Soul of Our Artillery", *Civil War Times Illustrated*, Volume 12, No.3, 1973.

Martin, Samuel J., "The Complex Confederate", *Civil War Times Illustrated*, Volume 25, No.2, 1986.

Mitchell, Adele, "Jackson's Engineer", *Civil War Times Illustrated*, Volume 7, No.3, 1968-69.

Motts, Wayne E., "To Gain a Second Star: The Forgotten George S. Greene", *Gettysburg Magazine*, Issue 3, 1990.

Musto, R.J., "The Treatment of the Wounded at Gettysburg: Jonathan Letterman: The Father of Modern Battlefield Medicine", *Gettysburg Magazine,* Issue 37, 2007.

Owen, Allison, "Record of an Old Artillery Organization", The Field Artillery Journal, Volume IV, No.1, 1914.

Ryan, Thomas, J., "A Battle of Wits: Intelligence Operations during the Gettysburg Campaign", *Gettysburg Magazine,* Issue 29, 2003.

Speicher, James L., "The Sumter Artillery: The 11th Battalion, Georgia Light Artillery", *Civil War Regiments,* Volume 3, No.2, 1993.

Tucker, Glenn, "Winfield S. Hancock", *Civil War Times Illustrated,* Volume 7, No. 5, 1968.

Wert, Jeffry D., "Old Artillery: William Nelson Pendleton"*, Civil War Times Illustrated,* Volume 13, No.3, 1974.

Winschel, Terrence J., "Heavy was Their Loss: Joe Davis' Brigade at Gettysburg", *Gettysburg Magazine,* Issue 2, 1990.

_____, "The Gettysburg Experience of James J. Kirkpatrick"*, Gettysburg Magazine,* Issue 8, 1993.

Wittenberg, Eric J., "John Buford and the Gettysburg Campaign", *Gettysburg Magazine,* Issue 11, 1994.

Encyclopedias, Dictionaries, Multi-Biographical and Photo Archives

Boatner, Mark Mayo, *The Civil War Dictionary,* David McKay Company, Inc., New York, 1959. Since it was first published Boatner's dictionary has been a regular resource for general information regarding the war. Included is biographical information on nearly every officer who attained the rank of general and a large number of those who did not. He also included information on campaigns, noteworthy commands, significant events and a host of other lesser topics. Boatner's work has stood the test of time and scrutiny and is an interesting book to read.

Eicher, John H., and Eicher, David J., *Civil War High Commands,* Stanford University Press, Stanford Californian, 2001. Simply a treasure trove of information on prominent generals from both the Union and Confederate service. Included for each general is a complete (or as complete as possible) service record, as well as a great deal of peripheral information regarding commission dates, congressional information, organizations of both Union and Confederate armies and strength numbers. Also included is a list of birth places and locations of internment of nearly every general from both North and South. Today efforts which includes biographical information for Civil War generals cannot afford to neglect this register.

Faust, Patricia L., *Historical Times Illustrated Encyclopedia of the Civil War,* Harper & Row, New York, 1986. Tragically, Faust died before her editorial work was published. Although her encyclopedia is a unique work in its own right, it is simply an expanded and illustrated volume much in the same vane as Boatner's work. Her work was built upon the submissions of a large number of learned scholars whose work she and her staff edited for inclusion.

Krick, Robert E. L., *Staff Officers in Gray: A Biographical Register of the Staff Officers in the Army of Northern Virginia*, University of North Carolina Press, Chapel Hill/London, 2003. An indispensable reference work for anyone researching the Army of Northern Virginia.

Krick, Robert K., *Lee's Colonels: A Biographical Register of the Field Officers of the Army of Northern Virginia*, Broadfoot Publishing Company, Wilmington North Carolina, 2005. Another fine reference work from the senior member of the Krick family duo.

Miller, Francis Trevelyan, ***The Photographic History of the Civil War*, 10 Volumes,** The Review of Reviews Company, New York, 1911. Miller's work is the seminal publication regarding period photographs of the war's events and its participants.

Perry, Thomas D., *Laurel Hill's Teachers Guide*, Ararat Virginia, 2005.

Rand, John C., *One of a Thousand: A Series of Biographical Sketches of One Thousand Representative Men Resident in the Commonwealth of Massachusetts*, First National Publishing Company, Boston, 1890.

Sifakis, Stewart, *Who was Who in the Civil War,* Facts on File, Inc., New York, 1988.

Tagg, Larry, *The Generals of Gettysburg*, Savas Publishing Company, Campbell California, 1998. Tagg's work is probably the best collection of biographical information on corps, division and brigade level commanders at Gettysburg.

Wakelyn, Jon L., *Biographical Dictionary of the Confederacy*, Greenwood Press, Westport Connecticut, 1977. Quite frankly a fine reference work consisting of an extensive collection of biographical sketches of not only Confederate military figures but also influential political figures, businessmen, newspaper editors and other prominent individuals.

Warner, Ezra J., *Generals in Blue*, Louisiana State University Press, Baton Rouge, 1964.

Warner, Ezra J., *Generals in Gray*, Louisiana State University Press, Baton Rouge, 1959. For years Warner's two volumes have been the staple for biographical information on Union and Confederate commanders who attained the rank of general.

Wilson, James Grant and Fiske, John, *Appletons' Cyclopædia of American Biography*, 6 Volumes, D. Appleton and Company, New York, 1988, 1989.

Atlases

Gottfried, Bradley M., *The Maps of Gettysburg: An Atlas of the Gettysburg Campaign, June 3 – July 13, 1863*, Savas Beatie, New York/California, 2007. Gottfried's work is extremely useful owing to the fact that each map is accompanied by a detailed text which describes the events depicted on each graphic.

Laino, Philip, *Gettysburg Campaign Atlas*, Gatehouse Press, Dayton Ohio, 2009. Laino, the cartographer for the Gettysburg Magazine, assembled his work for the magazine plus a great many additional maps to create possibly the best set of maps depicting the course of the battle ever assembled. Anyone truly interested in the course of the campaign and battle should never allow his work to be far from reach.

United States War Department, *Atlas to Accompany the Official Records of the Union and Confederate Armies*, Government Printing Office, Washington DC, 1891-1895; Reprint: Fairfax Press, Crown Publishers Inc., 1983. To augment the **OR**, the War Department published hundreds of period maps created by military engineers and topographers. The atlas is an indispensable work for anyone with a serious interest in the war in general and an excellent supporting publication when one is plowing through the reports and documents in the **OR**.

Electronic Sources

Since its explosive growth in the 1990's, the Internet has become a vehicle for the storage and retrieval of accurate and not so accurate information. Additionally, a great deal of the information has historical and social ramifications on our society, while much of it, to be quite frank, is simply excrement. Many sites, like *Wikipedia*, which began as a repository for the housing of accurate, and in many instances, inaccurate information, has evolved over the years to become a respectable and dependable *starting point* for investigative work. Other sites, like the *Internet Archive* (http://archive.org) provides access to scanned copies of literally tens of thousands of historical works which are out of copyright, allowing individuals access to historical publications housed at libraries and archives across the country and even the world.

Many historians still shy away from the internet as a resource but many are beginning to realize the benefits of the tool. However, one must still look at much of the information as suspect. An excellent rule of thumb for utilizing Internet data is to treat any information obtained as a starting point for investigative work and track the data back to its source. If the source of a specific piece of data is not cited by the site or available, then it should be treated as suspect until corroborating information can be located. If supporting data cannot be found then the information should be assumed to be suspect and not utilized or if used, cited as unconfirmed.

Nearly all libraries and archives are now online and provide access to some elements of their collections. Additionally, most have listings of their holdings and provide tools to locate and instructions on how to obtain copies. However, nothing is more refreshing to the historian/researcher then plowing through a stack of files looking for additional information on a specific subject. As a researcher, I have used some of these sites to plan visits to various libraries and archives and identify records or files I have interest in. The days of the Internet being snickered at by historians when a site is cited by other researches is over, but the use of the tool must still be treated as a starting point and not the termination of a search for historical data.

Augustus Pearl Martin Photo - (http://www.celebrateboston.com)
Battle of Palo Alto - (http://en.wikipedia.org/wiki/Battle_of_Palo_Alto)
Carl Schurz - (http://en.wikipedia.org/wiki/Carl_Schurz)
Cazenovia Seminary - (http://en.wikipedia.org/wiki/Cazenovia_Seminary)
David G. Birney - (http://en.wikipedia.org/wiki/James_G._Birney)
James G. Birney - (http://en.wikipedia.org/wiki/James_G._Birney)
Edward D. Muhlenberg - (http://en.wikipedia.org/wiki/Edward_D._Muhlenberg)
Frank Wheaton - (http://en.wikipedia.org/wiki/Frank_Wheaton)
Freedmen & Southern Society Project-The Second Confiscation Act - (http://www.history.umd.edu/Freedmen/conact2.htm)
Freeman McGilvery - (http://en.wikipedia.org/wiki/Freeman_McGilvery)
Gabriel R. Paul page on Arlington National Cemetery Site - (http://www.arlingtoncemetery.net/grpaul.htm)
George C. Cram page on Crossed Sabers website - (http://crossedsabers.blogspot.com/2009/05/fiddlers-green-george-c-cram.html)
George Sears Greene page on Warwick Rhode Island Digital History Project - (http://www.warwickhistory.com/index.php?option=com_content&view=article&id=103:apponaugs-george-sears-greene-&catid=43:apponaug-village&Itemid=96)
George Stoneman - (http://en.wikipedia.org/wiki/George_Stoneman)
Internet Archive - (http://archive.org) From the Internet Archive site: *"The Internet Archive is a 501(c)(3) non-profit that was founded to build an Internet library. Its purposes include offering permanent access for researchers, historians, scholars, people with disabilities, and the general public to historical collections that exist in digital format. Founded in 1996 and located in San Francisco, the Archive has been receiving data donations from Alexa Internet and others. In late 1999, the organization started to grow to include more well-rounded collections. Now the Internet Archive includes texts, audio, moving images, and software as well as archived web pages in our collections, and provides specialized services for adaptive reading and information access for the blind and other persons with disabilities."*
John Blair Dabney page on Ancestry.con - (http://worldconnect.rootsweb.ancestry.com/cgi-bin/igm.cgi?op=GET&db=adgedge&id=I32588&style=TABLE)
Jonathan Letterman - (http://en.wikipedia.org/wiki/Jonathan_Letterman)
Joseph Lane page on the Biographical Directory of the United States Congress website - (http://bioguide.congress.gov/scripts/biodisplay.pl?index=L000062)
Longstreet's Scout Henry Thomas Harrison - (http://home.comcast.net/~site002/Harrison/index.htm)
Mexican War Maps - Taylor's Northern Campaign, Scott's Campaign (2 maps) - (http://www.dean.usma.edu/departments/history/Atlases/MexicanWar)
Page dedicated to the genealogy of the Gibbon family - (http://www.shissem.com/Hissem_Heysham-Gibbon_Branch.html)

Pennsylvania State Archives, Civil War Veterans' Card File, 1861-1866 Indexes - (http://www.digitalarchives.state.pa.us/archive.asp)

Personal information on Alexander Schimmelfennig - (http://www.olypen.com/tinkers/74th%20Pennsylvania/Webpage/default.htm)

Reuben Lindsay Walker page on Virginia Military Institute website - (http://www.vmi.edu/archives.aspx?id=5673)

Stephen Hinsdale Weed - (http://en.wikipedia.org/wiki/Stephen_Weed)

Thomas Colepeper, 2nd Baron Colepeper - (http://en.wikipedia.org/wiki/Thomas_Colepeper,_2nd_Baron_Colepeper)

University of Virginia Department of Astronomy, Leander McCormick Observatory Museum - (http://www.astro.virginia.edu/research/observatories/26inch/history/venable.php)

William Irvine page on the Biographical Directory of the United States Congress website -(http://bioguide.congress.gov/scripts/biodisplay.pl?index=I000036)

Edwards Brothers Malloy
Thorofare, NJ USA
October 6, 2014